C0-ART-984

BASEBALL CARD

PRICE GUIDE
1994

Other **CONFIDENT COLLECTOR** *Titles*
by Allan Kaye and Michael McKeever
Coming Soon from Avon Books

BASKETBALL CARD PRICE GUIDE 1994
FOOTBALL CARD PRICE GUIDE 1994
HOCKEY CARD PRICE GUIDE 1994

Avon Books are available at special quantity discounts for bulk purchases for sales promotions, premiums, fund raising or educational use. Special books, or book excerpts, can also be created to fit specific needs.

For details write or telephone the office of the Director of Special Markets, Avon Books, Dept. FP, 1350 Avenue of the Americas, New York, New York 10019, 1-800-238-0658.

BASEBALL CARD

PRICE GUIDE
1994

ALLAN KAYE
AND
MICHAEL McKEEVER

AVON BOOKS ◆ NEW YORK

If you purchased this book without a cover, you should be aware that
this book is stolen property. It was reported as "unsold and destroyed"
to the publisher, and neither the author nor the publisher has received
any payment for this "stripped book."

THE CONFIDENT COLLECTOR: BASEBALL CARD PRICE
GUIDE (1994) is an original publication of Avon Books. This work
has never before appeared in book form.

AVON BOOKS
A division of
The Hearst Corporation
1350 Avenue of the Americas
New York, New York 10019

Copyright © 1993 by Michael McKeever
Cover art: Clifford Spohn
The Confident Collector and its logo are trademarked properties of
Avon Books.
Published by arrangement with the author
Library of Congress Catalog Card Number: 92-97140
ISBN: 0-380-77235-3

All rights reserved, which includes the right to reproduce this book or
portions thereof in any form whatsoever except as provided by the
U.S. Copyright Law. For information address Avon Books.

First Avon Books Printing: April 1993

AVON TRADEMARK REG. U.S. PAT. OFF. AND IN OTHER COUNTRIES,
MARCA REGISTRADA, HECHO EN U.S.A.

Printed in the U.S.A.

OPM   10 9 8 7 6 5 4 3 2 1

Important Notice: All of the information, including valuations, in this book has been compiled from the most reliable sources, and every effort has been made to eliminate errors and questionable data. Nevertheless, the possibility of error always exists in a work of such immense scope. The publisher and the author will not be held responsible for losses which may occur in the purchase, sale, or other transaction of property because of information contained herein. Readers who feel they have discovered errors are invited to *write* the authors in care of Avon Books, so that the errors may be corrected in subsequent editions.

TABLE OF CONTENTS

Acknowledgements

This book would not have been possible without the contributions of dozens of people whose imput and expertise in the areas of card evaluations, research and technical support have significantly enhanced this edition. We sincerely appreciate their efforts and want to thank each of them for their time, dedication and hard work.

Betty and Jonathan Abraham, Cape Coral Cards; Darren Adams, West Coast SportsCards; Michael Balser, Classic Games; Bill Boake, Hall Of Fame Cards; Tim Boyle, Lesnik Public Relations; Rich Bradley, The Upper Deck Company; Scott Bradshaw, Centerfield; John Brenner; Joie Casey, Field Of Dreams; Ken Cicola, Lou Costanza, Champion Sports; Mike Cramer; Pacific Trading Cards; Dick DeCourcy; Georgia Music & Sports; Larry Dluhy, Sports Collectibles of Houston; Lewis Early, Early Entertainment; Chris Eberheart; Joe Esposito, B & E Collectibles; Eddie Fisher, Batter's Box; Larry Fritsch, Larry Fritsch Cards; Richard Galasso, Home Plate Collectibles; Tony Galovich, American Card Exchange; Richard Gelman, Card Collector's Company; Dawn Marie Giargiari, Graphic Designer; Dick Gilkeson; Bill Goepner, San Diego Sports Collectibles; David Greenhill, New York Card Company; Wayne Grove, First Base Sports Nostalgia; Bill Goodwin, St. Louis Baseball Cards; Walter Hall, Hall's Nostalgia; Eric Handler, Lapin Public Relations; Don Harrison, The Tenth Inning; Bill Henderson (King Of The Commons); Neil Hoppenworth; Peter Hughes, NFL Properties; Bob Ibach, Lesnik Public Relations; Toby Johnson; Donn Jennings, Donn Jennings Cards; Bill Karaman; Bill Kennedy, No Gum Just Cards; Tim Kilbane, Ron Klasnick, JW International; Rick Kohl, The Strike Zone; David Kohler, SportsCards Plus; Chuck LaPaglia, The SportsCard Report Radio Show; Don Lepore; Lew Lipset; Kay Longmire, O-Pee-Chee of Canada; Greg Manning; Jane McKeever; Katherine McKeever; Jim Mayfield; Blake Meyer, Lone Star SportsCards; Chuck Miller; The SportsCard Report Radio Show; Mike Miller; Dick Millerd; Richard Morris; Steve Myland; Vince Nauss, Leaf/Donruss; Donovan Niemi; Joe Pasternack, Card Collectors Company; Frank and Steve Pemper, Ball Four Cards; Jack and Patti Petruzzelli, 59 Innings; Warren Power; Andy Rapoza; Peter Reeves (Our computer guru); Gavin Riley; Alan "Mr. Mint" Rosen; Steve Rotman, Rotman Productions; Murray Rubenfeld, The SportsCard Report Radio Show; Robert Rusnak; Ben Runyan; Kevin Savage, The Sports Gallery; Duke and Smokey Scheinman, Smokey's Baseball Cards; Michelle Serrio; Eric Slutsky, Edelman Public Relations Worldwide; Nigel Spill, Oldies And Goodies; Clifford Spohn, Jim Stevens; Ted Taylor, Fleer Corp.; Bud Tompkins, Minnesota Connection; Joe Valle, Cardboard Dreams; Eddie Vidal; Tom Wall; Virginia Webster; Bill Wesslund, Portland SportsCards; Katherine Wilkins, Del Mar Broadcasting and Publishing; Dean Winskill, Argyle SportsCards; Matt Wozniak, Kit Young. We especially want to thank our Editor, Dorothy Harris and all of the staff at Avon Books.

Introduction

Over the past several years baseball card collecting has surged in popularity and baseball card prices have soared in value. When we first started collecting cards there was only one company, Topps. When we published our first hobby magazine there were only three card companies, Donruss, Fleer and Topps. Today more than a dozen companies manufacture cards on an annual basis and collecting has grown from a passive, fun-filled hobby to a huge industry with investment grade cards selling for hundreds, even thousands of dollars.

The purpose of this edition is to provide you with an accurate, up-to-date listing of baseball card values. These prices don't reflect our opinions but are the result of extensive research throughout the marketplace. The prices listed in this volume are actual retail prices obtained by monitoring retail sports card shops, baseball card shows, memorabilia conventions and auctions, hobby publications and mail order catalogues. The card values were then entered in the book just prior to the press run.

We have also tried to make this edition as easy to use as possible. Since rookie cards are among the most popular in the hobby, and are usually a player's most valuable card, we've provided rookie card designations for thousands of players. Look for the (R) symbol next to the player's name.

Since bonus cards and limited edition inserts are among the hottest cards in the hobby we have provided a checklist and values for these special cards following the regular checklist for the set in which they were issued.

Finally, we have provided a complete card grading and conditioning guide to help you analyze the condition of your collection and a glossary with definitions to help you better understand the terminology of the hobby.

Over the past decade card collecting and sports memorabilia has grown from a cottage industry to a $5 billion a year business. It is estimated that 20 million people actively participate in what has become the most popular hobby in America. We sincerely hope this edition will enhance your enjoyment of the hobby and will serve as your official reference guide to the exciting world of baseball cards.

Glossary Of Terms

AS- All-Star. Cards with the AS designation are usually part of a subset and mean the player was chosen for the All-Star team the previous year.

AW-Award Winners. Cards that are usually part of a subset that honor a player's achievements from the previous season.

BC-Bonus card. Cards that are not part of a regular set but are often issued in conjunction with the set. Bonus cards are often issued in limited quantities and randomly inserted into selected wax or foil packs.

CL-Checklist. Cards that contain a numerical list of all the cards in a set.

Commons-Applies to the typical card in a set. A card that is not in demand. Most cards in any particular set are commons and have no significant value above the listing for all the common cards in a set.

COR-A card that's been reissued with corrections after an error was discovered on the original.

CY-Cy Young Award Winner

DP-Draft Pick

DK-Diamond King. Art cards of popular baseball stars found in Donruss issues and produced by Perez-Steele.

DS-Diamond Skills. A popular subset produced by Upper Deck.

DT-Dream Team. The title of a popular subset produced by Score.

EP-Elite Performers. A subset found in Fleer Ultra sets.

ER-Error Card. Signifies that an error exists on a baseball card. Covers such mistakes as misspelling, erroneous statistics or biographical information, wrong photograph or other graphics. The card has no significant value unless a corrected card is issued creating a variation. (See Variation)

FRAN-The Franchise. A popular subset produced by Score.

HL-Highlight Cards. These cards appear in various sets, primarily Topps, as part of subsets that depict selected players who are honored for special achievements.

IA-In-Action Cards. Usually appears as part of a subset and features an action photo of a player that differs from the player's regular card in the set.

INSERT-A card that's not part of a regular edition but usually produced in conjunction with that issue. Some insert cards are produced in limited quantities and packed randomly in wax or foil packs.

LL-League Leaders. A card in a subset that depicts leaders in various hitting, pitching and stolen base categories from the previous year.

MB-Master Blaster. A popular baseball subset produced by Score.

MVP-Most Valuable Player.

PV-Pro Visions. A popular subset produced by Fleer

R-Rookie Card. Indicates the player's first appearance on a card in a regular annual baseball card set, including update, traded and rookie sets. Rookie cards are usually a player's most valuable card.

RB-Record Breaker. A card that's usually part of a subset that honors a player for a particular milestone or record set the previous season.

RR-Rated Rookies. A subset found in Donruss issues that features promising prospects.

ROY-Rookie Of The Year.

SR-Star Rookies. A popular subset produced by Upper Deck.

TL-Team Leaders. The name of a popular subset or insert set.

UMP-Umpires. Part of a subset found in selected Topps sets.

USA-A card that's part of a subset that depicts players who performed for Team USA Baseball and the US Olympic team.

VAR-Variations. This symbol means that at least two versions of the same card exist. This usually happens when an error card is corrected in future print runs and then put in circulation by the card company.

WS-World Series cards.

Grading And Conditioning Guide

All prices quoted in this edition are retail prices, the price the card would sell for in established sports card stores. Buy prices, the price the dealer would pay for a card, range from about one-third of the price listed for common cards to one-half or more for higher valued cards. Regional interest and other factors may cause the value of a card to vary from one part of the country to another.

The values appearing in this edition are intended only to serve as an aid in evaluating your cards. They are not a solicitation to buy or sell on the part of the publisher or any other party.

Mint (MT): A perfect card. Well-centered, with equal borders. Four sharp, square corners. No nicks, creases, scratches, yellowing or fading. The printing must be flawless. No miscut cards or out of register photos. Cards with gum or wax stains cannot be considered truly mint, even when removed from brand new packs.

Near Mint (NR MT): A nearly perfect card that contains a minor flaw upon close inspection. Must be well-centered and three of the four corners must be perfectly sharp. A slightly off-centered card with four perfect corners would fit this grade. No creases, scratches, yellowing or fading. Card is valued at 50% to 60% of a mint card depending on the scarcity of the card and the demand for the player.

Excellent (EX): Moderate wear, corners still fairly sharp. Card borders might be off-center. No creases, scratches, gum or wax stains on front or back. Surface may show some lack of luster. Card is valued at 40% of mint.

Very Good (VG): Corners rounded or showing minor wear or light creases. Loss of surface luster. All printing must be perfect. No gum or wax stains, no major creases, no writing or markings on the card. Card is valued at 30% to 40% of mint.

Good (G): A well-worn card with rounded corners and a major crease. Could have a small tear, pencil, tape or glue marks on the back. Printing must be intact, but overall, the card shows excessive wear. Card is valued at 20% to 30% of mint.

Fair (F): Card shows major damage such as creases that break the cardboard or pin holes along the border. Shows tape and glue marks. May have a tear or missing a bit of paper. Could have writing or other markings on the back. Card has very little value, less than 10% of mint.

Poor (P): Card fronts have been defaced with pen and ink marks. Corners may be torn off or paper may be missing or ripped-off. Card may have pin holes, glue and tape marks and major cracks through the cardboard. Cards have little or no value, less than10% of the good (G) value.

Mickey Mantle Remembers

Mickey Mantle is a baseball legend and clearly the most popular figure in the history of the hobby. His rookie baseball card appears in the 1951 Bowman set and his 1952 Topps card is the most valuable card of the modern era.

In this exclusive interview for print, the former Yankee great talks about the 1961 Yankees and his relationship with former teammate, the late Roger Maris.

Q. You've often compared the 1961 Yankees to the 1927 Yankees, a team some call the greatest of all-time. How good were the '61 Yanks?

A. The best team I ever saw in my life, and I really believe this, was the 1961 Yankees. Everybody remembers how great our hitting was. We hit 240 home runs, which is a record that still stands. But we had great pitching too. Whitey Ford won 25 games and lost only four. We had Louis Arroyo in the bullpen and Bill Stafford, Ralph Terry and Art Ditmar. Everybody had a great year at the same time. Our infield was Cletus Boyer at third, Tony Kubek at shortstop, Bobby Richardson at second and Moose Skowron at first. Moose hit 27 home runs that year. Our catchers, Yogi Berra, John Blanchard and Elston Howard hit over 60 between them. And then, of course, Roger Maris and I had phenomenal years. It was just a great team. I never got to see the 1927 Yankees. Everybody says it was the greatest team ever. But it would have been a good series if we had gotten to play them.

Q. In 1961 you battled Roger Maris all season long for the home run record. What was it like playing with Roger?

A. In 1961, when Roger hit the 61 home runs there was a lot written that we didn't like each other, that we argued a lot, or fought a lot, or something. That's the farthest thing from the truth. In fact, we lived together in New York. Roger was one of my closest friends, and we used to just joke about all of the headlines that said we were fighting and arguing and mad at each other.

Q. At what point in the 1961 season did you feel that either you or Roger had a shot at breaking Babe Ruth's home run record?

A. I remember I took off like a ball of fire that year. I really did kind of carry the club for a while. Roger didn't hit a home run for quite a few games. I must have been 10 ahead of him at one time. Anyway, all of a sudden he got on fire and then the home run race really took off. Once it got far enough into the season, it looked like both Roger and I had a chance of breaking Babe Ruth's record. They called us the "M & M Boys" that year. Almost every paper the next day after a game would have the M & M Boys in the headline. I don't care if Kubek or Richardson or Boyer or Moose or Elston or Yogi or anyone had hit a home run that won the game, it would still say what the M & M Boys did in the headline. But the whole team was behind us. They made it a lot easier, especially for Roger after I fell out of the race. I mean, they helped him. The whole team did.

Q. You may have had a shot at the record yourself if it weren't for an untimely illness?

A. You know, I didn't get to finish the season that year. I had a really bad cold. We were in Boston and one of the announcers told me on the way back to New York, "You know Mick, those antibiotics you're taking aren't doing you any good." He said, "I know a doctor that you might be able to go to that can give you a shot that can get rid of that cold for you." So I said, "Well, I'll try anything because I want to stay in the race." I was only two or three home runs behind Roger at the time. Anyway, I went to this doctor and I got a shot in the hip and it turned bad. I got up the next morning and had a 104 degree temperature. I had to go to the hospital and have it lanced. So I spent the last week and a half of the season watching from my hospital bed.

Q. How were you guys able to cope with the pressure that year?

A. It wasn't bad really until the final month or six weeks. After I went down that made the pressure twice as bad on Roger, because there was only one guy that the reporters could come to. For Roger to have gone ahead and broken the record, I think was just unbelievable. It was the greatest thing I've ever seen in sports. I was so proud of him. And the way he acted. He never ran around the bases jumping up and down, or hit a home run and stood at home plate and watched it go out like they do nowadays. He was a real class act. When he hit his 61st home run he came into the dugout and the fans were all applauding. They wanted him to come back out. He wouldn't come out, so the players had to push him back out. They forced him to come out and take a bow. That's the kind of guy he was. He was great and I really liked him.

Q. Are you surprised Roger isn't in the Hall of Fame?

A. When you think about Roger, the first thing you think about is the home runs. I think it's the single hardest thing to do in sports. And to hit 61 of them in a season is really hard. There have been a lot of guys who have tried since then and nobody's even come close. But Roger was one of the greatest players I've ever seen. I mean, he was as good a fielder as I have ever seen. He had a great arm. He never made a mistake like throwing the ball too high or letting a guy take an extra base. He was a great baserunner. I never saw him make a mistake on the bases. He was always in the game. He was also a good team man. All the guys really liked him. I don't know why he hasn't been selected for the Hall of Fame. To me he's as good as there ever was. I have four boys of my own and if I could pick somebody for those boys to grow up and be like, it would be Roger. Out of all the trophies that I have, I think the one that I treasure more than anything else is a ball that Roger gave me. Its got his picture on it and he wrote on it, "To Mickey, the greatest of them all. Best always, Roger Maris."

Excerpted from "Mickey Mantle. The American Dream Comes To Life." The Mick tells his own story on video. 60 minutes. Early Entertainment, San Francisco, Ca.

1948 Bowman

This 48-card black and white set was the first major set issued after World War II. Cards measured 2-1/16"by 2-1/2". A dozen cards in the set were short-printed and are considered scarce (7 ,8, 13, 16, 20, 22, 24, 26, 28, 29,30,34).

	NR/MT	EX
Complete Set (48)	3,800.00	1900.00
Commons (1-36)	20.00	8.50
Commons (37-48)	28.00	12.50

		NR/MT	EX
1	Bob Elliott	110.00	25.00
2	Ewell Blackwell	45.00	20.00
3	Ralph Kiner (R)	165.00	80.00
4	Johnny Mize	100.00	45.00
5	Bob Feller	240.00	110.00
6	Yogi Berra (R)	600.00	275.00
7	Pete Reiser	65.00	30.00
8	Phil Rizzuto (R)	275.00	125.00
9	Walker Cooper	20.00	8.50
10	Buddy Rosar	20.00	8.50
11	Johnny Lindell	20.00	8.50
12	Johnny Sain	50.00	22.50
13	Willard Marshall	35.00	15.00
14	Allie Reynolds (R)	50.00	22.50
15	Eddie Joost	20.00	8.50
16	Jack Lohrke	35.00	15.00
17	Enos Slaughter	125.00	55.00
18	Warren Spahn (R)	325.00	150.00
19	Tommy Henrich	35.00	15.00
20	Buddy Kerr	35.00	15.00
21	Ferris Fain (R)	28.00	12.00
22	Floyd Bevins (Er)	45.00	20.00
23	Larry Jansen	28.00	12.00
24	Dutch Leonard	45.00	20.00
25	Barney McCosky	20.00	8.50
26	Frank Shea	35.00	15.00
27	Sid Gordon	20.00	8.50
28	Emil Verban	35.00	15.00
29	Joe Page (R)	55.00	25.00
30	Whitey Lockman (R)	45.00	20.00
31	Bill McCahan	20.00	8.50
32	Bill Rigney	28.00	12.00
33	Bill Johnson	20.00	8.50
34	Sheldon Jones	35.00	15.00
35	George Stirnweiss	25.00	10.00
36	Stan Musial (R)	975.00	450.00
37	Clint Hartung (R)	35.00	15.00
38	Red Schoendienst (R)	175.00	75.00
39	Augie Galan	28.00	12.00
40	Marty Marion (R)	90.00	40.00
41	Rex Barney (R)	35.00	15.00
42	Ray Poat	30.00	14.00
43	Bruce Edwards	30.00	14.00
44	Johnny Wyrostek	30.00	14.00
45	Hank Sauer (R)	45.00	20.00
46	Herman Wehmeier	30.00	14.00
47	Bobby Thomson (R)	90.00	40.00
48	George "Dave" Kosio	75.00	35.00

1949 Bowman

In this 240-card set Bowman tinted black and white photographs in various pastel shades to add color to the cards. Numerous variations exist and are noted in the checklist. Some names were printed on the card backs, others used script. Cards measure 2-1/16" by 2-1/2".

	NR/MT	EX
Complete Set (240)	16,750.00	8,250.00
Commons (1-36)	20.00	8.50
Commons (37-73)	22.00	9.50
Commons (74-144)	16.00	7.00
Commons (145-240)	80.00	38.00

		NR/MT	EX
1	Vernon Bickford	85.00	40.00
2	Whitey Lockman	20.00	8.50
3	Bob Porterfield	20.00	8.50
4a	Jerry Priddy (no name on front)	20.00	8.50
4b	Jerry Priddy(Name on front)	35.00	15.00

5	Hank Sauer	25.00	10.00
6	Phil Cavarretta	25.00	10.00
7	Joe Dobson	20.00	8.50
8	Murry Dickson	22.00	9.00
9	Ferris Fain	25.00	10.00
10	Ted Gray	20.00	8.50
11	Lou Boudreau	70.00	32.00
12	Cass Michaels	20.00	8.50
13	Bob Cesnes	20.00	8.50
14	Curt Simmons (R)	32.00	14.00
15	Ned Garver	20.00	8.50
16	Al Kozar	20.00	8.50
17	Earl Torgeson	20.00	8.50
18	Bobby Thomson	35.00	15.00
19	Bobby Brown (R)	50.00	22.50
20	Gene Hermanski	20.00	8.50
21	Frank Baumholtz	20.00	8.50
22	Harry Lowrey	20.00	8.50
23	Bobby Doerr	70.00	32.00
24	Stan Musial	600.00	275.00
25	Carl Scheib	20.00	8.50
26	George Kell	50.00	22.50
27	Bob Feller	175.00	75.00
28	Don Kolloway	20.00	8.50
29	Ralph Kiner	120.00	55.00
30	Andy Seminick	20.00	8.50
31	Dick Kokos	20.00	8.50
32	Eddie Yost (R)	25.00	10.00
33	Warren Spahn	190.00	90.00
34	Dave Koslo	20.00	8.50
35	Vic Raschi (R)	50.00	22.50
36	"Pee Wee" Reese	225.00	100.00
37	John Wyrostek	22.00	9.50
38	Emil Verban	22.00	9.50
39	Bill Goodman	25.00	10.00
40	George Munger	22.00	9.50
41	Lou Brissie	22.00	9.50
42	Walter Evers	22.00	9.50
43	Dale Mitchell	25.00	10.00
44	Dave Philley	22.00	9.50
45	Wally Westlake	22.00	9.50
46	Robin Roberts (R)	290.00	135.00
47	Johnny Sain	35.00	15.00
48	Willard Marshall	22.00	9.50
49	Frank Shea	22.00	9.50
50	Jackie Robinson	850.00	400.00
51	Herman Wehmeier	22.00	9.50
52	Johnny Schmitz	22.00	9.50
53	Jack Kramer	22.00	9.50
54	Marty Marion	30.00	12.50
55	Eddie Joost	22.00	9.50
56	Pat Mullin	22.00	9.50
57	Gene Bearden	22.00	9.50
58	Bob Elliott	22.00	9.50
59	Jack Lohrke	22.00	9.50
60	Yogi Berra	325.00	150.00
61	Rex Barney	22.00	9.50
62	Grady Hatton	22.00	9.50
63	Andy Pafko	25.00	10.00
64	Dom DiMaggio	30.00	12.50
65	Enos Slaughter	100.00	45.00
66	Elmer Valo	25.00	10.00
67	Alvin Dark	35.00	15.00
68	Sheldon Jones	22.00	9.50
69	Tommy Henrich	35.00	15.00
70	Carl Furillo (R)	75.00	35.00
71	Vern Stephens	25.00	10.00
72	Tommy Holmes	25.00	10.00
73	Billy Cox (R)	35.00	15.00
74	Tom McBride	16.00	7.00
75	Eddie Mayo	16.00	7.00
76	Bill Nicholson	25.00	10.00
77	Ernie Bonham	16.00	7.00
78a	Sam Zoldak (No name on front)	16.00	7.00
78b	Sam Zoldak (Name on front)	38.00	16.50
79	Ron Northey	16.00	7.00
80	Bill McCahan	16.00	7.00
81	Virgil Stallcup	16.00	7.00
82	Joe Page	28.00	12.00
83a	Bob Scheffing (No name on front)	16.00	7.00
83b	Bob Scheffing (Name on front)	38.00	16.50
84	Roy Campanella (R)	800.00	375.00
85a	Johnny Mize (No name on front)	100.00	45.00
85b	Johnny Mize (Name on front)	175.00	100.00
86	Johnny Pesky	28.00	12.00
87	Randy Gumpert	16.00	7.00
88a	Bill Salkeld (No name on front)	16.00	7.00
88b	Bill Salkeld (Name on front)	38.00	16.50
89	Mizell Platt	16.00	7.00
90	Gil Coan	16.00	7.00
91	Dick Wakefield	16.00	7.00
92	Willie Jones	16.00	7.00
93	Ed Stevens	16.00	7.00
94	Mickey Vernon (R)	35.00	15.00
95	Howie Pollett (R)	20.00	8.50
96	Taft Wright	16.00	7.00
97	Danny Litwhiler	16.00	7.00
98a	Phil Rizzuto (No name on front)	125.00	60.00
98b	Phil Rizzuto (Name on front)	200.00	90.00
99	Frank Gustine	16.00	7.00
100	Gil Hodges (R)	260.00	125.00
101	Sid Gordon	16.00	7.00
102	Stan Spence	16.00	7.00
103	Joe Tipton	16.00	7.00
104	Ed Stanky (R)	30.00	12.50

105	Bill Kennedy	16.00	7.00
106	Jake Early	16.00	7.00
107	Eddie Lake	16.00	7.00
108	Ken Heintzelman	16.00	7.00
109a	Ed Fitzgerald (Script)	16.00	7.00
109b	Ed Fitzgerald (Print)	35.00	15.00
110	Early Wynn (R)	140.00	65.00
111	Red Schoendienst	90.00	40.00
112	Sam Chapman	16.00	7.00
113	Ray Lamanno	16.00	7.00
114	Allie Reynolds	35.00	15.00
115	Dutch Leonard	16.00	7.00
116	Joe Hatten	16.00	7.00
117	Walker Cooper	16.00	7.00
118	Sam Mele	16.00	7.00
119	Floyd Baker	16.00	7.00
120	Cliff Fannin	16.00	7.00
121	Mark Christman	16.00	7.00
122	George Vico	16.00	7.00
123	Johnny Blatnick	16.00	7.00
124a	Danny Murtaugh (Script)	20.00	8.50
124b	Danny Murtaugh (Print)	45.00	20.00
125	Ken Keltner	16.00	7.00
126a	Al Brazie (Script)	16.00	7.00
126b	Al Brazie (Print)	35.00	15.00
127a	Henry Majeski (Script)	16.00	7.00
127b	Henry Majeski (Print)	35.00	15.00
128	Johnny VanderMeer	30.00	12.50
129	Bill Johnson	16.00	7.00
130	Harry Walker	16.00	7.00
131	Paul Lehner	16.00	7.00
132a	Al Evans (Script)	16.00	7.00
132b	Al Evans (Print)	35.00	15.00
133	Aaron Robinson	16.00	7.00
134	Hank Borowy	16.00	7.00
135	Stan Rojek	16.00	7.00
136	Henry Edwards	16.00	7.00
137	Ted Wilks	16.00	7.00
138	Warren Rosar	16.00	7.00
139	Hank Arft	16.00	7.00
140	Rae Scarborough	16.00	7.00
141	Ulysses Lupien	16.00	7.00
142	Eddie Waitkus	16.00	7.00
143a	Bob Dillinger (Script)	16.00	7.00
143b	Bob Dillinger (Print)	35.00	15.00
144	Milton Haefner	16.00	7.00
145	Sylvester Donnelly	85.00	40.00
146	Myron McCormick	80.00	38.00
147	Elmer Singleton	80.00	38.00
148	Bob Swift	85.00	40.00
149	Roy Partee	85.00	40.00
150	Alfred Clark	85.00	40.00
151	Maurice Harris	80.00	38.00
152	Clarence Maddern	85.00	40.00
153	Phil Masi	80.00	38.00
154	Clint Hartung	90.00	42.00
155	Fermin Guerra	80.00	38.00
156	Al Zarilla	85.00	40.00
157	Walt Masterson	85.00	40.00
158	Harry Brecheen	100.00	45.00
159	Glen Moulder	80.00	38.00
160	Jim Blackburn	80.00	38.00
161	John Thompson	80.00	38.00
162	Preacher Roe (R)	160.00	75.00
163	Clyde Mccullough	85.00	40.00
164	Vic Wertz (R)	125.00	60.00
165	George Stirnweiss	90.00	42.00
166	Mike Tresh	85.00	45.00
167	Boris Martin	80.00	38.00
168	Doyle Lade	80.00	38.00
169	Jeff Heath	80.00	38.00
170	Bill Rigney	100.00	45.00
171	Dick Fowler	85.00	40.00
172	Eddie Pelagrini	85.00	40.00
173	Eddie Stewart	80.00	38.00
174	Terry Moore (R)	125.00	60.00
175	Luke Appling	160.00	75.00
176	Ken Raffensberger	80.00	38.00
177	Stan Lopata	85.00	40.00
178	Tommy Brown	80.00	38.00
179	Hugh Casey	90.00	42.00
180	Connie Berry	80.00	38.00
181	Gus Niarhos	80.00	38.00
182	Hal Peck	80.00	38.00
183	Lou Stringer	80.00	38.00
184	Bob Chipman	80.00	38.00
185	Pete Reiser	100.00	45.00
186	John Kerr	80.00	38.00
187	Phil Marchildon	80.00	38.00
188	Karl Drews	80.00	38.00
189	Earl Wooten	80.00	38.00
190	Jim Hearn	80.00	38.00
191	Joe Haynes	80.00	38.00
192	Harry Gumbert	80.00	38.00
193	Ken Trinkle	80.00	38.00
194	Ralph Branca (R)	125.00	60.00
195	Eddie Bockman	80.00	38.00
196	Fred Hutchinson	90.00	42.00
197	Johnny Lindell	80.00	38.00
198	Steve Gromek	80.00	38.00
199	Cecil Hughson	80.00	38.00
200	Jess Dobernic	80.00	38.00
201	Sibby Sisti	80.00	38.00
202	Larry Jansen	100.00	45.00
203	Barney McCosky	80.00	38.00
204	Bob Savage	80.00	38.00
205	Dick Sisler	90.00	42.00
206	Bruce Edwards	80.00	38.00
207	Johnny Hopp	85.00	40.00
208	Dizzy Trout	100.00	45.00

		NR/MT	EX
209	Charlie Keller	100.00	45.00
210	Joe Gordon	100.00	45.00
211	Dave Ferris	80.00	38.00
212	Ralph Hamner	80.00	38.00
213	Charles Barrett	80.00	38.00
214	Richie Ashburn (R)	550.00	250.00
215	Kirby Higbe	80.00	38.00
216	Lynwood Rowe	90.00	42.00
217	Marino Pieretti	80.00	38.00
218	Dick Kryhoski	80.00	38.00
219	Virgil Trucks	100.00	45.00
220	Johnny McCarthy	80.00	38.00
221	Bob Muncrief	80.00	38.00
222	Alex Kellner	80.00	38.00
223	Bob Hofman	80.00	38.00
224	Satchel Paige (R)	1,350.00	650.00
225	Jerry Coleman (R)	110.00	50.00
226	Duke Snider (R)	1,250.00	600.00
227	Fritz Ostermueller	80.00	38.00
228	Jackie Mayo	80.00	38.00
229	Ed Lopat (R)	150.00	70.00
230	Augie Galan	80.00	38.00
231	Earl Johnson	80.00	38.00
232	George McQuinn	80.00	38.00
233	Larry Doby	190.00	90.00
234	Rip Sewell	85.00	40.00
235	Jim Russell	80.00	38.00
236	Fred Sanford	80.00	38.00
237	Monte Kennedy	80.00	38.00
238	Bob Lemon (R)	275.00	125.00
239	Frank McCormick	85.00	40.00
240	Norman Young (Wrong Photo)	175.00	75.00

1950 Bowman

The 252-cards in this set feature beautiful color portraits made from each player's black and white photograph. Cards measure 2-1/16"by 2-1/2". Card backs are horizontal. Cards 1-72 are considered scarce.

		NR/MT	EX
Complete Set (252)		10,250.00	4,800.00
Commons (1-72)		60.00	28.00
Commons (73-252)		18.00	8.00
1	Mel Parnell (R)	225.00	75.00
2	Vern Stephens	60.00	28.00
3	Dom DiMaggio	70.00	32.00
4	Gus Zernial (R)	70.00	32.00
5	Bob Kuzava	60.00	28.00
6	Bob Feller	225.00	100.00
7	Jim Hegan	60.00	28.00
8	George Kell	100.00	45.00
9	Vic Wertz	65.00	30.00
10	Tommy Henrich	70.00	32.00
11	Phil Rizzuto	175.00	85.00
12	Joe Page	70.00	32.00
13	Ferris Fain	65.00	30.00
14	Alex Kellner	60.00	28.00
15	Al Kozar	60.00	28.00
16	Roy Sievers (R)	70.00	32.00
17	Sid Hudson	60.00	28.00
18	Eddie Robinson	60.00	28.00
19	Warren Spahn	225.00	100.00
20	Bob Elliott	60.00	28.00
21	Pee Wee Reese	225.00	100.00
22	Jackie Robinson	700.00	325.00
23	Don Newcombe (R)	175.00	85.00
24	Johnny Schmitz	60.00	28.00
25	Hank Sauer	65.00	30.00
26	Grady Hatton	60.00	28.00
27	Herman Wehmeier	60.00	28.00
28	Bobby Thomson	75.00	35.00
29	Ed Stanky	65.00	30.00
30	Eddie Waitkus	60.00	28.00
31	Del Ennis	65.00	30.00
32	Robin Roberts	160.00	75.00
33	Ralph Kiner	125.00	60.00
34	Murry Dickson	60.00	28.00
35	Enos Slaughter	125.00	60.00
36	Eddie Kazak	60.00	28.00
37	Luke Appling	80.00	38.00
38	Bill Wright	60.00	28.00
39	Larry Doby	75.00	35.00
40	Bob Lemon	100.00	45.00
41	Walter Evers	60.00	28.00
42	Art Houtterman	60.00	28.00
43	Bobby Doerr	95.00	42.00
44	Joe Dobson	60.00	28.00
45	Al Zarilla	60.00	28.00
46	Yogi Berra	425.00	200.00
47	Jerry Coleman	70.00	32.00
48	Leland Brissie	60.00	28.00
49	Elmer Valo	65.00	30.00
50	Dick Kokos	60.00	28.00
51	Ned Garver	60.00	28.00
52	Sam Mele	60.00	28.00

No.	Name	Price 1	Price 2
53	Clyde Vollmer	60.00	28.00
54	Gil Coan	60.00	28.00
55	John Kerr	60.00	28.00
56	Del Crandall (R)	75.00	35.00
57	Vernon Bickford	60.00	28.00
58	Carl Furillo	75.00	35.00
59	Ralph Branca	65.00	30.00
60	Andy Pafko	65.00	30.00
61	Bob Rush	60.00	28.00
62	Ted Kluszewski	100.00	45.00
63	Ewell Blackwell	65.00	30.00
64	Alvin Dark	70.00	32.00
65	Dave Koslo	60.00	28.00
66	Larry Jansen	65.00	30.00
67	Willie Jones	60.00	28.00
68	Curt Simmons	65.00	30.00
69	Wally Westlake	60.00	28.00
70	Bob Chesnes	60.00	28.00
71	Al Schoendienst	100.00	45.00
72	Howie Pollet	60.00	28.00
73	Willard Mashall	18.00	8.00
74	Johnny Antonelli(R)	30.00	12.50
75	Roy Campanella	325.00	150.00
76	Rex Barney	20.00	8.50
77	Duke Snider	325.00	150.00
78	Mickey Owen	25.00	10.00
79	Johnny VanderMeer	30.00	12.50
80	Howard Fox	18.00	8.00
81	Ron Northey	20.00	8.50
82	Whitey Lockman	20.00	8.50
83	Sheldon Jones	18.00	8.00
84	Richie Ashburn	100.00	45.00
85	Ken Heintzelman	18.00	8.00
86	Stan Rojek	18.00	8.00
87	Bill Werle	18.00	8.00
88	Marty Marion	25.00	10.00
89	George Munger	18.00	8.00
90	Harry Brecheen	18.00	8.00
91	Cass Michaels	18.00	8.00
92	Hank Majeski	18.00	8.00
93	Gene Bearden	18.00	8.00
94	Lou Boudreau	50.00	22.50
95	Aaron Robinson	18.00	8.00
96	Virgil Trucks	20.00	8.50
97	Maurice McDermott	18.00	8.00
98	Ted Williams	850.00	400.00
99	Billy Goodman	18.00	8.00
100	Vic Raschi	30.00	12.50
101	Bobby Brown	30.00	12.50
102	Billy Johnson	18.00	8.00
103	Eddie Joost	18.00	8.00
104	Sam Chapman	18.00	8.00
105	Bob Dillinger	18.00	8.00
106	Cliff Fannin	18.00	8.00
107	Sam Dente	18.00	8.00
108	Rae Scarborough	18.00	8.00
109	Sid Gordon	18.00	8.00
110	Tommy Holmes	18.00	8.00
111	Walker Cooper	20.00	8.50
112	Gil Hodges	125.00	60.00
113	Gene Hermanski	18.00	8.00
114	Wayne Terwilliger	20.00	8.50
115	Roy Smalley	18.00	8.00
116	Virgil Stallcup	18.00	8.00
117	Bill Rigney	20.00	8.50
118	Clint Hartung	18.00	8.00
119	Dick Sisler	20.00	8.50
120	John Thompson	18.00	8.00
121	Andy Seminick	18.00	8.00
122	Johnny Hopp	18.00	8.00
123	Dino Restelli	18.00	8.00
124	Clyde McCullough	18.00	8.00
125	Del Rice	20.00	8.50
126	Al Brazle	18.00	8.00
127	Dave Philley	18.00	8.00
128	Phil Masi	18.00	8.00
129	Joe Gordon	20.00	8.50
130	Dale Mitchell	20.00	8.50
131	Steve Gromek	18.00	8.00
132	Mickey Vernon	25.00	10.00
133	Don Kolloway	18.00	8.00
134	Paul Trout	18.00	8.00
135	Pat Mullin	18.00	8.00
136	Warren Rosar	18.00	8.00
137	Johnny Pesky	20.00	8.50
138	Allie Reynolds	30.00	12.50
139	Johnny Mize	80.00	38.00
140	Pete Suder	18.00	8.00
141	Joe Coleman	20.00	8.50
142	Sherman Lollar (R)	28.00	12.00
143	Eddie Stewart	18.00	8.00
144	Al Evans	18.00	8.00
145	Jack Graham	18.00	8.00
146	Floyd Baker	18.00	8.00
147	Mike Garcia (R)	25.00	10.00
148	Early Wynn	75.00	35.00
149	Bob Swift	18.00	8.00
150	George Vico	18.00	8.00
151	Fred Hutchinson	20.00	8.50
152	Ellis Kinder	18.00	8.00
153	Walt Masterson	18.00	8.00
154	Gus Niarhos	18.00	8.00
155	Frank Shea	18.00	8.00
156	Fred Sanford	18.00	8.00
157	Mike Guerra	18.00	8.00
158	Paul Lehner	18.00	8.00
159	Joe Tipton	18.00	8.00
160	Mickey Harris	18.00	8.00
161	Sherry Robertson	18.00	8.00
162	Eddie Yost	20.00	8.50
163	Earl Torgeson	20.00	8.50
164	Sibby Sisti	18.00	8.00
165	Bruce Edwards	18.00	8.00
166	Joe Hatten	18.00	8.00
167	Preacher Roe	35.00	15.00
168	Bob Scheffing	18.00	8.00

169	Hank Edwards	18.00	8.00
170	Dutch Leonard	20.00	8.50
171	Harry Gumbert	18.00	8.00
172	Harry Lowrey	20.00	8.50
173	Lloyd Merriman	18.00	8.00
174	Henry Thompson(R)	25.00	10.00
175	Monte Kennedy	18.00	8.00
176	Sylvester Donnelly	18.00	8.00
177	Hank Borowy	18.00	8.00
178	Ed Fitzgerald	18.00	8.00
179	Charles Diering	18.00	8.00
180	Harry Walker	20.00	8.50
181	Marino Pieretti	18.00	8.00
182	Sam Zoldak	18.00	8.00
183	Mickey Haefner	18.00	8.00
184	Randy Gumpert	18.00	8.00
185	Howie Judson	18.00	8.00
186	Ken Keltner	20.00	8.50
187	Lou Stringer	18.00	8.00
188	Earl Johnson	18.00	8.00
189	Owen Friend	18.00	8.00
190	Ken Wood	18.00	8.00
191	Dick Starr	18.00	8.00
192	Bob Chipman	18.00	8.00
193	Pete Reiser	25.00	10.00
194	Billy Cox	25.00	10.00
195	Phil Cavaretta (Er)	25.00	10.00
196	Doyle Lade	18.00	8.00
197	Johnny Wyrostek	18.00	8.00
198	Danny Litwhiler	18.00	8.00
199	Jack Kramer	18.00	8.00
200	Kirby Higbe	18.00	8.00
201	Pete Castiglione	18.00	8.00
202	Cliff Chambers	18.00	8.00
203	Danny Murtaugh	20.00	8.50
204	Granny Hamner(R)	25.00	10.00
205	Mike Goliat	18.00	8.00
206	Stan Lopata	20.00	8.50
207	Max Lanier	18.00	8.00
208	Jim Hearn	18.00	8.00
209	Johnny Lindell	18.00	8.00
210	Ted Gray	18.00	8.00
211	Charlie Keller	20.00	8.50
212	Gerry Priddy	18.00	8.00
213	Carl Scheib	18.00	8.00
214	Dick Fowler	18.00	8.00
215	Ed Lopat	35.00	15.00
216	Bob Porterfield	18.00	8.00
217	Casey Stengel	150.00	70.00
218	Cliff Mapes	18.00	8.00
219	Hank Bauer (R)	80.00	38.00
220	Leo Durocher	75.00	35.00
221	Don Mueller (R)	30.00	12.50
222	Bobby Morgan	18.00	8.00
223	Jimmy Russell	18.00	8.00
224	Jack Banta	18.00	8.00
225	Eddie Sawyer	20.00	8.50
226	Jim Konstanty (R)	35.00	15.00

227	Bob Miller	18.00	8.00
228	Bill Nicholson	18.00	8.00
229	Frank Frisch	50.00	22.50
230	Bill Serena	18.00	8.00
231	Preston Ward	18.00	8.00
232	Al Rosen (R)	75.00	35.00
233	Allie Clark	18.00	8.00
234	Bobby Shantz (R)	35.00	15.00
235	Harold Gilbert	18.00	8.00
236	Bob Cain	18.00	8.00
237	Bill Salkeld	18.00	8.00
238	Vernal Jones	18.00	8.00
239	Bill Howerton	18.00	8.00
240	Eddie Lake	18.00	8.00
241	Neil Berry	18.00	8.00
242	Dick Kryhoski	18.00	8.00
243	Johnny Groth	18.00	8.00
244	Dale Coogan	18.00	8.00
245	Al Papal	18.00	8.00
246	Walt Dropo (R)	25.00	10.00
247	Irv Noren (R)	25.00	10.00
248	Sam Jethroe (R)	20.00	8.50
249	George Stirnweiss	20.00	8.50
250	Ray Coleman	18.00	8.00
251	John Moss	18.00	8.00
252	Billy DeMars (R)	90.00	25.00

1951 Bowman

Bowman enlarged the size of their cards to 2-1/16" by 3-1/8" and increased the size of their set to 324-cards. Card fronts depict colorful portraits drawn from actual player photos. High numbered cards (#253-324) are considered scarce. This set contains the true rookie cards of Mickey Mantle and Willie Mays.

	NR/MT	EX
Complete Set (324)	22,750.00	10,500.00
Commons (1-36)	20.00	8.50

Commons (37-252)	15.00	6.00		
Commons (253-324)	70.00	32.00		

#	Name			#	Name		
1	Whitey Ford (R)	1,350.00	650.00	55	Gene Hermanski	15.00	6.00
2	Yogi Berra	480.00	225.00	56	Ralph Branca	30.00	12.50
3	Robin Roberts	90.00	40.00	57	Alex Kellner	15.00	6.00
4	Del Ennis	25.00	10.00	58	Enos Slaughter	60.00	28.00
5	Dale Mitchell	20.00	8.50	59	Randy Gumpert	15.00	6.00
6	Don Newcombe	50.00	22.00	60	Chico Carrasquel	20.00	8.50
7	Gil Hodges	90.00	40.00	61	Jim Hearn	15.00	6.00
8	Paul Lehner	20.00	8.50	62	Lou Boudreau	50.00	22.50
9	Sam Chapman	20.00	8.50	63	Bob Dillinger	15.00	6.00
10	Al Schoendienst	75.00	35.00	64	Bill Werle	15.00	6.00
11	George Munger	20.00	8.50	65	Mickey Vernon	20.00	8.50
12	Hank Majeski	20.00	8.50	66	Bob Elliott	18.00	7.00
13	Ed Stanky	25.00	10.00	67	Roy Sievers	20.00	8.50
14	Alvin Dark	28.00	12.00	68	Dick Kokos	15.00	6.00
15	Johnny Pesky	25.00	10.00	69	Johnny Schmitz	15.00	6.00
16	Maurice McDermott	20.00	8.50	70	Ron Northey	15.00	6.00
17	Pete Castiglione	20.00	8.50	71	Jerry Priddy	15.00	6.00
18	Gil Coan	20.00	8.50	72	Lloyd Merriman	15.00	6.00
19	Sid Gordon	20.00	8.50	73	Tommy Byrne	15.00	6.00
20	Del Crandall	25.00	10.00	74	Billy Johnson	15.00	6.00
21	George Stirnweiss	22.00	9.00	75	Russ Meyer	15.00	6.00
22	Hank Sauer	25.00	10.00	76	Stan Lopata	15.00	6.00
23	Walter Evers	20.00	8.50	77	Mike Goliat	15.00	6.00
24	Ewell Blackwell	25.00	10.00	78	Early Wynn	55.00	25.00
25	Vic Raschi	30.00	12.50	79	Jim Hegan	15.00	6.00
26	Phil Rizzuto	125.00	60.00	80	Pee Wee Reese	160.00	75.00
27	Jim Konstanty	25.00	10.00	81	Carl Furillo	35.00	15.00
28	Eddie Waitkus	20.00	8.50	82	Joe Tipton	15.00	6.00
29	Allie Clark	20.00	8.50	83	Carl Scheib	15.00	6.00
30	Bob Feller	150.00	70.00	84	Barney McCosky	15.00	6.00
31	Roy Campanella	275.00	125.00	85	Eddie Kazak	15.00	6.00
32	Duke Snider	275.00	125.00	86	Harry Brecheen	15.00	6.00
33	Bob Hooper	20.00	8.50	87	Floyd Baker	15.00	6.00
34	Marty Marion	25.00	10.00	88	Eddie Robinson	15.00	6.00
35	Al Zarilla	20.00	8.50	89	Hank Thompson	15.00	6.00
36	Joe Dobson	20.00	8.50	90	Dave Koslo	15.00	6.00
37	Whitey Lockman	20.00	8.50	91	Clyde Vollmer	15.00	6.00
38	Al Evans	15.00	6.00	92	Vern Stephens	15.00	6.00
39	Ray Scarborough	15.00	6.00	93	Danny O'Connell	15.00	6.00
40	Gus Bell (R)	25.00	10.00	94	Clyde McCullough	15.00	6.00
41	Eddie Yost	18.00	7.00	95	Sherry Robertson	15.00	6.00
42	Vern Bickford	15.00	6.00	96	Sandy Consuegra	15.00	6.00
43	Billy DeMars	15.00	6.00	97	Bob Kuzava	15.00	6.00
44	Roy Smalley	15.00	6.00	98	Willard Marshall	15.00	6.00
45	Art Houtteman	15.00	6.00	99	Earl Torgeson	15.00	6.00
46	George Kell	50.00	22.50	100	Sherman Lollar	18.00	7.00
47	Grady Hatton	15.00	6.00	101	Owen Friend	15.00	6.00
48	Ken Raffensberger	15.00	6.00	102	Dutch Leonard	18.00	7.00
49	Jerry Colemen	25.00	10.00	103	Andy Pafko	18.00	7.00
50	Johnny Mize	65.00	30.00	104	Virgil Trucks	18.00	7.00
51	Andy Seminick	15.00	6.00	105	Don Kolloway	15.00	6.00
52	Dick Sisler	18.00	7.00	106	Pat Mullin	15.00	6.00
53	Bob Lemon	55.00	25.00	107	Johnny Wyrostek	15.00	6.00
54	Ray Boone (R)	28.00	12.00	108	Virgil Stallcup	15.00	6.00
				109	Allie Reynolds	35.00	15.00
				110	Bobby Brown	28.00	12.00
				111	Curt Simons	20.00	8.50
				112	Willie Jones	15.00	6.00

113	Bill Nicholson	15.00	6.00	171	Buddy Kerr	15.00	6.00
114	Sam Zoldak	15.00	6.00	172	Ned Garver	15.00	6.00
115	Steve Gromek	15.00	6.00	173	Hank Arft	15.00	6.00
116	Bruce Edwards	15.00	6.00	174	Mickey Owen	18.00	7.00
117	Eddie Miksis	15.00	6.00	175	Wayne Terwilliger	15.00	6.00
118	Preacher Roe	28.00	12.00	176	Vic Wertz	18.00	7.00
119	Eddie Joost	15.00	6.00	177	Charlie Keller	18.00	7.00
120	Joe Coleman	15.00	6.00	178	Ted Gray	15.00	6.00
121	Gerry Staley	15.00	6.00	179	Danny Litwhiler	15.00	6.00
122	Joe Garagiola (R)	160.00	75.00	180	Howie Fox	15.00	6.00
123	Howie Judson	15.00	6.00	181	Casey Stengel	110.00	48.00
124	Gus Niarhos	15.00	6.00	182	Tom Ferrick	15.00	6.00
125	Bill Rigney	18.00	7.00	183	Hank Bauer	30.00	12.50
126	Bobby Thomson	35.00	15.00	184	Eddie Sawyer	15.00	6.00
127	Sal Maglie (R)	50.00	22.50	185	Jimmy Bloodworth	15.00	6.00
128	Ellis Kinder	15.00	6.00	186	Richie Ashburn	65.00	30.00
129	Matt Batts	15.00	6.00	187	Al Rosen	28.00	12.00
130	Tom Saffell	15.00	6.00	188	Roberto Avila (R)	22.00	9.00
131	Cliff Chambers	15.00	6.00	189	Erv Palica	15.00	6.00
132	Cass Michaels	15.00	6.00	190	Joe Hatten	15.00	6.00
133	Sam Dente	15.00	6.00	191	Billy Hitchcock	15.00	6.00
134	Warren Spahn	135.00	65.00	192	Hank Wyse	15.00	6.00
135	Walker Cooper	15.00	6.00	193	Ted Wilks	15.00	6.00
136	Ray Coleman	15.00	6.00	194	Harry Lowrey	15.00	6.00
137	Dick Starr	15.00	6.00	195	Paul Richards	18.00	7.00
138	Phil Cavarretta	20.00	8.50	196	Bill Pierce (R)	28.00	12.00
139	Doyle Lade	15.00	6.00	197	Bob Cain	15.00	6.00
140	Eddie Lake	15.00	6.00	198	Monte Irvin (R)	125.00	60.00
141	Fred Hutchinson	18.00	7.00	199	Sheldon Jones	15.00	6.00
142	Aaron Robinson	15.00	6.00	200	Jack Kramer	15.00	6.00
143	Ted Kluszewski	38.00	18.00	201	Steve O'Neill	15.00	6.00
144	Herman Wehmeier	15.00	6.00	202	Mike Guerra	15.00	6.00
145	Fred Sanford	15.00	6.00	203	Vernon Law (R)	28.00	12.00
146	Johnny Hopp	15.00	6.00	204	Vic Lombardi	15.00	6.00
147	Ken Heintzelman	15.00	6.00	205	Mickey Brasso	15.00	6.00
148	Granny Hamner	15.00	6.00	206	Conrado Marrero	15.00	6.00
149	Emory Church	15.00	6.00	207	Billy Southworth	15.00	6.00
150	Mike Garcia	18.00	7.00	208	Blix Donnelly	15.00	6.00
151	Larry Doby	38.00	18.00	209	Ken Wood	15.00	6.00
152	Cal Abrams	15.00	6.00	210	Les Moss	15.00	6.00
153	Rex Barney	15.00	6.00	211	Hal Jeffcoat	15.00	6.00
154	Pete Suder	15.00	6.00	212	Bob Rush	15.00	6.00
155	Lou Brissie	15.00	6.00	213	Neil Berry	15.00	6.00
156	Del Rice	18.00	7.00	214	Bob Swift	15.00	6.00
157	Al Brazle	15.00	6.00	215	Kent Peterson	15.00	6.00
158	Chuck Diering	15.00	6.00	216	Connie Ryan	15.00	6.00
159	Eddie Stewart	15.00	6.00	217	Joe Page	20.00	8.50
160	Phil Masi	15.00	6.00	218	Ed Lopat	30.00	12.50
161	Wes Westrum (R)	20.00	8.50	219	Gene Woodling (R)	35.00	15.00
162	Larry Jansen	18.00	7.00	220	Bob Miller	15.00	6.00
163	Monte Kennedy	15.00	6.00	221	Dick Whitman	15.00	6.00
164	Bill Wight	15.00	6.00	222	Thurman Tucker	15.00	6.00
165	Ted Williams	700.00	325.00	223	Johnny VanderMeer	28.00	12.00
166	Stan Rojek	15.00	6.00	224	Billy Cox	18.00	7.00
167	Murry Dickson	15.00	6.00	225	Dan Bankhead	15.00	6.00
168	Sam Mele	15.00	6.00	226	Jimmy Dykes	18.00	7.00
169	Sid Hudson	15.00	6.00	227	Bobby Schantz (Er)	20.00	8.50
170	Sibby Sisti	15.00	6.00	228	Cloyd Boyer	18.00	7.00

229	Bill Howerton	15.00	6.00
230	Max Lanier	15.00	6.00
231	Luis Aloma	15.00	6.00
232	Nelson Fox (R)	160.00	75.00
233	Leo Durocher	50.00	22.50
234	Clint Hartung	15.00	6.00
235	Jack Lohrke	15.00	6.00
236	Warren Rosar	15.00	6.00
237	Billy Goodman	15.00	6.00
238	Pete Reiser	20.00	8.50
239	Bill MacDonald	15.00	6.00
240	Joe Haynes	15.00	6.00
241	Irv Noren	18.00	7.00
242	Sam Jethroe	15.00	6.00
243	John Antonelli	18.00	7.00
244	Cliff Fannin	15.00	6.00
245	John Berardino (R)	22.00	9.00
246	Bill Serena	15.00	6.00
247	Bob Ramazotti	15.00	6.00
248	Johnny Klippstein	15.00	6.00
249	Johnny Groth	15.00	6.00
250	Hank Borowy	15.00	6.00
251	Willard Ramsdell	15.00	6.00
252	Dixie Howell	15.00	6.00
253	Mickey Mantle (R)	10,000.00	5,200.00
254	Jackie Jensen (R)	150.00	70.00
255	Milo Candini	70.00	30.00
256	Ken Silvestri	70.00	30.00
257	Birdie Tebbetts (R)	75.00	35.00
258	Luke Easter (R)	75.00	35.00
259	Charlie Dressen	75.00	35.00
260	Carl Erskine (R)	125.00	60.00
261	Wally Moses	70.00	30.00
262	Gus Zernial	70.00	30.00
263	Howie Pollett (Er)	70.00	30.00
264	Don Richmond	70.00	30.00
265	Steve Bilko	70.00	30.00
266	Harry Dorish	70.00	30.00
267	Ken Holcombe	70.00	30.00
268	Don Mueller	70.00	30.00
269	Ray Noble	70.00	30.00
270	Willard Nixon	70.00	30.00
271	Tommy Wright	70.00	30.00
272	Billy Meyer	70.00	30.00
273	Danny Murtaugh	70.00	30.00
274	George Metkovich	70.00	30.00
275	Bucky Harris	75.00	35.00
276	Frank Quinn	70.00	30.00
277	Roy Hartsfield	70.00	30.00
278	Norman Roy	70.00	30.00
279	Jim Delsing	70.00	30.00
280	Frank Overmire	70.00	30.00
281	Al Widmar	70.00	30.00
282	Frank Frisch	100.00	45.00
283	Walt Dubiel	70.00	30.00
284	Gene Bearden	70.00	30.00
285	Johnny Lipon	70.00	30.00
286	Bob Usher	70.00	30.00
287	Jim Blackburn	70.00	30.00
288	Bobby Adams	70.00	30.00
289	Cliff Mapes	70.00	30.00
290	Bill Dickey	190.00	90.00
291	Tommy Henrich	80.00	38.00
292	Eddie Pellagrini	70.00	30.00
293	Ken Johnson	70.00	30.00
294	Jocko Thompson	70.00	30.00
295	Al Lopez	125.00	60.00
296	Bob Kennedy	70.00	30.00
297	Dave Philley	70.00	30.00
298	Joe Astroth	70.00	30.00
299	Clyde King	70.00	30.00
300	Hal Rice	70.00	30.00
301	Tommy Galviano	70.00	30.00
302	Jim Busby	70.00	30.00
303	Marv Rotblatt	70.00	30.00
304	Allen Gettel	70.00	30.00
305	Willie Mays (R)	3,750.00	2,000.00
306	Jim Piersall (R)	125.00	60.00
307	Walt Masterson	70.00	30.00
308	Ted Beard	70.00	30.00
309	Mel Queen	70.00	30.00
310	Erv Dusak	70.00	30.00
311	Mickey Harris	70.00	30.00
312	Gene Mauch (R)	80.00	38.00
313	Ray Mueller	70.00	30.00
314	Johnny Sain	75.00	35.00
315	Zack Taylor	70.00	30.00
316	Duane Pillette	70.00	30.00
317	Smoky Burgess (R)	80.00	38.00
318	Warren Hacker	70.00	30.00
319	Red Rolfe	75.00	35.00
320	Hal White	70.00	30.00
321	Earl Johnson	70.00	30.00
322	Luke Sewell	75.00	35.00
323	Joe Adcock (R)	110.00	48.00
324	Johnny Pramesa	125.00	60.00

1952 Bowman

Bowman cut back to 252-cards and employed a fascimile autograph on the card fronts in 1952. The card size remained the same as the previous year, 2-1/16" by 3-1/8", and the pictures were colorful art renditions of black and white photographs.

	NR/MT	EX
Complete Set (252)	9,250.00	4,500.00
Commons (1-36)	20.00	8.50
Commons (37-216)	18.00	7.00
Commons (217-252)	32.00	15.00

		NR/MT	EX
1	Yogi Berra	625.00	300.00
2	Bobby Thomson	35.00	15.00
3	Fred Hutchinson	22.00	9.00
4	Robin Roberts	75.00	35.00
5	Minnie Minoso (R)	110.00	48.00
6	Virgil Stallcup	20.00	8.50
7	Mike Garcia	22.00	9.00
8	Pee Wee Reese	110.00	48.00
9	Vern Stephens	20.00	8.50
10	Bob Hooper	20.00	8.50
11	Ralph Kiner	75.00	35.00
12	Max Surkont	20.00	8.50
13	Cliff Mapes	20.00	8.50
14	Cliff Chambers	20.00	8.50
15	Sam Mele	20.00	8.50
16	Omar Lown	20.00	8.50
17	Ed Lopat	38.00	18.00
18	Don Mueller	20.00	8.50
19	Bob Cain	20.00	8.50
20	Willie Jones	20.00	8.50
21	Nelson Fox	50.00	22.50
22	Willard Ramsdell	20.00	8.50
23	Bob Lemon	60.00	28.00
24	Carl Furillo	38.00	18.00
25	Mickey McDermott	20.00	8.50
26	Eddie Joost	20.00	8.50
27	Joe Garagiola	80.00	38.00
28	Roy Hartsfield	20.00	8.50
29	Ned Garver	20.00	8.50
30	Al Schoendienst	70.00	30.00
31	Eddie Yost	20.00	8.50
32	Eddie Miksis	20.00	8.50
33	Gil McDougald (R)	75.00	35.00
34	Al Dark	25.00	10.00
35	Granny Hamner	20.00	8.50
36	Cass Michaels	20.00	8.50
37	Vic Raschi	22.00	9.00
38	Whitey Lockman	20.00	8.50
39	Vic Wertz	20.00	8.50
40	Emory Church	18.00	7.00
41	Chico Carrasquel	20.00	8.50
42	Johnny Wyrostek	18.00	7.00
43	Bob Feller	130.00	65.00
44	Roy Campanella	240.00	110.00
45	Johnny Pesky	22.00	9.00
46	Carl Scheib	18.00	7.00
47	Pete Castiglione	18.00	7.00
48	Vern Bickford	18.00	7.00
49	Jim Hearn	18.00	7.00
50	Gerry Staley	18.00	7.00
51	Gil Coan	18.00	7.00
52	Phil Rizzuto	100.00	45.00
53	Richie Ashburn	60.00	28.00
54	Billy Pierce	25.00	10.00
55	Ken Raffensberger	18.00	7.00
56	Clyde King	18.00	7.00
57	Clyde Vollmer	18.00	7.00
58	Hank Majeski	18.00	7.00
59	Murray Dickson (Er)	18.00	7.00
60	Sid Gordon	18.00	7.00
61	Tommy Byrne	18.00	7.00
62	Joe Presko	18.00	7.00
63	Irv Noren	18.00	7.00
64	Roy Smalley	18.00	7.00
65	Hank Bauer	30.00	12.50
66	Sal Maglie	25.00	15.00
67	Johnny Groth	18.00	7.00
68	Jim Busby	20.00	8.50
69	Joe Adcock	25.00	10.00
70	Carl Erskine	35.00	15.00
71	Vernon Law	25.00	10.00
72	Earl Torgeson	18.00	7.00
73	Jerry Coleman	20.00	8.50
74	Wes Westrum	18.00	7.00
75	George Kell	42.00	20.00
76	Del Ennis	20.00	9.00
77	Eddie Robinson	18.00	7.00
78	Lloyd Merriman	18.00	7.00
79	Lou Brissie	18.00	7.00
80	Gil Hodges	90.00	40.00
81	Billy Goodman	18.00	7.00
82	Gus Zernial	18.00	7.00
83	Howie Pollet	18.00	7.00
84	Sam Jethroe	18.00	7.00
85	Marty Marion	20.00	8.50
86	Cal Abrams	18.00	7.00

87	Mickey Vernon	20.00	8.50
88	Bruce Edwards	18.00	7.00
89	Billy Hitchcock	18.00	7.00
90	Larry Jansen	20.00	8.50
91	Don Kolloway	18.00	7.00
92	Eddie Waitkus	18.00	7.00
93	Paul Richards	20.00	8.50
94	Luke Sewell	20.00	8.50
95	Luke Easter	20.00	8.50
96	Ralph Branca	20.00	8.50
97	Willard Marshall	18.00	7.00
98	Jimmy Dykes	20.00	8.50
99	Clyde McCullough	18.00	7.00
100	Sibby Sisti	18.00	7.00
101	Mickey Mantle	2,500.00	1,500.00
102	Peanuts Lowrey	18.00	7.00
103	Joe Haynes	18.00	7.00
104	Hal Jeffcoat	18.00	7.00
105	Bobby Brown	22.00	9.00
106	Randy Gumpert	18.00	7.00
107	Del Rice	18.00	7.00
108	George Metkovich	18.00	7.00
109	Tom Morgan	18.00	7.00
110	Max Lanier	18.00	7.00
111	Walter Evers	18.00	7.00
112	Smoky Burgess	20.00	8.50
113	Al Zarilla	18.00	7.00
114	Frank Hiller	18.00	7.00
115	Larry Doby	28.00	12.00
116	Duke Snider	225.00	100.00
117	Bill Wright	18.00	7.00
118	Ray Murray	18.00	7.00
119	Bill Howerton	18.00	7.00
120	Chet Nichols	18.00	7.00
121	Al Corwin	18.00	7.00
122	Billy Johnson	18.00	7.00
123	Sid Hudson	18.00	7.00
124	Birdie Tebbetts	20.00	8.50
125	Howie Fox	18.00	7.00
126	Phil Cavarretta	20.00	8.50
127	Dick Sisler	18.00	7.00
128	Don Newcombe	32.00	14.00
129	Gus Niarhos	18.00	7.00
130	Allie Clark	18.00	7.00
131	Bob Swift	18.00	7.00
132	Dave Cole	18.00	7.00
133	Dick Kryhoski	18.00	7.00
134	Al Brazle	18.00	7.00
135	Mickey Harris	18.00	7.00
136	Gene Hermanski	18.00	7.00
137	Stan Rojek	18.00	7.00
138	Ted Wilks	18.00	7.00
139	Jerry Priddy	18.00	7.00
140	Ray Scarborough	18.00	7.00
141	Hank Edwards	18.00	7.00
142	Early Wynn	50.00	22.50
143	Sandy Consuegra	18.00	7.00
144	Joe Hatten	18.00	7.00
145	Johnny Mize	60.00	28.00
146	Leo Durocher	45.00	20.00
147	Marlin Stuart	18.00	7.00
148	Ken Heintzelman	18.00	7.00
149	Howie Judson	18.00	7.00
150	Herman Wehmeier	18.00	7.00
151	Al Rosen	25.00	10.00
152	Billy Cox	20.00	8.50
153	Fred Hatfield	18.00	7.00
154	Ferris Fain	18.00	7.00
155	Billy Meyer	18.00	7.00
156	Warren Spahn	125.00	60.00
157	Jim Delsing	18.00	7.00
158	Bucky Harris	25.00	10.00
159	Dutch Leonard	18.00	7.00
160	Eddie Stanky	20.00	8.50
161	Jackie Jensen	35.00	15.00
162	Monte Irvin	50.00	22.50
163	Johnny Lipon	18.00	7.00
164	Connie Ryan	18.00	7.00
165	Saul Rogovin	18.00	7.00
166	Bobby Adams	18.00	7.00
167	Bob Avila	20.00	8.50
168	Preacher Roe	25.00	10.00
169	Walt Dropo	18.00	7.00
170	Joe Astroth	18.00	7.00
171	Mel Queen	18.00	7.00
172	Ebba St. Claire	18.00	7.00
173	Gene Bearden	18.00	7.00
174	Mickey Grasso	18.00	7.00
175	Ransom Jackson	18.00	7.00
176	Harry Brecheen	18.00	7.00
177	Gene Woodling	25.00	10.00
178	Dave Williams	18.00	7.00
179	Pete Suder	18.00	7.00
180	Ed Fitzgerald	18.00	7.00
181	Joe Collins (R)	18.00	7.00
182	Dave Koslo	18.00	7.00
183	Pat Mullin	18.00	7.00
184	Curt Simmons	18.00	7.00
185	Eddie Stewart	18.00	7.00
186	Frank Smith	18.00	7.00
187	Jim Hegan	18.00	7.00
188	Charlie Dressen	18.00	7.00
189	Jim Piersall	20.00	8.50
190	Dick Fowler	18.00	7.00
191	Bob Friend (R)	25.00	10.00
192	John Cusick	18.00	7.00
193	Bobby Young	18.00	7.00
194	Bob Porterfield	18.00	7.00
195	Frank Baumholtz	18.00	7.00
196	Stan Musial	550.00	250.00
197	Charlie Silvera	18.00	7.00
198	Chuck Diering	18.00	7.00
199	Ted Gray	18.00	7.00
200	Ken Silvestri	18.00	7.00
201	Ray Coleman	18.00	7.00
202	Harry Perkowski	18.00	7.00

203	Steve Gromek	18.00	7.00
204	Andy Pafko	20.00	8.50
205	Walt Masterson	18.00	7.00
206	Elmer Valo	18.00	7.00
207	George Strickland	18.00	7.00
208	Walker Cooper	18.00	7.00
209	Dick Littlefield	18.00	7.00
210	Archie Wilson	18.00	7.00
211	Paul Minner	18.00	7.00
212	Solly Hemus	18.00	7.00
213	Monte Kennedy	18.00	7.00
214	Ray Boone	20.00	8.50
215	Sheldon Jones	18.00	7.00
216	Matt Batts	18.00	7.00
217	Casey Stengel	175.00	80.00
218	Willie Mays	1,350.00	650.00
219	Neil Berry	32.00	15.00
220	Russ Meyer	32.00	15.00
221	Lou Kretlow	32.00	15.00
222	Dixie Howell	32.00	15.00
223	Harry Simpson	32.00	15.00
224	Johnny Schmitz	32.00	15.00
225	Del Wilber	32.00	15.00
226	Alex Kellner	32.00	15.00
227	Clyde Sukeforth	32.00	15.00
228	Bob Chipman	32.00	15.00
229	Hank Arft	32.00	15.00
230	Frank Shea	32.00	15.00
231	Dee Fondy	32.00	15.00
232	Enos Slaughter	100.00	45.00
233	Bob Kuzava	32.00	15.00
234	Fred Fitzsimmons	32.00	15.00
235	Steve Souchock	32.00	15.00
236	Tommy Brown	32.00	15.00
237	Sherman Lollar	32.00	15.00
238	Roy McMillan (R)	38.00	18.00
239	Dale Mitchell	32.00	15.00
240	Billy Loes (R)	38.00	18.00
241	Mel Parnell	32.00	15.00
242	Evertt Kell	32.00	15.00
243	George Munger	32.00	15.00
244	Lew Burdette (R)	65.00	30.00
245	George Schmees	32.00	15.00
246	Jerry Snyder	32.00	15.00
257	John Pramesa	32.00	15.00
248	Bill Werle	32.00	15.00
249	Hank Thompson	32.00	15.00
250	Ivan Delock	32.00	15.00
251	Jack Lohrke	32.00	15.00
252	Frank Crosetti	160.00	70.00

1953 Bowman Color

Bowman increased the size of their cards to 2-1/2" by 3-3/4" and, for the first time, used actual color photographs on the card fronts. No player names, team names or autographs appeared on the front making this one of the most desirable sets of all-time.

	NR/MT	EX
Complete Set (160)	11,500.00	5,200.00
Commons (1-112)	32.00	15.00
Commons (113-128)	55.00	25.00
Commons (129-160)	45.00	20.00

1	Davey Williams	90.00	35.00
2	Vic Wertz	38.00	18.00
3	Sam Jethroe	32.00	15.00
4	Art Houtteman	32.00	15.00
5	Sid Gordon	32.00	15.00
6	Joe Ginsberg	32.00	15.00
7	Harry Chiti	32.00	15.00
8	Al Rosen	50.00	22.50
9	Phil Rizzuto	125.00	60.00
10	Richie Ashburn	100.00	45.00
11	Bobby Shantz	35.00	16.50
12	Carl Erskine	45.00	20.00
13	Gus Zernial	35.00	16.50
14	Billy Loes	38.00	18.00
15	Jim Busby	32.00	15.00
16	Bob Friend	38.00	18.00
17	Gerry Staley	32.00	15.00
18	Nelson Fox	75.00	35.00
19	Al Dark	38.00	18.00
20	Don Lenhardt	32.00	15.00
21	Joe Garagiola	75.00	35.00
22	Bob Porterfield	32.00	15.00
23	Herman Wehmeier	32.00	15.00
24	Jackie Jensen	45.00	20.00
25	Walter Evers	32.00	15.00

No.	Player	Price	Price
26	Roy McMillan	32.00	15.00
27	Vic Raschi	38.00	18.00
28	Smoky Burgess	38.00	18.00
29	Roberto Avila	35.00	16.50
30	Phil Cavarretta	38.00	18.00
31	Jimmy Dykes	35.00	16.50
32	Stan Musial	575.00	275.00
33	Pee Wee Reese	475.00	225.00
34	Gil Coan	32.00	15.00
35	Maury McDermott	32.00	15.00
36	Minnie Minoso	65.00	30.00
37	Jim Wilson	32.00	15.00
38	Harry Byrd	32.00	15.00
39	Paul Richards	35.00	16.50
40	Larry Doby	48.00	20.00
41	Sammy White	32.00	15.00
42	Tommy Brown	32.00	15.00
43	Mike Garcia	35.00	16.50
44	H. Bauer, Y. Berra, M.Mantle	550.00	250.00
45	Walt Dropo	38.00	18.00
46	Roy Campanella	275.00	125.00
47	Ned Garver	32.00	15.00
48	Hank Sauer	35.00	16.50
49	Eddie Stanky	35.00	16.50
50	Lou Kretlow	32.00	15.00
51	Monte Irvin	65.00	30.00
52	Marty Marion	38.00	18.00
53	Del Rice	32.00	15.00
54	Chico Carrasquel	32.00	15.00
55	Leo Durocher	65.00	30.00
56	Bob Cain	32.00	15.00
57	Lou Boudreau	50.00	22.50
58	Willard Marshall	32.00	15.00
59	Mickey Mantle	2,750.00	1,500.00
60	Granny Hamner	32.00	15.00
61	George Kell	65.00	30.00
62	Ted Kluszewski	65.00	30.00
63	Gil McDougald	65.00	30.00
64	Curt Simmons	38.00	18.00
65	Robin Roberts	90.00	40.00
66	Mel Parnell	35.00	16.50
67	Mel Clark	32.00	15.00
68	Allie Reynolds	50.00	22.50
69	Charlie Grimm	35.00	16.50
70	Clint Courtney	32.00	15.00
71	Paul Minner	32.00	15.00
72	Ted Gray	32.00	15.00
73	Billy Pierce	38.00	18.00
74	Don Mueller	35.00	16.50
75	Saul Rogovin	32.00	15.00
76	Jim Hearn	32.00	15.00
77	Mickey Grasso	32.00	15.00
78	Carl Furillo	55.00	25.00
79	Ray Boone	38.00	18.00
80	Ralph Kiner	90.00	40.00
81	Enos Slaughter	95.00	42.50
82	Joe Astroth	32.00	15.00
83	Jack Daniels	32.00	15.00
84	Hank Bauer	55.00	25.00
85	Solly Hemus	32.00	15.00
86	Harry Simpson	32.00	15.00
87	Harry Perkowski	32.00	15.00
88	Joe Dobson	32.00	15.00
89	Sandy Consuegra	32.00	15.00
90	Joe Nuxhall	45.00	20.00
91	Steve Souchock	32.00	15.00
92	Gil Hodges	150.00	70.00
93	Billy Martin, Phil Rizzuto	260.00	125.00
94	Bob Addis	32.00	15.00
95	Wally Moses	35.00	16.50
96	Sal Maglie	45.00	20.00
97	Eddie Mathews	200.00	90.00
98	Hector Rodriquez	32.00	15.00
99	Warren Spahn	180.00	85.00
100	Bill Wright	32.00	15.00
101	Al Schoendienst	100.00	45.00
102	Jim Hegan	35.00	16.50
103	Del Ennis	38.00	18.00
104	Luke Easter	38.00	18.00
105	Eddie Joost	32.00	15.00
106	Ken Raffensberger	32.00	15.00
107	Alex Kellner	32.00	15.00
108	Bobby Adams	32.00	15.00
109	Ken Wood	32.00	15.00
110	Bob Rush	32.00	15.00
111	Jim Dyck	32.00	15.00
112	Toby Atwell	32.00	15.00
113	Karl Drews	55.00	25.00
114	Bob Feller	350.00	160.00
115	Cloyd Boyer	65.00	30.00
116	Eddie Yost	60.00	28.00
117	Duke Snider	650.00	300.00
118	Billy Martin	325.00	150.00
119	Dale Mitchell	65.00	30.00
120	Martin Stuart	55.00	25.00
121	Yogi Berra	600.00	275.00
122	Bill Serena	55.00	25.00
123	Johnny Lipon	55.00	25.00
124	Charle Dressen	60.00	28.00
125	Fred Hatfield	55.00	25.00
126	Al Corwin	55.00	25.00
127	Dick Kryhoski	55.00	25.00
128	Whitey Lockman	65.00	30.00
129	Russ Meyer	45.00	20.00
130	Cass Michaels	45.00	20.00
131	Connie Ryan	45.00	20.00
132	Fred Hutchinson	45.00	20.00
133	Willie Jones	45.00	20.00
134	Johnny Pesky	50.00	22.50
135	Bobby Morgan	45.00	20.00
136	Jim Brideweser	45.00	20.00
137	Sam Dente	45.00	20.00
138	Bubba Church	45.00	20.00
139	Pete Runnels	50.00	22.50

140	Al Brazle	45.00	20.00
141	Frank Shea	45.00	20.00
142	Larry Miggins	45.00	20.00
143	Al Lopez	65.00	30.00
144	Warren Hacker	45.00	20.00
145	George Shuba	45.00	20.00
146	Early Wynn	125.00	60.00
147	Clem Koshorek	45.00	20.00
148	Billy Goodman	45.00	20.00
149	Al Corwin	45.00	20.00
150	Carl Scheib	45.00	20.00
151	Joe Adcock	55.00	25.00
152	Clyde Vollmer	45.00	20.00
153	Whitey Ford	550.00	250.00
154	Omar Lown	45.00	20.00
155	Allie Clark	45.00	20.00
156	Max Surkont	45.00	20.00
157	Sherman Lollar	50.00	22.50
158	Howard Fox	45.00	20.00
159	Mickey Vernon (Er)	50.00	22.50
160	Cal Abrams	90.00	35.00

1953 Bowman Black & White

The design of this set is identical to the 1953 Bowman color set except for the black and white photographs. Cards measure 2-1/2" by 3-3/4".

		NR/MT	EX
Complete Set (64)		2,600.00	1,200.00
Commons		32.00	15.00

1	Gus Bell	125.00	50.00
2	Willard Nixon	32.00	15.00
3	Bill Rigney	32.00	15.00
4	Pat Mullin	32.00	15.00
5	Dee Fondy	32.00	15.00
6	Ray Murray	32.00	15.00
7	Andy Seminick	32.00	15.00
8	Pete Suder	32.00	15.00
9	Walt Masterson	32.00	15.00
10	Dick Sisler	32.00	15.00
11	Dick Gernert	32.00	15.00
12	Randy Jackson	32.00	15.00
13	Joe Tipton	32.00	15.00
14	Bill Nicholson	32.00	15.00
15	Johnny Mize	125.00	60.00
16	Stu Miller (R)	45.00	20.00
17	Virgil Trucks	38.00	18.00
18	Billy Hoeft	38.00	18.00
19	Paul LaPalme	32.00	15.00
20	Eddie Robinson	32.00	15.00
21	Clarence Podbielan	32.00	15.00
22	Matt Batts	32.00	15.00
23	Wilmer Mizell	38.00	18.00
24	Del Wilber	32.00	15.00
25	John Sain	60.00	28.00
26	Preacher Roe	50.00	22.50
27	Bob Lemon	140.00	65.00
28	Hoyt Wilhelm	125.00	60.00
29	Sid Hudson	32.00	15.00
30	Walker Cooper	32.00	15.00
31	Gene Wooding	45.00	20.00
32	Rocky Bridges	35.00	16.50
33	Bob Kuzava	32.00	15.00
34	Ebba St. Clair (Er)	32.00	15.00
35	Johnny Wyrostek	32.00	15.00
36	Jim Piersall	50.00	22.50
37	Hal Jeffcoat	32.00	15.00
38	Dave Cole	32.00	15.00
39	Casey Stengel	350.00	150.00
40	Larry Jansen	35.00	16.50
41	Bob Ramazotti	32.00	15.00
42	Howie Judson	32.00	15.00
43	Hal Bevan	32.00	15.00
44	Jim Delsing	32.00	15.00
45	Irv Noren	32.00	15.00
46	Bucky Harris	50.00	22.50
47	Jack Lohrke	32.00	15.00
48	Steve Ridzik	32.00	15.00
49	Floyd Baker	32.00	15.00
50	Dutch Leonard	35.00	16.50
51	Lew Burdette	50.00	22.50
52	Ralph Branca	45.00	20.00
53	Morris Martin	32.00	15.00
54	Bill Miller	32.00	15.00
55	Don Johnson	32.00	15.00
56	Roy Smalley	32.00	15.00
57	Andy Pafko	32.00	15.00
58	Jim Konstanty	38.00	18.00
59	Duane Pillette	32.00	15.00
60	Billy Cox	38.00	18.00
61	Tom Gorman	32.00	15.00

62	Keith Thomas	32.00	15.00
63	Steve Gromek	32.00	15.00
64	Andy Hansen	45.00	20.00

1954 Bowman

This full-color set contains 224 cards which measure 2-1/2" by 3-3/4". Card #66, Ted Williams, was pulled from the set shortly after its release and replaced by Jimmy Piersall. The set includes a number of variations involving statistical errors on the card backs which are noted in the checklist. In most cases, the variations are worth no more than the original. The set price does not include the scarce Ted Williams card.

		NR/MT	EX
Complete Set (224)		4,500.00	2,000.00
Commons (1-128)		10.00	5.00
Commons (129-224)		12.50	6.50

1	Phil Rizzuto	140.00	65.00
2	Jackie Jensen	15.00	7.00
3	Marion Fricano	10.00	5.00
4	Bob Hooper	10.00	5.00
5	William Hunter	10.00	5.00
6	Nelson Fox	25.00	12.00
7	Walter Dropo	12.50	6.50
8	Jim Busby	10.00	5.00
9	Davey Williams	10.00	5.00
10	Carl Erskine	15.00	7.00
11	Sid Gordon	10.00	5.00
12	Roy McMillan (Var)	12.50	6.50
13	Paul Minner	10.00	5.00
14	Gerald Staley	10.00	5.00
15	Richie Ashburn	38.00	18.00
16	Jim Wilson	10.00	5.00
17	Tom Gorman	10.00	5.00
18	Walter Evers	10.00	5.00
19	Bobby Shantz	12.50	6.50
20	Artie Houtteman	10.00	5.00
21	Vic Wertz	12.50	6.50
22	Sam Mele (Var)	10.00	5.00
23	Harvey Kuenn (R)	38.00	18.00
24	Bob Porterfield	10.00	5.00
25	Wes Westrum (Var)	10.00	5.00
26	Billy Cox (Var)	12.50	6.50
27	Richard Cole	10.00	5.00
28	Jim Greengrass (Var)	10.00	5.00
29	Johnny Klippstein	10.00	5.00
30	Del Rice Jr.	10.00	5.00
31	Smoky Burgess	15.00	7.00
32	Del Crandall	12.50	6.50
33a	Vic Raschi (No Trade)	25.00	12.00
33b	Vic Raschi (Traded)	35.00	16.50
34	Sammy White	10.00	5.00
35	Eddie Joost (Var)	10.00	5.00
36	George Strickland	10.00	5.00
37	Dick Kokos	10.00	5.00
38	Minnie Minoso (Var)	25.00	12.00
39	Ned Garver	10.00	5.00
40	Gil Coan	10.00	5.00
41	Alvin Dark (Var)	15.00	7.00
42	Billy Loes	12.50	6.50
43	Bob Friend (Var)	12.50	6.50
44	Harry Perkowski	10.00	5.00
45	Ralph Kiner	50.00	22.50
46	Rip Repulski	10.00	5.00
47	Granny Hamner (Var)	10.00	5.00
48	Jack Dittmer	10.00	5.00
49	Harry Byrd	10.00	5.00
50	George Kell	30.00	14.00
51	Alex Kellner	10.00	5.00
52	Myron Ginsberg	10.00	5.00
53	Don Lenhardt (Var)	10.00	5.00
54	Chico Carrasquel	10.00	5.00
55	Jim Delsing	10.00	5.00
56	Maurice McDermott	10.00	5.00
57	Hoyt Wilhelm	35.00	16.50
58	Pee Wee Reese	80.00	38.00
59	Bob Schultz	10.00	5.00
60	Fred Baczewski	10.00	5.00
61	Eddie Miksis (Var)	10.00	5.00
62	Enos Slaughter	50.00	22.50
63	Earl Torgeson	10.00	5.00
64	Ed Mathews	75.00	35.00
65	Mickey Mantle	1,000.00	500.00
66a	Ted Williams	4,500.00	2,400.00
66b	Jimmy Piersall	90.00	40.00
67	Carl Scheib (Var)	10.00	5.00
68	Bob Avila	10.00	5.00
69	Clinton Courtney	10.00	5.00
70	Willard Marshall	10.00	5.00

71	Ted Gray	10.00	5.00	129	Hank Bauer	25.00	12.00
72	Ed Yost	10.00	5.00	130	Milt Bolling	12.50	6.50
73	Don Mueller	10.00	5.00	131	Joe Astroth	12.50	6.50
74	Jim Gilliam	25.00	12.00	132	Bob Feller	100.00	50.00
75	Max Surkont	10.00	5.00	133	Duane Pillette	12.50	6.50
76	Joe Nuxhall	12.50	6.50	134	Luis Aloma	12.50	6.50
77	Bob Rush	10.00	5.00	135	Johnny Pesky	15.00	7.00
78	Sal Yvars	10.00	5.00	136	Clyde Vollmer	12.50	6.50
79	Curt Simmons	12.50	6.50	137	Al Corwin Jr.	12.50	6.50
80	John Logan (Var)	15.00	7.00	138	Gil Hodges (Var)	75.00	35.00
81	Jerry Coleman (Var)	12.50	6.50	139	Preston Ward (Var)	12.50	6.50
82	Bill Goodman (Var)	10.00	5.00	140	Saul Rogovin (Var)	12.50	6.50
83	Ray Murray	10.00	5.00	141	Joe Garagiola	50.00	22.50
84	Larry Doby	15.00	7.00	142	Al Brazle	12.50	6.50
85	Jim Dyck (Var)	10.00	5.00	143	Willie Jones	12.50	6.50
86	Harry Dorish	10.00	5.00	144	Ernie Johnson	20.00	8.50
87	Don Lund	10.00	5.00	145	Billy Martin (Var)	80.00	38.00
88	Tommy Umphlett	10.00	5.00	146	Dick Gernert	12.50	6.50
89	Willie Mays (Er)	400.00	200.00	147	Joe DeMaestri	12.50	6.50
90	Roy Campanella	150.00	70.00	148	Dale Mitchell	15.00	7.00
91	Cal Abrams	10.00	5.00	149	Bob Young	12.50	6.50
92	Ken Raffensberger	10.00	5.00	150	Cass Michaels	12.50	6.50
93	Bill Serena (Var)	10.00	5.00	151	Patrick Mullin	12.50	6.50
94	Solly Hemus (Var)	10.00	5.00	152	Mickey Vernon	15.00	7.00
95	Robin Roberts	45.00	20.00	153	Whitey Lockman	15.00	7.00
96	Joe Adcock	15.00	7.00	154	Don Newcombe	25.00	12.00
97	Gil McDougald	25.00	12.00	155	Frank Thomas (R)	20.00	8.50
98	Ellis Kinder	10.00	5.00	156	Rocky Bridges (Var)	12.50	6.50
99	Peter Suder (Var)	10.00	5.00	157	Omar Lown	12.50	6.50
100	Mike Garcia	12.50	6.50	158	Stu Miller	15.00	7.00
101	Don Larsen (R)	45.00	20.00	159	John Lindell	12.50	6.50
102	Bill Pierce	12.50	6.50	160	Danny O'Connell	12.50	6.50
103	Steve Souchock	10.00	5.00	161	Yogi Berra	200.00	100.00
104	Frank Shea	10.00	5.00	162	Ted Lepcio	12.50	6.50
105	Sal Maglie (Var)	15.00	7.00	163a	Dave Philley (No	15.00	7.00
106	Clem Labine	12.50	6.50		Trade)		
107	Paul LaPalme	10.00	5.00	163b	Dave Philley (Trade)	25.00	12.00
108	Bobby Adams	10.00	5.00	164	Early Wynn	50.00	22.50
109	Roy Smalley	10.00	5.00	165	Johnny Groth	12.50	6.50
110	Al Schoendienst	38.00	18.00	166	Sandy Consuegra	12.50	6.50
111	Murry Dickson	10.00	5.00	167	Bill Hoeft	12.50	6.50
112	Andy Pafko	12.50	6.50	168	Ed Fitzgerald	12.50	6.50
113	Allie Reynolds	20.00	8.50	169	Larry Jansen	15.00	7.00
114	Williard Nixon	10.00	5.00	170	Duke Snider	175.00	80.00
115	Don Bollweg	10.00	5.00	171	Carlos Bernier	12.50	6.50
116	Luke Easter	10.00	5.00	172	Andy Seminick	12.50	6.50
117	Dick Kryhoski	10.00	5.00	173	Dee Fondy Jr.	12.50	6.50
118	Robert Boyd	10.00	5.00	174	Pete Castiglione	12.50	6.50
119	Fred Hatfield	10.00	5.00	175	Melvin Clark	12.50	6.50
120	Mel Hoderlein	10.00	5.00	176	Vernon Bickford	12.50	6.50
121	Ray Katt	10.00	5.00	177	Whitey Ford	125.00	60.00
122	Carl Furillo	20.00	8.50	178	Del Wilber	12.50	6.50
123	Toby Atwell	10.00	5.00	179	Morris Martin (Var)	12.50	6.50
124	Gus Bell (Var)	12.50	6.50	180	Joe Tipton	12.50	6.50
125	Warren Hacker	10.00	5.00	181	Les Moss	12.50	6.50
126	Cliff Chambers	10.00	5.00	182	Sherman Lollar	15.00	7.00
127	Del Ennis	10.00	5.00	183	Matt Batts	12.50	6.50
128	Ebba St. Claire	10.00	5.00	184	Mickey Grasso	12.50	6.50

185	Daryl Spencer (Var)	12.50	6.50
186	Russell Meyer	12.50	6.50
187	Verne Law (Er)	20.00	8.50
188	Frank Smith	12.50	6.50
189	Ransom Jackson	12.50	6.50
190	Joe Presko	12.50	6.50
191	Karl Drews	12.50	6.50
192	Lew Burdette	20.00	8.50
193	Eddie Robinson	12.50	6.50
194	Sid Hudson	12.50	6.50
195	Bob Cain	12.50	6.50
196	Bob Lemon	45.00	20.00
197	Lou Kretlow	12.50	6.50
198	Virgil Trucks	15.00	7.00
199	Steve Gromek	12.50	6.50
200	Conrad Marrero	12.50	6.50
201	Bobby Thomson	20.00	8.50
202	George Shuba	12.50	6.50
203	Vic Janowicz	20.00	8.50
204	Jack Collum	12.50	6.50
205	Hal Jeffcoat	12.50	6.50
206	Steve Bilko	12.50	6.50
207	Stan Lopata	12.50	6.50
208	Johnny Antonelli	20.00	8.50
209	Gene Woodling (Er)	20.00	8.50
210	Jimmy Piersall	20.00	8.50
211	Al Robertson	12.50	6.50
212	Owen Friend (Var)	12.50	6.50
213	Dick Littlefield	12.50	6.50
214	Ferris Fain	15.00	7.00
215	Johnny Bucha	12.50	6.50
216	Jerry Snyder (Var)	12.50	6.50
217	Hank Thompson	15.00	7.00
218	Preacher Roe	20.00	8.50
219	Hal Rice	12.50	6.50
220	Hobie Landrith	12.50	6.50
221	Frank Baumholtz	12.50	6.50
222	Memo Luna	12.50	6.50
223	Steve Ridzik	12.50	6.50
224	Bill Bruton	40.00	15.00

1955 Bowman

This set proved to be one of Bowman's most popular issues primarily due to the design which featured player photos inside a television screen. Known as the "TV Set", the cards measure 2-1/2" by 3-3/4".

		NR/MT	EX
Complete Set (320)		5,450.00	2,600.00
Commons (1-224)		7.50	3.50
Commons (225-320)		20.00	8.50

1	Hoyt Wilhelm	100.00	45.00
2	Al Dark	12.50	6.50
3	Joe Coleman	7.50	3.50
4	Eddie Waitkus	7.50	3.50
5	Jim Robertson	7.50	3.50
6	Pete Suder	7.50	3.50
7	Gene Baker	7.50	3.50
8	Warren Hacker	7.50	3.50
9	Gil McDougald	20.00	8.50
10	Phil Rizzuto	60.00	28.00
11	Billy Bruton	7.50	3.50
12	Andy Pafko	10.00	5.00
13	Clyde Vollmer	7.50	3.50
14	Gus Keriazakos	7.50	3.50
15	Frank Sullivan	7.50	3.50
16	Jim Piersall	12.00	6.00
17	Del Ennis	8.50	4.00
18	Stan Lopata	7.50	3.50
19	Bobby Avila	8.50	4.00
20	Al Smith	7.50	3.50
21	Don Hoak	8.50	4.00
22	Roy Campanella	125.00	60.00
23	Al Kaline	175.00	80.00
24	Al Aber	7.50	3.50
25	Minnie Minoso	20.00	8.50
26	Virgil Trucks	10.00	5.00
27	Preston Ward	7.50	3.50
28	Dick Cole	7.50	3.50
29	Red Schoendienst	30.00	14.00
30	Bill Sarni	7.50	3.50
31	Johnny Temple (R)	12.00	6.00
32	Wally Post	10.00	5.00

33	Nelson Fox	25.00	12.00	90	Art Ditmar	7.50	3.50
34	Clint Courtney	7.50	3.50	91	Dick Marlowe	7.50	3.50
35	Bill Tuttle	7.50	3.50	92	George Zuverink	7.50	3.50
36	Wayne Belardi	7.50	3.50	93	Andy Seminick	7.50	3.50
37	Pee Wee Reese	80.00	38.00	94	Hank Thompson	7.50	3.50
38	Early Wynn	30.00	14.00	95	Sal Maglie	12.00	6.00
39	Bob Darnell	7.50	3.50	96	Ray Narleski (R)	12.00	6.00
40	Vic Wertz	8.50	4.00	97	John Podres	20.00	8.50
41	Mel Clark	7.50	3.50	98	Junior Gilliam	20.00	8.50
42	Bob Greenwood	7.50	3.50	99	Jerry Coleman	8.50	4.00
43	Bob Buhl	8.50	4.00	100	Tom Morgan	7.50	3.50
44	Danny O'Connell	7.50	3.50	101a	Don Johnson	8.50	4.00
45	Tom Umphlett	7.50	3.50		(Wrong Photo)		
46	Mickey Vernon	8.50	4.00	101b	Don Johnson (Cor)	20.00	8.50
47	Sammy White	7.50	3.50	102	Bobby Thomson	12.00	6.00
48a	Milt Bolling (Er)	8.50	4.00	103	Eddie Mathews	60.00	28.00
48b	Milt Bolling (Cor)	20.00	8.50	104	Bob Porterfield	7.50	3.50
49	Jim Greengrass	7.50	3.50	105	Johnny Schmitz	7.50	3.50
50	Hobie Landrith	7.50	3.50	106	Del Rice	7.50	3.50
51	Elvin Tappe	7.50	3.50	107	Solly Hemus	7.50	3.50
52	Hal Rice	7.50	3.50	108	Lou Kretlow	7.50	3.50
53	Alex Kellner	7.50	3.50	109	Vern Stephens	7.50	3.50
54	Don Bollweg	7.50	3.50	110	Bob Miller	7.50	3.50
55	Cal Abrams	7.50	3.50	111	Steve Ridzik	7.50	3.50
56	Billy Cox	8.50	4.00	112	Granny Hamner	7.50	3.50
57	Bob Friend	7.50	3.50	113	Bob Hall	7.50	3.50
58	Frank Thomas	10.00	5.00	114	Vic Janowicz	8.50	4.00
59	Whitey Ford	80.00	38.00	115	Roger Bowman	7.50	3.50
60	Enos Slaughter	30.00	14.00	116	Sandy Consuegra	7.50	3.50
61	Paul LaPalme	7.50	3.50	117	Johnny Groth	7.50	3.50
62	Royce Lint	7.50	3.50	118	Bobby Adams	7.50	3.50
63	Irv Noren	7.50	3.50	119	Joe Astroth	7.50	3.50
64	Curt Simmons	8.50	4.00	120	Ed Brutschy	7.50	3.50
65	Don Zimmer (R)	30.00	14.00	121	Rufus Crawford	7.50	3.50
66	George Shuba	7.50	3.50	122	Al Corwin	7.50	3.50
67	Don Larsen	20.00	8.50	123	Marv Grissom	7.50	3.50
68	Elston Howard (R)	75.00	35.00	124	Johnny Antonelli	10.00	5.00
69	Bill Hunter	7.50	3.50	125	Paul Giel	7.50	3.50
70	Lew Burdette	12.00	6.00	126	Billy Goodman	7.50	3.50
71	Dave Jolly	7.50	3.50	127	Hank Majeski	7.50	3.50
72	Chet Nichols	7.50	3.50	128	Mike Garcia	7.50	3.50
73	Eddie Yost	7.50	3.50	129	Hal Naragon	7.50	3.50
74	Jerry Snyder	7.50	3.50	130	Richie Ashburn	30.00	14.00
75	Brooks Lawrence	7.50	3.50	131	Willard Marshall	7.50	3.50
76	Tom Poholsky	7.50	3.50	132a	Harvey Kueen (Er)	12.00	6.00
77	Jim McDonald	7.50	3.50	132b	Harvey Kuenn (Cor)	25.00	12.00
78	Gil Coan	7.50	3.50	133	Charles King	7.50	3.50
79	Willie Miranda	7.50	3.50	134	Bob Feller	70.00	30.00
80	Lou Limmer	7.50	3.50	135	Lloyd Merriman	7.50	3.50
81	Bob Morgan	7.50	3.50	136	Rocky Bridges	7.50	3.50
82	Lee Walls	7.50	3.50	137	Bob Talbot	7.50	3.50
83	Max Surkont	7.50	3.50	138	Davey Williams	7.50	3.50
84	George Freese	7.50	3.50	139	Wil & Bobby Shantz	10.00	5.00
85	Cass Michaels	7.50	3.50	140	Bobby Shantz	8.50	4.00
86	Ted Gray	7.50	3.50	141	Wes Westrum	7.50	3.50
87	Randy Jackson	7.50	3.50	142	Rudy Regalado	7.50	3.50
88	Steve Bilko	7.50	3.50	143	Don Newcombe	20.00	8.50
89	Lou Boudreau	20.00	8.50	144	Art Houtteman	7.50	3.50

145	Bob Nieman	7.50	3.50
146	Don Liddle	7.50	3.50
147	Sam Mele	7.50	3.50
148	Bob Chakales	7.50	3.50
149	Cloyd Boyer	8.50	4.00
150	Bill Klaus	7.50	3.50
151	Jim Brideweser	7.50	3.50
152	Johnny Klippstein	7.50	3.50
153	Eddie Robinson	7.50	3.50
154	Frank Lary (R)	12.00	6.00
155	Gerry Staley	7.50	3.50
156	Jim Hughes	7.50	3.50
157a	Ernie Johnson	8.50	4.00
	(Wrong Photo)		
157b	Ernie Johnson (Cor)	20.00	8.50
158	Gil Hodges	45.00	20.00
159	Harry Byrd	7.50	3.50
160	Bill Skowron	25.00	12.00
161	Matt Batts	7.50	3.50
162	Charlie Maxwell	7.50	3.50
163	Sid Gordon	7.50	3.50
164	Toby Atwell	7.50	3.50
165	Maurice McDermott	7.50	3.50
166	Jim Busby	7.50	3.50
167	Bob Grim (R)	12.00	6.00
168	Yogi Berra	125.00	60.00
169	Carl Furillo	20.00	8.50
170	Carl Erskine	15.00	7.00
171	Robin Roberts	30.00	14.00
172	Willie Jones	7.50	3.50
173	Chico Carrasquel	7.50	3.50
174	Sherman Lollar	8.50	4.00
175	Wilmer Shantz	7.50	3.50
176	Joe DeMaestri	7.50	3.50
177	Willard Nixon	7.50	3.50
178	Tom Brewer	7.50	3.50
179	Hank Aaron	275.00	140.00
180	Johnny Logan	8.50	4.00
181	Eddie Miksis	7.50	3.50
182	Bob Rush	7.50	3.50
183	Ray Katt	7.50	3.50
184	Willie Mays	260.00	125.00
185	Vic Raschi	10.00	5.00
186	Alex Grammas	7.50	3.50
187	Fred Hatfield	7.50	3.50
188	Ned Garver	7.50	3.50
189	Jack Collum	7.50	3.50
190	Fred Baczewski	7.50	3.50
191	Bob Lemon	30.00	14.00
192	George Strickland	7.50	3.50
193	Howie Judson	7.50	3.50
194	Joe Nuxhall	8.50	4.00
195a	Erv Palica (No Trade)	8.50	4.00
195b	Erv Palica (Traded)	20.00	8.50
196	Russ Meyer	7.50	3.50
197	Ralph Kiner	30.00	14.00
198	Dave Pope	7.50	3.50
199	Vernon Law	8.50	4.00
200	Dick Littlefield	7.50	3.50
201	Allie Reynolds	15.00	7.00
202	Mickey Mantle	575.00	280.00
203	Steve Gromek	7.50	3.50
204a	Frank Bolling (Er)	8.50	4.00
204b	Frank Bolling (Cor)	20.00	8.50
205	Rip Repulski	7.50	3.50
206	Ralph Beard	7.50	3.50
207	Frank Shea	7.50	3.50
208	Ed Fitzgerald	7.50	3.50
209	Smoky Burgess	8.50	4.00
210	Earl Torgeson	7.50	3.50
211	John Dixon	7.50	3.50
212	Jack Dittmer	7.50	3.50
213	George Kell	25.00	12.00
214	Billy Pierce	10.00	5.00
215	Bob Kuzava	7.50	3.50
216	Preacher Roe	10.00	5.00
217	Del Crandall	8.50	4.00
218	Joe Adcock	10.00	5.00
219	Whitey Lockman	8.50	4.00
220	Jim Hearn	7.50	3.50
221	Hector Brown	7.50	3.50
222	Russ Kemmerer	7.50	3.50
223	Hal Jeffcoat	7.50	3.50
224	Dee Fondy	7.50	3.50
225	Paul Richards	20.00	8.50
226	W.F. McKinley(Ump)	28.00	13.00
227	Frank Baumholtz	20.00	8.50
228	John Phillips	20.00	8.50
229	Jim Brosnan (R)	25.00	12.00
230	Al Brazle	20.00	8.50
231	Jim Konstanty	25.00	12.00
232	Birdie Tebbetts	20.00	8.50
233	Bill Serena	20.00	8.50
234	Dick Bartell	20.00	8.50
235	J.A. Paparella (Ump)	25.00	12.00
236	Murray Dickson (Er)	20.00	8.50
237	Johnny Wyrostek	20.00	8.50
238	Eddie Stanky	20.00	8.50
239	Edwin Rommel	25.00	12.00
	(Ump)		
240	Billy Loes	20.00	8.50
241	John Pesky	20.00	8.50
242	Ernie Banks	450.00	225.00
243	Gus Bell	20.00	8.50
244	Duane Pillette	20.00	8.50
245	Bill Miller	20.00	8.50
246	Hank Bauer	38.00	18.00
247	Dutch Leonard	20.00	8.50
248	Harry Dorish	20.00	8.50
249	Billy Gardner	20.00	8.50
250	Larry Napp (Ump)	25.00	12.00
251	Stan Jok	20.00	8.50
252	Roy Smalley	20.00	8.50
253	Jim Wilson	20.00	8.50
254	Bennett Flowers	20.00	8.50
255	Pete Runnels	22.00	10.00

256	Owen Friend	20.00	8.50
257	Tom Alston	20.00	8.50
258	John W. Stevens (Ump)	25.00	12.00
259	Don Mossi (R)	25.00	12.00
260	Edwin Hurley (Ump)	25.00	12.00
261	Walt Moryn	20.00	8.50
262	Jim Lemon	22.00	10.00
263	Eddie Joost	20.00	8.50
264	Bill Henry	20.00	8.50
265	Albert Barlick (Ump)	28.00	13.00
266	Mike Fornieles	20.00	8.50
267	Jim Honochick (Ump)	75.00	35.00
268	Roy Lee Hawes	20.00	8.50
269	Joe Amalfitano (R)	22.00	10.00
270	Chico Fernandez	20.00	8.50
271	Bob Hooper	20.00	8.50
272	John Flaherty (Ump)	25.00	12.00
273	Emory Church	20.00	8.50
274	Jim Delsing	20.00	8.50
275	William Grieve(Ump)	25.00	12.00
276	Ivan Delock	20.00	8.50
277	Ed Runge (Ump)	30.00	14.00
278	Charles Neal (R)	30.00	14.00
279	Hank Soar (Ump)	25.00	12.00
280	Clyde McCullough	20.00	8.50
281	Charles Berry (Ump)	25.00	12.00
282	Phil Cavarretta	22.00	10.00
283	Nestor Chylak (Ump)	30.00	14.00
284	Wm. Jackowski (Ump)	25.00	12.00
285	Walt Dropo	20.00	8.50
286	Frank Secory (Ump)	30.00	14.00
287	Ron Mrozinski	20.00	8.50
288	Dick Smith	20.00	8.50
289	Arthur Gore (Ump)	25.00	12.00
290	Hershell Freeman	20.00	8.50
291	Frank Dascoli (Ump)	30.00	14.00
292	Marv Blaylock	20.00	8.50
293	Tom Gorman (Ump)	30.00	14.00
294	Wally Moses	20.00	8.50
295	Lee Ballanfant(Ump)	25.00	12.00
296	Bill Virdon (R)	38.00	18.00
297	Dusty Boggess (Ump)	30.00	14.00
298	Charlie Grimm	20.00	8.50
299	Lonnie Warneke (Ump)	30.00	14.00
300	Tommy Byrne	20.00	8.50
301	William Engeln(Ump)	25.00	12.00
302	Frank Malzone (R)	30.00	14.00
303	Jocko Conlan (Ump)	100.00	45.00
304	Harry Chiti	20.00	8.50
305	Frank Umont (Ump)	30.00	14.00
306	Bob Cerv	22.00	10.00
307	Babe Pinelli (Ump)	30.00	14.00
308	Al Lopez	45.00	20.00
309	Hal Dixon (Ump)	25.00	12.00
310	Ken Lehman	20.00	8.50
311	Lawrence Goetz (Ump)	25.00	12.00
312	Bill Wight	20.00	8.50
313	A.J. Donatelli (Ump)	35.00	15.00
314	Dale Mitchell	20.00	8.50
315	Cal Hubbard (Ump)	100.00	45.00
316	Marion Fricano	20.00	8.50
317	Wm. Summers(Ump)	25.00	12.00
318	Sid Hudson	20.00	8.50
319	Albert Schroll	20.00	8.50
320	George Susce, Jr.	55.00	20.00

1989 Bowman

After a 33 year layoff, Bowman returns under the Topps banner. The 484-card set was patterned after the 1953 Bowman set with full-color photos and a fascimile autograph on the front. Cards measure 2-1/2" by 3-3/4".

		MINT	NR/MT
Complete Set (484)		15.00	8.50
Commons		.05	.02
1	Oswald Peraza	.05	.02
2	Brian Holton	.05	.02
3	Jose Bautista	.05	.02
4	Pete Harnisch (R)	.15	.08
5	Dave Schmidt	.05	.02
6	Gregg Olson (R)	.20	.12
7	Jeff Ballard	.07	.04
8	Bob Melvin	.05	.02
9	Cal Ripken	.45	.28
10	Randy Milligan	.10	.06

11	Juan Bell (R)	.08	.05	69	Ron Kittle	.05	.02
12	Billy Ripken	.05	.02	70	Daryl Boston	.05	.02
13	Jim Trabor	.05	.02	71	Dave Gallagher	.05	.02
14	Pete Stanicek	.05	.02	72	Harold Baines	.08	.05
15	Steve Finley (R)	.20	.12	73	Charles Nagy (R)	.50	.30
16	Larry Sheets	.05	.02	74	John Farrell	.05	.02
17	Phil Bradley	.05	.02	75	Kevin Wickander	.05	.02
18	Brady Anderson (R)	.50	.30	76	Greg Swindell	.08	.05
19	Lee Smith	.10	.06	77	Mike Walker	.06	.03
20	Tom Fischer	.05	.02	78	Doug Jones	.05	.02
21	Mike Boddicker	.05	.02	79	Rich Yett	.05	.02
22	Rob Murphy	.05	.02	80	Tom Candiotti	.07	.04
23	Wes Gardner	.05	.02	81	Jesse Orosco	.05	.02
24	John Dopson	.05	.02	82	Bud Black	.07	.03
25	Bob Stanley	.05	.02	83	Andy Allanson	.05	.02
26	Roger Clemens	.40	.25	84	Pete O'Brien	.05	.02
27	Rich Gedman	.05	.02	85	Jerry Browne	.05	.02
28	Marty Barrett	.05	.02	86	Brook Jacoby	.05	.02
29	Luis Rivera	.05	.02	87	Mark Lewis (R)	.30	.18
30	Jody Reed	.06	.03	88	Luis Aguayo	.05	.02
31	Nick Esasky	.05	.02	89	Cory Snyder	.07	.04
32	Wade Boggs	.20	.12	90	Oddibe McDowell	.05	.02
33	Jim Rice	.07	.04	91	Joe Carter	.20	.12
34	Mike Greenwell	.08	.05	92	Frank Tanana	.07	.04
35	Dwight Evans	.08	.05	93	Jack Morris	.20	.12
36	Ellis Burks	.10	.06	94	Doyle Alexander	.05	.02
37	Chuck Finley	.10	.06	95	Steve Searcy	.07	.04
38	Kirk McCaskill	.06	.03	96	Randy Bockus	.05	.02
39	Jim Abbott (R)	.70	.40	97	Jeff Robinson	.05	.02
40	Bryan Harvey (R)	.20	.12	98	Mike Henneman	.05	.02
41	Bert Blyleven	.10	.06	99	Paul Gibson	.05	.02
42	Mike Witt	.08	.05	100	Frank Williams	.05	.02
43	Bob McClure	.05	.02	101	Matt Nokes	.08	.05
44	Bill Schroeder	.05	.02	102	Rico Brogna (R)	.25	.15
45	Lance Parrish	.08	.05	103	Lou Whitaker	.07	.04
46	Dick Schofield	.05	.02	104	Al Pedrique	.05	.02
47	Wally Joyner	.10	.06	105	Alan Trammell	.08	.05
48	Jack Howell	.05	.02	106	Chris Brown	.05	.02
49	Johnny Ray	.05	.02	107	Pat Sheridan	.05	.02
50	Chili Davis	.07	.04	108	Garry Pettis	.05	.02
51	Tony Armas	.05	.02	109	Keith Moreland	.05	.02
52	Claudell Washington	.05	.02	110	Mel Stottlemyre, Jr.	.07	.04
53	Brian Downing	.06	.03	111	Bret Saberhagen	.12	.07
54	Devon White	.07	.04	112	Floyd Bannister	.05	.02
55	Bobby Thigpen	.08	.05	113	Jeff Montgomery	.07	.04
56	Bill Long	.05	.02	114	Steve Farr	.05	.02
57	Jerry Reuss	.05	.02	115	Tom Gordon (R)	.10	.06
58	Shawn Hillegas	.05	.02	116	Charlie Leibrandt	.06	.03
59	Melido Perez	.08	.05	117	Mike Gubicza	.07	.04
60	Jeff Bittiger	.05	.02	118	Mike MacFarlane (R)	.10	.06
61	Jack McDowell	.40	.25	119	Bob Boone	.07	.04
62	Carlton Fisk	.15	.08	120	Kurt Stillwell	.05	.02
63	Steve Lyons	.05	.02	121	George Brett	.20	.12
64	Ozzie Guillen	.07	.04	122	Frank White	.05	.02
65	Robin Ventura (R)	1.00	.70	123	Keven Seitzer	.08	.05
66	Fred Manrique	.05	.02	124	Willie Wilson	.05	.02
67	Dan Pasqua	.05	.02	125	Pat Tabler	.05	.02
68	Ivan Calderon	.07	.04	126	Bo Jackson	.20	.12

127	Hugh Walker (R)	.10	.06	185	Gene Nelson	.05	.02
128	Danny Tartabull	.12	.07	186	Bob Welch	.07	.04
129	Teddy Higuera	.05	.02	187	Rick Honeycutt	.05	.02
130	Don August	.05	.02	188	Dave Stewart	.08	.05
131	Juan Nieves	.05	.02	189	Mike Moore	.07	.03
132	Mike Birkbeck	.05	.02	190	Dennis Eckersley	.20	.12
133	Dan Plesac	.05	.02	191	Eric Plunk	.05	.02
134	Chris Bosio	.08	.05	192	Storm Davis	.05	.02
135	Bill Wegman	.05	.02	193	Terry Steinbach	.08	.05
136	Chuck Crim	.05	.02	194	Ron Hassey	.05	.02
137	B.J. Surhoff	.07	.04	195	Stan Royer (R)	.10	.06
138	Joey Meyer	.05	.02	196	Walt Weiss	.07	.04
139	Dale Sveum	.05	.02	197	Mark McGwire	.40	.25
140	Paul Molitor	.08	.05	198	Carney Lansford	.07	.04
141	Jim Gantner	.05	.02	199	Glenn Hubbard	.05	.02
142	Gary Sheffield (R)	2.50	1.40	200	Dave Henderson	.07	.04
143	Greg Brock	.05	.02	201	Jose Canseco	.40	.25
144	Robin Yount	.25	.15	202	Dave Parker	.07	.04
145	Glenn Braggs	.05	.02	203	Scott Bankhead	.05	.02
146	Rob Deer	.08	.05	204	Tom Niedenfuer	.05	.02
147	Fred Toliver	.05	.02	205	Mark Langston	.10	.06
148	Jeff Reardon	.10	.06	206	Erik Hanson (R)	.15	.08
149	Allan Anderson	.05	.02	207	Mike Jackson	.07	.03
150	Frank Viola	.08	.05	208	Dave Valle	.05	.02
151	Shane Rawley	.05	.02	209	Scott Bradley	.05	.02
152	Juan Berenguer	.05	.02	210	Harold Reynolds	.07	.04
153	Johnny Ard (R)	.08	.05	211	Tino Martinez (R)	.40	.25
154	Tim Laudner	.05	.02	212	Rich Renteria	.05	.02
155	Brian Harper	.07	.04	213	Rey Quinones	.05	.02
156	Al Newman	.05	.02	214	Jim Presley	.05	.02
157	Kent Hrbek	.07	.04	215	Alvin Davis	.05	.02
158	Gary Gaetti	.07	.04	216	Edgar Martinez	.40	.25
159	Wally Backman	.05	.02	217	Darnell Coles	.05	.02
160	Gene Larkin	.05	.02	218	Jeffrey Leonard	.05	.02
161	Greg Gagne	.08	.05	219	Jay Buhner	.10	.06
162	Kirby Puckett	.35	.20	220	Ken Griffey, Jr. (R)	4.50	3.00
163	Danny Gladden	.05	.02	221	Drew Hall	.05	.02
164	Randy Bush	.05	.02	222	Bobby Witt	.08	.05
165	Dave LaPoint	.05	.02	223	Jamie Moyer	.05	.02
166	Andy Hawkins	.05	.02	224	Charlie Hough	.05	.02
167	Dave Righetti	.07	.04	225	Nolan Ryan	.60	.35
168	Lance McCullers	.05	.02	226	Jeff Russell	.07	.03
169	Jimmy Jones	.05	.02	227	Jim Sundberg	.05	.02
170	Al Leiter	.05	.02	228	Julio Franco	.10	.06
171	John Candelaria	.05	.02	229	Buddy Bell	.05	.02
172	Don Slaught	.05	.02	230	Scott Fletcher	.05	.02
173	Jamie Quirk	.05	.02	231	Jeff Kunkel	.05	.02
174	Rafael Santana	.05	.02	232	Steve Buechele	.06	.03
175	Mike Pagliarulo	.05	.02	233	Monty Fariss (R)	.15	.08
176	Don Mattingly	.20	.12	234	Rich Leach	.05	.02
177	Ken Phelps	.05	.02	235	Ruben Sierra	.30	.18
178	Steve Sax	.08	.05	236	Cecil Espy	.05	.02
179	Dave Winfield	.15	.08	237	Rafael Palmeiro	.15	.08
180	Stan Jefferson	.05	.02	238	Pete Incaviglia	.07	.04
181	Rickey Henderson	.25	.15	239	Dave Steib	.08	.05
182	Bob Brower	.05	.02	240	Jeff Musselman	.05	.02
183	Roberto Kelly	.25	.15	241	Mike Flanagan	.05	.02
184	Curt Young	.05	.02	242	Todd Stottlemyre	.12	.07

243	Jimmy Key	.08	.05	301	John Franco	.05	.02
244	Tony Castillo	.05	.02	302	Rich Mahler	.05	.02
245	Alex Sanchez	.05	.02	303	Ron Robinson	.05	.02
246	Tom Henke	.06	.03	304	Danny Jackson	.07	.03
247	John Cerutti	.05	.02	305	Rob Dibble (R)	.12	.07
248	Ernie Whitt	.05	.02	306	Tom Browning	.07	.04
249	Bob Brenly	.05	.02	307	Bo Diaz	.05	.02
250	Rance Mulliniks	.05	.02	308	Manny Trillo	.05	.02
251	Kelly Gruber	.08	.05	309	Chris Sabo (R)	.25	.15
252	Ed Sprague (R)	.15	.08	310	Ron Oester	.05	.02
253	Fred McGriff	.25	.15	311	Barry Larkin	.15	.08
254	Tony Fernandez	.07	.04	312	Todd Benzinger	.05	.02
255	Tom Lawless	.05	.02	313	Paul O'Neill	.08	.05
256	George Bell	.10	.06	314	Kal Daniels	.05	.02
257	Jesse Barfield	.07	.04	315	Joel Youngblood	.05	.02
258	R. Alomar/Dad	.20	.12	316	Eric Davis	.10	.06
259	Ken Griffey Jr & Sr	1.25	.80	317	Dave Smith	.05	.02
260	Cal Ripken Jr & Sr	.20	.12	318	Mark Portugal	.05	.02
261	Mel Stottlemyre Jr & Sr	.08	.05	319	Brian Meyer	.07	.04
262	Zane Smith	.07	.04	320	Jim Deshales	.05	.02
263	Charlie Puleo	.05	.02	321	Juan Agosto	.05	.02
264	Derek Lilliquist (R)	.08	.05	322	Mike Scott	.05	.02
265	Paul Assenmacher	.05	.02	323	Rick Rhoden	.05	.02
266	John Smoltz (R)	.75	.45	324	Jim Clancy	.05	.02
267	Tom Glavine	.70	.40	325	Larry Andersen	.05	.02
268	Steve Avery (R)	1.00	.70	326	Alex Trevino	.05	.02
269	Pete Smith	.12	.07	327	Alan Ashby	.05	.02
270	Jody Davis	.05	.02	328	Craig Reynolds	.05	.02
271	Bruce Benedict	.05	.02	329	Bill Doran	.05	.02
272	Andres Thomas	.05	.02	330	Rafael Ramirez	.05	.02
273	Gerald Perry	.05	.02	331	Glenn Davis	.10	.06
274	Ron Gant	.35	.20	332	Willie Ansley (R)	.15	.08
275	Darrell Evans	.07	.03	333	Gerald Young	.05	.02
276	Dale Murphy	.10	.06	334	Cameron Drew	.05	.02
277	Dion James	.05	.02	335	Jay Howell	.05	.02
278	Lonnie Smith	.05	.02	336	Tim Belcher	.07	.04
279	Geronimo Berroa	.05	.02	337	Fernando Valenzuela	.08	.05
280	Steve Wilson	.07	.04	338	Ricky Horton	.05	.02
281	Rick Sutcliffe	.07	.04	339	Tim Leary	.05	.02
282	Kevin Coffman	.05	.02	340	Bill Bene	.05	.02
283	Mitch Williams	.05	.02	341	Orel Hershiser	.08	.05
284	Greg Maddux	.15	.08	342	Mike Scioscia	.05	.02
285	Paul Kilgus	.05	.02	343	Rick Dempsey	.05	.02
286	Mike Harkey (R)	.12	.07	344	Willie Randolph	.07	.04
287	Lloyd McClendon	.05	.02	345	Alfredo Griffin	.05	.02
288	Damon Berryhill	.06	.03	346	Eddie Murray	.12	.07
289	Ty Griffin (R)	.07	.03	347	Mickey Hatcher	.05	.02
290	Ryne Sandberg	.35	.20	348	Mike Sharperson	.05	.02
291	Mark Grace	.20	.12	349	John Shelby	.05	.02
292	Curt Wilkerson	.05	.02	350	Mike Marshall	.05	.02
293	Vance Law	.05	.02	351	Kirk Gibson	.07	.04
294	Shawon Dunston	.08	.05	352	Mike Davis	.05	.02
295	Jerome Walton (R)	.08	.05	353	Bryn Smith	.05	.02
296	Mitch Webster	.05	.02	354	Pascual Perez	.05	.02
297	Dwight Smith (R)	.07	.04	355	Kevin Gross	.05	.02
298	Andre Dawson	.15	.08	356	Andy McGaffigan	.05	.02
299	Jeff Sellers	.05	.02	357	Brian Holman (R)	.12	.07
300	Jose Rijo	.08	.05	358	Dave Wainhouse (R)	.10	.06

359 Denny Martinez	.10	.06	417 Mike Lavalliere	.05	.02
360 Tim Burke	.05	.02	418 Ken Oberkfell	.05	.02
361 Nelson Santovenia	.05	.02	419 Sid Bream	.05	.02
362 Tim Wallach	.08	.05	420 Austin Manahan (R)	.10	.06
363 Spike Owen	.05	.02	421 Jose Lind	.05	.02
364 Rex Hudler	.05	.02	422 Bobby Bonilla	.12	.07
365 Andres Galarraga	.07	.04	423 Glenn Wilson	.05	.02
366 Otis Nixon	.05	.02	424 Andy Van Slyke	.12	.07
367 Hubie Brooks	.07	.04	425 Gary Redus	.05	.02
368 Mike Aldrete	.05	.02	426 Barry Bonds	.35	.20
369 Tim Raines	.08	.05	427 Don Heinkel	.05	.02
370 Dave Martinez	.05	.02	428 Ken Dayley	.05	.02
371 Bob Ojeda	.05	.02	429 Todd Worrel	.07	.04
372 Ron Darling	.05	.02	430 Brad DuVall	.07	.04
373 Wally Whitehurst	.07	.04	431 Jose DeLeon	.05	.02
374 Randy Myers	.05	.02	432 Joe Magrane	.07	.04
375 David Cone	.15	.10	433 John Ericks (R)	.12	.07
376 Doc Gooden	.15	.10	434 Frank DiPino	.05	.02
377 Sid Fernandez	.07	.04	435 Tony Pena	.06	.03
378 Dave Proctor (R)	.08	.05	436 Ozzie Smith	.15	.08
379 Gary Carter	.08	.05	437 Terry Pendleton	.15	.08
380 Keith Miller	.05	.02	438 Jose Oquendo	.05	.02
381 Gregg Jefferies (R)	.30	.18	439 Tim Jones	.08	.05
382 Tim Teufel	.05	.02	440 Pedro Guerrero	.07	.04
383 Kevin Elster	.05	.02	441 Milt Thompson	.05	.02
384 Dave Magaden	.07	.04	442 Willie McGee	.08	.05
385 Keith Hernandez	.07	.04	443 Vince Coleman	.08	.05
386 Mookie Wilson	.05	.02	444 Tom Brunansky	.07	.04
387 Darryl Strawberry	.20	.12	445 Walt Terrell	.05	.02
388 Kevin McReynolds	.07	.04	446 Eric Show	.05	.02
389 Mark Carreon	.05	.02	447 Mark Davis	.07	.04
390 Jeff Parrett	.05	.02	448 Andy Benes (R)	.40	.25
391 Mike Maddux	.05	.02	449 Eddie Whitson	.05	.02
392 Don Carman	.05	.02	450 Dennis Rasmussen	.05	.02
393 Bruce Ruffin	.05	.02	451 Bruce Hurst	.07	.04
394 Ken Howell	.05	.02	452 Pat Clements	.05	.02
395 Steve Bedrosian	.07	.04	453 Benito Santiago	.10	.06
396 Floyd Youmans	.05	.02	454 Sandy Alomar, Jr. (R)	.15	.08
397 Larry McWilliams	.05	.02	455 Garry Templeton	.05	.02
398 Pat Combs (R)	.10	.06	456 Jack Clark	.07	.04
399 Steve Lake	.05	.02	457 Tim Flannery	.05	.02
400 Dickie Thon	.05	.02	458 Roberto Alomar	.75	.45
401 Ricky Jordan (R)	.08	.05	459 Camelo Martinez	.05	.02
402 Mike Schmidt	.35	.20	460 John Kruk	.08	.05
403 Tom Herr	.05	.02	461 Tony Gwynn	.20	.12
404 Chris James	.05	.02	462 Jerald Clark (R)	.08	.05
405 Juan Samuel	.05	.02	463 Don Robinson	.05	.02
406 Von Hayes	.05	.02	464 Craig Lefferts	.05	.02
407 Ron Jones	.07	.04	465 Kelly Downs	.05	.02
408 Curt Ford	.05	.02	466 Rick Rueschel	.05	.02
409 Bob Walk	.05	.02	467 Scott Garrelts	.05	.02
410 Jeff Robinson	.05	.02	468 Wil Tejada	.05	.02
411 Jim Gott	.05	.02	469 Kirt Manwaring	.05	.02
412 Scott Medvin	.07	.04	470 Terry Kennedy	.05	.02
413 John Smiley	.10	.06	471 Jose Uribe	.05	.02
414 Bob Kipper	.05	.02	472 Royce Clayton (R)	.50	.30
415 Brian Fisher	.05	.02	473 Robby Thompson	.06	.03
416 Doug Drabek	.10	.06	474 Kevin Mitchell	.10	.06

		MINT	NR/MT
475	Ernie Riles	.05	.02
476	Will Clark	.40	.25
477	Donnell Nixon	.05	.02
478	Candy Maldonado	.05	.02
479	Tracy Jones	.05	.02
480	Brett Butler	.08	.05
481	Checklist	.05	.02
482	Checklist	.05	.02
483	Checklist	.05	.02
484	Checklist	.05	.02

1990 Bowman

In this 528-card Set Bowman converted to the current standard card size of 2-1/2" by 3-1/2". Card fronts feature full-color player photos surrounded by white borders. The checklist is organized by teams, in alphabetical order beginning with the National League.

		MINT	NR/MT
Complete Set (528)		15.00	8.00
Commons		.05	.02
1	Tommy Greene (R)	.20	.12
2	Tom Glavine	.40	.25
3	Andy Nezelek	.05	.02
4	Mike Stanton (R)	.08	.05
5	Rick Lueken	.08	.05
6	Kent Mercker (R)	.10	.06
7	Derek Lilliquist	.05	.02
8	Charlie Liebrandt	.05	.02
9	Steve Avery	.50	.30
10	John Smoltz	.25	.15
11	Mark Lemke	.05	.02
12	Lonnie Smith	.05	.02
13	Oddibe McDowell	.05	.02
14	Tyler Houston (R)	.10	.06

		MINT	NR/MT
15	Jeff Blauser	.05	.02
16	Ernie Whitt	.05	.02
17	Alexis Infante	.07	.04
18	Jim Presley	.05	.02
19	Dale Murphy	.10	.06
20	Nick Esasky	.05	.02
21	Rick Sutcliffe	.07	.04
22	Mike Bielecki	.05	.02
23	Steve Wilson	.05	.02
24	Kevin Blankenship	.05	.02
25	Mitch Williams	.05	.02
26	Dean Wilkins	.05	.02
27	Greg Maddux	.15	.08
28	Mike Harkey	.08	.05
29	Mark Grace	.10	.06
30	Ryne Sandberg	.30	.18
31	Greg Smith (R)	.08	.05
32	Dwight Smith	.07	.04
33	Damon Berryhill	.05	.02
34	Earl Cunningham (R)	.12	.07
35	Jerome Walton	.07	.04
36	Lloyd McClendon	.05	.02
37	Ty Griffin	.05	.02
38	Shawon Dunston	.08	.05
39	Andre Dawson	.12	.07
40	Luis Salazar	.05	.02
41	Tim Layana	.07	.04
42	Rob Dibble	.08	.05
43	Tom Browning	.07	.04
44	Danny Jackson	.06	.03
45	Jose Rijo	.08	.05
46	Scott Scudder (R)	.10	.06
47	Randy Myers	.05	.02
48	Brian Lane (R)	.10	.06
49	Paul O'Neill	.08	.05
50	Barry Larkin	.10	.06
51	Reggie Jefferson (R)	.20	.12
52	Jeff Branson (R)	.10	.06
53	Chris Sabo	.10	.06
54	Joe Oliver	.07	.04
55	Todd Benzinger	.05	.02
56	Rolando Roomes	.05	.02
57	Hal Morris	.20	.12
58	Eric Davis	.08	.05
59	Scott Bryant (R)	.12	.07
60	Ken Griffey	.07	.04
61	Darryl Kile (R)	.20	.12
62	Dave Smith	.05	.02
63	Mark Portugal	.05	.02
64	Jeff Juden (R)	.30	.18
65	Bill Gullickson	.05	.02
66	Danny Darwin	.05	.02
67	Larry Andersen	.05	.02
68	Jose Cano	.07	.04
69	Dan Schatzeder	.05	.02
70	Jim Deshaies	.05	.02
71	Mike Scott	.05	.02
72	Gerald Young	.05	.02

73	Ken Caminiti	.07	.04
74	Ken Oberkfell	.05	.02
75	Dave Rhode	.07	.04
76	Bill Doran	.05	.02
77	Andujar Cedeno (R)	.25	.15
78	Craig Biggio	.07	.04
79	Karl Rhodes	.12	.07
80	Glenn Davis	.08	.05
81	Eric Anthony (R)	.30	.18
82	John Wetteland	.15	.08
83	Jay Howell	.05	.02
84	Orel Hershiser	.07	.04
85	Tim Belcher	.07	.04
86	Kiki Jones (R)	.12	.07
87	Mike Hartley (R)	.10	.06
88	Ramon Martinez	.15	.08
89	Mike Scioscia	.05	.02
90	Willie Randolph	.05	.02
91	Juan Samuel	.05	.02
92	Jose Offerman (R)	.15	.08
93	Dave Hansen (R)	.12	.07
94	Jeff Hamilton	.05	.02
95	Alfredo Griffin	.05	.02
96	Tom Goodwin (R)	.12	.07
97	Kirk Gibson	.06	.03
98	Jose Vizcaino (R)	.07	.04
99	Kal Daniels	.05	.02
100	Hubie Brooks	.07	.04
101	Eddie Murray	.10	.06
102	Dennis Boyd	.05	.02
103	Tim Burke	.05	.02
104	Bill Sampen	.05	.02
105	Brett Gideon	.07	.04
106	Mark Gardner (R)	.12	.07
107	Howard Farmer	.08	.05
108	Mel Rojas (R)	.08	.05
109	Kevin Gross	.05	.02
110	Dave Schmidt	.05	.02
111	Denny Martinez	.08	.05
112	Jerry Goff	.05	.02
113	Andres Galarraga	.07	.04
114	Tim Welch	.07	.04
115	Marquis Grissom (R)	.60	.35
116	Spike Owen	.05	.02
117	Larry Walker (R)	.50	.30
118	Tim Raines	.07	.04
119	Delino DeShields (R)	.60	.35
120	Tom Foley	.05	.02
121	Dave Martinez	.05	.02
122	Frank Viola	.07	.04
123	Julio Valera (R)	.12	.07
124	Alejandro Pena	.05	.02
125	David Cone	.12	.07
126	Doc Gooden	.12	.07
127	Kevin Brown	.08	.05
128	John Franco	.05	.02
129	Terry Bross	.10	.06
130	Blaine Beatty	.10	.06
131	Sid Fernandez	.05	.02
132	Mike Marshall	.05	.02
133	Howard Johnson	.08	.05
134	Jaime Roseboro	.08	.05
135	Alan Zinter (R)	.10	.06
136	Keith Miller	.05	.02
137	Kevin Elster	.05	.02
138	Kevin McReynolds	.07	.04
139	Barry Lyons	.05	.02
140	Gregg Jefferies	.15	.08
141	Darryl Strawberry	.20	.12
142	Todd Hundley (R)	.10	.06
143	Scott Service	.05	.02
144	Chuck Malone	.08	.05
145	Steve Ontiveros	.05	.02
146	Roger McDowell	.05	.02
147	Ken Howell	.05	.02
148	Pat Combs	.08	.05
149	Jeff Parrett	.05	.02
150	Chuck McElroy (R)	.10	.06
151	Jason Grimsley (R)	.12	.07
152	Len Dykstra	.07	.04
153	Mickey Morandini (R)	.15	.08
154	John Kruk	.07	.04
155	Dickie Thon	.05	.02
156	Ricky Jordan	.05	.02
157	Jeff Jackson (R)	.12	.07
158	Darren Daulton	.12	.07
159	Tom Herr	.05	.02
160	Von Hayes	.05	.02
161	Dave Hollins (R)	.35	.20
162	Carmelo Martinez	.05	.02
163	Bob Walk	.05	.02
164	Doug Drabek	.10	.06
165	Walt Terrell	.05	.02
166	Bill Landrum	.05	.02
167	Scott Ruskin	.10	.06
168	Bob Patterson	.05	.02
169	Bobby Bonilla	.10	.06
170	Jose Lind	.05	.02
171	Andy Van Slyke	.10	.06
172	Mike Lavalliere	.05	.02
173	Willie Greene (R)	.20	.12
174	Jay Bell	.05	.02
175	Sid Bream	.05	.02
176	Tom Prince	.05	.02
177	Wally Backman	.05	.02
178	Moises Alou (R)	.35	.20
179	Steve Carter	.10	.06
180	Gary Redus	.05	.02
181	Barry Bonds	.25	.15
182	Don Slaught	.05	.02
183	Joe Magrane	.05	.02
184	Bryn Smith	.05	.02
185	Todd Worrell	.05	.02
186	Jose Deleon	.05	.02
187	Frank DiPino	.05	.02
188	John Tudor	.05	.02

189	Howard Hilton (R)	.08	.05
190	John Ericks	.10	.06
191	Ken Dayley	.05	.02
192	Ray Lankford (R)	.40	.25
193	Todd Zeile (R)	.15	.08
194	Willie McGee	.07	.04
195	Ozzie Smith	.08	.05
196	Milt Thompson	.05	.02
197	Terry Pendleton	.10	.06
198	Vince Coleman	.07	.04
199	Paul Coleman (R)	.10	.06
200	Jose Oquendo	.05	.02
201	Pedro Guerrero	.05	.02
202	Tom Brunansky	.06	.03
203	Roger Smithberg (R)	.08	.05
204	Ed Whitson	.05	.02
205	Dennis Rasmusen	.05	.02
206	Craig Lefferts	.05	.02
207	Andy Benes	.20	.12
208	Bruce Hurst	.07	.04
209	Eric Show	.05	.02
210	Rafael Valdez (R)	.12	.07
211	Joey Cora	.05	.02
212	Thomas Howard (R)	.10	.06
213	Rob Nelson	.05	.02
214	Jack Clark	.07	.04
215	Garry Templeton	.05	.02
216	Fred Lynn	.07	.04
217	Tony Gwynn	.15	.08
218	Benny Santiago	.08	.05
219	Mike Pagliarulo	.05	.02
220	Joe Carter	.15	.08
221	Roberto Alomar	.30	.18
222	Bip Roberts	.05	.02
223	Rick Reuschel	.05	.02
224	Russ Swan (R)	.08	.05
225	Eric Gunderson (R)	.08	.05
226	Steve Bedrosian	.05	.02
227	Mike Remlinger (R)	.07	.04
228	Scott Garrelts	.05	.02
229	Ernie Camacho	.05	.02
230	Andres Santana (R)	.15	.08
231	Will Clark	.25	.15
232	Kevin Mitchell	.08	.05
233	Robby Thompson	.05	.02
234	Bill Bathe	.05	.02
235	Tony Perezchica	.05	.02
236	Gary Carter	.07	.04
237	Brett Butler	.07	.04
238	Matt Williams	.12	.07
239	Ernie Riles	.05	.02
240	Kevin Bass	.05	.02
241	Terry Kennedy	.05	.02
242	Steve Hosey (R)	.35	.20
243	Ben McDonald (R)	.60	.35
244	Jeff Ballard	.05	.02
245	Joe Price	.05	.02
246	Curt Schilling	.10	.06
247	Pete Harnisch	.10	.06
248	Mark Williamson	.05	.02
249	Gregg Olson	.08	.05
250	Chris Myers (R)	.08	.05
251	David Segui (R)	.12	.07
252	Joe Orsulak	.05	.02
253	Craig Worthington	.05	.02
254	Mickey Tettleton	.07	.04
255	Cal Ripken	.35	.20
256	Billy Ripken	.05	.02
257	Randy Milligan	.06	.03
258	Brady Anderson	.15	.08
259	Chris Hoiles (R)	.30	.18
260	Mike Devereaux	.07	.04
261	Phil Bradley	.05	.02
262	Leo Gomez (R)	.40	.25
263	Lee Smith	.08	.05
264	Mike Rockford	.05	.02
265	Jeff Reardon	.07	.04
266	Wes Gardner	.05	.02
267	Mike Boddicker	.05	.02
268	Roger Clemens	.30	.18
269	Rob Murphy	.05	.02
270	Mickey Pina (R)	.07	.04
271	Tony Pena	.05	.02
272	Jody Reed	.05	.02
273	Kevin Romine	.05	.02
274	Mike Greenwell	.07	.04
275	Maurice Vaughn (R)	.30	.18
276	Danny Heep	.05	.02
277	Scott Cooper (R)	.25	.15
278	Greg Blosser (R)	.15	.08
279	Dwight Evans	.07	.04
280	Ellis Burks	.08	.05
281	Wade Boggs	.15	.08
282	Marty Barrett	.05	.02
283	Kirk McCaskill	.05	.02
284	Mark Langston	.07	.04
285	Bert Blyleven	.08	.05
286	Mike Fetters (R)	.08	.05
287	Kyle Abbott (R)	.10	.06
288	Jim Abbott	.20	.12
289	Chuck Finley	.08	.05
290	Gary DiSarcina (R)	.15	.08
291	Dick Schofield	.05	.02
292	Devon White	.05	.02
293	Bobby Rose (R)	.10	.06
294	Brian Downing	.05	.02
295	Lance Parrish	.05	.02
296	Jack Howell	.05	.02
297	Claudell Washington	.05	.02
298	John Orton (R)	.08	.05
299	Wally Joyner	.10	.06
300	Lee Stevens (R)	.12	.07
301	Chili Davis	.07	.04
302	Johnny Ray	.05	.02
303	Greg Hibbard (R)	.15	.08
304	Eric King	.05	.02

#	Player			#	Player		
305	Jack McDowell	.20	.12	363	Mark Gubicza	.05	.02
306	Bobby Thigpen	.07	.04	364	Bret Saberhagen	.07	.04
307	Adam Peterson	.05	.02	365	Tom Gordon	.05	.02
308	Scott Radinsky (R)	.15	.08	366	Steve Farr	.05	.02
309	Wayne Edwards	.07	.04	367	Kevin Appier (R)	.30	.18
310	Melido Perez	.06	.03	368	Storm Davis	.05	.02
311	Robin Ventura	.50	.30	369	Mark Davis	.05	.02
312	Sammy Sosa (R)	.15	.08	370	Jeff Montgomery	.05	.02
313	Dan Pasqua	.05	.02	371	Frank White	.05	.02
314	Carlton Fisk	.07	.04	372	Brent Mayne (R)	.10	.06
315	Ozzie Guillen	.07	.04	373	Bob Boone	.07	.04
316	Ivan Calderon	.07	.04	374	Jim Eisenreich	.05	.02
317	Daryl Boston	.05	.02	375	Danny Tartabull	.10	.06
318	Craig Grebeck (R)	.10	.06	376	Kurt Stillwell	.05	.02
319	Scott Fletcher	.05	.02	377	Bill Pecota	.05	.02
320	Frank Thomas (R)	3.00	2.00	378	Bo Jackson	.20	.12
321	Steve Lyons	.05	.02	379	Bob Hamelin (R)	.10	.06
322	Carlos Martinez	.07	.04	380	Kevin Seitzer	.05	.02
323	Joe Skalski	.07	.04	381	Rey Palacios	.05	.02
324	Tom Candiotti	.05	.02	382	George Brett	.20	.12
325	Greg Swindell	.07	.04	383	Gerald Perry	.05	.02
326	Steve Olin (R)	.12	.07	384	Teddy Higuera	.05	.02
327	Kevin Wickander	.05	.02	385	Tom Filer	.05	.02
328	Doug Jones	.05	.02	386	Dan Plesac	.05	.02
329	Jeff Shaw	.08	.05	387	Cal Eldred (R)	.50	.30
330	Kevin Bearse	.07	.04	388	Jaime Navarro (R)	.25	.15
331	Dion James	.05	.02	389	Chris Bosio	.50	.02
332	Jerry Browne	.05	.02	390	Randy Veres	.07	.04
333	Albert Belle (R)	.75	.45	391	Gary Sheffield	.50	.30
334	Felix Fermin	.05	.02	392	George Canale	.08	.05
335	Candy Maldonado	.05	.02	393	B.J. Surhoff	.05	.02
336	Cory Snyder	.05	.02	394	Tim McIntosh (R)	.12	.07
337	Sandy Alomar	.10	.06	395	Greg Brock	.05	.02
338	Mark Lewis	.15	.08	396	Greg Vaughn (R)	.25	.15
339	Carlos Baerga (R)	.80	.50	397	Darryl Hamilton (R)	.12	.07
340	Chris James	.05	.02	398	Dave Parker	.07	.04
341	Brook Jacoby	.05	.02	399	Paul Molitor	.08	.05
342	Keith Hernandez	.06	.03	400	Jim Gantner	.05	.02
343	Frank Tanana	.05	.02	401	Rob Deer	.05	.02
344	Scott Aldred (R)	.15	.08	402	Billy Spiers	.05	.02
345	Mike Henneman	.05	.02	403	Glenn Braggs	.05	.02
346	Steve Wapnick	.07	.04	404	Robin Yount	.20	.12
347	Greg Gohr (R)	.12	.07	405	Rick Aguilera	.07	.04
348	Eric Stone (R)	.10	.06	406	Johnny Ard	.07	.04
349	Brian DuBois	.07	.04	407	Kevin Tapani (R)	.20	.12
350	Kevin Ritz	.07	.04	408	Park Pittman	.08	.05
351	Rico Brogna	.15	.08	409	Allan Anderson	.05	.02
352	Mike Heath	.05	.02	410	Juan Berenguer	.05	.02
353	Alan Trammell	.07	.04	411	Willie Banks (R)	.25	.15
354	Chet Lemon	.05	.02	412	Rich Yett	.05	.02
355	Dave Bergman	.05	.02	413	Dave West	.05	.02
356	Lou Whitaker	.05	.02	414	Greg Gagne	.05	.02
357	Cecil Fielder	.20	.12	415	Chuck Knoblauch (R)	1.25	.80
358	Milt Cuyler (R)	.20	.12	416	Randy Bush	.05	.02
359	Tony Phillips	.05	.02	417	Gary Gaetti	.05	.02
360	Travis Fryman (R)	1.00	.70	418	Kent Hrbek	.05	.02
361	Ed Romero	.05	.02	419	Al Newman	.05	.02
362	Lloyd Moseby	.05	.02	420	Danny Gladden	.05	.02

421	Paul Sorrento (R)	.25	.15
422	Derek Parks (R)	.10	.06
423	Scott Leius (R)	.20	.12
424	Kirby Puckett	.25	.15
425	Willie Smith	.10	.06
426	Dave Righetti	.05	.02
427	Jeff Robinson	.05	.02
428	Alan Mills (R)	.12	.07
429	Tim Leary	.05	.02
430	Pascual Perez	.05	.02
431	Alvaro Espinoza	.05	.02
432	Dave Winfield	.10	.06
433	Jesse Barfield	.05	.02
434	Randy Velarde	.05	.02
435	Rick Cerone	.05	.02
436	Steve Balboni	.05	.02
437	Mel Hall	.05	.02
438	Bob Geren	.05	.02
439	Bernie Williams (R)	.25	.15
440	Kevin Maas (R)	.25	.15
441	Mike Blowers	.07	.04
442	Steve Sax	.07	.04
443	Don Mattingly	.12	.07
444	Roberto Kelly	.15	.08
445	Mike Moore	.05	.02
446	Reggie Harris (R)	.10	.06
447	Scott Sanderson	.05	.02
448	Dave Otto	.05	.02
449	Dave Stewart	.07	.04
450	Rick Honeycutt	.05	.02
451	Dennis Eckersley	.08	.05
452	Carney Lansford	.05	.02
453	Scott Hemond (R)	.07	.04
454	Mark McGwire	.25	.15
455	Felix Jose	.15	.08
456	Terry Steinbach	.07	.04
457	Rickey Henderson	.20	.12
458	Dave Henderson	.06	.03
459	Mike Gallego	.05	.02
460	Jose Canseco	.25	.15
461	Walt Weiss	.05	.02
462	Ken Phelps	.05	.02
463	Darren Lewis (R)	.15	.08
464	Ron Hassey	.05	.02
465	Roger Salkeld (R)	.35	.20
466	Scott Bankhead	.05	.02
467	Keith Comstock	.05	.02
468	Randy Johnson	.15	.08
469	Erik Hanson	.10	.06
470	Mike Schooler	.08	.05
471	Gary Eave	.08	.05
472	Jeffrey Leonard	.05	.02
473	Dave Valle	.05	.02
474	Omar Vizquel	.05	.02
475	Pete O'Brien	.05	.02
476	Henry Cotto	.05	.02
477	Jay Buhner	.08	.05
478	Harold Reynolds	.05	.02
479	Alvin Davis	.05	.02
480	Darnell Coles	.05	.02
481	Ken Griffey, Jr.	1.25	.80
482	Greg Briley	.07	.04
483	Scott Bradley	.05	.02
484	Tino Martinez	.25	.15
485	Jeff Russell	.05	.02
486	Nolan Ryan	.50	.30
487	Robb Nen (R)	.12	.07
488	Kevin Brown	.07	.04
489	Brian Bohanon (R)	.08	.05
490	Ruben Sierra	.20	.12
491	Pete Incaviglia	.05	.02
492	Juan Gonzalez (R)	2.00	1.25
493	Steve Buechele	.05	.02
494	Scott Coolbaugh	.05	.02
495	Geno Petralli	.05	.02
496	Rafael Palmeiro	.10	.06
497	Julio Franco	.10	.06
498	Gary Pettis	.05	.02
499	Donald Harris (R)	.10	.06
500	Monty Fariss	.07	.04
501	Harold Baines	.07	.04
502	Cecil Espy	.05	.02
503	Jack Daugherty	.07	.04
504	Willie Blair	.07	.04
505	Dave Steib	.07	.04
506	Tom Henke	.05	.02
507	John Cerutti	.05	.02
508	Paul Kilgus	.05	.02
509	Jimmy Key	.05	.02
510	John Olerud (R)	.30	.18
511	Ed Sprague	.08	.05
512	Manny Lee	.05	.02
513	Fred McGriff	.20	.12
514	Glenallen Hill	.08	.05
515	George Bell	.07	.04
516	Mookie Wilson	.05	.02
517	Luis Sojo (R)	.12	.07
518	Nelson Liriano	.05	.02
519	Kelly Gruber	.07	.04
520	Greg Myers	.05	.02
521	Pat Borders	.05	.02
522	Junior Felix	.05	.02
523	Eddie Zosky (R)	.15	.08
524	Tony Fernandez	.05	.02
525	Checklist	.05	.02
526	Checklist	.05	.02
527	Checklist	.05	.02
528	Checklist	.05	.02

1991 Bowman

The 1991 Bowman set is similar in design to the 1990 set and features 704-cards compared to 528 in 1990. Special subsets honor Hall of Famer Rod Carew and the winners of the NL and AL Silver Slugger Awards. The standard size cards measure 2-1/2" by 3-1/2" with full-color action photos on the card fronts.

		MINT	NR/MT
Complete Set (704)		16.00	9.00
Commons		.05	.02
1	Rod Carew	.15	.08
2	Rod Carew	.15	.08
3	Rod Carew	.15	.08
4	Rod Carew	.15	.08
5	Rod Carew	.15	.08
6	Willie Fraser	.05	.02
7	John Olerud	.12	.07
8	William Suero (R)	.10	.06
9	Roberto Alomar	.20	.12
10	Todd Stottlemyre	.07	.04
11	Joe Carter	.12	.07
12	Steve Karsay (R)	.15	.08
13	Mark Whiten	.15	.08
14	Pat Borders	.05	.02
15	Mike Timlin (R)	.10	.06
16	Tom Henke	.05	.02
17	Eddie Zosky	.07	.04
18	Kelly Gruber	.07	.04
19	Jimmy Key	.05	.02
20	Jerry Schunk (R)	.10	.06
21	Manny Lee	.05	.02
22	Dave Steib	.07	.04
23	Pat Hentgen (R)	.12	.07
24	Glenallen Hill	.08	.05
25	Rene Gonzales	.05	.02
26	Ed Sprague	.07	.04
27	Ken Dayley	.05	.02
28	Pat Tabler	.05	.02
29	Denis Boucher (R)	.10	.06
30	Devon White	.05	.02
31	Dante Bichette	.05	.02
32	Paul Molitor	.07	.04
33	Greg Vaughn	.10	.06
34	Dan Plesac	.05	.02
35	Chris George (R)	.10	.06
36	Tim McIntosh	.07	.04
37	Franklin Stubbs	.05	.02
38	Bo Dodson (R)	.15	.08
39	Ron Robinson	.05	.02
40	Ed Nunez	.05	.02
41	Greg Brock	.05	.02
42	Jaime Navarro	.08	.05
43	Chris Bosio	.07	.04
44	B.J. Surhoff	.05	.02
45	Chris Johnson (R)	.10	.06
46	Willie Randolph	.05	.02
47	Narciso Elvira (R)	.08	.05
48	Jim Gantner	.05	.02
49	Kevin Brown	.05	.02
50	Julio Machado	.05	.02
51	Chuck Crim	.05	.02
52	Gary Sheffield	.35	.20
53	Angel Miranda (R)	.08	.05
54	Teddy Higuera	.05	.02
55	Robin Yount	.15	.08
56	Cal Eldred	.15	.08
57	Sandy Alomar	.07	.04
58	Greg Swindell	.07	.04
59	Brook Jacoby	.05	.02
60	Efrain Valdez	.08	.05
61	Ever Magallanes (R)	.10	.06
62	Tom Candiotti	.05	.02
63	Eric King	.05	.02
64	Alex Cole	.07	.04
65	Charles Nagy	.20	.12
66	Mitch Webster	.05	.02
67	Chris James	.05	.02
68	Jim Thome (R)	.25	.15
69	Carlos Baerga	.20	.12
70	Mark Lewis	.10	.06
71	Jerry Browne	.05	.02
72	Jesse Orosco	.05	.02
73	Mike Huff	.05	.02
74	Jose Escobar (R)	.08	.05
75	Jeff Manto	.07	.04
76	Turner Ward (R)	.12	.07
77	Doug Jones	.05	.02
78	Bruce Egloff (R	.10	.06
79	Tim Costo (R)	.20	.12
80	Beau Allred	.08	.05
81	Albert Belle	.12	.07
82	John Farrell	.05	.02
83	Glenn Davis	.07	.04
84	Joe Orsulak	.05	.02
85	Mark Williamson	.05	.02
86	Ben McDonald	.12	.07

87	Billy Ripken	.05	.02
88	Leo Gomez	.12	.07
89	Bob Melvin	.05	.02
90	Jeff Robinson	.05	.02
91	Jose Mesa	.05	.02
92	Gregg Olson	.07	.04
93	Mike Devereaux	.10	.06
94	Luis Mercedes (R)	.20	.12
95	Arthur Rhodes (R)	.25	.15
96	Juan Bell	.05	.02
97	Mike Mussina (R)	1.00	.70
98	Jeff Ballard	.05	.02
99	Chris Hoiles	.12	.07
100	Brady Anderson	.20	.12
101	Bob Milacki	.05	.02
102	David Segui	.07	.04
103	Dwight Evans	.07	.04
104	Cal Ripken	.25	.15
105	Mike Linskey (R)	.08	.05
106	Jeff Tackett (R)	.10	.06
107	Jeff Reardon	.07	.04
108	Dana Kiecker	.05	.02
109	Ellis Burks	.07	.04
110	Dave Owen (R)	.08	.05
111	Danny Darwin	.05	.02
112	Mo Vaughn	.12	.07
113	Jeff McNeely (R)	.35	.20
114	Tom Bolton	.05	.02
115	Greg Blosser	.07	.04
116	Mike Greenwell	.08	.05
117	Phil Plantier (R)	.50	.30
118	Roger Clemens	.20	.12
119	John Marzano	.05	.02
120	Jody Reed	.05	.02
121	Scott Taylor (R)	.08	.05
122	Jack Clark	.07	.04
123	Derek Livernois (R)	.08	.05
124	Tony Pena	.05	.02
125	Tom Brunansky	.05	.02
126	Carlos Quintana	.07	.04
127	Tim Naehring	.10	.06
128	Matt Young	.05	.02
129	Wade Boggs	.08	.05
130	Kevin Morton (R)	.10	.06
131	Pete Incaviglia	.05	.02
132	Rob Deer	.05	.02
133	Bill Gullickson	.05	.02
134	Rico Brogna	.10	.06
135	Lloyd Moseby	.05	.02
136	Cecil Fielder	.12	.07
137	Tony Phillips	.05	.02
138	Mark Leiter (R)	.08	.05
139	John Cerutti	.05	.02
140	Mickey Tettleton	.05	.02
141	Milt Cuyler	.08	.05
142	Greg Gohr	.07	.04
143	Tony Bernazard	.05	.02
144	Dan Gakeler (R)	.08	.05
145	Travis Fryman	.20	.12
146	Dan Petry	.05	.02
147	Scott Aldred	.05	.02
148	John DeSilva (R)	.10	.06
149	Rusty Meacham (R)	.10	.06
150	Lou Whitaker	.05	.02
151	Dave Haas (R)	.08	.05
152	Luis de los Santos	.05	.02
153	Ivan Cruz (R)	.10	.06
154	Alan Trammell	.07	.04
155	Pat Kelly (R)	.15	.08
156	Carl Everett (R)	.20	.12
157	Greg Cadaret	.05	.02
158	Kevin Maas	.10	.06
159	Jeff Johnson (R)	.12	.07
160	Willie Smith	.07	.04
161	Gerald Williams (R)	.15	.08
162	Mike Humphreys (R)	.10	.06
163	Alvaro Espinoza	.05	.02
164	Matt Nokes	.05	.02
165	Wade Taylor	.10	.06
166	Roberto Kelly	.10	.06
167	John Habyan	.05	.02
168	Steve Farr	.05	.02
169	Jesse Barfield	.05	.02
170	Steve Sax	.07	.04
171	Jim Leyritz	.07	.04
172	Robert Eenhoorn (R)	.10	.06
173	Bernie Williams	.10	.06
174	Scott Lusader	.05	.02
175	Torey Lovullo	.05	.02
176	Chuck Cary	.05	.02
177	Scott Sanderson	.05	.02
178	Don Mattingly	.10	.06
179	Mel Hall	.07	.04
180	Juan Gonzalez	.35	.20
181	Hensley Meulens	.05	.02
182	Jose Offerman	.10	.06
183	Jeff Bagwell (R)	.80	.05
184	Jeff Conine (R)	.15	.08
185	Henry Rodriguez (R)	.20	.12
186	Jimmie Reese	.05	.02
187	Kyle Abbott	.08	.05
188	Lance Parrish	.05	.02
189	Rafael Montaivo (R)	.08	.05
190	Floyd Bannister	.05	.02
191	Dick Schofield	.05	.02
192	Scott Lewis (R)	.08	.05
193	Jeff Robinson	.05	.02
194	Kent Anderson	.05	.02
195	Wally Joyner	.07	.04
196	Chuck Finley	.07	.04
197	Luis Sojo	.05	.02
198	Jeff Richardson (R)	.08	.05
199	Dave Parker	.05	.02
200	Jim Abbott	.12	.07
201	Junior Felix	.05	.02
202	Mark Langston	.07	.04

203	Tim Salmon (R)	.40	.25	261	Bret Boone (R)	.50	.30
204	Cliff Young	.05	.02	262	Roger Salkeld	.12	.07
205	Scott Bailes	.05	.02	263	Dave Burba (R)	.08	.05
206	Bobby Rose	.07	.04	264	Kerry Woodson (R)	.08	.05
207	Gary Gaetti	.05	.02	265	Julio Franco	.07	.04
208	Ruben Amaro (R)	.12	.07	266	Dan Peltier (R)	.12	.07
209	Luis Polonia	.05	.02	267	Jeff Russell	.05	.02
210	Dave Winfield	.10	.06	268	Steve Buechele	.05	.02
211	Bryan Harvey	.05	.02	269	Donald Harris	.07	.04
212	Mike Moore	.05	.02	270	Robb Nen	.07	.04
213	Rickey Henderson	.12	.07	271	Rich Gossage	.05	.02
214	Steve Chitren (R)	.10	.06	272	Ivan Rodriguez (R)	1.00	.70
215	Bob Welch	.05	.02	273	Jeff Huson	.05	.02
216	Terry Steinbach	.05	.02	274	Kevin Brown	.08	.05
217	Ernie Riles	.05	.02	275	Dan Smith (R)	.10	.06
218	Todd Van Poppel (R)	.50	.30	276	Gary Pettis	.05	.02
219	Mike Gallego	.05	.02	277	Jack Daugherty	.05	.02
220	Curt Young	.05	.02	278	Mike Jeffcoat	.05	.02
221	Todd Burns	.05	.02	279	Brad Arnsbarg	.05	.02
222	Vance Law	.05	.02	280	Nolan Ryan	.35	.20
223	Eric Show	.05	.02	281	Eric McCray (R)	.08	.05
224	Don Peters (R)	.10	.06	282	Scott Chiamparino	.07	.04
225	Dave Stewart	.07	.04	283	Ruben Sierra	.15	.08
226	Dave Henderson	.05	.02	284	Geno Petralli	.05	.02
227	Jose Canseco	.20	.12	285	Monty Fariss	.05	.02
228	Walt Weiss	.05	.02	286	Rafael Palmeiro	.08	.05
229	Dann Howitt	.10	.06	287	Bobby Witt	.07	.04
230	Willie Wilson	.05	.02	288	Dean Palmer (R)	.35	.20
231	Harold Baines	.05	.02	289	Tony Scruggs (R)	.10	.06
232	Scott Hemond	.05	.02	290	Kenny Rogers	.05	.02
233	Joe Slusarsi	.07	.04	291	Bret Saberhagen	.07	.04
234	Mark McGwire	.20	.12	292	Brian McRae (R)	.20	.12
235	Kirk Dressendorfer (R)	.10	.06	293	Storm Davis	.05	.02
236	Craig Paquette (R)	.10	.06	294	Danny Tartabull	.07	.04
237	Dennis Eckersley	.10	.06	295	David Howard (R)	.08	.05
238	Dana Allison (R)	.08	.05	296	Mike Boddicker	.05	.02
239	Scott Bradley	.05	.02	297	Joel Johnston (R)	.10	.06
240	Brian Holman	.05	.02	298	Tim Spehr (R)	.08	.05
241	Mike Schooler	.05	.02	299	Hector Wagner	.07	.04
242	Rich Delucia	.08	.05	300	George Brett	.20	.12
243	Edgar Martinez	.20	.12	301	Mike Macfarlane	.05	.02
244	Henry Cotto	.05	.02	302	Kirk Gibson	.05	.02
245	Omar Vizquel	.05	.02	303	Harvey Pulliam (R)	.10	.06
246	Ken Griffey, Jr.	.35	.20	304	Jim Eisenreich	.05	.02
247	Jay Buhner	.07	.04	305	Kevin Seitzer	.07	.04
248	Bill Krueger	.05	.02	306	Mark Davis	.05	.02
249	Dave Fleming (R)	.80	.50	307	Kurt Stillwell	.05	.02
250	Patrick Lennon (R)	.20	.12	308	Jeff Montgomery	.05	.02
251	Dave Valle	.05	.02	309	Kevin Appier	.07	.04
252	Harold Reynolds	.05	.02	310	Bob Hamelin	.05	.02
253	Randy Johnson	.08	.05	311	Tom Gordon	.05	.02
254	Scott Bankhead	.05	.02	312	Kerwin Moore (R)	.10	.06
255	Ken Griffey	.07	.04	313	Hugh Walker	.07	.04
256	Greg Briley	.05	.02	314	Terry Shumpert	.07	.04
257	Tino Martinez	.10	.06	315	Warren Cromartie	.05	.02
258	Alvin Davis	.05	.02	316	Gary Thurman	.05	.02
259	Pete O'Brien	.05	.02	317	Steve Bedrosian	.05	.02
260	Erik Hanson	.07	.04	318	Danny Gladden	.05	.02

319	Jack Morris	.10	.06
320	Kirby Puckett	.15	.08
321	Kent Hrbek	.05	.02
322	Kevin Tapani	.07	.04
323	Denny Neagle (R)	.10	.06
324	Rich Garces (R)	.10	.06
325	Larry Casian	.07	.04
326	Shane Mack	.07	.04
327	Allan Anderson	.05	.02
328	Junior Ortiz	.05	.02
329	Paul Abbott (R)	.08	.05
330	Chuck Knolauch	.30	.18
331	Chili Davis	.05	.02
332	Todd Ritchie (R)	.10	.06
333	Brian Harper	.05	.02
334	Rick Aguilera	.05	.02
335	Scott Erickson (R)	.25	.15
336	Pedro Munoz (R)	.25	.15
337	Scott Leuis	.05	.02
338	Greg Gagne	.05	.02
339	Mike Pagliarulo	.05	.02
340	Terry Leach	.05	.02
341	Willie Banks	.08	.05
342	Bobby Thigpen	.05	.02
343	Roberto Hernandez	.08	.05
344	Melido Perez	.05	.02
345	Carlton Fisk	.10	.06
346	Norberto Martin (R)	.08	.05
347	Johnny Ruffin (R)	.15	.08
348	Jeff Carter (R)	.08	.05
349	Lance Johnson	.05	.02
350	Sammy Sosa	.07	.04
351	Alex Fernandez (R)	.12	.07
352	Jack McDowell	.15	.08
353	Bob Wickman (R)	.25	.15
354	Wilson Alvarez (R)	.10	.06
355	Charlie Hough	.05	.02
356	Ozzie Guillen	.05	.02
357	Cory Snyder	.05	.02
358	Robin Ventura	.15	.08
359	Scott Fletcher	.05	.02
360	Cesar Bernhardt (R)	.08	.05
361	Dan Pasqua	.05	.02
362	Tim Raines	.05	.02
363	Brian Drahman (R)	.08	.05
364	Wayne Edwards	.05	.02
365	Scott Radinsky	.07	.04
366	Frank Thomas	1.25	.80
367	Cecil Fielder (Slugger)	.10	.06
368	Julio Franco (Slugger)	.06	.03
369	Kelly Gruber (Slugger)	.06	.03
370	Alan Trammell (Slugger)	.06	.03
371	Rickey Henderson (Slugger)	.10	.06
372	Jose Canseco (Slugger)	.12	.07
373	Ellis Burks (Slugger)	.06	.03
374	Lance Parrish (Slugger)	.06	.03
375	Dave Parker (Slugger)	.06	.03
376	Eddie Murray (Slugger)	.06	.03
377	Ryne Sandberg (Slugger)	.10	.06
378	Matt Williams (Slugger)	.06	.03
379	Barry Larkin (Slugger)	.06	.03
380	Barry Bonds (Slugger)	.10	.06
381	Bobby Bonilla (Slugger)	.06	.03
382	D. Strawberry (Slugger)	.10	.06
383	Benny Santiago (Slugger)	.06	.03
384	Don Robinson (Slugger)	.05	.02
385	Paul Coleman	.07	.04
386	Milt Thompson	.05	.02
387	Lee Smith	.07	.04
388	Ray Lankford	.25	.15
389	Tom Pagnozzi	.05	.02
390	Ken Hill	.05	.02
391	Jamie Moyer	.05	.02
392	Greg Carmona (R)	.08	.05
393	John Ericks	.07	.04
394	Bob Tewksbury	.05	.02
395	Jose Oquendo	.05	.02
396	Rheal Cormier (R)	.15	.08
397	Mike Milchin (R)	.08	.05
398	Ozzie Smith	.10	.06
399	Aaron Holbert (R)	.08	.05
400	Jose DeLeon	.05	.02
401	Felix Jose	.07	.04
402	Juan Agosto	.05	.02
403	Pedro Guerrero	.05	.02
404	Todd Zeile	.10	.06
405	Gerald Perry	.05	.02
406	Donovan Osborne (R)	.30	.18
407	Bryn Smith	.05	.02
408	Bernard Gilkey (R)	.15	.08
409	Rex Hudler	.05	.02
410	Thomson/Branca	.10	.06
411	Lance Dickson (R)	.12	.07
412	Danny Jackson	.05	.02
413	Jerome Walton	.05	.02
414	Sean Cheetham (R)	.08	.05
415	Joe Girardi	.05	.02
416	Ryne Sandberg	.20	.12
417	Mike Harkey	.07	.04
418	George Bell	.07	.04
419	Rick Wilkins (R)	.08	.05
420	Earl Cunningham	.08	.05
421	Heathcliff Slocumb (R)	.10	.06
422	Mike Bieleci	.05	.02
423	Jessie Hollins (R)	.08	.05
424	Shawon Dunston	.05	.02
425	Dave Smith	.05	.02

#	Player			#	Player		
426	Greg Maddux	.10	.06	484	Dave Magadan	.05	.02
427	Jose Vizcaino	.05	.02	485	Andy Ashby (R)	.10	.06
428	Luis Salazar	.05	.02	486	Dale Murphy	.10	.06
429	Andre Dawson	.12	.07	487	Von Hayes	.05	.02
430	Rick Sutcliffe	.05	.02	488	Kim Batiste (R)	.12	.07
431	Paul Assenmacher	.05	.02	489	Tony Longmire (R)	.10	.06
432	Erik Pappas	.07	.04	490	Wally Backman	.05	.02
433	Mark Grace	.08	.05	491	Jeff Jackson	.08	.05
434	Denny Martinez	.08	.05	492	Mickey Morandini	.08	.05
435	Marquis Grissom	.15	.08	493	Darrel Akerfelds	.05	.02
436	Wilfredo Cordero (R)	.35	.20	494	Ricky Jordan	.05	.02
437	Tim Wallach	.07	.04	495	Randy Ready	.05	.02
438	Brian Barnes (R)	.12	.07	496	Darrin Fletcher	.05	.02
439	Barry Jones	.05	.02	497	Chuck Malone	.07	.04
440	Ivan Calderon	.05	.02	498	Pat Combs	.07	.04
441	Stan Spencer (R)	.08	.05	499	Dickie Thon	.05	.02
442	Larry Walker	.15	.08	500	Roger McDowell	.05	.02
443	Chris Haney (R)	.12	.07	501	Len Dykstra	.05	.02
444	Hector Rivera (R)	.08	.05	502	Joe Boever	.05	.02
445	Delino DeShields	.15	.08	503	John Kruk	.05	.02
446	Andres Galarraga	.05	.02	504	Terry Mulholland	.05	.02
447	Gilberto Reyes	.05	.02	505	Wes Chamberlain (R)	.15	.08
448	Willie Greene	.07	.04	506	Mike Lieberthal (R)	.20	.12
449	Greg Colbrunn (R)	.15	.08	507	Darren Daulton	.07	.04
450	Rondell White (R)	.35	.20	508	Charlie Hayes	.05	.02
451	Steve Frey	.05	.02	509	John Smiley	.08	.05
452	Shane Andrews (R)	.12	.07	510	Gary Varsho	.05	.02
453	Mike Fitzgerald	.05	.02	511	Curt Wilkerson	.05	.02
454	Spike Owen	.05	.02	512	Orlando Merced (R)	.15	.08
455	Dave Martinez	.05	.02	513	Barry Bonds	.20	.12
456	Dennis Boyd	.05	.02	514	Mike Lavalliere	.05	.02
457	Eric Bullock	.05	.02	515	Doug Drabek	.08	.05
458	Reid Cornelius (R)	.12	.07	516	Gary Redus	.05	.02
459	Chris Nabholz (R)	.15	.08	517	William Pennyfeather (R)	.15	.08
460	David Cone	.08	.05	518	Randy Tomlin (R)	.15	.08
461	Hubie Brooks	.05	.02	519	Mike Zimmerman (R)	.08	.05
462	Sid Fernandez	.05	.02	520	Jeff King	.07	.04
463	Doug Simons	.07	.04	521	Kurt Miller (R)	.20	.12
464	Howard Johnson	.08	.05	522	Jay Bell	.05	.02
465	Chris Donnels (R)	.08	.05	523	Bill Landrum	.05	.02
466	Anthony Young (R)	.25	.15	524	Zane Smith	.05	.02
467	Todd Hundley	.08	.05	525	Bobby Bonilla	.10	.06
468	Rick Cerone	.05	.02	526	Bob Walk	.05	.02
469	Kevin Elster	.05	.02	527	Austin Manahan	.07	.04
470	Wally Whitehurst	.05	.02	528	Joe Ausanio (R)	.08	.05
471	Vince Coleman	.05	.02	529	Andy Van Slyke	.10	.06
472	Doc Gooden	.10	.06	530	Jose Lind	.05	.02
473	Charlie O'Brien	.05	.02	531	Carlos Garcia (R)	.20	.12
474	Jeromy Burnitz (R)	.35	.20	532	Don Slaught	.05	.02
475	John Franco	.05	.02	533	Colin Powell	.10	.06
476	Daryl Boston	.05	.02	534	Frank Bolick	.12	.07
477	Frank Viola	.07	.04	535	Gary Scott (R)	.12	.07
478	D.J. Dozier	.10	.06	536	Nikco Riesgo (R)	.12	.07
479	Kevin McReynolds	.05	.02	537	Reggie Sanders (R)	1.00	.70
480	Tom Herr	.05	.02	538	Tim Howard (R)	.12	.07
481	Gregg Jefferies	.10	.06	539	Ryan Bowen (R)	.15	.08
482	Pete Schourek (R)	.08	.05	540	Eric Anthony	.12	.07
483	Ron Darling	.05	.02				

No.	Player		
541	Jim Deshales	.05	.02
542	Tom Nevers (R)	.10	.06
543	Ken Caminiti	.07	.04
544	Karl Rhodes	.07	.04
545	Xavier Hernandez	.07	.04
546	Mike Scott	.05	.02
547	Jeff Juden	.10	.06
548	Darryl Kile	.10	.06
549	Willie Ansley	.08	.05
550	Luis Gonzalez (R)	.20	.12
551	Mike Simms (R)	.08	.05
552	Mark Portugal	.05	.02
553	Jimmy Jones	.05	.02
554	Jim Clancy	.05	.02
555	Pete Harnisch	.07	.04
556	Craig Biggio	.10	.06
557	Eric Yelding	.07	.04
558	Dave Rohde	.05	.02
559	Casey Candaele	.05	.02
560	Curt Schilling	.05	.02
561	Steve Finley	.05	.02
562	Javier Ortiz	.05	.02
563	Andujar Cedeno	.15	.08
564	Rafael Ramirez	.05	.02
565	Kenny Lofton (R)	.75	.45
566	Steve Avery	.15	.08
567	Lonnie Smith	.05	.02
568	Kent Mercker	.05	.02
569	Chipper Jones (R)	.35	.20
570	Terry Pendleton	.10	.06
571	Otis Nixon	.05	.02
572	Juan Berenguer	.05	.02
573	Charlie Leibrandt	.05	.02
574	David Justice (R)	.35	.20
575	Keith Mitchell (R)	.10	.06
576	Tom Glavine	.20	.12
577	Greg Olson	.05	.02
578	Rafael Belliard	.05	.02
579	Ben Rivera (R)	.10	.06
580	John Smoltz	.12	.07
581	Tyler Houston	.07	.04
582	Mark Wohlers (R)	.12	.07
583	Ron Gant	.15	.08
584	Ramon Caraballo (R)	.10	.06
585	Sid Bream	.05	.02
586	Jeff Treadway	.05	.02
587	Javier Lopez (R)	.20	.12
588	Deion Sanders	.25	.15
589	Mike Heath	.05	.02
590	Ryan Klesko (R)	.80	.50
591	Bob Ojeda	.05	.02
592	Alfredo Griffin	.05	.02
593	Raul Mondesi (R)	.30	.18
594	Greg Smith	.05	.02
595	Orel Hershiser	.07	.04
596	Juan Samuel	.05	.02
597	Brett Butler	.07	.04
598	Gary Carter	.08	.05
599	Stan Javier	.05	.02
600	Kal Daniels	.05	.02
601	Jamie McAndrew (R)	.10	.06
602	Mike Sharperson	.05	.02
603	Jay Howell	.05	.02
604	Eric Karros (R)	.90	.60
605	Tim Belcher	.07	.04
606	Dan Opperman (R)	.08	.05
607	Lenny Harris	.05	.02
608	Tom Goodwin	.08	.05
609	Darryl Strawberry	.12	.07
610	Ramon Martinez	.08	.05
611	Kevin Gross	.05	.02
612	Zakary Shinall (R)	.15	.08
613	Mike Scioscia	.05	.02
614	Eddie Murray	.12	.07
615	Ronnie Walden (R)	.10	.06
616	Will Clark	.20	.12
617	Adam Hyzdu (R)	.15	.08
618	Matt Williams	.10	.06
619	Don Robinson	.05	.02
620	Jeff Brantley	.05	.02
621	Greg Litton	.05	.02
622	Steve Decker (R)	.12	.07
623	Robby Thompson	.05	.02
624	Mark Leonard (R)	.07	.04
625	Kevin Bass	.05	.02
626	Scott Garrelts	.05	.02
627	Jose Uribe	.05	.02
628	Eric Gunderson	.05	.02
629	Steve Hosey	.08	.05
630	Trevor Wilson	.05	.02
631	Terry Kennedy	.05	.02
632	Dave Righetti	.05	.02
633	Kelly Downs	.05	.02
634	Johnny Ard	.05	.02
635	Eric Christopherson(R)	.10	
636	Kevin Mitchell	.08	.05
637	John Burkett	.05	.02
638	Kevin Rogers (R)	.08	.05
639	Bud Black	.05	.02
640	Willie McGee	.05	.02
641	Royce Clayton	.12	.07
642	Tony Fernandez (R)	.05	.02
643	Ricky Bones (R)	.10	.06
644	Thomas Howard	.07	.04
645	Dave Staton (R)	.20	.12
646	Jim Presley	.05	.02
647	Tony Gwynn	.15	.08
648	Marty Barrett	.05	.02
649	Scott Coolbaugh	.05	.02
650	Craig Lefferts	.05	.02
651	Eddie Whitson	.05	.02
652	Oscar Azocar	.05	.02
653	Wes Gardner	.05	.02
654	Bip Roberts	.05	.02
655	Robbie Beckett (R)	.10	.06
656	Benny Santiago	.07	.04

657	Greg W. Harris	.05	.02
658	Jerald Clark	.05	.02
659	Fred McGriff	.15	.08
660	Larry Andersen	.05	.02
661	Bruce Hurst	.07	.04
662	Steve Martin (R)	.08	.05
663	Rafael Valdez	.07	.04
664	Paul Faries	.05	.02
665	Andy Benes	.08	.05
666	Randy Myers	.05	.02
667	Rob Dibble	.07	.04
668	Glenn Sutko (R)	.08	.05
669	Glenn Braggs	.05	.02
670	Billy Hatcher	.05	.02
671	Joe Oliver	.05	.02
672	Freddie Benavides	.05	.02
673	Barry Larkin	.08	.05
674	Chris Sabo	.07	.04
675	Mariano Duncan	.05	.02
676	Chris Jones	.12	.07
677	Gino Minutelli (R)	.10	.06
678	Reggie Jefferson	.08	.05
679	Jack Armstrong	.05	.02
680	Chris Hammond (R)	.12	.07
681	Jose Rijo	.07	.04
682	Bill Doran	.05	.02
683	Terry Lee (R)	.10	.06
684	Tom Browning	.07	.04
685	Paul O'Neill	.08	.05
686	Eric Davis	.08	.05
687	Dan Wilson (R)	.15	.08
688	Ted Power	.05	.02
689	Tim Layana	.05	.02
690	Norm Charlton	.05	.02
691	Hal Morris	.10	.06
692	Rickey Henderson	.15	.08
693	Sam Militello (R)	.35	.20
694	Matt Mieske (R)	.20	.12
695	Paul Russo (R)	.10	.06
696	Domingo Mota (R)	.10	.06
697	Todd Guggiana (R)	.08	.05
698	Marc Newfield (R)	.60	.35
699	Checklist	.05	.02
700	Checklist	.05	.02
701	Checklist	.05	.02
702	Checklist	.05	.02
703	Checklist	.05	.02
704	Checklist	.05	.02

1992 Bowman

The cards in this 705-card set measure 2-1/2" by 3-1/2" and feature full color photos on the card fronts. The quality of the 1992 set has been up-graded over previous years and uses a premium UV coated glossy card stock. The set includes 45-special Gold Foil insert cards and a group of 1991 Minor League MVP's and First Round Draft Picks.

		MINT	NR/MT
Complete Set (705)		20.00	14.00
Commons		.05	.02

1	Ivan Rodriquez	.40	.25
2	Kirk McCaskill	.05	.02
3	Scott Livingstone	.05	.02
4	Solomon Torres (R)	.30	.18
5	Carlos Hernandez	.07	.04
6	Dave Hollins	.10	.06
7	Scott Fletcher	.05	.02
8	Jorge Fabregas	.10	.06
9	Andujar Cedeno	.08	.05
10	Howard Johnson	.07	.04
11	Trevor Hoffman	.08	.05
12	Roberto Kelly	.12	.07
13	Gregg Jefferies	.10	.06
14	Marquis Grissom	.15	.08
15	Mike Ignasiak (R)	.10	.06
16	Jack Morris	.08	.05
17	William Pennyfeather	.08	.05
18	Todd Stottlemyre	.07	.04
19	Chito Martinez	.08	.05
20	Roberto Alomar	.20	.12
21	Sam Militello	.15	.08
22	Hector Fajardo	.12	.07
23	Paul Quantrill	.12	.07
24	Chuck Knoblauch	.20	.12
25	Reggie Jefferson	.08	.05
26	Jeremy McGarity (R)	.12	.07
27	Jerome Walton	.05	.02

28	Chipper Jones	.20	.12
29	Brain Barber	.15	.08
30	Ron Darling	.07	.04
31	Roberto Petrone (R)	.10	.06
32	Chuck Finley	.07	.04
33	Edgar Martinez	.15	.08
34	Napoleon Robinson(R)	.12	.07
35	Andy Van Slyke	.10	.06
36	Bobby Thigpen	.07	.04
37	Travis Fryman	.12	.08
38	Eric Christopherson	.08	.05
39	Terry Mulholland	.05	.02
40	Darryl Strawberry	.20	.12
41	Manny Alexander	.08	.05
42	Tracey Sanders (R)	.12	.07
43	Pete Incaviglia	.05	.02
44	Kim Batiste	.07	.04
45	Frank Rodriquez (R)	1.25	.80
46	Gregg Swindell	.07	.04
47	Delino DeShields	.12	.07
48	John Ericks	.08	.05
49	Franklin Stubbs	.05	.02
50	Tony Gwynn	.15	.08
51	Clifton Garrett (R)	.10	.06
52	Mike Gardella (R)	.08	.05
53	Scott Erickson	.12	.07
54	Gary Cababallo (R)	.08	.05
55	Jose Oliva (R)	.08	.05
56	Brook Fordyce (R)	.15	.08
57	Mark Whiten	.08	.05
58	Joe Slusarski	.07	.04
59	J. R. Phillips	.08	.05
60	Barry Bonds	.20	.12
61	Bob Milacki	.05	.02
62	Keith Mitchell	.07	.04
63	Angel Miranda	.05	.02
64	Raul Mondesi	.20	.12
65	Brian Koelling (R)	.10	.06
66	Brian McRae	.10	.06
67	John Patterson	.07	.04
68	John Wetteland	.10	.06
69	Wilson Alvarez	.07	.04
70	Wade Boggs	.12	.07
71	Darryl Ratliff	.08	.05
72	Jeff Jackson	.10	.06
73	Jeremy Hernandez	.05	.02
74	Darryl Hamilton	.05	.02
75	Rafeal Belliard	.05	.02
76	Ricky Talicek	.08	.05
77	Felipe Crespo	.08	.05
78	Carney Lansford	.07	.04
79	Ryan Long	.08	.05
80	Kirby Puckett	.15	.08
81	Earl Cunningham	.07	.04
82	Pedro Martinez (R)	.60	.35
83	Scott Hatteberg (R)	.20	.12
84	Juan Gonzalez	.30	.18
85	Robert Nutting (R)	.08	.05
86	Calvin Reese (R)	.25	.15
87	Dave Silvestri	.15	.08
88	Scott Ruffcorn (R)	.15	.08
89	Rick Aguilera	.05	.02
90	Cecil Fielder	.12	.07
91	Kirk Dressendorfer	.08	.05
92	Jerry Dipoto (R)	.08	.05
93	Mike Fielder	.05	.02
94	Craig Paquette	.08	.05
95	Elvin Paulino (R)	.08	.05
96	Donovan Osborne	.15	.08
97	Hubie Brooks	.05	.02
98	Derek Lowe (R)	.08	.05
99	David Zancanaro	.08	.05
100	Ken Griffey Jr.	.35	.20
101	Todd Hundley	.08	.05
102	Mike Trombley	.08	.05
103	Ricky Gutierrez	.08	.05
104	Braulio Castillo	.08	.05
105	Craig Lefferts	.05	.02
106	Rick Sutcliffe	.05	.02
107	Dean Palmer	.25	.15
108	Henry Rodriquez	.10	.06
109	Mark Clark	.08	.05
110	Kenny Lofton	.20	.12
111	Mark Carreon	.05	.02
112	J.T. Bruett (R)	.08	.05
113	Gerald Williams	.10	.06
114	Frank Thomas	.40	.25
115	Kevin Reimer	.08	.05
116	Sammy Sosa	.07	.04
117	Mickey Tettleton	.05	.02
118	Reggie Sanders	.20	.12
119	Trevor Wilson	.05	.02
120	Cliff Brantley	.05	.02
121	Spike Owen	.05	.02
122	Jeff Montgomery	.05	.02
123	Alex Sutherland	.07	.04
124	Brien Taylor (R)	2.00	1.25
125	Brian Williams	.15	.08
126	Kevin Seitzer	.07	.04
127	Carlos Delgado	.08	.05
128	Gary Scott	.07	.04
129	Scott Cooper	.12	.07
130	Domingo Jean	.08	.05
131	Pat Mahomes (R)	.40	.25
132	Mike Boddicker	.05	.02
133	Roberto Hernandez	.05	.02
134	Dave Valle	.05	.02
135	Kurt Stillwell	.05	.02
136	Brad Pennington (R)	.08	.05
137	Jermaine Swifton (R)	.10	.06
138	Ryan Hawblitzel (R)	.30	.18
139	Tito Navarro (R)	.08	.05
140	Sandy Alomar	.07	.04
141	Todd Benzinger	.05	.02
142	Danny Jackson	.05	.02
143	Melvin Nieves (R)	.08	.05

144	Jim Campanis (R)	.15	.08
145	Luis Gonzalez	.10	.06
146	Dave Doorneweerd (R)	.12	.07
147	Charlie Hayes	.05	.02
148	Greg Maddux	.10	.06
149	Brian Harper	.05	.02
150	Brent Miller (R)	.12	.07
151	Shawn Estes (R)	.20	.12
152	Mike Williams (R)	.12	.07
153	Charlie Hough	.05	.02
154	Randy Myers	.05	.02
155	Kevin Young	.05	.02
156	Rick Wilkins	.05	.02
157	Terry Schumpert	.05	.02
158	Steve Karsay	.08	.05
159	Gary DiSarcina	.08	.05
160	Deion Sanders	.25	.15
161	Tom Browning	.05	.02
162	Dickie Thon	.05	.02
163	Luis Mercedes	.07	.04
164	Riccardo Ingram	.12	.07
165	Tavo Alvarez	.08	.05
166	Rickey Henderson	.15	.08
167	Jaime Navarro	.12	.07
168	Billy Ashley (R)	.40	.25
169	Phil Dauphin (R)	.10	.06
170	Ivan Cruz (R)	.07	.04
171	Harold Baines	.05	.02
172	Bryan Harvey	.07	.04
173	Alex Cole	.07	.04
174	Curtis Shaw	.08	.05
175	Matt Williams	.08	.05
176	Felix Jose	.08	.05
177	Sam Horn	.05	.02
178	Randy Johnson	.10	.06
179	Ivan Calderon	.07	.04
180	Steve Avery	.15	.08
181	William Suero	.07	.04
182	Bill Swift	.05	.02
183	Howard Battle	.07	.04
184	Ruben Amaro	.07	.04
185	Jim Abbott	.12	.07
186	Mike Fitzgerald	.05	.02
187	Bruce Hurst	.07	.04
188	Jeff Juden	.07	.04
189	Jeromy Burnitz	.12	.08
190	Dave Burba	.05	.02
191	Kevin Brown	.10	.06
192	Patrick Lennon	.08	.05
193	Jeffrey McNeely	.20	.12
194	Wil Cordero	.25	.15
195	Chili Davis	.05	.02
196	Milt Cuyler	.07	.04
197	Von Hayes	.05	.02
198	Todd Revenig	.08	.05
199	Joel Johnson	.08	.05
200	Jeff Bagwell	.35	.20
201	Alex Fernandez	.10	.06
202	Todd Jones	.08	.05
203	Charles Nagy	.15	.08
204	Tim Raines	.07	.04
205	Kevin Maas	.08	.05
206	Julio Franco	.07	.04
207	Randy Velarde	.05	.02
208	Lance Johnson	.05	.02
209	Scott Leius	.07	.04
210	Derek Lee (R)	.08	.05
211	Joe Sondrini (R)	.08	.05
212	Royce Clayton	.10	.06
213	Chris George	.07	.04
214	Gary Sheffield	.25	.15
215	Mark Gubicza	.07	.04
216	Mike Moore	.05	.02
217	Rick Huisman (R)	.15	.08
218	Jeff Russell	.05	.02
219	D.J. Dozier	.05	.02
220	Dave Martinez	.05	.02
221	Alan Newman	.05	.02
222	Nolan Ryan	.30	.18
223	Teddy Higuera	.05	.02
224	Damon Buford (R)	.20	.12
225	Ruben Sierra	.12	.08
226	Tom Nevers	.05	.02
227	Tommy Greene	.10	.06
228	Nigel Wilson	.10	.06
229	John DeSilva	.08	.05
230	Bobby Witt	.07	.04
231	Greg Cadaret	.05	.02
232	John VanderWal	.07	.04
233	Jack Clark	.05	.02
234	Bill Doran	.05	.02
235	Bobby Bonilla	.08	.05
236	Steve Olin	.07	.04
237	Derek Bell	.08	.05
238	David Cone	.08	.05
239	Victor Cole	.05	.02
240	Rod Bolton	.05	.02
241	Tom Pagnozzi	.05	.02
242	Rob Dibble	.07	.04
243	Michael Carter (R)	.10	.06
244	Don Peters (R)	.15	.08
245	Mike LaValliere	.05	.02
246	Joe Perona	.08	.05
247	Mitch Williams	.05	.02
248	Jay Buhner	.07	.04
249	Andy Benes	.08	.05
250	Alex Ochoa (R)	.30	.18
251	Greg Blosser	.08	.05
252	Jack Armstrong	.05	.02
253	Juan Samuel	.05	.02
254	Terry Pendleton	.10	.06
255	Ramon Martinez	.10	.06
256	Rico Brogna	.10	.06
257	John Smiley	.08	.05
258	Carl Everett	.10	.06
259	Tim Salmon	.10	.06

260	Will Clark	.15	.08
261	Ugueth Urbina (R)	.08	.05
262	Jason Wood (R)	.10	.06
263	Dave Magadan	.05	.02
264	Dante Bichette	.05	.02
265	Jose DeLeon	.05	.02
266	Mike Neill (R)	.35	.20
267	Paul O'Neill	.08	.05
268	Anthony Young	.08	.05
269	Greg Harris	.05	.02
270	Todd Van Poppel	.15	.08
271	Pete Castellano	.05	.02
272	Tony Phillips	.05	.02
273	Mike Gallego	.05	.02
274	Steve Cooke	.07	.04
275	Robin Ventura	.15	.08
276	Kevin Mitchell	.08	.05
277	Doug Linton (R)	.08	.05
278	Robert Eenhorne	.08	.05
279	Gabe White	.08	.05
280	Dave Stewart	.08	.05
281	Mo Sanford	.08	.05
282	Greg Perschke	.07	.04
283	Kevin Flora (R)	.12	.07
284	Jeff Williams	.08	.05
285	Keith Miller	.05	.02
286	Andy Ashby	.05	.02
287	Doug Dascenzo	.05	.02
288	Eric Karros	.20	.12
289	Glenn Murray	.08	.05
290	Troy Percival (R)	.15	.08
291	Orlando Merced	.08	.05
292	Peter Hoy	.08	.05
293	Tony Fernandez	.05	.02
294	Juan Guzman	.25	.15
295	Jesse Barfield	.05	.02
296	Sid Fernandez	.07	.04
297	Scott Cepicky (R)	.20	.12
298	Garret Anderson	.08	.05
299	Cal Eldred	.25	.15
300	Ryne Sandberg	.15	.08
301	Jim Gantner	.05	.02
302	Mariano Rivera	.07	.04
303	Ron Lockett	.08	.05
304	Jose Offerman	.08	.05
305	Denny Martinez	.07	.04
306	Luis Ortiz	.05	.02
307	David Howard	.08	.05
308	Russ Springer	.05	.02
309	Chris Howard	.07	.04
310	Kyle Abbott	.07	.04
311	Aaron Sele (R)	.60	.35
312	David Justice	.25	.15
313	Pete O'Brien	.05	.02
314	Greg Hansell (R)	.08	.05
315	Dave Winfield	.10	.06
316	Lance Dickson	.10	.06
317	Eric King	.05	.02
318	Vaughn Eshelman	.08	.05
319	Tim Belcher	.07	.04
320	Andres Galarraga	.07	.04
321	Scott Bullett (R)	.12	.07
322	Doug Strange	.05	.02
323	Jerald Clark	.05	.02
324	Greg Hibbard	.05	.02
326	Eric Dillman	.08	.05
327	Shane Reynolds (R)	.10	.06
328	Chris Hammond	.08	.05
329	Albert Belle	.12	.07
330	Rich Becker	.08	.05
331	Eddie Williams	.05	.02
332	Donald Harris	.10	.06
333	Dave Smith	.05	.02
334	Steve Fireovid	.08	.05
335	Steve Buechele	.05	.02
336	Mike Schooler	.05	.02
337	Kevin McReynolds	.05	.02
338	Hensley Meulens	.07	.04
339	Benji Gil (R)	.20	.12
340	Don Mattingly	.15	.08
341	Alvin Davis	.05	.02
342	Alan Mills	.07	.04
343	Kelly Downs	.05	.02
344	Leo Gomez	.07	.04
345	Tarrik Brock (R)	.12	.07
346	Ryan Turner (R)	.08	.05
347	John Smoltz	.12	.07
348	Bill Sampen	.05	.02
349	Paul Byrd	.08	.05
350	Mike Bordick	.08	.05
351	Jose Lind	.05	.02
352	David Wells	.05	.02
353	Barry Larkin	.08	.05
354	Bruce Ruffin	.05	.02
355	Luis Rivera	.05	.02
356	Sid Bream	.05	.02
357	Julain Vasquez	.07	.04
358	Jason Bere	.10	.06
359	Ben McDonald	.12	.07
360	Scott Stahoviak	.12	.07
361	Kirt Manwaring	.05	.02
362	Jeff Johnson	.05	.02
363	Rob Deer	.05	.02
364	Tony Pena	.05	.02
365	Melido Perez	.05	.02
366	Clay Parker	.05	.02
367	Dale Sveum	.05	.02
368	Mike Scioscia	.05	.02
369	Roger Salkeld	.10	.06
370	Mike Stanley	.05	.02
371	Jack McDowell	.15	.08
372	Tim Wallach	.07	.04
373	Billy Ripken	.05	.02
374	Mike Christopher	.08	.05
375	Paul Molitor	.07	.04
376	Dave Stieb	.07	.04

377	Pedro Guerrero	.05	.02
378	Russ Swan	.05	.02
379	Bob Ojeda	.05	.02
380	Donn Pall	.05	.02
381	Eddie Zosky	.07	.04
382	Darnell Coles	.05	.02
383	Tom Smith	.08	.05
384	Mark McGwire	.15	.08
385	Gary Carter	.07	.04
386	Rich Amarel (R)	.08	.05
387	Alan Embree (R)	.10	.06
388	Jonathan Hurst (R)	.08	.05
389	Bobby Jones (R)	.25	.15
390	Rico Rossy (R)	.08	.05
391	Dan Smith (R)	.12	.07
392	Terry Steinbach	.07	.04
393	Jon Farrell	.07	.04
394	Dave Anderson	.05	.02
395	Benito Santiago	.07	.04
396	Mark Wohlers	.10	.06
397	Mo Vaughn	.12	.07
398	Randy Kramer	.08	.05
399	John Jaha	.08	.05
400	Cal Ripken	.15	.08
401	Ryan Bowen	.08	.05
402	Tim McIntosh	.08	.05
403	Bernard Gilkey	.08	.05
404	Junior Felix	.05	.02
405	Cris Colon	.08	.05
406	Marc Newfield	.20	.12
407	Bernie Williams	.10	.06
408	Jay Howell	.05	.02
409	Zane Smith	.05	.02
410	Jeff Shaw	.07	.04
411	Kerry Woodson	.08	.05
412	Wes Chamberlain	.08	.05
413	Dave Mulicki	.08	.05
414	Benny Distefano	.05	.02
415	Kevin Rogers	.05	.02
416	Tim Naehring	.07	.04
417	Clemente Nunez	.08	.05
418	Luis Sojo	.05	.02
419	Kevin Ritz	.05	.02
420	Omar Olivares	.05	.02
421	Manuel Lee	.05	.02
422	Julio Valera	.05	.02
423	Omar Vizquel	.05	.02
424	Darren Burton	.08	.05
425	Mel Hall	.07	.04
426	Dennis Powell	.07	.04
427	Lee Stevens	.08	.05
428	Glenn Davis	.05	.02
429	Willie Greene	.10	.06
430	Kevin Wickander	.05	.02
431	Dennis Eckersley	.12	.07
432	Joe Orsulak	.05	.02
433	Eddie Murray	.10	.06
434	Matt Stairs	.07	.04
435	Wally Joyner	.08	.05
436	Rondell White	.20	.12
437	Rob Mauer	.10	.06
438	Joe Redfield (R)	.08	.05
439	Mark Lewis	.08	.05
440	Darren Daulton	.08	.05
441	Mike Henneman	.05	.02
442	John Cangelosi	.05	.02
443	Vince Moore	.08	.05
444	John Wehner	.05	.02
445	Kent Hrbek	.07	.04
446	Mark McLemore	.05	.02
447	Bill Wegman	.05	.02
448	Robby Thompson	.05	.02
449	Mark Anthony	.07	.04
450	Archi Cianfrocco (R)	.20	.12
451	Johnny Ruffin	.12	.07
452	Javier Lopez	.20	.12
452	Greg Gohr	.10	.06
454	Tim Scott	.08	.05
455	Stan Belinda	.05	.02
456	Darrin Jackson	.05	.02
457	Chris Gardner	.05	.02
458	Esteban Beltre	.05	.02
459	Phil Plantier	.20	.12
460	Jim Thome	.15	.08
461	Mike Piazza (R)	.25	.15
462	Matt Sinatro	.05	.02
463	Scott Servais	.05	.02
464	Brian Jordan	.10	.06
465	Doug Drabek	.08	.05
466	Carl Willis	.05	.02
467	Bret Barberie	.07	.04
468	Hal Morris	.08	.05
469	Steve Sax	.07	.04
470	Jerry Willard	.05	.02
471	Dan Wilson	.07	.04
472	Chris Hoiles	.10	.06
473	Rheal Cormier	.08	.05
474	John Morris	.05	.02
475	Jeff Reardon	.08	.05
476	Mark Leiter	.05	.02
477	Tom Gordon	.05	.02
478	Kent Bottenfield	.05	.02
479	Gene Larkin	.05	.02
480	Dwight Gooden	.08	.05
481	B.J. Surhoff	.05	.02
482	Andy Stankiewicz	.07	.04
483	Tino Martinez	.08	.05
484	Craig Biggio	.07	.04
485	Denny Neagle	.07	.04
486	Rusty Meacham	.05	.02
487	Kal Daniels	.05	.02
488	Dave Henderson	.05	.02
489	Tim Costo	.08	.05
490	Doug Davis	.05	.02
491	Frank Viola	.07	.04
492	Cory Snyder	.05	.02

493	Chris Martin	.07	.04	551	Frank Thomas (Foil)	.25	.15
494	Dion James	.05	.02	552	Kevin Tapani	.08	.05
495	Randy Tomlin	.07	.04	553	Willie Banks	.07	.04
496	Greg Vaughn	.07	.04	554	B.J. Wallace	.07	.04
497	Dennis Cook	.05	.02	555	Orlando Miller (R)	.10	.06
498	Rosario Rodriguez	.05	.02	556	Mark Smith (R)	.25	.15
499	Dave Staton	.08	.05	557	Tim Wallach (Foil)	.10	.06
500	George Brett	.12	.07	558	Bill Gullickson	.05	.02
501	Brian Barnes	.08	.05	559	Derek Bell (Foil)	.12	.07
502	Butch Henry	.07	.04	560	Joe Randa (Foil)	.15	.08
503	Harold Reynolds	.05	.02	561	Frank Seminara (R)	.10	.06
504	Dave Nied (R)	.25	.15	562	Mark Gardner (R)	.12	.07
505	Lee Smith	.08	.05	563	Rick Greene (Foil)	.12	.07
506	Steve Chitren	.05	.02	564	Gary Gaetti	.05	.02
507	Ken Hill	.08	.05	565	Ozzie Guillen	.05	.02
508	Robbie Beckett	.07	.04	566	Charles Nagy (Foil)	.15	.08
509	Tony Afenir (R)	.12	.07	567	Mike Milchin (R)	.12	.07
510	Kelly Gruber	.07	.04	568	Ben Shelton (R)	.12	.07
511	Bret Boone	.15	.08	569	Chris Roberts (Foil)	.15	.08
512	Jeff Branson	.10	.06	570	Ellis Burks	.07	.04
513	Mike Jackson	.05	.02	571	Scott Scudder	.05	.02
514	Pete Harnisch	.07	.04	572	Jim Abbott (Foil)	.15	.08
515	Chad Kreuter	.05	.02	573	Joe Carter	.12	.07
516	Joe Vitko	.08	.05	574	Steve Finley	.05	.02
517	Orel Hershiser	.08	.05	575	Jim Olander (Foil)	.12	.07
518	John Doherty	.05	.02	576	Carlos Garcia	.15	.08
519	Jay Bell	.05	.02	577	Greg Olson	.05	.02
520	Mark Langston	.08	.05	578	Greg Swindell (Foil)	.12	.08
521	Dann Howitt	.07	.04	579	Matt Williams (Foil)	.15	.08
522	Bobby Reed	.07	.04	580	Mark Grace	.08	.05
523	Roberto Munoz	.07	.04	581	Howard House (Foil)	.15	.08
524	Todd Ritchie	.05	.02	582	Luis Polonia	.07	.04
525	Bip Roberts	.05	.02	583	Erik Hanson	.07	.04
526	Pat Listach	.30	.18	584	Salomon Torres (Foil)	.20	.12
527	Scott Brosius	.05	.02	585	Carlton Fisk	.10	.06
528	John Roper (R)	.12	.07	586	Bret Saberhagen	.08	.05
529	Phil Pratt (R)	.08	.05	587	Chad McDonnell (Foil)	.12	.07
530	Denny Walling	.05	.02	588	Jimmy Key	.05	.02
531	Carlos Baerga	.15	.08	589	Mike Macfarlane	.07	.04
532	Manny Ramirez (R)	1.50	.90	590	Barry Bonds (Foil)	.25	.15
533	Pat Clements	.05	.02	591	Jamie McAndrew	.10	.06
534	Ron Jam	.08	.05	592	Shane Mack	.08	.05
535	Pat Kelly	.07	.04	593	Kerwin Moore	.08	.05
536	Billy Spiers	.05	.02	594	Joe Oliver	.05	.02
537	Darren Reid	.05	.02	595	Chris Sabo	.07	.04
538	Ken Caminiti	.05	.02	596	Alex Gonzalez	.05	.02
539	Butch Hosky	.07	.04	597	Bret Butler	.07	.04
540	Matt Nokes	.05	.02	598	Mark Hutton	.07	.04
541	John Kruk	.07	.04	599	Andy Benes (Foil)	.12	.07
542	John Jaha (Foil)	.12	.07	600	Jose Canseco	.20	.12
543	Justin Thompson	.08	.05	601	Darryl Kile	.07	.04
544	Steve Hosey	.10	.06	602	Matt Stairs (Foil)	.12	.07
545	Joe Kmak	.07	.04	603	Robert Butler (Foil)	.12	.07
546	John Franco	.05	.02	604	Willie McGee	.07	.04
547	Devon White	.05	.02	605	Jack McDowell	.15	.08
548	Elston Hansen (Foil)	.12	.07	606	Tom Candiotti	.05	.02
549	Ryan Klesko	.35	.20	607	Ed Martel	.05	.02
550	Danny Tartabull	.08	.05	608	Matt Mieske (Foil)	.12	.07

609	Darrin Fletcher	.05	.02
610	Rafael Palmeiro	.08	.05
611	Bill Swift	.05	.02
612	Mike Mussina	.35	.20
613	Vince Coleman	.05	.02
614	Scott Cepicky (Foil)	.12	.07
615	Mike Greenwell	.07	.04
616	Kevin McGehee	.10	.06
617	Jeffrey Hammonds (Foil)	1.75	1.00
618	Scott Taylor	.08	.05
619	Dave Otto	.05	.02
620	Mark McGwire (Foil)	.25	.15
621	Kevin Tatar	.08	.05
622	Steve Farr	.05	.02
623	Ryan Klesko (Foil)	.50	.30
624	Dave Fleming	.25	.15
625	Andre Dawson	.10	.06
626	Tino Martinez (Foil)	.12	.07
627	Chad Curtis	.08	.05
628	Mickey Morandini	.08	.05
629	Gregg Olson (Foil)	.12	.07
630	Lou Whitaker	.07	.04
631	Arthur Rhodes	.10	.06
632	Brandon Wilson	.08	.05
633	Lance Jennings	.08	.05
634	Allen Watson	.08	.05
635	Len Dykstra	.07	.04
636	Joe Girardi	.05	.02
637	Kiki Hernandez (Foil)	.12	.07
638	Mike Hampton	.08	.05
639	Al Osuna	.05	.02
640	Kevin Appier	.08	.05
641	Rick Helling (Foil)	.12	.07
642	Jody Reed	.05	.02
643	Ray Lankford	.12	.07
644	John Olerud	.08	.05
645	Paul Molitor (Foil)	.15	.08
646	Pat Borders	.05	.02
647	Mike Morgan	.05	.02
648	Larry Walker	.10	.06
649	Pete Castellano	.05	.02
650	Fred McGriff	.12	.07
651	Walt Weiss	.05	.02
652	Calvin Murray (R)	.40	.25
653	Dave Nilsson	.12	.07
654	Greg Pirkl	.10	.06
655	Robin Ventura	.15	.08
656	Mark Portugal	.05	.02
657	Roger McDowell	.05	.02
658	Rick Hirtensteiner (Foil)	.12	.07
659	Glenallen Hill	.07	.04
660	Greg Gagne	.05	.02
661	Charles Johnson (Foil)	1.00	.70
662	Brian Hunter	.07	.04
663	Mark Lemke	.05	.02
664	Tim Belcher (Foil)	.12	.07
665	Rich DeLucia	.05	.02
666	Bob Walk	.05	.02
667	Joe Carter (Foil)	.25	.15
668	Jose Guzman	.05	.02
669	Otis Nixon	.05	.02
670	Phil Nevin (Foil)	3.00	2.00
671	Eric Davis	.08	.05
672	Damion Easley	.07	.04
673	Will Clark (Foil)	.25	.15
674	Mark Keifer	.07	.04
675	Ozzie Smith	.08	.05
676	Manny Ramirez (Foil)	1.00	.70
677	Gregg Olson	.07	.04
678	Cliff Floyd	.20	.12
679	Duane Singleton	.10	.06
680	Jose Rijo	.08	.05
681	Willie Randolph	.07	.04
682	Michael Tucker (Foil)	.12	.07
683	Darren Lewis	.05	.02
684	Dale Murphy	.08	.05
685	Mike Pagliarulo	.05	.02
686	Paul Miller	.08	.05
687	Mike Robertson	.08	.05
688	Mike Devereaux	.08	.05
689	Pedro Astacio (R)	.75	.45
690	Alan Trammell	.10	.06
691	Roger Clemens	.20	.12
692	Bud Black	.05	.02
693	Turk Wendell (R)	.15	.08
694	Barry Larkin (Foil)	.15	.08
695	Todd Zeile	.08	.05
696	Pat Hentgen	.07	.04
697	Eddie Taubensee	.07	.04
698	Guillermo Vasquez	.05	.02
699	Tom Glavine	.12	.07
700	Robin Yount	.15	.08
701	Checklist 1	.05	.02
702	Checklist 2	.05	.02
703	Checklist 3	.05	.02
704	Checklist 4	.05	.02
705	Checklist 5	.05	.02

CLASSIC

1987 Classic

This inaugural set was part of a baseball trivia board game produced by Game Time Ltd of Marietta, GA. The 100-card set featured full-color player photos on the front with career statistics and trivia questions on the card backs.

		MINT	NR/MT
Complete Set (100)		240.00	150.00
Commons		.10	.06

1	Pete Rose	3.50	2.00
2	Len Dykstra	1.50	.90
3	Darryl Strawberry	5.00	3.00
4	Keith Hernandez	.35	.20
5	Gary Carter	.50	.35
6	Wally Joyner	.90	.60
7	Andres Thomas	.15	.10
8	Pat Dobson	.15	.10
9	Kirk Gibson	.35	.20
10	Don Mattingly	4.50	2.75
11	Dave Winfield	.60	.35
12	Rickey Henderson	7.50	4.50
13	Dan Pasqua	.15	.10
14	Don Baylor	.20	.12
15	Bo Jackson	90.00	60.00
16	Pete Incaviglia	.25	.15
17	Kevin Bass	.15	.10
18	Barry Larkin	1.50	.90
19	Dave Magadan	.80	.50
20	Steve Sax	.25	.15
21	Eric Davis	1.50	.90
22	Mike Pagliarulo	.15	.10
23	Fred Lynn	.25	.15
24	Reggie Jackson	2.00	1.25
25	Lance Parrish	.12	.07
26	Tony Gwynn	2.50	1.50
27	Steve Garvey	.75	.45
28	Glenn Davis	.25	.15
29	Tim Raines	.35	.20
30	Vince Coleman	.25	.15
31	Willie McGee	.25	.15
32	Ozzie Smith	1.00	.70
33	Dave Parker	.25	.15
34	Tony Pena	.10	.06
35	Ryne Sandberg	10.00	6.00
36	Brett Butler	.12	.07
37	Dale Murphy	.60	.35
38	Bob Horner	.15	.10
39	Pedro Guerrero	.20	.12
40	Brook Jacoby	.10	.06
41	Carlton Fisk	.35	.20
42	Harold Baines	.25	.15
43	Rob Deer	.10	.06
44	Robin Yount	4.00	2.50
45	Paul Molitor	.35	.20
46	Jose Canseco	45.00	25.00
47	George Brett	1.75	1.00
48	Jim Presley	.10	.06
49	Rich Gedman	.10	.06
50	Lance Parrish	.20	.12
51	Eddie Murray	.75	.45
52	Cal Ripken Jr.	5.00	3.00
53	Kent Hrbek	.30	.18
54	Gary Gaetti	.20	.12
55	Kirby Puckett	4.00	2.50
56	George Bell	.50	.30
57	Tony Fernandez	.20	.12
58	Jesse Barfield	.15	.10
59	Jim Rice	.50	.30
60	Wade Boggs	2.00	1.25
61	Marty Barrett	.10	.06
62	Mike Schmidt	6.50	3.75
63	Von Hayes	.20	.12
64	Jeffrey Leonard	.15	.10
65	Chris Brown	.10	.06
66	Dave Smith	.10	.06
67	Mike Krukow	.10	.06
68	Ron Guidry	.30	.18
69	Rob Woodward	.10	.06
70	Rob Murphy	.10	.06
71	Andres Galarraga	.30	.18
72	Dwight Gooden	1.50	.90
73	Bob Ojeda	.12	.07
74	Sid Fernandez	.20	.12
75	Jesse Orosco	.10	.06
76	Roger McDowell	.12	.07
77	John Tudor (Er)	.15	.10
78	Tom Browning	.20	.12
79	Rick Aguilera	.15	.10
80	Lance McCullers	.10	.06
81	Mike Scott	.25	.15
82	Nolan Ryan	12.50	7.50
83	Bruce Hurst	.20	.12
84	Roger Clemens	3.00	2.00

85	Dennis "Oil Can" Boyd	.10	.06
86	Dave Righetti	.15	.10
87	Dennis Rasmussen	.10	.06
88	Bret Saberhagen (Er)	.40	.25
89	Mark Langston	.35	.20
90	Jack Morris	.25	.15
91	Fernando Valenzuela	.30	.18
92	Orel Hershiser	.35	.20
93	Rick Honeycutt	.10	.06
94	Jeff Reardon	.25	.15
95	John Habyan	.10	.06
96	Rich "Goose" Gossage	.20	.12
97	Todd Worrell	.20	.12
98	Floyd Youmans	.10	.06
99	Don Aase	.10	.06
100	John Franco	.15	.10

1987 Classic Travel Edition

This 50-card set is an update to the original Classic Baseball Trivia board game. Card backs feature all new trivia questions. Cards were issued without the game board.

	MINT	NR/MT
Complete Set (50)	32.00	20.00
Commons	.08	.05

101	Mike Schmidt	2.75	1.50
102	Eric Davis	1.00	.70
103	Pete Rose	1.25	.80
104	Don Mattingly	1.75	1.00
105	Wade Boggs	1.50	.90
106	Dale Murphy	.50	.30
107	Glenn Davis	.20	.12
108	Wally Joyner	1.50	.90

109	Bo Jackson	6.50	3.75
110	Cory Snyder	.25	.15
111	Jim Lindeman	.08	.05
112	Kirby Puckett	1.50	.90
113	Barry Bonds	5.00	3.00
114	Roger Clemens	1.75	1.00
115	Oddibe McDowell	.10	.06
116	Bret Saberhagen	.35	.20
117	Joe Magrane	.25	.15
118	Scott Fletcher	.10	.06
119	Mark McLemore	.08	.05
120	Joe Niekro (Who Me?)	.30	.18
121	Mark McGwire	3.00	1.75
122	Darryl Strawberry	1.25	.80
123	Mike Scott	.25	.15
124	Andre Dawson	.60	.35
125	Jose Canseco	6.50	3.75
126	Kevin McReynolds	.25	.15
127	Joe Carter	1.50	.90
128	Casey Candaele	.10	.06
129	Matt Nokes	.40	.25
130	Kal Daniels	.40	.25
131	Pete Incaviglia	.35	.20
132	Benito Santiago	1.00	.70
133	Barry Larkin	1.50	.90
134	Gary Pettis	.10	.06
135	B.J. Surhoff	.50	.30
136	Juan Nieves	.10	.06
137	Jim Deshaies	.12	.07
138	Pete O'Brien	.20	.12
139	Kevin Seitzer	.35	.20
140	Devon White	.30	.25
141	Rob Deer	.15	.10
142	Kurt Stillwell	.25	.15
143	Edwin Correa	.08	.05
144	Dion James	.08	.05
145	Danny Tartabull	.80	.50
146	Jerry Browne	.10	.06
147	Ted Higuera	.25	.15
148	Jack Clark	.25	.15
149	Ruben Sierra	2.75	1.65
150	E. Davis/M. McGwire	2.50	1.50

1988 Classic Travel Edition
Red Series

This 50-card update set is the second extension of Classic's original baseball trivia board game. Numbered from 151-200, cards feature red borders and all new trivia questions on the back.

		MINT	NR/MT
Complete Set (50)		12.00	7.00
Commons		.08	.05

		MINT	NR/MT
151	D. Mattingly/ M. McGwire	2.50	1.50
152	Don Mattingly	1.75	1.00
153	Mark McGwire	2.50	1.50
154	Eric Davis	1.00	.70
155	Wade Boggs	1.25	.80
156	Dale Murphy	.50	.30
157	Andre Dawson	.35	.20
158	Roger Clemens	.80	.50
159	Kevin Seitzer	.20	.12
160	Benito Santiago	.25	.15
161	Kal Daniels	.20	.12
162	John Kruk	.25	.15
163	Billy Ripkin (Er)	.10	.06
164	Kirby Puckett	.75	.45
165	Jose Canseco	2.50	1.50
166	Matt Nokes	.15	.10
167	Mike Schmidt	1.00	.70
168	Tim Raines	.40	.25
169	Ryne Sandberg	.75	.45
170	Dave Winfield	.40	.25
171	Dwight Gooden	.75	.45
172	Bret Saberhagen	.25	.15
173	Willie McGee	.20	.12
174	Jack Morris	.25	.15
175	Jeff Leonard	.10	.06
176	Cal Ripken Jr. (Er)	.80	.50
177	Pete Incaviglia	.10	.06
178	Devon White	.15	.10
179	Nolan Ryan	.80	.50
180	Ruben Sierra	.35	.20
181	Todd Worrell	.15	.10
182	Glenn Davis	.20	.12
183	Frank Viola	.25	.15
184	Cory Snyder	.10	.06
185	Tracy Jones	.15	.10
186	Terry Steinbach	.20	.12
187	Julio Franco	.25	.15
188	Larry Sheets	.10	.06
189	John Marzano	.08	.05
190	Kevin Elster	.20	.12
191	Vincente Palacios	.12	.07
192	Kent Hrbek	.25	.15
193	Eric Bell	.08	.05
194	Kelly Downs	.15	.10
195	Jose Lind	.25	.15
196	Dave Stewart	.40	.25
197	J. Canseco/M. McGwire (Er. No card number)	2.50	1.50
198	Phil Niekro (Indians)	.40	.25
199	Phil Niekro (Blue Jays)	.40	.25
200	Phil Niekro (Braves)	.40	.25

1988 Classic Travel Edition
Blue Series

This 50-card blue bordered set is an update of the Classic Travel Edition Red Series. Card backs feature new baseball trivia questions and a box for player's autographs.

	MINT	NR/MT
Complete Set (50)	24.00	14.00
Commons	.12	.07

201	E. Davis/D. Murphy	.50	.35
202	B.J. Surhoff	.15	.10
203	John Kruk	.25	.15
204	Sam Horn	.20	.12
205	Jack Clark	.25	.15
206	Wally Joiner	.40	.25
207	Matt Nokes	.25	.15
208	Bo Jackson	4.50	2.50
209	Darryl Strawberry	1.00	.70
210	Ozzie Smith	.30	.18
211	Don Mattingly	1.00	.70
212	Mark McGwire	1.50	.90
213	Eric Davis	.60	.35
214	Wade Boggs	1.50	.90
215	Dale Murphy	.25	.15
216	Andre Dawson	.35	.20
217	Roger Clemens	1.50	.90
218	Kevin Seitzer	.20	.12
219	Benito Santiago	.25	.15
220	Tony Gwynn	1.00	.70
221	Mike Scott	.15	.10
222	Steve Bedrosian	.15	.10
223	Vince Coleman	.20	.12
224	Rick Sutcliffe	.20	.12
225	Will Clark	8.00	5.00
226	Pete Rose	1.50	.90
227	Mike Greenwell	.75	.45
228	Ken Caminiti	.20	.12
229	Ellis Burks	.80	.50
230	Dave Magadan	.20	.12
231	Alan Trammell	.40	.25
232	Paul Molitor	.25	.15
233	Gary Gaetti	.20	.12
234	Rickey Henderson	1.50	.90
235	Danny Tartabull	.75	.45
236	Bobby Bonilla	1.00	.70
237	Mike Dunne	.12	.07
238	Al Leiter	.12	.07
239	John Farrell	.12	.07
240	Joe Magrane	.15	.10
241	Mike Henneman	.15	.10
242	George Bell	.35	.20
243	Gregg Jefferies	1.25	.80
244	Jay Buhner	.35	.20
245	Todd Benzinger	.25	.15
246	Matt Williams	2.50	1.50
247	D. Mattingly/M. McGwire	1.25	.80
	(Er No Card Number)		
248	George Brett	.75	.45
249	Jimmy Key	.25	.15
250	Mark Langston	.25	.15

1989 Classic

This 100-card set featured light blue borders and full color player photos on the fronts. Card backs included all new trivia questions. Card sets were packaged with a Baseball Trivia board game.

		MINT	NR/MT
Complete Set (100)		26.00	15.00
Commons		.08	.05
1	Orel Hershiser	.35	.20
2	Wade Boggs	.50	.30
3	Jose Canseco	1.75	1.00
4	Mark McGwire	.80	.50
5	Don Mattingly	.50	.30
6	Gregg Jefferies	1.00	.70
7	Dwight Gooden	.70	.40
8	Darryl Strawberry	.50	.30
9	Eric Davis	.40	.25
10	Joey Meyer	.08	.05
11	Joe Carter	.25	.15
12	Paul Molitor	.20	.12
13	Mark Grace	1.00	.70
14	Kurt Stillwell	.10	.06
15	Kirby Puckett	.75	.45
16	Keith Miller	.10	.06
17	Glenn Davis	.15	.10
18	Will Clark	1.75	1.00
19	Cory Snyder	.12	.07
20	Jose Lind	.10	.06
21	Andres Thomas	.08	.05
22	Dave Smith	.08	.05
23	Mike Scott	.15	.10
24	Kevin McReynolds	.15	.10
25	B.J. Surhoff	.15	.10
26	Mackey Sasser	.08	.05
27	Chad Kreuter	.12	.07
28	Hal Morris	1.25	.80
29	Wally Joyner	.20	.12
30	Tony Gwynn	.50	.30

31	Kevin Mitchell	1.25	.80
32	Dave Winfield	.30	.18
33	Billy Bean	.08	.05
34	Steve Bedrosian	.08	.05
35	Ron Gant	1.25	.80
36	Len Dykstra	.15	.10
37	Andre Dawson	.25	.15
38	Brett Butler	.20	.12
39	Rob Deer	.12	.07
40	Tommy John	.15	.10
41	Gary Gaetti	.20	.12
42	Tim Raines	.20	.12
43	George Bell	.25	.15
44	Dwight Evans	.20	.12
45	Dennis Martinez	.12	.07
46	Andres Galarraga	.25	.15
47	George Brett	.60	.35
48	Mike Schmidt	1.50	.90
49	Dave Steib	.25	.15
50	Rickey Henderson	.90	.60
51	Craig Biggio	.75	.45
52	Mark Lemke	.25	.15
53	Chris Sabo	.75	.45
54	Jeff Treadway	.15	.10
55	Kent Hrbek	.20	.12
56	Cal Ripken Jr.	1.50	.90
57	Tim Belcher	.25	.15
58	Ozzie Smith	.50	.30
59	Keith Hernandez	.20	.12
60	Pedro Guerrero	.15	.10
61	Greg Swindell	.25	.15
62	Bret Saberhagen	.35	.20
63	John Tudor	.10	.06
64	Gary Carter	.20	.12
65	Kevin Seitzer	.15	.10
66	Jesse Barfield	.15	.10
67	Luis Medina	.10	.06
68	Walt Weiss	.25	.15
69	Terry Steinbach	.30	.18
70	Barry Larkin	.35	.20
71	Pete Rose	1.00	.70
72	Luis Salazar	.12	.07
73	Benito Santiago	.35	.20
74	Kal Daniels	.15	.10
75	Kevin Elster	.12	.07
76	Rob Dibble	.50	.30
77	Bobby Witt	.40	.25
78	Steve Searcy	.15	.10
79	Sandy Alomar Jr.	.80	.50
80	Chili Davis	.25	.15
81	Alvin Davis	.20	.12
82	Charlie Leibrandt	.15	.10
83	Robin Yount	1.25	.80
84	Mark Carreon	.25	.15
85	Pascual Perez	.10	.06
86	Dennis Rasmussen	.08	.05
87	Ernie Riles	.08	.05
88	Melido Perez	.20	.12

89	Doug Jones	.15	.10
90	Dennis Eckersley	.25	.15
91	Bob Welch	.20	.12
92	Bob Milacki	.15	.10
93	Jeff Robinson	.12	.07
94	Mike Henneman	.12	.07
95	Randy Johnson	.50	.30
96	Ron Jones	.12	.07
97	Jack Armstrong	.20	.12
98	Willie McGee	.12	.07
99	Ryne Sandberg	1.00	.70
100	D. Cone/D. Jackson	.75	.45

1989 Classic Travel Edition
Orange Series

Andy Van Slyke

First update of the 1989 Classic Baseball Trivia board game. This 50-card set featured orange borders and was sold without the game board.

		MINT	NR/MT
Complete Set (50)		12.50	7.50
Commons		.08	.05

101	Gary Sheffield	4.00	2.50
102	Wade Boggs	.50	.30
103	Jose Canseco	1.25	.80
104	Mark McGwire	1.00	.70
105	Orel hershiser	.30	.18
106	Don Mattingly	1.00	.70
107	Dwight Gooden	.60	.35
108	Darryl Strawberry	.40	.25
109	Eric Davis	.30	.18
110	Bam Bam Meulens	.30	.18
111	Andy Van Slyke	.35	.20

112	Al Leiter	.08	.05
113	Matt Nokes	.15	.10
114	Mike Krukow	.08	.05
115	Tony Fernandez	.25	.15
116	Fred McGriff	.40	.25
117	Barry Bonds	.75	.45
118	Gerald Perry	.10	.06
119	Roger Clemens	.70	.40
120	Kirk Gibson	.15	.10
121	Greg Maddux	.50	.30
122	Bo Jackson	1.25	.80
123	Danny Jackson	.15	.10
124	Dale Murphy	.25	.15
125	David Cone	.40	.25
126	Tom Browning	.15	.10
127	Roberto Alomar	1.00	.70
128	Alan Trammell	.20	.12
129	Rickey Jordan	.15	.10
130	Ramon Martinez	1.00	.70
131	Ken Griffey Jr.	6.50	3.50
132	Gregg Olson	.60	.35
133	Carlos Quintana	.30	.18
134	Dave West	.25	.15
135	Cameron Drew	.10	.06
136	Ted Higuera	.20	.12
137	Sil Campusano	.12	.07
138	Mark Gubicza	.25	.15
139	Mike Boddicker	.10	.06
140	Paul Gibson	.08	.05
141	Jose Rijo	.35	.20
142	John Costello	.08	.05
143	Cecil Espy	.10	.06
144	Frank Viola	.25	.15
145	Erik Hanson	.35	.20
146	Juan Samuel	.10	.06
147	Harold Reynolds	.20	.12
148	Joe Magrane	.12	.07
149	Mike Greenwell	.25	.15
150	W. Clark/D. Strawberry	1.25	.80

1989 Classic Travel Edition Purple Series

This purple bordered set is the second update to the 1989 Classic Baseball Trivia board game. Also known as Travel Edition II, the set features special cards of Bo Jackson and Deion Sanders as two-sport stars.

		MINT	NR/MT
Complete Set (50)		16.50	10.50
Commons		.07	.04
151	Jim Abbott	.60	.35
152	Ellis Burks	.25	.15
153	Mike Schmidt	1.25	.80
154	Gregg Jefferies	.50	.30
155	Mark Grace	.35	.20
156	Jerome Walton	.30	.18
157	Bo Jackson	1.00	.70
158	Jack Clark	.08	.05
159	Tom Glavine	.80	.50
160	Eddie Murray	.15	.10
161	John Dopson	.07	.04
162	Ruben Sierra	.60	.35
163	Rafael Palmeiro	.40	.25
164	Nolan Ryan	1.50	.90
165	Barry Larkin	.30	.18
166	Tommy Herr	.07	.04
167	Roberto Kelly	.35	.20
168	Glenn Davis	.12	.07
169	Glenn Braggs	.08	.05
170	Juan Bell	.25	.15
171	Todd Burns	.07	.04
172	Derek Lilliquist	.07	.04
173	Orel Hershiser	.25	.15
174	John Smoltz	.50	.30
175	E. Burks/O. Guillen	.30	.18
176	Kirby Puckett	.70	.40

177	Robin Ventura	2.00	1.25
178	Allan Anderson	.07	.04
179	Steve Sax	.15	.10
180	Will Clark	1.00	.70
181	Mike Devereaux	.15	.10
182	Tom Gordon	.35	.20
183	Rob Murphy	.07	.04
184	Pete O'Brien	.08	.05
185	Cris Carpenter	.15	.10
186	Tom Brunansky	.12	.07
187	Bob Boone	.15	.10
188	Lou Whitaker	.10	.06
189	Dwight Gooden	.40	.25
190	Mark McGwire	.80	.50
191	John Smiley	.20	.12
192	Tommy Gregg	.07	.04
193	Ken Griffey Jr.	3.50	2.00
194	Bruce Hurst	.10	.06
195	Greg Swindell	.25	.15
196	Nelson Liriano	.07	.04
197	Randy Myers	.08	.05
198	Kevin Mitchell	.60	.35
199	Dante Bichette	.08	.05
200	Deion Sanders	1.00	.70

1990 Classic Baseball

John Smiley

The 1990 version of the Classic Baseball Trivia Game features 150 new cards with five new trivia questions on the card backs. Border colors are blue with colorful burgundy waves around the frame.

	MINT	NR/MT
Complete Set (150)	24.00	15.00
Commons	.06	.03

1	Nolan Ryan	2.50	1.50
2	Bo Jackson	.90	.60
3	Gregg Olson	.35	.20
4	Tom Gordon	.40	.25
5	Robin Ventura	1.00	.70
6	Will Clark	.75	.45
7	Ruben Sierra	.35	.20
8	Mark Grace	.25	.15
9	Luis de los Santos	.06	.03
10	Bernie Williams	.50	.30
11	Eric Davis	.12	.07
12	Carney Lansford	.10	.06
13	John Smoltz	.20	.12
14	Gary Sheffield	.80	.50
15	Kent Merker	.30	.18
16	Don Mattingly	.50	.30
17	Tony Gwynn	.25	.15
18	Ozzie Smith	.15	.10
19	Fred McGriff	.35	.20
20	Ken Griffey Jr.	2.50	1.50
21a	Prime Time (Deion Sanders)	12.00	7.50
21b	Deion "Prime Time" Sanders	1.75	1.00
22	Jose Canseco	.70	.40
23	Mitch Williams	.15	.10
24	Cal Ripken Jr.	.35	.20
25	Bob Geren	.10	.06
26	Wade Boggs	.20	.12
27	Ryne Sandberg	.40	.25
28	Kirby Puckett	.35	.20
29	Mike Scott	.06	.03
30	Dwight Smith	.15	.10
31	Craig Worthington	.06	.03
82	Ricky Jordan	.15	.10
33	Darryl Strawberry	.20	.12
34	Jerome Walton	.15	.10
35	John Olerud	1.00	.70
36	Tom Glavine	.30	.18
37	Rickey Henderson	.50	.30
38	Rolando Roomes	.06	.03
39	Mickey Tettleton	.12	.07
40	Jim Abbott	.50	.30
41	Dave Righetti	.06	.03
42	Mike LaValliere	.08	.05
43	Rob Dibble	.35	.20
44	Pete Harnisch	.25	.15
45	Jose Offerman	1.25	.80
46	Walt Weiss	.08	.05
47	Mike Greenwell	.25	.15
48	Barry Larkin	.15	.10
49	Dave Gallagher	.06	.03
50	Junior Felix	.20	.12
51	Roger Clemens	.30	.18
52	Lonnie Smith	.06	.03
53	Jerry Browne	.06	.03
54	Greg Briley	.20	.12
55	Delino DeShields	1.00	.70

No.	Player		
56	Carmelo Martinez	.06	.03
57	Craig Biggio	.20	.12
58	Dwight Gooden	.20	.12
59a	Bo, Ruben, Mark (Bo Jackson, Ruben Sierra, Mark McGwire)	5.00	3.00
59b	A.L. Fence Busters (Bo Jackson, Ruben Sierra, Mark McGwire)	.80	.50
60	Greg Vaughn	.75	.45
61	Roberto Alomar	.40	.25
62	Steve Bedrosian	.06	.03
63	Devon White	.06	.03
64	Kevin Mitchell	.30	.18
65	Marquis Grissom	.80	.50
66	Brian Holman	.10	.06
67	Julio Franco	.20	.12
68	Dave West	.08	.05
69	Harold Baines	.12	.07
70	Eric Anthony	.80	.50
71	Glenn Davis	.07	.04
72	Mark Langston	.20	.12
73	Matt Williams	.35	.20
74	Rafael Palmeiro	.10	.06
75	Pete Rose Jr.	.25	.15
76	Ramon Martinez	.50	.30
77	Dwight Evans	.10	.06
78	Mackey Sasser	.06	.03
79	Mike Schooler	.10	.06
80	Dennis Cook	.08	.05
81	Orel Hershiser	.20	.15
82	Barry Bonds	.40	.25
83	Geronimo Berroa	.06	.03
84	George Bell	.12	.07
85	Andre Dawson	.15	.10
86	John Franco	.10	.06
87a	W. Clark/T. Gwynn	4.00	2.50
87b	N.L. Hit Kings (Will Clark, Tony Gwynn)	.60	.35
88	Glenallen Hill	.30	.18
89	Jeff Ballard	.12	.07
90	Todd Zeile	1.00	.70
91	Frank Viola	.20	.12
92	Ozzie Guillen	.12	.07
93	Jeff Leonard	.06	.03
94	Dave Smith	.06	.03
95	Dave Parker	.15	.10
96	Jose Gonzalez	.12	.07
97	Dave Steib	.15	.10
98	Charlie Hayes	.12	.07
99	Jesse Barfield	.08	.05
100	Joey Belle	.75	.45
101	Jeff Reardon	.12	.07
102	Bruce Hurst	.08	.05
103	Luis Medina	.06	.03
104	Mike Moore	.08	.05
105	Vince Coleman	.10	.06
106	Alan Trammell	.12	.07
107	Randy Myers	.07	.04
108	Frank Tanana	.10	.06
109	Craig Lefferts	.08	.05
110	John Wetteland	.30	.18
111	Chris Gwynn	.10	.06
112	Mark Carreon	.10	.06
113	Von Hayes	.10	.06
114	Doug Jones	.10	.06
115	Andres Galarraga	.12	.07
116	Carlton Fisk	.12	.07
117	Paul O'Neill	.12	.07
118	Tim Raines	.10	.06
119	Tom Brunansky	.10	.06
120	Andy Benes	.50	.30
121	Mark Portugal	.06	.03
122	Willie Randolph	.10	.06
123	Jeff Blauser	.08	.05
124	Don August	.06	.03
125	Chuck Cary	.06	.03
126	John Smiley	.12	.07
127	Terry Mullholland	.10	.06
128	Harold Reynolds	.07	.04
129	Hubie Brooks	.08	.05
130	Ben McDonald	1.00	.70
131	Kevin Ritz	.15	.10
132	Luis Quinones	.06	.03
133	Bam Bam Meulens	.25	.15
134	Bill Spiers	.15	.10
135	Andy Hawkins	.06	.03
136	Alvin Davis	.08	.05
137	Lee Smith	.10	.06
138	Joe Carter	.15	.10
139	Bret Saberhagen	.12	.07
140	Sammy Sosa	.35	.20
141	Matt Nokes	.08	.05
142	Bert Blyleven	.12	.07
143	Bobby Bonilla	.30	.18
144	Howard Johnson	.15	.10
145	Joe Magrane	.06	.03
146	Pedro Guerrero	.08	.05
147	Robin Yount	.60	.35
148	Dan Gladden	.08	.05
149	Steve Sax	.10	.06
150a	W. Clark/K. Mitchell	4.00	2.50
150b	Bay Bombers (W. Clark, K. Mitchell)	.50	.30

1990 Classic II

This 50-card update set features all new trivia questions. Border colors are the reverse of Series I. Card numbers carry the "T" designation on the card backs.

		MINT	NR/MT
Complete Set (50)		12.50	7.50
Commons		.06	.03

		MINT	NR/MT
1	Gregg Jefferies	.30	.18
2	Steve Adkins	.08	.05
3	Sandy Alomar Jr.	.20	.12
4	Steve Avery	.40	.25
5	Mike Blowers	.08	.05
6	George Brett	.10	.06
7	Tom Browning	.08	.05
8	Ellis Burks	.10	.06
9	Joe Carter	.12	.07
10	Jerald Clark	.10	.06
11	Hot Corners (W. Clark, M. Williams)	.35	.20
12	Pat Combs	.15	.10
13	Scott Cooper	.40	.25
14	Mark Davis	.06	.03
15	Storm Davis	.06	.03
16	Larry Walker	.25	.15
17	Brian DuBois	.08	.05
18	Len Dykstra	.10	.06
19	John Franco	.10	.06
20	Kirk Gibson	.08	.05
21	Juan Gonzalez	3.00	1.75
22	Tommy Greene	.35	.20
23	Kent Hrbek	.10	.06
24	Mike Huff	.40	.25
25	Bo Jackson	1.25	.80
26	Nolan Knows Bo (Nolan Ryan)	3.50	2.00
27	Roberto Kelly	.15	.10
28	Mark Langston	.10	.06
29	Ray Lankford	1.00	.70
30	Kevin Maas	1.00	.70
31	Julio Machado	.20	.12
32	Greg Maddux	.15	.10
33	Mark McGwire	.30	.18
34	Paul Molitor	.08	.05
35	Hal Morris	.50	.30
36	Dale Murphy	.08	.05
37	Eddie Murray	.10	.06
38	Jaime Navarro	.15	.10
39	Dean Palmer	.80	.50
40	Derek Parks	.25	.15
41	Bobby Rose	.25	.15
42	Wally Joyner	.08	.05
43	Chris Sabo	.08	.05
44	Benito Santiago	.08	.05
45	Mike Stanton	.08	.05
46	Terry Steinbach	.10	.06
47	Dave Stewart	.10	.06
48	Greg Swindell	.10	.06
49	Jose Vizcaino	.15	.10
50	Royal Flush (M. Davis B. Saberhagen) (No number on card back)	.20	.12

1990 Classic III

This 100-card update set is Classic's third 1990 series. Cards feature yellow borders with blue highlights. Card backs consist of all-new trivia questions to go with Classic's Baseball Trivia board game. Card numbers 51 and 57 were never issued.

		MINT	NR/MT
Complete Set (100)		12.50	7.50
Commons		.06	.03

		MINT	NR/MT
1	Ken Griffey Jr.	1.25	.80

2	John Tudor	.06	.03
3	John Kruk	.10	.06
4	Mark Gardner	.15	.10
5	Scott Radinsky	.15	.10
6	John Burkett	.20	.12
7	Will Clark	.50	.30
8	Gary Carter	.08	.05
9	Ted Higuera	.08	.05
10	Dave Parker	.10	.06
11	Dante Bichette	.06	.03
12	Don Mattingly	.30	.18
13	Greg Harris	.12	.07
14	Dave Hollins	.25	.15
15	Matt Nokes	.06	.03
16	Kevin Tapani	.12	.07
17	Shane Mack	.25	.15
18	Randy Myers	.06	.03
19	Greg Olson	.12	.07
20	Shawn Abner	.08	.05
21	Jim Presley	.06	.03
22	Randy Johnson	.10	.06
23	Edgar Martinez	.35	.20
24	Scott Coolbaugh	.06	.03
25	Jeff Treadway	.06	.03
26	Joe Klink	.06	.03
27	Rickey Henderson	.35	.20
28	Sam Horn	.08	.05
29	Kurt Stillwell	.06	.03
30	Andy Van Slyke	.12	.07
31	Willie Banks	.35	.20
32	Jose Canseco	.50	.30
33	Felix Jose	.15	.10
34	Candy Maldonado	.06	.03
35	Carlos Baerga	.40	.25
36	Keith Hernandez	.06	.03
37	Frank Viola	.08	.05
38	Pete O'Brien	.06	.03
39	Pat Borders	.06	.03
40	Mike Heath	.06	.03
41	Kevin Brown	.20	.12
42	Chris Bosio	.08	.05
43	Shawn Boskie	.15	.10
44	Carlos Quintana	.08	.05
45	Juan Samuel	.06	.03
46	Tim Layana	.12	.07
47	Mike Harkey	.12	.07
48	Gerald Perry	.06	.03
49	Mike Witt	.06	.03
50	Joe Orsulak	.06	.03
51	Never Issued	.00	.00
52	Willie Blair	.08	.05
53	Gene Larkin	.06	.03
54	Jody Reed	.06	.03
55	Jeff Reardon	.08	.05
56	Kevin McReynolds	.06	.03
57	Never Issued	.00	.00
58	Eric Yelding	.08	.05
59	Fred Lynn	.06	.03
60	Jim Leyritz	.10	.06
61	John Orton	.08	.05
62	Mike Leiberthal	.75	.45
63	Mike Hartley	.10	.06
64	Kal Daniels	.06	.03
65	Terry Shumpert	.15	.10
66	Sil Campusano	.06	.03
67	Tony Pena	.06	.03
68	Barry Bonds	.30	.18
69	Oddibe McDowell	.06	.03
70	Kelly Gruber	.08	.05
71	Willie Randolph	.06	.03
72	Rick Parker	.08	.05
73	Bobby Bonilla	.12	.07
74	Jack Armstrong	.08	.05
75	Hubie Brooks	.08	.05
76	Sandy Alomar Jr.	.10	.06
77	Ruben Sierra	.15	.10
78	Erik Hanson	.08	.05
79	Tony Phillips	.06	.03
80	Rondell White	.60	.35
81	Bobby Thigpen	.12	.07
82	Ron Walden	.15	.10
83	Don Peters	.20	.2
84	Nolan Ryan's 6th	1.25	.80
85	Lance Dickson	.35	.20
86	Ryne Sandberg	.15	.10
87	Eric Christopherson	.25	.15
88	Shane Andrews	.20	.12
89	Marc Newfield	1.75	1.00
90	Adam Hyzdu	.40	.25
91	Texas Heat (Nolan and Reid Ryan)	2.50	1.50
92	Chipper Jones	.80	.50
93	Frank Thomas	3.50	2.00
94	Cecil Fielder	.50	.30
95	Delino DeShields	.35	.20
96	John Olerud	.75	.45
97	Dave Justice	1.50	.90
98	Joe Oliver	.12	.07
99	Alex Fernandez	.50	.30
100	Todd Hundley	.25	.15
___	Mike Marshall (Game instructions on back. No number)	.06	.03
___	Frank Viola (Micro)	.20	.12
___	Texas Heat (Micro)	.35	.20
___	Chipper Jones (Micro)	.35	.20
___	Don Mattingly (Micro)	.25	.15

1990 Classic Draft Picks

This set is not related to Classic's Baseball Trivia Game. Only 150,000 sets were issued featuring the first round draft picks from 1990. Card numbers 2 and 22 were never issued.

		MINT	NR/MT
Complete Set (25)		18.00	12.00
Commons		.20	.12

1	Chipper Jones	.70	.40
2	Never Issued	.00	.00
3	Mike Lieberthal	.40	.25
4	Alex Fernandez	.80	.50
5	Kurt Miller	.40	.25
6	Marc Newfield	1.50	.90
7	Dan Wilson	.50	.30
8	Tim Costo	.75	.45
9	Ron Walden	.25	.15
10	Carl Everett	.35	.20
11	Shane Andrews	.25	.15
12	Todd Richie	.25	.15
13	Donovan Osborne	.80	.50
14	Todd Van Poppel	2.50	1.50
15	Adam Hyzdu	.25	.15
16	Dan Smith	.20	.12
17	Jeromy Burnitz	1.25	.80
18	Aaron Holbert	.20	.12
19	Eric Christopherson	.25	.15
20	Mike Mussina	1.00	.70
21	Tom Nevers	.20	.12
22	Never Issued	.00	.00
23	Lance Dickson	.40	.25
24	Rondell White	.60	.35
25	Robbie Beckett	.20	.12
26	Don Peters	.25	.15
__	Checklist (Chipper Jones, Rondell White)	.50	.30

1991 Classic

The 1991 Classic set was issued with a game board and featured all new trivia questions on the card backs. Border colors are blue with red highlights.

		MINT	NR/MT
Complete Set (100)		11.00	7.00
Commons		.07	.04

1	John Olerud	.35	.20
2	Tino Martinez	.30	.18
3	Ken Griffey Jr.	1.00	.70
4	Jeromy Burnitz	.90	.60
5	Ron Gant	.30	.18
6	Mike Benjamin	.07	.04
7	Steve Decker	.20	.12
8	Matt Williams	.25	.15
9	Rafael Novoa	.10	.06
10	Kevin Mitchell	.10	.06
11	Dave Justice	.70	.40
12	Leo Gomez	.25	.15
13	Chris Hoiles	.35	.20
14	Ben McDonald	.25	.15
15	David Segui	.15	.10
16	Anthony Telford	.25	.15
17	Mike Mussina	1.00	.70
18	Roger Clemens	.60	.35
19	Wade Boggs	.30	.18
20	Tim Naehring	.20	.12
21	Joe Carter	.20	.12
22	Phil Plantier	.70	.40
23	Rob Dibble	.20	.12
24	Maurice Vaughn	.70	.40
25	Lee Stevens	.35	.20
26	Chris Sabo	.20	.12
27	Mark Grace	.20	.12
28	Derrick May	.25	.15
29	Ryne Sandberg	.60	.35
30	Matt Stark	.25	.15
31	Bobby Thigpen	.15	.10
32	Frank Thomas	1.00	.70

33	Don Mattingly	.40	.25
34	Eric Davis	.20	.12
35	Reggie Jefferson	.30	.18
36	Alex Cole	.25	.15
37	Mark Lewis	.25	.15
38	Tim Costo	.40	.25
39	Sandy Alomar Jr.	.20	.12
40	Travis Fryman	.90	.60
41	Cecil Fielder	.40	.25
42	Milt Cuyler	.30	.18
43	Andujar Cedeno	.25	.15
44	Danny Darwin	.07	.04
45	Randy Hennis	.10	.06
46	George Brett	.25	.15
47	Jeff Conine	.25	.15
48	Bo Jackson	.70	.40
49	Brian McRae	.30	.18
50	Brent Mayne	.20	.12
51	Eddie Murray	.20	.12
52	Ramon Martinez	.20	.12
53	Jim Neidlinger	.07	.04
54	Jim Poole	.07	.04
55	Tim McIntosh	.20	.12
56	Randy Veres	.07	.04
57	Kirby Puckett	.30	.18
58	Todd Ritchie	.10	.06
59	Rich Garces	.20	.12
60	Moises Alou	.25	.15
61	Delino DeShields	.30	.18
62	Oscar Azocar	.15	.10
63	Kevin Maas	.25	.15
64	Alan Mills	.10	.06
65	John Franco	.08	.05
66	Chris Jelic	.10	.06
67	Dave Magadan	.10	.06
68	Darryl Strawberry	.35	.20
69	Hensley Meulens	.15	.10
70	Juan Gonzalez	1.00	.70
71	Reggis Harris	.15	.10
72	Rickey Henderson	.35	.20
73	Mark McGwire	.40	.25
74	Willie McGee	.15	.10
75	Todd Van Poppel	.80	.50
76	Bob Welch	.10	.06
77	Future Aces	1.75	1.00
	(T. Van Poppel,		
	K. Dressendorfer		
	D. Peters,		
	D. Zancanaro)		
78	Len Dykstra	.12	.08
79	Mickey Morandini	.15	.10
80	Wes Chamberlain	.20	.12
81	Barry Bonds	.40	.25
82	Doug Drabek	.15	.10
83	Randy Tomlin	.15	.10
84	Scott Chiamparino	.15	.10
85	Rafael Palmiero	.20	.12
86	Nolan Ryan	.80	.50

87	Bobby Witt	.10	.06
88	Fred McGriff	.25	.15
89	Dave Stieb	.12	.07
90	Ed Sprague	.15	.10
91	Vince Coleman	.10	.06
92	Rod Brewer	.07	.04
93	Bernard Gilkey	.25	.15
94	Roberto Alomar	.50	.30
95	Chuck Finley	.15	.10
96	Dale Murphy	.15	.10
97	Jose Rijo	.15	.10
98	Hal Morris	.20	.12
99	Friendly Foes	.25	.15
	(D. Gooden,		
	D. Strawberry)		
___	Micro	.80	.50
	(D. Justice,		
	K. Maas,		
	R. Sandberg,		
	T. Van Poppel)		

1991 Classic II

Classic doubled the size of their second series in 1991 to 100 cards compared to 50-cards in 1990. Card fronts feature burgundy borders while card backs contain five new trivia questions to go along with Classic's Baseball Trivia board game.

	MINT	NR/MT
Complete Set (100)	10.00	6.50
Commons	.07	.04

1	Ken Griffey Jr.	.75	.45
2	Wilfredo Cordero	.80	.50
3	Cal Ripken, Jr.	.20	.12
4	D.J. Dozier	.15	.10

#	Player		
5	Darrin Fletcher	.07	.04
6	Glenn Davis	.10	.06
7	Alex Fernandez	.20	.12
8	Cory Snyder	.07	.04
9	Tim Raines	.07	.04
10	Greg Swindell	.12	.07
11	Mark Lewis	.15	.10
12	Rico Brogna	.30	.18
13	Gary Sheffield	.75	.45
14	Paul Molitor	.10	.06
15	Kent Hrbek	.07	.04
16	Scott Erickson	.30	.18
17	Steve Sax	.10	.06
18	Dennis Eckersley	.10	.06
19	Jose Canseco	.35	.20
20	Kirk Dressendorfer	.20	.12
21	Ken Griffey, Sr.	.07	.04
22	Erik Hanson	.10	.06
23	Dan Peltier	.20	.12
24	John Olerud	.12	.07
25	Eddie Zosky	.12	.07
26	Steve Avery	.25	.15
27	John Smoltz	.15	.10
28	Frank Thomas	.75	.45
29	Jerome Walton	.07	.04
30	George Bell	.10	.06
31	Jose Rijo	.10	.06
32	Randy Myers	.07	.04
33	Barry Larkin	.12	.07
34	Eric Anthony	.15	.10
35	Dave Hanson	.08	.05
36	Eric Karros	.40	.25
37	Jose Offerman	.10	.06
38	Marquis Grissom	.15	.10
39	Dwight Gooden	.10	.06
40	Greg Jefferies	.10	.06
41	Pat Combs	.10	.06
42	Todd Zeile	.10	.06
43	Benito Santiago	.10	.06
44	Dave Staton	.12	.07
45	Tony Fernandez	.07	.04
46	Fred McGriff	.15	.10
47	Jeff Brantley	.07	.04
48	Junior Felix	.07	.04
49	Jack Morris	.10	.06
50	Chris George	.07	.04
51	Henry Rodriquez	.40	.25
52	Paul Marak	.12	.07
53	Ryan Klesko	.75	.45
54	Darren Lewis	.10	.06
55	Lance Dickson	.15	.10
56	Anthony Young	.15	.10
57	Willie Banks	.15	.10
58	Mike Bordick	.35	.20
59	Roger Salkeld	.40	.25
60	Steve Karsay	.25	.15
61	Bernie Williams	.20	.12
62	Mickey Tettleton	.10	.06
63	Dave Justice	.25	.15
64	Steve Decker	.12	.07
65	Roger Clemens	.20	.12
66	Phil Plantier	.50	.30
67	Ryne Sandberg	.15	.10
68	Sandy Alomar Jr.	.10	.06
69	Cecil Fielder	.15	.10
70	George Brett	.12	.07
71	Delino DeShields	.12	.07
72	Dave Magadan	.07	.04
73	Darryl Strawberry	.12	.07
74	Juan Gonzalez	.40	.25
75	Rickey Henderson	.12	.07
76	Willie McGee	.07	.04
77	Todd Van Poppel	.80	.50
78	Barry Bonds	.15	.10
79	Doug Drabek	.10	.06
80	Nolan Ryan (300)	.50	.30
81	Roberto Alomar	.15	.10
82	Ivan Rodriguez	.70	.40
83	Dan Opperman	.15	.10
84	Jeff Bagwell	1.00	.70
85	Braulio Castillo	.10	.06
86	Doug Simons	.10	.06
87	Wade Taylor	.10	.06
88	Gary Scott	.25	.15
89	Dave Stewart	.10	.06
90	Mike Simms	.10	.06
91	Luis Gonzalez	.20	.12
92	Bobby Bonilla	.12	.07
93	Tony Gwynn	.12	.07
94	Will Clark	.15	.10
95	Rich Rowland	.08	.05
96	Alan Trammell	.10	.06
97	Strikeout Kings (N.Ryan R. Clemens)	.60	.35
98	Joe Carter	.10	.06
99	Jack Clark	.07	.04
100	Micro (S. Decker)	.15	.10

1991 Classic III

This is the third series of Classic's 1991 Baseball Trivia board game. The set features gray borders with green accents. Card backs contain five new baseball trivia questions.

		MINT	NR/MT
Complete Set (100)		10.00	6.50
Commons		.07	.04

1	Jim Abbott	.25	.15
2	Craig Biggio	.15	.10
3	Wade Boggs	.30	.18
4	Bobby Bonilla	.25	.15
5	Ivan Calderon	.07	.04
6	Jose Canseco	.40	.25
7	Andy Benes	.20	.12
8	Wes Chamberlain	.20	.12
9	Will Clark	.40	.25
10	Royce Clayton	.35	.20
11	Gerald Alexander	.08	.05
12	Chili Davis	.10	.06
13	Eric Davis	.12	.07
14	Andre Dawson	.20	.12
15	Rob Dibble	.15	.10
16	Chris Donnels	.15	.10
17	Scott Erickson	.30	.18
18	Monty Fariss	.15	.10
19	Ruben Amaro Jr.	.25	.15
20	Chuck Finley	.10	.06
21	Carlton Fiks	.15	.10
22	Carlos Baerga	.25	.15
23	Ron Gant	.25	.15
24	D. Justice/R. Gant	.50	.30
25	Mike Gardiner	.10	.06
26	Tom Glavine	.25	.15
27	Joe Grahe	.10	.06
28	Derek Bel	.35	.20l
29	Mike Greenwell	.10	.06
30	Ken Griffey Jr.	.70	.40
31	Leo Gomez	.12	.07
32	Tom Goodwin	.20	.12
33	Tony Gwynn	.30	.18
34	Mel Hall	.10	.06
35	Brian Harper	.07	.04
36	Dave Henderson	.10	.06
37	Albert Belle	.30	.18
38	Orel Hershiser	.12	.07
39	Brian Hunter	.30	.18
40	Howard Johnson	.15	.10
41	Felix Jose	.15	.10
42	Wally Joyner	.15	.10
43	Jeff Juden	.25	.15
44	Pat Kelly	.35	.20
45	Jimmy Key	.08	.05
46	Chuck Knoblauch	.80	.50
47	John Kruk	.08	.05
48	Ray Lankford	.25	.15
49	Cedric Landrum	.08	.05
50	Scott Livingstone	.15	.10
51	Kevin Maas	.20	.12
52	Greg Maddux	.15	.10
53	Dennis Martinez	.10	.06
54	Edgar Martinez	.35	.20
55	Pedro Martinez	.80	.50
56	Don Mattingly	.30	.18
57	Orlando Merced	.20	.12
58	Keith Mitchell	.20	.12
59	Kevin Mitchell	.10	.06
60	Paul Molitor	.10	.06
62	Hal Morris	.15	.10
63	Kevin Morton	.07	.04
64	Pedro Munoz	.30	.18
65	Eddie Murray	.15	.10
66	Jack McDowell	.25	.15
67	Jeff McNeely	.40	.25
68	Brian McRae	.15	.10
69	Kevin McReynolds	.08	.05
70	Gregg Olson	.10	.06
71	Rafael Palmeiro	.20	.12
72	Dean Palmer	.25	.15
73	Tony Phillips	.07	.04
74	Kirby Puckett	.30	.18
75	Carlos Quintana	.10	.06
76	Pat Rice	.10	.06
77	Cal Ripken Jr.	.60	.35
78	Ivan Rodriquez	.70	.40
79	Nolan Ryan (7th)	.70	.40
80	Bret Saberhagen	.10	.06
81	Tim Salmon	.80	.50
82	Juan Samuel	.07	.04
83	Ruben Sierra	.25	.15
84	Heathcliff Slocumb	.10	.06
85	Joe Slusarski	.15	.10
86	John Smiley	.15	.10
87	Dave Smith	.07	.04
88	Ed Sprague	.10	.06
89	Todd Stottlemyre	.10	.06
90	Mike Timlin	.10	.06

91	Greg Vaughn	.20	.12
92	Frank Viola	.12	.07
93	Chico Walker	.10	.06
94	Devon White	.07	.04
95	Matt Williams	.20	.12
96	Rick Wilkins	.10	.06
97	Bernie Williams	.20	.12
98	N. Ryan/G. Gossage	.40	.25
99	Gerald Williams	.25	.15
___	Micro (B. Bonilla, W. Clark, S. Erickson, C. Ripken Jr.)	.35	.20

1991 Classic Collectors Edition

Limited to just 100,000 individually numbered sets, Classic's Collector's Edition was packaged in a special collector's box and included game board, game pieces, spinner, scoreboard and a booklet offering baseball tips. Card fronts feature purple borders. Card backs include baseball trivia quesions.

		MINT	NR MT
Complete Set (200)		32.00	20.00
Commons		.08	.05

1	Frank Viola	.10	.06
2	Tim Wallach	.10	.06
3	Lou Whitaker	.08	.05
4	Bret Butler	.10	.06
5	Jim Abbott	.15	.10
6	Jack Armstrong	.08	.05
7	Craig Biggio	.10	.06
8	Brian Barnes	.15	.10
9	Dennis "Oil Can" Boyd	.08	.05

10	Tom Browning	.08	.05
11	Tom Brunansky	.08	.05
12	Ellis Burks	.10	.06
13	Harold Baines	.10	.06
14	Kal Daniels	.08	.05
15	Mark Davis	.08	.05
16	Storm Davis	.08	.05
17	Tom Glavine	.20	.12
18	Mike Greenwell	.15	.10
19	Kelly Gruber	.15	.10
20	Mark Gubicza	.10	.06
21	Pedro Guerrero	.10	.06
22	Mike Harkey	.10	.06
23	Orel Hershiser	.15	.10
24	Ted Higuera	.10	.06
25	Von Hayes	.08	.05
26	Andre Dawson	.20	.12
27	Shawon Dunston	.15	.10
28	Roberto Kelly	.20	.12
29	Joe Magrane	.08	.05
30	Dennis Martinez	.15	.10
31	Kevin McReynolds	.12	.07
32	Matt Nokes	.12	.07
33	Dan Plesac	.08	.05
34	Dave Parker	.12	.07
35	Randy Johnson	.15	.10
36	Bret Saberhagen	.20	.12
37	Mackey Sasser	.08	.05
38	Mike Scott	.08	.05
39	Ozzie Smith	.20	.12
40	Kevin Seitzer	.10	.06
41	Ruben Sierra	.20	.12
42	Kevin Tapani	.10	.06
43	Danny Tartabull	.20	.12
44	Robby Thompson	.10	.06
45	Andy Van Slyke	.20	.12
46	Greg Vaughn	.20	.12
47	Harold Reynolds	.10	.06
48	Will Clark	.50	.30
49	Gary Gaetti	.08	.05
50	Joe Grahe	.10	.06
51	Carlton Fisk	.20	.12
52	Robin Ventura	.40	.25
53	Ozzie Guillen	.15	.10
54	Tom Candiotti	.12	.07
55	Doug Jones	.10	.06
56	Eric King	.10	.06
57	Kirk Gibson	.10	.06
58	Tim Costo	.30	.18
59	Robin Yount	.50	.30
60	Sammy Sosa	.15	.10
61	Jesse Barfield	.10	.06
62	Marc Newfield	.75	.45
63	Jimmy Key	.10	.06
64	Felix Jose	.20	.12
65	Mark Whiten	.25	.15
66	Tommy Greene	.20	.12
67	Kent Mercker	.10	.06

68	Greg Maddux	.30	.18	126	Dennis Eckersley	.15	.10
69	Danny Jackson	.10	.06	127	Cecil Fielder	.25	.15
70	Reggie Sanders	.80	.50	128	Phil Plantier	.80	.50
71	Eric Yelding	.12	.07	129	Kevin Mitchell	.12	.07
72	Karl Rhodes	.15	.10	130	Kevin Maas	.25	.15
73	Fernando Valenzuela	.12	.07	131	Mark McGwire	.40	.25
74	Chris Nabholz	.15	.10	132	Ben McDonald	.30	.18
75	Andres Galarraga	.12	.07	133	Lenny Dykstra	.12	.07
76	Howard Johnson	.20	.12	134	Delino DeShields	.25	.15
77	Hubie Brooks	.12	.07	135	Jose Canseco	.60	.35
78	Terry Mulholland	.12	.07	136	Eric Davis	.15	.10
79	Paul Molitor	.15	.10	137	George Brett	.20	.12
80	Roger McDowell	.08	.05	138	Steve Avery	.50	.30
81	Darren Daulton	.15	.10	139	Eric Anthony	.20	.12
82	Zane Smith	.10	.06	140	Bobby Thigpen	.12	.07
83	Ray Lankford	.25	.15	141	Ken Griffey Sr.	.10	.06
84	Bruce Hurst	.12	.07	142	Barry Larkin	.20	.12
85	Andy Benes	.25	.15	143	Jeff Brantley	.10	.06
86	John Burkett	.10	.06	144	Bobby Bonilla	.20	.12
87	Dave Righetti	.10	.06	145	Jose Offerman	.20	.12
88	Steve Karsay	.20	.12	146	Mike Mussina	.70	.40
89	D.J. Dozier	.20	.12	147	Erik Hanson	.20	.12
90	Jeff Bagwell	1.75	1.00	148	Dale Murphy	.20	.12
91	Joe Carter	.20	.12	149	Roger Clemens	.60	.35
92	Wes Chamberlain	.35	.20	150	Tino Martinez	.25	.15
93	Vince Coleman	.10	.06	151	Todd Van Poppel	1.50	.90
94	Pat Combs	.15	.10	152	Maurice Vaughn	.80	.50
95	Jerome Walton	.08	.05	153	Derrick May	.25	.15
96	Jeff Conine	.20	.12	154	Jack Clark	.10	.06
97	Alan Trammell	.10	.06	155	Dave Hansen	.15	.10
98	Don Mattingly	.30	.18	156	Tony Gwynn	.35	.20
99	Ramon Martinez	.25	.15	157	Brian McRae	.25	.15
100	Dave Magadan	.10	.06	158	Matt Williams	.25	.15
101	Greg Swindell	.12	.07	159	Kirk Dressendorfer	.25	.15
102	Dave Stewart	.12	.07	160	Scott Erickson	.50	.30
103	Gary Sheffield	.80	.50	161	Tony Fernandez	.10	.06
104	George Bell	.15	.10	162	Willie McGee	.10	.06
105	Mark Grace	.20	.12	163	Fred McGriff	.30	.18
106	Steve Sax	.15	.10	164	Leo Gomez	.20	.12
107	Ryne Sandberg	.40	.25	165	Bernard Gilkey	.25	.15
108	Chris Sabo	.15	.10	166	Bobby Witt	.08	.05
109	Jose Rijo	.15	.10	167	Doug Drabek	.12	.07
110	Cal Ripken Jr.	.75	.45	168	Rob Dibble	.15	.10
111	Kirby Puckett	.30	.18	169	Glenn Davis	.10	.06
112	Eddie Murray	.20	.12	170	Danny Darwin	.08	.05
113	Roberto Alomar	.50	.30	171	Eric Karros	.75	.45
114	Randy Myers	.08	.05	172	Eddie Zosky	.20	.12
115	Rafael Palmeiro	.20	.12	173	Todd Zeile	.20	.12
116	John Olerud	.20	.12	174	Tim Raines	.10	.06
117	Gregg Jefferies	.20	.12	175	Benito Santiago	.15	.10
118	Kent Hrbek	.12	.07	176	Dan Peltier	.20	.12
119	Marquis Grissom	.30	.18	177	Darryl Strawberry	.40	.25
120	Ken Griffey Jr	1.50	.90	178	Hal Morris	.20	.12
121	Dwight Gooden	.15	.10	179	Hensley Meulens	.20	.12
122	Juan Gonzalez	.30	.18	180	John Smoltz	.15	.10
123	Ron Gant	.25	.15	181	Frank Thomas	2.00	1.25
124	Travis Fryman	.70	.40	182	Dave Staton	.25	.15
125	John Franco	.08	.05	183	Scott Chiamparino	.15	.10

184	Alex Fernandez	.20	.12
185	Mark Lewis	.20	.12
186	Bo Jackson	1.00	.70
187	Mickey Morandini	.15	.10
188	Cory Snyder	.08	.05
189	Rickey Henderson	.40	.25
190	Junior Felix	.15	.10
191	Milt Cuyler	.25	.15
192	Wade Boggs	.35	.20
193	Justice Prevails (Dave Justice)	1.50	.90
194	Sandy Alomar Jr.	.15	.10
195	Barry Bonds	.35	.20
196	Nolan Ryan	1.25	.80
197	Rico Brogna	.35	.20
198	Steve Decker	.15	.10
199	Bob Welch	.10	.06
200	Andujar Cedeno	.50	.30

1991 Classic Draft Picks

This edition features the top selections from the 1991 amateur baseball draft. Only 330,000 sets were produced, each shipped with a numbered certificate. Border colors are gray and burgundy. Only half of the sets contained the Frankie Rodriguez bonus card.

		MINT	NR/MT
Complete Set (51)		14.00	9.50
Commons		.15	.10
1	Brien Taylor	2.75	1.60
2	Mike Kelly	2.50	1.40
3	David McCarty	1.75	1.00
4	Dmitri Young	1.75	1.00

5	Joe Vitiello	1.25	.80
6	Mark Smith	.75	.45
7	Tyler Green	.75	.45
8	Shawn Estes	.50	.30
9	Doug Glanville	.75	.45
10	Manny Ramirez	1.25	.80
11	Cliff Floyd	.75	.45
12	Tyrone Hill	.50	.30
13	Eduardo Perez	.80	.50
14	Al Shirley	.75	.45
15	Benji Gil	.75	.45
16	Calvin Reese	.35	.20
17	Allen Watson	.30	.18
18	Brian Barber	.50	.30
19	Aaron Sele	.50	.30
20	John Farrell	.30	.18
21	Scott Ruffcorn	.35	.20
22	Brent Gates	.35	.20
23	Scott Stahoviak	.30	.18
24	Tom McKinnon	.25	.15
25	Shawn Livsey	.30	.18
26	Jason Pruitt	.30	.18
27	Greg Anthony	.25	.15
28	Justin Thompson	.25	.15
29	Steve Whitaker	.25	.15
30	Jorge Fabregas	.30	.18
31	Jeff Ware	.30	.18
32	Bobby Jones	.40	.25
33	J.J. Johnson	.25	.15
34	Mike Rossiter	.25	.15
35	Dan Chowlowsky	.25	.15
36	Jimmy Gonzalez	.25	.15
37	Trevor Miller	.25	.15
38	Scott Hatteberg	.30	.18
39	Mike Groppuso	.25	.15
40	Ryan Long	.20	.12
41	Eddie Williams	.25	.15
42	Mike Durant	.25	.15
43	Buck McNabb	.15	.10
44	Jimmy Lewis	.15	.10
45	Eddie Ramos	.15	.10
46	Terry Horn	.15	.10
47	Jon Barnes	.15	.10
48	Shawn Curran	.15	.10
49	Tommy Adams	.25	.15
50	Trevor Mallory	.15	.10
___	Bonus Card (Frankie Rodriquez)	2.00	1.25

1992 Classic I

The 1992 edition of Classic's Baseball Trivia board game features all new trivia questions and is packaged with a game board. Cards are printed on a glossy stock with white borders on the front.

		MINT	NR/MT
	Complete Set (100)	12.50	7.50
	Commons	.10	.06
1	Jim Abbott	.25	.15
2	Kyle Abbott	.25	.15
3	Scott Aldred	.12	.07
4	Roberto Alomar	.30	.18
5	Wilson Alvarez	.12	.07
6	Andy Ashby	.12	.07
7	Steve Avery	.25	.15
8	Jeff Bagwell	.60	.35
9	Bret Barberie	.25	.15
10	Kim Batiste	.20	.12
11	Derek Bell	.25	.15
12	Jay Bell	.10	.06
13	Albert Belle	.25	.15
14	Andy Benes	.15	.10
15	Sean Berry	.10	.06
16	Barry Bonds	.25	.15
17	Ryan Bowen	.15	.10
18	Trifecta (A. Pena, K. Mercker, M. Wohlers)	.12	.07
19	Scott Brosius		
20	Jay Buhner	.12	.07
21	David Burba	.10	.06
22	Jose Canseco	.50	.30
23	Andujar Cedeno	.20	.12
24	Will Clark	.40	.25
25	Royce Clayton	.25	.15
26	Roger Clemens	.40	.25
27	David Cone	.15	.10
28	Scott Cooper	.15	.10
29	Chris Cron	.10	.06
30	Len Dykstra	.12	.07
31	Cal Eldred	.20	.12
32	Hector Fajardo	.20	.12
33	Cecil Fielder	.25	.15
34	Dave Fleming	.50	.30
35	Steve Foster	.10	.06
36	Julio Franco	.15	.10
37	Carlos Garcia	.15	.10
38	Tom Glavine	.25	.15
39	Tom Goodwin	.20	.12
40	Ken Griffey Jr.	.60	.35
41	Chris Haney	.12	.07
42	Bryan Harvey	.12	.07
43	Rickey Henderson	.30	.18
44	Carlos Hernandez	.12	.07
45	Roberto Hernandez	.12	.07
46	Brook Jacoby	.10	.06
47	Howard Johnson	.15	.10
48	Pat Kelly	.15	.10
49	Darryl Kile	.12	.07
50	Chuck Knoblauch	.35	.20
51	Ray Lankford	.20	.12
52	Mark Leiter	.12	.07
53	Darren Lewis	.12	.07
54	Scott Livingstone	.12	.07
55	Shane Mack	.12	.07
56	Chito Martinez	.25	.15
57	Dennis Martinez	.12	.07
58	Don Mattingly	.30	.18
59	Paul McClellan	.12	.07
60	Chuck McElroy	.12	.07
61	Fred McGriff	.25	.15
62	Orlando Merced	.15	.10
63	Luis Mercedes	.20	.12
64	Kevin Mitchell	.12	.07
65	Hal Morris	.15	.10
66	Jack Morris	.12	.07
67	Mike Mussina	.35	.20
68	Denny Naegle	.20	.12
69	Tom Pagnozzi	.12	.07
70	Terry Pendleton	.15	.10
71	Phil Plantier	.30	.18
72	Kirby Puckett	.40	.25
73	Carlos Quintana	.12	.07
74	Willie Randolph	.10	.06
75	Arthur Rhodes	.25	.15
76	Cal Ripken Jr.	.35	.20
77	Ivan Rodriguez	.35	.20
78	Nolan Ryan	.60	.35
79	Ryne Sandberg	.40	.25
80	Deion Sanders	.35	.20
81	Reggie Sanders	.35	.20
82	Mo Sanford	.12	.07
83	Terry Shumpert	.10	.06
84	Tim Spehr	.12	.07
85	Lee Stevens	.12	.07
86	Darryl Strawberry	.25	.15
87	Kevin Tapani	.12	.07
88	Danny Tartabull	.20	.12
89	Frank Thomas	.80	.50
90	Jim Thome	.40	.25
91	Todd Van Poppel	.35	.20
92	Andy Van Slyke	.20	.12
93	John Wehner	.15	.10
94	John Wetteland	.15	.10
95	Devon White	.10	.06
96	Brian Williams	.35	.20

		MINT	NR/MT
97	Mark Wohlers	.15	.10
98	Robin Yount	.40	.25
99	Eddie Zosky	.12	.07
___	Micro (S. Avery, B. Bonds, R. Clemens, N. Ryan)	.75	.45

1992 Classic Draft Picks

The cards in this 125-card set feature the top draft picks from baseball's 1992 amateur draft. The cards measure 2-1/2" by 3-1/2". Card fronts include full color photos. 20-limited foil stamped bonus cards were issued in conjunction with the set. Those cards are listed at the end of the checklist but are not included in the checklist below.

		MINT	NR/MT
Complete Set (125)		15.00	10.00
Commons		.08	.05
1	Phil Nevin	3.50	2.50
2	Paul Shuey	2.00	1.25
3	B.J. Wallace	1.75	1.00
4	Jeffrey Hammonds	3.00	2.00
5	Chad Mottola	.80	.50
6	Derek Jeter	1.25	.80
7	Michael Tucker	1.25	.80
8	Derek Wallace	.75	.45
9	Kenny Felder	.80	.50
10	Chad McConnell	.80	.50
11	Sean Lowe	.60	.35
12	Ricky Greene	.80	.50
13	Chris Roberts	.75	.45
14	Shannon Stewart	.60	.35
15	Benji Grigsby	.75	.45
16	Jamie Arnold	.40	.25
17	Rick Helling	.40	.25
18	Jason Kendall	.40	.25
19	Todd Steverson	.20	.12
20	Dan Serafini	.35	.20
21	Jeff Schmidt	.15	.10
22	Sherard Clinkscales	.20	.12
23	Ryan Luzinski	.50	.30
24	Shon Walker	.25	.15
25	Brandon Cromer	.12	.07
26	Dave Landaker	.15	.10
27	Michael Mathews	.12	.07
28	Brian Sackinsky	.12	.07
29	Jon Lieber	.12	.07
30	Jim Rosenbohm	.12	.07
31	DeShawn Warren	.15	.10
32	Danny Clyburn	.12	.07
33	Chris Smith	.15	.10
34	Dwain Bostic	.08	.05
35	Bobby Hughes	.08	.05
36	Rick Magdellano	.12	.07
37	Bob Wolcott	.08	.05
38	Mike Gulan	.08	.05
39	Yuri Sanchez	.08	.05
40	Tony Sheffield	.12	.07
41	Dan Melendez	.35	.20
42	Jason Giambi	.75	.45
43	Ritchie Moody	.08	.05
44	Trey Beamon	.12	.07
45	Tim Crabtree	.08	.05
46	Chad Roper	.15	.10
47	Mark Thompson	.12	.07
48	Marquis Riley	.10	.06
49	Tom Krauss	.08	.05
50	Chris Holt	.10	.06
51	Jonathan Nunnally	.10	.06
52	Everett Stull	.08	.05
53	Billy Owens	.12	.07
54	Todd Etler	.08	.05
55	Benji Simonton	.20	.12
56	Dwight Maness	.15	.10
57	Chris Eddy	.12	.07
58	Brant Brown	.08	.05
59	Trevor Humphrey	.08	.05
60	Chris Widger	.15	.10
61	Steve Montgomery	.08	.05
62	Chris Gomez	.08	.05
63	Jared Baker	.12	.07
64	Doug Hecker	.08	.05
65	David Spykstra	.08	.05
66	Scott Miller	.08	.05
67	Carey Paige	.08	.05
68	Dave Manning	.08	.05
69	James Keefe	.08	.05
70	Levon Largusa	.08	.05
71	Roger Bailey	.08	.05
72	Rich Ireland	.08	.05
73	Matt Williams	.08	.05

74	Scott Gentile	.12	.07
75	Hut Smith	.12	.07
76	Rodney Henderson	.08	.05
77	Mike Buddie	.08	.05
78	Stephen Lyons	.08	.05
79	John Burke	.40	.25
80	Jim Pittsley	.08	.05
81	Donnie Leshnock	.20	.12
82	Cory Pearson	.12	.07
83	Kurt Ehmann	.08	.05
84	Bobby Bonds, Jr.	.25	.15
85	Steven Cox	.08	.05
86	Brien Taylor	1.25	.80
87	Mike Kelly	.75	.45
88	David McCarty	.80	.50
89	Dmitri Young	.60	.35
90	Joey Hamilton	.30	.18
91	Mark Smith	.35	.20
92	Doug Glanville	.25	.15
93	Mike Lieberthal	.25	.15
94	Joe Vitiello	.25	.15
95	Mike Mussina	.40	.25
96	Derek Hacopian	.15	.10
97	Ted Corbin	.15	.10
98	Carlton Pleming	.10	.06
99	Aaron Rounsifer	.15	.10
100	Chad Fox	.12	.07
101	Chris Sheff	.12	.07
102	Ben Jones	.15	.10
103	David Post	.08	.05
104	Jonnie Gendron	.08	.05
105	Bob Juday	.10	.06
106	David Becker	.08	.05
107	Brandon Pico	.08	.05
108	Tom Evans	.08	.05
109	Jeff Faino	.08	.05
110	Shawn Wills	.15	.10
111	Derrick Cantrell	.15	.10
112	Steve Rodriquez	.30	.18
113	Ray Suplee	.12	.07
114	Pat Leahy	.08	.05
115	Matt Luke	.08	.05
116	Jon McMullen	.08	.05
117	Preston Wilson	.75	.45
118	Gus Gandarillas	.25	.15
119	Pete Janicki	.15	.10
120	Byron Mathews	.08	.05
121	Eric Owens	.08	.05
122	John Lynch	.15	.10
123	Mike Hickey	.08	.05
124	Checklist I	.08	.05
125	Checklist 2	.08	.05
BC1	Phil Nevin	2.50	1.50
BC2	Paul Shuey	.75	.45
BC3	B.J. Wallace	1.00	.70
BC4	Jeffrey Hammonds	2.00	1.25
BC5	Chad Mottola	.75	.45
BC6	Derek Wallace	.75	.45
BC7	Michael Tucker	1.00	.70
BC8	Derek Wallace	.75	.45
BC9	Kenny Felder	.50	.30
BC10	Chad McConnell	.75	.45

BC11	Sean Lowe	.50	.30
BC12	Chris Roberts	.50	.30
BC13	Shannon Stewart	.50	.30
BC14	Benji Grigsby	.50	.30
BC15	Jamie Arnold	.50	.30
BC16	Ryan Luzinski	.50	.30
BC17	Bobby Bonds, Jr.	.50	.30
BC18	Brien Taylor	2.00	1.25
BC19	Mike Kelly	.75	.45
BC20	Mike Mussina	.75	.45

1993 Classic

This 99-card set is used as part of Classic Games Baseball Trivia Board Game. The card fronts feature full color action photos while the backs contain trivia questions. All cards measure 2-1/2" by 3-1/2".

		MINT	NR/MT
Complete Set (99)		11.00	7.50
Commons		.07	.04
1	Jim Abbott	.15	.10
2	Roberto Alomar	.20	.12
3	Moises Alou	.15	.10
4	Brady Anderson	.12	.07
5	Eric Anthony	.10	.06
6	Alex Arias	.15	.10
7	Pedro Astacio	.40	.25
8	Steve Avery	.20	.12
9	Carlos Baerga	.30	.18
10	Jeff Bagwell	.35	.20
11	George Bell	.10	.06
12	Albert Belle	.12	.07
13	Craig Biggio	.07	.04
14	Barry Bonds	.15	.10
15	Bobby Bonilla	.12	.07
16	Mike Bordick	.12	.07
17	George Brett	.15	.10
18	Jose Canseco	.35	.20
19	Joe Carter	.15	.10
20	Royce Clayton	.12	.07

21	Roger Clemens	.20	.12
22	Greg Colbrunn	.15	.10
23	David Cone	.10	.06
24	Darren Daulton	.10	.06
25	Delino DeShields	.12	.07
26	Rob Dibble	.07	.04
27	Dennis Eckersley	.15	.10
28	Cal Eldred	.60	.35
29	Scott Erickson	.15	.10
30	Junior Felix	.07	.04
31	Tony Fernandez	.08	.05
32	Cecil Fielder	.15	.10
33	Steve Finley	.07	.04
34	Dave Fleming	.60	.35
35	Travis Fryman	.20	.12
36	Tom Glavine	.20	.12
37	Juan Gonzalez	.40	.25
38	Ken Griffey, Jr.	.70	.40
39	Marquis Grissom	.15	.10
40	Juan Guzman	.35	.20
41	Tony Gwynn	.12	.07
42	Rickey Henderson	.12	.07
43	Felix Jose	.08	.05
44	Wally Joyner	.08	.05
45	David Justice	.25	.15
46	Eric Karros	.35	.20
47	Roberto Kelly	.12	.07
48	Ryan Klesko	.60	.35
49	Chuck Knoblauch	.25	.15
50	John Kruk	.08	.05
51	Ray Lankford	.15	.10
52	Barry Larkin	.12	.07
53	Pat Listach	.50	.30
54	Kenny Lofton	.30	.18
55	Shane Mack	.08	.05
56	Greg Maddux	.12	.07
57	Dave Magadan	.07	.04
58	Edgar Martinez	.12	.07
59	Don Mattingly	.20	.12
60	Ben McDonald	.12	.07
61	Jack McDowell	.12	.07
62	Fred McGriff	.20	.12
63	Mark McGwire	.25	.15
64	Kevin McReynolds	.07	.04
65	Sam Militello	.75	.45
66	Paul Molitor	.08	.05
67	Jeff Montgomery	.07	.04
68	Jack Morris	.12	.07
69	Eddie Murray	.12	.07
70	Mike Mussina	.40	.25
71	Otis Nixon	.08	.05
72	Donovan Osborne	.40	.25
73	Terry Pendleton	.12	.07
74	Mike Piazza	1.50	.90
75	Kirby Puckett	.25	.15
76	Cal Ripken, Jr.	.25	.15
77	Bip Roberts	.07	.04
78	Ivan Rodriquez	.35	.20

79	Nolan Ryan	.50	.30
80	Ryne Sandberg	.30	.18
81	Deion Sanders	.25	.15
82	Reggie Sanders	.25	.15
83	Frank Seminara	.15	.10
84	Gary Sheffield	.20	.12
85	Ruben Sierra	.20	.12
86	John Smiley	.08	.05
87	Lee Smith	.10	.06
88	Ozzie Smith	.12	.07
89	John Smoltz	.10	.06
90	Danny Tartabull	.10	.06
91	Frank Thomas	.75	.45
92	Bob Tewksbury	.07	.04
93	Andy Van Slyke	.10	.06
94	Mo Vaughn	.12	.07
95	Robin Ventura	.20	.12
96	Tim Wakefield	2.00	1.25
97	Larry Walker	.15	.10
98	Dave Winfield	.15	.10
99	Robin Yount	.20	.12

DONRUSS

1981 Donruss

JOHNNY BENCH

This 605-card set marks the first baseball edition from Donruss. The standard-size cards feature four-color photos on the fronts and career highlights in a vertical format on the card backs. The set contains more than three dozen errors which were later corrected in later print runs. Those variations are noted in the checklist but are not reflected in the set price.

		MINT	NR/MT
	Complete Set (605)	58.00	36.00
	Commons	.06	.03
1	Ozzie Smith	2.75	1.75
2	Rollie Fingers	1.00	.70
3	Rick Wise	.06	.03
4	Gene Richards	.06	.03
5	Alan Trammell	.75	.45
6	Tom Brookens	.06	.03
7	Duffy Dyer (Var)	.10	.06
8	Mark Fidrych	.15	.08
9	Dave Rozema	.06	.03
10	Ricky Peters	.06	.03
11	Mike Schmidt	3.00	2.00
12	Willie Stargell	.80	.50
13	Tim Foli	.06	.03
14	Manny Sanguillen	.06	.03
15	Grant Jackson	.06	.03
16	Eddie Solomon	.06	.03
17	Omar Moreno	.06	.03
18	Joe Morgan	.75	.45
19	Rafael Landestoy	.06	.03
20	Bruce Bochy	.06	.03
21	Joe Sambito	.06	.03
22	Manny Trillo	.06	.03
23	Dave Smith (R) (Var)	.25	.15
24	Terry Puhl	.06	.03
25	Bump Wills	.06	.03
26a	John Ellis (Wrong photo)	.40	.25
26b	John Ellis (Cor)	.06	.03
27	Jim Kern	.06	.03
28	Richie Zisk	.06	.03
29	John Mayberry	.06	.03
30	Bob Davis	.06	.03
31	Jackson Todd	.06	.03
32	Al Woods	.06	.03
33	Steve Carlton	2.00	1.25
34	Lee Mazzilli	.06	.03
35	John Stearns	.06	.03
36	Roy Jackson	.06	.03
37	Mike Scott	.20	.12
38	Lamar Johnson	.06	.03
39	Kevin Bell	.06	.03
40	Ed Farmer	.06	.03
41	Ross Baumgarten	.06	.03
42	Leo Sutherland	.06	.03
43	Dan Meyer	.06	.03
44	Ron Reed	.06	.03
45	Mario Mendoza	.06	.03
46	Rick Honeycutt	.06	.03
47	Glenn Abbott	.06	.03
48	Leon Roberts	.06	.03
49	Rod Carew	2.00	1.25
50	Bert Campaneris	.12	.07
51a	Tom Donahue (Er)	.10	.06
51b	Tom Donohue (Cor)	.06	.03
52	Dave Frost	.06	.03
53	Ed Halicki	.06	.03
54	Dan Ford	.06	.03
55	Garry Maddox	.06	.03
56a	Steve Garvey (25 Hr)	1.25	.80
56b	Steve Garvey (21 Hr)	.80	.50
57	Bill Russell	.08	.05
58	Don Sutton	.60	.35
59	Reggie Smith	.10	.06
60	Rick Monday	.08	.05
61	Ray Knight	.06	.03
62	Johnny Bench	2.50	1.50
63	Mario Soto	.06	.03
64	Doug Bair	.06	.03
65	George Foster	.25	.15
66	Jeff Burroughs	.08	.05
67	Keith Hernandez	.25	.15
68	Tom Herr	.08	.05
69	Bob Forsch	.06	.03
70	John Fulgham	.06	.03
71a	Bobby Bonds (lifetime HR 986)	.35	.20
71b	Bobby Bonds (lifetime HR 326)	.12	.07
72	Rennie Stennett (Var)	.08	.05
73	Joe Strain	.06	.03
74	Ed Whitson	.06	.03
75	Tom Griffin	.06	.03
76	Bill North	.06	.03
77	Gene Garber	.06	.03
78	Mike Hargrove	.08	.05
79	Dave Rosello	.06	.03
80	Ron Hassey	.10	.06
81	Sid Monge	.06	.03
82	Joe Charboneau (R)	.10	.06
83	Cecil Cooper	.12	.07
84	Sal Bando	.15	.08
85	Moose Haas	.06	.03
86	Mike Caldwell	.06	.03
87a	Larry Hisle (28 RBI)	.12	.07
87b	Larry Hisle (28 Hr)	.08	.05
88	Luis Gomez	.06	.03
89	Larry Parrish	.06	.03
90	Gary Carter	1.25	.80
91	Bill Gullickson (R)	.75	.45
92	Fred Norman	.06	.03
93	Tommy Hutton	.06	.03
94	Carl Yastrzemski	2.50	1.50
95	Glenn Hoffman	.06	.03
96	Dennis Eckersley	1.50	.90
97a	Tom Burgmeier (Throws:Right)	.08	.05
97b	Tom Burgmeier (Throws:Left)	.08	.05
98	Win Remmerswaal	.06	.30
99	Bob Horner	.12	.07
100	George Brett	3.50	2.50
101	Dave Chalk	.06	.03
102	Dennis Leonard	.06	.03
103	Renie Martin	.06	.03
104	Amos Otis	.10	.06
105	Graig Nettles	.15	.08
106	Eric Soderholm	.06	.03
107	Tommy John	.15	.08
108	Tom Underwood	.06	.03
109	Lou Piniella	.20	.12

110	Mickey Klutts	.06	.03
111	Bobby Murcer	.15	.08
112	Eddie Murray	3.00	2.00
113	Rick Dempsey	.06	.03
114	Scott McGregor	.06	.03
115	Ken Singleton	.06	.03
116	Gary Roenicke	.06	.03
117	Dave Revering	.06	.03
118	Mike Norris	.06	.03
119	Rickey Henderson	15.00	9.00
120	Mike Heath	.06	.03
121	Dave Cash	.06	.03
122	Randy Jones	.06	.03
123	Eric Rasmussen	.06	.03
124	Jerry Mumphrey	.06	.03
125	Richie Hebner	.08	.05
126	Mark Wagner	.06	.03
127	Jack Morris	1.75	1.00
128	Dan Petry	.10	.06
129	Bruce Robbins	.06	.03
130	Champ Summers	.06	.03
131a	Pete Rose ("see card 251.")	3.00	2.00
131b	Pete Rose ("see card 371.")	2.00	1.25
132	Willie Stargell	.80	.50
133	Ed Ott	.06	.03
134	Jim Bibby	.06	.03
135	Bert Blyleven	.50	.30
136	Dave Parker	.35	.20
137	Bill Robinson	.08	.05
138	Enos Cabell	.06	.03
139	Dave Bergman	.06	.03
140	J.R. Richard	.12	.07
141	Ken Forsch	.06	.03
142	Larry Bowa	.10	.06
143	Frank LaCorte (Wrong photo)	.06	.03
144	Dennis Walling	.06	.03
145	Buddy Bell	.12	.07
146	Ferguson Jenkins	.60	.35
147	Danny Darwin	.10	.06
148	John Grubb	.06	.03
149	Alfredo Griffin	.08	.05
150	Jerry Garvin	.06	.03
151	Paul Mirabella (R)	.08	.05
152	Rick Bosetti	.06	.03
153	Dick Ruthven	.06	.03
154	Frank Taveras	.06	.03
155	Craig Swan	.06	.03
156	Jeff Reardon (R)	8.50	5.50
157	Steve Henderson	.06	.03
158	Jim Morrison	.06	.03
159	Glenn Borgmann	.06	.03
160	LaMarr Hoyt (R)	.12	.07
161	Rich Wortham	.06	.03
162	Thad Bosley	.06	.03
163	Julio Cruz	.06	.03
164	Del Unser (Var)	.08	.05
165	Jim Anderson	.06	.03
166	Jim Beattie	.06	.03
167	Shane Rawley	.06	.03
168	Joe Simpson	.06	.03
169	Rod Carew	2.00	1.25
170	Fred Patek	.06	.03
171	Frank Tanana	.12	.07
172	Alfredo Martinez	.06	.03
173	Chris Knapp	.06	.03
174	Joe Rudi	.10	.06
175	Greg Luzinski	.20	.12
176	Steve Garvey	.80	.50
177	Joe Ferguson	.06	.03
178	Bob Welch	.35	.20
179	Dusty Baker	.12	.07
180	Rudy Law	.06	.03
181	Dave Concepcion	.25	.15
182	Johnny Bench	2.50	1.50
183	Mike LaCoss	.06	.03
184	Ken Griffey	.30	.18
185	Dave Collins	.06	.03
186	Brian Asselstine	.06	.03
187	Garry Templeton	.12	.07
188	Mike Phillips	.06	.03
189	Pete Vukovich	.06	.03
190	John Urrea	.06	.03
191	Tony Scott	.06	.03
192	Darrell Evans	.20	.12
193	Milt May	.06	.03
194	Bob Knepper	.06	.03
195	Randy Moffitt	.06	.03
196	Larry Herndon	.06	.03
197	Rick Camp	.06	.03
198	Andre Thornton	.12	.07
199	Tom Veryzer	.06	.03
200	Gary Alexander	.06	.03
201	Rick Waits	.06	.03
202	Rick Manning	.06	.03
203	Paul Molitor	1.50	.90
204	Jim Gantner	.08	.05
205	Paul Mitchell	.06	.03
206	Reggie Cleveland	.06	.03
207	Sixto Lezcano	.06	.03
208	Bruce Benedict	.06	.03
209	Rodney Scott	.06	.03
210	John Tamargo	.06	.03
211	Bill Lee	.06	.03
212	Andre Dawson	2.00	1.25
213	Rowland Office	.06	.03
214	Carl Yastrzemski	2.50	1.50
215	Jerry Remy	.06	.03
216	Mike Torrez	.06	.03
217	Skip Lockwood	.06	.03
218	Fred Lynn	.25	.15
219	Cris Chambliss	.10	.06
220	Willie Aikens	.06	.03
221	John Wathan	.10	.06
222	Dan Quisenberry	.20	.12
223	Willie Wilson	.25	.15
224	Clint Hurdle	.07	.04
225	Bob Watson	.08	.05
226	Jim Spencer	.06	.03
227	Ron Guidry	.30	.18
228	Reggie Jackson	3.00	2.00
229	Oscar Gamble	.07	.04

230	Jeff Cox	.06	.03
231	Luis Tiant	.12	.07
232	Rich Dauer	.06	.03
233	Dan Graham	.06	.03
234	Mike Flanagan	.08	.05
235	John Lowenstein	.06	.03
236	Benny Ayala	.06	.03
237	Wayne Gross	.06	.03
238	Rick Langford	.06	.03
239	Tony Armas	.06	.03
240	Bob Lacy (Er)	.12	.07
240	Bob Lacey (Cor)	.06	.03
241	Gene Tenace	.10	.06
242	Bob Shirley	.06	.03
243	Gary Lucas	.06	.03
244	Jerry Turner	.06	.03
245	John Wockenfuss	.06	.03
246	Stan Papi	.06	.03
247	Milt Wilcox	.06	.03
248	Dan Schatzeder	.06	.03
249	Steve Kemp	.06	.03
250	Jim Lentine	.06	.03
251	Pete Rose	2.00	1.25
252	Bill Madlock	.20	.12
253	Dale Berra	.06	.03
254	Kent Tekulve	.10	.06
255	Enrique Romo	.06	.03
256	Mike Easler	.06	.03
257	Chuck Tanner	.06	.03
258	Art Howe	.08	.05
259	Alan Ashby	.06	.03
260	Nolan Ryan	8.50	5.50
261a	Vern Ruhle(Wrong Photo)	.35	.20
261b	Vern Ruhle(Cor)	.06	.03
262	Bob Boone	.20	.12
263	Cesar Cedeno	.15	.08
264	Jeff Leonard	.10	.06
265	Pat Putnam	.06	.03
266	Jon Matlack	.06	.03
267	Dave Rajsich	.06	.03
268	Billy Sample	.06	.03
269	Damaso Garcia	.06	.03
270	Tom Buskey	.06	.03
271	Joey McLaughlin	.06	.03
272	Barry Bonnell	.06	.03
273	Tug McGraw	.20	.12
274	Mike Jorgensen	.06	.03
275	Pat Zachry	.06	.03
276	Neil Allen	.06	.03
277	Joel Youngblood	.06	.03
278	Greg Pryor	.06	.03
279	Britt Burns (R)	.10	.06
280	Rich Dotson (R)	.15	.08
281	Chet Lemon	.06	.03
282	Rusty Kuntz	.06	.03
283	Ted Cox	.06	.03
284	Sparky Lyle	.10	.06
285	Larry Cox	.06	.03
286	Floyd Bannister	.06	.03
287	Byron McLaughlin	.06	.03
288	Rodney Craig	.06	.03
289	Bobby Grich	.12	.07
290	Dickie Thon	.12	.07
291	Mark Clear	.06	.03
292	Dave Lemanczyk	.06	.03
293	Jason Thompson	.06	.03
294	Rick Miller	.06	.03
295	Lonnie Smith	.20	.12
296	Ron Cey	.12	.07
297	Steve Yeager	.06	.03
298	Bobby Castillo	.06	.03
299	Manny Mota	.10	.06
300	Jay Johnstone	.07	.04
301	Dan Driessen	.08	.05
302	Joe Nolan	.06	.03
303	Paul Householder	.06	.03
304	Harry Spilman	.06	.03
305	Cesar Geronimo	.06	.03
306a	Gary Mathews (Er)	.12	.07
306b	Gary Matthews (Cor)	.06	.03
307	Ken Reitz	.06	.03
308	Ted Simmons	.15	.08
309	John Littlefield	.06	.03
310	George Frazier	.06	.03
311	Dane Iorg	.06	.03
312	Mike Ivie	.06	.03
313	Dennis Littlejohn	.06	.03
314	Gary Lavelle	.06	.03
315	Jack Clark	.25	.15
316	Jim Wohlford	.06	.03
317	Rick Matula	.06	.03
318	Toby Harrah	.08	.05
319a	Dwane Kuiper (Er)	.08	.05
319b	Duane Kuiper(Cor)	.06	.03
320	Len Barker	.06	.03
321	Victor Cruz	.06	.03
322	Dell Alston	.06	.03
323	Robin Yount	3.50	2.50
324	Charlie Moore	.06	.03
325	Lary Sorensen	.06	.03
326a	Gorman Thomas (30 Hr 4th on back)	.25	.15
326b	Gorman Thomas (30 Hr 3rd on back)	.10	.06
327	Bob Rodgers	.06	.03
328	Phil Niekro	.75	.45
329	Chris Speier	.06	.03
330a	Steve Rodgers (Er)	.15	.08
330b	Steve Rogers(Cor)	.08	.05
331	Woodie Fryman	.06	.03
332	Warren Cromartie	.06	.03
333	Jerry White	.06	.03
334	Tony Perez	.70	.40
335	Carlton Fisk	2.00	1.25
336	Dick Drago	.06	.03
337	Steve Renko	.06	.03
338	Jim Rice	.25	.15
339	Jerry Royster	.06	.03
340	Frank White	.12	.07
341	Jamie Quirk	.06	.03
342a	Paul Spittorff (Er)	.10	.06
342b	Paul Splittorff (Cor)	.06	.03
343	Marty Pattin	.06	.03

#	Player		
344	Pete LaCock	.06	.03
345	Willie Randolph	.15	.08
346	Rick Cerone	.06	.03
347	Rich Gossage	.25	.15
348	Reggie Jackson	3.00	2.00
349	Ruppert Jones	.06	.03
350	Dave McKay	.06	.03
351	Yogi Berra	.35	.20
352	Doug DeCinces	.06	.03
353	Jim Palmer	2.00	1.25
354	Tippy Martinez	.06	.03
355	Al Bumbry	.06	.03
356	Earl Weaver	.15	.08
357a	Bob Picciolo (Er)	.08	.05
357b	Rob Picciolo (Cor)	.06	.03
358	Matt Keough	.06	.03
359	Dwayne Murphy	.06	.03
360	Brian Kingman	.06	.03
361	Bill Fahey	.06	.03
362	Steve Mura	.06	.03
363	Dennis Kinney	.06	.03
364	Dave Winfield	2.50	1.50
365	Lou Whitaker	.70	.40
366	Lance Parrish	.25	.15
367	Tim Corcoran	.06	.03
368	Pat Underwood	.06	.03
369	Al Cowens	.06	.03
370	Sparky Anderson	.10	.06
371	Pete Rose	2.00	1.25
372	Phil Garner	.08	.05
373	Steve Nicosia	.06	.03
374	John Candelaria	.15	.08
375	Don Robinson	.06	.03
376	Lee Lacy	.06	.03
377	John Milner	.06	.03
378	Craig Reynolds	.06	.03
379a	Luis Pujois (Er)	.08	.05
279b	Luis Pujols (Cor)	.06	.03
380	Joe Niekro	.08	.05
381	Joaquin Andujar	.10	.06
382	Keith Moreland (R)	.12	.07
383	Jose Cruz	.15	.08
384	Bill Virdon	.06	.03
385	Jim Sundberg	.06	.03
386	Doc Medich	.06	.03
387	Al Oliver	.12	.07
388	Jim Norris	.06	.03
389	Bob Bailor	.06	.03
390	Ernie Whitt	.06	.03
391	Otto Velez	.06	.03
392	Roy Howell	.06	.03
393	Bob Walk (R)	.25	.15
394	Doug Flynn	.06	.03
395	Pete Falcone	.06	.03
396	Tom Hausman	.06	.03
397	Elliott Maddox	.06	.03
398	Mike Squires	.06	.03
399	Marvis Foley	.06	.03
400	Steve Trout	.06	.03
401	Wayne Nordhagen	.06	.03
402	Tony LaRussa	.12	.07
403	Bruce Bochte	.06	.03
404	Bake McBride	.06	.03
405	Jerry Narron	.06	.03
406	Rob Dressler	.06	.03
407	Dave Heaverlo	.06	.03
408	Tom Paciorek	.06	.03
409	Carney Lansford	.20	.12
410	Brian Downing	.08	.05
411	Don Aase	.06	.03
412	Jim Barr	.06	.03
413	Don Baylor	.20	.12
414	Jim Fregosi	.06	.03
415	Dallas Green	.06	.03
416	Dave Lopes	.12	.07
417	Jerry Reuss	.06	.03
418	Rick Sutcliffe	.30	.18
419	Derrel Thomas	.06	.03
420	Tommy Lasorda	.12	.07
421	Charlie Leibrandt (R)	.70	.40
422	Tom Seaver	2.50	1.50
423	Ron Oester	.06	.03
424	Junior Kennedy	.06	.03
425	Tom Seaver	2.50	1.50
426	Bobby Cox	.06	.03
427	Leon Durham (R)	.12	.07
428	Terry Kenndey	.08	.05
429	Silvio Martiñez	.06	.03
430	George Hendrick	.08	.05
431	Red Schoendienst	.12	.07
432	John LeMaster	.06	.03
433	Vida Blue	.12	.07
434	John Montefusco	.06	.03
435	Terry Whitfield	.06	.03
436	Dave Bristol	.06	.03
437	Dale Murphy	1.25	.80
438	Jerry Dybzinski	.06	.03
439	Jorge Orta	.06	.03
440	Wayne Garland	.06	.03
441	Miguel Dilone	.06	.03
442	Dave Garcia	.06	.03
443	Don Money	.06	.03
444a	Buck Martinez (Photo reversed)	.10	.06
444b	Buck Martinez (Cor)	.06	.03
445	Jerry Augustine	.06	.03
446	Ben Oglivie	.06	.03
447	Jim Slaton	.06	.03
448	Doyle Alexander	.06	.03
449	Tony Bernazard	.06	.03
450	Scott Sanderson	.08	.05
451	Dave Palmer	.06	.03
452	Stan Bahnsen	.06	.03
453	Dick Williams	.06	.03
454	Rick Burleson	.08	.05
455	Gary Allenson	.06	.03
456	Bob Stanley	.06	.03
457	John Tudor(R)	.25	.15
458	Dwight Evans	.35	.20
459	Glenn Hubbard	.06	.03
460	U. L. Washington	.06	.03
461	Larry Gura	.06	.03
462	Rich Gale	.06	.03
463	Hal McRae	.20	.12

No.	Player		
464	Jim Frey	.06	.03
465	Bucky Dent	.10	.06
466	Dennis Werth	.06	.03
467	Ron Davis	.06	.03
468	Reggie Jackson	3.00	2.00
469	Bobby Brown	.06	.03
470	Mike Davis (R)	.12	.07
471	Gaylord Perry	.60	.35
472	Mark Belanger	.08	.05
473	Jim Palmer	2.00	1.25
474	Sammy Stewart	.06	.03
475	Tim Stoddard	.06	.03
476	Steve Stone	.06	.03
477	Jeff Newman	.06	.03
478	Steve McCatty	.06	.03
479	Billy Martin	.25	.15
480	Mitchell Page	.06	.03
481	Steve Carlton (Cy)	1.00	.70
482	Bill Buckner	.12	.07
483	Ivan DeJesus(Var)	.06	.03
484	Cliff Johnson	.06	.03
485	Lenny Randle	.06	.03
486	Larry Milbourne	.06	.03
487	Roy Smalley	.06	.03
488	John Castino	.06	.03
489	Ron Jackson	.06	.03
490	Dave Roberts (Var)	.06	.03
491	George Brett (MVP)	1.75	1.00
492	Mike Cubbage	.06	.03
493	Rob Wilfon	.06	.03
494	Danny Goodwin	.06	.03
495	Jose Morales	.06	.03
496	Mickey Rivers	.10	.06
497	Mike Edwards	.06	.03
498	Mike Sadek	.06	.03
499	Lenn Sakata	.06	.03
500	Gene Michael	.06	.03
501	Dave Roberts	.06	.03
502	Steve Dillard	.06	.03
503	Jim Essian	.06	.03
504	Rance Mulliniks	.06	.03
505	Darrell Porter	.06	.03
506	Joe Torre	.15	.08
507	Terry Crowley	.06	.03
508	Bill Travers	.06	.03
509	Nelson Norman	.06	.03
510	Bob McClure	.06	.03
511	Steve Howe (R)	.10	.06
512	Dave Rader	.06	.03
513	Mick Kelleher	.06	.03
514	Kiko Garcia	.06	.03
515	Larry Biittner	.06	.03
516	Willie Norwood (Var)	.06	.03
517	Bo Diaz	.06	.03
518	Juan Beniquez	.06	.03
519	Scot Thompson	.06	.03
520	Jim Tracy	.06	.03
521	Carlos Lezcano	.06	.03
522	Joe Amalfitano	.06	.03
523	Preston Hanna	.06	.03
524	Ray Burris (Var)	.08	.05
525	Broderick Perkins	.06	.03
526	Mickey Hatcher	.06	.03
527	John Goryl	.06	.03
528	Dick Davis	.06	.03
529	Butch Wynegar	.06	.03
530	Sal Butera	.06	.03
531	Jerry Koosman	.12	.07
532	Jeff Zahn (Var)	.06	.03
533	Dennis Martinez	.25	.15
534	Gary Thomasson	.06	.03
535	Steve Macko	.06	.03
536	Jim Kaat	.25	.15
537	Best Hitters(George Brett, Rod Carew	3.00	2.00
538	Tim Raines (R)	6.00	3.75
539	Keith Smith	.06	.03
540	Ken Macha	.06	.03
541	Burt Hooton	.06	.03
542	Butch Hobson	.08	.05
543	Bill Stein	.06	.03
544	Dave Stapleton	.06	.03
545	Bob Pate	.06	.03
546	Doug Corbett	.06	.03
547	Darrell Jackson	.06	.03
548	Pete Redfern	.06	.03
549	Roger Erickson	.06	.03
550	Al Hrabosky	.06	.03
551	Dick Tidrow	.06	.03
552	Dave Ford	.06	.03
553	Dave Kingman	.15	.08
554	Mike Vail (Var)	.06	.03
555	Jerry Martin (Var)	.06	.03
556	Jesus Figueroa (Var)	.06	.03
557	Don Stanhouse	.06	.03
558	Barry Foote	.06	.03
559	Tim Blackwell	.06	.03
560	Bruce Sutter	.15	.08
561	Rick Reuschel	.15	.08
562	Lynn McGlothen	.06	.03
563	Bob Owchinko (Var)	.06	.03
564	John Verhoeven	.06	.03
565	Ken Landreaux	.06	.03
566	Glenn Adams (Var)	.06	.03
567	Hosken Powell	.06	.03
568	Dick Noles	.06	.03
569	Danny Ainge (R)	1.50	.90
570	Bobby Mattick	.06	.03
571	Joe LeFebvre	.08	.05
572	Bobby Clark	.06	.03
573	Dennis Lamp	.06	.03
574	Randy Lerch	.06	.03
575	Mookie Wilson (R)	.40	.25
576	Ron LeFlore	.08	.05
577	Jim Dwyer	.06	.03
578	Bill Castro	.06	.03
579	Greg Minton	.06	.03
580	Mark Littell	.06	.03
581	Andy Hassler	.06	.03
582	Dave Stieb	.40	.25
583	Ken Oberkfell	.06	.03
584	Larry Bradford	.06	.03
585	Fred Stanley	.06	.03
586	Bill Caudill	.06	.03

587	Doug Capilla	.06	.03
588	George Riley	.06	.03
589	Willie Hernandez	.08	.05
590	Mike Schmidt (MVP)	1.75	1.00
591	Steve Stone (CY)	.08	.05
592	Rick Sofield	.06	.03
593	Bombo Rivera	.06	.03
594	Gary Ward	.06	.03
595	Dave Edwards (Var)	.06	.03
596	Mike Proly	.06	.03
597	Tommy Boggs	.06	.03
598	Greg Gross	.06	.03
599	Elias Sosa	.06	.03
600	Pat Kelly	.06	.03
___	Checklist (Er) (Tom Donohue)	1.00	.70
___	Checklist (Cor) (Tom Donahue)	.15	.08
___	Checklist (Er) (Gary Mathews)	.25	.15
___	Checklist (Cor) (Gary Matthews)	.15	.08
___	Checklist (Er) (Luis Pujois)	.25	.15
___	Checklist (Cor) (Luis Pujols)	.15	.08
___	Checklist (Er) Glen Adams)	.25	.15
___	Checklist (Cor) (Glenn Adams)	.15	.08

1982 Donruss

The second Donruss baseball set consists of 660-cards and marks the debut of the Donruss Diamond Kings subset. Donruss upgraded the quality of their paper stock over the previous year and included puzzle pieces instead of bubble gum in each pack. The standard-size cards measure 2-1/2" by 3-1/2".

		MINT	NR/MT
Complete Set (660)		110.00	75.00
Commons		.08	.05
1	Pete Rose (DK)	1.50	.90
2	Gary Carter (DK)	.50	.30
3	Steve Garvey (DK)	.50	.30
4	Vida Blue (DK)	.12	.07
5a	Alan Trammel (DK) (Er)	1.50	.90
5b	Alan Trammell (DK) (Cor)	.35	.20
6	Len Barker (DK)	.08	.05
7	Dwight Evans (DK)	.20	.12
8	Rod Carew (DK)	.80	.50
9	George Hendrick (DK)	.08	.05
10	Phil Niekro (DK)	.40	.25
11	Richie Zisk (DK)	.08	.05
12	Dave Parker (DK)	.15	.08
13	Nolan Ryan (DK)	3.00	2.00
14	Ivan DeJesus (DK)	.08	.05
15	George Brett (DK)	1.50	.90
16	Tom Seaver (DK)	1.75	1.00
17	Dave Kingman (DK)	.12	.07
18	Dave Winfield (DK)	1.25	.80
19	Mike Norris (DK)	.08	.05
20	Carlton Fisk (DK)	.80	.50
21	Ozzie Smith (DK)	1.00	.70
22	Roy Smalley (DK)	.08	.05
23	Buddy Bell (DK)	.08	.05
24	Ken Singleton (DK)	.08	.05
25	John Mayberry (DK)	.10	.06
26	Gorman Thomas (DK)	.10	.06
27	Earl Weaver	.12	.07
28	Rollie Fingers	.90	.60
29	Sparky Anderson	.10	.06
30	Dennis Eckersley	1.00	.70
31	Dave Winfield	2.00	1.25
32	Burt Hooton	.08	.05
33	Rick Waits	.08	.05
34	George Brett	3.00	2.00
35	Steve McCatty	.08	.05
36	Steve Rogers	.08	.05
37	Bill Stein	.08	.05
38	Steve Renko	.08	.05
39	Mike Squires	.08	.05
40	George Hendrick	.08	.05
41	Bob Knepper	.08	.05
42	Steve Carlton	1.75	1.00
43	Larry Biittner	.08	.05
44	Chris Welsh	.08	.05
45	Steve Nicosia	.08	.05
46	Jack Clark	.15	.08
47	Chris Chambliss	.10	.06
48	Ivan DeJesus	.08	.05
49	Lee Mazzilli	.08	.05
50	Julio Cruz	.08	.05
51	Pete Redfern	.08	.05

No.	Player		
52	Dave Stieb	.20	.12
53	Doug Corbett	.08	.05
54	Jorge Bell (R)	8.00	5.00
55	Joe Simpson	.08	.05
56	Rusty Staub	.15	.08
57	Hector Cruz	.08	.05
58	Claudell Washington	.08	.05
59	Enrique Romo	.08	.05
60	Gary Lavelle	.08	.05
61	Tim Flannery	.08	.05
62	Joe Nolan	.08	.05
63	Larry Bowa	.10	.06
64	Sixto Lezcano	.08	.05
65	Joe Sambito	.08	.05
66	Bruce Kison	.08	.05
67	Wayne Nordhagen	.08	.05
68	Woodie Fryman	.08	.05
69	Billy Sample	.08	.05
70	Amos Otis	.08	.05
71	Matt Keough	.08	.05
72	Toby Harrah	.08	.05
73	Dave Righetti(R)	.50	.30
74	Carl Yastrzemski	2.00	1.25
75	Bob Welch	.20	.12
76a	Alan Trammel(Er)	1.50	.90
76b	Alan Trammell (Cor)	.70	.40
77	Rick Dempsey	.08	.05
78	Paul Molitor	1.00	.70
79	Dennis Martinez	.25	.15
80	Jim Slaton	.08	.05
81	Champ Summers	.08	.05
82	Carney Lansford	.12	.07
83	Barry Foote	.08	.05
84	Steve Garvey	.70	.40
85	Rick Manning	.08	.05
86	John Wathan	.08	.05
87	Brian Kingman	.08	.05
88	Andre Dawson	2.00	1.25
89	Jim Kern	.08	.05
90	Bobby Grich	.12	.07
91	Bob Forsch	.08	.05
92	Art Howe	.08	.05
93	Marty Bystrom	.08	.05
94	Ozzie Smith	2.00	1.25
95	Dave Parker	.25	.15
96	Doyle Alexander	.08	.05
97	Al Hrabosky	.08	.05
98	Frank Taveras	.08	.05
99	Tim Blackwell	.08	.05
100	Floyd Bannister	.08	.05
101	Alfredo Griffin	.08	.05
102	Dave Engle	.08	.05
103	Mario Soto	.08	.05
104	Ross Baumgarten	.08	.05
105	Ken Singleton	.08	.05
106	Ted Simmons	.10	.06
107	Jack Morris	1.50	.90
108	Bob Watson	.10	.06
109	Dwight Evans	.25	.15
110	Tom Lasorda	.10	.06
111	Bert Blyleven	.35	.20
112	Dan Quisenberry	.10	.06
113	Rickey Henderson	5.00	3.00
114	Gary Carter	.80	.50
115	Brian Downing	.08	.05
116	Al Oliver	.12	.07
117	LaMarr Hoyt	.08	.05
118	Cesar Cedeno	.10	.06
119	Keith Moreland	.08	.05
120	Bob Shirley	.08	.05
121	Terry Kennedy	.08	.05
122	Frank Pastore	.08	.05
123	Gene Garber	.08	.05
124	Tony Pena	.25	.15
125	Allen Ripley	.08	.05
126	Randy Martz	.08	.05
127	Richie Zisk	.08	.05
128	Mike Scott	.20	.12
129	Lloyd Moseby	.12	.07
130	Rob Wilfong	.08	.05
131	Tim Stoddard	.08	.05
132	Gorman Thomas	.10	.06
133	Dan Petry	.08	.05
134	Bob Stanley	.08	.05
135	Lou Piniella	.10	.06
136	Pedro Guerrero	.25	.15
137	Len Barker	.08	.05
138	Richard Gale	.08	.05
139	Wayne Gross	.08	.05
140	Tim Wallach (R)	1.25	.80
141	Gene Mauch	.10	.06
142	Doc Medich	.08	.05
143	Tony Bernazard	.08	.05
144	Bill Virdon	.08	.05
145	John Littlefield	.08	.05
146	Dave Bergman	.08	.05
147	Dick Davis	.08	.05
148	Tom Seaver	2.50	1.50
149	Matt Sinatro	.08	.05
150	Chuck Tanner	.08	.05
151	Leon Durham	.08	.05
152	Gene Tenace	.08	.05
153	Al Bumbry	.08	.05
154	Mark Brouhard	.08	.05
155	Rick Peters	.08	.05
156	Jerry Remy	.08	.05
157	Rick Reuschel	.08	.05
158	Steve Howe	.08	.05
159	Alan Bannister	.08	.05
160	U.L. Washington	.08	.05
161	Rick Langford	.08	.05
162	Bill Gullickson	.15	.08
163	Mark Wagner	.08	.05

164	Geoff Zahn	.08	.05	226	Mike Parrott	.08	.05
165	Ron LeFlore	.08	.05	227	Jim Clancy	.08	.05
166	Dane Iorg	.08	.05	228	Hosken Powell	.08	.05
167	Joe Niekro	.08	.05	229	Tom Hume	.08	.05
168	Pete Rose	2.00	1.25	230	Britt Burns	.08	.05
169	Dave Collins	.08	.05	231	Jim Palmer	1.50	.90
170	Rick Wise	.08	.05	232	Bob Rodgers	.08	.05
171	Jim Bibby	.08	.05	233	Milt Wilcox	.08	.05
172	Larry Herndon	.08	.05	234	Dave Revering	.08	.05
173	Bob Horner	.10	.06	235	Mike Torrez	.08	.05
174	Steve Dillard	.08	.05	236	Robert Castillo	.08	.05
175	Mookie Wilson	.08	.05	237	Von Hayes (R)	.25	.15
176	Dan Meyer	.08	.05	238	Renie Martin	.08	.05
177	Fernando Arroyo	.08	.05	239	Dwayne Murphy	.08	.05
178	Jackson Todd	.08	.05	240	Rodney Scott	.08	.05
179	Darrell Jackson	.08	.05	241	Fred Patek	.08	.05
180	Al Woods	.08	.05	242	Mickey Rivers	.08	.05
181	Jim Anderson	.08	.05	243	Steve Trout	.08	.05
182	Dave Kingman	.12	.07	244	Jose Cruz	.10	.06
183	Steve Henderson	.08	.05	245	Manny Trillo	.08	.05
184	Brian Asselstine	.08	.05	246	Lary Sorensen	.08	.05
185	Rod Scurry	.08	.05	247	Dave Edwards	.08	.05
186	Fred Breining	.08	.05	248	Dan Driessen	.08	.05
187	Danny Boone	.08	.05	249	Tommy Boggs	.08	.05
188	Junior Kennedy	.08	.05	250	Dale Berra	.08	.05
189	Sparky Lyle	.10	.06	251	Ed Whitson	.08	.05
190	Whitey Herzog	.10	.06	252	Lee Smith (R)	9.00	6.00
191	Dave Smith	.08	.05	253	Tom Paciorek	.08	.05
192	Ed Ott	.08	.05	254	Pat Zachry	.08	.05
193	Greg Luzinski	.12	.07	255	Luis Leal	.08	.05
194	Bill Lee	.08	.05	256	John Castino	.08	.05
195	Don Zimmer	.08	.05	257	Rich Dauer	.08	.05
196	Hal McRae	.12	.07	258	Cecil Cooper	.10	.06
197	Mike Norris	.08	.05	259	Dave Rozema	.08	.05
198	Duane Kuiper	.08	.05	260	John Tudor	.08	.05
199	Rick Cerone	.08	.05	261	Jerry Mumphrey	.08	.05
200	Jim Rice	.25	.15	262	Jay Johnstone	.08	.05
201	Steve Yeager	.08	.05	263	Bo Diaz	.08	.05
202	Tom Brookens	.08	.05	264	Dennis Leonard	.08	.05
203	Jose Morales	.08	.05	265	Jim Spencer	.08	.05
204	Roy Howell	.08	.05	266	John Milner	.08	.05
205	Tippy Martinez	.08	.05	267	Don Aase	.08	.05
206	Moose Haas	.08	.05	268	Jim Sundberg	.08	.05
207	Al Cowens	.08	.05	269	Lamar Johnson	.08	.05
208	Dave Stapleton	.08	.05	270	Frank LaCorte	.08	.05
209	Bucky Dent	.10	.06	271	Barry Evans	.08	.05
210	Ron Cey	.10	.06	272	Enos Cabell	.08	.05
211	Jorge Orta	.08	.05	273	Del Unser	.08	.05
212	Jamie Quirk	.08	.05	274	George Foster	.15	.08
213	Jeff Jones	.08	.05	275	Brett Butler (R)	2.00	1.25
214	Tim Raines	1.00	.70	276	Lee Lacy	.08	.05
215	Jon Matlack	.08	.05	277	Ken Reitz	.08	.05
216	Rod Carew	1.50	.90	278	Keith Hernandez	.20	.12
217	Jim Kaat	.15	.08	279	Doug DeCinces	.08	.05
218	Joe Pittman	.08	.05	280	Charlie Moore	.08	.05
219	Larry Christenson	.08	.05	281	Lance Parrish	.25	.15
220	Juan Bonilla	.08	.05	282	Ralph Houk	.08	.08
221	Mike Easler	.08	.05	283	Rich Gossage	.25	.15
222	Vida Blue	.12	.07	284	Jerry Reuss	.08	.05
223	Rick Camp	.08	.05	285	Mike Stanton	.08	.05
224	Mike Jorgensen	.08	.05	286	Frank White	.08	.05
225	Jody Davis (R)	.12	.07	287	Bob Owchinko	.08	.05

288	Scott Sanderson	.08	.05	350	Alex Trevino	.08	.05
289	Bump Wills	.08	.05	351	Mike Krukow	.08	.05
290	Dave Frost	.08	.05	352a	Shane Rawley	.50	.30
291	Chet Lemon	.08	.05		(Wrong Photo)		
292	Tito Landrum	.08	.05	352b	Shane Rawley	.08	.05
293	Vern Ruhle	.08	.05		(Cor)		
294	Mike Schmidt	3.00	2.00	353	Garth Iorg	.08	.05
295	Sam Mejias	.08	.05	354	Pete Mackanin	.08	.05
296	Gary Lucas	.08	.05	355	Paul Moskau	.08	.05
297	John Candelaria	.08	.05	356	Richard Dotson	.08	.05
298	Jerry Martin	.08	.05	357	Steve Stone	.08	.05
299	Dale Murphy	1.00	.70	358	Larry Hisle	.08	.05
300	Mike Lum	.08	.05	359	Aurelio Lopez	.08	.05
301	Tom Hausman	.08	.05	360	Oscar Gamble	.08	.05
302	Glenn Abbott	.08	.05	361	Tom Burgmeier	.08	.05
303	Roger Erickson	.08	.05	362	Terry Forster	.08	.05
304	Otto Velez	.08	.05	363	Joe Charboneau	.08	.05
305	Danny Goodwin	.08	.05	364	Ken Brett	.08	.05
306	John Mayberry	.08	.05	365	Tony Armas	.08	.05
307	Lenny Randle	.08	.05	366	Chris Speier	.08	.05
308	Bob Bailor	.08	.05	367	Fred Lynn	.15	.08
309	Jerry Morales	.08	.05	368	Buddy Bell	.08	.05
310	Rufino Linares	.08	.05	369	Jim Essian	.08	.05
311	Kent Tekulve	.08	.05	370	Terry Puhl	.08	.05
312	Joe Morgan	.75	.45	371	Greg Gross	.08	.05
313	John Urrea	.08	.05	372	Bruce Sutter	.15	.08
314	Paul Householder	.08	.05	373	Joe Lefebvre	.08	.05
315	Garry Maddox	.08	.05	374	Ray Knight	.08	.05
316	Mike Ramsey	.08	.05	375	Bruce Benedict	.08	.05
317	Alan Ashby	.08	.05	376	Tim Foli	.08	.05
318	Bob Clark	.08	.05	377	Al Holland	.08	.05
319	Tony LaRussa	.10	.06	378	Ken Kravec	.08	.05
320	Charlie Lea	.08	.05	379	Jeff Burroughs	.08	.05
321	Danny Darwin	.08	.05	380	Pete Falcone	.08	.05
322	Cesar Geronimo	.08	.05	381	Ernie Whitt	.08	.05
323	Tom Underwood	.08	.05	382	Brad Havens	.08	.05
324	Andre Thornton	.10	.06	383	Terry Crowley	.08	.05
325	Rudy May	.08	.05	384	Don Money	.08	.05
326	Frank Tanana	.08	.05	385	Dan Schatzeder	.08	.05
327	Davey Lopes	.10	.06	386	Gary Allenson	.08	.05
328	Richie Hebner	.08	.05	387	Yogi Berra	.35	.20
329	Mike Flanagan	.08	.05	388	Ken Landreaux	.08	.05
330	Mike Caldwell	.08	.05	389	Mike Hargrove	.08	.05
331	Scott McGregor	.08	.05	390	Darryl Motley	.08	.05
332	Jerry Augustine	.08	.05	391	Dave McKay	.08	.05
333	Stan Papi	.08	.05	392	Stan Bahnsen	.08	.05
334	Rick Miller	.08	.05	393	Ken Forsch	.08	.05
335	Graig Nettles	.20	.12	394	Mario Mendoza	.08	.05
336	Dusty Baker	.10	.06	395	Jim Morrison	.08	.05
337	Dave Garcia	.08	.05	396	Mike Ivie	.08	.05
338	Larry Gura	.08	.05	397	Broderick Perkins	.08	.05
339	Cliff Johnson	.08	.05	398	Darrell Evans	.12	.07
340	Warren Cromartie	.08	.05	399	Ron Reed	.08	.05
341	Steve Comer	.08	.05	400	Johnny Bench	1.75	1.00
342	Rick Burleson	.08	.05	401	Steve Bedrosian (R)	.25	.15
343	John Martin	.08	.05	402	Bill Robinson	.08	.05
344	Craig Reynolds	.08	.05	403	Bill Buckner	.10	.06
345	Mike Proly	.08	.05	404	Ken Oberkfell	.08	.05
346	Ruppert Jones	.08	.05	405	Cal Ripken, Jr.	60.00	45.00
347	Omar Moreno	.08	.05		(R)		
348	Greg Minton	.08	.05	406	Jim Gantner	.08	.05
349	Rick Mahler (R)	.12	.07	407	Kirk Gibson	.60	.35

408	Tony Perez	.40	.25
409	Tommy John	.15	.08
410	Dave Stewart (R)	2.50	1.50
411	Dan Spillner	.08	.05
412	Willie Aikens	.08	.05
413	Mike Heath	.08	.05
414	Ray Burris	.08	.05
415	Leon Roberts	.08	.05
416	Mike Witt (R)	.15	.08
417	Bobby Molinaro	.08	.05
418	Steve Braun	.08	.05
419	Nolan Ryan	8.50	5.50
420	Tug McGraw	.20	.12
421	Dave Concepcion	.15	.08
422a	Juan Eickelberger (Er)(Wrong photo)	.50	.30
422b	Juan Eickelberger (Cor)	.08	.05
423	Rick Rhoden	.08	.05
424	Frank Robinson	.25	.15
425	Eddie Miller	.08	.05
426	Bill Caudill	.08	.05
427	Doug Flynn	.08	.05
428	Larry Anderson (Er)	.08	.05
429	Al Williams	.08	.05
430	Jerry Garvin	.08	.05
431	Glenn Adams	.08	.05
432	Barry Bonnell	.08	.05
433	Jerry Narron	.08	.05
434	John Stearns	.08	.05
435	Mike Tyson	.08	.05
436	Glenn Hubbard	.08	.05
437	Eddie Solomon	.08	.05
438	Jeff Leonard	.08	.05
439	Randy Bass	.08	.05
440	Mike LaCoss	.08	.05
441	Gary Matthews	.08	.05
442	Mark Littell	.08	.05
443	Don Sutton	.50	.30
444	John Harris	.08	.05
445	Vada Pinson	.08	.05
446	Elias Sosa	.08	.05
447	Charlie Hough	.08	.05
448	Willie Wilson	.10	.06
449	Fred Stanley	.08	.05
450	Tom Veryzer	.08	.05
451	Ron Davis	.08	.05
452	Mark Clear	.08	.05
453	Bill Russell	.10	.06
454	Lou Whitaker	.30	.18
455	Dan Graham	.08	.05
456	Reggie Cleveland	.08	.05
457	Sammy Stewart	.08	.05
458	Pete Vuckovich	.08	.05
459	John Wockenfuss	.08	.05
460	Glenn Hoffman	.08	.05
461	Willie Randolph	.15	.08
462	Fernando Valenzuela	.35	.20
463	Ron Hassey	.08	.05
464	Paul Splittorff	.08	.05
465	Rob Picciolo	.08	.05
466	Larry Parrish	.10	.06
467	Johnny Grubb	.08	.05
468	Dan Ford	.08	.05
469	Silvio Martinez	.08	.05
470	Kiko Garcia	.08	.05
471	Bob Boone	.12	.07
472	Luis Salazar	.08	.05
473	Randy Niemann	.08	.05
474	Tom Griffin	.08	.05
475	Phil Niekro	.50	.30
476	Hubie Brooks	.30	.18
477	Dick Tidrow	.08	.05
478	Jim Beattie	.08	.05
479	Damaso Garcia	.08	.05
480	Mickey Hatcher	.08	.05
481	Joe Price	.08	.05
482	Ed Farmer	.08	.05
483	Eddie Murray	2.00	3.00
484	Ben Oglivie	.08	.05
485	Kevin Saucier	.08	.05
486	Bobby Murcer	.10	.06
487	Bill Campbell	.08	.05
488	Reggie Smith	.08	.05
489	Wayne Garland	.08	.05
490	Jim Wright	.08	.05
491	Billy Martin	.25	.15
492	Jim Fanning	.08	.05
493	Don Baylor	.20	.12
494	Rick Honeycutt	.08	.05
495	Carlton Fisk	1.50	.90
496	Denny Walling	.08	.05
497	Bake McBride	.08	.05
498	Darrell Porter	.08	.05
499	Gene Richards	.08	.05
500	Ken Dayley (R)	.12	.07
501	Jason Thompson	.08	.05
503	Milt May	.08	.05
504	Doug Bird	.08	.05
505	Bruce Bochte	.08	.05
506	Neil Allen	.08	.05
507	Joey McLaughlin	.08	.05
508	Butch Wynegar	.08	.05
509	Gary Roenicke	.08	.05
510	Robin Yount	3.50	2.25
511	Dave Tobik	.08	.05
512	Rich Gedman (R)	.12	.07
513	Gene Nelson (R)	.08	.05
514	Rick Monday	.08	.05
515	Miguel Dilone	.08	.05
516	Clint Hurdle	.08	.05
517	Jeff Newman	.08	.05
518	Grant Jackson	.08	.05
519	Andy Hassler	.08	.05

Card	Player	Value	Value
520	Pat Putnam	.08	.05
521	Greg Pryor	.08	.05
522	Tony Scott	.08	.05
523	Steve Mura	.08	.05
524	Johnnie LeMaster	.08	.05
525	Dick Ruthven	.08	.05
526	John McNamara	.08	.05
527	Larry McWilliams	.08	.05
528	Johnny Ray (R)	.12	.07
529	Pat Tabler (R)	.20	.12
530	Tom Herr	.08	.05
531	San Diego Chicken (Var)	1.00	.70
532	Sal Butera	.08	.05
533	Mike Griffin	.08	.05
534	Kelvin Moore	.08	.05
535	Reggie Jackson	2.50	1.50
536	Ed Romero	.08	.05
537	Derrel Thomas	.08	.05
538	Mike O'Berry	.08	.05
539	Jack O'Connor	.08	.05
540	Bob Ojeda (R)	.35	.20
541	Roy Lee Jackson	.08	.05
542	Lynn Jones	.08	.05
543	Gaylord Perry	.50	.30
544a	Phil Garner(Photo reversed)	.50	.30
544b	Phil Garner (Cor)	.08	.05
545	Garry Templeton	.08	.05
546	Rafael Ramirez	.08	.05
547	Jeff Reardon	3.50	2.25
548	Ron Guidry	.25	.15
549	Tim Laudner (R)	.12	.07
550	John Henry Johnson	.08	.05
551	Chris Bando	.08	.05
552	Bobby Brown	.08	.05
553	Larry Bradford	.08	.05
554	Scott Fletcher (R)	.25	.15
555	Jerry Royster	.08	.05
556	Shooty Babbitt	.08	.05
557	Kent Hrbek (R)	2.50	1.50
558	Yankee Winners (Ron Guidry, Tommy John)	.20	.12
559	Mark Bomback	.08	.05
560	Julio Valdez	.08	.05
561	Buck Martinez	.08	.05
562	Mike Marshall (R)	.15	.08
563	Rennie Stennett	.08	.05
564	Steve Crawford	.08	.05
565	Bob Babcock	.08	.05
566	Johnny Podres	.12	.07
567	Paul Serna	.08	.05
568	Harold Baines	1.00	.70
569	Dave LaRoche	.08	.05
570	Lee May	.08	.05
571	Gary Ward	.08	.05
572	John Denny	.08	.05
573	Roy Smalley	.08	.05
574	Bob Brenly (R)	.15	.08
575	Bronx Bombers (Reggie Jackson, Dave Winfield)	2.50	1.50
576	Luis Pujols	.08	.05
577	Butch Hobson	.08	.05
578	Harvey Kuenn	.10	.06
579	Cal Ripken, Sr.	.12	.07
580	Juan Berenguer	.08	.05
581	Benny Ayala	.08	.05
582	Vance Law	.08	.05
583	Rick Leach (R)	.08	.05
584	George Frazier	.08	.05
585	Phillies Finest (Pete Rose, Mike Schmidt)	2.00	1.25
586	Joe Rudi	.10	.06
587	Juan Beniquez	.08	.05
588	Luis DeLeon (R)	.08	.05
589	Craig Swan	.08	.05
590	Dave Chalk	.08	.05
591	Billy Gardner	.08	.05
592	Sal Bando	.10	.06
593	Bert Campaneris	.08	.05
594	Steve Kemp	.08	.05
595a	Randy Lerch (Braves)	.50	.30
595b	Randy Lerch (Brewers)	.08	.05
596	Bryan Clark	.08	.05
597	Dave Ford	.08	.05
598	Mike Scioscia	.35	.20
599	John Lowenstein	.08	.05
600	Rene Lachemann	.08	.05
601	Mick Kelleher	.08	.05
602	Ron Jackson	.08	.05
603	Jerry Koosman	.10	.06
604	Dave Goltz	.08	.05
605	Ellis Valentine	.08	.05
606	Lonnie Smith	.12	.07
607	Joaquin Andujar	.10	.06
608	Garry Hancock	.08	.05
609	Jerry Turner	.08	.05
610	Bob Bonner	.08	.05
611	Jim Dwyer	.08	.05
612	Terry Bulling	.08	.05
613	Joel Youngblood	.08	.05
614	Larry Milbourne	.08	.05
615	Phil Roof (Er) (Gene)	.08	.05
616	Keith Drumright	.08	.05
617	Dave Rosello	.08	.05
618	Rickey Keeton	.08	.05
619	Dennis Lamp	.08	.05
620	Sid Monge	.08	.05
621	Jerry White	.08	.05

622	Luis Aguayo (R)	.08	.05
623	Jamie Easterly	.08	.05
624	Steve Sax (R)	2.75	1.75
625	Dave Roberts	.08	.05
626	Rick Bosetti	.08	.05
627	Terry Francona (R)	.10	.06
628	Pride of the Reds (Johnny Bench, Tom Seaver)	2.00	1.25
629	Paul Mirabella	.08	.05
630	Rance Mulliniks	.08	.05
631	Kevin Hickey	.08	.05
632	Reid Nichols	.08	.05
633	Dave Geisel	.08	.05
634	Ken Griffey	.20	.12
635	Bob Lemon	.15	.08
636	Orlando Sanchez	.08	.05
637	Bill Almon	.08	.05
638	Danny Ainge	.40	.25
639	Willie Stargell	.60	.30
640	Bob Sykes	.08	.05
641	Ed Lynch	.08	.05
642	John Ellis	.08	.05
643	Fergie Jenkins	.50	.30
644	Lenn Sakata	.08	.05
645	Julio Gonzales	.08	.05
646	Jesse Orosco	.08	.05
647	Jerry Dybzinski	.08	.05
648	Tommy Davis	.10	.06
649	Ron Gardenhire	.08	.05
650	Felipe Alou	.12	.07
651	Harvey Haddix	.08	.05
652	Willie Upshaw	.08	.05
653	Bill Madlock	.12	.07
___	Checklist (Er) (Alan Trammel)	.50	.30
___	Checklist (Cor) (Alan Trammell)	.15	.08
___	Checklist 27-130	.15	.08
___	Checklist 131-234	.15	.08
___	Checklist 235-338	.15	.08
___	Checklist 339-442	.15	.08
___	Checklist 443-544	.15	.08
___	Checklist 545-653	.15	.08

1983 Donruss

The 1983 Donruss set features 660 standard-size cards including seven unnumbered checklist cards. The first 26 cards in the set are Diamond Kings. Card backs consist of black type on a yellow and white background. The cards were sold with puzzle pieces featuring Ty Cobb.

		MINT	NR/MT
Complete Set (660)		140.00	100.00
Commons		.08	.05

1	Fernando Valenzuela (DK)	.25	.15
2	Rollie Fingers(DK)	.40	.25
3	Reggie Jackson(DK)	.90	.60
4	Jim Palmer(DK)	.50	.30
5	Jack Morris(DK)	.30	.18
6	George Foster(DK)	.12	.07
7	Jim Sundberg(DK)	.08	.05
8	Willie Stargell(DK)	.35	.20
9	Dave Stieb(DK)	.12	.07
10	Joe Niekro(DK)	.08	.05
11	Rickey Henderson (DK)	2.00	1.25
12	Dale Murphy(DK)	.35	.20
13	Toby Harrah(DK)	.08	.05
14	Bill Buckner(DK)	.10	.06
15	Willie Wilson(DK)	.08	.05
16	Steve Carlton(DK)	.75	.45
17	Ron Guidry(DK)	.15	.08
18	Steve Rogers(DK)	.08	.05
19	Kent Hrbek(DK)	.15	.08
20	Keith Hernandez(DK)	.15	.08
21	Floyd Bannister(DK)	.08	.05
22	Johnny Bench (DK)	.75	.45
23	Britt Burns (DK)	.08	.05
24	Joe Morgan (DK)	.40	.25
25	Carl Yastrzemski (DK)	.75	.45
26	Terry Kenndey (DK)	.08	.05
27	Gary Roenicke	.08	.05

#	Player		
28	Dwight Bernard	.08	.05
29	Pat Underwood	.08	.05
30	Gary Allenson	.08	.05
31	Ron Guidry	.15	.08
32	Burt Hooton	.08	.05
33	Chris Bando	.08	.05
34	Vida Blue	.12	.07
35	Rickey Henderson	2.50	1.50
36	Ray Burris	.08	.05
37	John Butcher	.08	.05
38	Don Aase	.08	.05
39	Jerry Koosman	.10	.06
40	Bruce Sutter	.12	.07
41	Jose Cruz	.12	.07
42	Pete Rose	1.75	1.00
43	Cesar Cedeno	.10	.06
44	Floyd Chiffer	.08	.05
45	Larry McWilliams	.08	.05
46	Alan Fowlkes	.08	.05
47	Dale Murphy	.70	.40
48	Doug Bird	.08	.05
49	Hubie Brooks	.15	.08
50	Floyd Bannister	.08	.05
51	Jack O'Connor	.08	.05
52	Steve Senteney	.08	.05
53	Gary Gaetti (R)	.30	.18
54	Damaso Garcia	.08	.05
55	Gene Nelson	.08	.05
56	Mookie Wilson	.08	.05
57	Allen Ripley	.08	.05
58	Bob Horner	.10	.06
59	Tony Pena	.08	.05
60	Gary Lavelle	.08	.05
61	Tim Lollar	.08	.05
62	Frank Pastore	.08	.05
63	Garry Maddox	.08	.05
64	Bob Forsch	.08	.05
65	Harry Spilman	.08	.05
66	Geoff Zahn	.08	.05
67	Salome Barojas	.08	.05
68	David Palmer	.08	.05
69	Charlie Hough	.08	.05
70	Dan Quisenberry	.08	.05
71	Tony Armas	.08	.05
72	Rick Sutcliffe	.12	.07
73	Steve Balboni	.08	.05
74	Jerry Remy	.08	.05
75	Mike Scioscia	.12	.07
76	John Wockenfuss	.08	.05
77	Jim Palmer	1.25	.80
78	Rollie Fingers	.80	.50
79	Joe Nolan	.08	.05
80	Pete Vuckovich	.08	.05
81	Rick Leach	.08	.05
82	Rick Miller	.08	.05
83	Graig Nettles	.12	.07
84	Ron Cey	.10	.06
85	Miguel Dilone	.08	.05
86	John Wathan	.08	.05
87	Kelvin Moore	.08	.05
88a	Byrn Smith(Er)	.50	.30
88b	Bryn Smith(Cor)	.10	.06
89	Dave Hostetler	.08	.05
90	Rod Carew	1.25	.80
91	Lonnie Smith	.08	.05
92	Bob Knepper	.08	.05
93	Marty Bystrom	.08	.05
94	Chris Welsh	.08	.05
95	Jason Thompson	.08	.05
96	Tom O'Malley	.08	.05
97	Phil Niekro	.60	.35
98	Neil Allen	.08	.05
99	Bill Buckner	.10	.06
100	Ed VandeBerg (R)	.08	.05
101	Jim Clancy	.08	.05
102	Robert Castillo	.08	.05
103	Bruce Berenyi	.08	.05
104	Carlton Fisk	1.25	.80
105	Mike Flanagan	.08	.05
106	Cecil Cooper	.08	.05
107	Jack Morris	1.00	.70
108	Mike Morgan	.20	.12
109	Luis Aponte	.08	.05
110	Pedro Guerrero	.25	.15
111	Len Barker	.08	.05
112	Willie Wilson	.08	.05
113	Dave Beard	.08	.05
114	Mike Gates	.08	.05
115	Reggie Jackson	2.50	1.50
116	George Wright	.08	.05
117	Vance Law	.08	.05
118	Nolan Ryan	7.50	4.50
119	Mike Krukow	.08	.05
120	Ozzie Smith	1.25	.80
121	Broderick Perkins	.08	.05
122	Tom Seaver	1.75	1.00
123	Chris Chambliss	.10	.06
124	Chuck Tanner	.08	.05
125	Johnnie LeMaster	.08	.05
126	Mel Hall (R)	2.50	1.50
127	Bruce Bochte	.08	.05
128	Charlie Puleo (R)	.08	.05
129	Luis Leal	.08	.05
130	John Pacella	.08	.05
131	Glenn Gulliver	.08	.05
132	Don Money	.08	.05
133	Dave Rozema	.08	.05
134	Bruce Hurst	.60	.35
135	Rudy May	.08	.05
136	Tom Lasorda	.10	.06
137	Dan Spillner (Er) (Wrong Photo)	.08	.05
138	Jerry Martin	.08	.05
139	Mike Norris	.08	.05
140	Al Oliver	.12	.07
141	Daryl Sconiers	.08	.05

142	Lamar Johnson	.08	.05	200	Dave Stapleton	.08	.05
143	Harold Baines	.40	.25	201	Steve Yeager	.08	.05
144	Alan Ashby	.08	.05	202	Enos Cabell	.08	.05
145	Garry Templeton	.08	.05	203	Sammy Stewart	.08	.05
146	Al Holland	.08	.05	204	Moose Haas	.08	.05
147	Bo Diaz	.08	.05	205	Lenn Sakata	.08	.05
148	Dave Concepcion	.12	.07	206	Charlie Moore	.08	.05
149	Rick Camp	.08	.05	207	Alan Trammell	.50	.30
150	Jim Morrison	.08	.05	208	Jim Rice	.25	.15
151	Randy Martz	.08	.05	209	Roy Smalley	.08	.05
152	Keith Hernandez	.20	.12	210	Bill Russell	.10	.06
153	John Lowenstein	.08	.05	211	Andre Thornton	.08	.05
154	Mike Caldwell	.08	.05	212	Willie Aikens	.08	.05
155	Milt Wilcox	.08	.05	213	Dave McKay	.08	.05
156	Rich Gedman	.08	.05	214	Tim Blackwell	.08	.05
157	Rich Gossage	.12	.07	215	Buddy Bell	.08	.05
158	Jerry Reuss	.08	.05	216	Doug DeCinces	.08	.05
159	Ron Hassey	.08	.05	217	Tom Herr	.08	.05
160	Larry Gura	.08	.05	218	Frank LaCorte	.08	.05
161	Dwayne Murphy	.08	.05	219	Steve Carlton	1.50	.90
162	Woodie Fryman	.08	.05	220	Terry Kennedy	.08	.05
163	Steve Comer	.08	.05	221	Mike Easler	.08	.05
164	Ken Forsch	.08	.05	222	Jack Clark	.15	.08
165	Dennis Lamp	.08	.05	223	Gene Garber	.08	.05
166	David Green	.08	.05	224	Scott Holman	.08	.05
167	Terry Puhl	.08	.05	225	Mike Proly	.08	.05
168	Mike Schmidt	2.50	1.50	226	Terry Bulling	.08	.05
169	Eddie Milner (R)	.08	.05	227	Jerry Garvin	.08	.05
170	John Curtis	.08	.05	228	Ron Davis	.08	.05
171	Don Robinson	.08	.05	229	Tom Hume	.08	.05
172	Richard Gale	.08	.05	230	Marc Hill	.08	.05
173	Steve Bedrosian	.08	.05	231	Dennis Martinez	.12	.07
174	Willie Hernandez	.08	.05	232	Jim Gantner	.08	.05
175	Ron Gardenhire	.08	.05	233	Larry Pashnick	.08	.05
176	Jim Beattie	.08	.05	234	Dave Collins	.08	.05
177	Tim Laudner	.08	.05	235	Tom Burgmeier	.08	.05
178	Buck Martinez	.08	.05	236	Ken Landreaux	.08	.05
179	Kent Hrbek	.40	.25	237	John Denny	.08	.05
180	Alfredo Griffin	.08	.05	238	Hal McRae	.12	.07
181	Larry Andersen	.08	.05	239	Matt Keough	.08	.05
182	Pete Falcone	.08	.05	240	Doug Flynn	.08	.05
183	Jody Davis	.08	.05	241	Fred Lynn	.12	.07
184	Glenn Hubbard	.08	.05	242	Billy Sample	.08	.05
185	Dale Berra	.08	.05	243	Tom Paciorek	.08	.05
186	Greg Minton	.08	.05	244	Joe Sambito	.08	.05
187	Gary Lucas	.08	.05	245	Sid Monge	.08	.05
188	Dave Van Gorder	.08	.05	246	Ken Oberkfell	.08	.05
189	Bob Dernier	.08	.05	247	Joe Pittman (Er)	.08	.05
190	Willie McGee (R)	3.50	2.25		(Wrong Photo)		
191	Dickie Thon	.08	.05	248	Mario Soto	.08	.05
192	Bob Boone	.12	.07	249	Claudell	.08	.05
193	Britt Burns	.08	.05		Washington		
194	Jeff Reardon	2.00	1.25	250	Rick Rhoden	.08	.05
195	Jon Matlack	.08	.05	251	Darrell Evans	.10	.06
196	Don Slaught (R)	.30	.18	252	Steve Henderson	.08	.05
197	Fred Stanley	.08	.05	253	Manny Castillo	.08	.05
198	Rick Manning	.08	.05	254	Craig Swan	.08	.05
199	Dave Righetti	.15	.08	255	Joey McLaughlin	.08	.05

256	Pete Redfern	.08	.05	312	Milt May	.08	.05
257	Ken Singleton	.08	.05	313	John Montefusco	.08	.05
258	Robin Yount	2.50	1.50	314	Wayne Krenchicki	.08	.05
259	Elias Sosa	.08	.05	315	George Vukovich	.08	.05
260	Bob Ojeda	.10	.06	316	Joaquin Andujar	.10	.06
261	Bobby Murcer	.12	.07	317	Craig Reynolds	.08	.05
262	Candy Maldonado (R)	.50	.30	318	Rick Burleson	.08	.05
				319	Richard Dotson	.08	.05
263	Rick Waits	.08	.05	320	Steve Rogers	.08	.05
264	Greg Pryor	.08	.05	321	Dave Schmidt	.10	.06
265	Bob Owchinko	.08	.05	322	Bud Black (R)	.30	.18
266	Chris Speier	.08	.05	323	Jeff Burroughs	.08	.05
267	Bruce Kison	.08	.05	324	Von Hayes	.08	.05
268	Mark Wagner	.08	.05	325	Butch Wynegar	.08	.05
269	Steve Kemp	.08	.05	326	Carl Yastrzemski	2.00	1.25
270	Phil Garner	.08	.05	327	Ron Roenicke	.08	.05
271	Gene Richards	.08	.05	328	Howard Johnson (R)	8.00	5.00
272	Renie Martin	.08	.05				
273	Dave Roberts	.08	.05	329	Rick Dempsey	.08	.05
274	Dan Driessen	.08	.05	330	Jim Slaton	.08	.05
275	Rufino Linares	.08	.05	331	Benny Ayala	.08	.05
276	Lee Lacy	.08	.05	332	Ted Simmons	.08	.05
277	Ryne Sandberg (R)	45.00	35.00	333	Lou Whitaker	.25	.15
				334	Chuck Rainey	.08	.05
278	Darrell Porter	.08	.05	335	Lou Piniella	.12	.07
279	Cal Ripken	20.00	14.00	336	Steve Sax	.70	.40
280	Jamie Easterly	.08	.05	337	Toby Harrah	.08	.05
281	Bill Fahey	.08	.05	338	George Brett	2.50	1.50
282	Glenn Hoffman	.08	.05	339	Davey Lopes	.10	.06
283	Willie Randolph	.10	.06	340	Gary Carter	.60	.35
284	Fernando Valenzuela	.12	.07	341	John Grubb	.08	.05
285	Alan Bannister	.08	.05	342	Tim Foli	.08	.05
286	Paul Splittorff	.08	.05	343	Jim Kaat	.15	.08
287	Joe Rudi	.10	.06	344	Mike LaCoss	.08	.05
288	Bill Gullickson	.12	.07	345	Larry Christenson	.08	.05
289	Danny Darwin	.08	.05	346	Juan Bonilla	.08	.05
290	Andy Hassler	.08	.05	347	Omar Moreno	.08	.05
291	Ernesto Escarrega	.08	.05	348	Chili Davis	.50	.30
292	Steve Mura	.08	.05	349	Tommy Boggs	.08	.05
293	Tony Scott	.08	.05	350	Rusty Staub	.12	.07
294	Manny Trillo	.08	.05	351	Bump Wills	.08	.05
295	Greg Harris	.10	.06	352	Rick Sweet	.08	.05
296	Luis DeLeon	.08	.05	353	Jim Gott (R)	.15	.08
297	Kent Tekulve	.08	.05	354	Terry Felton	.08	.05
298	Atlee Hammaker	.08	.05	355	Jim Kern	.08	.05
299	Bruce Benedict	.08	.05	356	Bill Almon	.08	.05
300	Fergie Jenkins	.40	.25	357	Tippy Martinez	.08	.05
301	Dave Kingman	.12	.07	358	Roy Howell	.08	.05
302	Bill Caudill	.08	.05	359	Dan Petry	.08	.05
303	John Castino	.08	.05	360	Jerry Mumphrey	.08	.05
304	Ernie Whitt	.08	.05	361	Mark Clear	.08	.05
305	Randy Johnson	.08	.05	362	Mike Marshall	.08	.05
306	Garth Iorg	.08	.05	363	Lary Sorensen	.08	.05
307	Gaylord Perry	.40	.25	364	Amos Otis	.10	.06
308	Ed Lynch	.08	.05	365	Rick Langford	.08	.05
309	Keith Moreland	.08	.05	366	Brad Mills	.08	.05
310	Rafael Ramirez	.08	.05	367	Brian Downing	.08	.05
311	Bill Madlock	.12	.07	368	Mike Richardt	.08	.05

369	Aurelio Rodriguez	.08	.05
370	Dave Smith	.08	.05
371	Tug McGraw	.12	.07
372	Doug Bair	.08	.05
373	Ruppert Jones	.08	.05
374	Alex Trevino	.08	.05
375	Ken Dayley	.08	.05
376	Rod Scurry	.08	.05
377	Bob Brenly	.08	.05
378	Scot Thompson	.08	.05
379	Julio Cruz	.08	.05
380	John Stearns	.08	.05
381	Dale Murray	.08	.05
382	Frank Viola (R)	4.50	2.75
383	Al Bumbry	.08	.05
384	Ben Oglivie	.08	.05
385	Dave Tobik	.08	.05
386	Bob Stanley	.08	.05
387	Andre Robertson	.08	.05
388	Jorge Orta	.08	.05
389	Ed Whitson	.08	.05
390	Don Hood	.08	.05
391	Tom Underwood	.08	.05
392	Tim Wallach	.20	.12
393	Steve Renko	.08	.05
394	Mickey Rivers	.08	.05
395	Greg Luzinski	.12	.07
396	Art Howe	.08	.05
397	Alan Wiggins	.08	.05
298	Jim Barr	.08	.05
399	Ivan DeJesus	.08	.05
400	Tom Lawless (R)	.08	.05
401	Bob Walk	.08	.05
402	Jimmy Smith	.08	.05
403	Lee Smith	3.50	2.25
404	George Hendrick	.08	.05
405	Eddie Murray	2.00	1.25
406	Marshall Edwards	.08	.05
407	Lance Parrish	.12	.07
408	Carney Lansford	.12	.07
409	Dave Winfield	2.00	1.25
410	Bob Welch	.15	.08
411	Larry Milbourne	.08	.05
412	Dennis Leonard	.08	.05
413	Dan Meyer	.08	.05
414	Charlie Lea	.08	.05
415	Rick Honeycutt	.08	.05
416	Mike Witt	.08	.05
417	Steve Trout	.08	.05
418	Glenn Brummer	.08	.05
419	Denny Walling	.08	.05
420	Gary Matthews	.08	.05
421	Charlie Liebrandt (Er)	.08	.05
422	Juan Eichelberger	.08	.05
423	Matt Guante (R) (Er) (Cecilio)	.08	.05
424	Bill Laskey	.08	.05
425	Jerry Royster	.08	.05
426	Dickie Noles	.08	.05
427	George Foster	.12	.07
428	Mike Moore (R)	.80	.50
429	Gary Ward	.08	.05
430	Barry Bonnell	.08	.05
431	Ron Washington	.08	.05
432	Rance Mulliniks	.08	.05
433	Mike Stanton	.08	.05
434	Jesse Orosco	.08	.05
435	Larry Bowa	.10	.06
436	Biff Pocoroba	.08	.05
437	Johnny Ray	.08	.05
438	Joe Morgan	.60	.35
439	Eric Show	.08	.05
440	Larry Biittner	.08	.05
441	Greg Gross	.08	.05
442	Gene Tenace	.10	.06
443	Danny Heep	.08	.05
444	Bobby Clark	.08	.05
445	Kevin Hickey	.08	.05
446	Scott Sanderson	.08	.05
447	Frank Tanana	.10	.06
448	Cesar Geronimo	.08	.05
449	Jimmy Sexton	.08	.05
450	Mike Hargrove	.08	.05
451	Doyle Alexander	.08	.05
452	Dwight Evans	.25	.15
453	Terry Forster	.08	.05
454	Tom Brookens	.08	.05
455	Rich Dauer	.08	.05
456	Rob Picciolo	.08	.05
457	Terry Crowley	.08	.05
458	Ned Yost	.08	.05
459	Kirk Gibson	.25	.15
460	Reid Nichols	.08	.05
461	Oscar Gamble	.08	.05
462	Dusty Baker	.10	.06
463	Jack Perconte	.08	.05
464	Frank White	.08	.05
465	Mickey Klutts	.08	.05
466	Warren Cromartie	.08	.05
467	Larry Parrish	.08	.05
468	Bobby Grich	.10	.06
469	Dane Iorg	.08	.05
470	Joe Niekro	.08	.05
471	Ed Farmer	.08	.05
472	Tim Flannery	.08	.05
473	Dave Parker	.25	.15
474	Jeff Leonard	.08	.05
475	Al Hrabosky	.08	.05
476	Ron Hodges	.08	.05
477	Leon Durham	.08	.05
478	Jim Essian	.08	.05
479	Roy Lee Jackson	.08	.05
480	Brad Havens	.08	.05
481	Joe Price	.08	.05

482	Tony Bernazard	.08	.05
483	Scott McGregor	.08	.05
484	Paul Molitor	.90	.60
485	Mike Ivie	.08	.05
486	Ken Griffey	.15	.08
487	Dennis Eckersley	1.00	.70
488	Steve Garvey	.50	.30
489	Mike Fischlin	.08	.05
490	U.L. Washington	.08	.05
491	Steve McCatty	.08	.05
492	Roy Johnson	.08	.05
493	Don Baylor	.12	.07
494	Bobby Johnson	.08	.05
495	Mike Squires	.08	.05
496	Bert Roberge	.08	.05
497	Dick Ruthven	.08	.05
498	Tito Landrum	.08	.05
499	Sixto Lezcano	.08	.05
500	Johnny Bench	1.50	.90
501	Larry Whisenton	.08	.05
502	Manny Sarmiento	.08	.05
503	Fred Breining	.08	.05
504	Bill Campbell	.08	.05
505	Todd Cruz	.08	.05
506	Bob Bailor	.08	.05
507	Dave Stieb	.15	.08
508	Al Williams	.08	.05
509	Dan Ford	.08	.05
510	Gorman Thomas	.08	.05
511	Chet Lemon	.08	.05
512	Mike Torrez	.08	.05
513	Shane Rawley	.08	.05
514	Mark Belanger	.10	.06
515	Rodney Craig	.08	.05
516	Onix Concepcion	.08	.05
517	Mike Heath	.08	.05
518	Andre Dawson	2.00	1.25
519	Luis Sanchez	.08	.05
520	Terry Bogener	.08	.05
521	Rudy Law	.08	.05
522	Ray Knight	.08	.05
523	Joe Lefebvre	.08	.05
524	Jim Wohlford	.08	.05
525	Julio Franco (R)	6.00	3.75
526	Ron Oester	.08	.05
527	Rick Mahler	.08	.05
528	Steve Nicosia	.08	.05
529	Junior Kenndey	.08	.05
530	Whitey Herzog (Var)	.10	.06
531	Don Sutton (Var)	.40	.25
532	Mark Brouhard	.08	.05
533	Sparky Anderson (Var)	.10	.06
534	Roger LaFrancois	.08	.05
535	George Frazier	.08	.05
536	Tom Niedenfuer	.08	.05
537	Ed Glynn	.08	.05
538	Lee May	.08	.05
539	Bob Kearney	.08	.05
540	Tim Raines	.50	.30
541	Paul Mirabella	.08	.05
542	Luis Tiant	.10	.06
543	Ron LeFlore	.08	.05
544	Dave LaPoint (R)	.10	.06
545	Randy Moffitt	.08	.05
546	Luis Aguayo	.08	.05
547	Brad Lesley	.08	.05
548	Luis Salazar	.08	.05
549	John Candelaria	.08	.05
550	Dave Bergman	.08	.05
551	Bob Watson	.10	.06
552	Pat Tabler	.08	.05
553	Brent Gaff	.08	.05
554	Al Cowens	.08	.05
555	Tom Brunansky	.35	.20
556	Lloyd Moseby	.08	.05
557a	Pascual Perez (Twins)	1.25	.80
557b	Pascual Perez (Braves)	.25	.15
558	Willie Upshaw	.08	.05
559	Richie Zisk	.08	.05
560	Pat Zachry	.08	.05
561	Jay Johnstone	.08	.05
562	Carlos Diaz	.08	.05
563	John Tudor	.08	.05
564	Frank Robinson	.25	.15
565	Dave Edwards	.08	.05
566	Paul Householder	.08	.05
567	Ron Reed	.08	.05
568	Mike Ramsey	.08	.05
569	Kiko Garcia	.08	.05
570	Tommy John	.15	.08
571	Tony LaRussa	.10	.06
572	Joel Youngblood	.08	.05
573	Wayne Tolleson (R)	.08	.05
574	Keith Creel	.08	.05
575	Billy Martin	.15	.08
576	Jerry Dybzinski	.08	.05
577	Rick Cerone	.08	.05
578	Tony Perez	.40	.25
579	Greg Brock (R)	.10	.06
580	Glenn Wilson (R)	.08	.05
581	Tim Stoddard	.08	.05
582	Bob McClure	.08	.05
583	Jim Dwyer	.08	.05
584	Ed Romero	.08	.05
585	Larry Herndon	.08	.05
586	Wade Boggs (R)	25.00	16.00
587	Jay Howell	.12	.07
588	Dave Stewart	.50	.30
589	Bert Blyleven	.40	.25
590	Dick Howser	.08	.05
591	Wayne Gross	.08	.05
592	Terry Francona	.08	.05
593	Don Werner	.08	.05
594	Bill Stein	.08	.05

595	Jesse Barfield	.35	.20
596	Bobby Molinaro	.08	.05
597	Mike Vail	.08	.05
598	Tony Gwynn (R)	28.00	18.50
599	Gary Rajsich	.08	.05
600	Jerry Ujdur	.08	.05
601	Cliff Johnson	.08	.05
602	Jerry White	.08	.05
603	Bryan Clark	.08	.05
604	Joe Ferguson	.08	.05
605	Guy Sularz	.08	.05
606	Ozzie Virgil (Var)	.08	.05
607	Terry Harper	.08	.05
608	Harvey Kuenn	.10	.06
609	Jim Sundberg	.08	.05
610	Willie Stargell	.60	.35
611	Reggie Smith	.08	.05
612	Rob Wilfong	.08	.05
613	Niekro Brothers	.25	.15
614	Lee Elia	.08	.05
615	Mickey Hatcher	.08	.05
616	Jerry Hairston	.08	.05
617	John Martin	.08	.05
618	Wally Backman	.10	.06
619	Storm Davis (R)	.15	.08
620	Alan Knicely	.08	.05
621	John Stuper	.08	.05
622	Matt Sinatro	.08	.05
623	Gene Petralli (R)	.10	.06
624	Duane Walker	.08	.05
625	Dick Williams	.08	.05
626	Pat Corrales	.08	.05
627	Vern Ruhle	.08	.05
628	Joe Torre	.10	.06
629	Anthony Johnson	.08	.05
630	Steve Howe	.08	.05
631	Gary Woods	.08	.05
632	LaMarr Hoyt	.08	.05
633	Steve Swisher	.08	.05
634	Terry Leach	.08	.05
635	Jeff Newman	.08	.05
636	Brett Butler	.50	.30
637	Gary Gray	.08	.05
638	Lee Mazzilli	.08	.05
639a	Ron Jackson (A's) (Er)	12.00	7.50
639b	Ron Jackson (Angels)	.10	.06
640	Juan Beniquez	.08	.05
641	Dave Rucker	.08	.05
642	Luis Pujols	.08	.05
643	Rick Monday	.08	.05
644	Hosken Powell	.08	.05
645	San Diego Chicken	.25	.15
646	Dave Engle	.08	.05
647	Dick Davis	.08	.05
648	MVP's(Vida Blue,Joe Morgan,Frank Robinson)	.40	.25

649	Al Chambers	.08	.05
650	Jesus Vega	.08	.05
651	Jeff Jones	.08	.05
652	Marvis Foley	.08	.05
653	Ty Cobb Puzzle Card	.08	.05
___	Checklist (DK)	.15	.08
___	Checklist 27-130	.15	.08
___	Checklist 131-234	.15	.08
___	Checklist 235-338	.15	.08
___	Checklist 339-442	.15	.08
___	Checklist 443-546	.15	.08
___	Checklist 547-653	.15	.08

1984 Donruss

Donruss changed the design of their card fronts for 1984 but maintained the horizontal style of the card backs which feature black type over a green and white background. The set includes 26 Diamond Kings and a new 20-card subset called Rated Rookies. Two "Living Legends" cards were randomly inserted into wax packs. Those cards marked A (Gaylord Perry and Rollie Fingers)and B (Johnny Bench and Carl Yastzremski) are listed at the end of the checklist. The set contains a total of 660 standard-size cards including 7 unnumbered checklist cards. A lower print run has created a scarcity of 1984 Donruss cards.

		MINT	NR/MT
Complete Set (660)		375.00	250.00
Commons		.20	.12
1a	Robin Yount(DK) (Perez-Steel on back)	2.50	1.50

1b	Robin Yount(DK) (Perez-Steele on back)	5.00	3.00	16a	Matt Young(DK)(Perez Steel on back)	.20	.12
2a	Dave Concepcion(DK) (Perez-Steel on back)	.25	.15	16b	Matt Young(DK)(Perez Steele on back)	.25	.12
2b	Dave Concepcion(DK) (Perez-Steele on back)	.30	.18	17a	Fred Lynn(DK)(Perez Steel on back)	.25	.15
3a	Dwayne Murphy(DK) (Perez-Steel on back)	.20	.12	17b	Fred Lynn(DK)(Perez Steele on back)	.30	.18
3b	Dwayne Murphy(DK) (Perez-Steele on back)	.25	.15	18a	Ron Kittle(DK)(Perez Steel on back)(FC)	.20	.12
4a	John Castino(DK) (Perez-Steel on back)	.20	.12	18b	Ron Kittle(DK)(Perez Steele on back)(FC)	.25	.12
4b	John Castino(DK) (Perez-Steele on back)	.25	.15	19a	Jim Clancy(DK)(Perez Steel on back)	.20	.12
5a	Leon Durham(DK) (Perez-Steel on back)	.20	.12	19b	Jim Clancy(DK)(Perez Steele on back)	.25	.15
5b	Leon Durham(DK) (Perez-Steele on back)	.25	.15	20a	Bill Madlock(DK) (Perez-Steel on back)	.20	.12
6a	Rusty Staub(DK) (Perez-Steel on back)	.25	.15	20b	Bill Madlock(DK) (Perez-Steele on back)	.25	.15
6b	Rusty Staub(DK) (Perez-Steele on back)	.30	.18	21a	Larry Parrish(DK) (Perez-Steel on back)	.20	.12
7a	Jack Clark(DK)(Perez Steel on back)	.25	.15	21b	Larry Parrish(DK) (Perez-Steele on back)	.25	.15
7b	Jack Clark(DK)(Perez Steele on back)	.30	.18	22a	Eddie Murray(DK) (Perez-Steel on back)	1.25	.80
8a	Dave Dravecky(DK) (Perez-Steel on back)	.20	.12	22b	Eddie Murray(DK) (Perez-Steele on back)	2.00	1.25
8b	Dave Dravecky(DK) (Perez-Steele on back)	.25	.15	23a	Mike Schmidt(DK) (Perez-Steel on back)	2.50	1.50
9a	Al Oliver(DK)(Perez Steel on back)	.20	.12	23b	Mike Schmidt(DK) (Perez-Steele on back)	4.00	2.75
9b	Al Oliver(DK)(Perez Steele on back)	.25	.15	24a	Pedro Guerrero(DK) (Perez-Steel on back)	.20	.12
10a	Dave Righetti(DK) (Perez-Steel on back)	.20	.12	24b	Pedro Guerrero(DK) (Perez-Steele on back)	.25	.15
10b	Dave Righetti(DK) (Perez-Steele on back)	.25	.15	25a	Andre Thornton(DK) (Perez-Steel on back)	.20	.12
11a	Hal McRae(DK)(Perez Steel on back)	.20	.12	25b	Andre Thornton(DK) (Perez-Steele on back)	.25	.15
11b	Hal McRae(DK)(Perez Steele on back)	.25	.15	26a	Wade Boggs(DK) (Perez-Steel on back)	2.00	1.25
12a	Ray Knight(DK)(Perez Steel on back)	.20	.12	26b	Wade Boggs(DK) (Perez-Steele on back)	3.00	2.00
12b	Ray Knight(DK)(Perez Steele on back)	.25	.15	27	Joel Skinner (R)	.20	.12
13a	Bruce Sutter(DK) (Perez-Steel on back)	.20	.12	28	Tom Dunbar (R)	.20	.12
13b	Bruce Sutter(DK) (Perez-Steele on back)	.25	.15	29a	Mike Stenhouse (R) (No number on back)	.20	.12
14a	Bob Horner(DK)(Perez Steel on back)	.20	.12	29b	Mike Stenhouse (R) (29 on back)	3.00	2.00
14b	Bob Horner(DK)(Perez Steele on back)	.25	.15	30a	Ron Darling (R) (No number on back)	2.00	1.25
15a	Lance Parrish(DK) (Perez-Steel on back)	.20	.12	30b	Ron Darling (R) (30 on back)	16.00	9.00
15b	Lance Parrish(DK) (Perez-Steele on back)	.25	.15	31	Dion James (R)	.20	.12
				32	Tony Fernandez (R)	6.00	3.75
				33	Angel Salazar (R)	.20	.12
				34	Kevin McReynolds(R)	4.00	2.75

35	Dick Schofield (R)	.30	.18	92	Juan Espino	.20	.12
36	Brad Kimminsk (R)	.20	.12	93	Candy Maldonado	.25	.15
37	Tim Teufel (R)	.25	.15	94	Andre Thornton	.20	.12
38	Doug Frobel (R)	.20	.12	95	Onix Concepcion	.20	.12
39	Greg Gagne (R)	.80	.50	96	Donnie Hill (R)	.20	.12
40	Mike Fuentes (R)	.20	.12	97	Andre Dawson	6.50	4.00
41	Joe Carter (R)	45.00	32.00	98	Frank Tanana	.25	.15
42	Mike Brown (R)	.20	.12	99	Curt Wilkerson (R)	.20	.12
43	Mike Jeffcoat (R)	.20	.12	100	Larry Gura	.20	.12
44	Sid Fernandez (R)	3.50	2.25	101	Dwayne Murphy	.20	.12
45	Brian Dayett (R)	.20	.12	102	Tom Brennan	.20	.12
46	Chris Smith (R)	.20	.12	103	Dave Righetti	.25	.15
47	Eddie Murray	7.50	4.50	104	Steve Sax	1.00	.70
48	Robin Yount	8.50	5.50	105	Dan Petry	.20	.12
49	Lance Parrish	.40	.25	106	Cal Ripken	35.00	25.00
50	Jim Rice	.35	.20	107	Paul Molitor	2.50	1.50
51	Dave Winfield	6.50	4.00	108	Fred Lynn	.25	.15
52	Fernando Valenzuela	.25	.15	109	Neil Allen	.20	.12
53	George Brett	8.50	5.50	110	Joe Niekro	.20	.12
54	Rickey Henderson	15.00	9.00	111	Steve Carlton	5.00	3.00
55	Gary Carter	1.75	1.00	112	Terry Kennedy	.20	.12
56	Buddy Bell	.20	.12	113	Bill Madlock	.25	.15
57	Reggie Jackson	7.50	4.50	114	Chili Davis	.25	.15
58	Harold Baines	.80	.50	115	Jim Gantner	.20	.12
59	Ozzie Smith	1.25	.80	116	Tom Seaver	8.00	5.00
60	Nolan Ryan	30.00	20.00	117	Bill Buckner	.25	.15
61	Pete Rose	6.00	3.75	118	Bill Caudill	.20	.12
62	Ron Oester	.20	.12	119	Jim Clancy	.20	.12
63	Steve Garvey	1.75	1.00	120	John Castino	.20	.12
64	Jason Thompson	.20	.12	121	Dave Concepcion	.25	.15
65	Jack Clark	.25	.15	122	Greg Luzinski	.25	.15
66	Dale Murphy	2.50	1.50	123	Mike Broddicker	.25	.15
67	Leon Durham	.20	.12	124	Pete Ladd	.20	.12
68	Darryl Strawberry (R)	60.00	42.00	125	Juan Berenguer	.20	.12
				126	John Montefusco	.20	.12
69	Richie Zisk	.20	.12	127	Ed Jurak	.20	.12
70	Kent Hrbek	1.00	.70	128	Tom Niedenfuer	.20	.12
71	Dave Stieb	.40	.25	129	Bert Blyleven	1.00	.70
72	Ken Schrom	.20	.12	130	Bud Black	.20	.12
73	George Bell	3.00	2.00	131	Gorman Heimueller	.20	.12
74	John Moses	.20	.12	132	Dan Schatzeder	.20	.12
75	Ed Lynch	.20	.12	133	Ron Jackson	.20	.12
76	Chuck Rainey	.20	.12	134	Tom Henke (R)	1.25	.80
77	Biff Pocoroba	.20	.12	135	Kevin Hickey	.20	.12
78	Cecilio Guante	.20	.12	136	Mike Scott	.25	.15
79	Jim Barr	.20	.12	137	Bo Diaz	.20	.12
80	Kurt Bevacqua	.20	.12	138	Glenn Brummer	.20	.12
81	Tom Foley	.20	.12	139	Sid Monge	.20	.12
82	Joe Lefebvre	.20	.12	140	Rich Gale	.20	.12
83	Andy Van Slyke (R)	12.00	8.50	141	Brett Butler	.70	.40
84	Bob Lillis	.20	.12	142	Brian Harper	.60	.35
85	Rick Adams	.20	.12	143	John Rabb	.20	.12
86	Jerry Hairston	.20	.12	144	Gary Woods	.20	.12
87	Bob James	.20	.12	145	Pat Putnam	.20	.12
88	Joe Altobelli	.20	.12	146	Jim Acker (R)	.20	.12
89	Ed Romero	.20	.12	147	Mickey Hatcher	.20	.12
90	John Grubb	.20	.12	148	Todd Cruz	.20	.12
91	John Henry Johnson	.20	.12	149	Tom Tellmann	.20	.12

150	John Wockenfuss	.20	.12
151	Wade Boggs	14.00	8.50
152	Don Baylor	.25	.15
153	Bob Welch	.40	.25
154	Alan Bannister	.20	.12
155	Willie Aikens	.20	.12
156	Jeff Burroughs	.20	.12
157	Bryan Little	.20	.12
158	Bob Boone	.30	.18
159	Dave Hostetler	.20	.12
160	Jerry Dybzinski	.20	.12
161	Mike Madden	.20	.12
162	Luis DeLeon	.20	.12
163	Willie Hernandez	.20	.12
164	Frank Pastore	.20	.12
165	Rick Camp	.20	.12
166	Lee Mazzilli	.20	.12
167	Scot Thompson	.20	.12
168	Bob Forsch	.20	.12
169	Mike Flanagan	.20	.12
170	Rick Manning	.20	.12
171	Chet Lemon	.20	.12
172	Jerry Remy	.20	.12
173	Ron Guidry	.35	.20
174	Pedro Guerrero	.30	.18
175	Willie Wilson	.20	.12
176	Carney Lansford	.25	.15
177	Al Oliver	.25	.15
178	Jim Sundberg	.20	.12
179	Bobby Grich	.25	.15
180	Richard Dotson	.20	.12
181	Joaquin Andujar	.20	.12
182	Jose Cruz	.20	.12
183	Mike Schmidt	15.00	9.00
184	Gary Redus (R)	.30	.18
185	Garry Templeton	.20	.12
186	Tony Pena	.20	.12
187	Greg Minton	.20	.12
188	Phil Niekro	1.50	.90
189	Ferguson Jenkins	1.50	.90
190	Mookie Wilson	.20	.12
191	Jim Beattie	.20	.12
192	Gary Ward	.20	.12
193	Jesse Barfield	.30	.18
194	Pete Filson	.20	.12
195	Roy Lee Jackson	.20	.12
196	Rick Sweet	.20	.12
197	Jesse Orosco	.20	.12
198	Steve Lake (R)	.20	.12
199	Ken Dayley	.20	.12
200	Manny Sarmiento	.20	.12
201	Mark Davis	.25	.15
202	Tim Flannery	.20	.12
203	Bill Scherrer	.20	.12
204	Al Holland	.20	.12
205	David Von Ohlen	.20	.12
206	Mike LaCoss	.20	.12
207	Juan Beniquez	.20	.12
208	Juan Agosto (R)	.25	.15
209	Bobby Ramos	.20	.12
210	Al Bumbry	.20	.12
211	Mark Brouhard	.20	.12
212	Howard Bailey	.20	.12
213	Bruce Hurst	.30	.18
214	Bob Shirley	.20	.12
215	Pat Zachry	.20	.12
216	Julio Franco	3.50	2.25
217	Mike Armstrong	.20	.12
218	Dave Beard	.20	.12
219	Steve Rogers	.20	.12
220	John Butcher	.20	.12
221	Mike Smithson (R)	.20	.12
222	Frank White	.20	.12
223	Mike Heath	.20	.12
224	Chris Bando	.20	.12
225	Roy Smalley	.20	.12
226	Dusty Baker	.25	.15
227	Lou Whitaker	.75	.45
228	John Lowenstein	.20	.12
229	Ben Oglivie	.20	.12
230	Doug DeCinces	.20	.12
231	Lonnie Smith	.25	.15
232	Ray Knight	.20	.12
233	Gary Matthews	.20	.12
234	Juan Bonilla	.20	.12
235	Rod Scurry	.20	.12
236	Atlee Hammaker	.20	.12
237	Mike Caldwell	.20	.12
238	Keith Hernandez	.30	.18
239	Larry Bowa	.25	.15
240	Tony Bernazard	.20	.12
241	Damaso Garcia	.20	.12
242	Tom Brunansky	.25	.15
243	Dan Driessen	.20	.12
244	Ron Kittle	.20	.12
245	Tim Stoddard	.20	.12
246	Bob Gibson	.20	.12
247	Marty Castillo	.20	.12
248	Don Mattingly (R)	48.00	32.00
249	Jeff Newman	.20	.12
250	Alejandro Pena (R)	.80	.50
251	Toby Harrah	.20	.12
252	Cesar Geronimo	.20	.12
253	Tom Underwood	.20	.12
254	Doug Flynn	.20	.12
255	Andy Hassler	.20	.12
256	Odell Jones	.20	.12
257	Rudy Law	.20	.12
258	Harry Spilman	.20	.12
259	Marty Bystrom	.20	.12
260	Dave Rucker	.20	.12
261	Ruppert Jones	.20	.12
262	Jeff Jones	.20	.12
263	Gerald Perry (R)	.25	.15
264	Gene Tenace	.25	.15
265	Brad Wellman	.20	.12

#	Player	Price 1	Price 2
266	Dickie Noles	.20	.12
267	Jamie Allen	.20	.12
268	Jim Gott	.20	.12
269	Ron Davis	.20	.12
270	Benny Ayala	.20	.12
271	Ned Yost	.20	.12
272	Dave Rozema	.20	.12
273	Dave Stapleton	.20	.12
274	Lou Piniella	.25	.15
275	Jose Morales	.20	.12
276	Broderick Perkins	.20	.12
277	Butch Davis	.20	.12
278	Tony Phillips(FC)	1.50	.90
279	Jeff Reardon	4.00	2.75
280	Ken Forsch	.20	.12
281	Pete O'Brien (R)	.70	.40
282	Tom Paciorek	.20	.12
283	Frank LaCorte	.20	.12
284	Tim Lollar	.20	.12
285	Greg Gross	.20	.12
286	Alex Trevino	.20	.12
287	Gene Garber	.20	.12
288	Dave Parker	1.00	.70
289	Lee Smith	4.00	2.75
290	Dave LaPoint	.20	.12
291	John Shelby (R)	.25	.15
292	Charlie Moore	.20	.12
293	Alan Trammell	2.00	1.25
294	Tony Armas	.20	.12
295	Shane Rawley	.20	.12
296	Greg Brock	.20	.12
297	Hal McRae	.25	.15
298	Mike Davis	.20	.12
299	Tim Raines	1.25	.80
300	Bucky Dent	.25	.15
301	Tommy John	.30	.18
302	Carlton Fisk	5.00	3.00
303	Darrell Porter	.20	.12
304	Dickie Thon	.20	.12
305	Garry Maddox	.20	.12
306	Cesar Cedeno	.25	.15
307	Gary Lucas	.20	.12
308	Johnny Ray	.20	.12
309	Andy McGaffigan	.20	.12
310	Claudell Washington	.20	.12
311	Ryne Sandberg	32.00	20.00
312	George Foster	.25	.15
313	Spike Owen (R)	.70	.40
314	Gary Gaetti	.25	.15
315	Willie Upshaw	.20	.12
316	Al Williams	.20	.12
317	Jorge Orta	.20	.12
318	Orlando Mercado	.20	.12
319	Junior Ortiz (R)	.20	.12
320	Mike Proly	.20	.12
321	Randy Johnson	.20	.12
322	Jim Morrison	.20	.12
323	Max Venable	.20	.12
324	Tony Gwynn	20.00	14.00
325	Duane Walker	.20	.12
326	Ozzie Virgil	.20	.12
327	Jeff Lahti	.20	.12
328	Bill Dawley (R)	.20	.12
329	Rob Wilfong	.20	.12
330	Marc Hill	.20	.12
331	Ray Burris	.20	.12
332	Allan Ramirez	.20	.12
333	Chuck Porter	.20	.12
334	Wayne Krenchicki	.20	.12
335	Gary Allenson	.20	.12
336	Bob Meacham (R)	.20	.12
337	Joe Beckwith	.20	.12
338	Rick Sutcliffe	.30	.18
339	Mark Huismann (R)	.20	.12
340	Tim Conroy (R)	.20	.12
341	Scott Sanderson	.20	.12
342	Larry Biittner	.20	.12
343	Dave Stewart	.80	.50
344	Darryl Motley	.20	.12
345	Chris Codiroli	.20	.12
346	Rick Behenna	.20	.12
347	Andre Robertson	.20	.12
348	Mike Marshall	.20	.12
349	Larry Herndon	.20	.12
350	Rich Dauer	.20	.12
351	Cecil Cooper	.20	.12
352	Rod Carew	5.00	3.00
353	Willie McGee	1.00	.70
354	Phil Garner	.20	.12
355	Joe Morgan	1.75	1.00
356	Luis Salazar	.20	.12
357	John Candelaria	.20	.12
358	Bill Laskey	.20	.12
359	Bob McClure	.20	.12
360	Dave Kingman	.25	.15
361	Ron Cey	.25	.15
362	Matt Young (R)	.25	.15
363	Lloyd Moseby	.20	.12
364	Frank Viola	1.50	.90
365	Eddie Milner	.20	.12
366	Floyd Bannister	.20	.12
367	Dan Ford	.20	.12
368	Moose Haas	.20	.12
369	Doug Bair	.20	.12
370	Ray Fontenot (R)	.20	.12
371	Luis Aponte	.20	.12
372	Jack Fimple	.20	.12
373	Neal Heaton (R)	.25	.15
374	Greg Pryor	.20	.12
375	Wayne Gross	.20	.12
376	Charlie Lea	.20	.12
377	Steve Lubratich	.20	.12
378	Jon Matlack	.20	.12
379	Julio Cruz	.20	.12
380	John Mizerock	.20	.12
381	Kevin Gross (R)	.70	.40

382	Mike Ramsey	.20	.12
383	Dough Gwosdz	.20	.12
384	Kelly Paris	.20	.12
385	Pete Falcone	.20	.12
386	Milt May	.20	.12
387	Fred Breining	.20	.12
388	Craig Lefferts (R)	.70	.40
389	Steve Henderson	.20	.12
390	Randy Moffitt	.20	.12
391	Ron Washington	.20	.12
392	Gary Roenicke	.20	.12
393	Tom Candiotti (R)	1.25	.80
394	Larry Pashnick	.20	.12
395	Dwight Evans	.80	.50
396	Goose Gossage	.50	.30
397	Derrel Thomas	.20	.12
398	Juan Eichelberger	.20	.12
399	Leon Roberts	.20	.12
400	Davey Lopes	.25	.15
401	Bill Gullickson	.20	.12
402	Geoff Zahn	.20	.12
403	Billy Sample	.20	.12
404	Mike Squires	.20	.12
405	Craig Reynolds	.20	.12
406	Eric Show	.20	.12
407	John Denny	.20	.12
408	Dann Bilardello	.20	.12
409	Bruce Benedict	.20	.12
410	Kent Tekulve	.20	.12
411	Mel Hall	.70	.40
412	John Stuper	.20	.12
413	Rich Dempsey	.20	.12
414	Don Sutton	1.50	.90
415	Jack Morris	3.50	2.25
416	John Tudor	.20	.12
417	Willie Randolph	.25	.15
418	Jerry Reuss	.20	.12
419	Don Slaught	.20	.12
420	Steve McCatty	.20	.12
421	Tim Wallach	.35	.20
422	Larry Parrish	.20	.12
423	Brian Downing	.20	.12
424	Britt Burns	.20	.12
425	David Green	.20	.12
426	Jerry Mumphrey	.20	.12
427	Ivan DeJesus	.20	.12
428	Mario Soto	.20	.12
429	Gene Richards	.20	.12
430	Dale Berra	.20	.12
431	Darrell Evans	.25	.15
432	Glenn Hubbard	.20	.12
433	Jody Davis	.20	.12
434	Danny Heep	.20	.12
435	Ed Nunez (R)	.25	.15
436	Bobby Castillo	.20	.12
437	Ernie Whitt	.20	.12
438	Scott Ullger	.20	.12
439	Doyle Alexander	.20	.12
440	Domingo Ramos	.20	.12
441	Craig Swan	.20	.12
442	Warren Brusstar	.20	.12
443	Len Barker	.20	.12
444	Mike Easler	.20	.12
445	Renie Martin	.20	.12
446	Dennis Rasmussen (R)	.25	.15
447	Ted Power	.20	.12
448	Charlie Hudson (R)	.20	.12
449	Danny Cox (R)	.30	.18
450	Kevin Bass	.25	.15
451	Daryl Sconiers	.20	.12
452	Scott Fletcher	.20	.12
453	Bryn Smith	.20	.12
454	Jim Dwyer	.20	.12
455	Rob Picciolo	.20	.12
456	Enos Cabell	.20	.12
457	Dennis "Oil Can" Boyd (R)	.25	.15
458	Butch Wynegar	.20	.12
459	Burt Hooton	.20	.12
460	Ron Hassey	.20	.12
461	Danny Jackson (R)	.50	.30
462	Bob Kearney	.20	.12
463	Terry Francona	.20	.12
464	Wayne Tolleson	.20	.12
465	Mickey Rivers	.20	.12
466	John Wathan	.20	.12
467	Bill Almon	.20	.12
468	George Vukovich	.20	.12
469	Steve Kemp	.20	.12
470	Ken Landreaux	.20	.12
471	Milt Wilcox	.20	.12
472	Tippy Martinez	.20	.12
473	Ted Simmons	.30	.18
474	Tim Foli	.20	.12
475	George Hendrick	.20	.12
476	Terry Puhl	.20	.12
477	Von Hayes	.20	.12
478	Bobby Brown	.20	.12
479	Lee Lacy	.20	.12
480	Joel Youngblood	.20	.12
481	Jim Slaton	.20	.12
482	Mike Fitzgerald (R)	.20	.12
483	Keith Moreland	.20	.12
484	Ron Roenicke	.20	.12
485	Luis Leal	.20	.12
486	Bryan Oelkers	.20	.12
487	Bruce Berenyi	.20	.12
488	LaMarr Hoyt	.20	.12
489	Joe Nolan	.20	.12
490	Marshall Edwards	.20	.12
491	Mike Laga	.20	.12
492	Rick Cerone	.20	.12
493	Mike Miller (Rick)	.20	.12
494	Rick Honeycutt	.20	.12
495	Mike Hargrove	.20	.12
496	Joe Simpson	.20	.12

No.	Player		
497	Keith Atherton (R)	.20	.12
498	Chris Welsh	.20	.12
499	Bruce Kison	.20	.12
500	Bob Johnson	.20	.12
501	Jerry Koosman	.25	.15
502	Frank DiPino	.20	.12
503	Tony Perez	1.25	.80
504	Ken Oberkfell	.20	.12
505	Mark Thurmond (R)	.20	.12
506	Joe Price	.20	.12
507	Pascual Perez	.20	.12
508	Marvell Wynne (R)	.20	.12
509	Mike Krukow	.20	.12
510	Dick Ruthven	.20	.12
511	Al Cowens	.20	.12
512	Cliff Johnson	.20	.12
513	Randy Bush	.25	.15
514	Sammy Stewart	.20	.12
515	Bill Schroeder (R)	.20	.12
516	Aurelio Lopez	.20	.12
517	Mike Brown	.20	.12
518	Graig Nettles	.25	.15
519	Dave Sax	.20	.12
520	Gerry Willard	.20	.12
521	Paul Splittorff	.20	.12
522	Tom Burgmeier	.20	.12
523	Chris Speier	.20	.12
524	Bobby Clark	.20	.12
525	George Wright	.20	.12
526	Dennis Lamp	.20	.12
527	Tony Scott	.20	.12
528	Ed Whitson	.20	.12
529	Ron Reed	.20	.12
530	Charlie Puleo	.20	.12
531	Jerry Royster	.20	.12
532	Don Robinson	.20	.12
533	Steve Trout	.20	.12
534	Bruce Sutter	.35	.20
535	Bob Horner	.25	.15
536	Pat Tabler	.20	.12
537	Chris Chambliss	.20	.12
538	Bob Ojeda	.25	.15
539	Alan Ashby	.20	.12
540	Jay Johnstone	.20	.12
541	Bob Dernier	.20	.12
542	Brook Jacoby (R)	.40	.25
543	U.L. Washington	.20	.12
544	Danny Darwin	.20	.12
545	Kiko Garcia	.20	.12
546	Vance Law	.20	.12
547	Tug McGraw	.20	.12
548	Dave Smith	.20	.12
549	Len Matuszek	.20	.12
550	Tom Hume	.20	.12
551	Dave Dravecky	.20	.12
552	Rick Rhoden	.20	.12
553	Duane Kuiper	.20	.12
554	Rusty Staub	.25	.15
555	Bill Campbell	.20	.12
556	Mike Torrez	.20	.12
557	Dave Henderson	1.50	.90
558	Len Whitehouse	.20	.12
559	Barry Bonnell	.20	.12
560	Rick Lysander	.20	.12
561	Garth Iorg	.20	.12
562	Bryan Clark	.20	.12
563	Brian Giles	.20	.12
564	Vern Ruhle	.20	.12
565	Steve Bedrosian	.20	.12
566	Larry McWilliams	.20	.12
567	Jeff Leonard	.20	.12
568	Alan Wiggins	.20	.12
569	Jeff Russell (R)	.80	.50
570	Salome Barojas	.20	.12
571	Dane Iorg	.20	.12
572	Bob Knepper	.20	.12
573	Gary Lavelle	.20	.12
574	Gorman Thomas	.20	.12
575	Manny Trillo	.20	.12
576	Jim Palmer	4.00	2.75
577	Dale Murray	.20	.12
578	Tom Brookens	.20	.12
579	Rich Gedman	.20	.12
580	Bill Doran (R)	.50	.30
581	Steve Yeager	.20	.12
582	Dan Spillner	.20	.12
583	Dan Quisenberry	.20	.12
584	Rance Mulliniks	.20	.12
585	Storm Davis	.20	.12
586	Dave Schmidt	.20	.12
587	Bill Russell	.25	.15
588	Pat Sheridan (R)	.25	.15
589	Rafael Ramirez	.20	.12
590	Bud Anderson	.20	.12
591	George Frazier	.20	.12
592	Lee Tunnell (R)	.20	.12
593	Kirk Gibson	.80	.50
594	Scott McGregor	.20	.12
595	Bob Bailor	.20	.12
596	Tom Herr	.20	.12
597	Luis Sanchez	.20	.12
598	Dave Engle	.20	.12
599	Craig McMurtry (R)	.20	.12
600	Carlos Diaz	.20	.12
601	Tom O'Malley	.20	.12
602	Nick Esasky (R)	.25	.15
603	Ron Hodges	.20	.12
604	Ed Vande Berg	.20	.12
605	Alfredo Griffin	.20	.12
606	Glenn Hoffman	.20	.12
607	Hubie Brooks	.25	.15
608	Richard Barnes (Er) (Wrong Photo)	.20	.12
609	Greg Walker (R)	.20	.12
610	Ken Singleton	.20	.12
611	Mark Clear	.20	.12

612	Buck Martinez	.20	.12
613	Ken Griffey	.25	.15
614	Reid Nichols	.20	.12
615	Doug Sisk (R)	.20	.12
616	Bob Brenly	.20	.12
617	Joey McLaughlin	.20	.12
618	Glenn Wilson	.20	.12
619	Bob Stoddard	.20	.12
620	Lenn Sakata	.20	.12
621	Mike Young (R)	.20	.12
622	John Stefero	.20	.12
623	Carmelo Martinez (R)	.25	.15
624	Dave Bergman	.20	.12
625	Runnin' Reds(David Green, Willie McGee, Lonnie Smith, Ozzie Smith)	1.00	.70
626	Rudy May	.20	.12
627	Matt Keough	.20	.12
628	Jose DeLeon (R)	.25	.15
629	Jim Essian	.20	.12
630	Darnell Coles (R)	.25	.15
631	Mike Warren	.20	.12
632	Del Crandall	.20	.12
633	Dennis Martinez	.30	.18
634	Mike Moore	.40	.25
635	Lary Sorensen	.20	.12
636	Ricky Nelson	.20	.12
637	Omar Moreno	.20	.12
638	Charlie Hough	.20	.12
639	Dennis Eckersley	3.00	2.00
640	Walt Terrell (R)	.25	.15
641	Denny Walling	.20	.12
642	Dave Anderson (R)	.25	.15
643	Jose Oquendo (R)	.30	.18
644	Bob Stanley	.20	.12
645	Dave Geisel	.20	.12
646	Scott Garrelts (R)	.25	.15
647	Gary Pettis (R)	.30	.18
648	Duke Snider Puzzle	.35	.20
649	Johnnie LeMaster	.20	.12
650	Dave Collins	.20	.12
651	San Diego Chicken	.40	.25
___	Checklist (DK)	.20	.12
___	Checklist 27-130	.20	.12
___	Checklist 131-234	.20	.12
___	Checklist 235-338	.20	.12
___	Checklist 339-442	.20	.12
___	Checklist 443-546	.20	.12
___	Checklist 547-651	.20	.12
___	Living Legends (A) (Fingers/Perry)	6.00	3.75
___	Living Legends (B) (Bench/Yastrzemski)	12.00	8.50

1985 Donruss

This 660-card set features black borders on the card fronts with action photos. Card backs are horizontal and contain player stats and personal data. Subsets include Diamond Kings (1-26) and Rated Rookies (27-46). The cards were issued with a Lou Gehrig puzzle.

		MINT	NR/MT
Complete Set (660)		200.00	135.00
Commons		.10	.06

1	Ryne Sandberg (DK)	3.50	2.25
2	Doug DeCinces (DK)	.10	.06
3	Rich Dotson (DK)	.10	.06
4	Bert Blyleven (DK)	.10	.06
5	Lou Whitaker (DK)	.12	.07
6	Dan Quisenberry (DK)	.10	.06
7	Don Mattingly (DK)	2.50	1.50
8	Carney Lansford (DK)	.15	.08
9	Frank Tanana (DK)	.12	.07
10	Willie Upshaw (DK)	.10	.06
11	Claudell Washington (DK)	.10	.06
12	Mike Marshall (DK)	.10	.06
13	Joaquin Andujar (DK)	.10	.06
14	Cal Ripken, Jr. (DK)	4.50	2.75
15	Jim Rice (DK)	.20	.12
16	Don Sutton (DK)	.25	.15
17	Frank Viola (DK)	.20	.12
18	Alvin Davis (DK)	.15	.08
19	Mario Soto (DK)	.10	.06
20	Jose Cruz (DK)	.12	.07
21	Charlie Lea (DK)	.10	.06
22	Jesse Orosco (DK)	.10	.06
23	Juan Samuel (DK)	.12	.07
24	Tony Pena (DK)	.12	.07
25	Tony Gwynn (DK)	2.50	1.50
26	Bob Brenly (DK)	.10	.06
27	Danny Tartabull (R)	9.00	6.00
28	Mike Bielecki (R)	.35	.20

29	Steve Lyons (R)	.15	.08
30	Jeff Reed(R)	.12	.07
31	Tony Brewer (R)	.10	.06
32	John Morris (R)	.10	.06
33	Daryl Boston (R)	.25	.15
34	Alfonso Pulido (R)	.10	.06
35	Steve Kiefer (R)	.10	.06
36	Larry Sheets (R)	.12	.07
37	Scott Bradley (R)	.12	.07
38	Calvin Schiraldi (R)	.12	.07
39	Shawon Dunston (R)	2.50	1.50
40	Charlie Mitchell (R)	.10	.06
41	Billy Hatcher (R)	.40	.25
42	Russ Stephans (R)	.10	.06
43	Alejandro Sanchez (R)	.10	.06
44	Steve Jeltz (R)	.12	.07
45	Jim Traber (R)	.12	.07
46	Doug Loman (R)	.10	.06
47	Eddie Murray	2.00	1.25
48	Robin Yount	3.50	2.25
49	Lance Parrish	.12	.07
50	Jim Rice	.15	.08
51	Dave Winfield	2.50	1.50
52	Fernando Valenzuela	.15	.08
53	George Brett	3.50	2.25
54	Dave Kingman	.12	.07
55	Gary Carter	.50	.30
56	Buddy Bell	.10	.06
57	Reggie Jackson	2.50	1.50
58	Harold Baines	.50	.30
59	Ozzie Smith	2.00	1.25
60	Nolan Ryan	12.00	8.00
61	Mike Schmidt	6.00	3.75
62	Dave Parker	.30	.18
63	Tony Gwynn	8.00	5.00
64	Tony Pena	.10	.06
65	Jack Clark	.12	.07
66	Dale Murphy	.80	.50
67	Ryne Sandberg	10.00	6.50
68	Keith Hernandez	.12	.07
69	Alvin Davis (R)	.30	.18
70	Kent Hrbek	.40	.25
71	Willie Upshaw	.10	.06
72	Dave Engle	.10	.06
73	Alfredo Griffin	.10	.06
74	Jack Perconte (Var)	.10	.06
75	Jesse Orosco	.10	.06
76	Jody Davis	.10	.06
77	Bob Horner	.12	.07
78	Larry McWilliams	.10	.06
79	Joel Youngblood	.10	.06
80	Alan Wiggins	.10	.06
81	Ron Oester	.10	.06
82	Ozzie Virgil	.10	.06
83	Ricky Horton (R)	.12	.07
84	Bill Doran	.12	.07
85	Rod Carew	2.00	1.25
86	LaMarr Hoyt	.10	.06
87	Tim Wallach	.15	.08
88	Mike Flanagan	.10	.06
89	Jim Sundberg	.10	.06
90	Chet Lemon	.10	.06
91	Bob Stanley	.10	.06
92	Willie Randolph	.12	.07
93	Bill Russell	.12	.07
94	Julio Franco	1.00	.70
95	Dan Quisenberry	.10	.06
96	Bill Caudill	.10	.06
97	Bill Gullickson	.10	.06
98	Danny Darwin	.10	.06
99	Curtis Wilkerson	.10	.06
100	Bud Black	.12	.07
101	Tony Phillips	.12	.07
102	Tony Bernazard	.10	.06
103	Jay Howell	.12	.07
104	Burt Hooton	.10	.06
105	Milt Wilcox	.10	.06
106	Rich Dauer	.10	.06
107	Don Sutton	.60	.35
108	Mike Witt	.10	.06
109	Bruce Sutter	.12	.07
110	Enos Cabell	.10	.06
111	John Denny	.10	.06
112	Dave Dravecky	.10	.06
113	Marvell Wynne	.10	.06
114	Johnnie LeMaster	.10	.06
115	Chuck Porter	.10	.06
116	John Gibbons	.10	.06
117	Keith Moreland	.10	.06
118	Darnell Coles	.10	.06
119	Dennis Lamp	.10	.06
120	Ron Davis	.10	.06
121	Nick Esasky	.10	.06
122	Vance Law	.10	.06
123	Gary Roenicke	.10	.06
124	Bill Schroeder	.10	.06
125	Dave Rozema	.10	.06
126	Bobby Meacham	.10	.06
127	Marty Barrett	.12	.07
128	R.J. Reynolds (R)	.10	.06
129	Ernie Camacho	.10	.06
130	Jorge Orta	.10	.06
131	Lary Sorensen	.10	.06
132	Terry Francona	.10	.06
133	Fred Lynn	.12	.07
134	Bobby Jones	.10	.06
135	Jerry Hairston	.10	.06
136	Kevin Bass	.12	.07
137	Garry Maddox	.10	.06
138	Dave LaPoint	.10	.06
139	Kevin McReynolds	.35	.20
140	Wayne Krenchicki	.10	.06
141	Rafael Ramirez	.10	.06
142	Rod Scurry	.10	.06
143	Greg Minton	.10	.06
144	Tim Stoddard	.10	.06

145	Steve Henderson	.10	.06
146	George Bell	.80	.50
147	Dave Meier	.10	.06
148	Sammy Stewart	.10	.06
149	Mark Brouhard	.10	.06
150	Larry Herndon	.10	.06
151	Oil Can Boyd	.10	.06
152	Brian Dayett	.10	.06
153	Tom Niedenfuer	.10	.06
154	Brook Jacoby	.12	.07
155	Onix Concepcion	.10	.06
156	Tim Conroy	.10	.06
157	Joe Hesketh	.20	.12
158	Brian Downing	.10	.06
159	Tommy Dunbar	.10	.06
160	Marc Hill	.10	.06
161	Phil Garner	.10	.06
162	Jerry Davis	.10	.06
163	Bill Campbell	.10	.06
164	John Franco (R)	1.50	.90
165	Len Barker	.10	.06
166	Benny Distefano (R)	.10	.06
167	George Frazier	.10	.06
168	Tito Landrum	.10	.06
169	Cal Ripken	12.00	8.00
170	Cecil Cooper	.10	.06
171	Alan Trammell	.50	.30
172	Wade Boggs	5.00	3.00
173	Don Baylor	.12	.07
174	Pedro Guerrero	.12	.07
175	Frank White	.10	.06
176	Rickey Henderson	4.00	2.75
177	Charlie Lea	.10	.06
178	Pete O'Brien	.10	.06
179	Doug DeCinces	.10	.06
180	Ron Kettle	.10	.06
181	George Hendrick	.10	.06
182	Joe Niekro	.10	.06
183	Juan Samuel	.20	.12
184	Mario Soto	.10	.06
185	Goose Gossage	.12	.07
186	Johnny Ray	.10	.06
187	Bob Brenly	.10	.06
188	Craig McMurtry	.10	.06
189	Leon Durham	.10	.06
190	Dwight Gooden (R)	10.00	6.50
191	Barry Bonnell	.10	.06
192	Tim Teufel	.10	.06
193	Dave Stieb	.15	.08
194	Mickey Hatcher	.10	.06
195	Jesse Barfield	.12	.07
196	Al Cowens	.10	.06
197	Hubie Brooks	.12	.07
198	Steve Trout	.10	.06
199	Glenn Hubbard	.10	.06
200	Bill Madlock	.12	.07
201	Jeff Robinson (R)	.12	.07
202	Eric Show	.10	.06
203	Dave Concepcion	.12	.07
204	Ivan DeJesus	.10	.06
205	Neil Allen	.10	.06
206	Jerry Mumphrey	.10	.06
207	Mike Brown	.10	.06
208	Carlton Fisk	1.75	1.00
209	Bryn Smith	.10	.06
210	Tippy Martinez	.10	.06
211	Dion James	.10	.06
212	Willie Hernandez	.10	.06
213	Mike Easler	.10	.06
214	Ron Guidry	.15	.08
215	Rick Honeycutt	.10	.06
216	Brett Butler	.20	.12
217	Larry Gura	.10	.06
218	Ray Burris	.10	.06
219	Steve Rogers	.10	.06
220	Frank Tanana	.10	.06
221	Ned Yost	.10	.06
222	Bret Saberhagen (R)	8.00	5.00
223	Mike Davis	.10	.06
224	Bert Blyleven	.30	.18
225	Steve Kemp	.10	.06
226	Jerry Reuss	.10	.06
227	Darrell Evans	.12	.07
228	Wayne Gross	.10	.06
229	Jim Gantner	.10	.06
230	Bob Boone	.15	.08
231	Lonnie Smith	.12	.07
232	Frank DePino	.10	.06
233	Jerry Koosman	.12	.07
234	Graig Nettles	.12	.07
235	John Tudor	.10	.06
236	John Rabb	.10	.06
237	Rick Manning	.10	.06
238	Mike Fitzgerald	.10	.06
239	Gary Matthews	.10	.06
240	Jim Presley (R)	.12	.07
241	Dave Collins	.10	.06
242	Gary Gaetti	.12	.07
243	Dann Bilardello	.10	.06
244	Rudy Law	.10	.06
245	John Lowenstein	.10	.06
246	Tom Tellmann	.10	.06
247	Howard Johnson	2.00	1.25
248	Ray Fontenot	.10	.06
249	Tony Armas	.10	.06
250	Candy Maldonado	.10	.06
251	Mike Jeffcoat	.10	.06
252	Dane Iorg	.10	.06
253	Bruce Bochte	.10	.06
254	Pete Rose	2.00	1.25
255	Don Aase	.10	.06
256	George Wright	.10	.06
257	Britt Burns	.10	.06
258	Mike Scott	.15	.08
259	Len Matuszek	.10	.06
260	Dave Rucker	.10	.06

#	Player	Price 1	Price 2
261	Craig Lefferts	.10	.06
262	Jay Tibbs (R)	.10	.06
263	Bruce Benedict	.10	.06
264	Don Robinson	.10	.06
265	Gary Lavelle	.10	.06
266	Scott Sanderson	.10	.06
267	Matt Young	.10	.06
268	Ernie Whitt	.10	.06
269	Houston Jimenez	.10	.06
270	Ken Dixon	.10	.06
271	Peter Ladd	.10	.06
272	Juan Berenguer	.10	.06
273	Roger Clemens (R)	60.00	45.00
274	Rick Cerone	.10	.06
275	Dave Anderson	.10	.06
276	George Vukovich	.10	.06
277	Greg Pryor	.10	.06
278	Mike Warren	.10	.06
279	Bob James	.10	.06
280	Bobby Grich	.12	.07
281	Mike Mason (R)	.10	.06
282	Ron Reed	.10	.06
283	Alan Ashby	.10	.06
284	Mark Thurmond	.10	.06
285	Joe Lefebvre	.10	.06
286	Ted Power	.10	.06
287	Chris Chambliss	.10	.06
288	Lee Tunnell	.10	.06
289	Rich Bordi	.10	.06
290	Glenn Brummer	.10	.06
291	Mike Boddicker	.10	.06
292	Rollie Fingers	.75	.45
293	Lou Whitaker	.35	.20
294	Dwight Evans	.20	.12
295	Don Mattingly	7.50	4.50
296	Mike Marshall	.10	.06
297	Willie Wilson	.10	.06
298	Mike Heath	.10	.06
299	Tim Raines	.30	.18
300	Larry Parrish	.10	.06
301	Geoff Zahn	.10	.06
302	Rich Dotson	.10	.06
303	David Green	.10	.06
304	Jose Cruz	.12	.07
305	Steve Carlton	1.75	1.00
306	Gary Redus	.10	.06
307	Steve Garvey	.50	.30
308	Jose DeLeon	.10	.06
309	Randy Lerch	.10	.06
310	Claudell Washington	.10	.06
311	Lee Smith	1.50	.90
312	Darryl Strawberry	10.00	6.50
313	Jim Beattie	.10	.06
314	John Butcher	.10	.06
315	Damaso Garcia	.10	.06
316	Mike Smithson	.10	.06
317	Luis Leal	.10	.06
318	Ken Phelps	.12	.07
319	Wally Backman	.10	.06
320	Ron Cey	.12	.07
321	Brad Komminsk	.10	.06
322	Jason Thompson	.10	.06
323	Frank Williams (R)	.10	.06
324	Tim Lollar	.10	.06
325	Eric Davis (R)	10.00	6.50
326	Von Hayes	.10	.06
327	Andy Van Slyke	1.00	.70
328	Craig Reynolds	.10	.06
329	Dick Schofield	.10	.06
330	Scott Fletcher	.10	.06
331	Jeff Reardon	1.50	.90
332	Rick Dempsey	.10	.06
333	Ben Oglivie	.10	.06
334	Dan Petry	.10	.06
335	Jackie Gutierrez	.10	.06
336	Dave Righetti	.12	.07
337	Alejandro Pena	.10	.06
338	Mel Hall	.15	.08
339	Pat Sheridan	.10	.06
340	Keith Atherton	.10	.06
341	David Palmer	.10	.06
342	Gary Ward	.10	.06
343	Dave Stewart	.35	.20
344	Mark Gubicza (R)	.75	.45
345	Carney Lansford	.12	.07
346	Jerry Willard	.10	.06
347	Ken Griffey	.12	.07
348	Franklin Stubbs (R)	.20	.12
349	Aurelio Lopez	.10	.06
350	Al Bumbry	.10	.06
351	Charlie Moore	.10	.06
352	Luis Sanchez	.10	.06
353	Darrell Porter	.10	.06
354	Bill Dawley	.10	.06
355	Charlie Hudson	.10	.06
356	Garry Templeton	.10	.06
357	Cecilio Guante	.10	.06
358	Jeff Leonard	.10	.06
359	Paul Molitor	.50	.30
360	Ron Gardenhire	.10	.06
361	Larry Bowa	.10	.06
362	Bob Kearney	.10	.06
363	Garth Iorg	.10	.06
364	Tom Brunansky	.12	.07
265	Brad Gulden	.10	.06
366	Greg Walker	.10	.06
367	Mike Young	.10	.06
368	Rick Waits	.10	.06
369	Doug Bair	.10	.06
370	Bob Shirley	.10	.06
371	Bob Ojeda	.12	.07
372	Bob Welch	.15	.08
373	Neal Heaton	.10	.06
374	Danny Jackson(Er) (Wrong Photo)	.12	.07
375	Donnie Hill	.10	.06

376	Mike Stenhouse	.10	.06
377	Bruce Kison	.10	.06
378	Wayne Tolleson	.10	.06
379	Floyd Bannister	.10	.06
380	Vern Ruhle	.10	.06
381	Tim Corcoran	.10	.06
382	Kurt Kepshire	.10	.06
383	Bobby Brown	.10	.06
384	Dave Van Gorder	.10	.06
385	Rick Mahler	.10	.06
386	Lee Mazzilli	.10	.06
387	Bill Laskey	.10	.06
388	Thad Bosley	.10	.06
389	Al Chambers	.10	.06
390	Tony Fernandez	.80	.50
391	Ron Washington	.10	.06
392	Bill Swaggerty	.10	.06
393	Bob Gibson	.10	.06
394	Marty Castillo	.10	.06
395	Steve Crawford	.10	.06
396	Clay Christiansen	.10	.06
397	Bob Bailor	.10	.06
398	Mike Hargrove	.10	.06
399	Charlie Leibrandt	.10	.06
400	Tom Burgmeier	.10	.06
401	Razor Shines	.10	.06
402	Rob Wilfong	.10	.06
403	Tom Henke	.12	.07
404	Al Jones	.10	.06
405	Mike LaCoss	.10	.06
406	Luis DeLeon	.10	.06
407	Greg Gross	.10	.06
408	Tom Hume	.10	.06
409	Rick Camp	.10	.06
410	Milt May	.10	.06
411	Henry Cotto (R)	.12	.07
412	Dave Von Ohlen	.10	.06
413	Scott McGregor	.10	.06
414	Ted Simmons	.12	.07
415	Jack Morris	1.00	.70
416	Bill Buckner	.12	.07
417	Butch Wynegar	.10	.06
418	Steve Sax	.50	.30
419	Steve Balboni	.10	.06
420	Dwayne Murphy	.10	.06
421	Andre Dawson	2.00	1.25
422	Charlie Hough	.10	.06
423	Tommy John	.12	.07
424a	Tom Seaver (Er) (Wrong Photo)	28.00	18.00
424b	Tom Seaver (Cor)	2.00	1.25
425	Tom Herr	.10	.06
426	Terry Puhl	.10	.06
427	Al Holland	.10	.06
428	Eddie Milner	.10	.06
429	Terry Kennedy	.10	.06
430	John Candelaria	.10	.06
431	Manny Trillo	.10	.06
432	Ken Oberkfell	.10	.06
433	Rick Sutcliffe	.10	.06
434	Ron Darling	.30	.18
435	Spike Owen	.10	.06
436	Frank Viola	.50	.30
437	Lloyd Moseby	.10	.06
438	Kirby Puckett (R)	60.00	45.00
439	Jim Clancy	.10	.06
440	Mike Moore	.30	.18
441	Doug Sisk	.10	.06
442	Dennis Eckersley	1.00	.70
443	Gerald Perry	.10	.06
444	Dale Berra	.10	.06
445	Dusty Baker	.12	.07
446	Ed Whitson	.10	.06
447	Cesar Cedeno	.12	.07
448	Rick Schu (R)	.10	.06
449	Joaquin Andujar	.10	.06
450	Mark Bailey (R)	.10	.06
451	Ron Romanick (R)	.10	.06
452	Julio Cruz	.10	.06
453	Miguel Dilone	.10	.06
454	Storm Davis	.10	.06
455	Jaime Cocanower	.10	.06
456	Barbaro Garbey	.10	.06
457	Rich Gedman	.10	.06
458	Phil Niekro	.70	.40
459	Mike Scioscia	.15	.08
460	Pat Tabler	.10	.06
461	Darryl Motley	.10	.06
462	Chris Codiroli	.10	.06
463	Doug Flynn	.10	.06
464	Billy Sample	.10	.06
465	Mickey Rivers	.10	.06
466	John Wathan	.10	.06
467	Bill Krueger	.10	.06
468	Andre Thornton	.10	.06
469	Rex Hudler	.12	.07
470	Sid Bream (R)	.50	.30
471	Kirk Gibson	.25	.15
472	John Shelby	.10	.06
473	Moose Haas	.10	.06
474	Doug Corbett	.10	.06
475	Willie McGee	.50	.30
476	Bob Knepper	.10	.06
477	Kevin Gross	.10	.06
478	Carmelo Martinez	.10	.06
479	Kent Tekulve	.10	.06
480	Chili Davis	.12	.07
481	Bobby Clark	.10	.06
482	Mookie Wilson	.10	.06
483	Dave Owen	.10	.06
484	Ed Nunez	.10	.06
485	Rance Mulliniks	.10	.06
486	Ken Schrom	.10	.06
487	Jeff Russell	.12	.07
488	Tom Paciorek	.10	.06
489	Dan Ford	.10	.06

No.	Name		
490	Mike Caldwell	.10	.06
491	Scottie Earl	.10	.06
492	Jose Rijo (R)	4.00	2.75
493	Bruce Hurst	.15	.08
494	Ken Landreaux	.10	.06
495	Mike Fischlin	.10	.06
496	Don Slaught	.10	.06
497	Steve McCatty	.10	.06
498	Gary Lucas	.10	.06
499	Gary Pettis	.10	.06
500	Marvis Foley	.10	.06
501	Mike Squires	.10	.06
502	Jim Pankovitz (R)	.10	.06
503	Luis Aguayo	.10	.06
504	Ralph Citarella	.10	.06
505	Bruce Bochy	.10	.06
506	Bob Owchinko	.10	.06
507	Pascual Perez	.12	.07
508	Lee Lacy	.10	.06
509	Atlee Hammaker	.10	.06
510	Bob Dernier	.10	.06
511	Ed Vande Berg	.10	.06
512	Cliff Johnson	.10	.06
513	Len Whitehouse	.10	.06
514	Dennis Martinez	.25	.15
515	Ed Romero	.10	.06
516	Rusty Kuntz	.10	.06
517	Rick Miller	.10	.06
518	Dennis Rasmussen	.10	.06
519	Steve Yeager	.10	.06
520	Chris Bando	.10	.06
521	U.L. Washington	.10	.06
522	Curt Young (R)	.12	.07
523	Angel Salazar	.10	.06
524	Curt Kaufman	.10	.06
525	Odell Jones	.10	.06
526	Juan Agosto	.10	.06
527	Denny Walling	.10	.06
528	Andy Hawkins	.12	.07
529	Sixto Lezcano	.10	.06
530	Skeeter Barnes	.10	.06
531	Randy Johnson	.10	.06
532	Jim Morrison	.10	.06
533	Warren Brusstar	.10	.06
534a	Jeff Pendleton (Er) (Wrong Name)	6.50	3.75
534b	Terry Pendleton (R)	20.00	14.00
535	Vic Rodriguez	.10	.06
536	Bob McClure	.10	.06
537	Dave Bergman	.10	.06
538	Mark Clear	.10	.06
539	Mike Pagliarulo (R)	.20	.12
540	Terry Whitfield	.10	.06
541	Joe Beckwith	.10	.06
542	Jeff Burroughs	.10	.06
543	Dan Schatzeder	.10	.06
544	Donnie Scott	.10	.06
545	Jim Slaton	.10	.06
546	Greg Luzinski	.12	.07
547	Mark Salas (R)	.10	.06
548	Dave Smith	.10	.06
549	John Wockenfuss	.10	.06
550	Frank Pastore	.10	.06
551	Tim Flannery	.10	.06
552	Rick Rhoden	.10	.06
553	Mark Davis	.10	.06
554	Jeff Dedmon (R)	.10	.06
555	Gary Woods	.10	.06
556	Danny Heep	.10	.06
557	Mark Langston (R)	3.50	2.25
558	Darrell Brown	.10	.06
559	Jimmy Key (R)	1.00	.70
560	Rick Lysander	.10	.06
561	Doyle Alexander	.10	.06
562	Mike Stanton	.10	.06
563	Sid Fernandez	.35	.20
564	Richie Hebner	.10	.06
565	Alex Trevino	.10	.06
566	Brian Harper	.25	.15
567	Dan Gladden (R)	.30	.18
568	Luis Salazar	.10	.06
569	Tom Foley	.10	.06
570	Larry Andersen	.10	.06
571	Danny Cox	.10	.06
572	Joe Sambito	.10	.06
573	Juan Beniquez	.10	.06
574	Joel Skinner	.10	.06
575	Randy St. Claire	.10	.06
576	Floyd Rayford	.10	.06
577	Roy Howell	.10	.06
578	John Grubb	.10	.06
579	Ed Jurak	.10	.06
580	John Montefusco	.10	.06
581	Orel Hershiser (R)	4.50	2.50
582	Tom Waddell	.10	.06
583	Mark Huismann	.10	.06
584	Joe Morgan	.50	.30
585	Jim Wohlford	.10	.06
586	Dave Schmidt	.10	.06
587	Jeff Kunkel (R)	.10	.06
588	Hal McRae	.12	.07
589	Bill Almon	.10	.06
590	Carmen Castillo	.10	.06
591	Omar Moreno	.10	.06
592	Ken Howell (R)	.12	.07
593	Tom Brookens	.10	.06
594	Joe Nolan	.10	.06
595	Willie Lozado	.10	.06
596	Tom Nieto	.10	.06
597	Walt Terrell	.10	.06
598	Al Oliver	.12	.07
599	Shane Rawley	.10	.06
600	Denny Gonzalez (R)	.10	.06
601	Mark Grant (R)	.10	.06
602	Mark Armstrong	.10	.06
603	George Foster	.12	.07

604	Davey Lopes	.12	.07
605	Salome Barojas	.10	.06
606	Roy Lee Jackson	.10	.06
607	Pete Filson	.10	.06
608	Duane Walker	.10	.06
609	Glenn Wilson	.10	.06
610	Rafael Santana (R)	.12	.07
611	Roy Smith	.10	.06
612	Ruppert Jones	.10	.06
613	Joe Cowley	.10	.06
614	Al Nippe	.12	.07
	(Wrong Photo)		
615	Gene Nelson	.10	.06
616	Joe Carter	8.00	5.00
617	Ray Knight	.10	.06
618	Chuck Rainey	.10	.06
619	Dan Driessen	.10	.06
620	Daryl Sconiers	.10	.06
621	Bill Stein	.10	.06
622	Roy Smalley	.10	.06
623	Ed Lynch	.10	.06
624	Jeff Stone (R)	.10	.06
625	Bruce Berenyi	.10	.06
626	Kelvin Chapman	.10	.06
627	Joe Price	.10	.06
628	Steve Bedrosian	.10	.06
629	Vic Mata	.10	.06
630	Mike Krukow	.10	.06
631	Phil Bradley (R)	.20	.12
632	Jim Gott	.10	.06
633	Randy Bush	.10	.06
634	Tom Browning (R)	.80	.50
635	Lou Gehrig	.15	.08
	Puzzle Card		
636	Reid Nichols	.10	.06
637	Dan Pasqua (R)	.35	.20
638	German Rivera	.10	.06
639	Don Schulze (R)	.10	.06
640	Mike Jones (Var)	.10	.06
641	Pete Rose	2.00	1.25
642	Wade Rowdon	.10	.06
643	Jerry Narron	.10	.06
644	Darrell Miller (R)	.10	.06
645	Tim Hulett (R)	.12	.07
646	Andy McGaffigan	.10	.06
647	Kurt Bevacqua	.10	.06
648	John Russell (R)	.12	.07
649	Ron Robinson (R)	.12	.07
650	Donnie Moore	.10	.06
651a	Two for the Title	9.00	5.00
	(Mattingly/Winfield)		
	(Yellow names)		
651b	Two for the Title	4.00	2.50
	(Mattingly/Winfield)		
	(White names)		
652	Tim Laudner	.10	.06
653	Steve Farr (R)	.50	.30
___	Checklist (DK)	.12	.07

___	Checklist 27-130	.12	.07
___	Checklist 131-234	.12	.07
___	Checklist 235-338	.12	.07
___	Checklist 339-442	.12	.07
___	Checklist 443-546	.12	.07
___	Checklist 547-653	.12	.07

1986 Donruss

This 660-card set features blue borders on the card fronts and horizontal card backs with black type on a blue and white background. Subsets include Diamond Kings (1-26) and Rated Rookies (27- 46). The standard-size cards measure 2-1/2" by 3-1/2". Wax packs include puzzle pieces featuring Hank Aaron.

		MINT	NR/MT
Complete Set (660)		180.00	125.00
Commons		.08	.05

1	Kirk Gibson (DK)	.12	.07
2	Goose Gossage (DK)	.12	.07
3	Willie McGee (DK)	.15	.08
4	George Bell (DK)	.15	.08
5	Tony Armas (DK)	.08	.05
6	Chili Davis (DK)	.10	.06
7	Cecil Cooper (DK)	.08	.05
8	Mike Boddicker (DK)	.08	.05
9	Davey Lopes (DK)	.10	.06
10	Bill Doran (DK)	.08	.05
11	Bret Saberhagen (DK)	.25	.15
12	Brett Butler (DK)	.15	.08
13	Harold Baines (DK)	.12	.07
14	Mike Davis (DK)	.08	.05
15	Tony Perez (DK)	.20	.12
16	Willie Randolph (DK)	.12	.07

17	Bob Boone (DK)	.12	.07
18	Orel Hershiser (DK)	.25	.15
19	Johnny Ray (DK)	.08	.05
20	Gary Ward (DK)	.08	.05
21	Rick Mahler (DK)	.08	.05
22	Phil Bradley (DK)	.10	.06
23	Jerry Koosman (DK)	.12	.07
24	Tom Brunansky (DK)	.12	.07
25	Andre Dawson (DK)	.30	.18
26	Dwight Gooden (DK)	.35	.20
27	Kal Daniels (R)	1.25	.80
28	Fred McGriff (R)	30.00	22.00
29	Cory Snyder (R)	.50	.30
30	Jose Guzman (R)	.30	.18
31	Ty Gainey (R)	.10	.06
32	Johnny Abrego (R)	.08	.05
33	Andres Galarraga (R)	1.25	.80
34	Dave Shipanoff (R)	.08	.05
35	Mark McLemore (R)	.10	.06
36	Marty Clary (R)	.10	.06
37	Paul O'Neill (R)	2.50	1.50
38	Danny Tartabull (R)	1.75	1.00
39	Jose Canseco (R)	60.00	45.00
40	Juan Nieves (R)	.15	.08
41	Lance McCullers (R)	.10	.06
42	Rick Surhoff (R)	.10	.06
43	Todd Worrell (R)	.25	.15
44	Bob Kipper (R)	.10	.06
45	John Habyan (R)	.15	.08
46	Mike Woodard (R)	.08	.05
47	Mike Boddicker	.08	.05
48	Robin Yount	2.00	1.25
49	Lou Whitaker	.20	.12
50	"Oil Can" Boyd	.08	.05
51	Rickey Henderson	2.50	1.50
52	Mike Marshall	.08	.05
53	George Brett	2.00	1.25
54	Dave Kingman	.10	.06
55	Hubie Brooks	.10	.06
56	Oddibe McDowell (R)	.10	.06
57	Doug DeCinces	.08	.05
58	Britt Burns	.08	.05
59	Ozzie Smith	.80	.05
60	Jose Cruz	.10	.06
61	Mike Schmidt	2.75	1.75
62	Pete Rose	1.25	.80
63	Steve Garvey	.40	.25
64	Tony Pena	.08	.05
65	Chili Davis	.10	.06
66	Dale Murphy	.40	.25
67	Ryne Sandberg	5.00	3.00
68	Gary Carter	.40	.25
69	Alvin Davis	.08	.05
70	Kent Hrbek	.15	.08
71	George Bell	.40	.25
72	Kirby Puckett	12.00	8.00
73	Lloyd Moseby	.08	.05
74	Bob Kearney	.08	.05
75	Dwight Gooden	1.25	.80
76	Gary Matthews	.08	.05
77	Rick Mahler	.08	.05
78	Benny Distefano	.08	.05
79	Jeff Leonard	.08	.05
80	Kevin McReynolds	.15	.08
81	Ron Oester	.08	.05
82	John Russell	.08	.05
83	Tommy Herr	.08	.05
84	Jerry Mumphrey	.08	.05
85	Ron Romanick	.08	.05
86	Daryl Boston	.08	.05
87	Andre Dawson	1.25	.80
88	Eddie Murray	1.25	.80
89	Dion James	.08	.05
90	Chet Lemon	.08	.05
91	Bob Stanley	.08	.05
92	Willie Randolph	.10	.06
93	Mike Scioscia	.10	.06
94	Tom Waddell	.08	.05
95	Danny Jackson	.08	.05
96	Mike Davis	.08	.05
97	Mike Fitzgerald	.08	.05
98	Gary Ward	.08	.05
99	Pete O'Brien	.08	.05
100	Bret Saberhagen	.80	.50
101	Alfredo Griffin	.08	.05
102	Brett Butler	.15	.08
103	Ron Guidry	.12	.07
104	Jerry Reuss	.08	.05
105	Jack Morris	.75	.45
106	Rick Dempsey	.08	.05
107	Ray Burris	.08	.05
108	Brian Downing	.08	.05
109	Willie McGee	.20	.12
110	Bill Doran	.08	.05
111	Kent Tekulve	.08	.05
112	Tony Gwynn	3.50	2.25
113	Marvell Wynne	.08	.05
114	David Green	.08	.05
115	Jim Gantner	.08	.05
116	George Foster	.10	.06
117	Steve Trout	.08	.05
118	Mark Langston	.50	.30
119	Tony Fernandez	.20	.12
120	John Butcher	.08	.05
121	Ron Robinson	.08	.05
122	Dan Spillner	.08	.05
123	Mike Young	.08	.05
124	Paul Molitor	.40	.25
125	Kirk Gibson	.12	.07
126	Ken Griffey	.12	.07
127	Tony Armas	.08	.05
128	Mariano Duncan (R)	.40	.25
129	Pat Tabler	.08	.05
130	Frank White	.08	.05
131	Carney Lansford	.10	.06
132	Vance Law	.08	.05

133	Dick Schofield	.08	.05
134	Wayne Tolleson	.08	.05
135	Greg Walker	.08	.05
136	Denny Walling	.08	.05
137	Ozzie Virgil	.08	.05
138	Ricky Horton	.08	.05
139	LaMarr Hoyt	.08	.05
140	Wayne Krenchicki	.08	.05
141	Glenn Hubbard	.08	.05
142	Cecilio Guante	.08	.05
143	Mike Krukow	.08	.05
144	Lee Smith	.75	.45
145	Edwin Nunez	.08	.05
146	Dave Steib	.12	.07
147	Mike Smithson	.08	.05
148	Ken Dixon	.08	.05
149	Danny Darwin	.08	.05
150	Chris Pittaro	.08	.05
151	Bill Buckner	.10	.06
152	Mike Pagliarulo	.08	.05
153	Bill Russell	.10	.06
154	Brook Jacoby	.08	.05
155	Pat Sheridan	.08	.05
156	Mike Gallego (R)	.15	.08
157	Jim Wohlford	.08	.05
158	Gary Pettis	.08	.05
159	Toby Harrah	.08	.05
160	Richard Dotson	.08	.05
161	Bob Knepper	.08	.05
162	Dave Dravecky	.08	.05
163	Greg Gross	.08	.05
164	Eric Davis	1.75	1.00
165	Gerald Perry	.08	.05
166	Rick Rhoden	.08	.05
167	Keith Moreland	.08	.05
168	Jack Clark	.12	.07
169	Storm Davis	.08	.05
170	Cecil Cooper	.08	.05
171	Alan Trammell	.50	.30
172	Roger Clemens	12.00	8.00
173	Don Mattingly	2.75	1.75
174	Pedro Guerrero	.10	.06
175	Willie Wilson	.08	.05
176	Dwayne Murphy	.08	.05
177	Tim Raines	.25	.15
178	Larry Parrish	.08	.05
179	Mike Witt	.08	.05
180	Harold Baines	.15	.08
181	Vince Coleman (R)	2.00	1.25
182	Jeff Heathcock (R)	.08	.05
183	Steve Carlton	1.00	.70
184	Mario Soto	.08	.05
185	Goose Gossage	.12	.07
186	Johnny Ray	.08	.05
187	Dan Gladden	.08	.05
188	Bob Horner	.10	.06
189	Rick Sutcliffe	.10	.06
190	Keith Hernandez	.12	.07
191	Phil Bradley	.08	.05
192	Tom Brunansky	.10	.06
193	Jesse Barfield	.12	.07
194	Frank Viola	.30	.18
195	Willie Upshaw	.08	.05
196	Jim Beattie	.08	.05
197	Darryl Strawberry	3.00	2.00
198	Ron Cey	.10	.06
199	Steve Bedrosian	.08	.05
200	Steve Kemp	.08	.05
201	Manny Trillo	.08	.05
202	Garry Templeton	.08	.05
203	Dave Parker	.15	.08
204	John Denny	.08	.05
205	Terry Pendleton	1.50	.90
206	Terry Puhl	.08	.05
207	Bobby Grich	.10	.06
208	Ozzie Guillen (R)	.60	.35
209	Jeff Reardon	.75	.45
210	Cal Ripken Jr.	5.00	3.00
211	Bill Schroeder	.08	.05
212	Dan Petry	.08	.05
213	Jim Rice	.12	.07
214	Dave Righetti	.10	.06
215	Fernando Valenzuela	.12	.07
216	Julio Franco	.40	.25
217	Darryl Motley	.08	.05
218	Dave Collins	.08	.05
219	Tim Wallach	.12	.07
220	George Wright	.08	.05
221	Tommy Dunbar	.08	.05
222	Steve Balboni	.08	.05
223	Jay Howell	.08	.05
224	Joe Carter	2.50	1.50
225	Ed Whitson	.08	.05
226	Orel Hershiser	.60	.35
227	Willie Hernandez	.08	.05
228	Lee Lacy	.08	.05
229	Rollie Fingers	.40	.25
230	Bob Boone	.12	.07
231	Joaquin Andujar	.08	.05
232	Craig Reynolds	.08	.05
233	Shane Rawley	.08	.05
234	Eric Show	.08	.05
235	Jose DeLeon	.08	.05
236	Jose Uribe (R)	.15	.08
237	Moose Haas	.08	.05
238	Wally Backman	.08	.05
239	Dennis Eckersley	.60	.35
240	Mike Moore	.12	.07
241	Damaso Garcia	.08	.05
242	Tim Teufel	.08	.05
243	Dave Concepcion	.12	.07
244	Floyd Bannister	.08	.05
245	Fred Lynn	.12	.07
246	Charlie Moore	.08	.05
247	Walt Terrell	.08	.05
248	Dave Winfield	1.50	.90

No.	Player		
249	Dwight Evans	.12	.07
250	Dennis Powell (R)	.08	.05
251	Andre Thornton	.08	.05
252	Onix Concepcion	.08	.05
253	Mike Heath	.08	.05
254a	David Palmer (Er)(2B)	.08	.05
254b	David Palmer (Cor)(P)	.75	.45
255	Donnie Moore	.08	.05
256	Curtis Wilkerson	.08	.05
257	Julio Cruz	.08	.05
258	Nolan Ryan	7.50	4.50
259	Jeff Stone	.08	.05
260	John Tudor (Var)	.08	.05
261	Mark Thurmond	.08	.05
262	Jay Tibbs	.08	.05
263	Rafael Ramirez	.08	.05
264	Larry McWilliams	.08	.05
265	Mark Davis	.08	.05
266	Bob Dernier	.08	.05
267	Matt Young	.08	.05
268	Jim Clancy	.08	.05
269	Mickey Hatcher	.08	.05
270	Sammy Stewart	.08	.05
271	Bob Gibson	.08	.05
272	Nelson Simmons	.08	.05
273	Rich Gedman	.08	.05
274	Butch Wynegar	.08	.05
275	Ken Howell	.08	.05
276	Mel Hall	.15	.08
277	Jim Sundberg	.08	.05
278	Chris Codiroli	.08	.05
279	Herm Winningham (R)	.12	.07
280	Rod Carew	1.00	.70
281	Don Slaught	.08	.05
282	Scott Fletcher	.08	.05
283	Bill Dawley	.08	.05
284	Andy Hawkins	.08	.05
285	Glenn Wilson	.08	.05
286	Nick Esasky	.08	.05
287	Claudell Washington	.08	.05
288	Lee Mazzilli	.08	.05
289	Jody Davis	.08	.05
290	Darrell Porter	.08	.05
291	Scott McGregor	.08	.05
292	Ted Simmons	.10	.06
293	Aurelio Lopez	.08	.05
294	Marty Barrett	.08	.05
295	Dale Berra	.08	.05
296	Greg Brock	.08	.05
297	Charlie Leibrandt	.08	.05
298	Bill Krueger	.08	.05
299	Bryn Smith	.08	.05
300	Burt Hooton	.08	.05
301	Stu Cliburn	.08	.05
302	Luis Salazar	.08	.05
303	Ken Dayley	.08	.05
304	Frank DiPino	.08	.05
305	Von Hayes	.08	.05
306	Gary Redus (Var)	.08	.05
307	Craig Lefferts	.08	.05
308	Sam Khalifa	.08	.05
309	Scott Garrelts	.08	.05
310	Rick Cerone	.08	.05
311	Shawon Dunston	.30	.18
312	Howard Johnson	.75	.45
313	Jim Presley	.08	.05
314	Gary Gaetti	.10	.06
315	Luis Leal	.08	.05
316	Mark Salas	.08	.05
317	Bill Caudill	.08	.05
318	Dave Henderson	.12	.07
319	Rafael Santana	.08	.05
320	Leon Durham	.08	.05
321	Bruce Sutter	.10	.06
322	Jason Thompson	.08	.05
323	Bob Brenly	.08	.05
324	Carmelo Martinez	.08	.05
325	Eddie Milner	.08	.05
326	Juan Samuel	.08	.05
327	Tom Nieto	.08	.05
328	Dave Smith	.08	.05
329	Urbano Lugo (R)	.08	.05
330	Joel Skinner	.08	.05
331	Bill Gullickson	.08	.05
332	Floyd Rayford	.08	.05
333	Ben Oglivie	.08	.05
334	Lance Parrish	.08	.05
335	Jackie Gutierrez	.08	.05
336	Dennis Rasmussen	.08	.05
337	Terry Whitfield	.08	.05
338	Neal Heaton	.08	.05
339	Jorge Orta	.08	.05
340	Donnie Hill	.08	.05
341	Joe Hesketh	.10	.06
342	Charlie Hough	.08	.05
343	Dave Rozema	.08	.05
344	Greg Pryor	.08	.05
345	Mickey Tettleton (R)	1.75	1.00
346	George Vukovich	.08	.05
347	Don Baylor	.10	.06
348	Carlos Diaz	.08	.05
349	Barbaro Garbey	.08	.05
350	Larry Sheets	.08	.05
351	Ted Higuera (R)	.20	.12
352	Juan Beniquez	.08	.05
353	Bob Forsch	.08	.05
354	Mark Bailey	.08	.05
355	Larry Andersen	.08	.05
356	Terry Kennedy	.08	.05
357	Don Robinson	.08	.05
358	Jim Gott	.08	.05
359	Earnest Riles (R)	.12	.07
360	John Christensen (R)	.08	.05
361	Ray Fontenot	.08	.05
362	Spike Owen	.08	.05
363	Jim Acker	.08	.05

364 Ron Davis (Var)	.08	.05
365 Tom Hume	.08	.05
366 Carlton Fisk	1.00	.70
367 Nate Snell	.08	.05
368 Rick Manning	.08	.05
369 Darrell Evans	.10	.06
370 Ron Hassey	.08	.05
371 Wade Boggs	2.50	1.50
372 Rick Honeycutt	.08	.05
373 Chris Bando	.08	.05
374 Bud Black	.08	.05
375 Steve Henderson	.08	.05
376 Charlie Lea	.08	.05
377 Reggie Jackson	1.75	1.00
378 Dave Schmidt	.08	.05
379 Bob James	.08	.05
380 Glenn Davis	.75	.45
381 Tim Corcoran	.08	.05
382 Danny Cox	.08	.05
383 Tim Flannery	.08	.05
384 Tom Browning	.15	.08
385 Rick Camp	.08	.05
386 Jim Morrison	.08	.05
387 Dave LaPoint	.08	.05
388 Davey Lopes	.10	.06
389 Al Cowens	.08	.05
390 Doyle Alexander	.08	.05
391 Tim Laudner	.08	.05
392 Don Aase	.08	.05
393 Jaime Cocanower	.08	.05
394 Randy O'Neal (R)	.08	.05
395 Mike Easler	.08	.05
396 Scott Bradley	.08	.05
397 Tom Niedenfuer	.08	.05
398 Jerry Willard	.08	.05
399 Lonnie Smith	.08	.05
400 Bruce Bochte	.08	.05
401 Terry Francona	.08	.05
402 Jim Slaton	.08	.05
403 Bill Stein	.08	.05
404 Tim Hulett	.08	.05
405 Alan Ashby	.08	.05
406 Tim Stoddard	.08	.05
407 Garry Maddox	.08	.05
408 Ted Power	.08	.05
409 Len Barker	.08	.05
410 Denny Gonzalez	.08	.05
411 George Frazier	.08	.05
412 Andy Van Slyke	.60	.35
413 Jim Dwyer	.08	.05
414 Paul Householder	.08	.05
415 Alejandro Sanchez	.08	.05
416 Steve Crawford	.08	.05
417 Dan Pasqua	.12	.07
418 Enos Cabell	.08	.05
419 Mike Jones	.08	.05
420 Steve Kiefer	.08	.05
421 Tim Burke (R)	.12	.07
422 Mike Mason	.08	.05
423 Ruppert Jones	.08	.05
424 Jerry Hairston	.08	.05
425 Tito Landrum	.08	.05
426 Jeff Calhoun	.08	.05
427 Don Carman (R)	.12	.07
428 Tony Perez	.35	.20
429 Jerry Davis	.08	.05
430 Bob Walk	.08	.05
431 Brad Wellman	.08	.05
432 Terry Forster	.08	.05
433 Billy Hatcher	.08	.05
434 Clint Hurdle	.08	.05
435 Ivan Calderon (R)	.75	.45
436 Pete Filson	.08	.05
437 Tom Henke	.10	.06
438 Dave Engle	.08	.05
439 Tom Filer	.08	.05
440 Gorman Thomas	.08	.05
441 Rick Aguilera (R)	1.00	.70
442 Scott Sanderson	.08	.05
443 Jeff Dedmon	.08	.05
444 Joe Orsulak (R)	.25	.15
445 Atlee Hammaker	.08	.05
446 Jerry Royster	.08	.05
447 Buddy Bell	.08	.05
448 Dave Rucker	.08	.05
449 Ivan DeJesus	.08	.05
450 Jim Pankovits	.08	.05
451 Jerry Narron	.08	.05
452 Bryan Little	.08	.05
453 Gary Lucas	.08	.05
454 Dennis Martinez	.15	.08
455 Ed Romero	.08	.05
456 Bob Melvin (R)	.10	.06
457 Glenn Hoffman	.08	.05
458 Bob Shirley	.08	.05
459 Bob Welch	.10	.06
460 Carmen Castillo	.08	.05
461 Dave Leeper	.08	.05
462 Tim Birtsas (R)	.10	.06
463 Randy St. Claire	.08	.05
464 Chris Welsh	.08	.05
465 Greg Harris	.08	.05
466 Lynn Jones	.08	.05
467 Dusty Baker	.10	.06
468 Roy Smith	.08	.05
469 Andre Robertson	.08	.05
470 Ken Landreaux	.08	.05
471 Dave Bergman	.08	.05
472 Gary Roenicke	.08	.05
473 Pete Vuckovich	.08	.05
474 Kirk McCaskill (R)	.25	.15
475 Jeff Lahti	.08	.05
476 Mike Scott	.10	.06
477 Darren Daulton (R)	1.75	1.00
478 Graig Nettles	.12	.07
479 Bill Almon	.08	.05

#	Player		
480	Greg Minton	.08	.05
481	Randy Ready	.10	.06
482	Lenny Dykstra (R)	1.50	.90
483	Thad Bosley	.08	.05
484	Harold Reynolds (R)	.75	.45
485	Al Oliver	.10	.06
486	Roy Smalley	.08	.05
487	John Franco	.12	.07
488	Juan Agosto	.08	.05
489	Al Pardo	.08	.05
490	Bill Wegman (R)	.40	.25
491	Frank Tanana	.10	.06
492	Brian Fisher (R)	.08	.05
493	Mark Clear	.08	.05
494	Len Matuszek	.08	.05
495	Ramon Romero	.08	.05
496	John Wathan	.08	.05
497	Rob Picciolo	.08	.05
498	U.L. Washington	.08	.05
499	John Candelaria	.08	.05
500	Duane Walker	.08	.05
501	Gene Nelson	.08	.05
502	John Mizerock	.08	.05
503	Luis Aguayo	.08	.05
504	Kurt Kepshire	.08	.05
505	Ed Wojna	.08	.05
506	Joe Price	.08	.05
507	Milt Thompson (R)	.25	.15
508	Junior Ortiz	.08	.05
509	Vida Blue	.12	.07
510	Steve Engel	.08	.05
511	Karl Best	.08	.05
512	Cecil Fielder (R)	25.00	18.00
513	Frank Eufemia	.08	.05
514	Tippy Martinez	.08	.05
515	Billy Robidoux (R)	.08	.05
516	Bill Scherrer	.08	.05
517	Bruce Hurst	.12	.07
518	Rich Bordi	.08	.05
519	Steve Yeager	.08	.05
520	Tony Bernazard	.08	.05
521	Hal McRae	.10	.06
522	Jose Rijo	.35	.20
523	Mitch Webster (R)	.15	.08
524	Jack Howell (R)	.10	.06
525	Alan Bannister	.08	.05
526	Ron Kittle	.08	.05
527	Phil Garner	.08	.05
528	Kurt Bevacqua	.08	.05
529	Kevin Gross	.08	.05
530	Bo Diaz	.08	.05
531	Ken Oberkfell	.08	.05
532	Rich Reuschel	.08	.05
533	Ron Meridith	.08	.05
534	Steve Braun	.08	.05
535	Wayne Gross	.08	.05
536	Ray Searage	.08	.05
537	Tom Brookens	.08	.05
538	Al Nipper	.08	.05
539	Billy Sample	.08	.05
540	Steve Sax	.25	.15
541	Dan Quisenberry	.08	.05
542	Tony Phillips	.08	.05
543	Floyd Youmans (R)	.10	.06
544	Steve Buechele (R)	.80	.50
545	Craig Gerber	.08	.05
546	Joe DeSa	.08	.05
547	Brian Harper	.12	.07
548	Kevin Bass	.10	.06
549	Tom Foley	.08	.05
550	Dave Van Gorder	.08	.05
551	Bruce Bochy	.08	.05
552	R.J. Reynolds	.08	.05
553	Chris Brown (R)	.08	.05
554	Bruce Benedict	.08	.05
555	Warren Brusstar	.08	.05
556	Danny Heep	.08	.05
558	Greg Gagne	.10	.06
559	Ernie Whitt	.08	.05
560	Ron Washington	.08	.05
561	Jimmy Key	.20	.12
562	Billy Swift	.40	.25
563	Ron Darling	.15	.08
564	Dick Ruthven	.08	.05
565	Zane Smith	.30	.18
566	Sid Bream	.10	.06
567a	Joel Youngblood (Er) (P on front)	.10	.06
567b	Joel Youngblood (Cor)	.75	.45
568	Mario Ramirez	.08	.05
569	Tom Runnells	.08	.05
570	Rick Schu	.08	.05
571	Bill Campbell	.08	.05
572	Dickie Thon	.08	.05
573	Al Holland	.08	.05
574	Reid Nichols	.08	.05
575	Bert Roberge	.08	.05
576	Mike Flanagan	.08	.05
577	Tim Leary (R)	.12	.07
578	Mike Laga	.08	.05
579	Steve Lyons	.08	.05
580	Phil Niekro	.35	.20
581	Gilberto Reyes	.10	.06
582	Jamie Easterly	.08	.05
583	Mark Gubicza	.12	.07
584	Stan Javier (R)	.12	.07
585	Bill Laskey	.08	.05
586	Jeff Russell	.10	.06
587	Dickie Noles	.08	.05
588	Steve Farr	.08	.05
589	Steve Ontiveros (R)	.08	.05
590	Mike Hargrove	.08	.05
591	Marty Bystrom	.08	.05
592	Franklin Stubbs	.08	.05
593	Larry Herndon	.08	.05
594	Bill Swaggerty	.08	.05

		MINT	NR/MT
595	Carlos Ponce	.08	.05
596	Pat Perry (R)	.08	.05
597	Ray Knight	.08	.05
598	Steve Lombardozzi (R)	.08	.05
599	Brad Havens	.08	.05
600	Pat Clements (R)	.10	.06
601	Joe Niekro	.08	.05
602	Hank Aaron Puzzle Card	.12	.07
603	Dwayne Henry (R)	.12	.07
604	Mookie Wilson	.08	.05
605	Buddy Biancalana	.08	.05
606	Rance Mulliniks	.08	.05
607	Alan Wiggins	.08	.05
608	Joe Cowley	.08	.05
609a	Tom Seaver (Green)	1.25	.80
609b	Tom Seaver (Yellow)	3.00	2.00
610	Neil Allen	.08	.05
611	Don Sutton	.35	.20
612	Fred Toliver (R)	.10	.06
613	Jay Baller	.08	.05
614	Marc Sullivan	.08	.05
615	John Grubb	.08	.05
616	Bruce Kison	.08	.05
617	Bill Madlock	.10	.06
618	Chris Chambliss	.08	.05
619	Dave Stewart	.20	.12
620	Tim Lollar	.08	.05
621	Gary Lavelle	.08	.05
622	Charles Hudson	.08	.05
623	Joel Davis (R)	.08	.05
624	Joe Johnson (R)	.10	.06
625	Sid Fernandez	.15	.08
626	Dennis Lamp	.08	.05
627	Terry Harper	.08	.05
628	Jack Lazorko	.08	.05
629	Roger McDowell (R)	.25	.15
630	Mark Funderburk	.08	.05
631	Ed Lynch	.08	.05
632	Rudy Law	.08	.05
633	Roger Mason (R)	.15	.08
634	Mike Felder (R)	.20	.12
635	Ken Schrom	.08	.05
637	Ed Vande Berg	.08	.05
638	Bobby Meacham	.08	.05
639	Cliff Johnson	.08	.05
640	Garth Iorg	.08	.05
641	Dan Driessen	.08	.05
642	Mike Brown	.08	.05
643	John Shelby	.08	.05
644	Ty-Breaker (Pete Rose)	.75	.45
645	Knuckle Brothers(Joe Niekro, Phil Niekro)	.20	.12
646	Jesse Orosco	.08	.05
647	Billy Beane (R)	.10	.06
648	Cesar Cedeno	.10	.06
649	Bert Blyleven	.20	.12

		MINT	NR/MT
650	Max Venable	.08	.05
651	Fleet Feet (Vince Coleman, Willie McGee)	.30	.18
652	Calvin Schiraldi	.08	.05
653	King of Kings(Pete Rose)	1.00	.70
___	Checklist (DK)	.08	.05
___a	Checklist 27-130 (Er) (45 Beane)	.08	.05
___b	Checklist 27-130 (Cor) (45 Habyan)	.40	.15
___	Checklist 131-234	.08	.05
___	Checklist 235-338	.08	.05
___	Checklist 339-442	.08	.05
___	Checklist 443-546	.08	.05
___	Checklist 547-653	.08	.05

1986 Donruss Rookies

This marks the first update set issued by Donruss. The 56-card set is similar to the regular edition except for bluish-green border colors and a small "rookies" logo in the lower left corner of the card front. The standard-size cards measure 2-1/2 by 3-1/2".

		MINT	NR/MT
	Complete Set (56)	55.00	40.00
	Commons	.12	.07
1	Wally Joyner (R)	2.50	1.50
2	Tracy Jones (R)	.15	.08
3	Allan Anderson (R)	.12	.07
4	Ed Correa (R)	.12	.07
5	Reggie Williams	.12	.07

6	Charlie Kerfeld (R)	.12	.07
7	Andres Galarraga	.15	.08
8	Bob Tewksbury (R)	.40	.25
9	Al Newman	.12	.07
10	Andres Thomas (R)	.15	.08
11	Barry Bonds (R)	15.00	9.00
12	Juan Nieves	.15	.08
13	Mark Eichhorn (R)	.20	.12
14	Dan Plesac (R)	.20	.12
15	Cory Snyder	.40	.25
16	Kelly Gruber	1.25	.80
17	Kevin Mitchell (R)	3.50	2.25
18	Steve Lombardozzi	.12	.07
19	Mitch Williams	.35	.20
20	John Cerutti (R)	.20	.12
21	Todd Worrell	.15	.08
22	Jose Canseco	10.00	6.50
23	Pete Incaviglia (R)	.35	.20
24	Jose Guzman	.15	.08
25	Scott Bailes (R)	.20	.12
26	Greg Mathews (R)	.15	.08
27	Eric King (R)	.12	.07
28	Paul Assenmacher	.15	.08
29	Jeff Sellers	.12	.07
30	Bobby Bonilla (R)	7.50	4.50
31	Doug Drabek (R)	1.50	.90
32	Will Clark (R)	16.00	10.00
33	Bip Roberts (R)	.80	.50
34	Jim Deshaies (R)	.15	.08
35	Mike LaValliere (R)	.20	.12
36	Scott Bankhead (R)	.15	.08
37	Dale Sveum (R)	.20	.12
38	Bo Jackson (R)	6.00	4.00
39	Rob Thompson (R)	.40	.25
40	Eric Plunk (R)	.20	.12
41	Bill Bathe	.12	.07
42	John Kruk (R)	1.50	.90
43	Andy Allanson (R)	.15	.08
44	Mark Portugal	.15	.08
45	Danny Tartabull	1.75	1.00
46	Bob Kipper	.15	.08
47	Gene Walter	.12	.07
48	Rey Quinonez	.15	.08
49	Bobby Witt (R)	.75	.45
50	Bill Mooneyham	.12	.07
51	John Cangelosi (R)	.15	.08
52	Ruben Sierra (R)	12.00	8.00
53	Rob Woodward	.12	.07
54	Ed Hearn	.12	.07
55	Joel McKeon	.12	.07
56	Checklist 1-56	.15	.08

1987 Donruss

This 660-card set features black borders with gold trim on the card fronts and horizontal card backs with black and gold print on a white stock. For the first time, Donruss has numbered the checklists. Subsets include Diamond Kings (1-26) and Rated Rookies (28-47). Cards measure 2-1/2" by 3-1/2" and the set was issued with puzzle pieces featuring Roberto Clemente.

		MINT	NR/MT
Complete Set (660)		65.00	42.00
Commons		.05	.02

1	Wally Joyner (DK)	.35	.20
2	Roger Clemens (DK)	1.00	.70
3	Dale Murphy (DK)	.15	.08
4	Darryl Strawberry (DK)	.40	.25
5	Ozzie Smith (DK)	.20	.12
6	Jose Canseco (DK)	1.25	.80
7	Charlie Hough (DK)	.07	.04
8	Brook Jacoby (DK)	.07	.04
9	Fred Lynn (DK)	.10	.06
10	Rick Rhoden (DK)	.07	.04
11	Chris Brown (DK)	.07	.04
12	Von Hayes (DK)	.07	.04
13	Jack Morris (DK)	.20	.12
14a	Kevin McReynolds (DK) (Er)	.60	.35
14b	Kevin McReynolds (DK) (Cor)	.10	.06
15	George Brett (DK)	.30	.18
16	Ted Higuera (DK)	.07	.04
17	Hubie Brooks (DK)	.07	.04
18	Mike Scott (DK)	.07	.04
19	Kirby Puckett (DK)	.80	.50
20	Dave Winfield (DK)	.30	.18
21	Lloyd Moseby (DK)	.07	.04
22a	Eric Davis (DK) (Er)	.80	.50

22b	Eric Davis(DK) (Cor)	.20	.12
23	Jim Presley(DK)	.07	.04
24	Keith Moreland (DK)	.07	.04
25a	Greg Walker (DK) (Er)	.25	.15
25b	Greg Walker (DK)(Cor)	.07	.04
26	Steve Sax (DK)	.15	.08
27	Checklist 1-27	.08	.05
28	B.J. Surhoff (R)	.15	.08
29	Randy Myers (R)	.20	.12
30	Ken Gerhart (R)	.05	.02
31	Benito Santiago (R)	.75	.45
32	Greg Swindell (R)	1.25	.80
33	Mike Birkbeck (R)	.07	.04
34	Terry Steinbach (R)	.35	.20
35	Bo Jackson (R)	5.00	3.00
36	Greg Maddux (R)	3.50	2.25
37	Jim Lindeman (R)	.07	.04
38	Devon White (R)	.60	.35
39	Eric Bell (R)	.07	.04
40	Will Fraser (R)	.07	.04
41	Jerry Browne (R)	.20	.12
42	Chris James (R)	.12	.07
43	Rafael Palmeiro (R)	4.50	2.75
44	Pat Dodson (R)	.07	.04
45	Duane Ward (R)	.30	.18
46	Mark McGwire (R)	10.00	6.50
47	Bruce Field (R) (Er)	.07	.04
	(Wrong Photo)		
48	Eddie Murray	.50	.30
49	Ted Higuera	.05	.02
50	Kirk Gibson	.08	.05
51	Oil Can Boyd	.05	.02
52	Don Mattingly	.80	.05
53	Pedro Guerrero	.08	.05
54	George Brett	.80	.50
55	Jose Rijo	.15	.08
56	Tim Raines	.15	.08
57	Ed Correa	.05	.02
58	Mike Witt	.05	.02
59	Greg Walker	.05	.02
60	Ozzie Smith	.35	.20
61	Glenn Davis	.15	.08
62	Glenn Wilson	.05	.02
63	Tom Browning	.08	.05
64	Tony Gwynn	1.00	.70
65	R.J. Reynolds	.05	.02
66	Will Clark	10.00	6.50
67	Ozzie Virgil	.05	.02
68	Rick Sutcliffe	.07	.04
69	Gary Carter	.25	.15
70	Mike Moore	.07	.04
71	Bert Blyleven	.20	.12
72	Tony Fernandez	.12	.07
73	Kent Krbek	.12	.07
74	Lloyd Moseby	.05	.02
75	Alvin Davis	.05	.02
76	Keith Hernandez	.08	.05
77	Ryne Sandberg	1.75	1.00
78	Dale Murphy	.25	.15
79	Sid Bream	.05	.02
80	Chris Brown	.05	.02
81	Steve Garvey	.25	.15
82	Mario Soto	.05	.02
83	Shane Rawley	.05	.02
84	Willie McGee	.10	.06
85	Jose Cruz	.08	.05
86	Brian Downing	.05	.02
87	Ozzie Guillen	.10	.06
88	Hubie Brooks	.10	.06
89	Cal Ripken	2.00	1.25
90	Juan Nieves	.05	.02
91	Lance Parrish	.07	.04
92	Jim Rice	.10	.06
93	Ron Guidry	.10	.06
94	Fernando Valenzuela	.10	.06
95	Andy Allanson	.05	.02
96	Willie Wilson	.05	.02
97	Jose Canseco	8.00	5.00
98	Jeff Reardon	.25	.15
99	Bobby Witt	.35	.20
100	Checklist 28-133	.08	.05
101	Jose Guzman	.07	.04
102	Steve Balboni	.05	.02
103	Tony Phillips	.05	.02
104	Brook Jacoby	.05	.02
105	Dave Winfield	.50	.30
106	Orel Hershiser	.15	.08
107	Lou Whitaker	.12	.07
108	Fred Lynn	.10	.06
109	Bill Wegman	.12	.08
110	Donnie Moore	.05	.02
111	Jack Clark	.10	.06
112	Bob Knepper	.05	.02
113	Von Hayes	.05	.02
114	Bip Roberts	.40	.25
115	Tony Pena	.05	.02
116	Scott Garrelts	.05	.02
117	Paul Molitor	.20	.12
118	Darryl Strawberry	1.00	.70
119	Shawon Dunston	.20	.12
120	Jim Presley	.05	.02
121	Jesse Barfield	.08	.05
122	Gary Gaetti	.07	.04
123	Kurt Stillwell	.08	.05
124	Joel Davis	.05	.02
125	Mike Boddicker	.05	.02
126	Robin Yount	.70	.04
127	Alan Trammell	.25	.15
128	Dave Righetti	.07	.04
129	Dwight Evans	.10	.06
130	Mike Scioscia	.07	.04
131	Julio Franco	.25	.15
132	Bret Saberhagen	.25	.15
133	Mike Davis	.05	.02
134	Joe Hesketh	.05	.02
135	Wally Joyner	1.25	.80

No.	Player		
136	Don Slaught	.05	.02
137	Daryl Boston	.05	.02
138	Nolan Ryan	3.00	2.00
139	Mike Schmidt	1.25	.80
140	Tommy Herr	.05	.02
141	Garry Templeton	.05	.02
142	Kal Daniels	.05	.02
143	Billy Sample	.05	.02
144	Johnny Ray	.05	.02
145	Rob Thompson	.20	.12
146	Bob Dernier	.05	.02
147	Danny Tartabull	.40	.25
148	Ernie Whitt	.05	.02
149	Kirby Puckett	2.00	1.25
150	Mike Young	.05	.02
151	Ernest Riles	.05	.02
152	Frank Tanana	.07	.04
153	Rich Gedman	.05	.02
154	Willie Randolph	.07	.04
155	Bill Madlock (Var)	.10	.06
156	Joe Carter (Var)	.80	.50
157	Danny Jackson	.07	.04
158	Carney Lansford	.07	.04
159	Bryn Smith	.05	.02
160	Gary Pettis	.05	.02
161	Oddibe McDowell	.05	.02
162	John Cangelosi	.07	.04
163	Mike Scott	.07	.04
164	Eric Show	.05	.02
165	Juan Samuel	.05	.02
166	Nick Esasky	.05	.02
167	Zane Smith	.07	.04
168	Mike Brown	.05	.02
169	Keith Moreland	.05	.02
170	John Tudor	.05	.02
171	Ken Dixon	.05	.02
172	Jim Gantner	.05	.02
173	Jack Morris	.30	.18
174	Bruce Hurst	.08	.05
175	Dennis Rasmussen	.05	.02
176	Mike Marshall	.05	.02
177	Dan Quisenberry	.05	.02
178	Eric Plunk	.08	.05
179	Tim Wallach	.08	.05
180	Steve Buechele	.07	.04
181	Don Sutton	.20	.12
182	Dave Schmidt	.05	.02
183	Terry Pendleton	.50	.30
184	Jim Deshaies	.08	.05
185	Steve Bedrosian	.05	.02
186	Pete Rose	.50	.30
187	Dave Dravecky	.05	.02
188	Rick Reuschel	.05	.02
189	Dan Gladden	.05	.02
190	Rick Mahler	.05	.02
191	Thad Bosley	.05	.02
192	Ron Darling	.08	.05
193	Matt Young	.05	.02
194	Tom Brunansky	.08	.05
195	Dave Steib	.10	.06
196	Frank Viola	.15	.08
197	Tom Henke	.05	.02
198	Karl Best	.05	.02
199	Dwight Gooden	.30	.18
200	Checklist 134-239	.08	.05
201	Steve Trout	.05	.02
202	Rafael Ramirez	.05	.02
203	Bob Walk	.05	.02
204	Roger Mason	.05	.02
205	Terry Kennedy	.05	.02
206	Ron Oester	.05	.02
207	John Russell	.05	.02
208	Greg Mathews	.05	.02
209	Charlie Kerfeld	.05	.02
210	Reggie Jackson	.60	.35
211	Floyd Bannister	.05	.02
212	Vance Law	.05	.02
213	Rich Bordi	.05	.02
214	Dan Plesac	.08	.05
215	Dave Collins	.05	.02
216	Bob Stanley	.05	.02
217	Joe Niekro	.05	.02
218	Tom Niedenfuer	.05	.02
219	Brett Butler	.10	.06
220	Charlie Leibrandt	.05	.02
221	Steve Ontiveros	.05	.02
222	Tim Burke	.05	.02
223	Curtis Wilkerson	.05	.02
224	Pete Incaviglia	.25	.15
225	Lonnie Smith	.05	.02
226	Chris Codiroli	.05	.02
227	Scott Bailes	.05	.02
228	Rickey Henderson	1.00	.70
229	Ken Howell	.05	.02
230	Darnell Coles	.05	.02
231	Don Aase	.05	.02
232	Tim Leary	.05	.02
233	Bob Boone	.10	.06
234	Ricky Horton	.05	.02
235	Mark Bailey	.05	.02
236	Kevin Gross	.05	.02
237	Lance McCullers	.05	.02
238	Cecilio Guante	.05	.02
239	Bob Melvin	.05	.02
240	Billy Jo Robidoux	.05	.02
241	Roger McDowell	.05	.02
242	Leon Durham	.05	.02
243	Ed Nunez	.05	.02
244	Jimmy Key	.08	.05
245	Mike Smithson	.05	.02
246	Bo Diaz	.05	.02
247	Carlton Fisk	.50	.30
248	Larry Sheets	.05	.02
249	Juan Castillo (R)	.08	.05
250	Eric King	.10	.06
251	Doug Drabek	1.00	.70

252	Wade Boggs	.50	.30
253	Mariano Duncan	.15	.08
254	Pat Tabler	.05	.02
255	Frank White	.05	.02
256	Alfredo Griffin	.05	.02
257	Floyd Youmans	.05	.02
258	Rob Wilfong	.05	.02
259	Pete O'Brien	.05	.02
260	Tim Hulett	.05	.02
261	Dickie Thon	.05	.02
262	Darren Daulton	.40	.25
263	Vince Coleman	.20	.12
264	Andy Hawkins	.05	.02
265	Eric Davis	.35	.20
266	Andres Thomas	.07	.04
267	Mike Diaz (R)	.08	.05
268	Chili Davis	.07	.04
269	Jody Davis	.05	.02
270	Phil Bradley	.05	.02
271	George Bell	.25	.15
272	Keith Atherton	.05	.02
273	Storm Davis	.05	.02
274	Rob Deer (R)	.25	.15
275	Walt Terrell	.05	.02
276	Roger Clemens	2.75	1.75
277	Mike Easler	.05	.02
278	Steve Sax	.12	.07
279	Andre Thornton	.05	.02
280	Jim Sundberg	.05	.02
281	Bill Bathe	.05	.02
282	Jay Tibbs	.05	.02
283	Dick Schofield	.05	.02
284	Mike Mason	.05	.02
285	Jerry Hairston	.05	.02
286	Bill Doran	.05	.02
287	Tim Flannery	.05	.02
288	Gary Redus	.05	.02
289	John Franco	.05	.02
290	Paul Assenmacher	.05	.02
291	Joe Orsulak	.07	.04
292	Lee Smith	.30	.18
293	Mike Laga	.05	.02
294	Rick Dempsey	.05	.02
295	Mike Felder	.07	.04
296	Tom Brookens	.05	.02
297	Al Nipper	.05	.02
298	Mike Pagliarulo	.05	.02
299	Franklin Stubbs	.08	.05
300	Checklist 240-345	.08	.05
301	Steve Farr	.07	.04
302	Bill Mooneyham	.05	.02
303	Andres Galarraga	.10	.06
304	Scott Fletcher	.05	.02
305	Jack Howell	.05	.02
306	Russ Morman (R)	.05	.02
307	Todd Worrell	.08	.05
308	Dave Smith	.05	.02
309	Jeff Stone	.05	.02
310	Ron Robinson	.05	.02
311	Bruce Bochy	.05	.02
312	Jim Winn	.05	.02
313	Mark Davis	.05	.02
314	Jeff Dedmon	.05	.02
315	Jamie Moyer (R)	.08	.05
316	Wally Backman	.05	.02
317	Ken Phelps	.05	.02
318	Steve Lombardozzi	.05	.02
319	Rance Mulliniks	.05	.02
320	Tim Laudner	.05	.02
321	Mark Eichhorn	.10	.06
322	Lee Guetterman	.07	.04
323	Sid Fernandez	.12	.07
324	Jerry Mumphrey	.05	.02
325	David Palmer	.05	.02
326	Bill Almon	.05	.02
327	Candy Maldonado	.07	.04
328	John Kruk	1.25	.80
329	John Denny	.05	.02
330	Milt Thompson	.05	.02
331	Mike LaValliere	.25	.15
332	Alan Ashby	.05	.02
333	Doug Corbett	.05	.02
334	Ron Karkovice (R)	.08	.05
335	Mitch Webster	.05	.02
336	Lee Lacy	.05	.02
337	Glenn Braggs (R)	.20	.12
338	Dwight Lowry	.05	.02
339	Don Baylor	.08	.05
340	Brian Fisher	.05	.02
341	Reggie Williams	.05	.02
342	Tom Candiotti	.07	.04
343	Rudy Law	.05	.02
344	Curt Young	.05	.02
345	Mike Fitzgerald	.05	.02
346	Ruben Sierra	7.00	4.00
347	Mitch Williams	.25	.15
348	Jorge Orta	.05	.02
349	Mickey Tettleton	.20	.12
350	Ernie Camacho	.05	.02
351	Ron Kittle	.05	.02
352	Ken Landreaux	.05	.02
353	Chet Lemon	.05	.02
354	John Shelby	.05	.02
355	Mark Clear	.05	.02
356	Doug DeCinces	.05	.02
357	Ken Dayley	.05	.02
358	Phil Garner	.05	.02
359	Steve Jeltz	.05	.02
360	Ed Whitson	.05	.02
361	Barry Bonds	8.50	5.50
362	Vida Blue	.07	.04
363	Cecil Cooper	.05	.02
364	Bob Ojeda	.07	.04
365	Dennis Eckersley	.35	.20
366	Mike Morgan	.05	.02
367	Willie Upshaw	.05	.02

368	Allan Anderson (R)	.12	.07	426	Al Newman	.05	.02
369	Bill Gullickson	.05	.02	427	Gary Ward	.05	.02
370	Bobby Thigpen (R)	.70	.40	428	Ruppert Jones	.05	.02
371	Juan Beniquez	.05	.02	429	Harold Baines	.12	.07
372	Charlie Moore	.05	.02	430	Pat Perry	.05	.02
373	Dan Petry	.05	.02	431	Terry Puhl	.05	.02
374	Rod Scurry	.05	.02	432	Don Carman	.05	.02
375	Tom Seaver	.50	.30	433	Eddie Milner	.05	.02
376	Ed Vande Berg	.05	.02	434	LaMarr Hoyt	.05	.02
377	Tony Bernazard	.05	.02	435	Rick Rhoden	.05	.02
378	Greg Pryor	.05	.02	436	Jose Uribe	.05	.02
379	Dwayne Murphy	.05	.02	437	Ken Oberkfell	.05	.02
380	Andy McGaffigan	.05	.02	438	Ron Davis	.05	.02
381	Kirk McCaskill	.05	.02	439	Jesse Orosco	.05	.02
382	Greg Harris	.05	.02	440	Scott Bradley	.05	.02
383	Rich Dotson	.05	.02	441	Randy Bush	.05	.02
384	Craig Reynolds	.05	.02	442	John Cerutti	.08	.05
385	Greg Gross	.05	.02	443	Roy Smalley	.05	.02
386	Tito Landrum	.05	.02	444	Kelly Gruber	.80	.05
387	Craig Lefferts	.05	.02	445	Bob Kearney	.05	.02
388	Dave Parker	.12	.07	446	Ed Hearn	.05	.02
389	Bob Horner	.08	.05	447	Scott Sanderson	.05	.02
390	Pat Clements	.05	.02	448	Bruce Benedict	.05	.02
391	Jeff Leonard	.05	.02	449	Junior Ortiz	.05	.02
392	Chris Speier	.05	.02	450	Mike Aldrete	.07	.04
393	John Moses	.05	.02	451	Kevin McReynolds	.10	.06
394	Garth Iorg	.05	.02	452	Rob Murphy (R)	.10	.06
395	Greg Gagne	.07	.04	453	Kent Tekulve	.05	.02
396	Nate Snell	.05	.02	454	Curt Ford (R)	.05	.02
397	Bryan Clutterbuck (R)	.05	.02	455	Davey Lopes	.07	.04
398	Darrell Evans	.07	.04	456	Bobby Grich	.07	.04
399	Steve Crawford	.05	.02	457	Jose DeLeon	.05	.02
400	Checklist 346-451	.08	.05	458	Andre Dawson	.50	.30
401	Phil Lombardi (R)	.07	.04	459	Mike Flanagan	.05	.02
402	Rick Honeycutt	.05	.02	460	Joey Meyer (R)	.10	.06
403	Ken Schrom	.05	.02	461	Chuck Cary (R)	.08	.05
404	Bud Black	.05	.02	462	Bill Buckner	.07	.04
405	Donnie Hill	.05	.02	463	Bob Shirley	.05	.02
406	Wayne Krenchicki	.05	.02	464	Jeff Hamilton (R)	.10	.06
407	Chuck Finley (R)	.70	.40	465	Phil Niekro	.20	.12
408	Toby Harrah	.05	.02	466	Mark Gubicza	.12	.07
409	Steve Lyons	.05	.02	467	Jerry Willard	.05	.02
410	Kevin Bass	.05	.02	468	Bob Sebra (R)	.07	.04
411	Marvell Wynne	.05	.02	469	Larry Parrish	.05	.02
412	Ron Roenicke	.05	.02	470	Charlie Hough	.05	.02
413	Tracy Jones	.07	.04	471	Hal McRae	.07	.04
414	Gene Garber	.05	.02	472	Dave Leiper (R)	.07	.04
415	Mike Bielecki	.07	.04	473	Mel Hall	.08	.05
416	Frank DiPino	.05	.02	474	Dan Pasqua	.07	.04
417	Andy Van Slyke	.25	.15	475	Bob Welch	.08	.05
418	Jim Dwyer	.05	.02	476	Johnny Grubb	.05	.02
419	Ben Oglivie	.05	.02	477	Jim Traber	.05	.02
420	Dave Bergman	.05	.02	478	Chris Bosio (R)	.40	.25
421	Joe Sambito	.05	.02	479	Mark McLemore	.05	.02
422	Bob Tewksbury	.25	.15	480	John Morris	.05	.02
423	Len Matuszek	.05	.02	481	Billy Hatcher	.05	.02
424	Mike Kingery (R)	.08	.05	482	Dan Schatzeder	.05	.02
425	Dave Kingman	.07	.04	483	Rich Gossage	.08	.05

#	Player		
484	Jim Morrison	.05	.02
485	Bob Brenly	.05	.02
486	Bill Schroeder	.05	.02
487	Mookie Wilson	.05	.02
488	Dave Martinez (R)	.25	.15
489	Harold Reynolds	.08	.05
490	Jeff Hearron	.05	.02
491	Mickey Hatcher	.05	.02
492	Barry Larkin (R)	3.50	2.25
493	Bob James	.05	.02
494	John Habyan	.05	.02
495	Jim Adduci (R)	.05	.02
496	Mike Heath	.05	.02
497	Tim Stoddard	.05	.02
498	Tony Armas	.05	.02
499	Dennis Powell	.05	.02
500	Checklist 452-557	.08	.05
501	Chris Bando	.05	.02
502	David Cone (R)	4.00	2.75
503	Jay Howell	.05	.02
504	Tom Foley	.05	.02
505	Ray Chadwick (R)	.05	.02
506	Mike Loynd (R)	.05	.02
507	Neil Allen	.05	.02
508	Danny Darwin	.05	.02
509	Rick Schu	.05	.02
510	Jose Oquendo	.05	.02
511	Gene Walter	.05	.02
512	Terry McGriff (R)	.05	.02
513	Ken Griffey	.08	.05
514	Benny Distefano	.05	.02
515	Terry Mulholland (R)	.40	.25
516	Ed Lynch	.05	.02
517	Bill Swift	.12	.07
518	Manny Lee (R)	.08	.05
519	Andre David	.05	.02
520	Scott McGregor	.05	.02
521	Rick Manning	.05	.02
522	Willie Hernandez	.05	.02
523	Marty Barrett	.05	.02
524	Wayne Tolleson	.05	.02
525	Jose Gonzalez (R)	.08	.05
526	Cory Snyder	.08	.05
527	Buddy Biancalana	.05	.02
528	Moose Haas	.05	.02
529	Wilfredo Tejada (R)	.07	.04
530	Stu Cliburn	.05	.02
531	Dale Mohorcic (R)	.08	.05
532	Ron Hassey	.05	.02
533	Ty Gainey	.05	.02
534	Jerry Royster	.05	.02
535	Mike Maddux (R)	.07	.04
536	Ted Power	.05	.02
537	Ted Simmons	.07	.04
538	Rafael Belliard (R)	.20	.12
539	Chico Walker	.08	.05
540	Bob Forsch	.05	.02
541	John Stefero	.05	.02
542	Dale Sveum	.08	.05
543	Mark Thurmond	.05	.02
544	Jeff Sellers	.07	.04
545	Joel Skinner	.05	.02
546	Alex Trevino	.05	.02
547	Randy Kutcher (R)	.07	.04
548	Joaquin Andujar	.05	.02
549	Casey Candaele (R)	.08	.05
550	Jeff Russell	.08	.05
551	John Candelaria	.05	.02
552	Joe Cowley	.05	.02
553	Danny Cox	.05	.02
554	Denny Walling	.05	.02
555	Bruce Ruffin (R)	.10	.06
556	Buddy Bell	.05	.02
557	Jimmy Jones (R)	.10	.06
558	Bobby Bonilla	4.50	2.75
559	Jeff Robinson	.05	.02
560	Ed Olwine	.05	.02
561	Glenallen Hill (R)	.30	.18
562	Lee Mazzilli	.05	.02
563	Mike Brown	.05	.02
564	George Frazier	.05	.02
565	Mike Sharperson (R)	.10	.06
566	Mark Portugal	.15	.08
567	Rick Leach	.05	.02
568	Mark Langston	.25	.15
569	Rafael Santana	.05	.02
570	Manny Trillo	.05	.02
571	Cliff Speck	.05	.02
572	Bob Kipper	.05	.02
573	Kelly Downs (R)	.12	.07
574	Randy Asadoor (R)	.05	.02
575	Dave Magadan (R)	.70	.40
576	Marvin Freeman (R)	.08	.05
577	Jeff Lahti	.05	.02
578	Jeff Calhoun	.05	.02
579	Gus Polidor (R)	.05	.02
580	Gene Nelson	.05	.02
581	Tim Teufel	.05	.02
582	Odell Jones	.05	.02
583	Mark Ryal	.05	.02
584	Randy O'Neal	.05	.02
585	Mike Greenwell (R)	1.50	.90
586	Ray Knight	.05	.02
587	Ralph Bryant (R)	.07	.04
588	Carmen Castillo	.05	.02
589	Ed Wojna	.05	.02
590	Stan Javier	.07	.04
591	Jeff Musselman (R)	.07	.04
592	Mike Stanley (R)	.10	.06
593	Darrell Porter	.05	.02
594	Drew Hall (R)	.07	.04
595	Rob Nelson (R)	.07	.04
596	Bryan Oelkers	.05	.02
597	Scott Nielsen (R)	.07	.04
598	Brian Holton (R)	.08	.05
599	Kevin Mitchell	3.00	2.00

600	Checklist 558-660	.08	.05
601	Jackie Gutierrez	.05	.02
602	Barry Jones (R)	.10	.06
603	Jerry Narron	.05	.02
604	Steve Lake	.05	.02
605	Jim Pankovits	.05	.02
606	Ed Romero	.05	.02
607	Dave LaPoint	.05	.02
608	Don Robinson	.05	.02
609	Mike Krukow	.05	.02
610	Dave Valle (R)	.07	.04
611	Len Dykstra	.20	.12
612	Roberto Clemente Puzzle Card	.15	.08
613	Mike Trujillo (R)	.05	.02
614	Damaso Garcia	.05	.02
615	Neal Heaton	.05	.02
616	Juan Berenguer	.05	.02
617	Steve Carlton	.60	.35
618	Gary Lucas	.05	.02
619	Geno Petralli	.05	.02
620	Rick Aguilera	.12	.07
621	Fred McGriff	4.50	3.00
622	Dave Henderson	.10	.06
623	Dave Clark (R)	.10	.06
624	Angel Salazar	.05	.02
625	Randy Hunt	.05	.02
626	John Gibbons	.05	.02
627	Kevin Brown (R)	2.00	1.25
628	Bill Dawley	.05	.02
629	Aurelio Lopez	.05	.02
630	Charlie Hudson	.05	.02
631	Ray Soff	.05	.02
632	Ray Hayward (R)	.05	.02
633	Spike Owen	.05	.02
634	Glenn Hubbard	.05	.02
635	Kevin Elster (R)	.12	.07
636	Mike LaCoss	.05	.02
637	Dwayne Henry	.05	.02
638	Rey Quinones	.05	.02
639	Jim Clancy	.05	.02
640	Larry Andersen	.05	.02
641	Calvin Schiraldi	.05	.02
642	Stan Jefferson (R)	.07	.04
643	Marc Sullivan	.05	.02
644	Mark Grant	.05	.02
645	Cliff Johnson	.05	.02
646	Howard Johnson	.25	.15
647	Dave Sax	.05	.02
648	Dave Stewart	.15	.08
649	Danny Heep	.05	.02
650	Joe Johnson	.05	.02
651	Bob Brower (R)	.05	.02
652	Rob Woodward	.05	.02
653	John Mizerock	.05	.02
654	Tim Pyznarski (R)	.05	.02
655	Luis Aquino (R)	.08	.05
656	Mickey Brantley (R)	.08	.05

657	Doyle Alexander	.05	.02
658	Sammy Stewart	.05	.02
659	Jim Acker	.05	.02
660	Pete Ladd	.05	.02

1987 Donruss Rookies

This 56-card update set features green borders on the card fronts and a small "rookies" logo at the bottom corner of the card. Cards measure 2-1/2" by 3-1/2".

		MINT	NR/MT
Complete Set (56)		24.00	16.00
Commons		.08	.05
1	Mark McGwire	5.00	3.00
2	Eric Bell	.08	.05
3	Mark Williamson (R)	.12	.07
4	Mike Greenwell	.80	.50
5	Ellis Burks (R)	.90	.60
6	DeWayne Buice (R)	.08	.05
7	Mark McLemore	.08	.05
8	Devon White	.25	.15
9	Willie Fraser	.08	.05
10	Les Lancaster (R)	.15	.08
11	Ken Williams (R)	.12	.07
12	Matt Nokes (R)	.35	.20
13	Jeff Robinson (R)	.10	.06
14	Bo Jackson	1.75	1.00
15	Kevin Seitzer (R)	.30	.18
16	Billy Ripken (R)	.15	.08
17	B.J. Surhoff	.12	.07
18	Chuck Crim (R)	.10	.06
19	Mike Birbeck	.08	.05
20	Chris Bosio	.20	.12
21	Les Straker (R)	.10	.06

22	Mark Davidson (R)	.10	.06
23	Gene Larkin (R)	.20	.12
24	Ken Gerhart	.08	.05
25	Luis Polonia (R)	.60	.35
26	Terry Steinbach	.20	.12
27	Mickey Brantley	.10	.06
28	Mike Stanley	.10	.06
29	Jerry Browne	.10	.06
30	Todd Benzinger (R)	.20	.12
31	Fred McGriff	4.50	2.75
32	Mike Henneman (R)	.25	.15
33	Casey Candaele	.10	.06
34	Dave Magadan	.20	.12
35	David Cone	2.00	1.25
36	Mike Jackson (R)	.20	.12
37	John Mitchell (R)	.08	.05
38	Mike Dunne (R)	.10	.06
39	John Smiley (R)	1.25	.80
40	Joe Magrane (R)	.25	.15
41	Jim Lindeman	.08	.05
42	Shane Mack (R)	1.00	.70
43	Stan Jefferson	.10	.06
44	Benito Santiago	.50	.30
45	Matt Williams (R)	3.50	2.25
46	Dave Meads (R)	.10	.06
47	Rafael Palmeiro	2.75	1.75
48	Bill Long (R)	.10	.06
49	Bob Brower	.08	.05
50	James Steels (R)	.08	.05
51	Paul Noce (R)	.08	.05
52	Greg Maddux	1.75	1.00
53	Jeff Musselman	.10	.06
54	Brian Holton	.10	.06
55	Chuck Jackson (R)	.10	.06
56	Checklist 1-56	.08	.05

1988 Donruss

The cards in this 660-card set feature black borders with blue and red accents. The cards measure 2-1/2" by 3-1/2". Diamond Kings (1-26) and Rated Rookies (28-47) are the two major subsets. The checklists are numbered for the second straight year and a variation exists reflecting the inclusion of Bonus MVP cards. The 26 MVP insert bonus cards were randomly packed into Donruss wax packs. Those bonus cards are listed at the end of the checklist. Puzzle pieces were distributed with the cards and feature Stan Musial.

		MINT	NR/MT
Complete Set (660)		20.00	14.00
Commons		.05	.02

1	Mark McGwire (DK)	.40	.25
2	Tim Raines (DK)	.08	.05
3	Benito Santiago (DK)	.10	.06
4	Alan Trammell (DK)	.10	.06
5	Danny Tartabull (DK)	.10	.06
6	Ron Darling (DK)	.07	.04
7	Paul Molitor (DK)	.08	.05
8	Devon White (DK)	.07	.04
9	Andre Dawson (DK)	.12	.07
10	Julio Franco (DK)	.10	.06
11	Scott Fletcher (DK)	.05	.02
12	Tony Fernandez (DK)	.07	.04
13	Shane Rawley (DK)	.05	.02
14	Kal Daniels (DK)	.07	.04
15	Jack Clark (DK)	.08	.05
16	Dwight Evans (DK)	.08	.05
17	Tommy John (DK)	.07	.04
18	Andy Van Slyke (DK)	.10	.06
19	Gary Gaetti (DK)	.05	.02
20	Mark Langston (DK)	.10	.06
21	Will Clark (DK)	.35	.20
22	Glenn Hubbard (DK)	.05	.02

#	Player		
23	Billy Hatcher (DK)	.05	.02
24	Bob Welch (DK)	.08	.05
25	Ivan Calderson (DK)	.07	.04
26	Cal Ripken, Jr. (DK)	.40	.25
27	Checklist 1-27	.05	.02
28	Mackey Sasser (R)	.10	.06
29	Jeff Treadway (R)	.10	.06
30	Mike Campbell (R)	.05	.02
31	Lance Johnson (R)	.20	.12
32	Nelson Liriano (R)	.08	.05
33	Shawn Abner (R)	.07	.04
34	Roberto Alomar (R)	7.50	4.50
35	Shawn Hillegas (R)	.07	.04
36	Joey Meyer	.05	.02
37	Kevin Elster	.07	.04
38	Jose Lind (R)	.12	.07
39	Kirt Manwaring	.10	.06
40	Mark Grace (R)	1.75	1.00
41	Jody Reed (R)	.25	.15
42	John Farrell (R)	.08	.05
43	Al Leiter (R)	.07	.04
44	Gary Thurman (R)	.10	.06
45	Vicente Palacios (R)	.10	.06
46	Eddie Williams (R)	.05	.02
47	Jack McDowell (R)	2.00	1.25
48	Ken Dixon	.05	.02
49	Mike Birkbeck	.05	.02
50	Eric King	.05	.02
51	Roger Clemens	.60	.35
52	Pat Clements	.05	.02
53	Fernando Valenzuela	.08	.05
54	Mrk Gubicza	.08	.05
55	Jay Howell	.05	.02
56	Floyd Youmans	.05	.02
57	Ed Correa	.05	.02
58	DeWayne Buice	.05	.02
59	Jose DeLeon	.05	.02
60	Danny Cox	.05	.02
61	Nolan Ryan	.80	.50
62	Steve Bedrosian	.05	.02
63	Tom Browning	.07	.04
64	Mark Davis	.05	.02
65	R.J. Reynolds	.05	.02
66	Kevin Mitchell	.20	.12
67	Ken Oberkfell	.05	.02
68	Rick Sutcliffe	.07	.04
69	Dwight Gooden	.15	.08
70	Scott Bankhead	.05	.02
71	Bert Blyleven	.15	.08
72	Jimmy Key	.07	.04
73	Les Straker	.05	.02
74	Jim Clancy	.05	.02
75	Mike Moore	.05	.02
76	Ron Darling	.07	.04
77	Ed Lynch	.05	.02
78	Dale Murphy	.12	.07
79	Doug Drabek	.12	.07
80	Scott Garrelts	.05	.02
81	Ed Whitson	.05	.02
82	Rob Murphy	.05	.02
83	Shane Rawley	.05	.02
84	Greg Mathews	.05	.02
85	Jim Deshaies	.05	.02
86	Mike Witt	.05	.02
87	Donnie Hill	.05	.02
88	Jeff Reed	.05	.02
89	Mike Boddicker	.05	.02
90	Ted Higuera	.05	.02
91	Walt Terrell	.05	.02
92	Bob Stanley	.05	.02
93	Dave Righetti	.07	.04
94	Orel Hershiser	.10	.06
95	Chris Bando	.05	.02
96	Bret Saberhagen	.15	.08
97	Curt Young	.05	.02
98	Tim Burke	.05	.02
99	Charlie Hough	.05	.02
100a	Checklist 28-137	.05	.02
100b	Checklist 28-133	.05	.02
101	Bobby Witt	.08	.05
102	George Brett	.35	.20
103	Mickey Tettleton	.10	.06
104	Scott Bailes	.05	.02
105	Mike Pagliarulo	.05	.02
106	Mike Scioscia	.05	.02
107	Tom Brookens	.05	.02
108	Ray Knight	.05	.02
109	Dan Plesac	.05	.02
110	Wally Joyner	.15	.08
111	Bob Forsch	.05	.02
112	Mike Scott	.07	.04
113	Kevin Gross	.05	.02
114	Benito Santiago	.10	.06
115	Bob Kipper	.05	.02
116	Mike Krukow	.05	.02
117	Chris Bosio	.10	.06
118	Sid Fernandez	.07	.04
119	Jody Davis	.05	.02
120	Mike Morgan	.05	.02
121	Mark Eichhorn	.05	.02
122	Jeff Reardon	.25	.15
123	John Franco	.05	.02
124	Richard Dotson	.05	.02
125	Eric Bell	.05	.02
126	Juan Nieves	.05	.02
127	Jack Morris	.12	.07
128	Rick Rhoden	.05	.02
129	Rich Gedman	.05	.02
130	Ken Howell	.05	.02
131	Brook Jacoby	.05	.02
132	Danny Jackson	.05	.02
133	Gene Nelson	.05	.02
134	Neal Heaton	.05	.02
135	Willie Fraser	.05	.02
136	Jose Guzman	.07	.04
137	Ozzie Guillen	.08	.05

138	Bob Knepper	.05	.02
139	Mike Jackson	.08	.05
140	Joe Magrane	.07	.04
141	Jimmy Jones	.07	.04
142	Ted Power	.05	.02
143	Ozzie Virgil	.05	.02
144	Felix Fermin (R)	.05	.02
145	Kelly Downs	.07	.04
146	Shawon Dunston	.12	.07
147	Scott Bradley	.05	.02
148	Dave Stieb	.07	.04
149	Frank Viola	.08	.05
150	Terry Kennedy	.05	.02
151	Bill Wegman	.05	.02
152	Matt Nokes	.15	.08
153	Wade Boggs	.25	.15
154	Wayne Tolleson	.05	.02
155	Mariano Duncan	.05	.02
156	Julio Franco	.12	.07
157	Charlie Leibrandt	.05	.02
158	Terry Steinbach	.07	.04
159	Mike Fitzgerald	.05	.02
160	Jack Lazorko	.05	.02
161	Mitch Williams	.05	.02
162	Greg Walker	.05	.02
163	Alan Ashby	.05	.02
164	Tony Gwynn	.30	.18
165	Bruce Ruffin	.05	.02
166	Ron Robinson	.05	.02
167	Zane Smith	.05	.02
168	Junior Ortiz	.05	.02
169	Jamie Moyer	.05	.02
170	Tony Pena	.05	.02
171	Cal Ripken	.70	.40
172	B.J. Surhoff	.07	.04
173	Lou Whitaker	.07	.04
174	Ellis Burks	.25	.15
175	Ron Guidry	.07	.04
176	Steve Sax	.08	.05
177	Danny Tartabull	.15	.08
178	Carney Lansford	.07	.04
179	Casey Candaele	.05	.02
180	Scott Fletcher	.05	.02
181	Mark McLemore	.05	.02
182	Ivan Calderon	.07	.04
183	Jack Clark	.07	.04
184	Glenn Davis	.07	.04
185	Luis Aguayo	.05	.02
186	Bo Diaz	.05	.02
187	Stan Jefferson	.05	.02
188	Sid Bream	.05	.02
189	Bob Brenly	.05	.02
190	Dion James	.05	.02
191	Leon Durham	.05	.02
192	Jesse Orosco	.05	.02
193	Alvin Davis	.05	.02
194	Gary Gaetti	.07	.04
195	Fred McGriff	.60	.35
196	Steve Lombardozzi	.05	.02
197	Rance Mulliniks	.05	.02
198	Rey Quinones	.05	.02
199	Gary Carter	.10	.06
200a	Checklist 138-247	.05	.02
200b	Checklist 134-239	.05	.02
201	Keith Moreland	.05	.02
202	Ken Griffey	.08	.05
203	Tommy Gregg (R)	.07	.04
204	Will Clark	.80	.50
205	John Kruk	.15	.08
206	Buddy Bell	.05	.02
207	Von Hayes	.05	.02
208	Tommy Herr	.05	.02
209	Craig Reynolds	.05	.02
210	Gary Pettis	.05	.02
211	Harold Baines	.07	.04
212	Vance Law	.05	.02
213	Ken Gerhart	.05	.02
214	Jim Gantner	.05	.02
215	Chet Lemon	.05	.02
216	Dwight Evans	.07	.04
217	Don Mattingly	.25	.15
218	Franklin Stubbs	.05	.02
219	Pat Tabler	.05	.02
220	Bo Jackson	.25	.15
221	Tony Phillips	.05	.02
222	Tim Wallach	.07	.04
223	Ruben Sierra	.40	.25
224	Steve Buechele	.05	.02
225	Frank White	.05	.02
226	Alfredo Griffin	.05	.02
227	Greg Swindell	.12	.07
228	Willie Randolph	.07	.04
229	Mike Marshall	.05	.02
230	Alan Trammell	.10	.06
231	Eddie Murray	.25	.15
232	Dale Sveum	.05	.02
233	Dick Schofield	.05	.02
234	Jose Oquendo	.05	.02
235	Bill Doran	.05	.02
236	Milt Thompson	.05	.02
237	Marvell Wynne	.05	.02
238	Bobby Bonilla	.25	.15
239	Chris Speier	.05	.02
240	Glenn Braggs	.05	.02
241	Wally Backman	.05	.02
242	Ryne Sandberg	.50	.30
243	Phil Bradley	.05	.02
244	Kelly Gruber	.10	.06
245	Tom Brunansky	.07	.04
246	Ron Oester	.05	.02
247	Bobby Thigpen	.07	.04
248	Fred Lynn	.07	.04
249	Paul Molitor	.12	.07
250	Darrell Evans	.07	.04
251	Gary Ward	.05	.02
252	Bruce Hurst	.08	.05

#	Player		
253	Bob Welch	.07	.04
254	Joe Carter	.25	.15
255	Willie Wilson	.05	.02
256	Mark McGwire	.60	.35
257	Mitch Webster	.05	.02
258	Brian Downing	.05	.02
259	Mike Stanley	.05	.02
260	Carlton Fisk	.20	.12
261	Billy Hatcher	.05	.02
262	Glenn Wilson	.05	.02
263	Ozzie Smith	.20	.12
264	Randy Ready	.05	.02
265	Kurt Stillwell	.05	.02
266	David Palmer	.05	.02
267	Mike Diaz	.05	.02
268	Robby Thompson	.07	.04
269	Andre Dawson	.25	.15
270	Lee Guetterman	.05	.02
271	Willie Upshaw	.05	.02
272	Randy Bush	.05	.02
273	Larry Sheets	.05	.02
274	Rob Deer	.07	.04
275	Kirk Gibson	.07	.04
276	Marty Barrett	.05	.02
277	Rickey Henderson	.35	.20
278	Pedro Guerrero	.05	.02
279	Brett Butler	.08	.05
280	Kevin Seitzer	.07	.04
281	Mike Davis	.05	.02
282	Andres Galarraga	.08	.05
283	Devon White	.07	.04
284	Pete O'Brien	.05	.02
285	Jerry Hairston	.05	.02
286	Kevin Bass	.05	.02
287	Carmelo Martinez	.05	.02
288	Juan Samuel	.05	.02
289	Kal Daniels	.07	.04
290	Albert Hall	.05	.02
291	Andy Van Slyke	.10	.06
292	Lee Smith	.20	.12
293	Vince Coleman	.07	.04
294	Tom Niedenfuer	.05	.02
295	Robin Yount	.35	.20
296	Jeff Robinson	.05	.02
297	Todd Benzinger	.12	.07
298	Dave Winfield	.25	.15
299	Mickey Hatcher	.05	.02
300a	Checklist 248-357	.05	.02
300b	Checklist 240-345	.05	.02
301	Bud Black	.05	.02
302	Jose Canseco	.75	.45
303	Tom Foley	.05	.02
304	Pete Incaviglia	.07	.04
305	Bob Boone	.07	.04
306	Bill Long	.05	.02
307	Willie McGee	.07	.04
308	Ken Caminiti (R)	.25	.15
309	Darren Daulton	.15	.08
310	Tracy Jones	.05	.02
311	Greg Booker	.05	.02
312	Mike LaValliere	.05	.02
313	Chili Davis	.07	.04
314	Glenn Hubbard	.05	.02
315	Paul Noce	.05	.02
316	Keith Hernandez	.07	.04
317	Mark Langston	.12	.07
318	Keith Atherton	.05	.02
319	Tony Fernandez	.08	.05
320	Kent Hrbek	.08	.05
321	John Cerutti	.05	.02
322	Mike Kingery	.05	.02
323	Dave Magadan	.07	.04
324	Rafael Palmeiro	.35	.20
325	Jeff Dedmon	.05	.02
326	Barry Bonds	.60	.35
327	Jeffrey Leonard	.05	.02
328	Tim Flannery	.05	.02
329	Dave Concepcion	.07	.04
330	Mike Schmidt	.50	.30
331	Bill Dawley	.05	.02
332	Larry Andersen	.05	.02
333	Jack Howell	.05	.02
334	Ken Williams	.05	.02
335	Bryn Smith	.05	.02
336	Billy Ripken	.07	.04
337	Greg Brock	.05	.02
338	Mike Heath	.05	.02
339	Mike Greenwell	.10	.06
340	Claudell Washington	.05	.02
341	Jose Gonzalez	.05	.02
342	Mel Hall	.07	.04
343	Jim Eisenreich	.05	.02
344	Tony Bernazard	.05	.02
345	Tim Raines	.07	.04
346	Bob Brower	.05	.02
347	Larry Parrish	.05	.02
348	Thad Bosley	.05	.02
349	Dennis Eckersley	.20	.12
350	Cory Snyder	.07	.04
351	Rick Cerone	.05	.02
352	John Shelby	.05	.02
353	Larry Herndon	.05	.02
354	John Habyan	.05	.02
355	Chuck Crim	.05	.02
356	Gus Polidor	.05	.02
357	Ken Dayley	.05	.02
358	Danny Darwin	.07	.04
359	Lance Parrish	.05	.02
360	James Steels	.05	.02
361	Al Pedrique (R)	.05	.02
362	Mike Aldrete	.05	.02
363	Juan Castillo	.05	.02
364	Len Dykstra	.07	.04
365	Luis Quinones	.05	.02
366	Jim Presley	.05	.02
367	Lloyd Moseby	.05	.02

368	Kirby Puckett	.50	.30	425	Luis Polonia	.25	.15
369	Eric Davis	.15	.08	426	Randy St. Claire	.05	.02
370	Gary Redus	.05	.02	427	Greg Harris	.05	.02
371	Dave Schmidt	.05	.02	428	Johnny Ray	.05	.02
372	Mark Clear	.05	.02	429	Ray Searage	.05	.02
373	Dave Bergman	.05	.02	430	Ricky Horton	.05	.02
374	Charles Hudson	.05	.02	431	Gerald Young (R)	.10	.06
375	Calvin Schiraldi	.05	.02	432	Rick Schu	.05	.02
376	Alex Trevino	.05	.02	433	Paul O'Neill	.10	.06
377	Tom Candiotti	.05	.02	434	Rich Gossage	.07	.04
378	Steve Farr	.05	.02	435	John Cangelosi	.05	.02
279	Mike Gallego	.05	.02	436	Mike LaCoss	.05	.02
380	Andy McGaffigan	.05	.02	437	Gerald Perry	.05	.02
381	Kirk McCaskill	.05	.02	438	Dave Martinez	.05	.02
382	Oddibe McDowell	.05	.02	439	Darryl Strawberry	.30	.18
383	Floyd Bannister	.05	.02	440	John Moses	.05	.02
384	Denny Walling	.05	.02	441	Greg Gagne	.05	.02
385	Don Carman	.05	.02	442	Jesse Barfield	.07	.04
386	Todd Worrell	.08	.05	443	George Frazier	.05	.02
387	Eric Show	.05	.02	444	Garth Iorg	.05	.02
388	Dave Parker	.07	.04	445	Ed Nunez	.05	.02
389	Rick Mahler	.05	.02	446	Rick Aguilera	.07	.04
390	Mike Dunne	.05	.02	447	Jerry Mumphrey	.05	.02
391	Candy Maldonado	.05	.02	448	Rafael Ramirez	.05	.02
392	Bob Dernier	.05	.02	449	John Smiley	.40	.25
393	Dave Valle	.05	.02	450	Atlee Hammaker	.05	.02
394	Ernie Whitt	.05	.02	451	Lance McCullers	.05	.02
395	Juan Berenguer	.05	.02	452	Guy Hoffman (R)	.05	.02
396	Mike Young	.05	.02	453	Chris James	.05	.02
397	Mike Felder	.05	.02	454	Terry Pendleton	.20	.12
398	Willie Hernandez	.05	.02	455	Dave Meads	.05	.02
399	Jim Rice	.07	.04	456	Bill Buckner	.07	.04
400a	Checklist 358-467	.05	.02	457	John Pawlowski (R)	.05	.02
400b	Checklist 346-451	.05	.02	458	Bob Sebra	.05	.02
401	Tommy John	.07	.04	459	Jim Dwyer	.05	.02
402	Brian Holton	.05	.02	460	Jay Aldrich (R)	.05	.02
403	Carmen Castillo	.05	.02	461	Frank Tanana	.07	.04
404	Jamie Quirk	.05	.02	462	Oil Can Boyd	.05	.02
405	Dwayne Murphy	.05	.02	463	Dan Pasqua	.07	.04
406	Jeff Parrett (R)	.07	.04	464	Tim Crews (R)	.12	.07
407	Don Sutton	.12	.07	465	Andy Allanson	.05	.02
408	Jerry Browne	.05	.02	466	Bill Pecota (R)	.10	.06
409	Jim Winn	.05	.02	467	Steve Ontiveros	.05	.02
410	Dave Smith	.05	.02	468	Hubie Brooks	.08	.05
411	Shane Mack	.20	.12	469	Paul Kilgus (R)	.07	.04
412	Greg Gross	.05	.02	470	Dale Mohorcic	.05	.02
413	Nick Esasky	.05	.02	471	Dan Quisenberry	.05	.02
414	Damaso Garcia	.05	.02	472	Dave Stewart	.08	.05
415	Brian Fisher	.05	.02	473	Dave Clark	.05	.02
416	Brian Dayett	.05	.02	474	Joel Skinner	.05	.02
417	Curt Ford	.05	.02	475	Dave Anderson	.05	.02
418	Mark Williamson	.08	.05	476	Dan Petry	.05	.02
419	Bill Schroeder	.05	.02	477	Carl Nichols (R)	.05	.02
420	Mike Henneman	.12	.08	478	Ernest Riles	.05	.02
421	John Marzano (R)	.07	.04	479	George Hendrick	.05	.02
422	Ron Kittle	.05	.02	480	John Morris	.05	.02
423	Matt Young	.05	.02	481	Manny Hernandez (R)	.05	.02
424	Steve Balboni	.05	.02	482	Jeff Stone	.05	.02

483	Chris Brown	.05	.02	540	Jim Lindeman	.05	.02
484	Mike Bielecki	.07	.04	541	Pete Stanicek (R)	.05	.02
485	Dave Dravecky	.05	.02	542	Steve Kiefer	.05	.02
486	Rick Manning	.05	.02	543	Jim Morrison	.05	.02
487	Bill Almon	.05	.02	544	Spike Owen	.05	.02
488	Jim Sundberg	.05	.02	545	Jan Buhner (R)	.35	.20
489	Ken Phelps	.05	.02	546	Mike Devereaux (R)	.60	.35
490	Tom Henke	.07	.04	547	Jerry Don Gleaton	.05	.02
491	Dan Gladden	.05	.02	548	Jose Rijo	.12	.07
492	Barry Larkin	.20	.12	549	Dennis Martinez	.10	.06
493	Fred Manrique (R)	.07	.04	550	Mike Loynd	.05	.02
494	Mike Griffin	.05	.02	551	Darrell Miller	.05	.02
495	Mark Knudson (R)	.10	.06	552	Dave LaPoint	.05	.02
496	Bill Madlock	.08	.05	553	John Tudor	.05	.02
497	Tim Stoddard	.05	.02	554	Rocky Childress (R)	.07	.04
498	Sam Horn (R)	.15	.08	555	Wally Ritchie (R)	.08	.05
499	Tracy Woodson (R)	.10	.06	556	Terry McGriff	.05	.02
500a	Checklist 468-577	.05	.02	557	Dave Leiper	.05	.02
500b	Checklist 452-557	.05	.02	558	Jeff Robinson	.05	.02
501	Ken Schrom	.05	.02	559	Jose Uribe	.05	.02
502	Angel Salazar	.05	.02	560	Ted Simmons	.07	.04
503	Eric Plunk	.07	.04	561	Les Lancaster	.07	.04
504	Joe Hesketh	.05	.02	562	Keith Miller (R)	.08	.05
505	Greg Minton	.05	.02	563	Harold Reynolds	.07	.04
506	Geno Petralli	.05	.02	564	Gene Larkin	.08	.05
507	Bob James	.05	.02	565	Cecil Fielder	.35	.20
508	Robbie Wine (R)	.05	.02	566	Roy Smalley	.05	.02
509	Jeff Calhoun	.05	.02	567	Duane Ward	.05	.02
510	Steve Lake	.05	.02	568	Bill Wilkinson (R)	.07	.04
511	Mark Grant	.05	.02	569	Howard Johnson	.15	.08
512	Frank Williams	.05	.02	570	Frank DiPino	.05	.02
513	Jeff Blauser (R)	.15	.08	571	Pete Smith (R)	.30	.18
514	Bob Walk	.05	.02	572	Darnell Coles	.05	.02
515	Craig Lefferts	.05	.02	573	Don Robinson	.05	.02
516	Manny Trillo	.05	.02	574	Rob Nelson	.05	.02
517	Jerry Reed	.05	.02	575	Dennis Rasmussen	.05	.02
518	Rick Leach	.05	.02	576	Steve Jeltz (Er)	.05	.02
519	Mark Davidson	.07	.04		(Wrong Photo)		
520	Jeff Ballard (R)	.10	.06	577	Tom Pagnozzi (R)	.35	.20
521	Dave Stapleton (R)	.07	.04	578	Ty Gainey	.05	.02
522	Pat Sheridan	.05	.02	579	Gary Lucas	.05	.02
523	Al Nipper	.05	.02	580	Ron Hassey	.05	.02
524	Steve Trout	.05	.02	581	Herm Winningham	.05	.02
525	Jeff Hamilton	.05	.02	582	Rene Gonzales (R)	.07	.04
526	Tommy Hinzo (R)	.05	.02	583	Brad Komminsk	.05	.02
527	Lonnie Smith	.05	.02	584	Doyle Alexander	.05	.02
528	Greg Cadaret (R)	.08	.05	585	Jeff Sellers	.05	.02
529	Rob McClure (Bob)	.05	.02	586	Bill Gullickson	.05	.02
530	Chuck Finley	.12	.07	587	Tim Belcher	.15	.08
531	Jeff Russell	.07	.04	588	Doug Jones (R)	.20	.12
532	Steve Lyons	.05	.02	589	Melido Perez (R)	.35	.20
533	Terry Puhl	.05	.02	590	Rick Honeycutt	.05	.02
534	Eric Nolte (R)	.07	.04	591	Pascual Perez	.05	.02
535	Kent Tekulve	.05	.02	592	Curt Wilkerson	.05	.02
536	Pat Pacillo (R)	.05	.02	593	Steve Howe	.05	.02
537	Charlie Puleo	.05	.02	594	John Davis (R)	.05	.02
538	Tom Prince (R)	.08	.05	595	Storm Davis	.05	.02
539	Greg Maddux	.30	.18	596	Sammy Stewart	.05	.02

597	Neil Allen	.05	.02
598	Alejandro Pena	.05	.02
599	Mark Thurmond	.05	.02
600a	Checklist 578-BC26	.05	.02
600b	Checklist 558-660	.05	.02
601	Jose Mesa (R)	.08	.05
602	Don August (R)	.07	.04
603	Terry Leach	.05	.02
604	Tom Newell (R)	.05	.02
605	Randall Byers (R)	.05	.02
606	Jim Gott	.05	.02
607	Harry Spilman	.05	.02
608	John Candelaria	.05	.02
609	Mike Brumley (R)	.07	.04
610	Mickey Brantley	.05	.02
611	Jose Nunez (R)	.07	.04
612	Tom Nieto	.05	.02
613	Rick Reuschel	.05	.02
614	Lee Mazzilli	.05	.02
615	Scott Lusader (R)	.07	.04
616	Bobby Meacham	.05	.02
617	Kevin McReynolds	.08	.05
618	Gene Garber	.05	.02
619	Barry Lyons (R)	.10	.06
620	Randy Myers	.05	.02
621	Donnie Moore	.05	.02
622	Domingo Ramos	.05	.02
623	Ed Romero	.05	.02
624	Greg Myers (R)	.08	.05
625	Ripken Family	.30	.18
626	Pat Perry	.05	.02
627	Andres Thomas	.05	.02
628	Matt Williams	1.50	.90
629	Dave Hengel (R)	.05	.02
630	Jeff Musselman	.05	.02
631	Tim Laudner	.05	.02
632	Bob Ojeda	.07	.04
633	Rafael Santana	.05	.02
634	Wes Gardner (R)	.10	.06
635	Roberto Kelly (R)	1.50	.90
636	Mike Flanagan	.05	.02
637	Jay Bell (R)	.25	.15
638	Bob Melvin	.05	.02
639	Damon Berryhill (R)	.10	.06
640	David Wells (R)	.15	.08
641	Stan Musial Puzzle	.15	.08
642	Doug Sisk	.05	.02
643	Keith Hughes (R)	.05	.02
644	Tom Glavine (R)	3.50	2.25
645	Al Newman	.05	.02
646	Scott Sanderson	.05	.02
647	Scott Terry	.05	.02
648	Tim Teufel	.05	.02
649	Garry Templeton	.05	.02
650	Manny Lee	.05	.02
651	Roger McDowell	.05	.02
652	Mookie Wilson	.05	.02
653	David Cone	.60	.35
654	Ron Gant (R)	4.00	2.75
655	Joe Price	.05	.02
656	George Bell	.15	.08
657	Gregg Jefferies (R)	1.25	.80
658	Todd Stottlemyre (R)	.30	.18
659	Geronimo Berroa (R)	.10	.06
660	Jerry Royster	.05	.02
B1	Cal Ripken (MVP)	.40	.25
B2	Eric Davis (MVP)	.12	.07
B3	Paul Molitor (MVP)	.10	.06
B4	Mike Schmidt (MVP)	.25	.15
B5	Ivan Calderon (MVP	.08	.05
B6	Tony Gwynn (MVP)	.15	.08
B7	Wade Boggs (MVP)	.15	.08
B8	Andy Van Slyke (MVP)	.12	.07
B9	Joe Carter (MVP)	.15	.08
B10	Andre Dawson (MVP)	.15	.08
B11	Alan Trammell (MVP)	.12	.07
B12	Mike Scott (MVP)	.07	.04
B13	Wally Joyner (MVP)	.10	.06
B14	Dale Murphy (MVP)	.12	.07
B15	Kirby Puckett (MVP)	.35	.20
B16	Pedro Guerrero (MVP)	.07	.04
B17	Kevin Seitzer (MVP)	.07	.04
B18	Tim Raines (MVP)	.08	.05
B19	George Bell (MVP)	.12	.07
B20	Darryl Strawberry (MVP)	.25	.15
B21	Don Mattingly (MVP)	.25	.15
B22	Ozzie Smith (MVP)	.15	.08
B23	Mark McGwire (MVP)	.50	.30
B24	Will Clark (MVP)	.50	.30
B25	Alvin Davis (MVP)	.07	.04
B26	Ruben Sierra (MVP)	.35	.20

1988 Donruss Rookies

This 56-card update set is similar to the Donruss regular 1988 edition except the border colors are black with green and red accents instead of black with blue and red accents. The standard-size cards measure 2-1/2" by 3-1/2".

		MINT	NR/MT
Complete Set (56)		20.00	14.00
Commons		.08	.05

1	Mark Grace	2.75	1.75
2	Mike Campbell	.08	.05
3	Todd Frowirth (R)	.10	.06
4	Dave Stapleton	.08	.05
5	Shawn Abner	.10	.06
6	Jose Cecena (R)	.08	.05
7	Dave Gallagher (R)	.10	.06
8	Mark Parent (R)	.10	.06
9	Cecil Espy (R)	.10	.06
10	Pete Smith	.40	.25
11	Jay Buhner	.40	.25
12	Pat Borders (R)	.25	.15
13	Doug Jennings (R)	.08	.05
14	Brady Anderson (R)	1.75	1.00
15	Pete Stanicek	.08	.05
16	Roberto Kelly	1.00	.70
17	Jeff Treadway	.12	.07
18	Walt Weiss (R)	.25	.15
19	Paul Gibson (R)	.08	.05
20	Tim Crews	.12	.07
21	Melido Perez	.40	.25
22	Steve Peters (R)	.10	.06
23	Craig Worthington (R)	.08	.05
24	John Trautwein (R)	.08	.05
25	DeWayne Vaughn (R)	.08	.05
26	David Wells	.10	.06
27	Al Leiter	.08	.05
28	Tim Belcher	.15	.08
29	Johnny Paredes (R)	.08	.05
30	Chris Sabo (R)	.80	.50
31	Damon Berryhill	.10	.06
32	Randy Milligan (R)	.40	.25
33	Gary Thurman	.08	.05
34	Kevin Elster	.12	.07
35	Roberto Alomar	12.00	8.00
36	Edgar Martinez (R)	2.50	1.50
37	Todd Stottlemyre	.30	.18
38	Joey Meyer	.10	.06
39	Carl Nichols	.08	.05
40	Jack McDowell	2.50	1.50
41	Jose Bautista (R)	.10	.06
42	Sil Campusano (R)	.10	.06
43	John Dopson (R)	.10	.06
44	Jody Reed	.25	.15
45	Darrin Jackson (R)	.50	.30
46	Mike Capel (R)	.08	.05
47	Ron Gant	3.50	2.25
48	John Davis	.08	.05
49	Kevin Coffman (R)	.08	.05
50	Cris Carpenter (R)	.15	.08
51	Mackey Sasser	.10	.06
52	Luis Alicea (R)	.20	.12
53	Bryan Harvey (R)	.40	.25
54	Steve Ellsworth (R)	.08	.05
55	Mike Macfarlane (R)	.35	.20
56	Checklist 1-56	.08	.05

1989 Donruss

This 660-card set is similar to the 1988 Donruss set except for the border colors on the card fronts. The 1989 edition consists of multi-colored top and bottom borders with black stripes on the sides. The card backs are orange and black. Subsets include Diamond King (1-26) and Rated Rookies (28-47). A Warren Spahn puzzle was included in the set. For the second straight year Donruss issued Bonus MVP cards which were randomly distributed in wax packs. Those cards are listed at the end of the checklist.

		MINT	NR/MT
Complete Set (660)		18.50	12.50
Commons		.05	.02

1	Mike Greenwell (DK)	.08	.05
2	Bobby Bonilla (DK)	.10	.06
3	Pete Incaviglia (DK)	.05	.02
4	Chris Sabo (DK)	.08	.05
5	Robin Yount (DK)	.15	.08
6	Tony Gwynn (DK)	.12	.07
7	Carlton Fisk (DK)	.10	.06
8	Cory Snyder (DK)	.05	.02
9	David Cone (DK)	.10	.06
10	Kevin Seitzer (DK)	.07	.04
11	Rick Reuschel (DK)	.05	.02
12	Johnny Ray (DK)	.05	.02
13	Dave Schmidt (DK)	.05	.02
14	Andres Galarraga (DK)	.07	.04
15	Kirk Gibson (DK)	.08	.05
16	Fred McGriff (DK)	.12	.07
17	Mark Grace (DK)	.10	.06
18	Jeff Robinson (DK)	.05	.02
19	Vince Coleman (DK)	.07	.04
20	Dave Henderson (DK)	.05	.02
21	Harold Reynolds (DK)	.05	.02
22	Gerald Perry (DK)	.05	.02
23	Frank Viola (DK)	.08	.05
24	Steve Bedrosian (DK)	.05	.02
25	Glenn Davis (DK)	.07	.04
26	Don Mattingly (DK)	.12	.07
27	Checklist 1-27	.05	.02
28	Sandy Alomar, Jr. (R)	.35	.20
29	Steve Searcy (R)	.08	.05
30	Cameron Drew (R)	.05	.02
31	Gary Sheffield (R)	2.50	1.50
32	Erik Hanson (R)	.25	.05
33	Ken Griffey, Jr. (R)	5.00	3.00
34	Greg Harris (R)	.10	.06
35	Gregg Jefferies (R)	.35	.20
36	Luis Medina (R)	.10	.06
37	Carlos Quintana (R)	.12	.07
38	Felix Jose (R)	.70	.40
39	Cris Carpenter (R)	.10	.06
40	Ron Jones (R)	.07	.04
41	Dave West	.10	.06
42	Randy Johnson (R)	.50	.30
43	Mike Harkey (R)	.15	.08
44	Pete Harnisch (R)	.15	.08
45	Tom Gordon (R)	.12	.07
46	Gregg Olson (R)	.25	.15
47	Alex Sanchez (R)	.07	.04
48	Ruben Sierra	.30	.18
49	Rafael Palmeiro	.25	.15
50	Ron Gant	.50	.30
51	Cal Ripken, Jr.	.60	.35
52	Wally Joyner	.10	.06
53	Gary Carter	.08	.05
54	Andy Van Slyke	.10	.06
55	Robin Yount	.30	.18
56	Pete Incaviglia	.05	.02
57	Greg Brock	.05	.02
58	Melido Perez	.07	.04
59	Craig Lefferts	.05	.02
60	Gary Pettis	.05	.02
61	Danny Tartabull	.15	.08
62	Guillermo Hernandez	.05	.02
63	Ozzie Smith	.05	.08
64	Gary Gaetti	.05	.02
65	Mark Davis	.05	.02
66	Lee Smith	.12	.07
67	Dennis Eckersley	.15	.08
68	Wade Boggs	.20	.12
69	Mike Scott	.07	.04
70	Fred McGriff	.25	.15
71	Tom Browning	.05	.02
72	Claudell Washington	.05	.02
73	Mel Hall	.07	.04
74	Don Mattingly	.20	.12
75	Steve Bedrosian	.05	.02
76	Juan Samuel	.05	.02
77	Mike Scioscia	.05	.02
78	Dave Righetti	.05	.02
79	Alfredo Griffin	.05	.02
80	Eric Davis	.12	.07
81	Juan Berenguer	.05	.02
82	Todd Worrell	.07	.04
83	Joe Carter	.20	.12
84	Steve Sax	.07	.04
85	Frank White	.05	.02
86	John Kruk	.07	.04
87	Rance Mulliniks	.05	.02
88	Alan Ashby	.05	.02
89	Charlie Leibrandt	.05	.02
90	Frank Tanana	.05	.02
91	Jose Canseco	.50	.30
92	Barry Bonds	.40	.25
93	Harold Reynolds	.05	.02
94	Mark McLemore	.05	.02
95	Mark McGwire	.40	.25
96	Eddie Murray	.15	.08
97	Tim Raines	.07	.04
98	Robby Thompson	.05	.02
99	Kevin McReynolds	.07	.04
100	Checklist 28-137	.05	.02
101	Carlton Fisk	.12	.07
102	Dave Martinez	.05	.02
103	Glenn Braggs	.05	.02
104	Dale Murphy	.12	.07
105	Ryne Sandberg	.35	.20

106	Dennis Martinez	.10	.06
107	Pete O'Brien	.05	.02
108	Dick Schofield	.05	.02
109	Henry Cotto	.05	.02
110	Mike Marshall	.05	.02
111	Keith Moreland	.05	.02
112	Tom Brunansky	.07	.04
113	Kelly Gruber	.08	.05
114	Brook Jacoby	.05	.02
115	Keith Brown (R)	.07	.04
116	Matt Nokes	.07	.04
117	Keith Hernandez	.07	.04
118	Bob Forsch	.05	.02
119	Bert Blyleven	.10	.06
120	Willie Wilson	.05	.02
121	Tommy Gregg	.05	.02
122	Jim Rice	.07	.04
123	Bob Knepper	.05	.02
124	Danny Jackson	.05	.02
125	Eric Plunk	.05	.02
126	Brian Fisher	.05	.02
127	Mike Pagliarulo	.05	.02
128	Tony Gwynn	.25	.15
129	Lance McCullers	.05	.02
130	Andres Galarraga	.07	.04
131	Jose Uribe	.05	.02
132	Kirk Gibson	.07	.04
133	David Palmer	.05	.02
134	R.J. Reynolds	.05	.02
135	Greg Walker	.05	.02
136	Kirk McCaskill	.05	.02
137	Shawon Dunston	.10	.06
138	Andy Allanson	.05	.02
139	Rob Murphy	.05	.02
140	Mike Aldrete	.05	.02
141	Terry Kennedy	.05	.02
142	Scott Fletcher	.05	.02
143	Steve Balboni	.05	.02
144	Bret Saberhagen	.12	.07
145	Ozzie Virgil	.05	.02
146	Dale Sveum	.05	.02
147	Darryl Strawberry	.30	.18
148	Harold Baines	.07	.04
149	George Bell	.10	.06
150	Dave Parker	.07	.04
151	Bobby Bonilla	.15	.08
152	Mookie Wilson	.05	.02
153	Ted Power	.05	.02
154	Nolan Ryan	.75	.45
155	Jeff Reardon	.12	.07
156	Tim Wallach	.07	.04
157	Jamie Moyer	.05	.02
158	Rich Gossage	.07	.04
159	Dave Winfield	.20	.12
160	Von Hayes	.05	.02
161	Willie McGee	.08	.05
162	Rich Gedman	.05	.02
163	Tony Pena	.05	.02
164	Mike Morgan	.05	.02
165	Charlie Hough	.05	.02
166	Mike Stanley	.05	.02
167	Andre Dawson	.20	.12
168	Joe Boever (R)	.08	.05
169	Pete Stanicek	.05	.02
170	Bob Boone	.08	.05
171	Ron Darling	.07	.04
172	Bob Walk	.05	.02
173	Rob Deer	.07	.04
174	Steve Buechele	.05	.02
175	Ted Higuera	.05	.02
176	Ozzie Guillen	.07	.04
177	Candy Maldonado	.05	.02
178	Doyle Alexander	.05	.02
179	Mark Gubicza	.07	.04
180	Alan Trammell	.10	.06
181	Vince Coleman	.07	.04
182	Kirby Puckett	.35	.20
183	Chris Brown	.05	.02
184	Marty Barrett	.05	.02
185	Stan Javier	.05	.02
186	Mike Greenwell	.08	.05
187	Billy Hatcher	.05	.02
188	Jimmy Key	.05	.02
189	Nick Esasky	.05	.02
190	Don Slaught	.05	.02
191	Cory Snyder	.05	.02
192	John Candelaria	.05	.02
193	Mike Schmidt	.40	.25
194	Kevin Gross	.05	.02
195	John Tudor	.05	.02
196	Neil Allen	.05	.02
197	Orel Hershiser	.08	.05
198	Kal Daniels	.05	.02
199	Kent Hrbek	.08	.05
200	Checklist 138-247	.05	.02
201	Joe Magrane	.07	.04
202	Scott Bailes	.05	.02
203	Tim Belcher	.07	.04
204	George Brett	.30	.18
205	Benito Santiago	.10	.06
206	Tony Fernandez	.05	.02
207	Gerald Young	.08	.05
208	Bo Jackson	.25	.15
209	Chet Lemon	.05	.02
210	Storm Davis	.05	.02
211	Doug Drabek	.10	.06
212	Mickey Brantley (Er) (Wrong Photo)	.05	.02
213	Devon White	.05	.02
214	Dave Stewart	.08	.05
215	Dave Schmidt	.05	.02
216	Bryn Smith	.05	.02
217	Brett Butler	.08	.05
218	Bob Ojeda	.05	.02
219	Steve Rosenberg (R)	.08	.05
220	Hubie Brooks	.07	.04

221	B.J. Surhoff	.05	.02
222	Rick Mahler	.05	.02
223	Rick Sutcliffe	.07	.04
224	Neal Heaton	.05	.02
225	Mitch Williams	.05	.02
226	Chuck Finley	.10	.06
227	Mark Langston	.10	.06
228	Jesse Orosco	.05	.02
229	Ed Whitson	.05	.02
230	Terry Pendleton	.15	.08
231	Lloyd Moseby	.05	.02
232	Greg Swindell	.07	.04
233	John Franco	.05	.02
234	Jack Morris	.12	.07
235	Howard Johnson	.12	.07
236	Glenn Davis	.05	.02
237	Frank Viola	.07	.04
238	Kevin Seitzer	.07	.04
239	Gerald Perry	.05	.02
240	Dwight Evans	.07	.04
241	Jim Deshaies	.05	.02
242	Bo Diaz	.05	.02
243	Carney Lansford	.07	.04
244	Mike LaValliere	.05	.02
245	Rickey Henderson	.30	.18
246	Roberto Alomar	.90	.60
247	Jimmy Jones	.05	.02
248	Pasquel Perez	.05	.02
249	Will Clark	.50	.30
250	Fernando Valenzuela	.08	.05
251	Shane Rawley	.05	.02
252	Sid Bream	.05	.02
253	Steve Lyons	.05	.02
254	Brian Downing	.05	.02
255	Mark Grace	.25	.15
256	Tom Candiotti	.05	.02
257	Barry Larkin	.20	.12
258	Mike Krukow	.05	.02
259	Billy Ripken	.05	.02
260	Cecilio Guante	.05	.02
261	Scott Bradley	.05	.02
262	Floyd Bannister	.05	.02
263	Pete Smith	.20	.12
264	Jim Gantner	.05	.02
265	Roger McDowell	.05	.02
266	Bobby Thigpen	.07	.04
267	Jim Clancy	.05	.02
268	Terry Steinbach	.07	.04
269	Mike Dunne	.05	.02
270	Dwight Gooden	.15	.08
271	Mike Heath	.05	.02
272	Dave Smith	.05	.02
273	Keith Atherton	.05	.02
274	Tim Burke	.05	.02
275	Damon Berryhill	.05	.02
276	Vance Law	.05	.02
277	Rich Dotson	.05	.02
278	Lance Parrish	.05	.02

279	Denny Walling		
		.05	.02
280	Roger Clemens	.50	.30
281	Greg Mathews	.05	.02
282	Tom Niedenfuer	.05	.02
283	Paul Kilgus	.05	.02
284	Jose Guzman	.05	.02
285	Calvin Schiraldi	.05	.02
286	Charlie Puleo	.05	.02
287	Joe Orsulak	.05	.02
288	Jack Howell	.05	.02
289	Kevin Elster	.05	.02
290	Jose Lind	.05	.02
291	Paul Molitor	.10	.06
292	Cecil Espy	.05	.02
293	Bill Wegman	.05	.02
294	Dan Pasqua	.05	.02
295	Scott Garrelts	.05	.02
296	Walt Terrell	.05	.02
297	Ed Hearn	.05	.02
298	Lou Whitaker	.07	.04
299	Ken Dayley	.05	.02
300	Checklist 248-357	.05	.02
301	Tommy Herr	.05	.02
302	Mike Brumley	.05	.02
303	Ellis Burks	.08	.05
304	Curt Young	.05	.02
305	Jody Reed	.05	.02
306	Bill Doran	.05	.02
307	David Wells	.07	.04
308	Ron Robinson	.05	.02
309	Rafael Santana	.05	.02
310	Julio Franco	.10	.06
311	Jack Clark	.07	.04
312	Chris James	.05	.02
313	Milt Thompson	.05	.02
314	John Shelby	.05	.02
315	Al Leiter	.05	.02
316	Mike Davis	.05	.02
317	Chris Sabo	.25	.15
318	Greg Gagne	.05	.02
319	Jose Oquendo	.05	.02
320	John Farrell	.05	.02
321	Franklin Stubbs	.05	.02
322	Kurt Stillwell	.05	.02
323	Shawn Abner	.05	.02
324	Mike Flanagan	.05	.02
325	Kevin Bass	.05	.02
326	Pat Tabler	.05	.02
327	Mike Henneman	.05	.02
328	Rick Honeycutt	.05	.02
329	John Smiley	.10	.06
330	Rey Quinones	.05	.02
331	Johnny Ray	.05	.02
332	Bob Welch	.07	.04
333	Larry Sheets	.05	.02
334	Jeff Parrett	.05	.02
335	Rick Reuschel	.05	.02

338	Andy McGaffigan	.05	.02
339	Joey Meyer	.05	.02
340	Dion James	.05	.02
341	Les Lancaster	.05	.02
342	Tom Foley	.05	.02
343	Geno Petralli	.05	.02
344	Dan Petry	.05	.02
345	Alvin Davis	.05	.02
346	Mickey Hatcher	.05	.02
347	Marvell Wynne	.05	.02
348	Danny Cox	.05	.02
349	Dave Stieb	.08	.05
350	Jay Bell	.08	.05
351	Jeff Treadway	.05	.02
352	Luis Salazar	.05	.02
353	Lenny Dykstra	.07	.04
354	Juan Agosto	.05	.02
355	Gene Larkin	.05	.02
356	Steve Farr	.05	.02
357	Paul Assenmacher	.05	.02
358	Todd Benzinger	.05	.02
359	Larry Andersen	.05	.02
360	Paul O'Neill	.10	.06
361	Ron Hassey	.05	.02
362	Jim Gott	.05	.02
363	Ken Phelps	.05	.02
364	Tim Flannery	.05	.02
365	Randy Ready	.05	.02
366	Nelson Santovenia (R)	.08	.05
367	Kelly Downs	.05	.02
368	Danny Heep	.05	.02
369	Phil Bradley	.05	.02
370	Jeff Robinson	.05	.02
371	Ivan Calderon	.07	.04
372	Mike Witt	.05	.02
373	Greg Maddux	.20	.12
374	Carmen Castillo	.05	.02
375	Jose Rijo	.08	.05
376	Joe Price	.05	.02
377	Rene Gonzalez	.05	.02
378	Oddibe McDowell	.05	.02
379	Jim Presley	.05	.02
380	Brad Wellman	.05	.02
381	Tom Glavine	.80	.50
382	Dan Plesac	.05	.02
383	Wally Backman	.05	.02
384	Dave Gallagher	.05	.02
385	Tom Henke	.05	.02
386	Luis Polonia	.08	.05
387	Junior Ortiz	.05	.02
388	David Cone	.12	.08
389	Dave Bergman	.05	.02
390	Danny Darwin	.05	.02
391	Dan Gladden	.05	.02
392	John Dopson	.05	.02
393	Frank DiPino	.05	.02
394	Al Nipper	.05	.02
395	Willie Randolph	.07	.04
396	Don Carman	.05	.02
397	Scott Terry	.05	.02
398	Rick Cerone	.05	.02
399	Tom Pagnozzi	.10	.06
400	Checklist 358-467	.05	.02
401	Mickey Tettleton	.07	.04
402	Curtis Wilkerson	.05	.02
403	Jeff Russell	.05	.02
404	Pat Perry	.05	.02
405	Jose Alvarez (R)	.07	.04
406	Rick Schu	.05	.02
407	Sherman Corbett (R)	.07	.04
408	Dave Magadan	.07	.04
409	Bob Kipper	.05	.02
410	Don August	.05	.02
411	Bob Brower	.05	.02
412	Chris Bosio	.08	.05
413	Jerry Reuss	.05	.02
414	Atlee Hammaker	.05	.02
415	Jim Walewander (R)	.05	.02
416	Mike Macfarlane	.08	.05
417	Pat Sheridan	.05	.02
418	Pedro Guerrero	.07	.04
419	Allan Anderson	.05	.02
420	Mark Parent	.05	.02
421	Bob Stanley	.05	.02
422	Mike Gallego	.05	.02
423	Bruce Hurst	.07	.04
424	Dave Meads	.05	.02
425	Jesse Barfield	.07	.04
426	Rob Dibble (R)	.20	.12
427	Joel Skinner	.05	.02
428	Ron Kittle	.05	.02
429	Rick Rhoden	.05	.02
430	Bob Dernier	.05	.02
431	Steve Jeltz	.05	.02
432	Rick Dempsey	.05	.02
433	Roberto Kelly	.25	.15
434	Dave Anderson	.05	.02
435	Herm Winningham	.05	.02
436	Al Newman	.05	.02
437	Jose DeLeon	.05	.02
438	Doug Jones	.05	.02
439	Brian Holton	.05	.02
440	Jeff Montgomery	.08	.05
441	Dickie Thon	.05	.02
442	Cecil Fielder	.30	.18
443	John Fishel (R)	.05	.02
444	Jerry Don Gleaton	.05	.02
445	Paul Gibson	.05	.02
446	Walt Weiss	.08	.05
447	Glenn Wilson	.05	.02
448	Mike Moore	.05	.02
449	Chili Davis	.07	.04
450	Dave Henderson	.05	.02
451	Jose Bautista	.05	.02
452	Rex Hudler	.05	.02
453	Bob Brenly	.05	.02

454	Mackey Sasser	.05	.02
455	Daryl Boston	.05	.02
456	Mike Fitzgerald	.05	.02
457	Jeffery Leonard	.05	.02
458	Bruce Sutter	.07	.04
459	Mitch Webster	.05	.02
460	Joe Hesketh	.05	.02
461	Bobby Witt	.08	.05
462	Stew Cliburn	.05	.02
463	Scott Bankhead	.05	.02
464	Ramon Martinez (R)	.50	.30
465	Dave Leiper	.05	.02
466	Luis Alicea	.08	.05
467	John Cerutti	.05	.02
468	Ron Washington	.05	.02
469	Jeff Reed	.05	.02
470	Jeff Robinson	.05	.02
471	Sid Fernandez	.07	.04
472	Terry Puhl	.05	.02
473	Charlie Lea	.05	.02
474	Israel Sanchez (R)	.07	.04
475	Bruce Benedict	.05	.02
476	Oil Can Boyd	.05	.02
477	Craig Reynolds	.05	.02
478	Frank Williams	.05	.02
479	Greg Cadaret	.05	.02
480	Randy Kramer (R)	.08	.05
481	Dave Eiland (R)	.10	.06
482	Eric Show	.05	.02
483	Garry Templeton	.05	.02
484	Wallace Johnson (R)	.05	.02
485	Kevin Mitchell	.12	.07
486	Tim Crews	.07	.04
487	Mike Maddux	.05	.02
488	Dave LaPoint	.05	.02
489	Fred Manrique	.05	.02
490	Greg Minton	.05	.02
491	Doug Dascenzo (R)	.10	.06
492	Willie Upshaw	.05	.02
493	Jack Armstrong (R)	.12	.07
494	Kirt Manwaring	.05	.02
495	Jeff Ballard	.05	.02
496	Jeff Kunkel	.05	.02
497	Mike Campbell	.05	.02
498	Gary Thurman	.05	.02
499	Zane Smith	.05	.02
500	Checklist 468-577	.05	.02
501	Mike Birkbeck	.05	.02
502	Terry Leach	.05	.02
503	Shawn Hillegas	.05	.02
504	Manny Lee	.05	.02
505	Doug Jennings	.05	.02
506	Ken Oberkfell	.05	.02
507	Tim Teufel	.05	.02
508	Tom Brookens	.05	.02
509	Rafael Ramirez	.05	.02
510	Fred Toliver	.05	.02
511	Brian Holman (R)	.12	.07
512	Mike Bielecki	.05	.02
513	Jeff Pico (R)	.07	.04
514	Charles Hudson	.05	.02
515	Bruce Ruffin	.05	.02
516	Larry McWilliams	.05	.02
517	Jeff Sellers	.05	.02
518	John Costello (R)	.08	.05
519	Brady Anderson	.75	.45
520	Craig McMurtry	.05	.02
521	Ray Hayward	.05	.02
522	Drew Hall	.05	.02
523	Mark Lemke (R)	.12	.07
524	Oswald Peraza (R)	.08	.05
525	Bryan Harvey	.15	.08
526	Rick Aguilera	.05	.02
527	Tom Prince	.05	.02
528	Mark Clear	.05	.02
529	Jerry Browne	.05	.02
530	Juan Castillo	.05	.02
531	Jack McDowell	.40	.25
532	Chris Speier	.05	.02
533	Darrell Evans	.07	.04
534	Luis Aquino	.05	.02
535	Eric King	.05	.02
536	Ken Hill (R)	.50	.30
537	Randy Bush	.05	.02
538	Shane Mack	.12	.07
539	Tom Bolton	.08	.05
540	Gene Nelson	.05	.02
541	Wes Gardner	.07	.04
542	Ken Caminiti	.07	.04
543	Duane Ward	.05	.02
544	Norm Charlton (R)	.20	.12
545	Hal Morris (R)	.40	.25
546	Rich Yett	.05	.02
547	Hensley Meulens (R)	.12	.07
548	Greg Harris	.05	.02
549	Darren Daulton	.12	.07
550	Jeff Hamilton	.05	.02
551	Luis Aguayo	.05	.02
552	Tim Leary	.05	.02
553	Ron Oester	.05	.02
554	Steve Lombardozzi	.05	.02
555	Tim Jones (R)	.07	.04
556	Bud Black	.05	.02
557	Alejandro Pena	.05	.02
558	Jose DeJesus (R)	.08	.05
559	Dennis Rasmussen	.05	.02
560	Pat Borders	.12	.07
561	Craig Biggio (R)	.40	.25
562	Luis de los Santos (R)	.07	.04
563	Fred Lynn	.07	.04
564	Todd Burns (R)	.10	.06
565	Felix Fermin	.05	.02
566	Darnell Coles	.05	.02
567	Willie Fraser	.05	.02
568	Glenn Hubbard	.05	.02
569	Craig Worthington	.05	.02

No.	Player		
570	Johnny Paredes	.05	.02
571	Don Robinson	.05	.02
572	Barry Lyons	.05	.02
573	Bill Long	.05	.02
574	Tracy Jones	.05	.02
575	Juan Nieves	.05	.02
576	Andres Thomas	.05	.02
577	Rolando Roomes (R)	.08	.05
578	Luis Rivera	.05	.02
579	Chad Kreuter (R)	.10	.06
580	Tony Armas	.05	.02
581	Jay Buhner	.12	.07
582	Ricky Horton	.05	.02
583	Andy Hawkins	.05	.02
584	Sil Campusano	.05	.02
585	Dave Clark	.05	.02
586	Van Snider (R)	.10	.06
587	Todd Frohwirth	.05	.02
588	Warren Spahn Puzzle	.12	.07
589	William Brennan (R)	.07	.04
590	German Gonzalez (R)	.07	.04
591	Ernie Whitt	.05	.02
592	Jeff Blauser	.07	.04
593	Spike Owen	.05	.02
594	Matt Williams	.25	.15
595	Lloyd McClendon	.07	.04
596	Steve Ontiveros	.05	.02
597	Scott Medvin (R)	.08	.05
598	Hipolito Pena (R)	.08	.05
599	Jerald Clark (R)	.12	.07
600	Checklist 578-BC26	.05	.02
601	Carmelo Martinez	.05	.02
602	Mike LaCoss	.05	.02
603	Mike Devereaux	.07	.04
604	Alex Madrid (R)	.08	.05
605	Gary Redus	.05	.02
606	Lance Johnson	.05	.02
607	Terry Clark (R)	.07	.04
608	Manny Trillo	.05	.02
609	Scott Jordan (R)	.08	.05
610	Jay Howell	.05	.02
611	Francisco Melendez (R)	.07	.04
612	Mike Boddicker	.05	.02
613	Kevin Brown	.30	.18
614	Dave Valle	.05	.02
615	Tim Laudner	.05	.02
616	Andy Nezelek (R)	.08	.05
617	Chuck Crim	.05	.02
618	Jack Savage	.08	.05
619	Adam Peterson	.08	.05
620	Todd Stottlemyre	.08	.05
621	Lance Blankenship (R)	.12	.07
622	Miguel Garcia (R)	.08	.05
623	Keith Miller	.05	.02
624	Ricky Jordan (R)	.20	.12
625	Ernest Riles	.05	.02
626	John Moses	.05	.02
627	Nelson Liriano	.05	.02
628	Mike Smithson	.05	.02
629	Scott Sanderson	.05	.02
630	Dale Mohorcic	.05	.02
631	Marvin Freeman	.05	.02
632	Mike Young	.05	.02
633	Dennis Lamp	.05	.02
634	Dante Bichette (R)	.15	.08
635	Curt Schilling (R)	.20	.12
636	Scott May (R)	.08	.05
637	Mike Schooler (R)	.15	.08
638	Rick Leach	.05	.02
639	Tom Lampkin (R)	.08	.05
640	Brian Meyer (R)	.10	.06
641	Brian Harper	.05	.02
642	John Smoltz (R)	.80	.50
643	Jose Canseco (40/40)	.25	.15
644	Bill Schroeder	.05	.02
645	Edgar Martinez	.60	.35
646	Dennis Cook (R)	.08	.05
647	Barry Jones	.05	.02
648	Orel Hershiser (59)	.12	.07
649	Rod Nichols (R)	.08	.05
650	Jody Davis	.05	.02
651	Bob Milacki (R)	.10	.06
652	Mike Jackson	.05	.02
653	Derek Lilliquist (R)	.10	.06
654	Paul Mirabella	.05	.02
655	Mike Diaz	.05	.02
656	Jeff Musselman	.05	.02
657	Jerry Reed	.05	.02
658	Kevin Blankenship (R)	.08	.05
659	Wayne Tolleson	.05	.02
660	Eric Hetzel (R)	.10	.06
B1	Kirby Puckett	.20	.12
B2	Mike Scott	.07	.04
B3	Joe Carter	.10	.06
B4	Orel Hershiser	.10	.06
B5	Jose Canseco	.25	.15
B6	Darryl Strawberry	.20	.12
B7	George Brett	.20	.12
B8	Andre Dawson	.12	.07
B9	Paul Molitor	.08	.05
B10	Andy Van Slyke	.08	.05
B11	Dave Winfield	.12	.07
B12	Kevin Gross	.07	.04
B13	Mike Greenwell	.08	.05
B14	Ozzie Smith	.12	.07
B15	Cal Ripken Jr.	.25	.15
B16	Andres Galarraga	.08	.05
B17	Alan Trammell	.10	.06
B18	Kal Daniels	.07	.04
B19	Fred McGriff	.15	.08
B20	Tony Gwynn	.15	.08
B21	Wally Joyner	.10	.06
B22	Will Clark	.20	.12
B23	Ozzie Guillen	.07	.04
B24	Gerald Perry	.07	.04
B25	Alvin Davis	.07	.04
B26	Ruben Sierra	.15	.08

1989 Donruss Rookies

Green and black borders highlight this 56-card update set from Donruss which is similar to their regular 1989 set. Cards measure 2-1/2" by 3-1/2".

		MINT	NR/MT
Complete Set (56)		16.50	10.50
Commons		.07	.04

1	Gary Sheffield	3.50	2.25
2	Gregg Jefferies	.35	.20
3	Ken Griffey, Jr.	7.50	4.50
4	Tom Gordon	.10	.06
5	Billy Spiers (R)	.12	.07
6	Deion Sanders (R)	1.50	1.00
7	Donn Pall (R)	.07	.04
8	Steve Carter (R)	.07	.04
9	Francisco Oliveras (R)	.08	.05
10	Steve Wilson (R)	.08	.05
11	Bob Geren (R)	.10	.06
12	Tony Castillo (R)	.07	.04
13	Kenny Rogers (R)	.10	.06
14	Carlos Martinez (R)	.10	.06
15	Edgar Martinez	.60	.35
16	Jim Abbott (R)	1.50	.90
17	Torey Lovullo (R)	.06	.05
18	Mark Carreon (R)	.10	.06
19	Geronimo Berroa	.07	.04
20	Luis Medina	.08	.05
21	Sandy Alomar, Jr.	.25	.15
22	Bob Milacki	.10	.06
23	Joe Girardi (R)	.10	.06
24	German Gonzalez	.07	.04
25	Craig Worthingtn	.07	.04
26	Jerome Walton (R)	.10	.06
27	Gary Wayne (R)	.08	.05
28	Tim Jones	.07	.04
29	Dante Bichette	.08	.05
30	Alexis Infante (R)	.08	.05
31	Ken Hill	.35	.20
32	Dwight Smith (R)	.10	.06
33	Luis de los Santos	.07	.04
34	Eric Yelding(FC)	.12	.07
35	Gregg Olson	.25	.15
36	Phil Stephenson (R)	.08	.05
37	Ken Patterson (R)	.08	.05
38	Rick Wrona (R)	.08	.05
39	Mike Brumley	.07	.04
40	Cris Carpenter	.08	.05
41	Jeff Brantley (R)	.12	.07
42	Ron Jones	.07	.04
43	Randy Johnson	.25	.15
44	Kevin Brown	.20	.12
45	Ramon Martinez	.50	.30
46	Greg Harris	.10	.06
47	Steve Finley (R)	.25	.15
48	Randy Kramer	.07	.04
49	Erik Hanson	.20	.12
50	Matt Merullo (R)	.12	.07
51	Mike Devereaux	.15	.08
52	Clay Parker (R)	.08	.05
53	Omar Vizquel (R)	.08	.05
54	Derek Lilliquist	.07	.04
55	Junior Felix (R)	.15	.08
56	Checklist	.07	.04

1990 Donruss

Donruss increased the size of their set to 716-cards in 1990 and added a new All-Star Subset to go along with Diamond Kings (1-26) and Rated Rookies (28-47). Bonus insert MVP cards were also distributed randomly in wax packs. Those cards are listed at the end of this checklist. The standard-size cards measure 2-1/2" by 3-1/2" and feature bright red borders. There are many variations in this set and those with significant differences in value are listed in the checklist.

		MINT	NR/MT
Complete Set (716)		16.00	10.00
Commons		.05	.02

		MINT	NR/MT
1	Bo Jackson (DK)	.15	.08
2	Steve Sax (DK)	.08	.05
3a	Ruben Sierra (DK) (Er)	.60	.35
3b	Ruben Sierra (DK) (Cor)	.15	.08
4	Ken Griffey, Jr. (DK)	.50	.30
5	Mickey Tettleton (DK)	.07	.04
6	Dave Stewart (DK)	.08	.05
7	Jim Deshaies (DK)	.05	.02
8	John Smoltz (DK)	.10	.06
9	Mike Bielecki (DK)	.05	.02
10a	Brian Downing (DK) (Reverse Negative)	.50	.30
10b	Brian Downing (DK) (Corrected)	.07	.04
11	Kevin Mitchell (DK)	.08	.05
12	Kelly Gruber (DK)	.07	.04
13	Joe Magrane (DK)	.07	.04
14	John Franco (DK)	.08	.05
15	Ozzie Guillen (DK)	.07	.04
16	Lou Whitaker (DK)	.08	.05
17	John Smiley (DK)	.08	.05
18	Howard Johnson (DK)	.08	.05
19	Willie Randolph (DK)	.07	.04
20	Chris Bosio (DK)	.07	.04
21	Tommy Herr (DK)	.05	.02
22	Dan Gladden (DK)	.05	.02
23	Ellis Burks (DK)	.08	.05
24	Pete O'Brien (DK)	.05	.02
25	Bryn Smith (DK)	.05	.02
26	Ed Whitson (DK)	.05	.02
27	Checklist 1-27	.05	.02
28	Robin Ventura (R)	.80	.05
29	Todd Zeile (R)	.25	.15
30	Sandy Alomar, Jr.	.08	.05
31	Kent Mercker (R)	.12	.07
32	Ben McDonald (R)	.75	.45
33a	Juan Gonzalez (R) (Reverse Negative)	4.00	2.75
33b	Juan Gonzalez (R) (Corrected)	2.50	1.50
34	Eric Anthony (R)	.40	.25
35	Mike Fetters (R)	.10	.06
36	Marquis Grissom (R)	.80	.50
37	Greg Vaughn (R)	.25	.15
38	Brian Dubois (R)	.10	.06
39	Steve Avery (R)	1.25	.80
40	Mark Gardner (R)	.15	.08
41	Andy Benes (R)	.40	.25
42	Delino Deshields (R)	.75	.45
43	Scott Coolbaugh	.07	.04
44	Pat Combs	.10	.06
45	Alex Sanchez	.07	.04
46	Kelly Mann (R)	.07	.04
47	Julio Machado (R)	.10	.06
48	Pete Incaviglia	.05	.02
49	Shawon Dunston	.08	.05
50	Jeff Treadway	.05	.02
51	Jeff Ballard	.05	.02
52	Claudell Washington	.05	.02
53	Juan Samuel	.05	.02
54	John Smiley	.10	.06
55	Rob Deer	.07	.04
56	Geno Petralli	.05	.02
57	Chris Bosio	.08	.05
58	Carlton Fisk	.10	.06
59	Kirt Manwaring	.05	.02
60	Chet Lemon	.05	.02
61	Bo Jackson	.20	.12
62	Doyle Alexander	.05	.02
63	Pedro Guerrero	.05	.02
64	Allan Anderson	.05	.02
65	Greg Harris	.05	.02
66	Mike Greenwell	.10	.06
67	Walt Weiss	.08	.05
68	Wade Boggs	.20	.12
69	Jim Clancy	.05	.02
70	Junior Felix	.07	.04
71	Barry Larkin	.12	.07
72	Dave LaPoint	.05	.02
73	Joel Skinner	.05	.02
74	Jesse Barfield	.07	.04
75	Tommy Herr	.05	.02
76	Ricky Jordan	.07	.04
77	Eddie Murray	.15	.08
78	Steve Sax	.08	.05
79	Tim Belcher	.07	.04
80	Danny Jackson	.05	.02
81	Kent Hrbek	.07	.04
82	Milt Thompson	.05	.02
83	Brook Jacoby	.05	.02
84	Mike Marshall	.05	.02
85	Kevin Seitzer	.07	.04
86	Tony Gwynn	.20	.12
87	Dave Steib	.08	.05
88	Dave Smith	.05	.02
89	Bret Saberhagen	.10	.06
90	Alan Trammell	.10	.06
91	Tony Phillips	.05	.02
92	Doug Drabek	.10	.06
93	Jeffrey Leonard	.05	.02
94	Wally Joyner	.08	.05
95	Carney Lansford	.07	.04
96	Cal Ripken	.50	.30
97	Andres Galarraga	.07	.04
98	Kevin Mitchell	.10	.06
99	Howard Johnson	.08	.05
100	Checklist	.05	.02
101	Melido Perez	.05	.02
102	Spike Owen	.05	.02

103	Paul Molitor	.08	.05
104	Geronimo Berroa	.05	.02
105	Ryne Sandberg	.35	.20
106	Bryn Smith	.05	.02
107	Steve Buechele	.05	.02
108	Jim Abbott	.25	.15
109	Alvin Davis	.05	.02
110	Lee Smith	.10	.06
111	Roberto Alomar	.40	.25
112	Rick Reuschel	.05	.02
113	Kelly Gruber	.07	.04
114	Joe Carter	.20	.12
115	Jose Rijo	.08	.05
116	Greg Minton	.05	.02
117	Bob Ojeda	.05	.02
118	Glenn Davis	.05	.02
119	Jeff Reardon	.08	.05
120	Kurt Stillwell	.05	.02
121	John Smoltz	.30	.18
122	Dwight Evans	.07	.04
123	Eric Yelding	.07	.04
124	John Franco	.05	.02
125	Jose Canseco	.35	.20
126	Barry Bonds	.30	.18
127	Lee Guetterman	.05	.02
128	Jack Clark	.07	.04
129	Dave Valle	.05	.02
130	Hubie Brooks	.07	.04
131	Ernest Riles	.05	.02
132	Mike Morgan	.05	.02
133	Steve Jeltz	.05	.02
134	Jeff Robinson	.05	.02
135	Ozzie Guillen	.07	.04
136	Chili Davis	.07	.04
137	Mitch Webster	.05	.02
138	Jerry Browne	.05	.02
139	Bo Diaz	.05	.02
140	Robby Thompson	.05	.02
141	Craig Worthington	.05	.02
142	Julio Franco	.10	.06
143	Brian Holman	.05	.02
144	George Brett	.20	.12
145	Tom Glavine	.40	.25
146	Robin Yount	.20	.12
147	Gary Carter	.08	.05
148	Ron Kittle	.05	.02
149	Tony Fernandez	.05	.02
150	Dave Stewart	.08	.05
151	Gary Gaetti	.05	.02
152	Kevin Elster	.05	.02
153	Gerald Perry	.05	.02
154	Jesse Orosco	.05	.02
155	Wally Backman	.05	.02
156	Dennis Martinez	.08	.05
157	Rick Sutcliffe	.05	.02
158	Greg Maddux	.10	.06
159	Andy Hawkins	.05	.02
160	John Kruk	.07	.04
161	Jose Oquendo	.05	.02
162	John Dopson	.05	.02
163	Joe Magrane	.05	.02
164	Billy Ripken	.05	.02
165	Fred Manrique	.05	.02
166	Nolan Ryan	.60	.35
167	Damon Berryhill	.05	.02
168	Dale Murphy	.10	.06
169	Mickey Tettleton	.07	.04
170	Kirk McCaskill	.05	.02
171	Dwight Gooden	.12	.07
172	Jose Lind	.05	.02
173	B.J. Surhoff	.05	.02
174	Ruben Sierra	.25	.15
175	Dan Plesac	.05	.02
176	Dan Pasqua	.05	.02
177	Kelly Downs	.05	.02
178	Matt Nokes	.05	.02
179	Luis Aquino	.05	.02
180	Frank Tanana	.05	.02
181	Tony Pena	.05	.02
182	Dan Gladden	.05	.02
183	Bruce Hurst	.07	.04
184	Roger Clemens	.35	.20
185	Mark McGwire	.40	.25
186	Rob Murphy	.05	.02
187	Jim Deshaies	.05	.02
188	Fred McGriff	.25	.15
189	Rob Dibble	.08	.05
190	Don Mattingly	.20	.12
191	Felix Fermin	.05	.02
192	Roberto Kelly	.15	.08
193	Dennis Cook	.05	.02
194	Darren Daulton	.10	.06
195	Alfredo Griffin	.05	.02
196	Eric Plunk	.05	.02
197	Orel Hershiser	.08	.05
198	Paul O'Neil	.08	.05
199	Randy Bush	.05	.02
200	Checklist	.05	.02
201	Ozzie Smith	.12	.07
202	Pete O'Brien	.05	.02
203	Jay Howell	.05	.02
204	Mark Gibicza	.07	.04
205	Ed Whitson	.05	.02
206	George Bell	.08	.05
207	Mike Scott	.05	.02
208	Charlie Leibrandt	.05	.02
209	Mike Heath	.05	.02
210	Dennis Eckersley	.12	.07
211	Mike LaValliere	.05	.02
212	Darnell Coles	.05	.02
213	Lance Parrish	.05	.02
214	Mike Moore	.05	.02
215	Steve Finley	.07	.04
216	Tim Raines	.07	.04
217	Scott Garrelts	.05	.02
218	Kevin McReynolds	.07	.04

219 Dave Gallagher	.05	.02
220 Tim Wallach	.07	.04
221 Chuck Crim	.05	.02
222 Lonnie Smith	.05	.02
223 Andre Dawson	.15	.08
224 Nelson Santovenia	.05	.02
225 Rafael Palmeiro	.10	.06
226 Devon White	.05	.02
227 Harold Reynolds	.05	.02
228 Ellis Burks	.08	.05
229 Mark Parent	.05	.02
230 Will Clark	.30	.18
231 Jimmy Key	.07	.04
232 John Farrell	.05	.02
233 Eric Davis	.10	.06
234 Johnny Ray	.05	.02
235 Darryl Strawberry	.25	.15
236 Bill Doran	.05	.02
237 Greg Gagne	.05	.02
238 Jim Eisenreich	.05	.02
239 Tommy Gregg	.05	.02
240 Marty Barrett	.05	.02
241 Rafael Ramirez	.05	.02
242 Chris Sabo	.10	.06
243 Dave Henderson	.05	.02
244 Andy Van Slyke	.10	.06
245 Alvaro Espinoza	.05	.02
246 Garry Templeton	.05	.02
247 Gene Harris	.05	.02
248 Kevin Gross	.05	.02
249 Brett Butler	.08	.05
250 Willie Randolph	.05	.02
251 Roger McDowell	.05	.02
252 Rafael Belliard	.05	.02
253 Steve Rosenberg	.05	.02
254 Jack Howell	.05	.02
255 Marvell Wynne	.05	.02
256 Tom Candiotti	.05	.02
257 Todd Benzinger	.05	.02
258 Don Robinson	.05	.02
259 Phil Bradley	.05	.02
260 Cecil Espy	.05	.02
261 Scott Bankhead	.05	.02
262 Frank White	.05	.02
263 Andres Thomas	.05	.02
264 Glenn Braggs	.05	.02
265 David Cone	.10	.06
266 Bobby Thigpen	.07	.04
267 Nelson Liriano	.05	.02
268 Terry Steinbach	.05	.02
269 Kirby Puckett	.30	.18
270 Gregg Jefferies	.12	.07
271 Jeff Blauser	.05	.02
272 Cory Snyder	.05	.02
273 Roy Smith	.05	.02
274 Tom Foley	.05	.02
275 Mitch Williams	.05	.02
276 Paul Kilgus	.05	.02

277 Don Slaught	.05	.02
278 Von Hayes	.05	.02
279 Vince Coleman	.07	.04
280 Mike Boddicker	.05	.02
281 Ken Dayley	.05	.02
282 Mike Devereaux	.08	.05
283 Kenny Rogers	.05	.02
284 Jeff Russell	.05	.02
285 Jerome Walton	.08	.05
286 Derek Lilliquist	.05	.02
287 Joe Orsulak	.05	.02
288 Dick Schofield	.05	.02
289 Ron Darling	.07	.04
290 Bobby Bonilla	.15	.08
291 Jim Gantner	.05	.02
292 Bobby Witt	.08	.05
293 Greg Brock	.05	.02
294 Ivan Calderon	.07	.04
295 Steve Bedrosian	.05	.02
296 Mike Henneman	.05	.02
297 Tom Gordon	.07	.04
298 Lou Whitaker	.07	.04
299 Terry Pendleton	.15	.08
300 Checklist	.05	.02
301 Juan Berenguer	.05	.02
302 Mark Davis	.05	.02
303 Nick Esasky	.05	.02
304 Rickey Henderson	.20	.12
305 Rick Cerone	.05	.02
306 Craig Biggio	.10	.06
307 Duane Ward	.05	.02
308 Tom Browning	.07	.04
309 Walt Terrell	.05	.02
310 Greg Swindell	.07	.04
311 Dave Righetti	.05	.02
312 Mike Maddux	.05	.02
131 Lenny Dykstra	.07	.04
314 Jose Gonzalez	.05	.02
315 Steve Balboni	.05	.02
316 Mike Scioscia	.05	.02
317 Ron Oester	.05	.02
318 Gary Wayne	.05	.02
319 Todd Worrell	.08	.05
320 Doug Jones	.05	.02
321 Jeff Hamilton	.05	.02
322 Danny Tartabull	.10	.06
323 Chris James	.05	.02
324 Mike Flanagan	.05	.02
325 Gerald Young	.05	.02
326 Bob Boone	.08	.05
327 Frank Williams	.05	.02
328 Dave Parker	.07	.04
329 Sid Bream	.05	.02
330 Mike Schooler	.05	.02
331 Bert Blyleven	.10	.06
332 Bob Welch	.07	.04
333 Bob Milacki	.05	.02
334 Tim Burke	.05	.02

335	Jose Uribe	.05	.02	393	Dwight Smith	.08	.05
336	Randy Myers	.05	.02	394	Steve Wilson	.07	.04
337	Eric King	.05	.02	395	Bob Geren	.05	.02
338	Mark Langston	.08	.05	396	Randy Ready	.05	.02
339	Ted Higuera	.05	.02	397	Ken Hill	.08	.05
340	Oddibe McDowell	.05	.02	398	Jody Reed	.05	.02
341	Lloyd McClendon	.05	.02	399	Tom Brunansky	.07	.04
342	Pasqual Perez	.05	.02	400	Checklist	.05	.02
343	Kevin Brown	.10	.06	401	Rene Gonzales	.05	.02
344	Chuck Finley	.08	.05	402	Harold Baines	.07	.04
345	Erik Hanson	.10	.06	403	Cecilio Guante	.05	.02
346	Rich Gedman	.05	.02	404	Joe Girardi	.07	.04
347	Bip Roberts	.05	.02	405	Sergio Valdez (R)	.10	.06
348	Matt Williams	.10	.06	406	Mark Williamson	.05	.02
349	Tom Henke	.05	.02	407	Glenn Hoffman	.05	.02
350	Brad Komminsk	.05	.02	408	Jeff Innis (R)	.10	.06
351	Jeff Reed	.05	.02	409	Randy Kramer	.05	.02
352	Brian Downing	.05	.02	410	Charlie O'Brien	.07	.04
353	Frank Viola	.08	.05	411	Charlie Hough	.05	.02
354	Terry Puhl	.05	.02	412	Gus Polidor	.05	.02
355	Brian Harper	.05	.02	413	Ron Karkovice	.05	.02
356	Steve Farr	.05	.02	414	Trevor Wilson (R)	.12	.07
357	Joe Boever	.05	.02	415	Kevin Ritz (R)	.10	.06
358	Danny Heep	.05	.02	416	Gary Thurman	.05	.02
359	Larry Andersen	.05	.02	417	Jeff Robinson	.05	.02
360	Rolando Roomes	.05	.02	418	Scott Terry	.05	.02
361	Mike Gallego	.05	.02	419	Tim Laudner	.05	.02
362	Bob Kipper	.05	.02	420	Dennis Rasmussen	.05	.02
363	Clay Parker	.05	.02	421	Luis Rivera	.05	.02
364	Mike Pagliarulo	.05	.02	422	Jim Corsi	.05	.02
365	Ken Griffey, Jr.	1.50	.90	423	Dennis Lamp	.05	.02
366	Rex Hudler	.05	.02	424	Ken Caminiti	.07	.04
367	Pat Sheridan	.05	.02	425	David Wells	.05	.02
368	Kirk Gibson	.07	.04	426	Norm Charlton	.07	.04
369	Jeff Parrett	.05	.02	427	Deion Sanders	.40	.25
370	Bob Walk	.05	.02	428	Dion James	.05	.02
371	Ken Patterson	.05	.02	429	Chuck Cary	.05	.02
372	Bryan Harvey	.08	.05	430	Ken Howell	.05	.02
373	Mike Bielecki	.05	.02	431	Steve Lake	.05	.02
374	Tom Magrann (R)	.08	.05	432	Kal Daniels	.05	.02
375	Rick Mahler	.05	.02	433	Lance McCullers	.05	.02
376	Craig Lefferts	.05	.02	434	Lenny Harris	.05	.02
377	Gregg Olson	.08	.05	435	Scott Scudder (R)	.12	.07
378	Jamie Moyer	.05	.02	436	Gene Larkin	.05	.02
379	Randy Johnson	.05	.02	437	Dan Quisenberry	.05	.02
380	Jeff Montgomery	.05	.02	438	Steve Olin (R)	.15	.08
381	Marty Clary	.05	.02	439	Mickey Hatcher	.05	.02
382	Bill Spiers	.07	.04	440	Willie Wilson	.05	.02
383	Dave Magadan	.07	.04	441	Mark Grant	.05	.02
384	Greg Hibbard (R)	.15	.08	442	Mookie Wilson	.05	.02
385	Ernie Whitt	.05	.02	443	Alex Trevino	.05	.02
386	Rick Honeycutt	.05	.02	444	Pat Tabler	.05	.02
387	Dave West	.05	.02	445	Dave Bergman	.05	.02
388	Keith Hernandez	.07	.04	446	Todd Burns	.05	.02
389	Jose Alvarez	.05	.02	447	R.J. Reynolds	.05	.02
390	Joey Belle (R)	.70	.40	448	Jay Buhner	.08	.05
391	Rick Aguilera	.05	.02	449	Lee Stevens (R)	.20	.12
392	Mike Fitzgerald	.05	.02	450	Ron Hassey	.05	.02

No.	Player		
451	Bob Melvin	.05	.02
452	Dave Martinez	.05	.02
453	Greg Litton (R)	.10	.06
454	Mark Carreon	.05	.02
455	Scott Fletcher	.05	.02
456	Otis Nixon	.05	.02
457	Tony Fossas (R)	.10	.06
458	John Russell	.05	.02
459	Paul Assenmacher	.05	.02
460	Zane Smith	.05	.02
461	Jack Daugherty (R)	.15	.08
462	Rich Monteleone (R)	.08	.05
463	Greg Briley (R)	.08	.05
464	Mike Smithson	.05	.02
465	Benito Santiago	.08	.05
466	Jeff Brantley	.07	.04
467	Jose Nunez	.05	.02
468	Scott Bailes	.05	.02
469	Ken Griffey, Sr.	.07	.04
470	Bob McClure	.05	.02
471	Mackey Sasser	.05	.02
472	Glenn Wilson	.05	.02
473	Kevin Tapani (R)	.30	.18
474	Bill Buckner	.07	.04
475	Ron Gant	.25	.15
476	Kevin Romine	.05	.02
477	Juan Agosto	.05	.02
478	Herm Winningham	.05	.02
479	Storm Davis	.05	.02
480	Jeff King (R)	.10	.06
481	Kevin Mmahat (R)	.10	.06
482	Carmelo Martinez	.05	.02
483	Omar Vizquel	.05	.02
484	Jim Dwyer	.05	.02
485	Bob Knepper	.05	.02
486	Dave Anderson	.05	.02
487	Ron Jones	.05	.02
488	Jay Bell	.07	.04
489	Sammy Sosa (R)	.25	.15
490	Kent Anderson (R)	.08	.05
491	Domingo Ramos	.05	.02
492	Dave Clark	.05	.02
493	Tim Birtsas	.05	.02
494	Ken Oberkfell	.05	.02
495	Larry Sheets	.05	.02
496	Jeff Kunkel	.05	.02
497	Jim Presley	.05	.02
498	Mike Macfarlane	.05	.02
499	Pete Smith	.12	.07
500	Checklist	.05	.02
501	Gary Sheffield	.50	.30
502	Terry Bross (R)	.12	.07
503	Jerry Kutzler (R)	.08	.05
504	Lloyd Moseby	.05	.02
505	Curt Young	.05	.02
506	Al Newman	.05	.02
507	Keith Miller	.05	.02
508	Mike Stanton (R)	.15	.08
509	Rich Yett	.05	.02
510	Tim Drummond (R)	.10	.06
511	Joe Hesketh	.05	.02
512	Rick Wrona	.07	.04
513	Luis Salazar	.05	.02
514	Hal Morris	.25	.15
515	Terry Mulholland	.08	.05
516	John Morris	.05	.02
517	Carlos Quintana	.07	.04
518	Frank DePino	.05	.02
519	Randy Milligan	.07	.04
520	Chad Kreuter	.05	.02
521	Mike Jeffcoat	.05	.02
522	Mike Harkey	.08	.05
523	Andy Nezelek	.05	.02
524	Dave Schmidt	.05	.02
525	Tony Armas	.05	.02
526	Barry Lyons	.05	.02
527	Rick Reed (R)	.10	.06
528	Jerry Reuss	.05	.02
529	Dean Palmer (R)	.75	.45
530	Jeff Peterek (R)	.08	.05
531	Carlos Martinez	.05	.02
532	Atlee Hammaker	.05	.02
533	Mike Brumley	.05	.02
534	Terry Leach	.05	.02
535	Doug Strange (R)	.10	.06
536	Jose DeLeon	.05	.02
537	Shane Rawley	.05	.02
538	Joey Cora	.08	.05
539	Eric Hetzel	.05	.02
540	Gene Nelson	.05	.02
541	Wes Gardner	.05	.02
542	Mark Portugal	.05	.02
543	Al Leiter	.05	.02
544	Jack Armstrong	.07	.04
545	Greg Cadaret	.05	.02
546	Rod Nichols	.05	.02
547	Luis Polonia	.05	.02
548	Charlie Hayes	.10	.06
549	Dickie Thon	.05	.02
550	Tim Crews	.05	.02
551	Dave Winfield	.15	.08
552	Mike Davis	.05	.02
553	Ron Robinson	.05	.02
554	Carmen Castillo	.05	.02
555	John Costello	.05	.02
556	Bud Black	.05	.02
557	Rick Dempsey	.05	.02
558	Jim Acker	.05	.02
559	Eric Show	.05	.02
560	Pat Borders	.05	.02
561	Danny Darwin	.05	.02
562	Rick Luecken (R)	.08	.05
563	Edwin Nunez	.05	.02
564	Felix Jose	.15	.08
565	John Cangelosi	.05	.02
566	Bill Swift	.07	.04

No.	Player		
567	Bill Schroeder	.05	.02
568	Stan Javier	.05	.02
569	Jim Traber	.05	.02
570	Wallace Johnson	.05	.02
571	Donell Nixon	.05	.02
572	Sid Fernandez	.05	.02
573	Lance Johnson	.05	.02
574	Andy McGaffigan	.05	.02
575	Mark Knudson	.05	.02
576	Tommy Greene (R)	.20	.12
577	Mark Grace	.15	.08
578	Larry Walker (R)	.75	.45
579	Mike Stanley	.05	.02
580	Mike Witt	.05	.02
581	Scott Bradley	.05	.02
582	Greg Harris	.05	.02
583	Kevin Hickey	.05	.02
584	Lee Mazzilli	.05	.02
585	Jeff Pico	.07	.04
586	Joe Oliver (R)	.15	.08
587	Willie Fraser	.05	.02
588	Puzzle Card	.07	.04
589	Kevin Bass	.05	.02
590	John Moses	.05	.02
591	Tom Pagnozzi	.08	.05
592	Tony Castillo	.05	.02
593	Jerald Clark	.07	.04
594	Dan Schatzeder	.05	.02
595	Luis Quinones	.05	.02
596	Pete Harnisch	.07	.04
597	Gary Redus	.05	.02
598	Mel Hall	.07	.04
599	Rick Schu	.05	.02
600	Checklist	.05	.02
601	Mike Kingery	.05	.02
602	Terry Kennedy	.05	.02
603	Mike Sharperson	.05	.02
604	Don Carman	.05	.02
605	Jim Gott	.05	.02
606	Donn Pall	.05	.02
607	Rance Mulliniks	.05	.02
608	Curt Wilkerson	.05	.02
609	Mike Felder	.05	.02
610	Guillermo Hernandez	.05	.02
611	Candy Maldonado	.05	.02
612	Mark Thurmond	.05	.02
613	Rick Leach	.05	.02
614	Jerry Reed	.05	.02
615	Franklin Stubbs	.05	.02
616	Billy Hatcher	.05	.02
617	Don August	.05	.02
618	Tim Teufel	.05	.02
619	Shawn Hillegas	.05	.02
620	Manny Lee	.05	.02
621	Gary Ward	.05	.02
622	Mark Guthrie (R)	.10	.06
623	Jeff Musselman	.05	.02
624	Mark Lemke	.08	.05
625	Fernando Valenzuela	.08	.05
626	Paul Sorrento (R)	.20	.12
627	Glenallen Hill	.08	.05
628	Les Lancaster	.05	.02
629	Vance Law	.05	.02
630	Randy Velarde	.07	.04
631	Todd Frohwirth	.05	.02
632	Willie McGee	.08	.05
633	Oil Can Boyd	.05	.02
634	Cris Carpenter	.05	.02
635	Brian Holton	.05	.02
636	Tracy Jones	.05	.02
637	Terry Steinbach (AS)	.07	.04
638	Brady Anderson	.10	.06
639	Jack Morris (R)	.30	.18
639	Jack Morris (Cor)	.12	.07
640	Jaime Navarro (R)	.35	.20
641	Darrin Jackson	.05	.02
642	Mike Dyer (R)	.10	.06
643	Mike Schmidt	.30	.18
644	Henry Cotto	.05	.02
645	John Cerutti	.05	.02
646	Francisco Cabrera (R)	.10	.06
647	Scott Sanderson	.05	.02
648	Brian Meyer	.05	.02
649	Ray Searage	.05	.02
650a	Bo Jackson AS (Er) (Major League Performance)	.40	.25
650b	Bo Jackson AS (Cor) (All-Star Performance)	.20	.12
651	Steve Lyons	.05	.02
652	Mike LaCoss	.05	.02
653	Ted Power	.05	.02
654	Howard Johnson (AS)	.08	.05
655	Mauro Gozzo (R)	.08	.05
656	Mike Blowers (R)	.08	.05
657	Paul Gibson	.05	.02
654	Neal Heaton	.05	.02
659a	Nolan Ryan (5000K) (Er)	3.50	2.25
659b	Nolan Ryan (5000K) (Cor)	.50	.30
660a	Harold Baines (AS)(Er)	2.00	1.25
660b	Harold Baines (AS)(Cor)	.08	.05
661	Gary Pettis	.05	.02
662	Clint Zavaras (R)	.10	.06
663	Rick Reuschel	.05	.02
664	Alejandro Pena	.05	.02
665a	Nolan Ryan (King)(Er) (Wrong Card Number)	2.50	1.50
665b	Nolan Ryan (King)(Er) (No Card Number)	1.00	.70
665c	Nolan Ryan (King)(Cor)	.50	.30
666	Ricky Horton	.05	.02

667	Curt Schilling	.05	.02
668	Bill Landrum	.05	.02
669	Todd Stottlemyre	.07	.04
670	Tim Leary	.05	.02
671	John Wetteland (R)	.15	.08
672	Calvin Schiraldi	.05	.02
673	Ruben Sierra(AS)	.12	.07
674	Pedro Guerrero(AS)	.05	.02
675	Ken Phelps	.05	.02
676	Cal Ripken(AS)	.20	.12
677	Denny Walling	.05	.02
678	Goose Gossage	.07	.04
679	Gary Mielke (R)	.08	.05
680	Bill Bathe	.05	.02
681	Tom Lawless	.05	.02
682	Xavier Hernandez (R)	.10	.06
683	Kirby Puckett(AS)	.15	.08
684	Mariano Duncan	.05	.02
685	Ramon Martinez	.25	.15
686	Tim Jones	.05	.02
687	Tom Filer	.05	.02
688	Steve Lombardozzi	.05	.02
689	Bernie Williams (R)	.25	.15
690	Chip Hale (R)	.10	.06
691	Beau Allred (R)	.12	.07
692	Ryne Sandberg(AS)	.15	.08
693	Jeff Huson (R)	.10	.06
694	Curt Ford	.05	.02
695	Eric Davis(AS)	.08	.05
696	Scott Lusader	.05	.02
697	Mark McGwire(AS)	.15	.08
698	Steve Cummings (R)	.10	.06
699	George Canale (R)	.12	.07
700	Checklist	.05	.02
701	Julio Franco(AS)	.10	.06
702	Dave Johnson (R)	.10	.06
703	Dave Stewart(AS)	.08	.05
704	Dave Justice (R)	1.25	.80
705	Tony Gwynn(AS)	.12	.07
706	Greg Myers	.05	.02
707	Will Clark(AS)	.15	.08
708	Benito Santiago(AS)	.10	.06
709	Larry McWilliams	.05	.02
710	Ozzie Smith(AS)	.10	.06
711	John Olerud (R)	.70	.40
712	Wade Boggs(AS)	.10	.06
713	Gary Eave (R)	.10	.06
714	Bob Tewksbury	.07	.04
715	Kevin Mitchell(AS)	.10	.06
716	A. Bartlett Giamatti	.15	.08
B1	Bo Jackson	.20	.12
B2	Howard Johnson	.08	.05
B3	Dave Stewart	.08	.05
B4	Tony Gwynn	.12	.07
B5	Orel Hershiser	.08	.05
B6	Pedro Guerrero	.07	.04
B7	Tim Raines	.07	.04
B8	Kirby Puckett	.15	.08

B9	Alvin Davis	.05	.02
B10	Ryne Sandberg	.12	.07
B11	Kevin Mitchell	.08	.05
B12	John Smoltz	.12	.07
B13	George Bell	.08	.05
B14	Julio Franco	.07	.04
B15	Paul Molitor	.08	.05
B16	Bobby Bonilla	.08	.05
B17	Mike Greenwell	.07	.04
B18	Cal Ripken	.15	.08
B19	Carlton Fisk	.08	.05
B20	Chili Davis	.07	.04
B21	Glenn Davis	.05	.02
B22	Steve Sax	.07	.04
B23	Eric Davis	.08	.05
B24	Greg Swindell	.07	.04
B25	Von Hayes	.05	.02
B26	Alan Trammell	.10	.06

1990 Donruss Rookies

This 56-card update set features green borders and a small "rookies" logo on the card front to distinguish it from the 1990 Donruss regular issue. Cards measure 2-1/2" by 3-1/2".

		MINT	NR/MT
Complete Set (56)		7.00	4.00
Commons		.05	.02

1	Sandy Alomar	.08	.05
2	John Olerud	.30	.18
3	Pat Combs	.10	.06
4	Brian Dubois	.15	.08
5	Felix Jose	.35	.20
6	Delino DeShields	.60	.35

1991 Donruss

For the first time Donruss issued their set in two series. Card fronts feature blue borders and the cards measure 2-1/2" by 3-1/2". Key subsets include Diamond Kings and Rated Rookies. 22 Bonus insert cards were given away randomly. Special limited edition Elite Series cards were randomly packed in series I wax packs. Those values can be found at the end of this checklist. 5,000 autographed Ryne Sandberg cards called The Signature Series were given away. 7,500 Nolan Ryan cards, called The Legend Series, also appeared randomly in wax packs.

		MINT	NR/MT
Complete Set (792)		16.50	10.50
Commons		.05	.02

1	Dave Steib (DK)	.08	.05
2	Craig Biggio (DK)	.07	.04
3	Cecil Fielder (DK)	.10	.06
4	Barry Bonds (DK)	.12	.07
5	Barry Larkin (DK)	.08	.05
6	Dave Parker (DK)	.07	.04
7	Len Dykstra (DK)	.07	.04
8	Bobby Thigpen (DK)	.07	.04
9	Roger Clemens (DK)	.12	.07
10	Ron Gant (DK)	.10	.06
11	Delino DeShields (DK)	.10	.06
12	Roberto Alomar (DK)	.10	.06
13	Sandy Alomar (DK)	.08	.05
14	Ryne Sandberg (DK)	.12	.08
15	Ramon Martinez (DK)	.08	.05
16	Edgar Martinez (DK)	.08	.05
17	Dave Magadan (DK)	.07	.04
18	Matt Williams (DK)	.10	.06
19	Rafael Palmeiro (DK)	.08	.05
20	Bon Welch (DK)	.07	.04
21	Dave Righetti (DK)	.07	.04

7	Mike Stanton	.08	.05
8	Mike Munoz (R)	.08	.05
9	Craig Grebeck (R))	.15	.08
10	Joe Kraemer (R)	.08	.05
11	Jeff Huson	.08	.05
12	Bill Sampen (R)	.15	.08
13	Brian Bohanon (R)	.08	.05
14	Dave Justice	1.00	.70
15	Robin Ventura	.80	.50
16	Greg Vaughn	.25	.15
17	Wayne Edwards (R)	.10	.06
18	Shawn Boskie	.10	.06
19	Carlos Baerga (R)	1.25	.80
20	Mark Gardner	.12	.07
21	Kevin Appier (R)	.50	.30
22	Mike Harkey	.10	.06
23	Tim Layana (R)	.10	.06
24	Glenallen Hill	.10	.06
25	Jerry Kutzler	.05	.02
26	Mike Blowers	.08	.05
27	Scott Ruskin (R)	.15	.08
28	Dana Kiecker (R)	.15	.08
29	Willie Blair (R)	.20	.12
30	Ben McDonald	.50	.30
31	Todd Zeile	.20	.12
32	Scott Coolbaugh	.05	.02
33	Xavier Hernandez	.05	.02
34	Mike Harley (R)	.08	.05
35	Kevin Tapani	.25	.15
36	Kevin Wickander	.05	.02
37	Carlos Hernandez	.08	.05
38	Brian Traxler (R)	.10	.06
39	Marty Brown (R)	.07	.04
40	Scott Radinsky	.12	.07
41	Julio Machado	.07	.04
42	Steve Avery	1.00	.70
43	Mark Lemke	.08	.05
44	Alan Mills	.10	.06
45	Marquis Grissom	.50	.30
46	Greg Olson (R)	.08	.05
47	Dave Hollins (R)	.50	.30
48	Jerald Clark	.08	.05
49	Eric Anthony	.35	.20
50	Tim Drummond	.08	.05
51	John Burkett	.10	.06
52	Brent Knackert (R)	.12	.07
53	Jeff Shaw (R)	.10	.06
54	John Orton (R)	.12	.07
55	Terry Shumpert	.12	.07
56	Checklist	.05	.02

22	Brian Harper (DK)	.07	.04	80	Kevin Reimer	.08	.05
23	Gregg Olson (DK)	.07	.04	81	Roger Clemens	.25	.15
24	Kurt Stillwell (DK)	.07	.04	82	Mike Fitzgerald	.05	.02
25	Pedro Guerrero (DK)	.07	.04	83	Bruce Hurst	.07	.04
26	Chuck Finley (DK)	.08	.05	84	Eric Davis	.08	.05
27	Checklist (DK)	.05	.02	85	Paul Molitor	.10	.06
28	Tino Martinez (R)	.20	.12	86	Will Clark	.20	.12
29	Mark Lewis (R)	.15	.08	87	Mike Bielecki	.05	.02
30	Bernard Gilkey (R)	.25	.15	88	Bret Saberhagen	.08	.05
31	Hensley Meulens	.07	.04	89	Nolan Ryan	.40	.25
32	Derek Bell (R)	.35	.20	90	Bobby Thigpen	.07	.04
33	Jose Offerman (R)	.20	.12	91	Dickie Thon	.05	.02
34	Terry Bross	.08	.05	92	Duane Ward	.05	.02
35	Leo Gomez (R)	.35	.20	93	Luis Polonia	.05	.02
36	Derrick May	.15	.08	94	Terry Kennedy	.05	.02
37	Kevin Morton (R)	.10	.06	95	Kent Hrbek	.07	.04
38	Moises Alou (R)	.20	.12	96	Danny Jackson	.05	.02
39	Julio Valera (R)	.12	.08	97	Sid Fernandez	.07	.04
40	Milt Cuyler (R)	.20	.12	98	Jimmy Key	.07	.04
41	Phil Plantier (R)	.60	.35	99	Franklin Stubbs	.05	.02
42	Scott Chiamparino (R)	.12	.07	100	Checklist	.05	.02
43	Ray Lankford (R)	.50	.30	101	R.J. Reynolds	.05	.02
44	Mickey Morandini (R)	.15	.07	102	Dave Stewart	.08	.05
45	Dave Hansen (R)	.25	.15	103	Dan Pasqua	.05	.02
46	Kevin Belcher (R)	.10	.06	104	Dan Plesac	.05	.02
47	Darrin Fletcher (R)	.10	.06	105	Mark McGwire	.20	.12
48	Steve Sax(AS)	.07	.04	106	John Farrell	.05	.02
49	Ken Griffey, Jr.(AS)	.20	.12	107	Don Mattingly	.12	.07
50	Jose Canseco(AS)	.15	.08	108	Carlton Fisk	.10	.06
51	Sandy Alomar(AS)	.07	.04	109	Ken Oberkfell	.05	.02
52	Cal Ripken(AS)	.20	.12	110	Darrell Akerfelds	.05	.02
53	Rickey Henderson(AS)	.12	.07	111	Gregg Olson	.07	.04
54	Bob Welch(AS)	.07	.04	112	Mike Scioscia	.05	.02
55	Wade Boggs(AS)	.10	.06	113	Bryn Smith	.05	.02
56	Mark McGwire(AS)	.15	.08	114	Bob Geren	.05	.02
57	Jack McDowell	.15	.08	115	Tom Candiotti	.05	.02
58	Jose Lind	.05	.02	116	Kevin Tapani	.08	.05
59	Alex Fernandez (R)	.20	.12	117	Jeff Treadway	.05	.02
60	Pat Combs	.08	.05	118	Alan Trammell	.08	.05
61	Mike Walker (R)	.08	.05	119	Pete O'Brien	.05	.02
62	Juan Samuel	.05	.02	120	Joel Skinner	.05	.02
63	Mike Blowers	.07	.04	121	Mike LaValliere	.05	.02
64	Mark Guthrie	.05	.02	122	Dwight Evans	.07	.04
65	Mark Salas	.05	.02	123	Jody Reed	.05	.02
66	Tim Jones	.05	.02	124	Lee Guetterman	.05	.02
67	Tim Leary	.05	.02	125	Tim Burke	.05	.02
68	Andres Galarraga	.07	.04	126	Dave Johnson	.05	.02
69	Bob Milacki	.05	.02	127	Fernando Valenzuela	.07	.04
70	Tim Belcher	.07	.04	128	Jose DeLeon	.05	.02
71	Todd Zeile	.10	.06	129	Andre Dawson	.12	.07
72	Jerome Walton	.07	.04	130	Gerald Perry	.05	.02
73	Kevin Seitzer	.07	.04	131	Greg Harris	.05	.02
74	Jerald Clark	.07	.04	132	Tom Glavine	.12	.07
75	John Smoltz	.15	.08	133	Lance McCullers	.05	.02
76	Mike Henneman	.05	.02	134	Randy Johnson	.12	.07
77	Ken Griffey, Jr.	.50	.30	135	Lance Parrish	.05	.02
78	Jim Abbott	.12	.07	136	Mackey Sasser	.05	.02
79	Gregg Jefferies	.10	.06	137	Geno Petralli	.05	.02

No.	Player		
138	Dennis Lamp	.05	.02
139	Dennis Martinez	.08	.05
140	Mike Pagliarulo	.05	.02
141	Hal Morris	.10	.06
142	Dave Parker	.07	.04
143	Brett Butler	.07	.04
144	Paul Assenmacher	.05	.02
145	Mark Gubicza	.07	.04
146	Charlie Hough	.05	.02
147	Sammy Sosa	.08	.05
148	Randy Ready	.05	.02
149	Kelly Gruber	.07	.04
150	Devon White	.05	.02
151	Gary Carter	.10	.06
152	Gene Larkin	.05	.02
153	Chris Sabo	.08	.05
154	David Cone	.10	.06
155	Todd Stottlemyre	.07	.04
156	Glenn Wilson	.07	.04
157	Bob Walk	.07	.04
158	Mike Gallego	.05	.02
159	Greg Hibbard	.05	.02
160	Chris Bosio	.07	.04
161	Mike Moore	.05	.02
162	Jerry Browne	.05	.02
163	Steve Sax	.07	.04
164	Melido Perez	.05	.02
165	Danny Darwin	.05	.02
166	Roger McDowell	.05	.02
167	Bill Ripken	.05	.02
168	Mike Sharperson	.05	.02
169	Lee Smith	.08	.05
170	Matt Nokes	.05	.02
171	Jesse Orosco	.05	.02
172	Rick Aguilera	.05	.02
173	Jim Presley	.05	.02
174	Lou Whitaker	.07	.04
175	Harold Reynolds	.05	.02
176	Brook Jacoby	.05	.02
177	Wally Backman	.05	.02
178	Wade Boggs	.10	.06
179	Chuck Cary	.05	.02
180	Tom Folen	.05	.02
181	Pete Harnisch	.07	.04
182	Mike Morgan	.05	.02
183	Bob Tewksbury	.05	.02
184	Joe Girardi	.05	.02
185	Storm Davis	.05	.02
186	Ed Whitson	.05	.02
187	Steve Avery	.25	.15
188	Lloyd Moseby	.05	.02
189	Scott Bankhead	.05	.02
190	Mark Langston	.08	.05
191	Kevin McReynolds	.07	.04
192	Julio Franco	.08	.05
193	John Dopson	.05	.02
194	Oil Can Boyd	.05	.02
195	Bip Roberts	.05	.02
196	Billy Hatcher	.05	.02
197	Edgar Diaz	.08	.05
198	Greg Litton	.05	.02
199	Mark Grace	.10	.06
200	Checklist	.05	.02
201	George Brett	.15	.08
202	Jeff Russell	.05	.02
203	Ivan Calderson	.07	.04
204	Ken Howell	.05	.02
205	Tom Henke	.05	.02
206	Bryan Harvey	.07	.04
207	Steve Bedrosian	.05	.02
208	Al Newman	.05	.02
209	Randy Myers	.05	.02
210	Daryl Boston	.05	.02
211	Manny Lee	.05	.02
212	Dave Smith	.05	.02
213	Don Slaught	.05	.02
214	Walt Weiss	.07	.04
215	Donn Pall	.05	.02
216	Jamie Navarro	.08	.05
217	Willie Randolph	.05	.02
218	Rudy Seanez (R)	.12	.07
219	Jim Leyritz (R)	.10	.06
220	Ron Karkovice	.05	.02
221	Ken Caminiti	.07	.04
222	Von Hayes	.05	.02
223	Cal Ripken	.25	.15
224	Lenny Harris	.05	.02
225	Milt Thompson	.05	.02
226	Alvaro Espinoza	.05	.02
227	Chris James	.05	.02
228	Dan Gladden	.05	.02
229	Jeff Blauser	.05	.02
230	Mike Heath	.05	.02
231	Omar Vizquel	.05	.02
232	Doug Jones	.05	.02
233	Jeff King	.07	.04
234	Luis Rivera	.05	.02
235	Ellis Burks	.08	.05
236	Greg Cadaret	.05	.02
237	Dave Martinez	.05	.02
238	Mark Williamson	.05	.02
239	Stan Javier	.05	.02
240	Ozzie Smith	.12	.07
241	Shawn Boskie	.05	.02
242	Tom Gordon	.07	.04
243	Tony Gwynn	.15	.08
244	Tommy Gregg	.05	.02
245	Jeff Robinson	.05	.02
246	Keith Comstock	.05	.02
247	Jack Howell	.05	.02
248	Keith Miller	.05	.02
249	Bobby Witt	.07	.04
250	Rob Murphy	.05	.02
251	Spike Owen	.05	.02
252	Garry Templeton	.05	.02
253	Glenn Braggs	.05	.02

254	Ron Robinson	.05	.02	312	Mitch Williams	.05	.02
255	Kevin Mitchell	.08	.05	313	Mike Macfarlane	.05	.02
256	Les Lancaster	.05	.02	314	Kevin Brown	.07	.04
257	Mel Stottlemyre (R)	.10	.06	315	Robin Ventura	.20	.12
258	Kenny Rogers	.05	.02	316	Darren Daulton	.08	.05
259	Lance Johnson	.05	.02	317	Pat Borders	.05	.02
260	John Kruk	.07	.04	318	Mark Eichhorn	.05	.02
261	Fred McGriff	.15	.08	319	Jeff Brantley	.05	.02
262	Dick Schofield	.05	.02	320	Shane Mack	.08	.05
263	Trevor Wilson	.05	.02	321	Rob Dibble	.07	.04
264	David West	.05	.02	322	John Franco	.05	.02
265	Scott Scudder	.07	.04	323	Junior Felix	.05	.02
266	Dwight Gooden	.12	.07	324	Casey Candaele	.05	.02
267	Willie Blair	.10	.06	325	Bobby Bonilla	.12	.07
268	Mark Portugal	.05	.02	326	Dave Henderson	.05	.02
269	Doug Drabek	.10	.06	327	Wayne Edwards	.05	.02
270	Dennis Eckersley	.12	.07	328	Mark Knudson	.05	.02
271	Eric King	.05	.02	329	Terry Steinbach	.05	.02
272	Robin Yount	.15	.08	330	Colby Ward (R)	.10	.06
273	Carney Lansford	.07	.04	331	Oscar Azocar (R)	.12	.07
274	Carlos Baerga	.25	.15	332	Scott Radinsky	.07	.04
275	Dave Righetti	.05	.02	333	Eric Anthony	.10	.06
276	Scott Fletcher	.05	.02	334	Steve Lake	.05	.02
277	Eric Yelding	.05	.02	335	Bob Melvin	.05	.02
278	Charlie Hayes	.05	.02	336	Kal Daniels	.05	.02
279	Jeff Ballard	.05	.02	337	Tom Pagnozzi	.07	.04
280	Orel Hershiser	.08	.05	338	Alan Mills	.05	.02
281	Jose Oquendo	.05	.02	339	Steve Olin	.05	.02
282	Mike Witt	.05	.02	340	Juan Berenguer	.05	.02
283	Mitch Webster	.05	.02	341	Francisco Cabrera	.07	.04
284	Greg Gagne	.05	.02	342	Dave Bergman	.05	.02
285	Greg Olson	.07	.04	343	Henry Cotto	.05	.02
286	Tony Phillips	.05	.02	344	Sergio Valdez	.05	.02
287	Scott Bradley	.05	.02	345	Bob Patterson	.05	.02
288	Cory Snyder	.05	.02	346	John Marzano	.05	.02
289	Jay Bell	.05	.02	347	Dana Kiecker	.07	.04
290	Kevin Romine	.05	.02	348	Dion James	.05	.02
291	Jeff Robinson	.05	.02	349	Hubie Brooks	.05	.02
292	Steve Frey	.07	.04	350	Bill Landrum	.05	.02
293	Craig Worthington	.05	.02	351	Bill Sampen	.05	.02
294	Tim Crews	.05	.02	352	Greg Briley	.05	.02
295	Joe Magrane	.07	.04	353	Paul Gibson	.05	.02
296	Hector Villanueva	.07	.04	354	Dave Eiland	.05	.02
297	Terry Shumpert	.07	.04	355	Steve Finley	.07	.04
298	Joe Carter	.15	.08	356	Bob Boone	.08	.05
299	Kent Mercker	.07	.04	357	Steve Buechele	.05	.02
300	Checklist	.05	.02	358	Chris Hoiles (R)	.25	.15
301	Chet Lemon	.05	.02	359	Larry Walker	.20	.12
302	Mike Schooler	.05	.02	360	Frank DiPino	.05	.02
303	Dante Bichette	.05	.02	361	Mark Grant	.05	.02
304	Kevin Elster	.05	.02	362	Dave Magadan	.05	.02
305	Jeff Huson	.05	.02	363	Robby Thompson	.05	.02
306	Greg Harris	.05	.02	364	Lonnie Smith	.05	.02
307	Marquis Grissom	.20	.12	365	Steve Farr	.05	.02
308	Calvin Schiraldi	.05	.02	366	Dave Valle	.05	.02
309	Mariano Duncan	.05	.02	367	Tim Naehring (R)	.20	.12
310	Bill Spiers	.05	.02	368	Jim Acker	.05	.02
311	Scott Garrelts	.05	.02	369	Jeff Reardon	.08	.05

370	Tim Teufel	.05	.02
371	Juan Gonzalez	.50	.30
372	Luis Salazar	.05	.02
373	Rick Honeycutt	.05	.02
374	Greg Maddux	.10	.06
375	Jose Uribe	.05	.02
376	Donnie Hill	.05	.02
377	Don Carman	.05	.02
378	Craig Grebeck	.07	.04
379	Willie Fraser	.05	.02
380	Glenallen Hill	.08	.05
381	Joe Oliver	.05	.02
382	Randy Bush	.05	.02
383	Alex Cole	.10	.06
384	Norm Charlton	.05	.02
385	Gene Nelson	.05	.02
386	Checklist	.05	.02
387	Rickey Henderson (MVP)	.10	.06
388	Lance Parrish(MVP)	.05	.02
389	Fred McGriff(MVP)	.10	.06
390	Dave Parker(MVP)	.07	.04
391	Candy Maldonado (MVP)	.07	.04
392	Ken Griffey, Jr.(MVP)	.25	.15
393	Gregg Olson(MVP)	.07	.04
394	Rafael Palmeiro(MVP)	.08	.05
395	Roger Clemens(MVP)	.12	.07
396	George Brett(MVP)	.12	.07
397	Cecil Fielder(MVP)	.10	.06
398	Brian Harper(MVP)	.05	.02
399	Bobby Thigpen(MVP)	.05	.02
400	Roberto Kelly(MVP)	.08	.05
401	Danny Darwin(MVP)	.05	.02
402	Dave Justice(MVP)	.12	.07
403	Lee Smith(MVP)	.08	.05
404	Ryne Sanberg(MVP)	.12	.07
405	Eddie Murray(MVP)	.10	.06
406	Tim Wallach(MVP)	.07	.04
407	Kevin Mitchell(MVP)	.07	.04
408	Darryl Strawberry (MVP)	.10	.06
409	Joe Carter(MVP)	.10	.06
410	Len Dykstra(MVP)	.07	.04
411	Doug Drabek(MVP)	.08	.05
412	Chris Sabo(MVP)	.07	.04
413	Paul Marak (R)	.10	.06
414	Tim McIntosh (R)	.12	.07
415	Brian Barnes (R)	.20	.12
416	Eric Gunderson (R)	.08	.05
417	Mike Gardiner (R)	.15	.08
418	Steve Carter (R)	.08	.05
419	Gerald Alexander (R)	.08	.05
420	Rich Garces (R)	.12	.07
421	Chuck Knoblauch (R)	.60	.35
422	Scott Aldred (R)	.10	.06
423	Wes Chamberlain (R)	.20	.12
424	Lance Dickson (R)	.15	.08
425	Greg Colbrunn (R)	.20	.12
426	Rich Delucia (R)	.12	.07
427	Jeff Conine (R)	.15	.08
428	Steve Decker (R)	.15	.08
429	Turner Ward (R)	.12	.07
430	Mo Vaughn (R)	.35	.20
431	Steve Chitren (R)	.10	.06
432	Mike Benjamin (R)	.10	.06
433	Ryne Sandberg (AS)	.12	.07
434	Len Dykstra (AS)	.07	.04
435	Andre Dawson (AS)	.10	.06
436	Mike Scioscia (AS)	.05	.02
437	Ozzie Smith (AS)	.10	.06
438	Kevin Mitchell (AS)	.08	.05
439	Jack Armstrong (AS)	.05	.02
440	Chris Sabo (AS)	.07	.04
441	Will Clark (AS)	.12	.07
442	Mel Hall	.07	.04
443	Mark Gardner	.05	.02
444	Mike Devereaux	.07	.04
445	Kirk Gibson	.07	.04
446	Terry Pendleton	.12	.07
447	Mike Harkey	.07	.04
448	Jim Eisenreich	.05	.02
449	Benito Santiago	.08	.05
450	Oddibe McDowell	.05	.02
451	Cecil Fielder	.12	.07
452	Ken Griffey, Sr.	.07	.04
453	Bert Blyleven	.08	.05
454	Howard Johnson	.07	.04
455	Monty Farris	.12	.07
456	Tony Pena	.05	.02
457	Tim Raines	.07	.04
458	Dennis Rasmussen	.05	.02
459	Luis Quinones	.05	.02
460	B.J. Surhoff	.05	.02
461	Ernest Riles	.05	.02
462	Rick Sutcliffe	.07	.04
463	Danny Tartabull	.10	.06
464	Pete Incaviglia	.05	.02
465	Carlos Martinez	.05	.02
466	Ricky Jordan	.07	.04
467	John Cerutti	.05	.02
468	Dave Winfield	.12	.07
469	Francisco Oliveras	.05	.02
470	Roy Smith	.05	.02
471	Barry Larkin	.08	.05
472	Ron Darling	.05	.02
473	David Wells	.05	.02
474	Glenn Davis	.05	.02
475	Neal Heaton	.05	.02
476	Ron Hassey	.05	.02
477	Frank Thomas (R)	1.25	.80
478	Greg Vaughn	.10	.06
479	Todd Burns	.05	.02
480	Candy Maldonado	.05	.02
481	Dave LaPoint	.05	.02
482	Alvin Davis	.05	.02

483	Mike Scott	.05	.02
484	Dale Murphy	.10	.06
485	Ben McDonald	.15	.08
486	Jay Howell	.05	.02
487	Vince Coleman	.07	.04
488	Alfredo Griffin	.05	.02
489	Sandy Alomar	.08	.05
490	Kirby Puckett	.25	.15
491	Andres Thomas	.05	.02
492	Jack Morris	.12	.07
493	Matt Young	.05	.02
494	Greg Myers	.05	.02
495	Barry Bonds	.20	.12
496	Scott Cooper (R)	.20	.12
497	Dan Schatzeder	.05	.02
498	Jesse Barfield	.07	.04
499	Jerry Goff	.07	.04
500	Checklist	.05	.02
501	Anthony Telford (R)	.15	.08
502	Eddie Murray	.12	.07
503	Omar Olivares (R)	.15	.08
504	Ryne Sandberg	.20	.12
505	Jeff Montgomery	.05	.02
506	Mark Parent	.05	.02
507	Ron Gant	.15	.08
508	Frank Tanana	.05	.02
509	Jay Buhner	.07	.04
510	Max Venable	.05	.02
511	Wally Whitehurst	.05	.02
512	Gary Pettis	.05	.02
513	Tom Brunansky	.07	.04
514	Tim Wallach	.07	.04
515	Craig Lefferts	.05	.02
516	Tim Layana	.05	.02
517	Darryl Hamilton	.07	.04
518	Rick Reuschel	.05	.02
519	Steve Wilson	.05	.02
520	Kurt Stillwell	.05	.02
521	Rafael Palmeiro	.08	.05
522	Ken Patterson	.05	.02
523	Len Dykstra	.07	.04
524	Tony Fernandez	.05	.02
525	Kent Anderson	.05	.02
526	Mark Leonard (R)	.12	.07
527	Allan Anderson	.05	.02
528	Tom Browning	.07	.04
529	Frank Viola	.08	.05
530	John Olerud	.15	.08
531	Juan Agosto	.05	.02
532	Zane Smith	.05	.02
533	Scott Sanderson	.05	.02
534	Barry Jones	.05	.02
535	Mike Felder	.05	.02
536	Jose Canseco	.25	.15
537	Felix Fermin	.05	.02
538	Roberto Kelly	.10	.06
539	Brian Holman	.05	.02
540	Mark Davidson	.05	.02
541	Terry Mulholland	.05	.02
542	Randy Milligan	.07	.04
543	Jose Gonzalez	.05	.02
544	Craig Wilson (R)	.10	.06
545	Mike Hartley	.05	.02
546	Greg Swindell	.07	.04
547	Gary Gaetti	.05	.02
548	Dave Justice	.25	.15
549	Steve Searcy	.05	.02
550	Erik Hanson	.07	.04
551	Dave Stieb	.07	.04
552	Andy Van Slyke	.10	.06
553	Mike Greenwell	.08	.05
554	Kevin Maas	.12	.07
555	Delino DeShields	.20	.12
556	Curt Schilling	.05	.02
557	Ramon Martinez	.12	.07
558	Pedro Guerrero	.05	.02
559	Dwight Smith	.05	.02
560	Mark Davis	.05	.02
561	Shawn Abner	.05	.02
562	Charlie Leibrandt	.05	.02
563	John Shelby	.05	.02
564	Bill Swift	.07	.04
565	Mike Fetters	.05	.02
566	Alejandro Pena	.05	.02
567	Ruben Sierra	.15	.08
568	Carlos Quintana	.07	.04
569	Kevin Gross	.05	.02
570	Derek Lilliquist	.05	.02
571	Jack Armstrong	.05	.02
572	Greg Brock	.05	.02
573	Mike Kingery	.05	.02
574	Greg Smith	.10	.06
575	Brian McRae (R)	.25	.15
576	Jack Daugherty	.05	.02
577	Ozzie Guillen	.05	.02
578	Joe Boever	.05	.02
579	Luis Sojo	.07	.04
580	Chili Davis	.07	.04
581	Don Robinson	.05	.02
582	Brian Harper	.05	.02
583	Paul O'Neill	.08	.05
584	Bob Ojeda	.05	.02
585	Mookie Wilson	.05	.02
586	Rafael Ramirez	.05	.02
587	Gary Redus	.05	.02
588	Jamie Quirk	.05	.02
589	Shawn Hilligas	.05	.02
590	Tom Edens (R)	.08	.05
591	Joe Klink	.07	.04
592	Charles Nagy (R)	.40	.25
593	Eric Plunk	.05	.02
594	Tracy Jones	.05	.02
595	Craig Biggio	.08	.05
596	Jose DeJesus	.05	.02
597	Mickey Tettleton	.07	.04
598	Chris Gwynn	.05	.02

599	Rex Hudler	.05	.02
600	Checklist	.05	.02
601	Jim Gott	.05	.02
602	Jeff Manto	.10	.06
603	Nelson Liriano	.05	.02
604	Mark Lemke	.07	.04
605	Clay Parker	.05	.02
606	Edgar Martinez	.12	.07
607	Mark Whiten (R)	.25	.15
608	Ted Power	.05	.02
609	Tom Bolton	.05	.02
610	Tom Herr	.05	.02
611	Andy Hawkins	.05	.02
612	Scott Ruskin	.05	.02
613	Ron Kittle	.05	.02
614	John Wetteland	.10	.06
615	Mike Perez (R)	.12	.07
616	Dave Clark	.05	.02
617	Brent Mayne	.10	.06
618	Jack Clark	.07	.04
619	Marvin Freeman	.05	.02
620	Edwin Nunez	.05	.02
621	Russ Swan	.08	.05
622	Johnny Ray	.05	.02
623	Charlie O'Brien	.05	.02
624	Joe Bitker	.08	.05
625	Mike Marshall	.05	.02
626	Otis Nixon	.05	.02
627	Andy Benes	.10	.06
628	Ron Oester	.05	.02
629	Ted Higuera	.05	.02
631	Damon Berryhill	.05	.02
632	Bo Jackson	.20	.12
633	Brad Arnsberg	.05	.02
634	Jerry Willard	.05	.02
635	Tommy Greene	.10	.06
636	Bob MacDonald (R)	.10	.06
637	Kirk McCaskill	.05	.02
638	John Burkett	.07	.04
639	Paul Abbott (R)	.12	.07
640	Todd Benzinger	.05	.02
641	Todd Hundley	.10	.06
642	George Bell	.10	.06
643	Javier Ortiz (R)	.10	.06
644	Sid Bream	.05	.02
645	Bob Welch	.05	.02
646	Phil Bradley	.05	.02
647	Bill Krueger	.05	.02
648	Rickey Henderson	.15	.08
649	Kevin Wickander	.05	.02
650	Steve Balboni	.05	.02
651	Gene Harris	.05	.02
652	Jim Deshaies	.05	.02
653	Jason Grimsley	.12	.07
654	Joe Orsulak	.05	.02
655	Jimmy Poole	.08	.05
656	Felix Jose	.10	.06
657	Dennis Cook	.05	.02
658	Tom Brookens	.05	.02
659	Junior Ortiz	.05	.02
660	Jeff Parrett	.05	.02
661	Jerry Don Gleaton	.05	.02
662	Brent Knackert	.07	.04
663	Rance Mulliniks	.05	.02
664	John Smiley	.08	.05
665	Larry Andersen	.05	.02
666	Willie McGee	.08	.05
667	Chris Nabholz (R)	.20	.12
668	Brady Anderson	.10	.06
669	Darren Holmes (R)	.10	.06
670	Ken Hill	.10	.06
671	Gary Varsho	.05	.02
672	Bill Pecota	.05	.02
673	Fred Lynn	.07	.04
674	Kevin Brown	.10	.06
675	Dan Petry	.05	.02
676	Mike Jackson	.05	.02
677	Wally Joyner	.08	.05
678	Danny Jackson	.05	.02
679	Bill Haselman	.10	.06
680	Mike Boddicker	.05	.02
681	Mel Rojas (R)	.15	.08
682	Roberto Alomar	.20	.12
683	Dave Justice (R.O.Y.)	.15	.08
684	Chuck Crim	.05	.02
685	Matt Williams	.10	.06
686	Shawon Dunston	.08	.05
687	Jeff Schulz (R)	.10	.06
688	John Barfield	.10	.06
689	Gerald Young	.05	.02
690	Luis Gonzalez (R)	.20	.12
691	Frank Wills	.07	.04
692	Chuck Finley	.08	.05
693	Sandy Alomar (R.O.Y.)	.07	.04
694	Tim Drummond	.05	.02
695	Herm Winningham	.05	.02
696	Darryl Strawberry	.15	.08
697	Al Leiter	.05	.02
698	Karl Rhodes	.12	.07
699	Stan Belinda	.10	.06
700	Checklist	.05	.02
701	Lance Blankenship	.05	.02
702	Puzzle Card (Stargell)	.08	.05
703	Jim Gantner	.05	.02
704	Reggie Harris (R)	.12	.07
705	Rob Ducey	.07	.04
706	Tim Hulett	.07	.04
707	Atlee Hammaker	.05	.02
708	Xavier Hernandez	.05	.02
709	Chuck McElroy	.08	.05
710	John Mitchell	.05	.02
711	Carlos Hernandez	.05	.02
712	Geronimo Pena	.08	.05
713	Jim Neidlinger (R)	.10	.06
714	John Orton	.08	.05
715	Terry Leach	.05	.02

716	Mike Stanton	.05	.02
717	Walt Terrel	.05	.02
718	Luis Aquino	.05	.02
719	Bud Black	.05	.02
720	Bob Kipper	.05	.02
721	Jeff Gray	.08	.05
722	Jose Rijo	.08	.05
723	Curt Young	.05	.02
724	Jose Vizcaino	.08	.05
725	Randy Tomlin (R)	.25	.15
726	Junior Noboa	.05	.02
727	Bob Welch (CY)	.07	.04
728	Gary Ward	.05	.02
729	Rob Deer	.07	.04
730	David Segui	.08	.05
731	Mark Carreon	.05	.02
732	Vicente Palacios	.05	.02
733	Sam Horn	.05	.02
734	Howard Farmer	.08	.05
735	Ken Dayley	.05	.02
736	Kelly Mann	.05	.02
737	Joe Grahe (R)	.15	.08
738	Kelly Downs	.05	.02
739	Jimmy Kremers (R)	.08	.05
740	Kevin Appier	.08	.05
741	Jeff Reed	.05	.02
742	Jose Rijo (WS)	.07	.04
743	Dave Rohde	.08	.05
744	Dr. Dirt/Mr. Clean	.07	.04
	(L.Dykstra/D. Murphy)		
745	Paul Sorrento	.08	.05
746	Thomas Howard	.12	.07
747	Matt Stark (R)	.10	.06
748	Harold Baines	.07	.04
749	Doug Dascenzo	.05	.02
750	Doug Drabek (CY)	.08	.05
751	Gary Sheffield	.30	.18
752	Terry Lee	.08	.05
753	Jim Vatcher	.08	.05
754	Lee Stevens	.12	.07
755	Randy Veres	.07	.04
756	Bill Doran	.05	.02
757	Gary Wayne	.05	.02
758	Pedro Munoz (R)	.30	.18
759	Chris Hammond (R)	.15	.08
760	Checklist	.05	.02
761	Rickey Henderson (MVP)	.12	.07
762	Barry Bonds (MVP)	.15	.08
763	Billy Hatcher (WS)	.05	.02
764	Julio Machado	.05	.02
765	Jose Mesa	.05	.02
766	Willie Randolph (WS)	.05	.02
767	Scott Erickson (R)	.40	.25
768	Travis Fryman (R)	.60	.35
769	Rich Rodriguez (R)	.12	.07
770	Checklist	.05	.02
B1	Langston/Witt (No-Hit)	.05	.02

B2	Randy Johnson (No-Hit)	.10	.06
B3	Nolan Ryan (No-Hit)	.25	.15
B4	Dave Stewart (No-Hit)	.07	.04
B5	Cecil Fielder (50 Hr)	.10	.06
B6	Carlton Fisk (RB)	.08	.05
B7	Ryne Sandberg (RB)	.10	.06
B8	Gary Carter (RB)	.08	.05
B9	Mark McGwire (RB)	.12	.07
B10	Bo Jackson (4 straight home runs)	.15	.08
B11	Fernando Valenzuela (No-Hit)	.08	.05
B12	Andy Hawkins (No-Hit)	.05	.02
B13	Melido Perez (No-Hit)	.05	.02
B14	Terry Mulholland (No-Hit)	.05	.02
B15	Nolan Ryan (300th)	.25	.15
B16	Delino DeShields (4 hits in debut)	.10	.06
B17	Cal Ripken (Errorless)	.15	.08
B18	Eddie Murray (RB)	.10	.06
B19	George Brett (RB)	.12	.07
B20	Bobby Thigpen (RB)	.07	.04
B21	Dave Stieb (No-Hit)	.07	.04
B22	Willie McGee (AW)	.08	.05
E1	Barry Bonds (Elite)	125.00	80.00
E2	George Brett (Elite)	140.00	90.00
E3	Jose Canseco (Elite)	175.00	125.00
E4	Andre Dawson (Elite)	90.00	60.00
E5	Doug Drabek (Elite)	75.00	45.00
E6	Cecil Fielder (Elite)	110.00	70.00
E7	Rickey Henderson (Elite)	150.00	110.00
E8	Matt Williams (Elite)	75.00	45.00
L1	Nolan Ryan (Legends)	500.00	375.00
S1	Ryne Sandberg (Signature)	450.00	325.00

1991 Donruss Rookies

This 56-card rookie update set features red borders with white frames around the photos. Card fronts feature "The Rookies" logo in the lower left corner. Cards measure 2-1/2" by 3-1/2".

		MINT	NR/MT
Complete Set (56)		5.00	3.00
Commons		.05	.02
1	Pat Kelly (R)	.25	.15
2	Rich DeLucia	.08	.05
3	Wes Chamberlain	.20	.12
4	Scott Leius (R)	.15	.08
5	Darryl Kile (R)	.15	.08
6	Milt Cuyler	.10	.06
7	Todd Van Poppel (R)	.80	.50
8	Ray Lankford	.25	.15
9	Brian Hunter (R)	.25	.15
10	Tony Perezchica	.05	.02
11	Ced Landrum (R)	.10	.06
12	Dave Burba (R)	.08	.05
13	Ramon Garcia (R)	.08	.05
14	Ed Sprague (R)	.12	.07
15	Warren Newson (R)	.10	.06
16	Paul Faries (R)	.05	.02
17	Luis Gonzalez	.15	.08
18	Charles Nagy	.25	.15
19	Chris Hammond	.08	.05
20	Frank Castillo (R)	.10	.06
21	Pedro Munoz	.25	.15
22	Orlando Merced (R)	.25	.15
23	Jose Melendez (R)	.10	.06
24	Kirk Dressendorfer(R)	.12	.07
25	Heathcliff Slocumb (R)	.10	.06
26	Doug Simons (R)	.10	.06
27	Mike Timlin (R)	.10	.06
28	Jeff Fassero (R)	.12	.07
29	Mark Leiter (R)	.08	.05
30	Jeff Bagwell (R)	1.00	.70
31	Brian McRae	.15	.08
32	Mark Whiten	.15	.08
33	Ivan Rodriguez (R)	1.25	.80
34	Wade Taylor (R)	.12	.07
35	Darren Lewis (R)	.12	.07
36	Mo Vaughn	.25	.15
37	Mike Remlinger (R)	.08	.05
38	Rick Wilkins (R)	.08	.05
39	Chuck Knoblauch	.50	.30
40	Kevin Morton	.08	.05
41	Carlos Rodriguez (R)	.10	.06
42	Mark Lewis	.15	.08
43	Brent Mayne	.08	.05
44	Chris Haney (R)	.12	.07
45	Denis Boucher (R)	.10	.06
46	Mike Gardiner	.10	.06
47	Jeff Johnson (R)	.10	.06
48	Dean Palmer	.35	.20
49	Chuck McElroy	.08	.05
50	Chris Jones (R)	.08	.05
51	Scott Kamieniecki (R)	.10	.06
52	Al Osuna (R)	.08	.05
53	Rusty Meacham (R)	.08	.05
54	Chito Martinez (R)	.15	.08
55	Reggie Jefferson (R)	.15	.08
56	Checklist	.05	.02

1992 Donruss

The 1992 Donruss set was issued in two series and included a new anti-counterfeit device on the card backs. Card fronts feature glossy white borders with two shades of blue stripes above and below the photograph. Donruss dropped Diamond Kings from the regular edition and randomly inserted them in foil packs. Once again, the company produced a limited edition Elite Series insert set along with 8 Bonus insert cards. 5,000 autographed Cal Ripken cards make up the Signature Series and were distributed randomly. Rickey Henderson is featured in the 7,500 card Legend Series. All cards measure 2-1/2" by 3-1/2" and all insert cards are listed at the end of this checklist.

		MINT	NR/MT
Complete Set (784)		18.50	12.50
Commons		.05	.02

1	Mark Wohlers (R)	.15	.08
2	Will Cordero (R)	.20	.12
3	Kyle Abbott (R)	.15	.08
4	Dave Nilsson (R)	.20	.12
5	Kenny Lofton (R)	.40	.25
6	Luis Mercedes (R)	.15	.08
7	Roger Salkeld (R)	.20	.12
8	Eddie Zosky (R)	.12	.08
9	Todd Van Poppel (R)	.30	.18
10	Frank Seminara (R)	.20	.12
11	Andy Ashby (R)	.12	.07
12	Reggie Jefferson	.15	.08
13	Ryan Klesko (R)	.50	.30
14	Carlos Garcia (R)	.20	.12
15	John Ramos (R)	.15	.08
16	Eric Karros (R)	.60	.35
17	Pat Lennon (R)	.25	.15
18	Eddie Taubensee (R)	.12	.07
19	Roberto Hernandez	.12	.07
20	D.J. Dozier (R)	.12	.07
21	Dave Henderson(AS)	.05	.02
22	Cal Ripken(AS)	.15	.08
23	Wade Boggs(AS)	.10	.06
24	Ken Griffey, Jr.(AS)	.25	.15
25	Jack Morris(AS)	.10	.06
26	Danny Tartabull(AS)	.10	.06
27	Cecil Fielder(AS)	.10	.06
28	Roberto Alomar(AS)	.12	.07
29	Sandy Alomar(AS)	.07	.04
30	Rickey Henderson(AS)	.10	.06
31	Ken Hill	.08	.05
32	John Habyan	.05	.02
33	Otis Nixon (HL)	.05	.02
34	Tim Wallach	.07	.04
35	Cal Ripken	.25	.15
36	Gary Carter	.10	.06
37	Juan Agosto	.05	.02
38	Doug Dascenzo	.05	.02
39	Kirk Gibson	.07	.04
40	Benito Santiago	.08	.05
41	Otis Nixon	.05	.02
42	Andy Allanson	.05	.02
43	Brian Holman	.05	.02
44	Dick Schofield	.05	.02
45	Dave Magadan	.05	.02
46	Rafael Palmeiro	.08	.05
47	Jody Reed	.05	.02
48	Ivan Calderon	.07	.04
49	Greg Harris	.05	.02
50	Chris Sabo	.07	.04
51	Paul Molitor	.08	.05
52	Robby Thompson	.05	.02
53	Dave Smith	.05	.02
54	Mark Davis	.05	.02
55	Kevin Brown	.08	.05
56	Donn Pall	.05	.02
57	Lenny Dykstra	.07	.04
58	Roberto Alomar	.20	.12
59	Jeff Robinson	.05	.02
60	Willie McGee	.08	.05
61	Jay Buhner	.07	.04
62	Mike Pagliarulo	.05	.02
63	Paul O'Neill	.08	.05
64	Hubie Brooks	.07	.04
65	Kelly Gruber	.07	.04
66	Ken Caminiti	.07	.04
67	Gary Redus	.05	.02
68	Harold Baines	.07	.04
69	Charlie Hough	.05	.02
70	B.J. Surhoff	.05	.02
71	Walt Weiss	.07	.04
72	Shawn Hillegas	.05	.02
73	Roberto Kelly	.10	.06
74	Jeff Ballard	.05	.02
75	Craig Biggio	.07	.04
76	Pat Combs	.05	.02
77	Jeff Robinson	.05	.02
78	Tim Belcher	.07	.04
79	Cris Carpenter	.05	.02
80	Checklist	.05	.02
81	Steve Avery	.20	.12
82	Chris James	.05	.02
83	Brian Harper	.05	.02
84	Charlie Leibrandt	.05	.02
85	Mickey Tettleton	.07	.04
86	Pete O'Brien	.05	.02
87	Danny Darwin	.05	.02
88	Bob Walk	.05	.02
89	Jeff Reardon	.08	.05
90	Bobby Rose	.08	.05
91	Danny Jackson	.05	.02
92	John Morris	.05	.02
93	Bud Black	.05	.02
94	Tommy Greene (HL)	.07	.04
95	Rick Aguilera	.05	.02
96	Gary Gaetti	.05	.02
97	David Cone	.10	.06
98	John Olerud	.10	.06
99	Joel Skinner	.05	.02
100	Jay Bell	.05	.02
101	Bob Milacki	.05	.02
102	Norm Charlton	.05	.02

103	Chuck Crim	.05	.02
104	Terry Steinbach	.05	.02
105	Juan Samuel	.05	.02
106	Steve Howe	.05	.02
107	Rafael Belliard	.05	.02
108	Joey Cora	.05	.02
109	Tommy Greene	.08	.05
110	Gregg Olson	.08	.05
111	Frank Tanana	.05	.02
112	Lee Smith	.10	.06
113	Greg Harris	.05	.02
114	Dwayne Henry	.05	.02
115	Chili Davis	.07	.04
116	Kent Mercker	.05	.02
117	Brian Barnes	.05	.02
118	Rich DeLucia	.05	.02
119	Andre Dawson	.10	.06
120	Carlos Baerga	.15	.08
121	Mike La Valliere	.05	.02
122	Jeff Gray	.05	.02
123	Bruce Hurst	.07	.04
124	Alvin Davis	.05	.02
125	John Candelaria	.05	.02
126	Matt Nokes	.05	.02
127	George Bell	.10	.06
128	Bret Saberhagen	.08	.05
129	Jeff Russell	.05	.02
130	Jim Abbott	.10	.06
131	Bill Gillickson	.05	.02
132	Todd Zeile	.08	.05
133	Dave Winfield	.10	.06
134	Wally Whitehurst	.05	.02
135	Matt Williams	.08	.05
136	Tom Browning	.07	.04
137	Marquis Grissom	.15	.08
138	Erik Hanson	.07	.04
139	Rob Dibble	.07	.04
140	Don August	.05	.02
141	Tom Henke	.05	.02
142	Dan Pasqua	.05	.02
143	George Brett	.15	.08
144	Jerald Clark	.07	.04
145	Robin Ventura	.15	.08
146	Dale Murphy	.08	.05
147	Dennis Eckersley	.10	.06
148	Eric Yelding	.05	.02
149	Mario Diaz	.05	.02
150	Casey Candaele	.05	.02
151	Steve Olin	.05	.02
152	Luis Salazar	.05	.02
153	Kevin Maas	.08	.05
154	Nolan Ryan (HL)	.25	.15
155	Barry Jones	.05	.02
156	Chris Hoiles	.10	.06
157	Bobby Ojeda	.05	.02
158	Pedro Guerrero	.05	.02
159	Paul Assenmacher	.05	.02
160	Checklist	.05	.02
161	Mike Macfarlane	.05	.02
162	Craig Lefferts	.05	.02
163	Brian Hunter	.08	.05
164	Alan Trammell	.10	.06
165	Ken Griffey, Jr.	.40	.25
166	Lance Parrish	.05	.02
167	Brian Downing	.05	.02
168	John Barfield	.05	.02
169	Jack Clark	.05	.02
170	Chris Nabholz	.08	.05
171	Tim Teufel	.05	.02
172	Chris Hammond	.05	.02
173	Robin Yount	.15	.08
174	Dave Righetti	.05	.02
175	Joe Girardi	.05	.02
176	Mike Boddicker	.05	.02
177	Dean Palmer	.15	.08
178	Greg Hibbard	.05	.02
179	Randy Ready	.05	.02
180	Devon White	.05	.02
181	Mark Eichhorn	.05	.02
182	Mike Felder	.05	.02
183	Joe Klink	.05	.02
184	Steve Bedrosian	.05	.02
185	Barry Larkin	.08	.05
186	John Franco	.05	.02
187	Ed Sprague	.07	.04
188	Mark Portugal	.05	.02
189	Jose Lind	.05	.02
190	Bob Welch	.07	.04
191	Alex Fernandez	.10	.06
192	Gary Sheffield	.30	.18
193	Rickey Henderson	.15	.08
194	Rod Nichols	.05	.02
195	Scott Kamieniecki	.08	.05
196	Mike Flanagan	.05	.02
197	Steve Finley	.05	.02
198	Darren Daulton	.10	.06
199	Leo Gomez	.12	.07
202	Mike Morgan	.05	.02
201	Bob Tewksbury	.05	.02
202	Sid Bream	.05	.02
203	Sandy Alomar	.08	.05
204	Greg Gagne	.05	.02
205	Juan Berenguer	.05	.02
206	Cecil Fielder	.12	.07
207	Randy Johnson	.10	.06
208	Tony Pena	.05	.02
209	Doug Drabek	.08	.05
210	Wade Boggs	.10	.06
211	Bryan Harvey	.07	.04
212	Jose Vizcaino	.05	.02
213	Alonzo Powell (R)	.10	.06
214	Will Clark	.15	.08
215	Rickey Henderson (HL)	.10	.06
216	Jack Morris	.10	.06
217	Junior Felix	.05	.02

218	Vince Coleman	.07	.04		276	Dennis Martinez (HL)	.07	.04
219	Jimmy Key	.05	.02		277	Delino DeShields	.15	.08
220	Alex Cole	.05	.02		278	Sam Horn	.05	.02
221	Bill Landrum	.05	.02		279	Kevin Gross	.05	.02
222	Randy Milligan	.05	.02		280	Jose Oquendo	.05	.02
223	Jose Rijo	.07	.04		281	Mark Grace	.10	.06
224	Greg Vaughn	.08	.05		282	Mark Gubicza	.07	.04
225	Dave Stewart	.08	.05		283	Fred McGriff	.15	.08
226	Lenny Harris	.05	.02		284	Ron Gant	.10	.06
227	Scott Sanderson	.05	.02		285	Lou Whitaker	.05	.02
228	Jeff Blauser	.05	.02		286	Edgar Martinez	.15	.08
229	Ozzie Guillen	.07	.04		287	Ron Tingley	.05	.02
230	John Kruk	.07	.04		288	Kevin McReynolds	.07	.04
231	Bob Melvin	.05	.02		289	Ivan Rodriguez	.50	.30
232	Milt Cuyler	.08	.05		290	Mike Gardiner	.08	.05
233	Felix Jose	.08	.05		291	Chris Haney	.08	.05
234	Ellis Burks	.07	.04		292	Darrin Jackson	.05	.02
235	Pete Harnisch	.07	.04		293	Bill Doran	.05	.02
236	Kevin Tapani	.07	.04		294	Ted Higuera	.05	.02
237	Terry Pendleton	.12	.07		295	Jeff Brantley	.05	.02
238	Mark Gardner	.05	.02		296	Les Lancaster	.05	.02
239	Harold Reynolds	.05	.02		297	Jim Eisenreich	.05	.02
240	Checklist	.05	.02		298	Ruben Sierra	.15	.08
241	Mike Harkey	.07	.04		299	Scott Radinsky	.05	.02
242	Felix Fermin	.05	.02		300	Jose DeJesus	.05	.02
243	Barry Bonds	.20	.12		301	Mike Timlin	.08	.05
244	Roger Clemens	.20	.12		302	Luis Sojo	.05	.02
245	Dennis Rasmussen	.05	.02		303	Kelly Downs	.05	.02
246	Jose DeLeon	.05	.02		304	Scott Bankhead	.05	.02
247	Orel Hershiser	.08	.05		305	Pedro Munoz	.08	.05
248	Mel Hall	.07	.04		306	Scott Scudder	.07	.04
249	Rick Wilkins	.07	.04		307	Kevin Elster	.05	.02
250	Tom Gordon	.07	.04		308	Duane Ward	.05	.02
251	Kevin Reimer	.07	.04		309	Darryl Kile	.08	.05
252	Luis Polonia	.05	.02		310	Orlando Merced	.12	.07
253	Mike Henneman	.05	.02		311	Dave Henderson	.05	.02
254	Tom Pagnozzi	.07	.04		312	Tim Raines	.07	.04
255	Chuck Finley	.07	.04		313	Mark Lee	.07	.04
256	Mackey Sasser	.05	.02		314	Mike Gallego	.05	.02
257	John Burkett	.05	.02		315	Charles Nagy	.15	.08
258	Hal Morris	.10	.06		316	Jesse Barfield	.05	.02
259	Larry Walker	.12	.07		317	Todd Frohwirth	.05	.02
260	Billy Swift	.05	.02		318	Al Osuna	.05	.02
261	Joe Oliver	.05	.02		319	Darrin Fletcher	.05	.02
262	Julio Machado	.05	.02		320	Checklist	.05	.02
263	Todd Stottlemyre	.07	.04		321	David Segui	.07	.04
264	Matt Merullo	.05	.02		322	Stan Javier	.05	.02
265	Brent Mayne	.07	.04		323	Bryn Smith	.05	.02
266	Thomas Howard	.07	.04		324	Jeff Treadway	.05	.02
267	Lance Johnson	.05	.02		325	Mark Whiten	.10	.06
268	Terry Mulholland	.05	.02		326	Kent Hrbek	.07	.04
269	Rick Honeycutt	.05	.02		327	David Justice	.20	.12
270	Luis Gonzalez	.12	.07		328	Tony Phillips	.05	.02
271	Jose Guzman	.05	.02		329	Rob Murphy	.05	.02
272	Jimmy Jones	.05	.02		330	Kevin Morton	.07	.04
273	Mark Lewis	.08	.05		331	John Smiley	.08	.05
274	Rene Gonzales	.05	.02		332	Luis Rivera	.05	.02
275	Jeff Johnson	.05	.02		333	Wally Joyner	.08	.05

334	Heathcliff Slocumb	.05	.02
335	Rick Cerone	.05	.02
336	Mike Remlinger	.07	.04
337	Mike Moore	.05	.02
338	Lloyd McClendon	.05	.02
339	Al Newman	.05	.02
340	Kirk McCaskill	.05	.02
341	Howard Johnson	.10	.06
342	Greg Myers	.05	.02
343	Kal Daniels	.05	.02
344	Bernie Williams	.10	.06
345	Shane Mack	.08	.05
346	Gary Thurman	.05	.02
347	Dante Bichette	.05	.02
348	Mark McGwire	.20	.12
349	Travis Fryman	.15	.08
350	Ray Lankford	.15	.08
351	Mike Jeffcoat	.05	.02
352	Jack McDowell	.15	.08
353	Mitch Williams	.05	.02
354	Mike Devereaux	.07	.04
355	Andres Galarraga	.07	.04
356	Henry Cotto	.05	.02
357	Scott Bailes	.05	.02
358	Jeff Bagwell	.40	.25
359	Scott Leius	.07	.04
360	Zane Smith	.05	.02
361	Bill Pecota	.05	.02
362	Tony Fernandez	.05	.02
363	Glenn Braggs	.05	.02
364	Bill Spiers	.05	.02
365	Vicente Palacios	.05	.02
366	Tim Burke	.05	.02
367	Randy Tomlin	.10	.06
368	Kenny Rogers	.05	.02
369	Brett Butler	.07	.04
370	Pat Kelly	.08	.05
371	Bip Roberts	.05	.02
372	Gregg Jefferies	.10	.06
373	Kevin Bass	.05	.02
374	Ron Karkovice	.05	.02
375	Paul Gibson	.05	.02
376	Bernard Gilkey	.10	.06
377	Dave Gallagher	.05	.02
378	Bill Wegman	.05	.02
379	Pat Borders	.05	.02
380	Ed Whitson	.05	.02
381	Gilberto Reyes	.05	.02
382	Russ Swan	.05	.02
383	Andy Van Slyke	.10	.06
384	Wes Chamberlain	.10	.06
385	Steve Chitren	.05	.02
386	Greg Olson	.05	.02
387	Brian McRae	.10	.06
388	Rich Rodriguez	.05	.02
389	Steve Decker	.10	.06
390	Chuck Knoblauch	.25	.15
391	Bobby Witt	.07	.04
392	Eddie Murray	.10	.06
393	Juan Gonzalez	.60	.35
394	Scott Ruskin	.05	.02
395	Jay Howell	.05	.02
396	Checklist	.05	.02
397	Royce Clayton (R)	.25	.15
398	John Jaha (R)	.20	.12
399	Dan Wilson	.10	.06
400	Archie Corbin (R)	.10	.06
401	Barry Manuel (R)	.10	.06
402	Kim Batiste	.10	.06
403	Pat Mahomes (R)	.30	.18
404	Dave Fleming	.80	.50
405	Jeff Juden	.15	.08
406	Jim Thome	.25	.15
407	Sam Militello	.25	.15
408	Jeff Nelson (R)	.12	.07
409	Anthony Young	.12	.07
410	Tino Martinez	.10	.06
411	Jeff Mutis (R)	.10	.06
412	Rey Sanchez (R)	.12	.07
413	Chris Gardner (R)	.12	.07
414	John VanderWal (R)	.12	.07
415	Reggie Sanders	.40	.25
416	Brian Williams (R)	.40	.25
417	Mo Sanford	.10	.06
418	David Weathers (R)	.15	.08
419	Hector Fajardo (R)	.20	.12
420	Steve Foster (R)	.10	.06
421	Lance Dickson	.10	.06
422	Andre Dawson (AS)	.08	.05
423	Ozzie Smith (AS)	.08	.05
424	Chris Sabo (AS)	.05	.02
425	Tony Gwynn (AS)	.10	.06
426	Tom Glavine (AS)	.10	.06
427	Bobby Bonilla (AS)	.07	.04
428	Will Clark (AS)	.10	.06
429	Ryne Sandberg (AS)	.10	.06
430	Benito Santiago (AS)	.07	.04
431	Ivan Calderon (AS)	.05	.02
432	Ozzie Smith	.10	.06
433	Tim Leary	.05	.02
434	Bret Saberhagen (HL)	.07	.04
435	Mel Rojas	.05	.02
436	Ben McDonald	.12	.07
437	Tim Crews	.05	.02
438	Rex Hudler	.05	.02
439	Chico Walker	.05	.02
440	Kurt Stillwell	.05	.02
441	Tony Gwynn	.12	.07
442	John Smoltz	.12	.07
443	Lloyd Moseby	.05	.02
444	Mike Schooler	.05	.02
445	Joe Grahe	.05	.02
446	Dwight Gooden	.10	.06
447	Oil Can Boyd	.05	.02
448	John Marzano	.05	.02
449	Bret Barberie	.07	.04

No.	Player		
450	Mike Maddux	.05	.02
451	Jeff Reed	.05	.02
452	Dale Sveum	.05	.02
453	Jose Uribe	.05	.02
454	Bob Scanlan	.05	.02
455	Kevin Appier	.08	.05
456	Jeff Huson	.05	.02
457	Ken Patterson	.05	.02
458	Ricky Jordan	.05	.02
459	Tom Candiotti	.05	.02
460	Lee Stevens	.07	.04
461	Rod Beck (R)	.10	.06
462	Dave Valle	.05	.02
463	Scott Erickson	.10	.06
464	Chris Jones	.05	.02
465	Mark Carreon	.05	.02
466	Rob Ducey	.05	.02
467	Jim Corsi	.05	.02
468	Jeff King	.05	.02
469	Curt Young	.05	.02
470	Bo Jackson	.15	.08
471	Chris Bosio	.05	.02
472	Jamie Quirk	.05	.02
473	Jesse Orosco	.05	.02
474	Alvaro Espinoza	.05	.02
475	Joe Orsulak	.05	.02
476	Checklist Card	.05	.02
477	Gerald Young	.05	.02
478	Wally Backman	.05	.02
479	Juan Bell	.05	.02
480	Mike Scioscia	.05	.02
481	Omar Olivares	.05	.02
482	Francisco Cabrera	.05	.02
483	Greg Swindell	.07	.04
484	Terry Leach	.05	.02
485	Tommy Gregg	.05	.02
486	Scott Aldred	.05	.02
487	Greg Briley	.05	.02
488	Phil Plantier	.25	.15
489	Curtis Wilkerson	.05	.02
490	Tom Brunansky	.05	.02
491	Mike Fetters	.05	.02
492	Frank Castillo	.07	.04
493	Joe Boever	.05	.02
494	Kirt Manwaring	.05	.02
495	Wilson Alvarez (HL)	.07	.04
496	Gene Larkin	.05	.02
497	Gary DiSarcina	.05	.02
498	Frank Viola	.07	.04
499	Manuel Lee	.05	.02
500	Albert Belle	.12	.08
501	Stan Belinda	.05	.02
502	Dwight Evans	.05	.02
503	Eric Davis	.07	.04
504	Darren Holmes	.05	.02
505	Mike Bordick	.10	.06
506	Dave Hansen	.08	.05
507	Lee Guetterman	.05	.02
508	Keith Mitchell	.08	.05
509	Melido Perez	.07	.04
510	Dickie Thon	.05	.02
511	Mark Williamson	.05	.02
512	Mark Salas	.05	.02
513	Milt Thompson	.05	.02
514	Mo Vaughn	.15	.08
515	Jim Deshaies	.05	.02
516	Rich Garces	.05	.02
517	Lonnie Smith	.05	.02
518	Spike Owen	.05	.02
519	Tracy Jones	.05	.02
520	Greg Maddux	.12	.07
521	Carlos Martinez	.05	.02
522	Neal Heaton	.05	.02
523	Mike Greenwell	.07	.04
524	Andy Benes	.08	.05
525	Jeff Schaefer	.05	.02
526	Mike Sharperson	.05	.02
527	Wade Taylor	.05	.02
528	Jerome Walton	.05	.02
529	Storm Davis	.05	.02
530	Jose Hernandez (R)	.10	.06
531	Mark Langston	.08	.05
532	Rob Deer	.05	.02
533	Geronimo Pena	.05	.02
534	Juan Guzman	.80	.50
535	Pete Schourek	.08	.04
536	Todd Benzinger	.05	.02
537	Billy Hatcher	.05	.02
538	Tom Foley	.05	.02
539	Dave Cochrane	.05	.02
540	Mariano Duncan	.05	.02
541	Edwin Nunez	.05	.02
542	Rance Mulliniks	.05	.02
543	Carlton Fisk	.10	.06
544	Luis Aquino	.05	.02
545	Ricky Bones	.08	.05
546	Craig Grebeck	.05	.02
547	Charlie Hayes	.05	.02
548	Jose Canseco	.25	.15
549	Andujar Cedeno	.08	.05
550	Geno Petralli	.05	.02
551	Javier Ortiz	.05	.02
552	Rudy Seanez	.05	.02
553	Rich Gedman	.05	.02
554	Eric Plunk	.05	.02
555	Nolan Ryan (HL)	.25	.15
556	Checklist Card	.05	.02
557	Greg Colbrunn	.08	.05
558	Chito Martinez	.10	.06
559	Darryl Strawberry	.15	.08
560	Luis Alicea	.05	.02
561	Dwight Smith	.05	.02
562	Terry Shumpert	.05	.02
563	Jim Vatcher	.05	.02
564	Deion Sanders	.20	.12
565	Walt Terrell	.05	.02

566	Dave Burba	.05	.02	622	Bob Kipper	.05	.02
567	Dave Howard	.05	.02	623	Anthony Telford	.05	.02
568	Todd Hundley	.07	.04	624	Randy Myers	.05	.02
569	Jack Daugherty	.05	.02	625	Willie Randolph	.05	.02
570	Scott Cooper	.10	.06	626	Joe Slusarski	.07	.04
571	Bill Sampen	.05	.02	627	John Wetteland	.08	.05
572	Jose Melendez	.05	.02	628	Greg Cadaret	.05	.02
573	Freddie Benavides	.05	.02	629	Tom Glavine	.25	.15
574	Jim Gantner	.05	.02	630	Wilson Alvarez	.08	.05
575	Trevor Wilson	.05	.02	631	Wally Ritchie	.05	.02
576	Ryne Sandberg	.15	.08	632	Mike Mussina	.50	.30
577	Kevin Seitzer	.07	.04	633	Mark Leiter	.05	.02
578	Gerald Alexander	.05	.02	634	Gerald Perry	.05	.02
579	Mike Huff	.05	.02	635	Matt Young	.05	.02
580	Von Hayes	.05	.02	636	Checklist Card	.05	.02
581	Derek Bell	.15	.08	637	Scott Hemond	.05	.02
582	Mike Stanley	.05	.02	638	David West	.05	.02
583	Kevin Mitchell	.08	.05	639	Jim Clancy	.05	.02
584	Mike Jackson	.05	.02	640	Doug Piatt (R)	.07	.04
585	Dan Gladden	.05	.02	641	Omar Vizquel	.05	.02
586	Ted Power	.05	.02	642	Rick Sutcliffe	.05	.02
587	Jeff Innis	.05	.02	643	Glenallen Hill	.08	.05
588	Bob MacDonald	.05	.02	644	Gary Varsho	.05	.02
589	Jose Tolentino (R)	.10	.06	645	Tony Fossas	.05	.02
590	Bob Patterson	.05	.02	646	Jack Howell	.05	.02
591	Scott Brosius (R)	.08	.05	647	Jim Campanis (R)	.10	.06
592	Frank Thomas	.80	.50	648	Chris Gwynn	.05	.02
593	Darryl Hamilton	.05	.02	649	Jim Leyritz	.05	.02
594	Kirk Dressendorfer	.08	.05	650	Chuck McElroy	.05	.02
595	Jeff Shaw	.05	.02	651	Sean Berry	.05	.02
596	Don Mattingly	.12	.07	652	Donald Harris	.08	.05
597	Glenn Davis	.05	.02	653	Don Slaught	.05	.02
598	Andy Mota	.05	.02	654	Rusty Meacham	.05	.02
599	Jason Grimsley	.05	.02	655	Scott Terry	.05	.02
600	Jimmy Poole	.05	.02	656	Ramon Martinez	.08	.05
601	Jim Gott	.05	.02	657	Keith Miller	.05	.02
602	Stan Royer	.07	.04	658	Ramon Garcia	.05	.02
603	Marvin Freeman	.05	.02	659	Milt Hill (R)	.08	.04
604	Denis Boucher	.05	.02	660	Steve Frey	.05	.02
605	Denny Neagle	.10	.06	661	Bob McClure	.05	.02
606	Mark Lemke	.05	.02	662	Ced Landrum	.08	.05
607	Jerry Don Gleaton	.05	.02	663	Doug Henry (R)	.20	.12
608	Brent Knackert	.05	.02	664	Candy Maldonado	.05	.02
609	Carlos Quintana	.07	.04	665	Carl Willis	.05	.02
610	Bobby Bonilla	.10	.06	666	Jeff Montgomery	.05	.02
611	Joe Hesketh	.05	.02	667	Craig Shipley	.07	.04
612	Daryl Boston	.05	.02	668	Warren Newsom	.05	.02
613	Shawon Dunston	.07	.04	669	Mickey Morandini	.07	.04
614	Danny Cox	.05	.02	670	Brook Jacoby	.05	.02
615	Darren Lewis	.07	.04	671	Ryan Bowen	.08	.05
616	Alejandro Pena (HL)	.08	.05	672	Bill Krueger	.05	.02
	Kent Mercker			673	Rob Mallicoat	.05	.02
	Mark Wohlers			674	Doug Jones	.05	.02
616	Kirby Puckett	.20	.12	675	Scott Livingstone	.08	.05
618	Franklin Stubbs	.05	.02	676	Danny Tartabull	.10	.06
619	Chris Donnels	.05	.02	677	Joe Carter (HL)	.10	.06
620	David Wells	.05	.02	678	Cecil Espy	.05	.02
621	Mike Aldrete	.05	.02	679	Randy Velarde	.05	.02

No.	Player		
680	Bruce Ruffin	.05	.02
681	Ted Wood	.08	.05
682	Dan Plesac	.05	.02
683	Eric Bullock	.05	.02
684	Junior Ortiz	.05	.02
685	Dave Hollins	.05	.02
686	Dennis Martinez	.07	.04
687	Larry Andersen	.05	.02
688	Doug Simmons	.05	.02
689	Tim Spehr	.05	.02
690	Calvin Jones (R)	.10	.06
691	Mark Guthrie	.05	.02
692	Alfredo Griffin	.05	.02
693	Joe Carter	.12	.07
694	Terry Matthews (R)	.08	.05
695	Pascual Perez	.05	.02
696	Gene Nelson	.05	.02
697	Gerald Williams	.10	.06
698	Chris Cron	.08	.05
699	Steve Buechele	.05	.02
700	Paul McClellan	.05	.02
701	Jim Lindeman	.05	.02
702	Francisco Oliveras	.05	.02
703	Rob Maurer	.15	.08
704	Pat Hentgen	.07	.04
705	Jaime Navarro	.08	.05
706	Mike Magnante (R)	.08	.05
707	Nolan Ryan	.40	.25
708	Bobby Thigpen	.07	.04
709	John Cerrutti	.05	.02
710	Steve Wilson	.05	.02
711	Hensley Meulens	.07	.04
712	Rheal Cormier	.10	.06
713	Scott Bradley	.05	.02
714	Mitch Webster	.05	.02
715	Roger Mason	.05	.02
716	Checklist Card	.05	.02
717	Jeff Fassero	.07	.04
718	Cal Eldred	.25	.15
719	Sid Fernandez	.07	.04
720	Bob Zupcic	.15	.08
721	Jose Offerman	.08	.05
722	Cliff Brantley	.08	.05
723	Ron Darling	.07	.04
724	Dave Stieb	.07	.04
725	Hector Villanueva	.05	.02
726	Mike Hartley	.05	.02
727	Arthur Rhodes	.10	.06
728	Randy Bush	.05	.02
729	Steve Sax	.07	.04
730	Dave Otto	.05	.02
731	John Wehner	.08	.05
732	Dave Martinez	.05	.02
733	Ruben Amaro	.08	.05
734	Billy Ripken	.05	.02
735	Steve Farr	.05	.02
736	Shawn Abner	.05	.02
737	Gil Heredia	.07	.04
738	Ron Jones	.05	.02
739	Tony Castillo	.05	.02
740	Sammy Sosa	.07	.04
741	Julio Franco	.07	.04
742	Tim Naehring	.07	.04
743	Steve Wapnick (R)	.08	.05
744	Craig Wilson	.05	.02
745	Darrin Chapin (R)	.12	.07
746	Chris George (R)	.10	.06
747	Mike Simms	.07	.04
748	Rosario Rodriguez	.05	.02
749	Skeeter Barnes	.05	.02
750	Roger McDowell	.05	.02
751	Dann Howitt	.08	.05
752	Paul Sorrento	.08	.05
753	Braulio Castillo (R)	.12	.07
754	Yorkis Perez (R)	.08	.05
755	Willie Fraser	.05	.02
756	Jeremy Hernandez (R)	.10	.06
757	Curt Schilling	.05	.02
758	Steve Lyons	.05	.02
759	Dave Anderson	.05	.02
760	Willie Banks	.10	.06
761	Mark Leonard	.05	.02
762	Jack Armstrong	.07	.04
763	Scott Servais	.07	.04
764	Ray Stephens	.05	.02
765	Junior Noboa	.05	.02
766	Jim Olander	.07	.04
767	Joe Magrane	.07	.04
768	Lance Blankenship	.05	.02
769	Mike Humphreys	.07	.04
770	Jarvis Brown	.08	.05
771	Damon Berryhill	.05	.02
772	Alejandro Pena	.05	.02
773	Jose Mesa	.05	.02
774	Gary Cooper	.08	.05
775	Carney Lansford	.05	.02
776	Mike Bielecki	.05	.02
777	Charlie O'Brien	.05	.02
778	Carlos Hernandez	.05	.02
779	Howard Farmer	.05	.02
780	Mike Stanton	.05	.02
781	Reggie Harris	.05	.02
782	Xavier Hernandez	.05	.02
783	Bryan Hickerson	.07	.04
784	Checklist Card	.05	.02
BC1	Cal Ripken (MVP)	.25	.15
BC2	Terry Pendleton (MVP)	.15	.08
BC3	Roger Clemens (CY)	.30	.18
BC4	Tom Glavine (CY)	.30	.18
BC5	Chuck Knoblauch (ROY)	.30	.18
BC6	Jeff Bagwell (ROY)	.40	.25
BC7	Colorado Rockies	.50	.30
BC8	Florida Marlins	.50	.30
DK1	Paul Molitor	1.75	1.00
DK2	Will Clark	4.00	2.50

DK3	Joe Carter	2.50	1.50
DK4	Julio Franco	1.50	.90
DK5	Cal Ripken	6.00	4.00
DK6	Dave Justice	5.00	3.00
DK7	George Bell	1.25	.80
DK8	Frank Thomas	8.50	5.50
DK9	Wade Boggs	2.00	1.25
DK10	Scott Sanderson	.80	.50
DK11	Jeff Bagwell	3.50	2.00
DK12	John Kruk	1.00	.70
DK13	Felix Jose	1.50	.90
DK14	Harold Baines	.80	.50
DK15	Dwight Gooden	1.00	.70
DK16	Brian McRae	1.00	.70
DK17	Jay Bell	.80	.50
DK18	Brett Butler	1.00	.70
DK19	Hal Morris	1.50	.90
DK20	Mark Langston	1.00	.80
DK21	Scott Erickson	2.00	1.25
DK22	Randy Johnson	1.75	1.00
DK23	Greg Swindell	1.00	.70
DK24	Dennis Martinez	1.00	.70
DK25	Tony Phillips	.80	.05
DK26	Fred McGriff	2.00	1.25
DK27	Checklist	.75	.45
E9	Wade Boggs (Elite)	100.00	70.00
E10	Joe Carter (Elite)	100.00	70.00
E11	Will Clark (Elite)	150.00	90.00
E12	Doc Gooden (Elite)	100.00	70.00
E13	Ken Griffey, Jr. (Elite)	300.00	200.00
E14	Tony Gwynn (Elite)	110.00	55.00
E15	Howard Johnson (Elite)	70.00	40.00
E16	Terry Pendleton (Elite)	70.00	40.00
E17	Kirby Puckett (Elite)	150.00	90.00
E18	Frank Thomas (Elite)	300.00	200.00
L1	Rickey Henderson	300.00	200.00
S1	Cal Ripken	450.00	325.00

1992 Donruss Rookies

At 132-cards this is the largest Donruss Rookies set issued to date. The card design is identical to the regular Donruss set except for the green borders at the top and bottom. The set includes 20 limited Bonus Cards called Phenoms which were randomly inserted in foil packs. Those cards are listed at the end of this checklist but are not included in the complete set price. All cards measure 2-1/2" by 3-1/2"

		MINT	NR/MT
Complete Set (132)		9.50	5.50
Commons		.05	.02
1	Kyle Abbott	.08	.05
2	Troy Afenir	.05	.02
3	Rich Amaral (R)	.10	.06
4	Ruben Amaro	.07	.04
5	Billy Ashley (R)	.30	.18
6	Pedro Astacio (R)	.35	.20
7	Jim Austin (R)	.08	.05
8	Robert Ayrault (R)	.07	.04
9	Kevin Baez (R)	.15	.10
10	Estaban Beltre (R)	.12	.07
11	Brian Bohanon	.05	.02
12	Kent Bottenfield (R)	.15	.10
13	Jeff Branson	.05	.02
14	Brad Brink (R)	.08	.05
15	John Briscoe	.07	.04
16	Doug Brocail (R)	.12	.07
17	Rico Brogna (R)	.15	.10
18	J.T. Bruett (R)	.08	.05
19	Jacob Brumfield (R)	.08	.05
20	Jim Bullinger	.05	.02
21	Kevin Campbell (R)	.10	.06
22	Pedro Castellano (R)	.15	.10
23	Mike Christopher (R)	.12	.07
24	Archi Cianfrocco (R)	.15	.10
25	Mark Clark (R)	.10	.06

26	Craig Colbert (R)	.10	.06	84	Rob Natal (R)	.08	.05
27	Victor Cole (R)	.12	.07	85	Troy Neel (R)	.08	.05
28	Steve Cooke (R)	.15	.10	86	David Nied (R)	2.50	1.25
29	Tim Costo	.15	.10	87	Jerry Nielsen (R)	.08	.05
30	Chad Curtis (R)	.20	.12	88	Donovan Osborne	.25	.15
31	Doug Davis (R)	.08	.05	89	John Patterson (R)	.12	.07
32	Gary DiSarcina	.08	.05	90	Roger Pavlik (R)	.10	.06
33	John Doherty (R)	.10	.06	91	Dan Peltier	.08	.05
34	Mike Draper (R)	.08	.05	92	Jim Pena (R)	.08	.05
35	Monty Fariss	.08	.05	93	William Pennyfeather	.10	.06
36	Bien Figueroa (R)	.08	.05	94	Mike Perez	.07	.04
37	John Flaherty (R)	.08	.05	95	Hipolito Pichardo (R)	.20	.12
38	Tim Fortugno (R)	.08	.05	96	Greg Pirkl (R)	.10	.06
39	Eric Fox (R)	.12	.07	97	Harvey Pulliam	.08	.05
40	Jeff Frye (R)	.10	.06	98	Manny Ramirez (R)	.90	.60
41	Ramon Garcia	.05	.02	99	Pat Rapp (R)	.15	.10
42	Brent Gates (R)	.75	.45	100	Jeff Reboulet (R)	.10	.06
43	Tom Goodwin	.10	.06	101	Darren Reed	.05	.02
44	Buddy Groom (R)	.08	.05	102	Shane Reynolds (R)	.08	.05
45	Jeff Grotewold (R)	.08	.05	103	Bill Risley (R)	.08	.05
46	Juan Guerrero (R)	.12	.07	104	Ben Rivera	.08	.05
47	Johnny Guzman (R)	.10	.06	105	Henry Rodriguez (R)	.15	.10
48	Shawn Hare (R)	.12	.07	106	Rico Rossy (R)	.12	.07
49	Ryan Hawblitzel (R)	.25	.15	107	Johnny Ruffin	.08	.05
50	Bert Heffernan (R)	.08	.05	108	Steve Scarsone (R)	.10	.06
51	Butch Henry (R)	.12	.07	109	Tim Scott (R)	.15	.10
52	Cesar Hernandez (R)	.08	.05	110	Steve Shifflett (R)	.10	.06
53	Vince Horsman (R)	.10	.06	111	Dave Silvestri	.12	.07
54	Steve Hosey	.25	.15	112	Matt Stairs (R)	.15	.10
55	Pat Howell (R)	.12	.07	113	William Suero (R)	.08	.05
56	Peter Hoy (R)	.12	.07	114	Jeff Tackett	.10	.06
57	Jon Hurst (R)	.15	.10	115	Eddie Taubensee	.07	.04
58	Mark Hutton (R)	.15	.10	116	Rick Trlicek (R)	.10	.06
59	Shawn Jeter (R)	.10	.06	117	Scooter Tucker (R)	.08	.05
60	Joel Johnston (R)	.15	.10	118	Shane Turner	.05	.02
61	Jeff Kent (R)	.15	.10	119	Julio Valera	.07	.04
62	Kurt Knudsen (R)	.08	.05	120	Paul Wagner (R)	.10	.06
63	Kevin Koslofski (R)	.07	.04	121	Tim Wakefield (R)	3.50	2.50
64	Danny Leon (R)	.07	.04	122	Mike Walker (R)	.08	.05
65	Jesse Levis (R)	.08	.05	123	Bruce Walton	.05	.02
66	Tom Marsh (R)	.08	.05	124	Lenny Webster	.05	.02
67	Ed Martel (R)	.12	.07	125	Bob Wickman	.20	.12
68	Al Martin (R)	.12	.07	126	Mike Williams (R)	.12	.07
69	Pedro Martinez	.30	.18	127	Kerry Woodson	.08	.05
70	Derrick May	.10	.06	128	Eric Young (R)	.15	.10
71	Matt Maysey (R)	.08	.05	129	Kevin Young (R)	.35	.20
72	Russ McGinnis (R)	.08	.05	130	Pete Young (R)	.08	.05
73	Tim McIntosh	.10	.06	131	Checklist	.05	.02
74	Jim McNamara (R)	.08	.05	132	Checklist	.05	.02
75	Jeff McNeely (R)	.12	.07	BC1	Moises Alou	2.00	1.25
76	Rusty Meacham	.05	.02	BC2	Bret Boone	3.50	2.50
77	Tony Menendez (R)	.08	.05	BC3	Jeff Conine	2.00	1.25
78	Henry Mercedes (R)	.10	.06	BC4	Dave Fleming	3.50	2.50
79	Paul Miller (R)	.12	.07	BC5	Tyler Green	1.50	.90
80	Joe Millette (R)	.08	.05	BC6	Eric Karros	6.00	3.75
81	Blas Minor (R)	.08	.05	BC7	Pat Listach	4.50	2.75
82	Dennis Moeller (R)	.08	.05	BC8	Kenny Lofton	5.00	3.00
83	Raul Mondesi	.40	.25	BC9	Mike Piazza	4.50	2.75

		MINT	NR/MT
BC10	Tim Salmon	3.00	2.00
BC11	Andy Stankiewicz	1.25	.80
BC12	Dan Walters	1.25	.80
BC13	Ramon Caraballo	1.25	.80
BC14	Brian Jordan	2.50	1.50
BC15	Ryan Klesko	4.50	2.75
BC16	Sam Militello	3.00	2.00
BC17	Frank Seminara	2.00	1.25
BC18	Salomon Torres	4.50	2.75
BC19	John Valentin	1.50	.90
BC20	Wilfredo Cordero	4.50	2.75

1993 Donruss

This set was issued in two 396-card series with each card measuring 2-1/2" by 3-1/2". Card fronts feature full color action shots. A color stripe reflecting the player's team colors appears below the photo and contains the player's name and position. Card backs include a large photo, stats and personal data. Special inserts include Diamond Kings, Spirit Of The Game, Elite, a Will Clark Signature Series and a Robin Yount Legends Series. Those inserts are listed at the end of this checklist but are not included in the complete set price below.

		MINT	NR/MT
Complete Set (792)		25.00	16.50
Commons		.05	.02
1	Craig Lefferts	.05	.02
2	Kent Mercker	.07	.04
3	Phil Plantier	.15	.10
4	Alex Arias	.08	.05
5	Julio Valera	.05	.02

6	Dan Wilson	.07	.04
7	Frank Thomas	.80	.50
8	Eric Anthony	.08	.05
9	Derek Lilliquist	.05	.02
10	Rafael Bournigal (R)	.15	.10
11	Manny Alexander	.15	.10
12	Bret Barberie	.07	.04
13	Mickey Tettleton	.05	.02
14	Anthony Young	.08	.05
15	Tim Spehr	.05	.02
16	Bob Ayrault	.08	.05
17	Bill Wegman	.05	.02
18	Jay Bell	.05	.02
19	Rick Aguilera	.05	.02
20	Todd Zeile	.07	.04
21	Steve Farr	.05	.02
22	Andy Benes	.08	.05
23	Lance Blankenship	.05	.02
24	Ted Wood	.07	.04
25	Omar Vizquel	.05	.02
26	Steve Avery	.15	.10
27	Brian Bohanon	.05	.02
28	Rick Wilkins	.05	.02
29	Devon White	.05	.02
30	Bobby Ayala (R)	.15	.10
31	Leo Gomez	.07	.04
32	Mike Simms	.05	.02
33	Ellis Burks	.07	.04
34	Steve Wilson	.05	.02
35	Jim Abbott	.15	.10
36	Tim Wallach	.05	.02
37	Wilson Alvarez	.07	.04
38	Daryl Boston	.05	.02
39	Sandy Alomar, Jr.	.07	.04
40	Mitch Williams	.05	.02
41	Rico Brogna	.10	.06
42	Gary Varsho	.05	.02
43	Kevin Appier	.08	.05
44	Eric Wedge (R)	.25	.15
45	Dante Bichette	.05	.02
46	Jose Oquendo	.05	.02
47	Mike Trombley	.07	.04
48	Dan Walters	.08	.05
49	Gerald Williams	.08	.05
50	Bud Black	.05	.02
51	Bobby Witt	.07	.04
52	Mark Davis	.05	.02
53	Shawn Barton (R)	.08	.05
54	Paul Assenmacher	.05	.02
55	Kevin Reimer	.07	.04
56	Billy Ashley	.25	.15
57	Eddie Zosky	.07	.04
58	Chris Sabo	.07	.04
59	Billy Ripken	.05	.02
60	Scooter Tucker	.07	.04
61	Tim Wakefield	.75	.45
62	Mitch Webster	.05	.02
63	Jack Clark	.07	.04

64	Mark Gardner	.05	.02	122	Checklist	.05	.02
65	Lee Stevens	.08	.05	123	Steve Sax	.07	.04
66	Todd Hundley	.05	.02	124	Chuck Carr	.05	.02
67	Bobby Thigpen	.05	.02	125	Mark Lewis	.07	.04
68	Dave Hollins	.10	.06	126	Tony Gwynn	.15	.10
69	Jack Armstrong	.05	.02	127	Travis Fryman	.15	.10
70	Alex Cole	.05	.02	129	Dave Burba	.05	.02
71	Mark Carreon	.05	.02	130	John Smoltz	.12	.07
72	Todd Worrell	.05	.02	131	Cal Eldred	.25	.15
73	Steve Shifflett	.05	.02	132	Checklist	.05	.02
74	Jerald Clark	.07	.04	133	Arthur Rhodes	.08	.05
75	Paul Molitor	.08	.05	134	Jeff Blauser	.05	.02
76	Larry Carter (R)	.10	.06	135	Scott Cooper	.08	.05
77	Rich Rowland	.08	.05	136	Doug Strange	.05	.02
78	Damon Berryhill	.05	.02	137	Luis Sojo	.05	.02
79	Willie Banks	.05	.02	138	Jeff Branson	.05	.02
80	Hector Villanueva	.05	.02	139	Alex Fernandez	.07	.04
81	Mike Gallego	.05	.02	140	Ken Caminiti	.07	.04
82	Tim Belcher	.07	.04	141	Charles Nagy	.15	.10
83	Mike Bordick	.07	.04	142	Tom Candiotti	.05	.02
84	Craig Biggio	.07	.04	143	Willie Green	.12	.07
85	Lance Parrish	.07	.04	144	John Vander Wal	.08	.05
86	Brett Butler	.07	.04	145	Kurt Knudsen	.08	.05
87	Mike Timlin	.07	.04	146	John Franco	.05	.02
88	Brian Barnes	.07	.04	147	Eddie Pierce (R)	.08	.05
89	Brady Anderson	.12	.07	148	Kim Batiste	.05	.02
90	D.J. Dozier	.07	.04	149	Darren Holmes	.05	.02
91	Frank Viola	.07	.04	150	Steve Cooke	.05	.02
92	Darren Daulton	.15	.10	151	Terry Jorgensen	.05	.02
93	Chad Curtis	.10	.06	152	Mark Clark	.05	.02
94	Zane Smith	.05	.02	153	Randy Velarde	.05	.02
95	George Bell	.08	.05	154	Greg Harris	.05	.02
96	Rex Hudler	.05	.02	155	Kevin Campbell	.05	.02
97	Mark Whiten	.07	.04	156	John Burkett	.05	.02
98	Tim Teufel	.05	.02	157	Kevin Mitchell	.08	.05
99	Kevin Ritz	.07	.04	158	Deion Sanders	.15	.10
100	Jeff Brantley	.05	.02	159	Jose Canseco	.25	.15
101	Jeff Conine	.10	.06	160	Jeff Hartsock (R)	.08	.05
102	Vinny Castilla	.05	.02	161	Tom Quinlan (R)	.08	.05
103	Greg Vaughn	.08	.05	162	Tim Pugh (R)	.20	.12
104	Steve Buechele	.05	.02	163	Glenn Davis	.07	.04
105	Darren Reed	.05	.02	164	Shane Reynolds	.05	.02
106	Bip Roberts	.05	.02	165	Jody Reed	.05	.02
107	John Habyan	.05	.02	166	Mike Sharperson	.05	.02
108	Scott Servais	.05	.02	167	Scott Lewis	.05	.02
109	Walt Weiss	.05	.02	168	Dennis Martinez	.08	.05
110	J.T. Snow (R)	.75	.45	169	Scott Radinsky	.05	.02
111	Jay Buhner	.07	.04	170	Dave Gallagher	.05	.02
112	Darryl Strawberry	.15	.10	171	Jim Thome	.08	.05
113	Roger Pavlik	.05	.02	172	Terry Mulholland	.05	.02
114	Chris Nabholz	.07	.04	173	Milt Cuyler	.07	.04
115	Pat Borders	.05	.02	174	Bob Patterson	.05	.02
116	Pat Howell	.05	.02	175	Jeff Montgomery	.05	.02
117	Gregg Olson	.07	.04	176	Tim Salmon	.20	.12
118	Curt Schilling	.05	.02	177	Franklin Stubbs	.05	.02
119	Roger Clemens	.25	.15	178	Donovan Osborne	.15	.10
120	Victor Cole	.05	.02	179	Jeff Reboulet	.07	.04
121	Gary DiSarcina	.07	.04	180	Jeremy Hernandez	.07	.04

181	Charlie Hayes	.05	.02	244	Dave Hansen	.05	.02
182	Matt Williams	.10	.06	245	Monty Fariss	.05	.02
183	Mike Raczka (R)	.08	.05	246	Archi Cianfrocco	.08	.05
184	Francisco Cabrera	.05	.02	247	Pat Hentgen	.07	.04
185	Rich DeLucia	.05	.02	248	Bill Pecota	.05	.02
186	Sammy Sosa	.07	.04	249	Ben McDonald	.15	.10
187	Ivan Rodriguez	.25	.15	250	Cliff Brantley	.07	.04
188	Bret Boone	.20	.12	251	John Valentin	.12	.07
189	Juan Guzman	.35	.20	252	Jeff King	.08	.05
190	Randy Milligan	.05	.02	253	Reggie Williams	.05	.02
191	Ivan Calderon	.07	.04	254	Checklist	.05	.02
197	Junior Felix	.05	.02	255	Ozzie Guillen	.05	.02
198	Pete Schourek	.05	.02	256	Mike Perez	.07	.04
199	Craig Grebeck	.05	.02	257	Thomas Howard	.07	.04
200	Juan Bell	.05	.02	258	Kurt Stillwell	.05	.02
201	Glenallen Hill	.07	.04	259	Mike Henneman	.05	.02
202	Danny Jackson	.05	.02	260	Steve Decker	.07	.04
203	John Kiely	.05	.02	261	Bret Mayne	.07	.04
204	Bob Tewksbury	.05	.02	262	Otis Nixon	.08	.05
205	Kevin Koslofski	.05	.02	263	Mark Keifer	.08	.05
206	Craig Shipley	.05	.02	264	Checklist	.05	.02
207	John Jaha	.12	.07	265	Richie Lewis (R)	.12	.07
208	Royce Clayton	.12	.07	266	Pat Gomez (R)	.10	.06
209	Mike Piazza	.30	.18	267	Scott Taylor	.05	.02
210	Ron Gant	.12	.07	268	Shawon Dunston	.07	.04
211	Scott Erickson	.12	.07	269	Greg Myers	.05	.02
212	Doug Dascenzo	.05	.02	270	Tim Costo	.08	.05
213	Andy Stankiewicz	.05	.02	271	Greg Hibbard	.07	.04
214	Geronimo Berroa	.05	.02	272	Pete Harnisch	.07	.04
215	Dennis Eckersley	.10	.06	273	Dave Mlicki	.08	.05
216	Al Osuna	.05	.02	274	Orel Hershiser	.08	.05
217	Tino Martinez	.07	.04	275	Sean Berry	.05	.02
218	Henry Rodriguez	.08	.05	276	Doug Simons	.05	.02
219	Ed Sprague	.07	.04	277	John Doherty	.05	.02
220	Ken Hill	.07	.04	278	Eddie Murray	.12	.07
221	Chito Martinez	.08	.05	279	Chris Haney	.07	.04
222	Bret Saberhagen	.08	.05	280	Stan Javier	.05	.02
223	Mike Greenwell	.07	.04	281	Jaime Navarro	.15	.10
224	Mickey Morandini	.07	.04	282	Orlando Merced	.07	.04
225	Chuck Finley	.07	.04	283	Kent Hrbek	.05	.02
226	Denny Neagle	.07	.04	284	Bernard Gilkey	.08	.05
227	Kirk McCaskill	.05	.02	285	Russ Springer	.12	.07
228	Rheal Cormier	.07	.04	286	Mike Maddux	.05	.02
229	Paul Sorrento	.10	.06	287	Eric Fox	.05	.02
230	Darrin Jackson	.05	.02	288	Mark Leonard	.05	.02
231	Rob Deer	.07	.04	289	Tim Leary	.05	.02
232	Bill Swift	.07	.04	290	Brian Hunter	.10	.06
233	Kevin McReynolds	.07	.04	291	Donald Harris	.10	.06
234	Terry Pendleton	.15	.10	292	Bob Scanlan	.05	.02
235	Dave Nilsson	.12	.07	293	Turner Ward	.05	.02
236	Chuck McElroy	.05	.02	294	Hal Morris	.10	.06
237	Derek Parks	.08	.05	295	Jimmy Poole	.05	.02
238	Norm Charlton	.05	.02	296	Doug Jones	.05	.02
239	Matt Nokes	.05	.02	297	Tony Pena	.05	.02
240	Juan Guerrero	.07	.04	298	Ramon Martinez	.10	.06
241	Jeff Parrett	.05	.02	299	Tim Fortugno	.07	.04
242	Ryan Thompson	.15	.10	300	Marquis Grissom	.15	.10
243	Dave Fleming	.20	.12	301	Lance Johnson	.05	.02

302	Jeff Kent	.07	.04
303	Reggie Jefferson	.08	.05
304	Wes Chamberlain	.08	.05
305	Shawn Hare	.08	.05
306	Mike LaValliere	.05	.02
307	Gregg Jefferies	.10	.06
308	Troy Neel	.07	.04
309	Pat Listach	.40	.25
310	Geronimo Pena	.05	.02
311	Pedro Munoz	.08	.05
312	Guillermo Pena	.08	.05
313	Roberto Kelly	.10	.06
314	Mike Jackson	.05	.02
315	Rickey Henderson	.15	.10
316	Mark Lemke	.05	.02
317	Erik Hanson	.05	.02
318	Derrick May	.07	.04
319	Geno Petralli	.05	.02
320	Melvin Nieves	.30	.18
321	Doug Linton	.08	.05
322	Rob Dibble	.07	.04
323	Chris Hoiles	.08	.05
324	Jimmy Jones	.05	.02
325	Dave Staton	.10	.06
326	Pedro Martinez	.15	.10
327	Paul Quantrill	.08	.05
328	Greg Colbrunn	.08	.05
329	Hilly Hathaway (R)	.15	.10
330	Jeff Innis	.05	.02
331	Ron Karkovice	.05	.02
332	Keith Shepherd (R)	.20	.12
333	Alan Embree	.10	.06
334	Paul Wagner	.07	.04
335	Dave Haas	.07	.04
336	Ozzie Canseco	.07	.04
337	Bill Sampen	.05	.02
338	Rich Rodriguez	.05	.02
339	Dean Palmer	.12	.07
340	Greg Litton	.05	.02
341	Jim Tatum (R)	.20	.12
342	Todd Haney (R)	.08	.05
343	Larry Casian	.05	.02
344	Ryne Sandberg	.25	.15
345	Sterling Hitchcock (R)	.20	.12
346	Chris Hammond	.07	.04
347	Vince Horsman	.08	.05
348	Butch Henry	.07	.04
349	Dan Howitt	.08	.05
350	Roger McDowell	.05	.02
351	Jack Morris	.12	.07
352	Bill Krueger	.05	.02
353	Cris Colon	.10	.06
354	Joe Vitko	.10	.06
355	Willie McGee	.08	.05
356	Jay Baller	.05	.02
357	Pat Mahomes	.15	.10
358	Roger Mason	.05	.02
359	Jerry Nielsen	.05	.02
360	Tom Pagnozzi	.07	.04
361	Kevin Baez	.07	.04
362	Tim Scott	.07	.04
363	Domingo Martinez (R)	.12	.07
364	Kirt Manwaring	.05	.02
365	Rafael Palmeiro	.08	.05
366	Ray Lankford	.15	.10
367	Tim McIntosh	.12	.07
368	Jessie Hollins	.07	.04
369	Scott Leius	.05	.02
370	Bill Doran	.05	.02
371	Sam Militello	.15	.10
372	Ryan Bowen	.07	.04
373	Dave Henderson	.07	.04
374	Dan Smith	.08	.05
375	Steve Reed (R)	.10	.06
376	Jose Offerman	.08	.05
377	Kevin Brown	.07	.04
378	Darrin Fletcher	.05	.02
379	Duane Ward	.05	.02
380	Wayne Kirby	.05	.02
381	Steve Scarsone	.07	.04
382	Mariano Duncan	.05	.02
383	Ken Ryan (R)	.10	.06
384	Lloyd McClendon	.05	.02
385	Brian Holman	.07	.04
386	Braulio Castillo	.07	.04
387	Danny Leon	.07	.04
388	Omar Olivares	.05	.02
389	Kevin Wickander	.05	.02
390	Fred McGriff	.20	.12
391	Phil Clark	.08	.05
392	Darren Lewis	.07	.04
393	Phil Hiatt	.12	.07
394	Mike Morgan	.05	.02
395	Shane Mack	.12	.07
396	Checklist	.05	.02
397	David Segui	.08	.05
398	Rafael Belliard	.05	.02
399	Tim Naehring	.08	.05
400	Frank Castillo	.05	.02
401	Joe Grahe	.07	.04
402	Reggie Sanders	.25	.15
403	Roberto Hernandez	.07	.04
404	Luis Gonzalez	.08	.05
405	Carlos Baerga	.20	.12
406	Carlos Hernandez	.10	.06
407	Pedro Astacio	.30	.12
408	Mel Rojas	.05	.02
409	Scott Livingstone	.07	.04
410	Chico Walker	.05	.02
411	Brian McRae	.08	.05
412	Ben Rivera	.07	.04
413	Ricky Bones	.08	.05
414	Andy Van Slyke	.10	.06
415	Chuck Knoblauch	.25	.15
416	Luis Alicea	.05	.02
417	Bob Wickman	.25	.15

418	Doug Brocail	.08	.05
419	Scott Brosius	.05	.02
420	Rod Beck	.08	.05
421	Edgar Martinez	.15	.10
422	Ryan Klesko	.50	.30
423	Nolan Ryan	.35	.20
424	Rey Sanchez	.10	.06
425	Roberto Alomar	.20	.12
426	Barry Larkin	.12	.07
427	Mike Mussina	.35	.20
428	Jeff Bagwell	.30	.18
429	Mo Vaughn	.12	.07
430	Eric Karros	.25	.15
431	John Orton	.05	.02
432	Wil Cordero	.25	.15
433	Jack McDowell	.15	.10
434	Howard Johnson	.08	.05
435	Albert Belle	.15	.10
436	John Kruk	.07	.04
437	Skeeter Barnes	.05	.02
438	Don Slaught	.05	.02
439	Rusty Meacham (R)	.20	.12
440	Tim Laker (R)	.15	.10
441	Robin Yount	.20	.12
442	Brian Jordan	.15	.10
443	Kevin Tapani	.08	.05
444	Gary Sheffield	.25	.15
445	Rich Monteleone	.05	.02
446	Will Clark	.20	.12
447	Jerry Browne	.05	.02
448	Jeff Treadway	.05	.02
449	Mike Schooler	.05	.02
450	Mike Harkey	.08	.05
451	Julio Franco	.07	.04
452	Kevin Young	.25	.15
453	Kelly Gruber	.07	.04
454	Jose Rijo	.08	.05
455	Mike Devereaux	.07	.04
456	Andujar Cedeno	.15	.10
457	Damion Easley (R)	.20	.12
458	Kevin Gross	.05	.02
459	Matt Young	.05	.02
460	Matt Stairs	.12	.07
461	Luis Polonia	.07	.04
462	Dwight Gooden	.15	.10
463	Warren Newson (R)	.12	.07
464	Jose DeLeon	.05	.02
465	Jose Mesa (R)	.15	.10
466	Danny Cox	.05	.02
467	Dan Gladden	.05	.02
468	Gerald Perry	.05	.02
469	Mike Boddicker	.05	.02
470	Jeff Gardner	.05	.02
471	Doug Henry	.07	.04
472	Mike Benjamin	.07	.04
473	Dan Peltier	.10	.06
474	Mike Stanton	.05	.02
475	John Smiley	.08	.05
476	Dwight Smith	.05	.02
477	Jim Leyritz	.05	.02
478	Dwayne Henry	.05	.02
479	Mark McGwire	.25	.15
480	Pete Incaviglia	.05	.02
481	Dave Cochrane (R)	.20	.12
482	Eric Davis	.08	.05
483	John Olerud	.10	.06
484	Ken Bottenfield	.05	.02
485	Mark McLemore	.05	.02
486	Dave Magadan	.07	.04
487	John Marzano	.05	.02
488	Ruben Amaro	.08	.05
489	Rob Ducey	.05	.02
490	Stan Belinda	.05	.02
491	Dan Pasqua	.05	.02
492	Joe Magrane	.07	.04
493	Brook Jacoby	.05	.02
494	Gene Harris	.05	.02
495	Mark Leiter	.05	.02
496	Bryan Hickerson	.05	.02
497	Tom Gordon	.08	.05
498	Pete Smith	.15	.10
499	Chris Bosio	.07	.04
500	Shawn Boskie	.07	.04
501	Dave West	.05	.02
502	Milt Hill	.05	.02
503	Pat Kelly	.08	.05
504	Joe Boever	.05	.02
505	Terry Steinbach	.07	.04
506	Butch Huskey (R)	.25	.15
507	Dave Valle	.05	.02
508	Mike Scioscia	.05	.02
509	Kenny Rogers	.05	.02
510	Moises Alou	.15	.10
511	David Wells	.05	.02
512	Mackey Sasser	.05	.02
513	Todd Frohwirth	.07	.04
514	Ricky Jordan	.07	.04
515	Mike Gardiner	.07	.04
516	Gary Redus	.05	.02
517	Gary Gaetti	.05	.02
518	Checklist	.05	.02
519	Carlton Fisk	.15	.10
520	Ozzie Smith	.15	.10
521	Rod Nichols	.05	.02
522	Benito Santiago	.10	.06
523	Bill Gullickson	.05	.02
524	Robby Thompson	.05	.02
525	Mike Macfarlane	.07	.04
526	Sid Bream	.05	.02
527	Darryl Hamilton (R)	.15	.10
528	Checklist	.05	.02
529	Jeff Tackett	.10	.06
530	Greg Olson	.05	.02
531	Bob Zupcic	.15	.10
532	Mark Grace	.10	.06
533	Steve Frey	.05	.02

534	Dave Martinez	.05	.02
535	Robin Ventura	.20	.12
536	Casey Candaele	.05	.02
537	Kenny Lofton	.30	.18
538	Jay Howell	.05	.02
539	Fernando Ramsey (R)	.15	.10
540	Larry Walker	.15	.10
541	Cecil Fielder	.15	.10
542	Lee Guetterman	.05	.02
543	Keith Miller	.05	.02
544	Lenny Dykstra	.07	.04
545	B.J. Surhoff	.05	.02
546	Bob Walk	.05	.02
547	Brian Harper	.05	.02
548	Lee Smith	.10	.06
549	Danny Tartabull	.12	.07
550	Frank Seminara	.15	.10
551	Henry Mercedes	.08	.05
552	Dave Righetti	.05	.02
553	Ken Griffey, Jr.	.50	.30
554	Tom Glavine	.20	.12
555	Juan Gonzalez	.35	.20
556	Jim Bullinger	.08	.05
557	Derek Bell	.15	.10
558	Cesar Hernandez	.08	.05
559	Cal Ripken, Jr.	.30	.18
560	Eddie Taubensee	.08	.05
561	John Flaherty	.08	.05
562	Todd Benzinger	.05	.02
563	Hubie Brooks	.07	.04
564	Delino DeShields	.15	.10
565	Tim Raines	.07	.04
566	Sid Fernandez	.07	.04
567	Steve Olin	.07	.04
568	Tommy Greene	.08	.05
569	Buddy Groom	.08	.05
570	Randy Tomlin	.10	.06
571	Hipolito Pichardo	.08	.05
572	Rene Arocha (R)	.20	.12
573	Mike Fetters	.05	.02
574	Felix Jose	.08	.05
575	Gene Larkin	.05	.02
576	Bruce Hurst	.08	.05
577	Bernie Williams	.12	.07
578	Trevor Wilson	.05	.02
579	Bob Welch	.07	.04
580	David Justice	.20	.12
581	Randy Johnson	.12	.07
582	Jose Vizcaino	.05	.02
583	Jeff Huson	.07	.04
584	Rob Maurer	.15	.10
585	Todd Stottlemyer	.07	.04
586	Joe Oliver	.05	.02
587	Bob Milacki	.05	.02
588	Rob Murphy	.05	.02
589	Greg Pirkl	.08	.05
590	Lenny Harris	.05	.02
591	Luis Rivera	.05	.02
592	John Wetteland	.08	.05
593	Mark Langston	.10	.06
594	Bobby Bonilla	.15	.10
595	Este Beltre	.08	.05
596	Mike Hartley	.08	.05
597	Felix Fermin	.05	.02
598	Carlos Garcia (R)	.40	.25
599	Frank Tanana	.05	.02
600	Pedro Guerrero	.08	.05
601	Terry Shumpert	.05	.02
602	Wally Whitehurst	.05	.02
603	Kevin Seitzer	.05	.02
604	Chris James	.05	.02
605	Greg Gohr (R)	.15	.10
606	Mark Wohlers	.12	.07
607	Kirby Puckett	.25	.15
608	Greg Maddux	.20	.12
609	Don Mattingly	.15	.10
610	Greg Cadaret	.05	.02
611	Dave Stewart	.08	.05
612	Mark Portugal	.05	.02
613	Pete O'Brien	.05	.02
614	Bobby Ojeda	.05	.02
615	Joe Carter	.25	.15
616	Pete Young	.08	.05
617	Sam Horn	.05	.02
618	Vince Coleman	.08	.05
619	Wade Boggs	.15	.10
620	Todd Pratt (R)	.12	.07
621	Ron Tingley (R)	.12	.07
622	Doug Drabek	.15	.10
623	Scott Hemond	.07	.04
624	Tim Jones (R)	.12	.07
625	Dennis Cook	.05	.02
626	Jose Melendez	.08	.05
627	Mike Munoz	.05	.02
628	Jim Pena	.08	.05
629	Gary Thurman	.08	.05
630	Charlie Leibrandt	.05	.02
631	Scott Fletcher	.05	.02
632	Andre Dawson	.15	.10
633	Greg Gagne	.05	.02
634	Greg Swindell	.08	.05
635	Kevin Maas	.10	.06
636	Xavier Hernandez	.07	.04
637	Ruben Sierra	.20	.12
638	Dmitri Young (R)	.50	.30
639	Harold Reynolds	.05	.02
640	Tom Goodwin	.08	.05
641	Todd Burns	.05	.02
642	Jeff Fassero	.05	.02
643	Dave Winfield	.15	.10
644	Willie Randolph	.07	.04
645	Luis Mercedes	.08	.05
646	Dale Murphy	.10	.06
647	Danny Darwin	.05	.02
648	Dennis Moeller	.08	.05
649	Chuck Crim	.08	.05

650 Checklist	.05	.02
651 Shawn Abner	.05	.02
652 Tracy Woodson	.05	.02
653 Scott Scudder	.05	.02
654 Tom Lampkin	.05	.02
655 Alan Trammell	.10	.06
656 Cory Snyder	.05	.02
657 Chris Gwynn	.07	.04
658 Lonnie Smith	.05	.02
659 Jim Austin	.08	.05
660 Checklist	.05	.02
661 Tim Hulett (R)	.20	.12
662 Marvin Freeman	.05	.02
663 Greg Harris	.05	.02
664 Heathcliff Slocumb	.05	.02
665 Mike Butcher (R)	.15	.10
666 Steve Foster	.08	.05
667 Donn Paul	.05	.02
668 Darryl Kile	.08	.05
669 Jesse Levis	.08	.05
670 Jim Gott	.05	.02
671 Mark Hutton	.12	.07
672 Brian Drahman (R)	.30	.18
673 Chad Kreuter	.05	.02
674 Tony Fernandez	.08	.05
675 Jose Lind	.05	.02
676 Kyle Abbott	.08	.05
677 Dan Plesac	.05	.02
678 Barry Bonds	.20	.12
679 Chili Davis	.07	.04
680 Stan Royer	.08	.05
681 Scott Kamieniecki	.08	.05
682 Carlos Martinez	.08	.05
683 Mike Moore	.05	.02
684 Candy Maldonado	.07	.04
685 Jeff Nelson (R)	.12	.07
686 Lou Whitaker	.07	.04
687 Jose Guzman	.05	.02
688 Manuel Lee	.05	.02
689 Bob MacDonald (R)	.12	.07
690 Scott Bankhead	.05	.02
691 Alan Mills	.07	.04
692 Brian Williams	.20	.12
693 Tom Brunansky	.07	.04
694 Lenny Webster	.05	.02
695 Greg Briley	.05	.02
696 Paul O'Neill	.10	.06
697 Joey Cora	.05	.02
698 Charlie O'Brien	.05	.02
699 Junior Ortiz	.05	.02
700 Ron Darling	.07	.04
701 Tony Phillips	.05	.02
702 William Pennyfeather	.12	.07
703 Mark Gubicza	.07	.04
704 Steve Hosey	.25	.15
705 Henry Cotto	.05	.02
706 David Hulse (R)	.12	.07
707 Mike Pagliarulo	.05	.02

708 Dave Stieb	.07	.04
709 Melido Perez	.07	.04
710 Jimmy Key	.05	.02
711 Jeff Russell	.05	.02
712 David Cone	.15	.10
713 Russ Swan	.05	.02
714 Mark Guthrie	.05	.02
715 Checklist	.05	.02
716 Al Martin	.08	.05
717 Randy Knorr	.05	.02
718 Mike Stanley	.05	.02
719 Rick Sutcliffe	.05	.02
720 Terry Leach	.05	.02
721 Chipper Jones	.50	.30
722 Jim Eisenrich	.05	.02
723 Tom Henke	.05	.02
724 Jeff Frye	.08	.05
725 Harold Baines	.07	.04
726 Scott Sanderson	.05	.02
727 Tom Foley	.05	.02
728 Bryan Harvey	.07	.04
729 Tom Edens (R)	.15	.10
730 Eric Young	.20	.12
731 Dave Weathers	.08	.05
732 Spike Owen	.05	.02
733 Scott Aldred (R)	.15	.10
734 Cris Carpenter	.07	.04
735 Dion James	.05	.02
736 Joe Girardi	.05	.02
737 Nigel Wilson (R)	1.25	.80
738 Scott Chiamparino	.07	.04
739 Jeff Reardon	.10	.06
740 Willie Blair	.08	.05
741 Jim Corsi	.05	.02
742 Ken Patterson	.05	.02
743 Andy Ashby	.08	.05
744 Rob Natal	.08	.05
745 Kevin Bass	.05	.02
746 Freddie Benavides	.05	.02
747 Chris Donnels	.08	.05
748 Kerry Woodson	.10	.06
749 Calvin Jones	.10	.06
750 Gary Scott	.07	.04
751 Joe Orsulak	.05	.02
752 Armondo Reynoso	.07	.04
753 Monty Fariss	.07	.04
754 Billy Hatcher	.05	.02
755 Denis Boucher	.07	.04
756 Walt Weiss	.05	.02
757 Mike Fitzgerald	.05	.02
758 Rudy Seanez	.08	.05
759 Bret Barberie	.08	.05
760 Mo Sanford	.08	.05
761 Pedro Castellano	.08	.05
762 Chuck Carr	.10	.06
763 Steve Howe	.05	.02
764 Andres Galarraga	.07	.04
765 Jeff Conine	.12	.07

766	Ted Power	.05	.02
767	Butch Henry	.08	.05
768	Steve Decker	.08	.05
769	Storm Davis	.05	.02
770	Vinny Castilla (R)	.15	.10
771	Junior Felix	.05	.02
772	Walt Terrell	.05	.02
773	Brad Ausmus (R)	.25	.15
774	Jamie McAndrew	.10	.06
775	Milt Thompson	.05	.02
776	Charlie Hayes	.05	.02
777	Jack Armstrong	.07	.04
778	Dennis Rasmussen	.05	.02
779	Darren Holmes	.08	.05
780	Alex Arias	.08	.05
781	Randy Bush	.05	.02
782	Javy Lopez (R)	.12	.07
783	Dante Bichette	.07	.04
784	John Johnstone (R)	.15	.10
785	Rene Gonzales	.08	.05
786	Alex Cole	.05	.02
787	Jeromy Burnitz (R)	.40	.25
788	Michael Huff	.08	.05
789	Anthony Telford	.12	.07
790	Jerald Clark	.08	.05
791	Joel Johnston	.08	.05
792	David Nied	1.75	1.00
E1	Fred McGriff	125.00	80.00
E2	Ryne Sandberg	250.00	150.00
E3	Eddie Murray	90.00	60.00
E4	Paul Molitor	60.00	35.00
E5	Barry Larkin	75.00	45.00
E6	Don Mattingly	150.00	90.00
E7	Dennis Eckersley	75.00	45.00
E8	Roberto Alomar	125.00	80.00
E9	Edgar Martinez	60.00	35.00
E10	Gary Sheffield	90.00	60.00
E11	Mark McGwire	200.00	125.00
E12	Cecil Fielder	125.00	80.00
E13	Dave Winfield	150.00	90.00
E14	Juan Gonzalez	175.00	100.00
E15	Darren Daulton	60.00	35.00
E16	Larry Walker	60.00	35.00
E17	Barry Bonds	150.00	90.00
E18	Andy Van Slyke	60.00	35.00
L1	Robin Yount	250.00	150.00
S1	Will Clark	300.00	200.00

1993 Donruss Diamond Kings

		MINT	NR/MT
Complete Set (30)		65.00	48.00
Commons		1.00	.70
1	Ken Griffey, Jr.	7.50	5.00
2	Ryne Sandberg	4.50	3.00
3	Roger Clemens	4.50	3.00
4	Kirby Puckett	4.50	3.00
5	Bill Swift	1.00	.70
6	Larry Walker	2.00	1.25
7	Juan Gonzalez	5.00	3.00
8	Wally Joyner	1.00	.70
9	Andy Van Slyke	1.00	.70
10	Robin Ventura	2.50	1.50
11	Bip Roberts	1.00	.70
12	Roberto Kelly	1.00	.70
13	Carlos Baerga	2.50	1.50
14	Orel Hershiser	1.00	.70
15	Cecil Fielder	3.00	2.00
16	Robin Yount	3.50	2.50
17	Darren Daulton	1.00	.70
18	Mark McGwire	4.50	3.00
19	Tom Glavine	2.50	1.50
20	Roberto Alomar	4.00	2.75
21	Gary Sheffield	3.50	2.50
22	Bob Tewksbury	1.00	.70
23	Brady Anderson	1.25	.80
24	Craig Biggio	1.00	.70
25	Eddie Murray	1.50	.90
26	Luis Polonia	1.00	.70
27	Nigel Wilson	7.00	5.00
28	David Nied	6.00	4.00
29	Pat Listach	4.00	2.75
30	Eric Karros	6.00	4.00

1993 Donruss Long Ball Leaders

		MINT	NR/MT
Complete Set (18)		35.00	24.00
Commons		.75	.45
1	Rob Deer	.75	.45
2	Fred McGriff	2.00	1.25
3	Albert Belle	1.50	.90
4	Mark McGwire	4.00	2.75
5	David Justice	2.00	1.25
6	Jose Canseco	4.00	2.75
7	Kent Hrbek	.75	.45
8	Roberto Alomar	2.00	1.25
9	Ken Griffey Jr	5.00	3.00
10	Frank Thomas	7.00	4.50
11	Darryl Strawberry	1.75	1.00
12	Felix Jose	.75	.45
13	Cecil Fielder	2.00	1.25
14	Juan Gonzalez	4.00	2.75
15	Ryne Sandberg	3.50	2.50
16	Gary Sheffield	2.00	1.25
17	Jeff Bagwell	1.75	1.00
18	Larry Walker	1.50	.90

1993 Donruss MVP's

		MINT	NR/MT
Complete Set (26)		50.00	35.00
Commons		.75	.45
1	Luis Polonia	.75	.45
2	Frank Thomas	7.00	4.00
3	George Brett	2.00	1.25
4	Paul Molitor	.75	.45
5	Don Mattingly	1.75	1.00
6	Roberto Alomar	2.00	1.25
7	Terry Pendleton	1.00	.70
8	Eric Karros	3.50	2.50
9	Larry Walker	1.25	.80
10	Eddie Murray	1.50	.90
11	Darren Daulton	.75	.45
12	Ray Lankford	1.50	.90
13	Will Clark	2.00	1.25
14	Cal Ripken	5.00	3.00
15	Roger Clemens	4.50	2.75
16	Carlos Baerga	1.50	.90
17	Cecil Fielder	2.00	1.25
18	Kirby Puckett	3.00	2.00
19	Mark McGwire	3.00	2.00
20	Ken Griffey, Jr.	6.00	4.00
21	Juan Gonzalez	4.50	2.75
22	Ryne Sandberg	3.00	2.00
23	Bip Roberts	.75	.45
24	Jeff Bagwell	1.75	1.00
25	Barry Bonds	2.50	1.50
26	Gary Sheffield	2.00	1.25

FLEER

1963 Fleer

This 67-card set was packaged with a cookie rather than bubble gum and was expected to be the first in a series. However, a lawsuit filed by Topps ended the series at 67 cards. Two cards in the set, #46 Joe Adcock and the unnumbered checklist are considered scarce. Both are included in the complete set price below. Cards measure 2-1/2" by 3-1/2".

		NR/MT	EX
Complete Set (67)		1,200.00	600.00
Commons		7.00	3.50
1	Steve Barber	10.00	5.00
2	Ron Hansen	7.00	3.50
3	Milt Pappas	7.00	3.50
4	Brooks Robinson	55.00	27.50
5	Willie Mays	125.00	62.50
6	Lou Clinton	7.00	3.50
7	Bill Monbouquette	7.00	3.50
8	Carl Yastrzemski	100.00	50.00
9	Ray Herbert	7.00	3.50
10	Jim Landis	7.00	3.50
11	Dick Donovan	7.00	3.50
12	Tito Francona	7.00	3.50
13	Jerry Kindall	7.00	3.50

14	Frank Lary	10.00	5.00
15	Dick Howser	8.50	4.25
16	Jerry Lumpe	7.00	3.50
17	Norm Siebern	7.00	3.50
18	Don Lee	7.00	3.50
19	Albie Pearson	7.00	3.50
20	Bob Rodgers	8.00	4.00
21	Leon Wagner	7.00	3.50
22	Jim Kaat	12.00	6.00
23	Vic Power	7.00	3.50
24	Rich Rollins	7.00	3.50
25	Bobby Richardson	12.00	6.00
26	Ralph Terry	8.00	4.00
27	Tom Cheney	7.00	3.50
28	Chuck Cottier	7.00	3.50
29	Jimmy Piersall	12.00	6.00
30	Dave Stenhouse	7.00	3.50
31	Glen Hobbie	7.00	3.50
32	Ron Santo	12.00	6.00
33	Gene Freese	7.00	3.50
34	Vada Pinson	12.00	6.00
35	Bob Purkey	7.00	3.50
36	Joe Amalfitano	7.00	3.50
37	Bob Aspromonte	7.00	3.50
38	Dick Farrell	7.00	3.50
39	Al Spangler	7.00	3.50
40	Tommy Davis	12.00	6.00
41	Don Drysdale	40.00	20.00
42	Sandy Koufax	125.00	62.50
43	Maury Wills (R)	75.00	37.50
44	Frank Bolling	7.00	3.50
45	Warren Spahn	40.00	20.00
46	Joe Adcock	150.00	75.00
47	Roger Craig	10.00	5.00
48	Al Jackson	7.00	3.50
49	Rod Kanehl	7.00	3.50
50	Ruben Amaro	7.00	3.50
51	John Callison	8.00	4.00
52	Clay Dalrymple	7.00	3.50
53	Don Demeter	7.00	3.50
54	Art Mahaffey	7.00	3.50
55	Smoky Burgess	8.50	4.25
56	Roberto Clemente	125.00	62.50
57	Elroy Face	10.00	5.00
58	Vernon Law	8.00	4.00
59	Bill Mazeroski	15.00	7.50
60	Ken Boyer	16.00	8.00
61	Bob Gibson	35.00	17.50
62	Gene Oliver	7.00	3.50
63	Bill White	12.00	6.00
64	Orlando Cepeda	15.00	7.50
65	Jimmy Davenport	7.00	3.50
66	Billy O'Dell	7.00	3.50
—	Checklist 1-66	375.00	150.00

1981 Fleer

For the first time since 1963 Fleer returned to the baseball card scene with a 660-card set. The standard size cards measure 2-1/2" by 3-1/2". The set is filled with numerous errors which were corrected creating many variations. Those variations are listed below with the lower price included in the complete set price. Players are grouped by team and each team group has its own border color that frames a full color player photo on the card fronts. Card backs are horizontal and feature statistical information printed in black, yellow and gray.

		MINT	NR/MT
Complete Set (660)		62.00	45.00
Commons		.07	.03
1	Pete Rose	3.00	2.00
2	Larry Bowa	.15	.10
3	Manny Trillo	.07	.04
4	Bob Boone	.20	.12
5	Mike Schmidt	4.50	3.00
6a	Steve Carlton	2.00	1.25
	(Date 1066 on back)		
6b	Steve Carlton	4.00	2.75
	(Date 1966 on back)		
7	Tug McGraw	.30	.18
8	Larry Christenson	.07	.03
9	Bake McBride	.07	.03
10	Greg Luzinski	.20	.12
11	Ron Reed	.07	.03
12	Dickie Noles	.07	.03
13	Keith Moreland (R)	.12	.07
14	Bob Walk (R)	.25	.15
15	Lonnie Smith	.15	.10
16	Dick Ruthven	.07	.03
17	Sparky Lyle	.15	.10
18	Greg Gross	.07	.03
19	Garry Maddox	.07	.03

#	Name		
20	Nino Espinosa	.07	.03
21	George Vukovich	.07	.03
22	John Vukovich	.07	.03
23	Ramon Aviles	.07	.03
24	Kevin Saucier	.07	.03
	(Ken Saucier on back)	.07	.03
25	Randy Lerch	.07	.03
26	Del Unser	.07	.03
27	Tim McCarver	.15	.10
28	George Brett	4.50	3.50
29	Willie Wilson	.20	.12
30	Paul Splittorff	.07	.03
31	Dan Quisenberry	.15	.10
32	Amos Otis	.20	.12
33	Steve Busby	.07	.03
34	U.L. Washington	.07	.03
35	Dave Chalk	.07	.03
36	Darrell Porter	.07	.03
37	Marty Pattin	.07	.03
38	Larry Gura	.07	.03
39	Renie Martin	.07	.03
40	Rich Gale	.07	.03
41a	Hal McRae(Black "Royals" on front)	.35	.20
41b	Hal McRae(Light blue "Royals" on front)	.20	.12
42	Dennis Leonard	.07	.03
43	Willie Aikens	.07	.03
44	Frank White	.10	.06
45	Clint Hurdle	.07	.03
46	John Wathan	.07	.03
47	Pete LaCock	.07	.03
48	Rance Mulliniks	.07	.03
49	Jeff Twitty	.07	.03
50	Jamie Quirk	.07	.03
51	Art Howe	.07	.03
52	Ken Forsch	.07	.03
53	Vern Ruhle	.07	.03
54	Joe Niekro	.10	.06
55	Frank LaCorte	.07	.03
56	J.R. Richard	.15	.10
57	Nolan Ryan	9.00	6.00
58	Enos Cabell	.07	.03
59	Cesar Cedeno	.12	.07
60	Jose Cruz	.15	.10
61	Bill Virdon	.07	.03
62	Terry Puhl	.07	.03
63	Joaquin Andujar	.10	.06
64	Alan Ashby	.07	.03
65	Joe Sambito	.07	.03
66	Denny Walling	.07	.03
67	Jeff Leonard	.10	.06
68	Luis Pujols	.07	.03
69	Bruce Bochy	.07	.03
70	Rafael Landestoy	.07	.03
71	Dave Smith (R)	.15	.10
72	Danny Heep (R)	.08	.05
73	Julio Gonzalez	.07	.03
74	Craig Reynolds	.07	.03
75	Gary Woods	.07	.03
76	Dave Bergman	.07	.03
77	Randy Niemann	.07	.03
78	Joe Morgan	1.00	.70
79	Reggie Jackson	4.50	3.50
80	Bucky Dent	.10	.06
81	Tommy John	.15	.10
82	Luis Tiant	.15	.10
83	Rick Cerone	.07	.03
84	Dick Howser	.07	.03
85	Lou Piniella	.15	.10
86	Ron Davis	.07	.03
87a	Graig Nettles (Graig on back)	12.00	8.50
87b	Graig Nettles (Graig on back)	.35	.20
88	Ron Guidry	.30	.18
89	Rich Gossage	.30	.18
90	Rudy May	.07	.03
91	Gaylord Perry	.80	.50
92	Eric Soderholm	.07	.03
93	Bob Watson	.12	.07
94	Bobby Murcer	.15	.10
95	Bobby Brown	.07	.03
96	Jim Spencer	.07	.03
97	Tom Underwood	.07	.03
98	Oscar Gamble	.07	.03
99	Johnny Oates	.07	.03
100	Fred Stanley	.07	.03
101	Ruppert Jones	.07	.03
102	Dennis Werth	.07	.03
103	Joe Lefebvre	.07	.03
104	Brian Doyle	.07	.03
105	Aurelio Rodriguez	.07	.03
106	Doug Bird	.07	.03
107	Mike Griffin	.07	.03
108	Tim Lollar	.07	.03
109	Willie Randolph	.12	.07
110	Steve Garvey	.80	.50
111	Reggie Smith	.08	.05
112	Don Sutton	.75	.45
113	Burt Hooton	.07	.03
114a	Dave Lopes (No finger on back)	.10	.06
114b	Dave Lopes (Small finger on back)	.40	.25
115	Dusty Baker	.10	.06
116	Tom Lasorda	.10	.06
117	Bill Russell	.12	.07
118	Jerry Reuss	.10	.06
119	Terry Forster	.07	.03
120	Robert Welch(Bob)	.35	.20
121	Don Stanhouse	.07	.03
122	Rick Monday	.10	.06
123	Derrel Thomas	.07	.03
124	Joe Ferguson	.07	.03
125	Rick Sutcliffe	.30	.18

Card	Player	Price 1	Price 2
126a	Ron Cey (No finger on back)	.10	.06
126b	Ron Cey (No finger on back)	.40	.25
127	Dave Goltz	.07	.03
128	Jay Johnstone	.08	.05
129	Steve Yeager	.07	.03
130	Gary Weiss	.07	.03
131	Mike Scioscia (R)	1.00	.70
132	Vic Davalillo	.07	.03
133	Doug Rau	.07	.03
134	Pepe Frias	.07	.03
135	Mickey Hatcher	.07	.03
136	Steve Howe (R)	.10	.06
137	Robert Castillo	.07	.03
138	Gary Thomasson	.07	.03
139	Rudy Law	.07	.03
140	Fernand Valenzuela (R) (Fernando)	1.75	1.00
141	Manny Mota	.10	.06
142	Gary Carter	1.25	.80
143	Steve Roberts	.07	.03
144	Warren Cromartie	.07	.03
145	Andre Dawson	2.50	1.50
146	Larry Parrish	.07	.03
147	Rowland Office	.07	.03
148	Ellis Valentine	.07	.03
149	Dick Williams	.07	.03
150	Bill Gullickson (R)	.60	.35
151	Elias Sosa	.07	.03
152	John Tamargo	.07	.03
153	Chris Speier	.07	.03
154	Ron LeFlore	.08	.05
155	Rodney Scott	.07	.03
156	Stan Bahnsen	.07	.03
157	Bill Lee	.08	.05
158	Fred Norman	.07	.03
159	Woodie Fryman	.07	.03
160	Dave Palmer	.07	.03
161	Jerry White	.07	.03
162	Roberto Ramos	.07	.03
163	John D'Acquisto	.07	.03
164	Tommy Hutton	.07	.03
165	Charlie Lea (R)	.10	.06
166	Scott Sanderson	.15	.10
167	Ken Macha	.07	.03
168	Tony Bernazard	.07	.03
169	Jim Palmer	2.00	1.25
170	Steve Stone	.08	.05
171	Mike Flanagan	.20	.12
172	Al Bumbry	.07	.03
173	Doug DeCinces	.07	.03
174	Scott McGregor	.07	.03
175	Mark Belanger	.20	.12
176	Tim Stoddard	.07	.03
177a	Rick Dempsey (No finger on front)	.10	.06
177b	Rick Dempsey (Small finger on front)	.35	.20
178	Earl Weaver	.10	.06
179	Tippy Martinez	.07	.03
180	Dennis Martinez	.30	.18
181	Sammy Stewart	.07	.03
182	Rich Dauer	.07	.03
183	Lee May	.07	.03
184	Eddie Murray	3.50	2.50
185	Benny Ayala	.07	.03
186	John Lowenstein	.07	.03
187	Gary Roenicke	.07	.03
188	Ken Singleton	.08	.05
189	Dan Graham	.07	.03
190	Terry Crowley	.07	.03
191	Kiko Garcia	.07	.03
192	Dave Ford	.07	.03
193	Mark Corey	.07	.03
194	Lenn Sakata	.07	.03
195	Doug DeCinces	.07	.03
196	Johnny Bench	2.50	1.50
197	Dave Concepcion	.25	.15
198	Ray Knight	.10	.06
199	Ken Griffey	.25	.15
200	Tom Seaver	3.00	2.00
201	Dave Collins	.07	.03
202	George Foster	.20	.12
203	Junior Kennedy	.07	.03
204	Frank Pastore	.07	.03
205	Dan Driessen	.08	.05
206	Hector Cruz	.07	.03
207	Paul Moskau	.07	.03
208	Charlie Leibrandt (R)	.75	.45
209	Harry Spilman	.07	.03
210	Joe Price (R)	.07	.03
211	Tom Hume	.07	.03
212	Joe Nolan	.07	.03
213	Doug Bair	.07	.03
214	Mario Soto	.08	.05
215	Bill Bonham	.07	.03
216	George Foster	.20	.12
217	Paul Householder	.07	.03
218	Ron Oester	.07	.03
219	Sam Mejias	.07	.03
220	Sheldon Burnside	.07	.03
221	Carl Yastrzemski	2.00	1.25
222	Jim Rice	.25	.15
223	Fred Lynn	.25	.15
224	Carlton Fisk	2.50	1.50
225	Rick Burleson	.08	.05
226	Dennis Eckersley	2.00	1.25
227	Butch Hobson	.07	.03
228	Tom Burgmeier	.07	.03
229	Garry Hancock	.07	.03
230	Don Zimmer	.07	.03
231	Steve Renko	.07	.03
232	Dwight Evans	.40	.25
233	Mike Torrez	.07	.03
234	Bob Stanley	.07	.03

235	Jim Dwyer	.07	.03
236	Dave Stapleton	.07	.03
237	Glenn Hoffman	.07	.03
238	Jerry Remy	.07	.03
239	Dick Drago	.07	.03
240	Bill Campbell	.07	.03
241	Tony Perez	.50	.30
242	Phil Niekro	.80	.50
243	Dale Murphy	1.25	.80
244	Bob Horner	.10	.06
245	Jeff Burroughs	.07	.03
246	Rick Camp	.07	.03
247	Bob Cox	.07	.03
248	Bruce Benedict	.07	.03
249	Gene Garber	.07	.03
250	Jerry Royster	.07	.03
251a	Gary Matthews (No finger on back)	.08	.05
251b	Gary Matthews (Small finger on back)	.35	.20
		.07	.03
252	Chris Cambliss	.10	.06
253	Luis Gomez	.07	.03
254	Bill Nahorodny	.07	.03
255	Doyle Alexander	.07	.03
256	Brian Asselstine	.07	.03
257	Biff Pocoroba	.07	.03
258	Mike Lum	.07	.03
259	Charlie Spikes	.07	.03
260	Glenn Hubbard	.07	.03
261	Tommy Boggs	.07	.03
262	Al Hrabosky	.10	.06
263	Rick Matula	.07	.03
264	Preston Hanna	.07	.03
265	Larry Bradford	.07	.03
266	Rafael Ramirez (R)	.12	.07
267	Larry McWilliams	.07	.03
268	Rod Carew	2.50	1.50
269	Bobby Grich	.10	.06
270	Carney Lansford	.15	.10
271	Don Baylor	.20	.12
272	Joe Rudi	.10	.06
273	Dan Ford	.07	.03
274	Jim Fregosi	.07	.03
275	Dave Frost	.07	.03
276	Frank Tanana	.10	.06
277	Dickie Thon	.08	.05
278	Jason Thompson	.07	.03
279	Rick Miller	.07	.03
280	Bert Campaneris	.12	.07
281	Tom Donohue	.07	.03
282	Brian Downing	.15	.10
283	Fred Patek	.07	.03
284	Bruce Kison	.07	.03
285	Dave LaRoche	.07	.03
286	Don Aase	.07	.03
287	Jim Barr	.07	.03
288	Alfredo Martinez	.07	.03
289	Larry Harlow	.07	.03
290	Andy Hassler	.07	.03
291	Dave Kingman	.15	.10
292	Bill Buckner	.15	.10
293	Rick Reuschel	.12	.07
294	Bruce Sutter	.20	.12
295	Jerry Martin	.07	.03
296	Scot Thompson	.07	.03
297	Ivan DeJesus	.07	.03
298	Steve Dillard	.07	.03
299	Dick Tidrow	.07	.03
300	Randy Martz	.07	.03
301	Lenny Randle	.07	.03
302	Lynn McGlothen	.07	.03
303	Cliff Johnson	.07	.03
304	Tim Blackwell	.07	.03
305	Dennis Lamp	.07	.03
306	Bill Caudill	.07	.03
307	Carlos Lezcano	.07	.03
308	Jim Tracy	.07	.03
309	Doug Capilla	.07	.03
310	Willie Hernandez	.10	.06
311	Mike Vail	.07	.03
312	Mike Krukow	.07	.03
313	Barry Foote	.07	.03
314	Larry Biittner	.07	.03
315	Mike Tyson	.07	.03
316	Lee Mazzilli	.07	.03
317	John Stearns	.07	.03
318	Alex Trevino	.07	.03
319	Craig Swan	.07	.03
320	Frank Taveras	.07	.03
321	Steve Henderson	.07	.03
322	Neil Allen	.07	.03
323	Mark Bomback	.07	.03
324	Mike Jorgensen	.07	.03
325	Joe Torre	.10	.06
326	Elliott Maddox	.07	.03
327	Pete Falcone	.07	.03
328	Ray Burris	.07	.03
329	Claudell Washington	.07	.03
330	Doug Flynn	.07	.03
331	Joel Youngblood	.07	.03
332	Bill Almon	.07	.03
333	Tom Hausman	.07	.03
334	Pat Zachry	.07	.03
335	Jeff Reardon (R)	8.50	5.50
336	Wally Backman (R)	.15	.10
337	Dan Norman	.07	.03
338	Jerry Morales	.07	.03
339	Ed Farmer	.07	.03
340	Bob Molinaro	.07	.03
341	Todd Cruz	.07	.03
342	Britt Burns (R)	.07	.03
343	Kevin Bell	.07	.03
344	Tony LaRussa	.10	.06
345	Steve Trout	.07	.03
346	Harold Baines (R)	2.00	1.25
347	Richard Wortham	.07	.03

348	Wayne Nordhagen	.07	.03	401	Mike Paxton	.07	.03
349	Mike Squires	.07	.03	402	Gary Gray	.07	.03
350	Lamar Johnson	.07	.03	403	Rick Manning	.07	.03
351	Rickey Henderson	8.50	5.50	404	Bo Diaz	.07	.03
352	Francisco Barrios	.07	.03	405	Ron Hassey	.07	.03
353	Thad Bosley	.07	.03	406	Ross Grimsley	.07	.03
354	Chet Lemon	.07	.03	407	Victor Cruz	.07	.03
355	Bruce Kimm	.07	.03	408	Len Barker	.07	.03
356	Richard Dotson (R)	.10	.06	409	Bob Bailor	.07	.03
357	Jim Morrison	.07	.03	410	Otto Velez	.07	.03
358	Mike Proly	.07	.03	411	Ernie Whitt	.07	.03
359	Greg Pryor	.07	.03	412	Jim Clancy	.07	.03
360	Dave Parker	.35	.20	413	Barry Bonnell	.07	.03
361	Omar Moreno	.07	.03	414	Dave Stieb	.35	.20
362a	Kent Tekulve	.12	.07	415	Damaso Garcia (R)	.08	.05
	(1971 on back)			416	John Mayberry	.10	.06
362b	Kent Tekulve	.07	.03	417	Roy Howell	.07	.03
	(1971 on back)			418	Dan Ainge (R)	1.25	.80
363	Willie Stargell	1.00	.70	419a	Jesse Jefferson	.10	.06
364	Phil Garner	.08	.05		(Pirates on back)		
365	Ed Ott	.07	.03	419b	Jesse Jefferson(Blue	.20	.12
366	Don Robinson	.07	.03		Jays on back)		
367	Chuck Tanner	.07	.03	420	Joey McLaughlin	.07	.03
368	Jim Rooker	.07	.03	421	Lloyd Moseby (R)	.25	.15
369	Dale Berra	.07	.03	422	Al Woods	.07	.03
370	Jim Bibby	.07	.03	423	Garth Iorg	.07	.03
371	Steve Nicosia	.07	.03	424	Doug Ault	.07	.03
372	Mike Easler	.07	.03	425	Ken Schrom	.07	.03
373	Bill Robinson	.10	.06	426	Mike Willis	.07	.03
374	Lee Lacy	.07	.03	427	Steve Braun	.07	.03
375	John Candelaria	.10	.06	428	Bob Davis	.07	.03
376	Manny Sanguillen	.10	.06	429	Jerry Garvin	.07	.03
377	Rick Rhoden	.07	.03	430	Alfredo Griffin	.07	.03
378	Grant Jackson	.07	.03	431	Bob Mattick	.07	.03
379	Tim Foli	.07	.03	432	Vida Blue	.15	.10
380	Rod Scurry (R)	.07	.03	433	Jack Clark	.20	.12
381	Bill Madlock	.15	.10	434	Willie McCovey	1.00	.70
382a	Kurt Bevacqua	.15	.10	435	Mike Ivie	.07	.03
	(Photo reversed)			436a	Darrel Evans(ER)	.50	.30
382b	Kurt Bevacqua(Cor)	.07	.03	436b	Darrell Evans(Cor)	.20	.12
383	Bert Blyleven	.50	.30	437	Terry Whitfield	.07	.03
384	Eddie Solomon	.07	.03	438	Rennie Stennett	.07	.03
385	Enrique Romo	.07	.03	439	John Montefusco	.07	.03
386	John Milner	.07	.03	440	Jim Wohlford	.07	.03
387	Mike Hargrove	.07	.03	441	Bill North	.07	.03
388	Jorge Orta	.07	.03	442	Milt May	.07	.03
389	Toby Harrah	.07	.03	443	Max Venable	.07	.03
390	Tom Veryzer	.07	.03	444	Ed Whitson	.07	.03
391	Miguel Dilone	.07	.03	445	Al Holland (R)	.07	.04
392	Dan Spillner	.07	.03	446	Randy Moffitt	.07	.03
393	Jack Brohamer	.07	.03	447	Bob Knepper	.07	.03
394	Wayne Garland	.07	.03	448	Gary Lavelle	.07	.03
395	Sid Monge	.07	.03	449	Greg Minton	.07	.03
396	Rick Waits	.07	.03	450	Johnnie LeMaster	.07	.03
397	Joe Charboneau (R)	.10	.06	451	Larry Herndon	.07	.03
398	Gary Alexander	.07	.03	452	Rich Murray	.07	.03
399	Jerry Dybzinski	.07	.03	453	Joe Pettini	.07	.03
400	Mike Stanton	.07	.03	454	Allen Ripley	.07	.03

455	Dennis Littlejohn	.07	.03
456	Tom Griffin	.07	.03
457	Alan Hargesheimer	.07	.03
458	Joe Strain	.07	.03
459	Steve Kemp	.07	.03
460	Sparky Anderson	.10	.06
461	Alan Trammell	1.00	.70
462	Mark Fidrych	.15	.10
463	Lou Whitaker	.75	.45
464	Dave Rozema	.07	.03
465	Milt Wilcox	.07	.03
466	Champ Summers	.07	.03
467	Lance Parrish	.20	.12
468	Dan Petry	.10	.06
469	Pat Underwood	.07	.03
470	Rick Peters	.07	.03
471	Al Cowens	.07	.03
472	John Wockenfuss	.07	.03
473	Tom Brookens	.07	.03
474	Richie Hebner	.07	.03
475	Jack Morris	2.50	1.50
476	Jim Lentine	.07	.03
477	Bruce Robbins	.07	.03
478	Mark Wagner	.07	.03
479	Tim Corcoran	.07	.03
480	Stan Papi(P)	.12	.07
480b	Stan Papi (SS)	.07	.03
481	Kirk Gibson (R)	2.00	1.25
482	Dan Schatzeder	.07	.03
483	Amos Otis	.20	.12
484	Dave Winfield	3.00	2.00
485	Rollie Fingers	1.25	.80
486	Gene Richards	.07	.03
487	Randy Jones	.08	.05
488	Ozzie Smith	2.75	1.40
489	Gene Tenace	.10	.06
490	Bill Fahey	.07	.03
491	John Curtis	.07	.03
492	Dave Cash	.07	.03
493a	Tim Flannery (Photo reversed)	.12	.07
493b	Tim Flannery(Cor)	.07	.03
494	Jerry Mumphrey	.07	.03
495	Bob Shirley	.07	.03
496	Steve Mura	.07	.03
497	Eric Rasmussen	.07	.03
498	Broderick Perkins	.07	.03
499	Barry Evans	.07	.03
500	Chuck Baker	.07	.03
501	Luis Salazar (R)	.10	.06
502	Gary Lucas	.07	.03
503	Mike Armstrong	.07	.03
504	Jerry Turner	.07	.03
505	Dennis Kinney	.07	.03
506	Willie Montanez	.07	.03
507	Gorman Thomas	.10	.06
508	Ben Oglivie	.07	.03
509	Larry Hisle	.07	.03

510	Sal Bando	.10	.06
511	Robin Yount	4.50	3.50
512	Mike Caldwell	.07	.03
513	Sixto Lezcano	.07	.03
514a	Jerry Augustine (Billy Travers photo)	.15	.10
514b	Billy Travers(Correct name with photo)	.07	.03
515	Paul Molitor	1.50	.90
516	Moose Haas	.07	.03
517	Bill Castro	.07	.03
518	Jim Slaton	.07	.03
519	Lary Sorensen	.07	.03
520	Bob McClure	.07	.03
521	Charlie Moore	.07	.03
522	Jim Gantner	.07	.03
523	Reggie Cleveland	.07	.03
524	Don Money	.07	.03
525	Billy Travers	.07	.03
526	Buck Martinez	.07	.03
527	Dick Davis	.07	.03
528	Ted Simmons	.20	.12
529	Garry Templeton	.10	.06
530	Ken Reitz	.07	.03
531	Tony Scott	.07	.03
532	Ken Oberkfell	.07	.03
533	Bob Sykes	.07	.03
534	Keith Smith	.07	.03
535	John Littlefield	.07	.03
536	Jim Kaat	.25	.15
537	Bob Forsch	.07	.03
538	Mike Phillips	.07	.03
539	Terry Landrum (R)	.07	.03
540	Leon Durham (R)	.12	.07
541	Terry Kennedy	.10	.06
542	George Hendrick	.10	.06
543	Dane Iorg	.07	.03
544	Mark Littell	.07	.03
545	Keith Hernandez	.20	.12
546	Silvio Martinez	.07	.03
547a	Pete Vuckovich (Don Hood photo)	.25	.15
547b	Don Hood (Correct photo)	.07	.03
548	Bobby Bonds	.15	.10
549	Mike Ramsey	.07	.03
550	Tom Herr	.07	.03
551	Roy Smalley	.07	.03
552	Jerry Koosman	.15	.10
553	Ken Landreaux	.07	.03
554	John Castino	.07	.03
555	Doug Corbett	.07	.03
556	Bombo Rivera	.07	.03
557	Ron Jackson	.07	.03
558	Butch Wynegar	.07	.03
559	Hosken Powell	.07	.03
560	Pete Redfern	.07	.03
561	Roger Erickson	.07	.03

No.	Player		
562	Glenn Adams	.07	.03
563	Rick Sofield	.07	.03
564	Geoff Zahn	.07	.03
565	Pete Mackanin	.07	.03
566	Mike Cubbage	.07	.03
567	Darrell Jackson	.07	.03
568	Dave Edwards	.07	.03
569	Rob Wilfong	.07	.03
570	Sal Butera	.07	.03
571	Jose Morales	.07	.03
572	Rick Langford	.07	.03
573	Mike Norris	.07	.03
574	Rickey Henderson	15.00	10.00
575	Tony Armas	.07	.03
576	Dave Revering	.07	.03
577	Jeff Newman	.07	.03
578	Bob Lacey	.07	.03
579	Brian Kingman	.07	.03
580	Mitchell Page	.07	.03
581	Billy Martin	.20	.12
582	Rob Piciolo	.07	.03
583	Mike Heath	.07	.03
584	Mickey Klutts	.07	.03
585	Orlando Gonzalez	.07	.03
586	Mike Davis (R)	.07	.03
587	Wayne Gross	.07	.03
588	Matt Keough	.07	.03
589	Steve McCatty	.07	.03
590	Dwayne Murphy	.07	.03
591	Mario Guerrero	.07	.03
592	Dave McKay	.07	.03
593	Jim Essian	.07	.03
594	Dave Heaverlo	.07	.03
595	Maury Wills	.10	.06
596	Juan Beniquez	.07	.03
597	Rodney Craig	.07	.03
598	Jim Anderson	.07	.03
599	Floyd Bannister	.07	.03
600	Bruce Bochte	.07	.03
601	Julio Cruz	.07	.03
602	Ted Cox	.07	.03
603	Dan Meyer	.07	.03
604	Larry Cox	.07	.03
605	Bill Stein	.07	.03
606	Steve Garvey	.80	.50
607	Dave Roberts	.07	.03
608	Leon Roberts	.07	.03
609	Reggie Walton	.07	.03
610	Dave Edler	.07	.03
611	Larry Milbourne	.07	.03
612	Kim Allen	.07	.03
613	Mario Mendoza	.07	.03
614	Tom Paciorek	.07	.03
615	Glenn Abbott	.07	.03
616	Joe Simpson	.07	.03
617	Mickey Rivers	.07	.03
618	Jim Kern	.07	.03
619	Jim Sundberg	.07	.03

No.	Player		
620	Richie Zisk	.07	.03
621	Jon Matlack	.07	.03
622	Ferguson Jenkins	.75	.45
623	Pat Corrales	.07	.03
624	Ed Figueroa	.07	.03
625	Buddy Bell	.07	.03
626	Al Oliver	.15	.10
627	Doc Medich	.07	.03
628	Bump Wills	.07	.03
629	Rusty Staub	.15	.10
630	Pat Putnam	.07	.03
631	John Grubb	.07	.03
632	Danny Darwin	.08	.05
633	Ken Clay	.07	.03
634	Jim Norris	.07	.03
635	John Butcher	.07	.03
636	Dave Roberts	.07	.03
637	Billy Sample	.07	.03
638	Carl Yastrzemski	2.00	1.00
639	Cecil Cooper	.20	.12
640	Mike Schmidt	4.50	3.00
641	Checklist 1-50	.15	.10
642	Checklist 51-109	.15	.10
643	Checklist 110-168	.15	.10
644	Checklist 169-220	.15	.10
645a	Triple Threat(Larry Bowa, Pete Rose, Mike Schmidt) (No Card Number)	3.50	2.50
645b	Triple Threat(Larry Bowa, Pete Rose, Mike Schmidt) (Cor)	2.00	1.25
646	Checklist 221-267	.15	.10
647	Checklist 268-315	.15	.10
648	Checklist 316-359	.15	.10
649	Checklist 360-408	.15	.10
650	Reggie Jackson	4.50	3.00
651	Checklist 409-458	.15	.10
652	Checklist 459-509	.15	.10
653	Willie Wilson	.15	.10
654	Checklist 507-550	.15	.10
655	George Brett	3.50	2.50
656	Checklist 551-593	.15	.10
657	Tug McGraw	.20	.12
658	Checklist 594-637	.15	.10
659	Checklist 640-660	.15	.10
660a	Steve Carlton (Date 1966 on back)	2.00	1.25
660b	Steve Carlton (Date 1966 on back)	3.50	2.50

1982 Fleer

This 660-card set features full color photos with multi-colored borders with each team assigned a different border color. Card backs are horizontal and printed in blue, yellow and white. The set is marked by poor photography and many variations. The lower priced variation is included in the complete set price below. Cards measure 2-1/2" by 3-1/2".

		MINT	NR/MT
Complete Set (660)		90.00	65.00
Commons		.08	.05
1	Dusty Baker	.12	.07
2	Robert Castillo	.08	.05
3	Ron Cey	.10	.06
4	Terry Forster	.08	.05
5	Steve Garvey	.75	.45
6	Dave Goltz	.08	.05
7	Pedro Guerrero	.25	.15
8	Burt Hooton	.08	.05
9	Steve Howe	.08	.05
10	Jay Johnstone	.08	.05
11	Ken Landreaux	.08	.05
12	Davey Lopes	.10	.06
13	Mike Marshall (R)	.10	.06
14	Bobby Mitchell	.08	.05
15	Rick Monday	.10	.06
16	Tom Niedenfuer (R)	.10	.06
17	Ted Power (R)	.12	.07
18	Jerry Reuss	.10	.06
19	Ron Roenicke	.08	.05
20	Bill Russell	.10	.06
21	Steve Sax (R)	2.75	1.75
22	Mike Scioscia	.30	.18
23	Reggie Smith	.08	.05
24	Dave Stewart (R)	2.50	1.50
25	Rick Sutcliffe	.15	.10
26	Derrel Thomas	.08	.05
27	Fernando Valenzuela	.20	.12
28	Bob Welch	.25	.15
29	Steve Yeager	.08	.05
30	Bobby Brown	.08	.05
31	Rick Cerone	.08	.05
32	Ron Davis	.08	.05
33	Bucky Dent	.10	.06
34	Barry Foote	.08	.05
35	George Frazier	.08	.05
36	Oscar Gamble	.08	.05
37	Rich Gossage	.25	.15
38	Ron Guidry	.25	.15
39	Reggie Jackson	3.00	2.00
40	Tommy John	.15	.10
41	Rudy May	.08	.05
42	Larry Milbourne	.08	.05
43	Jerry Mumphrey	.08	.05
44	Bobby Murcer	.10	.06
45	Gene Nelson (R)	.08	.05
46	Graig Nettles	.15	.10
47	Johnny Oates	.08	.05
48	Lou Piniella	.10	.06
49	Willie Randolph	.10	.06
50	Rick Reuschel	.10	.06
51	Dave Revering	.08	.05
52	Dave Righetti (R)	.40	.25
53	Aurelio Rodriguez	.08	.05
54	Bob Watson	.10	.06
55	Dennis Werth	.08	.05
56	Dave Winfield	2.00	1.25
57	Johnny Bench	.30	.18
58	Bruce Berenyi	.08	.05
59	Larry Biittner	.08	.05
60	Scott Brown	.08	.05
61	Dave Collins	.08	.05
62	Geoff Combe	.08	.05
63	Dave Concepcion	.20	.12
64	Dan Driessen	.10	.06
65	Joe Edelen	.08	.05
66	George Foster	.15	.10
67	Ken Griffey	.20	.12
68	Paul Householder	.08	.05
69	Tom Hume	.08	.05
70	Junior Kennedy	.08	.05
71	Ray Knight	.10	.06
72	Mike LaCoss	.08	.05
73	Rafael Landestoy	.08	.05
74	Charlie Leibrandt	.10	.06
75	Sam Mejias	.08	.05
76	Paul Moskau	.08	.05
77	Joe Nolan	.08	.05
78	Mike O'Berry	.08	.05
79	Ron Oester	.08	.05
80	Frank Pastore	.08	.05
81	Joe Price	.08	.05
82	Tom Seaver	2.50	1.50
83	Mario Soto	.10	.06
84	Mike Vail	.08	.05
85	Tony Armas	.08	.05

86	Shooty Babitt	.08	.05	144	Larry Hisle	.08	.05
87	Dave Beard	.08	.05	145	Roy Howell	.08	.05
88	Rick Bosetti	.08	.05	146	Rickey Keeton	.08	.05
89	Keith Drumright	.08	.05	147	Randy Lerch	.08	.05
90	Wayne Gross	.08	.05	148	Paul Molitor	1.00	.70
91	Mike Heath	.08	.05	149	Don Money	.08	.05
92	Rickey Henderson	4.50	3.50	150	Charlie Moore	.08	.05
93	Cliff Johnson	.08	.05	151	Ben Oglivie	.08	.05
94	Jeff Jones	.08	.05	152	Ted Simmons	.15	.10
95	Matt Keough	.08	.05	153	Jim Slaton	.08	.05
96	Brian Kingman	.08	.05	154	Gorman Thomas	.10	.06
97	Mickey Klutts	.08	.05	155	Robin Yount	3.00	2.00
98	Rick Langford	.08	.05	156	Pete Vukovich	.10	.06
99	Steve McCatty	.08	.05	157	Benny Ayala	.08	.05
100	Dave McKay	.08	.05	158	Mark Belanger	.10	.06
101	Dwayne Murphy	.08	.05	159	Al Bumbry	.08	.05
102	Jeff Newman	.08	.05	160	Terry Crowley	.08	.05
103	Mike Norris	.08	.05	161	Rich Dauer	.08	.05
104	Bob Owchinko	.08	.05	162	Doug DeCinces	.08	.05
105	Mitchell Page	.08	.05	163	Rick Dempsey	.08	.05
106	Rob Picciolo	.08	.05	164	Jim Dwyer	.08	.05
107	Jim Spencer	.08	.05	165	Mike Flanagan	.15	.10
108	Fred Stanley	.08	.05	166	Dave Ford	.08	.05
109	Tom Underwood	.08	.05	167	Dan Graham	.08	.05
110	Joaquin Andujar	.10	.06	168	Wayne Krenchicki	.08	.05
111	Steve Braun	.08	.05	169	John Lowenstein	.08	.05
112	Bob Forsch	.08	.05	170	Dennis Martinez	.25	.15
113	George Hendrick	.10	.06	171	Tippy Martinez	.08	.05
114	Keith Hernandez	.20	.12	172	Scott McGregor	.08	.05
115	Tom Herr	.08	.05	173	Jose Morales	.08	.05
116	Dane Iorg	.08	.05	174	Eddie Murray	2.50	1.50
117	Jim Kaat	.15	.10	175	Jim Palmer	1.50	.90
118	Tito Landrum	.08	.05	176	Cal Ripken, Jr. (R)	60.00	48.00
119	Sixto Lezcano	.08	.05	177	Gary Roenicke	.08	.05
120	Mark Littell	.08	.05	178	Lenn Sakata	.08	.05
121	John Martin	.08	.05	179	Ken Singleton	.08	.05
122	Silvio Martinez	.08	.05	180	Sammy Stewart	.08	.05
123	Ken Oberkfell	.08	.05	181	Tim Stoddard	.08	.05
124	Darrell Porter	.08	.05	182	Steve Stone	.10	.06
125	Mike Ramsey	.08	.05	183	Stan Bahnsen	.08	.05
126	Orlando Sanchez	.08	.05	184	Ray Burris	.08	.05
127	Bob Shirley	.08	.05	185	Gary Carter	.80	.50
128	Lary Sorensen	.08	.05	186	Warren Cromartie	.08	.05
129	Bruce Sutter	.15	.10	187	Andre Dawson	2.50	1.50
130	Bob Sykes	.08	.05	188	Terry Francona (R)	.08	.05
131	Garry Templeton	.10	.06	189	Woodie Fryman	.08	.05
132	Gene Tenace	.10	.06	190	Bill Gullickson	.10	.06
133	Jerry Augustine	.08	.05	191	Grant Jackson	.08	.05
134	Sal Bando	.10	.06	192	Wallace Johnson	.08	.05
135	Mark Brouhard	.08	.05	193	Charlie Lea	.08	.05
136	Mike Caldwell	.08	.05	194	Bill Lee	.08	.05
137	Reggie Cleveland	.08	.05	195	Jerry Manuel	.08	.05
138	Cecil Cooper	.12	.07	196	Brad Mills	.08	.05
139	Jamie Easterly	.08	.05	197	John Milner	.08	.05
140	Marshall Edwards	.08	.05	198	Rowland Office	.08	.05
141	Rollie Fingers	.80	.50	199	David Palmer	.08	.05
142	Jim Gantner	.08	.05	200	Larry Parrish	.08	.05
143	Moose Haas	.08	.05	201	Mike Phillips	.08	.05

202	Tim Raines (R)	1.50	.90	259	Lonnie Smith	.10	.06
203	Bobby Ramos	.08	.05	260	Manny Trillo	.08	.05
204	Jeff Reardon	3.00	2.00	261	Del Unser	.08	.05
205	Steve Rogers	.08	.05	262	George Vukovich	.08	.05
206	Scott Sanderson	.10	.06	263	Tom Brookens	.08	.05
207	Rodney Scott	.08	.05	264	George Cappuzzello	.08	.05
	(Wrong photo)			265	Marty Castillo	.08	.05
208	Elias Sosa	.08	.05	266	Al Cowens	.08	.05
209	Chris Speier	.08	.05	267	Kirk Gibson	.40	.25
210	Tim Wallach (R)	1.00	.70	268	Richie Hebner	.08	.05
211	Jerry White	.08	.05	269	Ron Jackson	.08	.05
212	Alan Ashby	.08	.05	270	Lynn Jones	.08	.05
213	Cesar Cedeno	.10	.06	271	Steve Kemp	.08	.05
214	Jose Cruz	.12	.07	272	Rick Leach (R)	.08	.05
215	Kiko Garcia	.08	.05	273	Aurelio Lopez	.08	.05
216	Phil Garner	.10	.06	274	Jack Morris	2.00	1.25
217	Danny Heep	.08	.05	275	Kevin Saucier	.08	.05
218	Art Howe	.08	.05	276	Lance Parrish	.15	.10
219	Bob Knepper	.08	.05	277	Rick Peters	.08	.05
220	Frank LaCorte	.08	.05	278	Dan Petry	.10	.06
221	Joe Niekro	.08	.05	279	Davis Rozema	.08	.05
222	Joe Pittman	.08	.05	280	Stan Papi	.08	.05
223	Terry Puhl	.08	.05	281	Dan Schatzeder	.08	.05
224	Luis Pujols	.08	.05	282	Champ Summers	.08	.05
225	Craig Reynolds	.08	.05	283	Alan Trammell	.75	.45
226	J.R. Richard	.12	.07	284	Lou Whitaker	.40	.25
227	Dave Roberts	.08	.05	285	Milt Wilcox	.08	.05
228	Vern Ruhle	.08	.05	286	John Wockenfuss	.08	.05
229	Nolan Ryan	8.50	5.50	287	Gary Allenson	.08	.05
230	Joe Sambito	.08	.05	288	Tom Burgmeier	.08	.05
231	Tony Scott	.08	.05	289	Bill Campbell	.08	.05
232	Dave Smith	.08	.05	290	Mark Clear	.08	.05
233	Harry Spilman	.08	.05	291	Steve Crawford	.08	.05
234	Don Sutton	.50	.30	292	Dennis Eckersley	1.50	.90
235	Dickie Thon	.08	.05	293	Dwight Evans	.25	.15
236	Denny Walling	.08	.05	294	Rich Gedman (R)	.12	.07
237	Gary Woods	.08	.05	295	Garry Hancock	.08	.05
238	Luis Aguayo (R)	.08	.05	296	Glenn Hoffman	.08	.05
239	Ramon Aviles	.08	.05	297	Bruce Hurst (R)	.75	.45
240	Bob Boone	.15	.10	298	Carney Lansford	.12	.07
241	Larry Bowa	.10	.06	299	Rick Miller	.08	.05
242	Warren Brusstar	.08	.05	300	Reid Nichols	.08	.05
243	Steve Carlton	2.00	1.25	301	Bob Ojeda (R)	.30	.18
244	Larry Christenson	.08	.05	302	Tony Perez	.50	.30
245	Dick Davis	.08	.05	303	Chuck Rainey	.08	.05
246	Greg Gross	.08	.05	304	Jerry Remy	.08	.05
247	Sparky Lyle	.10	.06	305	Jim Rice	.25	.15
248	Garry Maddox	.08	.05	306	Joe Rudi	.10	.06
249	Gary Matthews	.08	.05	307	Bob Stanley	.08	.05
250	Bake McBride	.08	.05	308	Dave Stapleton	.08	.05
251	Tug McGraw	.15	.10	309	Frank Tanana	.10	.06
252	Keith Moreland	.08	.05	310	Mike Torrez	.08	.05
253	Dickie Noles	.08	.05	311	John Tudor (R)	.15	.10
254	Mike Proly	.08	.05	312	Carl Yastrzemski	1.75	1.00
255	Ron Reed	.08	.05	313	Buddy Bell	.08	.05
256	Pete Rose	2.50	1.50	314	Steve Comer	.08	.05
257	Dick Ruthven	.08	.05	315	Danny Darwin	.08	.05
258	Mike Schmidt	3.50	2.50	316	John Ellis	.08	.05

317	John Grubb	.08	.05	375	Sid Monge	.08	.05
318	Rick Honeycutt	.08	.05	376	Jorge Orta	.08	.05
319	Charlie Hough	.10	.06	377	Dave Rosello	.08	.05
320	Ferguson Jenkins	.70	.40	378	Dan Spillner	.08	.05
321	John Henry Johnson	.08	.05	379	Mike Stanton	.08	.05
322	Jim Kern	.08	.05	380	Andre Thornton	.10	.06
323	Jon Matlack	.08	.05	381	Tom Veryzer	.08	.05
324	Doc Medich	.08	.05	382	Rick Waits	.08	.05
325	Mario Mendoza	.08	.05	383	Doyle Alexander	.08	.05
326	Al Oliver	.15	.10	384	Vida Blue	.15	.10
327	Pat Putnam	.08	.05	385	Fred Breining	.08	.05
328	Mickey Rivers	.08	.05	386	Enos Cabell	.08	.05
329	Leon Roberts	.08	.05	387	Jack Clark	.15	.10
330	Billy Sample	.08	.05	388	Darrell Evans	.10	.06
331	Bill Stein	.08	.05	389	Tom Griffin	.08	.05
332	Jim Sundberg	.08	.05	390	Larry Herndon	.08	.05
333	Mark Wagner	.08	.05	391	Al Holland	.08	.05
334	Bump Wills	.08	.05	392	Gary Lavelle	.08	.05
335	Bill Almon	.08	.05	393	Johnnie LeMaster	.08	.05
336	Harold Baines	.40	.25	394	Jerry Martin	.08	.05
337	Ross Baumgarten	.08	.05	395	Milt May	.08	.05
338	Tony Bernazard	.08	.05	396	Greg Minton	.08	.05
339	Britt Burns	.08	.05	397	Joe Morgan	.75	.45
340	Richard Dotson	.08	.05	398	Joe Pettini	.08	.05
341	Jim Essian	.08	.05	399	Alan Ripley	.08	.05
342	Ed Farmer	.08	.05	400	Billy Smith	.08	.05
343	Carlton Fisk	1.75	1.00	401	Rennie Stennett	.08	.05
344	Kevin Hickey	.08	.05	402	Ed Whitson	.08	.05
345	LaMarr Hoyt	.08	.05	403	Jim Wohlford	.08	.05
346	Lamar Johnson	.08	.05	404	Willie Aikens	.08	.05
347	Jerry Koosman	.10	.06	405	George Brett	3.50	2.50
348	Rusty Kuntz	.08	.05	406	Ken Brett	.08	.05
349	Dennis Lamp	.08	.05	407	Dave Chalk	.08	.05
350	Ron LeFlore	.08	.05	408	Rich Gale	.08	.05
351	Chet Lemon	.08	.05	409	Cesar Geronimo	.08	.05
352	Greg Luzinski	.12	.07	410	Larry Gura	.08	.05
353	Bob Molinaro	.08	.05	411	Clint Hurdle	.08	.05
354	Jim Morrison	.08	.05	412	Mike Jones	.08	.05
355	Wayne Nordhagen	.08	.05	413	Dennis Leonard	.08	.05
356	Greg Pryor	.08	.05	414	Renie Martin	.08	.05
357	Mike Squires	.08	.05	415	Lee May	.08	.05
358	Steve Trout	.08	.05	416	Hal McRae	.12	.07
359	Alan Bannister	.08	.05	417	Darryl Motley	.08	.05
360	Len Barker	.08	.05	418	Rance Mulliniks	.08	.05
361	Bert Blyleven	.40	.25	419	Amos Otis	.10	.06
362	Joe Charboneau	.08	.05	420	Ken Phelps (R)	.15	.10
363	John Denny	.08	.05	421	Jamie Quirk	.08	.05
364	Bo Diaz	.08	.05	422	Dan Quisenberry	.10	.06
365	Miguel Dilone	.08	.05	423	Paul Splittorff	.08	.05
366	Jerry Dybzinski	.08	.05	424	U.L. Washington	.08	.05
367	Wayne Garland	.08	.05	425	John Wathan	.08	.05
368	Mike Hargrove	.08	.05	426	Frank White	.10	.06
369	Toby Harrah	.08	.05	427	Willie Wilson	.10	.06
370	Ron Hassey	.08	.05	428	Brian Asselstine	.08	.05
371	Von Hayes (R)	.25	.15	429	Bruce Benedict	.08	.05
372	Pat Kelly	.08	.05	430	Tom Boggs	.08	.05
373	Duane Kuiper	.08	.05	431	Larry Bradford	.08	.05
374	Rick Manning	.08	.05	432	Rick Camp	.08	.05

433	Chris Chambliss	.10	.06
434	Gene Garber	.08	.05
435	Preston Hanna	.08	.05
436	Bob Horner	.10	.06
437	Glenn Hubbard	.08	.05
438a	Al Hrabosky (5'1")	20.00	14.00
438b	Al Hrabosky (5'10")	1.00	.70
439	Rufino Linares	.08	.05
440	Rick Mahler (R)	.10	.06
441	Ed Miller	.08	.05
442	John Montefusco	.08	.05
443	Dale Murphy	1.00	.70
444	Phil Niekro	.75	.45
445	Gaylord Perry	.75	.45
446	Biff Pocoroba	.08	.05
447	Rafael Ramirez	.08	.05
448	Jerry Royster	.08	.05
449	Claudell Washington	.08	.05
450	Don Aase	.08	.05
451	Don Baylor	.20	.12
452	Juan Beniquez	.08	.05
453	Rick Burleson	.08	.05
454	Bert Campaneris	.10	.06
455	Rod Carew	1.75	1.00
456	Bob Clark	.08	.05
457	Brian Downing	.10	.06
458	Dan Ford	.08	.05
459	Ken Forsch	.08	.05
460	Dave Frost	.08	.05
461	Bobby Grich	.10	.06
462	Larry Harlow	.08	.05
463	John Harris	.08	.05
464	Andy Hassler	.08	.05
465	Butch Hobson	.10	.06
466	Jesse Jefferson	.08	.05
467	Bruce Kison	.08	.05
468	Fred Lynn	.20	.12
469	Angel Moreno	.08	.05
470	Ed Ott	.08	.05
471	Fred Patek	.08	.05
472	Steve Renko	.08	.05
473	Mike Witt (R)	.10	.06
474	Geoff Zahn	.08	.05
475	Gary Alexander	.08	.05
476	Dale Berra	.08	.05
477	Kurt Bevacqua	.08	.05
478	Jim Bibby	.08	.05
479	John Candelaria	.08	.05
480	Victor Cruz	.08	.05
481	Mike Easler	.08	.05
482	Tim Foli	.08	.05
483	Lee Lacy	.08	.05
484	Vance Law (R)	.10	.06
485	Bill Madlock	.15	.10
486	Willie Montanez	.08	.05
487	Omar Moreno	.08	.05
488	Steve Nicosia	.08	.05
489	Dave Parker	.25	.15
490	Tony Pena (R)	.25	.15
491	Pascual Perez (R)	.15	.10
492	Johnny Ray (R)	.15	.10
493	Rick Rhoden	.08	.05
494	Bill Robinson	.10	.06
495	Don Robinson	.08	.05
496	Enrique Romo	.08	.05
497	Rod Scurry	.08	.05
498	Eddie Solomon	.08	.05
499	Willie Stargell	.75	.45
500	Kent Tekulve	.08	.05
501	Jason Thompson	.08	.05
502	Glenn Abbott	.08	.05
503	Jim Anderson	.08	.05
504	Floyd Bannister	.08	.05
505	Bruce Bochte	.08	.05
506	Jeff Burroughs	.08	.05
507	Bryan Clark	.08	.05
508	Ken Clay	.08	.05
509	Julio Cruz	.08	.05
510	Dick Drago	.08	.05
511	Gary Gray	.08	.05
512	Dan Meyer	.08	.05
513	Jerry Narron	.08	.05
514	Tom Paciorek	.08	.05
515	Casey Parsons	.08	.05
516	Lenny Randle	.08	.05
517	Shane Rawley	.08	.05
518	Joe Simpson	.08	.05
519	Richie Zisk	.08	.05
520	Neil Allen	.08	.05
521	Bob Bailor	.08	.05
522	Hubie Brooks (R)	.35	.20
523	Mike Cubbage	.08	.05
524	Pete Falcone	.08	.05
525	Doug Flynn	.08	.05
526	Tom Hausman	.08	.05
527	Ron Hodges	.08	.05
528	Randy Jones	.08	.05
529	Mike Jorgensen	.08	.05
530	Dave Kingman	.12	.07
531	Ed Lynch	.08	.05
532	Mike Marshall	.10	.06
533	Lee Mazzilli	.08	.05
534	Dyar Miller	.08	.05
535	Mike Scott (R)	.25	.15
536	Rusty Staub	.20	.12
537	John Stearns	.08	.05
538	Craig Swan	.08	.05
539	Frank Taveras	.08	.05
540	Alex Trevino	.08	.05
541	Ellis Valentine	.08	.05
542	Mookie Wilson (R)	.15	.10
543	Joel Youngblood	.08	.05
544	Pat Zachry	.08	.05
545	Glenn Adams	.08	.05
546	Fernando Arroyo	.08	.05
547	John Verhoeven	.08	.05

548	Sal Butera	.08	.05		596	Rawly Eastwick	.08	.05
549	John Castino	.08	.05		597	Steve Henderson	.08	.05
550	Don Cooper	.08	.05		598	Mike Krukow	.08	.05
551	Doug Corbett	.08	.05		599	Mike Lum	.08	.05
552	Dave Engle	.08	.05		600	Randy Martz	.08	.05
553	Roger Erickson	.08	.05		601	Jerry Morales	.08	.05
554	Danny Goodwin	.08	.05		602	Ken Reitz	.08	.05
555a	Darrell Jackson (Red cap)	.08	.05		603	Lee Smith (R)	8.50	5.50
					604	Dick Tidrow	.08	.05
555b	Darrell Jackson (Red cap, no logo)	3.50	2.50		605	Jim Tracy	.08	.05
					606	Mike Tyson	.08	.05
555c	Darrell Jackson (Black Cap)	.50	.30		607	Ty Waller	.08	.05
					608	Danny Ainge	.60	.35
556	Pete Mackanin	.08	.05		609	Jorge Bell (R)	7.50	4.50
557	Jack O'Connor	.08	.05		610	Mark Bomback	.08	.05
558	Hosken Powell	.08	.05		611	Barry Bonnell	.08	.05
559	Pete Redfern	.08	.05		612	Jim Clancy	.08	.05
560	Roy Smalley	.08	.05		613	Damaso Garcia	.08	.05
561	Chuck Baker	.08	.05		614	Jerry Garvin	.08	.05
562	Gary Ward	.08	.05		615	Alfredo Griffin	.08	.05
563	Rob Wilfong	.08	.05		616	Garth Iorg	.08	.05
564	Al Williams	.08	.05		617	Luis Leal	.08	.05
565	Butch Wynegar	.08	.05		618	Ken Macha	.08	.05
566	Randy Bass	.08	.05		619	John Mayberry	.10	.06
567	Juan Bonilla	.08	.05		620	Joey McLaughlin	.08	.05
568	Danny Boone	.08	.05		621	Lloyd Moseby	.08	.05
569	John Curtis	.08	.05		622	Dave Stieb	.25	.15
570	Juan Eichelberger	.08	.05		623	Jackson Todd	.08	.05
571	Barry Evans	.08	.05		624	Willie Upshaw (R)	.10	.06
572	Tim Flannery	.08	.05		625	Otto Velez	.08	.05
573	Ruppert Jones	.08	.05		626	Ernie Whitt	.08	.05
574	Terry Kennedy	.08	.05		627	Al Woods	.08	.05
575	Joe Lefebvre	.08	.05		628	1981 All-Star Game	.08	.05
576a	John Littlefield (Throwing Left-handed)	180.00	75.00		629	All-Star Infielders Bucky Dent, Frank White	.10	.06
576b	John Littlefield (Throwing Right-handed)	.08	.05		630	Big Red Machine Dave Concepcion, Dan Driessen, George Foster	.12	.07
577	Gary Lucas	.08	.05					
578	Steve Mura	.08	.05		631	N.L. Relief Pitcher Bruce Sutter	.10	.06
579	Broderick Perkins	.08	.05					
580	Gene Richards	.08	.05		632	Steve Carlton/Carlton Fisk	1.50	.90
581	Luis Salazar	.08	.05					
582	Ozzie Smith	2.00	1.25		633	Carl Yastrzemski (3,000th Game)	.50	.30
583	John Urrea	.08	.05					
584	Chris Welsh	.08	.05		634	Johnny Bench/Tom Seaver	1.50	.90
585	Rick Wise	.08	.05					
586	Doug Bird	.08	.05		635	Gary Carter/Fernando Valenzuela	.25	.15
587	Tim Blackwell	.08	.05					
588	Bobby Bonds	.15	.10		636	N.L. Strikeout King (Fernando Valenzuela)	.15	.08
589	Bill Buckner	.10	.06					
590	Bill Caudill	.08	.05		637	1981 Home Run King (Mike Schmidt)	2.00	1.25
591	Hector Cruz	.08	.05					
592	Jody Davis (R)	.10	.06		638	N.L. All-Stars(Gary Carter, Dave Parker)	.12	.07
593	Ivan DeJesus	.08	.05					
594	Steve Dillard	.08	.05		639	Perfect Game (Len Barker, Bo Diaz)	.08	.05
595	Leon Durham	.10	.06					

640	Pete & Re-Pete(Pete Rose, Pete Rose, Jr.)	1.75	1.00
641	Phillies' Finest(Steve Carlton, Mike Schmidt, Lonnie Smith)	1.25	.80
642	Red Sox Reunion (Dwight Evans, Fred Lynn)	.15	.10
643	1981 Most Hits, Runs (Rickey Henderson)	2.00	1.25
644	Most Saves (Rollie Fingers)	.50	.30
645	Most Wins (Tom Seaver)	.80	.50
646	Yankee Powerhouse (Reggie Jackson, Dave Winfield)	2.00	1.25
647	Checklist 1-56	.08	.05
648	Checklist 57-109	.08	.05
649	Checklist 110-156	.08	.05
650	Checklist 157-211	.08	.05
651	Checklist 212-262	.08	.05
652	Checklist 263-312	.08	.05
653	Checklist 313-358	.08	.05
654	Checklist 359-403	.08	.05
655	Checklist 404-449	.08	.05
656	Checklist 450-501	.08	.05
657	Checklist 502-544	.08	.05
658	Checklist 545-585	.08	.05
659	Checklist 586-627	.08	.05
660	Checklist 628-646	.08	.05

1983 Fleer

Willie Stargell

This 660-card set features full color photos surrounded by a brown border. Team logos appear in a small sphere in the lower left corner. Players' names and positions are printed across the bottom of the card. The reverse side is vertical and includes a small black and white head shot of the player. Cards measure 2-1/2" by 3-1/2".

		MINT	NR/MT
Complete Set (660)		125.00	85.00
Commons		.08	.05

1	Joaquin Andujar	.10	.06
2	Doug Bair	.08	.05
3	Steve Braun	.08	.05
4	Glenn Brummer	.08	.05
5	Bob Forsch	.08	.05
6	David Green	.08	.05
7	George Hendrick	.10	.06
8	Keith Hernandez	.15	.10
9	Tom Herr	.08	.05
10	Dan Iorg	.08	.05
11	Jim Kaat	.15	.10
12	Jeff Lahti	.08	.05
13	Tito Landrum	.08	.05
14	Dave LaPoint (R)	.08	.05
15	Willie McGee (R)	3.50	2.50
16	Steve Mura	.08	.05
17	Ken Oberkfell	.08	.05
18	Darrell Porter	.08	.05
19	Mike Ramsey	.08	.05
20	Gene Roof	.08	.05
21	Lonnie Smith	.10	.06
22	Ozzie Smith	1.75	1.00
23	John Stuper	.08	.05
24	Bruce Sutter	.15	.10
25	Gene Tenace	.10	.06
26	Jerry Augustine	.08	.05
27	Dwight Bernard	.08	.05
28	Mark Brouhard	.08	.05
29	Mike Caldwell	.08	.05
30	Cecil Cooper	.10	.06
31	Jamie Easterly	.08	.05
32	Marshall Edwards	.08	.05
33	Rollie Fingers	.75	.45
34	Jim Gantner	.08	.05
35	Moose Haas	.08	.05
36	Roy Howell	.08	.05
37	Peter Ladd	.08	.05
38	Bob McClure	.08	.05
39	Doc Medich	.08	.05
40	Paul Molitor	.80	.50
41	Don Money	.08	.05
42	Charlie Moore	.08	.05
43	Ben Oglivie	.08	.05
44	Ed Romero	.08	.05
45	Ted Simmons	.10	.06
46	Jim Slaton	.08	.05
47	Don Sutton	.45	.28
48	Gorman Thomas	.10	.06
49	Pete Vuckovich	.10	.06

50	Ned Yost	.08	.05
51	Robin Yount	2.75	1.75
52	Benny Ayala	.08	.05
53	Bob Bonner	.08	.05
54	Al Bumbry	.08	.05
55	Terry Crowley	.08	.05
56	Storm Davis (R)	.15	.10
57	Rich Dauer	.08	.05
58	Rick Dempsey	.08	.05
59	Jim Dwyer	.08	.05
60	Mike Flanagan	.15	.10
61	Dan Ford	.08	.05
62	Glenn Gulliver	.08	.05
63	John Lowenstein	.08	.05
64	Dennis Martinez	.20	.12
65	Tippy Martinez	.08	.05
66	Scott McGregor	.08	.05
67	Eddie Murray	1.75	1.00
68	Joe Nolan	.08	.05
69	Jim Palmer	1.00	.70
70	Cal Ripken, Jr.	22.00	15.00
71	Gary Roenicke	.08	.05
72	Lenn Sakata	.08	.05
73	Ken Singleton	.08	.05
74	Sammy Stewart	.08	.05
75	Tim Stoddard	.08	.05
76	Don Aase	.08	.05
77	Don Baylor	.12	.07
78	Juan Beniquez	.08	.05
79	Bob Boone	.15	.10
80	Rick Burleson	.08	.05
81	Rod Carew	1.25	.80
82	Bobby Clark	.08	.05
83	Doug Corbett	.08	.05
84	John Curtis	.08	.05
85	Doug DeCinces	.08	.05
86	Brian Downing	.10	.06
87	Joe Ferguson	.08	.05
88	Tim Foli	.08	.05
89	Ken Forsch	.08	.05
90	Dave Goltz	.08	.05
91	Bobby Grich	.10	.06
92	Andy Hassler	.08	.05
93	Reggie Jackson	2.50	1.50
94	Ron Jackson	.08	.05
95	Tommy John	.15	.10
96	Bruce Kison	.08	.05
97	Fred Lynn	.12	.07
98	Ed Ott	.08	.05
99	Steve Renko	.08	.05
100	Luis Sanchez	.08	.05
101	Rob Wilfong	.08	.05
102	Mike Witt	.08	.05
103	Geoff Zahn	.08	.05
104	Willie Aikens	.08	.05
105	Mike Armstrong	.08	.05
106	Vida Blue	.12	.07
107	Bud Black (R)	.35	.20
108	George Brett	2.75	1.75
109	Bill Castro	.08	.05
110	Onix Concepcion	.08	.05
111	Dave Frost	.08	.05
112	Cesar Geronimo	.08	.05
113	Larry Gura	.08	.05
114	Steve Hammond	.08	.05
115	Don Hood	.08	.05
116	Dennis Leonard	.08	.05
117	Jerry Martin	.08	.05
118	Lee May	.08	.05
119	Hal McRae	.12	.07
120	Amos Otis	.10	.06
121	Greg Pryor	.08	.05
122	Dan Quisenberry	.10	.06
123	Don Slaught (R)	.40	.25
124	Paul Splittorff	.08	.05
125	U.L. Washington	.08	.05
126	John Wathan	.08	.05
127	Frank White	.08	.05
128	Willie Wilson	.10	.06
129	Steve Bedrosian (R)	.20	.12
130	Bruce Benedict	.08	.05
131	Tommy Boggs	.08	.05
132	Brett Butler (R)	.80	.50
133	Rick Camp	.08	.05
134	Chris Chambliss	.10	.06
135	Ken Dayley (R)	.08	.05
136	Gene Garber	.08	.05
137	Terry Harper	.08	.05
138	Bob Horner	.10	.06
139	Glenn Hubbard	.08	.05
140	Rufino Linares	.08	.05
141	Rick Mahler	.08	.05
142	Dale Murphy	.90	.60
143	Phil Niekro	.60	.35
144	Pascual Perez	.10	.06
145	Biff Pocoroba	.08	.05
146	Rafael Ramirez	.08	.05
147	Jerry Royster	.08	.05
148	Ken Smith	.08	.05
149	Bob Walk	.08	.05
150	Claudell Washington	.08	.05
151	Bob Watson	.12	.07
152	Larry Whisenton	.08	.05
153	Porfirio Altamirano	.08	.05
154	Marty Bystrom	.08	.05
155	Steve Carlton	1.75	1.00
156	Larry Christenson	.08	.05
157	Ivan DeJesus	.08	.05
158	John Denny	.08	.05
159	Bob Dernier (R)	.10	.06
160	Bo Diaz	.08	.05
161	Ed Farmer	.08	.05
162	Greg Gross	.08	.05
163	Mike Krukow	.08	.05
164	Garry Maddox	.08	.05
165	Gary Matthews	.08	.05

166	Tug McGraw	.12	.07	224	Fernando Valenzuela	.15	.10
167	Bob Molinaro	.08	.05	225	Bob Welch	.20	.12
168	Sid Monge	.08	.05	226	Ricky Wright	.08	.05
169	Ron Reed	.08	.05	227	Steve Yeager	.08	.05
170	Bill Robinson	.10	.06	228	Bill Almon	.08	.05
171	Pete Rose	1.75	1.00	229	Harold Baines	.30	.18
172	Dick Ruthven	.08	.05	230	Salome Barojas	.08	.05
173	Mike Schmidt	3.00	2.00	231	Tony Bernazard	.08	.05
174	Manny Trillo	.08	.05	232	Britt Burns	.08	.05
175	Ozzie Virgil (R)	.08	.05	233	Richard Dotson	.08	.05
176	George Vukovich	.08	.05	234	Ernesto Escarrega	.08	.05
177	Gary Allenson	.08	.05	235	Carlton Fisk	1.50	.90
178	Luis Aponte	.08	.05	236	Jerry Hairston	.08	.05
179	Wade Boggs (R)	24.00	16.50	237	Kevin Hickey	.08	.05
180	Tom Burgmeier	.08	.05	238	LaMarr Hoyt	.08	.05
181	Mark Clear	.08	.05	239	Steve Kemp	.08	.05
182	Dennis Eckersley	1.00	.70	240	Jim Kern	.08	.05
183	Dwight Evans	.25	.15	241	Ron Kittle (R)	.20	.12
184	Rich Gedman	.08	.05	242	Jerry Koosman	.10	.06
185	Glenn Hoffman	.08	.05	243	Dennis Lamp	.08	.05
186	Bruce Hurst	.25	.15	244	Rudy Law	.08	.05
187	Carney Lansford	.15	.10	245	Vance Law	.08	.05
188	Rick Miller	.08	.05	246	Ron LeFlore	.08	.05
189	Reid Nichols	.08	.05	247	Greg Luzinski	.12	.07
190	Bob Ojeda	.10	.06	248	Tom Paciorek	.08	.05
191	Tony Perez	.50	.30	249	Aurelio Rodriguez	.08	.05
192	Chuck Rainey	.08	.05	250	Mike Squires	.08	.05
193	Jerry Remy	.08	.05	251	Steve Trout	.08	.05
194	Jim Rice	.15	.10	252	Jim Barr	.08	.05
195	Bob Stanley	.08	.05	253	Dave Bergman	.08	.05
196	Dave Stapleton	.08	.05	254	Fred Breining	.08	.05
197	Mike Torrez	.08	.05	255	Bob Brenly (R)	.08	.05
198	John Tudor	.10	.06	256	Jack Clark	.15	.10
199	Julio Valdez	.08	.05	257	Chili Davis (R)	.40	.25
200	Carl Yastrzemski	1.25	.80	258	Darrell Evans	.10	.06
201	Dusty Baker	.10	.06	259	Alan Fowlkes	.08	.05
202	Joe Beckwith	.08	.05	260	Rich Gale	.08	.05
203	Greg Brock (R)	.12	.07	261	Atlee Hammaker (R)	.08	.05
204	Ron Cey	.10	.06	262	Al Holland	.08	.05
205	Terry Forster	.08	.05	263	Duane Kuiper	.08	.05
206	Steve Garvey	.45	.28	264	Bill Laskey	.08	.05
207	Pedro Guerrero	.25	.15	265	Gary Lavelle	.08	.05
208	Burt Hooton	.08	.05	266	Johnnie LeMaster	.08	.05
209	Steve Howe	.08	.05	267	Renie Martin	.08	.05
210	Ken Landreaux	.08	.05	268	Milt May	.08	.05
211	Mike Marshall	.08	.05	269	Greg Minton	.08	.05
212	Candy Maldonado(R)	.60	.35	270	Joe Morgan	.60	.35
213	Rick Monday	.10	.06	271	Tom O'Malley	.08	.05
214	Tom Niedenfuer	.08	.05	272	Reggie Smith	.08	.05
215	Jorge Orta	.08	.05	273	Guy Sularz	.08	.05
216	Jerry Reuss	.12	.07	274	Champ Summers	.08	.05
217	Ron Roenicke	.08	.05	275	Max Venable	.08	.05
218	Vicente Romo	.08	.05	276	Jim Wohlford	.08	.05
219	Bill Russell	.10	.06	277	Ray Burris	.08	.05
220	Steve Sax	.50	.30	278	Gary Carter	.70	.40
221	Mike Scioscia	.10	.06	279	Warren Cromartie	.08	.05
222	Dave Stewart	.60	.35	280	Andre Dawson	2.00	1.25
223	Derrel Thomas	.08	.05	281	Terry Francona	.08	.05

No.	Player		
282	Doug Flynn	.08	.05
283	Woody Fryman	.08	.05
284	Bill Gullickson	.10	.06
285	Wallace Johnson	.08	.05
286	Charlie Lea	.08	.05
287	Randy Lerch	.08	.05
288	Brad Mills	.08	.05
289	Dan Norman	.08	.05
290	Al Oliver	.12	.07
291	David Palmer	.08	.05
292	Tim Raines	.45	.28
293	Jeff Reardon	2.00	1.25
294	Steve Rogers	.08	.05
295	Scott Sanderson	.08	.05
296	Dan Schatzeder	.08	.05
297	Bryn Smith	.12	.07
298	Chris Speier	.08	.05
299	Tim Wallach	.20	.12
300	Jerry White	.08	.05
301	Joel Youngblood	.08	.05
302	Ross Baumgarten	.08	.05
303	Dale Berra	.08	.05
304	John Candelaria	.08	.05
305	Dick Davis	.08	.05
306	Mike Easler	.08	.05
307	Richie Hebner	.08	.05
308	Lee Lacy	.08	.05
309	Bill Madlock	.15	.10
310	Larry McWilliams	.08	.05
311	John Milner	.08	.05
312	Omar Moreno	.08	.05
313	Jim Morrison	.08	.05
314	Steve Nicosia	.08	.05
315	Dave Parker	.30	.18
316	Tony Pena	.10	.06
317	Johnny Ray	.08	.05
318	Rick Rhoden	.08	.05
319	Don Robinson	.08	.05
320	Enrique Romo	.08	.05
321	Manny Sarmiento	.08	.05
322	Rod Scurry	.08	.05
323	Jim Smith	.08	.05
324	Willie Stargell	.75	.45
326	Kent Tekulve	.08	.05
327	Tom Brookens	.08	.05
328	Enos Cabell	.08	.05
329	Kirk Gibson	.08	.05
330	Larry Herndon	.08	.05
331	Mike Ivie	.08	.05
332	Howard Johnson(R)	7.50	4.50
333	Lynn Jones	.08	.05
334	Rick Leach	.08	.05
335	Chet Lemon	.08	.05
336	Jack Morris	1.25	.80
337	Lance Parrish	.10	.06
338	Larry Pashnick	.08	.05
339	Dan Petry	.08	.05
340	Dave Rozema	.08	.05
341	Dave Rucker	.08	.05
342	Elias Sosa	.08	.05
344	Alan Trammell	.60	.35
345	Jerry Turner	.08	.05
346	Jerry Ujdur	.08	.05
347	Pat Underwood	.08	.05
348	Lou Whitaker	.35	.20
349	Milt Wilcox	.08	.05
350	Glenn Wilson (R)	.10	.06
351	John Wockenfuss	.08	.05
352	Kurt Bevacqua	.08	.05
353	Juan Bonilla	.08	.05
354	Floyd Chiffer	.08	.05
355	Luis DeLeon	.08	.05
356	Dave Dravecky (R)	.50	.30
357	Dave Edwards	.08	.05
358	Juan Eichelberger	.08	.05
359	Tim Flannery	.08	.05
360	Tony Gwynn (R)	30.00	22.50
361	Ruppert Jones	.08	.05
362	Terry Kennedy	.08	.05
363	Joe Lefebvre	.08	.05
364	Sixto Lezcano	.08	.05
365	Tim Lollar	.08	.05
366	Gary Lucas	.08	.05
367	John Montefusco	.08	.05
368	Broderick Perkins	.08	.05
369	Joe Pittman	.08	.05
370	Gene Richards	.08	.05
371	Luis Salazar	.08	.05
372	Eric Show (R)	.10	.06
373	Garry Templeton	.10	.06
374	Chris Welsh	.08	.05
375	Alan Wiggins	.08	.05
276	Rick Cerone	.08	.05
377	Dave Collins	.08	.05
378	Roger Erickson	.08	.05
379	George Frazier	.08	.05
380	Oscar Gamble	.10	.06
381	Goose Gossage	.25	.15
382	Ken Griffey	.15	.10
383	Ron Guidry	.20	.12
384	Dave LaRoche	.08	.05
385	Rudy May	.08	.05
386	John Mayberry	.10	.06
387	Lee Mazzilli	.08	.05
388	Mike Morgan (R)	.35	.20
389	Jerry Mumphrey	.08	.05
390	Bobby Murcer	.10	.06
391	Graig Nettles	.12	.07
392	Lou Piniella	.10	.06
393	Willie Randolph	.10	.06
394	Shane Rawley	.08	.05
395	Dave Righetti	.12	.07
396	Andre Robertson	.08	.05
397	Roy Smalley	.08	.05
398	Dave Winfield	2.50	1.50
399	Butch Wynegar	.08	.05

400	Chris Bando	.08	.05
401	Alan Bannister	.08	.05
402	Len Barker	.08	.05
403	Tom Brennan	.08	.05
404	Carmelo Castillo (R)	.08	.05
405	Miguel Dilone	.08	.05
406	Jerry Dybzinski	.08	.05
407	Mike Fischlin	.08	.05
408	Ed Glynn	.08	.05
	(Wrong Photo)		
409	Mike Hargrove	.08	.05
410	Toby Harrah	.08	.05
411	Ron Hassey	.08	.05
412	Von Hayes	.10	.06
413	Rick Manning	.08	.05
414	Bake McBride	.08	.05
415	Larry Milbourne	.08	.05
416	Bill Nahorodny	.08	.05
417	Jack Perconte	.08	.05
418	Lary Sorensen	.08	.05
419	Dan Spillner	.08	.05
420	Rick Sutcliffe	.25	.15
421	Andre Thornton	.10	.06
422	Rick Waits	.08	.05
423	Eddie Whitson	.08	.05
424	Jesse Barfield (R)	.25	.15
425	Barry Bonnell	.08	.05
426	Jim Clancy	.08	.05
427	Damaso Garcia	.08	.05
428	Jerry Garvin	.08	.05
429	Alfredo Griffin	.08	.05
430	Garth Iorg	.08	.05
431	Roy Lee Jackson	.08	.05
432	Luis Leal	.08	.05
433	Buck Martinez	.08	.05
434	Joey McLaughlin	.08	.05
435	Lloyd Moseby	.08	.05
436	Rance Mulliniks	.08	.05
437	Dale Murray	.08	.05
438	Wayne Nordhagen	.08	.05
439	Gene Petralli (R)	.10	.06
440	Hosken Powell	.08	.05
441	Dave Stieb	.15	.10
442	Willie Upshaw	.08	.05
443	Ernie Whitt	.08	.05
444	Al Woods	.08	.05
445	Alan Ashby	.08	.05
446	Jose Cruz	.12	.07
447	Kiko Garcia	.08	.05
448	Phil Garner	.10	.06
449	Danny Heep	.08	.05
450	Art Howe	.08	.05
451	Bob Knepper	.08	.05
452	Alan Knicely	.08	.05
453	Ray Knight	.10	.06
454	Frank LaCorte	.08	.05
455	Mike LaCoss	.08	.05
456	Randy Moffitt	.08	.05
457	Joe Niekro	.08	.05
458	Terry Puhl	.08	.05
459	Luis Pujols	.08	.05
460	Craig Reynolds	.08	.05
461	Bert Roberge	.08	.05
462	Vern Ruhle	.08	.05
463	Nolan Ryan	7.50	4.50
464	Joe Sambito	.08	.05
465	Tony Scott	.08	.05
466	Dave Smith	.08	.05
467	Harry Spilman	.08	.05
468	Dickie Thon	.08	.05
469	Denny Walling	.08	.05
470	Larry Andersen	.08	.05
471	Floyd Bannister	.08	.05
472	Jim Beattie	.08	.05
473	Bruce Bochte	.08	.05
474	Manny Castillo	.08	.05
475	Bill Caudill	.08	.05
476	Bryan Clark	.08	.05
477	Al Cowens	.08	.05
478	Julio Cruz	.08	.05
479	Todd Cruz	.08	.05
480	Gary Gray	.08	.05
481	Dave Henderson (R)	.45	.28
482	Mike Moore (R)	.75	.45
483	Gaylord Perry	.50	.30
484	Dave Revering	.08	.05
485	Joe Simpson	.08	.05
486	Mike Stanton	.08	.05
487	Rick Sweet	.08	.05
488	Ed Vande Berg (R)	.08	.05
489	Richie Zisk	.08	.05
490	Doug Bird	.08	.05
491	Larry Bowa	.10	.06
492	Bill Buckner	.10	.06
493	Bill Campbell	.08	.05
494	Jody Davis	.08	.05
495	Leon Durham	.08	.05
496	Steve Henderson	.08	.05
497	Willie Hernandez	.10	.06
498	Ferguson Jenkins	.50	.30
499	Jay Johnstone	.10	.06
500	Junior Kennedy	.08	.05
501	Randy Martz	.08	.05
502	Jerry Morales	.08	.05
503	Keith Moreland	.08	.05
504	Dickie Noles	.08	.05
505	Mike Proly	.08	.05
506	Allen Ripley	.08	.05
507	Ryne Sandberg (R)	45.00	36.00
508	Lee Smith	2.50	1.50
509	Pat Tabler (R)	.10	.06
510	Dick Tidrow	.08	.05
511	Bump Wills	.08	.05
512	Gary Woods	.08	.05
513	Tony Armas	.08	.05
514	Dave Beard	.08	.05

515	Jeff Burroughs	.08	.05
516	John D'Acquisto	.08	.05
517	Wayne Gross	.08	.05
518	Mike Heath	.08	.05
519	Rickey Henderson	5.00	3.00
520	Cliff Johnson	.08	.05
521	Matt Keough	.08	.05
522	Brian Kingman	.08	.05
523	Rick Langford	.08	.05
524	Davey Lopes	.10	.06
525	Steve McCatty	.08	.05
526	Dave McKay	.08	.05
527	Dan Meyer	.08	.05
528	Dwayne Murphy	.08	.05
529	Jeff Newman	.08	.05
530	Mike Norris	.08	.05
531	Bob Owchinko	.08	.05
532	Joe Rudi	.10	.06
533	Jimmy Sexton	.08	.05
534	Fred Stanley	.08	.05
535	Tom Underwood	.08	.05
536	Neil Allen	.08	.05
537	Wally Backman	.08	.05
538	Bob Bailor	.08	.05
539	Hubie Brooks	.15	.10
540	Carlos Diaz	.08	.05
541	Pete Falcone	.08	.05
542	George Foster	.12	.07
543	Ron Gardenhire	.08	.05
544	Brian Giles	.08	.05
545	Ron Hodges	.08	.05
546	Randy Jones	.08	.05
547	Mike Jorgensen	.08	.05
548	Dave Kingman	.15	.10
549	Ed Lynch	.08	.05
550	Jesse Orosco (R)	.08	.05
551	Rick Ownbey	.08	.05
552	Charlie Puleo	.08	.05
553	Gary Rajsich	.08	.05
554	Mike Scott	.15	.10
555	Rusty Staub	.08	.05
556	John Stearns	.08	.05
557	Craig Swan	.08	.05
558	Ellis Valentine	.08	.05
559	Tom Veryzer	.08	.05
560	Mookie Wilson	.10	.06
561	Pat Zachry	.08	.05
562	Buddy Bell	.08	.05
563	John Butcher	.08	.05
564	Steve Comer	.08	.05
565	Danny Darwin	.08	.05
566	Bucky Dent	.10	.06
567	John Grubb	.08	.05
568	Rick Honeycutt	.08	.05
569	Dave Hostetler	.08	.05
570	Charlie Hough	.10	.06
571	Lamar Johnson	.08	.05
572	Jon Matlack	.08	.05
573	Paul Mirabella	.08	.05
574	Larry Parrish	.08	.05
575	Mike Richardt	.08	.05
576	Mickey Rivers	.08	.05
577	Billy Sample	.08	.05
578	Dave Schmidt (R)	.08	.05
579	Bill Stein	.08	.05
580	Jim Sundberg	.08	.05
581	Frank Tanana	.10	.06
582	Mark Wagner	.08	.05
583	George Wright	.08	.05
584	Johnny Bench	1.50	.90
585	Bruce Berenyi	.08	.05
586	Larry Biittner	.08	.05
587	Cesar Cedeno	.10	.06
588	Dave Concepcion	.15	.10
589	Dan Driessen	.08	.05
590	Greg Harris	.08	.05
591	Ben Hayes	.08	.05
592	Paul Householder	.08	.05
593	Tom Hume	.08	.05
594	Wayne Krenchicki	.08	.05
595	Rafael Landestoy	.08	.05
596	Charlie Leibrandt	.08	.05
597	Eddie Milner (R)	.10	.06
598	Ron Oester	.08	.05
599	Frank Pastore	.08	.05
600	Joe Price	.08	.05
601	Tom Seaver	1.75	1.00
602	Bob Shirley	.08	.05
603	Mario Soto	.08	.05
604	Alex Trevino	.08	.05
605	Mike Vail	.08	.05
606	Duane Walker	.08	.05
607	Tom Brunansky (R)	.35	.20
608	Bobby Castillo	.08	.05
609	John Castino	.08	.05
610	Ron Davis	.08	.05
611	Lenny Faedo	.08	.05
612	Terry Felton	.08	.05
613	Gary Gaetti (R)	.25	.15
614	Mickey Hatcher	.08	.05
615	Brad Havens	.08	.05
616	Kent Hrbek (R)	.70	.40
617	Randy Johnson	.08	.05
618	Tim Laudner (R)	.10	.06
619	Jeff Little	.08	.05
620	Bob Mitchell	.08	.05
621	Jack O'Connor	.08	.05
622	John Pacella	.08	.05
623	Pete Redfern	.08	.05
624	Jesus Vega	.08	.05
625	Frank Viola (R)	3.50	2.50
626	Ron Washington	.08	.05
627	Gary Ward	.08	.05
628	Al Williams	.08	.05
629	Red Sox All-Stars	.50	.30
	(Mark Clear, —		

	Dennis Eckersley, Carl Yastrzemski)		
630	300 Wins (Terry Bulling, Gaylord Perry)	.15	.10
631	Pride of Venezuela (Dave Concepcion, Manny Trillo)	.10	.06
632	All-Star Infielders (Buddy Bell, Robin Yount)	.80	.50
633	Mr. Vet & Mr. Rookie (Kent Hrbek, Dave Winfield)	.70	.40
634	Fountain of Youth (Pete Rose, Willie Stargell)	.80	.50
635	Big Chiefs (Toby Harrah, Andre Thornton)	.08	.05
636	Smith Bros. (Lonnie Smith, Ozzie Smith)	.35	.20
637	Base Stealers' Threat (Gary Carter, Bo Diaz)	.10	.06
638	All-Star Catchers (Gary Carter, Carlton Fisk)	.40	.25
639	The Silver Shoe (Rickey Henderson)	2.00	1.25
640	Home Run Threats (Reggie Jackson, Ben Oglivie)	.75	.45
641	Two Teams-Same Day (Joel Youngblood)	.08	.05
642	Last Perfect Game (Len Barker, Ron Hassey)	.08	.05
643	Black & Blue (Vida Blue)	.12	.07
644	Black & Blue (Bud Black)	.10	.06
645	Reggie Jackson (Power)	.80	.50
646	Rickey Henderson (Speed)	1.50	.90
647	Checklist 1-51	.08	.05
648	Checklist 52-103	.08	.05
649	Checklist 104-152	.08	.05
650	Checklist 153-200	.08	.05
651	Checklist 201-251	.08	.05
652	Checklist 252-301	.08	.05
653	Checklist 302-351	.08	.05
654	Checklist 352-399	.08	.05
655	Checklist 400-444	.08	.05
656	Checklist 445-489	.08	.05
657	Checklist 490-535	.08	.05
658	Checklist 536-583	.08	.05
659	Checklist 584-628	.08	.05
660	Checklist 629-646	.08	.05

1984 Fleer

This 660-card set features full color photos on the fronts framed by white borders on all sides and blue stripes at the top and bottom. A full color team logo is printed in the right corner of the card front. Card backs are vertical and printed in blue and white. All cards measure 2-1/2" by 3-1/2".

		MINT	NR/MT
Complete Set (660)		215.00	165.00
Commons		.10	.06
1	Mike Boddicker	.25	.15
2	Al Bumbry	.10	.06
3	Todd Cruz	.10	.06
4	Rich Dauer	.10	.06
5	Storm Davis	.12	.07
6	Rick Dempsey	.10	.06
7	Jim Dwyer	.10	.06
8	Mike Flanagan	.15	.10
9	Dan Ford	.10	.06
10	John Lowenstein	.10	.06
11	Dennis Martinez	.20	.12
12	Tippy Martinez	.10	.06
13	Scott McGregor	.10	.06
14	Eddie Murray	4.50	3.00
15	Joe Nolan	.10	.06
16	Jim Palmer	3.00	2.00
17	Cal Ripken, Jr.	24.00	16.00
18	Gary Roenicke	.10	.06
19	Lenn Sakata	.10	.06
20	John Shelby (R)	.15	.10
21	Ken Singleton	.10	.06

No.	Player		
22	Sammy Stewart	.10	.06
23	Tim Stoddard	.10	.06
24	Marty Bystrom	.10	.06
25	Steve Carlton	4.00	2.75
26	Ivan DeJesus	.10	.06
27	John Denny	.10	.06
28	Bob Dernier	.10	.06
29	Bo Diaz	.10	.06
30	Kiko Garcia	.10	.06
31	Greg Gross	.10	.06
32	Kevin Gross (R)	.30	.18
33	Von Hayes	.12	.07
34	Willie Hernandez	.15	.10
35	Al Holland	.10	.06
36	Charles Hudson (R)	.12	.07
37	Joe Lefebvre	.10	.06
38	Sixto Lezcano	.10	.06
39	Garry Maddox	.10	.06
40	Gary Matthews	.10	.06
41	Len Matuszek	.10	.06
42	Tug McGraw	.15	.10
43	Joe Morgan	.80	.50
44	Tony Perez	.90	.60
45	Ron Reed	.10	.06
46	Pete Rose	4.00	2.75
47	Juan Samuel (R)	1.00	.70
48	Mike Schmidt	10.00	7.00
49	Ozzie Virgil	.10	.06
50	Juan Agosto (R)	.12	.07
51	Harold Baines	.40	.25
52	Floyd Bannister	.10	.06
53	Salome Barojas	.10	.06
54	Britt Burns	.10	.06
55	Julio Cruz	.10	.06
56	Richard Dotson	.10	.06
57	Jerry Dybzinski	.10	.06
58	Carlton Fisk	3.50	2.50
59	Scott Fletcher (R)	.15	.10
60	Jerry Hairston	.10	.06
61	Kevin Hickey	.10	.06
62	Marc Hill	.10	.06
63	LaMarr Hoyt	.10	.06
64	Ron Kittle	.15	.10
65	Jerry Koosman	.15	.10
66	Dennis Lamp	.10	.06
67	Rudy Law	.10	.06
68	Vance law	.10	.06
69	Greg Luzinski	.12	.07
70	Tom Paciorek	.10	.06
71	Mike Squires	.10	.06
72	Dick Tidrow	.10	.06
73	Greg Walker (R)	.12	.07
74	Glenn Abbott	.10	.06
75	Howard Bailey	.10	.06
76	Doug Bair	.10	.06
77	Juan Berenguer	.10	.06
78	Tom Brookens	.10	.06
79	Enos Cabell	.10	.06
80	Kirk Gibson	.40	.25
81	John Grubb	.10	.06
82	Larry Herndon	.10	.06
83	Wayne Krenchicki	.10	.06
84	Rick Leach	.10	.06
85	Chet Lemon	.10	.06
86	Aurelio Lopez	.10	.06
87	Jack Morris	2.50	1.50
88	Lance Parrish	.20	.12
89	Dan Petry	.10	.06
90	Dave Rozema	.10	.06
91	Alan Trammell	1.50	.90
92	Lou Whitaker	.50	.30
93	Milt Wilcox	.10	.06
94	Glenn Wilson	.10	.06
95	John Wockenfuss	.10	.06
96	Dusty Baker	.12	.07
97	Joe Beckwith	.10	.06
98	Greg Brock	.10	.06
99	Jack Fimple	.10	.06
100	Pedro Guerrero	.20	.12
101	Rick Honeycutt	.10	.06
102	Burt Hooton	.10	.06
103	Steve Howe	.10	.06
104	Ken Landreaux	.10	.06
105	Mike Marshall	.10	.06
106	Rick Monday	.12	.07
107	Jose Morales	.10	.06
108	Tom Niedenfuer	.10	.06
109	Alejandro Pena (R)	.50	.30
110	Jerry Reuss	.12	.07
111	Bill Russell	.12	.07
112	Steve Sax	.50	.30
113	Mike Scioscia	.12	.07
114	Derrel Thomas	.10	.06
115	Fernando Valenzuela	.20	.12
116	Bob Welch	.20	.12
117	Steve Yeager	.10	.06
118	Pat Zachry	.10	.06
119	Don Baylor	.15	.10
120	Bert Campaneris	.15	.10
121	Rick Cerone	.10	.06
122	Ray Fontenot	.10	.06
123	George Frazier	.10	.06
124	Oscar Gamble	.12	.07
125	Goose Gossage	.35	.20
126	Ken Griffey	.20	.12
127	Ron Guidry	.25	.15
128	Jay Howell (R)	.15	.10
129	Steve Kemp	.10	.06
130	Matt Keough	.10	.06
131	Don Mattingly (R)	28.00	18.50
132	John Montefusco	.10	.06
133	Omar Moreno	.10	.06
134	Dale Murray	.10	.06
135	Graig Nettles	.20	.12
136	Lou Piniella	.15	.10
137	Willie Randolph	.15	.10

#	Player			#	Player		
138	Shane Rawley	.10	.06	196	Mike Caldwell	.10	.06
139	Dave Righetti	.15	.10	197	Tom Candiotti (R)	.80	.50
140	Andre Robertson	.10	.06	198	Cecil Cooper	.15	.10
141	Bob Shirley	.10	.06	199	Rollie Fingers	1.25	.80
142	Roy Smalley	.10	.06	200	Jim Gantner	.10	.06
143	Dave Winfield	4.50	3.00	201	Bob Gibson	.10	.06
144	Butch Wynegar	.10	.06	202	Moose Haas	.10	.06
145	Jim Acker (R)	.12	.07	203	Roy Howell	.10	.06
146	Doyle Alexander	.10	.06	204	Pete Ladd	.10	.06
147	Jesse Barfield	.25	.15	205	Rick Manning	.10	.06
148	Jorge Bell	2.00	1.25	206	Bob McClure	.10	.06
149	Barry Bonnell	.10	.06	207	Paul Molitor	1.50	.90
150	Jim Clancy	.10	.06	208	Don Money	.10	.06
151	Dave Collins	.10	.06	209	Charlie Moore	.10	.06
152	Tony Fernandez (R)	3.50	2.50	210	Ben Oglivie	.10	.06
153	Damaso Garcia	.10	.06	211	Chuck Porter	.10	.06
154	Dave Geisel	.10	.06	212	Ed Romero	.10	.06
155	Jim Gott (R)	.25	.15	213	Ted Simmons	.15	.10
156	Alfredo Griffin	.10	.06	214	Jim Slaton	.10	.06
157	Garth Iorg	.10	.06	215	Don Sutton	.80	.50
158	Roy Lee Jackson	.10	.06	216	Tom Tellmann	.10	.06
159	Cliff Johnson	.10	.06	217	Pete Vuckovich	.12	.07
160	Luis Leal	.10	.06	218	Ned Yost	.10	.06
161	Buck Martinez	.10	.06	219	Robin Yount	6.00	4.00
162	Joey McLaughlin	.10	.06	220	Alan Ashby	.10	.06
163	Randy Moffitt	.10	.06	221	Kevin Bass (R)	.20	.12
164	Lloyd Moseby	.10	.06	222	Jose Cruz	.15	.10
165	Rance Mulliniks	.10	.06	223	Bill Dawley	.10	.06
166	Jorge Orta	.10	.06	224	Frank DiPino	.10	.06
167	Dave Stieb	.25	.15	225	Bill Doran (R)	.40	.25
168	Willie Upshaw	.10	.06	226	Phil Garner	.12	.07
169	Ernie Whitt	.10	.06	227	Art Howe	.10	.06
170	Len Barker	.10	.06	228	Bob Knepper	.10	.06
171	Steve Bedrosian	.15	.10	229	Ray Knight	.12	.07
172	Bruce Benedict	.10	.06	230	Frank LaCorte	.10	.06
173	Brett Butler	.60	.35	231	Mike LaCoss	.10	.06
174	Rick Camp	.10	.06	232	Mike Madden	.10	.06
175	Chris Chambliss	.15	.10	233	Jerry Mumphrey	.10	.06
176	Ken Dayley	.10	.06	235	Terry Puhl	.10	.06
177	Pete Falcone	.10	.06	236	Luis Pujols	.10	.06
178	Terry Forster	.10	.06	237	Craig Reynolds	.10	.06
179	Gene Garber	.10	.06	238	Vern Ruhle	.10	.06
180	Terry Harper	.10	.06	239	Nolan Ryan	18.00	12.50
181	Bob Horner	.12	.07	240	Mike Scott	.15	.10
182	Glenn Hubbard	.10	.06	241	Tony Scott	.10	.06
183	Randy Johnson	.10	.06	242	Dave Smith	.10	.06
184	Craig McMurtry	.10	.06	243	Dickie Thon	.10	.06
185	Donnie Moore	.10	.06	244	Denny Walling	.10	.06
186	Dale Murphy	1.75	1.00	245	Dale Berra	.10	.06
187	Phil Niekro	1.25	.80	246	Jim Bibby	.10	.06
188	Pasqual Perez	.15	.10	247	John Candelaria	.10	.06
189	Biff Pocoroba	.10	.06	248	Jose DeLeon (R)	.15	.10
190	Rafael Ramirez	.10	.06	249	Mike Easler	.10	.06
191	Jerry Royster	.10	.06	250	Cecilio Guante (R)	.10	.06
192	Claudell Washington	.10	.06	251	Richie Hebner	.10	.06
193	Bob Watson	.15	.10	252	Lee Lacy	.10	.06
194	Jerry Augustine	.10	.06	253	Bill Madlock	.20	.12
195	Mark Brouhard	.10	.06	254	Milt May	.10	.06

#	Player		
255	Lee Mazzilli	.10	.06
256	Larry McWilliams	.10	.06
257	Jim Morrison	.10	.06
258	Dave Parker	.45	.28
259	Tony Pena	.12	.07
260	Johnny Ray	.10	.06
261	Rick Rhoden	.10	.06
262	Don Robinson	.10	.06
263	Manny Sarmiento	.10	.06
264	Rod Scurry	.10	.06
265	Kent Tekulve	.10	.06
266	Gene Tenace	.12	.07
267	Jason Thompson	.10	.06
268	Lee Tunnell	.10	.06
269	Marvell Wynne (R)	.12	.07
270	Ray Burris	.10	.06
271	Gary Carter	1.00	.70
272	Warren Cromartie	.10	.06
273	Andre Dawson	4.50	2.75
274	Doug Flynn	.10	.06
275	Terry Francona	.10	.06
276	Bill Gullickson	.12	.07
277	Bob James	.10	.06
278	Charlie Lea	.10	.06
279	Bryan Little	.10	.06
280	Al Oliver	.20	.12
281	Tim Raines	.70	.40
282	Bobby Ramos	.10	.06
283	Jeff Reardon	2.50	1.50
284	Steve Rogers	.10	.06
285	Scott Sanderson	.12	.07
286	Dan Schatzeder	.10	.06
287	Bryn Smith	.12	.07
288	Chris Speier	.10	.06
289	Manny Trillo	.10	.06
290	Mike Vail	.10	.06
291	Tim Wallach	.25	.15
292	Chris Welsh	.10	.06
293	Jim Wohlford	.10	.06
294	Kurt Bevacqua	.10	.06
295	Juan Bonilla	.10	.06
296	Bobby Brown	.10	.06
297	Luis DeLeon	.10	.06
298	Dave Dravecky	.15	.10
299	Tim Flannery	.10	.06
300	Steve Garvey	.80	.50
301	Tony Gwynn	14.00	8.50
302	Andy Hawkins (R)	.15	.10
303	Ruppert Jones	.10	.06
304	Terry Kennedy	.10	.06
305	Tim Lollar	.10	.06
306	Gary Lucas	.10	.06
307	Kevin McReynolds (R)	2.50	1.50
308	Sid Monge	.10	.06
309	Mario Ramirez	.10	.06
310	Gene Richards	.10	.06
311	Luis Salazar	.10	.06
312	Eric Show	.10	.06
313	Elias Sosa	.10	.06
314	Garry Templeton	.12	.07
315	Mark Thurmond (R)	.12	.07
316	Ed Whitson	.10	.06
317	Alan Wiggins	.10	.06
318	Neil Allen	.10	.06
319	Joaquin Andujar	.15	.10
320	Steve Braun	.10	.06
321	Glenn Brummer	.10	.06
322	Bob Forsch	.10	.06
323	David Green	.10	.06
324	George Hendrick	.12	.07
325	Tom Herr	.10	.06
326	Dane Iorg	.10	.06
327	Jeff Lahti	.10	.06
328	Dave LaPoint	.10	.06
329	Willie McGee	.75	.45
330	Ken Oberkfell	.10	.06
331	Darrell Porter	.10	.06
332	Jamie Quirk	.10	.06
333	Mike Ramsey	.10	.06
334	Floyd Rayford	.10	.06
335	Lonnie Smith	.12	.07
336	Ozzie Smith	4.00	2.75
337	John Stuper	.10	.06
338	Bruce Sutter	.20	.12
339	Andy Van Slyke (R)	7.50	4.50
340	Dave Von Ohlen	.10	.06
341	Willie Aikens	.10	.06
342	Mike Armstrong	.10	.06
343	Bud Black	.12	.07
344	George Brett	6.00	4.00
345	Onix Concepcion	.10	.06
346	Keith Creel	.10	.06
347	Larry Gura	.10	.06
348	Don Hood	.10	.06
349	Dennis Leonard	.10	.06
350	Hal McRae	.15	.10
351	Amos Otis	.12	.07
352	Gaylord Perry	.80	.50
353	Greg Pryor	.10	.06
354	Dan Quisenberry	.15	.10
355	Steve Renko	.10	.06
356	Leon Roberts	.10	.06
357	Pat Sheridan (R)	.12	.07
358	Joe Simpson	.10	.06
359	Don Slaught	.12	.07
360	Paul Splittorff	.10	.06
361	U.L. Washington	.10	.06
362	John Wathan	.10	.06
363	Frank White	.10	.06
364	Willie Wilson	.12	.07
365	Jim Barr	.10	.06
366	Dave Bergman	.10	.06
367	Fred Breining	.10	.06
368	Bob Brenly	.10	.06
369	Jack Clark	.15	.10
370	Chili Davis	.20	.12

371	Mark Davis (R)	.15	.10
372	Darrell Evans	.15	.10
373	Atlee Hammaker	.10	.06
374	Mike Krukow	.10	.06
ä375	Duane Kuiper	.10	.06
376	Bill Laskey	.10	.06
377	Gary Lavelle	.10	.06
378	Johnnie LeMaster	.10	.06
379	Jeff Leonard	.12	.07
380	Randy Lerch	.10	.06
381	Renie Martin	.10	.06
382	Andy McGaffigan	.10	.06
383	Greg Minton	.10	.06
384	Tom O'Malley	.10	.06
385	Max Venable	.10	.06
386	Brad Wellman	.10	.06
387	Joel Youngblood	.10	.06
388	Gary Allenson	.10	.06
389	Luis Aponte	.10	.06
390	Tony Armas	.10	.06
391	Doug Bird	.10	.06
392	Wade Boggs	8.50	4.50
393	Dennis Boyd (R)	.15	.10
394	Mike Brown	.10	.06
395	Mark Clear	.10	.06
396	Dennis Eckersley	2.50	1.50
397	Dwight Evans	.25	.15
298	Rich Gedman	.10	.06
399	Glenn Hoffman	.10	.06
400	Bruce Hurst	.20	.12
401	John Henry Johnson	.10	.06
402	Ed Jurak	.10	.06
403	Rick Miller	.10	.06
404	Jeff Newman	.10	.06
405	Reid Nichols	.10	.06
406	Bob Ojeda	.15	.10
407	Jerry Remy	.10	.06
408	Jim Rice	.25	.15
409	Bob Stanley	.10	.06
410	Dave Stapleton	.10	.06
411	John Tudor	.12	.07
412	Carl Yastrzemski	2.50	1.50
413	Buddy Bell	.10	.06
414	Larry Biittner	.10	.06
415	John Butcher	.10	.06
416	Danny Darwin	.10	.06
417	Bucky Dent	.12	.07
418	Dave Hostetler	.10	.06
419	Charlie Hough	.12	.07
420	Bobby Johnson	.10	.06
421	Odell Jones	.10	.06
422	Jon Matlack	.10	.06
423	Pete O'Brien (R)	.40	.25
424	Larry Parrish	.10	.06
425	Mickey Rivers	.10	.06
426	Billy Sample	.10	.06
427	Dave Schmidt	.10	.06
428	Mike Smithson	.10	.06
429	Bill Stein	.10	.06
430	Dave Stewart	.60	.35
431	Jim Sundberg	.10	.06
432	Frank Tanana	.12	.07
433	Dave Tobik	.10	.06
434	Wayne Tolleson (R)	.10	.06
435	George Wright	.10	.06
436	Bill Almon	.10	.06
437	Keith Atherton (R)	.10	.06
438	Dave Beard	.10	.06
439	Tom Burgmeier	.10	.06
440	Jeff Burroughs	.10	.06
441	Chris Codiroli (R)	.10	.06
442	Tim Conroy	.10	.06
443	Mike Davis	.10	.06
444	Wayne Gross	.10	.06
445	Garry Hancock	.10	.06
446	Mike Heath	.10	.06
447	Rickey Henderson	8.50	4.50
448	Don Hill (R)	.10	.06
449	Bob Kearney	.10	.06
450	Bill Krueger	.35	.20
451	Rick Langford	.10	.06
452	Carney Lansford	.20	.12
453	Davey Lopes	.12	.07
454	Steve McCatty	.10	.06
455	Dan Meyer	.10	.06
456	Dwayne Murphy	.10	.06
457	Mike Norris	.10	.06
458	Ricky Peters	.10	.06
459	Tony Phillips (R)	1.00	.70
460	Tom Underwood	.10	.06
461	Mike Warren	.10	.06
462	Johnny Bench	3.50	2.50
463	Bruce Berenyi	.10	.06
464	Dann Bilardello	.10	.06
465	Cesar Cedeno	.12	.07
466	Dave Concepcion	.25	.15
467	Dan Driessen	.10	.06
468	Nick Esasky (R)	.15	.10
469	Rich Gale	.10	.06
470	Ben Hayes	.10	.06
471	Paul Householder	.10	.06
472	Tom Hume	.10	.06
473	Alan Knicely	.10	.06
474	Eddie Milner	.10	.06
474	Ron Oester	.10	.06
476	Kelly Paris	.10	.06
477	Frank Pastore	.10	.06
478	Ted Power	.10	.06
479	Joe Price	.10	.06
480	Charlie Puleo	.10	.06
481	Gary Redus (R)	.20	.12
482	Bill Scherrer	.10	.06
483	Mario Soto	.10	.06
484	Alex Trevino	.10	.06
485	Duane Walker	.10	.06
486	Larry Bowa	.15	.10

487	Warren Brusstar	.10	.06		545	Ron Hassey	.10	.06
488	Bill Buckner	.15	.10		546	Neal Heaton (R)	.15	.10
489	Bill Campbell	.10	.06		547	Bake McBride	.10	.06
490	Ron Cey	.12	.07		548	Broderick Perkins	.10	.06
491	Jody Davis	.10	.06		549	Lary Sorensen	.10	.06
492	Leon Durham	.10	.06		550	Dan Spillner	.10	.06
493	Mel Hall (R)	1.25	.80		551	Rick Sutcliffe	.20	.12
494	Ferguson Jenkins	.80	.50		552	Pat Tabler	.10	.06
495	Jay Johnstone	.12	.07		553	Gorman Thomas	.15	.10
496	Craig Lefferts (R)	.60	.35		554	Andre Thornton	.15	.10
497	Carmelo Martinez(R)	.15	.10		555	George Vukovich	.12	.07
498	Jerry Morales	.10	.06		556	Darrell Brown	.10	.06
499	Keith Moreland	.10	.06		557	Tom Brunansky	.20	.12
500	Dickie Noles	.10	.06		558	Randy Bush (R)	.15	.10
501	Mike Proly	.10	.06		559	Bobby Castillo	.10	.06
502	Chuck Rainey	.10	.06		560	John Castino	.10	.06
503	Dick Ruthven	.10	.06		561	Ron Davis	.10	.06
504	Ryne Sandberg	24.00	18.00		562	Dave Engle	.10	.06
505	Lee Smith	2.00	1.25		563	Lenny Faedo	.10	.06
506	Steve Trout	.10	.06		564	Pete Filson	.10	.06
507	Gary Woods	.10	.06		565	Gary Gaetti	.15	.10
508	Juan Beniquez	.10	.06		566	Mickey Hatcher	.10	.06
509	Bob Boone	.20	.12		567	Kent Hrbek	.50	.30
510	Rick Burleson	.10	.06		568	Rusty Kuntz	.10	.06
511	Rod Carew	2.75	1.75		569	Tim Laudner	.10	.06
512	Bobby Clark	.10	.06		570	Rick Lysander	.10	.06
513	John Curtis	.10	.06		571	Bobby Mitchell	.10	.06
514	Doug DeCinces	.10	.06		572	Ken Schrom	.10	.06
515	Brian Downing	.12	.07		573	Ray Smith	.10	.06
516	Tim Foli	.10	.06		574	Tim Teufel (R)	.15	.10
517	Ken Forsch	.10	.06		575	Frank Viola	.80	.50
518	Bobby Grich	.12	.07		576	Gary Ward	.10	.06
519	Andy Hassler	.10	.06		577	Ron Washington	.10	.06
520	Reggie Jackson	4.00	2.75		578	Len Whitehouse	.10	.06
521	Ron Jackson	.10	.06		579	Al Williams	.10	.06
522	Tommy Jonn	.20	.12		580	Bob Bailor	.10	.06
523	Bruce Kison	.10	.06		581	Mark Bradley	.10	.06
524	Steve Lubratich	.10	.06		582	Hubie Brooks	.20	.12
525	Fred Lynn	.15	.10		583	Carlos Diaz	.10	.06
526	Gary Pettis (R)	.20	.12		584	George Foster	.15	.10
527	Luis Sanchez	.10	.06		585	Brian Giles	.10	.06
528	Daryl Sconiers	.10	.06		586	Danny Heep	.10	.06
529	Ellis Valentine	.10	.06		587	Keith Hernandez	.20	.12
530	Rob Wilfong	.10	.06		588	Ron Hodges	.10	.06
531	Mike Witt	.10	.06		589	Scott Holman	.10	.06
532	Geoff Zahn	.10	.06		590	Dave Kingman	.15	.10
533	Bud Anderson	.10	.06		591	Ed Lynch	.10	.06
534	Chris Bando	.10	.06		592	Jose Oquendo (R)	.20	.12
535	Alan Bannister	.10	.06		593	Jesse Orosco	.10	.06
536	Bert Blyleven	.75	.45		594	Junior Ortiz (R)	.12	.07
537	Tom Brennan	.10	.06		595	Tom Seaver	4.00	2.75
538	Jamie Easterly	.10	.06		596	Doug Sisk (R)	.10	.06
539	Juan Eichelberger	.10	.06		597	Rusty Staub	.15	.10
540	Jim Essian	.10	.06		598	John Stearns	.10	.06
541	Mike Fischlin	.10	.06		599	Darryl Strawberry(R)	32.00	24.00
542	Julio Franco (R)	2.50	1.50		600	Craig Swan	.10	.06
543	Mike Hargrove	.10	.06		601	Walt Terrell (R)	.15	.10
544	Toby Harrah	.10	.06		602	Mike Torrez	.10	.06

603	Mookie Wilson	.15	.10
604	Jamie Allen	.10	.06
605	Jim Beattie	.10	.06
606	Tony Bernazard	.10	.06
607	Manny Castillo	.10	.06
608	Bill Caudill	.10	.06
609	Bryan Clark	.10	.06
610	Al Cowens	.10	.06
611	Dave Henderson	.25	.15
612	Steve Henderson	.10	.06
613	Orlando Mercado	.10	.06
614	Mike Moore	.10	.06
615	Ricky Nelson	.25	.15
616	Spike Owen (R)	.25	.15
617	Pat Putnam	.10	.06
618	Ron Roenicke	.10	.06
619	Mike Stanton	.10	.06
620	Bob Stoddard	.10	.06
621	Rick Sweet	.10	.06
622	Roy Thomas	.10	.06
623	Ed Vande Berg	.10	.06
624	Matt Young	.20	.12
625	Richie Zisk	.10	.06
626	Fred Lynn (AS)(RB)	.15	.10
627	Manny Trillo (AS)(RB)	.10	.06
628	Steve Garvey (NL Iron Man)	.30	.18
629	Rod Carew (AL Batting Runner Up)	.50	.30
630	Wade Boggs (AL Batting Champ)	1.50	.90
631	Tim Raines	.25	.15
632	Al Oliver (Double Trouble)	.15	.10
633	All-Star Second Base (Steve Sax)	.15	.10
634	All-Star Shortstop (Dickie Thon)	.12	.07
635	Ace Firemen (Tippy Martinez, Dan Quisenberry)	.12	.07
636	Reds Reunited (Joe Morgan, Tony Perez, Pete Rose)	1.00	.70
637	Backstop Stars (Bob Boone, Lance Parrish)	.15	.10
638	The Pine Tar Incident George Brett, Gaylord Perry	1.50	.90
639	1983 No-Hitters (Bob Forsch, Dave Righetti, Mike Warren)	.15	.10
640	Retiring Superstars Johnny Bench, Carl Yastrzemski	3.50	2.50
641	Going Out In Style (Gaylord Perry)	.25	.15
642	300 Club & Strike Out	.80	.50

	Record (Steve Carlton)		
643	The Managers (Joe Altobelli, Paul Owens)	.10	.06
644	World Series MVP (Rick Dempsey)	.10	.06
645	Rookie Winner (Mike Boddicker)	.12	.07
646	The Clincher (Scott McGregor)	.10	.06
647	Checklist	.10	.06
648	Checklist	.10	.06
649	Checklist	.10	.06
650	Checklist	.10	.06
651	Checklist	.10	.06
652	Checklist	.10	.06
653	Checklist	.10	.06
654	Checklist	.10	.06
655	Checklist	.10	.06
656	Checklist	.10	.06
657	Checklist	.10	.06
658	Checklist	.10	.06
659	Checklist	.10	.06
660	Checklist	.10	.06

1984 Fleer Update

This 132-card set marks the first post-season set issued by Fleer. Like the Topps Traded Set, this set updates players who were traded during the year and introduces some promising rookies. Cards measure 2-1/2" by 3-1/2" and card numbers are preceeded by the letter "U" on the card backs to signify the Update Set. Due to a limited print run this set is considered scarce.

	MINT	NR/MT
Complete Set (132)	975.00	750.00
Commons	.35	.20

1	Willie Aikens	.35	.20	59	Ruppert Jones	.35	.20
2	Luis Aponte	.35	.20	60	Bob Kearney	.35	.20
3	Mark Bailey (R)	.35	.20	61	Jimmy Key (R)	7.50	4.50
4	Bob Bailor	.35	.20	62	Dave Kingman	.50	.30
5	Dusty Baker	.40	.25	63	Brad Komminsk (R)	.35	.20
6	Steve Balboni (R)	.40	.25	64	Jerry Koosman	.50	.30
7	Alan Bannister	.35	.20	65	Wayne Krenchicki	.35	.20
8	Marty Barrett (R)	.50	.30	66	Rusty Kuntz	.35	.20
9	Dave Beard	.35	.20	67	Frank LaCorte	.35	.20
10	Joe Beckwith	.35	.20	68	Dennis Lamp	.35	.20
11	Dave Bergman	.35	.20	69	Tito Landrum	.35	.20
12	Tony Bernazard	.35	.20	70	Mark Langston (R)	20.00	14.00
13	Bruce Bochte	.35	.20	71	Rick Leach	.35	.20
14	Barry Bonnell	.35	.20	72	Craig Lefferts	.75	.45
15	Phil Bradley (R)	.60	.35	73	Gary Lucas	.35	.20
16	Fred Breining	.35	.20	74	Jerry Martin	.35	.20
17	Mike Brown	.35	.20	75	Carmelo Martinez	.35	.20
18	Bill Buckner	.40	.25	76	Mike Mason (R)	.35	.20
19	Ray Burris	.35	.20	77	Gary Matthews	.35	.20
20	John Butcher	.35	.20	78	Andy McGaffigan	.35	.20
21	Brett Butler	3.00	2.00	79	Joey McLaughlin	.35	.20
22	Enos Cabell	.35	.20	80	Joe Morgan	10.00	7.00
23	Bill Campbell	.35	.20	81	Darryl Motley	.35	.20
24	Bill Caudill	.35	.20	82	Graig Nettles	.80	.50
25	Bobby Clark	.35	.20	83	Phil Niekro	8.50	5.50
26	Bryan Clark	.35	.20	84	Ken Oberkfell	.35	.20
27	Roger Clemens (R)	425.00	350.00	85	Al Oliver	.50	.30
28	Jaime Cocanower	.35	.20	86	Jorge Orta	.35	.20
29	Ron Darling (R)	8.50	5.50	87	Amos Otis	.40	.25
30	Alvin Davis (R)	3.00	2.00	88	Bob Owchinko	.35	.20
31	Bob Dernier	.35	.20	89	Dave Parker	3.50	2.50
32	Carlos Diaz	.35	.20	90	Jack Perconte	.35	.20
33	Mike Easler	.35	.20	91	Tony Perez	7.50	4.50
34	Dennis Eckersley	14.00	10.00	92	Gerald Perry (R)	.50	.30
35	Jim Essian	.35	.20	93	Kirby Puckett (R)	375.00	290.00
36	Darrell Evans	.75	.45	94	Shane Rawley	.35	.20
37	Mike Fitgerald (R)	.35	.20	ä95	Floyd Rayford	.35	.20
38	Tim Foli	.35	.20	96	Ron Reed	.35	.20
39	John Franco (R)	10.00	7.00	97	R.J. Reynolds (R)	.35	.20
40	George Frazier	.35	.20	98	Gene Richards	.35	.20
41	Rich Gale	.35	.20	99	Jose Rijo (R)	24.00	17.00
42	Barbaro Garbey	.35	.20	100	Jeff Robinson	.35	.20
43	Dwight Gooden (R)	95.00	72.00	101	Ron Romanick	.35	.20
44	Goose Gossage	1.50	.90	102	Pete Rose	28.00	20.00
45	Wayne Gross	.35	.20	103	Bret Saberhagen(R)	35.00	28.00
46	Mark Gubicza (R)	5.00	3.00	104	Scott Sanderson	.40	.25
47	Jackie Gutierrez	.35	.20	105	Dick Schofield (R)	1.00	.70
48	Toby Harrah	.35	.20	106	Tom Seaver	28.00	20.00
49	Ron Hassey	.35	.20	107	Jim Slaton	.35	.20
50	Richie Hebner	.35	.20	108	Mike Smithson	.35	.20
51	Willie Hernandez	.40	.25	109	Lary Sorensen	.35	.20
52	Ed Hodge	.35	.20	110	Tim Stoddard	.35	.20
53	Ricky Horton (R)	.35	.20	111	Jeff Stone (R)	.35	.20
54	Art Howe	.35	.20	112	Champ Summers	.35	.20
55	Dane Iorg	.35	.20	113	Jim Sundberg	.35	.20
56	Brook Jacoby (R)	.60	.35	114	Rick Sutcliffe	1.00	.70
57	Dion James (R)	.40	.25	115	Craig Swan	.35	.20
58	Mike Jeffcoat (R)	.35	.20	116	Derrel Thomas	.35	.20

117	Gorman Thomas	.40	.25
118	Alex Trevino	.35	.20
119	Manny Trillo	.35	.20
120	John Tudor	.40	.25
121	Tom Underwood	.35	.20
122	Mike Vail	.35	.20
123	Tom Waddell (R)	.35	.20
124	Gary Ward	.35	.20
125	Terry Whitfield	.35	.20
126	Curtis Wilkerson	.35	.20
127	Frank Williams (R)	.35	.20
128	Glenn Wilson	.35	.20
129	John Wockenfuss	.35	.20
130	Ned Yost	.35	.20
131	Mike Young	.40	.25
132	Checklist 1-132	.35	.20

1985 Fleer

This 660-card set features full color photos on the card fronts with various border colors that correspond to the player's team colors. Cards measure 2-1/2" by 3-1/2". Card backs are vertical and printed in red, light red and black on a white stock. Fleer introduced a new 10-card subset, called Major League Prospects, which feature two players on one card.

	MINT	NR/MT
Complete Set (660)	200.00	150.00
Commons	.08	.05

1	Doug Bair	.08	.05
2	Juan Berenguer	.08	.05
3	Dave Bergman	.08	.05
4	Tom Brookens	.08	.05

5	Marty Castillo	.08	.05
6	Darrell Evans	.12	.07
7	Barbaro Garbey	.08	.05
8	Kirk Gibson	.25	.15
9	John Grubb	.08	.05
10	Willie Hernandez	.12	.07
11	Larry Herndon	.08	.05
12	Howard Johnson	2.50	1.50
13	Ruppert Jones	.08	.05
14	Rusty Kuntz	.08	.05
15	Chet Lemon	.08	.05
16	Aurelio Lopez	.08	.05
17	Sid Monge	.08	.05
18	Jack Morris	1.25	.80
19	Lance Parrish	.12	.07
20	Dan Petry	.08	.05
21	Dave Rozema	.08	.05
22	Bill Scherrer	.08	.05
23	Alan Trammell	.70	.40
24	Lou Whitaker	.35	.20
25	Milt Wilcox	.08	.05
26	Kurt Bevacqua	.08	.05
27	Greg Booker (R)	.08	.05
28	Bobby Brown	.08	.05
29	Luis DeLeon	.08	.05
30	Dave Dravecky	.12	.07
31	Tim Flannery	.08	.05
32	Steve Garvey	.50	.30
33	Goose Gossage	.15	.10
34	Tony Gwynn	7.50	4.50
35	Greg Harris	.08	.05
36	Andy Hawkins	.08	.05
37	Terry Kennedy	.08	.05
38	Craig Lefferts	.10	.06
39	Tim Lollar	.08	.05
40	Carmelo Martinez	.08	.05
41	Kevin McReynolds	.35	.20
42	Graig Nettles	.15	.10
43	Luis Salazar	.08	.05
44	Eric Show	.08	.05
45	Garry Templeton	.10	.06
46	Mark Thurmond	.08	.05
47	Ed Whitson	.08	.05
48	Alan Wiggins	.08	.05
49	Rich Bordi	.08	.05
50	Larry Bowa	.10	.06
51	Warren Brusstar	.08	.05
52	Ron Cey	.08	.05
53	Henry Cotto (R)	.12	.07
54	Jody Davis	.08	.05
55	Bob Dernier	.08	.05
56	Leon Durham	.08	.05
57	Dennis Eckersley	1.00	.70
58	George Frazier	.08	.05
59	Richie Hebner	.08	.05
60	Dave Lopes	.10	.06
61	Gary Matthews	.08	.05
62	Keith Moreland	.08	.05

63	Rick Reuschel	.08	.05	121	Don Baylor	.15	.10
64	Dick Ruthven	.08	.05	122	Marty Bystrom	.08	.05
65	Ryne Sandberg	13.00	7.50	123	Rick Cerone	.08	.05
66	Scott Sanderson	.10	.06	124	Joe Cowley	.08	.05
67	Lee Smith	1.25	.80	125	Brian Dayett	.08	.05
68	Tim Stoddard	.08	.05	126	Tim Foli	.08	.05
69	Rick Sutcliffe	.15	.10	127	Ray Fontenot	.08	.05
70	Steve Trout	.08	.05	128	Ken Griffey	.15	.10
71	Gary Woods	.08	.05	129	Ron Guidry	.20	.12
72	Wally Backman	.08	.05	130	Toby Harrah	.08	.05
73	Bruce Berenyi	.08	.05	131	Jay Howell	.08	.05
74	Hubie Brooks	.12	.07	132	Steve Kemp	.08	.05
75	Kelvin Chapman	.08	.05	133	Don Mattingly	7.00	4.00
76	Ron Darling	.40	.25	134	Bobby Meacham	.08	.05
77	Sid Fernandez (R)	.50	.30	135	John Montefusco	.08	.05
78	Mike Fitgerald	.08	.05	136	Omar Moreno	.08	.05
79	George Foster	.10	.06	137	Dale Murray	.08	.05
80	Brent Gaff	.08	.05	138	Phil Niekro	.75	.45
81	Ron Gardenhire	.08	.05	139	Mike Pagliarulo (R)	.25	.15
82	Dwight Gooden	10.00	7.00	140	Willie Randolph	.15	.10
83	Tom Gorman	.08	.05	141	Dennis Rasmussen	.08	.05
84	Danny Heep	.08	.05	142	Dave Righetti	.12	.07
85	Keith Hernandez	.15	.10	143	Jose Rijo	4.50	3.00
86	Ray Knight	.10	.06	144	Andre Robertson	.08	.05
87	Ed Lynch	.08	.05	145	Bob Shirley	.08	.05
88	Jose Oquendo	.08	.05	146	Dave Winfield	3.50	2.50
89	Jesse Orosco	.08	.05	147	Butch Wynegar	.08	.05
90	Rafael Santana (R)	.12	.07	148	Gary Allenson	.08	.05
91	Doug Sisk	.08	.05	149	Tony Armas	.08	.05
92	Rusty Staub	.12	.07	150	Marty Barrett	.12	.07
93	Darryl Strawberry	10.00	7.00	151	Wade Boggs	5.00	3.00
94	Walt Terrell	.08	.05	152	Dennis Boyd	.08	.05
95	Mookie Wilson	.10	.06	153	Bill Buckner	.12	.07
96	Jim Acker	.08	.05	154	Mark Clear	.08	.05
97	Willie Aikens	.08	.05	155	Roger Clemens	75.00	60.00
98	Doyle Alexander	.08	.05	156	Steve Crawford	.08	.05
99	Jesse Barfield	.15	.10	157	Mike Easler	.08	.05
100	George Bell	.80	.50	158	Dwight Evans	.25	.15
101	Jim Clancy	.08	.05	159	Rich Gedman	.08	.05
102	Dave Collins	.08	.05	160	Jackie Gutierrez	.08	.05
103	Tony Fernandez	.80	.50	161	Bruce Hurst	.15	.10
104	Damaso Garcia	.08	.05	162	John Henry Johnson	.08	.05
105	Jim Gott	.08	.05	163	Rick Miller	.08	.05
106	Alfredo Griffin	.08	.05	164	Reid Nichols	.08	.05
107	Garth Iorg	.08	.05	165	Al Nipper (R)	.08	.05
108	Roy Lee Jackson	.08	.05	166	Bob Ojeda	.10	.06
109	Cliff Johnson	.08	.05	167	Jerry Remy	.08	.05
110	Jimmy Key	1.25	.80	168	Jim Rice	.20	.12
111	Dennis Lamp	.08	.05	169	Bob Stanley	.08	.05
112	Rick Leach	.08	.05	170	Mike Boddicker	.08	.05
113	Luis Leal	.08	.05	171	Al Bumbry	.08	.05
114	Buck Martinez	.08	.05	172	Todd Cruz	.08	.05
115	Lloyd Moseby	.10	.06	173	Rich Dauer	.08	.05
116	Rance Mulliniks	.08	.05	174	Storm Davis	.08	.05
117	Dave Stieb	.20	.15	175	Rick Dempsey	.08	.05
118	Willie Upshaw	.08	.05	176	Jim Dwyer	.08	.05
119	Ernie Whitt	.08	.05	177	Mike Flanagan	.12	.07
120	Mike Armstrong	.08	.05	178	Dan Ford	.08	.05

#	Name			#	Name		
179	Wayne Gross	.08	.05	237	Darrell Porter	.08	.05
180	John Lowenstein	.08	.05	238	Dave Rucker	.08	.05
181	Dennis Martinez	.20	.12	239	Lonnie Smith	.10	.06
182	Tippy Martinez	.08	.05	240	Ozzie Smith	2.75	1.75
183	Scott McGregor	.08	.05	241	Bruce Sutter	.15	.10
184	Eddie Murray	3.00	2.00	242	Andy Van Slyke	2.75	1.75
185	Joe Nolan	.08	.05	243	Dave Von Ohlen	.08	.05
186	Floyd Rayford	.08	.05	244	Larry Andersen	.08	.05
187	Cal Ripken, Jr.	14.00	9.50	245	Bill Campbell	.08	.05
188	Gary Roenicke	.08	.05	246	Steve Carlton	2.50	1.50
189	Lenn Sakata	.08	.05	247	Tim Corcoran	.08	.05
190	John Shelby	.08	.05	248	Ivan DeJesus	.08	.05
191	Ken Singleton	.08	.05	249	John Denny	.08	.05
192	Sammy Stewart	.08	.05	250	Bo Diaz	.08	.05
193	Bill Swaggerty	.08	.05	251	Greg Gross	.08	.05
194	Tom Underwood	.08	.05	252	Kevin Gross	.10	.06
195	Mike Young	.08	.05	253	Von Hayes	.10	.06
196	Steve Balboni	.08	.05	254	Al Holland	.08	.05
197	Joe Beckwith	.08	.05	255	Charles Hudson	.08	.05
198	Bud Black	.10	.06	256	Jerry Koosman	.10	.06
199	George Brett	4.50	3.00	257	Joe Lefebvre	.08	.05
200	Onix Concepcion	.08	.05	258	Sixto Lezcano	.08	.05
201	Mark Gubicza	.80	.50	259	Garry Maddox	.08	.05
202	Larry Gura	.08	.05	260	Len Matuszek	.08	.05
203	Mark Huismann	.08	.05	261	Tug McGraw	.12	.07
204	Dane Iorg	.08	.05	262	Al Oliver	.12	.07
205	Danny Jackson	.25	.15	263	Shane Rawley	.08	.05
206	Charlie Leibrandt	.08	.05	264	Juan Samuel	.12	.07
207	Hal McRae	.15	.10	265	Mike Schmidt	6.50	4.50
208	Darryl Motley	.08	.05	266	Jeff Stone	.08	.05
209	Jorge Orta	.08	.05	267	Ozzie Virgil	.08	.05
210	Greg Pryor	.08	.05	268	Glenn Wilson	.08	.05
211	Dan Quisenberry	.10	.06	269	John Wockenfuss	.08	.05
212	Bret Saberhagen	6.00	4.00	270	Darrell Brown	.08	.05
213	Pat Sheridan	.08	.05	271	Tom Brunansky	.12	.07
214	Don Slaught	.08	.05	272	Randy Bush	.08	.05
215	U.L. Washington	.08	.05	273	John Butcher	.08	.05
216	John Wathan	.08	.05	274	Bobby Castillo	.08	.05
217	Frank White	.08	.05	275	Ron Davis	.08	.05
218	Willie Wilson	.10	.06	276	Dave Engle	.08	.05
219	Neil Allen	.08	.05	277	Pete Filson	.08	.05
220	Joaquin Andujar	.10	.06	278	Gary Gaetti	.08	.05
221	Steve Braun	.08	.05	279	Mickey Hatcher	.08	.05
222	Danny Cox	.08	.05	280	Ed Hodge	.08	.05
223	Bob Forsch	.08	.05	281	Kent Hrbek	.30	.18
224	David Green	.08	.05	282	Houston Jimenez	.08	.05
225	George Hendrick	.10	.06	283	Tim Laudner	.08	.05
226	Tom Herr	.08	.05	284	Rick Lysander	.08	.05
227	Ricky Horton	.08	.05	285	Dave Meier	.08	.05
228	Art Howe	.08	.05	286	Kirby Puckett	65.00	50.00
229	Mike Jorgensen	.08	.05	287	Pat Putnam	.08	.05
230	Kurt Kepshire	.08	.05	288	Ken Schrom	.08	.05
231	Jeff Lahti	.08	.05	289	Mike Smithson	.08	.05
232	Tito Landrum	.08	.05	290	Tim Teufel	.08	.05
233	Dave LaPoint	.08	.05	291	Frank Viola	.50	.30
234	Willie McGee	.50	.30	292	Ron Washington	.08	.05
235	Tom Nieto (R)	.08	.05	293	Don Aase	.08	.05
236	Terry Pendleton (R)	9.00	6.00	294	Juan Beniquez	.08	.05

#	Player		
295	Bob Boone	.15	.10
296	Mike Brown	.08	.05
297	Rod Carew	2.00	1.25
298	Doug Corbett	.08	.05
299	Doug DeCinces	.08	.05
300	Brian Downing	.10	.06
301	Ken Forsch	.08	.05
302	Bobby Grich	.10	.06
303	Reggie Jackson	3.50	2.50
304	Tommy John	.15	.10
305	Curt Kaufman	.08	.05
306	Bruce Kison	.08	.05
307	Fred Lynn	.15	.10
308	Gary Pettis	.08	.05
309	Ron Romanick	.08	.05
310	Luis Sanchez	.08	.05
311	Dick Schofield	.10	.06
312	Daryl Sconiers	.08	.05
313	Jim Slaton	.08	.05
314	Derrel Thomas	.08	.05
315	Rob Wilfong	.08	.05
316	Mike Witt	.08	.05
317	Geoff Zahn	.08	.05
318	Len Barker	.08	.05
319	Steve Bedrosian	.12	.07
320	Bruce Benedict	.08	.05
321	Rick Camp	.08	.05
322	Chris Chambliss	.12	.07
323	Jeff Dedmon (R)	.10	.06
324	Terry Forster	.08	.05
325	Gene Garber	.08	.05
326	Albert Hall (R)	.08	.05
327	Terry Harper	.08	.05
328	Bob Horner	.10	.06
329	Glenn Hubbard	.08	.05
330	Randy Johnson	.08	.05
331	Brad Komminsk	.08	.05
332	Rick Mahler	.08	.05
333	Craig McMurtry	.08	.05
334	Donnie Moore	.08	.05
335	Dale Murphy	.80	.50
336	Ken Oberkfell	.08	.05
337	Pascual Perez	.10	.06
338	Gerald Perry	.08	.05
339	Rafael Ramirez	.08	.05
340	Jerry Royster	.08	.05
341	Alex Trevino	.08	.05
342	Claudell Washington	.08	.05
343	Alan Ashby	.08	.05
344	Mark Bailey	.08	.05
345	Kevin Bass	.12	.07
346	Enos Cabell	.08	.05
347	Jose Cruz	.12	.07
348	Bill Dawley	.08	.05
349	Frank DePino	.08	.05
350	Bill Doran	.10	.06
351	Phil Garner	.10	.06
352	Bob Knepper	.08	.05
353	Mike LaCoss	.08	.05
354	Jerry Mumphrey	.08	.05
355	Joe Niekro	.08	.05
356	Terry Puhl	.08	.05
357	Craig Reynolds	.08	.05
358	Vern Ruhle	.08	.05
359	Nolan Ryan	12.50	8.50
360	Joe Sambito	.08	.05
361	Mike Scott	.12	.07
362	Dave Smith	.08	.05
363	Julio Solano (R)	.08	.05
364	Dickie Thon	.08	.05
365	Denny Walling	.08	.05
366	Dave Anderson	.08	.05
367	Bob Bailor	.08	.05
368	Greg Brock	.08	.05
369	Carlos Diaz	.08	.05
370	Pedro Guerrero	.20	.12
371	Orel Hershiser (R)	4.50	3.50
372	Rick Honeycutt	.08	.05
373	Burt Hooton	.08	.05
374	Ken Howell (R)	.10	.06
375	Ken Landreaux	.08	.05
376	Candy Maldonado	.10	.06
377	Mike Marshall	.08	.05
378	Tom Niedenfuer	.08	.05
379	Alejandro Pena	.12	.07
380	Jerry Reuss	.12	.07
381	R.J. Reynolds	.08	.05
382	German Rivera	.08	.05
383	Bill Russell	.10	.06
384	Steve Sax	.45	.28
385	Mike Scioscia	.10	.06
386	Franklin Stubbs (R)	.20	.12
387	Fernando Valenzuela	.15	.10
388	Bob Welch	.15	.10
389	Terry Whitfield	.08	.05
390	Steve Yeager	.08	.05
391	Pat Zachry	.08	.05
392	Fred Breining	.08	.05
393	Gary Carter	.60	.35
394	Andre Dawson	3.50	2.50
395	Miguel Dilone	.08	.05
396	Dan Driessen	.08	.05
397	Doug Flynn	.08	.05
398	Terry Francona	.08	.05
399	Bill Gullickson	.10	.06
400	Bob James	.08	.05
401	Charlie Lea	.08	.05
402	Bryan Little	.08	.05
403	Gary Lucas	.08	.05
404	David Palmer	.08	.05
405	Tim Raines	.30	.18
406	Mike Ramsey	.08	.05
407	Jeff Reardon	1.50	.90
408	Steve Rogers	.08	.05
409	Dan Schatzeder	.08	.05
410	Bryn Smith	.10	.06

411	Mike Stenhouse	.08	.05	469	Lee Mazzilli	.08	.05
412	Tim Wallach	.20	.12	470	Larry McWilliams	.08	.05
413	Jim Wohlford	.08	.05	471	Jim Morrison	.08	.05
414	Bill Almon	.08	.05	472	Tony Pena	.10	.06
415	Keith Atherton	.08	.05	473	Johnny Ray	.08	.05
416	Bruce Bochte	.08	.05	474	Rick Rhoden	.08	.05
417	Tom Burgmeier	.08	.05	475	Don Robinson	.08	.05
418	Ray Burris	.08	.05	476	Rod Scurry	.08	.05
419	Bill Caudill	.08	.05	477	Kent Tekulve	.08	.05
420	Chris Codiroli	.08	.05	478	Jason Thompson	.08	.05
421	Tim Conroy	.08	.05	479	John Tudor	.10	.06
422	Mike Davis	.08	.05	480	Lee Tunnell	.08	.05
423	Jim Essian	.08	.05	481	Marvell Wynne	.08	.05
424	Mike Heath	.08	.05	482	Salome Barojas	.08	.05
425	Rickey Henderson	4.50	3.50	483	Dave Beard	.08	.05
426	Donnie Hill	.08	.05	484	Jim Beattie	.08	.05
427	Dave Kingman	.12	.07	485	Barry Bonnell	.08	.05
428	Bill Krueger	.08	.05	486	Phil Bradley	.12	.07
429	Carney Lansford	.12	.07	487	Al Cowens	.08	.05
430	Steve McCatty	.08	.05	488	Alvin Davis	.25	.15
431	Joe Morgan	.70	.40	489	Dave Henderson	.15	.10
432	Dwayne Murphy	.08	.05	490	Steve Henderson	.08	.05
433	Tony Phillips	.10	.06	491	Bob Kearney	.08	.05
434	Lary Sorensen	.08	.05	492	Mark Langston	3.50	2.50
435	Mike Warren	.08	.05	493	Larry Milbourne	.08	.05
436	Curt Young (R)	.20	.12	494	Paul Mirabella	.08	.05
437	Luis Aponte	.08	.05	495	Mike Moore	.08	.05
438	Chris Bando	.08	.05	496	Edwin Nunez	.08	.05
439	Tony Bernazard	.08	.05	497	Spike Owen	.08	.05
440	Bert Blyleven	.45	.28	498	Jack Perconte	.08	.05
441	Brett Butler	.40	.25	499	Ken Phelps	.08	.05
442	Ernie Camacho	.08	.05	500	Jim Presley (R)	.08	.05
443	Joe Carter (R)	12.00	8.00	501	Mike Stanton	.08	.05
444	Carmelo Castillo	.08	.05	502	Bob Stoddard	.08	.05
445	Jamie Easterly	.08	.05	503	Gorman Thomas	.10	.06
446	Steve Farr (R)	.12	.07	504	Ed Vande Berg	.08	.05
447	Mike Fischlin	.08	.05	505	Matt Young	.08	.05
448	Julio Franco	.70	.40	506	Juan Agosto	.08	.05
449	Mel Hall	.12	.07	507	Harold Baines	.30	.18
450	Mike Hargrove	.08	.05	508	Floyd Bannister	.08	.05
451	Neal Heaton	.08	.05	509	Britt Burns	.08	.05
452	Brook Jacoby	.08	.05	510	Julio Cruz	.08	.05
453	Mike Jeffcoat	.08	.05	511	Richard Dotson	.08	.05
454	Don Schulze (R)	.08	.05	512	Jerry Dybzinski	.08	.05
455	Roy Smith	.08	.05	513	Carlton Fisk	3.00	2.00
456	Pat Tabler	.08	.05	514	Scott Fletcher	.08	.05
457	Andre Thornton	.10	.06	515	Jerry Hairston	.08	.05
458	George Vukovich	.08	.05	516	Marc Hill	.08	.05
459	Tom Waddell	.08	.05	517	LaMarr Hoyt	.08	.05
460	Jerry Willard	.08	.05	518	Ron Kittle	.08	.05
461	Dale Berra	.08	.05	519	Rudy Law	.08	.05
462	John Candelaria	.08	.05	520	Vance Law	.08	.05
463	Jose DeLeon	.08	.05	521	Greg Luzinski	.12	.07
464	Doug Frobel	.08	.05	522	Gene Nelson	.08	.05
465	Cecilio Guante	.08	.05	523	Tom Paciorek	.08	.05
466	Brian Harper	.15	.10	524	Ron Reed	.08	.05
467	Lee Lacy	.08	.05	525	Bert Roberge	.08	.05
468	Bill Madlock	.15	.10	526	Tom Seaver	3.00	2.00

No.	Player		
527	Roy Smalley	.08	.05
528	Dan Spillner	.08	.05
529	Mike Squires	.08	.05
530	Greg Walker	.08	.05
531	Cesar Cedeno	.10	.06
532	Dave Concepcion	.20	.12
533	Eric Davis (R)	9.00	6.00
534	Nick Esasky	.08	.05
535	Tom Foley	.08	.05
536	John Franco	1.25	.80
537	Brad Gulden	.08	.05
538	Tom Hume	.08	.05
539	Wayne Krenchicki	.08	.05
540	Andy McGaffigan	.08	.05
541	Eddie Milner	.08	.05
542	Ron Oester	.08	.05
543	Bob Owchinko	.08	.05
544	Dave Parker	.30	.18
545	Frank Pastore	.08	.05
546	Tony Perez	.60	.35
547	Ted Power	.08	.05
548	Joe Price	.08	.05
549	Gary Redus	.08	.05
550	Pete Rose	2.50	1.50
551	Jeff Russell	.20	.12
552	Mario Soto	.08	.05
553	Jay Tibbs (R)	.10	.06
554	Duane Walker	.08	.05
555	Alan Bannister	.08	.05
556	Buddy Bell	.08	.05
557	Danny Darwin	.08	.05
558	Charlie Hough	.10	.06
559	Bobby Jones	.08	.05
560	Odell Jones	.08	.05
561	Jeff Kunkel (R)	.08	.05
562	Mike Mason	.08	.05
563	Pete O'Brien	.10	.06
564	Larry Parrish	.08	.05
565	Mickey Rivers	.08	.05
566	Billy Sample	.08	.05
567	Dave Schmidt	.08	.05
568	Donnie Scott	.08	.05
569	Dave Stewart	.40	.25
570	Frank Tanana	.10	.06
571	Wayne Tolleson	.08	.05
572	Gary Ward	.08	.05
573	Curtis Wilkerson	.08	.05
574	George Wright	.08	.05
575	Ned Yost	.08	.05
576	Mark Brouhard	.08	.05
577	Mike Caldwell	.08	.05
578	Bobby Clark	.08	.05
579	Jaime Cocanower	.08	.05
580	Cecil Cooper	.12	.07
581	Rollie Fingers	.75	.45
582	Jim Gantner	.08	.05
583	Moose Haas	.08	.05
584	Dion James	.08	.05
585	Pete Ladd	.08	.05
586	Rick Manning	.08	.05
587	Bob McClure	.08	.05
588	Paul Molitor	.80	.50
589	Charlie Moore	.08	.05
590	Ben Oglivie	.08	.05
591	Chuck Porter	.08	.05
592	Randy Ready (R)	.12	.07
593	Ed Romero	.08	.05
594	Bill Schroeder	.08	.05
595	Ray Searage	.08	.05
596	Ted Simmons	.12	.07
597	Jim Sundberg	.08	.05
598	Don Sutton	.60	.35
599	Tom Tellmann	.08	.05
600	Rick Waits	.08	.05
601	Robin Yount	4.50	3.00
602	Dusty Baker	.10	.06
603	Bob Brenly	.08	.05
604	Jack Clark	.12	.07
605	Chili Davis	.15	.10
606	Mark Davis	.08	.05
607	Dan Gladden (R)	.25	.15
608	Atlee Hammaker	.08	.05
609	Mike Krukow	.08	.05
610	Duane Kuiper	.08	.05
611	Bob Lacey	.08	.05
612	Bill Laskey	.08	.05
613	Gary Lavelle	.08	.05
614	Johnnie LeMaster	.08	.05
615	Jeff Leonard	.10	.06
616	Randy Lerch	.08	.05
617	Greg Minton	.08	.05
618	Steve Nocosia	.08	.05
619	Gene Richards	.08	.05
620	Jeff Robinson	.08	.05
621	Scot Thompson	.08	.05
622	Manny Trillo	.08	.05
623	Brad Wellman	.08	.05
624	Frank Williams	.08	.05
625	Joel Youngblood	.08	.05
626	Cal Ripken (IA)	4.50	3.00
627	Mike Schmidt (IA)	3.50	2.50
628	Sparky Anderson (Giving Signs)	.10	.06
629	Pitcher's Nightmare (Rickey Henderson, Dave Winfield)	2.50	1.50
630	Pitcher's Nightmare (Ryne Sandberg, Mike Schmidt)	2.50	1.50
631	N.L. All-Stars (Gary Carter, Steve Garvey, Ozzie Smith, Darryl Strawberry)	1.50	.90
632	All-Star Game Winning Battery (Gary Carter, Charlie Lea)	.10	.06

633	N.L. Pennant Clinchers (Steve Garvey, Goose Gossage)	.15	.10
634	N.L. Rookie Phenoms (Dwight Gooden, Juan Samuel)	.50	.30
635	Toronto's Big Guns (Willie Upshaw)	.08	.05
636	Toronto's Big Guns (Lloyd Moseby)	.08	.05
637	Holland (Al Holland)	.08	.05
638	Tunnell (Lee Tunnell)	.08	.05
639	Reggie Jackson (500th Homer)	1.25	.80
640	Pete Rose (4000th Hit)	1.00	.70
641	Father & Son (Cal Ripken Sr & Jr)	3.50	2.50
642	Cubs Team	.08	.05
643	1984's Two Perfect Games & One No-Hitter (Jack Morris, David Palmer, Mike Witt)	.10	.06
644	Major League Prospect Willie Lozado (R) Vic Mata (R)	.08	.05
645	Major League Prospect Kelly Gruber (R) Randy O'Neal (R)	7.00	4.00
646	Major League Prospect Jose Roman (R) Joel Skinner (R)	.08	.05
647	Major League Prospect Steve Kiefer (R) Danny Tartabull (R)	8.50	5.50
648	Major League Prospect Rob Deer (R) Alejandro Sanchez (R)	1.25	.80
649	Major League Prospect Shawon Dunston (R) Bill Hatcher (R)	2.50	1.50
650	Major League Prospect Mike Bielecki (R) Ron Robinson (R)	.25	.15
651	Major League Prospect Zane Smith (R) Paul Zuvella (R)	.80	.50
652	Major League Prospect Glenn Davis (R) Joe Hesketh (R)	5.00	3.00
653	Major League Prospect Steve Jeltz (R) John Russell (R)	.10	.06
654	Checklist 1-95	.10	.06
655	Checklist 96-195	.10	.06
656	Checklist 196-292	.10	.06
657	Checklist 293-391	.10	.06
658	Checklist 392-481	.10	.06
659	Checklist 482-575	.10	.06
660	Checklist 576-660	.10	.06

1985 Fleer Update

This 132-card update set is identical to Fleer's 1985 regular edition and features players who changed teams during the year and a number of rookie prospects. Card backs contain the letter "U" before the card number. Cards measure 2-1/2" by 3-1/2".

		MINT	NR/MT
Complete Set (132)		38.00	28.00
Commons		.10	.06
1	Don Aase	.12	.07
2	Bill Almon	.10	.06
3	Dusty Baker	.12	.07
4	Dale Berra	.10	.06
5	Karl Best (R)	.10	.06
6	Tim Birtsas (R)	.15	.10
7	Vida Blue	.20	.12
8	Rich Bordi	.10	.06
9	Daryl Boston (R)	.20	.12
10	Hubie Brooks	.20	.12
11	Chris Brown (R)	.10	.06
12	Tom Browning (R)	1.00	.70
13	Al Bumbry	.10	.06
14	Tim Burke (R)	.20	.12
15	Ray Burris	.10	.06
16	Jeff Burroughs	.10	.06
17	Ivan Calderon (R)	1.50	.90

18	Jeff Calhoun	.10	.06
19	Bill Campbell	.10	.06
20	Don Carman (R)	.15	.10
21	Gary Carter	1.00	.70
22	Bobby Castillo	.10	.06
23	Bill Caudill	.10	.06
24	Rick Cerone	.10	.06
25	Jack Clark	.25	.15
26	Pat Clements (R)	.15	.10
27	Stewart Cliburn (R)	.12	.07
28	Vince Coleman (R)	4.50	3.00
29	Dave Collins	.10	.06
30	Fritz Connally	.10	.06
31	Henry Cotto	.10	.06
32	Danny Darwin	.10	.06
33	Darren Daulton (R)	5.00	3.00
34	Jerry Davis	.10	.06
35	Brian Dayett	.10	.06
36	Ken Dixon	.10	.06
37	Tommy Dunbar	.10	.06
38	Mariano Duncan (R)	.60	.35
39	Bob Fallon	.10	.06
40	Brian Fisher (R)	.12	.07
41	Mike Fitzgerald	.10	.06
42	Ray Fontenot	.10	.06
43	Greg Gagne	.35	.20
44	Oscar Gamble	.12	.07
45	Jim Gott	.10	.06
46	David Green	.10	.06
47	Alfredo Griffin	.10	.06
48	Ozzie Guillen	1.50	.90
49	Toby Harrah	.10	.06
50	Ron Hassey	.10	.06
51	Rickey Henderson	4.50	3.00
52	Steve Henderson	.10	.06
53	George Hendrick	.12	.07
54	Teddy Higuera (R)	.35	.20
55	Al Holland	.10	.06
56	Burt Hooton	.10	.06
57	Jay Howell	.10	.06
58	LaMarr Hoyt	.12	.07
59	Tim Hulett (R)	.12	.07
60	Bob James	.10	.06
61	Cliff Johnson	.10	.06
62	Howard Johnson	2.00	1.25
63	Ruppert Jones	.10	.06
64	Steve Kemp	.10	.06
65	Bruce Kison	.10	.06
66	Mike LaCoss	.10	.06
67	Lee Lacy	.10	.06
68	Dave LaPoint	.10	.06
69	Gary Lavelle	.10	.06
70	Vance Law	.10	.06
71	Manny Lee (R)	.30	.18
72	Sixto Lezcano	.10	.06
73	Tim Lollar	.10	.06
74	Urbano Lugo (R)	.10	.06
75	Fred Lynn	.25	.15
76	Steve Lyons (R)	.15	.10
77	Mickey Mahler	.10	.06
78	Ron Mathis	.10	.06
79	Len Matuszek	.10	.06
80	Oddibe McDowell (R)	.15	.10
81	Roger McDowell (R)	.30	.18
82	Donnie Moore	.10	.06
83	Ron Musselman	.10	.06
84	Al Oliver	.25	.15
85	Joe Orsulak (R)	.60	.35
86	Dan Pasqua	.30	.18
87	Chris Pittaro	.10	.06
88	Rick Reuschel	.15	.10
89	Earnie Riles (R)	.15	.10
90	Jerry Royster	.10	.06
91	Dave Rozema	.10	.06
92	Dave Rucker	.10	.06
93	Vern Ruhle	.10	.06
94	Mark Salas (R)	.12	.07
95	Luis Salazar	.10	.06
96	Joe Sambito	.10	.06
97	Billy Sample	.10	.06
98	Alex Sanchez	.10	.06
99	Calvin Schiraldi (R)	.15	.10
100	Rick Schu (R)	.15	.10
101	Larry Sheets (R)	.12	.07
102	Ron Shepherd	.10	.06
103	Nelson Simmons (R)	.12	.07
104	Don Slaught	.10	.06
105	Roy Smalley	.10	.06
106	Lonnie Smith	.20	.12
107	Nate Snell (R)	.10	.06
108	Lary Sorensen	.10	.06
109	Chris Speier	.10	.06
110	Mike Stenhouse	.10	.06
111	Tim Stoddard	.10	.06
112	John Stuper	.10	.06
113	Jim Sundberg	.10	.06
114	Bruce Sutter	.25	.15
115	Don Sutton	.80	.50
116	Bruce Tanner (R)	.10	.06
117	Kent Tekulve	.10	.06
118	Walt Terrell	.10	.06
119	Mickey Tettleton (R)	4.50	3.00
120	Rich Thompson	.10	.06
121	Louis Thornton (R)	.10	.06
122	Alex Trevino	.10	.06
123	John Tudor	.15	.10
124	Jose Uribe (R)	.20	.12
125	Dave Valle (R)	.15	.10
126	Dave Von Ohlen	.10	.06
127	Curt Wardle	.10	.06
128	U.L. Washington	.10	.06
129	Ed Whitson	.10	.06
130	Herm Winningham (R)	.20	.12
131	Rich Yett	.10	.06
132	Checklist	.10	.06

1986 Fleer

The 1986 Fleer set contains 660-cards, each measuring 2-1/2" by 3-1/2". Card fronts feature full color photos framed by dark blue borders. Card backs are vertical with statistics and bio's printed in black and yellow on a white paper stock. The only subset of note is the 10-card Major League Prospects subset (644-653).

		MINT	NR/MT
Complete Set (660)		135.00	85.00
Commons		.08	.05

1	Steve Balboni	.08	.05
2	Joe Beckwith	.08	.05
3	Buddy Biancalana	.08	.05
4	Bud Black	.10	.06
5	George Brett	2.50	1.50
6	Onix Concepcion	.08	.05
7	Steve Farr	.08	.05
8	Mark Gubicza	.20	.12
9	Dane Iorg	.08	.05
10	Danny Jackson	.10	.06
11	Lynn Jones	.08	.05
12	Mike Jones	.08	.05
13	Charlie Leibrandt	.08	.05
14	Hal McRae	.12	.07
15	Omar Moreno	.08	.05
16	Darryl Motley	.08	.05
17	Jorge Orta	.08	.05
18	Dan Quisenberry	.10	.06
19	Bret Saberhagen	1.00	.70
20	Pat Sheridan	.08	.05
21	Lonnie Smith	.10	.06
22	Jim Sundberg	.08	.05
23	John Wathan	.08	.05
24	Frank White	.08	.05
25	Willie Wilson	.10	.06
26	Joaquin Andujar	.10	.06
27	Steve Braun	.08	.05
28	Bill Campbell	.08	.05
29	Cesar Cedeno	.10	.06
30	Jack Clark	.12	.07
31	Vince Coleman	2.00	1.25
32	Danny Cox	.08	.05
33	Ken Dayley	.08	.05
34	Ivan DeJesus	.08	.05
35	Bob Forsch	.08	.05
36	Brian Harper	.15	.10
37	Tom Herr	.08	.05
38	Ricky Horton	.08	.05
39	Kurt Kepshire	.08	.05
40	Jeff Lahti	.08	.05
41	Tito Landrum	.08	.05
42	Willie McGee	.30	.18
43	Tom Nieto	.08	.05
44	Terry Pendleton	2.00	1.25
45	Darrell Porter	.08	.05
46	Ozzie Smith	1.25	.80
47	John Tudor	.10	.06
48	Andy Van Slyke	.80	.50
49	Todd Worrell (R)	.25	.15
50	Jim Acker	.08	.05
51	Doyle Alexander	.08	.05
52	Jesse Barfield	.12	.07
53	George Bell	.75	.45
54	Jeff Burroughs	.08	.05
55	Bill Caudill	.08	.05
56	Jim Clancy	.08	.05
57	Tony Fernandez	.25	.15
58	Tom Filer	.08	.05
59	Damaso Garcia	.08	.05
60	Tom Henke	.20	.12
61	Garth Iorg	.08	.05
62	Cliff Johnson	.08	.05
63	Jimmy Key	.10	.06
64	Dennis Lamp	.08	.05
65	Gary Lavelle	.08	.05
66	Buck Martinez	.08	.05
67	Lloyd Moseby	.08	.05
68	Rance Mulliniks	.08	.05
69	Al Oliver	.15	.10
70	Dave Stieb	.20	.12
71	Louis Thornton	.08	.05
72	Willie Upshaw	.08	.05
73	Ernie Whitt	.08	.05
74	Rick Aguilera (R)	1.25	.80
75	Wally Backman	.08	.05
76	Gary Carter	.40	.25
77	Ron Darling	.15	.10
78	Len Dykstra (R)	1.50	.90
79	Sid Fernandez	.25	.15
80	George Foster	.10	.06
81	Dwight Gooden	1.50	.90
82	Tom Gorman	.08	.05
83	Danny Heep	.08	.05
84	Keith Hernandez	.15	.10
85	Howard Johnson	.80	.50
86	Ray Knight	.10	.06

87	Terry Leach	.08	.05	145	Fernando Valenzuela	.15	.10
88	Ed Lynch	.08	.05	146	Bob Welch	.12	.07
89	Roger McDowell	.20	.12	147	Terry Whitfield	.08	.05
90	Jesse Orosco	.08	.05	148	Juan Beniquez	.08	.05
91	Tom Paciorek	.08	.05	149	Bob Boone	.15	.10
92	Ronn Reynolds	.08	.05	150	John Candelaria	.08	.05
93	Rafael Santana	.08	.05	151	Rod Carew	1.00	.70
94	Doug Sisk	.08	.05	152	Stewart Cliburn	.08	.05
95	Rusty Staub	.12	.07	153	Doug DeCinces	.08	.05
96	Darryl Strawberry	3.50	2.50	154	Brian Downing	.10	.06
97	Mookie Wilson	.10	.06	155	Ken Forsch	.08	.05
98	Neil Allen	.08	.05	156	Craig Gerber	.08	.05
99	Don Baylor	.12	.07	157	Bobby Grich	.10	.06
100	Dale Berra	.08	.05	158	George Hendrick	.10	.06
101	Rich Bordi	.08	.05	159	Al Holland	.08	.05
102	Marty Bystrom	.08	.05	160	Reggie Jackson	1.75	1.00
103	Joe Cowley	.08	.05	161	Ruppert Jones	.08	.05
104	Brian Fisher	.08	.05	162	Urbano Lugo	.08	.05
105	Ken Griffey	.12	.07	163	Kirk McCaskill (R)	.25	.15
106	Ron Guidry	.20	.12	164	Donnie Moore	.08	.05
107	Ron Hassey	.08	.05	165	Gary Pettis	.08	.05
108	Rickey Henderson	3.00	2.00	166	Ron Romanick	.08	.05
109	Don Mattingly	2.75	1.75	167	Dick Schofield	.08	.05
110	Bobby Meacham	.08	.05	168	Daryl Sconiers	.08	.05
111	John Montefusco	.08	.05	169	Jim Slaton	.08	.05
112	Phil Niekro	.50	.30	170	Don Sutton	.30	.18
113	Mike Pagliarulo	.08	.05	171	Mike Witt	.08	.05
114	Dan Pasqua	.12	.07	172	Buddy Bell	.08	.05
115	Willie Randolph	.15	.10	173	Tom Browning	.25	.15
116	Dave Righetti	.12	.07	174	Dave Concepcion	.15	.10
117	Andre Robertson	.08	.05	175	Eric Davis	1.50	.90
118	Billy Sample	.08	.05	176	Bo Diaz	.08	.05
119	Bob Shirley	.08	.05	177	Nick Esasky	.08	.05
120	Ed Whitson	.08	.05	178	John Franco	.20	.12
121	Dave Winfield	1.75	1.00	179	Tom Hume	.08	.05
122	Butch Wynegar	.08	.05	180	Wayne Krenchicki	.08	.05
123	Dave Anderson	.08	.05	181	Andy McGaffigan	.08	.05
124	Bob Bailor	.08	.05	182	Eddie Milner	.08	.05
125	Greg Brock	.08	.05	183	Ron Oester	.08	.05
126	Enos Cabell	.08	.05	184	Dave Parker	.20	.12
127	Bobby Castillo	.08	.05	185	Frank Pastore	.08	.05
128	Carlos Diaz	.08	.05	186	Tony Perez	.40	.25
129	Mariano Duncan	.20	.12	187	Ted Power	.08	.05
130	Pedro Guerrero	.15	.10	188	Joe Price	.08	.05
131	Orel Hershiser	.50	.30	189	Gary Redus	.08	.05
132	Rick Honeycutt	.08	.05	190	Ron Robinson	.08	.05
133	Ken Howell	.08	.05	191	Pete Rose	1.25	.80
134	Ken Landreaux	.08	.05	192	Mario Soto	.08	.05
135	Bill Madlock	.12	.07	193	John Stuper	.08	.05
136	Candy Maldonado	.12	.07	194	Jay Tibbs	.08	.05
137	Mike Marshall	.08	.05	195	Dave Van Gorder	.08	.05
138	Len Matuszek	.08	.05	196	Max Venable	.08	.05
139	Tom Niedenfuer	.08	.05	197	Juan Agosto	.08	.05
140	Alejandro Pena	.12	.07	198	Harold Baines	.20	.12
141	Jerry Reuss	.10	.06	199	Floyd Bannister	.08	.05
142	Bill Russell	.10	.06	200	Britt Burns	.08	.05
143	Steve Sax	.25	.15	201	Julio Cruz	.08	.05
144	Mike Scioscia	.12	.07	202	Joel Davis (R)	.08	.05

203	Richard Dotson	.08	.05
204	Carlton Fisk	1.00	.70
205	Scott Fletcher	.08	.05
206	Ozzie Guillen	.50	.30
207	Jerry Hairston	.08	.05
208	Tim Hulett	.08	.05
209	Bob James	.08	.05
210	Ron Kittle	.08	.05
211	Rudy Law	.10	.06
212	Bryan Little	.08	.05
213	Gene Nelson	.08	.05
214	Reid Nichols	.08	.05
215	Luis Salazar	.08	.05
216	Tom Seaver	1.25	.80
217	Dan Spillner	.08	.05
218	Bruce Tanner	.08	.05
219	Greg Walker	.08	.05
220	Dave Wehrmeister	.08	.05
221	Juan Berenguer	.08	.05
222	Dave Bergman	.08	.05
223	Tom Brookens	.08	.05
224	Darrell Evans	.12	.07
225	Barbaro Garbey	.08	.05
226	Kirk Gibson	.12	.07
227	John Grubb	.08	.05
228	Willie Hernandez	.10	.06
229	Larry Herndon	.08	.05
230	Chet Lemon	.08	.05
231	Aurelio Lopez	.08	.05
232	Jack Morris	.80	.50
233	Randy O'Neal	.08	.05
234	Lance Parrish	.12	.07
235	Dan Petry	.08	.05
236	Alex Sanchez	.08	.05
237	Bill Scherrer	.08	.05
238	Nelson Simmons	.08	.05
239	Frank Tanana	.10	.06
240	Walt Terrell	.08	.05
241	Alan Trammell	.40	.25
242	Lou Whitaker	.20	.12
243	Milt Wilcox	.08	.05
244	Hubie Brooks	.12	.07
245	Tim Burke	.12	.07
246	Andre Dawson	1.25	.80
247	Mike Fitzgerald	.08	.05
248	Terry Francona	.08	.05
249	Bill Gullickson	.10	.06
250	Joe Hesketh	.08	.05
251	Bill Laskey	.08	.05
252	Vance Law	.08	.05
253	Charlie Lea	.08	.05
254	Gary Lucas	.08	.05
255	David Palmer	.08	.05
256	Tim Raines	.25	.15
257	Jeff Reardon	.75	.45
258	Bert Roberge	.08	.05
259	Dan Schatzeder	.08	.05
260	Bryn Smith	.10	.06
261	Randy St. Claire	.08	.05
262	Scot Thompson	.08	.05
263	Tim Wallach	.15	.10
264	U.L. Washington	.08	.05
265	Mitch Webster (R)	.20	.12
266	Herm Winningham	.15	.10
267	Floyd Youmans (R)	.08	.05
268	Don Aase	.08	.05
269	Mike Boddicker	.08	.05
270	Rich Dauer	.08	.05
271	Storm Davis	.08	.05
272	Rick Dempsey	.08	.05
273	Ken Dixon	.08	.05
274	Jim Dwyer	.08	.05
275	Mike Flanagan	.12	.07
276	Wayne Gross	.08	.05
277	Lee Lacy	.08	.05
278	Fred Lynn	.15	.10
279	Tippy Martinez	.08	.05
280	Dennis Martinez	.25	.15
281	Scott McGregor	.08	.05
282	Eddie Murray	1.25	.80
283	Floyd Rayford	.08	.05
284	Cal Ripken, Jr.	6.00	4.00
285	Gary Roenicke	.08	.05
286	Larry Sheets	.08	.05
287	John Shelby	.08	.05
288	Nate Snell	.08	.05
289	Sammy Stewart	.08	.05
290	Alan Wiggins	.08	.05
291	Mike Young	.08	.05
292	Alan Ashby	.08	.05
293	Mark Bailey	.08	.05
294	Kevin Bass	.10	.06
295	Jeff Calhoun	.08	.05
296	Jose Cruz	.12	.07
297	Glenn Davis	.50	.30
298	Bill Dawley	.08	.05
299	Frank DiPino	.08	.05
300	Bill Doran	.10	.06
301	Phil Garner	.10	.06
302	Jeff Heathcock (R)	.08	.05
303	Charlie Kerfeld (R)	.08	.05
304	Bob Knepper	.08	.05
305	Ron Mathis	.08	.05
306	Jerry Mumphrey	.08	.05
307	Jim Pankovits	.08	.05
308	Terry Puhl	.08	.05
309	Craig Reynolds	.08	.05
310	Nolan Ryan	7.50	5.00
311	Mike Scott	.12	.07
312	Dave Smith	.08	.05
313	Dickie Thon	.08	.05
314	Denny Walling	.08	.05
315	Kurt Bevacqua	.08	.05
316	Al Bumbry	.08	.05
317	Jerry Davis	.08	.05
318	Luis Deleon	.08	.05

319	Dave Dravecky	.10	.06	377	Dick Ruthven	.08	.05
320	Tim Flannery	.08	.05	378	Ryne Sandberg	6.00	4.00
321	Steve Garvey	.45	.28	379	Scott Sanderson	.10	.06
322	Goose Gossage	.20	.12	380	Lee Smith	.80	.50
323	Tony Gwynn	3.50	2.50	381	Lary Sorensen	.08	.05
324	Andy Hawkins	.08	.05	382	Chris Speier	.08	.05
325	LaMarr Hoyt	.08	.05	383	Rick Sutcliffe	.15	.10
326	Roy Lee Jackson	.08	.05	384	Steve Trout	.08	.05
327	Terry Kennedy	.08	.05	385	Gary Woods	.08	.05
328	Craig Lefferts	.12	.07	386	Bert Blyleven	.25	.15
329	Carmelo Martinez	.08	.05	387	Tom Brunansky	.12	.07
330	Lance McCullers (R)	.15	.10	388	Randy Bush	.08	.05
331	Kevin McReynolds	.20	.12	389	John Butcher	.08	.05
332	Graig Nettles	.12	.07	390	Ron Davis	.08	.05
333	Jerry Royster	.08	.05	391	Dave Engle	.08	.05
334	Eric Show	.08	.05	392	Frank Eufemia	.08	.05
335	Tim Stoddard	.08	.05	393	Pete Filson	.08	.05
336	Garry Templeton	.10	.06	394	Gary Gaetti	.08	.05
337	Mark Thurmond	.08	.05	395	Greg Gagne	.12	.07
338	Ed Wojna	.08	.05	396	Mickey Hatcher	.08	.05
339	Tony Armas	.08	.05	397	Kent Hrbek	.20	.12
340	Marty Barrett	.08	.05	398	Tim Laudner	.08	.05
341	Wade Boggs	2.00	1.25	399	Rick Lysander	.08	.05
342	Dennis Boyd	.08	.05	400	Dave Meier	.08	.05
343	Bill Buckner	.10	.06	401	Kirby Puckett	12.50	9.00
344	Mark Clear	.08	.05	402	Mark Salas	.08	.05
345	Roger Clemens	14.00	10.00	403	Ken Schrom	.08	.05
346	Steve Crawford	.08	.05	404	Roy Smalley	.08	.05
347	Mike Easler	.08	.05	405	Mike Smithson	.08	.05
348	Dwight Evans	.20	.12	406	Mike Stenhouse	.08	.05
349	Rich Gedman	.08	.05	407	Tim Teufel	.08	.05
350	Jackie Gutierrez	.08	.05	408	Frank Viola	.30	.18
351	Glenn Hoffman	.08	.05	409	Ron Washington	.08	.05
352	Bruce Hurst	.12	.07	410	Keith Atherton	.08	.05
353	Bruce Kison	.08	.05	411	Dusty Baker	.10	.06
354	Tim Lollar	.08	.05	412	Tim Birtsas	.08	.05
355	Steve Lyons	.08	.05	413	Bruce Bochte	.08	.05
356	Al Nipper	.08	.05	414	Chris Codiroli	.08	.05
357	Bob Ojeda	.10	.06	415	Dave Collins	.08	.05
358	Jim Rice	.20	.12	416	Mike Davis	.08	.05
359	Bob Stanley	.08	.05	417	Alfredo Griffin	.08	.05
360	Mike Trujillo	.08	.05	418	Mike Heath	.08	.05
361	Thad Bosley	.08	.05	419	Steve Henderson	.08	.05
362	Warren Brusstar	.08	.05	420	Donnie Hill	.08	.05
363	Ron Cey	.10	.06	421	Jay Howell	.08	.05
364	Jody Davis	.08	.05	422	Tommy John	.15	.10
365	Bob Dernier	.08	.05	423	Dave Kingman	.12	.07
366	Shawon Dunston	.35	.20	424	Bill Krueger	.08	.05
367	Leon Durham	.08	.05	425	Rick Langford	.08	.05
368	Dennis Eckersley	.75	.45	426	Carney Lansford	.12	.07
369	Ray Fontenot	.08	.05	427	Steve McCatty	.08	.05
370	George Frazier	.08	.05	428	Dwayne Murphy	.08	.05
371	Bill Hatcher	.10	.06	429	Steve Ontiveros (R)	.10	.06
372	Dave Lopes	.10	.06	430	Tony Phillips	.10	.06
373	Gary Matthews	.08	.05	431	Jose Rijo	.60	.35
374	Ron Meredith	.08	.05	432	Mickey Tettleton	1.75	1.00
375	Keith Moreland	.08	.05	433	Luis Aguayo	.08	.05
376	Reggie Patterson	.08	.05	434	Larry Andersen	.08	.05

435	Steve Carlton	1.50	.90
436	Don Carman	.08	.05
437	Tim Corcoran	.08	.05
438	Darren Daulton	2.50	1.50
439	John Denny	.08	.05
440	Tom Foley	.08	.05
441	Greg Gross	.08	.05
442	Kevin Gross	.08	.05
443	Von Hayes	.10	.06
444	Charles Hudson	.08	.05
445	Garry Maddox	.08	.05
446	Shane Rawley	.08	.05
447	Dave Rucker	.08	.05
448	John Russell	.08	.05
449	Juan Samuel	.12	.07
450	Mike Schmidt	3.50	2.50
451	Rick Schu	.08	.05
452	Dave Shipanoff	.08	.05
453	Dave Stewart	.20	.12
454	Jeff Stone	.08	.05
455	Kent Tekulve	.08	.05
456	Ozzie Virgil	.08	.05
457	Glenn Wilson	.08	.05
458	Jim Beattie	.08	.05
459	Karl Best	.08	.05
460	Barry Bonnell	.08	.05
461	Phil Bradley	.10	.06
462	Ivan Calderon	.75	.45
463	Al Cowens	.08	.05
464	Alvin Davis	.12	.07
465	Dave Henderson	.12	.07
466	Bob Kearney	.08	.05
467	Mark Langston	.50	.30
468	Bob Long	.08	.05
469	Mike Moore	.10	.06
470	Edwin Nunez	.08	.05
471	Spike Owen	.08	.05
472	Jack Perconte	.08	.05
473	Jim Presley	.08	.05
474	Donnie Scott	.08	.05
475	Bill Swift (R)	.40	.25
476	Danny Tartabull	2.00	1.25
477	Gorman Thomas	.10	.06
478	Roy Thomas	.08	.05
479	Ed Vande Berg	.08	.05
480	Frank Wills	.08	.05
481	Matt Young	.08	.05
482	Ray Burris	.08	.05
483	Jaime Cocanower	.08	.05
484	Cecil Cooper	.10	.06
485	Danny Darwin	.08	.05
486	Rollie Fingers	.60	.35
487	Jim Gantner	.08	.05
488	Bob Gibson	.08	.05
489	Moose Haas	.08	.05
490	Teddy Higuera	.20	.12
491	Paul Householder	.08	.05
492	Pete Ladd	.08	.05
493	Rick Manning	.08	.05
494	Bob McClure	.08	.05
495	Paul Molitor	.60	.35
496	Charlie Moore	.08	.05
497	Ben Oglivie	.08	.05
498	Randy Ready	.08	.05
499	Earnie Riles	.08	.05
500	Ed Romero	.08	.05
501	Bill Schroeder	.08	.05
502	Ray Searage	.08	.05
503	Ted Simmons	.15	.10
504	Pete Vuckovich	.10	.06
505	Rick Waits	.08	.05
506	Robin Yount	2.50	1.50
507	Len Barker	.08	.05
508	Steve Bedrosian	.10	.06
509	Bruce Benedict	.08	.05
510	Rick Camp	.08	.05
511	Rick Cerone	.08	.05
512	Chris Chambliss	.10	.06
513	Jeff Dedmon	.08	.05
514	Terry Forster	.08	.05
515	Gene Garber	.08	.05
516	Terry Harper	.08	.05
517	Bob Horner	.10	.06
518	Glenn Hubbard	.08	.05
519	Joe Johnson	.08	.05
520	Brad Komminsk	.08	.05
521	Rick Mahler	.08	.05
522	Dale Murphy	.60	.35
523	Ken Oberkfell	.08	.05
524	Pascual Perez	.10	.06
525	Gerald Perry	.08	.05
526	Rafael Ramirez	.08	.05
527	Steve Shields (R)	.10	.06
528	Zane Smith	.20	.12
529	Bruce Sutter	.15	.10
530	Milt Thompson (R)	.20	.12
531	Claudell Washington	.08	.05
532	Paul Zuvella	.08	.05
533	Vida Blue	.12	.07
534	Bob Brenly	.08	.05
535	Chris Brown	.08	.05
536	Chili Davis	.12	.07
537	Mark Davis	.08	.05
538	Rob Deer	.20	.12
539	Dan Driessen	.08	.05
540	Scott Garrelts	.08	.05
541	Dan Gladden	.08	.05
542	Jim Gott	.08	.05
543	David Green	.08	.05
544	Atlee Hammaker	.08	.05
545	Mike Jeffcoat	.08	.05
546	Mike Krukow	.08	.05
547	Dave LaPoint	.08	.05
548	Jeff Leonard	.08	.05
549	Greg Minton	.08	.05
550	Alex Trevino	.08	.05

551	Manny Trillo	.08	.05	609	Cecilio Guante	.08	.05
552	Jose Uribe	.15	.10	610	Steve Kemp	.08	.05
553	Brad Wellman	.08	.05	611	Sam Khalifa	.08	.05
554	Frank Williams	.08	.05	612	Lee Mazzilli	.08	.05
555	Joel Youngblood	.08	.05	613	Larry McWilliams	.08	.05
556	Alan Bannister	.08	.05	614	Jim Morrison	.08	.05
557	Glenn Brummer	.08	.05	615	Joe Orsulak	.25	.15
558	Steve Buechele (R)	.75	.45	616	Tony Pena	.10	.06
559	Jose Guzman (R)	.45	.28	617	Johnny Ray	.08	.05
560	Toby Harrah	.08	.05	618	Rick Reuschel	.08	.05
561	Greg Harris	.08	.05	619	R.J. Reynolds	.08	.05
562	Dwayne Henry (R)	.12	.07	620	Rick Rhoden	.08	.05
563	Burt Hooton	.08	.05	621	Don Robinson	.08	.05
564	Charlie Hough	.10	.06	622	Jason Thompson	.08	.05
565	Mike Mason	.08	.05	623	Lee Tunnell	.08	.05
566	Oddibe McDowell	.08	.05	624	Jim Winn	.08	.05
567	Dickie Noles	.08	.05	625	Marvell Wynne	.08	.05
568	Pete O'Brien	.08	.05	626	Dwight Gooden (IA)	.35	.20
569	Larry Parrish	.08	.05	627	Don Mattingly (IA)	1.00	.70
570	Dave Rozema	.08	.05	628	Pete Rose (4,192)	.80	.50
571	Dave Schmidt	.08	.05	629	Rod Carew	.50	.30
572	Don Slaught	.08	.05		(3,000 Hits)		
573	Wayne Tolleson	.08	.05	630	Phil Niekro/	.75	.45
574	Duane Walker	.08	.05		Tom Seaver		
575	Gary Ward	.08	.05		(300 Wins)		
576	Chris Welsh	.08	.05	631	Don Baylor (Ouch!)	.12	.07
577	Curtis Wilkerson	.08	.05	632	Tim Raines/Darryl	.50	.30
578	George Wright	.08	.05		Strawberry		
579	Chris Bando	.08	.05	633	Cal Ripken Jr./Alan	1.75	1.00
580	Tony Bernazard	.08	.05		Trammell		
581	Brett Butler	.25	.15	634	Wade Boggs/George	1.25	.80
582	Ernie Camacho	.08	.05		Brett		
583	Joe Carter	2.50	1.50	635	Bob Horner/Dale	.12	.07
584	Carmelo Castillo	.08	.05		Murphy		
585	Jamie Easterly	.08	.05	636	Vince Coleman/Willie	.20	.12
586	Julio Franco	.45	.28		McGee		
587	Mel Hall	.10	.06	637	Vince Coleman	.15	.10
588	Mike Hargrove	.08	.05		(Terror)		
589	Neal Heaton	.08	.05	638	Dwight Gooden/Pete	.80	.50
590	Brook Jacoby	.08	.05		Rose		
591	Otis Nixon (R)	1.00	.70	639	Wade Boggs/Don	1.00	.70
592	Jerry Reed	.08	.05		Mattingly		
593	Vern Ruhle	.08	.05	640	N.L. West Sluggers	.25	.15
594	Pat Tabler	.08	.05		(Steve Garvey, Dale		
595	Rich Thompson	.08	.05		Murphy, Dave Parker)		
596	Andre Thornton	.10	.06	641	Staff Aces	.15	.10
597	Dave Von Ohlen	.08	.05		(Doc Gooden		
598	George Vukovich	.08	.05		Fernando Valenzuela)		
599	Tom Waddell	.08	.05	642	Jimmy Key/Dave Stieb	.12	.07
600	Curt Wardle	.08	.05	643	Carlton Fisk/Rich	.25	.15
601	Jerry Willard	.08	.05		Gedman		
602	Bill Almon	.08	.05	644	Major League	3.00	2.00
603	Mike Bielecki	.08	.05		Prospect		
604	Sid Bream	.08	.05		Benito Santiago (R)		
605	Mike Brown	.08	.05		Gene Walter (R)		
606	Pat Clements	.08	.05	645	Major League Prospect	.08	.05
607	Jose DeLeon	.08	.05		Colin Ward (R)		
608	Denny Gonzalez	.08	.05		Mike Woodard (R)		

1986 Fleer Update

This 132-card update set mirrors the design of Fleer's regular edition. Cards measure 2-1/2" by 3-1/2" and the numbers on the card backs are preceeded by the letter "U". The set contains players who were traded during the season and a number of key rookie cards.

		MINT	NR/MT
Complete Set (132)		38.00	28.00
Commons		.08	.05
1	Mike Aldrete (R)	.12	.07
2	Andy Allanson (R)	.10	.06
3	Neil Allen	.08	.05
4	Joaquin Andujar	.10	.06
5	Paul Assenmacher (R)	.15	.10
6	Scott Bailes (R)	.10	.06
7	Jay Baller (R)	.10	.06
8	Scott Bankhead (R)	.12	.07
9	Bill Bathe (R)	.10	.06
10	Don Baylor	.12	.07
11	Billy Beane (R)	.10	.06
12	Steve Bedrosian	.10	.06
13	Juan Beniquez	.08	.05
14	Barry Bonds (R)	10.00	7.50
15	Bobby Bonilla (R)	5.00	3.00
16	Rich Bordi	.08	.05
17	Bill Campbell	.08	.05
18	Tom Candiotti	.15	.10
19	John Cangelosi (R)	.12	.07
20	Jose Canseco	8.50	5.50
21	Chuck Cary (R)	.12	.07
22	Juan Castillo (R)	.10	.06
23	Rick Cerone	.08	.05
24	John Cerutti (R)	.15	.10
25	Will Clark (R)	12.50	9.00
26	Mark Clear	.08	.05
27	Darnell Coles (R)	.12	.07
28	Dave Collins	.08	.05

646	Major League Prospect	3.00	2.00
	Kal Daniels (R)		
	Paul O'Neill (R)		
647	Major League Prospect	.40	.25
	Andres Galarraga (R)		
	Fred Toliver (R)		
648	Major League Prospect	.10	.06
	Curt Ford (R)		
	Bob Kipper (R)		
649	Major League Prospects	40.00	32.00
	Jose Canseco (R)		
	Eric Plunk (R)		
650	Major League Prospect	.12	.07
	Mark McLemore (R)		
	Gus Polidor (R)		
651	Major League Prospect	.10	.06
	Mickey Brantley (R)		
	Rob Woodward (R)		
652	Major League Prospect	.08	.05
	Mark Funderburk (R)		
	Billy Joe Robidoux (R)		
653	Major League Prospects	20.00	15.00
	Cecil Fielder (R)		
	Cory Snyder (R)		
654	Checklist 1-97	.10	.06
655	Checklist 98-196	.10	.06
656	Checklist 197-291	.10	.06
657	Checklist 292-385	.10	.06
658	Checklist 386-482	.10	.06
659	Checklist 483-578	.10	.06
660	Checklist 579-660	.10	.06

No.	Name		
29	Tim Conroy	.08	.05
30	Ed Correa (R)	.08	.05
31	Joe Cowley	.08	.05
32	Bill Dawley	.08	.05
33	Rob Deer	.25	.15
34	John Denny	.08	.05
35	Jim Deshaies (R)	.15	.10
36	Doug Drabek (R)	2.00	1.25
37	Mike Easler	.08	.05
38	Mark Eichhorn (R)	.12	.07
39	Dave Engle	.08	.05
40	Mike Fischlin	.08	.05
41	Scott Fletcher	.08	.05
42	Terry Forster	.08	.05
43	Terry Francona	.08	.05
44	Andres Galarraga	.15	.10
45	Lee Guetterman (R)	.12	.07
46	Bill Gullickson	.10	.06
47	Jackie Gutierrez	.08	.05
48	Moose Haas	.08	.05
49	Billy Hatcher	.10	.06
50	Mike Heath	.08	.05
51	Guy Hoffman (R)	.08	.05
52	Tom Hume	.08	.05
53	Pete Incaviglia (R)	.30	.18
54	Dane Iorg	.08	.05
55	Chris James (R)	.15	.10
56	Stan Javier (R)	.12	.07
57	Tommy John	.15	.10
58	Tracy Jones (R)	.10	.06
59	Wally Joyner (R)	1.50	.90
60	Wayne Krenchicki	.08	.05
61	John Kruk (R)	1.25	.80
62	Mike LaCoss	.08	.05
63	Pete Ladd	.08	.05
64	Dave LaPoint	.08	.05
65	Mike LaValliere (R)	.25	.15
66	Rudy Law	.08	.05
67	Dennis Leonard	.08	.05
68	Steve Lombardozzi (R)	.12	.07
69	Aurelio Lopez	.08	.05
70	Mickey Mahler	.08	.05
71	Candy Maldonado	.15	.10
72	Roger Mason (R)	.12	.07
73	Greg Mathews (R)	.10	.06
74	Andy McGaffigan	.08	.05
75	Joel McKeon (R)	.08	.05
76	Kevin Mitchell (R)	2.50	1.50
77	Bill Mooneyham (R)	.08	.05
78	Omar Moreno	.08	.05
79	Jerry Mumphrey	.08	.05
80	Al Newman (R)	.10	.06
81	Phil Niekro	.60	.35
82	Randy Niemann	.08	.05
83	Juan Nieves (R)	.10	.06
84	Bob Ojeda	.10	.06
85	Rick Ownbey	.08	.05
86	Tom Paciorek	.08	.05
87	David Palmer	.08	.05
88	Jeff Parrett (R)	.10	.06
89	Pat Perry (R)	.10	.06
90	Dan Plesac (R)	.15	.10
91	Darrell Porter	.08	.05
92	Luis Quinones (R)	.10	.06
93	Rey Quinonez (R)	.10	.06
94	Gary Redus	.08	.05
95	Jeff Reed (R)	.10	.06
96	Bip Roberts (R)	.80	.50
97	Billy Joe Robidoux (R)	.08	.05
98	Gary Roenicke	.08	.05
99	Ron Roenicke	.08	.05
100	Angel Salazar	.08	.05
101	Joe Sambito	.08	.05
102	Billy Sample	.08	.05
103	Dave Schmidt	.08	.05
104	Ken Schrom	.08	.05
105	Ruben Sierra (R)	8.00	5.50
106	Ted Simmons	.15	.10
107	Sammy Stewart	.08	.05
108	Kurt Stillwell (R)	.15	.10
109	Dale Sveum (R)	.15	.10
110	Tim Teufel	.08	.05
111	Bob Tewksbury (R)	.40	.25
112	Andres Thomas (R)	.10	.06
113	Jason Thompson	.08	.05
114	Milt Thompson	.10	.06
115	Robby Thompson (R)	.50	.30
116	Jay Tibbs	.08	.05
117	Fred Toliver	.08	.05
118	Wayne Tolleson	.08	.05
119	Alex Trevino	.08	.05
120	Manny Trillo	.08	.05
121	Ed Vande Berg	.08	.05
122	Ozzie Virgil	.08	.05
123	Tony Walker (R)	.10	.06
124	Gene Walter	.08	.05
125	Duane Ward (R)	.30	.18
126	Jerry Willard	.08	.05
127	Mitch Williams (R)	.30	.18
128	Reggie Williams (R)	.08	.05
129	Bobby Witt (R)	.70	.40
130	Marvell Wynne	.08	.05
131	Steve Yeager	.08	.05
132	Checklist	.08	.05

1987 Fleer

This 660-card set features full color player photos framed by a blue and white border. The vertical card backs are red, white and blue and includes a unique "scouting report" graphic that addresses the hitter's or pitcher's strengths. Cards measure 2-1/2" by 3-1/2".

		MINT	NR/MT
Complete Set (660)		100.00	70.00
Commons		.07	.04

1	Rick Aguilera	.30	.18
2	Richard Anderson	.07	.04
3	Wally Backman	.07	.04
4	Gary Carter	.30	.18
5	Ron Darling	.12	.07
6	Len Dykstra	.30	.18
7	Kevin Elster (R)	.15	.10
8	Sid Fernandez	.15	.10
9	Dwight Gooden	.90	.60
10	Ed Hearn (R)	.07	.04
11	Danny Heep	.07	.04
12	Keith Hernandez	.12	.07
13	Howard Johnson	.40	.25
14	Ray Knight	.10	.06
15	Lee Mazzilli	.07	.04
16	Roger McDowell	.07	.04
17	Kevin Mitchell	3.50	2.50
18	Randy Niemann	.07	.04
19	Bob Ojeda	.08	.05
20	Jesse Orosco	.07	.04
21	Rafael Santana	.07	.04
22	Doug Sisk	.07	.04
23	Darryl Strawberry	2.50	1.50
24	Tim Teufel	.07	.04
25	Mookie Wilson	.10	.06
26	Tony Armas	.07	.04
27	Marty Barrett	.07	.04
29	Wade Boggs	1.50	.90
30	Oil Can Boyd	.07	.04
31	Bill Buckner	.10	.06
32	Roger Clemens	6.00	4.00
33	Steve Crawford	.07	.04
34	Dwight Evans	.20	.12
36	Dave Henderson	.15	.10
37	Bruce Hurst	.15	.10
38	Tim Lollar	.07	.04
39	Al Nipper	.07	.04
40	Spike Owen	.07	.04
41	Jim Rice	.15	.10
42	Ed Romero	.07	.04
43	Joe Sambito	.07	.04
44	Calvin Schiraldi	.07	.04
45	Tom Seaver	1.25	.80
46	Jeff Sellers (R)	.08	.05
47	Bob Stanley	.07	.04
48	Sammy Stewart	.07	.04
49	Larry Andersen	.07	.04
50	Alan Ashby	.07	.04
51	Kevin Bass	.08	.05
52	Jeff Calhoun	.07	.04
53	Jose Cruz	.12	.07
54	Danny Darwin	.07	.04
55	Glenn Davis	.25	.15
56	Jim Deshaies	.12	.07
57	Bill Doran	.08	.05
58	Phil Garner	.08	.05
59	Billy Hatcher	.10	.06
60	Charlie Kerfeld	.07	.04
61	Bob Knepper	.07	.04
62	Dave Lopes	.10	.06
63	Aurelio Lopez	.07	.04
64	Jim Pankovits	.07	.04
65	Terry Puhl	.07	.04
66	Craig Reynolds	.07	.04
67	Nolan Ryan	6.50	4.50
68	Mike Scott	.12	.07
69	Dave Smith	.07	.04
70	Dickie Thon	.07	.04
71	Tony Walker	.07	.04
72	Denny Walling	.07	.04
73	Bob Boone	.12	.07
74	Rick Burleson	.07	.04
75	John Candelaria	.07	.04
76	Doug Corbett	.07	.04
77	Doug DeCinces	.07	.04
78	Brian Downing	.10	.06
79	Chuck Finley (R)	1.50	.90
80	Terry Forster	.07	.04
81	Bobby Grich	.10	.06
82	George Hendrick	.08	.05
83	Jack Howell (R)	.12	.07
84	Reggie Jackson	1.50	.90
85	Ruppert Jones	.07	.04
86	Wally Joyner	2.50	1.50
87	Gary Lucas	.07	.04
88	Kirk McCaskill	.07	.04
89	Donnie Moore	.07	.04

No.	Player		
90	Gary Pettis	.07	.04
91	Vern Ruhle	.07	.04
92	Dick Scholfield	.07	.04
93	Don Sutton	.40	.25
94	Rob Wilfong	.07	.04
95	Mike Witt	.07	.04
96	Doug Drabek	3.00	2.00
97	Mike Easler	.07	.04
98	Mike Fischlin	.07	.04
99	Brian Fisher	.07	.04
100	Ron Guidry	.15	.10
101	Rickey Henderson	2.00	1.25
102	Tommy John	.12	.07
103	Ron Kittle	.10	.06
104	Don Mattingly	1.75	1.00
105	Bobby Meacham	.07	.04
106	Joe Niekro	.07	.04
107	Mike Pagliarulo	.07	.04
108	Dan Pasqua	.08	.05
109	Willie Randolph	.12	.07
110	Dennis Rasmussen	.07	.04
111	Dave Righetti	.12	.07
112	Gary Roenicke	.07	.04
113	Rod Scurry	.07	.04
114	Bob Shirley	.07	.04
115	Joel Skinner	.07	.04
116	Tim Stoddard	.07	.04
117	Bob Tewksbury	.60	.35
118	Wayne Tolleson	.07	.04
119	Claudell Washington	.07	.04
120	Dave Winfield	1.50	.90
121	Steve Buechele	.10	.06
122	Ed Correa	.07	.04
123	Scott Fletcher	.07	.04
124	Jose Guzman	.08	.05
125	Toby Harrah	.07	.04
126	Greg Harris	.07	.04
127	Charlie Hough	.10	.06
128	Pete Incaviglia	.35	.20
129	Mike Mason	.07	.04
130	Oddibe McDowell	.07	.04
131	Dale Mohorcic (R)	.08	.05
132	Pete O'Brien	.07	.04
133	Tom Paciorek	.07	.04
134	Larry Parrish	.07	.04
135	Geno Petralli	.07	.04
136	Darrell Porter	.07	.04
137	Jeff Russell	.10	.06
138	Ruben Sierra	18.00	13.00
139	Don Slaught	.07	.04
140	Gary Ward	.07	.04
141	Curtis Wilkerson	.07	.04
142	Mitch Williams	.40	.25
143	Bobby Witt	1.00	.70
144	Dave Bergman	.07	.04
145	Tom Brookens	.07	.04
146	Bill Campbell	.07	.04
147	Chuck Cary	.07	.04
148	Darnell Coles	.07	.04
149	Dave Collins	.07	.04
150	Darrell Evans	.12	.07
151	Kirk Gibson	.12	.07
152	John Grubb	.07	.04
153	Willie Hernandez	.08	.05
154	Larry Herndon	.07	.04
155	Eric King	.07	.04
156	Chet Lemon	.07	.04
157	Dwight Lowry	.07	.04
158	Jack Morris	.90	.60
159	Randy O'Neal	.07	.04
160	Lance Parrish	.10	.06
161	Dan Petry	.07	.04
162	Pat Sheridan	.07	.04
163	Jim Slaton	.07	.04
164	Frank Tanana	.08	.05
165	Walt Terrell	.07	.04
166	Mark Thurmond	.07	.04
167	Alan Trammell	.40	.25
168	Lou Whitaker	.25	.15
169	Luis Aguayo	.07	.04
170	Steve Bedrosian	.08	.05
171	Don Carman	.07	.04
172	Darren Daulton	.75	.45
173	Greg Gross	.07	.04
174	Kevin Gross	.07	.04
175	Von Hayes	.07	.04
176	Charles Hudson	.07	.04
177	Tom Hume	.07	.04
178	Steve Jeltz	.07	.04
179	Mike Maddux (R)	.08	.05
180	Shane Rawley	.07	.04
181	Gary Redus	.07	.04
182	Ron Roenicke	.07	.04
183	Bruce Ruffin (R)	.10	.06
184	John Russell	.07	.04
185	Juan Samuel	.10	.06
186	Dan Schatzeder	.07	.04
187	Mike Schmidt	2.75	1.75
188	Rick Schu	.07	.04
189	Jeff Stone	.07	.04
190	Kent Tekulve	.07	.04
191	Milt Thompson	.08	.05
192	Glenn Wilson	.07	.04
193	Buddy Bell	.07	.04
194	Tom Browning	.15	.10
195	Sal Butera	.07	.04
196	Dave Concepcion	.15	.10
197	Kal Daniels	.12	.07
198	Eric Davis	.75	.45
199	John Denny	.07	.04
200	Bo Diaz	.07	.04
201	Nick Esasky	.07	.04
202	John Franco	.15	.10
203	Bill Gullickson	.08	.05
204	Barry Larkin (R)	8.50	5.50
205	Eddie Milner	.07	.04

206	Rob Murphy (R)	.08	.05
207	Ron Oester	.07	.04
208	Dave Parker	.15	.10
209	Tony Perez	.30	.18
210	Ted Power	.07	.04
211	Joe Price	.07	.04
212	Ron Robinson	.07	.04
213	Pete Rose	1.50	.90
214	Mario Soto	.07	.04
215	Kirt Stillwell	.20	.12
216	Max Venable	.07	.04
217	Chris Welsh	.07	.04
218	Carl Willis (R)	.10	.06
219	Jesse Barfield	.12	.07
220	George Bell	.60	.35
221	Bill Caudill	.07	.04
222	John Cerutti	.07	.04
223	Jim Clancy	.07	.04
224	Mark Eichhorn	.07	.04
225	Tony Fernandez	.25	.15
226	Damaso Garcia	.07	.04
227	Kelly Gruber	.40	.25
228	Tom Henke	.12	.07
229	Garth Iorg	.07	.04
230	Cliff Johnson	.07	.04
231	Joe Johnson	.07	.04
232	Jimmy Key	.10	.06
233	Dennis Lamp	.07	.04
234	Rick Leach	.07	.04
235	Buck Martinez	.07	.04
236	Lloyd Moseby	.07	.04
237	Rancy Mulliniks	.07	.04
238	Dave Stieb	.15	.10
239	Willie Upshaw	.07	.04
240	Ernie Whitt	.07	.04
241	Andy Allanson	.07	.04
242	Scott Bailes	.07	.04
243	Chris Bando	.07	.04
244	Tony Bernazard	.07	.04
245	John Butcher	.07	.04
246	Brett Butler	.25	.15
247	Ernie Camacho	.07	.04
248	Tom Candiotti	.10	.06
249	Joe Carter	1.75	1.00
240	Carmen Castillo	.07	.04
251	Julio Franco	.35	.20
252	Mel Hall	.10	.06
253	Brook Jacoby	.07	.04
254	Phil Niekro	.40	.28
255	Otis Nixon	.40	.25
256	Dickie Noles	.07	.04
257	Bryan Oelkers	.07	.04
258	Ken Schrom	.07	.04
259	Don Schulze	.07	.04
260	Cory Snyder	.12	.07
261	Pat Tabler	.07	.04
262	Andre Thornton	.08	.05
263	Rich Yett	.08	.05
264	Mike Aldrete	.08	.05
265	Juan Berenguer	.07	.04
266	Vida Blue	.12	.07
267	Bob Brenly	.07	.04
268	Chris Brown	.07	.04
269	Will Clark	27.00	20.00
270	Chili Davis	.10	.06
271	Mark Davis	.08	.05
272	Kelly Downs (R)	.15	.10
273	Scott Garrelts	.07	.04
274	Dan Gladden	.07	.04
275	Mike Krukow	.07	.04
276	Randy Kutcher	.08	.05
277	Mike LaCoss	.07	.04
278	Jeff Leonard	.07	.04
279	Candy Maldonado	.10	.06
280	Roger Mason	.07	.04
ä281	Bob Melvin (R)	.10	.06
282	Greg Minton	.07	.04
283	Jeff Robinson	.07	.04
284	Harry Spilman	.07	.04
285	Robby Thompson	.50	.30
286	Jose Uribe	.08	.05
287	Frank Williams	.07	.04
288	Joel Youngblood	.07	.04
289	Jack Clark	.15	.10
290	Vince Coleman	.30	.18
291	Tim Conroy	.07	.04
292	Danny Cox	.07	.04
293	Ken Dayley	.07	.04
294	Curt Ford	.07	.04
295	Bob Forsch	.07	.04
296	Tom Herr	.07	.04
297	Ricky Horton	.07	.04
298	Clint Hurdle	.07	.04
299	Jeff Lahti	.07	.04
300	Steve Lake	.07	.04
301	Tito Landrum	.07	.04
302	Mike LaValliere	.07	.04
303	Greg Mathews	.07	.04
304	Willie McGee	.25	.15
305	Jose Oquendo	.07	.04
306	Terry Pendleton	1.00	.70
307	Pat Perry	.07	.04
308	Ozzie Smith	1.00	.70
209	Ray Soff	.07	.04
310	John Tudor	.10	.06
311	Andy Van Slyke	.75	.45
312	Todd Worrell	.10	.06
313	Dann Bilardello	.07	.04
314	Hubie Brooks	.10	.06
315	Tim Burke	.08	.05
316	Andre Dawson	1.00	.70
317	Mike Fitzgerald	.07	.04
318	Tom Foley	.07	.04
319	Andres Galarraga	.12	.07
320	Joe Hesketh	.07	.04
321	Wallace Johnson	.07	.04

#	Name		
322	Wayne Krenchicki	.07	.04
323	Vance Law	.07	.04
324	Dennis Martinez	.20	.12
325	Bob McClure	.07	.04
326	Andy McGaffigan	.07	.04
327	Al Newman	.07	.04
328	Tim Raines	.25	.15
329	Jeff Reardon	.70	.40
330	Luis Rivera (R)	.07	.04
331	Bob Sebra (R)	.08	.05
332	Bryn Smith	.08	.05
333	Jay Tibbs	.07	.04
334	Tim Wallach	.15	.10
335	Mitch Webster	.07	.04
336	Jim Wohlford	.07	.04
337	Floyd Youmans	.07	.04
338	Chris Bosio (R)	.80	.50
339	Glenn Braggs (R)	.25	.15
340	Rick Cerone	.07	.04
341	Mark Clear	.07	.04
342	Bryan Clutterbuck	.07	.04
343	Cecil Cooper	.10	.06
344	Rob Deer	.15	.10
345	Jim Gantner	.07	.04
346	Ted Higuera	.08	.05
347	John Henry Johnson	.07	.04
348	Tim Leary (R)	.15	.10
349	Rick Manning	.07	.04
350	Paul Molitor	.50	.30
351	Charlie Moore	.07	.04
352	Juan Nieves	.07	.04
353	Ben Oglivie	.07	.04
354	Dan Plesac	.15	.10
355	Ernest Riles	.07	.04
356	Billy Joe Robidoux	.07	.04
357	Bill Schroeder	.07	.04
358	Dale Sveum	.10	.06
359	Gorman Thomas	.10	.06
360	Bill Wegman (R)	.15	.10
361	Robin Yount	2.00	1.25
362	Steve Balboni	.07	.04
363	Scott Bankhead	.10	.06
364	Buddy Biancalana	.07	.04
365	Bud Black	.08	.05
366	George Brett	2.00	1.25
367	Steve Farr	.07	.04
368	Mark Gubicza	.20	.12
369	Bo Jackson	7.50	4.50
370	Danny Jackson	.08	.05
371	Mike Kingery	.07	.04
372	Rudy Law	.07	.04
373	Charlie Leibrandt	.08	.05
374	Dennis Leonard	.07	.04
375	Hal McRae	.12	.07
376	Jorge Orta	.07	.04
377	Jamie Quirk	.07	.04
378	Dan Quisenberry	.08	.05
379	Bret Saberhagen	.40	.25
380	Angel Salazar	.07	.04
381	Lonnie Smith	.10	.06
382	Jim Sundberg	.07	.04
383	Frank White	.07	.04
384	Willie Wilson	.10	.06
385	Joaquin Andujar	.08	.05
386	Doug Bair	.07	.04
387	Dusty Baker	.08	.05
388	Bruce Bochte	.07	.04
389	Jose Canseco	10.00	7.00
390	Chris Codiroli	.07	.04
391	Mike Davis	.07	.04
392	Alfredo Griffin	.07	.04
393	Moose Haas	.07	.04
394	Donnie Hill	.07	.04
395	Jay Howell	.08	.05
396	Dave Kingman	.12	.07
397	Carney Lansford	.12	.07
398	David Leiper	.10	.06
399	Bill Mooneyham	.07	.04
400	Dwayne Murphy	.07	.04
401	Steve Ontiveros	.07	.04
402	Tony Phillips	.10	.06
403	Eric Plunk	.07	.04
404	Jose Rijo	.40	.25
405	Terry Steinbach (R)	.60	.35
406	Dave Steward	.25	.15
407	Mickey Tettleton	.30	.18
408	Dave Von Ohlen	.07	.04
409	Jerry Willard	.07	.04
410	Curt Young	.07	.04
411	Bruce Bochy	.07	.04
412	Dave Dravecky	.10	.06
413	Tim Flannery	.07	.04
414	Steve Garvey	.40	.25
415	Goose Gossage	.20	.12
416	Tony Gwynn	2.00	1.25
417	Andy Hawkins	.07	.04
418	LaMarr Hoyt	.07	.04
419	Terry Kennedy	.07	.04
420	John Kruk	3.00	2.00
421	Dave LaPoint	.07	.04
422	Craig Lefferts	.08	.05
423	Carmelo Martinez	.07	.04
424	Lance McCullers	.07	.04
425	Kevin McReynolds	.15	.10
426	Graig Nettles	.10	.06
427	Bip Roberts	1.00	.70
428	Jerry Royster	.07	.04
429	Benito Santiago	.45	.28
430	Eric Show	.07	.04
431	Bob Stoddard	.07	.04
432	Garry Templeton	.08	.05
433	Gene Walter	.07	.04
434	Ed Whitson	.07	.04
435	Marvell Wynne	.07	.04
436	Dave Anderson	.07	.04
437	Greg Brock	.07	.04

438	Enos Cabell	.07	.04
439	Mariano Duncan	.08	.05
440	Pedro Guerrero	.12	.07
441	Orel Hershiser	.30	.18
442	Rick Honeycutt	.07	.04
443	Ken Howell	.07	.04
444	Ken Landreaux	.07	.04
445	Bill Madlock	.12	.07
446	Mike Marshall	.07	.04
447	Len Matuszek	.07	.04
448	Tom Niedenfuer	.07	.04
449	Alejandro Pena	.07	.04
450	Dennis Powell	.08	.05
451	Jerry Reuss	.10	.06
452	Bill Russell	.08	.05
453	Steve Sax	.20	.12
454	Mike Scioscia	.08	.05
455	Franklin Stubbs	.08	.05
456	Alex Trevino	.07	.04
457	Fernando Valenzuela	.20	.12
458	Ed Vande Berg	.07	.04
459	Bob Welch	.12	.07
460	Reggie Williams	.07	.04
461	Don Aase	.07	.04
462	Juan Beniquez	.07	.04
463	Mike Boddicker	.07	.04
464	Juan Bonilla	.07	.04
465	Rich Bordi	.07	.04
466	Storm Davis	.07	.04
467	Rick Dempsey	.07	.04
468	Ken Dixon	.07	.04
469	Jim Dwyer	.07	.04
470	Mike Flanagan	.12	.07
471	Jackie Gutierrez	.07	.04
472	Brad Havens	.07	.04
473	Lee Lacy	.07	.04
474	Fred Lynn	.15	.10
475	Scott McGregor	.07	.04
476	Eddie Murray	1.00	.70
477	Tom O'Malley	.07	.04
478	Cal Ripken, Jr.	4.50	3.50
479	Larry Sheets	.07	.04
480	John Shelby	.07	.04
481	Nate Snell	.07	.04
482	Jim Traber (R)	.07	.04
483	Mike Young	.07	.04
484	Neil Allen	.07	.04
485	Harold Baines	.20	.12
486	Floyd Bannister	.07	.04
487	Daryl Boston	.07	.04
488	Ivan Calderon	.20	.12
489	John Cangelosi	.07	.04
490	Steve Carlton	1.25	.80
491	Joe Cowley	.07	.04
492	Julio Cruz	.07	.04
493	Bill Dawley	.07	.04
494	Jose DeLeon	.07	.04
495	Richard Dotson	.07	.04
496	Carlton Fisk	1.25	.80
497	Ozzie Guillen	.15	.10
498	Jerry Hairston	.07	.04
499	Ron Hassey	.07	.04
500	Tim Hulett	.07	.04
501	Bob James	.07	.04
502	Steve Lyons	.07	.04
503	Joel McKeon	.07	.04
504	Gene Nelson	.07	.04
505	Dave Schmidt	.07	.04
506	Ray Searage	.07	.04
507	Bobby Thigpen (R)	1.00	.70
508	Greg Walker	.07	.04
509	Jim Acker	.07	.04
510	Doyle Alexander	.07	.04
512	Bruce Benedict	.07	.04
513	Chris Chambliss	.10	.06
514	Jeff Dedmon	.07	.04
515	Gene Garber	.07	.04
516	Ken Griffey	.12	.07
517	Terry Harper	.07	.04
518	Bob Horner	.10	.06
520	Rick Mahler	.07	.04
521	Omar Moreno	.07	.04
522	Dale Murphy	.40	.25
523	Ken Oberkfell	.07	.04
524	Ed Olwine	.07	.04
525	David Palmer	.07	.04
526	Rafael Ramirez	.07	.04
527	Billy Sample	.07	.04
528	Ted Simmons	.10	.06
529	Zane Smith	.12	.07
530	Bruce Sutter	.15	.10
531	Andres Thomas	.07	.04
532	Ozzie Virgil	.07	.04
533	Allan Anderson (R)	.15	.10
534	Keith Atherton	.07	.04
535	Billy Beane	.07	.04
536	Bert Blyleven	.30	.18
537	Tom Brunansky	.15	.10
538	Randy Bush	.07	.04
539	George Frazier	.07	.04
540	Gary Gaetti	.07	.04
541	Greg Gagne	.08	.05
542	Mickey Hatcher	.07	.04
543	Neal Heaton	.07	.04
544	Kent Hrbek	.20	.12
545	Roy Lee Jackson	.07	.04
546	Tim Laudner	.07	.04
547	Steve Lombardozzi	.07	.04
548	Mark Portugal (R)	.15	.10
549	Kirby Puckett	5.00	3.00
550	Jeff Reed	.07	.04
551	Mark Salas	.07	.04
552	Roy Smalley	.07	.04
553	Mike Smithson	.07	.04
554	Frank Viola	.25	.15
555	Thad Bosley	.07	.04

556	Ron Cey	.08	.05
557	Jody Davis	.07	.04
558	Ron Davis	.07	.04
559	Bob Dernier	.07	.04
560	Frank DiPino	.07	.04
561	Shawon Dunston	.20	.12
562	Leon Durham	.07	.04
563	Dennis Eckersley	.70	.40
564	Terry Francona	.07	.04
565	Dave Gumpert	.07	.04
566	Guy Hoffman	.07	.04
567	Ed Lynch	.07	.04
568	Gary Matthews	.07	.04
569	Keith Moreland	.07	.04
570	Jamie Moyer	.08	.05
571	Jerry Mumphrey	.07	.04
572	Ryne Sandberg	3.50	2.50
573	Scott Sanderson	.07	.04
574	Lee Smith	.60	.35
575	Chris Speier	.07	.04
576	Rick Sutcliffe	.12	.07
577	Manny Trillo	.07	.04
578	Steve Trout	.07	.04
579	Karl Best	.07	.04
580	Scott Bradley	.07	.04
581	Phil Bradley	.07	.04
582	Mickey Brantley	.07	.04
583	Mike Brown	.07	.04
584	Alvin Davis	.10	.06
585	Lee Guetterman (R)	.12	.07
586	Mark Huismann	.07	.04
587	Bob Kearney	.07	.04
588	Pete Ladd	.07	.04
589	Mark Langston	.40	.25
590	Mike Moore	.10	.06
591	Mike Morgan	.10	.06
592	John Moses	.07	.04
593	Ken Phelps	.07	.04
594	Jim Presley	.07	.04
595	Rey Quinones	.07	.04
596	Harold Reynolds	.15	.10
597	Billy Swift	.15	.10
598	Danny Tartabull	.80	.50
599	Steve Yeager	.07	.04
600	Matt Young	.07	.04
601	Bill Almon	.07	.04
602	Rafael Belliard (R)	.20	.12
603	Mike Bielecki	.07	.04
604	Barry Bonds	18.00	12.50
605	Bobby Bonilla	8.50	5.50
606	Sid Bream	.07	.04
607	Mike Brown	.07	.04
608	Pat Clements	.07	.04
609	Mike Diaz	.07	.04
610	Cecilio Guante	.07	.04
611	Barry Jones (R)	.10	.06
612	Bob Kipper	.07	.04
613	Larry McWilliams	.07	.04
614	Jim Morrison	.07	.04
615	Joe Orsulak	.12	.07
616	Junior Ortiz	.07	.04
617	Tony Pena	.10	.06
618	Johnny Ray	.07	.04
619	Rick Reuschel	.07	.04
620	R.J. Reynolds	.07	.04
621	Rick Rhoden	.07	.04
622	Don Robinson	.07	.04
623	Bob Walk	.07	.04
624	Jim Winn	.07	.04
625	Jose Canseco/Pete Incaviglia	.80	.50
626	Phil Niekro/Don Sutton	.25	.15
627	Don Aase/Dave Righetti	.08	.05
628	Jose Canseco/Wally Joyner	1.25	.80
629	Magic Mets(Gary Carter, Sid Fernandez, Dwight Gooden, Keith Hernandez, Darryl Strawberry)	.25	.15
630	Mike Krukow/Mike Scott	.10	.06
631	John Franco/Fernando Valenzuela	.12 .07	.07 .04
632	Bob Horner(Count 'em)	.08	.05
633	Pitcher's Nightmare (Jose Canseco, Kirby Puckett, Jim Rice)	1.75	1.00
634	Gary Carter/Roger Clemens	.80	.50
635	Steve Carlton (4,000)	.40	.25
636	Glenn Davis/Eddie Murray	.25	.15
637	Wade Boggs/Keith Hernandez	.20	.12
638	Don Mattingly/Darryl Strawberry	.75	.45
639	Dave Parker/Ryne Sandberg	.35	.20
640	Roger Clemens/ Dwight Gooden	1.00	.70
641	Charlie Hough/Mike Witt	.07	.04
642	Tim Raines/Juan Samuel	.10	.06
643	Harold Baines/Jesse Barfield	.12	.07
644	Major League Prospects Dave Clark (R) Greg Swindell (R)	2.50	1.50
645	Major League Prospects Ron Karkovice (R) Russ Morman (R)	.08	.05

646	Major League Prospects Willie Fraser (R) Devon White (R)	.75	.45
647	Major League Prospects Jerry Browne (R) Mike Stanley (R)	.15	.10
648	Major League Prospects Phil Lombardi (R) Dave Magadan (R)	.35	.20
649	Major League Prospects Ralph Bryant (R) Jose Gonzalez (R)	.10	.06
650	Major League Prospects Randy Asadoor (R) Jimmy Jones (R)	.20	.12
651	Major League Prospects Marvin Freeman (R) Tracy Jones (R)	.12	.07
652	Major League Prospects Kevin Seitzer (R) John Stefero (R)	.75	.45
653	Major League Prospects Steve Fireovid (R) Rob Nelson (R)	.08	.05
654	Checklist 1-95	.08	.05
655	Checklist 96-192	.08	.05
656	Checklist 193-288	.08	.05
657	Checklist 289-384	.08	.05
658	Checklist 385-483	.08	.05
659	Checklist 484-578	.08	.05
660	Checklist 579-660	.08	.05

1987 Fleer Update

This 132-card update set is identical to Fleer's regular issue. The 2-1/2" by 3-1/2" cards feature players traded during the season and promising rookies. Card numbers carry the "U" prefix on the card backs.

		MINT	NR/MT
Complete Set (132)		18.00	12.00
Commons		.05	.03
1	Scott Bankhead	.08	.05
2	Eric Bell (R)	.08	.05
3	Juan Beniquez	.05	.03
4	Juan Berenguer	.05	.03
5	Mike Birkbeck (R)	.08	.05
6	Randy Bockus (R)	.10	.06
7	Rod Booker (R)	.07	.04
8	Thad Bosley	.05	.03
9	Greg Brock	.05	.03
10	Bob Brower (R)	.07	.04
11	Chris Brown	.05	.03
12	Jerry Browne	.10	.06
13	Ralph Bryant	.07	.04
14	DeWayne Buice (R)	.07	.04
15	Ellis Burks (R)	.80	.50
16	Casey Candaele (R)	.10	.06
17	Steve Carlton	.75	.45
18	Juan Castillo	.05	.03
19	Chuck Crim (R)	.10	.06
20	Mark Davidson (R)	.10	.06
21	Mark Davis	.08	.05
22	Storm Davis	.05	.03
23	Bill Dawley	.05	.03
24	Andre Dawson	.60	.35
25	Brian Dayett	.05	.03
26	Rick Dempsey	.05	.03
27	Ken Dowell	.05	.03
28	Dave Dravecky	.10	.06
29	Mike Dunne (R)	.10	.06
30	Dennis Eckersley	.50	.30

No.	Player		
31	Cecil Fielder	2.50	1.50
32	Brian Fisher	.05	.03
33	Willie Fraser	.05	.03
34	Ken Gerhart (R)	.05	.03
35	Jim Gott	.05	.03
36	Dan Gladden	.05	.03
37	Mike Greenwell (R)	.80	.50
38	Cecilio Guante	.05	.03
39	Albert Hall	.05	.03
40	Atlee Hammaker	.05	.03
41	Mickey Hatcher	.05	.03
42	Mike Heath	.05	.03
43	Neal Heaton	.05	.03
44	Mike Henneman (R)	.25	.15
45	Guy Hoffman	.05	.03
46	Charles Hudson	.05	.03
47	Chuck Jackson (R)	.10	.06
48	Mike Jackson (R)	.15	.10
49	Reggie Jackson	.90	.60
50	Chris James	.05	.03
51	Dion James	.05	.03
52	Stan Javier	.05	.03
53	Stan Jefferson (R)	.08	.05
54	Jimmy Jones	.05	.03
55	Tracy Jones	.05	.03
56	Terry Kennedy	.05	.03
57	Mike Kingery	.05	.03
58	Ray Knight	.10	.06
59	Gene Larkin (R)	.20	.12
60	Mike LaValliere	.05	.03
61	Jack Lazorko	.05	.03
62	Terry Leach	.05	.03
63	Rick Leach	.05	.03
64	Craig Lefferts	.05	.03
65	Jim Lindeman (R)	.12	.07
66	Bill Long (R)	.12	.07
67	Mike Loynd (R)	.08	.05
68	Greg Maddux (R)	5.00	3.50
69	Bill Madlock	.10	.06
70	Dave Magadan	.15	.10
71	Joe Magrane (R)	.15	.10
72	Fred Manrique (R)	.08	.05
73	Mike Mason	.05	.03
74	Lloyd McClendon (R)	.15	.10
75	Fred McGriff (R)	5.00	3.50
76	Mark McGwire (R)	6.50	4.50
77	Mark McLemore	.05	.03
78	Kevin McReynolds	.15	.10
79	Dave Meads	.07	.04
80	Greg Minton	.05	.03
81	John Mitchell (R)	.08	.05
82	Kevin Mitchell	.75	.45
83	John Morris	.05	.03
84	Jeff Musselman (R)	.10	.06
85	Randy Myers (R)	.15	.10
86	Gene Nelson	.05	.03
87	Joe Niekro	.05	.03
88	Tom Nieto	.05	.03
89	Reid Nichols	.05	.03
90	Matt Nokes (R)	.30	.18
91	Dickie Noles	.05	.03
92	Edwin Nunez	.05	.03
93	Jose Nunez (R)	.08	.05
94	Paul O'Neill	.25	.15
95	Jim Paciorek (R)	.08	.05
96	Lance Parrish	.10	.06
97	Bill Pecota (R)	.12	.07
98	Tony Pena	.10	.06
99	Luis Polonia (R)	.45	.28
100	Randy Ready	.05	.03
101	Jeff Reardon	.35	.20
102	Gary Redus	.05	.03
103	Rick Rhoden	.05	.03
104	Wally Ritchie (R)	.08	.05
105	Jeff Robinson (R)	.08	.05
106	Mark Salas	.05	.03
107	Dave Schmidt	.05	.03
108	Kevin Seitzer	.20	.12
109	John Shelby	.05	.03
110	John Smiley (R)	1.25	.80
111	Lary Sorensen	.05	.03
112	Chris Speier	.05	.03
113	Randy St. Claire	.05	.03
114	Jim Sundberg	.05	.03
115	B.J. Surhoff (R)	.25	.15
116	Greg Swindell	.80	.50
117	Danny Tartabull	.50	.30
118	Dorn Taylor (R)	.08	.05
119	Lee Tunnell	.05	.03
120	Ed Vande Berg	.05	.03
121	Andy Van Slyke	.30	.18
122	Gary Ward	.05	.03
123	Devon White	.25	.15
124	Alan Wiggins	.05	.03
125	Bill Wilkinson	.05	.03
126	Jim Winn	.05	.03
127	Frank Williams	.05	.03
128	Ken Williams (R)	.08	.05
129	Matt Williams (R)	2.50	1.50
130	Herm Winningham	.05	.03
131	Matt Young	.05	.03
132	Checklist 1-132	.05	.03

1988 Fleer

This set consists of 660-cards which measure 2-1/2" by 3-1/2". Card fronts feature full color player photos surrounded by a white frame with diagonal red and blue border stripes. Card backs are red and gray and printed vertically. A new feature at the bottom of the card backs, called "At Their Best", breaks down the player's statistics for home and road games as well as day and night games.

		MINT	NR/MT
Complete Set (660)		36.00	26.00
Commons		.05	.03
1	Keith Atherton	.05	.03
2	Don Baylor	.10	.06
3	Juan Berenguer	.05	.03
4	Bert Blyleven	.15	.10
5	Tom Brunansky	.08	.05
6	Randy Bush	.05	.03
7	Steve Carlton	.60	.35
8	Mark Davidson (R)	.07	.04
9	George Frazier	.05	.03
10	Gary Gaetti	.05	.03
11	Greg Gagne	.07	.04
12	Dan Gladden	.05	.03
13	Kent Hrbek	.12	.07
14	Gene Larkin	.10	.06
15	Tim Laudner	.05	.03
16	Steve Lombardozzi	.05	.03
17	Al Newman	.05	.03
18	Joe Niekro	.05	.03
19	Kirby Puckett	1.50	.90
20	Jeff Reardon	.30	.18
21	Dan Schatzader	.05	.03
22	Roy Smalley	.05	.03
23	Mike Smithson	.05	.03
24	Les Straker (R)	.07	.04
25	Frank Viola	.15	.10
26	Jack Clark	.10	.06
27	Vince Coleman	.12	.07
28	Danny Cox	.05	.03
29	Bill Dawley	.05	.03
30	Ken Dayley	.05	.03
31	Doug DeCinces	.05	.03
32	Curt Ford	.05	.03
33	Bob Forsch	.05	.03
34	David Green	.05	.03
35	Tom Herr	.05	.03
36	Ricky Horton	.05	.03
37	Lance Johnson (R)	.25	.15
38	Steve Lake	.05	.03
39	Jim Lindeman	.05	.03
40	Joe Magrane	.12	.07
41	Greg Mathews	.05	.03
42	Willie McGee	.12	.07
43	John Morris	.05	.03
44	Jose Oquendo	.05	.03
45	Tony Pena	.08	.05
46	Terry Pendleton	.45	.28
47	Ozzie Smith	.50	.30
48	John Tudor	.08	.05
49	Lee Tunnell	.05	.03
50	Todd Worrell	.08	.05
51	Doyle Alexander	.05	.03
52	Dave Bergman	.05	.03
53	Tom Brookens	.05	.03
54	Darrell Evans	.08	.05
55	Kirk Gibson	.12	.07
56	Mike Heath	.05	.03
57	Mike Henneman	.15	.10
58	Willie Hernandez	.07	.04
59	Larry Herndon	.05	.03
60	Eric King	.05	.03
61	Chet Lemon	.05	.03
62	Scott Lusader (R)	.08	.05
63	Bill Madlock	.10	.06
64	Jack Morris	.25	.15
65	Jim Morrison	.05	.03
66	Matt Nokes	.25	.15
67	Dan Petry	.05	.03
68	Jeff Robinson	.08	.05
69	Pat Sheridan	.05	.03
70	Nate Snell	.05	.03
ä71	Frank Tanana	.08	.05
72	Walt Terrell	.05	.03
73	Mark Thurmond	.05	.03
74	Alan Trammell	.25	.15
75	Lou Whitaker	.12	.07
76	Mike Aldrete	.05	.03
77	Bob Brenly	.05	.03
78	Will Clark	2.50	1.50
79	Chili Davis	.10	.06
80	Kelly Downs	.08	.05
81	Dave Dravecky	.08	.05
82	Scott Garrelts	.05	.03
83	Atlee Hammaker	.05	.03

84	Dave Henderson	.10	.06	142	Roger McDowell	.05	.03
85	Mike Krukow	.05	.03	143	Kevin McReynolds	.10	.06
86	Mike LaCoss	.05	.03	144	Keith Miller (R)	.25	.15
87	Craig Lefferts	.05	.03	145	John Mitchell (R)	.07	.04
88	Jeff Leonard	.05	.03	146	Randy Myers	.07	.04
89	Candy Maldonado	.08	.05	147	Bob Ojeda	.07	.04
90	Ed Milner	.05	.03	148	Jesse Orosco	.05	.03
91	Bob Melvin	.05	.03	149	Rafael Santana	.05	.03
92	Kevin Mitchell	.30	.18	150	Doug Sisk	.05	.03
93	Jon Perlman	.05	.03	151	Darryl Strawberry	.75	.45
94	Rick Reuschel	.05	.03	152	Tim Teufel	.05	.03
95	Don Robinson	.05	.03	153	Gene Walter	.05	.03
96	Chris Speier	.05	.03	154	Mookie Wilson	.07	.04
97	Harry Spilman	.05	.03	155	Jay Aldrich	.05	.03
98	Robbie Thompson	.08	.05	156	Chris Bosio	.08	.05
99	Jose Uribe	.05	.03	157	Glenn Braggs	.05	.03
100	Mark Wasinger (R)	.05	.03	158	Greg Brock	.05	.03
101	Matt Williams	2.75	1.75	159	Juan Castillo	.05	.03
102	Jesse Barfield	.08	.05	160	Mark Clear	.05	.03
103	George Bell	.15	.10	161	Cecil Cooper	.08	.05
104	Juan Beniquez	.05	.03	162	Chuck Crim	.05	.03
105	John Cerutti	.05	.03	163	Rob Deer	.07	.04
106	Jim Clancy	.05	.03	164	Mike Felder	.05	.03
107	Rob Ducey (R)	.10	.06	165	Jim Gantner	.05	.03
108	Mark Eichhorn	.05	.03	166	Ted Higuera	.07	.04
109	Tony Fernandez	.12	.07	167	Steve Kiefer	.05	.03
110	Cecil Fielder	.75	.45	168	Rick Manning	.05	.03
111	Kelly Gruber	.15	.10	169	Paul Molitor	.35	.20
112	Tom Henke	.08	.05	170	Juan Nieves	.05	.03
113	Garth Iorg	.05	.03	171	Dan Plesac	.07	.04
114	Jimmy Key	.07	.04	172	Earnest Riles	.05	.03
115	Rick Leach	.05	.03	173	Bill Schroeder	.05	.03
116	Manny Lee	.05	.03	174	Steve Stanicek (R)	.05	.03
117	Nelson Liriano (R)	.10	.06	175	B.J. Surhoff	.08	.05
118	Fred McGriff	2.75	1.75	176	Dale Sveum	.05	.03
119	Lloyd Moseby	.05	.03	177	Bill Wegman	.05	.03
120	Rance Mulliniks	.05	.03	178	Robin Yount	.80	.50
121	Jeff Musselman	.05	.03	179	Hubie Brooks	.08	.05
122	Jose Nunez	.05	.03	180	Tim Burke	.05	.03
123	Dave Stieb	.10	.06	181	Casey Candaele	.05	.03
124	Willie Upshaw	.05	.03	182	Mike Fitgerald	.05	.03
125	Duane Ward(R)	.20	.12	183	Tom Foley	.05	.03
126	Ernie Whitt	.05	.03	184	Andres Galarraga	.10	.06
127	Rick Aguilera	.08	.05	185	Neal Heaton	.05	.03
128	Wally Backman	.05	.03	186	Wallace Johnson	.05	.03
129	Mark Carreon (R)	.12	.07	187	Vance Law	.05	.03
130	Gary Carter	.15	.10	188	Dennis Martinez	.15	.10
131	David Cone (R)	1.50	.90	189	Bob McClure	.05	.03
132	Ron Darling	.08	.05	190	Andy McGaffigan	.05	.03
133	Len Dykstra	.08	.05	191	Reid Nichols	.05	.03
134	Sid Fernandez	.08	.05	192	Pascual Perez	.07	.04
135	Dwight Gooden	.25	.15	193	Tim Raines	.10	.06
136	Keith Hernandez	.08	.05	194	Jeff Reed	.05	.03
137	Gregg Jefferies (R)	2.00	1.25	195	Bob Sebra	.05	.03
138	Howard Johnson	.25	.15	196	Bryn Smith	.05	.03
139	Terry Leach	.05	.03	197	Randy St. Claire	.05	.03
140	Barry Lyons (R)	.08	.05	198	Tim Wallach	.10	.06
141	Dave Magadan	.12	.07	199	Mitch Webster	.05	.03

200	Herm Winningham	.05	.03
201	Floyd Youmans	.05	.03
202	Brad Arnsberg (R)	.08	.05
203	Rick Cerone	.05	.03
204	Pat Clements	.05	.03
205	Henry Cotto	.05	.03
206	Mike Easler	.05	.03
207	Ron Guidry	.10	.06
208	Bill Gullickson	.07	.04
209	Rickey Henderson	.75	.45
210	Charles Hudson	.05	.03
211	Tommy John	.10	.06
212	Roberto Kelly (R)	2.75	1.75
213	Ron Kittle	.07	.04
214	Don Mattingly	.70	.40
215	Bobby Meacham	.05	.03
216	Mike Pagliarulo	.05	.03
217	Dan Pasqua	.05	.03
218	Willie Randolph	.08	.05
219	Rick Rhoden	.05	.03
220	Dave Righetti	.08	.05
221	Jerry Royster	.05	.03
222	Tim Stoddard	.05	.03
223	Wayne Tolleson	.05	.03
224	Gary Ward	.05	.03
225	Claudell Washington	.05	.03
226	Dave Winfield	.75	.45
227	Buddy Bell	.05	.03
228	Tom Browning	.08	.05
229	Dave Concepcion	.12	.07
230	Kal Daniels	.10	.06
231	Eric Davis	.25	.15
232	Bob Diaz	.05	.03
233	Nick Esasky	.05	.03
234	John Franco	.07	.04
235	Guy Hoffman	.05	.03
236	Tom Hume	.05	.03
237	Tracy Jones	.05	.03
238	Bill Landrum (R)	.10	.06
239	Barry Larkin	.60	.35
240	Terry McGriff (R)	.05	.03
241	Rob Murphy	.05	.03
242	Ron Oester	.05	.03
243	Dave Parker	.12	.07
244	Pat Perry	.05	.03
245	Ted Power	.05	.03
246	Dennis Rasmussen	.05	.03
248	Kurt Stillwell	.07	.04
249	Jeff Treadway (R)	.15	.10
250	Frank Williams	.05	.03
251	Steve Balboni	.05	.03
252	Bud Black	.07	.04
253	Thad Bosley	.05	.03
254	George Brett	.80	.50
255	John Davis (R)	.05	.03
256	Steve Farr	.05	.03
257	Gene Garber	.05	.03
258	Jerry Gleaton	.05	.03
259	Mark Gubicza	.10	.06
260	Bo Jackson	.80	.50
261	Danny Jackson	.07	.04
262	Ross Jones	.05	.03
263	Charlie Leibrandt	.05	.03
264	Bill Pecota	.05	.03
265	Melido Perez (R)	.60	.35
266	Jamie Quirk	.05	.03
267	Dan Quisenberry	.07	.04
268	Bret Saberhagen	.20	.12
269	Angel Salazar	.05	.03
270	Kevin Seitzer	.10	.06
271	Danny Tartabull	.40	.25
272	Gary Thurman (R)	.15	.10
273	Frank White	.05	.03
274	Willie Wilson	.07	.04
275	Tony Bernazard	.05	.03
276	Jose Canseco	2.50	1.50
277	Mike Davis	.05	.03
278	Storm Davis	.05	.03
279	Dennis Eckersley	.50	.30
280	Alfredo Griffin	.05	.03
281	Rick Honeycutt	.05	.03
282	Jay Howell	.05	.03
283	Reggie Jackson	.80	.50
284	Dennis Lamp	.05	.03
285	Carney Lansford	.08	.05
286	Mark McGwire	3.50	2.50
287	Dwayne Murphy	.05	.03
288	Gene Nelson	.05	.03
289	Steve Ontiveros	.05	.03
290	Tony Phillips	.07	.04
291	Eric Plunk	.05	.03
292	Luis Polonia	.50	.30
293	Rick Rodriguez (R)	.08	.05
294	Terry Steinbach	.12	.07
295	Dave Stewart	.15	.10
296	Curt Young	.05	.03
297	Luis Aguayo	.05	.03
298	Steve Bedrosian	.05	.03
299	Jeff Calhoun	.05	.03
300	Don Carman	.05	.03
301	Todd Frohwirth (R)	.07	.04
302	Greg Gross	.05	.03
303	Kevin Gross	.05	.03
304	Von Hayes	.05	.03
305	Keith Hughes (R)	.07	.04
306	Mike Jackson	.12	.07
307	Chris James	.05	.03
308	Steve Jeltz	.05	.03
309	Mike Maddux	.05	.03
310	Lance Parrish	.08	.05
311	Shane Rawley	.05	.03
312	Wally Ritchie	.05	.03
313	Bruce Ruffin	.05	.03
314	Juan Samuel	.07	.04
315	Mike Schmidt	1.50	.90
316	Rick Schu	.05	.03

#	Player		
317	Jeff Stone	.05	.03
318	Kent Tekulve	.05	.03
319	Milt Thompson	.05	.03
320	Glenn Wilson	.05	.03
321	Rafael Belliard	.05	.03
322	Barry Bonds	1.50	.90
323	Bobby Bonilla	.70	.40
324	Sid Bream	.05	.03
325	John Cangelosi	.05	.03
326	Mike Diaz	.05	.03
327	Doug Drabek	.25	.15
328	Mike Dunne	.05	.03
329	Brian Fisher	.05	.03
330	Brett Gideon (R)	.05	.03
331	Terry Harper	.05	.03
332	Bob Kipper	.05	.03
333	Mike LaValliere	.05	.03
334	Jose Lind (R)	.25	.15
335	Junior Ortiz	.05	.03
336	Vicente Palacios (R)	.20	.12
338	Al Pedrique (R)	.05	.03
339	R.J. Reynolds	.05	.03
340	John Smiley	1.25	.80
341	Andy Van Slyke	.25	.15
342	Bob Walk	.05	.03
343	Marty Barrett	.05	.03
344	Todd Benzinger (R)	.15	.10
345	Wade Boggs	.60	.35
346	Tom Bolton (R)	.15	.10
347	Oil Can Boyd	.05	.03
348	Ellis Burks	.80	.50
349	Roger Clemens	1.50	.90
350	Steve Crawford	.05	.03
351	Dwight Evans	.12	.07
352	Wes Gardner (R)	.08	.05
353	Rich Gedman	.05	.03
354	Mike Greenwell	.50	.30
355	Sam Horn (R)	.15	.10
356	Bruce Hurst	.10	.06
357	John Marzano (R)	.08	.05
358	Al Nipper	.05	.03
359	Spike Owen	.05	.03
360	Jody Reed (R)	.45	.28
361	Jim Rice	.12	.07
362	Ed Romero	.05	.03
363	Kevin Romine (R)	.07	.04
364	Joe Sambito	.05	.03
365	Calvin Schiraldi	.05	.03
366	Jeff Sellers	.05	.03
367	Bob Stanley	.05	.03
368	Scott Bankhead	.05	.03
369	Phil Bradley	.05	.03
370	Scott Bradley	.05	.03
371	Mickey Brantley	.05	.03
372	Mike Campbell (R)	.05	.03
373	Alvin Davis	.08	.05
374	Lee Guetterman	.05	.03
375	Dave Hengel (R)	.05	.03
376	Mike Kingery	.05	.03
377	Mark Langston	.20	.12
378	Edgar Martinez (R)	4.00	2.75
379	Mike Moore	.05	.03
380	Mike Morgan	.07	.04
381	John Moses	.05	.03
382	Donnell Nixon (R)	.08	.05
383	Edwin Nunez	.05	.03
384	Ken Phelps	.05	.03
385	Jim Presley	.05	.03
386	Rey Quinones	.05	.03
387	Jerry Reed	.05	.03
388	Harold Reynolds	.08	.05
389	Dave Valle	.05	.03
390	Bill Wilkinson	.05	.03
391	Harold Baines	.08	.05
392	Floyd Bannister	.05	.03
393	Daryl Boston	.05	.03
394	Ivan Calderon	.12	.07
395	Jose DeLeon	.05	.03
396	Richard Dotson	.05	.03
397	Carlton Fisk	.60	.35
398	Ozzie Guillen	.10	.06
399	Ron Hassey	.05	.03
400	Donnie Hill	.05	.03
401	Bob James	.05	.03
402	Dave LaPoint	.05	.03
403	Bill Lindsey	.05	.03
404	Bill Long (R)	.07	.04
405	Steve Lyons	.05	.03
406	Fred Manrique	.05	.03
407	Jack McDowell (R)	5.50	4.00
408	Gary Redus	.05	.03
409	Ray Searage	.05	.03
410	Bobby Thigpen	.15	.10
411	Greg Walker	.05	.03
412	Kenny Williams	.05	.03
413	Jim Winn	.05	.03
414	Jody Davis	.05	.03
415	Andre Dawson	.60	.35
416	Brian Dayett	.05	.03
417	Bob Dernier	.05	.03
418	Frank DiPino	.05	.03
419	Shawon Dunston	.15	.10
420	Leon Durham	.05	.03
421	Les Lancaster (R)	.15	.10
422	Ed Lynch	.05	.03
423	Greg Maddux	1.75	1.00
424	Dave Martinez (R)	.12	.07
425a	Keith Moreland (Wrong Photo) (Bunting)	2.50	1.50
425b	Keith Moreland (Cor)	.10	.06
426	Jamie Moyer	.05	.03
427	Jerry Mumphrey	.05	.03
428	Paul Noce (R)	.07	.04
429	Rafael Palmeiro (R)	1.25	.80
430	Wade Rowdon (R)	.05	.03

431	Ryne Sandberg	1.50	.90
432	Scott Sanderson	.07	.04
433	Lee Smith	.35	.20
434	Jim Sundberg	.05	.03
435	Rick Sutcliffe	.08	.05
436	Manny Trillo	.05	.03
437	Juan Agosto	.05	.03
438	Larry Andersen	.05	.03
439	Alan Ashby	.05	.03
440	Kevin Bass	.07	.04
441	Ken Caminiti (R)	.35	.20
442	Rocky Childress (R)	.05	.03
443	Jose Cruz	.08	.05
444	Danny Darwin	.05	.03
445	Glenn Davis	.15	.10
446	Jim Deshaies	.05	.03
447	Bill Doran	.07	.04
448	Ty Gainey	.05	.03
449	Billy Hatcher	.07	.04
450	Jeff Heathcock	.05	.03
451	Bob Knepper	.05	.03
452	Rob Mallicoat (R)	.07	.04
453	Dave Meads	.05	.03
454	Craig Reynolds	.05	.03
455	Nolan Ryan	2.00	1.25
456	Mike Scott	.10	.06
457	Dave Smith	.05	.03
458	Denny Walling	.05	.03
459	Robbie Wine (R)	.05	.03
460	Gerald Young (R)	.12	.07
461	Bob Brower	.05	.03
462a	Jerry Browne	2.50	1.50
	(Wrong Photo)		
462b	Jerry Browne	.10	.06
463	Steve Buechele	.08	.05
464	Edwin Correa	.05	.03
465	Cecil Espy (R)	.15	.10
466	Scott Fletcher	.05	.03
467	Jose Guzman	.05	.03
468	Greg Harris	.05	.03
469	Charlie Hough	.07	.04
470	Pete Incaviglia	.10	.06
471	Paul Kilgus (R)	.07	.04
472	Mike Loynd	.05	.03
473	Oddibe McDowell	.05	.03
474	Dale Mohorcic	.05	.03
475	Pete O'Brien	.05	.03
476	Larry Parrish	.05	.03
477	Geno Petralli	.05	.03
478	Jeff Russell	.07	.04
479	Ruben Sierra	1.25	.80
480	Mike Stanley	.05	.03
481	Curtis Wilkerson	.05	.03
482	Mitch Williams	.07	.04
483	Bobby Witt	.12	.07
484	Tony Armas	.05	.03
485	Bob Boone	.10	.06
486	Bill Buckner	.08	.05
487	DeWayne Buice	.05	.03
488	Brian Downing	.07	.04
489	Chuck Finley	.20	.12
490	Willie Fraser	.05	.03
491	Jack Howell	.05	.03
492	Ruppert Jones	.05	.03
493	Wally Joyner	.25	.15
494	Jack Lazorko	.05	.03
495	Gary Lucas	.05	.03
496	Kirk McCaskill	.05	.03
497	Mark McLemore	.05	.03
498	Darrell Miller	.05	.03
499	Greg Minton	.05	.03
500	Donnie Moore	.05	.03
501	Gus Polidor	.05	.03
502	Johnny Ray	.05	.03
503	Mark Ryal (R)	.05	.03
504	Dick Schofield	.05	.03
505	Don Sutton	.20	.12
506	Devon White	.12	.07
507	Mike Witt	.05	.03
508	Dave Anderson	.05	.03
509	Tim Belcher	.35	.20
510	Ralph Bryant	.05	.03
511	Tim Crews (R)	.12	.07
512	Mike Devereaux (R)	1.50	.90
513	Mariano Duncan	.05	.03
514	Pedro Guerrero	.10	.06
515	Jeff Hamilton (R)	.08	.05
516	Mickey Hatcher	.05	.03
517	Brad Havens	.05	.03
518	Orel Hershiser	.15	.10
519	Shawn Hillegas (R)	.12	.07
520	Ken Howell	.05	.03
521	Tim Leary	.05	.03
522	Mike Marshall	.08	.05
523	Steve Sax	.15	.10
524	Mike Scioscia	.07	.04
525	Mike Sharperson (R)	.10	.06
526	John Shelby	.05	.03
527	Franklin Stubbs	.05	.03
528	Fernando Valenzuela	.12	.07
529	Bob Welch	.08	.05
530	Matt Young	.05	.03
531	Jim Acker	.05	.03
532	Paul Assenmacher	.05	.03
533	Jeff Blauser (R)	.30	.18
534	Joe Boever (R)	.08	.05
535	Martin Clary	.05	.03
536	Kevin Coffman	.05	.03
537	Jeff Dedmon	.05	.03
538	Ron Gant (R)	8.00	5.00
539	Tom Glavine (R)	10.00	7.50
540	Ken Griffey	.08	.05
541	Albert Hall	.05	.03
542	Glenn Hubbard	.05	.03
543	Dion James	.05	.03
544	Dale Murphy	.25	.15

No.	Player		
545	Ken Oberkfell	.05	.03
546	David Palmer	.05	.03
547	Gerald Perry	.05	.03
548	Charlie Puleo	.05	.03
549	Ted Simmons	.08	.05
550	Zane Smith	.10	.06
551	Andres Thomas	.05	.03
552	Ozzie Virgil	.05	.03
553	Don Aase	.05	.03
554	Jeff Ballard (R)	.10	.06
555	Eric Bell	.05	.03
556	Mike Boddicker	.05	.03
557	Ken Dixon	.05	.03
558	Jim Dwyer	.05	.03
559	Ken Gerhart	.05	.03
560	Rene Gonzales (R)	.12	.07
561	Mike Griffin	.05	.03
562	John Habyan	.07	.04
563	Terry Kennedy	.05	.03
564	Ray Knight	.08	.05
565	Lee Lacy	.05	.03
566	Fred Lynn	.15	.10
567	Eddie Murray	.60	.35
568	Tom Niedenfuer	.05	.03
569	Bill Ripken (R)	.15	.10
570	Cal Ripken, Jr.	1.50	.90
571	Dave Schmidt	.05	.03
572	Larry Sheets	.05	.03
573	Pete Stanicek	.05	.03
574	Mark Williamson (R)	.08	.05
575	Mike Young	.05	.03
576	Shawn Abner (R)	.07	.04
577	Greg Booker	.05	.03
578	Chris Brown	.05	.03
579	Keith Comstock	.07	.04
580	Joey Cora (R)	.08	.05
581	Mark Davis	.07	.04
582	Tim Flannery	.05	.03
583	Goose Gossage	.12	.07
584	Mark Grant	.05	.03
585	Tony Gwynn	.75	.45
586	Andy Hawkins	.05	.03
587	Stan Jefferson	.05	.03
588	Jimmy Jones	.05	.03
589	John Kruk	.40	.25
590	Shane Mack (R)	1.50	.90
591	Carmelo Martinez	.05	.03
592	Lance McCullers	.05	.03
593	Eric Nolte (R)	.07	.04
594	Randy Ready	.05	.03
595	Luis Salazar	.05	.03
596	Benito Santiago	.15	.10
597	Eric Show	.05	.03
598	Garry Templeton	.07	.04
599	Ed Whitson	.05	.03
600	Scott Bailes	.05	.03
601	Chris Bando	.05	.03
602	Jay Bell (R)	.75	.45
603	Brett Butler	.15	.10
604	Tom Candiotti	.07	.04
605	Joe Carter	.75	.45
606	Carmen Castillo	.05	.03
607	Brian Dorsett (R)	.07	.04
608	John Farrell (R)	.08	.05
609	Julio Franco	.15	.10
610	Mel Hall	.08	.05
611	Tommy Hinzo	.05	.03
612	Brook Jacoby	.05	.03
613	Doug Jones (R)	.40	.25
614	Ken Schrom	.05	.03
615	Cory Snyder	.07	.04
616	Sammy Stewart	.05	.03
617	Greg Swindell	.15	.10
618	Pat Tabler	.05	.03
619	Ed Vande Berg	.05	.03
620	Eddie Williams	.05	.03
621	Rich Yett	.05	.03
622	Wally Joyner/Cory Snyder	.12	.07
623	George Bell/Pedro Guerrero	.12	.07
624	Jose Canseco/Mark McGwire	1.00	.70
625	Dan Plesac/Dave Righetti	.08	.05
626	Jack Morris/Bret Saberhagen/Mike Witt	.12	.07
627	Steve Bedrosian/John Franco	.08	.05
628	Ryne Sandberg/Ozzie Smith	.75	.45
629	Mark McGwire (RB)	.75	.45
630	Todd Benzinger/Ellis Burks/Mike Greenwell	.15	.10
631	N.L. Batting Champs (Tony Gwynn, Tim Raines)	.25	.15
632	Orel Hershiser/Mike Scott	.12	.07
633	Mark McGwire/Pat Tabler	.40	.25
634	Vince Coleman/Tony Gwynn	.25	.15
635	Tony Fernandez/Cal Ripken, Jr./Alan Trammell	.50	.30
636	Gary Carter/Mike Schmidt	.50	.30
637	Eric Davis/Darryl Strawberry	.25	.15
638	A.L. All Stars(Matt Nokes, Kirby Puckett)	.30	.18
639	N.L. All Stars(Keith Hernandez, Dale Murphy)	.20	.12
640	Bill & Cal Ripken	.60	.35

641	Major League Prospects	4.50	3.50
	Mark Grace (R)		
	Darrin Jackson (R)		
642	Major League Prospects	.60	.35
	Damon Berryhill (R)		
	Jeff Montgomery (R)		
643	Major League Prospects	.05	.03
	Felix Fermin (R)		
	Jessie Reid (R)		
644	Major League Prospects	.05	.03
	Greg Myers (R)		
	Greg Tabor (R)		
645	Major League Prospects	.05	.03
	Jim Eppard (R)		
	Joey Meyer (R)		
646	Major League Prospects	.10	.06
	Adam Peterson (R)		
	Randy Velarde (R)		
647	Major League Prospects	.80	.50
	Chris Gwynn (R)		
	Pete Smith (R)		
648	Major League Prospects	.05	.03
	Greg Jelks (R)		
	Tom Newell (R)		
649	Major League Prospects	.10	.06
	Mario Diaz (R)		
	Clay Parker (R)		
650	Major League Prospects	.05	.03
	Jack Savage (R)		
	Todd Simmons (R)		
651	Major League Prospects	.30	.18
	John Burkett (R)		
	Kirt Manwaring (R)		
652	Major League Prospects	.30	.18
	Dave Otto (R)		
	Walt Weiss (R)		
653	Major League Prospects	.45	.28
	Randall Byers (R)		
	Jeff King (R)		
654	Checklist 1-101	.05	.03
655	Checklist 102-201	.05	.03
656	Checklist 202-296	.05	.03
657	Checklist 297-390	.05	.03
658	Checklist 391-483	.05	.03
659	Checklist 484-575	.05	.03
660	Checklist 576-660	.05	.03

1988 Fleer Update

As in previous years, this 132-card update set features players traded during the season and promising rookies. Cards are identical to the 1988 Fleer regular issue and the numbers on the card backs carry the prefix "U" for Update set. All cards measure 2-1/2" by 3-1/2".

		MINT	NR/MT
Complete Set (132)		17.00	12.00
Commons		.05	.03

1	Jose Bautista (R)	.07	.04
2	Joe Orsulak	.12	.07
3	Doug Sisk	.05	.03
4	Craig Worthington (R)	.07	.04
5	Mike Boddicker	.05	.03
6	Rick Cerone	.05	.03
7	Larry Parrish	.05	.03
8	Lee Smith	.30	.18
9	Mike Smithson	.05	.03
10	John Trautwein (R)	.05	.03
11	Sherman Corbett (R)	.07	.04
12	Chili Davis	.10	.06
13	Jim Eppard	.05	.03
14	Bryan Harvey (R)	.50	.30
15	John Davis	.05	.03
16	Dave Gallagher (R)	.10	.06
17	Ricky Horton	.05	.03
18	Dan Pasqua	.08	.05
19	Melido Perez	.30	.18
20	Jose Segura (R)	.10	.06
21	Andy Allanson	.05	.03
22	Jon Perlman	.05	.03
23	Domingo Ramos	.05	.03
24	Rick Rodriquez	.05	.03
25	Willie Upshaw	.05	.03
26	Paul Gibson (R)	.12	.07
27	Don Heinkel	.05	.03
28	Ray Knight	.08	.05
29	Gary Pettis	.05	.03

30	Luis Salazar	.05	.03
31	Mike Macfarlane	.35	.20
32	Jeff Montgomery	.12	.07
33	Ted Power	.05	.03
34	Israel Sanchez (R)	.05	.03
35	Kurt Stillwell	.08	.05
36	Pat Tabler	.05	.03
37	Don August (R)	.12	.07
38	Darryl Hamilton (R)	.35	.20
39	Jeff Leonard	.08	.05
40	Joey Meyer	.07	.04
41	Allan Anderson	.07	.04
42	Brian Harper	.08	.05
43	Tom Herr	.05	.03
44	Charlie Lea	.05	.03
45	John Moses	.05	.03
46	John Candelaria	.05	.03
47	Jack Clark	.08	.05
48	Richard Dotson	.05	.03
49	Al Leiter (R)	.08	.05
50	Rafael Santana	.05	.03
51	Don Slaught	.05	.03
52	Todd Burns (R)	.12	.07
53	Dave Henderson	.12	.07
54	Doug Jennings (R)	.10	.06
55	Dave Parker	.12	.07
56	Walt Weiss	.15	.10
57	Bob Welch	.10	.06
58	Henry Cotto	.05	.03
59	Mario Diaz	.07	.04
60	Mike Jackson	.12	.07
61	Bill Swift	.15	.10
62	Jose Cecena (R)	.08	.05
63	Ray Hayward (R)	.07	.04
64	Jim Steels (R)	.05	.03
65	Pat Borders (R)	.40	.25
66	Sil Campusano (R)	.10	.06
67	Mike Flanagan	.10	.06
68	Todd Stottlemyre (R)	.60	.35
69	David Wells (R)	.12	.07
70	Jose Alvarez (R)	.08	.05
71	Paul Runge	.05	.03
72	Cesar Jimenez (German) (R)	.05	.03
73	Pete Smith	.40	.25
74	John Smoltz (R)	5.00	3.50
75	Damon Berryhill	.05	.03
76	Goose Gossage	.15	.10
77	Mark Grace	2.00	1.25
78	Darrin Jackson	.20	.12
79	Vance Law	.05	.03
80	Jeff Pico	.10	.06
81	Gary Varsho (R)	.12	.07
82	Tim Birtsas	.05	.03
83	Rob Dibble (R)	.50	.30
84	Danny Jackson	.07	.04
85	Paul O'Neill	.15	.10
86	Jose Rijo	.15	.10
87	Chris Sabo (R)	.80	.50
88	John Fishel (R)	.05	.03
89	Craig Biggio (R)	1.50	.90
90	Terry Puhl	.05	.03
91	Rafael Ramirez	.05	.03
92	Louie Meadows (R)	.05	.03
93	Kirk Gibson	.10	.06
94	Alfredo Griffin	.05	.03
95	Jay Howell	.08	.05
96	Jesse Orosco	.05	.03
97	Alejandro Pena	.08	.05
98	Tracy Woodson	.08	.05
99	John Dopson	.10	.06
100	Brian Holman (R)	.20	.12
101	Rex Hudler (R)	.15	.10
102	Jeff Parrett	.08	.05
103	Nelson Santovenia (R)	.08	.05
104	Kevin Elster	.10	.06
105	Jeff Innis (R)	.10	.06
106	Mackey Sasser	.10	.06
107	Phil Bradley	.08	.05
108	Danny Clay (R)	.05	.03
109	Greg Harris	.05	.03
110	Ricky Jordan (R)	.25	.15
111	David Palmer	.05	.03
112	Jim Gott	.05	.03
113	Tommy Gregg (Wrong Photo)	.08	.05
114	Barry Jones	.08	.05
115	Randy Milligan	.30	.18
116	Luis Alicea (R)	.10	.06
117	Tom Brunansky	.08	.05
118	John Costello (R)	.08	.05
119	Jose DeLeon	.05	.03
120	Bob Horner	.08	.05
121	Scott Terry (R)	.10	.06
122	Roberto Alomar (R)	12.00	9.00
123	Dave Leiper	.05	.03
124	Keith Moreland	.05	.03
125	Mark Parent (R)	.10	.06
126	Dennis Rasmussen	.05	.03
127	Randy Bockus	.05	.03
128	Brett Butler	.12	.07
129	Donell Nixon	.05	.03
130	Earnest Riles	.05	.03
131	Roger Samuels(FC)	.05	.03
132	Checklist	.05	.03

1989 Fleer

This 660-card set features full color photos on the card fronts against a gray and white pinstripe background and yellow borders. The vertical card backs are black, yellow and gray on a white background. All cards measure 2-1/2" by 3-1/2". 12 Bonus All-Star cards were packed randomly in Fleer's wax packs. Those cards are listed at the end of this checklist and numbered B1-B12.

		MINT	NR/MT
Complete Set (660)		22.00	15.00
Commons		.05	.03

1	Don Baylor	.10	.06
2	Lance Blankenship(R)	.12	.07
3	Todd Burns	.07	.04
4	Greg Cadaret (R)	.10	.06
5	Jose Canseco	.50	.30
6	Storm Davis	.05	.03
7	Dennis Eckersley	.15	.10
8	Mike Gallego (R)	.10	.06
9	Ron Hassey	.05	.03
10	Dave Henderson	.08	.05
11	Rick Honeycutt	.05	.03
12	Glenn Hubbard	.05	.03
13	Stan Javier	.05	.03
14	Doug Jennings	.05	.03
15	Felix Jose (R)	.70	.40
16	Carney Lansford	.10	.06
17	Mark McGwire	.45	.28
18	Gene Nelson	.05	.03
19	Dave Parker	.08	.05
20	Eric Plunk	.05	.03
21	Luis Polonia	.08	.05
22	Terry Steinbach	.08	.05
23	Dave Stewart	.12	.07
24	Walt Weiss	.08	.05
25	Bob Welch	.08	.05
26	Curt Young	.05	.03
27	Rick Aguilera	.07	.04
28	Wally Backman	.05	.03
29	Mark Carreon	.08	.05
30	Gary Carter	.10	.06
31	David Cone	.25	.15
32	Ron Darling	.07	.04
33	Len Dykstra	.08	.05
34	Kevin Elster	.05	.03
35	Sid Fernandez	.08	.05
36	Dwight Gooden	.20	.12
37	Keith Hernandez	.08	.05
38	Gregg Jefferies	.25	.15
39	Howard Johnson	.12	.07
40	Terry Leach	.05	.03
41	Dave Magadan	.10	.06
42	Bob McClure	.05	.03
43	Roger McDowell	.05	.03
44	Kevin McReynolds	.10	.06
45	Keith Miller	.05	.03
46	Randy Myers	.07	.04
47	Bob Ojeda	.07	.04
48	Mackey Sasser	.05	.03
49	Darryl Strawberry	.30	.18
50	Tim Teufel	.05	.03
51	Dave West (R)	.12	.07
52	Mookie Wilson	.05	.03
53	Dave Anderson	.05	.03
54	Tim Belcher	.12	.07
55	Mike Davis	.05	.03
56	Mike Devereaux	.20	.12
57	Kirk Gibson	.08	.05
58	Alfredo Griffin	.05	.03
59	Chris Gwynn	.05	.03
60	Jeff Hamilton	.05	.03
61	Danny Heep	.07	.04
62	Orel Hershiser	.12	.07
63	Brian Holton	.05	.03
64	Jay Howell	.05	.03
65	Tim Leary	.05	.03
66	Mike Marshall	.05	.03
67	Ramon Martinez (R)	.50	.30
68	Jesse Orosco	.05	.03
69	Alejandro Pena	.05	.03
70	Steve Sax	.12	.07
71	Mike Scioscia	.07	.04
72	Mike Sharperson	.05	.03
73	John Shelby	.05	.03
74	Franklin Stubbs	.05	.03
75	John Tudor	.05	.03
76	Fernando Valenzuela	.12	.07
77	Tracy Woodson	.05	.03
78	Marty Barrett	.05	.03
79	Todd Benzinger	.05	.03
80	Mike Boddicker	.05	.03
81	Wade Boggs	.25	.15
82	Oil Can Boyd	.05	.03
83	Ellis Burks	.10	.06
84	Rick Cerone	.05	.03

85	Roger Clemens	.60	.35	138	Fred Lynn	.12	.07
86	Steve Curry (R)	.05	.03	139	Jack Morris	.20	.12
87	Dwight Evans	.12	.07	140	Matt Nokes	.07	.04
88	Wes Gardner	.05	.03	141	Gary Pettis	.05	.03
89	Rich Gedman	.05	.03	142	Ted Power	.05	.03
90	Mike Greenwell	.10	.06	143	Jeff Robinson	.05	.03
91	Bruce Hurst	.07	.04	144	Luis Salazar	.05	.03
92	Dennis Lamp	.05	.03	145	Steve Searcy	.07	.04
93	Spike Owen	.05	.03	146	Pat Sheridan	.05	.03
94	Larry Parrish	.05	.03	147	Frank Tanana	.07	.04
95	Carlos Quintana (R)	.15	.10	148	Alan Trammell	.20	.12
96	Jody Reed	.05	.03	149	Walt Terrell	.05	.03
97	Jim Rice	.12	.07	150	Jim Walewander (R)	.07	.04
98	Kevin Romine	.08	.05	151	Lou Whitaker	.10	.06
	(Wrong Photo)			152	Tim Birtsas	.05	.03
99	Lee Smith	.15	.10	153	Tom Browning	.08	.05
100	Mike Smithson	.05	.03	154	Keith Brown (R)	.05	.03
101	Bob Stanley	.05	.03	155	Norm Charlton (R)	.30	.18
102	Allan Anderson	.05	.03	156	Dave Concepcion	.12	.07
103	Keith Atherton	.05	.03	157	Kal Daniels	.07	.04
104	Juan Berenguer	.05	.03	158	Eric Davis	.12	.07
105	Bert Blyleven	.15	.10	159	Bo Diaz	.05	.03
106	Eric Bullock (R)	.07	.04	160	Rob Dibble	.20	.12
107	Randy Bush	.05	.03	161	Nick Esasky	.05	.03
108	John Christensen (R)	.05	.03	162	John Franco	.05	.03
109	Mark Davidson	.05	.03	163	Danny Jackson	.05	.03
110	Gary Gaetti	.05	.03	164	Barry Larkin	.20	.12
111	Greg Gagne	.07	.04	165	Rob Murphy	.05	.03
112	Dan Gladden	.05	.03	166	Paul O'Neill	.12	.07
113	German Gonzalez	.05	.03	167	Jeff Reed	.05	.03
114	Brian Harper	.07	.04	168	Jose Rijo	.12	.07
115	Tom Herr	.05	.03	169	Ron Robinson	.05	.03
116	Kent Hrbek	.10	.06	170	Chris Sabo	.25	.15
117	Gene Larkin	.05	.03	171	Candy Sierra (R)	.05	.03
118	Tim Laudner	.05	.03	172	Van Snider (R)	.08	.05
119	Charlie Lea	.05	.03	173	Jeff Treadway	.07	.04
120	Steve Lombardozzi	.05	.03	174	Frank Williams	.05	.03
121	John Moses	.05	.03	175	Herm Winningham	.05	.03
122	Al Newman	.05	.03	176	Jim Adduci (R)	.05	.03
123	Mark Portugal	.05	.03	177	Don August	.05	.03
124	Kirby Puckett	.50	.30	178	Mike Birkbeck	.05	.03
125	Jeff Reardon	.20	.12	179	Chris Bosio	.08	.05
126	Fred Toliver	.05	.03	180	Glenn Braggs	.05	.03
127	Frank Viola	.12	.07	181	Greg Brock	.05	.03
128	Doyle Alexander	.05	.03	182	Mark Clear	.05	.03
129	Dave Bergman	.05	.03	183	Check Crim	.05	.03
130a	Tom Brookens	.50	.30	184	Rob Deer	.07	.04
	(Wrong Stats On Back)			185	Tom Filer	.05	.03
130b	Tom Brookens(Cor)	.05	.03	186	Jim Gantner	.05	.03
131	Paul Gibson	.05	.03	187	Darryl Hamilton	.08	.05
132a	Mike Heath (Wrong	.50	.30	188	Ted Higuera	.07	.04
	Stats On Back)			189	Odell Jones	.05	.03
132b	Mike Heath (Cor)	.05	.03	190	Jeffrey Leonard	.05	.03
133	Don Heinkel	.05	.03	191	Joey Meyer	.05	.03
134	Mike Henneman	.05	.03	192	Paul Mirabella	.05	.03
135	Guillermo Hernandez	.05	.03	193	Paul Molitor	.15	.10
136	Eric King	.05	.03	194	Charlie O'Brien (R)	.08	.05
137	Chet Lemon	.05	.03	195	Dan Plesac	.05	.03

196	Gary Sheffield (R)	3.50	2.50
197	B.J. Surhoff	.05	.03
198	Dale Sveum	.05	.03
199	Bill Wegman	.05	.03
200	Robin Yount	.35	.20
201	Rafael Belliard	.05	.03
202	Barry Bonds	.50	.30
203	Bobby Bonilla	.20	.12
204	Sid Bream	.05	.03
205	Benny Distefano (R)	.05	.03
206	Doug Drabek	.15	.10
207	Mike Dunne	.05	.03
208	Felix Ferman	.05	.03
209	Brian Fisher	.05	.03
210	Jim Gott	.05	.03
211	Bob Kipper	.05	.03
212	Dave LaPoint	.05	.03
213	Mike LaValliere	.05	.03
214	Jose Lind	.05	.03
215	Junior Ortiz	.05	.03
216	Vicente Palacios	.07	.04
217	Tom Prince (R)	.08	.05
218	Gary Redus	.05	.03
219	R.J. Reynolds	.05	.03
220	Jeff Robinson	.05	.03
221	John Smiley	.15	.10
222	Andy Van Slyke	.15	.10
223	Bob Walk	.05	.03
224	Glenn Wilson	.05	.03
225	Jesse Barfield	.07	.04
226	George Bell	.12	.07
227	Pat Borders	.12	.07
228	John Cerutti	.05	.03
229	Jim Clancy	.05	.03
230	Mark Eichhorn	.05	.03
231	Tony Fernandez	.10	.06
232	Cecil Fielder	.35	.20
233	Mike Flanagan	.05	.03
234	Kelly Gruber	.12	.07
235	Tom Henke	.07	.04
236	Jimmy Key	.07	.04
237	Rick Leach	.05	.03
238	Manny Lee	.05	.03
239	Nelson Liriano	.05	.03
240	Fred McGriff	.35	.20
241	Lloyd Moseby	.05	.03
242	Rance Mulliniks	.05	.03
243	Jeff Musselman	.05	.03
244	Dave Stieb	.10	.06
245	Todd Stottlemyre	.15	.10
246	Duane Ward	.08	.05
247	David Wells	.08	.05
248	Ernie Whitt	.05	.03
249	Luis Aguayo	.05	.03
250	Neil Allen	.05	.03
251	John Candelaria	.05	.03
252	Jack Clark	.08	.05
253	Richard Dotson	.05	.03
254	Rickey Henderson	.35	.20
255	Tommy John	.08	.05
256	Roberto Kelly	.20	.12
257	Al Leiter	.05	.03
258	Don Mattingly	.25	.15
259	Dale Mohorcic	.05	.03
260	Hal Morris (R)	.60	.35
261	Scott Nielsen (R)	.05	.03
262	Mike Pagliarulo	.05	.03
263	Hipolito Pena (R)	.07	.04
264	Ken Phelps	.05	.03
265	Willie Randolph	.08	.05
266	Rick Rhoden	.05	.03
267	Dave Righetti	.07	.04
268	Rafael Santana	.05	.03
269	Steve Shields	.05	.03
270	Joel Skinner	.05	.03
271	Don Slaught	.05	.03
272	Claudell Washington	.05	.03
273	Gary Ward	.05	.03
274	Dave Winfield	.25	.15
275	Luis Aquino (R)	.05	.03
276	Floyd Bannister	.05	.03
277	George Brett	.35	.20
278	Bill Buckner	.08	.05
279	Nick Capra (R)	.05	.03
280	Jose DeJesus (R)	.08	.05
281	Steve Farr	.05	.03
282	Jerry Gleaton	.05	.03
283	Mark Gubicza	.10	.06
284	Tom Gordon (R)	.20	.12
285	Bo Jackson	.20	.12
286	Charlie Leibrandt	.05	.03
287	Mike Macfarlane	.08	.05
288	Jeff Montgomery	.08	.05
289	Bill Pecota	.05	.03
290	Jamie Quirk	.05	.03
291	Bret Saberhagen	.12	.07
292	Kevin Seitzer	.08	.05
293	Kurt Stillwell	.05	.03
294	Pat Tabler	.05	.03
295	Danny Tartabull	.15	.10
296	Gary Thurman	.05	.03
297	Frank White	.05	.03
298	Willie Wilson	.05	.03
299	Roberto Alomar	1.25	.80
300	Sandy Alomar Jr (R)	.20	.12
301	Chris Brown	.05	.03
302	Mike Brumley (R)	.07	.04
303	Mark Davis	.07	.04
304	Mark Grant	.05	.03
305	Tony Gwynn	.30	.18
306	Greg Harris(FC)	.15	.10
307	Andy Hawkins	.05	.03
308	Jimmy Jones	.05	.03
309	John Kruk	.10	.06
310	Dave Leiper	.05	.03
311	Carmelo Martinez	.05	.03

312	Lance McCullers	.05	.03
313	Keith Moreland	.05	.03
314	Dennis Rasmussen	.05	.03
315	Randy Ready	.05	.03
316	Benito Santiago	.12	.07
317	Eric Show	.05	.03
318	Todd Simmons	.05	.03
319	Garry Templeton	.07	.04
320	Dickie Thon	.05	.03
321	Ed Whitson	.05	.03
322	Marvell Wynne	.05	.03
323	Mike Aldrete	.05	.03
324	Brett Butler	.12	.07
325	Will Clark	.50	.30
327	Dave Dravecky	.07	.04
328	Scott Garrelts	.05	.03
329	Atlee Hammaker	.05	.03
330	Charlie Hayes (R)	.15	.10
331	Mike Krukow	.05	.03
332	Craig Lefferts	.05	.03
333	Candy Maldonado	.07	.04
334	Kirt Manwaring	.05	.03
335	Bob Melvin	.05	.03
336	Kevin Mitchell	.12	.07
337	Donell Nixon	.05	.03
338	Tony Perezchica (R)	.07	.04
339	Joe Price	.05	.03
340	Rick Reuschel	.05	.03
341	Earnest Riles	.05	.03
342	Don Robinson	.05	.03
343	Chris Speier	.05	.03
344	Robby Thompson	.07	.04
345	Jose Uribe	.05	.03
346	Matt Williams	.25	.15
347	Trevor Wilson (R)	.15	.10
348	Juan Agosto	.05	.03
349	Larry Andersen	.05	.03
350	Alan Ashby	.05	.03
351	Kevin Bass	.05	.03
352	Buddy Bell	.05	.03
353	Craig Biggio	.35	.20
354	Danny Darwin	.05	.03
355	Glenn Davis	.10	.06
356	Jim Deshaies	.05	.03
357	Bill Doran	.05	.03
358	John Fishel	.05	.03
359	Billy Hatcher	.05	.03
360	Bob Knepper	.05	.03
361	Louie Meadows	.05	.03
362	Dave Meads	.05	.03
363	Jim Pankovits	.05	.03
364	Terry Puhl	.05	.03
365	Rafael Ramirez	.05	.03
366	Craig Reynolds	.05	.03
367	Mike Scott	.08	.05
368	Nolan Ryan	.90	.60
369	Dave Smith	.05	.03
370	Gerald Young	.05	.03
371	Hubie Brooks	.07	.05
372	Tim Burke	.05	.03
373	John Dopson	.05	.03
374	Mike Fitzgerald	.05	.03
375	Tom Foley	.05	.03
376	Andres Galarraga	.08	.05
377	Neal Heaton	.05	.03
378	Joe Hesketh	.05	.03
379	Brian Holman	.08	.05
380	Rex Hudler	.05	.03
381	Randy Johnson (R)	.75	.45
382	Wallace Johnson	.05	.03
383	Tracy Jones	.05	.03
384	Dave Martinez	.05	.03
385	Dennis Martinez	.12	.07
386	Andy McGaffigan	.05	.03
387	Otis Nixon	.08	.05
388	Johnny Paredes (R)	.05	.03
389	Jeff Parrett	.05	.03
390	Pascual Perez	.05	.03
391	Tim Raines	.08	.05
392	Luis Rivera	.05	.03
393	Nelson Santovenia	.05	.03
394	Bryn Smith	.05	.03
395	Tim Wallach	.08	.05
396	Andy Allanson	.05	.03
297	Rod Allen	.05	.03
298	Scott Bailes	.05	.03
399	Tom Candiotti	.07	.04
400	Joe Carter	.25	.15
401	Carmen Castillo	.05	.03
402	Dave Clark	.05	.03
403	John Farrell	.05	.03
404	Julio Franco	.12	.07
405	Don Gordon	.05	.03
406	Mel Hall	.07	.04
407	Brad Havens	.05	.03
408	Brook Jacoby	.05	.03
409	Doug Jones	.05	.03
410	Jeff Kaiser (R)	.07	.04
411	Luis Medina (R)	.08	.05
412	Cory Snyder	.07	.04
413	Greg Swindell	.10	.06
414	Ron Tingley (R)	.08	.05
415	Willie Upshaw	.05	.03
416	Ron Washington	.05	.03
417	Rich Yett	.05	.03
418	Damon Berryhill	.05	.03
419	Mike Bielecki	.05	.03
420	Doug Dascenzo (R)	.12	.07
421	Jody Davis	.05	.03
422	Andre Dawson	.20	.12
423	Frank DiPino	.05	.03
424	Shawon Dunston	.10	.06
425	Goose Gossage	.08	.05
426	Mark Grace	.25	.15
427	Mike Harkey (R)	.20	.12
428	Darrin Jackson	.08	.05

429	Les Lancaster	.07	.04
430	Vance Law	.05	.03
431	Greg Maddux	.30	.18
432	Jamie Moyer	.05	.03
433	Al Nipper	.05	.03
434	Rafael Palmeiro	.25	.15
435	Pat Perry	.05	.03
436	Jeff Pico	.05	.03
437	Ryne Sandberg	.50	.30
438	Calvin Schiraldi	.05	.03
439	Rick Sutcliffe	.08	.05
440	Manny Trillo	.05	.03
441	Gary Varsho	.05	.03
442	Mitch Webster	.05	.03
443	Luis Alicea	.10	.06
444	Tom Brunansky	.08	.05
445	Vince Coleman	.10	.06
446	John Costello	.05	.03
447	Danny Cox	.05	.03
448	Ken Dayley	.05	.03
449	Jose DeLeon	.05	.03
450	Curt Ford	.05	.03
451	Pedro Guerrero	.10	.06
452	Bob Horner	.08	.05
453	Tim Jones (R)	.08	.05
454	Steve Lake	.05	.03
455	Joe Magrane	.08	.05
456	Greg Mathews	.05	.03
457	Willie McGee	.10	.06
458	Larry McWilliams	.05	.03
459	Jose Oquendo	.05	.03
460	Tony Pena	.07	.04
461	Terry Pendleton	.20	.12
462	Steve Peters (R)	.08	.05
463	Ozzie Smith	.20	.12
464	Scott Terry	.05	.03
465	Denny Walling	.05	.03
466	Todd Worrell	.07	.04
467	Tony Armas	.05	.03
468	Dante Bichette (R)	.15	.10
469	Bob Boone	.10	.06
470	Terry Clark (R)	.10	.06
471	Stew Cliburn	.05	.03
472	Mike Cook	.05	.03
473	Sherman Corbett	.05	.03
474	Chili Davis	.08	.05
475	Brian Downing	.07	.04
476	Jim Eppard	.05	.03
477	Chuck Finley	.15	.10
478	Willie Fraser	.05	.03
479	Bryan Harvey	.15	.10
480	Jack Howell	.05	.03
481	Wally Joyner	.12	.07
482	Jack Lazorko	.05	.03
483	Kirk McCaskill	.05	.03
484	Mark McLemore	.05	.03
485	Greg Minton	.05	.03
486	Dan Petry	.05	.03
487	Johnny Ray	.05	.03
488	Dick Schofield	.05	.03
489	Devon White	.07	.04
490	Mike Witt	.05	.03
491	Harold Baines	.08	.05
492	Daryl Boston	.05	.03
493	Ivan Calderon	.08	.05
494	Mike Diaz	.05	.03
495	Carlton Fisk	.20	.12
496	Dave Gallagher	.05	.03
497	Ozzie Guillen	.08	.05
498	Shawn Hillegas	.05	.03
499	Lance Johnson	.05	.03
500	Barry Jones	.05	.03
501	Bill Long	.05	.03
502	Steve Lyons	.05	.03
503	Fred Manrique	.05	.03
504	Jack McDowell	.50	.30
505	Donn Pall	.05	.03
506	Kelly Paris	.05	.03
507	Dan Pasqua	.05	.03
508	Ken Patterson	.05	.03
509	Melido Perez	.08	.05
510	Jerry Reuss	.05	.03
511	Mark Salas	.05	.03
512	Bobby Thigpen	.10	.06
513	Mike Woodard	.05	.03
514	Bob Brower	.05	.03
515	Steve Buechele	.07	.04
516	Jose Cecena	.05	.03
517	Cecil Espy	.05	.03
518	Scott Fletcher	.05	.03
519	Cecilio Guante	.05	.03
520	Jose Guzman	.05	.03
521	Ray Hayward	.05	.03
522	Charlie Hough	.07	.04
523	Pete Incaviglia	.08	.05
524	Mike Jeffcoat	.05	.03
525	Paul Kilgus	.05	.03
526	Chad Kreuter	.07	.04
527	Jeff Kunkel	.05	.03
528	Oddibe McDowell	.05	.03
529	Pete O'Brien	.05	.03
530	Geno Petralli	.05	.03
531	Jeff Russell	.07	.04
532	Ruben Sierra	.40	.25
533	Mike Stanley	.05	.03
534	Ed Vande Berg	.05	.03
535	Curtis Wilkerson	.05	.03
536	Mitch Williams	.05	.03
537	Bobby Witt	.10	.06
538	Steve Balboni	.05	.03
539	Scott Bankhead	.05	.03
540	Scott Bradley	.05	.03
541	Mickey Brantley	.05	.03
542	Jay Buhner (R)	.20	.12
543	Mike Campbell	.05	.03
544	Darnell Coles	.05	.03

545	Henry Cotto	.05	.03
546	Alvin Davis	.05	.03
547	Mario Diaz	.05	.03
548	Ken Griffey, Jr. (R)	8.00	5.50
549	Erik Hanson (R)	.25	.15
550	Mike Jackson	.05	.03
551	Mark Langston	.15	.10
552	Edgar Martinez	.75	.45
553	Bill McGuire	.05	.03
554	Mike Moore	.05	.03
555	Jim Presley	.05	.03
556	Rey Quinones	.05	.03
557	Jerry Reed	.05	.03
558	Harold Reynolds	.07	.04
559	Mike Schooler	.12	.07
560	Bill Swift	.08	.05
561	Dave Valle	.05	.03
562	Steve Bedrosian	.05	.03
563	Phil Bradley	.05	.03
564	Don Carman	.05	.03
565	Bob Dernier	.05	.03
566	Marvin Freeman	.05	.03
567	Todd Frohwirth	.05	.03
568	Greg Gross	.05	.03
569	Kevin Gross	.05	.03
570	Greg Harris	.05	.03
571	Von Hayes	.05	.03
572	Chris James	.05	.03
573	Steve Jeltz	.05	.03
574	Ron Jones (R)	.08	.05
575	Ricky Jordan	.12	.07
576	Mike Maddux	.05	.03
577	David Palmer	.05	.03
578	Lance Parrish	.07	.04
579	Shane Rawley	.05	.03
580	Bruce Ruffin	.05	.03
581	Juan Samuel	.05	.03
582	Mike Schmidt	.60	.35
583	Kent Tekulve	.05	.03
584	Milt Thompson	.05	.03
585	Jose Alvarez	.05	.03
586	Paul Assenmacher	.05	.03
587	Bruce Benedict	.05	.03
588	Jeff Blauser	.05	.03
589	Terry Blocker (R)	.05	.03
590	Ron Gant	.60	.35
591	Tom Glavine	.75	.45
592	Tommy Gregg	.05	.03
593	Albert Hall	.05	.03
594	Dion James	.05	.03
595	Rick Mahler	.05	.03
596	Dale Murphy	.15	.10
597	Gerald Perry	.05	.03
598	Charlie Puleo	.05	.03
599	Ted Simmons	.05	.03
600	Pete Smith	.15	.10
601	Zane Smith	.07	.04
602	John Smoltz	1.00	.70
603	Bruce Sutter	.10	.06
604	Andres Thomas	.05	.03
605	Ozzie Virgil	.05	.03
606	Brady Anderson (R)	.75	.45
607	Jeff Ballard	.05	.03
608	Jose Bautista	.05	.03
609	Ken Gerhart	.05	.03
610	Terry Kennedy	.05	.03
611	Eddie Murray	.20	.12
612	Carl Nichols (R)	.05	.03
613	Tom Niedenfuer	.05	.03
614	Joe Orsulak	.08	.05
615	Oswald Peraza (R)	.07	.04
616a	Bill Ripken (Er) (Obscenity on bat)	14.00	10.00
616b	Bill Ripken (Er) (Scratched out)	12.00	9.00
616c	Bill Ripken (Er) (Blacked out)	.50	.30
616d	Bill Ripken (Er) (Whiteout)	30.00	20.00
617	Cal Ripken, Jr.	.75	.45
618	Dave Schmidt	.05	.03
619	Rick Schu	.05	.03
620	Larry Sheets	.05	.03
621	Doug Sisk	.05	.03
622	Pete Stanicek	.05	.03
623	Mickey Tettleton	.08	.05
624	Jay Tibbs	.05	.03
625	Jim Traber	.05	.03
626	Mark Williamson	.05	.03
627	Craig Worthington	.05	.03
628	Speed and Power (Jose Canseco)	.30	.18
629	Pitcher Perfect (Tom Browning)	.05	.03
630	Roberto & Sandy Alomar Jr.	.60	.35
631	N.L. All-Stars (Will Clark, Rafael Palmeiro)	.25	.15
632	Will Clark/Darryl Strawberry	.30	.18
633	Wade Boggs/Carney Lansford	.15	.10
634	Jose Canseco/Mark McGwire/Terry Steinbach	.50	.30
635	Mark Davis/Dwight Gooden	.12	.07
636	David Cone/Danny Jackson	.12	.07
637	Bobby Bonilla/Chris Sabo	.12	.07
638	Andres Galarraga/ Gerald Perry	.08	.05
639	Eric Davis/Kirby Puckett	.25	.15

640	Major League Prospects Cameron Drew (R) Steve Wilson (R)	.08	.05
641	Major League Prospects Kevin Brown (R) Kevin Reimer (R)	.80	.50
642	Major League Prospects Jerald Clark (R) Brad Pounders (R)	.15	.10
643	Major League Prospects Mike Capel (R) Drew Hall (R)	.10	.06
644	Major League Prospects Joe Girardi (R) Rolando Roomes (R)	.12	.07
645	Major League Prospects Marty Brown (R) Lenny Harris (R)	.12	.07
646	Major League Prospects Luis de los Santos (R) Jim Campbell (R)	.07	.04
647	Major League Prospects Miguel Garcia (R) Randy Kramer	.08	.05
648	Major League Prospects Torey Lovullo (R) Robert Palacios (R)	.08	.05
649	Major League Prospects Jim Corsi Bob Milacki (R)	.15	.10
650	Major League Prospects Grady Hall (R) Mike Rochford (R)	.07	.04
651	Major League Prospects Vance Lovelace (R) Terry Taylor (R)	.07	.04
652	Major League Prospects Dennis Cook (R) Ken Hill (R)	.60	.35
653	Major League Prospects Scott Service (R) Shane Turner (R)	.08	.05
654	Checklist 1-101	.05	.03
655	Checklist 102-200	.05	.03
656	Checklist 201-298	.05	.03
657	Checklist 299-395	.05	.03
658	Checklist 396-490	.05	.03
659	Checklist 491-584	.05	.03
660	Checklist 585-660	.05	.03
B1	Bobby Bonilla (AS)	1.00	.70
B2	Jose Canseco (AS)	2.50	1.50
B3	Will Clark (AS)	2.00	1.25
B4	Dennis Eckersley(AS)	1.00	.70
B5	Julio Franco (AS)	.50	.30
B6	Mike Greenwell (AS)	.50	.30
B7	Orel Hershiser (AS)	.75	.45
B8	Paul Molitor (AS)	.75	.45
B9	Mike Scioscia (AS)	.25	.15
B10	Darryl Strawberry (AS)	1.50	.90
B11	Alan Trammell (AS)	.75	.45
B12	Frank Viola (AS)	.50	.30

1989 Fleer Update

This 132-card set updates players who were traded during the year and features a number of promising newcomers. The cards measure 2-1/2" by 3-1/2" and are identical to the design of Fleer's regular 1989 edition. Card backs are numbered with the letter "U" to distinguish the set from the regular issue.

		MINT	NR/MT
Complete Set (132)		12.00	8.00
Commons		.05	.03
1	Phil Bradley	.07	.04
2	Mike Devereaux	.20	.12
3	Steve Finley (R)	.25	.15
4	Kevin Hickey	.05	.03
5	Brian Holton	.07	.04

No.	Player		
6	Bob Milacki	.10	.06
7	Randy Milligan	.10	.06
8	John Dopson	.07	.04
9	Nick Esasky	.05	.03
10	Rob Murphy	.05	.03
11	Jim Abbott (R)	2.00	1.25
12	Bert Blyleven	.15	.10
13	Jeff Manto (R)	.10	.06
14	Bob McClure	.05	.03
15	Lance Parrish	.07	.04
16	Lee Stevens (R)	.20	.12
17	Claudell Washington	.05	.03
18	Mark Davis	.07	.04
19	Eric King	.05	.03
20	Ron Kittle	.05	.03
21	Matt Merullo (R)	.10	.06
22	Steve Rosenberg (R)	.07	.04
23	Robin Ventura (R)	3.00	2.00
24	Keith Atherton	.05	.03
25	Joey Belle (R)	2.50	1.50
26	Jerry Browne	.05	.03
27	Felix Fermin	.05	.03
28	Brad Komminsk	.05	.03
29	Pete O'Brien	.05	.03
30	Mike Brumley	.05	.03
31	Tracy Jones	.05	.03
32	Mike Schwabe (R)	.07	.04
33	Gary Ward	.05	.03
34	Frank Williams	.05	.03
35	Kevin Appier (R)	1.50	.90
36	Bob Boone	.12	.07
37	Luis de los Santos	.07	.04
38	Jim Eisenreich (R)	.12	.07
39	Jaime Navarro (R)	.80	.50
40	Bill Spiers (R)	.12	.07
41	Greg Vaughn (R)	.60	.35
42	Randy Veres (R)	.07	.04
43	Wally Backman	.05	.03
44	Shane Rawley	.05	.03
45	Steve Balboni	.05	.03
46	Jesse Barfield	.08	.05
47	Alvaro Espinoza (R)	.10	.06
48	Bob Geren (R)	.10	.06
49	Mel Hall	.08	.05
50	Andy Hawkins	.05	.03
51	Hensley Meulens (R)	.15	.10
52	Steve Sax	.15	.10
53	Deion Sanders (R)	2.00	1.25
54	Rickey Henderson	.40	.25
55	Mike Moore	.08	.05
56	Tony Phillips	.07	.04
57	Greg Briley	.08	.05
58	Gene Harris	.08	.05
59	Randy Johnson	.25	.15
60	Jeffrey Leonard	.05	.03
61	Dennis Powell	.05	.03
62	Omar Vizquel (R)	.08	.05
63	Kevin Brown	.35	.20
64	Julio Franco	.12	.07
65	Jamie Moyer	.05	.03
66	Rafael Palmeiro	.20	.12
67	Nolan Ryan	2.00	1.25
68	Francisco Cabrera (R)	.15	.10
69	Junior Felix (R)	.15	.10
70	Al Leiter	.05	.03
71	Alex Sanchez (R)	.08	.05
72	Geronimo Berroa	.05	.03
73	Derek Lilliquist (R)	.08	.05
74	Lonnie Smith	.10	.06
75	Jeff Treadway	.08	.05
76	Paul Kilgus	.05	.03
77	Lloyd McClendon	.05	.03
78	Scott Sanderson	.07	.04
79	Dwight Smith (R)	.10	.06
80	Jerome Walton (R)	.10	.06
81	Mitch Williams	.08	.05
82	Steve Wilson	.07	.04
83	Todd Benzinger	.08	.05
84	Ken Griffey	.12	.07
85	Rick Mahler	.05	.03
86	Rolando Roomes	.05	.03
87	Scott Scudder (R)	.15	.10
88	Jim Clancy	.05	.03
89	Rick Rhoden	.05	.03
90	Dan Schatzeder	.05	.03
91	Mike Morgan	.07	.04
92	Eddie Murray	.20	.12
93	Willie Randolph	.08	.05
94	Ray Searage	.05	.03
95	Mike Aldrete	.05	.03
96	Kevin Gross	.07	.04
97	Mark Langston	.12	.07
98	Spike Owen	.05	.03
99	Zane Smith	.08	.05
100	Don Aase	.05	.03
101	Barry Lyons	.05	.03
102	Juan Samuel	.05	.03
103	Wally Whitehurst (R)	.12	.07
104	Dennis Cook	.05	.03
105	Lenny Dykstra	.10	.06
106	Charlie Hayes	.10	.06
107	Tommy Herr	.05	.03
108	Ken Howell	.05	.03
109	John Kruk	.10	.06
110	Roger McDowell	.05	.03
111	Terry Mulholland	.12	.07
112	Jeff Parrett	.05	.03
113	Neal Heaton	.05	.03
114	Jeff King	.12	.07
115	Randy Kramer	.05	.03
116	Bill Landrum	.05	.03
117	Cris Carpenter (R)	.12	.07
118	Frank DiPino	.05	.03
119	Ken Hill	.25	.15
120	Dan Quisenberry	.07	.04
121	Milt Thompson	.05	.03

		MINT	NR/MT
122	Todd Zeile (R)	.80	.50
123	Jack Clark	.08	.05
124	Bruce Hurst	.07	.04
125	Mark Parent	.05	.03
126	Bip Roberts	.15	.10
127	Jeff Brantley (R)	.15	.10
128	Terry Kennedy	.05	.03
129	Mike LaCoss	.05	.03
130	Greg Litton (R)	.10	.06
131	Mike Schmidt	.80	.50
132	Checklist	.05	.03

1990 Fleer

1990 marks the tenth straight year that Fleer produced a baseball set, and like the others, it consists of 660-cards measuring 2-1/2" by 3-1/2" each. Card fronts feature full color action shots with an outer white border and a thin line around the photos that varies in color with each team assigned a different color. Card backs are vertical and printed in red, white and blue.

		MINT	NR/MT
Complete Set (660)		16.00	10.00
Commons		.05	.03
1	Lance Blankenship	.05	.03
2	Todd Burns	.05	.03
3	Jose Canseco	.40	.25
4	Jim Corsi	.05	.03
5	Storm Davis	.05	.03
6	Dennis Eckersley	.20	.12
7	Mike Gallego	.05	.03
8	Ron Hassey	.05	.03
9	Dave Henderson	.08	.05
10	Rickey Henderson	.25	.15

11	Rick Honeycutt	.05	.03
12	Stan Javier	.05	.03
13	Felix Jose	.20	.12
14	Carney Lansford	.08	.05
15	Mark McGwire	.35	.20
16	Mike Moore	.05	.03
17	Gene Nelson	.05	.03
18	Dave Parker	.08	.05
19	Tony Phillips	.05	.03
20	Terry Steinbach	.08	.05
21	Dave Stewart	.10	.06
22	Walt Weiss	.08	.05
23	Bob Welch	.05	.03
24	Curt Young	.05	.03
25	Paul Assenmacher	.05	.03
26	Damon Berryhill	.05	.03
27	Mike Bielecki	.05	.03
28	Kevin Blankenship	.05	.03
29	Andre Dawson	.15	.10
30	Shawon Dunston	.10	.06
31	Joe Girardi	.05	.03
32	Mark Grace	.15	.10
33	Mike Harkey	.10	.06
34	Paul Kilgus	.05	.03
35	Les Lancaster	.05	.03
36	Vance Law	.05	.03
37	Greg Maddux	.20	.12
38	Lloyd McClendon	.05	.03
39	Jeff Pico	.05	.03
40	Ryne Sandberg	.35	.20
41	Scott Sanderson	.05	.03
42	Dwight Smith	.08	.05
43	Rick Sutcliffe	.07	.04
44	Jerome Walton	.08	.05
45	Mitch Webster	.05	.03
46	Curt Wilkeron	.05	.03
47	Dean Wilkins (R)	.08	.05
48	Mitch Williams	.07	.04
49	Steve Wilson	.05	.03
50	Steve Bedrosian	.05	.03
51	Mike Benjamin (R)	.12	.07
52	Jeff Brantley	.08	.05
53	Brett Butler	.10	.06
54	Will Clark	.30	.18
55	Kelly Downs	.07	.04
56	Scott Garrelts	.05	.03
57	Atlee Hammaker	.05	.03
58	Terry Kennedy	.05	.03
59	Mike LaCoss	.05	.03
60	Craig Lefferts	.05	.03
61	Greg Litton	.05	.03
62	Candy Maldonado	.07	.04
63	Kirt Manwaring	.05	.03
64	Randy McCament (R)	.08	.05
65	Kevin Mitchell	.12	.07
66	Donell Nixon	.05	.03
67	Ken Oberkfell	.05	.03
68	Rick Reuschel	.05	.03

69	Ernest Riles	.05	.03	127	Dante Bichette	.07	.04
70	Don Robinson	.05	.03	128	Bert Blyleven	.10	.06
71	Pat Sheridan	.05	.03	129	Chili Davis	.07	.04
72	Chris Speier	.05	.03	130	Brian Downing	.05	.03
73	Robby Thompson	.07	.04	131	Mike Fetters	.07	.04
74	Jose Uribe	.05	.03	132	Chuck Finley	.10	.06
75	Matt Williams	.15	.10	133	Willie Fraser	.05	.03
76	George Bell	.10	.06	134	Bryan Harvey	.08	.05
77	Pat Borders	.05	.03	135	Jack Howell	.05	.03
78	John Cerutti	.05	.03	136	Wally Joyner	.10	.06
79	Junior Felix	.07	.04	137	Jeff Manto	.05	.03
80	Tony Fernandez	.10	.06	138	Kirk McCaskill	.05	.03
81	Mike Flanagan	.05	.03	139	Bob McClure	.05	.03
82	Mauro Gozzo (R)	.08	.05	140	Greg Minton	.05	.03
83	Kelly Gruber	.10	.06	141	Lance Parrish	.07	.04
84	Tom Henke	.07	.04	142	Dan Petry	.05	.03
85	Jimmy Key	.07	.04	143	Johnny Ray	.05	.03
86	Manny Lee	.05	.03	144	Dick Schofield	.05	.03
87	Nelson Liriano	.05	.03	145	Lee Stevens	.10	.06
88	Lee Mazzilli	.05	.03	146	Claudell Washington	.05	.03
89	Fred McGriff	.30	.18	147	Devon White	.05	.03
90	Lloyd Moseby	.05	.03	148	Roberto Alomar	.50	.30
91	Rance Mulliniks	.05	.03	150	Sandy Alomar, Jr.	.10	.06
92	Alex Sanchez	.05	.03	151	Andy Benes (R)	.30	.18
93	Dave Steib	.08	.05	152	Jack Clark	.08	.05
94	Todd Stottlemyre	.07	.04	153	Pat Clements	.05	.03
95	Duane Ward	.07	.04	154	Joey Cora	.05	.03
96	David Wells	.07	.04	155	Mark Davis	.05	.03
97	Ernie Whitt	.05	.03	156	Mark Grant	.05	.03
98	Frank Wills	.05	.03	157	Tony Gwynn	.25	.15
99	Mookie Wilson	.05	.03	158	Greg Harris	.05	.03
100	Kevin Appier	.40	.25	159	Bruce Hurst	.07	.04
101	Luis Aquino	.05	.03	160	Darrin Jackson	.05	.03
102	Bob Boone	.08	.05	161	Chris James	.05	.03
103	George Brett	.25	.15	162	Carmelo Martinez	.05	.03
104	Jose DeJesus	.05	.03	163	Mike Pagliarulo	.05	.03
105	Luis de los Santos	.05	.03	164	Mark Parent	.05	.03
106	Jim Eisenreich	.07	.04	165	Dennis Rasmussen	.05	.03
107	Steve Farr	.05	.03	166	Bip Roberts	.07	.04
108	Tom Gordon	.10	.06	167	Benito Santiago	.08	.05
109	Mark Gubicza	.10	.06	168	Calvin Schiraldi	.05	.03
110	Bo Jackson	.20	.12	169	Eric Show	.05	.03
111	Terry Leach	.05	.03	170	Garry Templeton	.05	.03
112	Charlie Leibrandt	.05	.03	171	Ed Whitson	.05	.03
113	Rick Luecken (R)	.08	.05	172	Brady Anderson	.15	.10
114	Mike Macfarlane	.07	.04	173	Jeff Ballard	.05	.03
115	Jeff Montgomery	.07	.04	174	Phil Bradley	.05	.03
116	Bret Saberhagen	.10	.06	175	Mike Devereaux	.05	.03
117	Kevin Seitzer	.07	.04	176	Steve Finley	.08	.05
118	Kurt Stillwell	.05	.03	177	Pete Harnisch (R)	.15	.10
119	Pat Tabler	.05	.03	178	Kevin Hickey	.05	.03
120	Danny Tartabull	.12	.07	179	Brian Holton	.05	.03
121	Gary Thurman	.05	.03	180	Ben McDonald (R)	.50	.30
122	Frank White	.05	.03	181	Bob Melvin	.05	.03
123	Willie Wilson	.05	.03	182	Bob Milacki	.05	.03
124	Matt Winters (R)	.08	.05	183	Randy Milligan	.08	.05
125	Jim Abbott	.25	.15	184	Gregg Olson (R)	.12	.06
126	Tony Armas	.05	.03	185	Joe Orsulak	.07	.04

186	Bill Ripken	.05	.03
187	Cal Ripken, Jr.	.50	.30
188	Dave Schmidt	.05	.03
189	Larry Sheets	.05	.03
190	Mickey Tettleton	.08	.05
191	Mark Thurmond	.05	.03
192	Jay Tibbs	.05	.03
193	Jim Traber	.05	.03
194	Mark Williamson	.05	.03
195	Craig Worthington	.05	.03
196	Don Aase	.05	.03
197	Blaine Beatty (R)	.10	.06
198	Mark Carreon	.05	.03
199	Gary Carter	.10	.06
200	David Cone	.20	.12
201	Ron Darling	.07	.04
202	Kevin Elster	.05	.03
203	Sid Fernandez	.07	.04
204	Dwight Gooden	.12	.07
205	Keith Hernandez	.07	.04
206	Jeff Innis	.05	.03
207	Gregg Jefferies	.12	.07
208	Howard Johnson	.12	.07
209	Barry Lyons	.05	.03
210	Dave Magadan	.07	.04
211	Kevin McReynolds	.07	.04
212	Jeff Musselman	.05	.03
213	Randy Myers	.05	.03
214	Bob Ojeda	.05	.03
215	Juan Samuel	.05	.03
216	Mackey Sasser	.05	.03
217	Darryl Strawberry	.25	.15
218	Tim Teufel	.05	.03
219	Frank Viola	.08	.05
220	Juan Agosto	.05	.03
221	Larry Anderson	.05	.03
222	Eric Anthony (R)	.40	.25
223	Kevin Bass	.05	.03
224	Craig Biggio	.10	.06
225	Ken Caminiti	.07	.04
226	Jim Clancy	.05	.03
227	Danny Darwin	.05	.03
228	Glenn Davis	.10	.06
229	Jim Deshaies	.05	.03
230	Bill Doran	.05	.03
231	Bob Forsch	.05	.03
233	Terry Puhl	.05	.03
234	Rafael Ramirez	.05	.03
235	Rick Rhoden	.05	.03
236	Dan Schatzeder	.05	.03
237	Mike Scott	.07	.04
238	Dave Smith	.05	.03
239	Alex Trevino	.05	.03
240	Glenn Wilson	.05	.03
241	Gerald Young	.05	.03
242	Tom Brunansky	.07	.04
243	Cris Carpenter	.05	.03
244	Alex Cole (R)	.15	.10
245	Vince Coleman	.10	.06
246	John Costello	.05	.03
247	Ken Dayley	.05	.03
248	Jose DeLeon	.05	.03
249	Frank DiPino	.05	.03
250	Pedro Guerrero	.08	.05
251	Ken Hill	.15	.10
252	Joe Magrane	.07	.04
253	Willie McGee	.08	.05
254	John Morris	.05	.03
255	Jose Oquendo	.05	.03
256	Tony Pena	.05	.03
257	Terry Pendleton	.15	.10
258	Ted Power	.05	.03
259	Dan Quisenberry	.05	.03
260	Ozzie Smith	.15	.10
261	Scott Terry	.05	.03
262	Milt Thompson	.05	.03
263	Denny Walling	.05	.03
264	Todd Worrell	.05	.03
265	Todd Zeile	.15	.10
266	Marty Barrett	.05	.03
267	Mike Boddicker	.05	.03
268	Wade Boggs	.15	.10
269	Ellis Burks	.08	.05
270	Rick Cerone	.05	.03
271	Roger Clemens	.45	.28
272	John Dopson	.05	.03
273	Nick Esasky	.05	.03
274	Dwight Evans	.08	.05
275	Wes Gardner	.05	.03
276	Rich Gedman	.05	.03
277	Mike Greenwell	.08	.05
278	Danny Heep	.05	.03
279	Eric Hetzel	.05	.03
280	Dennis Lamp	.05	.03
281	Rob Murphy	.05	.03
292	Joe Price	.05	.03
283	Carlos Quintana	.08	.05
284	Jody Reed	.05	.03
285	Luis Rivera	.05	.03
286	Kevin Romine	.05	.03
287	Lee Smith	.12	.07
288	Mike Smithson	.05	.03
289	Bob Stanley	.05	.03
290	Harold Baines	.07	.04
291	Kevin Brown	.10	.06
292	Steve Buechele	.07	.04
293	Scott Coolbaugh (R)	.07	.04
294	Jack Daugherty (R)	.10	.06
295	Cecil Espy	.05	.03
296	Julio Franco	.10	.06
297	Juan Gonzalez (R)	2.50	1.50
298	Cecilio Guante	.05	.03
299	Drew Hall	.05	.03
300	Charlie Hough	.05	.03
301	Pete Incaviglia	.05	.03
302	Mike Jeffcoat	.05	.03

No.	Player			No.	Player		
303	Chad Kreuter	.05	.03	361	Bryn Smith	.05	.03
304	Jeff Kunkel	.05	.03	362	Zane Smith	.05	.03
305	Rick Leach	.05	.03	363	Larry Walker (R)	.75	.45
306	Fred Manrique	.05	.03	364	Tim Wallach	.08	.05
307	Jamie Moyer	.05	.03	365	Rick Aguilera	.05	.03
308	Rafael Palmeiro	.10	.06	366	Allan Anderson	.05	.03
309	Geno Petralli	.05	.03	367	Wally Backman	.05	.03
310	Kevin Reimer	.05	.03	368	Doug Baker	.05	.03
311	Kenny Rogers	.05	.03	369	Juan Berenguer	.05	.03
312	Jeff Russell	.05	.03	370	Randy Bush	.05	.03
313	Nolan Ryan	.75	.45	371	Carmen Castillo	.05	.03
314	Ruben Sierra	.30	.18	372	Mike Dyer (R)	.08	.05
315	Bobby Witt	.08	.05	373	Gary Gaetti	.05	.03
316	Chris Bosio	.05	.03	374	Greg Gagne	.07	.04
317	Glenn Braggs	.05	.03	375	Dan Gladden	.05	.03
318	Greg Brock	.05	.03	376	German Gonzalez	.05	.03
319	Chuck Crim	.05	.03	377	Brian Harper	.05	.03
320	Rob Deer	.07	.04	378	Kent Hrbek	.10	.06
321	Mike Felder	.05	.03	379	Gene Larkin	.05	.03
322	Tom Filer	.05	.03	380	Tim Laudner	.05	.03
323	Tony Fossas (R)	.08	.05	381	John Moses	.05	.03
324	Jim Gantner	.05	.03	382	Al Newman	.05	.03
325	Darryl Hamilton	.05	.03	383	Kirby Puckett	.30	.18
326	Ted Higuera	.05	.03	384	Shane Rawley	.05	.03
327	Mark Knudson	.05	.03	385	Jeff Reardon	.12	.07
328	Bill Krueger	.05	.03	386	Roy Smith	.05	.03
329	Tim McIntosh (R)	.20	.12	387	Gary Wayne (R)	.08	.05
330	Paul Molitor	.15	.10	388	Dave West	.05	.03
331	Jaime Navarro	.10	.06	389	Tim Belcher	.08	.05
332	Charlie O'Brien	.05	.03	390	Tim Crews	.05	.03
333	Jeff Peterek (R)	.08	.05	391	Mike Davis	.05	.03
334	Dan Plesac	.05	.03	392	Rick Dempsey	.05	.03
335	Jerry Reuss	.05	.03	393	Kirk Gibson	.07	.04
336	Gary Sheffield	.80	.50	394	Jose Gonzalez	.05	.03
337	Bill Spiers	.05	.03	395	Alfredo Griffin	.05	.03
338	B.J. Surhoff	.05	.03	396	Jeff Hamilton	.05	.03
339	Greg Vaughn	.25	.15	397	Lenny Harris	.05	.03
340	Robin Yount	.25	.15	398	Mickey Hatcher	.05	.03
341	Hubie Brooks	.05	.03	399	Orel Hershiser	.10	.06
342	Tim Burke	.05	.03	400	Jay Howell	.05	.03
343	Mike Fitzgerald	.05	.03	401	Mike Marshall	.05	.03
344	Tom Foley	.05	.03	402	Ramon Martinez	.20	.12
345	Andres Galarraga	.08	.05	403	Mike Morgan	.05	.03
346	Damaso Garcia	.05	.03	404	Eddie Murray	.15	.10
347	Marquis Grissom (R)	.90	.60	405	Alejandro Pena	.05	.03
348	Kevin Gross	.05	.03	406	Willie Randolph	.07	.04
349	Joe Hesketh	.05	.03	407	Mike Scioscia	.05	.03
350	Jeff Huson (R)	.10	.06	408	Ray Searage	.05	.03
351	Wallace Johnson	.05	.03	409	Fernando Valenzuela	.10	.06
352	Mark Langston	.10	.06	410	Jose Vizcaino (R)	.10	.06
353	Dave Martinez	.05	.03	411	John Wetteland (R)	.15	.10
354	Dennis Martinez	.12	.07	412	Jack Armstrong	.08	.05
355	Andy McGaffigan	.05	.03	413	Todd Benzinger	.07	.04
356	Otis Nixon	.08	.05	414	Tim Birtsas	.05	.03
357	Spike Owen	.05	.03	415	Tom Browning	.07	.04
358	Pascual Perez	.05	.03	416	Norm Charlton	.08	.05
359	Tim Raines	.08	.05	417	Eric Davis	.12	.07
360	Nelson Santovenia	.05	.03	418	Rob Dibble	.10	.06

419	John Franco	.05	.03	477	Rick Reed (R)	.08	.05
420	Ken Griffey, Sr.	.08	.05	478	R.J. Reynolds	.05	.03
421	Chris Hammond (R)	.20	.12	479	Jeff Robinson	.05	.03
422	Danny Jackson	.05	.03	480	John Smiley	.10	.06
423	Barry Larkin	.15	.10	481	Andy Van Slyke	.15	.10
424	Tim Leary	.05	.03	482	Bob Walk	.05	.03
425	Rick Mahler	.05	.03	483	Andy Allanson	.05	.03
426	Joe Oliver (R)	.12	.07	484	Scott Bailes	.05	.03
427	Paul O'Neill	.10	.06	485	Albert Belle	.75	.45
428	Luis Quinones	.05	.03	486	Bud Black	.05	.03
429	Jeff Reed	.05	.03	487	Jerry Browne	.05	.03
430	Jose Rijo	.10	.06	488	Tom Candiotti	.05	.03
431	Ron Robinson	.05	.03	489	Joe Carter	.20	.12
432	Rolando Roomes	.05	.03	490	David Clark	.05	.03
433	Chris Sabo	.10	.06	491	John Farrell	.05	.03
434	Scott Scudder	.08	.05	492	Felix Fermin	.05	.03
435	Herm Winningham	.05	.03	493	Brook Jacoby	.05	.03
436	Steve Balboni	.05	.03	494	Dion James	.05	.03
437	Jesse Barfield	.07	.04	495	Doug Jones	.07	.04
438	Mike Blowers (R)	.10	.06	496	Brad Komminsk	.05	.03
439	Tom Brookens	.05	.03	497	Rod Nichols	.05	.03
440	Greg Cadaret	.05	.03	498	Pete O'Brien	.05	.03
441	Alvaro Espinoza	.05	.03	499	Steve Olin (R)	.15	.10
442	Bob Geren	.05	.03	500	Jesse Orosco	.05	.03
443	Lee Guetterman	.05	.03	501	Joel Skinner	.05	.03
444	Mel Hall	.07	.04	502	Cory Snyder	.07	.04
445	Andy Hawkins	.05	.03	503	Greg Swindell	.08	.05
446	Roberto Kelly	.15	.10	504	Rich Yett	.05	.03
447	Don Mattingly	.20	.12	505	Scott Bankhead	.05	.03
448	Lance McCullers	.05	.03	506	Scott Bradley	.05	.03
449	Hensley Meulens	.08	.05	507	Greg Briley	.05	.03
450	Dale Mohorcic	.05	.03	508	Jay Buhner	.12	.07
451	Clay Parker	.05	.03	509	Darnell Coles	.05	.03
452	Eric Plunk	.05	.03	510	Keith Comstock	.05	.03
453	Dave Righetti	.05	.03	511	Henry Cotto	.05	.03
454	Deion Sanders	.40	.25	512	Alvin Davis	.07	.04
455	Steve Sax	.10	.06	513	Ken Griffey, Jr.	1.50	.90
456	Don Slaught	.05	.03	514	Erik Hanson	.08	.05
457	Walt Terrell	.05	.03	515	Gene Harris	.05	.03
458	Dave Winfield	.20	.12	516	Brian Holman	.08	.05
459	Jay Bell	.07	.04	517	Mike Jackson	.05	.03
460	Rafael Belliard	.05	.03	518	Randy Johnson	.15	.10
461	Barry Bonds	.30	.18	519	Jeffrey Leonard	.05	.03
462	Bobby Bonilla	.15	.10	520	Edgar Martinez	.20	.12
463	Sid Bream	.05	.03	521	Dennis Powell	.05	.03
464	Benny Distefano	.05	.03	522	Jim Presley	.05	.03
465	Doug Drabek	.10	.06	523	Jerry Reed	.05	.03
466	Jim Gott	.05	.03	524	Harold Reynolds	.07	.04
467	Billy Hatcher	.05	.03	525	Mike Schooler	.07	.04
468	Neal Heaton	.05	.03	526	Bill Swift	.07	.04
469	Jeff King	.08	.05	527	David Valle	.05	.03
470	Bob Kipper	.05	.03	528	Omar Vizquel	.05	.03
471	Randy Kramer	.05	.03	529	Ivan Calderon	.08	.05
472	Bill Landrum	.05	.03	530	Carlton Fisk	.15	.10
473	Mike LaValliere	.05	.03	531	Scott Fletcher	.05	.03
474	Jose Lind	.05	.03	532	Dave Gallagher	.05	.03
475	Junior Ortiz	.05	.03	533	Ozzie Guillen	.07	.04
476	Gary Redus	.05	.03	534	Greg Hibbard (R)	.12	.07

535	Shawn Hillegas	.05	.03
536	Lance Johnson	.07	.04
537	Eric King	.05	.03
538	Ron Kittle	.05	.03
539	Steve Lyons	.05	.03
540	Carlos Martinez	.05	.03
541	Tom McCarthy (R)	.07	.04
542	Matt Merullo	.07	.04
543	Donn Pall	.05	.03
544	Dan Pasqua	.05	.03
545	Ken Patterson	.05	.03
546	Melido Perez	.08	.05
547	Steve Rosenberg	.05	.03
548	Sammy Sosa (R)	.20	.12
549	Bobby Thigpen	.08	.05
550	Robin Ventura	.80	.50
551	Greg Walker	.05	.03
552	Don Carman	.05	.03
553	Pat Combs (R)	.12	.07
554	Dennis Cook	.05	.03
555	Darren Daulton	.12	.07
556	Lenny Dykstra	.07	.04
557	Curt Ford	.05	.03
558	Charlie Hayes	.05	.03
559	Von Hayes	.05	.03
560	Tom Herr	.05	.03
561	Ken Howell	.05	.03
562	Steve Jeltz	.05	.03
563	Ron Jones	.05	.03
564	Ricky Jones	.05	.03
564	Ricky Jordan	.08	.05
565	John Kruk	.10	.06
566	Steve Lake	.05	.03
567	Roger McDowell	.05	.03
568	Terry Mulholland	.08	.05
569	Dwayne Murphy	.05	.03
570	Jeff Parrett	.05	.03
571	Randy Ready	.05	.03
572	Bruce Ruffin	.05	.03
573	Dickie Thon	.05	.03
574	Jose Alvarez	.05	.03
575	Geronimo Berroa	.05	.03
576	Jeff Blauser	.05	.03
577	Joe Boever	.05	.03
578	Marty Clary	.05	.03
579	Jody Davis	.05	.03
580	Mark Eichhorn	.05	.03
581	Darrell Evans	.07	.04
582	Ron Gant	.25	.15
583	Tom Glavine	.40	.25
584	Tommy Greene (R)	.12	.07
585	Tommy Gregg	.05	.03
586	David Justice (R)	1.75	1.00
587	Mark Lemke (R)	.08	.05
588	Derek Lilliquist	.05	.03
589	Oddibe McDowell	.05	.03
590	Kent Mercker (R)	.12	.07
591	Dale Murphy	.12	.07

592	Gerald Perry	.05	.03
593	Lonnie Smith	.08	.05
594	Pete Smith	.12	.07
595	John Smoltz	.35	.20
596	Mike Stanton (R)	.12	.07
597	Andres Thomas	.05	.03
598	Jeff Treadway	.05	.03
599	Doyle Alexander	.05	.03
600	Dave Bergman	.05	.03
601	Brian Dubois (R)	.08	.05
602	Paul Gibson	.05	.03
603	Mike Heath	.05	.03
604	Mike Henneman	.05	.03
605	Guillermo Hernandez	.05	.03
606	Shawn Holman (R)	.07	.04
607	Tracy Jones	.05	.03
608	Chet Lemon	.05	.03
609	Fred Lynn	.10	.06
610	Jack Morris	.15	.10
611	Matt Nokes	.05	.03
612	Gary Pettis	.05	.03
613	Kevin Ritz (R)	.10	.06
614	Jeff Robinson	.05	.03
615	Steve Searcy	.05	.03
616	Frank Tanana	.05	.03
617	Alan Trammell	.12	.07
618	Gary Ward	.05	.03
619	Lou Whitaker	.08	.05
620	Frank Williams	.05	.03
621a	Player of the Decade George Brett (1980) (Ten .390 seasons)(Er)	2.50	1.50
621b	Player of the Decade George Brett (1980) (Cor)	.25	.15
622	Player of the Decade Fernando Valenzuela (1981)	.10	.06
623	Player of the Decade Dale Murphy (1982)	.10	.06
624a	Player of the Decade Cal Ripken (1983) (Name misspelled on back)	3.50	2.50
624b	Player of the Decade Cal Ripken (1983) (Cor)	.35	.20
625	Player of the Decade Ryne Sandberg (1984)	.15	.10
626	Player of the Decade Don Mattingly (1985)	.12	.07
627	Player of the Decade Roger Clemens (1986)	.20	.12
628	Player of the Decade George Bell (1987)	.10	.06
629	Player of the Decade Jose Canseco (1988)	.20	.12
630a	Player of the Decade	1.50	.90

	Will Clark (1989)		
	(Total bases 32)		
630b	Player of the Decade	.15	.10
	Will Clark (1989)		
	(Total bases 321)		
631	Mark Davis/Mitch Williams	.08	.05
632	Wade Boggs/Mike Greenwell	.15	.10
633	Mark Gubicza/Jeff Russell	.08	.05
634	Tony Fernandez/Cal Ripken Jr.	.20	.12
635	Bo Jackson/Kirby Puckett	.20	.12
636	Nolan Ryan/Mike Scott	.25	.15
637	Will Clark/Kevin Mitchell	.15	.10
638	Don Mattingly/Mark McGwire	.20	.12
639	Howard Johnson/Ryne Sandberg	.15	.10
640	Major League Prospects	.15	.10
	Rudy Seanez (R)		
	Colin Charland (R)		
641	Major League Prospects	.25	.15
	George Canale (R)		
	Kevin Maas (R)		
642	Major League Prospects	.15	.10
	Kelly Mann (R)		
	Dave Hansen (R)		
643	Major League Prospects	.10	.06
	Greg Smith (R)		
	Stu Tate (R)		
644	Major League Prospects	.12	.07
	Tom Drees (R)		
	Dan Howitt (R)		
645	Major League Prospects	.25	.15
	Mike Roesler (R)		
	Derrick May (R)		
646	Major League Prospects	.20	.12
	Scott Hemond (R)		
	Mark Gardner (R)		
647	Major League Prospects	.20	.12
	John Orton (R)		
	Scott Leuis (R)		
648	Major League Prospects	.10	.06
	Rich Monteleone (R)		
	Dana Williams (R)		
649	Major League Prospects	.10	.06
	Mike Huff (R)		
	Steve Frey (R)		
650	Major League Prospects	.80	.50
	Chuck McElroy (R)		
	Moises Alou (R)		
651	Major League Prospects	.08	.05
	Bobby Rose (R)		
	Mike Hartley (R)		
652	Major League Prospects	.10	.06
	Matt Kinzer (R)		
	Wayne Edwards (R)		
653	Major League Prospects	.90	.60
	Delino DeShields (R)		
	Jason Grimsley (R)		
654	Team Checklists	.05	.02
655	Team Checklists	.05	.02
656	Team Checklists	.05	.03
657	Team Checklists	.05	.03
658	Team Checklists	.05	.03
659	Team Checklists	.05	.03
660	Team Checklists	.05	.03

1990 Fleer Update

This 132-card update set is identical in design to Fleer's 1990 regular edition. The set consists of cards of players traded to new teams since the beginning of the year and a number of promising rookies. Cards measure 2-1/2' by 3-1/2' and the set includes a special Nolan Ryan commemorative card.

		MINT	NR/MT
Complete Set (132)		10.00	7.00
Commons		.05	.03
1	Steve Avery (R)	.80	.50
2	Francisco Cabrera	.07	.04
3	Nick Esasky	.05	.03
4	Jim Kremers (R)	.10	.06
5	Greg Olson (R)	.10	.06
6	Jim Presley	.05	.03
7	Shawn Boskie (R)	.12	.07
8	Joe Kraemer (R)	.10	.06
9	Luis Salazar	.05	.03
10	Hector Villanueva (R)	.10	.06
11	Glenn Braggs	.05	.03
12	Mariano Duncan	.05	.03
13	Billy Hatcher	.07	.04
14	Tim Layana (R)	.12	.07
15	Hal Morris	.15	.10
16	Javier Ortiz	.20	.12
17	Dave Rohde (R)	.12	.07
18	Eric Yelding (R)	.12	.07
19	Hubie Brooks	.08	.05
20	Kal Daniels	.08	.05
21	Dave Hansen	.12	.07
22	Mike Hartley	.07	.04
23	Stan Javier	.05	.03
24	Jose Offerman (R)	.25	.15
25	Juan Samuel	.05	.03
26	Dennis Boyd	.05	.03
27	Delino DeShields	.75	.45
28	Steve Frey	.05	.03
29	Mark Gardner	.10	.06
30	Chris Nabholz (R)	.30	.18
31	Bill Sampen (R)	.10	.06
32	Dave Schmidt	.05	.03
33	Daryl Boston	.05	.03
34	Chuck Carr (R)	.08	.05
35	John Franco	.05	.03
36	Todd Hundley (R)	.15	.10
37	Julio Machado (R)	.10	.06
38	Alejandro Pena	.05	.03
39	Darren Reed (R)	.10	.06
40	Kelvin Torve (R)	.07	.04
41	Darrell Akerfelds (R)	.07	.04
42	Jose DeJesus	.05	.03
43	Dave Hollins (R)	.75	.45
44	Carmelo Martinez	.05	.03
45	Brad Moore (R)	.08	.05
46	Dale Murphy	.12	.07
47	Wally Backman	.05	.03
48	Stan Belinda (R)	.12	.07
49	Bob Patterson	.05	.03
50	Ted Power	.05	.03
51	Don Slaught	.05	.03
52	Geronimo Pena (R)	.15	.10
53	Lee Smith	.15	.10
54	John Tudor	.07	.04
55	Joe Carter	.20	.12
56	Tom Howard (R)	.20	.12
57	Craig Lefferts	.05	.03
58	Rafael Valdez (R)	.10	.06
59	Dave Anderson	.05	.03
60	Kevin Bass	.05	.03
61	John Burkett	.10	.06
62	Gary Carter	.10	.06
63	Rick Parker (R)	.07	.04
64	Trevor Wilson	.10	.06
65	Chris Hoiles (R)	.35	.20
66	Tim Hulett	.05	.03
67	Dave Johnson (R)	.10	.06
68	Curt Schilling (R)	.12	.07
69	David Segui (R)	.15	.10
70	Tom Brunansky	.08	.05
71	Greg Harris	.05	.03
72	Dana Kiecker (R)	.12	.07
73	Tim Naehring (R)	.12	.07
74	Tony Pena	.07	.04
75	Jeff Reardon	.15	.10
76	Jerry Reed	.05	.03
77	Mark Eichhorn	.05	.03
78	Mark Langston	.10	.06
79	John Orton	.10	.06
80	Luis Polonia	.08	.05
81	Dave Winfield	.20	.12
82	Cliff Young (R)	.10	.06
83	Wayne Edwards	.07	.04
84	Alex Fernandez (R)	.40	.25
85	Craig Grebeck (R)	.12	.07
86	Scott Radinsky (R)	.20	.12

87	Frank Thomas (R)	5.00	3.50
88	Beau Allred (R)	.12	.07
89	Sandy Alomar, Jr.	.10	.06
90	Carlos Baerga (R)	1.50	.90
91	Kevin Bearse (R)	.08	.05
92	Chris James	.05	.03
93	Candy Maldonado	.08	.05
94	Jeff Manto	.08	.05
95	Cecil Fielder	.25	.15
96	Travis Fryman (R)	1.25	.80
97	Lloyd Moseby	.05	.03
98	Edwin Nunez	.05	.03
99	Tony Phillips	.05	.03
100	Larry Sheets	.05	.03
101	Mark Davis	.07	.04
102	Strom Davis	.05	.03
103	Gerald Perry	.05	.03
104	Terry Shumpert (R)	.10	.06
105	Edgar Diaz (R)	.08	.05
106	Dave Parker	.08	.05
107	Tim Drummond (R)	.10	.06
108	Junior Ortiz	.05	.03
109	Park Pittman (R)	.08	.05
110	Kevin Tapani (R)	.35	.20
111	Oscar Azocar (R)	.10	.06
112	Jim Leyritz (R)	.10	.06
113	Kevin Maas	.20	.12
114	Alan Mills	.12	.07
115	Matt Nokes	.07	.04
116	Pascual Perez	.07	.04
117	Ozzie Canseco (R)	.12	.07
118	Scott Sanderson	.07	.04
119	Tino Martinez (R)	.30	.18
120	Jeff Schaefer (R)	.08	.05
121	Matt Young	.05	.03
122	Brian Bohanon (R)	.10	.06
123	Jeff Huson	.08	.05
124	Ramon Manon (R)	.08	.05
125	Gary Mielke (R)	.08	.05
126	Willie Blair (R)	.15	.10
127	Glenallen Hill (R)	.12	.07
128	John Olerud (R)	.75	.45
129	Luis Sojo (R)	.10	.06
130	Mark Whiten (R)	.45	.28
131	Three Decades of No Hitters(Nolan Ryan)	.80	.50
132	Checklist	.05	.03

1991 Fleer

For the first time since Fleer reentered the baseball card market they increased the size of their set to 720-cards. The fronts feature bright yellow borders with black type at the top and bottom. A thin black line frames full color action photos. Card backs are vertical and include a small head shot of the player in a circle at the top. Cards measure 2-1/2" by 3-1/2"

		MINT	NR/MT
Complete Set (720)		16.00	10.00
Commons		.05	.03

1	Troy Afenir (R)	.10	.06
2	Harold Baines	.07	.04
3	Lance Blankenship	.05	.03
4	Todd Burns	.05	.03
5	Jose Canseco	.25	.15
6	Dennis Eckersley	.15	.10
7	Mike Gallego	.05	.03
8	Ron Hassey	.05	.03
9	Dave Henderson	.07	.04
11	Rick Honeycutt	.05	.03
12	Doug Jennings	.05	.03
13	Joe Klink (R)	.08	.05
14	Carney Lansford	.08	.05
15	Darren Lewis (R)	.12	.07
16	Willie McGee	.08	.05
17	Mark McGwire	.20	.12
18	Mike Moore	.05	.03
19	Gene Nelson	.05	.03
20	Dave Otto	.05	.03
21	Jamie Quirk	.05	.03
22	Willie Randolph	.07	.04
23	Scott Sanderson	.05	.03
24	Terry Steinbach	.07	.04
25	Dave Stewart	.08	.05
26	Walt Weiss	.05	.03
27	Bob Welch	.07	.04
28	Curt Young	.05	.03
29	Wally Backman	.05	.03

No.	Player			No.	Player		
30	Stan Belinda	.05	.03	89	Ellis Burks	.08	.05
31	Jay Bell	.05	.03	90	Roger Clemens	.25	.15
32	Rafael Belliard	.05	.03	91	Scott Cooper (R)	.20	.12
33	Barry Bonds	.20	.12	92	John Dopson	.05	.03
34	Bobby Bonilla	.10	.06	93	Dwight Evans	.08	.05
35	Sid Bream	.05	.03	94	Wes Gardner	.05	.03
36	Doug Drabek	.10	.06	95	Jeff Gray (R)	.10	.06
37	Carlos Garcia (R)	.15	.10	96	Mike Greenwell	.08	.05
38	Neal Heaton	.05	.03	97	Greg Harris	.05	.03
39	Jeff King	.07	.04	98	Daryl Irvine (R)	.08	.05
40	Bob Kipper	.05	.03	99	Dana Kiecker	.05	.03
41	Bill Landrum	.05	.03	100	Randy Kutcher	.05	.03
42	Mike LaValliere	.05	.03	101	Dennis Lamp	.05	.03
43	Jose Lind	.05	.03	102	Mike Marshall	.05	.03
44	Carmelo Martinez	.05	.03	103	John Marzano	.05	.03
45	Bob Patterson	.05	.03	104	Rob Murphy	.05	.03
46	Ted Power	.05	.03	105	Tim Naehring	.07	.04
48	R.J. Reynolds	.05	.03	106	Tony Pena	.05	.03
49	Don Slaught	.05	.03	107	Phil Plantier (R)	.50	.30
50	John Smiley	.10	.06	108	Carlos Quintana	.08	.05
51	Zane Smith	.05	.03	109	Jeff Reardon	.10	.06
52	Randy Tomlin (R)	.20	.15	110	Jerry Reed	.05	.03
53	Andy Van Slyke	.12	.07	111	Jody Reed	.05	.03
54	Bob Walk	.05	.03	112	Luis Rivera	.05	.03
55	Jack Armstrog	.05	.03	113	Kevin Romine	.05	.03
56	Todd Benzinger	.05	.03	114	Phil Bradley	.05	.03
57	Glenn Braggs	.05	.03	115	Ivan Calderon	.08	.05
58	Keith Brown	.05	.03	116	Wayne Edwards	.05	.03
59	Tom Browning	.07	.04	117	Alex Fernandez	.12	.07
60	Norm Charlton	.07	.04	118	Carlton Fisk	.15	.10
61	Eric Davis	.10	.06	119	Scott Fletcher	.05	.03
62	Rob Dibble	.07	.04	120	Craig Grebeck	.05	.03
63	Bill Doran	.05	.03	121	Ozzie Guillen	.07	.04
64	Mariano Duncan	.05	.03	122	Greg Hibbard	.05	.03
65	Chris Hammond	.10	.06	123	Lance Johnson	.05	.03
66	Billy Hatcher	.05	.03	124	Barry Jones	.05	.03
67	Danny Jackson	.05	.03	125	Ron Karkovice	.05	.03
68	Barry Larkin	.12	.07	126	Eric King	.05	.03
69	Tim Layana	.05	.03	127	Steve Lyons	.05	.03
70	Terry Lee (R)	.10	.06	128	Carlos Martinez	.05	.03
71	Rick Mahler	.05	.03	129	Jack McDowell	.20	.12
72	Hal Morris	.12	.07	130	Donn Pall	.05	.03
73	Randy Myers	.05	.03	131	Dan Pasqua	.05	.03
74	Ron Oester	.05	.03	132	Ken Patterson	.05	.03
75	Joe Oliver	.07	.04	133	Melido Perez	.07	.04
76	Paul O'Neill	.10	.06	134	Adam Peterson	.05	.03
77	Luis Quinones	.05	.03	135	Scott Radinsky	.07	.04
78	Jeff Reed	.05	.03	136	Sammy Sosa	.08	.05
79	Jose Rojo	.10	.06	137	Bobby Thigpen	.07	.04
80	Chris Sabo	.08	.05	138	Frank Thomas	1.50	.90
81	Scott Scudder	.08	.05	139	Robin Ventura	.25	.15
82	Herm Winningham	.05	.03	140	Daryl Boston	.05	.03
83	Larry Anderson	.05	.03	141	Chuck Carr	.05	.03
84	Marty Barrett	.05	.03	142	Mark Carreon	.05	.03
85	Mike Boddicker	.05	.03	143	David Cone	.15	.10
86	Wade Boggs	.15	.10	144	Ron Darling	.07	.04
87	Tom Bolton	.05	.03	145	Kevin Elster	.05	.03
88	Tom Brunansky	.07	.04	146	Sid Fernandez	.07	.04

147	John Franco	.05	.03	205	Mike Hartley	.05	.03
148	Dwight Gooden	.10	.06	206	Mickey Hatcher	.05	.03
149	Tom Herr	.05	.03	207	Carlos Hernandez (R)	.12	.07
150	Todd Hundley	.08	.05	208	Orel Hershiser	.08	.05
151	Gregg Jefferies	.10	.06	209	Jay Howell	.05	.03
152	Howard Johnson	.10	.06	210	Mike Huff	.05	.03
153	Dave Magadan	.07	.04	211	Stan Javier	.05	.03
154	Kevin McReynolds	.07	.04	212	Ramon Martinez	.12	.07
155	Keith Miller	.05	.03	213	Mike Morgan	.05	.03
156	Bob Ojeda	.05	.03	214	Eddie Murray	.15	.10
157	Tom O'Malley	.05	.03	215	Jim Neidlinger	.05	.03
158	Alejandro Pena	.05	.03	216	Jose Offerman	.12	.07
159	Darren Reed	.05	.03	217	Jim Poole (R)	.08	.05
160	Mackey Sasser	.05	.03	218	Juan Samuel	.05	.03
161	Darryl Strawberry	.15	.10	219	Mike Scioscia	.05	.03
162	Tim Teufel	.05	.03	220	Ray Searage	.05	.03
163	Kelvin Torve	.05	.03	221	Mike Sharperson	.05	.03
164	Julio Valera	.10	.06	222	Fernando Valenzuela	.08	.05
165	Frank Viola	.08	.05	223	Jose Vizcaino	.05	.03
166	Wally Whitehurst	.05	.03	224	Mike Aldrete	.05	.03
167	Jim Acker	.05	.03	225	Scott Anderson (R)	.08	.05
168	Derek Bell (R)	.35	.20	226	Dennis Boyd	.05	.03
169	George Bell	.12	.07	227	Tim Burke	.05	.03
170	Willie Blair	.08	.05	228	Delino DeShields	.15	.10
171	Pat Borders	.05	.03	229	Mike Fitzgerald	.05	.03
172	John Cerutti	.05	.03	320	Tom Foley	.05	.03
173	Junior Felix	.05	.03	231	Steve Frey	.05	.03
174	Tony Fernandez	.08	.05	232	Andres Galarraga	.07	.04
175	Kelly Gruber	.07	.04	233	Mark Gardner	.08	.05
176	Tom Henke	.05	.03	234	Marquis Grissom	.15	.10
177	Glenallen Hill	.10	.06	235	Kevin Gross	.05	.03
178	Jimmy Key	.05	.03	236	Drew Hall	.05	.03
179	Manny Lee	.05	.03	237	Dave Martinez	.05	.03
180	Fred McGriff	.15	.10	238	Dennis Martinez	.08	.05
181	Rance Mulliniks	.05	.03	239	Dale Mohorcic	.05	.03
182	Greg Myers	.05	.03	240	Chris Nabholz	.10	.06
183	John Olerud	.12	.07	241	Otis Nixon	.07	.04
184	Luis Sojo	.05	.03	242	Junior Noboa	.05	.03
185	Dave Steib	.08	.05	243	Spike Owen	.05	.03
186	Todd Stottlemyre	.07	.04	244	Tim Raines	.07	.04
187	Duane Ward	.05	.03	245	Mel Rojas (R)	.10	.06
188	David Wells	.05	.03	246	Scott Ruskin (R)	.10	.06
189	Mark Whiten	.12	.07	247	Bill Sampen	.05	.03
190	Ken Williams	.05	.03	248	Nelson Santovenia	.05	.03
191	Frank Wills	.05	.03	249	Dave Schmidt	.05	.03
192	Mookie Wilson	.05	.03	250	Larry Walker	.15	.10
193	Don Aase	.05	.03	251	Tim Wallach	.08	.05
194	Tim Belcher	.07	.04	252	Dave Anderson	.05	.03
195	Hubie Brooks	.07	.04	253	Kevin Bass	.05	.03
196	Dennis Cook	.05	.03	254	Steve Bedrosian	.05	.03
197	Tim Crews	.05	.03	255	Jeff Brantley	.07	.04
198	Kal Daniels	.05	.03	256	John Burkett	.07	.04
199	Kirk Gibson	.07	.04	257	Brett Butler	.08	.05
200	Jim Gott	.05	.03	258	Gary Carter	.08	.05
201	Alfredo Griffin	.05	.03	259	Will Clark	.20	.12
202	Chris Gwynn	.05	.03	260	Steve Decker (R)	.12	.07
203	Dave Hansen	.08	.05	261	Kelly Downs	.05	.03
204	Lenny Harris	.05	.03	262	Scott Garrelts	.05	.03

263	Terry Kennedy	.05	.03	321	Lance Parrish	.05	.03
264	Mike LaCoss	.05	.03	322	Luis Polonia	.07	.04
265	Mark Leonard (R)	.08	.05	323	Johnny Ray	.05	.03
266	Greg Litton	.05	.03	324	Bobby Rose	.05	.03
267	Kevin Mitchell	.08	.05	325	Dick Schofield	.05	.03
268	Randy O'Neal (R)	.08	.05	326	Rick Schu	.05	.03
269	Rick Parker	.05	.03	327	Lee Stevens	.08	.05
270	Rick Reuschel	.05	.03	328	Devon White	.05	.03
271	Ernest Riles	.05	.03	329	Dave Winfield	.15	.10
272	Don Robinson	.05	.03	330	Cliff Young	.05	.03
273	Robby Thompson	.05	.03	331	Dave Bergman	.05	.03
274	Mark Thurmond	.05	.03	332	Phil Clark (R)	.12	.07
275	Jose Uribe	.05	.03	333	Darnell Coles	.05	.03
276	Matt Williams	.10	.06	334	Milt Cuyler (R)	.15	.10
277	Trevor Wilson	.07	.04	335	Cecil Fielder	.20	.12
278	Gerald Alexander (R)	.07	.04	336	Travis Fryman	.35	.20
279	Brad Arnsberg	.05	.03	337	Paul Gibson	.05	.03
280	Kevin Belcher (R)	.08	.05	338	Jerry Don Gleaton	.05	.03
281	Joe Bitker	.05	.03	339	Mike Heath	.05	.03
282	Kevin Brown	.07	.04	340	Mike Henneman	.05	.03
283	Steve Buechele	.05	.03	341	Chet Lemon	.05	.03
284	Jack Daugherty	.05	.03	342	Lance McCullers	.05	.03
285	Julio Franco	.08	.05	343	Jack Morris	.12	.07
286	Juan Gonzalez	.50	.30	344	Lloyd Moseby	.05	.03
287	Bill Haselman (R)	.07	.04	345	Edwin Nunez	.05	.03
288	Charlie Hough	.05	.03	346	Clay Parker	.05	.03
289	Jeff Huson	.05	.03	347	Dan Petry	.05	.03
290	Pete Incaviglia	.05	.03	348	Tony Phillips	.05	.03
291	Mike Jeffcoat	.05	.03	349	Jeff Robinson	.05	.03
292	Jeff Kunkel	.05	.03	350	Mark Salas	.05	.03
293	Gary Mielke	.05	.03	351	Mike Schwabe	.05	.03
294	Jamie Moyer	.05	.03	352	Larry Sheets	.05	.03
295	Rafael Palmeiro	.08	.05	353	John Shelby	.05	.03
296	Geno Petralli	.05	.03	354	Frank Tanana	.05	.03
297	Gary Pettis	.05	.03	355	Alan Trammell	.10	.06
298	Kevin Reimer	.05	.03	356	Gary Ward	.05	.03
299	Kenny Rogers	.05	.03	357	Lou Whitaker	.07	.04
300	Jeff Russell	.05	.03	358	Beau Allred	.07	.04
301	John Russell	.05	.03	359	Sandy Alomar, Jr.	.08	.05
302	Nolan Ryan	.50	.30	360	Carlos Baerga	.25	.15
303	Ruben Sierra	.20	.12	361	Kevin Bearse	.05	.03
304	Bobby Witt	.07	.04	362	Tom Brookens	.05	.03
305	Jim Abbott	.12	.07	363	Jerry Browne	.05	.03
306	Kent Anderson (R)	.08	.05	364	Tom Candiotti	.05	.03
307	Dante Bichette	.05	.03	365	Alex Cole	.05	.03
308	Bert Blyleven	.08	.05	366	John Farrell	.05	.03
309	Chili Davis	.07	.04	367	Felix Fermin	.05	.03
310	Brian Downing	.05	.03	368	Keith Hernandez	.07	.04
311	Mark Eichhorn	.05	.03	369	Brook Jacoby	.05	.03
312	Mike Fetters	.05	.03	370	Chris James	.05	.03
313	Chuck Finley	.08	.05	371	Dion James	.05	.03
314	Willie Fraser	.05	.03	372	Doug Jones	.05	.03
315	Bryan Harvey	.07	.04	373	Candy Maldonado	.05	.03
316	Donnie Hill	.05	.03	374	Steve Olin	.07	.04
317	Wally Joyner	.10	.06	375	Jesse Orosco	.05	.03
318	Mark Langston	.08	.05	376	Rudy Seanez	.10	.06
319	Kirk McCaskill	.05	.03	377	Joel Skinner	.05	.03
320	John Orton	.07	.04	378	Cory Snyder	.05	.03

379	Greg Swindell	.08	.05
380	Sergio Valdez	.07	.04
381	Mike Walker (R)	.08	.05
382	Colby Ward (R)	.08	.05
383	Turner Ward (R)	.10	.06
384	Mitch Webster	.05	.03
385	Kevin Wickander	.07	.04
386	Darrel Akerfelds	.05	.03
387	Joe Boever	.05	.03
388	Rod Booker	.05	.03
389	Sil Campusano	.05	.03
390	Don Carman	.05	.03
391	Wes Chamberlain (R)	.15	.10
392	Pat Combs	.07	.04
393	Darren Daulton	.10	.06
394	Jose DeJesus	.05	.03
395	Len Dykstra	.07	.04
396	Jason Grimsley	.05	.03
397	Charlie Hayes	.05	.03
398	Von Hayes	.05	.03
399	David Hollins	.20	.12
400	Ken Howell	.05	.03
401	Ricky Jordan	.05	.03
402	John Kruk	.08	.05
403	Steve Lake	.05	.03
404	Chuck Malone (R)	.10	.06
405	Roger McDowell	.05	.03
406	Chuck McElroy	.05	.03
407	Mickey Morandini (R)	.15	.10
408	Terry Mulholland	.05	.03
409	Dale Murphy	.08	.05
410	Randy Ready	.05	.03
411	Bruce Ruffin	.05	.03
412	Dickie Thon	.05	.03
413	Paul Assenmacher	.05	.03
414	Damon Berryhill	.05	.03
415	Mike Bielecki	.05	.03
416	Shawn Boskie	.05	.03
417	Dave Clark	.05	.03
418	Doug Dascenzo	.05	.03
419	Andre Dawson	.15	.10
420	Shawon Dunston	.08	.05
421	Joe Girardi	.05	.03
422	Mark Grace	.12	.07
423	Mike Harkey	.08	.05
424	Les Lancaster	.05	.03
425	Bill Long	.05	.03
426	Greg Maddux	.15	.10
427	Derrick May	.10	.06
428	Jeff Pico	.05	.03
429	Domingo Ramos	.05	.03
430	Luis Salazar	.05	.03
431	Ryne Sandberg	.25	.15
432	Dwight Smith	.07	.04
433	Greg Smith	.08	.05
434	Rick Sutcliffe	.07	.04
435	Gary Varsho	.05	.03
436	Hector Vallanueva	.07	.04
437	Jerome Walton	.08	.05
438	Curtis Wilkerson	.05	.03
439	Mitch Williams	.05	.03
440	Steve Wilson	.05	.03
441	Marvell Wynne	.05	.03
442	Scott Bankhead	.05	.03
443	Scott Bradley	.05	.03
444	Greg Briley	.05	.03
445	Mike Brumley	.05	.03
446	Jay Buhner	.08	.05
447	Dave Burba (R)	.10	.06
448	Henry Cotto	.05	.03
449	Alvin Davis	.05	.03
450	Ken Griffey, Jr.	.60	.35
451	Erik Hanson	.07	.04
452	Gene Harris	.05	.03
453	Brian Holman	.07	.04
454	Mike Jackson	.05	.03
455	Randy Johnson	.15	.10
456	Jeffrey Leonard	.05	.03
457	Edgar Martinez	.15	.10
458	Tino Martinez	.10	.06
459	Pete O'Brien	.05	.03
460	Harold Reynolds	.07	.04
461	Mike Schooler	.05	.03
462	Bill Swift	.05	.03
463	David Valle	.05	.03
464	Omar Vizquel	.05	.03
465	Matt Young	.05	.03
466	Brady Anderson	.12	.07
467	Jeff Ballard	.05	.03
468	Juan Bell (R)	.08	.05
469	Mike Devereaux	.08	.05
470	Steve Finley	.05	.03
471	Dave Gallagher	.05	.03
472	Leo Gomez (R)	.25	.15
473	Rene Gonzales	.07	.04
474	Pete Harnisch	.07	.04
475	Kevin Hickey	.05	.03
476	Chris Hoiles	.12	.07
477	Sam Horn	.07	.04
478	Tim Hulett	.05	.03
479	Dave Johnson	.05	.03
480	Ron Kittle	.05	.03
481	Ben McDonald	.15	.10
482	Bob Melvin	.05	.03
483	Bob Milacki	.05	.03
484	Randy Milligan	.07	.04
485	John Mitchell (R)	.08	.05
486	Gregg Olson	.07	.04
487	Joe Orsulak	.07	.04
488	Joe Price	.05	.03
489	Bill Ripken	.05	.03
490	Cal Ripken, Jr.	.35	.20
491	Curt Schilling	.05	.03
492	David Segui	.07	.04
493	Anthony Telford (R)	.12	.07
494	Mickey Tettleton	.07	.04

495	Mark Williamson	.05	.03
496	Craig Worthington	.05	.03
497	Juan Agosto	.05	.03
498	Eric Anthony	.12	.07
499	Craig Biggio	.08	.05
500	Ken Caminiti	.07	.04
501	Casey Candaele	.05	.03
502	Andujar Cedeno (R)	.15	.10
503	Danny Darwin	.05	.03
504	Mark Davidson	.05	.03
505	Glenn Davis	.07	.04
506	Jim Deshaies	.05	.03
507	Luis Gonzalez (R)	.15	.10
508	Bill Gullickson	.05	.03
509	Xavier Hernandez	.07	.04
510	Brian Meyer	.05	.03
511	Ken Oberkfell	.05	.03
512	Mark Portugal	.05	.03
513	Rafael Ramirez	.05	.03
514	Karl Rhodes (R)	.07	.04
515	Mike Scott	.07	.04
516	Mike Simms (R)	.07	.04
517	Dave Smith	.05	.03
518	Franklin Stubbs	.05	.03
519	Glenn Wilson	.05	.03
520	Eric Yelding	.05	.03
521	Gerald Young	.05	.03
522	Shawn Abner	.05	.03
523	Roberto Alomar	.25	.15
524	Andy Benes	.12	.07
525	Joe Carter	.12	.07
526	Jack Clark	.07	.04
527	Joey Cora	.05	.03
528	Paul Faries (R)	.07	.04
529	Tony Gwynn	.15	.10
530	Atlee Hammaker	.05	.03
531	Greg Harris	.05	.03
532	Thomas Howard	.07	.04
533	Bruce Hurst	.07	.04
534	Craig Lefferts	.05	.03
535	Derek Lilliquist	.05	.03
536	Fred Lynn	.08	.05
537	Mike Pagliarulo	.05	.03
538	Mark Parent	.05	.03
539	Dennis Rasmussen	.05	.03
540	Bip Roberts	.07	.04
541	Richard Rodriguez (R)	.10	.06
542	Benito Santiago	.08	.05
543	Calvin Schiraldi	.05	.03
544	Eric Show	.05	.03
545	Phil Stephenson	.05	.03
546	Garry Templeton	.05	.03
547	Ed Whitson	.05	.03
548	Eddie Williams	.05	.03
549	Kevin Appier	.12	.07
550	Luis Aquino	.05	.03
551	Bob Boone	.08	.05
552	George Brett	.20	.12
553	Jeff Conine (R)	.15	.10
554	Steve Crawford	.05	.03
555	Mark Davis	.05	.03
556	Storm Davis	.05	.03
557	Jim Eisenreich	.05	.03
558	Steve Farr	.05	.03
559	Tom Gordon	.07	.04
560	Mark Gubicza	.08	.05
561	Bo Jackson	.15	.10
562	Mike Macfarlane	.05	.03
563	Brian McRae (R)	.25	.15
564	Jeff Montgomery	.05	.03
565	Bill Pecota	.05	.03
566	Gerald Perry	.05	.03
567	Bret Saberhagen	.08	.05
568	Jeff Schulz (R)	.08	.05
569	Kevin Seitzer	.07	.04
570	Terry Shumpert	.05	.03
571	Kurt Stillwell	.05	.03
572	Danny Tartabull	.10	.06
573	Gary Thurman	.05	.03
574	Frank White	.05	.03
575	Willie Wilson	.05	.03
576	Chris Bosio	.05	.03
577	Greg Brock	.05	.03
578	George Canale	.05	.03
579	Chuck Crim	.05	.03
580	Rob Deer	.07	.04
581	Edgar Diaz	.05	.03
582	Tom Edens (R)	.08	.05
583	Mike Felder	.05	.03
584	Jim Gantner	.05	.03
585	Darryl Hamilton	.05	.03
586	Ted Higuera	.05	.03
587	Mark Knudson	.05	.03
588	Bill Krueger	.05	.03
589	Tim McIntosh	.10	.06
590	Pal Mirabella	.05	.03
591	Paul Molitor	.10	.06
592	Jaime Navarro	.10	.06
593	Dave Parker	.07	.04
594	Dan Plesac	.05	.03
595	Ron Robinson	.05	.03
596	Gary Sheffield	.35	.20
597	Bill Spiers	.05	.03
598	B.J. Surhoff	.05	.03
599	Greg Vaughn	.10	.06
600	Randy Veres	.05	.03
601	Robin Yount	.20	.12
602	Rick Aguilera	.05	.03
603	Allan Anderson	.05	.03
604	Juan Berenguer	.05	.03
605	Randy Bush	.05	.03
606	Carmen Castillo	.05	.03
607	Tim Drummond	.05	.03
608	Scott Erickson (R)	.25	.15
609	Gary Gaetti	.05	.03
610	Greg Gagne	.05	.03

611	Dan Gladden	.05	.03
612	Mark Guthrie (R)	.08	.05
613	Brian Harper	.05	.03
614	Kent Hrbek	.08	.05
615	Gene Larkin	.05	.03
616	Terry Leach	.05	.03
617	Nelson Liriano	.05	.03
618	Shane Mack	.10	.06
619	John Moses	.05	.03
620	Pedro Munoz	.20	.12
621	Al Newman	.05	.03
622	Junior Ortiz	.05	.03
623	Kirby Puckett	.20	.12
624	Roy Smith	.05	.03
625	Kevin Tapani	.08	.05
626	Gary Wayne	.05	.03
627	David West	.05	.03
628	Cris Carpenter	.05	.03
629	Vince Coleman	.07	.04
630	Ken Dayley	.05	.03
631	Jose DeLeon	.05	.03
632	Frank DePino	.05	.03
633	Bernard Gilkey (R)	.20	.12
634	Pedro Guerrero	.07	.04
635	Ken Hill	.10	.06
636	Felix Jose	.10	.06
637	Ray Lankford (R)	.35	.20
638	Joe Magrane	.05	.03
639	Tom Niedenfuer	.05	.03
640	Jose Oquendo	.05	.03
641	Tom Pagnozzi	.08	.05
642	Terry Pendleton	.15	.10
643	Mike Perez (R)	.12	.07
644	Bryn Smith	.05	.03
645	Lee Smith	.12	.07
646	Ozzie Smith	.15	.10
647	Scott Terry	.05	.03
648	Bob Tewksbury	.05	.03
649	Milt Thompson	.05	.03
650	John Tudor	.05	.03
651	Denny Walling	.05	.03
652	Craig Wilson (R)	.12	.07
653	Todd Worrell	.07	.04
654	Todd Zeile	.08	.05
655	Oscar Azocar	.05	.03
656	Steve Balboni	.05	.03
657	Jesse Barfield	.07	.04
658	Greg Cadaret	.05	.03
659	Chuck Cary	.05	.03
660	Rick Cerone	.05	.03
661	Dave Eiland	.07	.04
662	Alvaro Espinoza	.05	.03
663	Bob Geren	.05	.03
664	Lee Guetterman	.05	.03
665	Mel Hall	.07	.04
666	Andy Hawkins	.05	.03
667	Jimmy Jones	.05	.03
668	Roberto Kelly	.12	.07
669	Dave LaPoint	.05	.03
670	Tim Leary	.05	.03
671	Jim Leyritz	.05	.03
672	Kevin Maas	.10	.06
673	Don Mattingly	.12	.07
674	Matt Nokes	.05	.03
675	Pascual Perez	.05	.03
676	Eric Plunk	.05	.03
677	Dave Righetti	.05	.03
678	Jeff Robinson	.05	.03
679	Steve Sax	.08	.05
680	Mike Witt	.05	.03
681	Steve Avery	.25	.15
682	Mike Bell	.05	.03
683	Jeff Blauser	.05	.03
684	Francisco Cabrera	.05	.03
685	Tony Castillo	.07	.04
686	Marty Clary	.05	.03
687	Nick Esasky	.05	.03
688	Ron Gant	.12	.07
689	Tom Glavine	.25	.15
690	Mark Grant	.05	.03
691	Tommy Gregg	.05	.03
692	Dwayne Henry	.05	.03
693	Dave Justice	.25	.15
694	Jimmy Kremers	.05	.03
695	Charlie Leibrandt	.05	.03
696	Mark Lemke	.05	.03
697	Oddibe McDowell	.05	.03
698	Greg Olson	.07	.04
699	Jeff Parrett	.05	.03
700	Jim Presley	.05	.03
701	Victor Rosario (R)	.08	.05
702	Lonnie Smith	.07	.04
703	Pete Smith	.10	.06
704	John Smoltz	.15	.10
705	Mike Stanton	.05	.03
706	Andres Thomas	.05	.03
707	Jeff Treadway	.05	.03
708	Jim Vatcher (R)	.08	.05
709	Ryne Sandberg/Cecil Fielder	.15	.10
710	Barry Bonds/Ken Griffey, Jr.	.35	.20
711	Bobby Bonilla/Barry Larkin	.10	.06
712	Bobby Thigpen/John Franco	.07	.04
713	Andre Dawson/Ryne Sandberg	.15	.10
714	Team Checklists	.05	.03
715	Team Checklists	.05	.03
716	Team Checklists	.05	.03
717	Team Checklists	.05	.03
718	Team Checklists	.05	.03
719	Team Checklists	.05	.03
720	Team Checklists	.05	.03

1991 Fleer Update

The cards in this update set are identical to Fleer's regular 1991 edition and include players traded during the year and a number of up and coming rookie prospects. Cards measure 2-1/2" by 3-1/2" and the set contains 132-cards.

		MINT	NR/MT
Complete Set (132)		7.00	4.50
Commons		.05	.03
1	Glenn Davis	.10	.06
2	Dwight Evans	.08	.05
3	Jose Mesa (R)	.08	.05
4	Jack Clark	.07	.04
5	Danny Darwin	.05	.03
6	Steve Lyons	.05	.03
7	Mo Vaughn (R)	.20	.12
8	Floyd Bannister	.05	.03
9	Gary Gaetti	.05	.03
10	Dave Parker	.08	.05
11	Joey Cora	.05	.03
12	Charlie Hough	.05	.03
13	Matt Merullo	.07	.04
14	Warren Newson (R)	.12	.07
15	Tim Raines	.08	.05
16	Albert Belle	.20	.12
17	Glenallen Hill	.08	.05
18	Shawn Hillegas	.05	.03
19	Mark Lewis (R)	.15	.10
20	Charles Nagy (R)	.50	.30
21	Mark Whiten	.12	.07
22	John Cerutti	.05	.03
23	Rob Deer	.07	.04
24	Mickey Tettleton	.08	.05
25	Warren Cromartie	.05	.03
26	Kirk Gibson	.08	.05
27	David Howard (R)	.08	.05
28	Brent Mayne (R)	.10	.06
29	Dante Bichette	.05	.03
30	Mark Lee (R)	.08	.05
31	Julio Machado	.05	.03
32	Edwin Nunez	.05	.03
33	Willie Randolph	.07	.04
34	Franklin Stubbs	.05	.03
35	Bill Wegman	.05	.03
36	Chili Davis	.08	.05
37	Chuck Knoblauch (R)	.60	.35
38	Scott Leius	.05	.03
39	Jack Morris	.12	.07
40	Mike Pagliarulo	.05	.03
41	Lenny Webster (R)	.10	.06
42	John Habyan	.05	.03
43	Steve Howe	.05	.03
44	Jeff Johnson (R)	.10	.06
45	Scott Kamieniecki (R)	.10	.06
46	Pet Kelly (R)	.15	.10
47	Hensley Meulens	.08	.05
48	Wade Taylor (R)	.12	.07
49	Bernie Williams (R)	.20	.12
50	Kirk Dressendorfer (R)	.15	.10
51	Ernest Riles	.05	.03
52	Rich DeLucia (R)	.10	.06
53	Tracy Jones	.05	.03
54	Bill Krueger	.05	.03
55	Alonzo Powell	.07	.04
56	Jeff Schaefer	.05	.03
57	Russ Swan (R)	.08	.05
58	John Barfield (R)	.08	.05
59	Rich Gossage	.10	.06
60	Jose Guzman	.07	.04
61	Dean Palmer (R)	.35	.20
62	Ivan Rodriguez (R)	1.25	.80
63	Roberto Alomar	.30	.18
64	Tom Candiotti	.07	.04
65	Joe Carter	.20	.12
66	Ed Sprague	.12	.07
67	Pat Tabler	.05	.03
68	Mike Timlin (R)	.10	.06
69	Devon White	.07	.04
70	Rafael Belliard	.05	.03
71	Juan Berenguer	.05	.03
72	Sid Bream	.05	.03
73	Marvin Freeman	.05	.03
74	Kent Mercker	.08	.05
75	Otis Nixon	.07	.04
76	Terry Pendleton	.15	.10
77	George Bell	.12	.07
78	Danny Jackson	.07	.04
79	Chuck McElroy	.07	.04
80	Gary Scott (R)	.10	.06
81	Heathcliff Slocumb (R)	.12	.07
82	Dave Smith	.05	.03
83	Rick Wilkins (R)	.12	.07
84	Freddie Benavides (R)	.10	.06
85	Ted Power	.05	.03
86	Mo Sanford (R)	.15	.10
87	Jeff Bagwell (R)	1.50	.90
88	Steve Finley	.05	.03

1991 Fleer Ultra

This 400-card set marks Fleer's first venture into the upscale premium baseball card market. Cards measure 2-1/2" by 3-1/2" and feature full color photos on the card fronts with gray borders at the top and bottom. Card backs are vertical and consist of three photos and a band with 1990 and career statistics. Special subsets include "Elite Performers" (EP) (391-396) and Major League Prospects (373-390). A special limited edition 10-card Ultra Gold insert set was produced featuring cards with a gold background and three photos on the card fronts. Card backs contained highlights from the player's career in paragraph form. The Ultra Gold inserts are listed at the end of the checklist below but are not included in the complete set price.

		MINT	NR/MT
Complete Set(400)		32.00	22.00
Commons		.07	.04

89	Pete Harnisch	.07	.04
90	Darryl Kile (R)	.12	.07
91	Brett Butler	.10	.06
92	John Candelaria	.05	.03
93	Gary Carter	.10	.06
94	Kevin Gross	.05	.03
95	Bob Ojeda	.05	.03
96	Darryl Strawberry	.15	.10
97	Ivan Calderon	.08	.05
98	Ron Hassey	.05	.03
99	Gilberto Reyes	.05	.03
100	Hubie Brooks	.08	.05
101	Rick Cerone	.05	.03
102	Vince Coleman	.08	.05
103	Jeff Innis	.05	.03
104	Pete Schourek (R)	.12	.07
105	Andy Ashby (R)	.10	.06
106	Wally Backman	.05	.03
107	Darrin Fletcher (R)	.10	.06
108	Tommy Greene	.08	.05
109	John Morris	.05	.03
110	Mitch Williams	.08	.05
111	Lloyd McClendon	.05	.03
112	Orlando Merced (R)	.25	.15
113	Vicente Palacios	.05	.03
114	Gary Varsho	.05	.03
115	John Wehner (R)	.10	.06
116	Rex Hudler	.05	.03
117	Tim Jones	.05	.03
118	Geronimo Pena	.05	.03
119	Gerald Perry	.05	.03
120	Larry Andersen	.05	.03
121	Jerald Clark	.08	.05
122	Scott Coolbaugh	.05	.03
123	Tony Fernandez	.08	.05
124	Darrin Jackson	.07	.04
125	Fred McGriff	.20	.12
126	Jose Mota (R)	.10	.06
127	Tim Teufel	.05	.03
128	Bud Black	.07	.04
129	Mike Felder	.05	.03
130	Willie McGee	.08	.05
131	Dave Righetti	.07	.04
132	Checklist	.05	.03
1	Steve Avery	1.25	.80
2	Jeff Blauser	.07	.04
3	Francisco Cabrera	.07	.04
4	Ron Gant	.35	.20
5	Tom Glavine	.50	.30
6	Tommy Gregg	.07	.04
7	Dave Justice	1.50	.90
8	Oddibe McDowell	.07	.04
9	Greg Olson	.10	.06
10	Terry Pendleton	.25	.15
11	Lonnie Smith	.10	.06
12	John Smoltz	.30	.18
13	Jeff Treadway	.07	.04
14	Glenn Davis	.10	.06
15	Mike Devereaux	.15	.10
16	Leo Gomez	.40	.25

#	Player			#	Player		
17	Chris Hoiles	.25	.15	75	Greg Hibbard	.07	.04
18	Dave Johnson	.07	.04	76	Lance Johnson	.07	.04
19	Ben McDonald	.30	.18	77	Steve Lyons	.07	.04
20	Randy Milligan	.10	.06	78	Jack McDowell	.35	.20
21	Gregg Olson	.12	.07	79	Dan Pasqua	.07	.04
22	Joe Orsulak	.10	.06	80	Melido Perez	.10	.06
23	Bill Ripken	.07	.04	81	Tim Raines	.10	.06
24	Cal Ripken, Jr.	1.00	.70	82	Sammy Sosa	.10	.06
25	David Segui	.12	.07	83	Cory Snyder	.07	.04
26	Craig Worthington	.07	.04	84	Bobby Thigpen	.10	.06
27	Wade Boggs	.25	.15	85	Frank Thomas	5.00	3.50
28	Tom Bolton	.07	.04	86	Robin Ventura	.80	.50
29	Tom Brunansky	.10	.06	87	Todd Benzinger	.07	.04
30	Ellis Burks	.12	.07	88	Glenn Braggs	.07	.04
31	Roger Clemens	.80	.50	89	Tom Browning	.10	.06
32	Mike Greenwell	.12	.07	90	Norm Charlton	.10	.06
33	Greg Harris	.07	.04	91	Eric Davis	.12	.07
34	Daryl Irvine	.07	.04	92	Rob Dibble	.10	.06
35	Mike Marshall	.07	.04	93	Bill Doran	.07	.04
36	Tim Naehring	.10	.06	94	Mariano Duncan	.07	.04
37	Tony Pena	.07	.04	95	Billy Hatcher	.07	.04
38	Phil Plantier (R)	1.50	.90	96	Barry Larkin	.15	.10
39	Carlos Quintana	.12	.07	97	Randy Myers	.07	.04
40	Jeff Reardon	.20	.12	98	Hal Morris	.15	.10
41	Jody Reed	.07	.04	99	Joe Oliver	.10	.06
42	Luis Rivera	.07	.04	100	Paul O'Neill	.12	.07
43	Jim Abbott	.25	.15	101	Jeff Reed	.07	.04
44	Chuck Finley	.12	.07	102	Jose Rijo	.12	.07
45	Bryan Harvey	.10	.06	103	Chris Sabo	.10	.07
46	Donnie Hill	.07	.04	104	Beau Allred	.12	.07
47	Jack Howell	.07	.04	105	Sandy Alomar, Jr.	.12	.07
48	Wally Joyner	.12	.07	106	Carlos Baerga	.75	.45
49	Mark Langston	.12	.07	107	Albert Belle	.50	.30
50	Kirk McCaskill	.07	.04	108	Jerry Browne	.07	.04
51	Lance Parrish	.10	.06	109	Tom Candiotti	.07	.04
52	Dick Schofield	.07	.04	110	Alex Cole	.07	.04
53	Lee Stevens	.12	.07	111	John Farrell	.07	.04
54	Dave Winfield	.30	.18	112	Felix Fermin	.07	.04
55	George Bell	.15	.10	113	Brook Jacoby	.07	.04
56	Damon Berryhill	.07	.04	114	Chris James	.07	.04
57	Mike Bielecki	.07	.04	115	Doug Jones	.07	.04
58	Andre Dawson	.25	.15	116	Steve Olin	.10	.06
59	Shawon Dunston	.10	.06	117	Greg Swindell	.10	.06
60	Joe Girardi	.07	.04	118	Turner Warner	.07	.04
61	Mark Grace	.20	.12	119	Mitch Webster	.07	.04
62	Mike Harkey	.10	.06	120	Dave Bergman	.07	.04
63	Les Lancaster	.07	.04	121	Cecil Fielder	.40	.25
64	Greg Maddux	.25	.15	122	Travis Fryman	2.00	1.25
65	Derrick May	.15	.10	123	Mike Henneman	.07	.04
66	Ryne Sandberg	.75	.45	124	Lloyd Moseby	.07	.04
67	Luis Salazar	.07	.04	125	Dan Petry	.07	.04
68	Dwight Smith	.10	.06	126	Tony Phillips	.07	.04
69	Hector Villanueva	.10	.06	127	Mark Salas	.07	.04
70	Jerome Walton	.10	.06	128	Frank Tanana	.07	.04
71	Mitch Williams	.07	.04	129	Alan Trammell	.15	.10
72	Carlton Fisk	.20	.12	130	Lou Whitaker	.10	.06
73	Scott Fletcher	.07	.04	131	Eric Anthony	.15	.10
74	Ozzie Guillen	.07	.04	132	Craig Biggio	.15	.10

133	Ken Caminiti	.10	.06	191	Shane Mack	.12	.07
134	Casey Candaele	.07	.04	192	Pedro Munoz (R)	.80	.50
135	Andujar Cedeno	.30	.18	193	Al Newman	.07	.04
136	Mark Davidson	.07	.04	194	Junior Ortiz	.07	.04
137	Jim Deshaies	.07	.04	195	Kirby Puckett	.75	.45
138	Mark Portugal	.07	.04	196	Kevin Tapani	.10	.06
139	Rafael Ramirez	.07	.04	197	Dennis Boyd	.07	.04
140	Mike Scott	.10	.06	198	Tim Burke	.07	.04
141	Eric Yelding	.07	.04	199	Ivan Calderon	.10	.06
142	Gerald Young	.07	.04	200	Delino DeShields	.50	.30
143	Kevin Appier	.12	.07	201	Mike Fitzgerald	.07	.04
144	George Brett	.30	.18	202	Steve Frey	.07	.04
145	Jeff Conine (R)	.20	.12	203	Andres Galarraga	.10	.06
146	Jim Eisenreich	.07	.04	204	Marquis Grissom	.50	.30
147	Tom Gordon	.10	.06	205	Dave Martinez	.07	.04
148	Mark Gubicza	.10	.06	206	Dennis Martinez	.12	.07
149	Bo Jackson	.20	.12	207	Junior Noboa	.07	.04
150	Brent Mayne	.10	.06	208	Spike Owen	.07	.04
151	Mike Macfarlane	.07	.04	209	Scott Ruskin (R)	.07	.04
152	Brian McRae (R)	.30	.18	210	Tim Wallach	.12	.07
153	Jeff Montgomery	.07	.04	211	Daryl Boston	.07	.04
154	Bret Saberhagen	.15	.10	212	Vince Coleman	.10	.06
155	Kevin Seitzer	.07	.04	213	David Cone	.20	.12
156	Terry Shumpert	.07	.04	214	Ron Darling	.07	.04
157	Kurt Stillwell	.07	.04	215	Kevin Elster	.07	.04
158	Danny Tartabull	.15	.10	216	Sid Fernandez	.10	.06
159	Tim Belcher	.07	.04	217	John Franco	.07	.04
160	Kal Daniels	.07	.04	218	Dwight Gooden	.20	.12
161	Alfredo Griffin	.07	.04	219	Tom Herr	.07	.04
162	Lenny Harris	.07	.04	220	Todd Hundley	.10	.06
163	Jay Howell	.07	.04	221	Gregg Jefferies	.20	.12
164	Ramon Martinez	.15	.10	222	Howard Johnson	.12	.07
165	Mike Morgan	.07	.04	223	Dave Magadan	.10	.06
166	Eddie Murray	.15	.10	224	Kevin McReynolds	.10	.06
167	Jose Offerman	.12	.07	225	Keith Miller	.07	.04
168	Juan Samuel	.07	.04	226	Mackey Sasser	.07	.04
169	Mike Scioscia	.07	.04	227	Frank Viola	.10	.06
170	Mike Sharperson	.07	.04	228	Jesse Barfield	.10	.06
171	Darryl Strwberry	.25	.15	229	Greg Cadaret	.07	.04
172	Greg Brock	.07	.04	230	Alvaro Espinoza (R)	.07	.04
173	Chuck Crim	.07	.04	231	Bob Geren	.07	.04
174	Jim Gantner	.07	.04	232	Lee Guetterman	.07	.04
175	Ted Higuera	.07	.04	233	Mel Hall	.10	.06
176	Mark Knudson	.07	.04	234	Andy Hawkins	.07	.04
177	Tim McIntosh	.12	.07	235	Roberto Kelly	.15	.10
178	Paul Molitor	.15	.10	236	Tim Leary	.07	.04
179	Dan Plesac	.07	.04	237	Jim Leyritz	.07	.04
180	Gary Sheffield	1.50	.90	238	Kevin Maas	.12	.07
181	Bill Spiers	.07	.04	239	Don Mattingly	.25	.15
182	B.J. Surhoff	.07	.04	240	Hensley Meulens	.10	.06
183	Greg Vaughn	.12	.07	241	Eric Plunk	.07	.04
184	Robin Yount	.30	.18	242	Steve Sax	.10	.06
185	Rick Aguilera	.07	.04	243	Todd Burns	.07	.04
186	Greg Gagne	.07	.04	244	Jose Canseco	.75	.45
187	Dan Gladden	.07	.04	245	Dennis Eckersley	.15	.10
188	Brian Harper	.07	.04	246	Mike Gallego	.07	.04
189	Kent Hrbek	.10	.06	247	Dave Henderson	.07	.04
190	Gene Larkin	.07	.04	248	Rickey Henderson	.35	.20

No.	Player		
249	Rick Honeycutt	.07	.04
250	Carney Lansford	.10	.06
251	Mark McGwire	.60	.35
252	Mike Moore	.07	.04
253	Terry Steinbach	.10	.06
254	Dave Stewart	.12	.07
255	Walt Weiss	.07	.04
256	Bob Welch	.07	.04
257	Curt Young	.07	.04
258	Wes Chamberlain (R)	.35	.20
259	Pat Combs	.07	.04
260	Darren Daulton	.12	.07
261	Jose DeJesus	.07	.04
262	Len Dykstra	.10	.06
263	Charlie Hayes	.07	.04
264	Von Hayes	.07	.04
265	Ken Howell	.07	.04
266	John Kruk	.10	.06
267	Roger McDowell	.07	.04
268	Mickey Morandini (R)	.15	.10
269	Terry Mulholland	.07	.04
270	Dale Murphy	.15	.10
271	Randy Ready	.07	.04
272	Dickie Thon	.07	.04
273	Stan Belinda	.07	.04
274	Jay Bell	.07	.04
275	Barry Bonds	.50	.30
276	Bobby Bonilla	.20	.12
277	Doug Drabek	.15	.10
278	Carlos Garcia (R)	.20	.12
279	Neal Heaton	.07	.04
280	Jeff King	.10	.06
281	Bill Landrum	.07	.04
282	Mike LaValliere	.07	.04
283	Jose Lind	.07	.04
284	Orlando Merced (R)	.35	.20
285	Gary Redus	.07	.04
286	Don Slaught	.07	.04
287	Andy Van Slyke	.15	.10
288	Jose DeLeon	.07	.04
289	Pedro Guerrero	.10	.06
290	Ray Lankford	.60	.35
291	Joe Magrane	.07	.04
292	Jose Oquendo	.07	.04
293	Tom Pagnozzi	.07	.04
294	Bryn Smith	.07	.04
295	Lee Smith	.12	.07
296	Ozzie Smith	.20	.12
297	Milt Thompson	.07	.04
298	Craig Wilson (R)	.12	.07
299	Todd Zeile	.12	.07
300	Shawn Abner	.07	.04
301	Andy Benes	.15	.10
302	Paul Faries (R)	.07	.04
303	Tony Gwynn	.30	.18
304	Greg Harris	.07	.04
305	Thomas Howard	.10	.06
306	Bruce Hurst	.10	.06
307	Craig Lefferts	.07	.04
308	Fred McGriff	.45	.28
309	Dennis Rasmussen	.07	.04
310	Bip Roberts	.10	.06
311	Benito Santiago	.12	.07
312	Garry Templeton	.07	.04
313	Ed Whitson	.07	.04
314	Dave Anderson	.07	.04
315	Kevin Bass	.07	.04
316	Jeff Brantley	.07	.04
317	John Burkett	.07	.04
318	Will Clark	.60	.35
319	Steve Decker (R)	.12	.07
320	Scott Garrelts	.07	.04
321	Terry Kennedy	.07	.04
322	Mark Leonard (R)	.10	.06
323	Darren Lewis	.15	.10
324	Greg Litton	.07	.04
325	Willie McGee	.10	.06
326	Kevin Mitchell	.12	.07
327	Don Robinson	.07	.04
328	Andres Santana (R)	.12	.07
329	Robby Thompson	.07	.04
330	Jose Uribe	.07	.04
331	Matt Williams	.15	.10
332	Scott Bradley	.07	.04
334	Alvin Davis	.07	.04
335	Ken Griffey, Sr.	.10	.06
336	Ken Griffey, Jr.	2.50	1.50
337	Erik Hanson	.10	.06
338	Brian Holman	.10	.06
339	Randy Johnson	.25	.15
340	Edgar Martinez	.20	.12
341	Tino Martinez	.12	.07
342	Pete O'Brien	.07	.04
343	Harold Reynolds	.10	.06
344	David Valle	.07	.04
345	Omar Vizquel	.07	.04
346	Brad Arnsberg	.07	.04
347	Kevin Brown	.12	.07
348	Julio Franco	.12	.07
349	Jeff Huson	.07	.04
350	Rafael Palmeiro	.15	.10
351	Geno Petralli	.07	.04
352	Gary Pettis	.07	.04
353	Kenny Rogers	.07	.04
354	Jeff Russell	.07	.04
355	Nolan Ryan	1.50	.90
356	Ruben Sierra	.45	.28
357	Bobby Witt	.10	.06
358	Roberto Alomar	.70	.40
359	Pat Borders	.07	.04
360	Joe Carter	.25	.15
361	Kelly Gruber	.10	.06
362	Tom Henke	.07	.04
363	Glenallen Hill	.10	.06
364	Jimmy Key	.07	.04
365	Manny Lee	.07	.04

366	Rance Mulliniks	.07	.04
367	John Olerud	.15	.10
368	Dave Stieb	.10	.06
369	Duane Ward	.07	.04
370	David Wells	.07	.04
371	Mark Whiten	.15	.10
372	Mookie Wilson	.07	.04
373	Willie Banks (R)	.20	.12
374	Steve Carter (R)	.10	.06
375	Scott Chiamparino (R)	.12	.07
376	Steve Chitren (R)	.12	.07
377	Darrin Fletcher (R)	.10	.06
378	Rich Garces (R)	.12	.07
379	Reggie Jefferson (R)	.20	.12
380	Eric Karros (R)	3.50	2.50
381	Pat Kelly (R)	.20	.12
382	Chuck Knoblauch (R)	.50	.30
383	Denny Neagle (R)	.15	.10
384	Dan Opperman (R)	.12	.07
385	John Ramos (R)	.12	.07
386	Henry Rodriguez (R)	.35	.20
387	Maurice Vaughn (R)	.35	.20
388	Gerald Williams (R)	.50	.30
389	Mike York (R)	.10	.06
390	Eddie Zosky (R)	.12	.07
391	Barry Bonds (EP)	.20	.12
392	Cecil Fielder (EP)	.20	.12
393	Rickey Henderson(EP)	.20	.12
394	Dave Justice (EP)	.25	.15
395	Nolan Ryan (EP)	.60	.35
396	Bobby Thigpen (EP)	.12	.07
397	Checklist	.07	.04
398	Checklist	.07	.04
399	Checklist	.07	.04
400	Checklist	.07	.04
G1	Barry Bonds (Gold)	1.50	.90
G2	Will Clark (Gold)	1.75	1.00
G3	Doug Drabek (Gold)	.75	.45
G4	Ken Griffey Jr. (Gold)	3.50	2.50
G5	Rickey Henderson (Gold)	1.50	.90
G6	Bo Jackson (Gold)	1.00	.70
G7	Ramon Martinez(Gold)	.75	.45
G8	Kirby Puckett (Gold)	2.00	1.25
G9	Chris Sabo (Gold)	.50	.30
G10	Ryne Sandberg (Gold)	1.75	1.00

1991 Fleer Ultra Update

This 120-card update set is an extension of the Ultra set. Card fronts are identical to the regular edtion with a large action shot on the front and three small photos on the card backs. Cards measure 2-1/2" by 3-1/2" and the set features players who were traded during the year and a number of promising rookies.

		MINT	NR/MT
	Complete Set (120)	32.00	22.00
	Commons	.07	.04

1	Dwight Evans	.10	.06
2	Chito Martinez (R)	.25	.15
3	Bob Melvin	.07	.04
4	Mike Mussina (R)	7.50	5.00
5	Jack Clark	.10	.06
6	Dana Kiecker	.07	.04
7	Steve Lyons	.07	.04
8	Gary Gaetti	.07	.04
9	Dave Gallagher	.07	.04
10	Dave Parker	.10	.06
11	Luis Polonia	.10	.06
12	Luis Sojo	.10	.06
13	Wilson Alverez	.10	.06
14	Alex Fernandez	.35	.20
15	Craig Grebeck	.07	.04
16	Ron Karkovice	.07	.04
17	Warren Newson (R)	.20	.12
18	Scott Radinsky	.10	.06
19	Glenallen Hill	.10	.06
20	Charles Nagy	1.50	.90
21	Mark Whiten	.35	.20
22	Milt Cuyler (R)	.25	.15
23	Paul Gibson	.07	.04
24	Mickey Tettleton	.10	.06
25	Todd Benzinger	.07	.04

#	Player		
26	Storm Davis	.07	.04
27	Kirk Gibson	.10	.06
28	Bill Pecota	.07	.04
30	Darryl Hamilton	.10	.06
31	Jaime Navarro (R)	.50	.30
32	Willie Randolph	.10	.06
33	Bill Wegman	.07	.04
34	Randy Bush	.07	.04
35	Chili Davis	.10	.06
36	Scott Erickson (R)	.80	.50
37	Chuck Knoblauch	2.50	1.50
38	Scott Leius	.15	.10
39	Jack Morris	.15	.10
40	John Habyan	.07	.04
41	Pat Kelly	.35	.20
42	Matt Nokes	.07	.04
43	Scott Sanderson	.07	.04
44	Bernie Williams (R)	1.00	.70
45	Harold Baines	.10	.06
46	Brook Jacoby	.07	.04
47	Ernest Riles	.07	.04
48	Willie Wilson	.07	.04
49	Jay Buhner	.10	.06
50	Rich DeLucia (R)	.15	.10
51	Mike Jackson	.07	.04
52	Bill Krueger	.07	.04
53	Bill Swift	.10	.06
54	Brian Downing	.07	.04
55	Juan Gonzalez	8.50	5.50
56	Dean Palmer (R)	2.50	1.50
57	Kevin Reimer	.25	.15
58	Ivan Rodriguez (R)	4.50	3.50
59	Tom Candiotti	.07	.04
60	Juan Guzman (R)	8.50	5.50
61	Bob MacDonald (R)	.15	.10
62	Greg Myers	.07	.04
63	Ed Sprague	.25	.15
64	Devon White	.10	.06
65	Rafael Belliard	.07	.04
66	Juan Berenguer	.07	.04
67	Brian Hunter (R)	.60	.35
68	Kent Mercker	.10	.06
69	Otis Nixon	.10	.06
70	Danny Jackson	.10	.06
71	Chuck McElroy	.10	.06
72	Gary Scott (R)	.20	.12
73	Heathcliff Slocumb	.12	.07
74	Chico Walker	.10	.06
75	Rick Wilkins (R)	.15	.10
76	Chris Hammond (R)	.25	.15
77	Luis Quinones	.07	.04
78	Herm Winningham	.07	.04
79	Jeff Bagwell (R)	4.00	2.75
80	Jim Corsi	.07	.04
81	Steve Finley	.10	.06
82	Luis Gonzalez (R)	.30	.18
83	Pete Harnisch	.10	.06
84	Darryl Kile (R)	.20	.12
85	Brett Butler	.12	.07
86	Gary Carter	.12	.07
87	Tim Crews	.07	.04
88	Orel Hershiser	.12	.07
89	Bob Ojeda	.07	.04
90	Bret Barberie (R)	.30	.18
91	Barry Jones	.07	.04
92	Gilberto Reyes	.07	.04
93	Larry Walker	.75	.45
94	Hubie Brooks	.10	.06
95	Tim Burke	.07	.04
96	Rick Cerone	.07	.04
97	Jeff Innis	.07	.04
98	Wally Backman	.07	.04
99	Tommy Greene	.10	.06
100	Ricky Jordan	.10	.06
101	Mitch Williams	.10	.06
102	John Smiley	.15	.10
103	Randy Tomlin (R)	.80	.50
104	Gary Varsho	.07	.04
105	Cris Carpenter	.07	.04
106	Ken Hill	.20	.12
107	Felix Jose	.25	.15
108	Omar Oliveras (R)	.25	.15
109	Gerald Perry	.07	.04
110	Jerald Clark	.10	.06
111	Tony Fernandez	.10	.06
112	Darrin Jackson	.07	.04
113	Mike Maddux	.07	.04
114	Tim Teufel	.07	.04
115	Bud Black	.10	.06
116	Kelly Downs	.07	.04
117	Mike Felder	.07	.04
118	Willie McGee	.10	.06
119	Trevor Wilson	.07	.04
120	Checklist	.07	.04

1992 Fleer

This 720-card set features full color action photos framed by a blue border on the card fronts. The player's name, position and team are located in the wide border to the right of the photo. The top half of the card backs contain a full color action shot with statistics and bio's below the picture. Key subsets include Record Setters (RS)(681-687), League Leaders (LL)(688-697) and Pro Vision Art cards (PV)(708-713). Twelve special limited edition Roger Clemens cards were randomly inserted into Fleer wax packs. Three additonal Clemens cards were available through the mail. These 15-cards are listed at the end of this checklist but are not included in the complete set price.

		MINT	NR/MT
Complete Set (720)		22.50	15.00
Commons		.05	.03

1	Brady Anderson	.12	.07
2	Jose Bautista	.05	.03
3	Juan Bell	.05	.03
4	Glenn Davis	.08	.05
5	Mike Devereaux	.08	.05
6	Dwight Evans	.08	.05
7	Mike Flanagan	.05	.03
8	Leo Gomez	.10	.06
9	Chris Hoiles	.12	.07
10	Sam Horn	.07	.04
11	Tim Hulett	.05	.03
12	Dave Johnson	.05	.03
13	Chito Martinez	.20	.12
14	Ben McDonald	.12	.07
15	Bob Melvin	.05	.03
16	Luis Mercedes	.15	.10
17	Jose Mesa	.05	.03
18	Bob Milacki	.05	.03
19	Randy Milligan	.07	.04
20	Mike Mussina	.60	.35
21	Gregg Olson	.07	.04
22	Joe Orsulak	.05	.03
23	Jim Poole	.05	.03
24	Arthur Rhodes	.15	.10
25	Billy Ripken	.05	.03
26	Cal Ripken, Jr.	.25	.15
27	David Segui	.07	.04
28	Roy Smith	.05	.03
29	Anthony Telford	.07	.04
30	Mark Williamson	.05	.03
31	Craig Worthington	.05	.03
32	Wade Boggs	.12	.07
33	Tom Bolton	.05	.03
34	Tom Brunansky	.07	.04
35	Ellis Burks	.08	.05
36	Jack Clark	.07	.04
37	Roger Clemens	.25	.15
38	Danny Darwin	.05	.03
39	Mike Greenwell	.08	.05
40	Joe Hesketh	.05	.03
41	Daryl Irvine	.05	.03
42	Dennis Lamp	.05	.03
43	Tony Pena	.05	.03
44	Phil Plantier	.15	.10
45	Carlos Quintana	.07	.04
46	Jeff Reardon	.10	.06
47	Jody Reed	.05	.03
48	Luis Rivera	.05	.03
49	Mo Vaughn	.12	.07
50	Jim Abbott	.12	.07
51	Kyle Abbott	.07	.04
52	Ruben Amaro	.12	.07
53	Scott Bailes	.05	.03
54	Chris Beasley (R)	.08	.05
55	Mark Eichhorn	.05	.03
56	Mike Fetters	.05	.03
57	Chuck Finley	.08	.05
58	Gary Gaetti	.05	.03
59	Dave Gallagher	.05	.03
60	Donnie Hill	.05	.03
61	Bryan Harvey	.07	.04
62	Wally Joyner	.08	.05
63	Mark Langston	.08	.05
64	Kirk McCaskill	.05	.03
65	John Orton	.05	.03
66	Lance Parrish	.05	.03
67	Luis Polonia	.07	.04
68	Bobby Rose	.05	.03
69	Dick Schofield	.05	.03
70	Luis Sojo	.05	.03
71	Lee Stevens	.08	.05
72	Dave Winfield	.15	.10
73	Cliff Young	.05	.03
74	Wilson Alvarez	.10	.06
75	Estaban Beltre (R)	.12	.07
76	Joey Cora	.05	.03

77	Brian Drahman	.08	.05
78	Alex Fernandez	.12	.07
79	Carlton Fisk	.12	.07
80	Scott Fletcher	.05	.03
81	Craig Grebeck	.05	.03
82	Ozzie Guillen	.05	.03
83	Greg Hibbard	.05	.03
84	Charlie Hough	.05	.03
85	Mike Huff	.05	.03
86	Bo Jackson	.12	.07
87	Lance Johnson	.05	.03
88	Ron Karkovice	.05	.03
89	Jack McDowell	.12	.07
90	Matt Merullo	.05	.03
91	Warren Newson	.07	.04
92	Donn Pall	.05	.03
93	Dan Pasqua	.05	.03
94	Ken Patterson	.05	.03
95	Melido Perez	.07	.04
96	Scott Radinsky	.05	.03
97	Tim Raines	.07	.04
98	Sammy Sosa	.07	.04
99	Bobby Thigpen	.07	.04
100	Frank Thomas	.80	.50
101	Robin Ventura	.20	.12
102	Mike Aldrete	.05	.03
103	Sandy Alomar, Jr.	.08	.05
104	Carlos Baerga	.20	.12
105	Albert Belle	.15	.10
106	Willie Blair	.08	.05
107	Jerry Browne	.05	.03
108	Alex Cole	.05	.03
109	Felix Fermin	.05	.03
110	Glenallen Hill	.07	.04
111	Shawn Hillegas	.05	.03
112	Chris James	.05	.03
113	Reggie Jefferson	.12	.07
114	Doug Jones	.05	.03
115	Eric King	.05	.03
116	Mark Lewis	.08	.05
117	Carlos Martinez	.05	.03
118	Charles Nagy	.15	.10
119	Rod Nichols	.05	.03
120	Steve Olin	.05	.03
121	Jesse Orosco	.05	.03
122	Rudy Seanez	.08	.05
123	Joel Skinner	.05	.03
124	Greg Swindell	.08	.05
125	Jim Thome (R)	.20	.12
126	Mark Whiten	.08	.05
127	Scott Aldred	.05	.03
128	Andy Allanson	.05	.03
129	John Cerutti	.05	.03
130	Milt Cuyler	.08	.05
131	Mike Dalton (R)	.08	.05
132	Rob Deer	.07	.04
133	Cecil Fielder	.15	.10
134	Travis Fryman	.15	.10
135	Dan Gakeler (R)	.08	.05
136	Paul Gibson	.05	.03
137	Bill Gullickson	.05	.03
138	Mike Henneman	.05	.03
139	Pete Incaviglia	.05	.03
140	Mark Leiter	.07	.04
141	Scott Livingstone (R)	.20	.12
142	Lloyd Moseby	.05	.03
143	Tony Phillips	.05	.03
144	Mark Salas	.05	.03
145	Frank Tanana	.05	.03
146	Walt Terrell	.05	.03
147	Mickey Tettleton	.08	.05
148	Alan Trammell	.10	.06
149	Lou Whitaker	.07	.04
150	Kevin Appier	.08	.05
151	Luis Aquino	.05	.03
152	Todd Benzinger	.05	.03
153	Mike Boddicker	.05	.03
154	George Brett	.15	.10
155	Storm Davis	.05	.03
156	Jim Eisenreich	.05	.03
157	Kirk Gibson	.07	.04
158	Tom Gordon	.07	.04
159	Mark Gubicza	.07	.04
160	David Howard	.07	.04
161	Mike Macfarlane	.05	.03
162	Brent Mayne	.07	.04
163	Brian McRae	.12	.07
164	Jeff Montgomery	.05	.03
165	Bill Pecota	.05	.03
166	Harvey Pulliam (R)	.15	.10
167	Bret Saberhagen	.08	.05
168	Kevin Seitzer	.07	.04
169	Terry Shumpert	.05	.03
170	Kurt Stillwell	.05	.03
171	Danny Tartabull	.10	.06
172	Gary Thurman	.05	.03
173	Dante Bichette	.05	.03
174	Kevin Brown	.07	.04
175	Chuck Crim	.05	.03
176	Jim Gantner	.05	.03
177	Darryl Hamilton	.05	.03
178	Ted Higuera	.05	.03
179	Darren Holmes	.05	.03
180	Mark Lee	.05	.03
181	Julio Machado	.05	.03
182	Paul Molitor	.08	.05
183	Jaime Navarro	.10	.06
184	Edwin Nunez	.05	.03
185	Dan Plesac	.05	.03
186	Willie Randolph	.05	.03
187	Ron Robinson	.05	.03
188	Gary Sheffield	.30	.18
189	Bill Spiers	.05	.03
190	B.J. Surhoff	.05	.03
191	Dale Sveum	.05	.03
192	Greg Vaughn	.10	.06

193	Bill Wegman	.05	.03	251	Mike Bordick (R)	.12	.07
194	Robin Yount	.15	.10	252	Jose Canseco	.20	.12
195	Rick Aguilera	.05	.03	253	Steve Chitren	.05	.03
196	Allan Anderson	.05	.03	254	Ron Darling	.05	.03
197	Steve Bedrosian	.05	.03	255	Dennis Eckersley	.10	.06
198	Randy Bush	.05	.03	256	Mike Gallego	.05	.03
199	Larry Casian (R)	.08	.05	257	Dave Henderson	.05	.03
200	Chili Davis	.07	.04	258	Rickey Henderson	.15	.10
201	Scott Erickson	.12	.07	259	Rick Honeycutt	.05	.03
202	Greg Gagne	.05	.03	260	Brook Jacoby	.05	.03
203	Dan Gladden	.05	.03	261	Carney Lansford	.07	.04
204	Brian Harper	.05	.03	262	Mark McGwire	.20	.12
205	Kent Hrbek	.07	.04	263	Mike Moore	.05	.03
206	Chuck Knoblauch	.20	.12	264	Gene Nelson	.05	.03
207	Gene Larkin	.05	.03	265	Jamie Quirk	.05	.03
208	Terry Leach	.05	.03	266	Joe Slusarski (R)	.12	.07
209	Scott Leius	.07	.04	267	Terry Steinbach	.05	.03
210	Shane Mack	.10	.06	268	Dave Stewart	.08	.05
211	Jack Morris	.10	.06	269	Todd Van Poppel	.25	.15
212	Pedro Munoz	.10	.06	270	Walt Weiss	.05	.03
213	Denny Neagle	.10	.06	271	Bob Welch	.07	.04
214	Al Newman	.05	.03	272	Curt Young	.05	.03
215	Junior Ortiz	.05	.03	273	Scott Bradley	.05	.03
216	Mike Pagliarulo	.05	.03	274	Greg Briley	.05	.03
217	Kirby Puckett	.15	.10	275	Jay Buhner	.07	.04
218	Paul Sorrento	.08	.05	276	Henry Cotto	.05	.03
219	Kevin Tapani	.07	.04	277	Alvin Davis	.05	.03
220	Lenny Webster	.05	.03	278	Rich DeLucia	.05	.03
221	Jesse Barfield	.07	.04	279	Ken Griffey, Jr.	.50	.30
222	Greg Cadaret	.05	.03	280	Erik Hanson	.07	.04
223	Dave Eiland	.05	.03	281	Brian Holman	.07	.04
224	Alvaro Espinoza	.05	.03	282	Mike Jackson	.05	.03
225	Steve Farr	.05	.03	283	Randy Johnson	.12	.07
226	Bob Geren	.05	.03	284	Tracy Jones	.05	.03
227	Lee Guetterman	.05	.03	285	Bill Krueger	.05	.03
228	John Habyan	.05	.03	286	Edgar Martinez	.12	.07
229	Mel Hall	.07	.04	287	Tino Martinez	.08	.05
230	Steve Howe	.05	.03	288	Rob Murphy	.05	.03
231	Mike Humphreys (R)	.08	.05	289	Pete O'Brien	.05	.03
232	Scott Kamieniecki	.08	.05	290	Alonzo Powell	.05	.03
233	Pat Kelly	.10	.06	291	Harold Reynolds	.05	.03
234	Roberto Kelly	.12	.07	292	Mike Schooler	.05	.03
235	Tim Leary	.05	.03	293	Russ Swan	.05	.03
236	Kevin Maas	.10	.06	294	Bill Swift	.07	.04
237	Don Mattingly	.12	.07	295	Dave Valle	.05	.03
238	Hensley Meulens	.07	.04	296	Omar Vizquel	.05	.03
239	Matt Nokes	.05	.03	297	Gerald Alexander	.05	.03
240	Pascual Perez	.05	.03	298	Brad Arnsberg	.05	.03
241	Eric Plunk	.05	.03	299	Kevin Brown	.08	.05
242	John Ramos	.12	.07	300	Jack Daugherty	.05	.03
243	Scott Sanderson	.05	.03	301	Mario Diaz	.05	.03
244	Steve Sax	.08	.05	302	Brian Downing	.05	.03
245	Wade Taylor	.05	.03	303	Julio Franco	.08	.05
246	Randy Velarde	.05	.03	304	Juan Gonzalez	.50	.30
247	Bernie Williams	.12	.07	305	Rich Gossage	.07	.04
248	Troy Afenir	.05	.03	306	Jose Guzman	.05	.03
249	Harold Baines	.07	.04	307	Jose Hernandez (R)	.08	.05
250	Lance Blankenship	.05	.03	308	Jeff Huson	.05	.03

#	Player			#	Player		
309	Mike Jeffcoat	.05	.03	370	Pete Smith	.10	.06
310	Terry Mathews (R)	.08	.05	371	John Smoltz	.15	.10
311	Rafael Palmeiro	.08	.05	372	Mike Stanton	.05	.03
312	Dean Palmer	.12	.07	373	Jeff Treadway	.05	.03
313	Geno Petralli	.05	.03	374	Mark Wohlers (R)	.15	.10
314	Gary Pettis	.05	.03	375	Paul Assenmacher	.05	.03
315	Kevin Reimer	.07	.04	376	George Bell	.10	.06
316	Ivan Rodriguez	.45	.28	377	Shawn Boskie	.05	.03
317	Kenny Rogers	.05	.03	378	Frank Castillo	.05	.03
318	Wayne Rosenthal (R)	.08	.05	379	Andre Dawson	.15	.10
319	Jeff Russell	.05	.03	380	Shawon Dunston	.08	.05
320	Nolan Ryan	.50	.30	381	Mark Grace	.10	.06
321	Ruben Sierra	.15	.10	382	Mike Harkey	.07	.04
322	Jim Acker	.05	.03	383	Danny Jackson	.05	.03
323	Roberto Alomar	.20	.12	384	Les Lancaster	.05	.03
324	Derek Bell	.12	.07	385	Cedric Landrum (R)	.08	.05
325	Pat Borders	.05	.03	386	Greg Maddux	.12	.07
327	Joe Carter	.15	.10	387	Derrick May	.08	.05
328	Rob Ducey	.05	.03	388	Chuck McElroy	.05	.03
329	Kelly Gruber	.07	.04	389	Ryne Sanberg	.20	.12
330	Juan Guzman	.80	.50	390	Heathcliff Slocumb	.07	.04
331	Tom Henke	.05	.03	391	Dave Smith	.05	.03
332	Jimmy Key	.05	.03	392	Dwight Smith	.07	.04
333	Manny Lee	.05	.03	393	Rick Sutcliffe	.07	.04
334	Al Leiter	.05	.03	394	Hector Villanueva	.05	.03
335	Bob MacDonald	.07	.04	395	Chico Walker	.05	.03
336	Candy Maldonado	.05	.03	396	Jerome Walton	.07	.04
337	Rance Mulliniks	.05	.03	397	Rick Wilkins	.05	.03
338	Greg Myers	.05	.03	398	Jack Armstrong	.07	.04
339	John Olerud	.10	.06	399	Freddie Benavides	.05	.03
340	Ed Sprague	.10	.06	400	Glenn Braggs	.05	.03
341	Dave Stieb	.07	.04	401	Tom Browning	.07	.04
342	Todd Stottlemyre	.07	.04	402	Norm Charlton	.07	.04
343	Mike Timlin	.08	.05	403	Eric Davis	.08	.05
344	Duane Ward	.05	.03	404	Rob Dibble	.07	.04
345	David Wells	.05	.03	405	Bill Doran	.05	.03
347	Mookie Wilson	.05	.03	406	Mariano Duncan	.05	.03
348	Eddie Zosky	.12	.07	407	Kip Gross (R)	.08	.05
349	Steve Avery	.15	.10	408	Chris Hammond	.08	.05
350	Mike Bell	.08	.05	409	Billy Hatcher	.05	.03
351	Rafael Belliard	.05	.03	410	Chris Jones (R)	.08	.05
353	Jeff Blauser	.05	.03	411	Barry Larkin	.12	.07
354	Sid Bream	.05	.03	412	Hal Morris	.10	.06
355	Francisco Cabrera	.05	.03	413	Randy Myers	.05	.03
356	Marvin Freeman	.05	.03	414	Joe Oliver	.05	.03
357	Ron Gant	.12	.07	415	Paul O'Neill	.08	.05
358	Tom Glavine	.20	.12	416	Ted Power	.05	.03
359	Brian Hunter	.10	.06	417	Luis Quinones	.05	.03
360	Dave Justice	.20	.12	418	Jeff Reed	.05	.03
361	Charlie Leibrandt	.05	.03	419	Jose Rijo	.08	.05
362	Mark Lemke	.05	.03	420	Chris Sabo	.07	.04
363	Kent Mercker	.05	.03	421	Reggie Sanders	.25	.15
364	Keith Mitchell (R)	.12	.07	422	Scott Scudder	.08	.05
365	Greg Olson	.05	.03	423	Glenn Sutko	.05	.03
366	Terry Pendleton	.15	.10	424	Eric Anthony	.12	.07
367	Armando Reynoso (R)	.10	.06	425	Jeff Bagwell	.50	.30
368	Deion Sanders	.15	.10	426	Craig Biggio	.08	.05
369	Lonnie Smith	.07	.04	427	Ken Caminiti	.05	.03

428	Casey Candaele	.05	.03
429	Mike Capel	.05	.03
430	Andujar Cedeno	.10	.06
431	Jim Corsi	.05	.03
432	Mark Davidson	.05	.03
433	Steve Finley	.05	.03
434	Luis Gonzalez	.15	.10
435	Pete Harnisch	.07	.04
436	Dwayne Henry	.05	.03
437	Xavier Hernandez	.05	.03
438	Jimmy Jones	.05	.03
439	Darryl Kile	.08	.05
440	Rob Mallicoat	.05	.03
441	Andy Mota	.08	.05
442	Al Osuna	.05	.03
443	Mark Portugal	.05	.03
444	Scott Servais	.07	.04
445	Mike Simms	.05	.03
446	Gerald Young	.05	.03
447	Tim Belcher	.07	.04
448	Brett Butler	.08	.05
449	John Candelaria	.05	.03
450	Gary Carter	.08	.05
451	Dennis Cook	.05	.03
452	Tim Crews	.05	.03
453	Kal Daniels	.05	.03
454	Jim Gott	.05	.03
455	Alfredo Griffin	.05	.03
456	Kevin Gross	.05	.03
457	Chris Gwynn	.05	.03
458	Lenny Harris	.05	.03
459	Orel Hershiser	.08	.05
460	Jay Howell	.05	.03
461	Stan Javier	.05	.03
462	Eric Karros	.75	.45
463	Ramon Martinez	.10	.06
464	Roger McDowell	.05	.03
465	Mike Morgan	.05	.03
466	Eddie Murray	.15	.10
467	Jose Offerman	.08	.05
468	Bob Ojeda	.05	.03
469	Juan Samuel	.05	.03
470	Mike Scioscia	.05	.03
471	Darryl Strawberry	.15	.10
472	Bret Barberie (R)	.15	.10
473	Brian Barnes	.08	.05
474	Eric Bullock	.05	.03
475	Ivan Calderon	.07	.04
476	Delino DeShields	.15	.10
477	Jeff Fassero (R)	.08	.05
478	Mike Fitzgerald	.05	.03
479	Steve Frey	.05	.03
480	Andres Galarraga	.07	.04
481	Mark Gardner	.08	.05
482	Marquis Grissom	.15	.10
483	Chris Haney (R)	.12	.07
484	Barry Jones	.05	.03
485	Dave Martinez	.05	.03
486	Dennis Martinez	.08	.05
487	Chris Nabholz	.08	.05
488	Spike Owen	.05	.03
489	Gilberto Reyes	.05	.03
490	Mel Rojas	.07	.04
491	Scott Ruskin	.05	.03
492	Bill Sampen	.05	.03
493	Larry Walker	.15	.10
494	Tim Wallach	.07	.04
495	Daryl Boston	.05	.03
496	Hubie Brooks	.07	.04
497	Tim Burke	.05	.03
498	Mark Carreon	.05	.03
499	Tony Castillo	.05	.03
500	Vince Coleman	.07	.04
501	David Cone	.10	.06
502	Kevin Elster	.05	.03
503	Sid Fernandez	.07	.04
504	John Franco	.05	.03
505	Dwight Gooden	.12	.07
506	Todd Hundley	.08	.05
507	Jeff Innis	.05	.03
508	Gregg Jefferies	.12	.07
509	Howard Johnson	.10	.06
510	Dave Magadan	.07	.04
511	Terry McDaniel (R)	.10	.06
512	Kevin McReynolds	.07	.04
513	Keith Miller	.05	.03
514	Charlie O'Brien	.05	.03
515	Mackey Sasser	.05	.03
516	Pete Schourek	.07	.04
517	Julio Valera	.05	.03
518	Frank Viola	.08	.05
519	Wally Whitehurst	.05	.03
520	Anthony Young (R)	.20	.12
521	Andy Ashby	.05	.03
522	Kim Batiste	.10	.06
523	Joe Boever	.05	.03
524	Wes Chamberlain	.10	.06
525	Pat Combs	.07	.04
526	Danny Cox	.05	.03
527	Darren Daulton	.08	.05
528	Jose DeJesus	.05	.03
529	Lenny Dykstra	.07	.04
530	Darrin Fletcher	.05	.03
531	Tommy Greene	.07	.04
532	Jason Grimsley	.05	.03
533	Charlie Hayes	.05	.03
534	Von Hayes	.05	.03
535	Dave Hollins	.10	.06
536	Ricky Jordan	.07	.04
537	John Kruk	.08	.05
538	Jim Lindeman	.05	.03
539	Mickey Morandini	.08	.05
540	Terry Mulholland	.05	.03
541	Dale Murphy	.10	.06
542	Randy Ready	.05	.03
543	Wally Ritchie	.05	.03

No.	Player		
544	Bruce Ruffin	.05	.03
545	Steve Searcy	.05	.03
546	Dickie Thon	.05	.03
547	Mitch Williams	.05	.03
548	Stan Belinda	.05	.03
549	Jay Bell	.05	.03
550	Barry Bonds	.20	.12
551	Bobby Bonilla	.10	.06
552	Steve Buechele	.05	.03
553	Doug Drabek	.10	.06
554	Neal Heaton	.05	.03
555	Jeff King	.07	.04
556	Bob Kipper	.05	.03
557	Bill Landrum	.05	.03
558	Mike LaValliere	.05	.03
559	Jose Lind	.05	.03
560	Lloyd McClendon	.05	.03
561	Orlando Merced	.12	.07
562	Bob Patterson	.05	.03
563	Joe Redfield (R)	.08	.05
564	Gary Redus	.05	.03
565	Rosario Rodriguez	.05	.03
566	Don Slaught	.05	.03
567	John Smiley	.08	.05
568	Zane Smith	.05	.03
569	Randy Tomlin	.08	.05
570	Andy Van Slyke	.12	.07
571	Gary Varsho	.05	.03
572	Bob Walk	.05	.03
573	John Wehner (R)	.12	.07
574	Juan Agosto	.05	.03
575	Cris Carpenter	.05	.03
576	Jose DeLeon	.05	.03
577	Rich Gedman	.05	.03
578	Bernard Gilkey	.10	.06
579	Pedro Guerrero	.07	.04
580	Ken Hill	.08	.05
581	Rex Hudler	.05	.03
582	Felix Jose	.10	.06
583	Ray Lankford	.15	.10
584	Omar Olivares	.08	.05
585	Jose Oquendo	.05	.03
586	Tom Pagnozzi	.07	.04
587	Geronimo Pena	.05	.03
588	Mike Perez	.05	.03
589	Gerald Perry	.05	.03
590	Bryn Smith	.05	.03
591	Lee Smith	.08	.05
592	Ozzie Smith	.12	.07
593	Scott Terry	.05	.03
594	Bob Tewksbury	.05	.03
595	Milt Thompson	.05	.03
596	Todd Zeile	.10	.06
597	Larry Andersen	.05	.03
598	Oscar Azocar	.05	.03
599	Andy Benes	.12	.07
600	Ricky Bones (R)	.10	.06
601	Jerald Clark	.05	.03
602	Pat Clements	.05	.03
603	Paul Faries	.05	.03
604	Tony Fernandez	.07	.04
605	Tony Gwynn	.15	.10
606	Greg Harris	.05	.03
607	Thomas Howard	.05	.03
608	Bruce Hurst	.07	.04
609	Darrin Jackson	.05	.03
610	Tom Lampkin	.05	.03
611	Craig Lefferts	.05	.03
612	Jim Lewis (R)	.08	.05
613	Mike Maddux	.05	.03
614	Fred McGriff	.20	.12
615	Jose Melendez (R)	.08	.05
616	Jose Mota	.05	.03
617	Dennis Rasmussen	.05	.03
618	Bip Roberts	.05	.03
619	Rich Rodriguez	.05	.03
620	Benito Santiago	.08	.05
621	Craig Shipley (R)	.08	.05
622	Tim Teufel	.05	.03
623	Kevin Ward (R)	.08	.05
624	Ed Whitson	.05	.03
625	Dave Anderson	.05	.03
626	Kevin Bass	.05	.03
627	Rod Beck (R)	.10	.06
628	Bud Black	.05	.03
629	Jeff Brantley	.05	.03
630	John Burkett	.05	.03
631	Will Clark	.20	.12
632	Royce Clayton	.15	.10
633	Steve Decker	.07	.04
634	Kelly Downs	.05	.03
635	Mike Felder	.05	.03
636	Scott Garrelts	.05	.03
637	Eric Gunderson	.05	.03
638	Bryan Hickerson (R)	.08	.05
639	Darren Lewis	.07	.04
640	Greg Litton	.05	.03
641	Kirt Manwaring	.05	.03
642	Paul McClellan (R)	.07	.04
643	Willie McGee	.08	.05
644	Kevin Mitchell	.08	.05
645	Francisco Olivares	.05	.03
646	Mike Remlinger (R)	.08	.05
647	Dave Righetti	.05	.03
648	Robby Thompson	.05	.03
649	Jose Uribe	.05	.03
650	Matt Williams	.12	.07
651	Trevor Wilson	.05	.03
652	Tom Goodwin	.12	.07
653	Terry Bross	.08	.05
654	Mike Christopher (R)	.08	.05
655	Kenny Lofton (R)	.50	.30
656	Chris Cron (R)	.08	.05
657	Willie Banks	.12	.07
658	Pat Rice (R)	.08	.05
659	Rob Maurer (R)	.20	.12

660	Don Harris	.10	.06
661	Henry Rodriguez	.10	.06
662	Cliff Brantley (R)	.10	.06
663	Mike Linskey (R)	.07	.04
664	Gary Disarcina	.10	.06
665	Gil Heredia (R)	.10	.06
666	Vinny Castilla (R)	.08	.05
667	Paul Abbott	.10	.06
668	Monty Fariss	.08	.05
669	Jarvis Brown (R)	.08	.05
670	Wayne Kirby (R)	.08	.05
671	Scott Brosius (R)	.10	.06
672	Bob Hamelin	.10	.06
673	Joel Johnston (R)	.10	.06
674	Tim Spehr (R)	.08	.05
675	Jeff Gardner (R)	.08	.05
676	Rico Rossy (R)	.08	.05
677	Roberto Hernandez(R)	.08	.05
678	Ted Wood	.10	.06
679	Cal Eldred	.30	.18
680	Sean Berry	.08	.05
681	Rickey Henderson(RS)	.12	.07
682	Nolan Ryan(RS)	.35	.20
683	Dennis Martinez(RS)	.08	.05
684	Wilson Alvarez(RS)	.08	.05
685	Joe Carter(RS)	.12	.07
686	Dave Winfield(RS)	.15	.10
687	David Cone(RS)	.10	.06
688	Jose Canseco(LL)	.15	.10
689	Howard Johnson(LL)	.07	.04
690	Julio Franco(LL)	.07	.04
691	Terry Pendleton(LL)	.10	.06
692	Cecil Fielder(LL)	.10	.06
693	Scott Erickson(LL)	.10	.06
694	Tom Glavine(LL)	.12	.07
695	Dennis Martinez(LL)	.07	.04
696	Bryan Harvey(LL)	.07	.04
697	Lee Smith(LL)	.08	.05
698	Super Siblings(Roberto & Sandy Alomar)	.15	.10
699	The Indispensables (B. Bonilla & W. Clark)	.10	.06
700	Teamwork(Wohlers, Mercker & Pena)	.08	.05
701	Tiger Tandems (S. Jones,B. Jackson, G. Olson,F. Thomas)	.30	.18
702	The Ignitors(P. Molitor B. Butler)	.10	.06
703	The Indispensables II (C. Ripken, Jr., J. Carter)	.15	.10
704	Power Packs(B.Larkin, K. Puckett)	.15	.10
705	Today & Tomorrow (M. Vaughn, C. Fielder)	.12	.07
706	Teenage Sensations (R. Martinez, O. Guillen)	.10	.06

707	Designated Hitters (H. Baines, W. Boggs)	.10	.06
708	Robin Yount(PV)	.35	.20
709	Ken Griffey, Jr.(PV)	.60	.35
710	Nolan Ryan(PV)	.75	.45
711	Cal Ripken, Jr.(PV)	.50	.30
712	Frank Thomas(PV)	1.00	.70
713	Dave Justice(PV)	.40	.25
714	Checklist	.05	.03
715	Checklist	.05	.03
716	Checklist	.05	.03
717	Checklist	.05	.03
718	Checklist	.05	.03
719	Checklist	.05	.03
720	Checklist	.05	.03
BC1- BC15	Roger Clemens Inserts.	1.25ea	.80

1992 Fleer Update

This 132-card update set contains mostly rookies and players traded during the 1992 season. The card design is nearly identical to the regular Fleer edition except for the card numbers which carry the "U" designation. Factory sets contain 4 Bonus Cards called Headliners (H). Those cards are included at the end of this checklist but not in the complete set price below. All cards measure 2-1/2" by 3-1/2".

	MINT	NR/MT	
Complete Set (132)		12.50	8.50
Commons		.05	.02
1	Todd Frohwirth	.07	.04
2	Alan Mills	.07	.04
3	Rick Sutcliffe	.07	.04
4	John Valentin (R)	.20	.12
5	Frank Viola	.07	.04
6	Bob Zupcic (R)	.25	.15

No.	Player		
7	Mike Butcher (R)	.08	.05
8	Chad Curtis (R)	.20	.12
9	Damion Easley (R)	.25	.15
10	Tim Salmon	.35	.20
11	Julio Valera	.05	.02
12	George Bell	.07	.04
13	Roberto Hernandez	.10	.06
14	Shawn Jeter (R)	.12	.07
15	Thomas Howard	.08	.05
16	Jesse Levis (R)	.08	.05
17	Kenny Lofton	.35	.20
18	Paul Sorrento	.12	.07
19	Rico Brogna	.12	.07
20	John Doherty (R)	.10	.06
21	Dan Gladden	.05	.02
22	Buddy Groom (R)	.08	.05
23	Shawn Hare (R)	.12	.07
24	John Kiely (R)	.08	.05
25	Kurt Knudsen (R)	.08	.05
26	Gregg Jefferies	.10	.06
27	Wally Joyner	.10	.06
28	Kevin Koslofski (R)	.08	.05
29	Kevin McReynolds	.07	.04
30	Rusty Meacham	.07	.04
31	Keith Miller	.05	.02
32	Hipolito Pichardo (R)	.15	.10
33	James Austin (R)	.08	.05
34	Scott Fletcher	.05	.02
35	John Jaha (R)	.25	.15
36	Pat Listach (R)	1.25	.80
37	Dave Nilsson	.15	.10
38	Kevin Seitzer	.05	.02
39	Tom Edens	.07	.04
40	Pat Mahomes (R)	.35	.20
41	John Smiley	.08	.05
42	Charlie Hayes	.07	.04
43	Sam Militello (R)	.25	.15
44	Andy Stankiewicz (R)	.15	.10
45	Danny Tartabull	.15	.10
46	Bob Wickman	.20	.12
47	Jerry Browne	.05	.02
48	Kevin Campbell (R)	.08	.05
49	Vince Horsman (R)	.10	.06
50	Troy Neel (R)	.10	.06
51	Ruben Sierra	.20	.12
52	Bruce Walton	.05	.02
53	Willie Wilson	.05	.02
54	Bret Boone	.40	.25
55	Dave Fleming	.50	.30
56	Kevin Mitchell	.08	.05
57	Jeff Nelson (R)	.08	.05
58	Shane Turner	.07	.04
59	Jose Ccanseco	.25	.15
60	Jeff Frye (R)	.10	.06
61	Danilo Leon (R)	.08	.05
62	Roger Pavlik (R)	.10	.06
63	David Cone	.12	.07
64	Pat Hentgen	.08	.05
65	Randy Knorr (R)	.10	.06
66	Jack Morris	.12	.07
67	Dave Winfield	.15	.10
68	David Nied (R)	3.50	2.50
69	Otis Nixon	.08	.05
70	Alejandro Pena	.05	.02
71	Jeff Reardon	.08	.05
72	Alex Arias (R)	.10	.06
73	Jim Bullinger	.07	.04
74	Mike Morgan	.07	.04
75	Rey Sanchez (R)	.15	.10
76	Bob Scanlan	.05	.02
77	Sammy Sosa	.07	.04
78	Scott Bankhead	.05	.02
79	Tim Belcher	.07	.04
80	Steve Foster (R)	.10	.06
81	Willie Greene	.25	.15
82	Bip Roberts	.05	.02
83	Scott Ruskin	.05	.02
84	Greg Swindell	.07	.04
85	Juan Guerrero (R)	.10	.06
86	Butch Henry (R)	.12	.07
87	Doug Jones	.05	.02
88	Brian Williams (R)	.35	.20
89	Tom Candiotti	.05	.02
90	Eric Davis	.08	.05
91	Carlos Hernandez	.08	.05
92	Mike Piazza (R)	.60	.35
93	Mike Sharperson	.05	.02
94	Eric Young (R)	.20	.12
95	Moises Alou	.15	.10
96	Greg Colbrunn	.10	.06
97	Wil Cordero	.20	.12
98	Ken Hill	.08	.05
99	John Vander Wal (R)	.12	.07
100	John Wetteland	.08	.05
101	Bobby Bonilla	.12	.07
102	Eric Hillman (R)	.12	.07
103	Pat Howell (R)	.15	.10
104	Jeff Kent (R)	.20	.12
105	Dick Schofield	.05	.02
106	Ryan Thompson (R)	.50	.30
107	Chico Walker	.05	.02
108	Juan Bell	.05	.02
109	Mariano Duncan	.05	.02
110	Jeff Grotewold (R)	.10	.06
111	Ben Rivers	.08	.05
112	Curt Schilling	.05	.02
113	Victor Cole (R)	.12	.07
114	Albert Martin (R)	.15	.10
115	Roger Mason	.05	.02
116	Blas Minor (R)	.12	.07
117	Tim Wakefield (R)	3.50	2.50
118	Mark Clark (R)	.08	.05
119	Rheal Cormier	.08	.05
120	Donovan Osborne	.25	.15
121	Todd Worrell	.05	.02
122	Jeremy Hernandez (R)	.12	.07

123	Randy Myers	.05	.02
124	Frank Seminara (R)	.20	.12
125	Gary Sheffield	.35	.20
126	Dan Walters (R)	.15	.10
127	Steve Hosey	.25	.15
128	Mike Jackson	.05	.02
129	Jim Pena (R)	.08	.05
130	Cory Snyder	.05	.02
131	Bill Swift	.08	.05
132	Checklist	.05	.02
H1	Ken Griffey Jr.	6.50	3.75
H2	Robin Yount	1.50	.90
H3	Jeff Reardon	.25	.15
H4	Cecil Fielder	1.50	.90

1992 Fleer Ultra

For the second straight year Fleer produced a premium, upscale baseball card set. The 1992 edition contains 600 cards, each measuring 2-1/2" by 3-1/2". Card fronts feature full color action photos with marble-looking borders and a box at the bottom that holds the player's name, team and position. The horizontal card backs feature two photos and, through computer enhancement, the cards have a three-dimensional look. The set was issued in two series and includes a number of limited insert cards which were randomly issued in the foil packs. Those inserts consist of a 12-card Tony Gwynn set which includes two Gwynn cards available only by mail, a 20-card Ultra All-Stars Insert set, a 10-card All-Rookie Team Insert Set and a 25-card Ultra Award Winners Insert Set. Those insert cards are listed at the end of this checklist but are not included in the complete set price.

		MINT	NR/MT
Complete Set (600)		62.00	45.00
Commons		.10	.06

1	Glenn Davis	.12	.07
2	Mike Devereaux	.12	.07
3	Dwight Evans	.12	.07
4	Leo Gomez	.25	.15
5	Chris Hoiles	.30	.18
6	Sam Horn	.10	.06
7	Chito Martinez	.15	.10
8	Randy Milligan	.10	.06
9	Mike Mussina	3.00	2.00
10	Billy Ripken	.10	.06
11	Cal Ripken, Jr.	1.75	1.00
12	Tom Brunansky	.10	.06
13	Ellis Burks	.12	.07
14	Jack Clark	.12	.07
15	Roger Clemens	1.75	1.00
16	Mike Greenwell	.12	.07
17	Joe Hesketh	.10	.06
18	Tony Pena	.10	.06
19	Carlos Quintana	.12	.07
20	Jeff Reardon	.20	.12
21	Jody Reed	.10	.06
22	Luis Rivera	.10	.06
23	Mo Vaughn	.30	.18
24	Gary DiSarcina	.15	.10
25	Chuck Finley	.12	.07
26	Gary Gaetti	.10	.06
27	Bryan Harvey	.12	.07
28	Lance Parrish	.10	.06
29	Luis Polonia	.12	.07
30	Dick Schofield	.10	.06
31	Luis Sojo	.10	.06
32	Wilson Alvarez	.12	.07
33	Carlton Fisk	.40	.25
34	Craig Grebeck	.10	.06
35	Ozzie Guillen	.12	.07
36	Greg Hibbard	.10	.06
37	Charlie Hough	.10	.06
38	Lance Johnson	.10	.06
39	Ron Karkovice	.10	.06
40	Jack McDowell	.50	.30
41	Donn Pall	.10	.06
42	Melido Perez	.12	.07
43	Tim Raines	.15	.10
44	Frank Thomas	4.50	3.50
45	Sandy Alomar, Jr.	.12	.07
46	Carlos Baerga	.80	.50
47	Albert Belle	.90	.60
48	Jerry Browne	.10	.06
49	Felix Fermin	.10	.06
50	Reggie Jefferson	.15	.10
51	Mark Lewis	.20	.12
52	Carlos Martinez	.10	.06
53	Steve Olin	.10	.06
54	Jim Thome	.35	.20
55	Mark Whiten	.20	.12
56	Dave Bergman	.10	.06

No.	Player	Price 1	Price 2
57	Milt Culyler	.12	.07
58	Rob Deer	.12	.07
59	Cecil Fielder	.60	.35
60	Travis Fryman	1.25	.80
61	Scott Livingston	.20	.12
62	Tony Phillips	.10	.06
63	Mickey Tettleton	.12	.07
64	Alan Trammell	.20	.12
65	Lou Whitaker	.12	.07
66	Kevin Appier	.15	.10
67	Mike Boddicker	.10	.06
68	Geroge Brett	.80	.50
69	Jim Eisenreich	.10	.06
70	Mark Gubicza	.12	.07
71	Dave Howard	.12	.07
72	Joel Johnston	.15	.10
73	Mike Macfarlane	.10	.06
74	Brent Mayne	.15	.10
75	Brian McRae	.15	.10
76	Jeff Montgomery	.10	.06
77	Danny Tartabull	.20	.12
78	Don August	.10	.06
79	Dante Bichette	.10	.06
80	Ted Higuera	.10	.06
81	Paul Molitor	.15	.10
82	Jamie Navarro	.15	.10
83	Gary Sheffield	2.50	1.50
84	Bill Spiers	.10	.06
85	B.J. Surhoff	.10	.06
86	Greg Vaughn	.15	.10
87	Robin Yount	.80	.50
88	Rick Aguilera	.10	.06
89	Chili Davis	.12	.07
90	Scott Erickson	.30	.18
91	Brian Harper	.10	.06
92	Ken Hrbek	.12	.07
93	Chuck Knoblauch	.80	.50
94	Scott Leius	.15	.10
95	Shane Mack	.20	.12
96	Mike Pagliarulo	.10	.06
97	Kirby Puckett	1.75	1.00
98	Kevin Tapani	.12	.07
99	Jesse Barfield	.12	.07
100	Alvaro Espinoza	.10	.06
101	Mel Hall	.12	.07
102	Pat Kelly	.20	.12
103	Roberto Kelly	.25	.15
104	Kevin Maas	.15	.10
105	Don Mattingly	.60	.35
106	Hensley Meullens	.12	.07
107	Matt Nokes	.10	.06
108	Steve Sax	.15	.10
109	Harold Baines	.12	.07
110	Jose Canseco	2.00	1.25
111	Ron Darling	.10	.06
112	Mike Gallego	.10	.06
113	Dave Henderson	.12	.07
114	Rickey Henderson	.75	.45
115	Mark McGwire	1.50	.90
116	Terry Steinbach	.10	.06
117	Dave Stewart	.12	.07
118	Todd Van Poppel	.80	.50
119	Bob Welch	.12	.07
120	Greg Briley	.10	.06
121	Jay Buhner	.12	.07
122	Rich DeLucia	.12	.07
123	Ken Griffey, Jr.	4.00	3.00
124	Erik Hanson	.15	.10
125	Randy Johnson	.30	.18
126	Edgar Martinez	.25	.15
127	Tino Martinez	.12	.07
128	Pete O'Brien	.10	.06
129	Harold Reynolds	.10	.06
130	Dave Valle	.10	.06
131	Julio Franco	.15	.10
132	Juan Gonzalez	3.00	2.00
133	Jeff Huson	.12	.07
134	Mike Jeffcoat	.10	.06
135	Terry Matthews	.10	.06
136	Rafael Palmeiro	.20	.12
137	Dean Palmer	.80	.50
138	Geno Petralli	.10	.06
139	Ivan Rodriguez	2.00	1.25
140	Jeff Russell	.10	.06
141	Nolan Ryan	3.50	2.50
142	Ruben Sierra	1.25	.80
143	Roberto Alomar	1.75	1.00
144	Pat Borders	.10	.06
145	Joe Carter	.75	.45
146	Kelly Gruber	.12	.07
147	Jimmy Key	.10	.06
148	Manny Lee	.10	.06
149	Rance Mulliniks	.10	.06
150	Greg Myers	.10	.06
151	John Olerud	.40	.25
152	Dave Stieb	.12	.07
153	Todd Stottlemyre	.12	.07
154	Duane Ward	.10	.06
155	Devon White	.10	.06
156	Eddie Zosky	.20	.12
157	Steve Avery	1.00	.70
158	Rafael Belliard	.10	.06
159	Jeff Blauser	.10	.06
160	Sid Bream	.10	.06
161	Ron Gant	.50	.30
162	Tom Glavine	.75	.45
163	Brian Hunter	.25	.15
164	Dave Justice	1.50	.90
165	Mark Lemke	.10	.06
166	Greg Olson	.10	.06
167	Terry Pendleton	.35	.20
168	Lonnie Smith	.10	.06
169	John Smoltz	.50	.30
170	Mike Stanton	.12	.07
171	Jeff Treadway	.10	.06
172	Paul Assenmacher	.10	.06

173	George Bell	.20	.12
174	Shawon Dunston	.12	.07
175	Mark Grace	.20	.12
176	Danny Jackson	.10	.06
177	Les Lancaster	.10	.06
178	Greg Maddux	.35	.20
179	Luis Salazar	.10	.06
180	Rey Sanchez (R)	.25	.15
181	Ryne Sandberg	2.00	1.25
182	Jose Viscaino	.10	.06
183	Chico Walker	.10	.06
184	Jerome Walton	.12	.07
185	Glenn Braggs	.10	.06
186	Tom Browning	.12	.07
187	Rob Dibble	.12	.07
188	Bill Doran	.10	.06
189	Chris Hammond	.20	.12
190	Billy Hatcher	.10	.06
191	Barry Larkin	.50	.30
192	Hal Morris	.15	.10
193	Joe Oliver	.10	.06
194	Paul O'Neill	.12	.07
195	Jeff Reed	.10	.06
196	Jose Rijo	.15	.10
197	Chris Sabo	.12	.07
198	Jeff Bagwell	1.50	.90
199	Craig Biggio	.15	.10
200	Ken Caminiti	.12	.07
201	Andujar Cedeno	.25	.15
202	Steve Finley	.10	.06
203	Luis Gonzalez	.20	.12
204	Pete Harnisch	.12	.07
205	Xavier Hernandez	.15	.10
206	Darryl Kile	.15	.10
207	Al Osuna	.10	.06
208	Curt Schilling	.10	.06
209	Brett Butler	.20	.12
210	Kal Daniels	.10	.06
211	Lenny Harris	.10	.06
212	Stan Javier	.10	.06
213	Ramon Martinez	.20	.12
214	Roger McDowell	.10	.06
215	Jose Offerman	.15	.10
216	Juan Samuel	.10	.06
217	Mike Scioscia	.10	.06
218	Mike Sharperson	.10	.06
219	Darryl Strawberry	.50	.30
220	Delino DeShields	.75	.45
221	Tom Foley	.10	.06
222	Steve Frey	.10	.06
223	Dennis Martinez	.15	.10
224	Spike Owen	.10	.06
225	Gilbert Reyes	.10	.06
226	Tim Wallach	.12	.07
227	Daryl Boston	.10	.06
228	Tim Burke	.10	.06
229	Vince Coleman	.15	.10
230	David Cone	.25	.15
231	Kevin Elster	.10	.06
232	Dwight Gooden	.25	.15
233	Todd Hundley	.15	.10
234	Jeff Innis	.10	.06
235	Howard Johnson	.20	.12
236	Dave Magadan	.12	.07
237	Mackey Sasser	.10	.06
238	Anthony Young	.25	.15
239	Wes Chamberlain	.20	.12
240	Darren Daulton	.20	.12
241	Lenny Dykstra	.12	.07
242	Tommy Greene	.12	.07
243	Charlie Hayes	.10	.06
244	Dave Hollins	.40	.25
245	Ricky Jordan	.12	.07
246	John Kruk	.15	.10
247	Mickey Morandini	.15	.10
248	Terry Mulholland	.10	.06
249	Dale Murphy	.15	.10
250	Jay Bell	.10	.06
251	Barry Bonds	1.50	.90
252	Steve Buechele	.12	.07
253	Doug Drabek	.25	.15
254	Mike LaValliere	.10	.06
255	Jose Lind	.10	.06
256	Lloyd McClendon	.10	.06
257	Orlando Merced	.20	.12
258	Don Slaughter	.10	.06
259	John Smiley	.15	.10
260	Zane Smith	.12	.07
261	Randy Tomlin	.25	.10
262	Andy Van Slyke	.25	.10
263	Pedro Guerrero	.12	.07
264	Felix Jose	.20	.12
265	Ray Lankford	.70	.40
266	Omar Olivares	.15	.10
267	Jose Oquendo	.10	.06
268	Tom Pagnozzi	.12	.07
269	Bryn Smith	.10	.06
270	Lee Smith	.15	.10
271	Ozzie Smith	.40	.25
272	Milt Thompson	.10	.06
273	Todd Zeile	.15	.10
274	Andy Benes	.25	.15
275	Jerald Clark	.12	.07
276	Tony Fernandez	.12	.07
277	Tony Gwynn	1.00	.70
278	Gregg Harris	.12	.07
279	Thomas Howard	.15	.10
280	Bruce Hurst	.12	.07
281	Mike Maddux	.10	.06
282	Fred McGriff	.80	.50
283	Benito Santiago	.15	.10
284	Kevin Bass	.10	.06
285	Jeff Brantley	.10	.06
286	John Burkett	.10	.06
287	Will Clark	1.50	.90
288	Royce Clayton	.50	.30

289	Steve Decker	.15	.10	347	Glenallen Hill	.12	.07
290	Kelly Downs	.10	.06	348	Thomas Howard	.12	.07
291	Mike Felder	.10	.06	349	Brook Jacoby	.10	.06
292	Darren Lewis	.15	.10	350	Kenny Lofton	2.50	1.50
293	Kirt Manwaring	.10	.06	351	Charles Nagy	.60	.35
294	Willie McGee	.15	.10	352	Rod Nichols	.10	.06
295	Robby Thompson	.10	.06	353	Junior Ortiz	.10	.06
296	Matt Williams	.20	.12	354	Dave Otto	.10	.06
297	Trevor Wilson	.10	.06	355	Tony Perezchica	.10	.06
298	Checklist	.10	.06	356	Scott Scudder	.12	.07
299	Checklist	.10	.06	357	Paul Sorrento	.15	.10
300	Checklist	.10	.06	358	Skeeter Barnes	.10	.06
301	Brady Anderson	.35	.20	359	Mark Carreon	.10	.06
302	Todd Frohwirth	.10	.06	360	John Doherty (R)	.20	.12
303	Ben McDonald	.30	.18	361	Dan Gladden	.10	.06
304	Mark McLemore	.10	.06	362	Bill Gullickson	.10	.06
305	Jose Mesa	.10	.06	363	Shawn Hare (R)	.20	.12
306	Bob Milacki	.10	.06	364	Mike Henneman	.10	.06
307	Gregg Olson	.15	.10	365	Chad Kreuter	.12	.07
308	David Segui	.12	.07	366	Mark Leiter	.10	.06
309	Rick Sutcliffe	.12	.07	367	Mike Munoz	.10	.06
310	Jeff Tackett	.12	.07	368	Kevin Ritz	.12	.07
311	Wade Boggs	.75	.45	369	Mark Davis	.10	.06
312	Scott Cooper	.35	.20	370	Tom Gordon	.12	.07
313	John Flaherty (R)	.20	.12	371	Chris Gwynn	.10	.06
314	Wayne Housie (R)	.20	.12	372	Gregg Jefferies	.20	.12
315	Peter Hoy (R)	.15	.10	373	Wally Joyner	.20	.12
316	John Marzano	.10	.06	374	Kevin McReynolds	.15	.10
317	Tim Naehring	.15	.10	375	Keith Miller	.10	.06
318	Phil Plantier	1.00	.70	376	Rico Rossy (R)	.20	.12
319	Frank Viola	.15	.10	377	Curtis Wilkerson	.10	.06
320	Matt Young	.10	.06	378	Ricky Bones	.20	.12
321	Jim Abbott	.35	.20	379	Chris Bosio	.10	.06
322	Hubie Brooks	.12	.07	380	Cal Eldred	1.50	.90
323	Chad Curtis (R)	.75	.45	381	Scott Fletcher	.10	.06
324	Alvin Davis	.10	.06	382	Jim Gantner	.10	.06
325	Junior Felix	.10	.06	383	Darryl Hamilton	.12	.07
326	Von Hayes	.10	.06	384	Doug Henry (R)	.35	.20
327	Mark Langston	.20	.12	385	Pat Listach (R)	4.00	3.00
328	Scott Lewis	.12	.07	386	Tim McIntosh	.35	.20
329	Don Robinson	.10	.06	387	Edwin Nunez	.10	.06
330	Bobby Rose	.10	.06	388	Dan Plesac	.10	.06
331	Lee Stevens	.15	.10	389	Kevin Seitzer	.12	.07
332	George Bell	.15	.10	390	Franklin Stubbs	.10	.06
333	Esteban Beltre (R)	.20	.12	391	William Suero	.15	.10
334	Joey Cora	.10	.06	392	Bill Wegman	.10	.06
335	Alex Fernandez	.25	.15	393	Willie Banks	.25	.15
336	Roberto Hernandez	.25	.15	394	Jarvis Brown (R)	.20	.12
337	Mike Huff	.10	.06	395	Greg Gagne	.10	.06
338	Kirk McCaskill	.10	.06	396	Mark Guthrie (R)	.20	.12
339	Dan Pasqua	.10	.06	397	Bill Krueger	.12	.07
340	Scott Radinsky	.12	.07	398	Pat Mahomes (R)	.80	.50
341	Steve Sax	.15	.10	399	Pedro Munoz	.30	.18
342	Bobby Thigpen	.12	.07	400	John Smiley	.15	.10
343	Robin Ventura	1.00	.70	401	Gary Wayne (R)	.15	.10
344	Jack Armstrong	.12	.07	402	Lenny Webster	.10	.06
345	Alex Cole	.10	.06	403	Carl Willis	.10	.06
346	Dennis Cook	.10	.06	404	Greg Cadaret	.10	.06

405	Steve Farr	.10	.06
406	Mike Gallego	.10	.06
407	Charlie Hayes	.10	.06
408	Steve Howe	.10	.06
409	Dion James	.10	.06
410	Jeff Johnson	.10	.06
411	Tim Leary	.10	.06
412	Jim Leyritz	.10	.06
413	Melido Perez	.12	.07
414	Scott Sanderson	.10	.06
415	Andy Stankiewicz (R)	.25	.15
416	Mike Stanley	.10	.06
417	Danny Tartabull	.25	.15
418	Lance Blankenship	.10	.06
419	Mike Bordick	.30	.18
420	Scott Brosius (R)	.20	.12
421	Dennis Eckersley	.35	.20
422	Scott Hemond (R)	.15	.10
423	Carney Lansford	.12	.07
424	Henry Mercedes(R)	.20	.12
425	Mike Moore	.10	.06
426	Gene Nelson	.10	.06
427	Randy Ready	.10	.06
428	Bruce Wilson (R)	.15	.10
429	Willie Wilson	.10	.06
430	Rich Amaral (R)	.15	.10
431	Dave Cochrane (R)	.15	.10
432	Henry Cotto	.10	.06
433	Calvin Jones (R)	.20	.12
434	Kevin Mitchell	.25	.15
435	Clay Parker	.10	.06
436	Omar Vizquel	.10	.06
437	Floyd Bannister	.10	.06
438	Kevin Brown	.15	.10
439	John Cangelosi	.10	.06
440	Brian Downing	.12	.07
441	Monty Fariss	.20	.12
442	Jose Guzman	.10	.06
443	Donald Harris	.15	.10
444	Kevin Reimer	.12	.07
445	Kenny Rogers	.10	.06
446	Wayne Rosenthal (R)	.12	.07
447	Dickie Thon	.10	.06
448	Derek Bell	.40	.25
449	Juan Guzman	4.00	3.00
450	Tom Henke	.10	.06
451	Candy Maldonado	.10	.06
452	Jack Morris	.30	.18
453	David Wells	.10	.06
454	Dave Winfield	.60	.35
455	Juan Berenguer	.10	.06
456	Damon Berryhill	.10	.06
457	Mike Bielecki	.10	.06
458	Marvin Freeman	.10	.06
459	Charlie Leibrandt	.10	.06
460	Kent Mercker	.15	.10
461	Otis Nixon	.12	.07
462	Alejandro Pena	.10	.06
463	Ben Rivera	.15	.10
464	Deion Sanders	.80	.50
465	Mark Wohlers	.30	.18
466	Shawn Boskie	.12	.07
467	Frank Castillo	.10	.06
468	Andre Dawson	.50	.30
469	Joe Girardi	.10	.06
470	Chuck McElroy	.10	.06
471	Mike Morgan	.12	.07
472	Ken Patterson	.10	.06
473	Bob Scanlan	.10	.06
474	Gary Scott	.15	.10
475	Dave Smith	.10	.06
476	Sammy Sosa	.15	.10
477	Hector Villanueva	.10	.06
478	Scott Bankhead	.10	.06
479	Tim Belcher	.12	.07
480	Freddie Benavides	.10	.06
481	Jacob Brumfield (R)	.15	.10
482	Norm Charlton	.12	.07
483	Dwayne Henry	.12	.07
484	Dave Martinez	.10	.06
485	Bip Roberts	.12	.07
486	Reggie Sanders	1.75	1.00
487	Greg Swindell	.15	.10
488	Ryan Bowen	.15	.10
489	Casey Candaele	.10	.06
490	Juan Guerrero (R)	.30	.18
491	Pete Incaviglia	.10	.06
492	Jeff Juden	.30	.18
493	Rob Murphy	.10	.06
494	Mark Portugal	.10	.06
495	Rafael Ramirez	.10	.06
496	Scott Servais	.12	.07
497	Ed Taubensee (R)	.20	.12
498	Brian Williams (R)	.80	.50
499	Todd Benzinger	.10	.06
500	John Candelaria	.10	.06
501	Tom Candiotti	.10	.06
502	Tim Crews	.10	.06
503	Eric Davis	.20	.12
504	Jim Gott	.10	.06
505	Dave Hansen	.12	.07
506	Carlos Hernandez	.15	.10
507	Orel Hershiser	.20	.12
508	Eric Karros	3.50	2.50
509	Bob Ojeda	.10	.06
510	Steve Wilson	.10	.06
511	Moises Alou	.50	.30
512	Bret Barberie	.20	.12
513	Ivan Calderon	.12	.07
514	Gary Carter	.20	.12
515	Archi Cianfrocco (R)	.50	.30
516	Jeff Fassero	.15	.10
517	Darrin Fletcher	.15	.10
518	Marquis Grissom	.75	.45

519	Chris Haney	.25	.15
520	Ken Hill	.20	.12
521	Chris Nabholz	.20	.12
522	Bill Sampen	.10	.06
523	John Vander Wal (R)	.25	.15
524	Dave Wainhouse (R)	.15	.10
525	Larry Walker	.50	.30
526	John Wetteland	.20	.12
527	Bobby Bonilla	.35	.20
528	Sid Fernandez	.12	.07
529	John Franco	.10	.06
530	Dave Gallagher	.10	.06
531	Paul Gibson	.10	.06
532	Eddie Murray	.50	.30
533	Junior Noboa	.10	.06
534	Charlie O'Brien	.10	.06
535	Bill Pecota	.10	.06
536	Willie Randolph	.12	.07
537	Bret Saberhagen	.20	.12
538	Dick Schofield	.10	.06
539	Pete Schourek	.15	.10
540	Ruben Amaro	.15	.10
541	Andy Ashby	.15	.10
542	Kim Batiste	.20	.12
543	Cliff Brantley	.12	.07
544	Mariano Duncan	.10	.06
545	Jeff Grotewold (R)	.15	.10
546	Barry Jones	.10	.06
547	Julio Peguero (R)	.20	.12
548	Curt Schilling	.10	.06
549	Mitch Williams	.12	.07
550	Stan Belinda	.10	.06
551	Scott Bullett (R)	.25	.15
552	Cecil Espy	.10	.06
553	Jeff King	.15	.10
554	Roger Mason	.10	.06
555	Paul Miller (R)	.25	.15
556	Denny Neagle	.15	.10
557	Victor Palacios (R)	.15	.10
558	Bob Patterson	.10	.06
559	Tom Prince (R)	.12	.07
560	Gary Redus	.10	.06
561	Gary Varsho	.10	.06
562	Juan Agosto	.10	.06
563	Cris Carpenter	.12	.07
564	Mark Clark (R)	.25	.15
565	Jose DeLeon	.10	.06
566	Rich Gedman	.10	.06
567	Bernard Gilkey	.25	.15
568	Rex Hudler	.10	.06
569	Tim Jones	.12	.07
570	Donovan Osborne	.80	.50
571	Mike Perez	.10	.06
572	Gerald Perry	.10	.06
573	Bob Tweksbury	.10	.06
574	Todd Worrell	.12	.07
575	Dave Eiland	.10	.06

576	Jeremy Hernandez (R)	.20	.12
577	Craig Lefferts	.10	.06
578	Jose Melendez	.12	.07
579	Randy Myers	.10	.06
580	Gary Pettis	.10	.06
581	Rich Rodriquez	.12	.07
582	Gary Sheffield	2.50	1.50
583	Craig Shipley	.10	.06
584	Kurt Stillwell	.10	.06
585	Tim Teufel	.10	.06
586	Rod Beck (R)	.25	.15
587	Dave Burba (R)	.15	.10
588	Craig Colbert (R)	.15	.10
589	Bryan Hickerson (R)	.12	.07
590	Mike Jackson (R)	.12	.07
591	Mark Leonard (R)	.20	.12
592	Jim McNamara (R)	.20	.12
593	John Patterson (R)	.25	.15
594	Dave Righetti	.12	.07
595	Cory Snyder	.12	.07
596	Bill Swift	.15	.10
597	Ted Wood (R)	.20	.12
598	Checklist	.10	.06
599	Checklist	.10	.06
600	Checklist	.10	.06
BC1-	Tony Gwynn	2.00ea	1.25
BC10	Inserts Cards		
BC11	Tony Gwynn (Mail-in Bonus Card)	3.50	2.50
BC12	Tony Gwynn (Mail-in Bonus Card)	3.50	2.50

1992 Fleer Ultra Award Winners

		MINT	NR/MT
Complete Set (25)		120.00	85.00
Commons		3.00	2.00
1	Jack Morris	4.50	2.75
2	Chuck Knoblauch	6.00	3.75
3	Jeff Bagwell	7.00	4.50
4	Terry Pendleton	4.50	2.75
5	Cal Ripken Jr.	10.00	7.50
6	Roger Clemens	8.50	6.00
7	Tom Glavine	7.00	4.50
8	Tom Pagnozzi	3.00	2.00
9	Ozzie Smith	5.00	3.00
10	Andy Van Slyke	4.00	2.50

11	Barry Bonds	8.50	6.00
12	Tony Gwynn	6.00	3.75
13	Matt Williams	4.00	2.50
14	Will Clark	8.50	6.00
15	Robin Ventura	7.00	4.50
16	Mark Langston	3.50	2.25
17	Tony Pena	3.00	2.00
18	Devon White	3.00	2.00
19	Don Mattingly	6.00	3.75
20	Roberto Alomar	8.50	6.00
21	Cal Ripken Jr	12.00	9.00
22	Ken Griffey Jr.	10.00	7.50
23	Kirby Puckett	8.50	6.00
24	Greg Maddux	5.00	3.00
25	Ryne Sandberg	8.50	6.00

1992 Fleer Ultra All-Stars

		MINT	NR/MT
Complete Set (20)		95.00	75.00
Commons		3.00	2.00
1	Mark McGwire	8.00	5.50
2	Roberto Alomar	7.50	5.00
3	Cal Ripken Jr.	10.00	7.50
4	Wade Boggs	5.00	3.00
5	Mickey Tettleton	3.00	2.00
6	Ken Griffey Jr.	12.00	9.00
7	Roberto Kelly	4.50	2.75
8	Kirby Puckett	7.50	5.00
9	Frank Thomas	18.00	14.00
10	Jack McDowell	5.00	3.00
11	Will Clark	7.50	5.00
12	Ryne Sandberg	8.00	5.50
13	Barry Larkin	5.00	3.00
14	Gary Sheffield	7.50	5.00
15	Tom Pagnozzi	3.00	2.00
16	Barry Bonds	8.00	5.50
17	Deion Sanders	7.00	4.50
18	Darryl Strawberry	6.00	3.75
19	David Cone	4.50	2.75
20	Tom Glavine	7.50	5.00

1992 Fleer Ultra All-Rookies

		MINT	NR/MT
Complete Set (10)		55.00	45.00
Commons		3.00	2.00
1	Eric Karros	12.50	9.50
2	Andy Stankiewicz	4.00	2.50
3	Gary DiSarcina	3.00	2.00
4	Archi Cianfroco	4.00	2.50
5	Jim McNamara	3.00	2.00
6	Chad Curtis	4.00	2.50
7	Kenny Lofton	10.00	7.50
8	Reggie Sanders	7.50	5.00
9	Pat Mahomes	5.00	3.00
10	Donovan Osborne	5.00	3.00

1993 Fleer Series I

This set is the first of two series Fleer plans to release in 1993. The card fronts feature full color action photos framed by a silver border. Card backs include another action shot set against a silver background with the player's last name headlined across the top. Limited inserts include a 12-card Tom Glavine Signature series 3 Golden Moments and 3 new Pro-Visions cards. All cards measure 2-1/2" by 3-1/2"

	MINT	NR/MT
Complete Set (360)	15.00	10.00
Commons	.05	.02

1	Steve Avery	.15	.10	59	Brett Butler	.08	.05
2	Sid Bream	.05	.02	60	Tom Candiotti	.05	.02
3	Ron Gant	.12	.07	61	Lenny Harris	.05	.02
4	Tom Glavine	.15	.10	62	Carlos Hernandez	.08	.05
5	Brian Hunter	.10	.06	63	Orel Hershiser	.10	.06
6	Ryan Klesko (R)	1.25	.80	64	Eric Karros	.30	.18
7	Charlie Leibrandt	.05	.02	65	Ramon Martinez	.10	.06
8	Kent Mercker	.05	.02	66	Jose Offerman	.08	.05
9	David Nied	.50	.30	67	Mike Scioscia	.05	.02
10	Otis Nixon	.08	.05	68	Mike Sharperson	.05	.02
11	Greg Olson	.05	.02	69	Eric Young	.15	.10
12	Terry Pendleton	.12	.07	70	Moises Alou	.12	.07
13	Deion Sanders	.15	.10	71	Ivan Calderon	.07	.04
14	John Smoltz	.10	.06	72	Archi Cianfrocco (R)	.35	.20
15	Mike Stanton	.05	.02	73	Wil Cordero	.15	.10
16	Mark Wohlers	.08	.05	74	Delino DeShields	.12	.07
17	Paul Assenmacher	.05	.02	75	Mark Gardner	.05	.02
18	Steve Buechele	.05	.02	76	Ken Hill	.07	.04
19	Shawon Dunston	.08	.05	77	Tim Laker	.05	.02
20	Mark Grace	.10	.06	78	Chris Nabholz	.07	.04
21	Derrick May	.08	.05	79	Mel Rojas	.05	.02
22	Chuck McElroy	.05	.02	80	John Vander Wal	.10	.06
23	Mike Morgan	.05	.02	81	Larry Walker	.12	.07
24	Rey Sanchez	.08	.05	82	Tim Wallach	.07	.04
25	Ryne Sandberg	.20	.12	83	John Wetteland	.07	.04
26	Bob Scanlan	.05	.02	84	Bobby Bonilla	.12	.07
27	Sammy Sosa	.07	.04	85	Daryl Boston	.05	.02
28	Rick Wilkins	.05	.02	86	Sid Fernandez	.07	.04
29	Bobby Ayala	.05	.02	87	Eric Hillman	.10	.06
30	Tim Belcher	.07	.04	88	Todd Hundley	.08	.05
31	Jeff Branson	.05	.02	89	Howard Johnson	.08	.05
32	Norm Charlton	.05	.02	90	Jeff Kent	.15	.10
33	Steve Foster	.07	.04	91	Eddie Murray	.12	.07
34	Willie Greene	.15	.10	92	Bill Pecota	.05	.02
35	Chris Hammond	.05	.02	93	Bret Saberhagen	.10	.06
36	Milt Hill	.05	.02	94	Dick Schofield	.05	.02
37	Hal Morris	.08	.05	95	Pete Schourek	.05	.02
38	Joe Oliver	.05	.02	96	Anthony Young	.08	.05
39	Paul O'Neill	.08	.05	97	Ruben Amaro, Jr.	.08	.05
40	Tim Pugh (R)	.12	.07	98	Juan Bell	.05	.02
41	Jose Rijo	.08	.05	99	Wes Chanberlain	.10	.06
42	Bip Roberts	.05	.02	100	Darren Daulton	.10	.06
43	Chris Sabo	.07	.04	101	Mariano Duncan	.05	.02
44	Reggie Sanders	.20	.12	102	Mike Hartley	.05	.02
45	Eric Anthony	.10	.06	103	Ricky Jordan	.05	.02
46	Jeff Bagwell	.20	.12	104	John Kruk	.08	.05
47	Craig Biggio	.07	.04	105	Mickey Morandini	.07	.04
48	Joe Boever	.05	.02	106	Terry Mulholland	.05	.02
49	Casey Candaele	.05	.02	107	Ben Rivera	.05	.02
50	Steve Finley	.05	.02	108	Curt Schilling	.05	.02
51	Luis Gonzalez	.07	.04	109	Keith Shepherd (R)	.12	.07
52	Pete Harnisch	.07	.04	110	Stan Belinda	.05	.02
53	Xavier Hernandez	.05	.02	111	Jay Bell	.05	.02
54	Doug Jones	.05	.02	112	Barry Bonds	.15	.10
55	Eddie Taubensee	.07	.04	113	Jeff King	.07	.04
56	Brian Williams	.15	.10	114	Mike LaValliere	.05	.02
57	Pedro Astacio (R)	.25	.15	115	Jose Lind	.05	.02
58	Todd Benzinger	.05	.02	116	Roger Mason	.05	.02

117	Orlando Merced	.08	.05	175	David Segui	.08	.05
118	Bob Patterson	.05	.02	176	Ellis Burks	.07	.04
119	Don Slaught	.05	.02	177	Roger Clemens	.20	.12
120	Zane Smith	.05	.02	178	Scott Cooper	.12	.07
121	Randy Tomlin	.07	.04	179	Danny Darwin	.05	.02
122	Andy Van Slyke	.12	.07	180	Tony Fossas	.05	.02
123	Tim Wakefield	1.25	.80	181	Paul Quantrill (R)	.20	.12
124	Rheal Cormier	.05	.02	182	Jody Reed	.05	.02
125	Bernard Gilkey	.10	.06	183	John Valentin (R)	.25	.15
126	Felix Jose	.08	.05	184	Mo Vaughn	.12	.07
127	Ray Lankford	.15	.10	185	Frank Viola	.07	.04
128	Bob McClure	.05	.02	186	Bob Zupcic	.15	.10
129	Donovan Osborne	.20	.12	187	Jim Abbott	.12	.07
130	Tom Pagnozzi	.07	.04	188	Gary DiSarcina	.08	.05
131	Geronimo Pena	.05	.02	189	Damion Easley	.12	.07
132	Mike Perez	.08	.05	190	Junior Felix	.05	.02
133	Lee Smith	.10	.06	191	Chuck Finley	.08	.05
134	Bob Tewksbury	.05	.02	192	Joe Grahe	.05	.02
135	Todd Worrell	.05	.02	193	Bryan Harvey	.07	.04
136	Todd Zeile	.08	.05	194	Mark Langston	.10	.06
137	Jerald Clark	.08	.05	195	John Orton	.07	.04
138	Tony Gwynn	.15	.10	196	Luis Polonia	.07	.04
139	Greg Harris	.05	.02	197	Tim Salmon	.25	.15
140	Jeremy Hernandez	.08	.05	198	Luis Sojo	.05	.02
141	Darrin Jackson	.05	.02	199	Wilson Alvarez	.08	.05
142	Mike Maddux	.05	.02	200	George Bell	.10	.06
143	Fred McGriff	.15	.10	201	Alex Fernandez	.08	.05
144	Jose Melendez	.05	.02	202	Craig Grebeck	.05	.02
145	Rich Rodriquez	.05	.02	203	Ozzie Guillen	.05	.02
146	Frank Seminara	.12	.07	204	Lance Johnson	.05	.02
147	Gary Sheffield	.20	.12	205	Ron Karkovice	.05	.02
148	Kurt Stillwell	.05	.02	206	Kirk McCaskill	.05	.02
149	Dan Walters	.08	.05	207	Jack McDowell	.15	.10
150	Rod Beck (R)	.20	.12	208	Scott Radinsky	.05	.02
151	Bud Black	.05	.02	209	Tim Raines	.07	.04
152	Jeff Brantley	.05	.02	210	Frank Thomas	.75	.45
153	John Burkett	.05	.02	211	Robin Ventura	.15	.10
154	Will Clark	.20	.12	212	Sandy Alomar, Jr.	.07	.04
155	Royce Clayton	.12	.07	213	Carlos Baerga	.15	.10
156	Mike Jackson	.05	.02	214	Dennis Cook	.05	.02
157	Darren Lewis	.08	.05	215	Thomas Howard	.08	.05
158	Kirt Manwaring	.05	.02	216	Mark Lewis	.07	.04
159	Willie McGee	.08	.05	217	Derek Lilliquist	.05	.02
160	Cory Snyder	.05	.02	218	Kenny Lofton	.20	.12
161	Bill Swift	.07	.04	219	Charles Nagy	.10	.06
162	Trevor Wilson	.05	.02	220	Steve Olin	.05	.02
163	Brady Anderson	.10	.06	221	Paul Sorrento	.08	.05
164	Glenn Davis	.07	.04	222	Jim Thome	.10	.06
165	Mike Devereaux	.08	.05	223	Mark Whiten	.08	.05
166	Todd Frohwirth	.05	.02	224	Milt Cuyler	.07	.04
167	Leo Gomez	.08	.05	225	Rob Deer	.07	.04
168	Chris Hoiles	.08	.05	226	John Doherty	.10	.06
169	Ben McDonald	.10	.06	227	Cecil Fielder	.15	.10
170	Randy Milligan	.05	.02	228	Travis Fryman	.15	.10
171	Alan Mills	.05	.02	229	Mike Henneman	.05	.02
172	Mike Mussina	.25	.15	230	John Kiely	.08	.05
173	Gregg Olson	.07	.04	231	Kurt Knudsen	.08	.05
174	Arthur Rhodes	.10	.06	232	Scott Livingstone	.07	.04

233	Tony Phillips	.05	.02
234	Mickey Tettleton	.07	.04
235	Kevin Appier	.08	.05
236	George Brett	.12	.07
237	Tom Gordon	.07	.04
238	Gregg Jefferies	.10	.06
239	Wally Joyner	.08	.05
240	Kevin Koslofski	.08	.05
241	Mike Macfarlane	.05	.02
242	Brian McRae	.08	.05
243	Rusty Meacham (R)	.20	.12
244	Keith Miller	.05	.02
245	Jeff Montgomery	.05	.02
246	Hipolito Pichardo	.10	.06
247	Ricky Bones	.08	.05
248	Cal Eldred	.60	.35
249	Mike Fetters	.05	.02
250	Darryl Hamilton	.05	.02
251	Doug Henry	.05	.02
252	John Jaha	.20	.12
253	Pat Listach	1.00	.70
254	Paul Molitor	.08	.05
255	Jaime Navarro	.08	.05
256	Kevin Seitzer	.05	.02
257	B.J. Surhoff	.05	.02
258	Greg Vaughn	.08	.05
259	Bill Wegman	.05	.02
260	Robin Yount	.12	.07
261	Rick Aguilera	.05	.02
262	Chili Davis	.07	.04
263	Scott Erickson	.10	.06
264	Greg Gagne	.05	.02
265	Mark Guthrie	.05	.02
266	Brian Harper	.05	.02
267	Kent Hrbek	.07	.04
268	Terry Jorgensen	.05	.02
269	Gene Larkin	.05	.02
270	Scott Leius	.05	.02
271	Pat Mahomes	.20	.12
272	Pedro Munoz	.08	.05
273	Kirby Puckett	.20	.12
274	Kevin Tapani	.07	.04
275	Carl Willis	.05	.02
276	Steve Farr	.05	.02
277	John Habyan	.05	.02
278	Mel Hall	.07	.04
279	Charlie Hayes	.05	.02
280	Pat Kelly	.08	.05
281	Don Mattingly	.12	.07
282	Sam Militello	.20	.12
283	Matt Nokes	.05	.02
284	Melido Perez	.07	.04
285	Andy Stankiewicz	.10	.06
286	Danny Tartabull	.10	.06
287	Randy Velarde	.05	.02
288	Bob Wickman	.12	.07
289	Bernie Williams	.10	.06
290	Lance Blankenship	.05	.02
291	Mike Bordick	.08	.05
292	Jerry Browne	.05	.02
293	Dennis Eckersley	.12	.07
295	Vince Horsman	.08	.05
296	Mark McGwire	.20	.12
297	Jeff Parrett	.05	.02
298	Ruben Sierra	.15	.10
299	Terry Steinbach	.07	.04
300	Walt Weiss	.05	.02
301	Bob Welch	.07	.04
302	Willie Wilson	.05	.02
303	Bobby Witt	.07	.04
304	Bret Boone	.25	.15
305	Jay Buhner	.07	.04
306	Dave Fleming	.25	.15
307	Ken Griffey, Jr.	.50	.30
308	Erik Hanson	.05	.02
309	Edgar Martinez	.10	.06
310	Tino Martinez	.08	.05
311	Jeff Nelson	.08	.05
312	Dennis Powell	.05	.02
313	Mike Schooler	.05	.02
314	Russ Swan	.05	.02
315	Dave Valle	.05	.02
316	Omar Vizquel	.05	.02
317	Kevin Brown	.08	.05
318	Todd Burns	.05	.02
319	Jose Canseco	.25	.15
320	Julio Franco	.08	.05
321	Jeff Frye	.08	.05
322	Juan Gonzalez	.30	.18
323	Jose Guzman	.05	.02
324	Jeff Huson	.05	.02
325	Dean Palmer	.10	.06
326	Kevin Reimer	.07	.04
327	Ivan Rodriquez	.20	.12
328	Kenny Rogers	.05	.02
329	Dan Smith (R)	.15	.10
330	Roberto Alomar	.20	.12
331	Derek Bell	.10	.06
332	Pat Borders	.07	.04
333	Joe Carter	.20	.12
334	Kelly Gruber	.07	.04
335	Tom Henke	.05	.02
336	Jimmy Key	.05	.02
337	Manuel lee	.05	.02
338	Candy Maldonado	.05	.02
339	John Olerud	.10	.06
340	Todd Stottlemyre	.07	.04
341	Duane Ward	.05	.02
342	Devon White	.05	.02
343	Dave Winfield	.15	.10
344	Edgar Martinez (LL)	.07	.04
345	Ceci Fielder (LL)	.08	.05
346	Kenny Lofton (LL)	.10	.06
347	Jack Morris (LL)	.07	.04
348	Roger Clemens (LL)	.10	.06
349	Fred McGriff (RT)	.10	.06

350	Barry Bonds (RT)	.10	.06
351	Gary Sheffield (RT)	.08	.05
352	Darren Daulton (RT)	.07	.04
353	Dave Hollins (RT)	.07	.04
354	Pedro Martinez	.12	.07
	Ramon Martinez		
355	Ivan Rodriquez	.15	.10
	Kirby Puckett		
356	Ryne Sandberg	.15	.10
	Gary Sheffield		
357	Roberto Alomar	.12	.07
	Chuck Knoblauch		
	Carlos Baerga		
358	Checklist	.05	.02
359	Checklist	.05	.02
360	Checklist	.05	.02
GM1	George Brett	.30	.18
GM2	Mickey Morandini	.08	.05
GM3	Dave Winfield	.25	.15
PV1	Roberto Alomar	.60	.35
PV2	Dennis Eckersley	.25	.15
PV3	Gary Sheffield	.35	.20

1993 Fleer AL Team Leader Inserts

		MINT	NR/MT
Complete Set (10)		22.00	14.00
Commons		1.00	.70

1	Kirby Puckett	2.50	1.50
2	Mark McGwire	4.50	2.75
3	Pat Listach	1.50	.90
4	Roger Clemens	4.50	2.75
5	Frank Thomas	7.00	4.50
6	Carlos Baerga	1.75	1.00
7	Brady Anderson	1.00	.70
8	Juan Gonzalez	6.00	4.00
9	Roberto Alomar	2.50	1.50
10	Ken Griffey, Jr.	6.00	4.00

1993 Fleer Rookie Sensations

		MINT	NR/MT
Complete Set (10)		65.00	38.00
Commons		1.50	.90

1	Cal Eldred	6.00	3.75
2	Dave Fleming	6.00	3.75
3	Roberto Hernandez	1.50	.90
4	Eric Karros	18.00	12.00
5	Pat Listach	12.00	8.50
6	Kenny Lofton	10.00	6.50
7	Derrick May	2.00	1.25
8	Donovan Osborne	4.50	2.75
9	Mike Perez	1.50	.90
10	Reggie Sanders	10.00	6.50

1993 Fleer NL All-Stars

		MINT	NR/MT
Complete Set (12)		18.00	12.50
Commons		1.25	.80

1	Fred McGriff	2.00	1.25
2	Delino DeShields	1.50	.90
3	Gary Sheffield	2.00	1.25
4	Barry Larkin	1.50	.90
5	Felix Jose	1.25	.80
6	Larry Walker	1.25	.80
7	Barry Bonds	2.50	1.50
8	Andy Van Slyke	1.50	.90
9	Darren Daulton	1.25	.80
10	Greg Maddux	2.00	1.25
11	Tom Glavine	2.00	1.25
12	Lee Smith	1.25	.80

1993 Fleer Major League Prospects

		MINT	NR/MT
Complete Set (18)		58.00	40.00
Commons		1.25	.80

1	Melvin Nieves	6.00	4.00
2	Sterling Hitchcock	5.00	3.50
3	Tim Costo	3.00	2.00
4	Manny Alexander	1.75	1.00
5	Alan Embree	3.00	2.00

6	Kevin Young	2.50	1.50
7	J.T. Snow	5.00	3.50
8	Russ Springer	2.50	1.50
9	Billy Ashley	5.00	3.50
10	Kevin Rogers	2.50	1.50
11	Steve Hosey	5.00	3.50
12	Eric Wedge	4.00	2.75
13	Mike Piazza	8.50	5.50
14	Jesse Levis	3.00	2.00
15	Rico Brogna	3.00	2.00
16	Alex Arias	1.25	.80
17	Rod Brewer	2.50	1.50
18	Troy Neal	2.50	1.50

LEAF

1948 Leaf

This 98-card set is skip-numbered through card #168 and is very difficult to complete. Half of the cards in the set are short printed and tough to find. The cards were the first Post World War II set issued in color.

		NR/MT	EX
Complete Set (98)		32,000.00	16,500.00
Commons		28.00	12.00
Commons (Scarce)		325.00	150.00

1	Joe DiMaggio	2,200.00	1,000.00
3	Babe Ruth	2,400.00	1,200.00
4	Stan Musial (R)	800.00	350.00
5	Virgil Trucks	400.00	175.00
8	Satchel Paige (R)	2,000.00	950.00

10	Paul "Dizzy" Trout	28.00	12.00
11	Phil Rizzuto	180.00	80.00
13	Casimer Michaels	325.00	150.00
14	Billy Johnson	28.00	12.00
17	Frank Overmire	28.00	12.00
19	Johnny Wyrostek	325.00	150.00
20	Hank Sauer	425.00	190.00
22	Al Evans	28.00	12.00
26	Sam Chapman	28.00	12.00
27	Mickey Harris	28.00	12.00
28	Jim Hegan	35.00	15.00
29	Elmer Valo	30.00	12.50
30	Billy Goodman	375.00	160.00
31	Lou Brissie	28.00	12.00
32	Warren Spahn	250.00	100.00
33	Peanuts Lowrey	350.00	155.00
36	Al Zarilla	325.00	150.00
38	Ted Kluszewski	100.00	45.00
39	Ewell Blackwell	60.00	25.00
42	Kent Peterson	28.00	12.00
43	Ed Stevens	325.00	150.00
45	Ken Keltner	325.00	150.00
46	Johnny Mize	100.00	45.00
47	George Vico	28.00	12.00
48	Johnny Schmitz	325.00	150.00
49	Del Ennis	40.00	18.00
50	Dick Wakefield	28.00	12.00
51	Al Dark	425.00	190.00
53	Johnny VanderMeer	50.00	22.00
54	Bobby Adams	325.00	150.00
55	Tommy Henrich	450.00	200.00
56	Larry Jansen	30.00	12.50
57	Bob McCall	28.00	12.00
59	Luke Appling	100.00	45.00
61	Jake Early	28.00	12.00
62	Eddie Joost	325.00	150.00
63	Barney McCosky	325.00	150.00
65	Bob Elliot (ER)	28.00	12.00
66	Orval Grove	325.00	150.00
68	Eddie Miller	325.00	150.00
70	Honus Wagner	300.00	125.00
72	Hank Edwards	28.00	12.00
73	Pat Seerey	28.00	12.00
75	Dom DiMaggio	500.00	225.00
76	Ted Williams	850.00	400.00
77	Roy Smalley	28.00	12.00
78	Hoot Evers	325.00	150.00
79	Jackie Robinson (R)	800.00	375.00
81	Whitey Kurowski	325.00	150.00
82	Johnny Lindell	28.00	12.00
83	Bobby Doerr	150.00	60.00
84	Sid Hudson	28.00	12.00
85	Dave Philley	325.00	150.00
86	Ralph Weigel	28.00	12.00
88	Frank Gustine	325.00	150.00
91	Ralph Kiner	175.00	75.00
93	Bob Feller	1,500.00	650.00

1960 Leaf

95	George Stirnweiss	28.00	12.00
97	Marty Marion	50.00	22.00
98	Hal Newhouser	500.00	225.00
102a	Gene Hermansk (ER)	325.00	150.00
102b	Gene Hermanski	28.00	12.00
104	Edward Stewart	325.00	150.00
106	Lou Boudreau	100.00	45.00
108	Matt Batts	325.00	150.00
111	Jerry Priddy	28.00	12.00
113	Dutch Leonard	350.00	160.00
117	Joe Gordon	35.00	16.00
120	George Kell	600.00	275.00
121	Johnny Pesky	450.00	200.00
123	Cliff Fannin	325.00	150.00
125	Andy Pafko	30.00	12.50
127	Enos Slaughter	750.00	350.00
128	Buddy Rosar	28.00	12.00
129	Kirby Higbe	325.00	150.00
131	Sid Gordon	325.00	150.00
133	Tommy Holmes	400.00	175.00
136a	Cliff Aberson (Full Sleeve)	28.00	12.00
136b	Cliff Aberson (Short Sleeve)	250.00	100.00
137	Harry Walker	400.00	175.00
138	Larry Doby	600.00	275.00
139	Johnny Hopp	28.00	12.00
142	Danny Murtaugh	325.00	150.00
143	Dick Sisler	400.00	175.00
144	Bob Dillinger	325.00	150.00
146	Pete Reiser	500.00	225.00
149	Hank Majeski	325.00	150.00
153	Floyd Baker	325.00	150.00
158	Harry Brecheen	400.00	175.00
159	Mizell Platt	28.00	12.00
160	Bob Scheffing	325.00	150.00
161	Vern Stephens	400.00	175.00
163	Fred Hutchinson	400.00	175.00
165	Dale Mitchell	400.00	1750.00
168	Phil Cavarretta	500.00	225.00

HOYT WILHELM

This 144-card set was produced by Leaf for Sports Novelties, Inc., of Chicago. The cards were sold in wax packs with a marble rather than bubble gum. Cards feature black and white photos on the front and cards 73-144 are considered scarce.

		NR/MT	EX
Complete Set (144)		1,500.00	700.00
Commons (1-72)		3.00	1.25
Commons (73-144)		15.00	7.00
1	Luis Aparicio	24.00	10.00
2	Woody Held	3.00	1.25
3	Frank Lary	3.50	1.50
4	Camilo Pascual	3.50	1.50
5	Frank Herrera	3.00	1.25
6	Felipe Alou	4.00	1.75
7	Ben Daniels	3.00	1.25
8	Roger Craig	4.00	1.75
9	Eddie Kasko	3.00	1.25
10	Bob Grim	3.00	1.25
11	Jim Busby	3.00	1.25
12	Ken Boyer	5.00	2.25
13	Bob Boyd	3.00	1.25
14	Sam Jones	3.00	1.25
15	Larry Jackson	3.00	1.25
16	Roy Face	4.00	1.75
17	Walt Moryn	3.00	1.25
18	Jim Gilliam	4.00	1.75
19	Don Newcombe	4.00	1.75
20	Glen Hobbie	3.00	1.25
21	Pedro Ramos	3.00	1.25
22	Ryne Duran	3.50	1.50
23	Joey Jay	3.00	1.25
24	Lou Berberet	3.00	1.25
25a	Jim Grant (Wrong Photo)	15.00	7.00
25b	Jim Grant (Cor)	30.00	12.50
26	Tom Borland	3.00	1.25

27	Brooks Robinson	40.00	18.00
28	Jerry Adair	3.00	1.25
29	Ron Jackson	3.00	1.25
30	George Strickland	3.00	1.25
31	Rocky Bridges	3.50	1.50
32	Bill Tuttle	3.00	1.25
33	Ken Hunt	3.00	1.25
34	Hal Griggs	3.00	1.25
35	Jim Coates	3.00	1.25
36	Brooks Lawrence	3.00	1.25
37	Duke Snider	45.00	20.00
38	Al Spangler	3.00	1.25
39	Jim Owens	3.00	1.25
40	Bill Virdon	3.50	1.50
41	Ernie Broglio	3.50	1.50
42	Andre Rodgers	3.00	1.25
43	Julio Becquer	3.00	1.25
44	Tony Taylor	3.50	1.50
45	Jerry Lynch	3.50	1.50
46	Clete Boyer	3.50	1.50
47	Jerry Lumpe	3.00	1.25
48	Charlie Maxwell	3.00	1.25
49	Jim Perry	3.50	1.50
50	Danny McDevitt	3.00	1.25
51	Juan Pizarro	3.00	1.25
52	Dallas Green	5.00	2.25
53	Bob Friend	3.50	1.50
54	Jack Sanford	3.50	1.50
55	Jim Rivera	3.00	1.25
56	Ted Wills	3.00	1.25
57	Milt Pappas	3.50	1.50
58	Hal Smith	3.00	1.25
59	Bobby Avila	3.00	1.25
60	Clem Labine	3.50	1.50
61	Vic Rehm	3.00	1.25
62	John Gabler	3.00	1.25
63	John Tsitouris	3.00	1.25
64	Dave Sisler	3.00	1.25
65	Vic Power	3.50	1.50
66	Earl Battey	3.50	1.50
67	Bob Purkey	3.50	1.50
68	Moe Drabowsky	3.00	1.25
69	Hoyt Wilhelm	12.00	5.00
70	Humberto Robinson	3.00	1.25
71	Whitey Herzog	4.00	1.75
72	Dick Donovan	3.00	1.25
73	Gordon Jones	15.00	7.00
74	Joe Hicks	15.00	7.00
75	Ray Culp	16.50	7.50
76	Dick Drott	15.00	7.00
77	Bob Duliba	15.00	7.00
78	Art Ditmar	15.00	7.00
79	Steve Korcheck	15.00	7.00
80	Henry Mason	15.00	7.00
81	Harry Simpson	15.00	7.00
82	Gene Green	15.00	7.00
83	Bob Shaw	15.00	7.00
84	Howard Reed	15.00	7.00
85	Dick Stigman	15.00	7.00
86	Rip Repulski	15.00	7.00
87	Seth Morehead	15.00	7.00
88	Camilo Carreon	15.00	7.00
89	John Blanchard	20.00	8.50
90	Billy Hoeft	15.00	7.00
91	Fred Hopke	15.00	7.00
92	Joe Martin	15.00	7.00
93	Wally Shannon	15.00	7.00
94	Hal R. Smith/ Hal W. Smith	16.50	7.50
95	Al Schroll	15.00	7.00
96	John Kucks	15.00	7.00
97	Tom Morgan	15.00	7.00
98	Willie Jones	15.00	7.00
99	Marshall Renfroe	15.00	7.00
100	Willie Tasby	15.00	7.00
101	Irv Noren	15.00	7.00
102	Russ Snyder	15.00	7.00
103	Bob Turley	20.00	8.50
104	Jim Woods	15.00	7.00
105	Ronnie Kline	15.00	7.00
106	Steve Bilko	15.00	7.00
107	Elmer Valo	15.00	7.00
108	Tom McAvoy	15.00	7.00
109	Stan Williams	15.00	7.00
110	Earl Averill	15.00	7.00
111	Lee Walls	15.00	7.00
112	Paul Richards	16.50	8.50
113	Ed Sadowski	15.00	7.00
114	Stover McIlwain	15.00	7.00
115	Chuck Tanner (Wrong Photo)	18.00	8.00
116	Lou Klimchock	15.00	7.00
117	Neil Chrisley	15.00	7.00
118	John Callison	18.00	8.00
119	Hal Smith	15.00	7.00
120	Carl Sawatski	15.00	7.00
121	Frank Leja	15.00	7.00
122	Earl Torgeson	16.50	7.50
123	Art Schult	15.00	7.00
124	Jim Brosnan	16.50	7.50
125	George Anderson	40.00	18.00
126	Joe Pignatano	15.00	7.00
127	Rocky Nelson	15.00	7.00
128	Orlando Cepeda	48.00	22.00
129	Daryl Spencer	15.00	7.00
130	Ralph Lumenti	15.00	7.00
131	Sam Taylor	15.00	7.00
132	Harry Brecheen	16.50	7.50
133	Johnny Groth	15.00	7.00
134	Wayne Terwilliger	15.00	7.00
135	Kent Hadley	15.00	7.00
136	Faye Throneberry	15.00	7.00
137	Jack Meyer	15.00	7.00
138	Chuck Cottier	15.00	7.00
139	Joe DeMaestri	15.00	7.00
140	Gene Freese	15.00	7.00
141	Curt Flood	35.00	15.00
142	Gino Cimoli	15.00	7.00
143	Clay Dalrymple	15.00	7.00
144	Jim Bunning	60.00	25.00

1990 Leaf

This was the first premium set produced by Donruss. The cards are printed on glossy high quality paper stock and feature full color photos on both the front and back. The set was released in two 264-card series.

		MINT	NR/MT
Complete Set (528)		300.00	160.00
Commons		.25	.15
1.	Introductory Card	.25	.15
2	Mike Henneman	.25	.15
3	Steve Bedrosian	.25	.15
4	Mike Scott	.25	.15
5	Allan Anderson	.25	.15
6	Rick Sutcliffe	.25	.15
7	Gregg Olson	.30	.18
8	Kevin Elster	.25	.15
9	Pete O'Brien	.25	.15
10	Carlton Fisk	1.00	.70
11	Joe Magrane	.25	.15
12	Roger Clemens	3.50	2.00
13	Tom Glavine	2.00	1.25
14	Tom Gordon	.25	.15
15	Todd Benzinger	.25	.15
16	Hubie Brooks	.25	.15
17	Roberto Kelly	.35	.20
18	Barry Larkin	.75	.45
19	Mike Boddicker	.25	.15
20	Roger McDowell	.25	.15
21	Nolan Ryan	7.50	4.50
22	John Farrell	.25	.15
23	Bruce Hurst	.25	.15
24	Wally Joyner	.35	.20
25	Greg Maddux	.40	.25
26	Chris Bosio	.25	.15
27	John Cerutti	.25	.15
28	Tim Burke	.25	.15
29	Dennis Eckersley	.40	.25
30	Glenn Davis	.25	.15
31	Jim Abbott	2.00	1.25
32	Mike LaValliere	.25	.15
33	Andres Thomas	.25	.15
34	Lou Whitaker	.25	.15
35	Alvin Davis	.25	.15
36	Melido Perez	.25	.15
37	Craig Biggio	.35	.20
38	Rick Aguilera	.25	.15
39	Pete Harnisch	.30	.18
40	David Cone	.35	.20
41	Scott Garrelts	.25	.15
42	Jay Howell	.25	.15
43	Eric King	.25	.15
44	Pedro Guerrero	.25	.15
45	Mike Bielecki	.25	.15
46	Bob Boone	.30	.18
47	Kevin Brown	.35	.20
48	Jerry Browne	.25	.15
49	Mike Scioscia	.25	.15
50	Chuck Cary	.25	.15
51	Wade Boggs	2.50	1.50
52	Von Hayes	.25	.15
53	Tony Fernandez	.25	.15
54	Dennis Martinez	.25	.15
55	Tom Candiotti	.25	.15
56	Andy Benes	3.00	1.75
57	Rob Dibble	.30	.18
58	Chuck Crim	.25	.15
59	John Smoltz	3.00	1.75
60	Mike Heath	.25	.15
61	Kevin Gross	.25	.15
62	Mark McGwire	4.50	2.50
63	Bert Blyleven	.30	.18
64	Bob Walk	.25	.15
65	Mickey Tettleton	.25	.15
66	Sid Fernandez	.25	.15
67	Terry Kennedy	.25	.15
68	Fernando Valenzuela	.25	.15
69	Don Mattingly	2.00	1.25
70	Paul O'Neill	.35	.20
71	Robin Yount	2.50	1.50
72	Bret Saberhagen	.35	.20
73	Geno Petralli	.25	.15
74	Brook Jacoby	.25	.15
75	Roberto Alomar	10.00	6.00
76	Devon White	.25	.15
77	Jose Lind	.25	.15
78	Pat Combs	.25	.15
79	Dave Steib	.25	.15
80	Tim Wallach	.25	.15
81	Dave Stewart	.25	.15
82	Eric Anthony (R)	1.00	.70
83	Randy Bush	.25	.15
84	Checklist	.30	.18
85	Jaime Navarro	1.75	1.00
86	Tommy Gregg	.25	.15
87	Frank Tanana	.25	.15
88	Omar Vizquel	.25	.15
89	Ivan Calderon	.25	.15

90	Vince Coleman	.25	.15
91	Barry Bonds	4.00	2.25
92	Randy Milligan	.25	.15
93	Frank Viola	.30	.18
94	Matt Williams	.80	.50
95	Alfredo Griffin	.25	.15
96	Steve Sax	.35	.20
97	Gary Gaetti	.25	.15
98	Ryne Sandberg	4.50	2.50
99	Danny Tartabull	1.00	.70
100	Rafael Palmeiro	1.00	.70
101	Jesse Orasco	.25	.15
102	Garry Templeton	.25	.15
103	Frank DiPino	.25	.15
104	Tony Pena	.25	.15
105	Dickie Thon	.25	.15
106	Kelly Gruber	.25	.15
107	Marquis Grissom (R)	5.00	3.00
108	Jose Canseco	4.50	2.50
109	Mike Blowers	.25	.15
110	Tom Browning	.25	.15
111	Greg Vaughn	2.00	1.25
112	Oddibe McDowell	.25	.15
113	Gary Ward	.25	.15
114	Jay Buhner	.40	.25
115	Eric Show	.25	.15
116	Bryan Harvey	.35	.20
117	Andy Van Slyke	.75	.45
118	Jeff Ballard	.25	.15
119	Barry Lyons	.25	.15
120	Kevin Mitchell	.40	.25
121	Mike Gallego	.25	.15
122	Dave Smith	.25	.15
123	Kirby Puckett	4.50	2.50
124	Jerome Walton	.25	.15
125	Bo Jackson	2.00	1.25
126	Harold Baines	.30	.18
127	Scott Bankhead	.25	.15
128	Ozzie Guillen	.25	.15
129	Jose Oquendo	.25	.15
130	John Dopson	.25	.15
131	Charlie Hayes	.30	.18
132	Fred McGriff	3.00	1.75
133	Chet Lemon	.25	.15
134	Gary Carter	.35	.20
135	Rafael Ramirez	.25	.15
136	Shane Mack	.35	.20
137	Mark Grace	1.00	.70
138	Phil Bradley	.25	.15
139	Dwight Gooden	.70	.40
140	Harold Reynolds	.25	.15
141	Scott Fletcher	.25	.15
142	Ozzie Smith	1.00	.70
143	Mike Greenwell	.35	.20
144	Pete Smith	.35	.20
145	Mark Gubicza	.25	.15
146	Chris Sabo	.30	.18
147	Ramon Martinez	1.75	1.00

148	Tim Leary	.25	.15
149	Randy Myers	.25	.15
150	Jody Reed	.25	.15
151	Bruce Ruffin	.25	.15
152	Jeff Russell	.30	.18
153	Doug Jones	.30	.18
154	Tony Gwynn	3.00	1.75
155	Mark Langston	.30	.18
156	Mitch Williams	.25	.15
157	Gary Sheffield	10.00	6.00
158	Tom Henke	.25	.15
159	Oil Can Boyd	.25	.15
160	Rickey Henderson	2.50	1.50
161	Bill Doran	.25	.15
162	Chuck Finley	.30	.18
163	Jeff King	.25	.15
164	Nick Esasky	.25	.15
165	Cecil Fielder	2.50	1.50
166	Dave Valle	.25	.15
167	Robin Ventura	12.50	7.50
168	Jim DeShaies	.25	.15
169	Juan Berenguer	.25	.15
170	Craig Worthington	.25	.15
171	Gregg Jefferies	.50	.30
172	Will Clark	4.50	2.50
173	Kirk Gibson	.25	.15
174	Checklist	.30	.18
175	Bobby Thigpen	.25	.15
176	John Tudor	.25	.15
177	Andre Dawson	.75	.45
178	George Brett	2.50	1.50
179	Steve Buechele	.25	.15
180	Joey Belle	8.50	5.00
181	Eddie Murray	.75	.45
182	Bob Geren	.25	.15
183	Rob Murphy	.25	.15
184	Tom Herr	.25	.15
185	George Bell	.35	.20
186	Spike Owen	.25	.15
187	Cory Snyder	.25	.15
188	Fred Lynn	.25	.15
189	Eric Davis	.70	.40
190	Dave Parker	.30	.18
191	Jeff Blauser	.25	.15
192	Matt Nokes	.25	.15
193	Delino DeShields (R)	5.00	3.00
194	Scott Sanderson	.25	.15
195	Lance Parrish	.25	.15
196	Bobby Bonilla	1.25	.80
197	Cal Ripken	5.00	3.00
198	Kevin McReynolds	.25	.15
199	Robby Thompson	.25	.15
200	Tim Belcher	.25	.15
201	Jesse Barfield	.25	.15
202	Mariano Duncan	.25	.15
203	Bill Spiers	.25	.15
204	Frank White	.25	.15
205	Julio Franco	.35	.20

206 Greg Swindell	.25	.15
207 Benito Santiago	.30	.18
208 Johnny Ray	.25	.15
209 Gary Redus	.25	.15
210 Jeff Parrett	.25	.15
211 Jimmy Key	.25	.15
212 Tim Raines	.25	.15
213 Carney Lansford	.25	.15
214 Gerald Young	.25	.15
215 Gene Larkin	.25	.15
216 Dan Plesac	.25	.15
217 Lonnie Smith	.25	.15
218 Alan Trammell	.30	.18
219 Jeffrey Leonard	.25	.15
220 Sammy Sosa (R)	.60	.35
221 Todd Zeile	1.50	.90
222 Bill Landrum	.25	.15
223 Mike Devereaux	.35	.20
224 Mike Marshall	.25	.15
225 Jose Uribe	.25	.15
226 Juan Samuel	.25	.15
227 Mel Hall	.30	.18
228 Kent Hrbek	.25	.15
229 Shawon Dunston	.35	.20
230 Kevin Seitzer	.25	.15
231 Pete Incaviglia	.25	.15
232 Sandy Alomar	.35	.20
233 Bip Roberts	.25	.15
234 Scott Terry	.25	.15
235 Dwight Evans	.25	.15
236 Ricky Jordan	.25	.15
237 John Olerud (R)	3.00	1.75
238 Zane Smith	.25	.15
239 Walt Weiss	.25	.15
240 Alvaro Espinoza	.25	.15
241 Billy Hatcher	.25	.15
242 Paul Molitor	.40	.25
243 Dale Murphy	.50	.30
244 Dave Bergman	.25	.15
245 Ken Griffey Jr.	20.00	14.00
246 Ed Whitson	.25	.15
247 Kirk McCaskill	.25	.15
248 Jay Bell	.25	.15
249 Ben McDonald (R)	5.00	3.00
250 Darryl Strawberry	2.50	1.50
251 Bret Butler	.30	.18
252 Terry Steinbach	.25	.15
253 Ken Caminiti	.25	.15
254 Dan Gladden	.25	.15
255 Dwight Smith	.25	.15
256 Kurt Stillwell	.25	.15
257 Ruben Sierra	3.50	2.00
258 Mike Schooler	.25	.15
259 Lance Johnson	.25	.15
260 Terry Pendleton	.80	.50
261 Ellis Burks	.30	.18
262 Len Dykstra	.25	.15
263 Mookie Wilson	.25	.15
264 Checklist	.50	.30
265 No Hit King (Nolan Ryan)	7.00	4.00
266 Brian DuBois	.25	.15
267 Don Robinson	.25	.15
268 Glenn Wilson	.25	.15
269 Kevin Tapani (R)	1.75	1.00
270 Marvell Wynn	.25	.15
271 Billy Ripken	.25	.15
272 Howard Johnson	.40	.25
273 Brian Holman	.25	.15
274 Dan Pasqua	.25	.15
275 Ken Dayley	.25	.15
276 Jeff Reardon	.50	.30
277 Jim Presley	.25	.15
278 Jim Eisenreich	.25	.15
279 Danny Jackson	.25	.15
280 Orel Hershiser	.30	.18
281 Andy Hawkins	.25	.15
282 Jose Rijo	.30	.18
283 Luis Rivera	.25	.15
284 John Kruk	.35	.20
285 Jeff Huson (R)	.25	.15
286 Joel Skinner	.25	.15
287 Jack Clark	.25	.15
288 Chili Davis	.30	.18
289 Joe Girardi	.25	.15
290 B.J. Surhoff	.25	.15
291 Luis Sojo (R)	.30	.18
292 Tim Foley	.25	.15
293 Mike Moore	.25	.15
294 Ken Oberkfell	.25	.15
295 Luis Polonia	.25	.15
296 Doug Drabek	.35	.20
297 Dave Justice	32.00	22.00
298 Paul Gibson	.25	.15
299 Edgar Martinez	1.25	.80
300 Frank Thomas	60.00	45.00
301 Eric Yelding	.30	.18
302 Greg Gagne	.25	.15
303 Brad Komminsk	.25	.15
304 Ron Darling	.25	.15
305 Kevin Bass	.25	.15
306 Jeff Hamilton	.25	.15
307 Ron Karkovice	.25	.15
308 Milt Thompson	.30	.18
309 Mike Harkey	.30	.18
310 Mel Stottlemyre Jr.	.30	.18
311 Kenny Rogers	.25	.15
312 Mitch Webster	.25	.15
313 Kal Daniels	.25	.15
314 Matt Nokes	.25	.15
315 Dennis Lamp	.25	.15
316 Ken Howell	.25	.15
317 Glenallen Hill	.30	.18
318 Dave Martinez	.25	.15
319 Chris James	.25	.15
320 Mike Pagliarulo	.25	.15

321 Hal Morris	2.50	1.50
322 Rob Deer	.25	.15
323 Greg Olson (R)	.30	.18
324 Tony Phillips	.25	.15
325 Larry Walker (R)	4.00	2.25
326 Ron Hassey	.25	.15
327 Jack Howell	.25	.15
328 John Smiley	.30	.18
329 Steve Finley	.30	.18
330 Dave Magadan	.25	.15
331 Greg Litton	.25	.15
332 Mickey Hatcher	.25	.15
333 Lee Guetterman	.25	.15
334 Norm Charlton	.30	.18
335 Edgar Diaz	.25	.15
336 Willie Wilson	.25	.15
337 Bobby Witt	.25	.15
338 Candy Maldonado	.25	.15
339 Craig Lefferts	.25	.15
340 Dante Bichette	.25	.15
341 Wally Backman	.25	.15
342 Dennis Cook	.25	.15
343 Pat Borders	.25	.15
344 Wallace Johnson	.25	.15
345 Willie Randolph	.25	.15
346 Danny Darwin	.25	.15
347 Al Newman	.25	.15
348 Mark Knudson	.25	.15
349 Joe Boever	.25	.15
350 Larry Sheets	.30	.18
351 Mike Jackson	.25	.15
352 Wayne Edwards	.25	.15
353 Bernard Gilkey (R)	1.25	.80
354 Don Slaught	.25	.15
355 Joe Orsulak	.30	.18
356 John Franco	.25	.15
357 Jeff Brantley	.25	.15
358 Mike Morgan	.25	.15
359 Deion Sanders	7.50	4.50
360 Terry Leach	.25	.15
361 Les Lancaster	.25	.15
362 Storm Davis	.25	.15
363 Scott Coolbaugh	.25	.15
364 Checklist	.30	.18
365 Cecilio Guante	.25	.15
366 Joey Cora	.25	.15
367 Willie McGee	.30	.18
368 Jerry Reed	.25	.15
369 Darren Daulton	.35	.20
370 Manny Lee	.25	.15
371 Mark Gardner (R)	.60	.35
372 Rick Honeycutt	.25	.15
373 Steve Balboni	.25	.15
374 Jack Armstrong	.25	.15
375 Charlie O'Brien	.25	.15
376 Ron Gant	3.50	2.00
377 Lloyd Moseby	.25	.15
378 Gene Harris	.25	.15

379 Joe Carter	1.00	.70
380 Scott Bailes	.25	.15
381 R.J. Reynolds	.25	.15
382 Bob Melvin	.25	.15
383 Tim Teufel	.25	.15
384 John Burkett	.25	.15
385 Felix Jose	2.00	1.25
386 Larry Anderson	.25	.15
387 David West	.25	.15
388 Luis Salazar	.25	.15
389 Mike MacFarlane	.25	.15
390 Charlie Hough	.25	.15
391 Greg Briley	.25	.15
392 Donn Pall	.25	.15
393 Bryn Smith	.25	.15
394 Carlos Quintana	.30	.18
395 Steve Lake	.25	.15
396 Mark Whiten (R)	3.00	1.75
397 Edwin Nunez	.25	.15
398 Rick Parker	.25	.15
399 Mark Portugal	.25	.15
400 Roy Smith	.25	.15
401 Hector Villanueva (R)	.25	.15
402 Bob Milacki	.25	.15
403 Alejandro Pena	.25	.15
404 Scott Bradley	.25	.15
405 Ron Kittle	.25	.15
406 Bob Tewksbury	.25	.15
407 Wes Gardner	.25	.15
408 Ernie Whitt	.25	.15
409 Terry Shumpert (R)	.25	.15
410 Tim Layana (R)	.25	.15
411 Chris Gwynn (R)	.25	.15
412 Jeff Robinson	.25	.15
413 Scott Scudder	.25	.15
414 Kevin Romine	.25	.15
415 Jose DeJesus	.25	.15
416 Mike Jeffcoat	.25	.15
417 Rudy Seanez (R)	.40	.25
418 Mike Dunne	.25	.15
419 Dick Schofield	.25	.15
420 Steve Wilson	.25	.15
421 Bill Krueger	.25	.15
422 Junior Felix	.30	.18
423 Drew Hall	.25	.15
424 Curt Young	.25	.15
425 Franklin Stubbs	.25	.15
426 Dave Winfield	.75	.45
427 Rick Reed (R)	.25	.15
428 Charlie Leibrandt	.25	.15
429 Jeff Robinson	.25	.15
430 Erik Hanson	.30	.18
431 Barry Jones	.25	.15
432 Alex Trevino	.25	.15
433 John Moses	.25	.15
434 Dave Johnson	.25	.15
435 Mackey Sasser	.25	.15
436 Rick Leach	.25	.15

437 Lenny Harris	.25	.15
438 Carlos Martinez	.25	.15
439 Rex Hudler	.25	.15
440 Domingo Ramos	.25	.15
441 Gerald Perry	.25	.15
442 John Russell	.25	.15
443 Carlos Baerga	6.00	3.75
444 Checklist	.50	.30
445 Stan Javier	.25	.15
446 Kevin Maas (R)	3.00	1.75
447 Tom Brunansky	.25	.15
448 Carmelo Martinez	.25	.15
449 Willie Blair	.30	.18
450 Andres Galarraga	.25	.15
451 Bud Black	.25	.15
452 Greg Harris	.30	.18
453 Joe Oliver	.25	.15
454 Greg Brock	.25	.15
455 Jeff Treadway	.25	.15
456 Lance McCullers	.25	.15
457 Dave Schmidt	.25	.15
458 Todd Burns	.25	.15
459 Max Venable	.25	.15
460 Neal Heaton	.25	.15
461 Mark Williamson	.25	.15
462 Keith Miller	.25	.15
463 Mike LaCoss	.25	.15
464 Jose Offerman (R)	1.00	.70
465 Jim Leyritz (R)	.30	.18
466 Glenn Braggs	.25	.15
467 Ron Robinson	.25	.15
468 Mark Davis	.25	.15
469 Gary Pettis	.25	.15
470 Keith Hernandez	.25	.15
471 Dennis Rasmussen	.25	.15
472 Mark Eichhorn	.25	.15
473 Ted Power	.25	.15
474 Terry Mulholland	.30	.18
475 Todd Stottlemyre	.35	.20
476 Jerry Goff	.25	.15
477 Gene Nelson	.25	.15
478 Rich Gedman	.25	.15
479 Brian Harper	.25	.15
480 Mike Felder	.25	.15
481 Steve Avery	15.00	10.00
482 Jack Morris	.60	.35
483 Randy Johnson	.75	.45
484 Scott Radinsky (R)	.40	.25
485 Jose DeLeon	.25	.15
486 Stan Belinda (R)	.35	.20
487 Brian Holton	.30	.18
488 Mark Carreon	.25	.15
489 Trevor Wilson	.25	.15
490 Mike Sharperson	.25	.15
491 Alan Mills (R)	.50	.30
492 John Candelaria	.25	.15
493 Paul Assenmacher	.25	.15
494 Steve Crawford	.25	.15

495 Brad Arnsberg	.25	.15
496 Sergio Valdez	.25	.15
497 Mark Parent	.25	.15
498 Tom Pagnozzi	.30	.18
499 Greg Harris	.25	.15
500 Randy Ready	.25	.15
501 Duane Ward	.25	.15
502 Nelson Santovenia	.25	.15
503 Joe Klink	.25	.15
504 Eric Plunk	.25	.15
505 Jeff Reed	.25	.15
506 Ted Higuera	.25	.15
507 Joe Hesketh	.25	.15
508 Dan Petry	.25	.15
509 Matt Young	.25	.15
510 Jerald Clark (R)	.25	.15
511 John Orton (R)	.30	.18
512 Scott Ruskin (R)	.30	.18
513 Chris Hoiles (R)	2.50	1.50
514 Daryl Boston	.25	.15
515 Francisco Oliveras	.25	.15
516 Ozzie Canseco (R)	.35	.20
517 Xavier Hernandez (R)	.35	.20
518 Fred Manrique	.25	.15
519 Shawn Boskie (R)	.50	.30
520 Jeff Montgomery (R)	.25	.15
521 Jack Daugherty (R)	.25	.15
522 Keith Comstock	.25	.15
523 Greg Hibbard (R)	.50	.30
524 Lee Smith	.40	.25
525 Dana Kiecker	.25	.15
526 Darrel Akerfelds	.25	.15
527 Greg Myers	.25	.15
528 Checklist	.50	.25

1991 Leaf

This 528-card set was released in two 264-card series and features silver borders around four-color action photos. Numbered card backs consist of a small player photo, stat box and background information.

		MINT	NR/MT
	Complete Set (528)	50.00	35.00
	Commons	.07	.03
1	Leaf Card	.10	.06
2	Kurt Stillwell	.07	.03
3	Bobby Witt	.10	.06
4	Tony Phillips	.07	.03
5	Scott Garrelts	.07	.03
6	Greg Swindell	.12	.07
7	Billy Ripken	.07	.03
8	Dave Martinez	.07	.03
9	Kelly Gruber	.12	.07
10	Juan Samuel	.07	.03
11	Brian Holman	.10	.06
12	Craig Biggio	.25	.15
13	Lonnie Smith	.07	.03
14	Ron Robinson	.07	.03
15	Mike LaValliere	.07	.03
16	Mark Davis	.07	.03
17	Jack Daugherty	.07	.03
18	Mike Henneman	.07	.03
19	Mike Greenwell	.25	.15
20	Dave Magadan	.10	.06
21	Mark Williamson	.07	.03
22	Marquis Grissom	.70	.40
23	Pat Borders	.07	.03
24	Mike Scioscia	.07	.03
25	Shawon Dunston	.15	.10
26	Randy Bush	.07	.03
27	John Smoltz	.50	.30
28	Chuck Crim	.07	.03
29	Don Slaught	.07	.03
30	Mike Macfarlane	.10	.06
31	Wally Joyner	.15	.10
32	Pat Combs	.15	.10
33	Tony Pena	.10	.06
34	Howard Johnson	.20	.12
35	Leo Gomez (R)	1.00	.70
36	Spike Owen	.07	.03
37	Eric Davis	.20	.12
38	Roberto Kelly	.25	.15
39	Jerome Walton	.10	.06
40	Shane Mack	.20	.12
41	Kent Mercker	.12	.07
42	B.J. Surhoff	.07	.03
43	Jerry Browne	.07	.03
44	Lee Smith	.25	.15
45	Chuck Finley	.15	.10
46	Terry Mulholland	.10	.06
47	Tom Bolton	.07	.03
48	Tom Herr	.07	.03
49	Jim Deshaies	.07	.03
50	Walt Weiss	.10	.06
51	Hal Morris	.25	.15
52	Lee Guetterman	.07	.03
53	Paul Assenmacher	.07	.03
54	Brian Harper	.10	.06
55	Paul Gibson	.07	.03
56	John Burkett	.10	.06
57	Doug Jones	.12	.07
58	Jose Oquendo	.10	.06
59	Dick Schofield	.07	.03
60	Dickie Thon	.07	.03
61	Ramon Martinez	.25	.15
62	Jay Buhner	.15	.10
63	Mark Portugal	.07	.03
64	Bob Welch	.10	.06
65	Chris Sabo	.12	.07
66	Chuck Cary	.07	.03
67	Mark Langston	.15	.10
68	Joe Boever	.07	.03
69	Jody Reed	.10	.06
70	Alejandro Pena	.10	.06
71	Jeff King	.10	.06
72	Tom Pagnozzi	.15	.10
73	Joe Oliver	.10	.06
74	Mike Witt	.07	.03
75	Hector Villanueva	.10	.06
76	Dan Gladden	.07	.03
77	Dave Justice	2.75	1.75
78	Mike Gallego	.07	.03
79	Tom Candiotti	.10	.06
80	Ozzie Smith	.25	.15
81	Luis Polonia	.10	.06
82	Randy Ready	.07	.03
83	Greg Harris	.10	.06
84	Checklist (Justice)	.25	.15
85	Kevin Mitchell	.15	.10
86	Mark McLemore	.07	.03
87	Terry Steinbach	.10	.06
88	Tom Browning	.10	.06
89	Matt Nokes	.10	.06
90	Mike Harkey	.15	.10
91	Omar Vizquel	.07	.03
92	Dave Bergman	.07	.03
93	Matt Williams	.25	.15
94	Steve Olin	.07	.03
95	Craig Wilson	.15	.10
96	Dave Stieb	.10	.06
97	Ruben Sierra	.75	.45
98	Jay Howell	.07	.04
99	Scott Bradley	.07	.04
100	Eric Yelding	.07	.03
101	Rickey Henderson	.50	.30
102	Jeff Reed	.07	.03
103	Jimmy Key	.10	.06
104	Terry Shumpert	.15	.10
105	Kenny Rogers	.07	.03
106	Cecil Fielder	.70	.40
107	Robby Thompson	.10	.06

108 Alex Cole	.20	.12
109 Randy Milligan	.10	.06
110 Andres Galarraga	.10	.06
111 Bill Spiers	.07	.03
112 Kal Daniels	.10	.06
113 Henry Cotto	.07	.03
114 Casey Candaele	.07	.03
115 Jeff Blauser	.07	.03
116 Robin Yount	.70	.40
117 Ben McDonald	.50	.30
118 Bret Saberhagen	.15	.10
119 Juan Gonzalez (R)	7.00	4.00
120 Lou Whitaker	.10	.06
121 Ellis Burks	.15	.10
122 Charlie O'Brien	.07	.03
123 John Smiley	.15	.10
124 Tim Burke	.07	.03
125 John Olerud	.30	.18
126 Eddie Murray	.25	.15
127 Greg Maddux	.25	.15
128 Kevin Tapani	.25	.15
129 Ron Gant	.75	.45
130 Jay Bell	.10	.06
131 Chris Hoiles	.30	.18
132 Tom Gordon	.10	.06
133 Kevin Seitzer	.10	.06
134 Jeff Huson	.07	.03
135 Jerry Don Gleaton	.07	.03
136 Jeff Brantley	.07	.03
137 Felix Fermin	.07	.03
138 Mike Deavereaux	.15	.10
139 Delino DeShields	.70	.40
140 David Wells	.07	.03
141 Tim Crews	.07	.03
142 Erik Hanson	.15	.10
143 Mark Davidson	.07	.03
144 Tommy Gregg	.07	.03
145 Jim Gantner	.07	.03
146 Jose Lind	.07	.03
147 Danny Tartabull	.25	.15
148 Geno Petralli	.07	.03
149 Travis Fryman (R)	4.50	2.75
150 Tim Naehring (R)	.20	.12
151 Kevin McReynolds	.12	.07
152 Joe Orsulak	.10	.06
153 Steve Frey	.07	.03
154 Duane Ward	.07	.03
155 Stan Javier	.07	.03
156 Damon Berryhill	.07	.03
157 Gene Larkin	.07	.03
158 Greg Olson	.10	.06
159 Mark Knudson	.07	.03
160 Carmelo Martinez	.07	.03
161 Storm Davis	.07	.03
162 Jim Abbott	.30	.18
163 Len Dykstra	.12	.07
164 Tom Brunansky	.12	.07
165 Dwight Gooden	.25	.15

166 Jose Mesa	.07	.03
167 Oil Can Boyd	.07	.03
168 Barry Larkin	.25	.15
169 Scott Sanderson	.10	.06
170 Mark Grace	.25	.15
171 Mark Guthrie	.12	.07
172 Tom Glavine	.80	.50
173 Gary Sheffield	1.00	.70
174 Checklist (Clemens)	.20	.12
175 Chris James	.07	.03
176 Milt Thompson	.07	.03
177 Donnie Hill	.07	.03
178 Wes Chamberlain (R)	1.00	.70
179 John Marzano	.07	.03
180 Frank Viola	.12	.07
181 Eric Anthony	.35	.20
182 Jose Canseco	1.00	.70
183 Scott Scudder	.10	.06
184 Dave Eiland	.07	.03
185 Luis Salazar	.07	.03
186 Pedro Munoz (R)	1.25	.80
187 Steve Searcy	.07	.03
188 Don Robinson	.07	.03
189 Sandy Alomar Jr.	.15	.10
190 Jose DeLeon	.07	.03
191 John Orton	.10	.06
192 Darren Daulton	.25	.15
193 Mike Morgan	.10	.06
194 Greg Briley	.07	.03
195 Karl Rhodes (R)	.20	.12
196 Harold Baines	.10	.06
197 Bill Doran	.07	.03
198 Alvaro Espinoza	.07	.03
199 Kirk McCaskill	.07	.03
200 Jose DeJesus	.07	.03
201 Jack Clark	.10	.06
202 Daryl Boston	.07	.03
203 Randy Tomlin (R)	.80	.50
204 Pedro Guerrero	.10	.06
205 Billy Hatcher	.07	.03
206 Tim Leary	.07	.03
207 Ryne Sandberg	1.00	.70
208 Kirby Puckett	1.00	.70
209 Charlie Leibrandt	.10	.06
210 Rick Honeycutt	.07	.03
211 Joel Skinner	.07	.03
212 Rex Hudler	.07	.03
213 Bryan Harvey	.10	.06
214 Charlie Hayes	.07	.03
215 Matt Young	.07	.03
216 Terry Kennedy	.07	.03
217 Carl Nichols	.07	.03
218 Mike Moore	.10	.06
219 Paul O'Neill	.20	.12
220 Steve Sax	.12	.07
221 Shawn Boskie	.10	.06
222 Rich DeLucia (R)	.12	.07
223 Lloyd Moseby	.07	.03

224	Mike Kingery	.07	.03	282 Rob Dibble	.15	.10
225	Carlos Baerga	.70	.40	283 Mel Hall	.10	.06
226	Bryn Smith	.07	.03	284 Rick Mahler	.07	.03
227	Todd Stottlemyre	.10	.06	285 Dennis Eckersley	.35	.20
228	Julio Franco	.25	.15	286 Bernard Gilkey	.30	.18
229	Jim Gott	.07	.03	287 Dan Plesac	.07	.03
230	Mike Schooler	.07	.03	288 Jason Grimsley (R)	.10	.06
231	Steve Finley	.25	.15	289 Mark Lewis (R)	.60	.35
232	Dave Henderson	.10	.06	290 Tony Gwynn	.60	.35
233	Luis Quinones	.07	.03	291 Jeff Russell	.07	.03
234	Mark Whiten	.25	.15	292 Curt Schilling	.07	.03
235	Brian McRae (R)	.75	.45	293 Pascual Perez	.10	.06
236	Rich Gossage	.10	.06	294 Jack Morris	.20	.12
237	Rob Deer	.07	.03	295 Hubie Brooks	.10	.06
238	Will Clark	1.00	.70	296 Alex Fernandez (R)	.40	.25
239	Albert Belle	1.00	.70	297 Harold Reynolds	.10	.06
240	Bob Melvin	.07	.03	298 Craig Worthington	.07	.03
241	Larry Walker	.50	.30	299 Willie Wilson	.07	.03
242	Dante Bichette	.07	.03	300 Mike Maddux	.07	.03
243	Orel Hershiser	.15	.10	301 Dave Righetti	.10	.06
244	Pete O'Brien	.07	.03	302 Paul Molitor	.12	.07
245	Pete Harnisch	.10	.06	303 Gary Gaetti	.10	.06
246	Jeff Treadway	.07	.03	304 Terry Pendleton	.25	.15
247	Julio Machado	.07	.03	305 Kevin Elster	.07	.03
248	Dave Johnson	.07	.03	306 Scott Fletcher	.07	.03
249	Kirk Gibson	.10	.06	307 Jeff Robinson	.07	.03
250	Kevin Brown	.15	.10	308 Jesse Barfield	.10	.06
251	Milt Cuyler (R)	.35	.20	309 Mike LaCoss	.07	.03
252	Jeff Reardon	.20	.12	310 Andy Van Slyke	.20	.12
253	David Cone	.15	.10	311 Glenallen Hill	.15	.10
254	Gary Redus	.07	.03	312 Bud Black	.10	.06
255	Junior Noboa	.07	.03	313 Kent Hrbek	.10	.06
256	Greg Myers	.07	.03	314 Tim Teufel	.07	.03
257	Dennis Cook	.07	.03	315 Tony Fernandez	.10	.06
258	Joe Girardi	.10	.06	316 Beau Allred	.15	.10
259	Allan Anderson	.07	.03	317 Curtis Wilkerson	.07	.03
260	Paul Marak (R)	.15	.10	318 Bill Sampen	.10	.06
261	Barry Bonds	.70	.40	319 Randy Johnson	.15	.10
262	Juan Bell	.10	.06	320 Mike Heath	.07	.03
263	Russ Morman	.07	.03	321 Sammy Sosa	.10	.06
264	Checklist (Brett)	.20	.12	322 Mickey Tettleton	.10	.06
265	Jerald Clark	.15	.10	323 Jose Vizcaino	.12	.07
266	Dwight Evans	.10	.06	324 John Candelaria	.07	.03
267	Roberto Alomar	2.00	1.25	325 Dave Howard (R)	.12	.07
268	Danny Jackson	.10	.06	326 Jose Rijo	.12	.07
269	Brian Downing	.07	.03	327 Todd Zeile	.30	.18
270	John Cerutti	.07	.03	328 Gene Nelson	.07	.03
271	Robin Ventura	1.50	.90	329 Dwayne Henry	.07	.03
272	Gerald Perry	.07	.03	330 Mike Boddicker	.07	.03
273	Wade Boggs	.50	.30	331 Ozzie Guillen	.10	.06
274	Dennis Martinez	.15	.10	332 Sam Horn	.10	.06
275	Andy Benes	.40	.25	333 Wally Whitehurst	.07	.03
276	Tony Fossas	.07	.03	334 Dave Parker	.12	.07
277	Franklin Stubbs	.07	.03	335 George Brett	.50	.30
278	John Kruk	.15	.10	336 Bobby Thigpen	.10	.06
279	Kevin Gross	.07	.03	337 Ed Whitson	.07	.03
280	Von Hayes	.07	.03	338 Ivan Calderon	.10	.06
281	Frank Thomas	6.00	3.75	339 Mike Pagliarulo	.07	.03

No.	Player		
340	Jack McDowell	.50	.30
341	Dana Kiecker	.07	.03
342	Fred McGriff	.75	.45
343	Mark Lee (R)	.15	.10
344	Alfredo Griffin	.07	.03
345	Scott Bankhead	.07	.03
346	Darrin Jackson	.10	.06
347	Rafael Palmeiro	.25	.15
348	Steve Farr	.07	.03
349	Hensley Meulens	.15	.10
350	Danny Cox	.07	.03
351	Alan Trammell	.15	.10
352	Edwin Nunez	.07	.03
353	Joe Carter	.40	.25
354	Eric Show	.07	.03
355	Vance Law	.07	.03
356	Jeff Gray (R)	.12	.07
357	Bobby Bonilla	.30	.18
358	Ernest Riles	.07	.03
359	Ron Hassey	.07	.03
360	Willie McGee	.10	.06
361	Mackey Sasser	.07	.03
362	Glenn Braggs	.07	.03
363	Mario Diaz	.07	.03
364	Checklist (Bonds)	.20	.12
365	Kevin Bass	.07	.03
366	Pete Incaviglia	.07	.03
367	Luis Sojo	.10	.06
368	Lance Parrish	.10	.06
369	Mark Leonard (R)	.20	.12
370	Heathcliff Slocumb (R)	.15	.10
371	Jimmy Jones	.07	.03
372	Ken Griffey Jr.	3.75	2.25
373	Chris Hammond (R)	.25	.15
374	Chili Davis	.10	.06
375	Joey Cora	.07	.03
376	Ken Hill	.15	.10
377	Darryl Strawberry	.50	.30
378	Ron Darling	.10	.06
379	Sid Bream	.07	.03
380	Bill Swift	.20	.12
381	Shawn Abner	.07	.03
382	Eric King	.07	.03
383	Mickey Morandini	.20	.12
384	Carlton Fisk	.35	.20
385	Steve Lake	.07	.03
386	Mike Jeffcoat	.07	.03
387	Darren Holmes (R)	.12	.07
388	Tim Wallach	.12	.07
389	George Bell	.15	.10
390	Craig Lefferts	.07	.03
391	Ernie Whitt	.07	.03
392	Felix Jose	.25	.15
393	Kevin Maas	.25	.15
394	Devon White	.10	.06
395	Otis Nixon	.15	.10
396	Chuck Knoblauch (R)	2.75	1.75
397	Scott Coolbaugh	.07	.03
398	Glenn Davis	.12	.07
399	Manny Lee	.07	.03
400	Andre Dawson	.35	.20
401	Scott Chiamparino	.15	.10
402	Bill Gullickson	.10	.06
403	Lance Johnson	.07	.03
404	Juan Agosto	.07	.03
405	Danny Darwin	.07	.03
406	Barry Jones	.07	.03
407	Larry Andersen	.07	.03
408	Luis Rivera	.07	.03
409	Jaime Navarro	.15	.10
410	Roger McDowell	.07	.03
411	Brett Butler	.15	.10
412	Dale Murphy	.25	.15
413	Tim Raines	.10	.06
414	Norm Charlton	.15	.10
415	Greg Cadaret	.07	.03
416	Chris Nabholtz (R)	.15	.10
417	Dave Stewart	.12	.07
418	Rich Gedman	.07	.03
419	Willie Randolph	.10	.06
420	Mitch Williams	.10	.06
421	Brook Jacoby	.07	.03
422	Greg Harris	.10	.06
423	Nolan Ryan	3.75	2.25
424	Dave Rhode	.12	.07
425	Don Mattingly	.50	.30
426	Greg Gagne	.07	.03
427	Vince Coleman	.10	.06
428	Dan Pasqua	.07	.03
429	Alvin Davis	.07	.03
430	Cal Ripken	2.50	1.50
431	Jamie Quirk	.07	.03
432	Benito Santiago	.12	.07
433	Jose Uribe	.07	.03
434	Candy Maldonado	.07	.03
435	Junior Felix	.10	.06
436	Deion Sanders	1.25	.80
437	John Franco	.07	.03
438	Greg Hibbard	.07	.03
439	Floyd Bannister	.07	.03
440	Steve Howe	.07	.03
441	Steve Decker (R)	.30	.18
442	Vicente Palacious	.07	.03
443	Pat Tabler	.07	.03
444	Checklist (Strawberry)	.20	.12
445	Mike Felder	.07	.03
446	Al Newman	.07	.03
447	Chris Donnels (R)	.25	.15
448	Rich Rodriquez (R)	.15	.10
449	Turner Ward (R)	.15	.10
450	Bob Walk	.07	.03
451	Gilberto Reyes	.07	.03
452	Mike Jackson	.12	.07
453	Rafael Belliard	.07	.03
454	Wayne Edwards	.07	.03
455	Andy Allanson	.07	.03

456 Dave Smith	.07	.03
457 Gary Carter	.15	.10
458 Warren Cromartie	.07	.03
459 Jack Armstrong	.10	.06
460 Bob Tewksbury	.12	.07
461 Joe Klink	.07	.03
462 Xavier Hernandez	.07	.03
463 Scott Radinsky	.15	.10
464 Jeff Robinson	.07	.03
465 Gregg Jefferies	.15	.10
466 Denny Neagle (R)	.60	.35
467 Carmelo Martinez	.07	.03
468 Donn Paul	.07	.03
469 Bruce Hurst	.10	.06
470 Eric Bullock	.07	.03
471 Rick Aguilera	.10	.06
472 Charlie Hough	.07	.03
473 Carlos Quintana	.10	.06
474 Marty Barrett	.07	.03
475 Kevin Brown	.07	.03
476 Bobby Ojeda	.07	.03
477 Edgar Martinez	.25	.15
478 Bip Roberts	.07	.03
479 Mike Flanagan	.07	.03
480 John Habyan	.07	.03
481 Larry Casian (R)	.12	.07
482 Wally Backman	.07	.03
483 Doug Dascenzo	.07	.03
484 Rick Dempsey	.07	.03
485 Ed Sprague	.15	.10
486 Steve Chitren (R)	.15	.10
487 Mark McGwire	.80	.50
488 Roger Clemens	1.25	.80
489 Orlando Merced (R)	.60	.35
490 Rene Gonzalez	.07	.03
491 Mike Stanton	.07	.03
492 Al Osuna (R)	.20	.12
493 Rick Cerone	.07	.03
494 Mariano Duncun	.07	.03
495 Zane Smith	.10	.06
496 John Morris	.07	.03
497 Frank Tanana	.10	.06
498 Junior Ortiz	.07	.03
499 Dave Winfield	.35	.20
500 Gary Varsho	.07	.03
501 Chico Walker	.07	.03
502 Ken Caminiti	.12	.07
503 Ken Griffey Sr.	.10	.06
504 Randy Myers	.07	.03
505 Steve Bedrosian	.07	.03
506 Cory Snyder	.10	.06
507 Cris Carpenter	.10	.06
508 Tim Belcher	.10	.06
509 Jeff Hamilton	.07	.03
510 Steve Avery	1.75	1.00
511 Dave Valle	.07	.03
512 Tom Lampkin	.07	.03
513 Shawn Hillegas	.07	.03

514 Reggie Jefferson (R)	.50	.30
515 Ron Karkovice	.07	.03
516 Doug Drabek	.15	.10
517 Tom Henke	.07	.03
518 Chris Bosio	.07	.03
519 Gregg Olson	.12	.07
520 Bob Scanlan (R)	.15	.10
521 Alonzo Powell (R)	.20	.12
522 Jeff Ballard	.07	.03
523 Ray Lankford (R)	1.75	1.00
524 Tommy Greene	.12	.07
525 Mike Timlin (R)	.15	.10
526 Juan Berenguer	.07	.03
527 Scott Erickson (R)	1.00	.70
528 Checklist(S. Alomar)	.10	.06

1991 Leaf Gold Rookies

These bonus cards were randomly inserted into packs of 1991 Leaf cards and featured some of the hottest prospects in baseball. Though card numbers carry the BC designation, some variations numbered 265-276, have surfaced.

		MINT	NR/MT
Complete Set (26)		70.00	48.00
Commons		1.25	.80
1	Scott Leius	1.75	1.00
2	Luis Gonzalez	2.75	1.75
3	Wilfredo Cordero	4.50	2.75
4	Gary Scott	1.50	.90
5	Willie Banks	3.50	2.00
6	Arthur Rhodes	3.50	2.00
7	Mo Vaughn	3.50	2.00

8	Henry Rodriquez	2.75	1.75
9	Todd Van Poppel	6.00	3.75
10	Reggie Sanders	10.00	7.00
11	Rico Brogna	2.00	1.25
12	Mike Mussina	15.00	10.00
13	Kirk Dressendorfer	1.50	.90
14	Jeff Bagwell	12.00	8.50
15	Pete Schourek	1.25	.80
16	Wade Taylor	1.25	.80
17	Pat Kelly	2.00	1.25
18	Tim Costo	2.00	1.25
19	Roger Salkeld	5.00	3.00
20	Andujar Cedeno	2.75	1.75
21	Ryan Klesko	7.50	4.50
22	Mike Huff	1.25	.80
23	Anthony Young	2.75	1.75
24	Eddie Zosky	1.50	.90
25	Nolan Ryan (7th No-Hitter)	5.00	3.00
26	Rickey Henderson (Steals)	2.75	1.75

1991 Leaf Studio

This 264-card set is the first black and white set issued since 1960 and features close-up posed photos on the front framed in a maroon border. The set contained a puzzle of Rod Carew issued on 21 black and white cards with three puzzle pieces per card.

		MINT	NR/MT
Complete Set (264)		42.00	25.00
Commons		.07	.03
1	Glenn Davis	.12	.07
2	Dwight Evans	.10	.06
3	Leo Gomez	1.00	.70

4	Chris Hoiles	.35	.20
5	Sam Horn	.12	.07
6	Ben McDonald	.50	.35
7	Randy Milligan	.12	.07
8	Gregg Olson	.12	.07
9	Cal Ripken Jr.	2.50	1.50
10	David Segui	.15	.10
11	Wade Boggs	.70	.40
12	Ellis Burks	.15	.10
13	Jack Clark	.10	.06
14	Roger Clemens	1.25	.80
15	Mike Greenwell	.20	.12
16	Tim Naehring	.15	.10
17	Tony Pena	.10	.06
18	Phil Plantier	3.00	1.75
19	Jeff Reardon	.20	.12
20	Mo Vaughn	1.00	.70
21	Jimmy Reese	.07	.03
22	Jim Abbott	.40	.25
23	Bert Blyleven	.15	.10
24	Chuck Finley	.15	.10
25	Gary Gaetti	.10	.06
26	Wally Joyner	.15	.10
27	Mark Langston	.15	.10
28	Kirk McCaskill	.07	.03
29	Lance Parrish	.10	.06
30	Dave Winfield	.35	.20
31	Alex Fernandez	.40	.25
32	Carlton Fisk	.35	.20
33	Scott Fletcher	.07	.03
34	Greg Hibbard	.07	.03
35	Charlie Hough	.07	.03
36	Jack McDowell	.50	.30
37	Tim Raines	.12	.07
38	Sammy Sosa	.15	.10
39	Bobby Thigpen	.12	.07
40	Frank Thomas	7.50	4.50
41	Sandy Alomar	.12	.07
42	John Farrell	.07	.03
43	Glenallen Hill	.15	.10
44	Brook Jacoby	.07	.03
45	Chris James	.07	.03
46	Doug Jones	.12	.07
47	Eric King	.07	.03
48	Mark Lewis	.70	.40
49	Greg Swindell	.12	.07
50	Mark Whiten	.40	.25
51	Milt Cuyler	.35	.20
52	Rob Deer	.10	.06
53	Cecil Fielder	.80	.50
54	Travis Fryman	4.50	2.75
55	Bill Gullickson	.10	.06
56	Lloyd Moseby	.07	.03
57	Frank Tanana	.10	.06
58	Mickey Tettleton	.10	.06
59	Alan Trammell	.20	.12
60	Lou Whitaker	.10	.07
61	Mike Boddicker	.07	.03

62	George Brett	.50	.30
63	Jeff Conine (R)	.25	.15
64	Warren Cromartie	.07	.03
65	Storm Davis	.07	.03
66	Kirk Gibson	.10	.06
67	Mark Gubicza	.10	.06
68	Brian McRae	.75	.45
69	Bret Saberhagen	.12	.07
70	Kurt Stillwell	.07	.03
71	Tim McIntosh	.10	.06
72	Candy Maldonado	.07	.03
73	Paul Molitor	.15	.10
74	Willie Randolph	.07	.03
75	Ron Robinson	.07	.03
76	Gary Sheffield	1.00	.70
77	Franklin Stubbs	.07	.03
78	B.J. Surhoff	.07	.03
79	Greg Vaughn	.40	.25
80	Robin Yount	.75	.45
81	Rick Aguilera	.10	.06
82	Steve Bedrosian	.07	.03
83	Scott Erickson	1.25	.80
84	Greg Gagne	.07	.03
85	Dan Gladden	.07	.03
86	Brian Harper	.07	.03
87	Kent Hrbek	.10	.06
88	Shane Mack	.12	.07
89	Jack Morris	.25	.15
90	Kirby Puckett	1.00	.70
91	Jesse Barfield	.10	.06
92	Steve Farr	.07	.03
93	Steve Howe	.07	.03
94	Roberto Kelly	.35	.20
95	Tim Leary	.07	.03
96	Kevin Maas	.25	.15
97	Don Mattingly	.75	.45
98	Hensley Meulens	.15	.10
99	Scott Sanderson	.07	.03
100	Steve Sax	.10	.06
101	Jose Canseco	1.25	.80
102	Dennis Eckersley	.25	.15
103	Dave Henderson	.10	.06
104	Rickey Henderson	.50	.30
105	Rick Honeycutt	.07	.03
106	Mark McGwire	1.00	.70
107	Dave Stewart	.15	.10
108	Eric Show	.07	.03
109	Todd Van Poppel	3.00	1.75
110	Bob Welch	.10	.06
111	Alvin Davis	.07	.03
112	Ken Griffey Jr.	3.50	2.00
113	Ken Griffey Sr.	.10	.06
114	Eric Hanson	.15	.10
115	Brian Holman	.10	.06
116	Randy Johnson	.15	.10
117	Edgar Martinez	.35	.20
118	Tino Martinez	.30	.18
119	Harold Reynolds	.10	.06
120	David Valle	.07	.03
121	Kevin Belcher (R)	.10	.06
122	Scott Chiamparino	.12	.07
123	Julio Franco	.25	.15
124	Juan Gonzalez	4.50	2.75
125	Rich Gossage	.10	.06
126	Jeff Kunkel	.07	.03
127	Rafael Palmeiro	.20	.12
128	Nolan Ryan	4.00	2.50
129	Ruben Sierra	.75	.45
130	Bobby Witt	.10	.06
131	Roberto Alomar	2.00	1.25
132	Tom Candiotti	.10	.06
133	Joe Carter	.35	.20
134	Ken Dayley	.07	.03
135	Kelly Gruber	.12	.07
136	John Olerud	.35	.20
137	Dave Stieb	.10	.06
138	Turner Ward (R)	.15	.10
139	Devon White	.10	.06
140	Mookie Wilson	.07	.03
141	Steve Avery	1.75	1.00
142	Sid Bream	.07	.03
143	Nick Esasky	.07	.03
144	Ron Gant	.75	.45
145	Tom Glavine	1.00	.70
146	David Justice	2.50	1.50
147	Kelly Mann	.07	.03
148	Terry Pendleton	.25	.15
149	John Smoltz	.40	.25
150	Jeff Treadway	.07	.03
151	George Bell	.20	.12
152	Shawn Boskie	.10	.06
153	Andre Dawson	.35	.20
154	Lance Dickson (R)	.35	.20
155	Shawon Dunston	.15	.10
156	Joe Girardi	.10	.06
157	Mark Grace	.25	.15
158	Ryne Sandberg	1.25	.80
159	Gary Scott (R)	.35	.20
160	Dave Smith	.07	.03
161	Tom Browning	.10	.06
162	Eric Davis	.20	.12
163	Rob Dibble	.15	.10
164	Mariano Duncun	.07	.03
165	Chris Hammond	.12	.07
166	Billy Hatcher	.07	.03
167	Barry Larkin	.35	.20
168	Hal Morris	.30	.18
169	Paul O'Neill	.15	.10
170	Chris Sabo	.15	.10
171	Eric Anthony	.25	.15
172	Jeff Bagwell (R)	4.00	2.50
173	Craig Biggio	.25	.15
174	Ken Caminiti	.10	.06
175	Jim Deshaies	.07	.03
176	Steve Finley	.10	.06
177	Pete Harnisch	.15	.10

178	Darryl Kile	.25	.15
179	Curt Schilling	.07	.03
180	Mike Scott	.07	.03
181	Brett Butler	.12	.07
182	Gary Carter	.15	.10
183	Orel Hershiser	.15	.10
184	Ramon Martinez	.25	.15
185	Eddie Murray	.35	.20
186	Jose Offerman	.15	.10
187	Bob Ojeda	.07	.03
188	Juan Samuel	.07	.03
189	Mike Scioscia	.07	.03
190	Darryl Strawberry	.70	.40
191	Moises Alou	.35	.20
192	Brian Barnes (R)	.25	.15
193	Oil Can Boyd	.07	.03
194	Ivan Calderon	.10	.06
195	Delino DeShields	.60	.35
196	Mike Fitzgerald	.07	.03
197	Andres Galarraga	.10	.06
198	Marquis Grissom	.60	.35
199	Bill Sampen	.10	.06
200	Tim Wallach	.10	.06
201	Daryl Boston	.07	.03
202	Vince Coleman	.12	.07
203	John Franco	.07	.03
204	Dwight Gooden	.25	.15
205	Tom Herr	.07	.03
206	Grregg Jefferies	.20	.12
207	Howard Johnson	.20	.12
208	Dave Magadan	.12	.07
209	Kevin McReynolds	.10	.06
210	Frank Viola	.12	.07
211	Wes Chamberlain (R)	1.00	.70
212	Darren Daulton	.20	.12
213	Lenny Dykstra	.10	.06
214	Charlie Hayes	.07	.03
215	Ricky Jordan	.10	.06
216	Steve Lake	.07	.03
217	Roger McDowell	.07	.03
218	Terry Mulholland	.12	.07
219	Terry Mulholland	.12	.07
220	Dale Murphy	.25	.15
221	Jay Bell	.10	.06
222	Barry Bonds	.75	.45
223	Bobby Bonilla	.35	.20
224	Doug Drabek	.20	.12
225	Bill Landrum	.07	.03
226	Mike LaValliere	.07	.03
227	Jose Lind	.07	.03
228	Don Slaught	.07	.03
229	John Smiley	.15	.10
230	Andy Van Slyke	.25	.15
231	Bernard Gilkey	.35	.20
232	Pedro Guerrero	.10	.06
233	Rex Hudler	.07	.03
234	Ray Lankford	1.25	.80
235	Joe Magrane	.07	.03
236	Jose Oquendo	.07	.03
237	Lee Smith	.20	.12
238	Ozzie Smith	.35	.20
239	Milt Thompson	.07	.03
240	Todd Zeile	.25	.15
241	Larry Andersen	.07	.03
242	Andy Benes	.40	.25
243	Paul Faries (R)	.07	.03
244	Tony Fernandez	.10	.06
245	Tony Gwynn	.75	.45
246	Atlee Hammaker	.07	.03
247	Fred McGriff	.60	.35
248	Bip Roberts	.07	.03
249	Benito Santiago	.15	.10
250	Ed Whitson	.07	.03
251	Dave Anderson	.07	.03
252	Mike Benjamin	.07	.03
253	John Burkett	.10	.06
254	Will Clark	1.25	.80
255	Scott Garrelts	.07	.03
256	Willie McGee	.10	.06
257	Kevin Mitchell	.25	.15
258	Dave Righetti	.10	.06
259	Matt Williams	.25	.15
260	Black & Decker (Bud Black, Steve Decker)	.12	.07
261	Checklist	.10	.06
262	Checklist	.10	.06
263	Checklist	.10	.06
___	Cover Card	.10	.06

1992 Leaf

For the third straight year Donruss has produced a premium baseball set under the Leaf name. The cards feature full color player photos framed in silver borders. A gold bordered edition was also produced and is worth three to five times the value of the silver set.

		MINT	NR/MT
Complete Set (528)		52.00	38.00
Commons		.07	.03
1	Jim Abbott	.20	.12
2	Cal Eldred	.20	.12
3	Bud Black	.07	.03
4	Dave Howard	.07	.03
5	Luis Sojo	.07	.03
6	Gary Scott	.15	.10
7	Joe Oliver	.10	.06
8	Chris Gardner (R)	.20	.12
9	Sandy Alomar	.07	.03
10	Greg Harris	.07	.03
11	Doug Drabek	.10	.06
12	Darryl Hamilton	.10	.06
13	Mike Mussina	1.75	1.00
14	Kevin Tapani	.10	.06
15	Ron Gant	.40	.25
16	Mark McGwire	.50	.30
17	Robin Ventura	.40	.25
18	Pedro Guerrero	.07	.03
19	Roger Clemens	.80	.50
20	Steve Farr	.07	.03
21	Frank Tanana	.10	.06
22	Joe Hesketh	.07	.03
23	Erik Hanson	.10	.06
24	Greg Cadaret	.07	.03
25	Rex Hudler	.07	.03
26	Mark Grace	.15	.10
27	Kelly Gruber	.10	.06
28	Jeff Bagwell	1.25	.80
29	Darryl Strawberry	.35	.20
30	Dave Smith	.07	.03
31	Kevin Appier	.10	.06
32	Steve Chitren	.12	.07
33	Kevin Gross	.07	.03
34	Rick Aguilera	.10	.06
35	Juan Guzman	2.50	1.50
36	Joe Orsulak	.12	.07
37	Tim Raines	.10	.06
38	Harold Reynolds	.07	.03
39	Charlie Hough	.07	.03
40	Tony Phillips	.07	.03
41	Nolan Ryan	1.75	1.00
42	Vince Coleman	.10	.06
43	Andy Van Slyke	.20	.12
44	Tim Burke	.07	.03
45	Luis Polonia	.10	.06
46	Tom Browning	.10	.06
47	Willie McGee	.10	.06
48	Gary DiSarcina	.12	.07
49	Mark Lewis	.12	.07
50	Phil Plantier	.80	.50
51	Doug Dascenzo	.07	.03
52	Cal Ripken	1.00	.70
53	Pedro Munoz	.35	.20
54	Carlos Hernandez	.07	.03
55	Jerald Clark	.10	.06
56	Jeff Brantley	.10	.06
57	Don Mattingly	.30	.18
58	Roger McDowell	.07	.03
59	Steve Avery	.50	.30
60	John Olerud	.15	.10
61	Bill Gullickson	.07	.03
62	Juan Gonzalez	1.75	1.00
63	Felix Jose	.15	.10
64	Robin Yount	.35	.20
65	Greg Briley	.07	.03
66	Steve Finley	.07	.03
67	Checklist	.12	.07
68	Tom Gordon	.10	.06
69	Rob Dibble	.12	.07
70	Glenallen Hill	.10	.06
71	Calvin Jones (R)	.25	.15
72	Joe Girardi	.10	.06
73	Barry Larkin	.15	.10
74	Andy Benes	.15	.10
75	Milt Cuyler	.12	.07
76	Kevin Bass	.07	.03
77	Pete Harnisch	.10	.06
78	Wilson Alvarez	.10	.06
79	Mike Devereaux	.20	.12
80	Doug Henry (R)	.35	.20
81	Orel Hershiser	.10	.06
82	Shane Mack	.10	.06
83	Mike Macfarlane	.07	.03
84	Thomas Howard	.10	.06
85	Alex Fernandez	.12	.07
86	Reggie Jefferson	.12	.07
87	Leo Gomez	.15	.10

88	Mel Hall	.10	.06
89	Mike Greenwell	.10	.06
90	Jeff Russell	.10	.06
91	Steve Buechele	.10	.06
92	David Cone	.12	.07
93	Kevin Reimer	.10	.06
94	Mark Lemke	.07	.03
95	Bob Tewksbury	.10	.06
96	Zane Smith	.10	.06
97	Mark Eichhorn	.07	.03
98	Kirby Puckett	.60	.35
99	Paul O'Neill	.10	.06
100	Dennis Eckersley	.15	.10
101	Duane Ward	.12	.07
102	Matt Nokes	.07	.03
103	Mo Vaughn	.25	.15
104	Pat Kelly	.15	.10
105	Ron Karkovice	.07	.03
106	Bill Spiers	.07	.03
107	Gary Gaetti	.07	.03
108	Mackey Sasser	.07	.03
109	Robby Thompson	.10	.06
110	Marvin Freeman	.07	.03
111	Jimmy Key	.07	.03
112	Dwight Gooden	.12	.07
113	Charlie Leibrandt	.07	.03
114	Devon White	.07	.03
115	Charles Nagy	.40	.25
116	Rickey Henderson	.40	.25
117	Paul Assenmacher	.07	.03
118	Junior Felix	.07	.03
119	Julio Franco	.10	.06
120	Norm Charlton	.12	.07
121	Scott Servais	.10	.06
122	Gerald Perry	.07	.03
123	Brian McRae	.15	.10
124	Don Slaught	.07	.03
125	Juan Samuel	.07	.03
126	Harold Baines	.10	.06
127	Scott Livingstone	.15	.10
128	Jay Buhner	.12	.07
129	Darrin Jackson	.10	.06
130	Luis Mercedes	.12	.07
131	Brian Harper	.10	.06
132	Howard Johnson	.10	.06
133	Checklist	.12	.07
134	Dante Bichette	.07	.03
135	Dave Righetti	.07	.03
136	Jeff Montgomery	.07	.03
137	Joe Grahe	.07	.03
138	Delino DeShields	.30	.18
139	Jose Rijo	.12	.07
140	Ken Caminiti	.10	.06
141	Steve Olin	.07	.03
142	Kurt Stillwell	.07	.03
143	Jay Bell	.07	.03
144	Jaime Navarro	.20	.12
145	Ben McDonald	.25	.15
146	Greg Gagne	.10	.06
147	Jeff Blauser	.07	.03
148	Carney Lansford	.10	.06
149	Ozzie Guillen	.10	.06
150	Milt Thompson	.07	.03
151	Jeff Reardon	.12	.07
152	Scott Sanderson	.07	.03
153	Cecil Fielder	.50	.30
154	Greg Harris	.10	.06
155	Rich DeLucia	.07	.03
156	Roberto Kelly	.15	.10
157	Bryn Smith	.07	.03
158	Chuck McElroy	.07	.03
159	Tom Henke	.07	.03
160	Luis Gonzalez	.15	.10
161	Steve Wilson	.07	.03
162	Shawn Boskie	.10	.06
163	Mark Davis	.07	.03
164	Mike Moore	.07	.03
165	Mike Scioscia	.07	.03
166	Scott Erickson	.20	.12
167	Todd Stottlemyre	.07	.03
168	Alvin Davis	.07	.03
169	Greg Hibbard	.07	.03
170	David Valle	.07	.03
171	Dave Winfield	.25	.15
172	Alan Trammell	.10	.06
173	Kenny Rogers	.10	.06
174	John Franco	.10	.06
175	Jose Lind	.07	.03
176	Pete Schourek	.10	.06
177	Von Hayes	.07	.03
178	Chris Hammond	.10	.06
179	John Burkett	.07	.03
180	Dickie Thon	.07	.03
181	Joel Skinner	.07	.03
182	Scott Cooper	.25	.15
183	Andre Dawson	.15	.10
184	Billy Ripken	.07	.03
185	Kevin Mitchell	.10	.06
186	Brett Butler	.10	.06
187	Tony Fernandez	.07	.03
188	Cory Snyder	.07	.03
189	John Habyan	.07	.03
190	Dennis Martinez	.10	.06
191	John Smoltz	.20	.12
192	Greg Myers	.07	.03
193	Rob Deer	.07	.03
194	Ivan Rodriquez	1.75	1.00
195	Ray Lankford	.30	.18
196	Bill Wegman	.07	.03
197	Edgar Martinez	.25	.15
198	Darryl Kile	.12	.07
199	Checklist	.12	.07
200	Brent Mayne	.07	.03
201	Larry Walker	.30	.18
202	Carlos Baerga	.35	.20
203	Russ Swan	.07	.03

204 Mike Morgan	.07	.03		262 Bob Milacki	.07	.03
205 Hal Morris	.12	.07		263 Mark Guthrie	.07	.03
206 Tony Gwynn	.60	.35		264 Darrin Fletcher	.07	.03
207 Mark Leiter	.07	.03		265 Omar Vizquel	.07	.03
208 Kirt Manwaring	.07	.03		266 Chris Bosio	.08	.05
209 Al Osuna	.07	.03		267 Jose Canseco	.80	.50
210 Bobby Thigpen	.10	.06		268 Mike Boddicker	.07	.03
211 Chris Hoiles	.20	.12		269 Lance Parrish	.07	.03
212 B.J. Surhoff	.07	.03		270 Jose Vizcaino	.07	.03
213 Lenny Harris	.07	.03		271 Chris Sabo	.08	.05
214 Scott Leius	.10	.06		272 Royce Clayton	.40	.25
215 Gregg Jefferies	.12	.07		273 Marquis Grissom	.25	.15
216 Bruce Hurst	.10	.06		274 Fred McGriff	.35	.20
217 Steve Sax	.10	.06		275 Barry Bonds	.75	.45
218 Dave Otto	.07	.03		276 Greg Vaughn	.10	.06
219 Sam Horn	.07	.03		277 Gregg Olson	.08	.05
220 Charlie Hayes	.07	.03		278 Dave Hollins	.25	.15
221 Frank Viola	.10	.06		279 Tom Glavine	.35	.20
222 Jose Guzman	.10	.06		280 Bryan Hickerson	.07	.03
223 Gary Redus	.07	.03		281 Scott Radinsky	.08	.05
224 Dave Gallagher	.07	.03		282 Omar Olivares	.07	.03
225 Dean Palmer	.70	.40		283 Ivan Calderon	.08	.05
226 Greg Olson	.10	.06		284 Kevin Maas	.15	.08
227 Jose DeLeon	.07	.03		285 Mickey Tettleton	.08	.05
228 Mike LaValliere	.07	.03		286 Wade Boggs	.30	.18
229 Mark Langston	.10	.06		287 Stan Belinda	.07	.03
230 Chuck Knoblauch	.50	.30		288 Bret Barberie	.10	.06
231 Bill Doran	.07	.03		289 Jose Oquendo	.07	.03
232 Dave Henderson	.07	.03		290 Frank Castillo	.10	.06
233 Roberto Alomar	.80	.50		291 Dave Stieb	.08	.05
234 Scott Fletcher	.07	.03		292 Tommy Greene	.12	.07
235 Tim Naehring	.10	.06		293 Eric Karros	1.25	.80
236 Mike Gallego	.07	.03		294 Greg Maddux	.15	.08
237 Lance Johnson	.07	.03		295 Jim Eisenreich	.07	.03
238 Paul Molitor	.10	.06		296 Rafael Palmeiro	.12	.07
239 Dan Gladden	.07	.03		297 Ramon Martinez	.15	.08
240 Willie Randolph	.07	.03		298 Tim Wallach	.08	.05
241 Will Clark	.75	.45		299 Jim Thome	.35	.20
242 Sid Bream	.07	.03		300 Chito Martinez	.10	.06
243 Derek Bell	.35	.20		301 Mitch Williams	.07	.03
244 Bill Pecota	.07	.03		302 Randy Johnson	.15	.08
245 Terry Pendleton	.10	.06		303 Carlton Fisk	.20	.12
246 Randy Ready	.07	.03		304 Travis Fryman	.80	.50
247 Jack Armstrong	.07	.03		305 Bobby Witt	.10	.06
248 Todd Van Poppel	.75	.45		306 Dave Magadan	.07	.03
249 Shawon Dunston	.10	.06		307 Alex Cole	.08	.05
250 Bobby Rose	.10	.06		308 Bobby Bonilla	.20	.12
251 Jeff Huson	.07	.03		309 Bryan Harvey	.08	.05
252 Bip Roberts	.07	.03		310 Rafael Belliard	.07	.03
253 Doug Jones	.10	.06		311 Mariano Duncan	.07	.03
254 Lee Smith	.15	.10		312 Chuck Crim	.07	.03
255 George Brett	.35	.20		313 John Kruk	.08	.05
256 Randy Tomlin	.12	.07		314 Ellis Burks	.10	.06
257 Todd Benzinger	.07	.03		315 Craig Biggio	.08	.05
258 Dave Stewart	.10	.06		316 Glenn Davis	.07	.03
259 Mark Carreon	.07	.03		317 Ryne Sandberg	.80	.50
260 Pete O'Brien	.07	.03		318 Mike Sharperson	.07	.03
261 Tim Teufel	.07	.03		319 Rich Rodriquez	.10	.06

320 Lee Guetterman	.07	.03	378 Hubie Brooks	.08	.05
321 Benito Santiago	.10	.06	379 Eric Bell	.07	.03
322 Jose Offerman	.10	.06	380 Walt Weiss	.07	.03
323 Tony Pena	.07	.03	381 Danny Jackson	.08	.05
324 Pat Borders	.07	.03	382 Manuel Lee	.07	.03
325 Mike Henneman	.07	.03	383 Ruben Sierra	.60	.35
326 Kevin Brown	.12	.07	384 Greg Swindell	.10	.06
327 Chris Nabholtz	.12	.07	385 Ryan Bowen	.12	.07
328 Franklin Stubbs	.07	.03	386 Kevin Ritz	.08	.05
329 Tino Martinez	.12	.07	387 Curtis Wilkerson	.07	.03
330 Mickey Morandini	.10	.06	388 Gary Varsho	.07	.03
331 Checklist	.07	.03	389 Dave Hansen	.12	.07
332 Mark Gubicza	.08	.05	390 Bob Welch	.08	.05
333 Bill Landrum	.07	.03	391 Lou Whitaker	.08	.05
334 Mark Whiten	.15	.08	392 Ken Griffey Jr.	2.00	1.25
335 Darren Daulton	.12	.07	393 Mike Maddux	.07	.03
336 Rick Wilkins	.07	.03	394 Arthur Rhodes	.25	.15
337 Brian Jordan	.50	.30	395 Chili Davis	.08	.05
338 Kevin Ward	.10	.06	396 Eddie Murray	.15	.08
339 Ruben Amaro	.12	.07	397 Checklist	.07	.03
340 Trevor Wilson	.08	.05	398 Dave Cochrane	.08	.05
341 Andujar Cedeno	.15	.08	399 Kevin Seitzer	.08	.05
342 Michael Huff	.10	.06	400 Ozzie Smith	.15	.08
343 Brady Anderson	.25	.15	401 Paul Sorrento	.25	.15
344 Craig Grebeck	.07	.03	402 Les Lancaster	.07	.03
345 Bobby Ojeda	.07	.03	403 Junior Noboa	.07	.03
346 Mike Pagliarulo	.07	.03	404 David Justice	.50	.30
347 Terry Shumpert	.07	.03	405 Andy Ashby	.10	.06
348 Dann Bilardello	.07	.03	406 Danny Tartabull	.15	.08
349 Frank Thomas	3.50	2.50	407 Bill Swift	.08	.05
350 Albert Belle	.30	.18	408 Craig Lefferts	.07	.03
351 Jose Mesa	.07	.03	409 Tom Candiotti	.07	.03
352 Rich Monteleone	.07	.03	410 Lance Blankenship	.07	.03
353 Bob Walk	.07	.03	411 Jeff Tackett	.07	.03
354 Monty Fariss	.07	.03	412 Sammy Sosa	.10	.06
355 Luis Rivera	.07	.03	413 Jody Reed	.07	.03
356 Anthony Young	.12	.07	414 Bruce Ruffin	.07	.03
357 Geno Petralli	.07	.03	415 Gene Larkin	.07	.03
358 Otis Nixon	.08	.05	416 John Vanderwal	.10	.06
359 Tom Pagnozzi	.08	.05	417 Tim Belcher	.08	.05
360 Reggie Sanders	1.50	.90	418 Steve Frey	.07	.03
361 Lee Stevens	.08	.05	419 Dick Schofield	.07	.03
362 Kent Hrbek	.08	.05	420 Jeff King	.07	.03
363 Orlando Merced	.15	.08	421 Kim Batiste	.12	.07
364 Mike Bordick	.15	.08	422 Jack McDowell	.30	.18
365 Dion James	.07	.03	423 Damon Berryhill	.07	.03
366 Jack Clark	.08	.05	424 Gary Wayne	.10	.06
367 Mike Stanley	.07	.03	425 Jack Morris	.15	.08
368 Randy Velarde	.07	.03	426 Moises Alou	.20	.12
369 Dan Pasqua	.07	.03	427 Mark McLemore	.07	.03
370 Pat Listach (R)	1.50	.90	428 Juan Guerrero (R)	.20	.12
371 Mike Fitzgerald	.07	.03	429 Scott Scudder	.07	.03
372 Tom Foley	.07	.03	430 Eric Davis	.10	.06
373 Matt Williams	.12	.07	431 Joe Slusarski	.08	.05
374 Brian Hunter	.15	.08	432 Todd Zeile	.10	.06
375 Joe Carter	.25	.15	433 Dwayne Henry	.08	.05
376 Bret Saberhagen	.10	.06	434 Cliff Brantley (R)	.12	.07
377 Mike Stanton	.07	.03	435 Butch Henry	.08	.05

436	Todd Worrell	.08	.05	494	Dave Fleming	1.50	.90
437	Bob Scanlan	.08	.05	495	Kyle Abbott	.12	.07
438	Wally Joyner	.10	.06	496	Chad Kreuter	.08	.05
439	John Flaherty (R)	.10	.06	497	Chris James	.07	.03
440	Brian Downing	.07	.03	498	Donnie Hill	.07	.03
441	Darren Lewis	.10	.06	499	Jacob Brumfield (R)	.12	.07
442	Gary Carter	.10	.06	500	Ricky Bones	.12	.07
443	Wally Ritchie	.07	.03	501	Terry Steinbach	.08	.05
444	Chris Jones	.08	.05	502	Bernard Gilkey	.15	.08
445	Jeff Kent (R)	.25	.15	503	Dennis Cook	.07	.03
446	Gary Sheffield	.80	.50	504	Lenny Dykstra	.08	.05
447	Ron Darling	.08	.05	505	Mike Bielecki	.07	.03
448	Deion Sanders	.35	.20	506	Bob Kipper	.07	.03
449	Andres Galarraga	.08	.05	507	Jose Melendez	.08	.05
450	Chuck Finley	.10	.06	508	Rick Sutcliffe	.08	.05
451	Derek Lilliquist	.07	.03	509	Ken Patterson	.07	.03
452	Carl Willis	.07	.03	510	Andy Allanson	.07	.03
453	Wes Chamberlain	.15	.08	511	Al Newman	.07	.03
454	Roger Mason	.07	.03	512	Mark Gardner	.08	.05
455	Spike Owen	.07	.03	513	Jeff Schaefer	.08	.05
456	Thomas Howard	.10	.06	514	Jim McNamara	.12	.07
457	Dave Martinez	.07	.03	515	Peter Hoy (R)	.12	.07
458	Pete Incaviglia	.07	.03	516	Curt Schilling	.07	.03
459	Keith Miller	.07	.03	517	Kirk McCaskill	.07	.03
460	Mike Fetters	.07	.03	518	Chris Gwynn	.07	.03
461	Paul Gibson	.07	.03	519	Sid Fernandez	.08	.05
462	George Bell	.15	.08	520	Jeff Parrett	.07	.03
463	Checklist	.07	.03	521	Scott Ruskin	.07	.03
464	Terry Mulholland	.07	.03	522	Kevin McReynolds	.08	.05
465	Storm Davis	.07	.03	523	Rick Cerone	.07	.03
466	Gary Pettis	.07	.03	524	Jesse Orosco	.07	.03
467	Randy Bush	.07	.03	525	Troy Afenir	.10	.06
468	Ken Hill	.10	.06	526	John Smiley	.10	.06
469	Rheal Cormier	.12	.07	527	Dale Murphy	.12	.08
470	Andy Stankiewicz (R)	.30	.18	528	Leaf Cover Card	.15	.08
471	Dave Burba	.07	.03				
472	Henry Cotto	.07	.03				
473	Dale Sveum	.07	.03				
474	Rich Gossage	.07	.03				
475	William Suero	.08	.05				
476	Doug Strange	.07	.03				
477	Bill Krueger	.07	.03				
478	John Wetteland	.10	.06				
479	Melido Perez	.08	.05				
480	Lonnie Smith	.07	.03				
481	Mike Jackson	.07	.03				
482	Mike Gardiner	.12	.07				
483	David Wells	.07	.03				
484	Barry Jones	.07	.03				
485	Scott Bankhead	.07	.03				
486	Terry Leach	.07	.03				
487	Vince Horsman (R)	.12	.07				
488	Dave Eiland	.07	.03				
489	Alejandro Pena	.07	.03				
490	Julio Valera	.07	.03				
491	Joe Boever	.07	.03				
492	Paul Miller (R)	.15	.08				
493	Archi Cianfrocco (R)	.50	.30				

1992 Leaf Gold Rookies

		MINT	NR/MT
Complete Set (24)		65.00	48.00
Commons		2.00	1.40
1	Chad Curtis	3.50	2.50
2	Brent Gates	3.00	2.00
3	Pedro Martinez	6.00	4.00
4	Kenny Lofton	7.00	5.00
5	Turk Wendell	2.00	1.40
6	Mark Hutton	2.00	1.40
7	Todd Hundley	2.00	1.40

8	Matt Stairs	2.50	1.75
9	Eddie Taubensee	2.00	1.40
10	David Nied	4.00	3.00
11	Salomon Torres	4.00	3.00
12	Bret Boone	6.00	4.00
13	Johnny Ruffin	2.50	1.75
14	Ed Martel	2.00	1.40
15	Rick Tricek	2.00	1.40
16	Raul Mondesi	4.00	3.00
17	Pat Mahomes	4.00	3.00
18	Dan Wilson	2.50	1.75
19	Donovan Osborne	4.00	3.00
20	Dave Silvestri	2.00	1.40
21	Gary DiSarcina	2.00	1.40
22	Denny Neagle	2.00	1.40
23	Steve Hosey	3.00	2.00
24	John Doherty	2.00	1.40

1992 Leaf Studio

This 264-card set combines dramatic black and white action photos with small four-color portrait shots on the card fronts. Special limited bonus cards called "The Heritage Series" were randomly inserted into packs. The bonus cards feature portrait photos of current players wearing historic uniforms.

		MINT	NR/MT
Complete Set (264)		34.00	25.00
Commons		.08	.05

1	Steve Avery	.40	.25
2	Sid Bream	.08	.05
3	Ron Gant	.25	.15
4	Tom Glavine	.50	.30
5	David Justice	.80	.50
6	Mark Lemke	.08	.05

7	Greg Olson	.08	.05
8	Terry Pendleton	.20	.12
9	Deion Sanders	.40	.25
10	John Smoltz	.20	.12
11	Doug Dascenzo	.08	.05
12	Andre Dawson	.25	.15
13	Joe Girardi	.08	.05
14	Mark Grace	.20	.12
15	Greg Maddux	.20	.12
16	Chuck McElroy	.08	.05
17	Mike Morgan	.08	.05
18	Ryne Sandberg	.50	.30
19	Gary Scott	.15	.08
20	Sammy Sosa	.10	.06
21	Norm Charlton	.08	.05
22	Rob Dibble	.10	.06
23	Barry Larkin	.25	.15
24	Hal Morris	.15	.08
25	Paul O'Neill	.10	.06
26	Jose Rijo	.10	.06
27	Bip Roberts	.08	.05
28	Chris Sabo	.10	.06
29	Reggie Sanders	1.50	.90
30	Greg Swindell	.10	.06
31	Jeff Bagwell	1.00	.70
32	Craig Biggio	.10	.06
33	Ken Caminiti	.08	.05
34	Andujar Cedeno	.30	.18
35	Steve Finley	.08	.05
36	Pete Harnisch	.10	.06
37	Butch Henry	.08	.05
38	Doug Jones	.08	.05
39	Darryl Kile	.15	.08
40	Eddie Taubensee	.15	.08
41	Brett Butler	.12	.07
42	Tom Candiotti	.08	.05
43	Eric Davis	.12	.07
44	Orel Hershiser	.12	.07
45	Eric Karros	2.00	1.25
46	Ramon Martinez	.15	.08
47	Jose Offerman	.12	.07
48	Mike Scioscia	.08	.05
49	Mike Sharperson	.08	.05
50	Darryl Strawberry	.30	.18
51	Bret Barberie	.15	.08
52	Ivan Calderon	.10	.06
53	Gary Carter	.12	.07
54	Delino DeShields	.35	.20
55	Marquis Grissom	.40	.28
56	Ken Hill	.10	.06
57	Dennis Martinez	.10	.06
58	Spike Owen	.08	.05
59	Larry Walker	.35	.20
60	Tim Wallach	.10	.06
61	Bobby Bonilla	.25	.15
62	Tim Burke	.08	.05
63	Vince Coleman	.10	.06
64	John Franco	.08	.05

No.	Player		
65	Dwight Gooden	.15	.08
66	Todd Hundley	.12	.07
67	Howard Johnson	.15	.08
68	Eddie Murray	.25	.15
69	Bret Saberhagen	.12	.08
70	Anthony Young	.40	.25
71	Kim Batiste	.20	.12
72	Wes Chamberlain	.25	.15
73	Darren Daulton	.15	.08
74	Mariano Duncan	.08	.05
75	Lenny Dykstra	.10	.06
76	John Kruk	.10	.06
77	Mickey Morandini	.12	.07
78	Terry Mulholland	.08	.05
79	Dale Murphy	.15	.08
80	Mitch Williams	.08	.05
81	Jay Bell	.08	.05
82	Barry Bonds	.75	.45
83	Steve Buechele	.08	.05
84	Doug Drabek	.20	.12
85	Mike LaValliere	.08	.05
86	Jose Lind	.08	.05
87	Denny Neagle	.12	.07
88	Randy Tomlin	.10	.06
89	Andy Van Slyke	.15	.08
90	Gary Varsho	.08	.05
91	Pedro Guerrero	.08	.05
92	Rex Hudler	.08	.05
93	Brian Jordan	.60	.35
94	Felix Jose	.15	.08
95	Donovan Osborne	.50	.30
96	Tom Pagnozzi	.10	.06
97	Lee Smith	.12	.08
98	Ozzie SMith	.25	.15
99	Todd Worrell	.10	.06
100	Todd Zeile	.12	.07
101	Andy Benes	.20	.12
102	Jerald Clark	.08	.05
103	Tony Fernandez	.10	.06
104	Tony Gwynn	.30	.18
105	Greg Harris	.08	.05
106	Fred McGriff	.30	.18
107	Benito Santiago	.10	.06
108	Gary Sheffield	1.00	.70
109	Kurt Stillwell	.08	.05
110	Tim Teufel	.08	.05
111	Kevin Bass	.08	.05
112	Jeff Brantley	.10	.06
113	John Burkett	.10	.06
114	Will Clark	.75	.45
115	Royce Clayton	.40	.25
116	Mike Jackson	.08	.05
117	Darren Lewis	.20	.12
118	Bill Swift	.10	.06
119	Robby Thompson	.08	.05
120	Matt Williams	.15	.08
121	Brady Anderson	.40	.25
122	Glenn Davis	.10	.06
123	Mike Devereaux	.15	.08
124	Chris Hoiles	.15	.08
125	Sam Horn	.10	.06
126	Ben McDonald	.30	.18
127	Mike Mussina	.80	.50
128	Gregg Olson	.10	.06
129	Cal Ripken Jr.	.80	.50
130	Rick Sutcliffe	.10	.06
131	Wade Boggs	.25	.15
132	Roger Clemens	.80	.50
133	Greg Harris	.08	.05
134	Tim Naehring	.10	.06
135	Tony Pena	.08	.05
136	Phil Plantier	.75	.45
137	Jeff Reardon	.12	.07
138	Jody Reed	.08	.05
139	Mo Vaughn	.25	.15
140	Frank Viola	.10	.06
141	Jim Abbott	.25	.15
142	Hubie Brooks	.08	.05
143	Chad Curtis	.20	.12
144	Gary DiSarcina	.15	.08
145	Chuck Finley	.12	.07
146	Bryan Harvey	.10	.06
147	Von Hayes	.08	.05
148	Mark Langston	.12	.07
149	Lance Parrish	.08	.05
150	Lee Stevens	.12	.07
151	George Bell	.20	.12
152	Alex Fernandez	.15	.08
153	Greg Hibbard	.08	.05
154	Lance Johnson	.08	.05
155	Kirk McCaskill	.08	.05
156	Tim Raines	.12	.07
157	Steve Sax	.12	.07
158	Bobby Thigpen	.10	.06
159	Frank Thomas	3.00	2.00
160	Robin Ventura	.50	.30
161	Sandy Alomar Jr.	.15	.08
162	Jack Armstrong	.08	.05
163	Carlos Baerga	.75	.45
164	Albert Belle	.35	.20
165	Alex Cole	.12	.07
166	Glenallen Hill	.12	.07
167	Mark Lewis	.15	.08
168	Kenny Lofton	1.25	.80
169	Paul Sorrento	.40	.25
170	Mark Whiten	.15	.08
171	Milt Cuyler	.15	.08
172	Rob Deer	.10	.06
173	Cecil Fielder	.30	.18
174	Travis Fryman	.75	.45
175	Mike Henneman	.08	.05
176	Tony Phillips	.08	.05
177	Frank Tanana	.08	.05
178	Mickey Tettleton	.10	.06
179	Alan Trammell	.15	.08
180	Lou Whitaker	.10	.06

181 George Brett	.35	.20
182 Tom Gordon	.10	.06
183 Mark Gubicza	.10	.06
184 Gregg Jefferies	.15	.08
185 Wally Joyner	.15	.08
186 Brent Mayne	.12	.07
187 Brian McRae	.15	.08
188 Kevin McReynolds	.10	.06
189 Keith Miller	.08	.05
190 Jeff Montgomery	.08	.05
191 Dante Bichette	.08	.05
192 Ricky Bones	.15	.08
193 Scott Fletcher	.08	.05
194 Paul Molitor	.15	.08
195 Jaime Navarro	.20	.12
196 Franklin Stubbs	.08	.05
197 B.J. Surhoff	.08	.05
198 Greg Vaughn	.15	.08
199 Bill Wegman	.08	.05
200 Robin Yount	.35	.20
201 Rick Aguilera	.08	.05
202 Scott Erickson	.40	.25
203 Greg Gagne	.08	.05
204 Brian Harper	.08	.05
205 Kent Hrbek	.10	.06
206 Scott Leius	.08	.05
207 Shane Mack	.12	.07
208 Pat Mahomes	.60	.35
209 Kirby Puckett	.75	.45
210 John Smiley	.12	.07
211 Mike Gallego	.08	.05
212 Charlie Hayes	.08	.05
213 Pat Kelly	.20	.12
214 Roberto Kelly	.20	.12
215 Kevin Maas	.15	.08
216 Don Mattingly	.40	.25
217 Matt Nokes	.08	.05
218 Melido Perez	.08	.05
219 Scott Sanderson	.08	.05
220 Danny Tartabull	.15	.08
221 Harold Baines	.10	.06
222 Jose Canseco	.80	.50
223 Dennis Eckersley	.25	.15
224 Dave Henderson	.08	.05
225 Carney Lansford	.10	.06
226 Mark McGwire	.75	.45
227 Mike Moore	.08	.05
228 Randy Ready	.08	.05
229 Terry Steinbach	.10	.06
230 Dave Stewart	.12	.07
231 Jay Buhner	.12	.07
232 Ken Griffey Jr.	2.00	1.25
233 Erik Hanson	.12	.07
234 Randy Johnson	.25	.15
235 Edgar Martinez	.20	.12
236 Tino Martinez	.20	.12
237 Kevin Mitchell	.10	.06
238 Pete O'Brien	.08	.05

239 Harold Reynolds	.10	.06
240 David Valle	.08	.05
241 Julio Franco	.15	.08
242 Juan Gonzalez	3.00	2.00
243 Jose Guzman	.08	.05
244 Rafael Palmeiro	.20	.12
245 Dean Palmer	.25	.15
246 Ivan Rodriquez	1.25	.80
247 Jeff Russell	.08	.05
248 Nolan Ryan	1.75	1.00
249 Ruben Sierra	.50	.30
250 Dickie Thon	.08	.05
251 Roberto Alomar	.75	.45
252 Derek Bell	.25	.15
253 Pat Borders	.08	.05
254 Joe Carter	.25	.15
255 Kelly Gruber	.10	.06
256 Juan Guzman	1.50	.90
257 Jack Morris	.20	.12
258 John Olerud	.20	.12
259 Devon White	.08	.05
260 Dave Winfield	.25	.15
261 Checklist	.08	.05
262 Checklist	.08	.05
263 Checklist	.08	.05
264 History Card	.20	.12
BC1 Ryne Sandberg	5.00	3.50
BC2 Carlton Fisk	2.00	1.25
BC3 Wade Boggs	2.00	1.25
BC4 Jose Canseco	4.00	2.75
BC5 Don Mattingly	3.00	2.00
BC6 Darryl Strawberry	3.00	2.00
BC7 Cal Ripken Jr	5.00	3.50
BC8 Will Clark	3.50	2.50

O-PEE-CHEE

1991 O-Pee-Chee Premier

This 132-card set is the first premium issue from Canadian based O-Pee-Chee. Card fronts feature four-color action photos framed in white with multi-colored border stripes. Horizontal card backs are numbered and include small head shots, player stats and bio's.

		MINT	NR/MT
Complete Set (132)		23.00	15.00
Commons		.07	.03
1	Roberto Alomar	1.00	.70
2	Sandy Alomar	.12	.07
3	Moises Alou	.20	.12
4	Brian Barnes	.20	.12
5	Steve Bedrosian	.07	.03
6	George Bell	.20	.12
7	Juan Bell	.10	.06
8	Albert Belle	.80	.50
9	Bud Black	.07	.03
10	Mike Boddicker	.07	.03
11	Wade Boggs	.70	.40
12	Barry Bonds	.75	.45
13	Denis Boucher	.20	.12
14	George Brett	.60	.35
15	Hubie Brooks	.10	.06
16	Brett Butler	.10	.06
17	Ivan Calderon	.10	.06
18	Jose Canseco	1.50	.90
19	Gary Carter	.12	.07
20	Joe Carter	.30	.18
21	Jack Clark	.10	.06
22	Will Clark	1.25	.80
23	Roger Clemens	1.00	.70
24	Alex Cole	.15	.10
25	Vince Coleman	.12	.07
26	Jeff Conine (R)	.25	.15
27	Milt Cuyler	.40	.25
28	Danny Darwin	.07	.03
29	Eric Davis	.35	.20
30	Glenn Davis	.10	.06
31	Andre Dawson	.25	.15
32	Ken Dayley	.07	.03
33	Steve Decker (R)	.40	.25
34	Delino DeShields	.60	.35
35	Lance Dickson (R)	.40	.25
36	Kirk Dressendorfer (R)	.40	.25
37	Shawon Dunston	.15	.10
38	Dennis Eckersley	.20	.12
39	Dwight Evans	.10	.06
40	Howard Farmer	.12	.07
41	Junior Felix	.10	.06
42	Alex Fernandez	.40	.25
43	Tony Fernandez	.10	.06
44	Cecil Fielder	.60	.35
45	Carlton Fisk	.25	.15
46	Willie Fraser	.07	.03
47	Gary Gaetti	.10	.06
48	Andres Galarraga	.10	.06
49	Ron Gant	.50	.30
50	Kirk Gibson	.10	.06
51	Bernard Gilkey	.30	.18
52	Leo Gomez	.80	.50
53	Rene Gonzalez	.07	.03
54	Juan Gonzalez	4.00	2.75
55	Dwight Gooden	.35	.20
56	Ken Griffey Jr.	6.00	4.00
57	Kelly Gruber	.12	.07
58	Pedro Guerrero	.10	.06
59	Tony Gwynn	.60	.35
60	Chris Hammond	.15	.10
61	Ron Hassey	.07	.03
62	Rickey Henderson	.50	.30
63	Tom Henke	.10	.06
64	Orel Hershiser	.12	.07
65	Chris Hoiles	.25	.15
66	Todd Hundley	.25	.15
67	Pete Incaviglia	.10	.06
68	Danny Jackson	.10	.06
69	Barry Jones	.07	.03
70	David Justice	2.50	1.50
71	Jimmy Key	.10	.06
72	Ray Lankford	1.25	.80
73	Darren Lewis	.35	.20
74	Kevin Maas	.50	.30
75	Denny Martinez	.15	.10
76	Tino Martinez	.40	.25
77	Don Mattingly	.50	.30
78	Willie McGee	.10	.06
79	Fred McGriff	.35	.20
80	Hensley Meulens	.15	.10

81	Kevin Mitchell	.15	.10
82	Paul Molitor	.12	.07
83	Mickey Morandini	.30	.18
84	Jack Morris	.15	.10
85	Dale Murphy	.20	.12
86	Eddie Murray	.25	.15
87	Chris Nabholz	.15	.10
88	Tim Naehring	.15	.10
89	Otis Nixon	.10	.06
90	Jose Offerman	.25	.15
91	Bob Ojeda	.07	.03
92	John Olerud	.50	.30
93	Gregg Olson	.12	.07
94	Dave Parker	.10	.06
95	Terry Pendleton	.25	.15
96	Kirby Puckett	.60	.35
97	Tim Raines	.15	.10
98	Jeff Reardon	.15	.10
99	Dave Righetti	.10	.06
100	Cal Ripken	2.00	1.25
101	Mel Rojas	.07	.03
102	Nolan Ryan	3.00	2.00
103	Ryne Sandberg	1.00	.70
104	Scott Sanderson	.07	.03
105	Benito Santiago	.15	.10
106	Pete Schourek	.25	.15
107	Gary Scott (R)	.40	.25
108	Terry Shumpert	.10	.06
109	Ruben Sierra	.70	.40
110	Doug Simons	.20	.12
111	Dave Smith	.07	.03
112	Ozzie Smith	.40	.25
113	Cory Snyder	.10	.06
114	Luis Sojo	.10	.06
115	Dave Stewart	.15	.10
116	Dave Stieb	.12	.07
117	Darryl Strawberry	.70	.40
118	Pat Tabler	.07	.03
119	Wade Taylor	.20	.12
120	Bobby Thigpen	.10	.06
121	Frank Thomas	8.50	5.50
122	Mike Timlin	.20	.12
123	Alan Trammell	.25	.15
124	Mo Vaughn	1.00	.70
125	Tim Wallach	.10	.06
126	Devon White	.07	.03
127	Mark Whiten	.70	.40
128	Bernie Williams	.80	.50
129	Willie Wilson	.10	.06
130	Dave Winfield	.40	.25
131	Robin Yount	.80	.50
132	Checklist	.10	.06

1992 O-Pee-Chee Premier

BOBBY BONILLA

This second year premium set from O-Pee-Chee of Canada is similar to their 1991 set but larger with 198-cards compared to 132-cards in 1991. The cards feature four-color action photos on the front with a small head shot on the back with career statistics.

		MINT	NR/MT
Complete Set (198)		24.00	15.00
Commons		.05	.02

1	Wade Boggs	.20	.12
2	John Smiley	.12	.07
3	Checklist	.08	.04
4	Ron Gant	.30	.18
5	Mike Bordick	.15	.10
6	Charlie Hayes	.05	.02
7	Kevin Morton	.05	.02
8	Checklist	.08	.04
9	Chris Gwynn	.05	.02
10	Melido Perez	.10	.06
11	Dan Gladden	.05	.02
12	Brian McRae	.15	.10
13	Denny Martinez	.10	.06
14	Bob Scanlan	.10	.06
15	Julio Franco	.12	.07
16	Ruben Amaro (R)	.30	.18
17	Mo Sanford	.15	.10
18	Scott Bankhead	.05	.02
19	Dickie Thon	.05	.03
20	Chris James	.05	.02
21	Mike Huff (R)	.20	.12
22	Orlando Merced	.15	.10
23	Chris Sabo	.10	.06
24	Jose Canseco	.75	.45
25	Reggie Sanders (R)	.80	.50
26	Chris Nabholz	.15	.10
27	Kevin Seitzer	.07	.03

28	Ryan Bowen	.12	.07
29	Gary Carter	.10	.06
30	Wayne Rosenthal	.15	.10
31	Alan Trammell	.10	.06
32	Doug Drabek	.12	.07
33	Craig Shipley	.05	.02
34	Ryne Sandberg	.50	.30
35	Chuck Knoblauch	.50	.30
36	Bret Barberie	.25	.15
37	Tim Naehring	.10	.06
38	Omar Oliveres	.10	.06
39	Royce Clayton	.35	.20
40	Brent Mayne	.07	.03
41	Darrin Fletcher	.12	.07
42	Howard Johnson	.10	.06
43	Steve Sax	.10	.06
44	Greg Swindell	.10	.06
45	Andre Dawson	.15	.10
46	Kent Hrbek	.07	.03
47	Dwight Gooden	.10	.06
48	Mark Leiter	.12	.07
49	Tom Glavine	.35	.20
50	Mo Vaughn	.50	.30
51	Doug Jones	.12	.07
52	Brian Barnes	.15	.10
53	Rob Dibble	.12	.07
54	Kevin McReynolds	.05	.03
55	Ivan Rodriguez	1.25	.80
56	Scott Livingstone	.30	.18
57	Mike Magnante	.20	.12
58	Pete Schourek	.12	.07
59	Frank Thomas	2.50	1.50
60	Kirk McCaskill	.05	.02
61	Wally Joyner	.15	.10
62	Rick Aguilera	.10	.06
63	Eric Karros (R)	1.75	1.00
64	Tino Martinez	.20	.12
65	Bryan Hickerson	.12	.07
66	Ruben Sierra	.25	.15
67	Willie Randolph	.05	.02
68	Bill Landrum	.05	.02
69	Bip Roberts	.07	.03
70	Cecil Fielder	.30	.18
71	Pat Kelly	.12	.07
72	Kenny Lofton (R)	1.25	.80
73	John Franco	.07	.03
74	Phil Plantier	1.50	.90
75	Dave Martinez	.05	.02
76	Warren Newson	.10	.06
77	Chito Martinez	.12	.07
78	Brian Hunter	.25	.15
79	Jack Morris	.10	.06
80	Eric King	.07	.03
81	Nolan Ryan	1.00	.70
82	Bret Saberhagen	.10	.06
83	Roberto Kelly	.25	.15
84	Ozzie Smith	.25	.15
85	Chuck McElroy	.10	.06
86	Carlton Fisk	.15	.10
87	Mike Mussina	.80	.50
88	Mark Carreon	.05	.02
89	Ken Hill	.12	.07
90	Rick Cerone	.07	.03
91	Deion Sanders	.75	.45
92	Don Mattingly	.25	.15
93	Danny Tartabull	.20	.12
94	Keith Miller	.07	.03
95	Gregg Jefferies	.15	.10
96	Barry Larkin	.15	.10
97	Kevin Mitchell	.10	.06
98	Rick Sutcliffe	.07	.03
99	Mark McGwire	.70	.40
100	Albert Belle	.30	.18
101	Gregg Olson	.10	.06
102	Kirby Puckett	.30	.18
103	Luis Gonzalez	.12	.07
104	Randy Myers	.05	.02
105	Roger Clemens	.40	.25
106	Tony Gwynn	.25	.15
107	Jeff Bagwell	1.25	.80
108	John Wetteland	.20	.12
109	Bernie Williams	.15	.10
110	Scott Kamienecki	.12	.07
111	Robin Yount	.35	.20
112	Dean Palmer	.70	.40
113	Tim Belcher	.07	.03
114	George Brett	.25	.15
115	Frank Viola	.10	.06
116	Kelly Gruber	.07	.03
117	David Justice	1.00	.70
118	Scott Leius	.12	.07
119	Jeff Fassero	.15	.10
120	Sammy Sosa	.10	.06
121	Al Osuna	.07	.03
122	Wilson Alvarez	.07	.03
123	Jose Offerman	.15	.10
124	Mel Rojas	.05	.02
125	Shawon Dunston	.10	.06
126	Pete Incaviglia	.07	.03
127	Von Hayes	.05	.02
128	Dave Gallagher	.05	.02
129	Eric Davis	.12	.07
130	Roberto Alomar	.80	.50
131	Mike Gallego	.05	.02
132	Robin Ventura	.70	.40
133	Bill Swift	.15	.10
134	John Kruk	.12	.07
135	Craig Biggio	.10	.06
136	Eddie Taubensee	.10	.06
137	Cal Ripken	.80	.50
138	Charles Nagy	.25	.15
139	Jose Melendez	.15	.10
140	Jim Abbott	.25	.15
141	Paul Molitor	.10	.06
142	Tom Candiotti	.05	.02
143	Bobby Bonilla	.20	.12

144	Matt Williams	.15	.10
145	Brett Butler	.10	.06
146	Will Clark	.50	.30
147	Rickey Henderson	.30	.18
148	Ray Lankford	.25	.15
149	Bill Pecota	.05	.02
150	Dave Winfield	.20	.12
151	Darren Lewis	.07	.03
152	Bob MacDonald	.12	.07
153	David Segui	.10	.06
154	Benito Santiago	.07	.03
155	Chuck Finley	.10	.06
156	Andujar Cedeno	.35	.20
157	Barry Bonds	.35	.20
158	Joe Grahe	.07	.03
159	Frank Castillo	.05	.02
160	Dave Burba	.07	.03
161	Leo Gomez	.25	.15
162	Orel Hershiser	.10	.06
163	Delino DeShields	.25	.15
164	Sandy Alomar	.10	.06
165	Denny Neagle	.10	.06
166	Fred McGriff	.25	.15
167	Ken Griffey Jr.	1.75	1.00
168	Juan Guzman	2.50	1.50
169	Bobby Rose (R)	.15	.10
170	Steve Avery	.50	.30
171	Rich DeLucia	.07	.03
172	Mike Timlin	.07	.03
173	Randy Johnson	.10	.06
174	Paul Gibson	.07	.03
175	David Cone	.10	.06
176	Marquis Grissom	.30	.18
177	Kurt Stillwell	.05	.02
178	Mark Whiten	.15	.10
179	Darryl Strawberry	.20	.12
180	Mike Morgan	.05	.02
181	Scott Scudder	.10	.06
182	George Bell	.07	.03
183	Alvin Davis	.05	.02
184	Len Dykstra	.07	.03
185	Kyle Abbott	.10	.06
186	Chris Haney	.20	.12
187	Junior Naboa	.05	.02
188	Dennis Eckersley	.12	.07
189	Derek Bell	.60	.35
190	Lee Smith	.12	.07
191	Andres Galarraga	.07	.03
192	Jack Armstrong	.07	.03
193	Eddie Murray	.20	.12
194	Joe Carter	.25	.15
195	Terry Pendleton	.20	.12
196	Darryl Kile	.15	.10
197	Rod Beck	.10	.06
198	Hubie Brooks	.07	.03

SCORE

1988 Score

The premier set from Score featured four-color fronts and backs. The standard-size cards, 2-1/2" by 3-1/2", used six different border colors to frame game-action photos on the front while the card backs contained a small head shot of each player. Reggie Jackson is featured in a special 5-card subset.

		MINT	NR/MT
Complete Set (660)		20.00	14.00
Commons		.05	.02
1	Don Mattingly	.25	.15
2	Wade Boggs	.20	.12
3	Tim Raines	.07	.04
4	Andre Dawson	.20	.12
5	Mark McGwire	.60	.35
6	Kevin Seitzer	.07	.04
7	Wally Joyner	.15	.08
8	Jesse Barfield	.07	.04
9	Pedro Guerrero	.07	.04
10	Eric Davis	.10	.06
11	George Brett	.35	.20
12	Ozzie Smith	.20	.12
13	Rickey Henderson	.30	.18
14	Jim Rice	.07	.04
15	Matt Nokes (R)	.12	.07
16	Mike Schmidt	.50	.30
17	Dave Parker	.10	.06
18	Eddie Murray	.20	.12
19	Andres Galarraga	.07	.04
20	Tony Fernandez	.07	.04
21	Kevin McReynolds	.07	.04
22	B.J. Surhoff	.05	.02
23	Pat Tabler	.05	.02
24	Kirby Puckett	.50	.30

#	Player			#	Player		
25	Benny Santiago	.15	.08	83	Alvin Davis	.05	.02
26	Ryne Sandberg	.50	.30	84	Tom Herr	.05	.02
27	Kelly Downs	.07	.04	85	Vance Law	.05	.02
28	Jose Cruz	.07	.04	86	Kal Daniels	.05	.02
29	Pete O'Brien	.05	.02	87	Rick Honeycutt	.05	.02
30	Mark Langston	.10	.06	88	Alfredo Griffin	.05	.02
31	Lee Smith	.15	.08	89	Bret Saberhagen	.12	.07
32	Juan Samuel	.05	.02	90	Bert Blyleven	.12	.07
33	Kevin Bass	.05	.02	91	Jeff Reardon	.20	.12
34	R.J. Reynolds	.05	.02	92	Cory Snyder	.05	.02
35	Steve Sax	.10	.06	93	Greg Walker	.05	.02
36	John Kruk	.15	.08	94	Joe Magrane (R)	.10	.06
37	Alan Trammell	.15	.08	95	Rob Deer	.05	.02
38	Chris Bosio	.08	.05	96	Ray Knight	.05	.02
39	Brook Jacoby	.05	.02	97	Casey Candaele	.05	.02
40	Willie McGee	.10	.06	98	John Cerutti	.05	.02
41	Dave Magadan	.05	.02	99	Buddy Bell	.05	.02
42	Fred Lynn	.08	.05	100	Jack Clark	.07	.04
43	Kent Hrbek	.08	.05	101	Eric Bell	.05	.02
44	Brian Downing	.05	.02	102	Willie Wilson	.05	.02
45	Jose Canseco	.80	.50	103	Dave Schmidt	.05	.02
46	Jim Presley	.05	.02	104	Dennis Eckersley	.20	.12
47	Mike Stanley	.05	.02	105	Don Sutton	.12	.07
48	Tony Pena	.05	.02	106	Danny Tartabull	.15	.08
49	David Cone	.35	.20	107	Fred McGriff	.75	.45
50	Rick Sutcliffe	.07	.04	108	Les Straker (R)	.05	.02
51	Doug Drabek	.15	.08	109	Lloyd Moseby	.05	.02
52	Bill Doran	.05	.02	110	Roger Clemens	.60	.35
53	Mike Scioscia	.05	.02	111	Glenn Hubbard	.05	.02
54	Candy Maldonado	.05	.02	112	Ken Williams (R)	.05	.02
55	Dave Winfield	.20	.12	113	Ruben Sierra	.50	.30
56	Lou Whitaker	.07	.04	114	Stan Jefferson	.05	.02
57	Tom Henke	.05	.02	115	Milt Thompson	.05	.02
58	Ken Gerhart	.05	.02	116	Bobby Bonilla	.25	.15
59	Glenn Braggs	.05	.02	117	Wayne Tolleson	.05	.02
60	Julio Franco	.12	.07	118	Matt Williams (R)	1.25	.80
61	Charlie Leibrandt	.05	.02	119	Chet Lemon	.05	.02
62	Gary Gaetti	.05	.02	120	Dale Sveum	.05	.02
63	Bob Boone	.08	.05	121	Dennis Boyd	.05	.02
64	Louis Polonia (R)	.12	.07	122	Brett Butler	.08	.05
65	Dwight Evans	.08	.05	123	Terry Kennedy	.05	.02
66	Phil Bradley	.05	.02	124	Jack Howell	.05	.02
67	Mike Boddicker	.05	.02	125	Curt Young	.05	.02
68	Vince Coleman	.08	.05	126a	Dale Valle (Er)	.10	.06
69	Howard Johnson	.15	.08	126b	Dave Valle (Correct)	.05	.02
70	Tim Wallach	.10	.06	127	Curt Wilkerson	.05	.02
71	Keith Moreland	.05	.02	128	Tim Teufel	.05	.02
72	Barry Larkin	.20	.12	129	Ozzie Virgil	.05	.02
73	Alan Ashby	.05	.02	130	Brian Fisher	.05	.02
74	Rick Rhoden	.05	.02	131	Lance Parrish	.07	.04
75	Darrell Evans	.07	.04	132	Tom Browning	.07	.04
76	Dave Stieb	.07	.04	133a	Larry Anderson (Er)	.10	.06
77	Dan Plesac	.05	.02	133b	Larry Andersen (Cor)	.05	.02
78	Will Clark	.80	.50	134a	Bob Brenley (Er)	.10	.06
79	Frank White	.05	.02	134b	Bob Brenly (Cor)	.05	.02
80	Joe Carter	.25	.15	135	Mike Marshall	.05	.02
81	Mike Witt	.05	.02	136	Gerald Perry	.05	.02
82	Terry Steinbach	.05	.02	137	Bobby Meacham	.05	.02

138	Larry Herndon	.05	.02
139	Fred Manrique (R)	.05	.02
140	Charlie Hough	.05	.02
141	Ron Darling	.07	.04
142	Herm Winningham	.05	.02
143	Mike Diaz	.05	.02
144	Mike Jackson (R)	.12	.07
145	Denny Walling	.05	.02
146	Rob Thompson	.05	.02
147	Franklin Stubbs	.05	.02
148	Albert Hall	.05	.02
149	Bobby Witt	.10	.06
150	Lance McCullers	.05	.02
151	Scott Bradley	.05	.02
152	Mark McLemore	.05	.02
153	Tim Laudner	.05	.02
154	Greg Swindell	.08	.05
155	Marty Barrett	.05	.02
156	Mike Heath	.05	.02
157	Gary Ward	.05	.02
158a	Lee Mazilli (Er)	.10	.06
158b	Lee Mazzilli (Cor)	.05	.02
159	Tom Foley	.05	.02
160	Robin Yount	.35	.20
161	Steve Bedrosian	.05	.02
162	Bob Walk	.05	.02
163	Nick Esasky	.05	.02
164	Ken Caminiti (R)	.25	.12
165	Jose Uribe	.05	.02
166	Dave Anderson	.05	.02
167	Ed Whitson	.05	.02
168	Ernie Whitt	.05	.02
169	Cecil Cooper	.05	.02
170	Mike Pagliarulo	.05	.02
171	Pat Sheridan	.05	.02
172	Chris Bando	.05	.02
173	Lee Lacy	.05	.02
174	Steve Lonbardozzi	.05	.02
175	Mike Greenwell	.12	.07
176	Greg Minton	.05	.02
177	Moose Haas	.05	.02
178	Mike Kingery	.05	.02
179	Greg Harris	.05	.02
180	Bo Jackson	.35	.20
181	Carmelo Martinez	.05	.02
182	Alex Trevino	.05	.02
183	Ron Oester	.05	.02
184	Danny Darwin	.05	.02
185	Mike Krukow	.05	.02
186	Rafael Palmeiro	.20	.12
187	Tim Burke	.05	.02
188	Roger McDowell	.05	.02
189	Garry Templeton	.05	.02
190	Terry Pendleton	.20	.12
191	Larry Parrish	.05	.02
192	Rey Quinones	.05	.02
193	Joaqin Andujar	.05	.02
194	Tom Brunansky	.07	.04
195	Donnie Moore	.05	.02
196	Dan Pasqua	.05	.02
197	Jim Gantner	.05	.02
198	Mark Eichhorn	.05	.02
199	John Grubb	.05	.02
200	Bill Ripken (R)	.10	.06
201	Sam Horn (R)	.15	.08
202	Todd Worrell	.05	.02
203	Terry Leach	.05	.02
204	Garth Iorg	.05	.02
205	Brian Dayett	.05	.02
206	Bo Diaz	.05	.02
207	Craig Reynolds	.05	.02
208	Brian Holton	.07	.04
209	Marvelle Wynne (Er)	.05	.02
210	Dave Concepcion	.10	.06
211	Mike Davis	.05	.02
212	Devon White	.05	.02
213	Mickey Brantley	.05	.02
214	Greg Gagne	.05	.02
215	Oddibe McDowell	.05	.02
216	Jimmy Key	.07	.04
217	Dave Bergman	.05	.02
218	Calvin Schiraldi	.05	.02
219	Larry Sheets	.05	.02
220	Mike Easler	.05	.02
221	Kurt Stillwell	.05	.02
222	Chuck Jackson	.05	.02
223	Dave Martinez	.05	.02
224	Tim Leary	.05	.02
225	Steve Garvey	.15	.08
226	Greg Mathews	.05	.02
227	Doug Sisk	.05	.02
228	Dave Henderson	.05	.02
229	Jimmy Dwyer	.05	.02
230	Larry Owen	.05	.02
231	Andre Thornton	.05	.02
232	Mark Salas	.05	.02
233	Tom Brookens	.05	.02
234	Greg Brock	.05	.02
235	Rance Mulliniks	.05	.02
236	Bob Brower	.05	.02
237	Joe Niekro	.05	.02
238	Scott Bankhead	.05	.02
239	Doug DeCinces	.05	.02
240	Tommy John	.07	.04
241	Rich Gedman	.05	.02
242	Ted Power	.05	.02
243	Dave Meads (R)	.05	.02
244	Jim Sundberg	.05	.02
245	Ken Oberkfell	.05	.02
246	Jimmy Jones	.05	.02
247	Ken Landreaux	.05	.02
248	Jose Oquendo	.05	.02
249	John Mitchell	.05	.02
250	Don Baylor	.07	.04
251	Scott Fletcher	.05	.02
252	Al Newman (R)	.05	.02

253	Carney Lansford	.07	.04	308	George Hendrick	.05	.02
254	Johnny Ray	.05	.02	309	John Moses	.05	.02
255	Gary Pettis	.05	.02	310	Ron Guidry	.10	.06
256	Ken Phelps	.05	.02	311	Bill Schroeder	.05	.02
257	Rick Leach	.05	.02	312	Jose Nunez (R)	.08	.05
258	Tim Stoddard	.05	.02	313	Bud Black	.07	.04
259	Ed Romero	.05	.02	314	Joe Sambito	.05	.02
260	Sid Bream	.05	.02	315	Scott McGregor	.05	.02
261a	Tom Neidenfuer (Er)	.10	.06	316	Rafael Santana	.05	.02
261b	Tom Niedenfuer (Cor)	.05	.02	317	Frank Williams	.05	.02
262	Rick Dempsey	.05	.02	318	Mike Fitzgerald	.05	.02
263	Lonnie Smith	.05	.02	319	Rick Mahler	.05	.02
264	Bob Forsch	.05	.02	320	Jim Gott	.05	.02
265	Barry Bonds	.50	.30	321	Mariano Duncan	.05	.02
266	Willie Randolph	.05	.02	322	Jos Guzman	.05	.02
267	Mike Ramsey	.05	.02	323	Lee Guetterman	.05	.02
268	Don Slaught	.05	.02	324	Dan Gladden	.05	.02
269	Mickey Tettleton	.08	.05	325	Gary Carter	.10	.06
270	Jerry Reuss	.05	.02	326	Tracy Jones	.05	.02
271	Marc Sullivan	.05	.02	327	Floyd Youmans	.05	.02
272	Jim Morrison	.05	.02	328	Bill Dawley	.05	.02
273	Steve Balboni	.05	.02	329	Paul Noce (R)	.05	.02
274	Dick Schofield	.05	.02	330	Angel Salazar	.05	.02
275	John Tudor	.05	.02	331	Goose Gossage	.07	.04
276	Gene Larkin (R)	.10	.06	332	George Frazier	.05	.02
277	Harold Reynolds	.07	.04	333	Ruppert Jones	.05	.02
278	Jerry Browne	.05	.02	334	Billy Jo Robidoux	.05	.02
279	Willie Upshaw	.05	.02	335	Mike Scott	.05	.02
280	Ted Higuera	.05	.02	336	Randy Myers	.05	.02
281	Terry McGriff	.05	.02	337	Bob Sebra	.05	.02
282	Terry Puhl	.05	.02	338	Eric Show	.05	.02
283	Mark Wasinger	.05	.02	339	Mitch Williams	.05	.02
284	Luis Salazar	.05	.02	340	Paul Molitor	.10	.06
285	Ted Simmons	.07	.04	341	Gus Polidor	.05	.02
286	John Shelby	.05	.02	342	Steve Trout	.05	.02
287	John Smiley (R)	.35	.20	343	Jerry Don Gleaton	.05	.02
288	Curt Ford	.05	.02	344	Bob Knepper	.05	.02
289	Steve Crawford	.05	.02	345	Mitch Webster	.05	.02
290	Dan Quisenberry	.05	.02	346	John Morris	.05	.02
291	Alan Wiggins	.05	.02	347	Andy Hawkins	.05	.02
292	Randy Bush	.05	.02	348	Dave Leiper	.05	.02
293	John Candelaria	.05	.02	349	Ernest Riles	.05	.02
294	Tony Phillips	.05	.02	350	Dwight Gooden	.12	.07
295	Mike Morgan	.05	.02	351	Dave Righetti	.05	.02
296	Bill Wegman	.05	.02	352	Pat Dodson	.05	.02
297a	Terry Franconia (Er)	.10	.06	353	John Habyan	.05	.02
297b	Terry Francona (Cor)	.05	.02	354	Jim Deshaies	.05	.02
298	Mickey Hatcher	.05	.02	355	Butch Wynegar	.05	.02
299	Andres Thomas	.05	.02	356	Bryn Smith	.05	.02
300	Bob Stanley	.05	.02	357	Matt Young	.05	.02
301	Al Pedrique (R)	.05	.02	358	Tom Pagnozzi (R)	.20	.12
302	Jim Lindeman	.05	.02	359	Floyd Rayford	.05	.02
303	Wally Backman	.05	.02	360	Darryl Strawberry	.35	.20
304	Paul O'Neill	.10	.06	361	Sal Butera	.05	.02
305	Hubie Brooks	.08	.05	362	Domingo Ramos	.05	.02
306	Steve Buechele	.07	.04	363	Chris Brown	.05	.02
307	Bobby Thigpen	.08	.05	364	Jose Gonzalez	.05	.02
				365	Dave Smith	.05	.02

366	Andy McGaffigan	.05	.02
367	Stan Javier	.05	.02
368	Henry Cotto	.05	.02
369	Mike Birkbeck	.05	.02
370	Len Dykstra	.07	.04
371	Dave Collins	.05	.02
372	Spike Owen	.05	.02
373	Geno Petralli	.05	.02
374	Ron Karkovice	.05	.02
375	Shane Rawley	.05	.02
376	DeWayne Buice (R)	.05	.02
377	Bill Pecota (R)	.08	.05
378	Leon Durham	.05	.02
379	Ed Olwine	.05	.02
380	Bruce Hurst	.07	.04
381	Bob McClure	.05	.02
382	Mark Thurmond	.05	.02
383	Buddy Biancalana	.05	.02
384	Tim Conroy	.05	.02
385	Tony Gwynn	.30	.18
386	Greg Gross	.05	.02
387	Barry Lyons (R)	.05	.02
388	Mike Felder	.05	.02
389	Pat Clements	.05	.02
390	Ken Griffey	.08	.05
391	Mark Davis	.05	.02
392	Jos Rijo	.08	.05
393	Mike Young	.05	.02
394	Willie Fraser	.05	.02
395	Dion James	.05	.02
396	Steve Shields (R)	.05	.02
397	Randy St. Claire	.05	.02
398	Danny Jackson	.07	.04
399	Cecil Fielder	.35	.20
400	Keith Hernandez	.07	.04
401	Don Carman	.05	.02
402	Chuck Crim (R)	.07	.04
403	Rob Woodward	.05	.02
404	Junior Ortiz	.05	.02
405	Glenn Wilson	.05	.02
406	Ken Howell	.05	.02
407	Jeff Kunkel	.05	.02
408	Jeff Reed	.05	.02
409	Chris James	.05	.02
410	Zane Smith	.07	.04
411	Ken Dixon	.05	.02
412	Ricky Horton	.05	.02
413	Frank DiPino	.05	.02
414	Shane Mack (R)	.30	.18
415	Danny Cox	.05	.02
416	Andy Van Slyke	.15	.08
417	Danny Heep	.05	.02
418	John Cangelosi	.05	.02
419a	John Christiansen (Er)	.10	.06
419b	John Christensen (Cor)	.05	.02
420	Joey Cora	.05	.02
421	Mike LaValliere	.05	.02
422	Kelly Gruber	.10	.06
423	Bruce Benedict	.05	.02
424	Len Matuszek	.05	.02
425	Kent Tekulve	.05	.02
426	Rafael Ramirez	.05	.02
427	Mike Flanagan	.05	.02
428	Mike Gallego	.05	.02
429	Juan Castillo	.05	.02
430	Neal Heaton	.05	.02
431	Phil Garner	.05	.02
432	Mike Dunne (R)	.05	.02
433	Wallace Johnson	.05	.02
434	Jack O'Connor	.05	.02
435	Steve Jeltz	.05	.02
436	Donnell Nixon (R)	.07	.04
437	Jack Lazorko	.05	.02
438	Keith Comstock (R)	.05	.02
439	Jeff Robinson	.05	.02
440	Graig Nettles	.07	.04
441	Mel Hall	.07	.04
442	Gerald Young (R)	.08	.05
443	Gary Redus	.05	.02
444	Charlie Moore	.05	.02
445	Bill Madlock	.07	.04
446	Mark Clear	.05	.02
447	Greg Booker	.05	.02
448	Rick Schu	.05	.02
449	Ron Kittle	.05	.02
450	Dale Murphy	.15	.08
451	Bob Dernier	.05	.02
452	Dale Mohorcic	.05	.02
453	Rafael Belliard	.05	.02
454	Charlie Puleo	.05	.02
455	Dwayne Murphy	.05	.02
456	Jim Eisenreich	.05	.02
457	David Palmer	.05	.02
458	Dave Stewart	.10	.06
459	Pascual Perez	.05	.02
460	Glenn Davis	.08	.05
461	Dan Petry	.05	.02
462	Jim Winn	.05	.02
463	Darrell Miller	.05	.02
464	Mike Moore	.05	.02
465	Mike LaCoss	.05	.02
466	Steve Farr	.05	.02
467	Jerry Mumphrey	.05	.02
468	Kevin Gross	.05	.02
469	Bruce Bochy	.05	.02
470	Orel Hershiser	.10	.06
471	Eric King	.05	.02
472	Ellis Burks (R)	.25	.15
473	Darren Daulton	.15	.08
474	Mookie Wilson	.05	.02
475	Frank Viola	.07	.04
476	Ron Robinson	.05	.02
477	Bob Melvin	.05	.02
478	Jeff Musselman	.05	.02

479	Charlie Kerfeld	.05	.02	535	John Franco	.05	.02
480	Richard Dotson	.05	.02	536	Paul Kilgus (R)	.07	.04
481	Kevin Mitchell	.20	.12	537	Darrell Porter	.05	.02
482	Gary Roenicke	.05	.02	538	Walt Terrell	.05	.02
483	Tim Flannery	.05	.02	539	Bill Long (R)	.05	.02
484	Rich Yett	.05	.02	540	George Bell	.10	.06
485	Pete Incaviglia	.07	.04	541	Jeff Sellers	.05	.02
486	Rick Cerone	.05	.02	542	Joe Boever (R)	.05	.02
487	Tony Armas	.05	.02	543	Steve Howe	.05	.02
488	Jerry Reed	.05	.02	544	Scott Sanderson	.05	.02
489	Davey Lopes	.07	.04	545	Jack Morris	.12	.07
490	Frank Tanana	.07	.04	546	Todd Benzinger (R)	.12	.07
491	Mike Loynd	.05	.02	547	Steve Henderson	.05	.02
492	Bruce Ruffin	.05	.02	548	Eddie Milner	.05	.02
493	Chris Speier	.05	.02	549	Jeff Robinson (R)	.08	.05
490	Tom Hume	.05	.02	550	Cal Ripkin, Jr.	.75	.45
495	Jesse Orosco	.05	.02	551	Jody Davis	.05	.02
496	Robby Wine, Jr. (R)	.05	.02	552	Kirk McCaskill	.05	.02
497	Jeff Mongomery (R)	.20	.12	553	Craig Lefferts	.05	.02
498	Jeff Dedmon	.05	.02	554	Darnell Coles	.05	.02
499	Luis Aguayo	.05	.02	555	Phil Niekro	.20	.12
500	Reggie Jackson (A'S)	.25	.15	556	Mike Aldrete	.05	.02
501	Reggie Jackson (O's)	.25	.15	557	Pat Perry	.05	.02
502	Reggie Jackson (Yanks)	.25	.15	558	Juan Agosto	.05	.02
				559	Rob Murphy	.05	.02
503	Reggie Jackson (Angels)	.25	.15	560	Dennis Rasmussen	.05	.02
				561	Manny Lee	.05	.02
504	Reggie Jackson (A's)	.25	.15	562	Jeff Blauser (R)	.10	.06
505	Billy Hatcher	.05	.02	563	Bob Ojeda	.05	.02
506	Ed Lynch	.05	.02	564	Dave Dravecky	.05	.02
507	Willie Hernandez	.05	.02	565	Gene Garber	.05	.02
508	Jose DeLeon	.05	.02	566	Ron Roenicke	.05	.02
509	Joel Youngblood	.05	.02	567	Tommy Hinzo (R)	.08	.05
510	Bob Welch	.07	.04	568	Eric Nolte (R)	.05	.02
511	Steve Ontiveros	.05	.02	569	Ed Hearn	.05	.02
512	Randy Ready	.05	.02	570	Mark Davidson (R)	.07	.04
513	Juan Nieves	.05	.02	571	Jim Walewander (R)	.07	.04
514	Jeff Russell	.05	.02	572	Donnie Hill	.05	.02
515	Von Hayes	.05	.02	573	Jamie Moyer	.05	.02
516	Mark Gubicza	.07	.04	574	Ken Schrom	.05	.02
517	Ken Dayley	.05	.02	575	Nolan Ryan	.80	.50
518	Don Aase	.05	.02	576	Jim Acker	.05	.02
519	Rick Reuschel	.05	.02	577	Jamie Quirk	.05	.02
520	Mike Henneman (R)	.10	.06	578	Jay Aldrich (R)	.05	.02
512	Rick Aguilera	.05	.02	579	Claudell Washington	.05	.02
522	Jay Howell	.05	.02	580	Jeff Leonard	.05	.02
523	Ed Correa	.05	.02	581	Carmen Castillo	.05	.02
524	Manny Trillo	.05	.02	582	Daryl Boston	.05	.02
525	Kirk Gibson	.07	.04	583	Jeff DeWillis (R)	.07	.04
526	Wally Ritchie (R)	.07	.04	584	John Marzano (R)	.07	.04
527	Al Nipper	.05	.02	585	Bill Gullickson	.05	.02
528	Atlee Hammaker	.05	.02	586	Andy Allanson	.05	.02
529	Shawon Dunston	.08	.05	587	Lee Tunnell	.05	.02
530	Jim Clancy	.05	.02	588	Gene Nelson	.05	.02
531	Tom Paciorek	.05	.02	589	Dave LaPoint	.05	.02
532	Joel Skinner	.05	.02	590	Harold Baines	.08	.05
533	Scott Garrelts	.05	.02	591	Bill Buckner	.07	.04
534	Tom O'Malley	.05	.02	592	Carlton Fisk	.20	.12

593	Rick Manning	:05	.02
594	Doug Jones (R)	.20	.12
595	Tom Candiotti	.07	.04
596	Steve Lake	.05	.02
597	Jose Lind (R)	.20	.12
598	Ross Jones (R)	.05	.02
599	Gary Matthews	.05	.02
600	Fernando Valezuela	.07	.04
601	Dennis Martinez	.10	.06
602	Les Lancaster (R)	.08	.05
603	Ozzie Guillen	.08	.05
604	Tony Bernazard	.05	.02
605	Chili Davis	.07	.04
606	Roy Smalley	.05	.02
607	Ivan Calderon	.07	.04
608	Jay Tibbs	.05	.02
609	Guy Hoffman	.05	.02
610	Doyle Alexander	.05	.02
611	Mike Bielecki	.05	.02
612	Shawn Hillegas (R)	.12	.07
613	Keith Atherton	.05	.02
614	Eric Plunk	.05	.02
615	Sid Fernandez	.07	.04
616	Dennis Lamp	.05	.02
617	Dave Engle	.05	.02
618	Harry Spillman	.05	.02
619	Don Robinson	.05	.02
620	John Farrell (R)	.07	.04
621	Nelson Liriano (R)	.10	.06
622	Floyd Bannister	.05	.02
623	Randy Milligan (R)	.25	.15
624	Kevin Elster (R)	.08	.05
625	Jody Reed (R)	.15	.08
626	Shawn Abner (R)	.07	.04
627	Kirt Manwaring (R)	.08	.05
628	Pete Stanicek (R)	.07	.04
629	Rob Ducey (R)	.07	.04
630	Steve Kiefer (R)	.07	.04
631	Gary Thurman (R)	.08	.05
632	Darrel Akerfelds (R)	.07	.04
633	Dave Clark (R)	.07	.04
634	Roberto Kelly (R)	.90	.60
635	Keith Hughes (R)	.05	.02
636	John Davis (R)	.05	.02
637	Mike Devereaux (R)	.60	.35
638	Tom Glavine (R)	3.00	2.00
639	Keith Miller (R)	.15	.08
640	Chris Gwynn (R)	.08	.05
641	Tim Crews (R)	.08	.05
642	Mackey Sasser (R)	.08	.05
643	Vicente Palacios (R)	.08	.05
644	Kevin Romine (R)	.07	.05
645	Gregg Jefferies (R)	.80	.50
646	Jeff Treadway (R)	.10	.06
647	Ron Gant (R)	2.75	1.75
648	M. McGwire, M. Nokes	.25	.15
649	Eric Davis,	.10	.06

	Tim Raines		
650	J. Clark, D. Mattingly	.10	.06
651	T.Fernandez, C.Ripken,A.Trammell	.20	.12
652	Vince Coleman (HL)	.08	.05
653	Kirby Puckett (HL)	.25	.15
654	Benito Santiago (HL)	.07	.04
655	Juan Nieves (HL)	.07	.04
656	Steve Bedrosian (HL)	.07	.04
657	Mike Schmidt (HL)	.25	.15
658	Don Mattingly (HL)	.15	.08
659	Mark McGwire (HL)	.25	.15
660	Paul Molitor (HL)	.07	.04

1988 Score Traded

Score's first update set consists of 110-cards featuring rookie and traded players. The orange borders on the card fronts distinguish it from Score's regular set. Card numbers contain the letter "T". The set was underproduced and is considered scarce.

	MINT	NR/MT
Complete Set (110)	95.00	62.50
Commons	.15	.08

1T	Jack Clark	.20	.12
2T	Danny Jackson	.15	.08
3T	Brett Butler	.35	.20
4T	Kurt Stillwell	.15	.08
5T	Tom Burnansky	.20	.12
6T	Dennis Lamp	.15	.08
7T	Jose DeLeon	.15	.08
8T	Tom Herr	.15	.08
9T	Keith Moreland	.15	.08
10T	Kirk Gibson	.20	.12

11T Bud Black	.15	.08	69T Tommy Gregg (R)	.20	.12
12T Rafael Ramirez	.15	.08	70T Brady Anderson (R)	7.50	4.50
13T Luis Salazar	.15	.08	71T Jeff Montgomery	.20	.12
14T Goose Gossage	.20	.12	72T Darryl Hamilton (R)	1.25	.80
15T Bob Welch	.25	.15	73T Cecil Espy (R)	.20	.12
16T Vance Law	.15	.08	74T Greg Briley (R)	.30	.18
17T Ray Knight	.20	.12	75T Joey Meyer (R)	.20	.12
18T Dan Quisenberry	.15	.08	76T Mike Macfarlane (R)	.80	.50
19T Don Slaught	.15	.08	77T Oswald Peraza (R)	.20	.12
20T Lee Smith	.80	.50	78T Jack Armstrong (R)	.50	.30
21T Rick Cerone	.15	.08	79T Don Heinkel (R)	.15	.08
22T Pat Tabler	.15	.08	80T Mark Grace (R)	18.00	12.00
23T Larry McWilliams	.15	.08	81T Steve Curry (R)	.20	.12
24T Rick Horton	.15	.08	82T Damon Berryhill (R)	.25	.15
25T Graig Nettles	.20	.12	83T Steve Ellsworth (R)	.15	.08
26T Dan Petry	.15	.08	84T Pete Smith (R)	1.00	.70
27T Joe Rijo	.30	.18	85T Jack McDowell (R)	14.00	8.50
28T Chili Davis	.20	.12	86T Rob Dibble (R)	3.00	2.00
29T Dicki Thon	.15	.08	87T Brian Harvey (R)	2.00	1.25
30T Mackey Sasser	.20	.12	88T John Dopson (R)	.20	.12
31T Mickey Tettleton	.30	.18	89T Dave Gallagher (R)	.20	.12
32T Rick Dempsey	.15	.08	90T Todd Stottlemyre (R)	2.00	1.25
33T Ron Hassey	.15	.08	91T Mike Schooler (R)	.35	.20
34T Phil Bradley	.15	.08	92T Don Gordon (R)	.15	.08
35T Jay Howell	.15	.08	93T Sil Campusano (R)	.25	.15
36T Bill Buckner	.20	.12	94T Jeff Pico (R)	.15	.08
37T Alfredo Griffin	.15	.08	95T Jay Buhner (R)	2.50	1.50
38T Gary Pettis	.15	.08	96T Nelson Santovenia (R)	.20	.12
39T Calvin Schiraldi	.15	.08	97T Al Leiter (R)	.20	.12
40T John Candelaria	.15	.08	98T Luis Alicea (R)	.25	.15
41T Joe Orsulak	.20	.12	99T Pat Borders (R)	1.00	.70
42T Willie Upshaw	.15	.08	100T Chris Sabo (R)	5.00	3.00
43T Herm Winningham	.15	.08	101T Tim Becher (R)	.40	.25
44T Ron Kittle	.15	.08	102T Walt Weiss (R)	.50	.30
45T Bob Dernier	.15	.08	103T Craig Biggio (R)	5.00	3.00
46T Steve Balboni	.15	.08	104T Don August (R)	.15	.08
47T Steve Shields	.15	.08	105T Roberto Alomar (R)	65.00	40.00
48T Henry Cotto	.15	.08	106T Todd Burns (R)	.40	.25
49T Dave Henderson	.20	.12	107T John Costello (R)	.20	.12
50T Dave Parker	.25	.15	108T Melido Perez (R)	2.00	1.25
51T Mike Young	.15	.08	109T Darrin Jackson (R)	1.25	.80
52T Mark Salas	.15	.08	110T Orestes Destrade (R)	.20	.12
53T Mike Davis	.15	.08			
54T Rafael Santana	.15	.08			
55T Don Baylor	.20	.12			
56T Dan Pasqua	.15	.08			
57T Ernest Riles	.15	.08			
58T Glenn Hubbard	.15	.08			
59T Mike Smithson	.15	.08			
60T Richard Dotson	.15	.08			
61T Jerry Reuss	.15	.08			
62T Mike Jackson	.15	.08			
63T Floyd Bannister	.15	.08			
64T Jesse Orosco	.15	.08			
65T Larry Parrish	.15	.08			
66T Jeff Bittiger	.15	.08			
67T Ray Hayward	.15	.08			
68T Ricky Jordan (R)	.35	.20			

1989 Score

Score's second set consists of 660-cards with six different border colors on the card fronts framed in white. Card backs contain full-color head shots of the players. The standard-size cards measure 2-1/2' by 3-1/2".

		MINT	NR/MT
Complete Set (660)		18.00	12.00
Commons		.05	.02
1	Jose Canseco	.35	.20
2	Andre Dawson	.15	.08
3	Mark McGwire	.30	.18
4	Benny Santiago	.07	.04
5	Rick Reuschel	.05	.02
6	Fred McGriff	.25	.15
7	Kal Daniels	.05	.02
8	Gary Gaetti	.05	.02
9	Ellis Burks	.08	.05
10	Darryl Strawberry	.25	.15
11	Julio Franco	.12	.07
12	Lloyd Moseby	.05	.02
13	Jeff Pico	.12	.07
14	Johnny Ray	.05	.02
15	Cal Ripken, Jr.	.50	.30
16	Dick Schofield	.05	.02
17	Mel Hall	.07	.04
18	Bill Ripken	.05	.02
19	Brook Jacoby	.05	.02
20	Kirby Puckett	.35	.20
21	Bill Doran	.05	.02
22	Pete O'Brien	.05	.02
23	Matt Nokes	.05	.02
24	Brian Fisher	.05	.02
25	Jack Clark	.07	.04
26	Gary Pettis	.05	.02
27	Dave Valle	.05	.02
28	Willie Wilson	.05	.02
29	Curt Young	.05	.02
30	Dale Murphy	.10	.06
31	Barry Larkin	.15	.08
32	Dave Stewart	.07	.04
33	Mike LaValliere	.05	.02
34	Glen Hubbard	.05	.02
35	Ryne Sandberg	.40	.25
36	Tony Pena	.05	.02
37	Greg Walker	.05	.02
38	Von Hayes	.05	.02
39	Kevin Mitchell	.10	.06
40	Tim Raines	.08	.05
41	Keith Hernandez	.05	.02
42	Keith Moreland	.05	.02
43	Ruben Sierra	.35	.20
44	Chet Lemon	.05	.02
45	Willie Randolph	.05	.02
46	Andy Allanson	.05	.02
47	Candy Maldonado	.05	.02
48	Sid Bream	.05	.02
49	Denny Walling	.05	.02
50	Dave Winfield	.15	.08
51	Alvin Davis	.05	.02
52	Cory Snyder	.05	.02
53	Hubie Brooks	.05	.02
54	Chili Davis	.05	.02
55	Kevin Seitzer	.07	.04
56	Jose Uribe	.05	.02
57	Tony Fernandez	.05	.02
58	Tim Teufel	.05	.02
59	Oddibe McDowell	.05	.02
60	Les Lancaster	.05	.02
61	Billy Hatcher	.05	.02
62	Dan Gladden	.05	.02
63	Marty Barrett	.05	.02
64	Nick Esasky	.05	.02
65	Wally Joyner	.10	.06
66	Mike Greenwell	.08	.05
67	Ken Williams	.05	.02
68	Bob Horner	.07	.04
69	Steve Sax	.08	.05
70	Rickey Henderson	.25	.12
71	Mitch Webster	.05	.02
72	Rob Deer	.05	.02
73	Jim Presley	.05	.02
74	Albert Hall	.05	.02
75a	George Brett (Er)	.80	.50
75b	George Brett (Cor)	.35	.20
76	Brian Downing	.05	.02
77	Dave Martinez	.05	.02
78	Scott Fletcher	.05	.02
79	Phil Bradley	.05	.02
80	Ozzie Smith	.12	.07
81	Larry Sheets	.05	.02
82	Mike Aldrete	.05	.02
83	Darnell Coles	.05	.02
84	Len Dykstra	.05	.02
85	Jim Rice	.07	.04
86	Jeff Treadway	.05	.02
87	Jose Lind	.05	.02

88 Willie McGee	.07	.04
89 Mickey Brantley	.05	.02
90 Tony Gwynn	.25	.15
91 R.J. Reynolds	.05	.02
92 Milt Thompson	.05	.02
93 Kevin McReynolds	.07	.04
94 Eddie Murray	.15	.08
95 Lance Parrish	.05	.02
96 Ron Kittle	.05	.02
97 Gerald Young	.05	.02
98 Ernie Whitt	.05	.02
99 Jeff Reed	.05	.02
100 Don Mattingly	.20	.12
101 Gerald Perry	.50	.02
102 Vance Law	.05	.02
103 John Shelby	.05	.02
104 Chris Sabo	.25	.15
105 Danny Tartabull	.15	.08
106 Glenn Wilson	.05	.02
107 Mark Davidson	.05	.02
108 Dave Parker	.07	.04
109 Eric Davis	.12	.07
110 Alan Trammell	.10	.06
111 Ozzie Virgil	.05	.02
112 Frank Tanana	.05	.02
113 Rafael Ramirez	.05	.02
114 Dennis Martinez	.08	.05
115 Jose DeLeon	.05	.02
116 Bob Ojeda	.05	.02
117 Doug Drabek	.10	.06
118 Andy Hawkins	.05	.02
119 Greg Maddux (R)	.20	.12
120 Cecil Fielder (Er)	.30	.18
121 Mike Scioscia	.05	.02
122 Dan Petry	.05	.02
123 Terry Kennedy	.05	.02
124 Kelly Downs	.05	.02
125 Greg Gross (Er)	.05	.02
126 Fred Lynn	.07	.04
127 Barry Bonds	.35	.20
128 Harold Baines	.07	.04
129 Doyle Alexander	.05	.02
130 Kevin Elster	.05	.02
131 Mike Heath	.05	.02
132 Teddy Higuera	.05	.02
133 Charlie Leibrandt	.05	.02
134 Tim Laudner	.05	.02
135aRay Knight (Er)	.50	.30
135bRay Knight (Cor)	.08	.05
136 Howard Johnson	.10	.06
137 Terry Pendleton	.15	.08
138 Andy McGaffigan	.05	.02
139 Ken Oberkfell	.05	.02
140 Butch Wynegar	.05	.02
141 Rob Murphy	.05	.02
142 Rich Renteria (R)	.07	.04
143 Jose Guzman	.05	.02
144 Andres Galarraga	.05	.02
145 Rick Horton	.05	.02
146 Frank DiPino	.05	.02
147 Glenn Braggs	.05	.02
148 John Kruk	.08	.05
149 Mike Schmidt	.40	.25
150 Lee Smith	.12	.07
151 Robin Yount	.30	.18
152 Mark Eichhorn	.05	.02
153 DeWayne Buice	.05	.02
154 B.J. Surhoff	.05	.02
155 Vince Coleman	.07	.04
156 Tony Phillips	.05	.02
157 Willie Fraser	.05	.02
158 Lance McCullers	.05	.02
159 Greg Gagne	.05	.02
160 Jesse Barfield	.05	.02
161 Mark Langston	.08	.05
162 Kurt Sttillwell	.05	.02
163 Dion James	.05	.02
164 Glenn Davis	.07	.04
165 Walt Weiss	.07	.04
166 Dave Concepcion	.07	.04
167 Alfredo Griffin	.05	.02
168 Don Heinkel	.05	.02
169 Luis Riveral (R)	.05	.02
170 Shane Rawley	.05	.02
171 Darrell Evans	.05	.02
172 Robby Thompson	.05	.02
173 Jody Davis	.05	.02
174 Andy Van Slyke	.12	.07
175 Wade Boggs (Er)	.20	.12
176 Garry Templeton	.05	.02
177 Gary Redus	.05	.02
178 Craig Lefferts	.05	.02
179 Carney Lansford	.05	.02
180 Ron Darling	.05	.02
181 Kirk McCaskill	.05	.02
182 Tony Armas	.05	.02
183 Steve Farr	.05	.02
184 Tom Brunansky	.05	.02
185 Bryan Harvey	.20	.12
186 Mike Marshall	.05	.02
187 Bo Diaz	.05	.02
188 Willie Upshaw	.05	.02
189 Mike Pagliarulo	.05	.02
190 Mike Krukow	.05	.02
191 Tommy Herr	.05	.02
192 Jim Pankovits	.05	.02
193 Dwight Evans	.05	.02
194 Kelly Gruber	.07	.04
195 Bobby Bonilla	.15	.07
196 Wallace Johnson	.05	.02
197 Dave Sieb	.05	.02
198 Pat Borders	.12	.07
199 Rafael Palmeiro	.15	.07
200 Doc Gooden	.12	.07
201 Pete Incaviglia	.05	.02
202 Chris James	.05	.02

203 Marvell Wynne	.05	.02
204 Pat Sheridan	.05	.02
205 Don Baylor	.05	.02
206 Paul O'Neill	.08	.05
207 Pete Smith	.10	.06
208 Mark McLemore	.05	.02
209 Henry Cotto	.05	.02
210 Kirk Gibson	.07	.04
211 Claudell Washington	.05	.02
212 Randy Bush	.05	.02
213 Joe Carter	.15	.07
214 Bill Buckner	.05	.02
215 Bert Blyleven	.08	.05
216 Brett Butler	.07	.04
217 Lee Mazzilli	.05	.02
218 Spike Owen	.05	.02
219 Bill Swift	.07	.04
220 Tim Wallach	.07	.04
221 David Cone	.12	.07
222 Don Carman	.05	.02
223 Rich Gossage	.07	.04
224 Bob walk	.05	.02
225 Dave Righetti	.05	.02
226 Kevin Bass	.05	.02
227 Kevin Gross	.05	.02
228 Tim Burke	.05	.02
229 Rick Mahler	.05	.02
230 Lou Whitaker	.05	.02
231 Luis Alicea	.07	.04
232 Roberto Alomar	1.00	.70
233 Bob Boone	.07	.04
234 Dickie Thon	.05	.02
235 Shawon Dunston	.07	.04
236 Pete Stanicek	.05	.02
237 Craig Biggio	.30	.18
238 Dennis Boyd	.05	.02
239 Tom Candiotti	.05	.02
240 Gary Carter	.10	.06
241 Mike Stanley	.05	.02
242 Ken Phelps	.05	.02
243 Chris Bosio	.07	.04
244 Les Straker	.05	.02
245 Dave Smith	.05	.02
246 John Candelaria	.05	.02
247 Joe Orsulak	.05	.02
248 Storm Davis	.05	.02
249 Floyd Bannister	.05	.02
250 Jack Morris	.12	.07
251 Bret Saberhagen	.10	.06
252 Tom Niedenfuer	.05	.02
253 Neal Heaton	.05	.02
254 Eric Show	.05	.02
255 Juan Samuel	.05	.02
256 Dale Sveum	.05	.02
257 Jim Gott	.05	.02
258 Scott Garrelts	.05	.02
259 Larry McWilliams	.05	.02
260 Steve Bedrosian	.05	.02
261 Jack Howell	.05	.02
262 Jay Tibbs	.05	.02
263 Jamie Moyer	.05	.02
264 Doug Sisk	.05	.02
265 Todd Worrell	.07	.04
266 John Farrell	.05	.02
267 Dave Collins	.05	.02
268 Sid Fernandez	.05	.02
276 Dennis Eckersley	.12	.07
277 Graig Nettles	.05	.02
278 Rich Dotson	.05	.02
279 Larry Herndon	.05	.02
280 Gene Larkin	.05	.02
281 Roger McDowell	.05	.02
282 Greg Swindell	.07	.04
283 Juan Agosto	.05	.02
284 Jeff Robinson	.05	.02
285 Mike Dunne	.05	.02
286 Greg Mathews	.05	.02
287 Kent Tekulve	.05	.02
288 Jerry Mumphrey	.05	.02
289 Jack McDowell	.50	.30
290 Frank Viola	.08	.05
291 Mark Gubicza	.07	.04
292 Dave Schmidt	.05	.02
293 Mike Henneman	.05	.02
294 Jimmy Jones	.05	.02
295 Charlie Hough	.05	.02
296 Rafael Santana	.05	.02
297 Chris Speier	.05	.02
298 Mike Witt	.05	.02
299 Pascual Perez	.05	.02
300 Nolan Ryan	.70	.40
301 Mitch Williams	.05	.02
302 Mookie Wilson	.05	.02
303 Mackey Sasser	.05	.02
304 John Cerutti	.05	.02
305 Jeff Reardon	.10	.06
306 Randy Myers	.05	.02
308 Bob Welch	.07	.04
309 Jeff Robinson	.05	.02
310 Harold Reynolds	.05	.02
311 Jim Walewander	.05	.02
312 Dave Magadan	.05	.02
313 Jim Gantner	.05	.02
314 Walt Terrell	.05	.02
315 Wally Backman	.05	.02
316 Luis Salazar	.05	.02
317 Rick Rhoden	.05	.02
318 Tom Henke	.05	.02
319 Mike Macfarlane	.15	.08
320 Dan Plesac	.05	.02
321 Calvin Schiraldi	.05	.02
322 Stan Javier	.05	.02
323 Devon White	.05	.02
324 Scott Bradley	.05	.02
325 Bruce Hurst	.07	.04
326 Manny Lee	.05	.02

327 Rick Aguilera	.05	.02
328 Bruce Ruffin	.05	.02
329 Ed Whitson	.05	.02
330 Bo Jackson	.30	.18
331 Ivan Calderon	.05	.02
332 Mickey Hatcher	.05	.02
333 Barry Jones	.05	.02
334 Ron Hassey	.05	.02
335 Bill Wegman	.05	.02
336 Damon Berryhill	.05	.02
337 Steve Ontiveros	.05	.02
338 Dan Pasqua	.05	.02
339 Bill Pecota	.05	.02
340 Greg Cadaret	.05	.02
341 Scott Bankhead	.05	.02
342 Ron Guidry	.08	.05
343 Danny Heep	.05	.02
344 Bob Brower	.05	.02
345 Rich Gedman	.05	.02
346 Nelson Santovenia	.07	.04
347 George Bell	.10	.06
348 Ted Power	.05	.02
349 Mark Grant	.05	.02
350a Roger Clemens (Er)	3.50	2.00
350b Roger Clemens (Cor)	.50	.30
351 Bill Long	.05	.02
352 Jay Bell (R)	.15	.08
353 Steve Balboni	.05	.02
354 Bob Kipper	.05	.02
355 Steve Jeltz	.05	.02
356 Jesse Orosco	.05	.02
357 Bob Dernier	.05	.02
358 Mickey Tettleton	.05	.02
359 Duane Ward (R)	.08	.05
360 Darrin Jackson	.08	.05
361 Rey Quinones	.05	.02
362 Mark Grace	.40	.25
363 Steve Lake	.05	.05
364 Pat Perry	.05	.02
365 Terry Steinbach	.05	.02
366 Alan Ashby	.05	.02
367 Jeff Montgomery	.07	.04
368 Steve Buechele	.05	.02
369 Chris Brown	.05	.02
370 Orel Hershiser	.08	.05
371 Todd Benzinger	.05	.02
372 Ron Gant	.50	.30
373 Paul Assenmacher (R)	.10	.06
374 Joey Meyer	.05	.02
375 Neil Allen	.05	.02
376 Mike Davis	.05	.02
377 Jeff Parrett (R)	.07	.04
378 Jay Howell	.05	.02
379 Rafael Belliard	.05	.02
380 Luis Polonia	.08	.05
381 Keith Atherton	.05	.02
382 Kent Hrbek	.07	.04
383 Bob Stanley	.05	.02
384 Dave LaPoint	.05	.02
385 Rance Mulliniks	.05	.02
386 Melido Perez	.10	.06
387 Doug Jones	.05	.02
388 Steve Lyons	.05	.02
389 Alejandro Pena	.05	.02
390 Frank White	.05	.02
391 Pat Tabier	.05	.02
392 Eric Plunk (R)	.08	.05
393 Mike Maddux (R)	.05	.02
394 Allan Anderson (R)	.07	.04
395 Bob Brenly	.05	.02
396 Rick Cerone	.05	.02
397 Scott Terry (R)	.07	.04
398 Mike Jackson	.05	.02
399 Bobby Thigpen	.05	.02
400 Don Sutton	.10	.06
401 Cecil Espey	.05	.02
402 Junio Ortiz	.05	.02
403 Mike Smithson	.05	.02
404 Bud Black	.05	.02
405 Tom Foley	.05	.02
406 Andres Thomas	.05	.02
407 Rick Sutcliffe	.05	.02
408 Brian Harper	.05	.02
409 John Smiley	.10	.06
410 Juan Nieves	.05	.02
411 Shawn Abner	.05	.02
412 Wes Gardner (R)	.08	.05
413 Darren Daulton	.12	.07
414 Juan Berenguer	.05	.02
415 Charles Hudson	.05	.02
416 Rick Honeycutt	.05	.02
417 Greg Booker	.05	.02
418 Tim Belcher	.07	.04
419 Don August	.05	.02
420 Dale Mohorcic	.05	.02
421 Steve Lombardozzi	.05	.02
422 Atlee Hammaker	.05	.02
423 Jerry Don Gleaton	.05	.02
424 Scott Bailes (R)	.10	.06
425 Bruce Sutter	.08	.05
426 Randy Ready	.05	.02
427 Gerry Reed	.05	.02
428 Bryn Smith	.05	.02
429 Tim Leary	.05	.02
430 Mark Clear	.05	.02
431 Terry Leach	.05	.02
432 John Moses	.05	.02
433 Ozzie Guillen	.07	.04
434 Gene Nelson	.05	.02
435 Gary Ward	.05	.02
436 Luis Aguayo	.05	.02
437 Fernando Valenzuela	.07	.04
438 Jeff Russell	.05	.02
439 Cecilio Guante	.05	.02
440 Don Robinson	.05	.02
441 Rick Anderson (R)	.07	.04

442 Tom Glavine	1.00	.70
443 Daryl Boston	.05	.02
444 Joe Price	.05	.02
445 Stewart Cliburn	.05	.02
446 Manny Trillo	.05	.02
447 Joel Skinner	.05	.02
448 Charlie Puleo	.05	.02
449 Carlton Fisk	.15	.08
450 Will Clark	.50	.30
451 Otis Nixon	.05	.02
452 Rick Schu	.05	.02
453 Todd Stottlemyre	.12	.07
454 Tim Birtsas	.05	.02
455 Dave Gallagher	.07	.04
456 Barry Lyons	.05	.02
457 Fred Manrique	.05	.02
458 Ernest Riles	.05	.02
459 Doug Jennings (R)	.08	.05
460 Joe Magrane	.07	.04
461 Jamie Quirk	.05	.02
462 Jack Armstrong	.10	.06
463 Bobby Witt	.07	.04
464 Keith Miller	.05	.02
465 Todd Burns	.05	.02
466 John Dopson (R)	.12	.07
467 Rich Yett	.05	.02
468 Craig Reynolds	.05	.02
469 Dave Bergman	.05	.02
470 Rex Hudler	.07	.04
471 Eric King	.05	.02
472 Joaquin Andujar	.05	.02
473 Sil Campusano	.08	.05
474 Terry Mulholland (R)	.12	.07
475 Mike Flanagan	.05	.02
476 Greg Harris	.05	.02
477 Tommy John	.07	.04
478 Dave Anderson	.05	.02
479 Fred Toliver	.05	.02
480 Jimmy Key	.05	.02
481 Donell Nixon	.05	.02
482 Mark Portugal (R)	.07	.04
483 Tom Pagnozzi	.08	.05
484 Jeff Kunkel	.05	.02
485 Frank Williams	.05	.02
486 Jody Reed	.07	.04
487 Roberto Kelly	.30	.18
488 Shawn Hillegas	.05	.02
489 Jerry Reuss	.05	.02
490 Mark Davis	.05	.02
491 Jeff Sellers	.05	.02
492 Zane Smith	.07	.04
493 Al Newman	.05	.02
494 Mike Young	.05	.02
495 Larry Parrish	.05	.02
496 Herm Winningham	.05	.02
497 Carmen Castillo	.05	.02
498 Joe Hesketh	.05	.02
499 Darrell Miller	.05	.02
500 Mike LaCoss	.05	.02
501 Charlie Lea	.05	.02
502 Bruce Benedict	.05	.02
503 Chuck Finley (R)	.25	.15
504 Brad Wellman (R)	.07	.04
505 Tim Crews	.05	.02
506 Ken Gerhart	.05	.02
507 Brian Holton (Er)	.07	.04
508 Dennis Lamp	.05	.02
509 Bobby Meacham (Er)	.07	.04
510 Tracy Jones	.05	.02
511 Mike Fitzgerald	.05	.02
512 Jeff Bittiger	.05	.02
513 Tim Flannery	.05	.02
514 Ray Hayward (R	.07	.04
515 Dave Leiper	.05	.02
516 Rod Scurry	.05	.02
517 Carmelo Martinez	.05	.02
518 Curtis Wilkerson	.05	.02
519 Stan Jefferson	.05	.02
520 Dan Quisenberry	.05	.02
521 Lloyd McClendon (R)	.07	.04
522 Steve Trout	.05	.02
523 Larry Andersen	.05	.02
524 Don Aase	.05	.02
525 Bob Forsch	.05	.02
526 Geno Petralli	.05	.02
527 Angel Salazar	.05	.02
529 Jose Oquendo	.05	.02
530 Jay Buhner	.15	.08
531 Tom Bolton (R)	.08	.05
532 Al Nipper	.05	.02
533 Dave Henderson	.05	.02
534 John Costello (R)	.07	.04
535 Donnie Moore	.05	.02
536 Mike Laga	.05	.02
537 Mike Gallego	.05	.02
538 Jim Clancy	.05	.02
539 Joel Youngblood	.05	.02
540 Rick Leach	.05	.02
541 Kevin Romine	.05	.02
542 Mark Salas	.05	.02
543 Greg Minton	.05	.02
544 Dave Palmer	.05	.02
545 Dwayne Murphy	.05	.02
546 Jim Deshaies	.05	.02
547 Don Gordon	.05	.02
548 Ricky Jordan	.08	.05
549 Mike Boddicker	.05	.02
550 Mike Scott	.05	.02
551 Jeff Ballard	.07	.04
552a Jose Rijo (Uniform #27 on card back)	.40	.25
552b Jose Rijo (Uniform #24 on card back)	.12	.07
553 Danny Darwin	.05	.02

554 Tom Browning	.07	.04
555 Danny Jackson	.07	.04
556 Rick Dempsey	.05	.02
557 Jeffrey Leonard	.05	.02
558 Jeff Musselman	.05	.02
559 Ron Robinson	.05	.02
560 John Tudor	.05	.02
561 Don Slaught	.05	.02
562 Dennis Rasmussen	.05	.02
563 Brady Anderson	.75	.45
564 Pedro Guerrero	.05	.02
565 Paul Molitor	.10	.06
566 Terry Clark	.07	.04
567 Terry Puhl	.05	.02
568 Mike Campbell	.05	.02
569 Paul Mirabella	.05	.02
570 Jeff Hamilton (R)	.07	.04
571 Oswald Peraza	.07	.04
572 Bob McClure	.05	.02
573 Jose Bautista (R)	.08	.05
574 Alex Trevino	.05	.02
575 John Franco	.05	.02
576 Mark Parent	.07	.04
577 Nelson Liriano	.05	.02
578 Steve Shields	.05	.02
579 Odell Jones	.05	.02
580 Al Leiter	.05	.02
581 Dave Stapleton (R)	.08	.05
582 1988 World Series (J.	.12	.07
Canseco, O. Hershiser,		
K. Gibons. D. Stewart)		
583 Donnie Hill	.05	.02
584 Chuck Jackson	.05	.02
585 Rene Gonzales	.05	.02
586 Tracy Woodson (R)	.07	.04
587 Jim Adduci (R)	.07	.04
588 Mario Soto	.05	.02
589 Jeff Blauser	.05	.02
590 Jim Traber	.05	.02
591 Jon Perlman (R)	.05	.02
592 Mark Williamson	.05	.02
593 Dave Meads	.05	.02
594 Jim Eisenreich	.05	.02
595 Paul Gibson	.05	.02
596 Mike Birkbeck	.05	.02
597 Terry Francona	.05	.02
598 Paul Zuvella (R)	.07	.04
599 Franklin Stubbs	.05	.02
600 Gregg Jefferies	.30	.18
601 John Cangelosi	.05	.02
602 Mike Sharperson (R)	.08	.05
603 Mike Diaz	.05	.02
604 Gary Varsho (R)	.07	.04
605 Terry Blocker (R)	.07	.04
606 Charlie O'Brien (R)	.07	.04
607 Jim Eppard (R)	.07	.04
608 John Davis	.05	.02
609 Ken Griffey, Sr.	.07	.04

610 Buddy Bell	.05	.02
611 Ted Simmons	.07	.04
612 Matt Williams	.20	.12
613 Danny Cox	.05	.02
614 Al Pedrique	.05	.02
615 Ron Oester	.05	.02
616 John Smoltz (R)	.80	.50
617 Bob Melvin	.05	.02
618 Rob Dibble	.20	.12
619 Kirt Manwaring	.05	.02
620 Felix Fermin (R)	.07	.04
621 Doug Descenzo (R)	.10	.06
622 Bill Brennan (R)	.07	.04
623 Carlos Quintana (R)	.15	.08
624 Mike Harkey (R)	.12	.07
625 Gary Sheffield (R)	3.00	2.00
626 Tom Prince (R)	.07	.04
627 Steve Searcy (R)	.07	.04
628 Charlie Hayes (R)	.15	.08
629 Felix Jose (R)	.60	.35
630 Sandy Alomar Jr. (R)	.25	.15
631 Derek Lilliquist (R)	.10	.06
632 Geronimo Berroa (R)	.07	.04
633 Luis Medina (R)	.07	.04
634 Tom Gordon (R)	.15	.08
635 Ramon Martinez (R)	.50	.30
636 Craig Worthington (R)	.07	.04
637 Edgar Martinez (R)	.70	.40
638 Chad Kreuter (R)	.10	.06
639 Ron Jones (R)	.07	.04
640 Van Snyder (R)	.07	.04
641 Lance Blankenship (R)	.10	.06
642 Dwight Smith (R)	.10	.06
643 Cameron Drew (R)	.07	.04
644 Jerald Clark (R)	.10	.06
645 Randy Johnson (R)	.40	.25
646 Norm Charlton (R)	.15	.08
647 Todd Frohwirth (R)	.10	.06
648 Luis de los Santos (R)	.07	.04
649 Tim Jones (R)	.07	.04
650 Dave West (R)	.12	.07
651 Bob Milacki (R)	.08	.05
652 Wrigley Field (Night)	.05	.02
653 Orel Hershiser (HL)	.08	.05
654a Wade Boggs	2.50	1.50
(HL) (Er)		
654b Wade Boggs	.10	.06
(HL) (Cor)		
655 Jose Canseco (HL)	.25	.15
656 Doug Jones (HL)	.05	.02
657 Rickey Henderson	.12	.07
(HL)		
658 Tom Browning (HL)	.07	.04
659 Mike Greenwell (HL)	.07	.04
660 Red Sox Steak (HL)	.07	.04

1989 Score Traded

Score's second straight update set is similar in design to their regular edition. Card fronts feature blue-green borders, Vertical card backs contain full-color head shots of the players. Cards measure 2-1/2" by 3-1/2" and the set contains rookies plus players traded during the regular 1989 season.

		MINT	NR/MT
	Complete Set (110)	12.00	8.00
	Commons	.05	.02
1T	Rafael Palmeiro	.20	.12
2T	Nolan Ryan	1.75	1.00
3T	Jack Clark	.08	.05
4T	Dave LaPoint	.05	.02
5T	Mike Moore	.05	.02
6T	Pete O'Brien	.05	.02
7T	Jeffrey Leonard	.05	.02
8T	Rob Murphy	.05	.02
9T	Tom Herr	.05	.02
10T	Claudell Washington	.05	.02
11T	Mike Pagliarulo	.05	.02
12T	Steve Lake	.05	.02
13T	Spike Owen	.05	.02
14T	Andy Hawkins	.05	.02
15T	Todd Benzinger	.05	.02
16T	Mookie Wilson	.05	.02
17T	Bert Blyleven	.12	.07
18T	Jeff Treadway	.05	.02
19T	Bruce Hurst	.10	.06
20T	Steve Sax	.12	.07
21T	Juan Samuel	.05	.02
22T	Jesse Barfield	.07	.04
23T	Carmelo Castillo	.05	.02
24T	Terry Leach	.05	.02
25T	Mark Langston	.12	.07
26T	Eric King	.07	.04
27T	Steve Balboni	.05	.02
28T	Len Dykstra	.10	.06
29T	Keith Moreland	.05	.02
30T	Terry Kennedy	.05	.02
31T	Eddie Murray	.15	.08
32T	Mitch Williams	.07	.04
33T	Jeff Parrett	.05	.02
34T	Wally Backman	.05	.02
35T	Julio Franco	.10	.06
36T	Lance Parrish	.07	.04
37T	Nick Esasky	.05	.02
38T	Luis Polonia	.07	.04
39T	Kevin Gross	.05	.02
40T	John Dopson	.05	.02
41T	Willie Randolph	.05	.02
42T	Jim Clancy	.05	.02
43T	Tracy Jones	.05	.02
44T	Phil Bradley	.05	.02
45T	Mil Thompson	.05	.02
46T	Chris James	.05	.02
47T	Scott Fletcher	.05	.02
48T	Kal Daniels	.07	.04
49T	Steve Bedrosian	.05	.02
50T	Rickey Henderson	.35	.20
51T	Dion James	.05	.02
52T	Tim Leary	.05	.02
53T	Roger McDowell	.05	.02
54T	Mel Hall	.08	.05
55T	Dickie Thon	.05	.02
56T	Zane Smith	.07	.04
57T	Danny Heep	.05	.02
58T	Bob McClure	.05	.02
59T	Brian Holton	.05	.02
60T	Randy Ready	.05	.02
61T	Bob Melvin	.05	.02
62T	Harold Baines	.08	.05
63T	Lance McCullers	.05	.02
64T	Jody Davis	.05	.02
65T	Darrell Evans	.07	.04
66T	Joel Youngblood	.05	.02
67T	Frank Viola	.08	.05
68T	Mike Aldrete	.05	.02
69T	Greg Cadaret	.07	.04
70T	John Kruk	.12	.07
71T	Pat Sheridan	.05	.02
72T	Oddibe McDowell	.05	.02
73T	Tom Brookens	.05	.02
74T	Bob Boone	.10	.06
75T	Walt Terrell	.05	.02
76T	Joel Skinner	.05	.02
77T	Randy Johnson	.15	.08
78T	Felix Fermin	.05	.02
79T	Rick Mahler	.05	.02
80T	Rich Dotson	.05	.02
81T	Cris Carpenter (R)	.12	.07
82T	Bill Spiers (R)	.10	.06
83T	Junior Felix (R)	.12	.07
84T	Joe Girardi (R)	.08	.05
85T	Jerome Walton (R)	.10	.06
86T	Greg Litton (R)	.08	.05
87T	Greg Harris (R)	.12	.07

88T	Jim Abbott (R)	1.50	.90
89T	Kevin Brown (R)	.30	.18
90T	John Wetteland (R)	.40	.25
91T	Gary Wayne (R)	.08	.05
92T	Rich Monteleone (R)	.07	.04
93T	Bob Geren (R)	.10	.06
94T	Clay Parker (R)	.08	.05
95T	Steve Finley (R)	.30	.18
96T	Gregg Olson (R)	.40	.25
97T	Ken Patterson (R)	.08	.05
98T	Ken Hill (R)	.50	.30
99T	Scott Scudder (R)	.15	.08
100T	Ken Griffey, Jr. (R)	6.00	4.00
101T	Jeff Brantley (R)	.10	.06
102T	Donn Pall (R)	.10	.06
103T	Carlos Martinez (R)	.12	.07
104T	Joe Oliver (R)	.12	.07
105T	Omar Vizquel (R)	.10	.06
106T	Joey Belle (R)	2.50	1.50
107T	Kenny Rogers (R)	.10	.06
108T	Mark Carreon (R)	.10	.06
109T	Rolando Roomes (R)	.08	.05
110T	Pete Harnisch (R)	.30	.18

1990 Score

Score increased the size of their 1990 set to 704-cards and introduced several new subsets including First Round Draft Picks and the Dream Team (DT). Card fronts feature four different border colors, red, white, green and blue. Card backs contain a full-color head shot. Cards measure 2-1/2' by 3-1/2". 10 bonus Dream Team cards were inserted in Score's Factory sets. These cards carry the BC prefix at the end of the checklist.

		MINT	NR/MT
Complete Set (704)		22.00	15.00
Commons:		.05	.02
1	Don Mattingly	.20	.12
2	Cal Ripken, Jr.	.35	.20
3	Dwight Evans	.07	.04
4	Barry Bonds	.30	.18
5	Kevin McReynolds	.05	.02
6	Ozzie Guillen	.05	.02
7	Terry Kennedy	.05	.02
8	Bryan Harvey	.08	.05
9	Alan Trammell	.08	.05
10	Cory Snyder	.05	.02
11	Jody Reed	.05	.02
12	Roberto Alomar	.50	.30
13	Pedro Guerrero	.05	.02
14	Gary Redus	.05	.02
15	Marty Barrett	.05	.02
16	Ricky Jordan	.07	.04
17	Joe Magrane	.07	.04
18	Sid Fernandez	.05	.02
19	Rich Dotson	.05	.02
20	Jack Clark	.05	.02
21	Bob Walk	.05	.02
22	Ron Karkovice	.05	.02
23	Lenny Harris	.08	.05
24	Phil Bradley	.05	.02
25	Andres Galarraga	.05	.02
26	Brian Downing	.05	.02
27	Dave Martinez	.05	.02
28	Eric King	.05	.02
29	Barry Lyons	.05	.02
30	Dave Schmidt	.05	.02
31	Mike Boddicker	.05	.02
32	Tom Foley	.05	.02
33	Brady Anderson	.15	.07
34	Jim Presley	.05	.02
35	Lance Parrish	.05	.02
36	Von Hayes	.05	.02
37	Lee Smith	.07	.04
38	Herm Winningham	.05	.02
39	Alejandro Pena	.05	.02
40	Mike Scott	.05	.02
41	Joe Orsulak	.05	.02
42	Rafael Ramirez	.05	.02
43	Gerald Young	.05	.02
44	Dick Schofield	.05	.02
45	Dave Smith	.05	.02
46	Dave Magadan	.05	.02
47	Dennis Martinez	.05	.02
48	Greg Minton	.05	.02
49	Milt Thompson	.05	.02
50	Orel Hershiser	.07	.04
51	Bip Roberts	.12	.07
52	Jerry Browne	.05	.02
53	Bob Ojeda	.05	.02
54	Fernando Valenzuela	.07	.04

#	Player			#	Player		
55	Matt Nokes	.05	.02	113	Danny Heep	.05	.02
56	Brook Jacoby	.05	.02	114	Carmelo Martinez	.05	.02
57	Frank Tanana	.05	.02	115	Dave Gallagher	.05	.02
58	Scott Fletcher	.05	.02	116	Mike LaValliere	.05	.02
59	Ron Oester	.05	.02	117	Bob McClure	.05	.02
60	Bob Boone	.07	.04	118	Rene Gonzales	.05	.02
61	Dan Gladden	.05	.02	119	Mark Parent	.05	.02
62	Darnell Coles	.05	.02	120	Wally Joyner	.08	.05
63	Gregg Olson	.10	.06	121	Mark Gubicza	.05	.02
64	Todd Burns	.07	.04	122	Tony Pena	.05	.02
65	Todd Benzinger	.05	.02	123	Carmen Castillo	.05	.02
66	Dale Murphy	.10	.06	124	Howard Johnson	.08	.05
67	Mike Flanagan	.05	.02	125	Steve Sax	.07	.04
68	Jose Oquendo	.05	.02	126	Tim Belcher	.05	.02
69	Cecil Espy	.05	.02	127	Tim Burke	.05	.02
70	Chris Sabo	.08	.05	128	Al Newman	.05	.02
71	Shane Rawley	.05	.02	129	Dennis Rasmussen	.05	.02
72	Tom Brunansky	.05	.02	130	Doug Jones	.05	.02
73	Vance Law	.05	.02	131	Fred Lynn	.07	.04
74	B.J. Surhoff	.05	.02	132	Jeff Hamilton	.05	.02
75	Lou Whitaker	.05	.02	133	German Gonzalez	.05	.02
76	Ken Caminiti	.07	.04	134	John Morris	.05	.02
77	Nelson Liriano	.05	.02	135	Dave Parker	.05	.02
78	Tommy Gregg	.05	.02	136	Gary Pettis	.05	.02
79	Don Slaught	.05	.02	137	Dennis Boyd	.05	.02
80	Eddie Murray	.10	.06	138	Candy Maldonado	.05	.02
81	Joe Boever	.05	.02	139	Rick Cerone	.05	.02
82	Charlie Leibrandt	.05	.02	140	George Brett	.15	.08
83	Jose Lind	.05	.02	141	Dave Clark	.05	.02
84	Tony Phillips	.05	.02	142	Dickie Thon	.05	.02
85	Mitch Webster	.05	.02	143	Junior Ortiz	.05	.02
86	Dan Plesac	.05	.02	144	Don August	.05	.02
87	Rick Mahler	.05	.02	145	Gary Gaetti	.05	.02
88	Steve Lyons	.05	.02	146	Kirt Manwaring	.05	.02
89	Tony Fernandez	.05	.02	147	Jeff Reed	.05	.02
90	Ryne Sandberg	.35	.20	148	Jose Alvarez (R)	.07	.04
91	Nick Esasky	.05	.02	149	Mike Schooler	.05	.02
92	Luis Salazar	.05	.02	150	Mark Grace	.15	.08
93	Pete Incaviglia	.05	.02	151	Geronimo Berroa	.05	.02
94	Ivan Calderon	.05	.02	152	Barry Jones	.05	.02
95	Jeff Treadway	.05	.02	153	Geno Petralli	.05	.02
96	Kurt Stillwell	.05	.02	154	Jim Deshaies	.05	.02
97	Gary Sheffield	.50	.30	155	Barry Larkin	.12	.07
98	Jeffrey Leonard	.05	.02	156	Alredo Griffin	.05	.02
99	Andres Thomas	.05	.02	157	Tom Henke	.05	.02
100	Roberto Kelly	.20	.12	158	Mike Jeffcoat (R)	.07	.04
101	Alvaro Espinoza (R)	.07	.04	159	Bob Welch	.05	.02
102	Greg Gagne	.05	.02	160	Julio Franco	.08	.05
103	John Farrell	.05	.02	161	Henry Cotto	.05	.02
104	Willie Wilson	.05	.02	162	Terry Steinbach	.05	.02
105	Glenn Braggs	.05	.02	163	Damon Berryhill	.05	.02
106	Chet Lemon	.05	.02	164	Tim Crews	.05	.02
107	Jamie Moyer	.05	.02	165	Tom Browning	.05	.02
108	Chuck Crim	.05	.02	166	Fred Manrique	.05	.02
109	Dave Valle	.05	.02	167	Harold Reynolds	.05	.02
110	Walt Weiss	.07	.04	168	Ron Hassey	.05	.02
111	Larry Sheets	.05	.02	169	Shawon Dunston	.08	.05
112	Don Robinson	.05	.02	170	Bobby Bonilla	.12	.07

171 Tom Herr	.05	.02	225 Pete Smith	.05	.02
172 Mike Heath	.05	.02	226 Mike Witt	.05	.02
173 Rich Gedman	.05	.02	227 Jay Howell	.05	.02
174 Bill Ripken	.05	.02	228 Scott Bradley	.05	.02
175 Pete O'Brien	.05	.02	229 Jerome Walton	.07	.04
176aLloyd McClendon (Er)	.40	.25	230 Greg Swindell	.07	.04
176bLloyd McClendon (Cor)	.05	.02	231 Atlee Hammaker	.05	.02
			232 Mike Deveraux	.10	.06
177 Brian Holton	.07	.04	233 Ken Hill	.30	.18
178 Jeff Blauser	.05	.02	234 Craig Worthington	.05	.02
179 Jim Eisenreich	.05	.02	235 Scott Henry	.05	.02
180 Bert Blyleven	.07	.04	236 Brett Butler	.06	.03
181 Rob Murphy	.05	.02	237 Doyle Alexander	.05	.02
182 Bill Doran	.05	.02	238 Dave Anderson	.05	.02
183 Curt Ford	.05	.02	239 Bob Milacki	.05	.02
184 Mike Henneman	.05	.02	240 Dwight Smith	.07	.04
185 Eric Davis	.10	.06	241 Otis Nixon	.05	.02
186 Lance McCullers	.05	.02	242 Pat Tabler	.05	.02
187 Steve Davis (R)	.07	.04	243 Derek Lilliquist	.05	.02
188 Bill Wegman	.05	.02	244 Danny Tartabull	.10	.06
189 Brian Harper	.05	.02	245 Wade Boggs	.15	.08
190 Mike Moore	.05	.02	246 Scott Garrelts	.05	.02
191 Dale Mohorcic	.05	.02	247 Spike Owen	.05	.02
192 Tim Wallach	.07	.04	248 Norm Charlton	.05	.02
193 Keith Hernandez	.05	.02	249 Gerald Perry	.05	.02
194 Dave Righetti	.05	.02	250 Nolan Ryan	.60	.35
195aBret Saberhagen (Er)	.10	.06	251 Kevin Gross	.05	.02
195bBret Saberhagen (Cor)	.25	.15	252 Randy Milligan	.05	.02
			253 Mike LaCoss	.05	.02
196 Paul Kilgus	.05	.02	254 Dave Bergman	.05	.02
197 Bud Black	.05	.02	255 Tony Gwynn	.20	.12
198 Juan Samuel	.05	.02	256 Felix Fermin	.05	.02
199 Kevin Seitzer	.05	.02	257 Greg Harris	.05	.02
200 Darryl Strawberry	.20	.12	258 Junior Felix (R)	.05	.02
201 Dave Steib	.07	.04	259 Mark Davis	.05	.02
202 Charlie Hough	.05	.02	260 Vince Coleman	.07	.04
203 Jack Morris	.10	.06	261 Paul Gibson	.05	.02
204 Rance Mulliniks	.05	.02	262 Mitch Williams	.05	.02
205 Alvin Davis	.05	.02	263 Jeff Russell	.05	.02
206 Jack Howell	.05	.02	264 Omar Vizquel (R)	.05	.02
207 Ken Patterson	.07	.04	265 Andre Dawson	.12	.07
208 Terry Pendleton	.12	.07	266 Storm Davis	.05	.02
209 Craig Lefferts	.05	.02	267 Guillermo Hernandez	.05	.02
210 Kevin Brown	.08	.05	268 Mike Felder	.05	.02
211 Dan Petry	.05	.02	269 Tom Candiotti	.05	.02
212 Dave Leiper	.05	.02	270 Bruce Hurst	.06	.03
213 Daryl Boston	.05	.02	271 Fred McGriff	.25	.15
214 Kevin Hickey	.07	.04	272 Glenn Davis	.05	.02
215 Mike Krukow	.05	.02	273 John Franco	.05	.02
216 Terry Francona	.05	.02	274 Rich Yett	.05	.02
217 Kirk McCaskill	.05	.02	275 Craig Biggio	.08	.05
218 Scott Bailes	.05	.02	276 Gene Larkin	.05	.02
219 Bob Forsch	.05	.02	277 Rob Dibble	.07	.04
220 Mike Aldrete	.05	.02	278 Randy Bush	.05	.02
221 Steve Buechele	.05	.02	279 Kevin Bass	.05	.02
222 Jesse Barfield	.05	.02	280aBo Jackson (Er)	.25	.15
223 Juan Berenguer	.05	.02	280bBo Jackson (Cor)	.70	.40
224 Andy McGaffigan	.05	.02	281 Wally Backman	.05	.02

282 Larry Andersen	.05	.02
283 Chris Bosio	.05	.02
284 Juan Agosto	.05	.02
285 Ozzie Smith	.10	.06
286 George Bell	.10	.06
287 Rex Hudler	.05	.02
288 Pat Borders	.05	.02
289 Danny Jackson	.05	.02
290 Carlton Fisk	.10	.06
291 Tracy Jones	.05	.02
292 Allan Anderson	.05	.02
293 Johnny Ray	.05	.02
294 Lee Guetterman	.05	.02
295 Paul O'Neill	.07	.04
296 Carney Lansford	.05	.02
297 Tom Brookens	.05	.02
298 Claudell Washington	.05	.02
299 Hubie Brooks	.05	.02
300 Will Clark	.35	.20
301 Kenny Rogers (R)	.05	.02
302 Darrell Evans	.05	.02
303 Greg Briley	.05	.02
304 Donn Pall	.05	.02
305 Teddy Higuera	.05	.02
306 Dan Pasqua	.05	.02
307 Dave Winfield	.10	.06
308 Dennis Powell	.05	.02
309 Jose DeLeon	.05	.02
310 Roger Clemens	.25	.15
311 Melido Perez	.05	.02
312 Devon White	.05	.02
313 Doc Gooden	.10	.06
314 Carlos Martinez (R)	.12	.08
315 Dennis Eckersley	.10	.06
316 Clay Parker	.05	.02
317 Rick Honeycutt	.05	.02
318 Tim Laudner	.05	.02
319 Joe Carter	.15	.08
320 Robin Yount	.20	.12
321 Felix Jose	.15	.08
322 Mickey Tettleton	.05	.02
323 Mike Gallego	.05	.02
324 Edgar Martinez	.30	.18
325 Dave Henderson	.05	.02
326 Chili Davis	.05	.02
327 Steve Balboni	.05	.02
328 Jody Davis	.05	.02
329 Shawn Hillegas	.05	.02
330 Jim Abbott	.20	.12
331 John Dopson	.05	.02
332 Mark Williamson	.05	.02
333 Jeff Robinson	.05	.02
334 John Smiley	.08	.05
335 Bobby Thigpen	.05	.02
336 Garry Templeton	.05	.02
337 Marvell Wynne	.05	.02
338a Ken Griffey, Sr. (#25 uniform on back)	.08	.05
338b Ken Griffey, Sr. (#30 uniform on back)	2.00	1.25
339 Steve Finley (R)	.07	.04
340 Ellis Burks	.08	.05
341 Frank Williams	.05	.02
342 Mike Morgan	.05	.02
343 Kevin Mitchell	.08	.05
344 Joel Youngblood	.05	.02
345 Mike Greenwell	.10	.06
346 Glenn Wilson	.05	.02
347 John Costello	.05	.02
348 Wes Gardner	.05	.02
349 Jeff Ballard	.05	.02
350 Mark Thurmond	.05	.02
351 Randy Myers	.05	.02
352 Shawn Abner	.05	.02
353 Jesse Orosco	.05	.02
354 Greg Walker	.05	.02
355 Pete Harnisch	.08	.05
356 Steve Farr	.05	.02
357 Dave LaPoint	.05	.02
358 Willie Fraser	.05	.02
359 Mickey Hatcher	.05	.02
360 Rickey Henderson	.25	.15
361 Mike Fitzgerald	.05	.02
362 Bill Schroeder	.05	.02
363 Mark Carreon	.05	.02
364 Ron Jones	.05	.02
365 Jeff Montgomery	.07	.04
366 Bill Krueger	.05	.02
367 John Cangelosi	.05	.02
368 Jose Gonzalez	.05	.02
369 Greg Hibbard (R)	.20	.12
370 John Smoltz	.35	.20
371 Jeff Brantley (R)	.05	.02
372 Frank White	.05	.02
373 Ed Whitson	.05	.02
374 Willie McGee	.07	.04
375 Jose Canseco	.35	.20
376 Randy Ready	.05	.02
377 Don Aase	.05	.02
378 Tony Armas	.05	.02
379 Steve Bedrosian	.05	.02
380 Chuck Finley	.08	.05
381 Kent Hrbek	.07	.04
382 Jim Gantner	.05	.02
383 Mel Hall	.07	.04
384 Mike Marshall	.05	.02
385 Mark McGwire	.30	.18
386 Wayne Tolleson	.05	.02
387 Brian Holton	.08	.05
388 John Wetteland (R)	.40	.25
389 Darren Daulton	.10	.06
390 Rob Deer	.05	.02
391 John Moses	.05	.02
392 Todd Worrell	.05	.02
393 Chuck Cary	.07	.04
394 Stan Javier	.05	.02

395 Willie Randolph	.05	.02	452 Andy Allanson	.05	.02
396 Bill Buckner	.05	.02	453 Bob Melvin	.05	.02
397 Robby Thompson	.05	.02	454 Benny Santiago	.07	.04
398 Mike Scioscia	.05	.02	455 Jose Uribe	.05	.02
399 Lonnie Smith	.05	.02	456 Bill Landrum	.07	.04
400 Kirby Puckett	.25	.15	457 Bobby Witt	.08	.05
401 Mark Langston	.08	.05	458 Kevin Romine	.05	.02
402 Danny Darwin	.05	.02	459 Lee Mazzilli	.05	.02
403 Greg Maddux	.12	.07	460 Paul Molitor	.08	.05
404 Lloyd Moseby	.05	.02	461 Ramon Martinez	.20	.12
405 Rafael Palmeiro	.10	.06	462 Frank DiPino	.05	.02
406 Chad Kreuter	.05	.02	463 Walt Terrell	.05	.02
407 Jimmy Key	.05	.02	464 Bob Geren (R)	.12	.07
408 Tim Birtsas	.05	.02	465 Rick Reuchel	.05	.02
409 Tim Raines	.07	.04	466 Mark Grant	.05	.02
410 Dave Stewart	.08	.05	467 John Kruk	.05	.02
411 Eric Yelding (R)	.12	.07	468 Gregg Jefferies	.15	.08
412 Kent Anderson (R)	.07	.04	469 R.J. Reynolds	.05	.02
413 Les Lancaster	.05	.02	470 Harold Baines	.05	.02
414 Rick Dempsey	.05	.02	471 Dennis Lamp	.05	.02
415 Randy Johnson	.10	.06	472 Tom Gordon	.07	.04
416 Gary Carter	.10	.06	473 Terry Puhl	.05	.02
417 Rolando Roomes	.05	.02	474 Curtis Wilkerson	.05	.02
418 Dan Schatzeder	.05	.02	475 Dan Quisenberry	.05	.02
419 Bryn Smith	.05	.02	476 Oddibe McDowell	.05	.02
420 Ruben Sierra	.25	.15	477 Zane Smith	.05	.02
421 Steve Jeltz	.05	.02	478 Franklin Stubbs	.05	.02
422 Ken Oberkfell	.05	.02	479 Wallace Johnson	.05	.02
423 Sid Bream	.05	.02	480 Jay Tibbs	.05	.02
424 Jim Clancy	.05	.02	481 Tom Glavine	.50	.30
425 Kelly Gruber	.08	.05	482 Manny Lee	.05	.02
426 Rick Leach	.05	.02	483 Joe Hesketh	.05	.02
427 Lenny Dykstra	.07	.04	484 Mike Bielecki	.05	.02
428 Jeff Pico	.05	.02	485 Greg Brock	.05	.02
429 John Cerutti	.05	.02	486 Pascual Perez	.05	.02
430 David Cone	.08	.05	487 Kirk Gibson	.06	.03
431 Jeff Kunkel	.05	.02	488 Scott Sanderson	.05	.02
432 Luis Aquino	.05	.02	489 Domingo Ramos	.05	.02
433 Ernie Whitt	.05	.02	490 Kal Daniels	.05	.02
434 Bo Diaz	.05	.02	491aDavid Wells (Reverse	2.00	1.25
435 Steve Lake	.05	.02	negative on card back)		
436 Pat Perry	.05	.02	491bDavid Wells (Cor)	.07	.04
437 Mike Davis	.05	.02	492 Jerry Reed	.05	.02
438 Cecilio Guante	.05	.02	493 Eric Show	.05	.02
439 Duane Ward	.05	.02	494 Mike Pagliarulo	.05	.02
440 Andy Van Slyke	.10	.06	495 Ron Robinson	.05	.02
441 Gene Nelson	.05	.02	496 Brad Komminsk	.05	.02
442 Luis Polonia	.07	.04	497 Greg Litton (R)	.10	.06
443 Kevin Elster	.05	.02	498 Chris James	.05	.02
444 Keith Moreland	.05	.02	499 Luis Quinones (R)	.08	.05
445 Roger McDowell	.05	.02	500 Frank Viola	.07	.04
446 Ron Darling	.05	.02	501 Tim Teufel	.05	.02
447 Ernest Riles	.05	.02	502 Terry Leach	.05	.02
448 Mookie Wilson	.05	.02	503 Matt Williams	.10	.06
449aBill Spiers (R) (Er)	.80	.50	504 Tim Leary	.05	.02
449bBill Spiers (R) (Cor)	.15	.08	505 Doug Drabek	.08	.05
450 Rick Sutcliffe	.05	.02	506 Mariano Duncan	.05	.02
451 Nelson Santovenia	.05	.02	507 Charlie Hayes	.05	.02

508 Albert Belle (R)	.75	.45
509 Pat Sheridan	.05	.02
510 Mackey Sasser	.05	.02
511 Jose Rijo	.08	.05
512 Mike Smithson	.05	.02
513 Gary Ward	.05	.02
514 Dion James	.05	.02
515 Jim Gott	.05	.02
516 Drew Hall (R)	.07	.04
517 Doug Bair	.05	.02
518 Scott Scudder (R)	.15	.08
519 Rick Aguilera	.05	.02
520 Rafael Belliard	.05	.02
521 Jay Buhner	.08	.05
522 Jeff Reardon	.10	.06
523 Steve Rosenberg (R)	.07	.04
524 Randy Velarde (R)	.08	.05
525 Jeff Musselman	.05	.02
526 Bill Long	.05	.02
527 Gary Wayne	.05	.02
528 Dave Johnson (R)	.07	.04
529 Ron Kittle	.05	.02
530 Erik Hanson (R)	.15	.07
531 Steve Wilson (R)	.07	.04
532 Joey Meyer	.05	.02
533 Curt Young	.05	.02
534 Kelly Downs	.05	.02
535 Joe Girardi	.05	.02
536 Lance Blankenship	.07	.04
537 Greg Mathews	.05	.02
538 Donell Nixon	.05	.02
539 Mark Knudson (R)	.08	.05
540 Jeff Wetherby (R)	.08	.05
541 Darrin Jackson	.07	.04
542 Terry Mulholland	.07	.04
543 Eric Hetzel (R)	.08	.05
544 Rick Reed (R)	.10	.06
545 Dennis Cook (R)	.07	.04
546 Mike Jackson	.05	.02
547 Brian Fisher	.05	.02
548 Gene Harris (R)	.07	.04
549 Jeff King (R)	.20	.12
550 Dave Dravecky (Salute)	.05	.02
551 Randy Kutcher (R)	.07	.04
552 Mark Portugal	.05	.02
553 Jim Corsi (R)	.07	.04
554 Todd Stottlemyre	.07	.04
555 Scott Bankhead	.05	.02
556 Ken Dayley	.05	.02
557 Rick Wrona (R)	.07	.04
558 Sammy Sosa (R)	.25	.15
559 Keith Miller	.05	.02
560 Ken Griffey, Jr.	1.50	.90
561a Ryne Sandberg (Er 3B)	10.00	7.00
561b Ryne Sandberg (Cor)	.35	.20
562 Billy Hatcher	.05	.02

563 Jay Bell	.07	.04
564 Jack Daugherty (R)	.10	.06
565 Rich Monteleone	.05	.02
566 Bo Jackson (AS- MVP)	.20	.12
567 Tony Fossas (R)	.10	.06
568 Roy Smith (R)	.07	.04
569 Jaime Navarro (R)	.35	.20
570 Lance Johnson (R)	.07	.04
571 Mike Dyer (R)	.07	.04
572 Kevin Ritz (R)	.08	.05
573 Dave West	.05	.02
574 Gary Mielke (R)	.08	.05
575 Scott Lusader (R)	.08	.05
576 Joe Oliver (R)	.15	.08
577 Sandy Alomar, Jr.	.10	.06
578 Andy Benes (R)	.30	.18
579 Tim Jones	.05	.02
580 Randy McCament (R)	.07	.04
581 Curt Schilling (R)	.08	.05
582 John Orton (R)	.12	.07
583a Milt Cuyler (R) (Er)	.80	.50
583b Milt Cuyler (R) (Cor)	.25	.15
584 Eric Anthony (R)	.50	.30
585 Greg Vaughn (R)	.40	.25
586 Deion Sanders (R)	.70	.40
587 Jose DeJesus (R)	.07	.04
588 Chip Hale((R)	.07	.04
589 John Olerud (R)	.60	.35
590 Steve Olin (R)	.25	.15
591 Marquis Grissom (R)	.75	.45
592 Moises Alou (R)	.60	.35
593 Mark Lemke (R)	.10	.06
594 Dean Palmer (R)	.70	.40
595 Robin Ventura (R)	.80	.50
596 Tino Martinez (R)	.35	.20
597 Mike Huff (R)	.12	.07
598 Scott Hemond (R)	.10	.06
599 Wally Whitehurst (R)	.10	.06
600 Todd Zeile (R)	.20	.12
601 Glenallen Hill (R)	.25	.15
602 Hal Morris (R)	.25	.15
603 Juan Bell (R)	.08	.05
604 Bobby Rose (R)	.12	.07
605 Matt Merullo (R)	.10	.06
606 Kevin Maas (R)	.35	.20
607 Randy Nosek (R)	.07	.04
608 Billy Bates (R)	.12	.07
609 Mike Stanton (R)	.12	.07
610 Mauro Gozzo (R)	.08	.05
611 Charles Nagy (R)	.60	.35
612 Scott Coolbaugh (R)	.07	.04
613 Jose Vizcaino (R)	.15	.08
614 Greg Smith (R)	.10	.06
615 Jeff Huson (R)	.10	.06
616 Mickey Weston (R)	.08	.05
617 John Pawlowski (R)	.08	.05
618a Joe Skalski (R) (#27 uniform on back)	.12	.07

618b Joe Skalski (R) (#67 uniform on back)	1.00	.70
619 Bernie Williams (R)	.35	.20
620 Shawn Holman (R)	.08	.05
621 Gary Eave (R)	.10	.06
622 Darrin Fletcher (R)	.12	.07
623 Pat Combs (R)	.15	.07
624 Mike Blowers (R)	.10	.06
625 Kevin Appier (R)	.25	.15
626 Pat Austin (R)	.10	.06
627 Kelly Mann (R)	.08	.05
628 Matt Kinzer (R)	.08	.05
629 Chris Hammond (R)	.35	.20
630 Dean Wilkins (R)	.12	.07
631 Larry Walker (R)	.75	.45
632 Blaine Beatty (R)	.12	.07
633a Tom Barrett (R) (#29 uniform on back)	.08	.05
633b Tom Barrett (R) (#14 uniform on back)	3.00	2.00
634 Stan Belinda (R)	.12	.07
635 Tex Smith (R)	.10	.06
636 Hensley Meulens (R)	.10	.06
637 Juan Gonzalez (R)	2.50	1.50
638 Lenny Webster (R)	.10	.06
639 Mark Gardner (R)	.15	.08
640 Tommy Greene (R)	.15	.08
641 Mike Hartley (R)	.15	.08
642 Phil Stephenson (R)	.08	.05
643 Kevin Mmahat (R)	.15	.08
644 Ed Whited (R)	.10	.06
645 Delino DeShields (R)	.80	.50
646 Kevin Blankenship (R)	.08	.05
647 Paul Sorrento (R)	.25	.15
648 Mike Roesler (R)	.10	.06
649 Jason Grimsley (R)	.12	.07
650 Dave Justice (R)	1.25	.80
651 Scott Cooper (R)	.30	.18
652 Dave Eiland (R)	.10	.06
653 Mike Munoz (R)	.08	.05
654 Jeff Fischer (R)	.08	.05
655 Terry Jorgenson (R)	.08	.05
656 George Canale (R)	.10	.06
657 Brian DuBois (R)	.12	.07
658 Carlos Quintana	.08	.05
659 Luis De los santos	.05	.02
660 Jerald Clark	.07	.04
661 Donald Harris (R)	.15	.08
662 Paul Coleman (R)	.15	.08
663 Frank Thomas (R)	5.00	3.50
664 Brent Mayne (R)	.15	.08
665 Eddie Zosky (R)	.15	.08
666 Steve Hosey (R)	.50	.30
667 Scott Bryant (R)	.15	.08
668 Tom Goodwin (R)	.20	.12
669 Cal Eldred (R)	.75	.45
670 Earl Cunningham (R)	.20	.12
671 Alan Zinter (R)	.15	.08
672 Chuck Knoblauch (R)	2.00	1.25
673 Kyle Abbott (R)	.20	.12
674 Roger Salkeld (R)	.60	.35
675 Mo Vaughn (R)	.50	.30
676 Kiki Jones (R)	.15	.08
677 Tyler Houston (R)	.12	.07
678 Jeff Jackson (R)	.15	.08
679 Greg Gohr (R)	.15	.08
680 Ben McDonald (R)	.60	.35
681 Greg Blosser (R)	.25	.15
682 Willie Greene (R)	.30	.18
683 Wade Boggs (DT)	.10	.06
684 Will Clark (DT)	.20	.12
685 Tony Gwynn (DT)	.15	.08
686 Rickey Henderson (DT)	.15	.08
687 Bo Jackson (DT)	.20	.12
688 Mark Langston (DT)	.08	.05
689 Barry Larkin (DT)	.10	.06
690 Kirby Puckett (DT)	.15	.08
691 Ryne Sandberg (DT)	.20	.12
692 Mike Scott (DT)	.07	.04
693 Terry Steinbach (DT)	.07	.04
694 Bobby Thigpen (DT)	.07	.04
695 Mitch Williams (DT)	.07	.04
696 Nolan Ryan (5,000 K)	.25	.15
697 Bo Jackson (BB/FB)	2.50	1.50
698 Rickey Henderson (HL)	.12	.07
699 Will Clark (HL)	.15	.08
700 World Series (1,2)	.08	.05
701 Candlestick Park	.12	.07
702 World Series (3)	.08	.05
703 World Series (Wrap up)	.08	.05
704 Wade Boggs (HL)	.12	.07
BC1 Bart Giamatti (DT)	1.50	.90
BC2 Pat Combs (DT)	.30	.18
BC3 Todd Zeile (DT)	1.00	.70
BC4 Luis de los Santos (DT)	.20	.12
BC5 Mark Lemke (DT)	.30	.18
BC6 Robin Ventura (DT)	6.00	4.00
BC7 Jeff Huson (DT)	.20	.12
BC8 Greg Vaughn (DT)	1.50	.90
BC9 Marquis Grissom (DT)	5.00	3.50
BC10 Eric Anthony (DT)	1.50	.90

1990 Score Traded

Similar in design to Score's 1990 regular edition, this update set contains cards of rookies and players who changed teams during the regular season. The standard-size cards feature a yellow and orange border. Card backs contain a small headshot of the player. The set contains a card of hockey player Eric Lindros.

		MINT	NR/MT
Complete Set (110)		18.00	12.00
Commons		.05	.02

1T	Dave Winfield	.15	.08
2T	Kevin Bass	.05	.02
3T	Nick Esasky	.05	.02
4T	Mitch Webster	.05	.02
5T	Pascual Perez	.05	.02
6T	Gary Pettis	.05	.02
7T	Tony Pena	.05	.02
8T	Candy Maldonado	.05	.02
9T	Cecil Fielder	.15	.08
10T	Carmelo Martinez	.05	.02
11T	Mark Langston	.10	.06
12T	Dave Parker	.08	.05
13T	Don Slaught	.05	.02
14T	Tony Phillips	.05	.02
15T	John Franco	.05	.02
16T	Randy Myers	.05	.02
17T	Jeff Reardon	.15	.08
18T	Sandy Alomar, Jr.	.12	.07
19T	Joe Carter	.20	.12
20T	Fred Lynn	.07	.04
21T	Storm Davis	.05	.02
22T	Craig Lefferts	.05	.02
23T	Pete O'Brien	.05	.02
24T	Dennis Boyd	.05	.02
25T	Lloyd Moseby	.05	.02
26T	Mark Davis	.05	.02
27T	Tim Leary	.05	.02
28T	Gerald Perry	.05	.02
29T	Don Aase	.05	.02
30T	Ernie Whitt	.05	.02
31T	Dale Murphy	.12	.07
32T	Alejandro Pena	.05	.02
33T	Juan Samuel	.05	.02
34T	Hubie Brooks	.05	.02
35T	Gary Carter	.10	.06
36T	Jim Presley	.05	.02
37T	Wally Backman	.05	.02
38T	Matt Nokes	.05	.02
39T	Dan Petry	.05	.02
40T	Franklin Stubbs	.05	.02
41T	Jeff Huson	.07	.04
42T	Billy Hatcher	.05	.02
43T	Terry Leach	.05	.02
44T	Phil Bradley	.05	.02
45T	Claudell Washington	.05	.02
46T	Luis Polonia	.05	.02
47T	Daryl Boston	.05	.02
48T	Lee Smith	.10	.06
49T	Tom Brunansky	.07	.04
50T	Mike Witt	.05	.02
51T	Willie Randolph	.05	.02
52T	Stan Javier	.05	.02
53T	Brad Komminsk	.05	.02
54T	John Candelaria	.05	.02
55T	Bryn Smith	.05	.02
56T	Glenn Braggs	.05	.02
57T	Keith Hernandez	.07	.04
58T	Ken Oberkfell	.05	.02
59T	Steve Jeltz	.05	.02
60T	Chris James	.05	.02
61T	Scott Sanderson	.05	.02
62T	Bill Long	.05	.02
63T	Rick Cerone	.05	.02
64T	Scott Bailes	.05	.02
65T	Larry Sheets	.05	.02
66T	Junior Ortiz	.05	.02
67T	Francisco Cabrera (R)	.15	.08
68T	Gary DiSarcina (R)	.15	.08
69T	Greg Olson (R)	.12	.07
70T	Beau Allred (R)	.12	.07
71T	Oscar Azocar (R)	.12	.07
72T	Kent Mercker (R)	.15	.07
73T	John Burkett (R)	.12	.07
74T	Carlos Baerga (R)	.80	.50
75T	Dave Hollin (R)	.40	.25
76T	Todd Hundley (R)	.15	.08
77T	Rick Parker (R)	.10	.06
78T	Steve Cummings (R)	.10	.06
79T	Bill Sampen (R)	.15	.07
80T	Jerry Kutzier (R)	.10	.06
81T	Derek Bell (R)	.80	.50
82T	Kevin Tapani (R)	.25	.15
83T	Jim Leyritz (R)	.12	.07
84T	Ray Lankford (R)	.60	.35
85T	Wayne Edwards (R)	.10	.06

		MINT	NR/MT
86T Frank Thomas		7.50	5.00
87T Tim Naehring (R)		.12	.07
88T Willie Blair (R)		.12	.07
89T Alan Mills (R)		.10	.06
90T Scott Radinsky (R)		.15	.08
91T Howard Farmer (R)		.12	.07
92T Julio Machado (R)		.12	.07
93T Rafael Valdez (R)		.10	.06
94T Shawn Boskie (R)		.12	.07
95T David Segui (R)		.12	.07
96T Chris Hoiles (R)		.40	.25
97T D.J. Dozier (R)		.15	.08
98T Hector Villanueva (R)		.12	.07
99T Eric Gunderson (R)		.10	.06
100TEric Lindros (R)		8.50	6.00
101TDave Otto (R)		.10	.06
102TDana Kiecker (R)		.10	.06
103TTim Drummond (R)		.08	.05
104TMickey Pina (R)		.10	.06
105TCraig Grebeck (R)		.12	.07
106TBernard Gilkey (R)		.40	.25
107TTim Layana (R)		.12	.07
108TScott Chiamparino (R)		.12	.07
109TSteve Avery (R)		1.50	.90
110TTerry Shumpert (R)		.15	.08

1991 Score

Score increased the size of their set in 1991 and, for the first time, issued the cards in two series. Card fronts feature multiple solid color borders and game action photos. Card backs contain close-up head shots of the player. In addition to the Dream Team, Score introduced a number of new subsets including K-Men, Master Blasters, Riflemen and Franchise. Score's Factory Set contained 7 Bonus Cooperstown Cards. Those cards are listed at the end of this checklist.

		MINT	NR/MT
	Complete Set (893)	21.00	14.50
	Commons	.05	.02
1	Jose Canseco	.25	.15
2	Ken Griffey, Jr.	.50	.30
3	Ryne Sandberg	.20	.12
4	Nolan Ryan	.40	.25
5	Bo Jackson	.20	.12
6	Bret Saberhagen	.08	.05
7	Will Clark	.20	.12
8	Ellis Burks	.07	.04
9	Joe Carter	.12	.07
10	Rickey Henderson	.15	.08
11	Ozzie Guillen	.05	.02
12	Wade Boggs	.12	.07
13	Jerome Walton	.07	.04
14	John Franco	.05	.02
15	Ricky Jordan	.05	.02
16	Wally Backman	.05	.02
17	Rob Dibble	.07	.04
18	Glenn Braggs	.05	.02
19	Cory Snyder	.05	.02
20	Kal Daniels	.05	.02
21	Mark Langston	.08	.05
22	Kevin Gross	.05	.02
23	Don Mattingly	.12	.07
24	Dave Righetti	.05	.02
25	Roberto Alomar	.20	.12
26	Robby Thompson	.05	.02
27	Jack McDowell	.15	.08
28	Bip Roberts	.05	.02
29	Jay Howell	.05	.02
30	Dave Steib	.05	.02
31	Johnny Ray	.05	.02
32	Steve Sax	.07	.04
33	Terry Mulholland	.07	.04
34	Lee Guetterman	.05	.02
35	Tim Raines	.07	.04
36	Scott Fletcher	.05	.02
37	Lance Parrish	.05	.02
38	Tony Phillips	.05	.02
39	Todd Stottlemyre	.07	.04
40	Alan Trammell	.08	.05
41	Todd Burns	.05	.02
42	Mookie Wilson	.05	.02
43	Chris Bosio	.05	.02
44	Jeffrey Leonard	.05	.02
45	Doug Jones	.05	.02
46	Mike Scott	.05	.02
47	Andy Hawkins	.05	.02
48	Harold Reynolds	.05	.02
49	Paul Molitor	.08	.05
50	John Farrell	.05	.02
51	Danny Darwin	.05	.02
52	Jeff Blauser	.05	.02
53	John Tudor	.05	.02
54	Milt Thompson	.05	.02

55	Dave Justice	.25	.15
56	Greg Olson	.06	.03
57	Willie Blair	.07	.04
58	Rick Parker	.05	.02
59	Shawn Boskie	.05	.02
60	Kevin Tapani	.07	.04
61	Dave Hollins	.15	.08
62	Scott Radinsky	.07	.04
63	Francisco Cabrera	.05	.02
64	Tim Layana	.05	.02
65	Jim Leyritz	.05	.02
66	Wayne Edwards	.05	.02
67	Lee Stevens	.12	.07
68	Bill Sampen	.05	.02
69	Craig Grebeck	.05	.02
70	John Burkett	.05	.02
71	Hector Villanueva	.05	.02
72	Oscar Azocar	.05	.02
73	Alan Mills	.05	.02
74	Carlos Baerga	.30	.18
75	Charles Nagy	.25	.15
76	Tim Drummond	.05	.02
77	Dana Kiecker	.05	.02
78	Tom Edens (R)	.08	.05
79	Kent Mercker	.07	.04
80	Steve Avery	.20	.12
81	Lee Smith	.10	.06
82	Dave Martinez	.05	.02
83	Dave Winfield	.10	.06
84	Bill Spiers	.05	.02
85	Dan Pasqua	.05	.02
86	Randy Milligan	.05	.02
87	Tracy Jones	.05	.02
88	Greg Myers	.05	.02
89	Keith Hernandez	.05	.02
90	Todd Benzinger	.05	.02
91	Mike Jackson	.05	.02
92	Mike Stanley	.05	.02
93	Candy Maldonado	.05	.02
94	John Kruk	.05	.02
95	Cal Ripken, Jr.	.35	.20
96	Willie Fraser	.05	.02
97	Mike Felder	.05	.02
98	Bill Landrum	.05	.02
99	Chuck Crim	.05	.02
100	Chuck Finley	.07	.04
101	Kirt Manwaring	.05	.02
102	Jaime Navarro	.07	.04
103	Dickie Thon	.05	.02
104	Brian Downing	.05	.02
105	Jim Abbott	.12	.07
106	Tom Brookens	.05	.02
107	Darryl Hamilton	.05	.02
108	Bryan Harvey	.07	.04
109	Greg Harris	.05	.02
110	Greg Swindell	.07	.04
111	Juan Berenguer	.05	.02
112	Mike Heath	.05	.02
113	Scott Bradley	.05	.02
114	Jack Morris	.08	.05
115	Barry Jones	.05	.02
116	Kevin Romine	.05	.02
117	Gary Templeton	.05	.02
118	Scott Sanderson	.05	.02
119	Roberto Kelly	.10	.06
120	George Brett	.15	.08
121	Oddibe McDowell	.05	.02
122	Jim Acker	.05	.02
123	Bill Swift	.05	.02
124	Eric King	.05	.02
125	Jay Buhner	.07	.04
126	Matt Young	.05	.02
127	Alvaro Espinoza	.05	.02
128	Greg Hibbard	.05	.02
129	Jeff Robinson	.05	.02
130	Mike Greenwell	.08	.05
131	Dion James	.05	.02
132	Donn Pall	.05	.02
133	Lloyd Moseby	.05	.02
134	Randy Velarde	.05	.02
135	Allan Anderson	.05	.02
136	Mark Davis	.05	.02
137	Eric Davis	.08	.05
138	Phil Stephenson	.05	.02
139	Felix Fermin	.05	.02
140	Pedro Guerrero	.05	.02
141	Charlie Hough	.05	.02
142	Mike Henneman	.05	.02
143	Jeff Montgomery	.05	.02
144	Lenny Harris	.05	.02
145	Bruce Hurst	.06	.03
146	Eric Anthony	.12	.07
147	Paul Assenmacher	.05	.02
148	Jesse Barfield	.07	.04
149	Carlos Quintana	.07	.04
150	Dave Stewart	.07	.04
151	Roy Smith	.05	.02
152	Paul Gibson	.05	.02
153	Mickey Hatcher	.05	.02
154	Jim Eisenreich	.05	.02
155	Kenny Rogers	.05	.02
156	Dave Schmidt	.05	.02
157	Lance Johnson	.05	.02
158	Dave West	.05	.02
159	Steve Balboni	.05	.02
160	Jeff Brantley	.05	.02
161	Craig Biggio	.07	.04
162	Brook Jacoby	.05	.02
163	Dan Gladden	.05	.02
164	Jeff Reardon	.08	.05
165	Mark Carreon	.05	.02
166	Mel Hall	.05	.02
167	Gary Mielke	.05	.02
168	Cecil Fielder	.15	.08
169	Darrin Jackson	.05	.02
170	Rick Aguilera	.05	.02

171 Walt Weiss	.05	.02	
172 Steve Farr	.05	.02	
173 Jody Reed	.05	.02	
174 Mike Jeffcoat	.05	.02	
175 Mark Grace	.08	.05	
176 Larry Sheets	.05	.02	
177 Bill Gullickson	.05	.02	
178 Chris Gwynn	.05	.02	
179 Melido Perez	.05	.02	
180 Sid Fernandez	.05	.02	
181 Tim Burke	.05	.02	
182 Gary Pettis	.05	.02	
183 Rob Murphy	.05	.02	
184 Craig Lefferts	.05	.02	
185 Howard Johnson	.08	.05	
186 Ken Caminiti	.07	.04	
187 Tim Belcher	.07	.04	
188 Greg Cadaret	.05	.02	
189 Matt Williams	.08	.05	
190 Dave Magadan	.05	.02	
191 Geno Petralli	.05	.02	
192 Jeff Robinson	.05	.02	
193 Jim Deshaies	.05	.02	
194 Willie Randolph	.05	.02	
195 George Bell	.08	.05	
196 Hubie Brooks	.05	.02	
197 Tom Gordon	.07	.04	
198 Mike Fitzgerald	.05	.02	
199 Mike Pagliarulo	.05	.02	
200 Kirby Puckett	.20	.12	
201 Shawon Dunston	.07	.04	
202 Dennis Boyd	.05	.02	
203 Junior Felix	.05	.02	
204 Alejandro Pena	.05	.02	
205 Pete Smith	.10	.06	
206 Tom Glavine	.30	.18	
207 Luis Salazar	.05	.02	
208 John Smoltz	.20	.12	
209 Doug Dascenzo	.05	.02	
210 Tim Wallach	.07	.04	
211 Greg Gagne	.05	.02	
212 Mark Gubicza	.05	.02	
213 Mark Parent	.05	.02	
214 Ken Oberkfell	.05	.02	
215 Gary Carter	.08	.05	
216 Rafael Palmeiro	.08	.05	
217 Tom Niedenfuer	.05	.02	
218 Dave LaPoint	.05	.02	
219 Jeff Treadway	.05	.02	
220 Mitch Williams	.05	.02	
221 Jose DeLeon	.05	.02	
222 Mike LaValliere	.05	.02	
223 Darrel Akerfelds	.05	.02	
224 Kent Anderson	.05	.02	
225 Dwight Evans	.07	.04	
226 Gary Redus	.05	.02	
227 Paul O'Neill	.07	.04	
228 Marty Barrett	.05	.02	

229 Tom Browning	.07	.04
230 Terry Pendleton	.10	.06
231 Jack Armstrong	.05	.02
232 Mike Boddicker	.05	.02
233 Neal Heaton	.05	.02
234 Marquis Grissom	.20	.12
235 Bert Blyleven	.08	.05
236 Curt Young	.05	.02
237 Don Carman	.05	.02
238 Charlie Hayes	.05	.02
239 Mark Knudson	.05	.02
240 Todd Zeile	.10	.06
241 Larry Walker	.20	.12
242 Jerald Clark	.05	.02
243 Jeff Ballard	.05	.02
244 Jeff King	.07	.04
245 Tom Brunansky	.05	.02
246 Darren Daulton	.10	.06
247 Scott Terry	.05	.02
248 Rob Deer	.05	.02
249 Brady Anderson	.12	.07
250 Lenny Dykstra	.05	.02
251 Greg Harris	.05	.02
252 Mike Hartley	.05	.02
253 Joey Cora	.05	.02
254 Ivan Calderon	.05	.02
255 Ted Power	.05	.02
256 Sammy Sosa	.08	.05
257 Steve Buechele	.05	.02
258 Mike Devereaux	.08	.05
259 Brad Komminsk	.05	.02
260 Teddy Higuera	.05	.02
261 Shawn Abner	.05	.02
262 Dave Valle	.05	.02
263 Jeff Huson	.05	.02
264 Edgar Martinez	.12	.07
265 Carlton Fisk	.10	.06
266 Steve Finley	.07	.04
267 John Wetteland	.12	.07
268 Kevin Appier	.07	.04
269 Steve Lyons	.05	.02
270 Mickey Tettleton	.05	.02
271 Luis Rivera	.05	.02
272 Steve Jeltz	.05	.02
273 R.J. Reynolds	.05	.02
274 Carlos Martinez	.05	.02
275 Dan Plesac	.05	.02
276 Mike Morgan	.05	.02
277 Jeff Russell	.05	.02
278 Pete Incaviglia	.05	.02
279 Kevin Seitzer	.05	.02
280 Bobby Thigpen	.05	.02
281 Stan Javier	.05	.02
282 Henry Cotto	.05	.02
283 Gary Wayne	.05	.02
284 Shane Mack	.07	.04
285 Brian Holman	.07	.04
286 Gerald Perry	.05	.02

287 Steve Crawford	.05	.02
288 Nelson Liriano	.05	.02
289 Don Aase	.05	.02
290 Randy Johnson	.08	.05
291 Harold Baines	.07	.04
292 Kent Hrbek	.07	.04
293 Les Lancaster	.05	.02
294 Jeff Musselman	.05	.02
295 Kurt Stillwell	.05	.02
296 Stan Belinda	.07	.04
297 Lou Whitaker	.05	.02
298 Glenn Wilson	.05	.02
299 Omar Vizquel	.05	.02
300 Ramon Martinez	.12	.07
301 Dwight Smith	.05	.02
302 Tim Crews	.05	.02
303 Lance Blankenship	.05	.02
304 Sid Bream	.05	.02
305 Rafael Ramirez	.05	.02
306 Steve Wilson	.05	.02
307 Mackey Sasser	.05	.02
308 Franklin Stubbs	.05	.02
309 Jack Daugherty	.05	.02
310 Eddie Murray	.10	.06
311 Bob Welch	.07	.04
312 Brian Harper	.05	.02
313 Lance McCullers	.05	.02
314 Dave Smith	.05	.02
315 Bobby Bonilla	.10	.06
316 Jerry Don Gleaton	.05	.02
317 Greg Maddux	.12	.07
318 Keith Miller	.05	.02
319 Mark Portugal	.05	.02
320 Robin Ventura	.25	.15
321 Bob Ojeda	.05	.02
322 Mike Harkey	.08	.05
323 Jay Bell	.05	.02
324 Mark McGwire	.25	.15
325 Gary Gaetti	.05	.02
326 Jeff Pico	.05	.02
327 Kevin McReynolds	.05	.02
328 Frank Tanana	.05	.02
329 Eric Yelding	.05	.02
330 Barry Bonds	.25	.15
331 Brian McRae (R)	.20	.12
332 Pedro Munoz (R)	.25	.15
333 Daryl Irvine (R)	.08	.05
334 Chris Hoiles	.15	.08
335 Thomas Howard	.10	.06
336 Jeff Schultz (R)	.08	.05
337 Jeff Manto (R)	.10	.06
338 Beau Allred	.08	.05
339 Mike Bordick (R)	.30	.18
340 Todd Hundley	.08	.05
341 Jim Vatcher (R)	.10	.06
342 Luis Sojo	.10	.06
343 Jose Offerman	.15	.07
344 Pete Coachman (R)	.10	.06

345 Mike Benjamin	.07	.04
346 Ozzie Canseco (R)	.10	.06
347 Tim McIntosh	.10	.06
348 Phil Plantier (R)	.75	.45
349 Terry Shumper	.07	.04t
350 Darren Lewis	.10	.06
351 David Walsh (R)	.10	.06
352 Scott Chiamparino	.10	.06
353 Julio Valera	.07	.04
354 Anthony Telford (R)	.20	.12
355 Kevin Wickander	.08	.05
356 Tim Naehring	.10	.06
357 Jim Poole (R)	.10	.06
358 Mark Whiten(R)	.25	.15
359 Terry Wells (R)	.10	.06
360 Rafael Valdez	.07	.04
361 Mel Stottlemyre	.07	.04
362 David Segui	.07	.04
363 Paul Abbott (R)	.10	.06
364 Steve Howard	.08	.05
365 Karl Rhodes	.10	.06
366 Rafael Novoa (R)	.10	.06
367 Joe Grahe (R)	.12	.07
368 Darren Reed	.10	.06
369 Jeff McKnight	.10	.06
370 Scott Leius	.10	.06
371 Mark Dewey (R)	.10	.06
372 Mark Lee (R)	.10	.06
373 Rosario Rodriguez (R)	.10	.06
374 Chuck McElroy	.07	.04
375 Mike Bell (R)	.08	.05
376 Mickey Morandini	.12	.07
377 Bill Haselman	.08	.05
378 Dave Pavlas	.08	.05
379 Derrick May	.20	.12
380 Jeromy Burnitz (R)	.35	.20
381 Donald Peters (R)	.15	.08
382 Alex Fernandez	.12	.07
383 Michael Mussina (R)	1.25	.80
384 Daniel Smith (R)	.12	.07
385 Lance Dickson (R)	.15	.08
386 Carl Everett (R)	.20	.12
387 Thomas Nevers (R)	.15	.08
388 Adam Hyzdu (R)	.20	.12
389 Todd Van Poppel (R)	.80	.50
390 Rondell White (R)	.75	.45
391 Marc Newfield (R)	.80	.50
392 Julio Franco (AS)	.05	.02
393 Wade Boggs (AS)	.10	.06
394 Ozzie Guillen (AS)	.05	.02
395 Cecil Fielder (AS)	.10	.06
396 Ken Griffey, Jr. (AS)	.25	.15
397 Rickey Henderson (AS)	.15	.08
398 Jose Canseco (AS)	.25	.15
399 Roger Clemens (AS)	.15	.08
400 Sandy Alomar, Jr. (AS)	.07	.04
401 Bobby Thigpen (AS)	.05	.02

402	Bobby Bonilla (MB)	.08	.05	459 Steve Bedrosian	.05	.02
403	Eric Davis (MB)	.07	.04	460 Frank Viola	.07	.04
404	Fred McGriff (MB)	.12	.07	461 Jose Lind	.05	.02
405	Glenn Davis (MB)	.05	.02	462 Chris Sabo	.07	.04
406	Kevin Mitchell (MB)	.08	.05	463 Dante Bichette	.05	.02
407	Rob Dibble (KM)	.05	.02	464 Rick Mahler	.05	.02
408	Ramon Martinez (KM)	.08	.05	465 John Smiley	.08	.05
409	David Cone (KM)	.08	.05	466 Devon White	.05	.02
410	Bobby Witt (KM)	.05	.02	467 John Orton	.05	.02
411	Mark Langston (KM)	.08	.05	468 Mike Stanton	.05	.02
412	Bo Jackson (Rifle)	.15	.08	469 Billy Hatcher	.05	.02
413	Shawon Dunston (Rifle)	.05	.02	470 Wally Joyner	.08	.05
414	Jesse Barfield (Rifle)	.05	.02	471 Gene Larkin	.05	.02
415	Ken Caminiti (Rifle)	.05	.02	472 Doug Drabek	.08	.05
416	Benito Santiago (Rifle)	.07	.04	473 Gary Sheffield	.35	.20
417	Nolan Ryan (HL)	.30	.18	474 David Wells	.05	.02
418	Bobby Thigpen (HL)	.05	.02	475 Andy Van Slyke	.08	.05
419	Ramon Martinez (HL)	.07	.04	476 Mike Gallego	.05	.02
420	Bo Jackson (HL)	.15	.08	477 B.J. Surhoff	.05	.02
421	Carlton Fisk (HL)	.10	.06	478 Gene Nelson	.05	.02
422	Jimmy Key	.05	.02	479 Mariano Duncan	.05	.02
423	Junior Noboa (R)	.05	.02	480 Fred McGriff	.15	.08
424	Al Newman	.05	.02	481 Jerry Browne	.05	.02
425	Pat Borders	.05	.02	482 Alvin Davis	.05	.02
426	Von Hayes	.05	.02	483 Bill Wegman	.05	.02
427	Tim Teufel	.05	.02	484 Dave Parker	.07	.04
428	Eric Plunk	.05	.02	485 Dennis Eckersley	.10	.06
429	John Moses	.05	.02	486 Erik Hanson	.08	.05
430	Mike Witt	.05	.02	487 Bill Ripken	.05	.02
431	Otis Nixon	.05	.02	488 Tom Candiotti	.05	.02
432	Tony Fernandez	.05	.02	489 Mike Schooler	.05	.02
433	Rance Mulliniks	.05	.02	490 Gregg Olson	.05	.02
434	Dan Petry	.05	.02	491 Chris James	.05	.02
435	Bob Geren	.05	.02	492 Pete Harnisch	.08	.05
436	Steve Frey	.07	.04	493 Julio Franco	.07	.04
437	Jamie Moyer	.05	.02	494 Greg Briley	.05	.02
438	Junio Ortiz	.05	.02	495 Ruben Sierra	.15	.08
439	Tom O'Malley	.05	.02	496 Steve Olin	.05	.02
440	Pat Combs	.07	.04	497 Mike Fetters	.05	.02
441	Jose Canseco (DT)	1.50	.90	498 Mark Williamson	.05	.02
442	Alfredo Griffin	.05	.02	499 Bob Tewksbury	.05	.02
443	Andres Galarraga	.05	.02	500 Tony Gwynn	.20	.12
444	Bryn Smith	.05	.02	501 Randy Myers	.05	.02
445	Andre Dawson	.10	.06	502 Keith Comstock	.05	.02
446	Juan Samuel	.05	.02	503 Craig Worthington	.05	.02
447	Mike Aldrete	.05	.02	504 Mark Eichhorn	.05	.02
448	Ron Gant	.15	.08	505 Barry Larkin	.08	.05
449	Fernando Valenzuela	.05	.02	506 Dave Johnson	.05	.02
450	Vince Coleman	.05	.02	507 Bobby Witt	.07	.04
451	Kevin Mitchell	.08	.05	508 Joe Orsulak	.05	.02
452	Spike Owen	.05	.02	509 Pete O'Brien	.05	.02
453	Mike Bielecki	.05	.02	510 Brad Arnsberg	.05	.02
454	Dennis Martinez	.08	.05	511 Storm Davis	.05	.02
455	Brett Butler	.07	.04	512 Bob Milacki	.05	.02
456	Ron Darling	.05	.02	513 Bill Pecota	.05	.02
457	Dennis Rasmussen	.05	.02	514 Glenallen Hill	.08	.05
458	Ken Howell	.05	.02	515 Danny Tartabull	.10	.06
				516 Mike Moore	.05	.02

517 Ron Robinson	.05	.02
518 Mark Gardner	.07	.04
519 Rick Wrona	.05	.02
520 Mike Scioscia	.05	.02
521 Frank Willis	.05	.02
522 Greg Brock	.05	.02
523 Jack Clark	.05	.02
524 Bruce Ruffin	.05	.02
525 Robin Yount	.25	.15
526 Tom Foley	.05	.02
527 Pat Perry	.05	.02
528 Greg Vaughn	.10	.06
529 Wally Whitehurst	.05	.02
530 Norm Charlton	.05	.02
531 Marvell Wynne	.05	.02
532 Jim Gantner	.05	.02
533 Greg Litton	.05	.02
534 Manny Lee	.05	.02
535 Scott Bailes	.05	.02
536 Charlie Leibrandt	.05	.02
537 Roger McDowell	.05	.02
538 Andy Benes	.12	.07
539 Rick Honeycutt	.05	.02
540 Doc Gooden	.10	.06
541 Scott Garrelts	.05	.02
542 Dave Clark	.05	.02
543 Lonnie Smith	.05	.02
544 Rick Rueschel	.05	.02
545 Delino DeShields	.15	.08
546 Mike Sharperson	.05	.02
547 Mike Kingery	.05	.02
548 Terry Kennedy	.05	.02
549 David Cone	.10	.06
550 Orel Hershiser	.08	.05
551 Matt Nokes	.05	.02
552 Eddie Williams	.05	.02
553 Frank DiPino	.05	.02
554 Fred Lynn	.07	.04
555 Alex Cole	.12	.07
556 Terry Leach	.05	.02
557 Chet Lemon	.05	.02
558 Paul Mirabella	.05	.02
559 Bill Long	.05	.02
560 Phil Bradley	.05	.02
561 Duane Ward	.05	.02
562 Dave Bergman	.05	.02
563 Eric Show	.05	.02
564 Xavier Hernandez	.08	.05
565 Jeff Parrett	.05	.02
566 Chuck Cary	.05	.02
567 Ken Hill	.08	.05
568 Bob Welch	.07	.04
569 John Mitchell	.05	.02
570 Travis Fryman (R)	.60	.35
571 Derek Lilliquist	.05	.02
572 Steve Lake	.05	.02
573 John Barfield (R)	.10	.06
574 Randy Bush	.05	.02
575 Joe Magrane	.05	.02
576 Edgar Diaz	.05	.02
577 Casy Candaele	.05	.02
578 Jesse Orosco	.05	.02
579 Tom Henke	.05	.02
580 Rick Cerone	.05	.02
581 Drew Hall	.05	.02
582 Tony Castillo	.05	.02
583 Jimmy Jones	.05	.02
584 Rick Reed	.05	.02
585 Joe Girardi	.05	.02
586 Jeff Gray (R)	.12	.07
587 Luis Polonia	.05	.02
588 Joe Klink	.07	.04
589 Rex Hudler	.05	.02
590 Kirk McCaskill	.05	.02
591 Juan Agosto	.05	.02
592 Wes Gardner	.05	.02
593 Rich Rodriguez (R)	.10	.06
594 Mitch Webster	.05	.02
595 Kelly Gruber	.07	.04
596 Dale Mohorcic	.05	.02
597 Willie McGee	.07	.04
598 Bill Krueger	.05	.02
599 Bob Walk	.05	.02
600 Kevin Mass	.10	.06
601 Danny Jackson	.05	.02
602 Craig McMurtry	.05	.02
603 Curtis Wilkerson	.05	.02
604 Adam Peterson	.05	.02
605 Sam Horn	.05	.02
606 Tommy Gregg	.05	.02
607 Ken Dayley	.05	.02
608 Carmelo Castillo	.05	.02
609 John Shelby	.05	.02
610 Don Slaught	.05	.02
611 Calvin Schiraldi	.05	.02
612 Dennis Lamp	.05	.02
613 Andres Thomas	.05	.02
614 Jose Gonzalez	.05	.02
615 Randy Ready	.05	.02
616 Kevin Bass	.05	.02
617 Mike Marshall	.05	.02
618 Daryl Boston	.05	.02
619 Andy McGaffigan	.05	.02
620 Joe Oliver	.07	.04
621 Jim Gott	.05	.02
622 Jose Oquendo	.05	.02
623 Jose DeJesus	.05	.02
624 Mike Brumley	.05	.02
625 John Olerud	.15	.08
626 Ernest Riles	.05	.02
627 Gene Harris	.05	.02
628 Jose Uribe	.05	.02
629 Darnell Coles	.05	.02
630 Carney Lansford	.07	.04
631 Tim Leary	.05	.02
632 Tim Hulett	.05	.02

No.	Player	Val1	Val2
633	Kevin Elster	.05	.02
634	Tony Fossas	.05	.02
635	Francisco Oliveras	.05	.02
636	Bob Patterson	.05	.02
637	Gary Ward	.05	.02
638	Rene Gonzales	.05	.02
639	Don Robinson	.05	.02
640	Darryl Strawberry	.15	.08
641	Dave Anderson	.05	.02
642	Scott Scudder	.05	.02
643	Reggie Harris (R)	.10	.06
644	Dave Henderson	.05	.02
645	Ben McDonald	.15	.08
646	Bob Kipper	.05	.02
647	Hal Morris	.10	.06
648	Tim Birtsas	.05	.02
649	Steve Searcy	.05	.02
650	Dale Murphy	.10	.06
651	Ron Oester	.05	.02
652	Mike LaCoss	.05	.02
653	Ron Jones	.05	.02
654	Kelly Downs	.05	.02
655	Roger Clemens	.25	.15
656	Herm Winningham	.05	.02
657	Trevor Wilson	.05	.02
658	Jose Rijo	.07	.04
659	Dann Bilardello	.05	.02
660	Gregg Jefferies	.10	.06
661	Doug Drabek (AS)	.08	.05
662	Randy Myers (AS)	.05	.02
663	Benito Santiago (AS)	.07	.04
664	Will Clark (AS)	.12	.07
665	Ryne Sandberg (AS)	.12	.07
666	Barry Larkin (AS)	.08	.05
667	Matt Williams (AS)	.07	.04
668	Barry Bonds (AS)	.12	.07
669	Eric Davis (AS)	.07	.04
670	Bobby Bonilla (AS)	.08	.05
671	Chipper Jones (R)	.50	.30
672	Eric Christopherson (R	.10	.06
673	Robbie Beckett (R)	.12	.07
674	Shane Andrews (R)	.12	.07
675	Steve Karsay (R)	.15	.08
676	Aaron Holbert (R)	.10	.06
677	Donovan Osborne (R)	.60	.35
678	Todd Ritchie (R)	.15	.08
679	Ron Walden (R)	.10	.06
680	Tim Costo (R)	.25	.15
681	Dan Wilson (R)	.15	.08
682	Kurt Miller (R)	.25	.15
683	Mike Lieberthal (R)	.25	.15
684	Roger Clemens (KM)	.15	.08
685	Doc Gooden (KM)	.10	.06
686	Nolan Ryan (KM)	.30	.18
687	Frank Viola (KM)	.07	.04
688	Erik Hanson (KM)	.07	.04
689	Matt Williams (MB)	.07	.04
690	Jose Canseco (MB)	.15	.08
691	Darryl Strawberry (MB)	.10	.06
692	Bo Jackson (MB)	.12	.07
693	Cecil Fielder (MB)	.12	.07
694	Sandy Alomar, Jr.(Rifle)	.07	.04
695	Cory Snyder (Rifle)	.05	.02
696	Eric Davis (Rifle)	.08	.05
697	Ken Griffey, Jr. (Rifle)	.20	.12
698	Andy Van Slyke (Rifle)	.07	.04
699	Langston/Witt (No-Hit)	.08	.05
700	Randy Johnson (No-Hit)	.10	.06
701	Nola Ryan (No-Hit)	.30	.18
702	Dave Stewart (No-Hit)	.07	.04
703	Fernando Valenzuela (No-Hit)	.07	.04
704	Andy Hawkins (No-Hit)	.05	.02
705	Melido Perez (No-Hit)	.05	.02
706	Terry Mulholland (NH)	.05	.02
707	Dave Stieb (No-Hit)	.07	.04
708	Brian Barnes (R)	.15	.08
709	Bernard Gilkey (R)	.15	.08
710	Steve Decker (R)	.12	.08
711	Paul Faries (R)	.07	.04
712	Paul Marak (R)	.08	.05
713	Wes Chamberlain (R)	.25	.15
714	Kevin Belcher (R)	.10	.06
715	Dan Boone (R)	.08	.05
716	Steve Adkins (R)	.10	.06
717	Geronimo Pena (R)	.10	.06
718	Howard Farmer	.07	.04
719	Mark Leonard (R)	.10	.06
720	Tom Lampkin	.05	.02
721	Mike Gardiner (R)	.15	.08
722	Jeff Conine (R)	.15	.08
723	Efrain Valdez (R)	.08	.05
724	Chuck Malone	.07	.04
725	Leo Gomez (R)	.40	.25
726	Paul McClellan (R)	.08	.05
727	Mark Leiter (R)	.10	.06
728	Rich DeLucia (R)	.10	.06
729	Mel Rojas	.10	.06
730	Hector Wagner (R)	.10	.06
731	Ray Lankford	.35	.20
732	Turner Ward (R)	.12	.07
733	Gerald Alexander (R)	.08	.05
734	Scott Anderson (R)	.08	.05
735	Tony Perezchica	.07	.04
736	Jimmy Kremers	.07	.04
737	American Flag	.25	.15
738	Mike York (R)	.07	.04
739	Mike Rochford (R)	.07	.04
740	Scott Aldred	.10	.06
741	Rico Brogna (R)	.20	.12
742	Dave Burba (R)	.12	.07
743	Ray Stephens (R)	.08	.05
744	Eric Gunderson	.07	.04
745	Troy Afenir (R)	.12	.07

746 Jeff Shaw (R)	.08	.05	804 Chris Nabholz	.10	.06
747 Orlando Merced (R)	.25	.15	805 Juan Gonzalez	.50	.30
748 Omar Oliveras (R)	.12	.07	806 Ron Hassey	.05	.02
749 Jerry Kutzier	.07	.04	807 Todd Worrell	.05	.02
750 Maurice Vaughn	.30	.18	808 Tommy Greene	.05	.02
751 Matt Stark (R)	.12	.07	809 Joel Skinner	.05	.02
752 Randy Hennis (R)	.08	.05	810 Benito Santiago	.07	.04
753 Andujar Cedeno (R)	.35	.20	811 Pat Tabler	.05	.02
754 Kevin Torve	.08	.05	812 Scott Erickson (R)	.75	.45
755 Joe Kraemer	.08	.05	813 Moises Alou	.25	.15
756 Phil Clark (R)	.12	.07	814 Dale Sveum	.05	.02
757 Ed Vosberg (R)	.10	.06	815 Ryne Sandberg	.20	.12
758 Mike Perez (R)	.10	.06	(Man of the year)		
759 Scott Lewis (R)	.10	.06	816 Rick Dempsey	.05	.02
760 Steve Chitren (R)	.12	.07	817 Scott Bankhead	.05	.02
761 Ray Young (R)	.08	.05	818 Jason Grimsley	.05	.02
762 Andres Santana	.15	.08	819 Doug Jennings	.05	.02
763 Rodney McCray (R)	.08	.05	820 Tom Herr	.05	.02
764 Sean Berry (R)	.10	.06	821 Rob Ducey	.05	.02
765 Brent Mayne	.07	.04	822 Luis Quinones	.05	.02
766 Mike Simms (R)	.08	.05	823 Greg Minton	.05	.02
767 Glenn Sutko (R)	.08	.05	824 Mark Grant	.05	.02
768 Gary Disarcina	.07	.04	825 Ozzie Smith	.10	.06
769 George Brett (HL)	.10	.06	826 Dave Eiland	.05	.02
770 Cecil Fielder (HL)	.10	.06	827 Danny Heep	.05	.02
771 Jim Presley	.05	.02	828 Hensley Meulens	.07	.04
772 John Dopson	.05	.02	829 Charlie O'Brien	.05	.02
773 Bo Jackson (Breaker)	.15	.08	830 Glenn Davis	.05	.02
774 Brent Knackert	.07	.04	831 John Marzano	.05	.02
775 Bill Doran	.05	.02	832 Steve Ontiveros	.05	.02
776 Dick Schofield	.05	.02	833 Ron Karkovice	.05	.02
777 Nelson Santovenia	.05	.02	834 Jerry Goff	.07	.04
778 Mark Guthrie	.07	.04	835 Ken Griffey, Sr.	.05	.02
779 Mark Lemke	.05	.02	836 Kevin Reimer	.10	.06
780 Terry Steinbach	.05	.02	837 Randy Kutcher	.05	.02
781 Tom Bolton	.05	.02	838 Mike Blowers	.05	.02
782 Randy Tomlin (R)	.20	.12	839 Mike McFarlane	.05	.02
783 Jeff Kunkel	.05	.02	840 Frank Thomas	1.50	.90
784 Felix Jose	.10	.06	841 Ken Griffey, Jr. & Sr.	.50	.30
785 Rick Sutcliffe	.05	.02	842 Jack Howell	.05	.02
786 John Cerutti	.05	.02	843 Mauro Gozzo	.07	.04
787 Jose Vizcaino	.05	.02	844 Gerald Young	.05	.02
788 Curt Schilling	.05	.02	845 Zane Smith	.05	.02
789 Ed Whitson	.05	.02	846 Kevin Brown	.10	.06
790 Tony Pena	.05	.02	847 Sil Campusano	.05	.02
791 John Candelaria	.05	.02	848 Larry Andersen	.05	.02
792 Carmelo Martinez	.05	.02	849 Cal Ripken, Jr. (Fran)	.20	.12
793 Sandy Alomar, Jr.	.07	.04	850 Roger Clemens (Fran)	.15	.08
794 Jim Neidinger (R)	.08	.05	851 Sandy Alomar, Jr (Fr)	.07	.04
795 Red's October	.07	.04	852 Alan Trammell (Fran)	.08	.05
796 Paul Sorrento	.05	.02	853 George Brett (Fran)	.15	.08
797 Tom Pagnozzi	.05	.02	854 Robin Yount (Fran)	.15	.08
798 Tino Martinez	.10	.06	855 Kirby Puckett (Fran)	.15	.08
799 Scott Ruskin (R)	.08	.05	856 Don Mattingly (Fran)	.10	.06
800 Kirk Gibson	.05	.02	857 Rickey Henderson (Fr)	.10	.06
801 Walt Terrell	.05	.02	858 Ken Griffey, Jr. (Fran)	.25	.15
802 John Russell	.05	.02	859 Ruben Sierra (Fran)	.12	.07
803 Chili Davis	.05	.02	860 John Olerud (Fran)	.08	.05

861	Dave Justice (Fran)	.15	.08
862	Ryne Sandberg (Fran)	.15	.08
863	Eric Davis (Fran)	.08	.05
864	Darryl Strawberry (Fr)	.12	.07
865	Tim Wallach (Fran)	.08	.05
866	Doc Gooden (Fran)	.12	.07
867	Lenny Dykstra (Fran)	.08	.05
868	Barry Bonds (Fran)	.15	.08
869	Todd Zeile (Fran)	.07	.04
870	Benito Santiago (Fran)	.07	.04
871	Will Clark (Fran)	.15	.08
872	Craig Biggio (Fran)	.07	.04
873	Wally Joyner (Fran)	.08	.05
874	Frank Thomas (FR)	.70	.40
875	Rickey Henderson (MVP)	.10	.06
876	Barry Bonds (MVP)	.12	.07
877	Bob Welch (Cy Young)	.07	.04
878	Dou Drabek(Cy Young)	.07	.04
879	Sandy Alomar, Jr (ROY)	.08	.05
880	Dave Justice (ROY)	.12	.07
881	Damon Berryhill	.05	.02
882	Frank Viola (DT)	.08	.05
883	Dave Stewart (DT)	.08	.05
884	Doug Jones (DT)	.07	.04
885	Randy Myers (DT)	.07	.04
886	Will Clark (DT)	.50	.30
887	Robert Alomar (DT)	.40	.25
888	Barry Larkin (DT)	.10	.06
889	Wade Boggs (DT)	.20	.12
890	Rickey Henderson (DT)	.50	.30
891	Kirby Puckett (DT)	.40	.25
892	Ken Griffey, Jr. (DT)	1.50	.90
893	Benito Santiago (DT)	.08	.05
BC1	Wade Boggs	.75	.45
BC2	Barry Larkin	.50	.30
BC3	Ken Griffey Jr.	3.00	2.00
BC4	Rickey Henderson	1.50	.90
BC5	George Brett	2.00	1.25
BC6	Will Clark	1.50	.90
BC7	Nolan Ryan	3.00	2.00

1991 Score Traded

Score's 110-card update set is similar in design to their regular issue except for purple and white border colors. The set features rookies and players who were traded during the regular season. The standard-size cards measure 2-1/2" by 3-1/2"

		MINT	NR/MT
Complete Set (110)		6.50	3.50
Commons		.05	.02
1	Bo Jackson	.25	.15
2	Mike Flanagan	.05	.02
3	Pete Incaviglia	.05	.02
4	Jack Clark	.05	.02
5	Hubie Brooks	.05	.02
6	Ivan Calderon	.05	.02
7	Glenn Davis	.05	.02
8	Wally Backman	.05	.02
9	Dave Smith	.05	.02
10	Tim Raines	.05	.02
11	Joe Carter	.12	.07
12	Sid Bream	.05	.02
13	George Bell	.08	.05
14	Steve Bedrosian	.05	.02
15	Willie Wilson	.05	.02
16	Darryl Strawberry	.15	.08
17	Danny Jackson	.05	.02
18	Kirk Gibson	.05	.02
19	Willie McGee	.07	.04
20	Junior Felix	.05	.02
21	Steve Farr	.05	.02
22	Pat Tabler	.05	.02
23	Brett Butler	.07	.04
24	Danny Darwin	.05	.02
25	Mikey Tettleton	.07	.04
26	Gary Carter	.08	.05
27	Mitch Williams	.05	.02
28	Candy Maldonado	.05	.02
29	Otis Nixon	.05	.02

30	Brian Downing	.05	.02
31	Tom Candiotti	.05	.02
32	John Candelaria	.05	.02
33	Rob Murphy	.05	.02
34	Deion Sanders	.25	.15
35	Willie Randolph	.05	.02
36	Pete Harnisch	.07	.04
37	Dante Bichette	.05	.02
38	Garry Templeton	.05	.02
39	Gary Gaetti	.05	.02
40	John Cerutti	.05	.02
41	Rick Cerone	.05	.02
42	Mike Pagliarulo	.05	.02
43	Ron Hassey	.05	.02
44	Roberto Alomar	.30	.18
45	Mike Boddicker	.05	.02
46	Bud Black	.05	.02
47	Rob Deer	.05	.02
48	Devon White	.05	.02
49	Luis Sojo	.05	.02
50	Terry Pendleton	.12	.07
51	Kevin Gross	.05	.02
52	Mike Huff	.05	.02
53	Dave Righetti	.05	.02
54	Matt Young	.05	.02
55	Ernest Riles	.05	.02
56	Bill Gullickson	.05	.02
57	Vince Coleman	.07	.04
58	Fred McGriff	.15	.08
59	Franklin Stubbs	.05	.02
60	Eric King	.05	.02
61	Cory Snyder	.05	.02
62	Dwight Evans	.07	.04
63	Gerald Perry	.05	.02
64	Eric Show	.05	.02
65	Shawn Hillegas	.05	.02
66	Tony Fernandez	.05	.02
67	Tim Teufel	.05	.02
68	Mitch Webster	.05	.02
69	Mike Heath	.05	.02
70	Chili Davis	.05	.02
71	Larry Andersen	.05	.02
72	Gary Varsho	.05	.02
73	Juan Berenguer	.05	.02
74	Jack Morris	.10	.06
75	Barry Jones	.05	.02
76	Rafael Belliard	.05	.02
77	Steve Buechele	.05	.02
78	Scott Sanderson	.05	.02
79	Bob Ojeda	.05	.02
80	Curt Schilling	.05	.02
81	Brian Drahman (R)	.08	.05
82	Ivan Rodriguez (R)	1.50	.90
83	David Howard (R)	.10	.06
84	Healthcliff Slocumb (R)	.10	.06
85	Mike Timlin (R)	.10	.06
86	Darryl Kile	.10	.06
87	Pete Schourek (R)	.10	.06
88	Bruce Walton (R)	.08	.05
89	Al Osuna (R)	.08	.05
90	Gary Scott (R)	.12	.07
91	Doug Simon	.07	.04
92	Chris Jones	.07	.04
93	Chuck Knoblauch	.40	.25
94	Dana Allison (R)	.08	.05
95	Erik Pappas (R)	.08	.05
96	Jeff Bagwell (R)	1.00	.70
97	Kirk Dressendorfer (R)	.12	.07
98	Freddie Benavides (R)	.08	.05
99	Luis Gonzalez (R)	.20	.12
100	Wade Taylor (R)	.15	.08
101	Ed Sprague	.10	.06
102	Bob Scanlan (R)	.10	.06
103	Rick Wilkins (R)	.08	.05
104	Chris Donnels (R)	.08	.05
105	Joe Slusarski (R)	.10	.06
106	Mark Lewis	.25	.15
107	Pat Kelly (R)	.20	.12
108	John Briscoe (R)	.10	.06
109	Luis Lopez (R)	.10	.06
110	Jeff Johnson (R)	.12	.07

1992 Score

For the second straight year Score issued their baseball set in two series which totalled 893-cards. The company redesigned the card fronts using thick border stripes on the left side with smaller borders on the top and bottom. The standard-size cards measure 2-1/2" by 3-1/2". The set is loaded with unique subsets plus a 5-card insert set honoring Joe DiMaggio. Those listings follow the checklist under the prefix BC. A special 4-card Franchise insert set featuring

Musial, Mantle and Yaz are also listed at the end of the checklist under the prefix SP.

		MINT	NR/MT
Complete Set (893)		20.00	14.00
Commons		.05	.02
1	Ken Griffey, Jr.	.40	.25
2	Nolan Ryan	.40	.25
3	Will Clark	.20	.12
4	Dave Justice	.20	.12
5	Dave Henderson	.05	.02
6	Bret Saberhagen	.07	.04
7	Fred McGriff	.15	.08
8	Erik Hanson	.08	.05
9	Darryl Strawberry	.15	.08
10	Doc Gooden	.10	.06
11	Juan Gonzalez	.50	.30
12	Mark Langston	.07	.04
13	Lonnie Smith	.05	.02
14	Jeff Montgomery	.05	.02
15	Robert Alomar	.20	.12
16	Delino DeShields	.15	.08
17	Steve Bedrosian	.05	.02
18	Terry Pendleton	.10	.06
19	Mark Carreon	.05	.02
20	Mark McGwire	.25	.15
21	Roger Clemens	.20	.12
22	Chuck Crim	.05	.02
23	Don Mattingly	.12	.07
24	Dickie Thon	.05	.02
25	Ron Gant	.15	.08
26	Milt Cuyler	.08	.05
27	Mike Macfarlane	.05	.02
28	Dan Gladden	.05	.02
29	Melido Perez	.05	.02
30	Willie Randolph	.05	.02
31	Albert Belle	.12	.07
32	Dave Winfield	.10	.06
33	Jimmy Jones	.05	.02
34	Kevin Gross	.05	.02
35	Andres Galarraga	.05	.02
36	Mike Deveraux	.05	.02
37	Chris Bosio	.05	.02
38	Mike LaValliere	.05	.02
39	Gary Gaetti	.05	.02
40	Felix Jose	.08	.05
41	Alvaro Espinoza	.05	.02
42	Rick Aguilera	.05	.02
43	Mike Gallego	.05	.02
44	Eric Davis	.07	.04
45	George Bell	.08	.05
46	Tom Brunansky	.05	.02
47	Steve Farr	.05	.02
48	Duane Ward	.05	.02
49	David Wells	.05	.02
50	Cecil Fielder	.15	.08
51	Walt Weiss	.05	.02
52	Todd Zeile	.08	.05
53	Doug Jones	.05	.02
54	Bob Walk	.05	.02
55	Rafael Palmeiro	.08	.05
56	Rob Deer	.05	.02
57	Paul O'Neill	.07	.04
58	Jeff Reardon	.08	.05
59	Randy Ready	.05	.02
60	Scott Erickson	.12	.07
61	Paul Molitor	.07	.04
62	Jack McDowell	.15	.08
63	Jim Acker	.05	.02
64	Jay Buhner	.07	.04
65	Travis Fryman	.15	.08
66	Marquis Grisson	.20	.12
67	Mike Harkey	.07	.04
68	Luis Polonia	.05	.02
69	Ken Caminiti	.07	.04
70	Chris Sabo	.08	.05
71	Gregg Olson	.07	.04
72	Carlton Fisk	.08	.05
73	Juan Samuel	.05	.02
74	Todd Stottlemyre	.07	.04
75	Andre Dawson	.10	.06
76	Alvin Davis	.05	.02
77	Bill Doran	.05	.02
78	B.J. Surhoff	.05	.02
79	Kirk McCaskill	.05	.02
80	Dale Murphy	.10	.06
81	Jose DeLeon	.05	.02
82	Alex Fernandez	.08	.05
83	Ivan Calderon	.05	.02
84	Brent Mayne	.05	.02
85	Jody Reed	.05	.02
86	Randy Tomlin	.08	.05
87	Randy Milligan	.05	.02
88	Pascual Perez	.05	.02
89	Hensley Meulens	.05	.02
90	Joe Carter	.12	.07
91	Mike Moore	.05	.02
92	Ozzie Guillen	.05	.02
93	Shawn Hillegas	.05	.02
94	Chili Davis	.05	.02
95	Vince Coleman	.07	.04
96	Jimmy Key	.05	.02
97	Billy Ripken	.05	.02
98	Dave Smith	.05	.02
99	Tom Bolton	.05	.02
100	Barry Larkin	.08	.05
101	Kenny Rogers	.05	.02
102	Mike Boddicker	.05	.02
103	Kevin Elster	.05	.02
104	Ken Hill	.05	.02
105	Charlie Leibrandt	.05	.02
106	Pat Combs	.05	.02

107	Hubie Brooks	.05	.02	165	Scott Lewis	.05	.02
108	Julio Franco	.08	.05	166	Bill Sampen	.05	.02
109	Vicente Palacios	.05	.02	167	Dave Anderson	.05	.02
110	Kal Daniels	.05	.02	168	Kevin McReynolds	.05	.02
111	Bruce Hurst	.07	.04	169	Jose Vizcaino	.05	.02
112	Willie McGee	.07	.04	170	Bob Geren	.05	.02
113	Ted Power	.05	.02	171	Mike Morgan	.05	.02
114	Milt Thompson	.05	.02	172	Jim Gott	.05	.02
115	Doug Drabek	.08	.05	173	Mike Pagliarulo	.05	.02
116	Rafael Belliard	.05	.02	174	Mike Jeffcoat	.05	.02
117	Scott Garrelts	.05	.02	175	Craig Lefferts	.05	.02
118	Terry Mulholland	.05	.02	176	Steve Finley	.05	.02
119	Jay Howell	.05	.02	177	Wally Backman	.05	.02
120	Danny Jackson	.05	.02	178	Kent Mercker	.05	.02
121	Scott Ruskin	.05	.02	179	John Cerutti	.05	.02
122	Robin Ventura	.20	.12	180	Jay Bell	.05	.02
123	Bip Roberts	.05	.02	181	Dale Sveum	.05	.02
124	Jeff Russell	.05	.02	182	Greg Gagne	.05	.02
125	Hal Morris	.10	.06	183	Donnie Hill	.05	.02
126	Teddy Higuera	.05	.02	184	Rex Hudler	.05	.02
127	Luis Sojo	.05	.02	185	Pat Kelly	.10	.06
128	Carlos Baerga	.20	.12	186	Jeff Robinson	.05	.02
129	Jeff Ballard	.05	.02	187	Jeff Gray	.05	.02
130	Tom Gordon	.05	.02	188	Jerry Willard	.05	.02
131	Sid Bream	.05	.02	189	Carlos Quintana	.07	.04
132	Rance Mulliniks	.05	.02	190	Dennis Eckersley	.10	.06
133	Andy Benes	.10	.06	191	Kelly Downs	.05	.02
134	Mickey Tettleton	.05	.02	192	Gregg Jefferies	.10	.06
135	Rich DeLucia	.05	.02	193	Darrin Fletcher	.05	.02
136	Tom Pagnozzi	.05	.02	194	Mike Jackson	.05	.02
137	Harold Baines	.05	.02	195	Eddie Murray	.10	.06
138	Danny Darwin	.05	.02	196	Billy Landrum	.05	.02
139	Kevin Bass	.05	.02	197	Eric Yelding	.05	.02
140	Chris Nabholtz	.07	.04	198	Devon White	.05	.02
141	Pete O'Brien	.05	.02	199	Larry Walker	.12	.07
142	Jeff Treadway	.05	.02	200	Ryne Sandberg	.20	.12
143	Mickey Morandini	.07	.04	201	Dave Magadan	.05	.02
144	Eric King	.05	.02	202	Steve Chitren	.05	.02
145	Danny Tartabull	.10	.06	203	Scott Fletcher	.05	.02
1465	Lance Johnson	.05	.02	204	Dwayne Henry	.05	.02
147	Casey Candaele	.05	.02	205	Scott Coolbaugh	.05	.02
148	Felix Fermin	.05	.02	206	Tracy Jones	.05	.02
149	Rich Rodriguez	.05	.02	207	Von Hayes	.05	.02
150	Dwight Evans	.07	.04	208	Bob Melvin	.05	.02
151	Joe Klink	.05	.02	209	Scott Scudder	.05	.02
152	Kevin Reimer	.07	.04	210	Luis Gonzalez	.12	.07
153	Orlando Merced	.10	.06	211	Scott Sanderson	.05	.02
154	Mel Hall	.07	.04	212	Chris Donnels	.08	.05
155	Randy Myers	.05	.02	213	Heathcliff Slocumb	.07	.04
156	Greg Harris	.05	.02	214	Mike Timlin	.07	.04
157	Jeff Brantley	.05	.02	215	Brian Harper	.05	.02
158	Jim Eisenreich	.05	.02	216	Juan Berenguer	.05	.02
159	Luis Rivera	.05	.02	217	Mike Henneman	.05	.02
160	Cris Carpenter	.05	.02	218	Bill Spiers	.05	.02
161	Bruce Ruffin	.05	.02	219	Scott Terry	.05	.02
162	Omar Vizquel	.05	.02	220	Frank Viola	.07	.04
163	Gerald Alexander	.05	.02	221	Mark Eichhorn	.05	.02
164	Mark Guthrie	.05	.02	222	Ernest Riles	.05	.02

#	Player		
223	Ray Lankford	.20	.12
224	Pete Harnisch	.07	.04
225	Bobby Bonilla	.10	.06
226	Mike Scioscia	.05	.02
227	Joel Skinner	.05	.02
228	Brian Holman	.05	.02
229	Gilberto Reyes	.07	.04
230	Matt Williams	.08	.05
231	Jaime Navarro	.08	.05
232	Jose Rijo	.08	.05
233	Atlee Hammaker	.05	.02
234	Tim Teufel	.05	.02
235	John Kruk	.07	.04
236	Kurt Stillwell	.05	.02
237	Dan Pasqua	.05	.02
238	Tim Crews	.05	.02
239	Dave Gallagher	.05	.02
240	Leo Gomez	.15	.08
241	Steve Avery	.20	.12
242	Bill Gullickson	.05	.02
243	Mark Portugal	.05	.02
244	Lee Guetterman	.05	.02
245	Benny Santiago	.07	.04
246	Jim Gantner	.05	.02
247	Robby Thompson	.05	.02
248	Terry Shumpert	.05	.02
249	Mike Bell (R)	.12	.07
250	Harold Reynolds	.05	.02
251	Mike Felder	.05	.02
252	Bill Pecota	.05	.02
253	Bill Krueger	.05	.02
254	Alfredo Griffin	.05	.02
255	Lou Whitaker	.05	.02
256	Roy Smith	.05	.02
257	Jerald Clark	.05	.02
258	Sammy Sosa	.07	.04
259	Tim Naehring	.07	.04
260	Dave Righetti	.05	.02
261	Paul Gibson	.05	.02
262	Chris James	.05	.02
263	Larry Andersen	.05	.02
264	Storm Davis	.05	.02
265	Jose Lind	.05	.02
266	Greg Hibbard	.05	.02
267	Norm Charlton	.05	.02
268	Paul Kilgus	.05	.02
269	Greg Maddux	.10	.06
270	Ellis Burks	.07	.04
271	Frank Tanana	.05	.02
272	Gene Larkin	.05	.02
273	Ron Hassey	.05	.02
274	Jeff Robinson	.05	.02
275	Steve Howe	.05	.02
276	Daryl Boston	.05	.02
277	Mark Lee	.05	.02
278	Jose Segura (R)	.10	.06
279	Lance Blankenship	.05	.02
280	Don Slaught	.05	.02
281	Russ Swan	.05	.02
282	Bob Tewksbury	.05	.02
283	Geno Petralli	.05	.02
284	Shane Mack	.08	.05
285	Bob Scanlan	.05	.02
286	Tim Leary	.05	.02
287	John Smoltz	.12	.07
288	Pat Borders	.05	.02
289	Mark Davidson	.05	.02
290	Sam Horn	.05	.02
291	Lenny Harris	.05	.02
292	Franklin Stubbs	.05	.02
293	Thomas Howard	.08	.05
294	Steve Lyons	.05	.02
295	Francisco Oliveras	.05	.02
296	Terry Leach	.05	.02
297	Barry Jones	.05	.02
298	Lance Parrish	.05	.02
299	Wally Whitehurst	.05	.02
300	Bob Welch	.07	.04
301	Charlie Hayes	.05	.02
302	Charlie Hough	.05	.02
303	Gary Redus	.05	.02
304	Scott Bradley	.05	.02
305	Jose Oquendo	.05	.02
306	Pete Incaviglia	.05	.02
307	Marvin Freeman	.05	.02
308	Gary Pettis	.05	.02
309	Joe Slusarski	.07	.04
310	Kevin Seitzer	.07	.04
311	Jeff Reed	.05	.02
312	Pat Tabler	.05	.02
313	Mike Maddux	.05	.02
314	Bob Milacki	.05	.02
315	Eric Anthony	.08	.05
316	Dante Bichette	.05	.02
317	Steve Decker	.08	.05
318	Jack Clark	.05	.02
319	Doug Dascenzo	.05	.02
320	Scott Leius	.05	.02
321	Jim Lindeman	.05	.02
322	Bryan Harvey	.07	.04
323	Spike Owen	.05	.02
324	Roberto Kelly	.10	.06
325	Stan Belinda	.05	.02
326	Joe Cora	.05	.02
327	Jeff Innis	.05	.02
328	Willie Wilson	.05	.02
329	Juan Agosto	.05	.02
330	Charles Nagy	.15	.08
331	Scott Bailes	.05	.02
332	Pete Schourek	.07	.04
333	Mike Flanagan	.05	.02
334	Omar Olivares	.05	.02
335	Dennis Lamp	.05	.02
336	Tommy Greene	.07	.04
337	Randy Velarde	.05	.02
338	Tom Lampkin	.05	.02

339	John Russell	.05	.02
340	Bob Kipper	.05	.02
341	Todd Burns	.05	.02
342	Ron Jones	.05	.02
343	Dave Valle	.05	.02
344	Mike Heath	.05	.02
345	John Olerud	.12	.07
346	Gerald Young	.05	.02
347	Ken Patterson	.05	.02
348	Les Lancaster	.05	.02
349	Steve Crawford	.05	.02
350	John Candelaria	.05	.02
351	Mike Aldrete	.05	.02
352	Mariano Duncan	.05	.02
353	Julio Machado	.05	.02
354	Ken Williams	.05	.02
355	Walt Terrell	.05	.02
356	Mitch Williams	.05	.02
357	Al Newman	.05	.02
358	Bud Black	.05	.02
359	Joe Hesketh	.05	.02
360	Paul Assenmacher	.05	.02
361	Bo Jackson	.15	.08
362	Jeff Blauser	.05	.02
363	Mike Brumley	.05	.02
364	Jim Deshaies	.05	.02
365	Brady Anderson	.10	.06
366	Chuck McElroy	.05	.02
367	Matt Merullo	.05	.02
368	Tim Belcher	.07	.04
369	Luis Aquino	.05	.02
370	Joe Oliver	.05	.02
371	Greg Swindell	.07	.04
372	Lee Stevens	.08	.05
373	Mark Knudson	.05	.02
374	Bill Wegman	.05	.02
375	Jerry Don Gleaton	.05	.02
376	Pedro Guerrero	.05	.02
377	Randy Bush	.05	.02
378	Greg Harris	.05	.02
379	Eric Plunk	.05	.02
380	Jose DeJesus	.05	.02
381	Bobby Witt	.07	.04
382	Curtis Wilkerson	.05	.02
383	Gene Nelson	.05	.02
384	Wes Chamberlain	.10	.06
385	Tom Henke	.05	.02
386	Mark Lemke	.05	.02
387	Greg Briley	.05	.02
388	Rafael Ramirez	.05	.02
389	Tony Fossas	.05	.02
390	Henry Cotto	.05	.02
391	Tim Hulett	.05	.02
392	Dean Palmer	.15	.08
393	Glen Braggs	.05	.02
394	Mark Salas	.05	.02
395	Rusty Meacham (R)	.10	.06
396	Andy Ashby (R)	.12	.07
397	Jose Melendez (R)	.12	.07
398	Warren Newson (R)	.10	.06
399	Frank Castillo (R)	.12	.07
400	Chito Martinez (R)	.12	.07
401	Bernie Williams	.12	.07
402	Derek Bell	.15	.08
403	Javier Ortiz (R)	.08	.05
404	Tim Sherrill (R)	.08	.05
405	Rob MacDonald (R)	.08	.05
406	Phil Plantier	.20	.12
407	Troy Afenir	.07	.04
408	Gino Minutelli (R)	.08	.05
409	Reggie Jefferson (R)	.20	.12
410	Mike Remlinger (R)	.07	.04
411	Carlos Rodriguez (R)	.07	.04
412	Joe Redfield (R)	.08	.05
413	Alfonzo Powell (R)	.12	.07
414	Scott Livingstone (R)	.12	.07
415	Scott Kamieniecki (R)	.08	.05
416	Tim Spehr (R)	.08	.05
417	Brian Hunter (R)	.12	.07
418	Ced Landrum (R)	.08	.05
419	Bret Barberie	.12	.07
420	Kevin Morton	.08	.05
421	Doug Henry (R)	.15	.08
422	Doug Piatt (R)	.08	.05
423	Pat Rice (R)	.08	.05
424	Juan Guzman (R)	.80	.50
425	Nolan Ryan (No-Hit)	.25	.15
426	Tommy Greene (No-Hit)	.08	.05
427	Milacki/Flanagan/ Williamson (No-Hit)	.07	.04
428	Wilson Alvarez (NH)	.08	.05
429	Otis Nixon (HL)	.05	.02
430	Rickey Henderson (HL)	.10	.06
431	Cecil Fielder (AS)	.10	.06
432	Julio Franco (AS)	.08	.05
433	Cal Ripken, Jr. (AS)	.15	.08
434	Wade Boggs (AS)	.08	.05
435	Joe Carter (AS)	.10	.06
436	Ken Griffey, Jr. (AS)	.25	.15
437	Ruben Sierra (AS)	.10	.06
438	Scott Erickson (AS)	.08	.05
439	Tom Henke (AS)	.05	.02
440	Terry Steinbach (AS)	.05	.02
441	Ricky Henderson (DT)	.15	.08
442	Ryne Sandberg (DT)	.30	.18
443	Otis Nixon	.05	.02
444	Scott Radinsky	.05	.02
445	Mark Grace	.08	.05
446	Tona Pena	.05	.02
447	Billy Hatcher	.05	.02
448	Glenallen Hill	.08	.05
449	Chris Gwynn	.05	.02
450	Tom Glavine	.20	.12
451	John Habyan	.05	.02

452	Al Osuna	.05	.02
453	Tony Phillips	.05	.02
454	Greg Cadaret	.05	.02
455	Rob Dibble	.07	.04
456	Rick Honeycutt	.05	.02
457	Jerome Walton	.07	.04
458	Mookie Wilson	.05	.02
459	Mark Gubicza	.05	.02
460	Craig Biggio	.07	.04
461	Dave Cochrane	.05	.02
462	Keith Miller	.05	.02
463	Alex Cole	.05	.02
464	Pete Smith	.08	.05
465	Brett Butler	.07	.04
466	Jeff Huson	.05	.02
467	Steve Lake	.05	.02
468	Lloyd Moseby	.05	.02
469	Tim McIntosh	.07	.04
470	Dennis Martinez	.08	.05
471	Greg Myers	.05	.02
472	Mackey Sasser	.05	.02
473	Junior Ortiz	.05	.02
474	Greg Olson	.05	.02
475	Steve Sax	.07	.04
476	Ricky Jordan	.05	.02
477	Max Venable	.05	.02
478	Brian McRae	.15	.08
479	Doug Simons	.05	.02
480	Rickey Henderson	.15	.08
481	Gary Varsho	.05	.02
482	Carl Willis	.05	.02
483	Rick Wilkins	.05	.02
484	Donn Pall	.05	.02
485	Edgar Martinez	.10	.06
486	Tom Foley	.05	.02
487	Mark Williamson	.05	.02
488	Jack Armstrong	.05	.02
489	Gary Carter	.08	.05
490	Ruben Sierra	.15	.08
491	Gerald Perry	.05	.02
492	Rob Murphy	.05	.02
493	Zane Smith	.05	.02
494	Darryl Kile	.08	.05
495	Kelly Gruber	.07	.04
496	Jerry Browne	.05	.02
497	Darryl Hamilton	.05	.02
498	Mike Stanton	.05	.02
499	Mark Leonard	.05	.02
500	Jose Canseco	.25	.15
501	Dave Martinez	.05	.02
502	Jose Guzman	.05	.02
503	Terry Kennedy	.05	.02
504	Ed Sprague	.07	.04
505	Frank Thomas	.80	.50
506	Darren Daulton	.10	.06
507	Kevin Tapani	.07	.04
508	Luis Salazar	.05	.02
509	Paul Faries	.05	.02
510	Sandy Alomar Jr.	.08	.05
511	Jeff King	.07	.04
512	Gary Thurman	.05	.02
513	Chris Hammond	.07	.04
514	Pedro Munoz	.08	.05
515	Alan Trammell	.08	.05
516	Geronimo Pena	.05	.02
517	Rodney McCray	.05	.02
518	Manny Lee	.05	.02
519	Junior Felix	.05	.02
520	Kirk Gibson	.05	.02
521	Darrin Jackson	.05	.02
522	John Burkett	.05	.02
523	Jeff Johnson	.07	.04
524	Jim Corsi	.05	.02
525	Robin Yount	.15	.08
526	Jamie Quirk	.05	.02
527	Bob Ojeda	.05	.02
528	Mark Lewis	.10	.06
529	Bryn Smith	.05	.02
530	Kent Hrbek	.05	.02
531	Dennis Boyd	.05	.02
532	Ron Karkovice	.05	.02
533	Don August	.05	.02
534	Todd Frohwirth	.05	.02
535	Wally Joyner	.08	.05
536	Dennis Rasmussen	.05	.02
537	Andy Allanson	.05	.02
538	Goose Gossage	.05	.02
539	John Marzano	.05	.02
540	Cal Ripken	.35	.20
541	Bill Swift	.05	.02
542	Kevin Appier	.07	.04
543	Dave Bergman	.05	.02
544	Bernard Gilkey	.12	.07
545	Mike Greenwell	.08	.05
546	Jose Uribe	.05	.02
547	Jesse Orasco	.05	.02
548	Bob Patterson	.05	.02
549	Mike Stanley	.05	.02
550	Howard Johnson	.08	.05
551	Joe Orsulak	.05	.02
552	Dick Schofield	.05	.02
553	Dave Hollins	.07	.04
554	David Segui	.07	.04
555	Barry Bonds	.20	.12
556	Mo Vaughn	.15	.08
557	Craig Wilson	.10	.06
558	Bobby Rose	.05	.02
559	Rod Nichols	.05	.02
560	Len Dykstra	.05	.02
561	Craig Grebeck	.05	.02
562	Darren Lewis	.07	.04
563	Todd Benzinger	.05	.02
564	Ed Whitson	.05	.02
565	Jesse Barfield	.05	.02
566	Lloyd McClendon	.05	.02
567	Dan Plesac	.05	.02

568	Danny Cox	.05	.02
569	Skeeter Barnes	.05	.02
570	Bobby Thigpen	.05	.02
571	Deion Sanders	.20	.12
572	Chuck Knoblauch	.20	.12
573	Matt Nokes	.05	.02
574	Herm Winningham	.05	.02
575	Tom Candiotti	.05	.02
576	Jeff Bagwell	.35	.20
577	Brook Jacoby	.05	.02
578	Chico Walker	.05	.02
579	Brian Downing	.05	.02
580	Dave Stewart	.07	.04
581	Francisco Cabrera	.05	.02
582	Rene Gonzales	.05	.02
583	Stan Javier	.05	.02
584	Randy Johnson	.08	.05
585	Chuck Finley	.07	.04
586	Mark Gardner	.05	.02
587	Mark Whiten	.10	.06
588	Garry Templeton	.05	.02
589	Gary Sheffield	.30	.18
590	Ozzie Smith	.10	.06
591	Candy Maldonado	.05	.02
592	Mike Sharperson	.05	.02
593	Carlos Martinez	.05	.02
594	Scott Bankhead	.05	.02
595	Tim Wallach	.05	.02
596	Tino Martinez	.10	.06
597	Roger McDowell	.05	.02
598	Cory Snyder	.05	.02
599	Andujar Cedeno	.12	.07
600	Kirby Puckett	.25	.15
601	Rick Parker	.05	.02
602	Todd Hundley	.07	.04
603	Greg Litton	.05	.02
604	Dave Johnson	.05	.02
605	John Franco	.05	.02
606	Mike Fetters	.05	.02
607	Luis Alicea	.05	.02
608	Trevor Wilson	.05	.02
609	Rob Ducey	.05	.02
610	Ramon Martinez	.10	.06
611	Dave Burba	.07	.04
612	Dwight Smith	.07	.04
613	Kevin Maas	.12	.07
614	John Costello	.05	.02
615	Glenn Davis	.05	.02
616	Shawn Abner	.05	.02
617	Scott Hemond	.08	.05
618	Tom Prince	.07	.04
619	Wally Ritchie	.07	.04
620	Jim Abbott	.12	.07
621	Charlie O'Brien	.05	.02
622	Jack Daugherty	.05	.02
623	Tommy Gregg	.05	.02
624	Jeff Shaw	.05	.02
625	Tony Gwynn	.15	.08
626	Mark Leiter	.07	.04
627	Jim Clancy	.05	.02
628	Tim Layana	.05	.02
629	Jeff Shaefer	.05	.02
630	Lee Smith	.10	.06
631	Wade Taylor	.08	.05
632	Mike Simms	.07	.04
633	Terry Steinbach	.05	.02
634	Shawon Dunston	.07	.04
635	Tim Raines	.05	.02
636	Kirt Manwaring	.05	.02
637	Warren Cromartie	.05	.02
638	Luis Quinones	.05	.02
639	Greg Vaughn	.10	.06
640	Kevin Mitchell	.10	.06
641	Chris Hoiles	.10	.06
642	Tom Browning	.07	.04
643	Mitch Webster	.05	.02
644	Steve Olin	.05	.02
645	Tony Fernandez	.05	.02
646	Juan Bell	.05	.02
647	Joe Boever	.05	.02
648	Carney Lansford	.07	.04
649	Mike Benjamin	.05	.02
650	George Brett	.20	.12
651	Tim Burke	.05	.02
652	Jack Morris	.10	.06
653	Orel Hershiser	.08	.05
654	Mike Schooler	.05	.02
655	Andy Van Slyke	.08	.05
656	Dave Stieb	.07	.04
657	Dave Clark	.05	.02
658	Ben McDonald	.12	.07
659	John Smiley	.08	.05
660	Wade Boggs	.12	.07
661	Eric Bullock	.05	.02
662	Eric Show	.05	.02
663	Lenny Webster	.05	.02
664	Mike Huff	.05	.02
665	Rick Sutcliffe	.05	.02
666	Jeff Manto	.05	.02
667	Mike Fitzgerald	.05	.02
668	Matt Young	.05	.02
669	Dave West	.05	.02
670	Mike Hartley	.05	.02
671	Curt Schilling	.05	.02
672	Brian Bohanon	.05	.02
673	Cecil Espy	.05	.02
674	Joe Grahe	.05	.02
675	Sid Fernandez	.05	.02
676	Edwin Nunez	.05	.02
677	Hector Villanueva	.07	.04
678	Sean Berry	.08	.05
679	Dave Eiland	.05	.02
680	David Cone	.10	.06
681	Mike Bordick	.12	.07
682	Tony Castillo	.05	.02
683	John Barfield	.05	.02

684	Jeff Hamilton	.05	.02
685	Ken Dayley	.05	.02
686	Carmelo Martinez	.05	.02
687	Mike Capel	.05	.02
688	Scott Chiamparino	.07	.04
689	Rich Gedman	.05	.02
690	Rich Monteleone	.05	.02
691	Alejandro Pena	.05	.02
692	Oscar Azocar	.05	.02
693	Jim Poole	.08	.05
694	Mark Gardiner	.07	.04
695	Steve Buechele	.05	.02
696	Rudy Seanez	.10	.06
697	Paul Abbott	.05	.02
698	Steve Searcy	.05	.02
699	Jose Offerman	.08	.05
700	Ivan Rodriquez	.50	.30
701	Joe Girardi	.05	.02
702	Tony Perezchica	.05	.02
703	Paul McClellan	.05	.02
704	David Howard	.05	.02
705	Dan Petry	.05	.02
706	Jack Howell	.05	.02
707	Jose Mesa	.05	.02
708	Randy St. Claire	.05	.02
709	Kevin Brown	.07	.04
710	Ron Darling	.05	.02
711	Jason Grimsley	.05	.02
712	John Orton	.05	.02
713	Shawn Boskie	.05	.02
714	Pat Clements	.05	.02
715	Brian Barnes	.07	.04
716	Luis Lopez	.07	.04
717	Bob McClure	.05	.02
718	Mark Davis	.05	.02
719	Dann Bilardello	.05	.02
720	Tom Edens	.05	.02
721	Willie Fraser	.05	.02
722	Curt Young	.05	.02
723	Neal Heaton	.05	.02
724	Craig Worthington	.05	.02
725	Mel Rojas	.08	.05
726	Daryl Irvine	.05	.02
727	Roger Mason	.05	.02
728	Kirk Dressendorfer	.08	.05
729	Scott Aldred	.05	.02
730	Willie Blair	.05	.02
731	Allan Anderson	.05	.02
732	Dana Kiecker	.05	.02
733	Jose Gonzalez	.05	.02
734	Brian Drahman	.07	.04
735	Brad Komminsk	.05	.02
736	Arthur Rhodes	.15	.08
737	Terry Matthews (R)	.10	.06
738	Jeff Fassero (R)	.10	.06
739	Mike Magnante (R)	.10	.06
740	Kip Gross (R)	.08	.05
741	Jim Hunter (R)	.10	.06
742	Jose Mota (R)	.10	.06
743	Joe Bitker (R)	.08	.05
744	Tim Mauser (R)	.10	.06
745	Ramon Garcia (R)	.08	.05
746	Rod Beck (R)	.12	.07
747	Jim Austin (R)	.08	.05
748	Keith Mitchell	.10	.06
749	Wayne Rosenthal	.08	.05
750	Bryan Hickerson (R)	.10	.06
751	Bruce Egloff	.08	.05
752	John Wehner (R)	.10	.06
753	Darren Holmes (R)	.10	.06
754	Dave Hansen	.10	.06
755	Mike Mussina	.50	.30
756	Anthony Young	.10	.06
757	Ron Tingley	.07	.04
758	Ricky Bones	.08	.05
759	Mark Wohlers	.12	.07
760	Wilson Alvarez	.07	.04
761	Harvey Pulliam	.08	.05
762	Ryan Bowen	.10	.06
763	Terry Bross	.08	.05
764	Joel Johnston	.08	.05
765	Terry McDaniel (R)	.08	.05
766	Esteban Beltre (R)	.10	.06
767	Rob Maurer (R)	.15	.08
768	Ted Wood (R)	.15	.08
769	Mo Sanford	.10	.06
770	Jeff Carter	.08	.05
771	Gil Heredia (R)	.10	.06
772	Monty Fariss	.10	.06
773	Will Clark AS	.12	.07
774	Ryne Sandberg AS	.12	.07
775	Barry Larkin AS	.08	.05
776	Howard Johnson AS	.08	.05
777	Barry Bonds AS	.12	.07
778	Brett Butler AS	.07	.04
779	Tony Gwynn AS	.10	.06
780	Ramon Martinez AS	.08	.05
781	Lee Smith AS	.07	.04
782	Mike Scioscia AS	.05	.02
783	Dennis Martinez HL	.07	.04
784	Dennis Martinez (No-Hit)	.07	.04
785	Mark Gardner (No-Hit)	.08	.05
786	Bret Saberhagen No-Hit)	.08	.05
787	Kent Mercker, Mark Wohlers, Alejandro Pena (No-Hit)	.08	.05
788	Cal Ripken (MVP)	.15	.08
789	Terry Pendleton (MVP)	.10	.06
790	Roger Clemens (CY)	.12	.07
791	Tom Glavine (CY)	.10	.06
792	Chuck Knoblauch (ROY)	.12	.07
793	Jeff Bagwell (ROY)	.25	.15
794	Cal Ripken (Man of	.15	.08

	the Year)		
795	David Cone (HL)	.10	.06
796	Kirby Puckett (HL)	.12	.07
797	Steve Avery (HL)	.12	.07
798	Jack Morris (HL)	.10	.06
799	Allen Watson (R)	.12	.07
800	Manny Ramirez (R)	.70	.40
801	Cliff Floyd (R)	.40	.25
802	Al Shirley (R)	.35	.20
803	Brian Barber (R)	.30	.18
804	Jon Farrell (R)	.10	.06
805	Brent Gates (R)	.30	.18
806	Scott Ruffcorn (R)	.30	.18
807	Tyrone Hill (R)	.30	.18
808	Benji Gil (R)	.25	.15
809	Aaron Sele (R)	.30	.18
810	Tyler Green (R)	.40	.25
811	Chris Jones	.07	.04
812	Steve Wilson	.07	.04
813	Freddie Benavides	.05	.02
814	Don Wakamatsu (R)	.08	.05
815	Mike Humphreys (R)	.08	.05
816	Scott Servais (R)	.10	.06
817	Rico Rossy (R)	.10	.06
818	John Ramos (R)	.08	.05
819	Rob Mallicoat (R)	.08	.05
820	Milt Hill (R)	.08	.05
821	Carlos Garcia (R)	.15	.08
822	Stan Royer (R)	.10	.06
823	Jeff Plympton (R)	.08	.05
824	Braulio Castillo (R)	.15	.08
825	David Haas (R)	.08	.05
826	Luis Mercedes	.12	.07
827	Eric Karros	.50	.03
828	Shawn Hare (R)	.10	.06
829	Reggie Sanders	.40	.25
830	Tom Goodwin	.10	.06
831	Dan Gakeler (R)	.08	.05
832	Stacy Jones (R)	.08	.05
833	Kim Batiste	.10	.06
834	Cal Eldred	.20	.12
835	Chris George	.08	.05
836	Wayne Housie (R)	.08	.05
837	Mike Ignasiak (R)	.08	.05
838	Jose Manzanillo (R)	.10	.06
839	Jim Olander (R)	.08	.05
840	Gary Cooper (R)	.08	.05
841	Royce Clayton	.15	.08
842	Hector Fajardo (R)	.15	.08
843	Blaine Beatty	.07	.04
844	Jorge Pedre (R)	.08	.05
845	Kenny Lofton	.40	.25
846	Scott Brosius (R)	.10	.06
847	Chris Cron (R)	.10	.06
848	Denis Boucher	.07	.04
849	Kyle Abbott	.12	.07
850	Robert Zupcic (R)	.25	.15
851	Rheal Cormier	.12	.07

852	Jim Lewis (R)	.08	.05
853	Anthony Telford	.08	.05
854	Cliff Brantley (R)	.08	.05
855	Kevin Campbell (R)	.08	.05
856	Craig Shipley (R)	.08	.05
857	Chuck Carr	.07	.04
858	Tony Eusebio (R)	.08	.05
859	Jim Thome	.15	.08
860	Vinny Castilla (R)	.08	.05
861	Dann Howitt	.08	.05
862	Kevin Ward (R)	.08	.05
863	Steve Wapnick (R)	.08	.05
864	Rod Brewer	.07	.04
865	Todd Van Poppel	.25	.15
866	Jose Hernandez (R)	.12	.07
867	Amalio Carreno (R)	.08	.05
868	Calvin Jones (R)	.10	.06
869	Jeff Gardner (R)	.08	.05
870	Jarvis Brown (R)	.08	.05
871	Eddie Taubensee (R)	.12	.07
872	Andy Mota	.10	.06
873	Chris Haney	.12	.07
874	Roberto Hernandez	.10	.06
875	Laddie Renfroe (R)	.08	.05
876	Scott Cooper	.12	.07
877	Armando Reynoso	.07	.04
878	Ty Cobb	.25	.15
879	Babe Ruth	.50	.30
880	Honus Wagner	.25	.15
881	Lou Gehrig	.35	.20
882	Satchel Page	.25	.15
883	Will Clark DT	.30	.18
884	Cal Ripken DT	.40	.25
885	Wade Boggs DT	.20	.12
886	Tony Gwynn DT	.25	.15
887	Kirby Puckett DT	.25	.15
888	Craig Biggio DT	.10	.06
889	Scott Erikson DT	.20	.12
890	Tom Glavine DT	.20	.12
891	Rob Dibble DT	.08	.05
892	Mitch Williams DT	.08	.05
893	Frank Thomas DT	1.25	.80
BC1	Joe DiMaggio	35.00	20.00
BC2	Joe DiMaggio	40.00	25.00
BC3	Joe DiMaggio	35.00	20.00
BC4	Joe DiMaggio	40.00	25.00
BC5	Joe DiMaggio	35.00	20.00
SP1	Stan Musial	15.00	10.00
SP2	Mickey Mantle	25.00	15.00
SP3	Carl Yastzremski	15.00	10.00
SP4	S. Musial, M. Mantle,	25.00	15.00
	C. Yastzremski		

1992 Score Traded

This 110-card set features player's traded during the year and a number of 1992 rookies. Cards measure 2-1/2" by 3-1/2" and are patterned after the 1992 Score regular edition.

	MINT	NR/MT
Complete Set (110)	11.00	7.50
Commons	.05	.02

		MINT	NR/MT
1	Gary Sheffield	.25	.15
2	Kevin Seitzer	.05	.02
3	Danny Tartabull	.10	.06
4	Steve Sax	.07	.04
5	Bobby Bonilla	.12	.07
6	Frank Viola	.07	.04
7	Dave Winfield	.12	.07
8	Rick Sutcliffe	.05	.02
9	Jose Canseco	.25	.15
10	Greg Swindell	.05	.02
11	Eddie Murray	.12	.07
12	Randy Myers	.05	.02
13	Wally Joyner	.08	.05
14	Kenny Lofton	.25	.15
15	Jack Morris	.10	.06
16	Charlie Hayes	.05	.02
17	Pete Incaviglia	.05	.02
18	Kevin Mitchell	.08	.05
19	Kurt Stillwell	.05	.02
20	Bret Saberhagen	.08	.05
21	Steve Buechele	.05	.02
22	John Smiley	.07	.04
23	Sammy Sosa	.05	.02
24	George Bell	.08	.05
25	Curt Schilling	.05	.02
26	Dick Schofield	.05	.02
27	David Cone	.08	.05
28	Dan Gladden	.05	.02
29	Kirk McCaskill	.05	.02
30	Mike Gallego	.05	.02
31	Kevin McReynolds	.07	.04
32	Bill Swift	.07	.04
33	Dave Martinez	.05	.02
34	Storm Davis	.05	.02
35	Willie Randolph	.07	.04
36	Melido Perez	.07	.04
37	Mark Carreon	.05	.02
38	Doug Jones	.05	.02
39	Gregg Jefferies	.10	.06
40	Mike Jackson	.05	.02
41	Dickie Thon	.05	.02
42	Eric King	.05	.02
43	Herm Winningham	.05	.02
44	Derek Lilliquist	.05	.02
45	Dave Anderson	.05	.02
46	Jeff Reardon	.10	.06
47	Scott Bankhead	.05	.02
48	Cory Snyder	.05	.02
49	Al Newman	.05	.02
50	Keith Miller	.05	.02
51	Dave Burba	.05	.02
52	Bill Pecota	.05	.02
53	Chuck Crim	.05	.02
54	Mariano Duncan	.05	.02
55	Dave Gallagher	.05	.02
56	Chris Gwynn	.05	.02
57	Scott Ruskin	.05	.02
58	Jack Armstrong	.05	.02
59	Gary Carter	.10	.06
60	Andres Galarraga	.07	.04
61	Ken Hill	.07	.04
62	Eric Davis	.08	.05
63	Ruben Sierra	.20	.12
64	Darrin Fletcher	.05	.02
65	Tim Belcher	.07	.04
66	Mike Morgan	.05	.02
67	Scott Scudder	.05	.02
68	Tom Candiotti	.05	.02
69	Hubie Brooks	.05	.02
70	Kal Daniels	.05	.02
71	Bruce Ruffin	.05	.02
72	Billy Hatcher	.05	.02
73	Bob Melvin	.05	.02
74	Lee Guetterman	.05	.02
75	Rene Gonzales	.05	.02
76	Kevin Bass	.05	.02
77	Tom Bolton	.05	.02
78	John Wetteland	.07	.04
79	Bip Roberts	.05	.02
80	Pat Listach (R)	1.25	.80
81	John Doherty (R)	.10	.06
82	Sam Militello (R)	.35	.20
83	Brian Jordan (R)	.25	.15
84	Jeff Kent (R)	.20	.12
85	Dave Fleming	.50	.30
86	Jeff Tackett	.08	.05
87	Chad Curtis (R)	.25	.15
88	Eric Fox (R)	.10	.06

#	Player	MINT	NR/MT
89	Denny Neagle	.08	.05
90	Donovan Osborne	.25	.15
91	Carlos Hernandez	.08	.05
92	Tim Wakefield (R)	3.50	2.00
93	Tim Salmon	.40	.25
94	Dave Nilsson	.20	.12
95	Mike Perez	.08	.05
96	Pat Hentgen	.08	.05
97	Frank Seminara (R)	.20	.12
98	Ruben Amaro, Jr.	.08	.05
99	Archi Cianfrocco	.15	.10
100	Andy Stankiewicz (R)	.12	.07
101	Jim Bullinger	.08	.05
102	Pat Mahomes (R)	.40	.25
103	Hipolito Pichardo (R)	.15	.10
104	Bret Boone	.50	.30
105	John Vander Wal (R)	.12	.07
106	Vince Horsman (R)	.10	.06
107	James Austin (R)	.08	.05
108	Brian Williams (R)	.30	.18
109	Dan Walters (R)	.10	.06
110	Wil Cordero (R)	.40	.25

1992 Score Impact

The cards in this 90-card set were available in Score cello packs and feature both superstars and prospects. Different photos and border colors were used to distinguish the set from Score's regular issue. Cards measure 2-1/2" by 3-1/2".

	MINT	NR/MT
Complete Set (90)	18.00	12.50
Commons	.08	.05

#	Player	MINT	NR/MT
1	Chuck Knoblauch	.40	.25
2	Jeff Bagwell	.80	.50
3	Juan Guzman	1.50	.90
4	Milt Cuyler	.12	.07
5	Ivan Rodriguez	1.00	.70
6	Rich DeLucia	.10	.06
7	Orlando Merced	.15	.08
8	Ray Lankford	.25	.15
9	Brian Hunter	.12	.07
10	Roberto Alomar	.50	.30
11	Wes Chamberlain	.12	.07
12	Steve Avery	.40	.25
13	Scott Erickson	.25	.15
14	Jim Abbott	.15	.08
15	Mark Whiten	.15	.08
16	Leo Gomez	.15	.08
17	Doug Henry	.15	.08
18	Brent Mayne	.08	.05
19	Charles Nagy	.20	.12
20	Phil Plantier	.80	.50
21	Mo Vaughn	.25	.15
22	Craig Biggio	.08	.05
23	Derek Bell	.25	.15
24	Royce Clayton	.35	.20
25	Gary Cooper	.10	.06
26	Scott Cooper	.20	.12
27	Juan Gonzalez	1.75	1.00
28	Ken Griffey Jr.	2.00	1.25
29	Larry Walker	.25	.15
30	John Smoltz	.25	.15
31	Todd Hundley	.10	.06
32	Kenny Lofton	.75	.45
33	Andy Mota	.08	.05
34	Todd Zeile	.10	.06
35	Arthur Rhodes	.20	.12
36	Jim Thome	.20	.12
37	Todd Van Poppel	.60	.35
38	Mark Wohlers	.15	.08
39	Anthony Young	.15	.08
40	Sandy Alomar Jr.	.10	.06
41	John Olerud	.15	.08
42	Robin Ventura	.50	.30
43	Frank Thomas	2.75	1.75
44	Dave Justice	.75	.45
45	Hal Morris	.15	.08
46	Ruben Sierra	.35	.20
47	Travis Fryman	.40	.25
48	Mike Mussina	1.25	.80
49	Tom Glavine	.50	.30
50	Barry Larkin	.15	.08
51	Will Clark	.50	.30
52	Jose Canseco	.60	.35
53	Bo Jackson	.25	.15
54	Dwight Gooden	.12	.07
55	Barry Bonds	.35	.20
56	Fred McGriff	.30	.18
57	Roger Clemens	.50	.30
58	Benito Santiago	.12	.07
59	Darryl Strawberry	.25	.15
60	Cecil Fielder	.30	.18
61	John Franco	.08	.05
62	Matt Williams	.15	.08
63	Marquis Grissom	.25	.15
64	Danny Tartabull	.15	.08
65	Ron Gant	.20	.12
66	Paul O'Neill	.12	.07
67	Devon White	.08	.05
68	Rafael Palmeiro	.12	.07
69	Tom Gordon	.08	.05
70	Shawon Dunston	.10	.06
71	Rob Dibble	.08	.05
72	Eddie Zosky	.12	.07
73	Jack McDowell	.25	.15
74	Lenny Dykstra	.08	.05
75	Ramon Martinez	.10	.06

76	Reggie Sanders	1.00	.70
77	Greg Maddux	.20	.12
78	Ellis Burks	.10	.06
79	John Smiley	.10	.06
80	Roberto Kelly	.15	.08
81	Ben McDonald	.20	.12
82	Mark Lewis	.12	.07
83	Jose Rijo	.10	.06
84	Ozzie Guillen	.08	.05
85	Lance Dickson	.15	.08
86	Kim Batiste	.15	.08
87	Gregg Olson	.10	.06
88	Andy Benes	.12	.07
89	Cal Eldred	.40	.25
90	David Cone	.15	.08

1992 Score Pinnacle

Score entered the premium card market with their first upscale baseball set. The 620-card set was released in two series and featured a number of inventive subsets such as Idols, Sidelines, Technicians and Shades. Random insert subsets include the 12 card Team Pinnacle set and the 18-card Rookie Idols set. Cello packs contain a special 40-card insert set dubbed Team 2000 featuring projected stars in the year 2000. The standard-size cards measure 2-1/2" by 3-1/2"

		MINT	NR/MT
Complete Set (620)		70.00	50.00
Commons		.07	.04
1	Frank Thomas	3.50	2.25
2	Benito Santiago	.10	.06

3	Carlos Baerga	.35	.20
4	Cecil Fielder	.50	.30
5	Barry Larkin	.15	.08
6	Ozzie Smith	.20	.12
7	Willie McGee	.10	.06
8	Paul Molitor	.10	.06
9	Andy Van Slyke	.10	.06
10	Ryne Sandberg	.80	.50
11	Kevin Seitzer	.07	.04
12	Lenny Dykstra	.08	.05
13	Edgar Martinez	.20	.12
14	Ruben Sierra	.50	.30
15	Howard Johnson	.15	.08
16	Dave Henderson	.07	.04
17	Devon White	.07	.04
18	Terry Pendleton	.15	.08
19	Steve Finley	.08	.05
20	Kirby Puckett	.75	.45
21	Orel Hershiser	.12	.07
22	Hal Morris	.15	.08
23	Don Mattingly	.30	.18
24	Delino DeShields	.30	.18
25	Dennis Eckersley	.15	.08
26	Ellis Burks	.08	.05
27	Jay Buhner	.10	.06
28	Matt Williams	.12	.07
29	Lou Whitaker	.07	.04
30	Alex Fernandez	.12	.07
31	Albert Belle	.35	.20
32	Todd Zeile	.12	.07
33	Tony Pena	.07	.04
34	Jay Bell	.07	.04
35	Rafael Palmeiro	.10	.06
36	Wes Chamberlain	.12	.07
37	George Bell	.10	.06
38	Robin Yount	.30	.18
39	Vince Coleman	.08	.05
40	Bruce Hurst	.08	.05
41	Harold Baines	.08	.05
42	Chuck Finley	.08	.05
43	Ken Caminiti	.07	.04
44	Ben McDonald	.20	.15
45	Roberto Alomar	.70	.40
46	Chili Davis	.07	.04
47	Bill Doran	.07	.04
48	Jerald Clark	.08	.05
49	Jose Lind	.07	.04
50	Nolan Ryan	1.75	1.00
51	Phil Plantier	.50	.30
52	Gary DiSarcina	.08	.05
53	Kevin Bass	.07	.04
54	Pat Kelly	.12	.07
55	Mark Wohlers	.20	.12
56	Walt Weiss	.07	.04
57	Lenny Harris	.07	.04
58	Ivan Calderon	.07	.04
59	Harold Reynolds	.07	.04
60	George Brett	.30	.18

61	Gregg Olson	.08	.05
62	Orlando Merced	.12	.07
63	Steve Decker	.10	.06
64	John Franco	.07	.04
65	Greg Maddux	.15	.08
66	Alex Cole	.08	.05
67	Dave Hollins	.12	.07
68	Kent Hrbek	.07	.04
69	Tom Pagnozzi	.07	.04
70	Jeff Bagwell	.80	.50
71	Jim Gantner	.07	.04
72	Matt Nokes	.07	.04
73	Brian Harper	.07	.04
74	Andy Benes	.12	.07
75	Tom Glavine	.50	.30
76	Terry Steinbach	.07	.04
77	Dennis Martinez	.08	.05
78	John Olerud	.20	.12
79	Ozzie Guillen	.07	.04
80	Darryl Strawberry	.25	.15
81	Gary Gaetti	.07	.04
82	Dave Righetti	.07	.04
83	Chris Hoiles	.12	.07
84	Andujar Cedeno	.15	.08
85	Jack Clark	.07	.04
86	David Howard	.07	.04
87	Bill Gullickson	.07	.04
88	Bernard Gilkey	.15	.08
89	Kevin Elster	.07	.04
90	Kevin Maas	.15	.07
91	Mark Lewis	.12	.07
92	Greg Vaughn	.12	.07
93	Bret Barberie	.10	.06
94	Dave Smith	.07	.04
95	Roger Clemens	.80	.50
96	Doug Drabek	.12	.07
97	Omar Vizquel	.07	.04
98	Jose Guzman	.07	.04
99	Juan Samuel	.07	.04
100	Dave Justice	.80	.50
101	Tom Browning	.07	.04
102	Mark Gubicza	.07	.04
103	Mickey Morandini	.08	.05
104	Ed Whitson	.07	.04
105	Lance Parrish	.07	.04
106	Scott Erickson	.20	.12
107	Jack McDowell	.25	.15
108	Dave Stieb	.08	.05
109	Mike Moore	.07	.04
110	Travis Fryman	.75	.45
111	Dwight Gooden	.12	.07
112	Fred McGriff	.25	.15
113	Alan Trammell	.08	.05
114	Roberto Kelly	.15	.08
115	Andre Dawson	.15	.08
116	Bill Landrum	.07	.04
117	Brian McRae	.12	.07
118	B.J. Surhoff	.07	.04
119	Chuck Knoblauch	.40	.25
120	Steve Olin	.07	.04
121	Robin Ventura	.50	.30
122	Will Clark	.80	.05
123	Tino Martinez	.20	.12
124	Dale Murphy	.12	.07
125	Pete O'Brien	.07	.04
126	Ray Lankford	.25	.15
127	Juan Gonzalez	1.75	1.00
128	Ron Gant	.25	.15
129	Marquis Grissom	.35	.20
130	Jose Canseco	.80	.50
131	Mike Greenwell	.12	.07
132	Mark Langston	.12	.07
133	Brett Butler	.10	.06
134	Kelly Gruber	.08	.05
135	Chris Sabo	.08	.05
136	Mark Grace	.15	.08
137	Tony Fernandez	.08	.05
138	Glenn Davis	.08	.05
139	Pedro Munoz	.12	.07
140	Craig Biggio	.10	.06
141	Pete Schourek	.10	.06
142	Mike Boddicker	.07	.04
143	Robby Thompson	.07	.04
144	Mel Hall	.08	.05
145	Bryan Harvey	.08	.05
146	Mike LaValliere	.07	.04
147	John Kruk	.08	.05
148	Joe Carter	.25	.15
149	Greg Olson	.08	.05
150	Julio Franco	.12	.07
151	Darryl Hamilton	.07	.04
152	Felix Fermin	.07	.04
153	Jose Offerman	.12	.07
154	Paul O'Neill	.10	.06
155	Tommy Greene	.10	.06
156	Ivan Rodriguez	1.00	.70
157	Dave Stewart	.08	.05
158	Jeff Reardon	.10	.06
159	Felix Jose	.20	.12
160	Doug Dascenzo	.07	.04
161	Tim Wallach	.08	.05
162	Dan Plesac	.07	.04
163	Luis Gonzalez	.12	.07
164	Mike Henneman	.07	.05
165	Mike Devereaux	.10	.06
166	Luis Polonia	.07	.04
167	Mike Sharperson	.07	.04
168	Chris Donnels	.08	.05
169	Greg Harris	.07	.04
170	Deion Sanders	.35	.20
171	Mike Schooler	.07	.04
172	Jose DeJesus	.07	.04
173	Jeff Montgomery	.07	.04
174	Milt Cuyler	.12	.07
175	Wade Boggs	.25	.15
176	Kevin Tapani	.08	.05

177	Bill Spiers	.07	.04	235	Gary Sheffield	.80	.50
178	Tim Raines	.07	.04	236	Steve Chitren	.08	.05
179	Randy Milligan	.07	.04	237	Zane Smith	.07	.04
180	Rob Dibble	.08	.05	238	Tom Gordon	.08	.05
181	Kirt Manwaring	.07	.04	239	Jose Oquendo	.07	.04
182	Pascual Perez	.07	.04	240	Todd Stottlemyre	.08	.05
183	Juan Guzman	1.75	1.00	241	Darren Daulton	.10	.06
184	John Smiley	.12	.07	242	Tim Naehring	.10	.06
185	David Segui	.08	.05	243	Tony Phillips	.07	.04
186	Omar Oliveras	.07	.04	244	Shawon Dunston	.10	.06
187	Joe Slusarski	.08	.05	245	Manuel Lee	.07	.04
188	Erik Hanson	.08	.05	246	Mike Pagliarulo	.07	.04
189	Mark Portugal	.07	.04	247	Jim Thome	.30	.18
190	Walt Terrell	.07	.04	248	Luis Mercedes	.15	.08
191	John Smoltz	.25	.15	249	Cal Eldred	.35	.20
192	Wilson Alvarez	.08	.05	250	Derek Bell	.30	.18
193	Jimmy Key	.07	.04	251	Arthur Rhodes	.25	.15
194	Larry Walker	.30	.18	252	Scott Cooper	.25	.15
195	Lee Smith	.12	.07	253	Roberto Hernandez	.12	.07
196	Pete Harnisch	.10	.06	254	Mo Sanford	.15	.08
197	Mike Harkey	.10	.06	255	Scott Servais	.10	.06
198	Frank Tanana	.07	.04	256	Eric Karros	1.75	1.00
199	Terry Mulholland	.07	.04	257	Andy Mota	.08	.05
200	Cal Ripken Jr.	1.25	.80	258	Keith Mitchell	.12	.07
201	Dave Magadan	.08	.05	259	Joel Johnson	.12	.07
202	Bud Black	.07	.04	260	John Wehner	.10	.06
203	Terry Shumpert	.08	.05	261	Gino Minutelli	.10	.06
204	Mike Mussina	2.00	1.25	262	Greg Gagne	.08	.05
205	Mo Vaughn	.25	.15	263	Stan Royer	.08	.05
206	Steve Farr	.07	.04	264	Carlos Garcia	.25	.15
207	Darrin Jackson	.07	.04	265	Andy Ashby	.08	.05
208	Jerry Browne	.07	.04	266	Kim Batiste	.12	.07
209	Jeff Russell	.07	.04	267	Julio Velera	.10	.06
210	Mike Scioscia	.07	.04	268	Royce Clayton	.40	.25
211	Rick Aguilera	.07	.04	269	Gary Scott	.10	.06
212	Jaime Navarro	.15	.08	270	Kirk Dressendorfer	.10	.06
213	Randy Tomlin	.15	.08	271	Sean Berry	.12	.07
214	Bobby Thigpen	.08	.05	272	Lance Dickson	.12	.07
215	Mark Gardner	.08	.05	273	Rob Maurer (R)	.25	.15
216	Norm Charlton	.07	.04	274	Scott Brosius (R)	.12	.07
217	Mark McGwire	.75	.45	275	Dave Fleming	1.75	1.00
218	Skeeter Barnes	.07	.04	276	Lenny Webster	.07	.04
219	Bob Tewksbury	.07	.04	277	Mike Humphries	.08	.05
220	Junior Felix	.07	.04	278	Fred Benavides	.07	.04
221	Sam Horn	.07	.04	279	Harvey Pulliam	.12	.07
222	Jody Reed	.07	.04	280	Joe Carter	.10	.06
223	Luis Sojo	.07	.04	281	Jim Abbott (ID)	.35	.20
224	Jerome Walton	.08	.05	282	Wade Boggs (ID)	.20	.12
225	Darryl Kile	.10	.06	283	Ken Griffey Jr. (ID)	.70	.40
226	Mickey Tettleton	.08	.05	284	Wally Joyner (ID)	.10	.06
227	Dan Pasqua	.07	.04	285	Chuck Knoblauch (ID)	.20	.12
228	Jim Gott	.07	.04	286	Robin Ventura (ID)	.35	.20
229	Bernie Williams	.15	.08	287	Robin Yount (SL)	.25	.15
230	Shane Mack	.20	.12	288	Bob Tewksbury (SL)	.07	.04
231	Steve Avery	.50	.30	289	Kirby Puckett (SL)	.35	.20
232	Dave Valle	.07	.04	290	Kenny Lofton (SL)	.25	.15
233	Mark Leonard	.07	.04	291	Jack McDowell SL)	.20	.12
234	Spike Owen	.07	.04	292	John Burkett (SL)	.07	.04

293	Dwight Smith (SL)	.07	.04
294	Nolan Ryan (SL)	.80	.50
295	Manny Ramirez (R)	1.50	.90
296	Cliff Floyd (R)	1.00	.70
297	Al Shirley (R)	.75	.45
298	Brian Barber (R)	.40	.25
299	Jon Farrell (R)	.25	.15
300	Scott Ruffcorn (R)	.30	.18
301	Tyrone Hill (R)	.50	.30
302	Benji Gil (R)	.30	.18
303	Tyler Green (R)	.90	.60
304	Allen Watson (R)	.25	.15
305	Jay Buhner	.10	.06
306	Roberto Alomar (SH)	.30	.18
307	Chuck Knoblauch (SH)	.20	.12
308	Darryl Strawberry (SH)	.20	.12
309	Danny Tartabull (SH)	.15	.08
310	Bobby Bonilla (SH)	.15	.08
311	Mike Felder	.08	.05
312	Storm Davis	.07	.04
313	Tim Teufel	.07	.04
314	Tom Brunansky	.07	.04
315	Rex Hudler	.07	.04
316	Dave Otto	.07	.04
317	Jeff King	.10	.06
318	Dan Gladden	.07	.04
319	Bill Pecota	.07	.04
320	Franklin Stubbs	.07	.04
321	Gary Carter	.12	.07
322	Melido Perez	.08	.05
323	Eric Davis	.12	.07
324	Greg Myers	.07	.04
325	Pete Incaviglia	.07	.04
326	Von Hayes	.07	.04
327	Greg Swindell	.08	.05
328	Steve Sax	.08	.05
329	Chuck McElroy	.08	.05
330	Gregg Jefferies	.15	.08
331	Joe Oliver	.08	.05
332	Paul Faries	.07	.04
333	David West	.07	.04
334	Craig Grebeck	.08	.05
335	Chris Hammond	.10	.06
336	Billy Ripken	.07	.04
337	Scott Sanderson	.07	.04
338	Dick Schofield	.07	.04
339	Bob Milacki	.07	.04
340	Kevin Reimer	.10	.06
341	Jose DeLeon	.07	.04
342	Henry Cotto	.07	.04
343	Daryl Boston	.07	.04
344	Kevin Gross	.07	.04
345	Milt Thompson	.07	.04
346	Luis Rivera	.07	.04
347	Al Osuna	.07	.04
348	Rob Deer	.07	.04
349	Tim Leary	.07	.04
350	Mike Stanton	.07	.04
351	Dean Palmer	.20	.12
352	Trevor Wilson	.08	.05
353	Mark Eichhorn	.07	.04
354	Scott Aldred	.10	.06
355	Mark Whiten	.15	.08
356	Leo Gomez	.15	.08
357	Rafael Belliard	.07	.04
358	Carlos Quintana	.08	.05
359	Mark Davis	.07	.04
360	Chris Nabholz	.10	.06
361	Carlton Fisk	.20	.12
362	Joe Orsulak	.08	.05
363	Eric Anthony	.25	.15
364	Greg Hibbard	.08	.05
365	Scott Leius	.07	.04
366	Hensley Meulens	.08	.05
367	Chris Bosio	.07	.04
368	Brian Downing	.07	.04
369	Sammy Sosa	.12	.07
370	Stan Belinda	.08	.05
371	Joe Grahe	.08	.05
372	Luis Salazar	.07	.04
373	Lance Johnson	.07	.04
374	Kal Daniels	.07	.04
375	Dave Winfield	.20	.12
376	Brook Jacoby	.07	.04
377	Mariano Duncan	.07	.04
378	Ron Darling	.07	.04
379	Randy Johnson	.15	.08
380	Chito Martinez	.12	.07
381	Andres Galarraga	.07	.04
382	Willie Randolph	.07	.04
383	Charles Nagy	.25	.15
384	Tim Belcher	.08	.05
385	Duane Ward	.07	.04
386	Vicente Palacios	.07	.04
387	Mike Gallego	.07	.04
388	Rich DeLucia	.08	.05
389	Scott Radinsky	.10	.06
390	Damon Berryhill	.07	.04
391	Kirk McCaskill	.07	.04
392	Pedro Guerrero	.08	.05
393	Kevin Mitchell	.12	.07
394	Dickie Thon	.07	.04
395	Bobby Bonilla	.15	.08
396	Bill Wegman	.07	.04
397	Dave Martinez	.07	.04
398	Rick Sutcliffe	.08	.05
399	Larry Anderson	.07	.04
400	Tony Gwynn	.30	.18
401	Rickey Henderson	.40	.25
402	Greg Cadaret	.07	.04
403	Keith Miller	.07	.04
404	Bip Roberts	.07	.04
405	Kevin Brown	.10	.06
406	Mitch Williams	.08	.05
407	Frank Viola	.10	.06
408	Darren Lewis	.12	.07

409	Bob Welch	.10	.06	467	Alvin Davis	.07	.04
410	Bob Walk	.07	.04	468	Jim Eisenreich	.07	.04
411	Todd Frohwirt	.10	.06	469	Brent Mayne	.08	.05
412	Brian Hunter	.15	.08	470	Jeff Brantley	.08	.05
413	Ron Karkovice	.07	.04	471	Tim Burke	.07	.04
414	Mike Morgan	.07	.04	472	Pat Mahomes (R)	.25	.15
415	Joe Hesketh	.07	.04	473	Ryan Bowen	.15	.08
416	Don Slaught	.07	.04	474	Bryn Smith	.07	.04
417	Tom Henke	.07	.04	475	Mike Flanagan	.07	.04
418	Kurt Stillwell	.07	.04	476	Reggie Jefferson	.12	.07
419	Hector Villanueva	.08	.05	477	Jeff Blauser	.07	.04
420	Glenallen Hill	.10	.06	478	Craig Lefferts	.07	.04
421	Pat Borders	.07	.04	479	Todd Worrell	.08	.05
422	Charlie Hough	.07	.04	480	Scott Scudder	.08	.05
423	Charlie Leibrandt	.07	.04	481	Kirk Gibson	.07	.04
424	Eddie Murray	.15	.08	482	Kenny Rogers	.07	.04
425	Jesse Barfield	.07	.04	483	Jack Morris	.15	.08
426	Mark Lemke	.07	.04	484	Russ Swann	.07	.04
427	Kevin McReynolds	.08	.05	485	Mike Huff	.07	.04
428	Gilberto Reyes	.07	.04	486	Ken Hill	.12	.07
429	Ramon Martinez	.15	.08	487	Geronimo Pena	.10	.06
430	Steve Buechele	.07	.04	488	Charlie O'Brien	.07	.04
431	David Wells	.07	.04	489	Mike Maddux	.07	.04
432	Kyle Abbott	.12	.07	490	Scott Livingstone	.15	.08
433	John Habyan	.07	.04	491	Carl Willis	.07	.04
434	Kevin Appier	.10	.06	492	Kelly Downs	.07	.04
435	Gene Larkin	.07	.04	493	Dennis Cook	.07	.04
436	Sandy Alomar, Jr.	.12	.07	494	Joe Magrane	.08	.05
437	Mike Jackson	.08	.05	495	Bob Kipper	.07	.04
438	Todd Benzinger	.07	.04	496	Jose Mesa	.07	.04
439	Teddy Higuera	.07	.04	497	Charlie Hayes	.07	.04
440	Reggie Sanders	1.25	.80	498	Joe Girardi	.07	.04
441	Mark Carreon	.07	.04	499	Doug Jones	.07	.04
442	Bret Saberhagen	.15	.08	500	Barry Bonds	.60	.35
443	Gene Nelson	.07	.04	501	Bill Krueger	.07	.04
444	Jay Howell	.07	.04	502	Glenn Braggs	.07	.04
445	Roger McDowell	.07	.04	503	Eric King	.07	.04
446	Sid Bream	.07	.04	504	Frank Castillo	.10	.06
447	Mackey Sasser	.07	.04	505	Mike Gardiner	.10	.06
448	Bill Swift	.08	.05	506	Cory Snyder	.07	.04
449	Hubie Brooks	.08	.05	507	Steve Howe	.07	.04
450	David Cone	.20	.12	508	Jose Rijo	.10	.06
451	Bobby Witt	.12	.07	509	Sid Fernandez	.08	.05
452	Brady Anderson	.30	.18	510	Archi Cianfrocco (R)	.40	.25
453	Lee Stevens	.10	.06	511	Mark Guthrie	.08	.05
454	Luis Aquino	.07	.04	512	Bob Ojeda	.07	.04
455	Carney Lansford	.08	.05	513	John Doherty	.07	.04
456	Carlos Hernandez	.08	.05	514	Dante Bichette	.07	.04
457	Danny Jackson	.07	.04	515	Juan Berenguer	.07	.04
458	Gerald Young	.08	.05	516	Jeff Robinson	.07	.04
459	Tom Candiotti	.07	.04	517	Mike McFarlane	.08	.05
460	Billy Hatcher	.07	.04	518	Matt Young	.07	.04
461	John Wetteland	.20	.12	519	Otis Nixon	.07	.04
462	Mike Bordick	.15	.08	520	Brian Holman	.08	.05
463	Don Robinson	.07	.04	521	Chris Haney	.15	.08
464	Jeff Johnson	.10	.06	522	Jeff Kent (R)	.35	.20
465	Lonnie Smith	.15	.08	523	Chad Curtis (R)	.25	.15
466	Paul Assenmacher	.07	.04	524	Vince Horsman (R)	.15	.08

525	Rod Nichols (R)	.10	.06
526	Peter Hoy (R)	.10	.06
527	Shawn Boskie	.10	.06
528	Alejandro Pena	.07	.04
529	Dave Burba	.07	.04
530	Ricky Jordan	.07	.04
531	Dave Silvestri (R)	.15	.08
532	John Patterson (R)	.12	.07
533	Jeff Branson (R)	.10	.06
534	Derrick May (R)	.15	.08
535	Esteban Beltre (R)	.15	.08
536	Jose Melendez	.12	.07
537	Wally Joyner	.12	.07
538	Eddie Taubensee (R)	.12	.07
539	Jim Abbott	.20	.12
540	Brian Williams (R)	.75	.45
541	Donovan Osborne	.40	.25
542	Patrick Lennon	.15	.08
543	Mike Groppuso (R)	.12	.07
544	Jarvis Brown (R)	.15	.08
545	Shawn Livsey (R)	.25	.15
546	Jeff Ware	.25	.15
547	Danny Tartabull	.15	.08
548	Bobby Jones (R)	.50	.30
549	Ken Griffey Jr.	2.50	1.50
550	Rey Sanchez (R)	.20	.12
551	Eric Wedge (R)	.25	.15
552	Juan Guerrero (R)	.25	.15
553	Jacob Brumfield (R)	.12	.07
554	Ben Rivera	.10	.06
555	Brian Jordan	.50	.30
556	Denny Neagle	.12	.07
557	Cliff Brantley	.12	.07
558	Anthony Young	.15	.08
559	John Vander Wal (R)	.15	.08
560	Monty Fariss	.12	.07
561	Russ Springer (R)	.15	.08
562	Pat Listach (R)	1.50	.90
563	Pat Hentgen	.12	.07
564	Andy Stankiewicz (R)	.30	.18
565	Mike Perez	.12	.07
566	Mike Bielecki	.07	.04
567	Butch Henry (R)	.20	.12
568	Dave Nilsson (R)	.60	.35
569	Scott Hatteberg (R)	.15	.08
570	Ruben Amaro Jr.	.15	.08
571	Todd Hundley	.12	.07
572	Moises Alou	.20	.12
573	Hector Fajardo (R)	.20	.12
574	Todd Van Poppel (R)	.70	.40
575	Willie Banks	.15	.08
576	Eddie Zosky (R)	.25	.15
577	J.J. Johnson (R)	.25	.15
578	John Burkett (R)	.25	.15
579	Trevor Miller (R)	.15	.08
580	Scott Bankhead	.07	.04
581	Rich Amaral (R)	.10	.06
582	Kenny Lofton	.70	.04
583	Matt Stairs (R)	.35	.20
584	Don Mattingly (ID)	.20	.12
585	Steve Avery (ID)	.25	.15
586	Roberto Alomar (ID)	.30	.18
587	Scott Sanderson (ID)	.07	.04
588	Dave Justice (ID)	.35	.20
589	Rex Hudler (ID)	.10	.06
590	David Cone (ID)	.15	.08
591	Tony Gwynn (ID)	.20	.12
592	Orel Hershiser (SL)	.10	.06
593	John Wetteland (SL)	.10	.06
594	Tom Glavine (SL)	.20	.12
595	Randy Johnson (SL)	.15	.08
596	Jim Gott (SL)	.07	.04
597	Dave Weathers (R)	.12	.07
598	Shawn Hare (R)	.12	.07
599	Chris Gardner (R)	.20	.12
600	Rusty Meacham	.08	.05
601	Benito Santiago (SH)	.08	.05
602	Eric Davis (SH)	.10	.06
603	Jose Lind (SH)	.07	.04
604	Dave Justice (SH)	.30	.18
605	Tim Raines (SH)	.08	.05
606	Randy Tomlin (G)	.08	.05
607	Jack McDowell (G)	.15	.08
608	Greg Maddux (G)	.08	.05
609	Charles Nagy (G)	.08	.05
610	Tom Candiotti (G)	.07	.04
611	David Cone (G)	.08	.05
612	Steve Avery (G)	.12	.07
613	Rod Beck (R)	.12	.07
614	Rickey Henderson	.20	.12
615	Benito Santiago	.10	.06
616	Ruben Sierra	.25	.15
617	Ryne Sandberg	.30	.18
618	Nolan Ryan	.70	.40
619	Brett Butler	.08	.05
620	Dave Justice	.30	.18

1992 Score Team Pinnacle

These All-Star cards were randomly inserted into Pinnacle foil packs and consist of side-by-side drawings of two players on the card fronts. The cards feature the artwork of noted illustrator Chris Greco. The set contains 12 standard-size cards measuring 2-1/2" by 3-1/2".

		MINT	NR/MT
	Complete Set (12)	400.00	300.00
	Commons	15.00	10.00
1B	Frank Thomas/Will Clark	80.00	55.00
2B	Roberto Alomar/ Ryne Sandberg	60.00	40.00
3B	Robin Ventura/Matt Williams	30.00	20.00
SS	Cal Ripken/Barry Larkin	60.00	40.00
LF	Danny Tartabull/ Barry Bonds	50.00	35.00
CF	Ken Griffey Jr./ Brett Butler	60.00	40.00
RF	Ruben Sierra/Dave Justice	50.00	35.00
C	Ivan Rodriguez/ Benito Santiago	30.00	20.00
RP	Roger Clemens/ Ramon Martinez	50.00	35.00
LP	Jim Abbott/Steve Avery	30.00	20.00
RRP	Dennis Eckersley/ Rob Dibble	25.00	15.00
LRP	Scott Radinsky/ John Franco	15.00	10.00

			MINT	NR/MT
		George Brett		
4	Mark Wohlers/ Roger Clemens		30.00	20.00
5	Luis Mercedes/ Julio Franco		14.00	9.00
6	Willie Banks/ Doc Gooden		14.00	9.00
7	Kenny Lofton/ Rickey Henderson		30.00	20.00
8	Keith Mitchell/ Dave Henderson		14.00	9.00
9	Kim Batiste/ Barry Larkin		14.00	9.00
10	Todd Hundley/ Thurman Munson		14.00	9.00
11	Eddie Zosky/Cal Ripken Jr.		35.00	25.00
12	Todd Van Poppel/ Nolan Ryan		40.00	30.00
13	Jim Thome/Ryne Sandberg		25.00	15.00
14	Dave Fleming/ Bobby Murcer		25.00	15.00
15	Royce Clayton/ Ozzie Smith		20.00	12.50
16	Donald Harris/ Darryl Strawberry		25.00	15.00
17	Chad Curtis/ Alan Trammell		14.00	9.00
18	Derek Bell/Dave Winfield		25.00	15.00

1992 Score Pinnacle Rookie Idols

This 18-card insert set features dual pictures on the card fronts featuring rookies and their idols. The standard-size cards were randomly distributed in Pinnacle foil packs.

		MINT	NR/MT
	Complete Set (18)	275.00	175.00
	Commons	14.00	9.00
1	Reggie Sanders/ Eric Davis	25.00	15.00
2	Hector Fajardo/ Jim Abbott	14.00	9.00
3	Gary Cooper/	25.00	15.00

1992 Score Pinnacle Rookies

This 30-card update set features some of baseball's top 1992 rookies. Card fronts include full-bleed, full color action photos with the player's name printed in gold in a color bar under the photo. His team logo appears opposite his name. The words "1992 Rookie" is located in a black border under his name. The horizontal card backs contain another full color action photo and a brief description of the player. All cards measure 2-1/2" by 3-1/2".

		MINT	NR/MT
Complete Set (30)		12.00	8.50
Commons		.08	.05

1	Luis Mercedes	.20	.12
2	Scott Cooper	.15	.10
3	Kenny Lofton	1.50	.90
4	John Doherty	.20	.12
5	Pat Listach	2.00	1.25
6	Andy Stankiewicz	.15	.10
7	Derek Bell	.40	.25
8	Gary DiSarcina	.08	.05
9	Roberto Hernandez	.15	.10
10	Joel Johnston	.08	.05
11	Pat Mahomes	.50	.30
12	Todd Van Poppel	.75	.45
13	Dave Fleming	1.25	.80
14	Monty Fariss	.12	.07
15	Gary Scott	.10	.06
16	Moises Alou	.35	.20
17	Todd Hundley	.10	.06
18	Kim Batiste	.15	.10
19	Denny Neagle	.10	.06
20	Donovan Osborne	.80	.50
21	Mark Wohlers	.20	.12
22	Reggie Sanders	1.25	.80
23	Brian Williams	.40	.25
24	Eric Karros	3.00	2.00
25	Frank Seminara	.40	.25
26	Royce Clayton	.40	.25
27	Dave Nilsson	.50	.30
28	Matt Stairs	.20	.12
29	Chad Curtis	.35	.20
30	Carlos Hernandez	.10	.06

1993 Score Select

This 405-card set is the premier edition of Score's newest baseball set. Card fronts feature full color action photos on a green card stock. The player's name appears in yellow in the bottom corner of the card. A Score Select logo is located in a corner of the photograph. Card backs contain a full color photo, stats and a brief description of the player. All cards measure 2-1/2" by 3-1/2".

		MINT	NR/MT
Complete Set (405)		24.00	16.50
Commons		.06	.03

1	Barry Bonds	.30	.18
2	Ken Griffey, Jr.	.80	.50
3	Will Clark	.30	.18
4	Kirby Puckett	.30	.18
5	Tony Gwynn	.20	.12
6	Frank Thomas	1.00	.70
7	Tom Glavine	.20	.12
8	Roberto Alomar	.30	.18
9	Andre Dawson	.15	.10
10	Ron Darling	.06	.03
11	Bobby Bonilla	.15	.10
12	Danny Tartabull	.12	.07
13	Darren Daulton	.10	.06
14	Roger Clemens	.40	.25
15	Ozzie Smith	.15	.10
16	Mark McGwire	.35	.20
17	Terry Pendleton	.15	.10
18	Cal Ripken, Jr.	.50	.30
19	Fred McGriff	.25	.15
20	Cecil Fielder	.25	.15
21	Darryl Strawberry	.25	.15
22	Robin Yount	.20	.12
23	Barry Larkin	.15	.10
24	Don Mattingly	.20	.12
25	Craig Biggio	.08	.05
26	Sandy Alomar, Jr.	.07	.04

27	Larry Walker	.15	.10	85	Bill Gullickson	.06	.03
28	Junior Felix	.06	.03	86	Paul O'Neill	.10	.06
29	Eddie Murray	.15	.10	87	Kevin Seitzer	.06	.03
30	Robin Ventura	.20	.12	88	Steve Finley	.06	.03
31	Greg Maddux	.20	.12	89	Mel Hall	.07	.04
32	Dave Winfield	.20	.12	90	Nolan Ryan	.75	.45
33	John Kruk	.07	.04	91	Eric Davis	.10	.06
34	Wally Joyner	.08	.05	92	Mike Mussina	.35	.20
35	Andy Van Slyke	.08	.05	93	Tony Fernandez	.08	.05
36	Chuck Knoblauch	.25	.15	94	Frank Viola	.08	.05
37	Tom Pagnozzi	.07	.04	95	Matt Williams	.15	.10
38	Dennis Eckersley	.15	.10	96	Joe Carter	.25	.15
39	Dave Justice	.35	.15	97	Ryne Sandberg	.40	.25
40	Juan Gonzalez	.40	.25	98	Jim Abbott	.20	.12
41	Gary Sheffield	.30	.18	99	Marquis Grissom	.15	.10
42	Paul Molitor	.10	.06	100	George Bell	.12	.07
43	Delino DeShields	.12	.07	101	Howard Johnson	.10	.06
44	Travis Fryman	.20	.12	102	Kevin Appier	.08	.05
45	Hal Morris	.08	.05	103	Dale Murphy	.10	.06
46	Gregg Olson	.07	.04	104	Shane Mack	.08	.05
47	Ken Caminiti	.06	.03	105	Jose Lind	.06	.03
48	Wade Boggs	.20	.12	106	Rickey Henderson	.25	.15
49	Orel Hershiser	.08	.05	107	Bob Tewksbury	.06	.03
50	Albert Belle	.25	.15	108	Kevin Mitchell	.10	.06
51	Bill Swift	.07	.04	109	Steve Avery	.20	.12
52	Mark Langston	.08	.05	110	Candy Maldonado	.06	.03
53	Joe Girardi	.06	.03	111	Bip Roberts	.06	.03
54	Keith Miller	.06	.03	112	Lou Whitaker	.06	.03
55	Gary Carter	.12	.07	113	Jeff Bagwell	.25	.15
56	Brady Anderson	.15	.10	114	Dante Bichette	.06	.03
57	Doc Gooden	.15	.10	115	Brett Butler	.08	.05
58	Julio Franco	.06	.03	116	Melido Perez	.07	.04
59	Lenny Dykstra	.06	.03	117	Andy Benes	.12	.07
60	Mickey Tettleton	.07	.04	118	Randy Johnson	.12	.07
61	Randy Tomlin	.06	.03	119	Willie McGee	.10	.06
62	B.J. Surhoff	.06	.03	120	Jody Reed	.06	.03
63	Todd Zeile	.08	.05	121	Shawon Dunston	.08	.05
64	Roberto Kelly	.10	.06	122	Carlos Baerga	.20	.12
65	Rob Dibble	.07	.04	123	Bret Saberhagen	.12	.07
66	Leo Gomez	.08	.05	124	John Olerud	.12	.07
67	Doug Jones	.06	.03	125	Ivan Calderon	.07	.04
68	Ellis Burks	.08	.05	126	Bryan Harvey	.06	.03
69	Mike Scioscia	.06	.03	127	Terry Mulholland	.06	.03
70	Charles Nagy	.12	.07	128	Ozzie Guillen	.06	.03
71	Cory Snyder	.06	.03	129	Steve Buechele	.06	.03
72	Devon White	.06	.03	130	Kevin Tapani	.07	.04
73	Mark Grace	.15	.10	131	Felix Jose	.10	.06
74	Luis Polonia	.06	.03	132	Terry Steinbach	.08	.05
75	John Smiley	.08	.05	133	Ron Gant	.20	.12
76	Carlton Fisk	.20	.12	134	Harold Reynolds	.06	.03
77	Luis Sojo	.06	.03	135	Chris Sabo	.07	.04
78	George Brett	.20	.12	136	Ivan Rodriquez	.25	.15
79	Mitch Williams	.06	.03	137	Eric Anthony	.10	.06
80	Kent Hrbek	.06	.03	138	Mike Henneman	.06	.03
81	Jay Bell	.06	.03	139	Robby Thompson	.06	.03
82	Edgar Martinez	.15	.10	140	Scott Fletcher	.06	.03
83	Lee Smith	.08	.05	141	Bruce Hurst	.08	.05
84	Deion Sanders	.25	.15	142	Kevin Maas	.12	.07

143	Tom Candiotti	.06	.03	201	John Wetteland	.07	.04
144	Chris Hoiles	.08	.05	202	Jay Buhner	.08	.05
145	Mike Morgan	.06	.03	203	Mike LaValliere	.06	.03
146	Mark Whiten	.08	.05	204	Kevin Brown	.08	.05
147	Dennis Martinez	.08	.05	205	Luis Gonzalez	.08	.05
148	Tony Pena	.06	.03	206	Rick Aguilera	.06	.03
149	Dave Magadan	.06	.03	207	Norm Charlton	.06	.03
150	Mark Lewis	.08	.05	208	Mike Bordick	.08	.05
151	Mariano Duncan	.06	.03	209	Charlie Leibrandt	.06	.03
152	Gregg Jefferies	.12	.07	210	Tom Brunansky	.07	.04
153	Doug Drabek	.10	.06	211	Tom Henke	.06	.03
154	Brian Harper	.06	.03	212	Randy Milligan	.06	.03
155	Ray Lankford	.15	.10	213	Ramon Martinez	.10	.06
156	Carney Lansford	.06	.03	214	Mo Vaughn	.15	.10
157	Mike Sharperson	.06	.03	215	Randy Myers	.06	.03
158	Jack Morris	.15	.10	216	Greg Hibbard	.06	.03
159	Otis Nixon	.08	.05	217	Wes Chamberlain	.12	.07
160	Steve Sax	.07	.04	218	Tony Phillips	.06	.03
161	Mark Lemke	.06	.03	219	Pete Harnisch	.07	.04
162	Rafael Palmeiro	.08	.05	220	Mike Gallego	.06	.03
163	Jose Rijo	.10	.06	221	Bud Black	.06	.03
164	Omar Visquel	.06	.03	222	Greg Vaughn	.12	.07
165	Sammy Sosa	.07	.04	223	Milt Thompson	.06	.03
166	Milt Cuyler	.08	.05	224	Ben McDonald	.15	.10
167	John Franco	.06	.03	225	Billy Hatcher	.06	.03
168	Darryl Hamilton	.06	.03	226	Paul Sorrento	.10	.06
169	Ken Hill	.08	.05	227	Mark Gubicza	.07	.04
170	Mike Devereaux	.08	.05	228	Mike Greenwell	.10	.06
171	Don Slaught	.06	.03	229	Curt Schilling	.06	.03
172	Steve Farr	.06	.03	230	Alan Trammell	.10	.06
173	Bernard Gilkey	.12	.07	231	Zane Smith	.06	.03
174	Mike Fetters	.06	.03	232	Bobby Thigpen	.07	.04
175	Vince Coleman	.07	.04	233	Greg Olson	.06	.03
176	Kevin McReynolds	.07	.04	234	Joe Orsulak	.06	.03
177	John Smoltz	.20	.12	235	Joe Oliver	.07	.04
178	Greg Gagne	.06	.03	236	Tim Raines	.08	.05
179	Greg Swindell	.07	.04	237	Juan Samuel	.06	.03
180	Juan Guzman	.30	.18	238	Chili Davis	.08	.05
181	Kal Daniels	.06	.03	239	Spike Owen	.06	.03
182	Rick Sutcliffe	.06	.03	240	Dave Stewart	.08	.05
183	Orlando Merced	.08	.05	241	Jim Eisenreich	.06	.03
184	Bill Wegman	.06	.03	242	Phil Plantier	.15	.10
185	Mark Gardner	.06	.03	243	Sid Fernandez	.08	.05
186	Rob Deer	.08	.05	244	Dan Gladden	.06	.03
187	Dave Hollins	.12	.07	245	Mickey Morandini	.08	.05
188	Jack Clark	.08	.05	246	Tino Martinez	.08	.05
189	Brian Hunter	.12	.07	247	Kirt Manwaring	.06	.03
190	Tim Wallach	.07	.04	248	Dean Palmer	.12	.07
191	Tim Belcher	.07	.04	249	Tom Browning	.07	.04
192	Walt Weiss	.06	.03	250	Brian McRae	.10	.06
193	Kurt Stillwell	.06	.03	251	Scott Leius	.06	.03
194	Charlie Hayes	.06	.03	252	Bert Blyleven	.10	.06
195	Willie Randolph	.07	.04	253	Scott Erickson	.15	.10
196	Jack McDowell	.15	.10	254	Bob Welch	.07	.04
197	Jose Offerman	.10	.06	255	Pat Kelly	.08	.05
198	Chuck Finley	.08	.05	256	Felix Fermin	.06	.03
199	Darrin Jackson	.06	.03	257	Harold Baines	.07	.04
200	Kelly Gruber	.07	.04	258	Duane Ward	.06	.03

259	Bill Spiers	.06	.03
260	Jamie Navarro	.10	.06
261	Scott Sanderson	.06	.03
262	Gary Gaetti	.06	.03
263	Bob Ojeda	.06	.03
264	Jeff Montgomery	.06	.03
265	Scott Bankhead	.06	.03
266	Lance Johnson	.06	.03
267	Rafael Belliard	.06	.03
268	Kevin Reimer	.08	.05
269	Benito Santiago	.10	.06
270	Mike Moore	.06	.03
271	Dave Fleming	.30	.18
272	Moises Alou	.12	.07
273	Pat Listach	.50	.30
274	Reggie Sanders	.20	.12
275	Kenny Lofton	.35	.20
276	Donovan Osborne	.20	.12
277	Rusty Meacham	.10	.06
278	Eric Karros	.75	.45
279	Andy Stankiewicz	.10	.06
280	Brian Jordan	.20	.12
281	Gary DiSarcina	.08	.05
282	Mark Wohlers	.08	.05
283	Dave Nilsson	.15	.10
284	Anthony Young	.10	.06
285	Jim Bullinger	.07	.04
286	Derek Bell	.15	.10
287	Brian Williams	.20	.12
288	Julio Valera	.06	.03
289	Dan Walters	.10	.06
290	Chad Curtis	.15	.10
291	Michael Tucker (R)	.80	.50
292	Bob Zupcic	.08	.05
293	Todd Hundley	.08	.05
294	Jeff Tackett	.10	.06
295	Greg Colbrunn	.10	.06
296	Cal Eldred	.40	.25
297	Chris Roberts (R)	.35	.20
298	John Doherty	.10	.06
299	Denny Neagle	.08	.05
300	Arthur Rhodes	.12	.07
301	Mark Clark	.10	.06
302	Scott Cooper	.12	.07
303	Jamie Arnold (R)	.25	.15
304	Jim Thome	.08	.05
305	Frank Seminara	.15	.10
306	Kurt Knudsen	.08	.05
307	Tim Wakefield (R)	1.25	.80
308	John Jaha	.15	.10
309	Pat Hentgen	.08	.05
310	B.J. Wallace (R)	.50	.30
311	Roberto Hernandez	.08	.05
312	Hipolito Pachardo	.15	.10
313	Eric Fox	.10	.06
314	Willie Banks	.08	.05
315	Sam Militello	.40	.25
316	Vince Horsman	.15	.10
317	Carlos Hernandez	.07	.04
318	Jeff Kent	.15	.10
319	Mike Perez	.08	.05
320	Scott Livingstone	.07	.04
321	Jeff Conine	.15	.10
322	James Austin	.10	.06
323	John Vander Wal	.12	.07
324	Pat Mahomes	.25	.15
325	Pedro Astacio	.25	.15
326	Bret Boone	.40	.25
327	Matt Stairs	.12	.07
328	Damion Easley	.15	.10
329	Ben Rivera	.07	.04
330	Reggie Jefferson	.10	.06
331	Luis Mercedes	.10	.06
332	Kyle Abbott	.10	.06
333	Eddie Taubensee	.08	.05
334	Tim McIntosh	.10	.06
335	Phil Clark	.08	.05
336	Wil Cordero	.30	.18
337	Russ Springer	.12	.07
338	Craig Colbert	.08	.05
339	Tim Salmon	.30	.18
340	Braulio Castillo	.08	.05
341	Donald Harris	.10	.06
342	Eric Young	.15	.10
343	Bob Wickman	.20	.12
344	John Valentin	.15	.10
345	Dan Wilson	.12	.07
346	Steve Hosey	.20	.12
347	Mike Piazza	.50	.30
348	Willie Greene	.25	.15
349	Tom Goodwin	.12	.07
350	Eric Hillman	.12	.07
351	Steve Reed (R)	.15	.10
352	Dan Serafini (R)	.30	.18
353	Todd Steverson (R)	.25	.15
354	Benji Grigsby (R)	.30	.18
355	Shannon Stewart (R)	.30	.18
356	Sean Lowe (R)	.20	.12
357	Derek Wallace (R)	.25	.15
358	Rick Helling	.15	.10
359	Jason Kendall (R)	.25	.15
360	Derek Jeter (R)	.40	.25
361	David Cone	.15	.10
362	Jeff Reardon	.10	.06
363	Bobby Witt	.08	.05
364	Jose Canseco	.40	.25
365	Jeff Russell	.06	.03
366	Ruben Sierra	.25	.15
367	Alan Mills	.07	.04
368	Matt Nokes	.07	.04
369	Pat Borders	.07	.04
370	Pedro Munoz	.10	.06
371	Danny Jackson	.06	.03
372	Geronimo Pena	.06	.03
373	Craig Lefferts	.06	.03
374	Joe Grahe	.06	.03

375	Roger McDowell	.06	.03
376	Jimmy Key	.07	.04
377	Steve Olin	.07	.04
378	Glenn Davis	.08	.05
379	Rene Gonzales	.07	.04
380	Manuel Lee	.06	.03
381	Ron Karkovice	.06	.03
382	Sid Bream	.06	.03
383	Gerald Williams	.15	.10
384	Lenny Harris	.06	.03
385	J.T. Snow (R)	.75	.45
386	Dave Steib	.10	.06
387	Kirk McCaskill	.06	.03
388	Lance Parrish	.07	.04
389	Craig Grebeck	.06	.03
390	Rick Wilkins	.06	.03
391	Manny Alexander	.10	.06
392	Mike Schooler	.06	.03
393	Bernie Williams	.12	.07
394	Kevin Koslofski (R)	.12	.07
395	Willie Wilson	.06	.03
396	Jeff Parrett	.06	.03
397	Mike Harkey	.08	.05
398	Frank Tanana	.06	.03
399	Doug Henry	.06	.03
400	Royce Clayton	.15	.10
401	Eric Wedge (R)	.25	.15
402	Derrick May	.12	.07
403	Carlos Garcia (R)	.25	.15
404	Henry Rodriquez	.12	.07
405	Ryan Klesko	.50	.30

6	Andy Van Slyke	1.00	.70
7	Barry Bonds	2.50	1.50
8	Tony Gwynn	1.50	.90
9	Greg Maddux	1.00	.70
10	Tom Glavine	1.75	1.00
11	John Franco	.50	.30
12	Lee Smith	.60	.35
13	Cecil Fielder	1.75	1.00
14	Roberto Alomar	1.75	1.00
15	Cal Ripken, Jr.	4.50	3.00
16	Edgar Martinez	1.00	.70
17	Ivan Rodriquez	1.25	.80
18	Kirby Puckett	2.50	1.50
19	Ken Griffey, Jr.	6.00	3.75
20	Joe Carter	2.00	1.25
21	Roger Clemens	3.50	2.50
22	Dave Fleming	1.25	.80
23	Paul Molitor	.50	.30
24	Dennis Eckersley	1.00	.70

1993 Score Select Rookies

The cards in this limited edition 24-card set were available through the hobby trade and feature some of the most promising rookies in baseball and three Triple Crown Winners, Mickey Mantle, Carl Yastzremski and Frank Robinson. Cards measure 2-1/2" by 3-1/2".

		MINT	NR/MT
Complete Set (24)		90.00	65.00
Commons		1.50	.90
1	Pat Listach	4.00	2.75
2	Moises Alou	2.50	1.50
3	Reggie Sanders	3.00	2.00
4	Kenny Lofton	5.00	3.50
5	Eric Karros	8.50	5.50
6	Brian Williams	1.75	1.00
7	Donovan Osborne	3.50	2.50
8	Sam Militello	3.50	2.50
9	Chad Curtis	3.50	2.50
10	Bob Zupcic	1.75	1.00
11	Tim Salmon	5.00	3.50
12	Jeff Conine	3.00	2.00
13	Pedro Astacio	3.50	2.50
14	Arthur Rhodes	1.75	1.00

1993 Score Select Stars

This 24-card limited edtion set features bonus cards packed randomly in Score Select packs. Cards measure 2-1/2" by 3-1/2".

		MINT	NR/MT
Complete Set (24)		35.00	22.00
Commons		.50	.30
1	Fred McGriff	2.00	1.25
2	Ryne Sandberg	3.00	2.00
3	Ozzie Smith	1.25	.80
4	Gary Sheffield	1.50	.90
5	Darren Daulton	.60	.35

15	Cal Eldred	6.00	4.00
16	Tim Wakefield	6.50	4.50
17	Andy Stankiewicz	1.50	.90
18	Wil Cordero	3.00	2.00
19	Todd Hundley	1.50	.90
20	Dave Fleming	2.50	1.50
21	Bret Boone	4.50	3.00
22	Mickey Mantle	25.00	18.50
23	Carl Yastzremski	6.50	4.50
24	Frank Robinson	6.50	4.50

1993 Score

Score goes back to the basics with this single series 660-card set. White borders frame full color action shots on the card fronts. The backs contain a small color photo, the player's personal data and stats. Key subsets include Award Winners, Draft Picks, All-Stars, Highlights and Dream Team. All cards measure 2-1/2" by 3-1/2".

1993 Score Select Diamond Aces

The cards in this limited edition 24-card set were only available in Score Select Cello packs. Cards measure 2-1/2" by 3-1/2" and feature some of the top pitchers in the Majors.

		MINT	NR/MT
Complete Set (24)		50.00	30.00
Commons		.75	.45

1	Roger Clemens	7.50	5.00
2	Tom Glavine	3.50	2.50
3	Jack McDowell	2.00	1.25
4	Greg Maddux	2.50	1.50
5	Jack Morris	3.00	2.00
6	Dennis Martinez	1.00	.70
7	Kevin Brown	.75	.45
8	Dwight Gooden	2.50	1.50
9	Kevin Appier	1.00	.70
10	Mike Morgan	.75	.45
11	Juan Guzman	6.50	4.50
12	Charles Nagy	3.00	2.00
13	John Smiley	1.25	.80
14	Ken Hill	.75	.45
15	Bob Tewksbury	.75	.45
16	Doug Drabek	1.50	.90
17	John Smoltz	1.75	1.00
18	Greg Swindell	1.00	.70
19	Bruce Hurst	1.00	.70
20	Mike Mussina	6.00	4.00
21	Cal Eldred	5.00	3.00
22	Melido Perez	1.00	.70
23	Dave Fleming	2.50	1.50
24	Kevin Tapani	1.50	.90

		MINT	NR/MT
Complete Set (660)		18.00	12.00
Commons		.05	.02

1	Ken Griffey, Jr.	.50	.30
2	Gary Sheffield	.20	.12
3	Frank Thomas	.75	.45
4	Ryne Sandberg	.25	.15
5	Larry Walker	.15	.10
6	Cal Ripken, Jr.	.25	.15
7	Roger Clemens	.25	.15
8	Bobby Bonilla	.12	.07
9	Carlos Baerga	.20	.12
10	Darren Daulton	.10	.06
11	Travis Fryman	.20	.12
12	Andy Van Slyke	.10	.06
13	Jose Canseco	.25	.15
14	Roberto Alomar	.20	.12
15	Tom Glavine	.15	.10
16	Barry Larkin	.10	.06
17	Gregg Jefferies	.10	.06
18	Craig Biggio	.07	.04
19	Shane Mack	.08	.05
20	Brett Butler	.08	.05
21	Dennis Eckersley	.12	.07
22	Will Clark	.20	.12
23	Don Mattingly	.20	.12
24	Tony Gwynn	.15	.10
25	Ivan Rodriquez	.25	.15
26	Shawon Dunston	.08	.05

27	Mike Mussina	.40	.25
28	Marquis Grissom	.15	.10
29	Charles Nagy	.20	.12
30	Lenny Dykstra	.07	.04
31	Cecil Fielder	.15	.10
32	Jay Bell	.05	.02
33	B.J. Surhoff	.05	.02
34	Bob Tewksbury	.05	.02
35	Danny Tartabull	.10	.06
36	Terry Pendleton	.12	.07
37	Jack Morris	.12	.07
38	Hal Morris	.08	.05
39	Luis Polonia	.07	.04
40	Ken Caminiti	.05	.02
41	Robin Ventura	.15	.10
42	Darryl Strawberry	.15	.10
43	Wally Joyner	.08	.05
44	Fred McGriff	.20	.12
45	Kevin Tapani	.07	.04
46	Matt Williams	.10	.06
47	Robin Yount	.20	.12
48	Ken Hill	.07	.04
49	Edgar Martinez	.12	.07
50	Mark Grace	.10	.06
51	Juan Gonzalez	.30	.18
52	Curt Schilling	.05	.02
53	Dwight Gooden	.12	.07
54	Chris Hoiles	.08	.05
55	Frank Viola	.08	.05
56	Ray Lankford	.15	.10
57	George Brett	.20	.12
58	Kenny Lofton	.30	.18
59	Nolan Ryan	.40	.25
60	Mickey Tettleton	.07	.04
61	John Smoltz	.10	.06
62	Howard Johnson	.08	.05
63	Eric Karros	.40	.25
64	Rick Aguilera	.05	.02
65	Steve Finley	.05	.02
66	Mark Langston	.10	.06
67	Bill Swift	.07	.04
68	John Olerud	.10	.06
69	Kevin McReynolds	.07	.04
70	Jack McDowell	.15	.10
71	Rickey Henderson	.20	.12
72	Brian Harper	.05	.02
73	Mike Morgan	.05	.02
74	Rafael Palmeiro	.08	.05
75	Dennis Martinez	.08	.05
76	Tino Martinez	.08	.05
77	Eddie Murray	.12	.07
78	Ellis Burks	.08	.05
79	John Kruk	.08	.05
80	Gregg Olson	.07	.04
81	Bernard Gilkey	.10	.06
82	Milt Cuyler	.08	.05
83	Mike LaValliere	.05	.02
84	Albert Belle	.15	.10
85	Bip Roberts	.05	.02
86	Melido Perez	.07	.04
87	Otis Nixon	.08	.05
88	Bill Spiers	.05	.02
89	Jeff Bagwell	.25	.15
90	Orel Hershiser	.10	.06
91	Andy Benes	.10	.06
92	Devon White	.05	.02
93	Willie McGee	.08	.05
94	Ozzie Guillen	.05	.02
95	Ivan Calderon	.07	.04
96	Keith Miller	.05	.02
97	Steve Buechele	.05	.02
98	Kent Hrbek	.07	.04
99	Dave Hollins	.12	.07
100	Mike Bordick	.10	.06
101	Randy Tomlin	.08	.05
102	Omar Vizquel	.05	.02
103	Lee Smith	.10	.06
104	Leo Gomez	.08	.05
105	Jose Rijo	.08	.05
106	Mark Whiten	.10	.06
107	Dave Justice	.20	.12
108	Eddie Taubensee	.08	.05
109	Lance Johnson	.05	.02
110	Felix Jose	.08	.05
111	Mike Harkey	.07	.04
112	Randy Milligan	.05	.02
113	Anthony Young	.10	.06
114	Rico Brogna	.10	.06
115	Bret Saberhagen	.10	.06
116	Sandy Alomar, Jr.	.08	.05
117	Terry Mulholland	.05	.02
118	Darryl Hamilton	.07	.04
119	Todd Zeile	.08	.05
120	Bernie Williams	.10	.06
121	Zane Smith	.05	.02
122	Derek Bell	.15	.10
123	Deion Sanders	.15	.10
124	Luis Sojo	.05	.02
125	Joe Oliver	.05	.02
126	Craig Grebeck	.05	.02
127	Andujar Cedeno	.10	.06
128	Brian McRae	.08	.05
129	Jose Offerman	.10	.06
130	Pedro Munoz	.08	.05
131	Bud Black	.05	.02
132	Mo Vaughn	.12	.07
133	Bruce Hurst	.08	.05
134	Dave Henderson	.08	.05
135	Tom Pagnozzi	.08	.05
136	Erik Hanson	.05	.02
137	Orlando Merced	.08	.05
138	Dean Palmer	.10	.06
139	John Franco	.07	.04
140	Brady Anderson	.10	.06
141	Ricky Jordan	.07	.04
142	Jeff Blauser	.05	.02

143	Sammy Sosa	.07	.04	201	Mariano Duncan	.05	.02
144	Bob Walk	.05	.02	202	Ben McDonald	.12	.07
145	Delino DeShields	.15	.10	203	Darren Lewis	.08	.05
146	Kevin Brown	.10	.06	204	Kenny Rogers	.05	.02
147	Mark Lemke	.05	.02	205	Manuel Lee	.05	.02
148	Chuck Knoblauch	.20	.12	206	Scott Erickson	.12	.07
149	Chris Sabo	.07	.04	207	Dan Gladden	.05	.02
150	Bobby Witt	.07	.04	208	Bob Welch	.07	.04
151	Luis Gonzalez	.08	.05	209	Greg Olson	.05	.02
152	Ron Karkovice	.05	.02	210	Dan Pasqua	.05	.02
153	Jeff Brantley	.05	.02	211	Tim Wallach	.08	.05
154	Kevin Appier	.08	.05	212	Jeff Montgomery	.05	.02
155	Darrin Jackson	.07	.04	213	Derrick May	.10	.06
156	Kelly Gruber	.07	.04	214	Ed Sprague	.08	.05
157	Royce Clayton	.15	.10	215	David Haas	.05	.02
158	Chuck Finley	.08	.05	216	Darrin Fletcher	.08	.05
159	Jeff King	.07	.04	217	Brian Jordan	.10	.06
160	Greg Vaughn	.10	.06	218	Jaime Navarro	.10	.06
161	Geronimo Pena	.05	.02	219	Randy Velarde	.05	.02
162	Steve Farr	.05	.02	220	Ron Gant	.12	.07
163	Jose Oquendo	.05	.02	221	Paul Quantrill (R)	.20	.12
164	Mark Lewis	.07	.04	222	Damion Easley (R)	.20	.12
165	John Wetteland	.07	.04	223	Charlie Hough	.05	.02
166	Mike Henneman	.05	.02	224	Brad Brink (R)	.15	.10
167	Todd Hundley	.08	.05	225	Barry Manuel (R)	.20	.12
168	Wes Chamberlain	.10	.06	226	Kevin Koslofski (R)	.20	.12
169	Steve Avery	.15	.10	227	Ryan Thompson (R)	.35	.20
170	Mike Devereaux	.08	.05	228	Mike Munoz (R)	.15	.10
171	Reggie Sanders	.20	.12	229	Dan Wilson	.12	.07
172	Jay Buhner	.07	.04	230	Peter Hoy (R)	.15	.10
173	Eric Anthony	.10	.06	231	Pedro Astacio (R)	.50	.30
174	John Burkett	.05	.02	232	Matt Stairs (R)	.15	.10
175	Tom Candiotti	.05	.02	233	Jeff Reboulet (R)	.15	.10
176	Phil Plantier	.15	.10	234	Manny Alexander (R)	.15	.10
177	Doug Henry	.08	.05	235	Willie Banks (R)	.15	.10
178	Scott Leius	.05	.02	236	John Jaha (R)	.20	.12
179	Kirt Manwaring	.05	.02	237	Scooter Tucker (R)	.15	.10
180	Jeff Parrett	.05	.02	238	Russ Springer (R)	.15	.10
181	Don Slaught	.05	.02	239	Paul Miller (R)	.20	.12
182	Scott Radinsky	.05	.02	240	Dan Peltier (R)	.15	.10
183	Luis Alicea	.05	.02	241	Ozzie Canseco	.10	.06
184	Tom Gordon	.07	.04	242	Ben Rivera (R)	.12	.07
185	Rick Wilkins	.05	.02	243	John Valentin (R)	.20	.12
186	Todd Stottlemyre	.07	.04	244	Henry Rodriguez (R)	.20	.12
187	Moises Alou	.15	.10	245	Derek Parks (R)	.15	.10
188	Joe Grahe	.05	.02	246	Carlos Garcia	.15	.10
189	Jeff Kent	.20	.12	247	Tim Pugh (R)	.15	.10
190	Bill Wegman	.05	.02	248	Melvin Nieves (R)	.40	.25
191	Kim Batiste	.07	.04	249	Rich Amaral (R)	.15	.10
192	Matt Nokes	.05	.02	250	Willie Greene	.35	.20
193	Mark Wohlers	.08	.05	251	Tim Scott (R)	.20	.12
194	Paul Sorrento	.10	.06	252	Dave Silvestri (R)	.15	.10
195	Chris Hammond	.08	.05	253	Rob Mallicoat (R)	.12	.07
196	Scott Livingstone	.07	.04	254	Donald Harris	.10	.06
197	Doug Jones	.05	.02	255	Craig Colbert (R)	.15	.10
198	Scott Cooper	.08	.05	256	Jose Guzman	.40	.25
199	Ramon Martinez	.10	.06	257	Domingo Martinez (R)	.25	.15
200	Dave Valle	.05	.02	258	William Suero (R)	.15	.10

259	Juan Guerrero (R)	.15	.10
260	J.T. Snow (R)	.50	.35
261	Tony Pena	.05	.02
262	Tim Fortugno (R)	.15	.10
263	Tom Marsh (R)	.15	.10
264	Kurt Knudsen (R)	.15	.10
265	Tim Costo	.15	.10
266	Steve Shifflett (R)	.15	.10
267	Billy Ashley (R)	.30	.18
268	Jerry Nielsen (R)	.15	.10
269	Pete Young (R)	.15	.10
270	Johnny Guzman (R)	.15	.10
271	Greg Colbrunn (R)	.25	.15
272	Jeff Nelson (R)	.15	.10
273	Kevin Young (R)	.20	.12
274	Jeff Frye (R)	.20	.12
275	J.T. Bruett (R)	.15	.10
276	Todd Pratt (R)	.15	.10
277	Mike Butcher (R)	.15	.10
278	John Flaherty (R)	.20	.12
279	John Patterson (R)	.15	.10
280	Eric Hillman (R)	.25	.15
281	Bien Figueroa (R)	.15	.10
282	Shane Reynolds (R)	.15	.10
283	Rich Rowland (R)	.20	.12
284	Steve Foster (R)	.15	.10
285	Dave Mlicki (R)	.15	.10
286	Mike Piazza (R)	.80	.50
287	Mike Trombley (R)	.15	.10
288	Jim Pena (R)	.15	.10
289	Bob Ayrault (R)	.15	.10
290	Henry Mercedes (R)	.15	.10
291	Bob Wickman (R)	.30	.18
292	Jacob Brumfield (R)	.20	.12
293	David Hulse (R)	.20	.12
294	Ryan Klesko (R)	.75	.45
295	Doug Linton (R)	.15	.10
296	Steve Cooke (R)	.20	.12
297	Eddie Zosky	.12	.07
298	Gerald Williams (R)	.30	.18
299	Jonathan Hurst (R)	.15	.10
300	Larry Carter (R)	.15	.10
301	Wm. Pennyfeather (R)	.20	.12
302	Cesar Hernandez (R)	.15	.10
303	Steve Hosey	.40	.25
304	Blas Minor (R)	.20	.12
305	Jeff Grotewald (R)	.15	.10
306	Bernardo Brito (R)	.15	.10
307	Rafael Bournigal (R)	.15	.10
308	Jeff Branson (R)	.15	.10
309	Tom Quinlan (R)	.15	.10
310	Pat Gomez (R)	.15	.10
311	Sterling Hitchcock (R)	.35	.20
312	Kent Bottenfield (R)	.15	.10
313	Alan Trammell	.10	.06
314	Cris Colon (R)	.20	.12
315	Paul Wagner (R)	.20	.12
316	Matt Maysey (R)	.15	.10
317	Mike Stanton	.05	.02
318	Rick Trlicek (R)	.15	.10
319	Kevin Rogers (R)	.15	.10
320	Mark Clark (R)	.20	.12
321	Pedro Martinez (R)	.35	.20
322	Al Martin (R)	.20	.12
323	Mike Macfarlane	.07	.04
324	Rey Sanchez (R)	.25	.15
325	Roger Pavlik (R)	.15	.10
326	Troy Neel (R)	.15	.10
327	Kerry Woodson (R)	.15	.10
328	Wayne Kirby (R)	.15	.10
329	Ken Ryan (R)	.15	.10
330	Jesse Levis (R)	.15	.10
331	James Austin	.08	.05
332	Dan Walters	.08	.05
333	Brian Williams	.20	.12
334	Wil Cordero	.20	.12
335	Bret Boone	.35	.20
336	Hipolito Pichardo	.10	.06
337	Pat Mahomes	.25	.15
338	Andy Stankiewicz	.08	.05
339	Jim Bullinger	.08	.05
340	Archi Cianfrocco	.12	.07
341	Ruben Amaro Jr.	.10	.06
342	Frank Seminara	.12	.07
343	Pat Hentgen	.07	.04
344	Dave Nilsson	.15	.10
345	Mike Perez	.08	.05
346	Tim Salmon	.30	.18
347	Tim Wakefield	1.75	1.00
348	Carlos Hernandez	.08	.05
349	Donovan Osborne	.25	.15
350	Denny Neagle	.08	.05
351	Sam Militello	.25	.15
352	Eric Fox	.10	.06
353	John Doherty	.08	.05
354	Chad Curtis	.10	.06
355	Jeff Tackett	.08	.05
356	Dave Fleming	.30	.18
357	Pat Listach	.80	.50
358	Kevin Wickander	.08	.05
359	John Vander Wal	.10	.06
360	Arthur Rhodes	.08	.05
361	Bob Scanlan	.08	.05
362	Bob Zupcic	.08	.05
363	Mel Rojas	.07	.04
364	Jim Thome	.12	.07
365	Bill Pecota	.05	.02
366	Mark Carreon	.05	.02
367	Mitch Williams	.05	.02
368	Cal Eldred	.30	.18
369	Stan Belinda	.05	.02
370	Pat Kelly	.08	.05
371	Rheal Cormier	.07	.04
372	Juan Guzman	.45	.28
373	Damon Berryhill	.05	.02
374	Gary DiSarcina	.08	.05

375	Norm Charlton	.05	.02
376	Roberto Hernandez	.07	.04
377	Scott Kamieniecki	.07	.04
378	Rusty Meacham	.08	.05
379	Kurt Stillwell	.05	.02
380	Lloyd McClendon	.05	.02
381	Mark Leonard	.05	.02
382	Jerry Browne	.05	.02
383	Glenn Davis	.08	.05
384	Randy Johnson	.12	.07
385	Mike Greenwell	.08	.05
386	Scott Chiamparino	.07	.04
387	George Bell	.10	.06
388	Steve Olin	.07	.04
389	Chuck McElroy	.05	.02
390	Mark Gardner	.07	.04
391	Rod Beck	.07	.04
392	Dennis Rasmussen	.05	.02
393	Charlie Leibrandt	.05	.02
394	Julio Franco	.08	.05
395	Pete Harnisch	.08	.05
396	Sid Bream	.05	.02
397	Milt Thompson	.05	.02
398	Glenallen Hill	.08	.05
399	Chico Walker	.05	.02
400	Alex Cole	.05	.02
401	Trevor Wilson	.05	.02
402	Jeff Conine	.12	.07
403	Kyle Abbott	.08	.05
404	Tom Browning	.07	.04
405	Jerald Clark	.08	.05
406	Vince Horsman	.10	.06
407	Kevin Mitchell	.10	.06
408	Pete Smith	.15	.10
409	Jeff Innis	.05	.02
410	Mike Timlin	.07	.04
411	Charlie Hayes	.05	.02
412	Alex Fernandez	.08	.05
413	Jeff Russell	.05	.02
414	Jody Reed	.05	.02
415	Mickey Morandini	.08	.05
416	Darnell Coles	.05	.02
417	Xavier Hernandez	.07	.04
418	Steve Sax	.07	.04
419	Joe Girardi	.05	.02
420	Mike Fetters	.05	.02
421	Danny Jackson	.07	.04
422	Jim Gott	.05	.02
423	Tim Belcher	.07	.04
424	Jose Mesa	.07	.04
425	Junior Felix	.05	.02
426	Thomas Howard	.08	.05
427	Julio Valerz	.05	.02
428	Dante Bichette	.05	.02
429	Mike Sharperson	.05	.02
430	Darryl Kile	.07	.04
431	Lonnie Smith	.07	.04
432	Monty Fariss	.07	.04
433	Reggie Jefferson	.10	.06
434	Bob McClure	.05	.02
435	Craig Lefferts	.05	.02
436	Duane Ward	.05	.02
437	Shawn Abner	.05	.02
438	Roberto Kelly	.10	.06
439	Paul O'Neill	.10	.06
440	Alan Mills	.07	.04
441	Roger Mason	.05	.02
442	Gary Pettis	.05	.02
443	Steve Lake	.05	.02
444	Gene Larkin	.05	.02
445	Larry Andersen	.05	.02
446	Doug Dascenzo	.05	.02
447	Daryl Boston	.05	.02
448	John Candelaria	.05	.02
449	Storm Davis	.05	.02
450	Tom Edens	.07	.04
451	Mike Maddux	.05	.02
452	Tim Naehring	.08	.05
453	John Orton	.07	.04
454	Joey Cora	.05	.02
455	Chuck Crim	.05	.02
456	Dan Plesac	.05	.02
457	Mike Bielecki	.05	.02
458	Terry Jorgensen (R)	.12	.07
459	John Habyan	.05	.02
460	Pete O'Brien	.05	.02
461	Jeff Treadway	.05	.02
462	Frank Castillo	.05	.02
463	Jimmy Jones	.05	.02
464	Tommy Greene	.08	.05
465	Tracy Woodson	.05	.02
466	Rich Rodriguez	.08	.05
467	Joe Hesketh	.05	.02
468	Greg Myers	.05	.02
469	Kirk McCaskill	.05	.02
470	Ricky Bones	.08	.05
471	Lenny Webster	.05	.02
472	Francisco Cabrera	.05	.02
473	Turner Ward	.05	.02
474	Dwayne Henry	.05	.02
475	Al Osuna	.05	.02
476	Craig Wilson	.05	.02
477	Chris Nabholz	.07	.04
478	Rafael Belliard	.05	.02
479	Terry Leach	.05	.02
480	Tim Teufel	.05	.02
481	Dennis Eckersley (MVP)	.08	.05
482	Barry Bonds (MVP)	.12	.07
483	Dennis Eckersley (CY)	.08	.05
484	Greg Maddux (CY)	.08	.05
485	Pat Listach (ROY)	.15	.10
486	Eric Karros (ROY)	.25	.15
487	Jamie Arnold (R)	.25	.15
488	B.J. Wallace (R)	.25	.15
489	Derek Jeter (R)	.40	.25

490	Jason Kendall (R)	.30	.18
491	Rick Helling (R)	.20	.12
492	Derek Wallace (R)	.20	.12
493	Sean Lowe (R)	.25	.15
494	Shannon Stewart (R)	.25	.15
495	Benji Grigsby (R)	.35	.20
496	Todd Steverson (R)	.20	.12
497	Dan Serafini (R)	.25	.15
498	Michael Tucker (R)	.25	.15
499	Chris Roberts (R)	.40	.25
500	Pete Janicki (R)	.25	.15
501	Jeff Schmidt (R)	.25	.15
502	Edgar Martinez (AS)	.08	.05
503	Omar Vizquel (AS)	.05	.02
504	Ken Griffey Jr. (AS)	.25	.15
505	Kirby Puckett (AS)	.15	.10
506	Joe Carter (AS)	.12	.07
507	Ivan Rodriguez (AS)	.15	.10
508	Jack Morris (AS)	.08	.05
509	Dennis Eckersley (AS)	.08	.05
510	Frank Thomas (AS)	.30	.18
511	Roberto Alomar (AS)	.15	.10
512	Mickey Morandini (HL)	.07	.04
513	Dennis Eckersley (HL)	.08	.05
514	Jeff Reardon (HL)	.07	.04
515	Danny Tartabull (HL)	.07	.04
516	Bip Roberts (HL)	.05	.02
517	George Brett (HL)	.12	.07
518	Robin Yount (HL)	.12	.07
519	Kevin Gross (HL)	.07	.04
520	Ed Sprague (HL)	.07	.04
521	Dave Winfield (HL)	.10	.06
522	Ozzie Smith (AS)	.07	.04
523	Barry Bonds (AS)	.10	.06
524	Andy Van Slyke (AS)	.07	.04
525	Tony Gwynn (AS)	.08	.05
526	Darren Daulton (AS)	.05	.02
527	Greg Maddux (AS)	.07	.04
528	Fred McGriff (AS)	.08	.05
529	Lee Smith (AS)	.05	.02
530	Ryne Sandberg (AS)	.10	.06
531	Gary Sheffield (AS)	.08	.05
532	Ozzie Smith (DT)	.20	.12
533	Kirby Puckett (DT)	.25	.15
534	Gary Sheffield (DT)	.20	.12
535	Andy Van Slyke (DT)	.12	.07
537	Ivan Rodriguez (DT)	.20	.12
539	Tom Glavine (DT)	.20	.12
540	Dennis Eckersley (DT)	.20	.12
541	Frank Thomas (DT)	.80	.50
542	Roberto Alomar (DT)	.25	.15
543	Sean Berry	.10	.06
544	Mike Schooler	.05	.02
545	Chuck Carr	.10	.06
546	Lenny Harris	.05	.02
547	Gary Scott	.08	.05
548	Derek Lilliquist	.05	.02
549	Brian Hunter	.10	.06

550	Kirby Puckett (Man Of The year)	.15	.10
551	Jim Eisenreich	.05	.02
552	Andre Dawson	.12	.07
553	David Nied (R)	3.00	2.00
554	Spike Owen	.05	.02
555	Greg Gagne	.05	.02
556	Sid Fernandez	.07	.04
557	Mark McGwire	.20	.12
558	Bryan Harvey	.07	.04
559	Harold Reynolds	.05	.02
560	Barry Bonds	.20	.12
561	Eric Wedge (R)	.30	.18
562	Ozzie Smith	.12	.07
563	Rick Sutcliffe	.05	.02
564	Jeff Reardon	.08	.05
565	Alex Arias (R)	.15	.10
566	Greg Swindell	.07	.04
567	Brook Jacoby	.05	.02
568	Pete Incaviglia	.05	.02
569	Butch Henry (R)	.15	.10
570	Eric Davis	.08	.05
571	Kevin Seitzer	.05	.02
572	Tony Fernandez	.08	.05
573	Steve Reed (R)	.20	.12
574	Cory Snyder	.05	.02
575	Joe Carter	.20	.12
576	Greg Maddux	.12	.07
577	Bert Blyleven	.08	.05
578	Kevin Bass	.05	.02
579	Carlton Fisk	.15	.10
580	Doug Drabek	.12	.07
581	Mark Gubicza	.07	.04
582	Bobby Thigpen	.07	.04
583	Chili Davis	.07	.04
584	Scott Bankhead	.05	.02
585	Harold Baines	.07	.04
586	Eric Young (R)	.20	.12
587	Lance Parrish	.07	.04
588	Juan Bell	.05	.02
589	Bob Ojeda	.05	.02
590	Joe Orsulak	.05	.02
591	Benito Santiago	.08	.05
592	Wade Boggs	.12	.07
593	Robby Thompson	.05	.02
594	Eric Plunk	.05	.02
595	Hensley Meulens	.07	.04
596	Lou Whitaker	.07	.04
597	Dale Murphy	.10	.06
598	Paul Molitor	.08	.05
599	Greg W. Harris	.05	.02
600	Darren Holmes	.07	.04
601	Dave Martinez	.05	.02
602	Tom Henke	.05	.02
603	Mike Benjamin	.07	.04
604	Rene Gonzales	.08	.05
605	Roger McDowell	.05	.02
606	Kirby Puckett	.20	.12

607	Randy Myers	.05	.02
608	Ruben Sierra	.15	.10
609	Wilson Alvarez	.07	.04
610	David Segui	.07	.04
611	Juan Samuel	.05	.02
612	Tom Brunansky	.07	.04
613	Willie Randolph	.07	.04
614	Tony Phillips	.05	.02
615	Candy Maldonado	.05	.02
616	Chris Bosio	.07	.04
617	Bret Barberie	.10	.06
618	Scott Sanderson	.05	.02
619	Ron Darling	.07	.04
620	Dave Winfield	.15	.10
621	Mike Felder	.05	.02
622	Greg Hibbard	.07	.04
623	Mike Scioscia	.05	.02
624	John Smiley	.08	.05
625	Alejandro Pena	.05	.02
626	Terry Steinbach	.07	.04
627	Freddie Benavides	.05	.02
628	Kevin Reimer	.07	.04
629	Braulio Castillo	.08	.05
630	Dave Stieb	.07	.04
631	Dave Magadan	.07	.04
632	Scott Fletcher	.05	.02
633	Cris Carpenter	.07	.04
634	Kevin Maas	.08	.05
635	Todd Worrell	.05	.02
636	Rob Deer	.07	.04
637	Dwight Smith	.05	.02
638	Chito Martinez	.08	.05
639	Jimmy Key	.05	.02
640	Greg Harris	.05	.02
641	Mike Moore	.05	.02
642	Pat Borders	.07	.04
643	Bill Gullickson	.05	.02
644	Gary Gaetti	.05	.02
645	David Howard	.07	.04
646	Jim Abbott	.10	.06
647	Willie Wilson	.05	.02
648	David Wells	.05	.02
649	Andres Galarraga	.07	.04
650	Vince Coleman	.07	.04
651	Rob Dibble	.07	.04
652	Frank Tanana	.05	.02
653	Steve Decker	.08	.05
654	David Cone	.12	.07
655	Jack Armstrong	.07	.04
656	Dave Stewart	.10	.06
657	Billy Hatcher	.05	.02
658	Tim Raines	.07	.04
659	Walt Weiss	.05	.02
660	Jose Lind	.05	.02

1993 Score Pinnacle I

For the second straight year Score issued a premium baseball card set under the Pinnacle name. Series I contains 310-cards. The cards feature full color photos on the front and back. Key subsets include Rookies (R), Now and Then (289-296), Idols (ID) and Hometown Hero (HH). All cards measure 2-1/2" by 3-1/2".

		MINT	NR/MT
Complete Set (310)		38.00	26.00
Commons		.08	.05
1	Gary Sheffield	.75	.45
2	Cal Eldred	.60	.35
3	Larry Walker	.25	.15
4	Deion Sanders	.30	.18
5	Dave Fleming	.75	.45
6	Carlos Baerga	.30	.18
7	Bernie Williams	.20	.12
8	John Kruk	.08	.05
9	Jimmy Key	.08	.05
10	Jeff Bagwell	.50	.30
11	Jim Abbott	.20	.12
12	Terry Steinbach	.10	.06
13	Bob Tewksbury	.08	.05
14	Eric Karros	1.25	.80
15	Ryne Sandberg	.60	.35
16	Will Clark	.50	.30
17	Edgar Martinez	.25	.15
18	Eddie Murray	.20	.12
19	Andy Van Slyke	.15	.10
20	Cal Ripken Jr.	.75	.45
21	Ivan Rodriguez	.60	.35
22	Barry Larkin	.15	.10
23	Don Mattingly	.25	.15
24	Gregg Jefferies	.12	.07
25	Roger Clemens	.60	.35

#	Player		
26	Cecil Fielder	.30	.18
27	Kent Hrbek	.10	.06
28	Robin Ventura	.30	.18
29	Rickey Henderson	.25	.15
30	Roberto Alomar	.40	.25
31	Luis Polonia	.08	.05
32	Andujar Cedeno	.12	.07
33	Pat Listach	.80	.50
34	Mark Grace	.20	.12
35	Otis Nixon	.10	.06
36	Felix Jose	.10	.06
37	Mike Sharperson	.08	.05
38	Dennis Martinez	.10	.06
39	Willie McGee	.10	.06
40	Kenny Lofton	.80	.50
41	Randy Johnson	.12	.07
42	Andy Benes	.12	.07
43	Bobby Bonilla	.20	.12
44	Mike Mussina	1.00	.70
45	Lenny Dykstra	.08	.05
46	Ellis Burks	.10	.06
47	Chris Sabo	.10	.06
48	Jay Bell	.08	.05
49	Jose Canseco	.60	.35
50	Craig Biggio	.10	.06
51	Wally Joyner	.12	.07
52	Mickey Tettleton	.10	.06
53	Tim Raines	.10	.06
54	Brian Harper	.08	.05
55	Rene Gonzales	.12	.07
56	Mark Langston	.15	.10
57	Jack Morris	.20	.12
58	Mark McGwire	.60	.35
59	Ken Caminiti	.08	.05
60	Terry Pendleton	.20	.12
61	Dave Nilsson	.30	.18
62	Tom Pagnozzi	.10	.06
63	Mike Morgan	.08	.05
64	Darryl Strawberry	.30	.18
65	Charles Nagy	.20	.12
66	Ken Hill	.10	.06
67	Matt Williams	.20	.12
68	Jay Buhner	.10	.06
69	Vince Coleman	.10	.06
70	Brady Anderson	.20	.12
71	Fred McGriff	.30	.18
72	Ben McDonald	.15	.10
73	Terry Mulholland	.08	.05
74	Randy Tomlin	.10	.06
75	Nolan Ryan	1.25	.80
76	Frank Viola	.12	.07
77	Jose Rijo	.12	.07
78	Shane Mack	.12	.07
79	Travis Fryman	.30	.18
80	Jack McDowell	.20	.12
81	Mark Gubicza	.08	.05
82	Matt Nokes	.08	.05
83	Bert Blyleven	.15	.10
84	Eric Anthony	.12	.07
85	Mike Bordick	.12	.07
86	John Olerud	.15	.10
87	B.J. Surhoff	.08	.05
88	Bernard Gilkey	.15	.10
89	Shawon Dunston	.12	.07
90	Tom Glavine	.25	.15
91	Brett Butler	.10	.06
92	Moises Alou	.30	.18
93	Albert Belle	.25	.15
94	Darren Lewis	.10	.06
95	Omar Vizquel	.08	.05
96	Doc Gooden	.20	.12
97	Gregg Olson	.10	.06
98	Tony Gwynn	.30	.18
99	Darren Daulton	.12	.07
100	Dennis Eckersley	.25	.15
101	Rob Dibble	.10	.06
102	Mike Greenwell	.10	.06
103	Jose Lind	.08	.05
104	Julio Franco	.10	.06
105	Tom Gordon	.10	.06
106	Scott Livingstone	.10	.06
107	Chuck Knoblauch	.30	.18
108	Frank Thomas	2.50	1.50
109	Melido Perez	.10	.06
110	Ken Griffey Jr.	1.75	1.00
111	Harold Baines	.10	.06
112	Gary Gaetti	.08	.05
113	Pete Harnisch	.10	.06
114	David Wells	.08	.05
115	Charlie Leibrandt	.08	.05
116	Ray Lankford	.30	.18
117	Kevin Seitzer	.08	.05
118	Robin Yount	.25	.15
119	Lenny Harris	.08	.05
120	Chris James	.08	.05
121	Delino DeShields	.20	.12
122	Kirt Manwaring	.08	.05
123	Glenallen Hill	.12	.07
124	Hensley Meulens	.10	.06
125	Darrin Jackson	.10	.06
126	Todd Hundley	.10	.06
127	Dave Hollins	.15	.10
128	Sam Horn	.08	.05
129	Roberto Hernandez	.10	.06
130	Vicente Palacios	.08	.05
131	George Brett	.25	.15
132	Dave Martinez	.08	.05
133	Kevin Appier	.10	.06
134	Pat Kelly	.10	.06
135	Pedro Munoz	.12	.07
136	Mark Carreon	.08	.05
137	Lance Johnson	.08	.05
138	Devon White	.08	.05
139	Julio Valera	.08	.05
140	Eddie Taubensee	.10	.06
141	Willie Wilson	.08	.05

#	Player		
142	Stan Belinda	.08	.05
143	John Smoltz	.20	.12
144	Darryl Hamilton	.10	.06
145	Sammy Sosa	.10	.06
146	Carlos Hernandez	.12	.07
147	Tom Candiotti	.08	.05
148	Mike Felder	.08	.05
149	Rusty Meacham	.12	.07
150	Ivan Calderon	.10	.06
151	Pete O'Brien	.08	.05
152	Erik Hanson	.08	.05
153	Billy Ripken	.08	.05
154	Kurt Stillwell	.08	.05
155	Jeff Kent	.15	.10
156	Mickey Morandini	.10	.06
157	Randy Milligan	.08	.05
158	Reggie Sanders	.50	.30
159	Luis Rivera	.10	.06
160	Orlando Merced	.10	.06
161	Dean Palmer	.15	.10
162	Mike Perez	.12	.07
163	Scott Erickson	.20	.12
164	Kevin McReynolds	.10	.06
165	Kevin Maas	.12	.07
166	Ozzie Guillen	.08	.05
167	Rob Deer	.10	.06
168	Danny Tartabull	.20	.12
169	Lee Stevens	.20	.12
170	Dave Henderson	.10	.06
171	Derek Bell	.25	.15
172	Steve Finley	.08	.05
173	Greg Olson	.08	.05
174	Geronimo Pena	.08	.05
175	Paul Quantrill (R)	.30	.18
176	Steve Buechele	.08	.05
177	Kevin Gross	.08	.05
178	Tim Wallach	.10	.06
179	Dave Valle	.08	.05
180	Dave Silvestri	.20	.12
181	Bud Black	.08	.05
182	Henry Rodriguez	.15	.10
183	Tim Teufel	.08	.05
184	Mark McLemore	.08	.05
185	Bret Saberhagen	.15	.10
186	Chris Hoiles	.15	.10
187	Ricky Jordan	.10	.06
188	Don Slaught	.08	.05
189	Mo Vaughn	.20	.12
190	Joe Oliver	.08	.05
191	Juan Gonzalez	1.00	.70
192	Scott Leius	.08	.05
193	Milt Cuyler	.10	.06
194	Chris Haney	.10	.06
195	Ron Karkovice	.08	.05
196	Steve Farr	.08	.05
197	John Orton	.10	.06
198	Kelly Gruber	.10	.06
199	Ron Darling	.10	.06
200	Ruben Sierra	.40	.25
201	Chuck Finley	.12	.07
202	Mike Moore	.08	.05
203	Pat Borders	.10	.06
204	Sid Bream	.08	.05
205	Todd Zeile	.12	.07
206	Rick Wilkins	.08	.05
207	Jim Gantner	.08	.05
208	Frank Castillo	.08	.05
209	Dave Hansen	.10	.06
210	Trevor Wilson	.08	.05
211	Sandy Alomar Jr.	.12	.07
212	Sean Berry	.15	.10
213	Tino Martinez	.12	.07
215	Dan Walters	.15	.10
216	John Franco	.10	.06
217	Glenn Davis	.10	.06
218	Mariano Duncan	.08	.05
219	Mike LaValliere	.08	.05
220	Rafael Palmeiro	.15	.10
221	Jack Clark	.12	.07
222	Hal Morris	.15	.10
223	Ed Sprague	.15	.10
224	John Valentin (R)	.25	.15
225	Sam Militello	.75	.45
226	Bob Wickman	.25	.15
227	Damion Easley	.20	.12
228	John Jaha	.15	.10
229	Bob Ayrault	.15	.10
230	Mo Sanford	.15	.10
231	Walt Weiss	.08	.05
232	Dante Bichette	.08	.05
233	Steve Decker	.12	.07
234	Jerald Clark	.12	.07
235	Bryan Harvey	.10	.06
236	Joe Girardi	.08	.05
237	Dave Magadan	.08	.05
238	David Nied (R)	3.50	2.50
239	Eric Wedge (R)	.40	.25
240	Rico Brogna (R)	.25	.15
241	J.T. Bruett (R)	.20	.12
242	Jonathan Hurst (R)	.20	.12
243	Bret Boone (R)	1.25	.80
244	Manny Alexander (R)	.20	.12
245	Scooter Tucker (R)	.20	.12
246	Troy Neel (R)	.20	.12
247	Eddie Zosky (R)	.25	.15
248	Melvin Nieves (R)	1.00	.70
249	Ryan Thompson (R)	.40	.25
250	Shawn Barton (R)	.20	.12
251	Ryan Klesko (R)	2.00	1.25
252	Mike Piazza (R)	1.75	1.00
253	Steve Hosey (R)	.75	.45
254	Shane Reynolds (R)	.25	.15
255	Dan Wilson (R)	.30	.18
256	Tom Marsh (R)	.20	.12
257	Barry Manuel (R)	.20	.12
258	Paul Miller (R)	.25	.15

259	Pedro Martinez (R)	.60	.35
260	Steve Cooke (R)	.20	.12
261	Johnny Guzman (R)	.15	.10
262	Mike Butcher (R)	.25	.15
263	Bien Figueroa (R)	.20	.12
264	Rich Rowland (R)	.20	.12
265	Shawn Jeter (R)	.30	.18
266	Gerald Williams (R)	.40	.25
267	Derek Parks (R)	.25	.15
268	Henry Mercedes (R)	.25	.15
269	David Hulse (R)	.25	.15
270	Tim Pugh (R)	.25	.15
271	Williams Suero (R)	.20	.12
272	Ozzie Canseco (R)	.40	.25
273	Fernando Ramsey (R)	.25	.15
274	Bernardo Brito (R)	.15	.10
275	Dave Mlicki (R)	.20	.12
276	Tim Salmon (R)	1.25	.80
277	Mike Raczka (R)	.20	.12
278	Ken Ryan (R)	.20	.12
279	Rafael Bournigal (R)	.30	.18
280	Wil Cordero (R)	.80	.50
281	Billy Ashley (R)	.75	.45
282	Paul Wagner (R)	.20	.12
283	Blas Minor (R)	.20	.12
284	Rick Trlicek (R)	.20	.12
285	Willie Greene (R)	.75	.45
286	Ted Wood	.15	.10
287	Phil Clark	.15	.10
288	Jesse Levis (R)	.15	.10
289	Tony Gwynn	.15	.10
290	Nolan Ryan	.80	.50
291	Dennis Martinez	.10	.06
292	Eddie Murray	.20	.12
293	Robin Yount	.20	.12
294	George Brett	.20	.12
295	Dave Winfield	.20	.12
296	Bert Blyleven	.12	.07
297	Jeff Bagwell (ID)	.40	.25
298	John Smoltz (ID)	.10	.06
299	Larry Walker (ID)	.10	.06
300	Gary Sheffield (ID)	.15	.10
301	Ivan Rodriguez (ID)	.15	.10
302	Delino DeShields (ID)	.15	.10
303	Tim Salmon (ID)	.25	.15
304	Bernard Gilkey (HH)	.08	.05
305	Cal Ripken Jr. (HH)	.25	.15
306	Barry Larkin (HH)	.10	.06
307	Kent Hrbek (HH)	.08	.05
308	Rickey Henderson (HH)	.12	.07
309	Darryl Strawberry(HH)	.15	.10
310	John Franco (HH)	.08	.05

TOPPS

1951 Topps Blue Backs

This is the first card set to carry the Topps name. The 56-card set featured black and white photos on the card fronts surrounded by a red, green, yellow and white background. Card backs were printed in blue on a white backgrund. The cards were used as a baseball card game and came packaged two to a pack with a piece of candy. Cards measured 2" by 2-5/8".

		NR/MT	EX
Complete Set (52)		2,200.00	1,000.00
Commons		35.00	20.00
1	Eddie Yost	55.00	30.00
2	Hank Majeski	35.00	20.00
3	Richie Ashburn	175.00	75.00
4	Del Ennis	40.00	22.00
5	Johnny Pesky	45.00	25.00
6	Red Schoendienst	125.00	65.00
7	Gerald Staley	35.00	20.00
8	Dick Sisler	40.00	22.00
9	Johnny Sain	50.00	28.00
10	Joe Page	40.00	22.00
11	Johnny Groth	35.00	20.00
12	Sam Jethroe	35.00	20.00
13	Mickey Vernon	40.00	22.00
14	George Munger	35.00	20.00
15	Eddie Joost	35.00	20.00
16	Murry Dickson	35.00	20.00
17	Roy Smalley	35.00	20.00
18	Ned Garver	35.00	20.00
19	Phil Masi	35.00	20.00

		NR/MT	EX
20	Ralph Branca	50.00	28.00
21	Billy Johnson	35.00	20.00
22	Bob Kuzava	35.00	20.00
23	Paul "Dizzy" Trout	35.00	20.00
24	Sherman Lollar	40.00	22.00
25	Sam Mele	35.00	20.00
26	Chico Carrasquel	35.00	20.00
27	Andy Pafko	40.00	22.00
28	Harry Brecheen	35.00	20.00
29	Granny Hamner	35.00	20.00
30	Enos Slaughter	135.00	70.00
31	Lou Brissie	35.00	20.00
32	Bob Elliott	35.00	20.00
33	Don Lenhardt	35.00	20.00
34	Earl Torgeson	35.00	20.00
35	Tommy Byrne	40.00	22.00
36	Cliff Fannin	35.00	20.00
37	Bobby Doerr	125.00	65.00
38	Irv Noren	40.00	22.00
39	Ed Lopat	45.00	25.00
40	Vic Wertz	40.00	22.00
41	Johnny Schmitz	35.00	20.00
42	Bruce Edwards	35.00	20.00
43	Willie Jones	35.00	20.00
44	Johnny Wyrostek	35.00	20.00
45	Bill Pierce	50.00	28.00
46	Gerry Priddy	35.00	20.00
47	Herman Wehmeier	35.00	20.00
48	Billy Cox	40.00	22.00
49	Hank Sauer	40.00	22.00
50	Johnny Mize	175.00	75.00
51	Eddie Waitkus	35.00	20.00
52	Sam Chapman	45.00	25.00

1951 Topps
Red Backs

This 52-card set is identical to the Blue Backs except the black and white photos on the front are framed by blue, red, yellow and white backgrounds and the card backs feature red type on a white background. Cards measure 2" by 2-5/8".

		NR/MT	EX
Complete Set (52)		800.00	450.00
Commons		7.50	4.50
1	Yogi Berra	150.00	80.00
2	Sid Gordon	7.50	4.50
3	Ferris Fain	8.50	5.00
4	Vern Stephens	10.00	6.00
5	Phil Rizzuto	40.00	22.00
6	Allie Reynolds	15.00	8.00
7	Howie Pollet	7.50	4.50
8	Early Wynn	25.00	14.00
9	Roy Sievers	10.00	6.00
10	Mel Parnell	8.50	5.00
11	Gene Hermanski	7.50	4.50
12	Jim Hegan	8.50	5.00
13	Dale Mitchell	10.00	6.00
14	Wayne Terwilliger	7.50	4.50
15	Ralph Kiner	35.00	20.00
16	Preacher Roe	10.00	6.00
17	Gus Bell	12.00	7.00
18	Jerry Coleman	12.00	7.00
19	Dick Kokos	7.50	4.50
20	Dom DiMaggio	12.00	7.00
21	Larry Jansen	8.50	5.00
22	Bob Feller	55.00	30.00
23	Ray Boone	12.00	7.00
24	Hank Bauer	16.00	9.00
25	Cliff Chambers	7.50	4.50
26	Luke Easter	10.00	6.00
27	Wally Westlake	7.50	4.50
28	Elmer Valo	7.50	4.50
29	Bob Kennedy	7.50	4.50
30	Warren Spahn	55.00	30.00
31	Gil Hodges	40.00	22.00
32	Hank Thompson	10.00	6.00
33	William Werle	7.50	4.50
34	Grady Hatton	7.50	4.50
35	Al Rosen	15.00	8.00
36a	Gus Zernial (Chicago)	35.00	20.00
36b	Gus Zernial (Philly)	20.00	12.00
37	Wes Westrum	7.50	4.50
38	Duke Snider	90.00	55.00
39	Ted Kluszewski	20.00	12.00
40	Mike Garcia	10.00	6.00
41	Whitey Lockman	8.50	5.00
42	Ray Scarborough	7.50	4.50
43	Maurice McDermott	7.50	4.50
44	Sid Hudson	7.50	4.50
45	Andy Seminick	7.50	4.50
46	Billy Goodman	8.50	5.00
47	Tommy Glaviano	7.50	4.50
48	Eddie Stanky	12.00	7.00
49	Al Zarilla	7.50	4.50
50	Monte Irvin	50.00	28

51	Eddie Robinson	7.50	4.50
52a	Tommy Holmes (Boston)	35.00	20.00
52b	Tommy Holmes (Hartford)	20.00	12.00

1952 Topps

This 407-card set is considered the father of modern day card sets. Cards measure 2-5/8" by 3-3/4". Card fronts feature colorized black and white photos. The card backs were the first to utilize player stats. Card numbers 311 through 407 are considered scarce due to shorter print runs. The set contains the first ever Mickey Mantle Topps card and the set is considered the most sought after set in the hobby.

	NR/MT	EX
Complete Set (407)	75,000.00	35,000.00
Commons (1-80)	65.00	30.00
Commons (81-250)	28.00	12.00
Commons (251-280)	48.00	20.00
Commons (281-300)	55.00	25.00
Commons (310-310)	48.00	20.00
Commons (311-407	180.00	85.00

1	Andy Pafko	1,250.00	400.00
2	Pete Runnels (R)	75.00	35.00
3	Hank Thompson	70.00	32.00
4	Don Lenhardt	65.00	30.00
5	Larry Jansen	65.00	30.00
6	Grady Hatton	65.00	30.00
7	Wayne Terwilliger	65.00	30.00
8	Fred Marsh	65.00	30.00
9	Bobby Hogue	65.00	30.00
10	Al Rosen	100.00	48.00
11	Phil Rizzuto	200.00	95.00
12	Monty Basgall	65.00	30.00
13	Johnny Wyrostek	65.00	30.00
14	Bob Elliott	65.00	30.00
15	Johnny Pesky	75.00	35.00
16	Gene Hermanski	65.00	30.00
17	Jim Hegan	65.00	30.00
18	Merrill Combs	65.00	30.00
19	Johnny Bucha	65.00	30.00
20	Bill Loes (R)	110.00	50.00
21	Ferris Fain	60.00	28.00
22	Dom DiMaggio	100.00	48.00
23	Billy Goodman	65.00	30.00
24	Luke Easter	65.00	30.00
25	Johnny Groth	65.00	30.00
26	Monty Irvin	125.00	60.00
27	Sam Jethroe	65.00	30.00
28	Jerry Priddy	65.00	30.00
29	Ted Kluszewski	110.00	50.00
30	Mel Parnell	70.00	32.00
31	Gus Zernial	70.00	32.00
32	Eddie Robinson	65.00	30.00
33	Warren Spahn	280.00	130.00
34	Elmer Valo	60.00	28.00
35	Hank Sauer	75.00	35.00
36	Gil Hodges	200.00	95.00
37	Duke Snider	340.00	160.00
38	Wally Westlake	65.00	30.00
39	"Dizzy" Trout	65.00	30.00
40	Irv Noren	65.00	30.00
41	Bob Wellman	65.00	30.00
42	Lou Kretlow	65.00	30.00
43	Ray Scarborough	65.00	30.00
44	Con Dempsey	65.00	30.00
45	Eddie Joost	65.00	30.00
46	Gordon Goldsberry	65.00	30.00
47	Willie Jones	65.00	30.00
48a	Joe Page (Er)	300.00	125.00
48b	Joe Page (Cor)	75.00	35.00
49a	Johnny Sain (Er)	325.00	140.00
49b	Johnny Sain (Cor)	90.00	42.00
50	Marv Rickert	65.00	30.00
51	Jim Russell	65.00	30.00
52	Don Mueller	65.00	30.00
53	Chris Van Cuyk	65.00	30.00
54	Leo Kiely	65.00	30.00
55	Ray Boone	70.00	32.00
56	Tommy Glaviano	65.00	30.00
57	Ed Lopat	110.00	50.00
58	Bob Mahoney	65.00	30.00
59	Robin Roberts	180.00	85.00
60	Sid Hudson	65.00	30.00
61	"Tookie" Gilbert	65.00	30.00
62	Chuck Stobbs	65.00	30.00
63	Howie Pollet	65.00	30.00
64	Roy Sievers	70.00	32.00
65	Enos Slaughter	180.00	85.00
66	"Preacher" Roe	110.00	50.00

67	Allie Reynolds	110.00	50.00
68	Cliff Chambers	65.00	30.00
69	Virgil Stallcup	65.00	30.00
70	Al Zarilla	65.00	30.00
71	Tom Upton	65.00	30.00
72	Karl Olson	65.00	30.00
73	William Werle	65.00	30.00
74	Andy Hansen	65.00	30.00
75	Wes Westrum	65.00	30.00
76	Eddie Stanky	75.00	35.00
77	Bob Kennedy	65.00	30.00
78	Ellis Kinder	65.00	30.00
79	Gerald Staley	65.00	30.00
80	Herman Wehmeier	65.00	30.00
81	Vernon Law	35.00	15.00
82	Duane Pillette	28.00	12.00
83	Billy Johnson	28.00	12.00
84	Vern Stephens	32.00	13.50
85	Bob Kuzava	28.00	12.00
86	Ted Gray	28.00	12.00
87	Dale Coogan	28.00	12.00
88	Bob Feller	175.00	80.00
89	Johnny Lipon	28.00	12.00
90	Mickey Grasso	28.00	12.00
91	Al Schoendienst	100.00	48.00
92	Dale Mitchell	32.00	13.50
93	Al Sima	28.00	12.00
94	Sam Mele	28.00	12.00
95	Ken Holcombe	28.00	12.00
96	Willard Marshall	28.00	12.00
97	Earl Torgeson	28.00	12.00
98	Bill Pierce	32.00	13.50
99	Gene Woodling (R)	65.00	30.00
100	Del Rice	28.00	12.00
101	Max Lanier	28.00	12.00
102	Bill Kennedy	28.00	12.00
103	Cliff Mapes	28.00	12.00
104	Don Kolloway	28.00	12.00
105	John Pramesa	28.00	12.00
106	Mickey Vernon	35.00	15.00
107	Connie Ryan	28.00	12.00
108	Jim Konstanty	35.00	15.00
109	Ted Wilks	28.00	12.00
110	Dutch Leonard	28.00	12.00
111	Harry Lowrey	28.00	12.00
112	Henry Majeski	28.00	12.00
113	Dick Sisler	32.00	13.50
114	Willard Ramsdell	28.00	12.00
115	George Munger	28.00	12.00
116	Carl Scheib	28.00	12.00
117	Sherman Lollar	32.00	13.50
118	Ken Raffensberger	28.00	12.00
119	Maurice McDermott	28.00	12.00
120	Bob Chakales	28.00	12.00
121	Gus Niarhos	28.00	12.00
122	Jack Jensen (R)	80.00	38.00
123	Eddie Yost	32.00	13.50
124	Monte Kennedy	28.00	12.00
125	Bill Rigney	32.00	13.50
126	Fred Hutchinson	32.00	13.50
127	Paul Minner	28.00	12.00
128	Don Bollweg	28.00	12.00
129	Johnny Mize	100.00	48.00
130	Sheldon Jones	28.00	12.00
131	Morrie Martin	28.00	12.00
132	Clyde Kluttz	28.00	12.00
133	Al Widmar	28.00	12.00
134	Joe Tipton	28.00	12.00
135	Dixie Howell	28.00	12.00
136	Johnny Schmitz	28.00	12.00
137	Roy McMillan (R)	35.00	15.00
138	Bill MacDonald	28.00	12.00
139	Ken Wood	28.00	12.00
140	John Antonelli	32.00	13.50
141	Clint Hartung	28.00	12.00
142	Harry Perkowski	28.00	12.00
143	Les Moss	28.00	12.00
144	Ed Blake	28.00	12.00
145	Joe Haynes	28.00	12.00
146	Frank House	28.00	12.00
147	Bob Young	28.00	12.00
148	Johnny Klippstein	28.00	12.00
149	Dick Kryhoski	28.00	12.00
150	Ted Beard	28.00	12.00
151	Wally Post (R)	32.00	13.50
152	Al Evans	28.00	12.00
153	Bob Rush	28.00	12.00
154	Joe Muir	28.00	12.00
155	Frank Overmire	28.00	12.00
156	Frank Hiller	28.00	12.00
157	Bob Usher	28.00	12.00
158	Eddie Waitkus	28.00	12.00
159	Saul Rogovin	28.00	12.00
160	Owen Friend	28.00	12.00
161	Bud Byerly	28.00	12.00
162	Del Crandall	32.00	13.50
163	Stan Rojek	28.00	12.00
164	Walt Dubiel	28.00	12.00
165	Eddie Kazak	28.00	12.00
166	Paul LaPalme	28.00	12.00
167	Bill Howerton	28.00	12.00
168	Charlie Silvera	32.00	13.50
169	Howie Judson	28.00	12.00
170	Gus Bell	35.00	15.00
171	Ed Erautt	28.00	12.00
172	Eddie Miksis	28.00	12.00
173	Roy Smalley	28.00	12.00
174	Clarence Marshall	28.00	12.00
175	Billy Martin	400.00	190.00
176	Hank Edwards	28.00	12.00
177	Bill Wight	28.00	12.00
178	Cass Michaels	28.00	12.00
179	Frank Smith	28.00	12.00
180	Charley Maxwell (R)	32.00	13.50
181	Bob Swift	28.00	12.00
182	Billy Hitchcock	28.00	12.00

183	Erv Dusak	28.00	12.00	241	Tommy Byrne	28.00	12.00
184	Bob Ramazzotti	28.00	12.00	242	Tom Poholsky	28.00	12.00
185	Bill Nicholson	28.00	12.00	243	Larry Doby	50.00	22.00
186	Walt Masterson	28.00	12.00	244	Vic Wertz	32.00	13.50
187	Bob Miller	28.00	12.00	245	Sherry Robertson	28.00	12.00
188	Clarence Podbielan	28.00	12.00	246	George Kell	80.00	38.00
189	Pete Reiser	35.00	15.00	247	Randy Gumpert	28.00	12.00
190	Don Johnson	28.00	12.00	248	Frank Shea	28.00	12.00
191	Yogi Berra	500.00	240.00	249	Bobby Adams	28.00	12.00
192	Myron Ginsberg	28.00	12.00	250	Carl Erskine	75.00	35.00
193	Harry Simpson	28.00	12.00	251	Chico Carrasquel	48.00	20.00
194	Joe Hatten	28.00	12.00	252	Vern Bickford	48.00	20.00
195	Minnie Minoso	150.00	70.00	253	Johnny Berardino	55.00	25.00
196	Solly Hemus	32.00	13.50	254	Joe Dobson	48.00	20.00
197	George Strickland	32.00	13.50	255	Clyde Vollmer	48.00	20.00
198	Phil Haugstad	28.00	12.00	256	Pete Suder	48.00	20.00
199	George Zuverink	28.00	12.00	257	Bobby Avila	50.00	22.00
200	Ralph Houk	60.00	28.00	258	Steve Gromek	48.00	20.00
201	Alex Kellner	28.00	12.00	259	Bob Addis	48.00	20.00
202	Joe Collins	35.00	15.00	260	Pete Castiglione	48.00	20.00
203	Curt Simmons	32.00	13.50	261	Willie Mays	2,500.00	1,200.00
204	Ron Northey	28.00	12.00	262	Virgil Trucks	50.00	22.00
205	Clyde King	28.00	12.00	263	Harry Brecheen	50.00	22.00
206	Joe Ostrowski	28.00	12.00	264	Roy Hartsfield	48.00	20.00
207	Mickey Harris	28.00	12.00	265	Chuck Diering	48.00	20.00
208	Marlin Stuart	28.00	12.00	266	Murry Dickson	48.00	20.00
209	Howie Fox	28.00	12.00	267	Sid Gordon	48.00	20.00
210	Dick Fowler	28.00	12.00	268	Bob Lemon	200.00	95.00
211	Ray Coleman	28.00	12.00	269	Willard Nixon	48.00	20.00
212	Ned Garver	28.00	12.00	270	Lou Brissie	48.00	20.00
213	Nippy Jones	28.00	12.00	271	Jim Delsing	48.00	20.00
214	Johnny Hopp	28.00	12.00	272	Mike Garcia	55.00	25.00
215	Hank Bauer	60.00	28.00	273	Erv Palica	48.00	20.00
216	Richie Ashburn	125.00	60.00	274	Ralph Branca	80.00	38.00
217	George Stirnweiss	32.00	13.50	275	Pat Mullin	48.00	20.00
218	Clyde McCullough	28.00	12.00	276	Jim Wilson	48.00	20.00
219	Bobby Shantz	35.00	15.00	277	Early Wynn	200.00	95.00
220	Joe Presko	28.00	12.00	278	Al Clark	48.00	20.00
221	Granny Hamner	28.00	12.00	279	Ed Stewart	48.00	20.00
222	"Hoot" Evers	28.00	12.00	280	Cloyd Boyer	48.00	20.00
223	Del Ennis	28.00	12.00	281	Tommy Brown	55.00	25.00
224	Bruce Edwards	28.00	12.00	282	Birdie Tebbetts	65.00	30.00
225	Frank Baumholtz	28.00	12.00	283	Phil Masi	55.00	25.00
226	Dave Philley	28.00	12.00	284	Hank Arft	55.00	25.00
227	Joe Garagiola	140.00	65.00	285	Cliff Fannin	55.00	25.00
228	Al Brazle	28.00	12.00	286	Joe DeMaestri	55.00	25.00
229	Gene Bearden	28.00	12.00	287	Steve Bilko	55.00	25.00
230	Matt Batts	28.00	12.00	288	Chet Nichols	55.00	25.00
231	Sam Zoldak	28.00	12.00	289	Tommy Holmes	60.00	28.00
232	Billy Cox	35.00	15.00	290	Joe Astroth	55.00	25.00
233	Bob Friend (R)	35.00	15.00	291	Gil Coan	55.00	25.00
234	Steve Souchock	28.00	12.00	292	Floyd Baker	55.00	25.00
235	Walt Dropo	35.00	13.50	293	Sibby Sisti	55.00	25.00
236	Ed FitzGerald	28.00	12.00	294	Walker Cooper	55.00	25.00
237	Jerry Coleman	32.00	13.50	295	Phil Cavarretta	65.00	30.00
238	Art Houtteman	28.00	12.00	296	Red Rolfe	60.00	28.00
239	Rocky Bridges	28.00	12.00	297	Andy Seminick	60.00	28.00
240	Jack Phillips	28.00	12.00	298	Bob Ross	55.00	25.00

299	Ray Murray	55.00	25.00
300	Barney McCosky	55.00	25.00
301	Bob Porterfield	48.00	20.00
302	Max Surkont	48.00	20.00
303	Harry Dorish	48.00	20.00
304	Sam Dente	48.00	20.00
305	Paul Richards	55.00	25.00
306	Lou Sleator	48.00	20.00
307	Frank Campos	48.00	20.00
308	Luis Aloma	48.00	20.00
309	Jim Busby	48.00	20.00
310	George Metkovich	48.00	20.00
311	Mickey Mantle	40,000.00	22000.00
312	Jackie Robinson	1,400.00	650.00
313	Bobby Thomson	275.00	130.00
314	Roy Campanella	1,850.00	850.00
315	Leo Durocher	350.00	160.00
316	Davey Williams	225.00	100.00
317	Connie Marrero	180.00	85.00
318	Hal Gregg	180.00	85.00
319	Al Walker	180.00	85.00
320	John Rutherford	180.00	85.00
321	Joe Black (R)	275.00	130.00
322	Randy Jackson	180.00	85.00
323	Bubba Church	180.00	85.00
324	Warren Hacker	180.00	85.00
325	Bill Serena	180.00	85.00
326	George Shuba	225.00	100.00
327	Archie Wilson	180.00	85.00
328	Bob Borkowski	180.00	85.00
329	Ivan Delock	180.00	85.00
330	Turk Lown	180.00	85.00
331	Tom Morgan	180.00	85.00
332	Tony Bartirome	180.00	85.00
333	Pee Wee Reese	1,250.00	600.00
334	Wilmer Mizell	210.00	95.00
335	Ted Lepcio	180.00	85.00
336	Dave Koslo	180.00	85.00
337	Jim Hearn	180.00	85.00
338	Sal Yvars	180.00	85.00
339	Russ Meyer	180.00	85.00
340	Bob Hooper	180.00	85.00
341	Hal Jeffcoat	180.00	85.00
342	Clem Labine (R)	250.00	120.00
343	Dick Gernert	180.00	85.00
344	Ewell Blackwell	200.00	95.00
345	Sam White	180.00	85.00
346	George Spencer	180.00	85.00
347	Joe Adcock	225.00	100.00
348	Bob Kelly	180.00	85.00
349	Bob Cain	180.00	85.00
350	Cal Abrams	180.00	85.00
351	Al Dark	210.00	95.00
352	Karl Drews	180.00	85.00
353	Bob Del Greco	180.00	85.00
354	Fred Hatfield	180.00	85.00
355	Bobby Morgan	180.00	85.00
356	Toby Atwell	180.00	85.00
357	Smoky Burgess	240.00	110.00
358	John Kucab	180.00	85.00
359	Dee Fondy	180.00	85.00
360	George Crowe	180.00	85.00
361	Bill Posedel	180.00	85.00
362	Ken Heintzelman	180.00	85.00
363	Dick Rozek	180.00	85.00
364	Clyde Sukeforth	180.00	85.00
365	Cookie Lavagetto	200.00	95.00
366	Dave Madison	180.00	85.00
367	Bob Thorpe	180.00	85.00
368	Ed Wright	180.00	85.00
369	Dick Groat (R)	300.00	140.00
370	Billy Hoeft	180.00	85.00
371	Bob Hofman	180.00	85.00
372	Gil McDougald (R)	325.00	150.00
373	Jim Turner	180.00	85.00
374	Al Benton	180.00	85.00
375	Jack Merson	180.00	85.00
376	Faye Throneberry	180.00	85.00
377	Chuck Dressen	200.00	95.00
378	Les Fusselman	180.00	85.00
379	Joe Rossi	180.00	85.00
380	Clem Koshorek	180.00	85.00
381	Milton Stock	180.00	85.00
382	Sam Jones	200.00	95.00
383	Del Wilber	180.00	85.00
384	Frank Crosetti	250.00	120.00
385	Herman Franks	200.00	95.00
386	Eddie Yuhas	180.00	85.00
387	Billy Meyer	180.00	85.00
388	Bob Chipman	180.00	85.00
389	Ben Wade	180.00	85.00
390	Glenn Nelson	180.00	85.00
391	Ben Chapman (Wrong Photo)	180.00	85.00
392	Hoyt Wilhelm	675.00	325.00
393	Ebba St. Claire	180.00	85.00
394	Billy Herman	280.00	130.00
395	Jake Pitler	180.00	85.00
396	Dick Williams (R)	240.00	110.00
397	Forrest Main	180.00	85.00
398	Hal Rice	180.00	85.00
399	Jim Fridley	180.00	85.00
400	Bill Dickey	650.00	320.00
401	Bob Schultz	180.00	85.00
402	Earl Harrist	180.00	85.00
403	Bill Miller	180.00	85.00
404	Dick Brodowski	180.00	85.00
405	Eddie Pellagrini	180.00	85.00
406	Joe Nuxhall (R)	250.00	120.00
407	Ed Mathews	2,850.00	1,300.00

1953 Topps

YOGI BERRA

The 1953 Topps set consists of 274-cards measuring 2-5/8" by 3-3/4". Card fronts feature colorful drawings of players. Although the checklist is numbered to 280, 6-cards are missing from the set. 253, 261, 267, 268, 271, and 275 were never issued. Short prints account for a scarcity of cards 221-280. A number of high number cards were double printed. Those are marked with the symbol (DP).

	NR/MT	EX
Complete Set (274)	15,000.00	9,000.00
Commons (1-165)	25.00	12.00
Commons (166-220)	20.00	8.50
Commons (221-280)	95.00	45.00
Commons (DP)	50.00	22.00

		NR/MT	EX
1	Jackie Robinson	675.00	325.00
2	Luke Easter	25.00	12.00
3	George Crowe	25.00	12.00
4	Ben Wade	25.00	12.00
5	Joe Dobson	25.00	12.00
6	Sam Jones	25.00	12.00
7	Bob Borkowski	25.00	12.00
8	Clem Koshorek	25.00	12.00
9	Joe Collins	35.00	15.00
10	Smoky Burgess	40.00	18.00
11	Sal Yvars	25.00	12.00
12	Howie Judson	25.00	12.00
13	Connie Marrero	25.00	12.00
14	Clem Labine	25.00	12.00
15	Bobo Newsom	30.00	13.50
16	Harry Lowrey	25.00	12.00
17	Billy Hitchcock	25.00	12.00
18	Ted Lepcio	25.00	12.00
19	Mel Parnell	25.00	12.00
20	Hank Thompson	25.00	12.00
21	Billy Johnson	25.00	12.00
22	Howie Fox	25.00	12.00
23	Toby Atwell	25.00	12.00
24	Ferris Fain	25.00	12.00
25	Ray Boone	30.00	13.50
26	Dale Mitchell	25.00	12.00
27	Roy Campanella	225.00	110.00
28	Eddie Pellagrini	25.00	12.00
29	Hal Jeffcoat	25.00	12.00
30	Willard Nixon	25.00	12.00
31	Ewell Blackwell	45.00	20.00
32	Clyde Vollmer	25.00	12.00
33	Bob Kennedy	25.00	12.00
34	George Shuba	25.00	12.00
35	Irv Noren	25.00	12.00
36	Johnny Groth	25.00	12.00
37	Ed Mathews	125.00	60.00
38	Jim Hearn	25.00	12.00
39	Eddie Miksis	25.00	12.00
40	John Lipon	25.00	12.00
41	Enos Slaughter	100.00	48.00
42	Gus Zernial	25.00	12.00
43	Gil McDougald	50.00	22.00
44	Ellis Kinder	35.00	15.00
45	Grady Hatton	25.00	12.00
46	Johnny Klippstein	25.00	12.00
47	Bubba Church	25.00	12.00
48	Bob Del Greco	25.00	12.00
49	Faye Throneberry	25.00	12.00
50	Chuck Dressen	25.00	12.00
51	Frank Campos	25.00	12.00
52	Ted Gray	25.00	12.00
53	Sherman Lollar	25.00	12.00
54	Bob Feller	125.00	60.00
55	Maurice McDermott	25.00	12.00
56	Gerald Staley	25.00	12.00
57	Carl Scheib	25.00	12.00
58	George Metkovich	25.00	12.00
59	Karl Drews	25.00	12.00
60	Cloyd Boyer	25.00	12.00
61	Early Wynn	100.00	48.00
62	Monte Irvin	45.00	20.00
63	Gus Niarhos	25.00	12.00
64	Dave Philley	25.00	12.00
65	Earl Harrist	25.00	12.00
66	Orestes Minoso	45.00	20.00
67	Roy Sievers	25.00	12.00
68	Del Rice	25.00	12.00
69	Dick Brodowski	25.00	12.00
70	Ed Yuhas	25.00	12.00

#	Player			#	Player		
71	Tony Baritrome	25.00	12.00	129	Keith Thomas	25.00	12.00
72	Fred Hutchinson	35.00	15.00	130	Turk Lown	25.00	12.00
73	Eddie Robinson	25.00	12.00	131	Harry Byrd	25.00	12.00
74	Joe Rossi	25.00	12.00	132	Tom Morgan	25.00	12.00
75	Mike Garcia	30.00	13.50	133	Gil Coan	25.00	12.00
76	Pee Wee Reese	180.00	85.00	134	Rube Walker	25.00	12.00
77	John Mize	75.00	35.00	135	Al Rosen	35.00	15.00
78	Red Schoendienst	75.00	35.00	136	Ken Heintzelman	25.00	12.00
79	Johnny Wyrostek	25.00	12.00	137	John Rutherford	25.00	12.00
80	Jim Hegan	25.00	12.00	138	George Kell	60.00	28.00
81	Joe Black	70.00	32.00	139	Sammy White	25.00	12.00
82	Mickey Mantle	4,200.00	2,000.00	140	Tommy Glaviano	25.00	12.00
83	Howie Pollet	25.00	12.00	141	Allie Reynolds	35.00	15.00
84	Bob Hooper	25.00	12.00	142	Vic Wertz	30.00	13.50
85	Bobby Morgan	25.00	12.00	143	Billy Pierce	30.00	13.50
86	Billy Martin	160.00	75.00	144	Bob Schultz	25.00	12.00
87	Ed Lopat	45.00	20.00	145	Harry Dorish	25.00	12.00
88	Willie Jones	25.00	12.00	146	Granville Hamner	25.00	12.00
89	Chuck Stobbs	25.00	12.00	147	Warren Spahn	160.00	75.00
90	Hank Edwards	25.00	12.00	148	Mickey Grasso	25.00	12.00
91	Ebba St. Claire	25.00	12.00	149	Dom DiMaggio	35.00	15.00
92	Paul Minner	25.00	12.00	150	Harry Simpson	25.00	12.00
93	Hal Rice	25.00	12.00	151	Hoyt Wilhelm	75.00	35.00
94	William Kennedy	25.00	12.00	152	Bob Adams	25.00	12.00
95	Willard Marshall	25.00	12.00	153	Andy Seminick	25.00	12.00
96	Virgil Trucks	25.00	12.00	154	Dick Groat	45.00	20.00
97	Don Kolloway	25.00	12.00	155	Dutch Leonard	25.00	12.00
98	Cal Abrams	25.00	12.00	156	Jim Rivera	25.00	12.00
99	Dave Madison	25.00	12.00	157	Bob Addis	25.00	12.00
100	Bill Miller	25.00	12.00	158	John Logan (R)	35.00	15.00
101	Ted Wilks	25.00	12.00	159	Wayne Terwilliger	25.00	12.00
102	Connie Ryan	25.00	12.00	160	Bob Young	25.00	12.00
103	Joe Astroth	25.00	12.00	161	Vern Bickford	25.00	12.00
104	Yogi Berra	350.00	160.00	162	Ted Kluszewski	55.00	25.00
105	Joe Nuxhall	25.00	12.00	163	Fred Hatfield	25.00	12.00
106	Johnny Antonelli	30.00	13.50	164	Frank Shea	25.00	12.00
107	Danny O'Connell	25.00	12.00	165	Billy Hoeft	30.00	13.50
108	Bob Porterfield	25.00	12.00	166	Bill Hunter	20.00	8.50
109	Alvin Dark	35.00	15.00	167	Art Schult	20.00	8.50
110	Herman Wehmeier	25.00	12.00	168	Willard Schmidt	20.00	8.50
111	Hank Sauer	25.00	12.00	169	Dizzy Trout	20.00	8.50
112	Ned Garver	25.00	12.00	170	Bill Werle	20.00	8.50
113	Jerry Priddy	25.00	12.00	171	Bill Glynn	20.00	8.50
114	Phil Rizzuto	140.00	65.00	172	Rip Repulski	20.00	8.50
115	George Spencer	25.00	12.00	173	Preston Ward	20.00	8.50
116	Frank Smith	25.00	12.00	174	Billy Loes	25.00	12.00
117	Sid Gordon	25.00	12.00	175	Ron Kline (R)	20.00	8.50
118	Gus Bell	25.00	12.00	176	Don Hoak (R)	30.00	13.50
119	John Sain	50.00	22.00	177	Jim Dyck	20.00	8.50
120	Davey Williams	25.00	12.00	178	Jim Waugh	20.00	8.50
121	Walt Dropo	30.00	13.50	179	Gene Hermanski	20.00	8.50
122	Elmer Valo	25.00	12.00	180	Virgil Stallcup	20.00	8.50
123	Tommy Byrne	25.00	12.00	181	Al Zarilla	20.00	8.50
124	Sibby Sisti	25.00	12.00	182	Bob Hofman	20.00	8.50
125	Dick Williams	25.00	12.00	183	Stu Miller (R)	25.00	12.00
126	Bill Connelly	25.00	12.00	184	Hal Brown (R)	20.00	8.50
127	Clint Courtney	25.00	12.00	185	Jim Pendleton	20.00	8.50
128	Wilmer Mizell	25.00	12.00	186	Charlie Bishop	20.00	8.50

187 Jim Fridley	20.00	8.50	
188 Andy Carey (R)	35.00	15.00	
189 Ray Jablonski	20.00	8.50	
190 Dixie Walker	20.00	8.50	
191 Ralph Kiner	65.00	30.00	
192 Wally Westlake	20.00	8.50	
193 Mike Clark	20.00	8.50	
194 Eddie Kazak	20.00	8.50	
195 Ed McGhee	20.00	8.50	
196 Bob Keegan	20.00	8.50	
197 Del Crandall	25.00	12.00	
198 Forrest Main	20.00	8.50	
199 Marrion Fricano	20.00	8.50	
200 Gordon Goldsberry	20.00	8.50	
201 Paul LaPalme	20.00	8.50	
202 Carl Sawatski	20.00	8.50	
203 Cliff Fannin	20.00	8.50	
204 Dick Bokelmann	20.00	8.50	
205 Vern Benson	20.00	8.50	
206 Ed Bailey (R)	25.00	12.00	
207 Whitey Ford	200.00	95.00	
208 Jim Wilson	20.00	8.50	
209 Jim Greengrass	20.00	8.50	
210 Bob Cerv (R)	25.00	12.00	
211 J.W. Porter	20.00	8.50	
212 Jack Dittmer	20.00	8.50	
213 Ray Scaborough	20.00	8.50	
214 Bill Bruton (R)	25.00	12.00	
215 Gene Conley (R)	30.00	13.50	
216 Jim Hughes	20.00	8.50	
217 Murray Wall	20.00	8.50	
218 Les Fusselman	20.00	8.50	
219 Pete Runnels (Er) (Wrong Photo)	25.00	12.00	
220 Satchell Paige	500.00	240.00	
221 Bob Milliken	95.00	45.00	
222 Vic Janowicz(R)(DP)	60.00	28.00	
223 John O'Brien (DP)	50.00	22.00	
224 Lou Sleater (DP)	50.00	22.00	
225 Bobby Shantz	100.00	48.00	
226 Ed Erautt	95.00	45.00	
227 Morris Martin	95.00	45.00	
228 Hal Newhouser	160.00	75.00	
229 Rocky Krsnich	95.00	45.00	
230 Johnny Lindell (DP)	50.00	22.00	
231 Solly Hemus(DP	50.00	22.00	
232 Dick Kokos	95.00	45.00	
233 Al Aber	95.00	45.00	
234 Ray Murray (DP)	50.00	22.00	
235 John Hetki (DP)	50.00	22.00	
236 Harry Perkowski (DP)	50.00	22.00	
237 Clarence Podbielan (DP)	50.00	22.00	
238 Cal Hogue (DP)	50.00	22.00	
239 Jim Delsing	95.00	45.00	
240 Freddie Marsh	95.00	45.00	
241 Al Sima (DP)	50.00	22.00	
242 Charlie Silvera	95.00	45.00	
243 Carlos Bernier (DP)	50.00	22.00	
244 Willie Mays	2,650.00	1,300.00	
245 Bill Norman	95.00	45.00	
246 Roy Face (R) (DP)	100.00	48.00	
247 Mike Sandlock (DP)	50.00	22.00	
248 Gene Stephens (DP)	50.00	22.00	
249 Ed O'Brien (DP)	50.00	22.00	
250 Bob Wilson	95.00	45.00	
251 Sid Hudson	95.00	45.00	
252 Henry Foiles	95.00	45.00	
253 No Card	00.00	00.00	
254 Preacher Roe (DP)	95.00	45.00	
255 Dixie Howell	95.00	45.00	
256 Les Peden	95.00	45.00	
257 Bob Boyd	95.00	45.00	
258 Jim Gilliam (R)	350.00	165.00	
259 Roy McMillan (DP)	95.00	45.00	
260 Sam Calderone	95.00	45.00	
261 No Card	00.00	00.00	
262 Bob Oldis	95.00	45.00	
263 John Podres (R)	260.00	125.00	
264 Gene Woodling (DP)	80.00	38.00	
265 Jackie Jensen	110.00	50.00	
266 Bob Cain	95.00	45.00	
267 No Card	00.00	00.00	
268 No Card	00.00	00.00	
269 Duane Pillette	95.00	45.00	
270 Vern Stephens	95.00	45.00	
271 No Card	00.00	00.00	
272 Bill Antonello	95.00	45.00	
273 Harvey Haddix (R)	125.00	60.00	
274 John Riddle	95.00	45.00	
275 No Card	00.00	00.00	
276 Ken Raffensberger	95.00	45.00	
277 Don Lund	95.00	45.00	
278 Willie Miranda	95.00	45.00	
279 Joe Coleman (DP)	50.00	22.00	
280 Milt Bolling	350.00	160.00	

1954 Topps

This 250-card set measures 2-5/8" by 3-3/4" and remains one of Topps most popular issues. Card fronts were the first to use two player images, a small head and shoulder shot in color and a larger black and white action photo. Card backs contained a small cartoon and player stats and a brief biography.

		NR/MT	EX
Complete Set (250)		8,500.00	4,200.00
Commons (1-50)		15.00	9.00
Commons (51-75)		30.00	14.00
Commons (76-250)		15.00	9.00

		NR/MT	EX
1	Ted Williams	750.00	300.00
2	Gus Zernial	15.00	9.00
3	Monte Irvin	40.00	22.00
4	Hank Sauer	15.00	9.00
5	Ed Lopat	20.00	12.00
6	Pete Runnels	15.00	9.00
7	Ted Kluszewski	30.00	16.00
8	Bobby Young	15.00	9.00
9	Harvey Haddix	18.00	10.00
10	Jackie Robinson	350.00	180.00
11	Paul Smith	15.00	9.00
12	Del Crandall	15.00	9.00
13	Billy Martin	100.00	55.00
14	Preacher Roe	25.00	14.00
15	Al Rosen	25.00	14.00
16	Vic Janowicz	18.00	10.00
17	Phil Rizzuto	80.00	42.00
18	Walt Dropo	15.00	9.00
19	Johnny Lipon	15.00	9.00
20	Warren Spahn	125.00	65.00
21	Bobby Shantz	18.00	10.00
22	Jim Greengrass	15.00	9.00
23	Luke Easter	15.00	9.00
24	Granny Hamner	15.00	9.00
25	Harvey Kuenn (R)	40.00	22.00
26	Ray Jablonski	15.00	9.00
27	Ferris Fain	15.00	9.00
28	Paul Minner	15.00	9.00
29	Jim Hegan	15.00	9.00
30	Ed Mathews	125.00	65.00
31	Johnny Klippstein	15.00	9.00
32	Duke Snider	175.00	90.00
33	Johnny Schmitz	15.00	9.00
34	Jim Rivera	15.00	9.00
35	Junior Gilliam	30.00	16.00
36	Hoyt Wilhelm	50.00	27.00
37	Whitey Ford	110.00	60.00
38	Eddie Stanky	18.00	10.00
39	Sherm Lollar	15.00	9.00
40	Mel Parnell	15.00	9.00
41	Willie Jones	15.00	9.00
42	Don Mueller	15.00	9.00
43	Dick Great	20.00	12.00
44	Ned Garver	15.00	9.00
45	Richie Ashburn	50.00	27.00
46	Ken Raffensberger	15.00	9.00
47	Ellis Kinder	15.00	9.00
48	Billy Hunter	15.00	9.00
49	Ray Murray	15.00	9.00
50	Yogi Berra	275.00	140.00
51	Johnny Lindell	30.00	14.00
52	Vic Power (R)	35.00	18.50
53	Jack Dittmer	30.00	14.00
54	Vern Stephens	32.00	17.00
55	Phil Cavarretta	35.00	18.50
56	Willie Miranda	30.00	14.00
57	Luis Aloma	30.00	14.00
58	Bob Wilson	30.00	14.00
59	Gene Conley	35.00	18.50
60	Frank Baumholtz	30.00	14.00
61	Bob Cain	30.00	14.00
62	Eddie Robinson	30.00	14.00
63	Johnny Pesky	35.00	18.50
64	Hank Thompson	32.00	17.00
65	Bob Swift	30.00	14.00
66	Ted Lepcio	30.00	14.00
67	Jim Willis	30.00	14.00
68	Sammy Calderone	30.00	14.00
69	Bud Podbielan	30.00	14.00
70	Larry Doby	75.00	38.00
71	Frank Smith	30.00	14.00
72	Preston Ward	30.00	14.00
73	Wayne Terwilliger	30.00	14.00
74	Bill Taylor	30.00	14.00
75	Fred Haney	30.00	14.00
76	Bob Scheffing	15.00	9.00
77	Ray Boone	18.00	10.00
78	Ted Kazanski	15.00	9.00
79	Andy Pafko	18.00	10.00
80	Jackie Jensen	25.00	14.00
81	Dave Hoskins	15.00	9.00
82	Milt Bolling	15.00	9.00
83	Joe Collins	18.00	10.00
84	Dick Cole	15.00	9.00
85	Bob Turley (R)	28.00	15.00

86	Billy Herman	25.00	14.00
87	Roy Face	18.00	10.00
88	Matt Batts	15.00	9.00
89	Howie Pollet	15.00	9.00
90	Willie Mays	550.00	280.00
91	Bob Oldis	15.00	9.00
92	Wally Westlake	15.00	9.00
93	Sid Hudson	15.00	9.00
94	Ernie Banks (R)	850.00	450.00
95	Hal Rice	15.00	9.00
96	Charlie Silvera	15.00	9.00
97	Jerry Lane	15.00	9.00
98	Joe Black	20.00	12.00
99	Bob Hofman	15.00	9.00
100	Bob Keegan	15.00	9.00
101	Gene Woodling	20.00	12.00
102	Gil Hodges	90.00	48.00
103	Jim Lemon (R)	20.00	12.00
104	Mike Sandlock	15.00	9.00
105	Andy Carey	18.00	10.00
106	Dick Kokos	15.00	9.00
107	Duane Pillette	15.00	9.00
108	Thornton Kipper	15.00	9.00
109	Bill Bruton	15.00	9.00
110	Harry Dorish	15.00	9.00
111	Jim Delsing	15.00	9.00
112	Bill Renna	15.00	9.00
113	Bob Boyd	15.00	9.00
114	Dean Stone	15.00	9.00
115	Rip Repulski	15.00	9.00
116	Steve Bilko	15.00	9.00
117	Solly Hemus	15.00	9.00
118	Carl Scheib	15.00	9.00
119	Johnny Antonelli	18.00	10.00
120	Roy McMillan	15.00	9.00
121	Clem Labine	18.00	10.00
122	Johnny Logan	18.00	10.00
123	Bobby Adams	15.00	9.00
124	Marion Fricano	15.00	9.00
125	Harry Perkowski	15.00	9.00
126	Ben Wade	15.00	9.00
127	Steve O'Neill	15.00	9.00
128	Henry Aaron (R)	2,000.00	975.00
129	Forrest Jacobs	15.00	9.00
130	Hank Bauer	30.00	16.00
131	Reno Bertoia	15.00	9.00
132	Tom Lasorda (R)	150.00	80.00
133	Del Baker	15.00	9.00
134	Cal Hogue	15.00	9.00
135	Joe Presko	15.00	9.00
136	Connie Ryan	15.00	9.00
137	Wally Moon (R)	25.00	14.00
138	Bob Borkowski	15.00	9.00
139	Ed & Johnny O'Brien	30.00	16.00
140	Tom Wright	15.00	9.00
141	Joe Jay (R)	18.00	10.00
142	Tom Poholski	15.00	9.00
143	Rollie Hemsley	15.00	9.00
144	Bill Werle	15.00	9.00
145	Elmer Valo	15.00	9.00
146	Don Johnson	15.00	9.00
147	John Riddle	15.00	9.00
148	Bob Trice	15.00	9.00
149	Jim Robertson	15.00	9.00
150	Dick Kryhoski	15.00	9.00
151	Alex Grammas	15.00	9.00
152	Mike Blyzka	15.00	9.00
153	Rube Walker	15.00	9.00
154	Mike Fornieles	15.00	9.00
155	Bob Kennedy	15.00	9.00
156	Joe Coleman	15.00	9.00
157	Don Lenhardt	15.00	9.00
158	Peanuts Lowrey	15.00	9.00
159	Dave Philley	15.00	9.00
160	Red Kress	15.00	9.00
161	John Hetki	15.00	9.00
162	Herman Wehmeier	15.00	9.00
163	Frank House	15.00	9.00
164	Stu Miller	18.00	10.00
165	Jim Pendleton	15.00	9.00
166	Johnny Podres	30.00	16.00
167	Don Lund	15.00	9.00
168	Morrie Martin	15.00	9.00
169	Jim Hughes	15.00	9.00
170	Dusty Rhodes (R)	20.00	12.00
171	Leo Kiely	15.00	9.00
172	Hal Brown	15.00	9.00
173	Jack Harshman	15.00	9.00
174	Tom Qualters	15.00	9.00
175	Frank Leja	15.00	9.00
176	Bob Keely	15.00	9.00
177	Bob Milliken	15.00	9.00
178	Bill Glynn	15.00	9.00
179	Gair Allie	15.00	9.00
180	Wes Westrum	15.00	9.00
181	Mel Roach	15.00	9.00
182	Chuck Harmon	15.00	9.00
183	Earle Combs	30.00	16.00
184	Ed Bailey	18.00	10.00
185	Chuck Stobbs	15.00	9.00
186	Karl Olson	15.00	9.00
187	Heinie Manush	30.00	16.00
188	Dave Jolly	15.00	9.00
189	Bob Ross	15.00	9.00
190	Ray Herbert	15.00	9.00
191	Dick Schofield (R)	18.00	10.00
192	Ellis Deal	15.00	9.00
193	Johnny Hopp	15.00	9.00
194	Bill Sarni	15.00	9.00
195	Bill Consolo	15.00	9.00
196	Stank Jok	15.00	9.00
197	Schoolboy Rowe	15.00	9.00
198	Carl Sawatski	15.00	9.00
199	Rocky Nelson	15.00	9.00
200	Larry Jansen	18.00	10.00
201	Al Kaline (R)	850.00	450.00

202	Bob Purkey (R)	18.00	10.00
203	Harry Brecheen	15.00	9.00
204	Angel Scull	15.00	9.00
205	Johnny Sain	28.00	15.00
206	Ray Crone	15.00	9.00
207	Tom Oliver	15.00	9.00
208	Grady Hatton	15.00	9.00
209	Charlie Thompson	15.00	9.00
210	Bob Buhl (R)	18.00	10.00
211	Don Hoak	18.00	10.00
212	Mickey Micelotta	15.00	9.00
213	John Fitzpatrick	15.00	9.00
214	Arnold Portocarrero	15.00	9.00
215	Ed McGhee	15.00	9.00
216	Al Sima	15.00	9.00
217	Paul Schreiber	15.00	9.00
218	Fred Marsh	15.00	9.00
219	Charlie Kress	15.00	9.00
220	Ruben Gomez	15.00	9.00
221	Dick Brodowski	15.00	9.00
222	Bill Wilson	15.00	9.00
223	Joe Haynes	15.00	9.00
224	Dick Weik	15.00	9.00
225	Don liddle	15.00	9.00
226	Jehosie Heard	15.00	9.00
227	Buster Mills	15.00	9.00
228	Gene Hermanski	15.00	9.00
229	Bob Talbot	15.00	9.00
230	Bob Kuzava	15.00	9.00
231	Roy Smalley	15.00	9.00
232	Lou Limmer	15.00	9.00
233	Augie Galan	15.00	9.00
234	Jerry Lynch (R)	18.00	10.00
235	Vern Law	18.00	10.00
236	Paul Penson	15.00	9.00
237	Mike Ryba	15.00	9.00
238	Al Aber	15.00	9.00
239	Bill Skowron (R)	80.00	42.00
240	Sam Mele	15.00	9.00
241	Bob Miller	15.00	9.00
242	Curt Roberts	15.00	9.00
243	Ray Blades	15.00	9.00
244	Leroy Wheat	15.00	9.00
245	Roy Sievers	15.00	9.00
246	Howie Fox	15.00	9.00
247	Eddie Mayo	15.00	9.00
248	Al Smith (R)	18.00	10.00
249	Wilmer Mizell	15.00	9.00
250	Ted Williams	800.00	350.00

1955 Topps

For the first time, Topps introduced a horizontal format on the card fronts. The design is similar to the 1954 set with two photos on the front, a large head shot and a smaller action shot. The card fronts are in color and the card size is 3-3/4" by 2-5/8". Although the checklist is numbered to 210, four cards were never issued, 175, 186, 203 and 209.

		NR/MT	EX
Complete Set (206)		7,800.00	3,800.00
Commons (1-150)		9.00	4.50
Commons (151-160)		18.00	9.00
Commons (161-210)		28.00	14.00
1	Dusty Rhodes	48.00	24.00
2	Ted Williams	500.00	250.00
3	Art Fowler	9.00	4.50
4	Al Kaline	250.00	125.00
5	Jim Gilliam	18.00	9.00
6	Stan Hack	12.00	6.00
7	Jim Hegan	9.00	4.50
8	Hal Smith	9.00	4.50
9	Bob Miller	9.00	4.50
10	Bob Keegan	9.00	4.50
11	Ferris Fain	9.00	4.50
12	Jake Thies	9.00	4.50
13	Fred Marsh	9.00	4.50
14	Jim Finigan	9.00	4.50
15	Jim Pendleton	9.00	4.50
16	Roy Sievers	12.00	6.00
17	Bobby Hofman	9.00	4.50
18	Russ Kemmerer	9.00	4.50
19	Billy Herman	12.00	6.00
20	Andy Carey	12.00	6.00
21	Alex Grammas	9.00	4.50
22	Bill Skowron	20.00	10.00
23	Jack Parks	9.00	4.50
24	Hal Newhouser	25.00	12.50
25	Johnny Podres	20.00	10.00
26	Dick Groat	12.00	6.00
27	Billy Gardner	9.00	4.50
28	Ernie Banks	240.00	120.00
29	Herman Wehmeier	9.00	4.50
30	Vic Power	10.00	5.00
31	Warren Spahn	90.00	45.00

#	Player			#	Player		
32	Ed McGhee	9.00	4.50	90	Karl Spooner (R)	12.00	6.00
33	Tom Qualters	9.00	4.50	91	Milt Bolling	9.00	4.50
34	Wayne Terwilliger	9.00	4.50	92	Don Zimmer (R)	35.00	18.00
35	Dave Jolly	9.00	4.50	93	Steve Bilko	9.00	4.50
36	Leo Kiely	9.00	4.50	94	Reno Bertoia	9.00	4.50
37	Joe Cunningham (R)	10.00	5.00	95	Preston Ward	9.00	4.50
38	Bob Turley	15.00	7.50	96	Charlie Bishop	9.00	4.50
39	Bill Glynn	9.00	4.50	97	Carlos Paula	9.00	4.50
40	Don Hoak	10.00	5.00	98	Johnny Riddle	9.00	4.50
41	Chuck Stobbs	9.00	4.50	99	Frank Leja	9.00	4.50
42	Windy McCall	9.00	4.50	100	Monte Irvin	35.00	18.00
43	Harvey Haddix	12.00	6.00	101	Johnny Gray	9.00	4.50
44	Corky Valentine	9.00	4.50	102	Wally Westlake	9.00	4.50
45	Hank Sauer	10.00	5.00	103	Charlie White	9.00	4.50
46	Ted Kazanski	9.00	4.50	104	Jack Harshman	9.00	4.50
47	Hank Aaron	9.00	4.50	105	Chuck Diering	9.00	4.50
48	Bob Kennedy	9.00	4.50	106	Frank Sullivan	9.00	4.50
49	J.W. Porter	9.00	4.50	107	Curt Roberts	9.00	4.50
50	Jackie Robinson	275.00	140.00	108	Rube Walker	9.00	4.50
51	Jim Hughes	9.00	4.50	109	Ed Lopat	15.00	7.50
52	Bill Tremel	9.00	4.50	110	Gus Zernial	10.00	5.00
53	Bill Taylor	9.00	4.50	111	Bob Milliken	9.00	4.50
54	Lou Limmer	9.00	4.50	112	Nelson King	9.00	4.50
55	"Rip" Repulski	9.00	4.50	113	Harry Brecheen	9.00	4.50
56	Ray Jablonski	9.00	4.50	114	Lou Ortiz	9.00	4.50
57	Billy O'Dell	9.00	4.50	115	Ellis Kinder	9.00	4.50
58	Jim Rivera	9.00	4.50	116	Tom Hurd	9.00	4.50
59	Gair Allie	9.00	4.50	117	Mel Roach	9.00	4.50
60	Dean Stone	9.00	4.50	118	Bob Purkey	9.00	4.50
61	Forrest Jacobs	9.00	4.50	119	Bob Lennon	9.00	4.50
62	Thornton Kipper	9.00	4.50	120	Ted Kluszewski	30.00	15.00
63	Joe Collins	12.00	6.00	121	Bill Renna	9.00	4.50
64	Gus Triandos (R)	12.00	6.00	122	Carl Sawatski	9.00	4.50
65	Ray Boone	10.00	6.00	123	Sandy Koufax (R)	1,300.00	650.00
66	Ron Jackson	9.00	4.50	124	Harmon Killebrew (R)	400.00	200.00
67	Wally Moon	12.00	6.00				
68	Jim Davis	9.00	4.50	125	Ken Boyer (R)	80.00	40.00
69	Ed Bailey	9.00	4.50	126	Dick Hall	9.00	4.50
70	Al Rosen	12.00	6.00	127	Dale Long (R)	12.00	6.00
71	Ruben Gomez	9.00	4.50	128	Ted Lepcio	9.00	4.50
72	Karl Olson	9.00	4.50	129	Elvin Tappe	9.00	4.50
73	Jack Shepard	9.00	4.50	130	Mayo Smith	9.00	4.50
74	Bob Borkowski	9.00	4.50	131	Grady Hatton	9.00	4.50
75	Sandy Amoros (R)	25.00	12.50	132	Bob Trice	9.00	4.50
76	Howie Pollet	9.00	4.50	133	Dave Hoskins	9.00	4.50
77	Arnold Portcarrero	9.00	4.50	134	Joe Jay	9.00	4.50
78	Gordon Jones	9.00	4.50	135	Johnny O'Brien	9.00	4.50
79	Danny Schell	9.00	4.50	136	Bunky Stewart	9.00	4.50
80	Bob Grim (R)	15.00	7.50	137	Harry Elliott	9.00	4.50
81	Gene Conley	12.00	6.00	138	Ray Herbert	9.00	4.50
82	Chuck Harmon	9.00	4.50	139	Steve Kraly	9.00	4.50
83	Tom Brewer	9.00	4.50	140	Mel Parnell	10.00	5.00
84	Camilo Pascual (R)	12.00	6.00	141	Tom Wright	9.00	4.50
85	Don Mossi (R)	12.00	6.00	142	Jerry Lynch	9.00	4.50
86	Bill Wilson	9.00	4.50	143	Dick Schofield	9.00	4.50
87	Frank House	9.00	4.50	144	Joe Amalfitano (R)	12.00	6.00
88	Bob Skinner (R)	12.00	6.00	145	Elmer Valo	9.00	4.50
89	Joe Frazier	9.00	4.50	146	Dick Donovan (R)	10.00	5.00

		NR/MT	EX
147	Laurin Pepper	9.00	4.50
148	Hal Brown	9.00	4.50
149	Ray Crone	9.00	4.50
150	Mike Higgins	9.00	4.50
151	Red Kress	18.00	9.00
152	Harry Agganis (R)	100.00	50.00
153	Bud Podbielan	18.00	9.00
154	Willie Miranda	18.00	9.00
155	Ed Mathews	140.00	70.00
156	Joe Black	30.00	15.00
157	Bob Miller	18.00	9.00
158	Tom Carroll	18.00	9.00
159	Johnny Schmitz	18.00	9.00
160	Ray Narleski (R)	25.00	12.50
161	Chuck Tanner (R)	30.00	15.00
162	Joe Coleman	28.00	14.00
163	Faye Throneberry	28.00	14.00
164	Roberto Clemente (R)	1,650.00	825.00
165	Don Johnson	28.00	14.00
166	Hank Bauer	50.00	25.00
167	Tom Casagrande	28.00	14.00
168	Duane Pillette	28.00	14.00
169	Bob Oldis	28.00	14.00
170	Jim Pearce	28.00	14.00
171	Dick Brodowski	28.00	14.00
172	Frank Baumholtz	28.00	14.00
173	Bob Kline	28.00	14.00
174	Rudy Minarcin	28.00	14.00
175	Not issued	28.00	14.00
176	Norm Zauchin	28.00	14.00
177	Jim Robertson	28.00	14.00
178	Bobby Adams	28.00	14.00
179	Jim Bolger	28.00	14.00
180	Clem Labine	35.00	18.00
181	Roy McMillan	30.00	15.00
182	Humberto Robinson	28.00	14.00
183	Tony Jacobs	28.00	14.00
184	Harry Perkowski	28.00	14.00
185	Don Ferrarese	28.00	14.00
186	No Card	00.00	00.00
187	Gil Hodges	175.00	90.00
188	Charlie Silvera	28.00	14.00
189	Phil Rizzuto	175.00	90.00
190	Gene Woodling	35.00	18.00
191	Ed Stanky	30.00	15.00
192	Jim Delsing	28.00	14.00
193	Johnny Sain	40.00	20.00
194	Willie Mays	600.00	300.00
195	Ed Roebuck (R)	35.00	18.00
196	Gale Wade	28.00	14.00
197	Al Smith	28.00	14.00
198	Yogi Berra	275.00	140.00
199	Bert Hamric	28.00	14.00
200	Jack Jensen	50.00	25.00
201	Sherm Lollar	30.00	15.00
202	Jim Owens	28.00	14.00
203	No Card	00.00	00.00
204	Frank Smith	28.00	14.00
205	Gene Freese (R)	30.00	15.00
206	Pete Daley	28.00	14.00
207	Bill Consolo	28.00	14.00
208	Ray Moore	28.00	14.00
209	No Card	00.00	00.00
210	Duke Snider	600.00	275.00

1956 Topps

This 340-card set is similar to Topp's 1955 set with horizontal fronts with two player photos. Cards measure 2-5/8" by 3-3/4". Card backs contain a three panel cartoon. For the first time Topps created team cards and also included cards of the league presidents. Two unnumbered check-lists were issued as part of the set. Though they are not included in the set price, the checklists are included at the end of this listing.

		NR/MT	EX
Complete Set (340)		7,600.00	3,800.00
Commons (1-100)		9.00	4.50
Commons (101-180)		10.00	5.00
Commons (181-260)		16.00	8.00
Commons (261-340)		12.00	6.00
1	William Harridge	110.00	40.00
2	Warren Giles	18.00	9.00
3	Elmer Valo	9.00	4.50
4	Carlos Paula	9.00	4.50
5	Ted Williams	350.00	175.00
6	Ray Boone	10.00	5.00
7	Ron Negray	9.00	4.50
8	Walter Alston	40.00	20.00
9	Ruben Gomez	9.00	4.50
10	Warren Spahn	90.00	45.00
11a	Cubs Team (Date)	55.00	25.00
11b	Cubs Team (No Date)	18.00	9.00

12	Andy Carey	10.00	5.00
13	Roy Face	12.00	6.00
14	Ken Boyer	18.00	9.00
15	Ernie Banks	100.00	50.00
16	Hector Lopez (R)	12.00	6.00
17	Gene Conley	10.00	5.00
18	Dick Donovan	9.00	4.50
19	Chuck Diering	9.00	4.50
20	Al Kaline	140.00	70.00
21	Joe Collins	9.00	4.50
22	Jim Finigan	9.00	4.50
23	Freddie Marsh	9.00	4.50
24	Dick Groat	12.00	5.00
25	Ted Kluszewski	28.00	14.00
26	Grady Hatton	9.00	4.50
27	Nelson Burbrink	9.00	4.50
28	Bobby Hofman	9.00	4.50
29	Jack Harshman	9.00	4.50
30	Jackie Robinson	180.00	90.00
31	Hank Aaron	300.00	150.00
32	Frank House	9.00	4.50
33	Roberto Clemente	450.00	225.00
34	Tom Brewer	9.00	4.50
35	Al Rosen	12.00	6.00
36	Rudy Minarcin	9.00	4.50
37	Alex Grammas	9.00	4.50
38	Bob Kennedy	9.00	4.50
39	Don Mossi	10.00	5.00
40	Bob Turley	10.00	5.00
41	Hank Sauer	12.00	6.00
42	Sandy Amoros	12.00	6.00
43	Ray Moore	9.00	4.50
44	Windy McCall	9.00	4.50
45	Gus Zernial	9.00	4.50
46	Gene Freese	9.00	4.50
47	Art Fowler	9.00	4.50
48	Jim Hegan	9.00	4.50
49	Pedro Ramos	9.00	4.50
50	Dusty Rhodes	10.00	5.00
51	Ernie Oravetz	9.00	4.50
52	Bob Grim	9.00	4.50
53	Arnold Portocarrero	9.00	4.50
54	Bob Keegan	9.00	4.50
55	Wally Moon	10.00	5.00
56	Dale Long	10.00	5.00
57	Duke Maas	9.00	4.50
58	Ed Roebuck	10.00	5.00
59	Jose Santiago	9.00	4.50
60	Mayo Smith	9.00	4.50
61	Bill Skowron	18.00	9.00
62	Hal Smith	9.00	4.50
63	Roger Craig (R)	30.00	15.00
64	Luis Arroyo (R)	10.00	5.00
65	Johnny O'Brien	9.00	4.50
66	Bob Speake	9.00	4.50
67	Vic Power	9.00	4.50
68	Chuck Stobbs	9.00	4.50
69	Chuck Tanner	10.00	5.00
70	Jim Rivera	9.00	4.50
71	Frank Sullivan	9.00	4.50
72a	Phillies Team (Date)	55.00	25.00
72b	Phillies Team (No Date)	18.00	9.00
73	Wayne Terwilliger	9.00	4.50
74	Jim King	9.00	4.50
75	Roy Sievers	9.00	4.50
76	Ray Crone	9.00	4.50
77	Harvey Haddix	9.00	4.50
78	Herman Wehmeier	9.00	4.50
79	Sandy Koufax	450.00	225.00
80	Gus Triandos	9.00	4.50
81	Wally Westlake	9.00	4.50
82	Bill Renna	9.00	4.50
83	Karl Spooner	9.00	4.50
84	"Babe" Birrer	9.00	4.50
85a	Indians Team (Date)	55.00	25.00
85b	Indians Team (No Date)	18.00	9.00
86	Ray Jablonski	9.00	4.50
87	Dean Stone	9.00	4.50
88	Johnny Kucks (R)	10.00	5.00
89	Norm Zauchin	9.00	4.50
90a	Reds Team (Date)	55.00	25.00
90b	Reds Team (No date)	18.00	9.00
91	Gail Harris	9.00	4.50
92	Red Wilson	9.00	4.50
93	George Susce, Jr.	9.00	4.50
94	Ronnie Kline	9.00	4.50
95a	Braves Team (Date)	60.00	28.00
95b	Braves Team (No Date)	20.00	10.00
96	Bill Tremel	9.00	4.50
97	Jerry Lynch	9.00	4.50
98	Camilo Pascual	9.00	4.50
99	Don Zimmer	15.00	7.50
100a	Orioles Team (Date)	55.00	25.00
100b	Orioles Team (No Date)	18.00	9.00
101	Roy Campanella	150.00	75.00
102	Jim Davis	10.00	5.00
103	Willie Miranda	10.00	5.00
104	Bob Lennon	10.00	5.00
105	Al Smith	10.00	5.00
106	Joe Astroth	10.00	5.00
107	Ed Mathews	70.00	35.00
108	Laurin Pepper	10.00	5.00
109	Enos Slaughter	35.00	18.00
110	Yogi Berra	160.00	80.00
111	Red Sox Team	25.00	12.50
112	Dee Fondy	10.00	5.00
113	Phil Rizzuto	60.00	30.00
114	Jim Owens	10.00	5.00
115	Jackie Jensen	15.00	7.50
116	Eddie O'Brien	10.00	5.00
117	Virgil Trucks	10.00	5.00

118 Nellie Fox	35.00	18.00	176 Alex Kellner	10.00	5.00
119 Larry Jackson (R)	15.00	7.50	177 Hank Bauer	18.00	9.00
120 Richie Ashburn	38.00	19.00	178 Joe Black	15.00	7.50
121 Pirates Team	25.00	12.50	179 Harry Chiti	10.00	5.00
122 Willard Nixon	10.00	5.00	180 Robin Roberts	45.00	22.50
123 Roy McMillan	10.00	5.00	181 Billy Martin	110.00	55.00
124 Don Kaiser	10.00	5.00	182 Paul Minner	16.00	8.00
125 Minnie Minoso	25.00	12.50	183 Stan Lopata	16.00	8.00
126 Jim Brady	10.00	5.00	184 Don Bessent	16.00	8.00
127 Willie Jones	10.00	5.00	185 Bill Bruton	16.00	8.00
128 Eddie Yost	10.00	5.00	186 Ron Jackson	16.00	8.00
129 Jake Martin	10.00	5.00	187 Early Wynn	45.00	22.50
130 Willie Mays	380.00	200.00	188 White Sox Team	35.00	18.00
131 Bob Roselli	10.00	5.00	189 Ned Garver	16.00	8.00
132 Bobby Avila	12.00	6.00	190 Carl Furillo	30.00	15.00
133 Ray Narleski	12.00	6.00	191 Frank Lary (R)	20.00	10.00
134 Cardinals Team	25.00	12.50	192 Smoky Burgess	18.00	9.00
135 Mickey Mantle	1,250.00	650.00	193 Wilmer Mizell	16.00	8.00
136 Johnny Logan	12.00	6.00	194 Monte Irvin	35.00	18.00
137 Al Silvera	10.00	5.00	195 George Kell	35.00	18.00
138 Johnny Antonelli	12.00	6.00	196 Tom Poholsky	16.00	8.00
139 Tommy Carrol	10.00	5.00	197 Granny Hamner	16.00	8.00
140 Herb Score (R)	35.00	18.00	198 Ed Fitzgerald	16.00	8.00
141 Joe Frazier	10.00	5.00	199 Hank Thompson	18.00	9.00
142 Gene Baker	10.00	5.00	200 Bob Feller	150.00	75.00
143 Jim Piersall	15.00	7.50	201 Rip Repulski	16.00	8.00
144 Leroy Powell	10.00	5.00	202 Jim Hearn	16.00	8.00
145 Gil Hodges	60.00	30.00	203 Bill Tuttle	16.00	8.00
146 Senators Team	25.00	12.50	204 Art Swanson	16.00	8.00
147 Earl Torgeson	10.00	5.00	205 Whitey Lockman	18.00	9.00
148 Alvin Dark	12.00	6.00	206 Erv Palica	16.00	8.00
149 Dixie Howell	10.00	5.00	207 Jim Small	16.00	8.00
150 Duke Snider	160.00	80.00	208 Elston Howard	60.00	30.00
151 Spook Jacobs	10.00	5.00	209 Max Surkont	16.00	8.00
152 Billy Hoeft	10.00	5.00	210 Mike Garcia	18.00	9.00
153 Frank Thomas	12.00	6.00	211 Murry Dickson	16.00	8.00
154 Dave Pope	10.00	5.00	212 Johnny Temple	18.00	9.00
155 Harvey Kuenn	18.00	9.00	213 Tigers Team	35.00	18.00
156 Wes Westrum	10.00	5.00	214 Bob Rush	16.00	8.00
157 Dick Brodowski	10.00	5.00	215 Tommy Byrne	16.00	8.00
158 Wally Post	12.00	6.00	216 Jerry Schoonmaker	16.00	8.00
159 Clint Courtney	12.00	6.00	217 Billy Klaus	16.00	8.00
160 Billy Pierce	12.00	6.00	218 Joe Nuxhall	20.00	10.00
161 Joe DeMaestri	10.00	5.00	219 Lew Burdette	25.00	12.50
162 Gus Bel	12.00	6.00	220 Del Ennis	18.00	9.00
163 Gene Woodling	15.00	7.50	221 Bob Friend	18.00	9.00
164 Harmon Killebrew	160.00	80.00	222 Dave Philley	16.00	8.00
165 Red Schoendienst	35.00	18.00	223 Randy Jackson	16.00	8.00
166 Dodgers Team	180.00	90.00	224 Bud Podbielan	16.00	8.00
167 Harry Dorish	10.00	5.00	225 Gil McDougald	30.00	15.00
168 Sammy White	10.00	5.00	226 Giants Team	60.00	30.00
169 Bob Nelson	10.00	5.00	227 Russ Meyer	16.00	8.00
170 Bill Virdon	12.00	6.00	228 Mickey Vernon	18.00	9.00
171 Jim Wilson	10.00	5.00	229 Harry Brecheen	16.00	8.00
172 Frank Torre (R)	15.00	7.50	230 Chico Carrasquel	16.00	8.00
173 Johnny Podres	15.00	7.50	231 Bob Hale	16.00	8.00
174 Glen Gorbous	10.00	5.00	232 Toby Atwell	16.00	8.00
175 Del Crandall	12.00	6.00	233 Carl Erskine	25.00	12.50

234 Pete Runnels	18.00	9.00	
235 Don Newcombe	60.00	30.00	
236 Athletics Team	30.00	15.00	
237 Jose Valdivielso	16.00	8.00	
238 Walt Dropo	18.00	9.00	
239 Harry Simpson	16.00	8.00	
240 Whitey Ford	160.00	80.00	
241 Don Mueller	16.00	8.00	
242 Hershell Freeman	16.00	8.00	
243 Sherm Lollar	18.00	9.00	
244 Bob Buhl	18.00	9.00	
245 Billy Goodman	16.00	8.00	
246 Tom Gorman	16.00	8.00	
247 Bill Sarni	16.00	8.00	
248 Bob Porterfield	16.00	8.00	
249 Johnny Klippstein	16.00	8.00	
250 Larry Doby	28.00	14.00	
251 Yankees Team	250.00	125.00	
252 Vernon Law	18.00	9.00	
253 Irv Noren	18.00	9.00	
254 George Crowe	16.00	8.00	
255 Bob Lemon	40.00	20.00	
256 Tom Hurd	16.00	8.00	
257 Bobby Thomson	25.00	12.50	
258 Art Ditmar	18.00	9.00	
259 Sam Jones	16.00	8.00	
260 Pee Wee Reese	125.00	60.00	
261 Bobby Shantz	15.00	7.50	
262 Howie Pollet	12.00	6.00	
263 Bob Miller	12.00	6.00	
264 Ray Monzant	12.00	6.00	
265 Sandy Consuegra	12.00	6.00	
266 Don Ferrarese	12.00	6.00	
267 Bob Nieman	12.00	6.00	
268 Dale Mitchell	15.00	7.50	
269 Jack Meyer	12.00	6.00	
270 Billy Loes	12.00	6.00	
271 Foster Castleman	12.00	6.00	
272 Danny O'Connell	12.00	6.00	
273 Walker Cooper	12.00	6.00	
274 Frank Baumholtz	12.00	6.00	
275 Jim Greengrass	12.00	6.00	
276 George Zuverink	12.00	6.00	
277 Daryl Spencer	12.00	6.00	
278 Chet Nichols	12.00	6.00	
279 Johnny Groth	12.00	6.00	
280 Jim Gilliam	20.00	10.00	
281 Art Houtteman	12.00	6.00	
282 Warren Hacker	12.00	6.00	
283 Hal Smith	12.00	6.00	
284 Ike Delock	12.00	6.00	
285 Eddie Miksis	12.00	6.00	
286 Bill Wright	12.00	6.00	
287 Bobby Adams	12.00	6.00	
288 Bob Cerv	25.00	12.50	
289 Hal Jeffcoat	12.00	6.00	
290 Curt Simmons	15.00	7.50	
291 Frank Kellert	12.00	6.00	
292 Luis Aparicio (R)	160.00	80.00	
293 Stu Miller	15.00	7.50	
294 Ernie Johnson	12.00	6.00	
295 Clem Labine	15.00	7.50	
296 Andy Seminick	12.00	6.00	
297 Bob Skinner	15.00	9.00	
298 Johnny Schmitz	12.00	6.00	
299 Charley Neal	28.00	14.00	
300 Vic Wertz	15.00	7.50	
301 Marv Grissom	12.00	6.00	
302 Eddie Robinson	12.00	6.00	
303 Jim Dyck	12.00	6.00	
304 Frank Malzone	18.00	9.00	
305 Brooks Lawrence	12.00	6.00	
306 Curt Roberts	12.00	6.00	
307 Hoyt Wilhelm	35.00	18.00	
308 Chuck Harmon	12.00	6.00	
309 Don Blasingame (R)	18.00	9.00	
310 Steve Gromek	12.00	6.00	
311 Hal Naragon	12.00	6.00	
312 Andy Pafko	12.00	6.00	
313 Gene Stephens	12.00	6.00	
314 Hobie Landrith	12.00	6.00	
315 Milt Bolling	12.00	6.00	
316 Jerry Coleman	15.00	7.50	
317 Al Aber	12.00	6.00	
318 Fred Hatfield	12.00	6.00	
319 Jack Crimian	12.00	6.00	
320 Joe Adcock	15.00	7.50	
321 Jim Konstanty	15.00	7.50	
322 Karl Olson	12.00	6.00	
323 Willard Schmidt	12.00	6.00	
324 Rocky Bridges	12.00	6.00	
325 Don Liddle	12.00	6.00	
326 Connie Johnson	12.00	6.00	
327 Bob Wiesler	12.00	6.00	
328 Preston Ward	12.00	6.00	
329 Lou Berberet	12.00	6.00	
330 Jim Busby	12.00	6.00	
331 Dick Hall	12.00	6.00	
332 Don Larsen	50.00	25.00	
333 Rube Walker	12.00	6.00	
334 Bob Miller	12.00	6.00	
335 Don Hoak	12.00	6.00	
336 Ellis Kinder	12.00	6.00	
337 Bobby Morgan	12.00	6.00	
338 Jim Delsing	12.00	6.00	
339 Rance Pless	12.00	6.00	
340 Mickey McDermott	45.00	20.00	
___ Checklist 1/3	250.00	110.00	
___ Checklist 2/4	250.00	110.00	

1957 Topps

Starting in 1957 Topps adopted a smaller card size, 2-1/2" by 3-1/2", a size that's become the standard in the hobby. Card fronts feature full-color photos and, for the first time, Topps introduced multi-player card fronts. The 407-card set does not include four unnumbered checklists. Those values are listed at the end of this checklist.

	NR/MT	EX
Complete Set (407)	7,800.00	3,850.00
Commons (1-264)	8.00	4.00
Commons (265-352)	20.00	10.00
Commons (353-407)	6.50	3.25

#	Player	NR/MT	EX
1	Ted Williams	475.00	175.00
2	Yogi Berra	160.00	80.00
3	Dale Long	8.00	4.00
4	Johnny Logan	10.00	5.00
5	Sal Maglie	12.00	6.00
6	Hector Lopez	8.00	4.00
7	Luis Aparicio	45.00	22.50
8	Don Mossi	10.00	5.00
9	Johnny Temple	10.00	5.00
10	Willie Mays	260.00	130.00
11	George Zuverink	8.00	4.00
12	Dick Groat	12.00	6.00
13	Wally Burnette	8.00	4.00
14	Bob Nieman	8.00	4.00
15	Robin Roberts	30.00	15.00
16	Walt Moryn	8.00	4.00
17	Billy Gardner	8.00	4.00
18	Don Drysdale (R)	260.00	130.00
19	Bob Wilson	8.00	4.00
20	Hank Aaron (Photo Reversed)	275.00	140.00
21	Frank Sullivan	8.00	4.00
22	Jerry Snyder (Wrong Photo)	8.00	4.00
23	Sherm Lollar	8.00	4.00
24	Bill Mazeroski (R)	70.00	35.00
25	Whitey Ford	75.00	38.00
26	Bob Boyd	8.00	4.00
27	Ted Kazanski	8.00	4.00
28	Gene Conley	8.00	4.00
29	Whitey Herzog (R)	30.00	15.00
30	Pee Wee Reese	70.00	35.00
31	Ron Northey	8.00	4.00
32	Hersh Freeman	8.00	4.00
33	Jim Small	8.00	4.00
34	Tom Sturdivant	8.00	4.00
35	Frank Robinson (R)	325.00	160.00
36	Bob Grim	10.00	5.00
37	Frank Torre	10.00	5.00
38	Nellie Fox	25.00	12.50
39	Al Worthington	8.00	4.00
40	Early Wynn	25.00	12.50
41	Hal Smith	8.00	4.00
42	Dee Fondy	8.00	4.00
43	Connie Johnson	8.00	4.00
44	Joe DeMaestri	8.00	4.00
45	Carl Furillo	18.00	9.00
46	Bob Miller	8.00	4.00
47	Don Blasingame	8.00	4.00
48	Bill Bruton	8.00	4.00
49	Daryl Spencer	8.00	4.00
50	Herb Score	18.00	9.00
51	Clint Courtney	8.00	4.00
52	Lee Walls	8.00	4.00
53	Clem Labine	12.00	6.00
54	Elmer Valo	8.00	4.00
55	Ernie Banks	125.00	65.00
56	Dave Sisler	8.00	4.00
57	Jim Lemon	8.00	4.00
58	Ruben Gomez	8.00	4.00
59	Dick Williams	8.00	4.00
60	Billy Hoeft	8.00	4.00
61	Dusty Rhodes	8.00	4.00
62	Billy Martin	50.00	25.00
63	Ike Delock	8.00	4.00
64	Pete Runnels	10.00	5.00
65	Wally Moon	10.00	5.00
66	Brooks Lawrence	8.00	4.00
67	Chico Carrasquel	8.00	4.00
68	Ray Crone	8.00	4.00
69	Roy McMillan	8.00	4.00
70	Richie Ashburn	25.00	15.00
71	Murry Dickson	8.00	4.00
72	Bill Tuttle	8.00	4.00
73	George Crowe	8.00	4.00
74	Vito Valentinetti	8.00	4.00
75	Jim Piersall	12.00	6.00
76	Roberto Clemente	250.00	125.00
77	Paul Foytack	8.00	4.00
78	Vic Wertz	10.00	5.00
79	Lindy McDaniel (R)	12.00	6.00
80	Gil Hodges	60.00	30.00
81	Herm Wehmeier	8.00	4.00

82	Elston Howard	25.00	12.50
83	Lou Skizas	8.00	4.00
84	Moe Drabowsky	8.00	4.00
85	Larry Doby	12.00	6.00
86	Bill Sarni	8.00	4.00
87	Tom Gorman	8.00	4.00
88	Harvey Kuenn	12.00	6.00
89	Roy Sievers	8.00	4.00
90	Warren Spahn	80.00	40.00
91	Mack Burk	8.00	4.00
92	Mickey Vernon	8.00	4.00
93	Hal Jeffcoat	8.00	4.00
94	Bobby Del Greco	8.00	4.00
95	Mickey Mantle	1,250.00	650.00
96	Hank Aguirre	8.00	4.00
97	Yankees Team	60.00	30.00
98	Al Dark	8.00	4.00
99	Bob Keegan	8.00	4.00
100	League Presidents	10.00	5.00
	(Giles/Harridge)		
101	Chuck Stobbs	8.00	4.00
102	Ray Boone	8.00	4.00
103	Joe Nuxhall	8.00	4.00
104	Hank Foiles	8.00	4.00
105	Johnny Antonelli	8.00	4.00
106	Ray Moore	8.00	4.00
107	Jim Rivera	8.00	4.00
108	Tommy Byrne	8.00	4.00
109	Hank Thompson	8.00	4.00
110	Bill Virdon	10.00	5.00
111	Hal Smith	8.00	4.00
112	Tom Brewer	8.00	4.00
113	Wilmer Mizell	8.00	4.00
114	Braves Team	15.00	7.50
115	Jim Gilliam	15.00	7.50
116	Mike Fornieles	8.00	4.00
117	Joe Adcock	10.00	5.00
118	Bob Porterfield	8.00	4.00
119	Stan Lopata	8.00	4.00
120	Bob Lemon	25.00	12.50
121	Cletis Boyer (R)	25.00	12.50
122	Ken Boyer	18.00	9.00
123	Steve Ridzik	8.00	4.00
124	Dave Philley	8.00	4.00
125	Al Kaline	110.00	55.00
126	Bob Wiesler	8.00	4.00
127	Bob Buhl	8.00	4.00
128	Ed Bailey	8.00	4.00
129	Saul Rogovin	8.00	4.00
130	Don Newcombe	15.00	7.50
131	Milt Bolling	8.00	4.00
132	Art Ditmar	8.00	4.00
133	Del Crandall	8.00	4.00
134	Don Kaiser	8.00	4.00
135	Bill Skowron	18.00	9.00
136	Jim Hegan	8.00	4.00
137	Bob Rush	8.00	4.00
138	Minnie Minoso	18.00	9.00
139	Lou Kretlow	8.00	4.00
140	Frank Thomas	8.00	4.00
141	Al Aber	8.00	4.00
142	Charley Thompson	8.00	4.00
143	Andy Pafko	8.00	4.00
144	Ray Narleski	8.00	4.00
145	Al Smith	8.00	4.00
146	Don Ferrarese	8.00	4.00
147	Al Walker	8.00	4.00
148	Don Mueller	8.00	4.00
149	Bob Kennedy	8.00	4.00
150	Bob Friend	8.00	4.00
151	Willie Miranda	8.00	4.00
152	Jack Harshman	8.00	4.00
153	Karl Olson	8.00	4.00
154	Red Schoendienst	28.00	14.00
155	Jim Brosnan	8.00	4.00
156	Gus Triandos	8.00	4.00
157	Wally Post	8.00	4.00
158	Curt Simmons	8.00	4.00
159	Solly Drake	8.00	4.00
160	Billy Pierce	8.00	4.00
161	Pirates Team	15.00	7.50
162	Jack Meyer	8.00	4.00
163	Sammy White	8.00	4.00
164	Tommy Carroll	8.00	4.00
165	Ted Kluszewski	35.00	18.00
166	Roy Face	10.00	5.00
167	Vic Power	8.00	4.00
168	Frank Lary	8.00	4.00
169	Herb Plews	8.00	4.00
170	Duke Snider	125.00	65.00
171	Red Sox Team	15.00	7.50
172	Gene Woodling	10.00	5.00
173	Roger Craig	15.00	7.50
174	Willie Jones	8.00	4.00
175	Don Larsen	20.00	10.00
176	Gene Baker	8.00	4.00
177	Eddie Yost	8.00	4.00
178	Don Bessent	8.00	4.00
179	Ernie Oravetz	8.00	4.00
180	Gus Bell	8.00	4.00
181	Dick Donovan	8.00	4.00
182	Hobie Landrith	8.00	4.00
183	Cubs Team	15.00	7.50
184	Tito Francona (R)	8.00	4.00
185	Johnny Kucks	8.00	4.00
186	Jim King	8.00	4.00
187	Virgil Trucks	8.00	4.00
188	Felix Mantilla (R)	8.00	4.00
189	Willard Nixon	8.00	4.00
190	Randy Jackson	8.00	4.00
191	Joe Margoneri	8.00	4.00
192	Jerry Coleman	8.00	4.00
193	Del Rice	8.00	4.00
194	Hal Brown	8.00	4.00
195	Bobby Avila	8.00	4.00
196	Larry Jackson	8.00	4.00

197 Hank Sauer	8.00	4.00	255 Charlie Silvera	8.00	4.00
198 Tigers Team	15.00	7.50	256 Ronnie Kline	8.00	4.00
199 Vernon Law	8.00	4.00	257 Walt Dropo	8.00	4.00
200 Gil McDougald	18.00	9.00	258 Steve Gromek	8.00	4.00
201 Sandy Amoros	10.00	5.00	259 Eddie O'Brien	8.00	4.00
202 Dick Gernert	8.00	4.00	260 Del Ennis	8.00	4.00
203 Hoyt Wilhelm	25.00	12.50	261 Bob Chakales	8.00	4.00
204 Athletics Team	15.00	7.50	262 Bobby Thomson	12.00	6.00
205 Charley Maxwell	8.00	4.00	263 George Strickland	8.00	4.00
206 Willard Schmidt	8.00	4.00	264 Bob Turley	12.00	6.00
207 Billy Unter	8.00	4.00	265 Harvey Haddix	20.00	10.00
208 Lew Burdette	12.00	6.00	266 Ken Kuhn	20.00	10.00
209 Bob Skinner	8.00	4.00	267 Danny Kravitz	20.00	10.00
210 Roy Campanella	125.00	65.00	268 Jackie Collum	20.00	10.00
211 Camilo pascual	8.00	4.00	269 Bob Cerv	20.00	10.00
212 Rocky Colavito (R)	140.00	70.00	270 Senators Team	45.00	22.50
213 Les Moss	8.00	4.00	271 Danny O'Connell	20.00	10.00
214 Phillies Team	15.00	7.50	272 Bobby Shantz	28.00	14.00
215 Enos Slaughter	30.00	15.00	273 Jim Davis	20.00	10.00
216 Marv Grissom	8.00	4.00	274 Don Hoak	20.00	10.00
217 Gene Stephens	8.00	4.00	275 Indians Team	45.00	22.50
218 Ray Jablonski	8.00	4.00	276 Jim Pyburn	20.00	10.00
219 Tom Acker	8.00	4.00	277 Johnny Podres	50.00	25.00
220 Jackie Jensen	12.00	6.00	278 Fred Hatfield	20.00	10.00
221 Dixie Howell	8.00	4.00	279 Bob Thurman	20.00	10.00
222 Alex Grammas	8.00	4.00	280 Alex Kellner	20.00	10.00
223 Frank House	8.00	4.00	281 Gail Harris	20.00	10.00
224 Marv Blaylock	8.00	4.00	282 Jack Dittmer	20.00	10.00
225 Harry Simpson	8.00	4.00	283 Wes Covington	20.00	10.00
226 Preston Ward	8.00	4.00	284 Don Zimmer	30.00	15.00
227 Jerry Staley	8.00	4.00	285 Ned Garver	20.00	10.00
228 Smoky Burgess	8.00	4.00	286 Bobby Richardson(R)	140.00	70.00
229 George Susce	8.00	4.00	287 Sam Jones	20.00	10.00
230 George Kell	20.00	10.00	288 Ted Lepcio	20.00	10.00
231 Solly Hemus	8.00	4.00	289 Jim Bolger	20.00	10.00
232 Whitey Lockman	10.00	5.00	290 Andy Carey	20.00	10.00
233 Art Fowler	8.00	4.00	291 Windy McCall	20.00	10.00
234 Dick Cole	8.00	4.00	292 Billy Klaus	20.00	10.00
235 Tom Poholsky	8.00	4.00	293 Ted Abernathy	20.00	10.00
236 Joe Ginsberg	8.00	4.00	294 Rocky Bridges	20.00	10.00
237 Foster Castleman	8.00	4.00	295 Joe Collins	20.00	10.00
238 Eddie Robinson	8.00	4.00	296 Johnny Klippstein	20.00	10.00
239 Tom Morgan	8.00	4.00	297 Jack Crimian	20.00	10.00
240 Hank Bauer	15.00	7.50	298 Irv Noren	20.00	10.00
241 Joe Lonnett	8.00	4.00	299 Chuck Harmon	20.00	10.00
242 Charley Neal	8.00	4.00	300 Mike Garcia	20.00	10.00
243 Cardinals Team	15.00	7.50	301 Sam Esposito	20.00	10.00
244 Billy Loes	8.00	4.00	302 Sandy Koufax	375.00	190.00
245 Rip Repulski	8.00	4.00	303 Billy Goodman	20.00	10.00
246 Jose Valdivielso	8.00	4.00	304 Joe Cunningham	20.00	10.00
247 Turk Lown	8.00	4.00	305 Chico Fernandez	20.00	10.00
248 Jim Finigan	8.00	4.00	306 Darrell Johnson	20.00	10.00
249 Dave Pope	8.00	4.00	307 Jack Phillips	20.00	10.00
250 Eddie Mathews	48.00	24.00	308 Dick Hall	20.00	10.00
251 Orioles Team	15.00	7.50	309 Jim Busby	20.00	10.00
252 Carl Erskine	12.00	6.00	310 Max Surkont	20.00	10.00
253 Gus Zernial	8.00	4.00	311 Al Pilarcik	20.00	10.00
254 Ron Negray	8.00	4.00	312 Tony Kubek (R)	125.00	65.00

313 Mel Parnell	20.00	10.00	
314 Ed Bouchee	20.00	10.00	
315 Lou Berberet	20.00	10.00	
316 Billy O'Dell	20.00	10.00	
317 Giants Team	50.00	25.00	
318 Mickey McDermott	20.00	10.00	
319 Gino Cimoli (R)	22.00	11.00	
320 Neil Chrisley	20.00	10.00	
321 Red Murff	20.00	10.00	
322 Redlegs Team	50.00	25.00	
323 Wes Westrum	20.00	10.00	
324 Dodgers Team	125.00	65.00	
325 Frank Bolling	20.00	10.00	
326 Pedro Ramos	20.00	10.00	
327 Jim Pendleton	20.00	10.00	
328 Brooks Robinson(R)	450.00	225.00	
329 White Sox Team	50.00	25.00	
330 Jim Wilson	20.00	10.00	
331 Ray Katt	20.00	10.00	
332 Bob Bowman	20.00	10.00	
333 Ernie Johnson	20.00	10.00	
334 Jerry Schoonmaker	20.00	10.00	
335 Granny Hamner	20.00	10.00	
336 Haywood Sullivan (R)	24.00	12.00	
337 Rene Valdes	20.00	10.00	
338 Jim Bunning (R)	150.00	75.00	
339 Bob Speake	20.00	10.00	
340 Bill Wight	20.00	10.00	
341 Don Gross	20.00	10.00	
342 Gene Mauch	25.00	12.50	
343 Taylor Phillips	20.00	10.00	
344 Paul LaPalme	20.00	10.00	
345 Paul Smith	20.00	10.00	
346 Dick Littlefield	20.00	10.00	
347 Hal Naragon	20.00	10.00	
348 Jim Hearn	20.00	10.00	
349 Nelson King	20.00	10.00	
350 Eddie Miksis	20.00	10.00	
351 Dave Hillman	20.00	10.00	
352 Ellis Kinder	20.00	10.00	
353 Cal Neeman	6.50	3.25	
354 Rip Coleman	6.50	3.25	
355 Frank Malzone	6.50	3.25	
356 Faye Throneberry	6.50	3.25	
357 Earl Torgeson	6.50	3.25	
358 Jerry Lynch	6.50	3.25	
359 Tom Cheney (R)	6.50	3.25	
360 Johnny Groth	6.50	3.25	
361 Curt Barclay	6.50	3.25	
362 Roman Mejias	6.50	3.25	
363 Eddie Kasko	6.50	3.25	
364 Cal McLish	6.50	3.25	
365 Ossie Virgil	6.50	3.25	
366 Ken Lehman	6.50	3.25	
367 Ed FitzGerald	6.50	3.25	
368 Bob Purkey	6.50	3.25	
369 Milt Graff	6.50	3.25	
370 Warren Hacker	6.50	3.25	
371 Bob Lennon	6.50	3.25	
372 Norm Zauchin	6.50	3.25	
373 Pete Whisenant	6.50	3.25	
374 Don Cardwell	6.50	3.25	
375 Jim Landis	6.50	3.25	
376 Don Elston	6.50	3.25	
377 Andre Rodgers	6.50	3.25	
378 Elmer Singleton	6.50	3.25	
379 Don Lee	6.50	3.25	
380 Walker Cooepr	6.50	3.25	
381 Dean Stone	6.50	3.25	
382 Jim Brideweser	6.50	3.25	
383 Juan Pizarro	6.50	3.25	
384 Bobby Gene Smith	6.50	3.25	
385 Art Houtteman	6.50	3.25	
386 Lyle Luttrell	6.50	3.25	
387 Jack Sanford (R)	8.50	4.25	
388 Pete Daley	6.50	3.25	
389 Dave Jolly	6.50	3.25	
390 Reno Bertoia	6.50	3.25	
391 Ralph Terry	8.50	4.25	
392 Chuck Tanner	8.50	4.25	
393 Raul Sanchez	6.50	3.25	
394 Luis Arroyo	6.50	3.25	
395 Bubba Phillips	6.50	3.25	
396 Casey Wise	6.50	3.25	
397 Roy Smalley	6.50	3.25	
398 Al Cicotte	6.50	3.25	
399 Billy Consolo	6.50	3.25	
400 Dodgers' Sluggers	225.00	110.00	
(Campanella,			
Furillo,Hodges,			
Snider)			
401 Earl Battey (R)	8.50	4.25	
402 Jim Pisoni	6.50	3.25	
403 Dick Hyde	6.50	3.25	
404 Harry Anderson	6.50	3.25	
405 Duke Maas	6.50	3.25	
406 Bob Hale	6.50	3.25	
407 Yankee Power	450.00	225.00	
(Y. Berra,			
M. Mantle)			
___ Checklist 1-2	225.00	110.00	
___ Checklist 2-3	350.00	150.00	
___ Checklist 3-4	650.00	300.00	
___ Checklist 4-5	800.00	375.00	

1958 Topps

Sandy Koufax

L. A. DODGERS

Topps expanded their baseball set in 1958 to 494-cards. Although the checklist below is numbered to 495, card number 145 was never issued. The larger set contains Topps first All-Star subset (#475-#495). For the first time Topps began numbering their checklist cards which appear on the back of the team cards. Color variations exist on the lettering of some cards with yellow (Y) being the most scarce and white more common. Those variations are listed below.

		NR/MT	EX
Complete Set (494)		5,600.00	2,800.00
Commons (1-110)		8.00	4.00
Commons (111-495)		5.00	2.50

		NR/MT	EX
1	Ted Williams	400.00	125.00
2a	Bob Lemon (Y)	40.00	20.00
2b	Bob Lemon	24.00	12.00
3	Alex Kellner	8.00	4.00
4	Hank Foiles	8.00	4.00
5	Willie Mays	200.00	100.00
6	George Zuverink	8.00	4.00
7	Dale Long	8.00	4.00
8a	Eddie Kasko (Y)	25.00	12.50
8b	Eddie Kasko	8.00	4.00
9	Hank Bauer	12.00	6.00
10	Lou Burdette	10.00	5.00
11a	Jim Rivera (Y)	20.00	10.00
11b	Jim Rivera	8.00	4.00
12	George Crowe	8.00	4.00
13a	Billy Hoeft (Y)	24.00	12.00
13b	Billy Hoeft	8.00	4.00
14	Rip Repulski	8.00	4.00
15	Jim Lemon	8.00	4.00
16	Charley Neal	8.00	4.00
17	Felix Mantilla	8.00	4.00
18	Frank Sullivan	8.00	4.00
19	Giants Team (Checklist 1-88)	25.00	12.50
20a	Gil McDougald (Y)	30.00	15.00
20b	Gil McDougald	18.00	9.00
21	Curt Barclay	8.00	4.00
22	Hal Naragon	8.00	4.00
23a	Bill Tuttle (Y)	24.00	12.00
23b	Bill Tuttle	8.00	4.00
24a	Hobie Landrith(Y)	24.00	12.00
24b	Hobie Landrith	8.00	4.00
25	Don Drysdale	80.00	40.00
26	Ron Jackson	8.00	4.00
27	Bud Freeman	8.00	4.00
28	Jim Busby	8.00	4.00
29	Ted Lepcio	8.00	4.00
30a	Hank Aaron (Y)	350.00	175.00
30b	Hank Aaron	200.00	100.00
31	Tex Clevenger	8.00	4.00
32a	J.W. Porter (Y)	24.00	12.00
32b	J.W. Porter	8.00	4.00
33a	Cal Neeman (Y)	20.00	10.00
33b	Cal Neeman	8.00	4.00
34	Bob Thurman	8.00	4.00
35a	Don Mossi (Y)	24.00	12.00
35b	Don Mossi	8.00	4.00
36	Ted Kazanski	8.00	4.00
37	Mike McCormick (R) (Wrong Photo)	10.00	5.00
38	Dick Gernert	8.00	4.00
39	Bob Martyn	8.00	4.00
40	George Kell	15.00	7.50
41	Dave Hillman	8.00	4.00
42	John Roseboro (R)	18.00	9.00
43	Sal Maglie	12.00	6.00
44	Senators Team (Checklist 1-88)	12.00	6.00
		8.00	4.00
45	Dick Groat	10.00	5.00
46a	Lou Sleater (Y)	24.00	12.00
46b	Lou Sleater	8.00	4.00
47	Roger Marix	8.00	4.00
48	Chuck Harmon	8.00	4.00
49	Smoky Burgess	10.00	5.00
50a	Billy Pierce (Y)	25.00	12.50
50b	Billy Pierce	10.00	5.00
51	Del Rice	8.00	4.00
52a	Bob Clemente (Y)	325.00	165.00
52b	Bob Clemente	185.00	95.00
53a	Morrie Martin (Y)	24.00	12.00
53b	Morrie Martin	8.00	4.00
54	Norm Siebern (R)	10.00	5.00
55	Chico Carrasquel	8.00	4.00
56	Bill Fischer	8.00	4.00
57a	Tim Thompson (Y)	24.00	12.00
57b	Tim Thompson	8.00	4.00
58a	Art Schult (Y)	20.00	10.00
58b	Art Schult	8.00	4.00
59	Dave Sisler	8.00	4.00
60a	Del Ennis (Y)	8.00	4.00

60b	Del Ennis	8.00	4.00
61a	Darrell Johnson (Y)	24.00	12.00
61b	Darrell Johnson	8.00	4.50
62	Joe DeMaestri	8.00	4.00
63	Joe Nuxhall	8.00	4.00
64	Joe Lonnett	8.00	4.00
65a	Von McDaniel (Y) (R)	28.00	14.00
65b	Von McDaniel(R)	10.00	5.00
66	Lee Walls	8.00	4.00
67	Joe Ginsberg	8.00	4.00
68	Daryl Spencer	8.00	4.00
69	Wally Burnette	8.00	4.00
70a	Al Kaline (Y)	175.00	90.00
70b	Al Kaline	75.00	38.00
71	Dodgers Team (Checklist 1-88)	38.00	20.00
72	Bud Byerly	8.00	4.00
73	Pete Daley	8.00	4.00
74	Roy Face	10.00	5.00
75	Gus Bell	8.00	4.00
76a	Dick Farrell (Y)	25.00	12.50
76b	Dick Farrell	8.00	4.00
77a	Don Zimmer (Y)	28.00	14.00
77b	Don Zimmer	10.00	5.00
78a	Ernie Johnson (Y)	24.00	12.00
78b	Ernie Johnson	8.00	4.00
79a	Dick Williams (Y)	24.00	12.00
79b	Dick Williams	8.00	4.00
80	Dick Drott	8.00	4.00
81a	Steve Boros (Y)	20.00	10.00
81b	Steve Boros	8.00	4.00
82	Ronnie Kline	8.00	4.00
83	Bob Hazle (R)	10.00	5.00
84	Billy O'Dell	8.00	4.00
85a	Luis Aparicio (Y)	50.00	25.00
85b	Luis Aparicio	28.00	14.00
86	Valmy Thomas	8.00	4.00
87	Johnny Kucks	8.00	4.00
88	Duke Snider	80.00	40.00
89	Billy Klaus	8.00	4.00
90	Robin Roberts	24.00	12.00
91	Chuck Tanner	8.00	4.00
92a	Clint Courtney (Y)	24.00	12.00
92b	Clint Courtney	8.00	4.00
93	Sandy Amoros	10.00	5.00
94	Bob Skinner	8.00	4.00
95	Frank Bolling	8.00	4.00
96	Joe Durham	8.00	4.00
97a	Larry Jackson (Y)	24.00	12.00
97b	Larry Jackson	8.00	4.00
98a	Billy Hunter (Y)	24.00	12.00
98b	Billy Hunter	8.00	4.00
99	Bobby Adams	8.00	4.00
100a	Early Wynn (Y)	40.00	20.00
100b	Early Wynn	24.00	12.00
101a	Bobby Richardson (Y)	40.00	20.00
101b	Bobby Richardson	20.00	10.00
102	George Strickland	8.00	4.00
103	Jerry Lynch	8.00	4.00
104	Jim Pendleton	8.00	4.00
105	Billy Gardner	8.00	4.00
106	Dick Schofield	8.00	4.00
107	Ossie Virgil	8.00	4.00
108a	Jim Landis (Y)	20.00	10.00
108b	Jim Landis	8.00	4.00
109	Herb Plews	8.00	4.00
110	Johnny Logan	8.00	4.00
111	Stu Miller	5.00	2.50
112	Gus Zernial	5.00	2.50
113	Jerry Walker	5.00	2.50
114	Irv Noren	5.00	2.50
115	Jim Bunning	24.00	12.00
116	Dave Philley	5.00	2.50
117	Frank Torre	5.00	2.50
118	Harvey Haddix	7.00	3.50
119	Harry Chiti	5.00	2.50
120	Johnny Podres	10.00	5.00
121	Eddie Miksis	5.00	2.50
122	Walt Moryn	5.00	2.50
123	Dick Tomanek	5.00	2.50
124	Bobby Usher	5.00	2.50
125	Al Dark	7.00	3.50
126	Stan Palys	5.00	2.50
127	Tom Sturdivant	5.00	2.50
128	Willie Kirkland	7.00	3.50
129	Jim Derrington	5.00	2.50
130	Jackie Jensen	12.00	6.00
131	Bob Henrich	5.00	2.50
132	Vernon Law	7.00	3.50
133	Russ Nixon (R)	7.00	3.50
134	Phillies Team (Checklist 89-176)	10.00	5.00
135	Moe Drabowsky	7.00	3.50
136	Jim Finingan	5.00	2.50
137	Russ Kemmerer	5.00	2.50
138	Earl Torgeson	5.00	2.50
139	George Brunet	5.00	2.50
140	Wes Covington	7.00	3.50
141	Ken Lehman	5.00	2.50
142	Enos Slaughter	25.00	12.50
143	Billy Muffett	5.00	2.50
144	Bobby Morgan	5.00	2.50
145	No Card	5.00	2.50
146	Dick Gray	5.00	2.50
147	Don McMahon (R)	7.00	3.50
148	Billy Consolo	5.00	2.50
149	Tom Acker	5.00	2.50
150	Mickey Mantle	650.00	350.00
151	Buddy Pritchard	5.00	2.50
152	Johnny Antonelli	7.00	3.50
153	Les Moss	5.00	2.50
154	Harry Byrd	5.00	2.50
155	Hector Lopez	5.00	2.50
156	Dick Hyde	5.00	2.50
157	Dee Fondy	5.00	2.50

158 Indians Team (Checklist 177-264)	10.00	5.00	
159 Taylor Phillips	5.00	2.50	
160 Don Hoak	5.00	2.50	
161 Don Larsen	10.00	5.00	
162 Gil Hodges	30.00	15.00	
163 Jim Wilson	5.00	2.50	
164 Bob Taylor	5.00	2.50	
165 Bob Nieman	5.00	2.50	
166 Danny O'Connell	5.00	2.50	
167 Frank Baumann	5.00	2.50	
168 Joe Cunningham	5.00	2.50	
169 Ralph Terry	7.00	3.50	
170 Vic Wertz	5.00	2.50	
171 Harry Anderson	5.00	2.50	
172 Don Gross	5.00	2.50	
173 Eddie Yost	5.00	2.50	
174 A's Team (Checklist 89-176)	10.00	5.00	
175 Marv Throneberry	10.00	5.00	
176 Bob Buhl	7.00	3.50	
177 Al Smith	5.00	2.50	
178 Ted Kluszewski	12.00	6.00	
179 Willy Miranda	5.00	2.50	
180 Lindy McDaniel	7.00	3.50	
181 Willie Jones	5.00	2.50	
182 Joe Cafie	5.00	2.50	
183 Dave Jolly	5.00	2.50	
184 Elvin Tappe	5.00	2.50	
185 Ray Boone	5.00	2.50	
186 Jack Meyer	5.00	2.50	
187 Sandy Koufax	225.00	110.00	
188 Milt Bolling (Wrong Photo)	5.00	2.50	
189 George Susce	5.00	2.50	
190 Red Schoendienst	25.00	12.50	
191 Art Ceccarelli	5.00	2.50	
192 Milt Graff	5.00	2.50	
193 Jerry Lumpe (R)	6.00	3.00	
194 Roger Craig	8.50	4.25	
195 Whitey Lockman	6.00	3.00	
196 Mike Garcia	6.00	3.00	
197 Haywood Sullivan	5.00	2.50	
198 Bill Virdon	7.00	3.50	
199 Don Blasingame	5.00	2.50	
200 Bob Keegan	5.00	2.50	
201 Jim Bolger	5.00	2.50	
202 Woody Held (R)	6.00	3.00	
203 Al Walker	5.00	2.50	
204 Leo Kiely	5.00	2.50	
205 Johnny Temple	5.00	2.50	
206 Bob Shaw	5.00	2.50	
207 Solly Hemus	5.00	2.50	
208 Cal McLish	5.00	2.50	
209 Bob Anderson	5.00	2.50	
210 Wally Moon	6.00	3.00	
211 Pete Burnside	5.00	2.50	
212 Bubba Phillips	5.00	2.50	
213 Red Wilson	5.00	2.50	
214 Willard Schmidt	5.00	2.50	
215 Jim Gilliam	12.00	6.00	
216 Cards Team (Checklist 177-264)	10.00	5.00	
217 Jack Harshman	5.00	2.50	
218 Dick Rand	5.00	2.50	
219 Camilo Pascual	5.00	2.50	
220 Tom Brewer	5.00	2.50	
221 Jerry Kindall	5.00	2.50	
222 Bud Daley	5.00	2.50	
223 Andy Pafko	6.00	3.00	
224 Bob Grim	5.00	2.50	
225 Billy Goodman	5.00	2.50	
226 Bob Smith	5.00	2.50	
227 Gene Stephens	5.00	2.50	
228 Duke Maas	5.00	2.50	
229 Frank Zupo	5.00	2.50	
230 Richie Ashburn	20.00	10.00	
231 Lloyd Merritt	5.00	2.50	
232 Reno Bertoia	5.00	2.50	
233 Mickey Vernon	6.00	3.00	
234 Carl Sawatski	5.00	2.50	
235 Tom Gorman	5.00	2.50	
236 Ed FitzGerald	5.00	2.50	
237 Bill Wight	5.00	2.50	
238 Bill Mazeroski	18.00	9.00	
239 Chuck Stobbs	5.00	2.50	
240 Moose Skowron	12.00	6.00	
241 Dick Littlefield	5.00	2.50	
242 Johnny Klippstein	5.00	2.50	
243 Larry Raines	5.00	2.50	
244 Don Demeter (R)	5.00	2.50	
245 Frank Lary	7.00	3.50	
246 Yankees Team (Checklist 177-264)	48.00	24.00	
247 Casey Wise	5.00	2.50	
248 Herm Wehmeier	5.00	2.50	
249 Ray Moore	5.00	2.50	
250 Roy Sievers	6.00	3.00	
251 Warren Hacker	5.00	2.50	
252 Bob Trowbridge	5.00	2.50	
253 Don Mueller	5.00	2.50	
254 Alex Grammas	5.00	2.50	
255 Bob Turley	8.50	4.50	
256 White Sox Team (Checklist 265-353)	10.00	5.00	
257 Hal Smith	5.00	2.50	
258 Carl Erskine	10.00	5.00	
259 Al Pilarcik	5.00	2.50	
260 Frank Malzone	6.00	3.00	
261 Turk Lown	5.00	2.50	
262 Johnny Groth	5.00	2.50	
263 Eddie Bressoud	5.00	2.50	
264 Jack Sanford	5.00	2.50	
265 Pete Runnels	7.00	3.50	
266 Connie Johnson	5.00	2.50	
267 Sherm Lollar	5.00	2.50	

268	Granny Hamner	5.00	2.50	320	Whitey Ford	60.00	30.00
269	Paul Smith	5.00	2.50	321	Sluggers Supreme	50.00	25.00
270	Warren Spahn	65.00	35.00		(Kluszewski/Williams)		
271	Billy Martin	24.00	12.00	322	Harding Peterson	5.00	2.50
272	Ray Crone	5.00	2.50	323	Elmer Valo	5.00	2.50
273	Hal Smith	5.00	2.50	324	Hoyt Wilhelm	20.00	10.00
274	Rocky Bridges	5.00	2.50	325	Joe Adcock	7.00	3.50
275	Elston Howard	15.00	7.50	326	Bob Miller	5.00	2.50
276	Bobby Avila	5.00	2.50	327	Cubs Team	10.00	5.00
277	Virgil Trucks	5.00	2.50		(Checklist 265-352)		
278	Mack Burk	5.00	2.50	328	Ike Delock	5.00	2.50
279	Bob Boyd	5.00	2.50	329	Bob Cerv	5.00	2.50
280	Jim Piersall	7.00	3.50	330	Ed Bailey	5.00	2.50
281	Sam Taylor	5.00	2.50	331	Pedro Ramos	5.00	2.50
282	Paul Foytack	5.00	2.50	332	Jim King	5.00	2.50
283	Ray Shearer	5.00	2.50	333	Andy Carey	5.00	2.50
284	Ray Katt	5.00	2.50	334	Mound Aces	6.00	3.00
285	Frank Robinson	100.00	50.00		(Friend/Pierce)		
286	Gino Cimoli	5.00	2.50	335	Ruben Gomez	5.00	2.50
287	Sam Jones	5.00	2.50	336	Bert Hamric	5.00	2.50
288	Harmon Killebrew	90.00	45.00	337	Hank Aguirre	6.00	3.00
289	Series Hurling Rivals	6.00	3.00	338	Walt Dropo	6.00	3.00
	(Burdette/Shantz)			339	Fred Hatfield	5.00	2.50
290	Dick Donovan	5.00	2.50	340	Don Newcombe	12.00	6.00
291	Don Landrum	5.00	2.50	341	Pirates Team	10.00	5.00
292	Ned Garver	5.00	2.50		(Checklist 265-352)		
293	Gene Freese	5.00	2.50	342	Jim Brosnan	6.00	3.00
294	Hal Jeffcoat	5.00	2.50	343	Orlando Cepeda (R)	80.00	40.00
295	Minnie Minoso	12.00	6.00	344	Bob Porterfield	5.00	2.50
296	Ryne Duren (R)	15.00	7.50	345	Jim Hegan	5.00	2.50
297	Don Buddin	5.00	2.50	346	Steve Bilko	5.00	2.50
298	Jim Hearn	5.00	2.50	347	Don Rudolph	5.00	2.50
299	Harry Simpson	5.00	2.50	348	Chico Fernandez	5.00	2.50
300	League Presidents	7.00	3.50	349	Murry Dickson	5.00	2.50
	(Giles/Harridge)	5.00	2.50	350	Ken Boyer	15.00	7.50
301	Randy Jackson	5.00	2.50	351	Braves Fence	30.00	15.00
302	Mike Baxes	5.00	2.50		Busters (Aaron/		
303	Neil Chrisley	5.00	2.50		Crandall/Mathews)		
304	Tigers' Big Bats	20.00	10.00	352	Herb Score	10.00	5.00
	(Kaline/Kuenn)			353	Stan Lopata	5.00	2.50
305	Clem Labine	6.00	3.00	354	Art Ditmar	5.00	2.50
306	Whammy Douglas	5.00	2.50	355	Bill Bruton	5.00	2.50
307	Brooks Robinson	125.00	65.00	356	Bob Malkmus	5.00	2.50
308	Paul Giel	5.00	2.50	357	Danny McDevitt	5.00	2.50
309	Gail Harris	5.00	2.50	358	Gene Baker	5.00	2.50
310	Ernie Banks	100.00	50.00	359	Billy Loes	5.00	2.50
311	Bob Purkey	5.00	2.50	360	Roy McMillan	5.00	2.50
312	Red Sox Team	10.00	5.00	361	Mike Fornieles	5.00	2.50
	(Checklist 353-440)			362	Ray Jablonski	5.00	2.50
313	Bob Rush	5.00	2.50	363	Don Elston	5.00	2.50
314	Dodgers'			364	Earl Battey	5.00	2.50
	Boss&Power	20.00	10.00	365	Tom Morgan	5.00	2.50
	(Alston/Snider)	5.00	2.50	366	Gene Green	5.00	2.50
315	Bob Friend	6.00	3.00	367	Jack Urban	5.00	2.50
316	Tito Francona	5.00	2.50	368	Rocky Colavito	35.00	18.00
317	Albie Pearson	5.00	2.50	369	Ralph Lumenti	5.00	2.50
318	Frank House	5.00	2.50	370	Yogi Berra	180.00	90.00
319	Lou Skizas	5.00	2.50	371	Marty Keough	5.00	2.50

372	Don Cardwell	5.00	2.50	412	Jerry Staley	5.00	2.50
373	Joe Pignatano	5.00	2.50	413	Jim Davenport (R)	7.50	3.50
374	Brooks Lawrence	5.00	2.50	414	Sammy White	5.00	2.50
375	Pee Wee Reese	60.00	30.00	415	Bob Bowman	5.00	2.50
376	Charley Rabe	5.00	2.50	416	Foster Castleman	5.00	2.50
377a	Braves Team (Alphabetical Checklist)	10.00	5.00	417	Carl Furillo	10.00	5.00
				418	World Series Foes (Aaron/Mantle)	200.00	100.00
377b	Braves Team (Numerical Check-list)	60.00	28.00	419	Bobby Shantz	6.00	3.00
				420	Vada Pinson (R)	30.00	15.00
378	Hank Sauer	6.00	3.00	421	Dixie Howell	5.00	2.50
379	Ray Herbert	5.00	2.50	422	Norm Zauchin	5.00	2.50
380	Charley Maxwell	5.00	2.50	423	Phil Clark	5.00	2.50
381	Hal Brown	5.00	2.50	424	Larry Doby	7.50	3.50
382	Al Cicotte	5.00	2.50	425	Sam Esposito	5.00	2.50
383	Lou Berberet	5.00	2.50	426	Johnny O'Brien	5.00	2.50
384	John Goryl	5.00	2.50	427	Al Worthington	5.00	2.50
385	Wilmer Mizell	5.00	2.50	428a	Redlegs Team (Alphabetical Checklist)	10.00	5.00
386	Birdie's Sluggers (Ed Bailey/Frank Robinson/Birdie Tebbetts)	10.00	5.00	428b	Redlegs Team (Numerical Checklist)	60.00	28.00
387	Wally Post	6.00	3.00	429	Gus Triandos	5.00	2.50
388	Billy Moran	5.00	2.50	430	Bobby Thomson	6.00	3.00
389	Bill Taylor	5.00	2.50	431	Gene Conley	5.00	2.50
390	Del Crandall	7.00	3.50	432	John Powers	5.00	2.50
391	Dave Melton	5.00	2.50	433	Pancho Herrera	5.00	2.50
392	Bennie Daniels	5.00	2.50	434	Harvey Kuenn	7.00	3.50
393	Tony Kubek	24.00	12.00	435	Ed Roebuck	5.00	2.50
394	Jim Grant (R)	7.00	3.50	436	Rivals (Mays/Snider)	75.00	38.00
395	Willard Nixon	5.00	2.50	437	Bob Speake	5.00	2.50
396	Dutch Dotterer	5.00	2.50	438	Whitey Herzog	7.00	3.50
397a	Tigers Team (Alphabetical Checklist)	10.00	5.00	439	Ray Narleski	5.00	2.50
				440	Ed Mathews	40.00	20.00
397b	Tigers Team (Numerical Checklist)	60.00	28.00	441	Jim Marshall	5.00	2.50
				442	Phil Paine	5.00	2.50
				443	Billy Harrell	5.00	2.50
398	Gene Woodling	6.00	3.00	444	Danny Kravitz	5.00	2.50
399	Marv Grissom	5.00	2.50	445	Bob Smith	5.00	2.50
400	Nellie Fox	18.00	9.00	446	Carroll Hardy	5.00	2.50
401	Don Bessent	5.00	2.50	447	Ray Monzant	5.00	2.50
402	Bobby Gene Smith	5.00	2.50	448	Charlie Lau (R)	6.00	3.00
403	Steve Korcheck	5.00	2.50	449	Gene Fodge	5.00	2.50
404	Curt Simmons	6.00	3.00	450	Preston Ward	5.00	2.50
405	Ken Aspromonte	5.00	2.50	451	Joe Taylor	5.00	2.50
406	Vic Power	5.00	2.50	452	Roman Mejias	5.00	2.50
407	Carlton Willey	5.00	2.50	453	Tom Qualters	5.00	2.50
408a	Orioles Team (Alphabetical Checklist)	10.00	5.00	454	Harry Hanebrink	5.00	2.50
				455	Hal Griggs	5.00	2.50
				456	Dick Brown	5.00	2.50
				457	Milt Pappas (R)	7.00	3.50
408b	Orioles Team (Numerical Checklist)	60.00	28.00	458	Julio Becquer	5.00	2.50
				459	Ron Blackburn	5.00	2.50
				460	Chuck Essegian	5.00	2.50
409	Frank Thomas	5.00	2.50	461	Ed Mayer	5.00	2.50
410	Murray wall	5.00	2.50	462	Gary Geiger	5.00	2.50
411	Tony Taylor (R)	7.50	3.50	463	Vito Valentinetti	5.00	2.50

464	Curt Flood	28.00	14.00
465	Arnie Portocarrero	5.00	2.50
466	Pete Whisenant	5.00	2.50
467	Glen Hobbie	5.00	2.50
468	Bob Schmidt	5.00	2.50
469	Don Ferrarese	5.00	2.50
470	R.C. Stevens	5.00	2.50
471	Lenny Green	5.00	2.50
472	Joe Jay	5.00	2.50
473	Bill Renna	5.00	2.50
474	Roman Semproch	5.00	2.50
475	All-Star Managers (Haney/Stengel)	16.00	8.00
476	Stan Musial AS	45.00	22.50
477	Bill Skowron AS	7.00	3.50
478	Johnny Temple AS	5.00	2.50
479	Nellie Fox AS	8.00	4.00
480	Eddie Mathews AS	18.00	9.00
481	Frank Malzone AS	5.00	2.50
482	Ernie Banks AS	28.00	14.00
483	Luis Aparicio AS	15.00	7.50
484	Frank Robinson AS	28.00	14.00
485	Ted Williams AS	80.00	40.00
486	Willie Mays AS	60.00	30.00
487	Mickey Mantle AS	125.00	65.00
488	Hank Aaron AS	60.00	30.00
489	Jackie Jensen AS	6.00	3.00
490	Ed Bailey AS	5.00	2.50
491	Sherm Lollar AS	5.00	2.50
492	Bob Friend AS	5.00	2.50
493	Bob Turley AS	5.00	2.50
494	Warren Spahn AS	20.00	10.00
495	Herb Score AS	12.00	6.00
___	Contest Card	15.00	7.50

1959 Topps

gil hodges

This 572-card set is Topps largest to date. Card fronts feature player photos in a circle with a fascimile autograph across the front of the photograph. For the first time Topps included a Rookie Subset (116-146). Other Subsets include All-Stars (551-572) and Highlights (461-470). Cards measure 2-1/2" by 3-1/2".

		NR/MT	EX
Complete Set (572)		5,500.00	2,750.00
Commons (1-110)		6.00	3.00
Commons (111-506)		4.00	2.00
Commons (507-572)		16.00	8.00

1	Ford Frick	75.00	20.00
2	Eddie Yost	6.00	3.00
3	Don McMahon	6.00	3.00
4	Albie Pearson	6.00	3.00
5	Dick Donovan	6.00	3.00
6	Alex Grammas	6.00	3.00
7	Al Pilarcik	6.00	3.00
8	Phillies Team Checklist 1-88	28.00	14.00
9	Paul Giel	6.00	3.00
10	Mickey Mantle	500.00	250.00
11	Billy Hunter	6.00	3.00
12	Vern Law	6.00	3.00
13	Dick Gernert	6.00	3.00
14	Pete Whisenant	6.00	3.00
15	Dick Drott	6.00	3.00
16	Joe Pignatano	6.00	3.00
17	Danny's All-Stars (Ted Kluszewski, Danny Murtaugh, Frank Thomas)	7.00	3.50
18	Jack Urban	6.00	3.00
19	Ed Bressoud	6.00	3.00
20	Duke Snider	75.00	38.00
21	Connie Johnson	6.00	3.00
22	Al Smith	6.00	3.00
23	Murry Dickson	6.00	3.00
24	Red Wilson	6.00	3.00
25	Don Hoak	6.00	3.00
26	Chuck Stobbs	6.00	3.00
27	Andy Pafko	6.00	3.00
28	Red Worthington	6.00	3.00
29	Jim Bolger	6.00	3.00
30	Nellie Fox	15.00	7.50
31	Ken Lehman	6.00	3.00
32	Don Buddin	6.00	3.00
33	Ed Fitz Gerald	6.00	3.00
34	Al Kaline/ Charlie Maxwell	12.00	6.00 l
35	Ted Kluszewski	12.00	6.00
36	Hank Aguirre	6.00	3.00
37	Gene Green	6.00	3.00
38	Morrie Martin	6.00	3.00
39	Ed Bouchee	6.00	3.00
40	Warren Spahn	60.00	30.00

41	Bob Martyn	6.00	3.00		Checklist 89-176		
42	Murry Wall	6.00	3.00	95	Carl Willey	6.00	3.00
43	Steve Bilko	6.00	3.00	96	Lou Berberet	6.00	3.00
44	Vito Valentinetti	6.00	3.00	97	Jerry Lynch	6.00	3.00
45	Andy Carey	6.00	3.00	98	Arnie Portocarrero	6.00	3.00
46	Bill Henry	6.00	3.00	99	Ted Kazanski	6.00	3.00
47	Jim Finigan	6.00	3.00	100	Bob Cerv	6.00	3.00
48	Orioles Team	18.00	9.00	101	Alex Kellner	6.00	3.00
	Checklist 1-88			102	Felipe Alou (R)	25.00	12.50
49	Bill Hall	6.00	3.00	103	Billy Goodman	6.00	3.00
50	Willie Mays	190.00	95.00	104	Del Rice	6.00	3.00
51	Rip Coleman	6.00	3.00	105	Lee Walls	6.00	3.00
52	Coot Veal	6.00	3.00	106	Hal Woodeshick	6.00	3.00
53	Stan Williams (R)	7.00	3.50	107	Norm Larker	6.00	3.00
54	Mel Roach	6.00	3.00	108	Zack Monroe	6.00	3.00
55	Tom Brewer	6.00	3.00	109	Bob Schmidt	6.00	3.00
56	Carl Sawatski	6.00	3.00	110	George Witt	6.00	3.00
57	Al Cicotte	6.00	3.00	111	Redlegs Team	10.00	5.00
58	Eddie Miksis	6.00	3.00		Checklist 89-176		
59	Irv Noren	6.00	3.00	112	Billy Consolo	4.00	2.00
60	Bob Turley	8.50	4.25	113	Taylor Phillips	4.00	2.00
61	Dick Brown	6.00	3.00	114	Earl Battey	4.00	2.00
62	Tony Taylor	6.00	3.00	115	Mickey Vernon	5.00	2.25
63	Jim Hearn	6.00	3.00	116	Bob Allison (R)	8.00	4.00
64	Joe DeMaestri	6.00	3.00	117	John Blanchard (R)	8.00	4.00
65	Frank Torre	6.00	3.00	118	John Buzhardt (R)	4.00	2.00
66	Joe Ginsberg	6.00	3.00	119	John Callison (R)	8.00	4.00
67	Brooks Lawrence	6.00	3.00	120	Chuck Coles	4.00	2.00
68	Dick Schofield	6.00	3.00	121	Bob Conley	4.00	2.00
69	Giants Team	18.00	9.00	122	Bennie Daniels	4.00	2.00
	Checklist 89-176			123	Don Dillard	4.00	2.00
70	Harvey Kuenn	10.00	5.00	124	Dan Dobbek	4.00	2.00
71	Don Bessent	6.00	3.00	125	Ron Fairly	8.00	4.00
72	Bill Renna	6.00	3.00	126	Eddie Haas	4.00	2.00
73	Ron Jackson	6.00	3.00	127	Kent Hadley	4.00	2.00
74	Directing the Power	7.00	3.50	128	Bob Hartman	4.00	2.00
	(Cookie Lavagetto, Jim			129	Frank Herrera	4.00	2.00
	Lemon, Roy Sievers)			130	Lou Jackson	4.00	2.00
75	Sam Jones	6.00	3.00	131	Deron Johnson (R)	8.00	4.00
76	Bobby Richardson	18.00	9.00	132	Don Lee	4.00	2.00
77	John Goryl	6.00	3.00	133	Bob Lillis (R)	4.00	2.00
78	Pedro Ramos	6.00	3.00	134	Jim McDaniel	4.00	2.00
79	Harry Chiti	6.00	3.00	135	Gene Oliver	4.00	2.00
80	Minnie Minoso	10.00	5.00	136	Jim O'Toole (R)	6.00	3.00
81	Hal Jeffcoat	6.00	3.00	137	Dick Ricketts	4.00	2.00
82	Bob Boyd	6.00	3.00	138	John Romano	4.00	2.00
83	Bob Smith	6.00	3.00	139	Ed Sadowski	4.00	2.00
84	Reno Bertoia	6.00	3.00	140	Charlie Secrest	4.00	2.00
85	Harry Anderson	6.00	3.00	141	Joe Shipley	4.00	2.00
86	Bob Keegan	6.00	3.00	142	Dick Stigman	4.00	2.00
87	Danny O'Connell	6.00	3.00	143	Willie Tasby	4.00	2.00
88	Herb Score	8.50	4.25	144	Jerry Walker	4.00	2.00
89	Billy Gardner	6.00	3.00	145	Dom Zanni	4.00	2.00
90	Bill Skowron	12.00	6.00	146	Jerry Zimmerman	4.00	2.00
91	Herb Moford	6.00	3.00	147	Cub's Clubbers	15.00	7.50
92	Dave Philley	6.00	3.00		Ernie Banks, Dale		
93	Julio Becquer	6.00	3.00		Long, Walt Moryn)	4.00	2.00
94	White Sox Team	18.00	9.00	148	Mike McCormick	4.00	2.00

149 Jim Bunning	15.00	7.50	203 Ozzie Virgil	4.00	2.00
150 Stan Musial	190.00	95.00	204 Casey Wise	4.00	2.00
151 Bob Malkmus	4.00	2.00	205 Don Larsen	7.00	3.50
152 Johnny Klippstein	4.00	2.00	206 Carl Furillo	6.00	3.00
153 Jim Marshall	4.00	2.00	207 George Strickland	4.00	2.00
154 Ray Herbert	4.00	2.00	208 Willie Jones	4.00	2.00
155 Enos Slaughter	20.00	10.00	209 Lenny Green	4.00	2.00
156 Ace Hurlers (Billy	7.00	3.50	210 Ed Bailey	4.00	2.00
Pierce, Robin Roberts)			211 Bob Blaylock	4.00	2.00
157 Felix Mantilla	4.00	2.00	212 Fence Busters	50.00	25.00
158 Walt Dropo	4.00	2.00	(Aaron/Mathews)		
159 Bob Shaw	4.00	2.00	213 Jim Rivera	4.00	2.00
160 Dick Groat	6.00	3.00	214 Marcelino Solis	4.00	2.00
161 Frank Baumann	4.00	2.00	215 Jim Lemon	4.00	2.00
162 Bobby G. Smith	4.00	2.00	216 Andre Rodgers	4.00	2.00
163 Sandy Koufax	180.00	90.00	217 Carl Erskine	5.00	2.50
164 Johnny Groth	4.00	2.00	218 Roman Mejiaas	4.00	2.00
165 Bill Bruton	4.00	2.00	219 George Zuverink	4.00	2.00
166 Destruction Crew	8.00	4.00	220 Frank Malzone	5.00	2.50
(Rocky Colavito, Larry			221 Bob Bowman	4.00	2.00
Doby, Minnie Minoso)			222 Bobby Shantz	6.00	3.00
167 Duke Maas	4.00	2.00	223 Cards Team	10.00	5.00
168 Carroll Hardy	4.00	2.00	Checklist 265-352		
169 Ted Abernathy	4.00	2.00	224 Claude Osteen (R)	7.00	3.50
170 Gene Woodling	5.00	2.50	225 Johnny Logan	4.00	2.00
171 Willard Schmidt	4.00	2.00	226 Art Ceccarelli	4.00	2.00
172 A's Team	10.00	5.00	227 Hal Smith	4.00	2.00
Checklist 177-242			228 Don Gross	4.00	2.00
173 Bill Monbouquette (R)	4.00	2.00	229 Vic Power	4.00	2.00
174 Jim Pendleton	4.00	2.00	230 Bill Fischer	4.00	2.00
175 Dick Farrell	4.00	2.00	231 Ellis Burton	4.00	2.00
176 Preston Ward	4.00	2.00	232 Eddie Kasko	4.00	2.00
177 Johnny Briggs	4.00	2.00	233 Paul Foytack	4.00	2.00
178 Ruben Amaro (R)	5.00	2.50	234 Chuck Tanner	4.00	2.00
179 Don Rudolph	4.00	2.00	235 Valmy Thomas	4.00	2.00
180 Yogi Berra	110.00	55.00	236 Ted Bowsfield	4.00	2.00
181 Bob Porterfield	4.00	2.00	237 McDougald, Turley,	7.00	3.50
182 Milt Graff	4.00	2.00	Richardson		
183 Stu Miller	4.00	2.00	238 Gene Baker	4.00	2.00
184 Harvey Haddix	5.00	2.50	239 Bob Trowbridge	4.00	2.00
185 Jim Busby	4.00	2.00	240 Hank Bauer	6.00	3.00
186 Mudcat Grant	4.00	2.00	241 Billy Muffett	4.00	2.00
187 Bubba Phillips	4.00	2.00	242 Ron Samford	4.00	2.00
188 Juan Pizarro	4.00	2.00	243 Marv Grissom	4.00	2.00
189 Neil Chrisley	4.00	2.00	244 Dick Gray	4.00	2.00
190 Bill Virdon	5.00	2.50	245 Ned Garver	4.00	2.00
191 Russ Kemmerer	4.00	2.00	246 J.W. Porter	4.00	2.00
192 Charley Beamon	4.00	2.00	247 Don Ferrarese	4.00	2.00
193 Sammy Taylor	4.00	2.00	248 Red Sox Team	10.00	5.00
194 Jim Brosnan	4.00	2.00	Checklist 177-264		
195 Rip Repulski	4.00	2.00	249 Bobby Adams	4.00	2.00
196 Billy Moran	4.00	2.00	250 Billy O'Dell	4.00	2.00
197 Ray Semproch	4.00	2.00	251 Cletis Boyer	5.00	2.50
198 Jim Davenport	4.00	2.00	252 Ray Boone	4.00	2.00
199 Leo Kiely	4.00	2.00	253 Seth Morehead	4.00	2.00
200 Warren Giles	5.00	2.50	254 Zeke Bella	4.00	2.00
201 Tom Acker	4.00	2.00	255 Del Ennis	4.00	2.00
202 Roger Maris	170.00	85.00	256 Jerry Davie	4.00	2.00

257 Leon Wagner (R)	5.00	2.50
258 Fred Kipp	4.00	2.00
259 Jim Pisoni	4.00	2.00
260 Early Wynn	18.00	9.00
261 Gene Stephens	4.00	2.00
262 Hitters' Foes (Don	8.50	4.25
Drysdale, Clem Labine,		
Johnny Podres)		
263 Buddy Daley	4.00	2.00
264 Chico Carrasquel	4.00	2.00
265 Ron Kline	4.00	2.00
266 Woody Held	4.00	2.00
267 John Romonosky	4.00	2.00
268 Tito Francona	4.00	2.00
269 Jack Meyer	4.00	2.00
270 Gil Hodges	25.00	12.50
271 Orlando Pena (R)	4.00	2.00
272 Jerry Lumpe	4.00	2.00
273 Joe Jay	4.00	2.00
274 Jerry Kindall	4.00	2.00
275 Jack Sanford	4.00	2.00
276 Pete Daley	4.00	2.00
277 Turk Lown	4.00	2.00
278 Chuck Essegian	4.00	2.00
279 Ernie Johnson	4.00	2.00
280 Frank Bolling	4.00	2.00
281 Walt Craddock	4.00	2.00
282 R.C. Stevens	4.00	2.00
283 Russ Heman	4.00	2.00
284 Steve Korcheck	4.00	2.00
285 Joe Cunningham	4.00	2.00
286 Dean Stone	4.00	2.00
287 Don Zimmer	5.00	2.50
288 Dutch Dotterer	4.00	2.00
289 Johnny Kucks	4.00	2.00
290 Wes Covington	5.00	2.50
291 Pitching Partners	4.00	2.00
(Camilo Pascual,		
Pedro Ramos)		
292 Dick Williams	4.00	2.00
293 Ray Moore	4.00	2.00
294 Hank Foiles	4.00	2.00
295 Billy Martin	18.00	9.00
296 Ernie Broglio (R)	6.00	3.00
297 Jackie Brandt	4.00	2.00
298 Tex Clevenger	4.00	2.00
299 Billy Klaus	4.00	2.00
300 Richie Ashburn	15.00	7.50
301 Earl Averill	4.00	2.00
302 Don Mossi	4.00	2.00
303 Marty Keough	4.00	2.00
304 Cubs Team	10.00	5.00
Checklist 265-352		
305 Curt Raydon	4.00	2.00
306 Jim Gilliam	7.00	3.50
307 Curt Barclay	4.00	2.00
308 Norm Siebern	4.00	2.00
309 Sal Maglie	5.00	2.50
310 Luis Aparicio	20.00	10.00
311 Norm Zauchin	4.00	2.00
312 Don Newcombe	6.00	3.00
313 Frank House	4.00	2.00
314 Don Cardwell	4.00	2.00
315 Joe Adcock	5.00	2.50
316aRalph Lumenti	90.00	45.00
(No Option)		
316b Ralph Lumenti	4.00	2.00
(With Option)		
317 N.L. Hitting Kings	28.00	14.00
(Ashburn/Mays)		
318 Rocky Bridges	4.00	2.00
319 Dave Hillman	4.00	2.00
320 Bob Skinner	4.00	2.00
321aBob Giallombardo	90.00	45.00
(No Option)		
321bBob Giallombardo	4.00	2.00
(With Option)		
322aHarry Hanebrink	90.00	45.00
(No Trader		
Statement)		
322bHarry Hanebrink	4.00	2.00
(With Trade)		
323 Frank Sullivan	4.00	2.00
324 Don Demeter	4.00	2.00
325 Ken Boyer	10.00	5.00
326 Marv Throneberry	4.00	2.00
327 Gary Bell	4.00	2.00
328 Lou Skizas	4.00	2.00
329 Tigers Team	10.00	5.00
Checklist 353-429		
330 Gus Triandos	4.00	2.00
331 Steve Boros	4.00	2.00
332 Ray Monzant	4.00	2.00
333 Harry Simpson	4.00	2.00
334 Glen Hobbie	4.00	2.00
335 Johnny Temple	4.00	2.00
336aBilly Loes	90.00	45.00
(No Trade)		
336bBilly Loes (With trade)	4.00	2.00
337 George Crowe	4.00	2.00
338 George Anderson	45.00	22.50
339 Roy Face	5.00	2.50
340 Roy Sievers	4.00	2.00
341 Tom Qualters	4.00	2.00
342 Roy Jablonski	4.00	2.00
343 Billy Hoeft	4.00	2.00
344 Russ Nixon	4.00	2.00
345 Gil McDougald	8.00	4.00
346 Batter Bafflers (Tom	4.00	2.00
Brewer, Dave Sisler)		
347 Bob Buhl	4.00	2.00
348 Ted Lepcio	4.00	2.00
349 Hoyt Wilhelm	20.00	10.00
350 Ernie Banks	80.00	40.00
351 Earl Torgeson	4.00	2.00
352 Robin Roberts	18.00	9.00

353 Curt Flood	6.00	3.00		405 Roy McMillan	4.00	2.00
354 Pete Burnside	4.00	2.00		406 Solly Drake	4.00	2.00
355 Jim Piersall	5.00	2.50		407 Moe Drabowsky	4.00	2.00
356 Bob Mabe	4.00	2.00		408 Keystone Combo	10.00	5.00
357 Dick Stuart (R)	5.00	2.50		(Luis Aparicio,		
358 Ralph Terry	5.00	2.50		Nellie Fox		
359 Bill White (R)	24.00	12.00		409 Gus Zernial	4.00	2.00
360 Al Kaline	70.00	35.00		410 Billy Pierce	4.00	2.00
361 Willard Nixon	4.00	2.00		411 Whitey Lockman	4.00	2.00
362aDolan Nichols	90.00	45.00		412 Stan Lopata	4.00	2.00
(No Option)				413 Camilo Pascual	4.00	2.00
362bDolan Nichols	4.00	2.00		414 Dale Long	4.00	2.00
(With Option)				415 Bill Mazeroski	8.00	4.00
363 Bobby Avila	4.00	2.00		416 Haywood Sullivan	4.00	2.00
364 Danny McDevitt	4.00	2.00		417 Virgil Trucks	4.00	2.00
365 Gus Bell	4.00	2.00		418 Gino Cimoli	4.00	2.00
366 Humberto Robinson	4.00	2.00		419 Braves Team	10.00	5.00
367 Cal Neeman	4.00	2.00		Checklist 353-429		
368 Don Mueller	4.00	2.00		420 Rocky Colavito	20.00	10.00
369 Dick Tomanek	4.00	2.00		421 Herm Wehmeier	4.00	2.00
370 Pete Runnels	5.00	2.50		422 Hobie Landrith	4.00	2.00
371 Dick Brodowski	4.00	2.00		423 Bob Grim	4.00	2.00
372 Jim Hegan	4.00	2.00		424 Ken Aspromonte	4.00	2.00
373 Herb Plews	4.00	2.00		425 Del Crandall	4.00	2.00
374 Art Ditmar	4.00	2.00		426 Jerry Staley	4.00	2.00
375 Bob Nieman	4.00	2.00		427 Charlie Neal	4.00	2.00
376 Hal Naragon	4.00	2.00		428 Buc Hill Aces	5.00	2.50
377 Johnny Antonelli	5.00	2.50		(Roy Face,		
378 Gail Harris	4.00	2.00		Bob Friend,		
379 Bob Miller	4.00	2.00		Ron Kline, Vern Law)		
380 Hank Aaron	140.00	70.00		429 Bobby Thompson	5.00	2.50
381 Mike Baxes	4.00	2.00		430 Whitey Ford	50.00	25.00
382 Curt Simmons	4.00	2.00		431 Whammy Douglas	4.00	2.00
383 Words of Wisdom	8.00	4.00		432 Smoky Burgess	5.00	2.50
(Don Larsen,				433 Billy Harrell	4.00	2.00
Casey Stengel)				434 Hal Griggs	4.00	2.00
384 Dave Sisler	4.00	2.00		435 Frank Robinson	55.00	28.00
385 Sherm Lollar	4.00	2.00		436 Granny Hamner	4.00	2.00
286 Jim Delsing	4.00	2.00		437 Ike Delock	4.00	2.00
387 Don Drysdale	50.00	25.00		438 Sam Esposito	4.00	2.00
388 Bob Will	4.00	2.00		439 Brooks Robinson	60.00	30.00
389 Joe Nuxhall	4.00	2.00		440 Lou Burdette	6.00	3.00
390 Orlando Cepeda	24.00	12.00		441 John Roseboro	6.00	3.00
391 Milt Pappas	4.00	2.00		442 Ray Narleski	4.00	2.00
392 Whitey Herzog	6.00	3.00		443 Daryl Spencer	4.00	2.00
393 Frank Lary	4.00	2.00		444 Ronnie Hansen	4.00	2.00
394 Randy Jackson	4.00	2.00		445 Cal McLish	4.00	2.00
395 Elston Howard	10.00	5.00		446 Rocky Nelson	4.00	2.00
396 Bob Rush	4.00	2.00		447 Bob Anderson	4.00	2.00
397 Senators Team	10.00	5.00		448 Vada Pinson	8.00	4.00
Checklist 430-495				449 Tom Gorman	4.00	2.00
398 Wally Post	4.00	2.00		450 Ed Mathews	28.00	14.00
399 Larry Jackson	4.00	2.00		451 Jimmy Constable	4.00	2.00
400 Jackie Jensen	5.00	2.50		452 Chico Fernandez	4.00	2.00
401 Ron Blackburn	4.00	2.00		453 Les Moss	4.00	2.00
402 Hector Lopez	4.00	2.00		454 Phil Clark	4.00	2.00
403 Clem Labine	5.00	2.50		455 Larry Doby	7.00	3.50
404 Hank Sauer	4.00	2.00		456 Jerry Casale	4.00	2.00

#	Player	Price	Price
457	Dodgers Team Checklist 430-495	15.00	7.50
458	Gordon Jones	4.00	2.00
459	Bill Tuttle	4.00	2.00
460	Bob Friend	4.00	2.00
461	Mickey Mantle (HL)	50.00	25.00
462	Rocky Colavito (HL)	10.00	5.00
463	Al Kaline (HL)	15.00	7.50
464	Willie Mays (HL)	25.00	12.50
465	Roy Sievers (HL)	5.00	2.50
466	Billy Pierce (HL)	5.00	2.50
467	Hank Aaron (HL)	25.00	12.50
468	Duke Snider (HL)	18.00	9.00
469	Ernie Banks (HL)	15.00	7.50
470	Stan Musial (HL)	25.00	12.50
471	Tom Sturdivant	4.00	2.00
472	Gene Freese	4.00	2.00
473	Mike Fornieles	4.00	2.00
474	Moe Thacker	4.00	2.00
475	Jack Harshman	4.00	2.00
476	Indians Team Checklist 496-572	10.00	5.00
477	Barry Latman	4.00	2.00
478	Bob Clemente	140.00	70.00
479	Lindy McDaniel	4.00	2.00
480	Red Schoendienst	15.00	7.50
481	Charley Maxwell	4.00	2.00
482	Russ Meyer	4.00	2.00
483	Clint Courtney	4.00	2.00
484	Willie Kirkland	4.00	2.00
485	Ryne Duren	5.00	2.50
486	Sammy White	4.00	2.00
487	Hal Brown	4.00	2.00
488	Walt Moryn	4.00	2.00
489	John C. Powers	4.00	2.00
490	Frank Thomas	4.00	2.00
491	Don Blasingame	4.00	2.00
492	Gene Conley	4.00	2.00
493	Jim Landis	4.00	2.00
494	Don Pavletich	4.00	2.00
495	Johnny Podres	5.00	2.50
496	Wayne Terwilliger	4.00	2.00
497	Hal R. Smith	4.00	2.00
498	Dick Hyde	4.00	2.00
499	Johnny O'Brien	4.00	2.00
500	Vic Wertz	5.00	2.50
501	Bobby Tiefenauer	4.00	2.00
502	Al Dark	5.00	2.50
503	Jim Owens	4.00	2.00
504	Ossie Alvarez	4.00	2.00
505	Tony Kubek	12.00	6.00
506	Bob Purkey	4.00	2.00
507	Bob Hale	16.00	8.00
508	Art Fowler	16.00	8.00
509	Norm Cash (R)	75.00	38.00
510	Yankees Team Checklist 496-572	75.00	38.00
511	George Susce	16.00	8.00
512	George Altman	16.00	8.00
513	Tom Carroll	16.00	8.00
514	Bob Gibson (R)	400.00	200.00
515	Harmon Killebrew	160.00	80.00
516	Mike Garcia	18.00	9.00
517	Joe Koppe	16.00	8.00
518	Mike Cuellar (R)	24.00	12.00
519	Infield Power (Dick Gernert, Frank Malzone, Pete Runnells)	18.00	9.00
520	Don Elston	16.00	8.00
521	Gary Geiger	16.00	8.00
522	Gene Snyder	16.00	8.00
523	Harry Bright	16.00	8.00
524	Larry Osborne	16.00	8.00
525	Jim Coates	16.00	8.00
526	Bob Speake	16.00	8.00
527	Solly Hemus	16.00	8.00
528	Pirates Team Checklist 496-572	40.00	20.00
529	George Bamberger (R)	18.00	9.00
530	Wally Moon	20.00	10.00
531	Ray Webster	16.00	8.00
532	Mark Freeman	16.00	8.00
533	Darrel Johnson	16.00	8.00
534	Fay Throneberry	16.00	8.00
535	Ruben Gomez	16.00	8.00
536	Dan Kravitz	16.00	8.00
537	Rodolfo Arias	16.00	8.00
538	Chick King	16.00	8.00
539	Gary Blaylock	16.00	8.00
540	Willy Miranda	16.00	8.00
541	Bob Thurman	16.00	8.00
542	Jim Perry (R)	20.00	10.00
543	Corsair Outfield (Clemente, Skinner, Virdon)	75.00	38.00
544	Lee Tate	16.00	8.00
545	Tom Morgan	16.00	8.00
546	Al Schroll	16.00	8.00
547	Jim Baxes	16.00	8.00
548	Elmer Singleton	16.00	8.00
549	Howie Nunn	16.00	8.00
550	Roy Campanella	175.00	90.00
551	Fred Haney As	16.00	8.00
552	Casey Stengel AS	30.00	15.00
553	Orlando Cepeda AS	25.00	12.50
554	Bill Skowron AS	25.00	12.50
555	Bill Mazeroski AS	25.00	12.50
556	Nellie Fox AS	25.00	12.50
557	Ken Boyer AS	25.00	12.50
558	Frank Malzone AS	18.00	9.00
559	Ernie Banks AS	60.00	30.00
560	Luis Aparicio AS	35.00	18.00
561	Hank Aaron AS	140.00	70.00
562	Al Kaline AS	60.00	30.00

		NR/MT	EX
563	Willie Mays AS	140.00	70.00
564	Mickey Mantle AS	310.00	155.00
565	Wes Covington AS	18.00	9.00
566	Roy Sievers As	18.00	9.00
567	Del Crandall AS	18.00	9.00
568	Gus Triandos AS	18.00	9.00
569	Bob Friend AS	18.00	9.00
570	Bob Turley AS	18.00	9.00
571	Warren Spahn AS	40.00	20.00
572	Billy Pierce AS	28.00	14.00

1960 Topps

Topps reverted to a horizontal format in 1960. Card fronts consist of a small color photo and a larger black and white action shot. Subsets include rookie prospects, managers, coaches and, for the first time Topps included a World Series subset. The cards in this 572-card set are 2-1/2" by 3-1/2"

		NR/MT	EX
Complete Set (572)		4,000.00	2,000.00
Commons (1-440)		3.50	1.75
Commons (441-506)		5.00	2.50
Commons (507-572)		12.00	6.00
1	Early Wynn	40.00	18.00
2	Roman Mejias	3.50	1.75
3	Joe Adcock	5.00	2.50
4	Bob Purkey	3.50	1.75
5	Wally Moon	5.00	2.50
6	Lou Berberet	3.50	1.75
7	Master & Mentor	24.00	12.00
	(Willie Mays/		
	Bill Rigney)		
8	Bud Daley	3.50	1.75
9	Faye Thronesberry	3.50	1.75
10	Ernie Banks	60.00	30.00
11	Norm Siebern	3.50	1.75
12	Milt Pappas	3.50	1.75
13	Wally Post	3.50	1.75
14	Jim Grant	3.50	1.75
15	Pete Runnels	5.00	2.50
16	Ernie Broglio	5.00	2.50
17	Johnny Callison	5.00	2.50
18	Dodgers Team	15.00	7.50
	Checklist 1-88		
19	Felix Mantilla	3.50	1.75
20	Roy Face	5.00	2.50
21	Dutch Dotterer	3.50	1.75
22	Rocky Bridges	3.50	1.75
23	Eddie Fisher	3.50	1.75
24	Dick Gray	3.50	1.75
25	Roy Sievers	5.00	2.50
26	Wayne Terwilliger	3.50	1.75
27	Dick Drott	3.50	1.75
28	Brooks Robinson	60.00	30.00
29	Clem Labine	4.00	2.00
30	Tito Francona	3.50	1.75
31	Sammy Esposito	3.50	1.75
32	Sophomore Stalwarts	4.00	2.00
	(Jim O'Toole/		
	Vada Pinson)		
33	Tom Morgan	3.50	1.75
34	George Anderson	10.00	5.00
35	Whitey Ford	48.00	24.00
36	Russ Nixon	3.50	1.75
37	Bill Bruton	3.50	1.75
38	Jerry Casale	3.50	1.75
39	Earl Averill	3.50	1.75
40	Joe Cunningham	3.50	1.75
41	Barry Latman	3.50	1.75
42	Hobie Landrith	3.50	1.75
43	Senators Team	7.00	3.50
	Checklist 1-88		
44	Bobby Locke	3.50	1.75
45	Roy McMillan	3.50	1.75
46	Jack Fisher	3.50	1.75
47	Don Zimmer	5.00	2.50
48	Hal Smith	3.50	1.75
49	Curt Raydon	3.50	1.75
50	Al Kaline	60.00	30.00
51	Jim Coates	3.50	1.75
52	Dave Philley	3.50	1.75
53	Jackie Brandt	3.50	1.75
54	Mike Fornieles	3.50	1.75
55	Bill Mazeroski	7.00	3.50
56	Steve Korcheck	3.50	1.75
57	Win-Savers (Turk	3.50	1.75
	Lown/Jerry Staley)		
58	Gino Cimoli	3.50	1.75
59	Juan Pizarro	3.50	1.75
60	Gus Triandos	3.50	1.75
61	Eddie Kasko	3.50	1.75
62	Roger Craig	5.00	2.50
63	George Strickland	3.50	1.75

No.	Name		
64	Jack Meyer	3.50	1.75
65	Elston Howard	8.00	4.00
66	Bob Trowbridge	3.50	1.75
67	Jose Pagan (R)	4.00	2.00
68	Dave Hillman	3.50	1.75
69	Billy Goodman	3.50	1.75
70	Lou Burdette	6.00	3.00
71	Marty Keough	3.50	1.75
72	Tigers Team Checklist 89-176)	7.00	3.50
73	Bob Gibson	75.00	38.00
74	Walt Moryn	3.50	1.75
75	Vic Power	3.50	1.75
76	Bill Bisher	3.50	1.75
77	Hank Foiles	3.50	1.75
78	Bob Grim	3.50	1.75
79	Walt Dropo	3.50	1.75
80	Johnny Antonelli	4.00	2.00
81	Russ Snyder	3.50	1.75
82	Ruben Gomez	3.50	1.75
83	Tony Kubek	7.00	3.50
84	Hal Smith	3.50	1.75
85	Frank Lary	4.00	2.00
86	Dick Gernert	3.50	1.75
87	John Romonosky	3.50	1.75
88	John Roseboro	5.00	2.50
89	Hal Brown	3.50	1.75
90	Bobby Avila	3.50	1.75
91	Bennie Daniels	3.50	1.75
92	Whitey Herzog	5.00	2.50
93	Art Schult	3.50	1.75
94	Leo Kiely	3.50	1.75
95	Frank Thomas	3.50	1.75
96	Ralph Terry	4.00	2.00
97	Ted Lepcio	3.50	1.75
98	Gordon Jones	3.50	1.75
99	Lenny Green	3.50	1.75
100	Nellie Fox	10.00	5.00
101	Bob Miller	3.50	1.75
102	Kent Hadley	3.50	1.75
103	Dick Farrell	3.50	1.75
104	Dick Schofield	3.50	1.75
105	Larry Sherry	5.00	2.50
106	Billy Gardner	3.50	1.75
107	Carl Willey	3.50	1.75
108	Pete Daley	3.50	1.75
109	Cletis Boyer	5.00	2.50
110	Cal McLish	3.50	1.75
111	Vic Wertz	3.50	1.75
112	Jack Harshman	3.50	1.75
113	Bob Skinner	3.50	1.75
114	Ken Aspromonte	3.50	1.75
115	Fork & Knuckler (Roy Face, Hoyt Wilhelm)	7.00	3.50
116	Jim Rivera	3.50	1.75
117	Tom Borland	3.50	1.75
118	Bob Bruce	3.50	1.75
119	Chico Cardenas	3.50	1.75
120	Duke Carmel	3.50	1.75
121	Camilo Carreon	3.50	1.75
122	Don Dillad	3.50	1.75
123	Dan Dobbek	3.50	1.75
124	Jim Donohue	3.50	1.75
125	Dick Ellsworth (R)	5.00	2.50
126	Chuck Estrada (R)	4.00	2.00
127	Ronnie Hansen	5.00	2.50
128	Bill Harris	3.50	1.75
129	Bob Hartman	3.50	1.75
130	Frank Herrera	3.50	1.75
131	Ed Hobaugh	3.50	1.75
132	Frank Howard (R)	15.00	7.50
133	Julian Javier (R)	4.00	2.00
134	Deron Johnson	3.50	1.75
135	Ken Johnson	3.50	1.75
136	Jim Kaat	38.00	20.00
137	Lou Klimchock	3.50	1.75
138	Art Mahaffey (R)	3.50	1.75
139	Carl Mathias	3.50	1.75
140	Julio Navarro	3.50	1.75
141	Jim Proctor	3.50	1.75
142	Bill Short	3.50	1.75
143	Al Spangler	3.50	1.75
144	Al Stieglitz	3.50	1.75
145	Jim Umricht	3.50	1.75
146	Ted Wieand	3.50	1.75
147	Bob Will	3.50	1.75
148	Carl Yastrzemski (R)	325.00	165.00
149	Bob Nieman	3.50	1.75
150	Billy Pierce	3.50	1.75
151	Giants Team Checklist 177-264	10.00	5.00
152	Gail Harris	3.50	1.75
153	Bobby Thompson	4.00	2.00
154	Jim Davenport	3.50	1.75
155	Charlie Neal	3.50	1.75
156	Art Ceccarelli	3.50	1.75
157	Rocky Nelson	3.50	1.75
158	Wes Covington	3.50	1.75
159	Jim Piersall	4.00	2.00
160	Rival All Stars (Ken Boyer/Mickey Mantle)	50.00	25.00
161	Ray Narleski	3.50	1.75
162	Sammy Taylor	3.50	1.75
163	Hector Lopez	3.50	1.75
164	Reds Team Checklist 89-176	7.00	3.50
165	Jack Sanford	3.50	1.75
166	Chuck Essegian	3.50	1.75
167	Valmy Thomas	3.50	1.75
168	Alex Grammas	3.50	1.75
169	Jake Striker	3.50	1.75
170	Del Crandall	3.50	1.75
171	Johnny Groth	3.50	1.75
172	Willie Kirkland	3.50	1.75
173	Billy Martin	14.00	7.00

174	Indians Team Checklist 89-176	7.00	3.50
175	Pedro Ramos	3.50	1.75
176	Vada Pinson	7.00	3.50
177	Johnny Kucks	3.50	1.75
178	Woody Held	3.50	1.75
179	Rip Coleman	3.50	1.75
180	Harry Simpson	3.50	1.75
181	Billy Loes	3.50	1.75
182	Glen Hobbie	3.50	1.75
183	Eli Grba	3.50	1.75
184	Gary Geiger	3.50	1.75
185	Jim Owens	3.50	1.75
186	Dave Sisler	3.50	1.75
187	Jay Hook	3.50	1.75
188	Dick Williams	3.50	1.75
189	Don McMahon	3.50	1.75
190	Gene Woodling	4.00	2.00
191	Johnny Klippstein	3.50	1.75
192	Danny O'Connell	3.50	1.75
193	Dick Hyde	3.50	1.75
194	Bobby Gene Smith	3.50	1.75
195	Lindy McDaniel	3.50	1.75
196	Andy Carey	3.50	1.75
197	Ron Kline	3.50	1.75
198	Jerry Lynch	3.50	1.75
199	Dick Donovan	3.50	1.75
200	Willie Mays	125.00	65.00
201	Larry Osborne	3.50	1.75
202	Fred Kipp	3.50	1.75
203	Sammy White	3.50	1.75
204	Ryne Duren	4.00	2.00
205	Johnny Logan	3.50	1.75
206	Claude Osteen	4.00	2.00
207	Bob Boyd	3.50	1.75
208	White Sox Team Checklist 177-264	7.00	3.50
209	Ron Blackburn	3.50	1.75
210	Harmon Killebrew	32.00	16.00
211	Taylor Phillips	3.50	1.75
212	Walt Alston	10.00	5.00
213	Chuck Dressen	3.50	1.75
214	Jimmie Dykes	3.50	1.75
215	Bob Elliott	3.50	1.75
216	Joe Gordon	3.50	1.75
217	Charley Grimm	3.50	1.75
218	Solly Hemus	3.50	1.75
219	Fred Hutchinson	3.50	1.75
220	Billy Jurges	3.50	1.75
221	Cookie Lavagetto	3.50	1.75
222	Al Lopez	5.00	2.50
223	Danny Murtaugh	3.50	1.75
224	Paul Richards	3.50	1.75
225	Bill Rigney	3.50	1.75
226	Eddie Sawyer	3.50	1.75
227	Casey Stengel	20.00	10.00
228	Ernie Johnson	3.50	1.75
229	Joe Morgan	3.50	1.75
230	Mound Magicians (Bob Buhl, Lou Burdette, Warren Spahn)	8.00	4.00
231	Hal Naragon	3.50	1.75
233	Don Elston	3.50	1.75
234	Don Demeter	3.50	1.75
235	Gus Bell	3.50	1.75
236	Dick Ricketts	3.50	1.75
237	Elmer Valo	3.50	1.75
238	Danny Kravitz	3.50	1.75
239	Joe Shipley	3.50	1.75
240	Luis Aparicio	15.00	7.50
241	Albie Pearson	3.50	1.75
242	Cards Team Checklist 265-352	7.00	3.50
243	Bubba Phillips	3.50	1.75
244	Hal Griggs	3.50	1.75
245	Eddie Yost	3.50	1.75
246	Lee Maye	3.50	1.75
247	Gil McDougald	5.00	2.50
248	Del Rice	3.50	1.75
249	Earl Wilson (R)	4.00	2.00
250	Stan Musial	125.00	65.00
251	Bobby Malkmus	3.50	1.75
252	Ray Herbert	3.50	1.75
253	Eddie Berssoud	3.50	1.75
254	Arnie Portocarrero	3.50	1.75
255	Jim Gilliam	6.00	3.00
256	Dick Brown	3.50	1.75
257	Gordy Coleman (R)	4.00	2.00
258	Dick Groat	5.00	2.50
259	George Altman	3.50	1.75
260	Power Plus (Rocky Colavito/Tito Francona)	5.00	2.50
261	Pete Burnside	3.50	1.75
262	Hank Bauer	4.00	2.00
263	Darrell Johnson	3.50	1.75
264	Robin Roberts	15.00	7.50
265	Rip Repulski	3.50	1.75
266	Joe Jay	3.50	1.75
267	Jim Marshall	3.50	1.75
268	Al Worthington	3.50	1.75
269	Gene Green	3.50	1.75
270	Bob Turley	4.00	2.00
271	Julio Becquer	3.50	1.75
272	Fred Green	3.50	1.75
273	Neil Chrisley	3.50	1.75
274	Tom Acker	3.50	1.75
275	Curt Flood	5.00	2.50
276	Ken McBride	3.50	1.75
277	Harry Bright	3.50	1.75
278	Stan Williams	3.50	1.75
279	Chuck Tanner	3.50	1.75
280	Frank Sullivan	3.50	1.75
281	Ray Boone	3.50	1.75
282	Joe Nuxhall	3.50	1.75
283	John Blanchard	4.00	2.00

No.	Player		
284	Don Gross	3.50	1.75
285	Harry Anderson	3.50	1.75
286	Ray Semproch	3.50	1.75
287	Felipe Alou	7.00	3.50
288	Bob Mabe	3.50	1.75
289	Willie Jones	3.50	1.75
290	Jerry Lumpe	3.50	1.75
291	Bob Keegan	3.50	1.75
292	Dodger Backstops	4.00	2.00
	(Joe Pignatano,		
	John Roseboro)	3.50	1.75
293	Gene Conley	3.50	1.75
294	Tony Taylor	3.50	1.75
295	Gil Hodges	24.00	12.00
296	Nelson Chittum	3.50	1.75
297	Reno Bertoia	3.50	1.75
298	George Witt	3.50	1.75
299	Earl Torgeson	3.50	1.75
300	Hank Aaron	130.00	65.00
301	Jerry Davie	3.50	1.75
302	Phillies Team	7.00	3.50
	Checklist 353-429		
303	Billy O'Dell	3.50	1.75
304	Joe Ginsberg	3.50	1.75
305	Richie Ashburn	10.00	5.00
306	Frank Baumann	3.50	1.75
307	Gene Oliver	3.50	1.75
308	Dick Hall	3.50	1.75
309	Bob Hale	3.50	1.75
310	Frank Malzone	3.50	1.75
311	Raul Sanchez	3.50	1.75
312	Charlie Lau	3.50	1.75
313	Turk Lown	3.50	1.75
314	Chico Fernandez	3.50	1.75
315	Bobby Shantz	4.00	2.00
316	Willie McCovey (R)	275.00	140.00
317	Pumpsie Green	3.50	1.75
318	Jim Baxes	3.50	1.75
319	Joe Koppe	3.50	1.75
320	Bob Allison	6.00	3.00
321	Ron Fairly	5.00	2.50
322	Willie Tasby	3.50	1.75
323	Johnny Romano	3.50	1.75
324	Jim Perry	5.00	2.50
325	Jim O'Toole	4.00	2.00
326	Roberto Clemente	140.00	70.00
327	Ray Sadecki (R)	4.00	2.00
328	Earl Battey	3.50	1.75
329	Zack Monroe	3.50	1.75
330	Harvey Kuenn	5.00	2.50
331	Henry Mason	3.50	1.75
332	Yankees Team	25.00	12.50
	Checklist 265-352		
333	Danny McDevitt	3.50	1.75
334	Ted Abernathy	3.50	1.75
335	Red Schoendienst	12.00	6.00
336	Ike Delock	3.50	1.75
337	Cal Neeman	3.50	1.75
338	Ray Monzant	3.50	1.75
339	Harry Chiti	3.50	1.75
340	Harvey Haddix	4.00	2.00
341	Carroll Hardy	3.50	1.75
342	Casey Wise	3.50	1.75
343	Sandy Koufax	140.00	70.00
344	Clint Courtney	3.50	1.75
345	Don Newcombe	5.00	2.50
346	J.C. Martin (Wrong	3.50	1.75
	Photo)		
347	Ed Bouchee	3.50	1.75
348	Barry Shetrone	3.50	1.75
349	Moe Drabowsky	3.50	1.75
350	Micky Mantle	425.00	215.00
351	Don Nottebart	3.50	1.75
352	Cincy Clouters (Gus	8.00	4.00
	Bell, Jerry Lynch		
	Frank Robinson)	3.50	1.75
353	Don Larsen	5.00	2.50
354	Bob Lillis	3.50	1.75
355	Bill White	6.00	3.00
356	Joe Amalfitano	3.50	1.75
357	Al Schroll	3.50	1.75
358	Joe DeMaestri	3.50	1.75
359	Buddy Gilbert	3.50	1.75
360	Herb Score	4.00	2.00
361	Bob Oldis	3.50	1.75
362	Russ Kemmerer	3.50	1.75
363	Gene Stephens	3.50	1.75
364	Paul Foytack	3.50	1.75
365	Minnie Minoso	7.00	3.50
366	Dallas Green (R)	8.50	4.25
367	Bill Tuttle	3.50	1.75
368	Daryl Spencer	3.50	1.75
369	Billy Hoeft	3.50	1.75
370	Bill Skowron	7.00	3.50
371	Bud Byerly	3.50	1.75
372	Frank House	3.50	1.75
373	Don Hoak	3.50	1.75
374	Bob Buhl	3.50	1.75
375	Dale Long	3.50	1.75
376	Johnny Briggs	3.50	1.75
377	Roger Maris	125.00	65.00
378	Stu Miller	3.50	1.75
379	Red Wilson	3.50	1.75
380	Bob Shaw	3.50	1.75
381	Braves Team	7.00	3.50
	Checklist 353-429		
382	Ted Bowsfield	3.50	1.75
383	Leon Wagner	3.50	1.75
384	Don Cardwell	3.50	1.75
385	World Series Game 1	5.00	2.50
386	World Series Game 2	5.00	2.50
387	World Series Game 3	5.00	2.50
388	World Series Game 4	10.00	5.00
389	World Series Game 5	8.00	4.00
390	World Series Game 6	5.00	2.50
391	W. S. Summary	5.00	2.50

No.	Player		
392	Tex Clevenger	3.50	1.75
393	Smoky Burgess	4.00	2.00
394	Norm Larker	3.50	1.75
395	Hoyt Wilhelm	12.00	6.00
396	Steve Bilko	3.50	1.75
397	Don Blasingame	3.50	1.75
398	Mike Cuellar	4.00	2.00
399	Young Hill Stars	3.50	1.75
	(Jack Fisher, Milt		
	Pappas, Jerry Walker)		
400	Rocky Colavito	12.00	6.00
401	Bob Duliba	5.00	2.50
402	Dick Stuart	5.00	2.50
403	Ed Sadowski	5.00	2.50
404	Bob Rush	5.00	2.50
405	Bobby Richardson	8.00	4.00
406	Billy Klaus	5.00	2.50
407	Gary Peters (R)	5.00	2.50
	(Wrong Photo)		
408	Carl Furillo	6.00	3.00
409	Ron Samford	5.00	2.50
410	Sam Jones	5.00	2.50
411	Ed Bailey	5.00	2.50
412	Bob Anderson	5.00	2.50
413	A's Team	7.00	3.50
	Checklist 430-495		
414	Don Williams	5.00	2.50
415	Bob Cerv	5.00	2.50
416	Humberto Robinso	5.00	2.50
417	Chuck Cottier (R)	5.00	2.50
418	Don Mossi	5.00	2.50
419	George Crowe	5.00	2.50
420	Ed Mathews	38.00	20.00
421	Duke Maas	5.00	2.50
422	Johnny Powers	5.00	2.50
423	Ed FitzGerald	5.00	2.50
424	Pete Whisenant	5.00	2.50
425	Johnny Podres	5.00	2.50
426	Ron Jackson	5.00	2.50
427	Al Grunwald	5.00	2.50
428	Al Smith	5.00	2.50
429	AL Kings (Nellie Fox,	7.00	3.50
	Harvey Kuenn)		
430	Art Ditmar	5.00	2.50
431	Andre Rodgers	5.00	2.50
432	Chuck Stobbs	5.00	2.50
433	Irv Noren	5.00	2.50
434	Brooks Lawrence	5.00	2.50
435	Gene Freese	5.00	2.50
436	Marv Throneberry	5.00	2.50
437	Bob Friend	5.00	2.50
438	Jim Coker	5.00	2.50
439	Tom Brewer	5.00	2.50
440	Jim Lemon	5.00	2.50
441	Gary Bell	5.00	2.50
442	Joe Pignatano	5.00	2.50
443	Charlie Maxwell	5.00	2.50
444	Jerry Kindall	5.00	2.50
445	Warren Spahn	55.00	28.00
446	Ellis Burton	5.00	2.50
447	Ray Moore	5.00	2.50
448	Jim Gentile (R)	12.00	6.00
449	Jim Brosnan	5.00	2.50
450	Orlando Cepeda	16.00	8.00
451	Curt Simmons	5.00	2.50
452	Ray Webster	5.00	2.50
453	Vern Law	6.00	3.00
454	Hal Woodeshick	5.00	2.50
455	Orioles Coaches	5.00	2.50
456	Red Sox Coaches	7.00	3.50
457	Cubs Coaches	5.00	2.50
458	White Sox Coaches	5.00	2.50
459	Reds Coaches	5.00	2.50
460	Indians Coaches	7.00	3.50
461	Tigers Coaches	7.00	3.50
462	A's Coaches	5.00	2.50
463	Dodgers Coaches	5.00	2.50
464	Braves Coaches	5.00	2.50
465	Yankees Coaches	10.00	5.00
466	Phillies Coaches	5.00	2.50
467	Pirates Coaches	5.00	2.50
468	Cardinals Coaches	5.00	2.50
469	Giants Coaches	5.00	2.50
470	Senators Coaches	5.00	2.50
471	Ned Garver	5.00	2.50
472	Al Dark	5.00	2.50
473	Al Cicotte	5.00	2.50
474	Haywood Sullivan	5.00	2.50
475	Don Drysdale	50.00	25.00
476	Lou Johnson	5.00	2.50
477	Don Ferrarese	5.00	2.50
478	Frank Torre	5.00	2.50
479	Georges Maranda	5.00	2.50
480	Yogi Berra	90.00	45.00
481	Wes Stock	5.00	2.50
482	Frank Bolling	5.00	2.50
483	Camilo Pascual	5.00	2.50
484	Pirates Team	20.00	10.00
	Checklist 430-495		
485	Ken Boyer	12.00	6.00
486	Bobby Del Greco	5.00	2.50
487	Tom Sturdivant	5.00	2.50
488	Norm Cash	14.00	7.00
489	Steve Ridzik	5.00	2.50
490	Frank Robinson	60.00	30.00
491	Mel Roach	5.00	2.50
492	Larry Jackson	5.00	2.50
493	Duke Snider	70.00	35.00
494	Orioles Team	10.00	5.00
	Checklist 496-572		
495	Sherm Lollar	5.00	2.50
496	Bill Virdon	6.00	3.00
497	John Tsitouris	5.00	2.50
498	Al Pilarcik	5.00	2.50
499	Johnny James	5.00	2.50
500	Johnny Temple	5.00	2.50

501	Bob Schmidt	5.00	2.50
502	Jim Bunning	14.00	7.00
503	Don Lee	5.00	2.50
504	Seth Morehead	5.00	2.50
505	Ted Kluszewski	10.00	5.00
506	Lee Walls	5.00	2.50
507	Dick Stigman	12.00	6.00
508	Billy Consolo	12.00	6.00
509	Tommy Davis (R)	28.00	14.00
510	Jerry Staley	12.00	6.00
511	Ken Walters	12.00	6.00
512	Joe Gibbon	12.00	6.00
513	Cubs Team Checklist 496-572	32.00	16.00
514	Steve Barber (R)	14.00	7.00
515	Stan Lopata	12.00	6.00
516	Marty Kutyna	12.00	6.00
517	Charley James	12.00	6.00
518	Tony Gonzalez (R)	14.00	7.00
519	Ed Roebuck	12.00	6.00
520	Don Buddin	12.00	6.00
521	Mike Lee	12.00	6.00
522	Ken Hunt	12.00	6.00
523	Clay Dalrymple (R)	12.00	6.00
524	Bill Henry	12.00	6.00
525	Marv Breeding	12.00	6.00
526	Paul Giel	12.00	6.00
527	Jose Valdivielso	12.00	6.00
528	Ben Johnson	12.00	6.00
529	Norm Sherry (R)	15.00	7.50
530	Mike McCormick	12.00	6.00
531	Sandy Amoros	12.00	6.00
532	Mike Garcia	12.00	6.00
533	Lu Clinton	12.00	6.00
534	Ken MacKenzie	12.00	6.00
535	Whitey Lockman	12.00	6.00
536	Wynn Hawkins	12.00	6.00
537	Red Sox Team Checklist 496-572	32.00	16.00
538	Frank Barnes	12.00	6.00
539	Gene Baker	12.00	6.00
540	Jerry Walker	12.00	6.00
541	Tony Curry	12.00	6.00
542	Ken Hamlin	12.00	6.00
543	Elio Chacon	12.00	6.00
544	Bill Monbouquette	12.00	6.00
545	Carl Sawatski	12.00	6.00
546	Hank Aguirre	12.00	6.00
547	Bob Aspromonte	12.00	6.00
548	Don Mincher	12.00	6.00
549	John Buzhardt	12.00	6.00
550	Jim Landis	12.00	6.00
551	Ed Rakow	12.00	6.00
552	Walt Bond	12.00	6.00
553	Bill Skowron AS	15.00	7.50
554	Willie McCovey As	75.00	38.00
555	Nellie Fox AS	18.00	9.00
556	Charlie Neal AS	12.00	6.00

557	Frank Malzone AS	12.00	6.00
558	Eddie Mathews AS	35.00	18.00
559	Luis Aparicio AS	25.00	12.50
560	Ernie Banks AS	60.00	30.00
561	Al Kaline AS	60.00	30.00
562	Joe Cunningham AS	12.00	6.00
563	Mickey Mantle AS	325.00	165.00
564	Willie Mays AS	130.00	65.00
565	Roger Maris AS	125.00	60.00
566	Hank Aaron AS	130.00	65.00
567	Sherm Lollar AS	12.00	6.00
568	Del Crandall AS	12.00	6.00
569	Camilo Pascual AS	12.00	6.00
570	Don Drysdale AS	38.00	20.00
571	Billy Pierce AS	12.00	6.00
572	Johnny Antonelli AS	24.00	12.00

1961 Topps

For 1961 Topps returned to a vertical design on the card fronts which feature large color close up shots. Although the checklist is numbered through #589, only 587 cards were issued. Numbers 587 and 588 were never issued. For the first time Topps included a League Leaders subset (41-50). Cards measure 2-1/2" by 3-1/2".

	NR/MT	EX
Complete (Set 587)	5,800.00	2,900.00
Commons (1-370)	3.00	1.50
Commons (371-522)	4.50	2.25
Commons (523-589)	32.00	16.00

1	Dick Groat	20.00	8.50
2	Roger Maris	190.00	95.00
3	John Buzhardt	3.00	1.50
4	Lenny Green	3.00	1.50

5	Johnny Romano	3.00	1.50
6	Ed Roebuck	3.00	1.50
7	White Sox Team	5.00	2.50
8	Dick Williams	3.00	1.50
9	Bob Purkey	3.00	1.50
10	Brooks Robinson	40.00	20.00
11	Curt Simmons	3.00	1.50
12	Moe Thacker	3.00	1.50
13	Chuck Cottier	3.00	1.50
14	Don Mossi	3.00	1.50
15	Willie Kirkland	3.00	1.50
16	Billy Muffett	3.00	1.50
17	Checklist 1-88	8.00	4.00
18	Jim Grant	3.00	1.50
19	Cletis Boyer	3.00	1.50
20	Robin Roberts	12.50	6.25
21	Zoilo Versalles (R)	5.00	2.50
22	Clem Labine	3.00	1.50
23	Don Demeter	3.00	1.50
24	Ken Johnson	3.00	1.50
25	Red's Artillery (Gus Bell, Vada Pinson, Frank Robinson)	8.00	4.00
26	Wes Stock	3.00	1.50
27	Jerry Kindall	3.00	1.50
28	Hector Lopez	3.00	1.50
29	Don Nottebart	3.00	1.50
30	Nellie Fox	8.00	4.00
31	Bob Schmidt	3.00	1.50
32	Ray Sadecki	3.00	1.50
33	Gary Geiger	3.00	1.50
34	Wynn Hawkins	3.00	1.50
35	Ron Santo (R)	50.00	25.00
36	Jack Kralick	3.00	1.50
37	Charlie Maxwell	3.00	1.50
38	Bob Lillis	3.00	1.50
39	Leo Posada	3.00	1.50
40	Bob Turley	3.00	1.50
41	N.L. Batting Leaders	12.00	6.00
42	A.L. Batting Leaders	6.00	3.00
43	N.L. HR Leaders	15.00	7.50
44	A.L. HR Leaders	38.00	20.00
45	N.L. E.R.A. Leaders	6.00	3.00
46	A.L. E.R.A. Leaders	6.00	3.00
47	N.L. Pitching Leaders	7.00	3.50
48	A.L. Pitching Leaders	6.00	3.00
49	N.L. Strikeout Ldrs	10.00	5.00
50	A.L. Strkeout Leaders	7.00	3.50
51	Tigers Team	5.00	2.50
52	George Crowe	3.00	1.50
53	Russ Nixon	3.00	1.50
54	Earl Francis	3.00	1.50
55	Jim Davenport	3.00	1.50
56	Russ Kemmerer	3.00	1.50
57	Marv Throneberry	3.00	1.50
58	Joe Schaffernoth	3.00	1.50
59	Jim Woods	3.00	1.50
60	Woodie Held	3.00	1.50
61	Ron Piche	3.00	1.50
62	Al Pilarcik	3.00	1.50
63	Jim Kaat	10.00	5.00
64	Alex Grammas	3.00	1.50
65	Ted Kluszewski	7.00	3.50
66	Bill Henry	3.00	1.50
67	Ossie Virgil	3.00	1.50
68	Deron Johnson	3.00	1.50
69	Earl Wilson	3.00	1.50
70	Bill Virdon	4.00	2.00
71	Jerry Adair	3.00	1.50
72	Stu Miller	3.00	1.50
73	Al Spangler	3.00	1.50
74	Joe Pignatano	3.00	1.50
75	Larry Jackson/Lindy McDaniel)	3.00	1.50
76	Harry Anderson	3.00	1.50
77	Dick Stigman	3.00	1.50
78	Lee Walls	3.00	1.50
79	Joe Ginsberg	3.00	1.50
80	Harmon Killebrew	25.00	12.50
81	Tracy Stallard	3.00	1.50
82	Joe Christopher	3.00	1.50
83	Bob Bruce	3.00	1.50
84	Lee Maye	3.00	1.50
85	Jerry Walker	3.00	1.50
86	Dodgers Team	7.00	3.50
87	Joe Amalfitano	3.00	1.50
88	Richie Ashburn	8.50	4.25
89	Billy Martin	10.00	5.00
90	Jerry Staley	3.00	1.50
91	Walt Moryn	3.00	1.50
92	Hal Naragon	3.00	1.50
93	Tony Gonzalez	3.00	1.50
94	Johnny Kucks	3.00	1.50
95	Norm Cash	8.00	4.00
96	Billy O'Dell	3.00	1.50
97	Jerry Lynch	3.00	1.50
98a	Checklist 89-176	8.00	4.00
99	Don Buddin	3.00	1.50
100	Harvey Haddix	4.00	2.00
101	Bubba Phillips	3.00	1.50
102	Gene Stephens	3.00	1.50
103	Ruben Amaro	3.00	1.50
104	John Blanchard	3.00	1.50
105	Carl Willey	3.00	1.50
106	Whitey Herzog	4.00	2.00
107	Seth Morehead	3.00	1.50
108	Dan Dobbek	3.00	1.50
109	Johnny Podres	4.00	2.00
110	Vada Pinson	6.00	3.00
111	Jack Meyer	3.00	1.50
112	Chico Fernandez	3.00	1.50
113	Mike Fornieles	3.00	1.50
114	Hobie Landrith	3.00	1.50
115	Johnny Antonelli	4.00	2.00
116	Joe DeMaestri	3.00	1.50
117	Dale Long	3.00	1.50

118	Chris Cannizzaro	3.00	1.50
119	A's Big Armor (Hank Bauer, Jerry Lumpe, Norm Siebern)	3.00	1.50
120	Ed Mathews	30.00	15.00
121	Eli Grba	3.00	1.50
122	Cubs Team	5.00	2.50
123	Billy Gardner	3.00	1.50
124	J.C. Martin	3.00	1.50
125	Steve Barber	3.00	1.50
126	Dick Stuart	3.00	1.50
127	Ron Kline	3.00	1.50
128	Rip Repulski	3.00	1.50
129	Ed Hobaugh	3.00	1.50
130	Norm Larker	3.00	1.50
131	Paul Richards	3.00	1.50
132	Al Lopez	4.00	2.00
133	Ralph Houk	4.00	2.00
134	Mickey Vernon	3.00	1.50
135	Fred Hutchinson	4.00	2.00
136	Walt Alston	5.00	2.50
137	Chuck Dressen	3.00	1.50
138	Danny Murtaugh	4.00	2.00
139	Solly Hemus	3.00	1.50
140	Gus Triandos	3.00	1.50
141	Billy Williams (R)	125.00	65.00
142	Luis Arroyo	3.00	1.50
143	Russ Snyder	3.00	1.50
144	Jim Coker	3.00	1.50
145	Bob Buhl	3.00	1.50
146	Marty Keough	3.00	1.50
147	Ed Rakow	3.00	1.50
148	Julian Javier	3.00	1.50
149	Bob Oldis	3.00	1.50
150	Willie Mays	140.00	70.00
151	Jim Donohue	3.00	1.50
152	Earl Torgeson	3.00	1.50
153	Don Lee	3.00	1.50
154	Bobby Del Greco	3.00	1.50
155	Johnny Temple	3.00	1.50
156	Ken Hunt	3.00	1.50
157	Cal McLish	3.00	1.50
158	Pete Daley	3.00	1.50
159	Orioles Team	5.00	2.50
160	Whitey Ford	40.00	20.00
161	Sherman Jones (Wrong Photo)	3.00	1.50
162	Jay Hook	3.00	1.50
163	Ed Sadowsi	3.00	1.50
164	Felix Mantilla	3.00	1.50
165	Gino Cimoli	3.00	1.50
166	Danny Kravitz	3.00	1.50
167	Giants Team	5.00	2.50
168	Tommy Davis	8.00	4.00
169	Don Elston	3.00	1.50
170	Al Smith	3.00	1.50
171	Paul Foytack	3.00	1.50
172	Don Dillard	3.00	1.50
173	Beantown Bombers (Jackie Jensen, Frank Malzone, Vic Wertz)	4.00	2.00
174	Ray Semproch	3.00	1.50
175	Gene Freese	3.00	1.50
176	Ken Aspromonte	3.00	1.50
177	Don Larsen	4.50	2.25
178	Bob Nieman	3.00	1.50
179	Joe Koppe	3.00	1.50
180	Bobby Richardson	8.00	4.00
181	Fred Green	3.00	1.50
182	Dave Nicholson	3.00	1.50
183	Andre Rodgers	3.00	1.50
184	Steve Bilko	3.00	1.50
185	Herb Score	4.00	2.00
186	Elmer Valo	3.00	1.50
187	Billy Klaus	3.00	1.50
188	Jim Marshall	3.00	1.50
189	Checklist 177-264	8.00	5.00
190	Stan Williams	3.00	1.50
191	Mike de la Hoz	3.00	1.50
192	Dick Brown	3.00	1.50
193	Gene Conley	3.00	1.50
194	Gordy Coleman	3.00	1.50
195	Jerry Casale	3.00	1.50
196	Ed Bouchee	3.00	1.50
197	Dick Hall	3.00	1.50
198	Carl Sawatski	3.00	1.50
199	Bob Boyd	3.00	1.50
200	Warren Spahn	38.00	20.00
201	Pete Whisenant	3.00	1.50
202	Al Neiger	3.00	1.50
203	Eddie Bressoud	3.00	1.50
204	Bob Skinner	3.00	1.50
205	Bill Pierce	3.00	1.50
206	Gene Green	3.00	1.50
207	Dodger Southpaws (Sandy Koufax, Johnny Podres)	24.00	12.00
208	Larry Osborne	3.00	1.50
209	Ken McBride	3.00	1.50
210	Pete Runnels	4.00	2.00
211	Bob Gibson	45.00	22.50
212	Haywood Sullivan	3.00	1.50
213	Bill Stafford	3.00	1.50
214	Danny Murphy	3.00	1.50
215	Gus Bell	3.00	1.50
216	Ted Bowsfield	3.00	1.50
217	Mel Roach	3.00	1.50
218	Hal Brown	3.00	1.50
219	Gene Mauch	4.00	2.00
220	Al Dark	3.00	1.50
221	Mike Higgins	3.00	1.50
222	Jimmie Dykes	4.00	2.00
223	Bob Scheffing	3.00	1.50
224	Joe Gordon	4.00	2.00
225	Bill Rigney	3.00	1.50
226	Harry Lavagetto	3.00	1.50

227	Juan Pizarro	3.00	1.50
228	Yankees Team	24.00	12.00
229	Rudy Hernandez	3.00	1.50
230	Don Hoak	3.00	1.50
231	Dick Drott	3.00	1.50
232	Bill White	4.00	2.00
233	Joe Jay	3.00	1.50
234	Ted Lepcio	3.00	1.50
235	Camilo Pascual	3.00	1.50
236	Don Gile	3.00	1.50
237	Billy Loes	3.00	1.50
238	Jim Gilliam	5.00	2.50
239	Dave Sisler	3.00	1.50
240	Ron Hansen	3.00	1.50
241	Al Cicotte	3.00	1.50
242	Hal W. Smith	3.00	1.50
243	Frank Lary	4.00	2.00
244	Chico Cardenas	3.00	1.50
245	Joe Adcock	4.00	2.00
246	Bob Davis	3.00	1.50
247	Billy Goodman	3.00	1.50
248	Ed Keegan	3.00	1.50
249	Reds Team	5.00	2.50
250	Buc Hill Aces (Roy Face, Vern Law)	4.00	2.00
251	Bill Bruton	3.00	1.50
252	Bill Short	3.00	1.50
253	Sammy Taylor	3.00	1.50
254	Ted Sadowski	3.00	1.50
255	Vic Power	3.00	1.50
256	Billy Hoeft	3.00	1.50
257	Carroll Hardy	3.00	1.50
258	Jack Sanford	3.00	1.50
259	John Schaive	3.00	1.50
260	Don Drysdale	30.00	15.00
261	Charlie Lau	3.00	1.50
262	Tony Curry	3.00	1.50
263	Ken Hamlin	3.00	1.50
264	Glen Hobbie	3.00	1.50
265	Tony Kubek	8.00	4.00
266	Lindy McDaniel	3.00	1.50
267	Norm Siebern	3.00	1.50
268	Ike Delock	3.00	1.50
269	Harry Chiti	3.00	1.50
270	Bob Friend	3.00	1.50
271	Jim Landis	3.00	1.50
272	Tom Morgan	3.00	1.50
273	Checklist 265-352	8.00	4.00
274	Gary Bell	3.00	1.50
275	Gene Woodling	3.00	1.50
276	Ray Rippelmeyer	3.00	1.50
277	Hank Foiles	3.00	1.50
278	Don McMahon	3.00	1.50
279	Jose Pagan	3.00	1.50
280	Frank Howard	6.00	3.00
281	Frank Sullivan	3.00	1.50
282	Faye Throneberry	3.00	1.50
283	Bob Anderson	3.00	1.50
284	Dick Gernert	3.00	1.50
285	Sherm Lollar	3.00	1.50
286	George Witt	3.00	1.50
287	Carl Yastrzemski	140.00	70.00
288	Albie Pearson	3.00	1.50
289	Ray Moore	3.00	1.50
290	Stan Musial	120.00	60.00
291	Tex Clevenger	3.00	1.50
292	Jim Baumer	3.00	1.50
293	Tom Sturdivant	3.00	1.50
294	Don Blasingame	3.00	1.50
295	Milt Pappas	3.00	1.50
296	Wes Covington	3.00	1.50
297	Athletics Team	5.00	2.50
298	Jim Golden	3.00	1.50
299	Clay Dalrymple	3.00	1.50
300	Mickey Mantle	475.00	240.00
301	Chet Nichols	3.00	1.50
302	Al Heist	3.00	1.50
303	Gary Peters	3.00	1.50
304	Rocky Nelson	3.00	1.50
305	Mike McCormick	3.00	1.50
306	World Series Game 1	6.00	3.00
307	World Series Game 2	40.00	20.00
308	World Series Game 3	6.00	3.00
309	World Series Game 4	6.00	3.00
310	World Series Game 5	6.00	3.00
311	World Series Game 6	10.00	5.00
312	World Series Game 7	12.00	6.00
313	WS Celebration	8.00	4.00
314	Bob Miller	3.00	1.50
315	Earl Battey	3.00	1.50
316	Bobby Gene Smith	3.00	1.50
317	Jim Brewer	3.00	1.50
318	Danny O'Connell	3.00	1.50
319	Valmy Thoms	3.00	1.50
320	Lou Burdette	4.00	2.00
321	Marv Breeding	3.00	1.50
322	Bill Kunkel	3.00	1.50
323	Sammy Esposito	3.00	1.50
324	Hank Aguirre	3.00	1.50
325	Wally Moon	3.50	1.75
326	Dave Hillman	3.00	1.50
327	Matty Alou (R)	6.00	3.00
328	Jim O'Toole	3.00	1.50
329	Julio Becquer	3.00	1.50
330	Rocky Colavito	12.00	6.00
331	Ned Garver	3.00	1.50
332	Dutch Dotterer	3.00	1.50
333	Fritz Brickell	3.00	1.50
334	Walt Bond	3.00	1.50
335	Frank Bolling	3.00	1.50
336	Don Mincher	3.00	1.50
337	Al's Aces (Al Lopez, Herb Score, Early Wynn)	8.00	4.00
338	Don Landrum	3.00	1.50
339	Gene Baker	3.00	1.50

340	Vic Wertz	3.00	1.50
341	Jim Owens	3.00	1.50
342	Clint Courtney	3.00	1.50
343	Earl Robinson	3.00	1.50
344	Sandy Koufax	125.00	65.00
345	Jim Piersall	4.00	2.00
346	Howie Nunn	3.00	1.50
347	Cardinals Team	5.00	2.50
348	Steve Boros	3.00	1.50
349	Danny McDevitt	3.00	1.50
350	Ernie Banks	40.00	20.00
351	Jim King	3.00	1.50
352	Bob Shaw	3.00	1.50
353	Howie Bedell	3.00	1.50
354	Billy Harrell	3.00	1.50
355	Bob Allison	3.00	1.50
356	Ryne Duren	4.00	2.00
357	Daryl Spencer	3.00	1.50
358	Earl Averill	3.00	1.50
359	Dallas Green	4.00	2.00
360	Frank Robinson	48.00	24.00
361	Checklist 353-429	8.00	4.00
362	Frank Funk	3.00	1.50
363	John Roseboro	3.00	1.50
364	Moe Drabowsky	3.00	1.50
365	Jerry Lumpe	3.00	1.50
366	Eddie Fisher	3.00	1.50
367	Jim Rivera	3.00	1.50
368	Bennie Daniels	3.00	1.50
369	Dave Philley	3.00	1.50
370	Roy Face	4.00	2.00
371	Bill Skowron	6.00	3.00
372	Bob Hendley	4.50	2.25
373	Red Sox Team	5.00	2.50
374	Paul Giel	4.50	2.25
375	Ken Boyer	8.00	4.00
376	Mike Roarke	4.50	2.25
377	Ruben Gomez	4.50	2.25
378	Wally Post	4.50	2.25
379	Bobby Shantz	4.50	2.25
380	Minnie Minoso	7.00	3.50
381	Dave Wickersham	4.50	2.25
382	Frank Thomas	4.50	2.25
383	Frisco First Liners (Mike McCormick, Billy O'Dell, Jack Sanford)	5.00	2.50
384	Chuck Essegian	4.50	2.25
385	Jim Perry	4.50	2.25
386	Joe Hicks	4.50	2.25
387	Duke Maas	4.50	2.25
388	Bob Clemente	125.00	65.00
389	Ralph Terry	5.00	2.50
390	Del Crandall	4.50	2.25
391	Winston Brown	4.50	2.25
392	Reno Bertoia	4.50	2.25
393	Batter Bafflers (Don Cardwell, Glen Hobbie)	4.50	2.25
394	Ken Walters	4.50	2.25
395	Chuck Estrada	4.50	2.25
396	Bob Aspromonte	4.50	2.25
397	Hal Woodeshick	4.50	2.25
398	Hank Bauer	5.00	2.50
399	Cliff Cook	4.50	2.25
400	Vern Law	4.50	2.25
401	Babe Ruth Hits 60th	32.00	16.00
402	Larsen' Perfect Game	16.00	8.00
403	26 Inning Tie	5.00	2.50
404	Hornsby Tops N.L.	10.00	5.00
405	Gehrig 2,130 Games	20.00	10.00
406	Mantle's 565' HR	60.00	30.00
407	Chesbro's 41st Win	5.00	2.50
408	Mathewson's K's	8.00	4.00
409	Johnson's Shutout's	10.00	5.00
410	Haddix 12 Perfect Innings	7.00	3.50
411	Tony Taylor	4.50	2.25
412	Larry Sherry	4.50	2.25
413	Eddie Yost	4.50	2.25
414	Dick Donovan	4.50	2.25
415	Hank Aaron	150.00	90.00
416	Dick Howser (R)	7.50	3.25
417	Juan Marichal (R)	150.00	90.00
418	Ed Bailey	4.50	2.25
419	Tom Borland	4.50	2.25
420	Ernie Broglio	4.50	2.25
421	Ty Cline	4.50	2.25
422	Bud Daley	4.50	2.25
423	Charlie Neal	4.50	2.25
424	Turk Lown	4.50	2.25
425	Yogi Berra	75.00	38.00
426	No Card	00.00	00.00
427	Dick Ellsworth	4.50	2.25
428	Ray Barker	4.50	2.25
429	Al Kaline	48.00	24.00
430	Bill Mazeroski	15.00	7.50
431	Chuck Stobbs	4.50	2.25
432	Coot Veal	4.50	2.25
433	Art Mahaffey	4.50	2.25
434	Tom Brewer	4.50	2.25
435	Orlando Cepeda	10.00	5.00
436	Jim Maloney (R)	6.00	3.00
437	Checklist 430-506	8.00	4.00
438	Curt Flood	5.00	2.50
439	Phil Regan (R)	5.00	2.50
440	Luis Aparicio	18.00	9.00
441	Dick Bertell	4.50	2.25
442	Gordon Jons	4.50	2.25
443	Duke Snider	48.00	24.00
444	Joe Nuxhall	4.50	2.25
445	Frank Malzone	4.50	2.25
446	Bob Taylor	4.50	2.25
447	Harry Bright	4.50	2.25

448	Del Rice	4.50	2.25	502	Clarence Coleman (R)	7.00	3.50
449	Bobby Bolin	4.50	2.25	503	Tito Francona	4.50	2.25
450	Jim Lemon	4.50	2.25	504	Billy Consolo	4.50	2.25
451	Power For Ernie	5.00	2.50	505	Red Schoendienst	16.00	8.00
	(Ernie Broglio, Daryl			506	Willie Davis (R)	18.00	9.00
	Spencer, Bill White)			507	Pete Burnside	4.50	2.25
452	Bob Allen	4.50	2.25	508	Rocky Bridges	4.50	2.25
453	Dick Schofield	4.50	2.25	509	Camilo Carreon	4.50	2.25
454	Pumpsie Green	4.50	2.25	510	Art Ditmar	4.50	2.25
455	Early Wynn	15.00	7.50	511	Joe Morgan	4.50	2.25
456	Hal Bevan	4.50	2.25	512	Bob Will	4.50	2.25
457	Johnny James	4.50	2.25	513	Jim Brosnan	4.50	2.25
458	Willie Tasby	4.50	2.25	514	Jake Wood	4.50	2.25
459	Terry Fox	4.50	2.25	515	Jackie Brandt	4.50	2.25
460	Gil Hodges	18.00	9.00	516	Checklist 507-587	10.00	5.00
461	Smoky Burgess	5.00	2.50	517	Willie McCovey	70.00	35.00
462	Lou Klimchock	4.50	2.25	518	Andy Carey	4.50	2.25
463	Braves Team	5.00	2.50	519	Jim Pagliaroni	4.50	2.25
463	Jack Fisher	4.50	2.25	520	Joe Cunningham	4.50	2.25
464	Lee Thomas (R)	5.00	2.50	521	Larry & Norm	5.00	2.50
465	Roy McMillan	4.50	2.25		Sherry		
466	Ron Moeller	4.50	2.25	522	Dick Farrell	4.50	2.25
467	Indians Team	5.00	2.50	523	Joe Gibbon	32.00	16.00
468	Johnny Callison	4.50	2.25	524	Johnny Logan	36.00	18.00
469	Ralph Lumenti	4.50	2.25	525	Ron Perranoski (R)	40.00	20.00
470	Roy Sievers	5.00	2.50	526	R.C. Stevens	32.00	16.00
471	Phil Rizzuto MVP	15.00	7.50	527	Gene Leek	32.00	16.00
472	Yogi Berra MVP	55.00	28.00	528	Pedro Ramos	32.00	16.00
473	Bobby Shantz MVP	5.00	2.50	529	Bob Roselli	32.00	16.00
474	Al Rosen MVP	6.00	3.00	530	Bobby Malkmus	32.00	16.00
475	Mickey Mantle MVP	140.00	70.00	531	Jim Coates	32.00	16.00
476	Jackie Jensen MVP	6.00	3.00	532	Bob Hale	32.00	16.00
477	Nellie Fox MVP	8.00	4.00	533	Jack Curtis	32.00	16.00
478	Roger Maris MVP	48.00	24.00	534	Eddie Kasko	32.00	16.00
479	Jim Konstanty MVP	5.00	2.50	535	Larry Jackson	32.00	16.00
480	Roy Campanella	40.00	20.00	536	Bill Tuttle	32.00	16.00
	MVP			537	Bobby Locke	32.00	16.00
481	Hank Sauer MVP	5.00	2.50	538	Chuck Hiller	32.00	16.00
482	Willie Mays MVP	50.00	25.00	539	Johnny Klippstein	32.00	16.00
483	Don Newcombe MVP	6.00	3.00	540	Jackie Jensen	38.00	20.00
484	Hank Aaron MVP	50.00	25.00	541	Roland Sheldon	32.00	16.00
485	Ernie Banks MVP	35.00	18.00	542	Twins Team	60.00	30.00
486	Dick Groat MVP	5.00	2.50	543	Roger Craig	36.00	18.00
487	Gene Oliver	4.50	2.25	544	George Thomas	32.00	16.00
488	Joe McClain	4.50	2.25	545	Hoyt Wilhelm	70.00	35.00
489	Walt Dropo	4.50	2.25	546	Marty Kutyna	32.00	16.00
490	Jim Bunning	10.00	5.00	547	Leon Wagner	32.00	16.00
491	Phillies Team	5.00	2.50	548	Ted Wills	32.00	16.00
492	Ron Fairly	4.50	2.25	549	Hal R. Smith	32.00	16.00
493	Don Zimmer	6.00	3.00	550	Frank Baumann	32.00	16.00
494	Tom Cheney	4.50	2.25	551	George Altman	32.00	16.00
495	Elston Howard	10.00	5.00	552	Jim Archer	32.00	16.00
496	Ken MacKenzie	4.50	2.25	553	Bill Fischer	32.00	16.00
497	Willie Jones	4.50	2.25	554	Pirates Team	60.00	30.00
498	Ray Herbert	4.50	2.25	555	Sam Jones	32.00	16.00
499	Chuck Schilling	4.50	2.25	556	Ken R. Hunt	32.00	16.00
500	Harvey Kuenn	7.00	3.50	557	Jose Valdivielso	32.00	16.00
501	John DeMerit	4.50	2.25	558	Don Ferrarese	32.00	16.00

559	Jim Gentile	36.00	18.00
560	Barry Latman	32.00	16.00
561	Charley James	32.00	16.00
562	Bill Monbouquette	32.00	16.00
563	Bob Cerv	36.00	18.00
564	Don Cardwell	32.00	16.00
565	Felipe Alou	40.00	20.00
566	Paul Richards AS	32.00	16.00
567	Danny Murtaugh AS	36.00	18.00
568	Bill Skowron AS	38.00	20.00
569	Frank Herrera AS	32.00	16.00
570	Nellie Fox As	48.00	24.00
571	Bill Mazeroski AS	40.00	20.00
572	Brooks Robinson AS	110.00	55.00
573	Ken Boyer AS	48.00	24.00
574	Luis Aparicio AS	50.00	25.00
575	Ernie Banks AS	110.00	55.00
576	Roger Maris AS	175.00	90.00
577	Hank Aaron AS	190.00	95.00
578	Mickey Mantle AS	450.00	225.00
579	Willie Mays AS	190.00	95.00
580	Al Kaline AS	110.00	55.00
581	Frank Robinson AS	110.00	55.00
582	Earl Battey AS	32.00	16.00
583	Del Crandall AS	32.00	16.00
584	Jim Perry AS	32.00	16.00
585	Bob Friend AS	32.00	16.00
586	Whitey Ford AS	100.00	50.00
587	No Card	00.00	00.00
588	No Card	00.00	00.00
589	Warren Spahn AS	175.00	80.00

1962 Topps

This 598-card set features a vertical format on the front with large color photos set against a wood grain background. Cards measure 2-1/2" by 3-1/2". The Topps set contains a special 10-card Babe Ruth subset, a new In-Action

Subset (IA) plus League Leaders, World Series, All-Stars and Rookies. For the first time, Topps introduced multi-player rookie cards.

		NR/MT	EX
Complete Set (598)		5,500.00	2,750.00
Commons (1-370)		2.50	1.25
Commons (371-522)		5.00	2.50
Commons (523-598)		15.00	7.50

1	Roger Maris	240.00	75.00
2	Jim Brosnan	2.50	1.25
3	Pete Runnels	2.50	1.25
4	John DeMerit	2.50	1.25
5	Sandy Koufax	125.00	65.00
6	Marv Breeding	2.50	1.25
7	Frank Thomas	2.50	1.25
8	Ray Herbert	2.50	1.25
9	Jim Davenport	2.50	1.25
10	Bob Clemente	125.00	65.00
11	Tom Morgan	2.50	1.25
12	Harry Craft	2.50	1.25
13	Dick Howser	3.00	1.50
14	Bill White	3.50	1.75
15	Dick Donovan	2.50	1.25
16	Darrell Johnson	2.50	1.25
17	Johnny Callison	2.50	1.25
18	Manager's Dream (Mantle/Mays)	140.00	70.00
19	Ray Washburn (R)	2.50	1.25
20	Rocky Colavito	10.00	5.00
21	Jim Kaat	7.50	3.50
22a	Checklist 1-88	8.00	4.00
23	Norm Larker	2.50	1.25
24	Tigers Team	6.00	3.00
25	Ernie Banks	48.00	24.00
26	Chris Cannizzaro	2.50	1.25
27	Chuck Cottier	2.50	1.25
28	Minnie Minoso	6.00	3.00
29	Casey Stengel	18.00	9.00
30	Ed Mathews	24.00	12.00
31	Tom Tresh (R)	18.00	9.00
32	John Roseboro	2.50	1.25
33	Don Larsen	3.50	1.75
34	Johnny Temple	2.50	1.25
35	Don Schwall	2.50	1.25
36	Don Leppert	2.50	1.25
37	Tribe Hill Trio (Barry Latman, Jim Perry, Dick Stigman)	2.50	1.25
38	Gene Stephens	2.50	1.25
39	Joe Koppe	2.50	1.25
40	Orlando Cepeda	10.00	5.00
41	Cliff Cook	2.50	1.25
42	Jim King	2.50	1.25

43	Dodgers Team	6.00	3.00
44	Don Tausig	2.50	1.25
45	Brooks Robinson	40.00	20.00
46	Jack Baldschun	2.50	1.25
47	Bob Will	2.50	1.25
48	Ralph Terry	3.00	1.50
49	Hal Jones	2.50	1.25
50	Stan Musial	125.00	65.00
51	A.L. Batting Leaders	5.00	2.50
52	N.L. Batting Leaders	8.00	4.00
53	A.L. HR Leaders	50.00	25.00
54	N.L. HR Leaders	10.00	5.00
55	A.L. E.R.A. Leaders	3.00	1.50
56	N.L. E.R.A. Leaders	5.00	2.50
57	A.L. Win Leaders	5.00	2.50
58	N.L. Win Leaders	5.00	2.50
59	A.L. Strikeout Ldrs	5.00	2.50
60	N.L. Strikeout Ldrs	8.00	4.00
61	Cardinals Team	6.00	3.00
62	Steve Boros	2.50	1.25
63	Tony Cloninger (R)	4.00	2.00
64	Russ Snyder	2.50	1.25
65	Bobby Richardson	7.00	3.50
66	Cuno Barragan	2.50	1.25
67	Harvey Haddix	3.00	1.50
68	Ken L. Hunt	2.50	1.25
69	Phil Ortega	2.50	1.25
70	Harmon Killebrew	24.00	12.00
71	Dick LeMay	2.50	1.25
72	Bob's Pupils (Steve	2.50	1.25
	Boros, Bob Scheffing,		
	Jake Wood)		
73	Nellie Fox	8.00	4.00
74	Bob Lillis	2.50	1.25
75	Milt Pappas	2.50	1.25
76	Howie Bedell	2.50	1.25
77	Tony Taylor	2.50	1.25
78	Gene Green	2.50	1.25
79	Ed Hobaugh	2.50	1.25
80	Vada Pinson	4.00	2.00
81	Jim Pagliaroni	2.50	1.25
82	Deron Johnson	2.50	1.25
83	Larry Jackson	2.50	1.25
84	Lenny Green	2.50	1.25
85	Gil Hodges	15.00	7.50
86	Donn Clendenon (R)	5.00	2.50
87	Mike Roarke	2.50	1.25
88	Ralph Houk	3.00	1.50
89	Barney Schultz	2.50	1.25
90	Jim Piersall	3.00	1.50
91	J.C. Martin	2.50	1.25
92	Sam Jones	2.50	1.25
93	John Blanchard	2.50	1.25
94	Jay Hook	2.50	1.25
95	Don Hoak	2.50	1.25
96	Eli Grba	2.50	1.25
97	Tito Francona	2.50	1.25
98	Checklist 89-176	8.00	4.00
99	Boog Powell (R)	24.00	12.00
100	Warren Spahn	36.00	18.00
101	Carroll Hardy	2.50	1.25
102	Al Schroll	2.50	1.25
103	Don Blasingame	2.50	1.25
104	Ted Savage	2.50	1.25
105	Don Mossi	2.50	1.25
106	Carl Sawatski	2.50	1.25
107	Mike McCormick	2.50	1.25
108	Willie Davis	4.00	2.00
109	Bob Shaw	2.50	1.25
110	Bill Skowron	5.00	2.50
111	Dallas Green	3.00	1.50
112	Hank Foiles	2.50	1.25
113	White Sox Team	6.00	3.00
114	Howie Koplitz	2.50	1.25
115	Bob Skinner	2.50	1.25
116	Herb Score	3.00	1.50
117	Gary Geiger	2.50	1.25
118	Julian Javier	2.50	1.25
119	Danny Murphy	2.50	1.25
120	Bob Purkey	2.50	1.25
121	Billy Hitchcock	2.50	1.25
122	Norm Bass	2.50	1.25
123	Mike de la Hoz	2.50	1.25
124	Bill Pleis	2.50	1.25
125	Gene Woodling	2.50	1.25
126	Al Cicotte	2.50	1.25
127	Pride of the A's	3.00	1.50
	(Hank Bauer, Jerry		
	Lumpe, Norm Siebern)		
128	Art Fowler	2.50	1.25
129a	Lee Walls (Left)	18.00	9.00
129b	Lee Walls (Right)	2.50	1.25
130	Frank Bolling	2.50	1.25
131	Pete Richert (R)	3.00	1.50
132a	Angels Team (With	18.00	9.00
	inset photos)		
132b	Angels Team (W/O	4.00	2.00
	inset photos)		
133	Felipe Alou	5.00	2.50
134a	Billy Hoeft (Green	18.00	9.00
	Sky)		
134b	Billy Hoeft (Blue sky)	3.00	1.50
135	Babe as a Boy	10.00	5.00
136	Babe Joins Yanks	10.00	5.00
137	Babe and Huggins	10.00	5.00
138	The Famous Slugger	10.00	5.00
139a	Babe Hits 60	18.00	9.00
139b	Hal Reniff (Pitching)	50.00	25.00
139c	Hal Reniff (portrait)	12.00	6.00
140	Gehrig and Ruth	20.00	10.00
141	Babe Ruth (Twilight)	10.00	5.00
142	Babe Coaching	10.00	5.00
	Dodgers		
143	Greatest Sports Hero	10.00	5.00
144	Babe's Farewell	10.00	5.00
145	Barry Latman	2.50	1.25

No.	Player		
146	Don Demeter	2.50	1.25
147a	Bill Kunkel (Pitching)	18.00	9.00
147b	Bill Kunkel (Portrait)	2.50	1.25
148	Wally Post	2.50	1.25
149	Bob Duliba	2.50	1.25
150	Al Kaline	40.00	20.00
151	Johnny Klippstein	2.50	1.25
152	Mickey Vernon	2.50	1.25
153	Pumpsie Green	2.50	1.25
154	Lee Thomas	2.50	1.25
155	Stu Miller	2.50	1.25
156	Merritt Ranew	2.50	1.25
157	Wes Covington	2.50	1.25
158	Braves Team	6.00	3.00
159	Hal Reniff	2.50	1.25
160	Dick Stuart	2.50	1.25
161	Frank Baumann	2.50	1.25
162	Sammy Drake	2.50	1.25
163	Hot Corner (Cletis Boyer, Billy Gardner)	3.00	1.50
164	Hal Naragon	2.50	1.25
165	Jackie Brandt	2.50	1.25
166	Don Lee	2.50	1.25
167	Tim McCarver (R)	32.00	16.00
168	Leo Posada	2.50	1.25
169	Bob Cerv	2.50	1.25
170	Ron Santo	14.00	7.00
171	Dave Sisler	2.50	1.25
172	Fred Hutchinson	2.50	1.25
173	Chico Fernandez	2.50	1.25
174a	Carl Willey (Cap)	18.00	9.00
174b	Carl Willey (No cap)	2.50	1.25
175	Frank Howard	6.00	3.00
176a	Eddie Yost (Batting)	18.00	9.00
176b	Eddie Yost (Portrait)	2.50	1.25
177	Bobby Shantz	3.00	1.50
178	Camilo Carreon	2.50	1.25
179	Tom Sturdivant	2.50	1.25
180	Bob Allison	3.00	1.50
181	Paul Brown	2.50	1.25
182	Bob Nieman	2.50	1.25
183	Roger Craig	3.00	1.50
184	Haywood Sullivan	2.50	1.25
185	Roland Sheldon	2.50	1.25
186	Mack Jones	2.50	1.25
187	Gene Conley	2.50	1.25
188	Chuck Hiller	2.50	1.25
189	Dick Hall	2.50	1.25
190a	Wally Moon (Cap)	18.00	9.00
190b	Wally Moon (No Cap)	3.50	1.75
191	Jim Brewer	2.50	1.25
192	Checklist 177-264	8.00	4.00
193	Eddie Kasko	2.50	1.25
194	Dean Chance (R)	5.00	2.50
195	Joe Cunningham	2.50	1.25
196	Terry Fox	2.50	1.25
197	Daryl Spencer	2.50	1.25
198	Johnny Keane	2.50	1.25
199	Gaylord Perry (R)	200.00	100.00
200	Mickey Mantle	550.00	275.00
201	Ike Delock	2.50	1.25
202	Carl Warwick	2.50	1.25
203	Jack Fisher	2.50	1.25
204	Johnny Weekly	2.50	1.25
205	Gene Freese	2.50	1.25
206	Senators Team	6.00	3.00
207	Pete Burnside	2.50	1.25
208	Billy Martin	10.00	5.00
209	Jim Fregosi (R)	10.00	5.00
210	Roy Face	3.00	1.50
211	Midway Masters (Frank Bolling, Roy McMillan)	2.50	1.25
212	Jim Owens	2.50	1.25
213	Richie Ashburn	8.00	4.00
214	Dom Zanni	2.50	1.25
215	Woody Held	2.50	1.25
216	Ron Kline	2.50	1.25
217	Walt Alston	4.00	2.00
218	Joe Torre (R)	25.00	12.50
219	Al Downing	2.50	1.25
220	Roy Sievers	2.50	1.25
221	Bill Short	2.50	1.25
222	Jerry Zimmerman	2.50	1.25
223	Alex Grammas	2.50	1.25
224	Don Rudolph	2.50	1.25
225	Frank Malzone	3.50	1.75
226	Giants Team	6.00	3.00
227	Bobby Tiefenauer	2.50	1.25
228	Dale Long	2.50	1.25
229	Jesus McFarlane	2.50	1.25
230	Camilo Pascual	2.50	1.25
231	Ernie Bowman	2.50	1.25
232	World Series Game 1	5.00	2.50
233	World Series Game 2	5.00	2.50
234	World Series Game 3	12.00	6.00
235	World Series Game 4	8.00	4.00
236	World Series Game 5	5.00	2.50
237	WS (Yanks Celebrate)	5.00	2.50
238	Norm Sherry	2.50	1.25
239	Cecil Butler	2.50	1.25
240	George Altman	2.50	1.25
241	Johnny Kucks	2.50	1.25
242	Mel McGaha	2.50	1.25
243	Robin Roberts	12.00	6.00
244	Don Gile	2.50	1.25
245	Ron Hansen	2.50	1.25
246	Art Ditmar	2.50	1.25
247	Joe Pignatano	2.50	1.25
248	Bob Aspromonte	2.50	1.25
249	Ed Keegan	2.50	1.25
250	Norm Cash	7.00	3.50
251	Yankees Team	18.00	9.00
252	Earl Francis	2.50	1.25
253	Harry Chiti	2.50	1.25
254	Gordon Windhorn	2.50	1.25

255	Juan Pizarro	2.50	1.25
256	Elio Chacon	2.50	1.25
257	Jack Spring	2.50	1.25
258	Marty Keough	2.50	1.25
259	Lou Klimchock	2.50	1.25
260	Bill Piece	2.50	1.25
261	George Alusik	2.50	1.25
262	Bob Schmidt	2.50	1.25
263	The Right Pitch (Joe Jay, Bob Purkey, Jim Turner)	3.00	1.50
264	Dick Ellsworth	2.50	1.25
265	Joe Adcock	3.00	1.50
266	John Anderson	2.50	1.25
267	Dan Dobbek	2.50	1.25
268	Ken McBride	2.50	1.25
269	Bob Oldis	2.50	1.25
270	Dick Groat	3.00	1.50
271	Ray Rippelmeyer	2.50	1.25
272	Earl Robinson	2.50	1.25
273	Gary Bell	2.50	1.25
274	Sammy Taylor	2.50	1.25
275	Norm Siebern	2.50	1.25
276	Hal Kostad	2.50	1.25
277	Checklist 265-352	8.00	4.00
278	Ken Johnson	2.50	1.25
279	Hobie Landrith	2.50	1.25
280	Johnny Podres	3.00	1.50
281	Jake Gibbs (R)	3.00	1.50
282	Dave Hillman	2.50	1.25
283	Charlie Smith	2.50	1.25
284	Ruben Amaro	2.50	1.25
285	Curt Simmons	2.50	1.25
286	Al Lopez	4.00	2.00
287	George Witt	2.50	1.25
288	Billy Williams	45.00	22.50
289	Mike Krsnich	2.50	1.25
290	Jim Gentile	6.00	3.00
291	Hal Stowe	2.50	1.25
292	Jerry Kindall	2.50	1.25
293	Bob Miller	2.50	1.25
294	Phillies Team	6.00	3.00
295	Vern Law	3.00	1.50
296	Ken Hamlin	2.50	1.25
297	Ron Perranoski	4.00	2.00
298	Bill Tuttle	2.50	1.25
299	Don Wert	2.50	1.25
300	Willie Mays	175.00	90.00
301	Galen Cisco (R)	4.00	2.00
302	John Edwards (R)	3.50	1.75
303	Frank Torre	2.50	1.25
304	Dick Farrell	2.50	1.25
305	Jerry Lumpe	2.50	1.25
306	Redbird Rippers (Larry Jackson, Lindy McDaniel)	3.00	1.50
307	Jim Grant	3.00	1.50
308	Neil Chrisley	2.50	1.25
309	Moe Morhardt	2.50	1.25
310	Whitey Ford	45.00	22.50
311	Tony Kubek (IA)	7.00	3.50
312	Warren Spahn (IA)	12.00	6.00
313	Roger Maris (IA)	24.00	12.00
314	Rocky Colavito (IA)	7.00	3.50
315	Whitey Ford (IA)	10.00	5.00
316	Harmon Killebrew(IA)	8.00	4.00
317	Stan Musial (IA)	20.00	10.00
318	Mickey Mantle (IA)	65.00	35.00
319	Mike McCormick (IA)	3.00	1.50
320	Hank Aaron	160.00	80.00
321	Lee Stange	2.50	1.25
322	Al Dark	2.50	1.25
323	Don Landrum	2.50	1.25
324	Joe McClain	2.50	1.25
325	Luis Aparicio	15.00	7.50
326	Tom Parsons	2.50	1.25
327	Ozzie Virgil	2.50	1.25
328	Ken Walters	2.50	1.25
329	Bob Bolin	2.50	1.25
330	Johnny Romano	2.50	1.25
331	Moe Drabowsky	2.50	1.25
332	Don Buddin	2.50	1.25
333	Frank Cipriani	2.50	1.25
334	Red Sox Team	6.00	3.00
335	Bill Bruton	2.50	1.25
336	Billy Muffett	2.50	1.25
337	Jim Marshall	2.50	1.25
338	Billy Gardner	2.50	1.25
339	Jose Valdivielso	2.50	1.25
340	Don Drysdale	40.00	20.00
341	Mike Hershberger	2.50	1.25
342	Ed Rakow	2.50	1.25
343	Albie Pearson	2.50	1.25
344	Ed Bauta	2.50	1.25
345	Chuck Schilling	2.50	1.25
346	Jack Kralick	2.50	1.25
347	Chuck Hinton	2.50	1.25
348	Larry Burright	2.50	1.25
349	Paul Foytack	2.50	1.25
350	Frank Robinson	55.00	28.00
351	Braves' Backstops (Crandall/Torre)		
352	Frank Sullivan	2.50	1.25
353	Bill Mazeroski	7.00	3.50
354	Roman Mejias	2.50	1.25
355	Steve Barber	2.50	1.25
356	Tom Haller (R)	4.00	2.00
357	Jerry Walker	2.50	1.25
358	Tommy Davis	8.00	4.00
359	Bobby Locke	2.50	1.25
360	Yogi Berra	90.00	45.00
361	Bob Hendley	2.50	1.25
362	Ty Cline	2.50	1.25
363	Bob Roselli	2.50	1.25
364	Ken Hunt	2.50	1.25
365	Charley Neal	2.50	1.25

366	Phil Regan	2.50	1.25
367	Checklist 353-429	8.00	4.00
368	Bob Tillman	2.50	1.25
369	Ted Bowsfield	2.50	1.25
370	Ken Boyer	9.00	4.50
371	Earl Battey	5.00	2.50
372	Jack Curtis	5.00	2.50
373	Al Heist	5.00	2.50
374	Gene Mauch	5.00	2.50
375	Ron Fairly	5.00	2.50
376	Bud Daley	5.00	2.50
377	Johnny Orsino	5.00	2.50
378	Bennie Daniels	5.00	2.50
379	Chuck Essegian	5.00	2.50
380	Lou Burdette	6.00	3.00
381	Chico Cardenas	5.00	2.50
382	Dick Williams	5.00	2.50
383	Ray Sadecki	5.00	2.50
384	Athletics Team	6.00	3.00
385	Early Wynn	20.00	10.00
386	Don Mincher	5.00	2.50
387	Lou Brock (R)	225.00	110.00
388	Ryne Duren	6.00	3.00
389	Smoky Burgess	6.00	3.00
390	Orlando Cepeda AS	8.00	4.00
391	Bill Mazeroski As	7.00	3.50
392	Ken Boyer AS	8.00	4.00
393	Roy McMillan As	5.00	2.50
394	Hank Aaron AS	42.00	21.00
395	Willie Mays AS	42.00	21.00
396	Frank Robinson AS	18.00	9.00
397	John Roseboro AS	5.00	2.50
398	Don Drysdale AS	15.00	7.50
399	Warren Spahn AS	15.00	7.50
400	Elston Howard	10.00	5.00
401	AL & NL HR Kings	35.00	18.00
	(Orlando Cepeda,		
	Roger Maris)		
402	Gino Cimoli	5.00	2.50
403	Chet Nichols	5.00	2.50
404	Tim Harkness	5.00	2.50
405	Jim Perry	5.00	2.50
406	Bob Taylor	5.00	2.50
407	Hank Aguirre	5.00	2.50
408	Gus Bell	5.00	2.50
409	Pirates Team	6.00	3.00
410	Al Smith	5.00	2.50
411	Danny O'Connell	5.00	2.50
412	Charlie James	5.00	2.50
413	Matty Alou	6.00	3.00
414	Joe Gaines	5.00	2.50
415	Bill Virdon	6.00	3.00
416	Bob Scheffing	5.00	2.50
417	Joe Azcue	5.00	2.50
418	Andy Carey	5.00	2.50
419	Bob Bruce	5.00	2.50
420	Gus Triandos	5.00	2.50
421	Ken MacKenzie	5.00	2.50
422	Steve Bilko	5.00	2.50
423	Rival Relief Aces	8.00	4.00
	(Roy Face, Hoyt		
	Wilhelm)		
424	Al McBean	5.00	2.50
425	Carl Yastrzemski	210.00	100.00
426	Bob Farley	5.00	2.50
427	Jake Wood	5.00	2.50
428	Joe Hicks	5.00	2.50
429	Bill O'Dell	5.00	2.50
430	Tony Kubek	10.00	5.00
431	Bob Rodgers (R)	7.00	3.50
432	Jim Pendleton	5.00	2.50
433	Jim Archer	5.00	2.50
434	Clay Dalrymple	5.00	2.50
435	Larry Sherry	5.00	2.50
436	Felix Mantilla	5.00	2.50
437	Ray Moore	5.00	2.50
438	Dick Brown	5.00	2.50
439	Jerry Buchek	5.00	2.50
440	Joe Jay	5.00	2.50
441	Checklist 430-506	8.00	4.00
442	Wes Stock	5.00	2.50
443	Del Crandall	5.00	2.50
444	Ted Wills	5.00	2.50
445	Vic Power	5.00	2.50
446	Don Elston	5.00	2.50
447	Willie Kirkland	5.00	2.50
448	Joe Gibbon	5.00	2.50
449	Jerry Adair	5.00	2.50
450	Jim O'Toole	6.00	3.00
451	Jose Tartabull (R)	7.00	3.50
452	Earl Averill	5.00	2.50
453	Cal McLish	5.00	2.50
454	Floyd Robinsn	5.00	2.50
455	Luis Arroyo	5.00	2.50
456	Joe Amalfitano	5.00	2.50
457	Lou Clinton	5.00	2.50
458a	Bob Buhl ("M" on cap)	5.00	2.50
458b	Bob Buhl (No "M")	50.00	25.00
459	Ed Bailey	5.00	2.50
460	Jim Bunning	12.00	6.00
461	Ken Hubbs (R)	16.00	8.00
462a	Willie Tasby ("W"	5.00	2.50
	on cap)		
462b	Willie Tasby(No "W")	50.00	25.00
463	Hank Bauer	6.00	3.00
464	Al Jackson (R)	8.00	4.00
465	Reds Team	6.00	3.00
466	Norm Cash AS	8.00	4.00
467	Chuck Schilling AS	5.00	2.50
468	Brooks Robinson AS	20.00	10.00
469	Luis Aparicio AS	12.00	6.00
470	Al Kaline AS	20.00	10.00
471	Mickey Mantle AS	150.00	75.00
472	Rocky Colavito AS	10.00	5.00
473	Elston Howard AS	8.00	4.00
474	Frank Lary AS	6.00	3.00

475	Whitey Ford AS	15.00	7.50	533	Charley Lau	15.00	7.50
476	Orioles Team	6.00	3.00	534	Tony Gonzalez	18.00	9.00
477	Andre Rodgers	5.00	2.50	535	Ed Roebuck	15.00	7.50
478	Don Zimmer	7.00	3.50	536	Dick Gernert	15.00	7.50
479	Joel Horlen	5.00	2.50	537	Indians Team	24.00	12.00
480	Harvey Kuenn	7.00	3.50	538	Jack Sanford	15.00	7.50
481	Vic Wertz	5.00	2.50	539	Billy Moran	15.00	7.50
482	Sam Mele	5.00	2.50	540	Jim Landis	15.00	7.50
483	Don McMahon	5.00	2.50	541	Don Nottebart	15.00	7.50
484	Dick Schofield	5.00	2.50	542	Dave Philley	15.00	7.50
485	Pedro Ramos	5.00	2.50	543	Bob Allen	15.00	7.50
486	Jim Gilliam	8.00	4.00	544	Willie McCovey	150.00	75.00
487	Jerry Lynch	5.00	2.50	545	Hoyt Wilhelm	50.00	25.00
488	Hal Brown	5.00	2.50	546	Moe Thacker	15.00	7.50
489	Julio Gotay	5.00	2.50	547	Don Ferrarese	15.00	7.50
490	Clete Boyer	6.00	3.00	548	Bobby Del Greco	15.00	7.50
491	Leon Wagner	5.00	2.50	549	Bill Rigney	15.00	7.50
492	Hal Smith	5.00	2.50	550	Art Mahaffey	15.00	7.50
493	Danny McDevitt	5.00	2.50	551	Harry Bright	15.00	7.50
494	Sammy White	5.00	2.50	552	Cubs Team	35.00	18.00
495	Don Cardwell	5.00	2.50	553	Jim Coates	15.00	7.50
496	Wayne Causey	5.00	2.50	554	Bubba Morton	15.00	7.50
497	Ed Bouchee	5.00	2.50	555	John Buzhardt	15.00	7.50
498	Jim Donohue	5.00	2.50	556	Al Spangler	15.00	7.50
499	Zoilo Versalles	5.00	2.50	557	Bob Anderson	15.00	7.50
500	Duke Snider	55.00	28.00	558	John Goryl	15.00	7.50
501	Claude Osteen	6.00	3.00	559	Mike Higgins	15.00	7.50
502	Hector Lopez	5.00	2.50	560	Chuck Estrada	15.00	7.50
503	Danny Murtaugh	5.00	2.50	561	Gene Oliver	15.00	7.50
504	Eddie Bressoud	5.00	2.50	562	Bill Henry	15.00	7.50
505	Juan Marichal	45.00	22.50	563	Ken Aspromonte	15.00	7.50
506	Charley Maxwell	5.00	2.50	564	Bob Grim	15.00	7.50
507	Ernie Broglio	5.00	2.50	565	Jose Pagan	15.00	7.50
508	Gordy Coleman	5.00	2.50	566	Marty Kutyna	15.00	7.50
509	Dave Giusti (R)	7.00	3.50	567	Tracy Stallard	15.00	7.50
510	Jim Lemon	5.00	2.50	568	Jim Golden	15.00	7.50
511	Bubba Phillips	5.00	2.50	569	Ed Sadowski	15.00	7.50
512	Mike Fornieles	5.00	2.50	570	Bill Stafford	15.00	7.50
513	Whitey Herzog	7.00	3.50	571	Billy Klaus	15.00	7.50
514	Sherm Lollar	5.00	2.50	572	Bob Miller	15.00	7.50
515	Stan Williams	5.00	2.50	573	Johnny Logan	15.00	7.50
516	Checklist 507-598	12.00	6.00	574	Dean Stone	15.00	7.50
517	Dave Wickersham	5.00	2.50	575	Red Schoendienst	45.00	22.50
518	Lee Maye	5.00	2.50	576	Russ Kemmerer	15.00	7.50
519	Bob Johnson	5.00	2.50	577	Dave Nicholson	15.00	7.50
520	Bob Friend	5.00	2.50	578	Jim Duffalo	15.00	7.50
521	Jacke Davis	5.00	2.50	579	Jim Schaffer	15.00	7.50
522	Lindy McDaniel	5.00	2.50	580	Bill Monbouquette	15.00	7.50
523	Russ Nixon	15.00	7.50	581	Mel Roach	15.00	7.50
524	Howie Nunn	15.00	7.50	582	Ron Piche	15.00	7.50
525	George Thomas	15.00	7.50	583	Larry Osborne	15.00	7.50
526	Hal Woodeshick	15.00	7.50	584	Twins Team	35.00	18.00
527	Dick McAuliffe (R)	15.00	7.50	585	Glen Hobbie	15.00	7.50
528	Turk Lown	15.00	7.50	586	Sammy Esposito	15.00	7.50
529	John Schaive	15.00	7.50	587	Frank Funk	15.00	7.50
530	Bob Gibson	190.00	95.00	588	Birdie Tebbetts	15.00	7.50
531	Bobby G. Smith	15.00	7.50	589	Bob Turley	15.00	7.50
532	Dick Stigman	15.00	7.50	590	Curt Flood	18.00	9.00

591	Rookie Pitchers	50.00	25.00
	Sam McDowell		
	Ron Taylor		
	Dick Radatz		
	Ron Nischwitz		
	Art Quirk		
592	Rookie Pitchers	75.00	38.00
	Bo Belinsky		
	Joe Bonikowski		
	Jim Bouton		
	Dan Pfister		
	Dave Stenhouse		
593	Rookie Pitchers	28.00	14.00
	Craig Anderson		
	Jack Hamilton		
	Jack Lamabe		
	Bob Moorhead		
	Bob Veale		
594	Rookie Catchers	120.00	60.00
	Doug Camilli		
	Doc Edwards		
	Don Pavletich		
	Ken Retzer		
	Bob Uecker		
595	Rookie Infielders	24.00	12.00
	Ed Charles		
	Marlin Coughtry		
	Bob Sadowski		
	Felix Torres		
596	Rookie Infielders	60.00	30.00
	Bernie Allen		
	Phil Linz		
	Joe Pepitone		
	Rich Rollins		
597	Rookie Infielders	30.00	15.00
	Rod Kanehl		
	Jim McKnight		
	Denis Menke		
	Amado Samuel		
598	Rookie Outfielders	60.00	30.00
	Howie Goss		
	Jim Hickman		
	Manny Jimenez		
	Al Luplow		
	Ed Olivares		

1963 Topps

The 1963 Topps set is one of Topp's most popular sets. There's a major improvement in the quality of the color reproduction over previous years. The 576-card set features two photos on the front, a large portrait shot and a smaller black and white photo in the bottom right corner. The set contains the popular League Leaders, World Series and Rookies subsets. Cards measure 2-1/2" by 3-1/2".

Complete Set (576)		5,200.00	2,600.00
Commons (1-283)		2.50	1.25
Commons (284-446)		3.50	1.75
Commons (447-522)		12.00	6.00
Commons (523-576)		9.00	4.50

1	N.L. Batting Leaders	40.00	15.00
2	A.L. Batting Leaders	28.00	14.00
3	N.L. HR Leaders	20.00	10.00
4	A.L. HR Leaders	7.00	3.50
5	N.L. E.R.A. Leaders	8.00	4.00
6	A.L. E.R.A. Leaders	4.00	2.00
7	N.L. Pitching Leaders	4.00	2.00
8	A.L. Pitching Leaders	4.00	2.00
9	N.L. Strikeout Ldrs	8.00	4.00
10	A.L. Strikeout Ldrs	3.50	1.75
11	Lee Walls	2.50	1.25
12	Steve Barber	2.50	1.25
13	Phillies Team	4.00	2.00
14	Pedro Ramos	2.50	1.25
15	Ken Hubbs	3.00	1.50
16	Al Smith	2.50	1.25
17	Ryne Duren	3.00	1.50
18	Buc Blasters	15.00	7.50
	(Smokey Burgess, Bob Clemente, Bob Skinner, Dick Stuart)		
19	Pete Burnside	2.50	1.25

20	Tony Kubek	5.00	2.50
21	Marty Keough	2.50	1.25
22	Curt Simmons	2.50	1.25
23	Ed Lopat	2.50	1.25
24	Bob Bruce	2.50	1.25
25	Al Kaline	35.00	18.00
26	Ray Moore	2.50	1.25
27	Choo Choo Coleman	2.50	1.25
28	Mike Fornieles	2.50	1.25
29a	1962 Rookie Stars (John Boozer, Ray Culp, Sammy Ellis, Jesse Gonder)	4.00	2.00
29b	1963 Rookie Stars (John Boozer, Ray Culp, Sammy Ellis, Jesse Gonder)	3.00	1.50
30	Harvey Kuenn	3.50	1.75
31	Cal Koonce	2.50	1.25
32	Tony Gonzalez	2.50	1.25
33	Bo Belinsky	2.50	1.25
34	Dick Schofield	2.50	1.25
35	John Buzhardt	2.50	1.25
36	Jerry Kindall	2.50	1.25
37	Jerry Lynch	2.50	1.25
38	Bud Daley	2.50	1.25
39	Angels Team	4.00	2.00
40	Vic Power	2.50	1.25
41	Charlie Lau	2.50	1.25
42	Stan Williams	2.50	1.25
43	Veteran Masters (Casey Stengel, Gene Woodling)	4.00	2.00
44	Terry Fox	2.50	1.25
45	Bob Aspromonte	2.50	1.25
46	Tommie Aaron (R)	3.00	1.50
47	Don Lock	2.50	1.25
48	Birdie Tebbetts	2.50	1.25
49	Dal Maxvill (R)	4.00	2.00
50	Bill Pierce	2.50	1.25
51	George Alusik	2.50	1.25
52	Chuck Schilling	2.50	1.25
53	Joe Moeller	2.50	1.25
54a	1962 Rookie Stars (Jack Cullen, Dave DeBusscher, Harry Fanok, Nelson Mathews)	15.00	7.50
54b	1963 Rookie Stars (Jack Cullen, Dave DeBusscher, Harry Fanok, Nelson Mathews)	4.00	2.00
55	Bill Virdon	3.00	1.50
56	Dennis Bennett	2.50	1.25
57	Billy Moran	2.50	1.25
58	Bob Will	2.50	1.25
59	Craig Anderson	2.50	1.25
60	Elston Howard	7.00	3.50
61	Ernie Bowman	2.50	1.25
62	Bob Hendley	2.50	1.25
63	Reds Team	4.00	2.00
64	Dick McAuliffe	2.50	1.25
65	Jackie Brandt	2.50	1.25
66	Mike Joyce	2.50	1.25
67	Ed Charles	2.50	1.25
68	Friendly Foes (Gil Hodges, Duke Snider)	14.00	7.00
69	Bud Zipfel	2.50	1.25
70	Jim O'Toole	2.50	1.25
71	Bobby Wine (R)	2.50	1.25
72	Johnny Romano	2.50	1.25
73	Bobby Bragan	2.50	1.25
74	Denny Lemaster (R)	2.50	1.25
75	Bob Allison	2.50	1.25
76	Earl Wilson	2.50	1.25
77	Al Spangler	2.50	1.25
78	Marv Throneberry	2.50	1.25
79	Checklist 1-88	8.00	4.00
80	Jim Gilliam	4.00	2.00
81	Jimmie Schaffer	2.50	1.25
82	Ed Rakow	2.50	1.25
83	Charley James	2.50	1.25
84	Ron Kline	2.50	1.25
85	Tom Haller	2.50	1.25
86	Charley Maxwell	2.50	1.25
87	Bob Veale	2.50	1.25
88	Ron Hansen	2.50	1.25
89	Dick Stigman	2.50	1.25
90	Gordy Coleman	2.50	1.25
91	Dallas Green	3.00	1.50
92	Hector Lopez	2.50	1.25
93	Galen Cisco	2.50	1.25
94	Bob Schmidt	2.50	1.25
95	Larry Jackson	2.50	1.25
96	Lou Clinton	2.50	1.25
97	Bob Duliba	2.50	1.25
98	George Thomas	2.50	1.25
99	Jim Umbricht	2.50	1.25
100	Joe Cunningham	2.50	1.25
101	Joe Gibbon	8.00	4.00
103	Chuck Essegian	2.50	1.25
104	Lew Krausse	2.50	1.25
105	Ron Fairly	2.50	1.25
106	Bob Bolin	2.50	1.25
107	Jim Hickman	2.50	1.25
108	Hoyt Wilhelm	12.00	6.00
109	Lee Maye	2.50	1.25
110	Rich Rollins	2.50	1.25
111	Al Jackson	2.50	1.25
112	Dick Brown	2.50	1.25
113	Don Landrum (Wrong Photo)	3.00	1.50
114	Dan Osinski	2.50	1.25
115	Carl Yastrzemski	75.00	38.00
116	Jim Brosnan	2.50	1.25

117	Jack Davis	2.50	1.25		Dick Egan		
118	Sherm Lollar	2.50	1.25		Julio Navarro		
119	Bob Lillis	2.50	1.25		Gaylord Perry		
120	Roger Maris	70.00	35.00		Tommy Sisk		
121	Jim Hannan	2.50	1.25	170	Joe Adcock	3.00	1.50
122	Julio Gotay	2.50	1.25	171	Steve Hamilton	2.50	1.25
123	Frank Howard	4.00	2.00	172	Gene Oliver	2.50	1.25
124	Dick Howser	3.00	1.50	173	Bomber's Best	70.00	35.00
125	Robin Roberts	12.00	6.00		Mickey Mantle		
126	Bob Uecker	30.00	15.00		Bobby Richardson		
127	Bill Tuttle	2.50	1.25		Tom Tresh)		
128	Matty Alou	3.00	1.50	174	Larry Burright	2.50	1.25
129	Gary Bell	2.50	1.25	175	Bob Buhl	2.50	1.25
130	Dick Groat	3.00	1.50	176	Jim King	2.50	1.25
131	Senators Team	4.00	2.00	177	Bubba Phillips	2.50	1.25
132	Jack Hamilton	2.50	1.25	178	Johnny Edwards	2.50	1.25
133	Gene Freese	2.50	1.25	179	Ron Piche	2.50	1.25
134	Bob Scheffing	2.50	1.25	180	Bill Skowron	3.00	1.50
135	Richie Ashburn	10.00	5.00	181	Sammy Esposito	2.50	1.25
136	Ike Delock	2.50	1.25	182	Albie Pearson	2.50	1.25
137	Mack Jones	2.50	1.25	183	Joe Pepitone	3.50	1.75
138	Pride of N.L. (Willie	38.00	20.00	184	Vern Law	3.00	1.50
	Mays, Stan Musial)			185	Chuck Hiller	2.50	1.25
139	Earl Averill	2.50	1.25	186	Jerry Zimmerman	2.50	1.25
140	Frank Lary	3.00	1.50	187	Willie Kirkland	2.50	1.25
141	Manny Mota (R)	7.00	3.50	188	Eddie Bressoud	2.50	1.25
142	World Series Game 1	6.00	3.00	189	Dave Giusti	2.50	1.25
143	World Series Game 2	5.00	2.50	190	Minnie Minoso	5.00	2.50
144	World Series Game 3	10.00	5.00	191	Checklist 177-264	8.00	4.00
145	World Series Game 4	5.00	2.50	192	Clay Dalrymple	2.50	1.25
146	World Series Game 5	5.00	2.50	193	Andre Rodgers	2.50	1.25
147	World Series Game 6	5.00	2.50	194	Joe Nuxhall	2.50	1.25
148	World Series Game 7	5.00	2.50	195	Manny Jimenez	2.50	1.25
149	Marv Breeding	2.50	1.25	196	Doug Camilli	2.50	1.25
150	Johnny Podres	3.00	1.50	197	Roger Craig	3.00	1.50
151	Pirates Team	4.00	2.00	198	Lenny Green	2.50	1.25
152	Ron Nischwitz	2.50	1.25	199	Joe Amalfitano	2.50	1.25
153	Hal Smith	2.50	1.25	200	Mickey Mantle	475.00	240.00
154	Walt Alston	3.00	1.50	201	Cecil Butler	2.50	1.25
155	Bill Stafford	2.50	1.25	202	Red Sox Team	5.00	2.00
156	Roy McMillan	2.50	1.25	203	Chico Cardenas	2.50	1.25
157	Diego Segui (R)	2.50	1.25	204	Don Nottebart	2.50	1.25
158	1963 Rookie Stars	3.00	1.50	205	Luis Aparicio	15.00	7.50
	Rogelio Alvarez			206	Ray Washburn	2.50	1.25
	Tommy Harper			207	Ken Hunt	2.50	1.25
	Dave Roberts			208	1963 Rookie Stars	2.50	1.25
	Bob Saverine				Ron Herbel		
159	Jim Pagliaroni	2.50	1.25		John Miller		
160	Juan Pizarro	2.50	1.25		Ron Taylor		
161	Frank Torre	2.50	1.25		Wally Wolf		
162	Twins Team	4.00	2.00	209	Hobie Landrith	2.50	1.25
163	Don Larsen	3.50	1.75	210	Sandy Koufax	175.00	90.00
164	Bubba Morton	2.50	1.25	211	Fred Whitfield	2.50	1.25
165	Jim Kaat	3.50	1.75	212	Glen Hobbie	2.50	1.25
166	Johnny Keane	2.50	1.25	213	Billy Hitchcock	2.50	1.25
167	Jim Fregosi	3.00	1.50	214	Orlando Pena	2.50	1.25
168	Russ Nixon	2.50	1.25	215	Bob Skinner	2.50	1.25
169	1963 Rookie Stars	32.00	16.00				

216	Gene Conley	2.50	1.25
217	Joe Christopher	2.50	1.25
218	Tiger Twirlers (Jim Bunning, Frank Lary Don Mossi)	4.00	2.00
219	Chuck Cottier	2.50	1.25
220	Camilo Pascual	2.50	1.25
221	Cookie Rojas (R)	4.00	2.00
222	Cubs Team	5.00	2.50
223	Eddie Fisher	2.50	1.25
224	Mike Roarke	2.50	1.25
225	Joe Jay	2.50	1.25
226	Julian Javier	2.50	1.25
227	Jim Grant	3.00	1.50
228	1963 Rookie Stars Max Alvis Bob Bailey Ed Kranepool Tony Oliva	55.00	28.00
229	Willie Davis	3.00	1.50
230	Pete Runnels	3.00	1.50
231	Eli Grba (Wrong Photo)	2.50	1.25
232	Frank Malzone	3.00	1.50
233	Casey Stengel	15.00	7.50
234	Dave Nicholson	2.50	1.25
235	Billy O'Dell	2.50	1.25
236	Bill Bryan	2.50	1.25
237	Jim Coates	2.50	1.25
238	Lou Johnson	2.50	1.25
239	Harvey Haddix	3.00	1.50
240	Rocky Colavito	10.00	5.00
241	Billy Smith	2.50	1.25
242	Power Plus (Hank Aaron, Ernie Banks)	38.00	20.00
243	Don Leppert	2.50	1.25
244	John Tsitouris	2.50	1.25
245	Gil Hodges	20.00	10.00
246	Lee Stange	2.50	1.25
247	Yankees Team	15.00	7.50
248	Tito Francona	2.50	1.25
249	Leo Burke	2.50	1.25
250	Stan Musial	125.00	65.00
251	Jack Lamabe	2.50	1.25
252	Ron Santo	8.00	4.00
253	1963 Rookie Stars Len Gabrielson Pete Jerrigan Deacon Jones John Wojcik	2.50	1.25
254	Mike Hershberger	2.50	1.25
255	Bob Shaw	2.50	1.25
256	Jerry Lumpe	2.50	1.25
257	Hank Aguirre	2.50	1.25
258	Alvin Dark	2.50	1.25
259	Johnny Logan	2.50	1.25
260	Jim Gentile	3.50	1.75
261	Bob Miller	2.50	1.25
262	Ellis Burton	2.50	1.25
263	Dave Stenhouse	2.50	1.25
264	Phil Linz	2.50	1.25
265	Vada Pinson	4.00	2.00
266	Bob Allen	2.50	1.25
267	Carl Sawatski	2.50	1.25
268	Don Demeter	2.50	1.25
269	Don Mincher	2.50	1.25
270	Felipe Alou	4.00	2.00
271	Dean Stone	2.50	1.25
272	Danny Murphy	2.50	1.25
273	Sammy Taylor	2.50	1.25
274	Checklist 265-352	8.00	4.00
275	Ed Mathews	24.00	12.00
276	Barry Shetrone	2.50	1.25
277	Dick Farrell	2.50	1.25
278	Chico Fernandez	2.50	1.25
279	Wally Moon	3.00	1.50
280	Bob Rodgers	3.00	1.50
281	Tom Sturdivant	2.50	1.25
282	Bob Del Greco	2.50	1.25
283	Roy Sievers	3.00	1.50
284	Dave Sisler	3.50	1.75
285	Dick Stuart	3.50	1.75
286	Stu Miller	3.50	1.75
287	Dick Bertell	3.50	1.75
288	White Sox Team	7.00	3.50
289	Hal Brown	3.50	1.75
290	Bill White	4.00	2.00
291	Don Rudolph	3.50	1.75
292	Pumpsie Green	3.50	1.75
293	Bill Pleis	3.50	1.75
294	Bill Rigney	3.50	1.75
295	Ed Roebuck	3.50	1.75
296	Doc Edwards	3.50	1.75
297	Jim Golden	3.50	1.75
298	Don Dillard	3.50	1.75
299	1963 Rookie Stars Tom Butters Bob Dustal Dave Morehead Dan Schneider	3.50	1.75
300	Willie Mays	180.00	90.00
301	Bill Fischer	3.50	1.75
302	Whitey Herzog	5.00	2.50
303	Earl Francis	3.50	1.75
304	Harry Bright	3.50	1.75
305	Don Hoak	3.50	1.75
306	Star Receivers (Earl Battey, Elston Howard)	5.00	2.50
307	Chet Nichols	3.50	1.75
308	Camilo Carreon	3.50	1.75
309	Jim Brewer	3.50	1.75
310	Tommy Davis	6.00	3.00
311	Joe McClain	3.50	1.75
312	Colt .45s Team	7.00	3.50
313	Ernie Broglio	3.50	1.75
314	John Goryl	3.50	1.75

315	Ralph Terry	4.00	2.00
316	Norm Sherry	3.50	1.75
317	Sam McDowell	5.00	2.50
318	Gene Mauch	4.00	2.00
319	Joe Gaines	3.50	1.75
320	Warren Spahn	45.00	22.50
321	Gino Cimoli	3.50	1.75
322	Bob Turley	3.50	1.75
323	Bill Mazeroski	6.00	3.00
324	1963 Rookie Stars	5.00	2.50
	Vic Davalillo		
	Phil Roof		
	Pete Ward		
	George Williams		
325	Jack Sanford	3.50	1.75
326	Hank Foiles	3.50	1.75
327	Paul Foytack	3.50	1.75
328	Dick Williams	3.50	1.75
329	Lindy McDaniel	3.50	1.75
330	Chuck Hinton	3.50	1.75
331	Series Foes (Bill	4.00	2.00
	Pierce, Bill Stafford)		
332	Joel Horlen	3.50	1.75
333	Carl Warwick	3.50	1.75
334	Wynn Hawkins	3.50	1.75
335	Leon Wagner	3.50	1.75
336	Ed Bauta	3.50	1.75
337	Dodgers Team	10.00	5.00
338	Russ Kemmerer	3.50	1.75
339	Ted Bowsfield	3.50	1.75
340	Yogi Berra	80.00	40.00
341	Jack Baldschun	3.50	1.75
342	Gene Woodling	4.00	2.00
343	Johnny Pesky	3.50	1.75
344	Don Schwall	3.50	1.75
345	Brooks Robinson	55.00	28.00
346	Billy Hoeft	3.50	1.75
347	Joe Torre	8.00	4.00
348	Vic Wertz	3.50	1.75
349	Zoilo Versalles	4.00	2.00
350	Bob Purkey	3.50	1.75
351	Al Luplow	3.50	1.75
352	Ken Johnson	3.50	1.75
353	Billy Williams	24.00	12.00
354	Dom Zanni	3.50	1.75
355	Dean Chance	4.00	2.00
356	John Schaive	3.50	1.75
357	George Altman	3.50	1.75
358	Milt Pappas	3.50	1.75
359	Haywood Sullivan	3.50	1.75
360	Don Drysdale	40.00	20.00
361	Clete Boyer	5.00	2.50
362	Checklist 353-429	8.00	4.00
363	Dick Radatz	3.50	1.75
364	Howie Goss	3.50	1.75
365	Jim Bunning	10.00	5.00
366	Tony Taylor	3.50	1.75
367	Tony Cloninger	3.50	1.75
368	Ed Bailey	3.50	1.75
369	Jim Lemon	3.50	1.75
370	Dick Donovan	3.50	1.75
371	Rod Kanehl	3.50	1.75
372	Don Lee	3.50	1.75
373	Jim Campbell	3.50	1.75
374	Claude Osteen	4.00	2.00
375	Ken Boyer	8.00	4.00
376	Johnnie Wyatt	3.50	1.75
377	Orioles Team	7.00	3.50
378	Bill Henry	3.50	1.75
379	Bob Anderson	3.50	1.75
380	Ernie Banks	65.00	32.50
381	Frank Baumann	3.50	1.75
382	Ralph Houk	5.00	2.50
383	Pete Richert	3.50	1.75
384	Bob Tillman	3.50	1.75
385	Art Mahaffey	3.50	1.75
386	1963 Rookie Stars	4.00	2.00
	John Bateman		
	Larry Bearnarth		
	Ed Kirkpatrick		
	Garry Roggenburk		
387	Al McBean	3.50	1.75
388	Jim Davenport	3.50	1.75
389	Frank Sullivan	3.50	1.75
390	Hank Aaron	165.00	85.00
391	Bill Dailey	3.50	1.75
392	Tribe Thumpers	3.50	1.75
	Tito Francona, Johnny		
	Romano)		
393	Ken MacKenzie	3.50	1.75
394	Tim McCarver	12.00	6.00
395	Don McMahon	4.00	2.00
396	Joe Koppe	3.50	1.75
397	Athletics Team	7.00	3.50
398	Boog Powell	20.00	10.00
399	Dick Ellsworth	3.50	1.75
400	Frank Robinson	55.00	28.00
401	Jim Bouton	8.00	4.00
402	Mickey Vernon	3.50	1.75
403	Ron Perranoski	4.00	2.00
404	Bob Oldis	3.50	1.75
405	Floyd Robinson	3.50	1.75
406	Howie Koplitz	3.50	1.75
407	1963 Rookie Stars	3.50	1.75
	Larry Elliot		
	Frank Kostro		
	Chico Ruiz		
	Dick Simpson		
408	Billy Gardner	3.50	1.75
409	Roy Face	5.00	2.50
410	Earl Battey	4.00	2.00
411	Jim Constable	3.50	1.75
412	Dodgers' Big Three	40.00	20.00
	Don Drysdale, Sandy		
	Koufax, Johnny Podres		
413	Jerry Walker	3.50	1.75

414	Ty Cline	3.50	1.75
415	Bob Gibson	45.00	22.50
416	Alex Grammas	3.50	1.75
417	Giants team	7.00	3.50
418	Johnny Orsino	3.50	1.75
419	Tracy Stallard	3.50	1.75
420	Bobby Richardson	10.00	5.00
421	Tom Morgan	3.50	1.75
422	Fred Hutchinson	4.00	2.00
423	Ed Hobaugh	3.50	1.75
424	Charley Smith	3.50	1.75
425	Smoky Burgess	4.00	2.00
426	Barry Latman	3.50	1.75
427	Bernie Allen	3.50	1.75
428	Carl Boles	3.50	1.75
429	Lew Burdette	5.00	2.50
430	Norm Siebern	4.00	2.00
431	Checklist 430-506	8.00	4.00
432	Roman Mejias	3.50	1.75
433	Denis Menke	3.50	1.75
434	Johnny Callison	3.50	1.75
435	Woody Held	3.50	1.75
436	Tim Harkness	3.50	1.75
437	Bill Bruton	3.50	1.75
438	Wes Stock	3.50	1.75
439	Don Zimmer	5.00	2.50
440	Juan Marichal	28.00	14.00
441	Lee Thomas	3.50	1.75
442	J.C. Hartman	3.50	1.75
443	Jim Piersall	5.00	2.50
444	Jim Maloney	4.00	2.00
445	Norm Cash	7.00	3.50
446	Whitey Ford	40.00	20.00
447	Felix Mantilla	12.00	6.00
448	Jack Kralick	12.00	6.00
449	Jose Tartabull	12.00	6.00
451	Indians Team	18.00	9.00
452	Barney Schultz	12.00	6.00
453	Jake Wood	12.00	6.00
454	Art Fowler	12.00	6.00
455	Ruben Amaro	12.00	6.00
456	Jim Coker	12.00	6.00
457	Tex Clevenger	12.00	6.00
458	Al Lopez	15.00	7.50
459	Dick LeMay	12.00	6.00
460	Del Crandall	14.00	7.00
461	Norm Bass	12.00	6.00
462	Wally Post	12.00	6.00
463	Joe Schaffernoth	12.00	6.00
464	Ken Aspromonte	12.00	6.00
465	Chuck Estrada	12.00	6.00
466	1963 Rookie Stars	40.00	20.00
	Bill Freehan		
	Tony Martinez		
	Nate Oliver		
	Jerry Robinson		
467	Phil Ortega	12.00	6.00
468	Carroll Hardy	12.00	6.00
469	Jay Hook	12.00	6.00
470	Tom Tresh	24.00	12.00
471	Ken Retzer	12.00	6.00
472	Lou Brock	150.00	90.00
473	Mets Team	100.00	50.00
474	Jack Fisher	12.00	6.00
475	Gus Triandos	12.00	6.00
476	Frank Funk	12.00	6.00
477	Donn Clendenon	12.00	6.00
478	Paul Brown	12.00	6.00
479	Ed Brinkman	12.00	6.00
480	Bill Monbouquette	12.00	6.00
481	Bob Taylor	12.00	6.00
482	Felix Torres	12.00	6.00
483	Jim Owens	12.00	6.00
484	Dale Long	12.00	6.00
385	Jim Landis	12.00	6.00
486	Ray Sadecki	12.00	6.00
487	John Roseboro	14.00	7.00
488	Jerry Adair	12.00	6.00
489	Paul Toth	12.00	6.00
490	Willie McCovey	150.00	90.00
491	Harry Craft	12.00	6.00
492	Dave Wickersham	12.00	6.00
493	Walt Bond	12.00	6.00
494	Phil Regan	12.00	6.00
495	Frank Thomas	12.00	6.00
496	1963 Rookie Stars	12.00	6.00
	Carl Bouldin		
	Steve Dalkowski		
	Fred Newman		
	Jack Smith		
497	Bennie Daniels	12.00	6.00
498	Eddie Kasko	12.00	6.00
499	J.C. Martin	12.00	6.00
500	Harmon Killebrew	110.00	55.00
501	Joe Azcue	12.00	6.00
502	Daryl Spencer	12.00	6.00
503	Braves Team	20.00	10.00
504	Bob Johnson	12.00	6.00
505	Curt Flood	18.00	12.00
506	Gene Green	12.00	6.00
507	Roland Sheldon	12.00	6.00
508	Ted Savage	12.00	6.00
509	Checklist 507-576	18.00	9.00
510	Ken McBride	12.00	6.00
511	Charlie Neal	12.00	6.00
512	Cal McLish	12.00	6.00
513	Gary Geiger	12.00	6.00
514	Larry Osborne	12.00	6.00
515	Don Elston	12.00	6.00
516	Purnell Goldy	12.00	6.00
517	Hal Woodeshick	12.00	6.00
518	Don Blasingame	12.00	6.00
519	Claude Raymond (R)	14.00	7.00
520	Orlando Cepeda	24.00	12.00
521	Dan Pfister	12.00	6.00
522	1963 Rookie Stars	12.00	6.00

	Mel Nelson		
	Gary Peters		
	Art Quirk		
	Jim Roland		
523	Bill Kunkel	9.00	4.50
524	Cardinals Team	18.00	9.00
525	Nellie Fox	20.00	10.00
526	Dick Hall	9.00	4.50
527	Ed Sadowski	9.00	4.50
528	Carl Willey	9.00	4.50
529	Wes Covington	10.00	5.00
530	Don Mossi	9.00	4.50
531	Sam Mele	9.00	4.50
532	Steve Boros	9.00	4.50
533	Bobby Shantz	12.00	6.00
534	Ken Walters	9.00	4.50
535	Jim Perry	10.00	5.00
536	Norm Larker	9.00	4.50
537	1963 Rookie Stars	750.00	375.00
	Pedro Gonzalez		
	Ken McMullen		
	Pete Rose		
	Al Weis		
538	George Brunet	9.00	4.50
539	Wayne Causey	9.00	4.50
540	Bob Clemente	225.00	110.00
541	Ron Moeller	9.00	4.50
542	Lou Klimchock	9.00	4.50
543	Russ Snyder	9.00	4.50
544	1963 Rookie Stars	40.00	20.00
	Duke Carmel		
	Bill Haas		
	Dick Phillips		
	Rusty Staub		
545	Jose Pagan	9.00	4.50
546	Hal Reniff	9.00	4.50
547	Gus Bell	9.00	4.50
548	Tom Satriano	9.00	4.50
549	1963 Rookie Stars	9.00	4.50
	Marcelino Lopez		
	Pete Lovrich		
	Elmo Plaskett		
	Paul Ratliff	9.00	4.50
550	Duke Snider	75.00	38.00
551	Billy Klaus	9.00	4.50
552	Tigers Team	18.00	9.00
553	1963 Rookie Stars	290.00	150.00
	Brock Davis		
	Jim Gosger		
	John Herrnstein		
	Willie Stargell		
554	Hank Fischer	9.00	4.50
555	John Blanchard	9.00	4.50
556	Al Worthington	9.00	4.50
557	Cuno Barragan	9.00	4.50
558	1963 Rookie Stars	10.00	5.00
	Bill Faul		
	Ron Hunt		
	Bob Lipski		
	Al Moran		
559	Danny Murtaugh	9.00	4.50
560	Ray Herbert	9.00	4.50
561	Mike de la Hoz	9.00	4.50
562	1963 Rookie Stars	14.00	7.00
	Randy Cardinal		
	Dave McNally		
	Don Rowe		
	Ken Rowe		
563	Mike McCormick	9.00	4.50
564	George Banks	9.00	4.50
565	Larry Sherry	10.00	5.00
566	Cliff Cook	9.00	4.50
567	Jim Duffalo	9.00	4.50
568	Bob Sadowski	9.00	4.50
569	Luis Arroyo	10.00	5.00
570	Frank Bolling	9.00	4.50
571	Johnny Klippstein	9.00	4.50
572	Jack Spring	9.00	4.50
573	Coot Veal	9.00	4.50
574	Hal Kolstad	9.00	4.50
575	Don Cardwell	9.00	4.50
576	Johnny Temple	12.00	6.00

1964 Topps

This 587-card set features large color photos on the card fronts with a panel above the picture containing team names in large block letters. Cards measure 2-1/2" by 3-1/2". The orange colored card backs contain a baseball trivia question in which the answer is revealed by scratching off a small white panel. Subsets include League Leaders, World Series Highlights and Rookie Prospects.

		NR/MT	EX
Complete Set (587)		3,300.00	1,650.00
Commons (1-370)		2.50	1.25
Commons (371-522)		4.00	2.00
Commons (523-587)		9.00	4.50
1	N.L. E.R.A. Leaders	18.00	7.00
2	A.L. E.R.A. Leaders	3.00	1.50
3	N.L. Pitching Ldrs	12.00	6.00
4	A.L. Pitching Leaders	3.00	1.50
5	N.L. Strikeout Ldrs	10.00	5.00
6	A.L. Strikeout Leaders	3.00	1.50
7	N.L. Batting Leaders	7.00	3.50
8	A.L. Batting Leaders	7.00	3.50
9	N.L. Home Run Ldrs	15.00	7.50
10	A.L. Home Run Ldrs	4.00	2.00
11	N.L. R.B.I. Leaders	7.00	3.50
12	A.L. R.B.I. Leaders	4.00	2.00
13	Hoyt Wilhelm	10.00	5.00
14	Dodgers Rookies	2.50	1.25
	Dick Nen (R)		
	Nick Willhite (R)		
15	Zoilo Versalles	2.50	1.25
16	John Boozer	2.50	1.25
17	Willie Kirkland	2.50	1.25
18	Billy O'Dell	2.50	1.25
19	Don Wert	2.50	1.25
20	Bob Friend	2.50	1.25
21	Yogi Berra	45.00	22.50
22	Jerry Adair	2.50	1.25
23	Chris Zachary	2.50	1.25
24	Carl Sawatski	2.50	1.25
25	Bill Monbouquette	2.50	1.25
26	Gino Cimoli	2.50	1.25
27	Mets Team	7.00	3.50
28	Claude Osteen	2.50	1.25
29	Lou Brock	40.00	20.00
30	Ron Perranoski	2.50	1.25
31	Dave Nicholson	2.50	1.25
32	Dean Chance	2.50	1.25
33	Reds Rookies	2.50	1.75
	Sammy Ellis (R)		
	Mel Queen (R)		
34	Jim Perry	2.50	1.25
35	Ed Mathews	2.50	1.25
36	Hal Reniff	2.50	1.25
37	Smoky Burgess	2.50	1.25
38	Jim Wynn (R)	8.00	4.00
39	Hank Aguirre	2.50	1.25
40	Dick Groat	2.50	1.25
41	Friendly Foes	6.00	3.00
	Willie McCovey		
	Leon Wagner		
42	Moe Drabowsky	2.50	1.25
43	Roy Sievers	3.00	1.50
44	Duke Carmel	2.50	1.25
45	Milt Pappas	2.50	1.25
46	Ed Brinkman	2.50	1.25
47	Giants Rookies	3.00	1.50
	Jesus Alou (R)		
	Ron Herbel (R)		
48	Bob Perry	2.50	1.25
49	Bill Henry	2.50	1.25
50	Mickey Mantle	260.00	130.00
51	Pete Richert	2.50	1.25
52	Chuck Hinton	2.50	1.25
53	Denis Menke	2.50	1.25
54	Sam Mele	2.50	1.25
55	Ernie Banks	30.00	15.00
56	Hal Brown	2.50	1.25
57	Tim Harkness	2.50	1.25
58	Don Demeter	2.50	1.25
59	Ernie Broglio	2.50	1.25
60	Frank Malzone	2.50	1.25
61	Angel Backstops	2.50	1.25
	Bob Rodgers		
	Ed Sadowski		
62	Ted Savage	2.50	1.25
63	Johnny Orsino	2.50	1.25
64	Ted Abernathy	2.50	1.25
65	Felipe Alou	3.50	1.75
66	Eddie Fisher	2.50	1.25
67	Tigers Team	3.50	1.75
68	Willie Davis	3.00	1.50
69	Clete Boyer	3.00	1.50
70	Joe Torre	4.00	2.00
71	Jack Spring	2.50	1.25
72	Chico Cardenas	2.50	1.25
73	Jimmie Hall	2.50	1.25
74	Pirates Rookies	2.50	1.25
	Tom Butlers (R)		
	Bob Priddy (R)		
75	Wayne Causey	2.50	1.25
76	Checklist 1-88	7.00	3.50
77	Jerry Walker	2.50	1.25
78	Merritt Ranew	2.50	1.25
79	Bob Heffner	2.50	1.25
80	Vada Pinson	4.00	2.00
81	All-Star Vets	8.00	4.00
	Nellie Fox		
	Harmon Killebrew		
82	Jim Davenport	2.50	1.25
83	Gus Triandos	2.50	1.25
84	Carl Willey	2.50	1.25
85	Pete Ward	2.50	1.25
86	Al Downing	3.00	1.50
87	Cardinals Team	3.50	1.75
88	John Roseboro	3.00	1.50
89	Boog Powell	5.00	2.50
90	Earl Battey	2.50	1.25
91	Bob Bailey	2.50	1.25
92	Steve Ridzik	2.50	1.25
93	Gary Geiger	2.50	1.25
94	Braves Rookies	2.50	1.25
	Jim Britton (R)		

	Larry Maxie (R)		
95	George Altman	2.50	1.25
96	Bob Buhl	2.50	1.25
97	Jim Fregosi	3.00	1.50
98	Bill Bruton	2.50	1.25
99	Al Stanek	2.50	1.25
100	Elston Howard	6.00	3.00
101	Walt Alston	3.00	1.50
102	Checklist 89-176	7.00	3.50
103	Curt Flood	3.00	1.50
104	Art Mahaffey	2.50	1.25
105	Woody Held	2.50	1.25
106	Joe Nuxhall	2.50	1.25
107	White Sox Rookies	2.50	1.25
	Bruce Howard (R)		
	Frank Kreutzer (R)		
108	John Wyatt	2.50	1.25
109	Rusty Staub	8.00	4.00
110	Albie Pearson	2.50	1.25
111	Don Elston	2.50	1.25
112	Bob Tillman	2.50	1.25
113	Grover Powell	2.50	1.25
114	Don Lock	2.50	1.25
115	Frank Bolling	2.50	1.25
116	Twins Rookies	18.00	9.00
	Tony Oliva		
	Jay Ward (R)		
117	Earl Francis	2.50	1.25
118	John Blanchard	2.50	1.25
119	Gary Kolb	2.50	1.25
120	Don Drysdale	20.00	10.00
121	Pete Runnels	3.00	1.50
122	Don McMahon	2.50	1.25
123	Jose Pagan	2.50	1.25
124	Orlando Pena	2.50	1.25
125	Pete Rose	190.00	95.00
126	Russ Snyder	2.50	1.25
127	Angels Rookies	2.50	1.25
	Aubrey Gatewood (R)		
	Dick Simpson (R)		
128	Mickey Lolich (R)	15.00	7.50
129	Amado Samuel	2.50	1.25
130	Gary Peters	2.50	1.25
131	Steve Boros	2.50	1.25
132	Braves Team	3.50	1.75
133	Jim Grant	2.50	1.25
134	Don Zimmer	3.00	1.50
135	Johnny Callison	2.50	1.25
136	World Series Game	110.00	5.00
137	World Series Game 2	3.50	1.75
138	World Series Game 3	3.50	1.75
139	World Series Game 4	3.50	1.75
140	WS Celebration	3.50	1.75
141	Danny Murtaugh	2.50	1.25
142	John Bateman	2.50	1.25
143	Bubba Phillips	2.50	1.25
144	Al Worthington	2.50	1.25
145	Norm Siebern	2.50	1.25
146	Indians Rookies	70.00	35.00
	Bob Chance (R)		
	Tommy John (R)		
147	Ray Sadecki	2.50	1.25
148	J.C. Martin	2.50	1.25
149	Paul Foytack	2.50	1.25
150	Willie Mays	125.00	65.00
151	Athletics Team	3.50	1.75
152	Denver Lemaster	2.50	1.25
153	Dick Williams	2.50	1.25
154	Dick Tracewski	2.50	1.25
155	Duke Snider	2.50	1.25
156	Billy Dailey	2.50	1.25
157	Gene Mauch	3.00	1.50
158	Ken Johnson	2.50	1.25
159	Charlie Dees	2.50	1.25
160	Ken Boyer	6.00	3.00
161	Dave McNalley	3.50	1.75
162	Hitting Area	3.00	1.50
	Vada Pinson		
	Dick Sisler		
163	Donn Clendenon	2.50	1.25
164	Bud Daley	2.50	1.25
165	Jerry Lumpe	2.50	1.25
166	Marty Keough	2.50	1.25
167	Senators Rookies	30.00	15.00
	Mike Brumley (R)		
	Lou Piniella (R)		
168	Al Weis	2.50	1.25
169	Del Crandall	2.50	1.25
170	Dick Radatz	2.50	1.25
171	Ty Cline	2.50	1.25
172	Indians Team	3.50	1.75
173	Ryne Duren	2.50	1.25
174	Doc Edwards	2.50	1.25
175	Billy Williams	16.00	8.00
176	Tracy Stallard	2.50	1.25
177	Harmon Killebrew	24.00	12.00
178	Hank Bauer	2.50	1.25
179	Carl Warwick	2.50	1.25
180	Tommy Davis	3.50	1.75
181	Dave Wickersham	2.50	1.25
182	Sox Sockers	15.00	7.50
	Chuck Schilling		
	Carl Yastrzemski		
183	Ron Taylor	2.50	1.25
184	Al Luplow	2.50	1.25
185	Jim O'Toole	2.50	1.25
186	Roman Mejias	2.50	1.25
187	Ed Roebuck	2.50	1.25
188	Checklist 177-264	7.00	3.50
189	Bob Hendley	2.50	1.25
190	Bobby Richardson	5.00	2.50
191	Clay Dalrymple	2.50	1.25
192	Cubs Rookies	2.50	1.25
	John Boccabella (R)		
	Billy Cowan (R)		
193	Jerry Lynch	2.50	1.25

194	John Goryl	2.50	1.25
195	Floyd Robinson	2.50	1.25
196	Jim Gentile	3.50	1.75
197	Frank Lary	2.50	1.25
198	Len Gabrielson	2.50	1.25
199	Joe Azcue	2.50	1.25
200	Sandy Koufax	125.00	65.00
201	Orioles Rookies	2.50	1.25
	Sam Bowens (R)		
	Wally Bunker (R)		
202	Galen Cisco	2.50	1.25
203	John Kennedy	2.50	1.25
204	Matty Alou	4.00	2.00
205	Nellie Fox	8.00	4.00
206	Steve Hamilton	2.50	1.25
207	Fred Hutchinson	2.50	1.25
208	Wes Covington	2.50	1.25
209	Bob Allen	2.50	1.25
210	Carl Yastrzemski	70.00	35.00
211	Jim Coker	2.50	1.25
212	Pete Lovrich	2.50	1.25
213	Angels Team	3.50	1.75
214	Ken McMullen	2.50	1.25
215	Ray Herbert	2.50	1.25
216	Mike de la Hoz	2.50	1.25
217	Jim King	2.50	1.25
218	Hank Fischer	2.50	1.25
219	Young Aces (Jim	3.50	1.75
	Bouton/Al Downing)		
220	Dick Ellsworth	2.50	1.25
221	Bob Saverine	2.50	1.25
222	Bill Pierce	2.50	1.25
223	George Banks	2.50	1.25
224	Tommie Sisk	2.50	1.25
225	Roger Maris	70.00	35.00
226	Colts Rookies	4.00	2.00
	Jerry Grote (R)		
	Larry Yellen (R)		
227	Barry Latman	2.50	1.25
228	Felix Mantilla	2.50	1.25
229	Charley Lau	2.50	1.25
230	Brooks Robinson	38.00	20.00
231	Dick Calmus	2.50	1.25
232	Al Lopez	3.50	1.75
233	Hal Smith	2.50	1.25
234	Gary Bell	2.50	1.25
235	Ron Hunt	2.50	1.25
236	Bill Faul	2.50	1.25
237	Cubs Team	3.50	1.75
238	Roy McMillan	2.50	1.25
239	Herm Starrette	2.50	1.25
240	Bill White	3.50	1.75
241	Jim Owens	2.50	1.25
242	Harvey Kuenn	3.50	1.75
243	Phillies Rookies	25.00	12.50
	Richie Allen (R)		
	John Hernstein (R)		
244	Tony LaRussa (R)	15.00	7.50
245	Dick Stigman	2.50	1.25
246	Manny Mota	4.00	2.00
247	Dave DeBusschere	4.00	2.00
248	Johnny Pesky	2.50	1.25
249	Doug Camilli	2.50	1.25
250	Al Kaline	35.00	18.00
251	Choo Choo Coleman	2.50	1.25
252	Ken Aspromonte	2.50	1.25
253	Wally Post	2.50	1.25
254	Don Hoak	2.50	1.25
255	Lee Thomas	2.50	1.25
256	Johnny Weekly	2.50	1.25
257	Giants Team	3.50	1.75
258	Garry Roggenburk	2.50	1.25
259	Harry Bright	2.50	1.25
260	Frank Robinson	30.00	15.00
261	Jim Hannan	2.50	1.25
262	Cardinals Rookie	4.00	2.00
	Stars Harry Fanok (R)		
	Mike Shannon (R)		
263	Chuck Estrada	2.50	1.25
264	Jim Landis	2.50	1.25
265	Jim Bunning	7.00	3.50
266	Gene Freese	2.50	1.25
267	Wilbur Wood (R)	4.00	2.00
268	Bill's Got It	3.00	1.50
	Danny Murtaugh		
	Bill Virdon		
269	Ellis Burton	2.50	1.25
270	Rich Rollins	2.50	1.25
271	Bob Sadowski	2.50	1.25
272	Jake Wood	2.50	1.25
273	Mel Nelson	2.50	1.25
274	Checklist 265-352	7.00	3.50
275	John Tsitouris	2.50	1.25
276	Jose Tartabull	2.50	1.25
277	Ken Retzer	2.50	1.25
278	Bobby Shantz	3.00	1.50
279	Joe Koppe	2.50	1.25
280	Juan Marichal	14.00	7.00
281	Yankees Rookies	2.50	1.25
	Jake Gibbs (R)		
	Tom Metcalf (R)		
282	Bob Bruce	2.50	1.25
283	Tommy McCraw	2.50	1.25
284	Dick Schofield	2.50	1.25
285	Robin Roberts	10.00	5.00
286	Don Landrum	2.50	1.25
287	Red Sox Rookies	28.00	14.00
	Tony Conigliaro (R)		
	Bill Spanswick (R)		
288	Al Moran	2.50	1.25
289	Frank Funk	2.50	1.25
290	Bob Allison	2.50	1.25
291	Phil Ortega	2.50	1.25
292	Mike Roarke	2.50	1.25
293	Phillies Team	3.50	1.75
294	Ken Hunt	2.50	1.25

295	Roger Craig	3.50	1.75		343	Senators Team	3.50	1.75
296	Ed Kirkpatrick	2.50	1.25		344	Phil Linz	2.50	1.25
297	Ken MacKenzie	2.50	1.25		345	Frank Thomas	2.50	1.25
298	Harry Craft	2.50	1.25		346	Joe Jay	2.50	1.25
299	Bill Stafford	2.50	1.25		347	Bobby Wine	2.50	1.25
300	Hank Aaron	140.00	70.00		348	Ed Lopat	2.50	1.25
301	Larry Brown	2.50	1.25		349	Art Fowler	2.50	1.25
302	Dan Pfister	2.50	1.25		350	Willie McCovey	28.00	14.00
303	Jim Campbell	2.50	1.25		351	Dan Schneider	2.50	1.25
304	Bob Johnson	2.50	1.25		352	Eddie Bressoud	2.50	1.25
305	Jack Lamabe	2.50	1.25		353	Wally Moon	2.50	1.25
306	Giant Gunners	25.00	12.50		354	Dave Giusti	2.50	1.25
	Orlando Cepeda				355	Vic Power	2.50	1.25
	Willie Mays				356	Reds Rookies	2.50	1.25
307	Joe Gibbon	2.50	1.25			Bill McCool (R)		
308	Gene Stephens	2.50	1.25			Chico Ruiz (R)		
309	Paul Toth	2.50	1.25		357	Charley James	2.50	1.25
310	Jim Gilliam	5.00	2.50		358	Ron Kline	2.50	1.25
311	Tom Brown	2.50	1.25		359	Jim Schaffer	2.50	1.25
312	Tigers Rookies	2.50	1.25		360	Joe Pepitone	4.00	2.00
	Fritz Fisher (R)				361	Jay Hook	2.50	1.25
	Fred Gladding (R)				362	Checklist 353-429	7.00	3.50
313	Chuck Hiller	2.50	1.25		363	Dick McAuliffe	2.50	1.25
314	Jerry Buchek	2.50	1.25		364	Joe Gaines	2.50	1.25
315	Bo Belinsky	4.00	2.00		365	Cal McLish	2.50	1.25
316	Gene Oliver	2.50	1.25		366	Nelson Mathews	2.50	1.25
317	Al Smith	2.50	1.25		367	Fred Whitfield	2.50	1.25
318	Twins Team	3.50	1.75		368	White Sox Rookies	2.50	1.25
319	Paul Brown	2.50	1.25			Fritz Ackley (R)		
320	Rocky Colavito	8.00	4.00			Don Buford (R)		
321	Bob Lillis	2.50	1.25		369	Jerry Zimmerman	2.50	1.25
322	George Brunet	2.50	1.25		370	Hal Woodeshick	2.50	1.25
323	John Buzhardt	2.50	1.25		371	Frank Howard	7.00	3.50
324	Casey Stengel	15.00	7.50		372	Howie Koplitz	4.00	2.00
325	Hector Lopez	2.50	1.25		373	Pirates Team	7.00	3.50
326	Ron Brand	2.50	1.25		374	Bobby Bolin	4.00	2.00
327	Don Blasingame	2.50	1.25		375	Ron Santo	7.00	3.50
328	Bob Shaw	2.50	1.25		376	Dave Morehead	4.00	2.00
329	Russ Nixon	2.50	1.25		377	Bob Skinner	4.00	2.00
330	Tommy Harper	3.00	1.50		378	Braves Rookies	5.00	2.50
331	A.L. Bombers	125.00	65.00			Jack Smith (R)		
	Norm Cash					Woody Woodward (R)		
	Al Kaline				379	Tony Gonzalez	2.50	2.50
	Mickey Mantle				380	Whitey Ford	28.00	14.00
	Roger Maris				381	Bob Taylor	4.00	2.00
332	Ray Washburn	2.50	1.25		382	Wes Stock	4.00	2.00
333	Billy Moran	2.50	1.25		383	Bill Rigney	4.00	2.00
334	Lew Krausse	2.50	1.25		384	Ron Hansen	4.00	2.00
335	Don Mossi	2.50	1.25		385	Curt Simmons	4.00	2.00
336	Andre Rodgers	2.50	1.25		386	Lenny Green	4.00	2.00
337	Dodgers Rookies	7.00	3.50		387	Terry Fox	4.00	2.00
	Al Ferrara (R)				388	Athletics Rookies	4.00	2.00
	Jeff Torborg (R)					John O'Donoghue (R)		
338	Jack Kralick	2.50	1.25			George Williams (R)		
339	Walt Bond	2.50	1.25		389	Jim Umbricht	4.00	2.00
340	Joe Cunningham	2.50	1.25		390	Orlando Cepeda	8.00	4.00
341	Jim Roland	2.50	1.25		391	Sam McDowell	5.00	2.50
342	Willie Stargell	48.00	24.00		392	Jim Pagliaroni	4.00	2.00

393	Casey Teaches	6.00	3.00
	Ed Kranepool		
	Casey Stengel		
394	Bob Miller	4.00	2.00
395	Tom Tresh	5.00	2.50
396	Dennis Bennett	4.00	2.00
397	Chuck Cottier	4.00	2.00
398	Mets Rookies	4.00	2.00
	Bill Haas		
	Dick Smith		
399	Jackie Brandt	4.00	2.00
400	Warren Spahn	38.00	20.00
401	Charlie Maxwell	4.00	2.00
402	Tom Sturdivant	4.00	2.00
403	Reds Team	7.00	3.50
404	Tony Martinez	4.00	2.00
405	Ken McBride	4.00	2.00
406	Al Spangler	4.00	2.00
407	Bill Freehan	7.00	3.50
408	Cubs Rookies	4.00	2.00
	Fred Burdette (R)		
	Jim Stewart (R)		
409	Bill Fischer	4.00	2.00
410	Dick Stuart	5.00	2.50
411	Lee Walls	4.00	2.00
412	Ray Culp	4.00	2.00
413	Johnny Keane	4.00	2.00
414	Jack Sanford	4.00	2.00
415	Tony Kubek	7.00	3.50
416	Lee Maye	4.00	2.00
417	Don Cardwell	4.00	2.00
418	Orioles Rookies	5.00	2.50
	Darold Knowles (R)		
	Les Narum (R)		
419	Ken Harrelson (R)	8.00	4.00
420	Jim Maloney	4.00	2.00
421	Camilo Carreon	4.00	2.00
422	Jack Fisher	4.00	2.00
423	Tops in NL	110.00	55.00
	Hank Aaron		
	Willie Mays		
424	Dick Bertell	4.00	2.00
425	Norm Cash	8.00	4.00
426	Bob Rodgers	4.00	2.00
427	Don Rudolph	4.00	2.00
428	Red Sox Rookies	4.00	2.00
	Archie Skeen (R)		
	Pete Smith (R)		
429	Tim McCarver	8.00	4.00
430	Juan Pizarro	4.00	2.00
431	George Alusik	4.00	2.00
432	Ruben Amaro	4.00	2.00
433	Yankees Team	12.00	6.00
434	Don Nottebart	4.00	2.00
435	Vic Davalillo	4.00	2.00
436	Charlie Neal	4.00	2.00
437	Ed Bailey	4.00	2.00
438	Checklist 430-506	7.00	3.50
439	Harvey Haddix	4.00	2.00
440	Roberto Clemente	150.00	75.00
441	Bob Duliba	4.00	2.00
442	Pumpsie Green	4.00	2.00
443	Chuck Dressen	4.00	2.00
444	Larry Jackson	4.00	2.00
445	Bill Skowron	6.00	3.00
446	Julian Javier	4.00	2.00
447	Ted Bowsfield	4.00	2.00
448	Cookie Rojas	5.00	2.50
449	Deron Johnson	5.00	2.50
450	Steve Barber	4.00	2.00
451	Joe Amalfitano	4.00	2.00
452	Giants Rookies	8.00	4.00
	Gil Garrido (R)		
	Jim Ray Hart (R)		
453	Frank Baumann	4.00	2.00
454	Tommie Aaron	4.00	2.00
455	Bernie Allen	4.00	2.00
456	Dodgers Rookies	7.00	3.50
	Wes Parker (R)		
	John Werhas (R)		
457	Jesse Gonder	4.00	2.00
458	Ralph Terry	5.00	2.50
459	Red Sox Rookies	4.00	2.00
	Pete Charton (R)		
	Dalton Jones (R)		
460	Bob Gibson	40.00	20.00
461	George Thomas	4.00	2.00
462	Birdie Tebbetts	4.00	2.00
463	Don Leppert	4.00	2.00
464	Dallas Green	5.00	2.50
465	Mike Hershberger	4.00	2.00
466	Athletics Rookies	4.00	2.00
	Dick Green (R)		
	Aurelio Monteagudo (R)		
467	Bob Aspromonte	4.00	2.00
468	Gaylord Perry	48.00	24.00
469	Cubs Rookies	4.00	2.00
	Fred Norman (R)		
	Sterling Slaughter (R)		
470	Jim Bouton	5.00	2.50
471	Gates Brown (R)	6.00	3.00
472	Vern Law	5.00	2.50
473	Orioles Team	7.00	3.50
474	Larry Sherry	4.00	2.00
475	Ed Charles	4.00	2.00
476	Braves Rookies	8.00	4.00
	Rico Carty (R)		
	Dick Kelley (R)		
477	Mike Joyce	4.00	2.00
478	Dick Howser	4.00	2.00
479	Cardinals Rookies	4.00	2.00
	Dave Bakenhaster (R)		
	Johnny Lewis (R)		
480	Bob Purkey	4.00	2.00
481	Chuck Schilling	4.00	2.00
482	Phillies Rookies	4.00	2.00

	John Briggs (R)		
	Danny Cater (R)		
483	Fred Valentine	4.00	2.00
484	Bill Pleis	4.00	2.00
485	Tom Haller	4.00	2.00
486	Bob Kennedy	4.00	2.00
487	Mike McCormick	4.00	2.00
488	Yankees Rookies	4.00	2.00
	Bob Meyer (R)		
	Pete Mikkelsen (R)		
489	Julio Navarro	4.00	2.00
490	Ron Fairly	4.00	2.00
491	Ed Rakow	4.00	2.00
492	Colts Rookies	4.00	2.00
	Jim Beauchamp (R)		
	Mike White (R)		
493	Don Lee	4.00	2.00
494	Al Jackson	4.00	2.00
495	Bill Virdon	5.00	2.50
496	White Sox Team	7.00	3.50
497	Jeoff Long	4.00	2.00
498	Dave Stenhouse	4.00	2.00
499	Indians Rookies	4.00	2.00
	Chico Salmon (R)		
	Gordon Seyfried (R)		
500	Camilo Pascual	4.00	2.00
501	Bob Veale	4.00	2.00
502	Angels Rookies	4.00	2.00
	Bobby Knoop (R)		
	Bob Lee (R)		
503	Earl Wilson	4.00	2.00
504	Claude Raymond	4.00	2.00
505	Stan Williams	4.00	2.00
506	Bobby Bragan	4.00	2.00
507	John Edwards	4.00	2.00
508	Diego Segui	4.00	2.00
509	Pirates Rookies	7.00	3.50
	Gene Alley (R)		
	Orlando McFarlane (R)		
510	Lindy McDaniel	4.00	2.00
511	Lou Jackson	4.00	2.00
512	Tigers Rookies	10.00	5.00
	Willie Horton (R)		
	Joe Sparma (R)		
513	Don Larsen	4.00	2.00
514	Jim Hickman	4.00	2.00
515	Johnny Romano	4.00	2.00
516	Twins Rookies	4.00	2.00
	Jerry Arrigo (R)		
	Dwight Siebler (R)		
517	Checklist 507-587	7.00	3.50
518	Carl Bouldin	4.00	2.00
519	Charlie Smith	4.00	2.00
520	Jack Baldschun	4.00	2.00
521	Tom Satriano	4.00	2.00
522	Bobby Tiefenauer	4.00	2.00
523	Lew Burdette	10.00	5.00
524	Reds Rookies	9.00	4.50

	Jim Dickson (R)		
	Bobby Klaus (R)		
525	Al McBean	9.00	4.50
526	Lou Clinton	9.00	4.50
527	Larry Bearnarth	9.00	4.50
528	Athletics Rookies	10.00	5.00
	Dave Duncan (R)		
	Tom Reynolds (R)		
529	Al Dark	9.00	4.50
530	Leon Wagner	9.00	4.50
531	Dodgers Team	12.00	6.00
532	Twins Rookies	9.00	4.50
	Bud Bloomfield (R)		
	Joe Nossek (R)		
533	Johnny Klippstein	9.00	4.50
534	Gus Bell	9.00	4.50
535	Phil Regan	9.00	4.50
536	Mets Rookies	9.00	4.50
	Larry Elliot (R)		
	John Stephenson (R)		
537	Dan Osinski	9.00	4.50
538	Minnie Minoso	14.00	7.00
539	Roy Face	10.00	5.00
540	Luis Aparicio	20.00	10.00
541	Braves Rookies	250.00	125.00
	Phil Niekro (R)		
	Phil Roof (R)		
542	Don Mincher	9.00	4.50
543	Bob Uecker	70.00	35.00
544	Colts Rookies	9.00	4.50
	Steve Hertz (R)		
	Joe Hoerner (R)		
545	Max Alvis	9.00	4.50
546	Joe Christopher	9.00	4.50
547	Gil Hodges	18.00	9.00
548	N.L. Rookies	9.00	4.50
	Wayne Schurr (R)		
	Paul Speckenbach (R)		
549	Joe Moeller	9.00	4.50
550	Ken Hubbs Memorial	10.00	5.00
551	Billy Hoeft	9.00	4.50
552	Indians Rookies	10.00	5.00
	Tom Kelley (R)		
	Sonny Siebert (R)		
553	Jim Brewer	9.00	4.50
554	Hank Foiles	9.00	4.50
555	Lee Stange	9.00	4.50
556	Mets Rookies	9.00	4.50
	Steve Dillon (R)		
	Ron Locke (R)		
557	Leo Burke	9.00	4.50
558	Don Schwall	9.00	4.50
559	Dick Phillips	9.00	4.50
560	Dick Farrell	9.00	4.50
561	Phillies Rookies	12.00	6.00
	Dave Bennett (R)		
	Rick Wise (R)		
562	Pedro Ramos	9.00	4.50

563	Dal Maxvill	9.00	4.50
564	A.L. Rookies	9.00	4.50
	Joe McCabe (R)		
	Jerry McNertney (R)		
565	Stu Miller	9.00	4.50
566	Ed Kranepool	10.00	5.00
567	Jim Kaat	14.00	7.00
568	N.L. Rookies	9.00	4.50
	Phil Gagliano (R)		
	Cap Peterson (R)		
569	Fred Newman	9.00	4.50
570	Bill Mazeroski	12.00	6.00
571	Gene Conley	9.00	4.50
572	A.L. Rookies	9.00	4.50
	Dick Egan (R)		
	Dave Gray (R)		
573	Jim Duffalo	9.00	4.50
574	Manny Jimenez	9.00	4.50
575	Tony Cloninger	9.00	4.50
576	Mets Rookies	9.00	4.50
	Jerry Hinsley (R)		
	Bill Wakefield (R)		
577	Gordy Coleman	9.00	4.50
578	Glen Hobbie	9.00	4.50
579	Red Sox Team	15.00	7.50
580	Johnny Podres	10.00	5.00
581	Yankees Rookies	9.00	4.50
	Pedro Gonzalez (R)		
	Archie Moore (R)		
582	Rod Kanehl	9.00	4.50
583	Tito Francona	9.00	4.50
584	Joel Horlen	9.00	4.50
585	Tony Taylor	9.00	4.50
586	Jim Piersall	10.00	5.00
587	Bennie Daniels	10.00	5.00

1965 Topps

This 598-card set features large color photos on the card fronts with team names in a pennant-shaped design in the bottom corner. Player names are in a horizonal bar at the bottom of the card. Cards measure 2-1/2" by 3-1/2" and subsets include League Leaders, World Series Highlights and Rookies.

		NR/MT	EX
Complete Set (598)		3,750.00	1,950.00
Commons (1-198)		1.50	.75
Commons (199-446)		3.50	1.75
Commons (447-522)		5.00	2.50
Commons (523-598)		6.00	3.00

1	A.L. Batting Leaders	14.00	6.00
2	N.L. Batting Leaders	10.00	5.00
3	A.L. HR Leaders	18.00	9.00
4	N.L. HR Leaders	8.00	4.00
5	A.L. RBI Leaders	18.00	9.00
6	N.L. RBI Leaders	6.00	3.00
7	A.L. ERA Leaders	3.00	1.50
8	N.L. ERA Leaders	10.00	5.00
9	A.L. Pitching Leaders	3.00	1.50
10	N.L. Pitching Leaders	3.00	1.50
11	A.L. Strikeout Ldrs	3.00	1.50
12	N.L. Strikeout Ldrs	5.00	2.50
13	Pedro Ramos	1.50	.75
14	Len Gabrielson	1.50	.75
15	Robin Roberts	9.00	4.50
16	Astros Rookies	180.00	90.00
	Sonny Jackson (R)		
	Joe Morgan (R)		
17	Johnny Romano	1.50	.75
18	Bill McCool	1.50	.75
19	Gates Brown	2.00	1.00
20	Jim Bunning	5.00	2.50
21	Don Blasingame	1.50	.75
22	Charlie Smith	1.50	.75
23	Bob Tiefenauer	1.50	.75
24	Twins Team	2.50	1.25
25	Al McBean	1.50	.75
26	Bobby Knoop	1.50	.75
27	Dick Bertell	1.50	.75
28	Barney Schultz	1.50	.75
29	Felix Mantilla	1.50	.75
30	Jim Bouton	2.00	1.00
31	Mike White	1.50	.75
32	Harman Franks	1.50	.75
33	Jackie Brandt	1.50	.75
34	Cal Koonce	1.50	.75
35	Ed Charles	1.50	.75
36	Bobby Wine	1.50	.75
37	Fred Gladding	1.50	.75
38	Jim King	1.50	.75
39	Gerry Arrigo	1.50	.75
40	Frank Howard	3.00	1.50
41	White Sox Rookies	1.50	.75

#	Player		
	Bruce Howard (R)		
	Marv Staehle (R)		
42	Earl Wilson	1.50	.75
43	Mike Shannon	1.50	.75
44	Wade Blasingame	1.50	.75
45	Roy McMillan	1.50	.75
46	Bob Lee	1.50	.75
47	Tommy Harper	2.00	1.00
48	Claude Raymond	1.50	.75
49	Orioles Rookies	1.50	.75
	Curt Blefary (R)		
	John Miller (R)		
50	Juan Marichal	12.00	6.00
51	Billy Bryan	1.50	.75
52	Ed Roebuck	1.50	.75
53	Dick McAuliffe	1.50	.75
54	Joe Gibbon	1.50	.75
55	Tony Conigliaro	7.00	3.50
56	Ron Kline	1.50	.75
57	Cardinals Team	2.50	1.25
58	Fred Talbot	1.50	.75
59	Nate Oliver	1.50	.75
60	Jim O'Toole	1.50	.75
61	Chris Cannizzaro	1.50	.75
62	Jim Katt (Kaat)	5.00	2.50
63	Ty Cline	1.50	.75
64	Lou Burdette	2.00	1.00
65	Tony Kubek	3.00	1.50
66	Bill Rigney	1.50	.75
67	Harvey Haddix	1.50	.75
68	Del Crandall	1.50	.75
69	Bill Virdon	2.00	1.00
70	Bill Skowron	2.00	1.00
71	John O'Donoghue	1.50	.75
72	Tony Gonzalez	1.50	.75
73	Dennis Ribant	1.50	.75
74	Red Sox Rookies	5.00	2.50
	Rico Petrocelli (R)		
	Jerry Stephenson (R)		
75	Deron Johnson	2.00	1.00
76	Sam McDowell	2.50	1.25
77	Doug Camilli	1.50	.75
78	Dal Maxvill	1.50	.75
79	Checklist 1-88	7.00	3.50
80	Turk Farrell	1.50	.75
81	Don Buford	1.50	.75
82	Braves Rookies	4.00	2.00
	Sandy Alomar (R)		
	John Braun (R)		
83	George Thomas	1.50	.75
84	Ron Herbel	1.50	.75
85	Willie Smith	1.50	.75
86	Les Narum	1.50	.75
87	Nelson Mathews	1.50	.75
88	Jack Lamabe	1.50	.75
89	Mike Hershberger	1.50	.75
90	Rich Rollins	1.50	.75
91	Cubs Team	2.50	1.25
92	Dick Howser	1.50	.75
93	Jack Fisher	1.50	.75
94	Charlie Lau	1.50	.75
95	Bill Mazeroski	3.00	1.50
96	Sonny Siebert	1.50	.75
97	Pedro Gonzalez	1.50	.75
98	Bob Miller	1.50	.75
99	Gil Hodges	7.00	3.50
100	Ken Boyer	4.00	2.00
101	Fred Newman	1.50	.75
102	Steve Boros	1.50	.75
103	Harvey Kuenn	2.00	1.00
104	Checklist 89-176	7.00	3.50
105	Chico Salmon	1.50	.75
106	Gene Oliver	1.50	.75
107	Phillies Rookies	2.00	1.00
	Pat Corrales (R)		
	Costen Shockley (R)		
108	Don Mincher	1.50	.75
109	Walt Bond	1.50	.75
110	Ron Sant0	3.50	1.75
111	Lee Thomas	1.50	.75
112	Derrell Griffith	1.50	.75
113	Steve Barber	1.50	.75
114	Jim Hickman	1.50	.75
115	Bobby Richardson	3.00	1.50
116	Cardinals Rookies	2.50	1.25
	Dave Dowling (R)		
	Bob Tolan (R)		
117	Wes Stock	1.50	.75
118	Hal Lanier (R)	2.50	1.25
119	John Kennedy	1.50	.75
120	Frank Robinson	30.00	15.00
121	Gene Alley	1.50	.75
122	Bill Pleis	1.50	.75
123	Frank Thomas	1.50	.75
124	Tom Satriano	1.50	.75
125	Juan Pizarro	1.50	.75
126	Dodgers Team	3.50	1.75
127	Frank Lary	1.50	.75
128	Vic Davalillo	1.50	.75
129	Bennie Daniels	1.50	.75
130	Al Kaline	30.00	15.00
131	Johnny Keane	1.50	.75
132	World Series Game 1	3.00	1.50
133	World Series Game 2	3.00	1.50
134	World Series Game 3	40.00	20.00
135	World Series Game 4	3.50	1.75
136	World Series Game 5	3.00	1.50
137	World Series Game 6	3.00	1.50
138	World Series Game 7	10.00	5.00
139	WS Celebration	3.00	1.50
140	Dean Chance	1.75	.90
141	Charlie James	1.50	.75
142	Bill Monbouquette	1.50	.75
143	Pirates Rookies	1.50	.75
	John Gelnar (R)		
	Jerry May (R)		

144	Ed Kranepool	2.00	1.00
145	Luis Tiant (R)	15.00	7.50
146	Ron Hansen	1.50	.75
147	Dennis Bennett	1.50	.75
148	Willie Kirkland	1.50	.75
149	Wayne Schurr	1.50	.75
150	Brooks Robinson	34.00	17.00
151	Athletics Team	2.50	1.25
152	Phil Ortega	1.50	.75
153	Norm Cash	4.00	2.00
154	Bob Humphreys	1.50	.75
155	Roger Maris	65.00	32.50
156	Bob Sadowski	1.50	.75
157	Zoilo Versalles	1.75	.90
158	Dick Sisler	1.50	.75
159	Jim Duffalo	1.50	.75
160	Roberto Clemente	90.00	45.00
161	Frank Baumann	1.50	.75
162	Russ Nixon	1.50	.75
163	John Briggs	1.50	.75
164	Al Spangler	1.50	.75
165	Dick Ellsworth	1.50	.75
166	Indians Rookies	3.00	1.50
	Tommie Agee (R)		
	George Culver (R)		
167	Bill Wakefield	1.50	.75
168	Dick Green	1.50	.75
169	Dave Vineyard	1.50	.75
170	Hank Aaron	125.00	.65.00
171	Jim Roland	1.50	.75
172	Jim Piersall	2.00	1.00
173	Tigers Team	2.50	1.25
174	Joey Jay	1.50	.75
175	Bob Aspromonte	1.50	.75
176	Willie McCovey	20.00	10.00
177	Pete Mikkelsen	1.50	.75
178	Dalton Jones	1.50	.75
179	Hal Woodeshick	1.50	.75
180	Bob Allison	1.50	.75
181	Senators Rookies	1.50	.75
	Don Loun		
	Joe McCabe		
182	Mike de la Hoz	1.50	.75
183	Dave Nicholson	1.50	.75
184	John Boozer	1.50	.75
185	Max Alvis	1.50	.75
186	Billy Cowan	1.50	.75
187	Casey Stengel	15.00	7.50
188	Sam Bowens	1.50	.75
189	Checklist 177-264	7.00	3.50
190	Bill White	2.50	1.25
191	Phil Regan	1.50	.75
192	Jim Coker	1.50	.75
193	Gaylord Perry	20.00	10.00
194	Angels Rookies	2.00	1.00
	Bill Kelso (R)		
	Rick Reichardt (R)		
195	Bob Veale	1.50	.75
196	Ron Fairly	1.50	.75
197	Diego Segui	1.50	.75
198	Smoky Burgess	1.75	.90
199	Bob Heffner	3.50	1.75
200	Joe Torre	4.00	2.00
201	Twins Rookies	3.50	1.75
	Cesar Tovar (R)		
	Sandy Valdespino (R)		
202	Leo Burke	3.50	1.75
203	Dallas Green	3.50	1.75
204	Russ Snyder	3.50	1.75
205	Warren Spahn	28.00	14.00
206	Willie Horton	4.50	2.25
207	Pete Rose	180.00	90.00
208	Tommy John	12.00	6.00
209	Pirates Team	4.00	2.00
210	Jim Fregosi	3.50	1.75
211	Steve Ridzik	3.50	1.75
212	Ron Brand	3.50	1.75
213	Jim Davenport	3.50	1.75
214	Bob Purkey	3.50	1.75
215	Pete Ward	3.50	1.75
216	Al Worthington	3.50	1.75
217	Walt Alston	4.00	2.00
218	Dick Schofield	3.50	1.75
219	Bob Meyer	3.50	1.75
220	Billy Williams	14.00	7.00
221	John Tsitouris	3.50	1.75
222	Bob Tillman	3.50	1.75
223	Dan Osinski	3.50	1.75
224	Bob Chance	3.50	1.75
225	Bo Belinsky	3.50	1.75
226	Yankees Rookies	3.50	1.75
	Jake Gibbs		
	Elvio Jimenez (R)		
227	Bobby Klaus	3.50	1.75
228	Jack Sanford	3.50	1.75
229	Lou Clinton	3.50	1.75
230	Ray Sadecki	3.50	1.75
231	Jerry Adair	3.50	1.75
232	Steve Blass (R)	4.50	2.25
233	Don Zimmer	3.50	1.75
234	White Sox Team	4.00	2.00
235	Chuck Hinton	3.50	1.75
236	Dennis McLain (R)	24.00	12.00
237	Bernie Allen	3.50	1.75
238	Joe Moeller	3.50	1.75
239	Doc Edwards	3.50	1.75
240	Bob Bruce	3.50	1.75
241	Mack Jones	3.50	1.75
242	George Brunet	3.50	1.75
243	Reds Rookies	3.50	1.75
	Ted Davidson (R)		
	Tommy Helms (R)		
244	Lindy McDaniel	3.50	1.75
245	Joe Pepitone	3.50	1.75
246	Tom Butters	3.50	1.75
247	Wally Moon	3.50	1.75

#	Player		
248	Gus Triandos	3.50	1.75
249	Dave McNally	3.50	1.75
250	Willie Mays	120.00	60.00
251	Billy Herman	3.50	1.75
252	Pete Richert	3.50	1.75
253	Danny Carter	3.50	1.75
254	Roland Sheldon	3.50	1.75
255	Camilo Pascual	3.50	1.75
256	Tito Francona	3.50	1.75
257	Jim Wynn	4.00	2.00
258	Larry Bearnarth	3.50	1.75
259	Tigers Rookies	4.50	2.25
	Jim Northrup (R)		
	Ray Oyler (R)		
260	Don Drysdale	20.00	10.00
261	Duke Carmel	3.50	1.75
262	Bud Daley	3.50	1.75
263	Marty Keough	3.50	1.75
264	Bob Buhl	3.50	1.75
265	Jim Pagliaroni	3.50	1.75
266	Bert Campaneris (R)	7.00	3.50
267	Senators Team	4.00	2.00
268	Ken McBride	3.50	1.75
269	Frank Bolling	3.50	1.75
270	Milt Pappas	3.50	1.75
271	Don Wert	3.50	1.75
272	Chuck Schilling	3.50	1.75
273	Checklist 265-352	7.00	3.50
274	Lum Harris	3.50	1.75
275	Dick Groat	3.50	1.75
276	Hoyt Wilhelm	8.00	4.00
277	Johnny Lewis	3.50	1.75
278	Ken Retzer	3.50	1.75
279	Dick Tracewski	3.50	1.75
280	Dick Stuart	3.50	1.75
281	Bill Stafford	3.50	1.75
282	Giants Rookies	3.50	1.75
	Dick Estelle (R)		
	Masanori Murakami (R)		
283	Fred Whitfield	3.50	1.75
284	Nick Willhite	3.50	1.75
285	Ron Hunt	3.50	1.75
286	Athletics Rookies	3.50	1.75
	Jim Dickson (R)		
	Aurelio Monteagudo		
287	Gary Kolb	3.50	1.75
288	Jack Hamilton	3.50	1.75
289	Gordy Coleman	3.50	1.75
290	Wally Bunker	3.50	1.75
291	Jerry Lynch	3.50	1.75
292	Larry Yellen	3.50	1.75
293	Angels Team	4.00	2.00
294	Tim McCarver	5.00	2.50
295	Dick Radatz	3.50	1.75
296	Tony Taylor	3.50	1.75
297	Dave DeBusschere	4.00	2.00
298	Jim Stewart	3.50	1.75
299	Jerry Zimmerman	3.50	1.75
300	Sandy Koufax	140.00	70.00
301	Birdie Tebbetts	3.50	1.75
302	Al Stanek	3.50	1.75
303	Johnny Orsino	3.50	1.75
304	Dave Stenhouse	3.50	1.75
305	Rico Carty	3.50	1.75
306	Bubba Phillips	3.50	1.75
307	Barry Latman	3.50	1.75
308	Mets Rookies	6.00	3.00
	Cleon Jones (R)		
	Tom Parsons (R)		
309	Steve Hamilton	3.50	1.75
310	Johnny Callison	3.50	1.75
311	Orlanda Pena	3.50	1.75
312	Joe Nuxhall	3.50	1.75
313	Jimmie Schaffer	3.50	1.75
314	Sterling Slaughter	3.50	1.75
315	Frank Malzone	3.50	1.75
316	Reds Team	4.00	2.00
317	Don McMahon	3.50	1.75
318	Matty Alou	4.00	2.00
319	Ken McMullen	3.50	1.75
320	Bob Gibson	34.00	17.00
321	Rusty Staub	6.00	3.00
322	Rick Wise	3.50	1.75
323	Hank Bauer	3.50	1.75
324	Bobby Locke	3.50	1.75
325	Donn Clendenon	3.50	1.75
326	Dwight Siebler	3.50	1.75
327	Denis Menke	3.50	1.75
328	Eddie Fisher	3.50	1.75
329	Hawk Taylor	3.50	1.75
330	Whitey Ford	30.00	15.00
331	Dodgers Rookies	3.50	1.75
	Al Ferrara (R)		
	John Purdin (R)		
332	Ted Abernathy	3.50	1.75
333	Tommie Reynolds	3.50	1.75
334	Vic Roznovsky	3.50	1.75
335	Mickey Lolich	6.00	3.00
336	Woody Held	3.50	1.75
337	Mike Cuellar	3.50	1.75
338	Phillies Team	4.00	2.00
339	Ryne Duren	3.50	1.75
340	Tony Oliva	12.00	6.00
341	Bobby Bolin	3.50	1.75
342	Bob Rodgers	3.50	1.75
343	Mike McCormick	3.50	1.75
344	Wes Parker	3.50	1.75
345	Floyd Robinson	3.50	1.75
346	Bobby Bragan	3.50	1.75
347	Roy Face	4.00	2.00
348	George Banks	3.50	1.75
349	Larry Miller	3.50	1.75
350	Mickey Mantle	480.00	240.00
351	Jim Perry	3.50	1.75
352	Alex Johnson (R)	4.00	2.00
353	Jerry Lumpe	3.50	1.75

#			
354	Cubs Rookies	3.50	1.75
	Billy Ott (R)		
	Jack Warner (R)		
355	Vada Pinson	4.00	2.00
356	Bill Spanswick	3.50	1.75
357	Carl Warwick	3.50	1.75
358	Albie Pearson	3.50	1.75
359	Ken Johnson	3.50	1.75
360	Orlando Cepeda	8.00	4.00
361	Checklist 353-429	7.00	3.50
362	Don Schwall	3.50	1.75
363	Bob Johnson	3.50	1.75
364	Galen Cisco	3.50	1.75
365	Jim Gentile	3.50	1.75
366	Dan Schneider	3.50	1.75
367	Leon Wagner	3.50	1.75
368	White Sox Rookies	3.50	1.75
	Ken Berry (R)		
	Joel Gibson (R)		
369	Phil Linz	3.50	1.75
370	Tommy Davis	4.50	2.25
371	Frank Kreutzer	3.50	1.75
372	Clay Dalrymple	3.50	1.75
373	Curt Simmons	3.50	1.75
374	Angels Rookies	5.00	2.50
	Jose Cardenal (R)		
	Dick Simpson (R)		
375	Dave Wickersham	3.50	1.75
376	Jim Landis	3.50	1.75
377	Willie Stargell	32.00	16.00
378	Chuck Estrada	3.50	1.75
379	Giants Team	5.00	2.50
380	Rocky Colavito	8.00	4.00
381	Al Jackson	3.50	1.75
382	J.C. Martin	3.50	1.75
383	Felipe Alou	4.50	2.25
384	Johnny Klippstein	3.50	1.75
385	Carl Yastrzemski	90.00	45.00
386	Cubs Rookies	3.50	1.75
	Paul Jaeckel (R)		
	Fred Norman		
387	Johnny Podres	5.00	2.50
388	John Blanchard	3.50	1.75
389	Don Larsen	5.00	2.50
390	Bill Freehan	6.00	3.00
391	Mel McGaha	3.50	1.75
392	Bob Friend	3.50	1.75
393	Ed Kirkpatrick	3.50	1.75
394	Jim Hannan	4.50	2.25
396	Frank Bertaina	3.50	1.75
397	Jerry Buchek	3.50	1.75
398	Reds Rookies	3.50	1.75
	Dan Neville (R)		
	Art Shamsky (R)		
399	Ray Herbert	3.50	1.75
400	Harmon Killebrew	38.00	20.00
401	Carl Willey	3.50	1.75
402	Joe Amalfitano	3.50	1.75
403	Red Sox Team	5.00	2.50
404	Stan Williams	3.50	1.75
405	John Roseboro	4.00	2.00
406	Ralph Terry	4.00	2.00
407	Lee Maye	3.50	1.75
408	Larry Sherry	3.50	1.75
409	Astros Rookies	6.00	3.00
	Jim Beauchamp		
	Larry Dierker (R)		
410	Luis Aparicio	10.00	5.00
411	Roger Craig	4.50	2.25
412	Bob Bailey	3.50	1.75
413	Hal Reniff	3.50	1.75
414	Al Lopez	5.00	2.50
415	Curt Flood	6.00	3.00
416	Jim Brewer	3.50	1.75
417	Ed Brinkman	3.50	1.75
418	Johnny Edwards	3.50	1.75
419	Ruben Amaro	3.50	1.75
420	Larry Jackson	3.50	1.75
421	Twins Rookies	3.50	1.75
	Gary Dotter (R)		
	Jay Ward		
422	Aubrey Gatewood	3.50	1.75
423	Jesse Gonder	3.50	1.75
424	Gary Bell	3.50	1.75
425	Wayne Causey	3.50	1.75
426	Braves Team	5.00	2.50
427	Bob Saverine	3.50	1.75
428	Bob Shaw	3.50	1.75
429	Don Demeter	3.50	1.75
430	Gary Peters	3.50	1.75
431	Cardinals Rookies	5.00	2.50
	Nelson Briles (R)		
	Wayne Spiezio (R)		
432	Jim Grant	3.50	1.75
433	John Bateman	3.50	1.75
434	Dave Morehead	3.50	1.75
435	Willie Davis	4.00	2.00
436	Don Elston	3.50	1.75
437	Chico Cardenas	3.50	1.75
438	Harry Walker	3.50	1.75
439	Moe Drabowsky	3.50	1.75
440	Tom Tresh	6.00	3.00
441	Denver Lemaster	3.50	1.75
442	Vic Power	3.50	1.75
443	Checklist 430-506	7.00	3.50
444	Bob Hendley	3.50	1.75
445	Don Lock	3.50	1.75
446	Art Mahaffey	3.50	1.75
447	Julian Javier	5.00	2.50
448	Lee Stange	5.00	2.50
449	Mets Rookies	5.00	2.50
	Jerry Hinsley (R)		
	Gary Kroll (R)		
450	Elston Howard	8.00	4.00
451	Jim Owens	5.00	2.50
452	Gary Geiger	5.00	2.50

453	Dodgers Rookies	6.00	3.00
	Willie Crawford (R)		
	John Werhas		
454	Ed Rakow	5.00	2.50
455	Norm Siebern	5.00	2.50
456	Bill Henry	5.00	2.50
457	Bob Kennedy	5.00	2.50
458	John Buzhardt	5.00	2.50
459	Frank Kostro	5.00	2.50
460	Richie Allen	25.00	12.50
461	Braves Rookies	60.00	30.00
	Clay Carroll (R)		
	Phil Niekro		
462	Lew Krausse	5.00	2.50
463	Manny Mota	6.00	3.00
464	Ron Piche	5.00	2.50
465	Tom Haller	5.00	2.50
466	Senators Rookies	5.00	2.50
	Pete Craig (R)		
	Dick Nen		
467	Ray Washburn	5.00	2.50
468	Larry Brown	5.00	2.50
469	Don Nottebart	5.00	2.50
470	Yogi Berra	60.00	30.00
471	Billy Hoeft	5.00	2.50
472	Don Pavletich	5.00	2.50
473	Orioles Rookies	14.00	7.00
	Paul Blair (R)		
	Dave Johnson (R)		
474	Cookie Rojas	6.00	3.00
475	Clete Boyer	6.00	3.00
476	Billy O'Dell	5.00	2.50
477	Cardinals Rookies	575.00	285.00
	Fritz Ackley (R)		
	Steve Carlton (R)		
478	Wilbur Wood	6.00	3.00
479	Ken Harrelson	6.00	3.00
480	Joel Horlen	5.00	2.50
481	Indians Team	7.00	3.50
482	Bob Priddy	5.00	2.50
483	George Smith	5.00	2.50
484	Ron Perranoski	6.00	3.00
485	Nellie Fox	12.00	6.00
486	Angels Rookis	5.00	2.50
	Tom Egan (R)		
	Pat Rogan (R)		
487	Woody Woodward	5.00	2.50
488	Ted Wills	5.00	2.50
489	Gene Mauch	5.00	2.50
490	Earl Batte	5.00	2.50
491	Tracy Stallard	5.00	2.50
492	Gene Freese	5.00	2.50
493	Tigers Rookies	5.00	2.50
	Bruce Brubaker (R)		
	Bill Roman (R)		
494	Jay Ritchie	5.00	2.50
495	Joe Christopher	5.00	2.50
496	Joe Cunningham	5.00	2.50
497	Giants Rookies	5.00	2.50
	Ken Henderson (R)		
	Jack Hiatt (R)		
498	Gene Stephens	5.00	2.50
499	Stu Miller	5.00	2.50
500	Ed Mathews	38.00	20.00
501	Indians Rookies	5.00	2.50
	Ralph Gagliano (R)		
	Jim Rittwage (R)		
502	Don Cardwell	5.00	2.50
503	Phil Gagliano	5.00	2.50
504	Jerry Grote	6.00	3.00
505	Ray Culp	5.00	2.50
506	Sam Mele	5.00	2.50
507	Sammy Ellis	5.00	2.50
508	Checklist 507-598	10.00	5.00
509	Red Sox Rookies	5.00	2.50
	Bob Guindon (R)		
	Gerry Vezendy (R)		
510	Ernie Banks	90.00	45.00
511	Ron Lock	5.00	2.50
512	Cap Peterson	5.00	2.50
513	Yankees Team	15.00	7.50
514	Joe Azcue	5.00	2.50
515	Vern Law	5.00	2.50
516	Al Weis	5.00	2.50
517	Angels Rookies	5.00	2.50
	(Paul Schaal,		
	JackWarner)		
518	Ken Rowe	5.00	2.50
519	Bob Uecker	45.00	22.50
520	Tony Cloninger	5.00	2.50
521	Phillies Rookies	5.00	2.50
	Dave Bennett (R)		
	Morrie Stevens (R)		
522	Hank Aguirre	5.00	2.50
523	Mike Brumley	6.00	3.00
524	Dave Giusti	6.00	3.00
525	Eddie Ressoud	6.00	3.00
526	Athletics Rookies	175.00	85.00
	Catfish Hunter(R)		
	Rene Lachemann (R)		
	Skip Lockwood (R)		
	John Odom (R)		
527	Jeff Torborg	7.00	3.50
528	George Altman	6.00	3.00
529	Jerry Fosnow	6.00	3.00
530	Jim Maloney	6.00	3.00
531	Chuck Hiller	6.00	3.00
532	Hector Lopez	6.00	3.00
533	Mets Rookies	32.00	16.00
	Jim Bethke (R)		
	Tug McGraw (R)		
	Dan Napolean (R)		
	Ron Swoboda (R)		
534	John Herrnstein	6.00	3.00
535	Jack Kralick	6.00	3.00
536	Andre Rodgers	6.00	3.00

537	Angels Rookies	6.00	3.00
	Marcelino Lopez		
	Rudy May (R)		
	Phil Roof		
538	Chuck Dressen	6.00	3.00
539	Herm Starrette	6.00	3.00
540	Lou Brock	55.00	27.50
541	White Sox Rookies	6.00	3.00
	Greg Bollo		
	Bob Locker (R)		
542	Lou Klimchock	6.00	3.00
543	Ed Connolly	6.00	3.00
544	Howie Reed	6.00	3.00
545	Jesus Alou	7.00	3.50
546	Indians Rookies	6.00	3.00
	Ray Barker (R)		
	Bill Davis (R)		
	Mike Hedlund (R)		
	Floyd Weaver (R)		
547	Jake Wood	6.00	3.00
548	Dick Stigman	6.00	3.00
549	Cubs Rookies	9.00	4.50
	Glenn Beckert (R)		
	Roberto Pena (R)		
550	Mel Stottlemyre (R)	35.00	18.00
551	Mets Team	18.00	9.00
552	Julio Gotay	6.00	3.00
553	Astros Rookies	6.00	3.00
	Dan Coombs (R)		
	Jack McClure (R)		
	Gene Ratliff (R)		
554	Chico Ruiz	6.00	3.00
555	Jack Baldschun	6.00	3.00
556	Red Schoendienst	18.00	9.00
557	Jose Santiago	6.00	3.00
558	Tommie Sisk	6.00	3.00
559	Ed Bailey	6.00	3.00
560	Boog Powell	16.00	8.00
561	Dodgers Rookies	8.00	4.00
	Dennis Daboll (R)		
	Mike Kekich (R)		
	Jim Lefebvre (R)		
	Hector Valle (R)		
562	Billy Moran	6.00	3.00
563	Julio Navarro	6.00	3.00
564	Mel Nelson	6.00	3.00
565	Ernie Broglio	6.00	3.00
566	Yankees Rookies	6.00	3.00
	Gil Blanco (R)		
	ArtLopez (R)		
	Ross Moschitto (R)		
567	Tommie Aaron	6.00	3.00
568	Ron Taylor	6.00	3.00
569	Gino Cimoli	6.00	3.00
570	Claude Osteen	6.00	3.00
571	Ossie Virgil	6.00	3.00
572	Orioles Team	6.00	3.00
573	Red Sox Rookies	14.00	7.00
	Jim Lonborg (R)		
	Gerry Moses (R)		
	Mike Ryan (R)		
	Bill Schlesinger (R)		
574	Roy Sievers	6.00	3.00
575	Jose Pagan	6.00	3.00
576	Terry Fox	6.00	3.00
577	A.L. Rookies	8.00	4.00
	Jim Buschhorn (R)		
	Darold Knowles (R)		
	Richie Scheinblum (R)		
578	Camilo Carreon	6.00	3.00
579	Dick Smith	6.00	3.00
580	Jimmie Hall	6.00	3.00
581	N.L. Rookies	180.00	90.00
	Kevin Collins (R)		
	Tony Perez (R)		
	Dave Ricketts (R)		
582	Bob Schmidt	6.00	3.00
583	Wes Covington	6.00	3.00
584	Harry Bright	6.00	3.00
585	Hank Fischer	6.00	3.00
586	Tommy McCraw	6.00	3.00
587	Joe Sparma	6.00	3.00
588	Lenny Green	6.00	3.00
589	Giants Rookies	6.00	3.00
	Frank Linzy (R)		
	Bob Schroder (R)		
590	Johnnie Wyatt	6.00	3.00
591	Bob Skinner	6.00	3.00
592	Frank Bork	6.00	3.00
593	Tigers Rookies	7.00	3.50
	Jackie Moore (R)		
	John Sullivan (R)		
594	Joe Gaines	6.00	3.00
595	Don Lee	6.00	3.00
596	Don Landrum	6.00	3.00
597	Twins Rookies	6.00	3.00
	Joe Nossek		
	Dick Reese (R)		
	John Sevcik (R)		
598	Al Downing	14.00	7.00

1966 Topps

This 598-card set features color photos on the card fronts with team names appearing in a small diagonal stripe in the top left corner. Player's names and positions are printed across the bottom of the card fronts. Cards measure 2-1/2" by 3-1/2". Major subsets include League Leaders and Managers. Several variations exists in the set. Those cards are noted in the checklist below with the smaller valued card included in the complete set price.

		NR/MT	EX
Complete Set (598)		4,750.00	2,300.00
Commons (1-110)		1.50	.75
Commons (111-446)		2.50	1.25
Commons (447-522)		7.00	3.50
Commons (523-598)		24.00	12.00

		NR/MT	EX
1	Willie Mays	175.00	65.00
2	Ted Abernathy	1.50	.75
3	Sam Mele	1.50	.75
4	Ray Culp	1.50	.75
5	Jim Fregosi	2.00	1.00
6	Chuck Schilling	1.50	.75
7	Tracy Stallard	1.50	.75
8	Floyd Robinson	1.50	.75
9	Clete Boyer	2.00	1.00
10	Tony Cloninger	1.50	.75
11	Senators Rookies	1.50	.75
	Brant Alyea (R)		
	Pete Craig		
12	John Tsitouris	1.50	.75
13	Lou Johnson	1.50	.75
14	Norm Siebern	1.50	.75
15	Vern Law	1.50	.75
16	Larry Brown	1.50	.75
17	Johnny Stephenson	1.50	.75
18	Roland Sheldon	1.50	.75
19	Giants Team	3.50	1.75
20	Willie Horton	2.00	1.00
21	Don Nottebart	1.50	.75
22	Joe Nossek	1.50	.75
23	Jack Sanford	1.50	.75
24	Don Kessinger (R)	3.50	1.75
25	Pete Ward	1.50	.75
26	Ray Sadecki	1.50	.75
27	Orioles Rookies	1.50	.75
	Andy Etchebarren (R)		
	Darold Knowles		
28	Phil Niekro	24.00	12.00
29	Mike Brumley	1.50	.75
30	Pete Rose	55.00	27.50
31	Jack Cullen	1.50	.75
32	Adolfo Phillips	1.50	.75
33	Jim Pagliaroni	1.50	.75
34	Checklist 1-88	6.50	3.25
35	Ron Swoboda	2.00	1.00
36	Jim Hunter	32.00	16.00
37	Billy Herman	2.00	1.00
38	Ron Nischwitz	1.50	.75
39	Ken Henderson	1.50	.75
40	Jim Grant	1.50	.75
41	Don LeJohn	1.50	.75
42	Aubrey Gatewood	1.50	.75
43	Don Landrum	1.50	.75
44	Indians Rookies	1.50	.75
	Bill Davis (R)		
	Tom Kelley		
45	Jim Gentile	2.00	1.00
46	Howie Koplitz	1.50	.75
47	J.C. Martin	1.50	.75
48	Paul Blair	2.00	1.00
49	Woody Woodward	1.50	.75
50	Mickey Mantle	240.00	120.00
51	Gordon Richardson	1.50	.75
52	Power Plus	2.00	1.00
	Johnny Callison		
	Wes Covington		
53	Bob Duliba	1.50	.75
54	Jose Pagan	1.50	.75
55	Ken Harrelson	1.50	.75
56	Sandy Valdespino	1.50	.75
57	Jim Lefebvre	1.50	.75
58	Dave Wickersham	1.50	.75
59	Reds Team	3.50	1.75
60	Curt Flood	2.00	1.00
61	Bob Bolin	1.50	.75
62a	Merritt Ranew (no sold statement)	24.00	12.00
62b	Merritt Ranew (Sold Statement)	1.50	.75
63	Jim Stewart	1.50	.75
64	Bob Bruce	1.50	.75
65	Leon Wagner	1.50	.75
66	Al Weis	1.50	.75
67	Mets Rookies	2.00	1.25
	Cleon Jones		

	Dick Selma (R)		
68	Hal Reniff	1.50	.75
69	Ken Hamlin	1.50	.75
70	Carl Yastrzemski	45.00	22.50
71	Frank Carpin	1.50	.75
72	Tony Perez	35.00	17.50
73	Jerry Zimmerman	1.50	.75
74	Don Mossi	1.50	.75
75	Tommy Davis	3.00	1.50
76	Red Schoendienst	4.00	2.00
77	Johnny Orsino	1.50	.75
78	Frank Linzy	1.50	.75
79	Joe Pepitone	2.50	1.25
80	Richie Allen	5.00	2.50
81	Ray Oyler	1.50	.75
82	Bob Hendley	1.50	.75
83	Albie Pearson	1.50	.75
84	Braves Rookies	1.50	.75
	Jim Beauchamp		
	Dick Kelley (R)		
85	Eddie Fisher	1.50	.75
86	John Bateman	1.50	.75
87	Dan Napoleon	1.50	.75
88	Fred Whitfield	1.50	.75
89	Ted Davidson	1.50	.75
90	Luis Aparicio	8.00	4.00
91a	Bob Uecker (No	70.00	35.00
	trade statement)		
91b	Bob Uecker (Trade	20.00	10.00
	statement)		
92	Yankees Team	5.00	2.50
93	Jim Lonborg	2.50	1.25
94	Matty Alou	2.50	1.25
95	Pete Richert	1.50	.75
96	Felipe Alou	3.00	1.50
97	Jim Merritt	1.50	.75
98	Don Demeter	1.50	.75
99	Buc Belters	5.00	2.50
	Donn Clendenon		
	Willie Stargell		
100	Sandy Koufax	125.00	65.00
101a	Checklist 89-176	12.00	6.00
	(#115 is Spahn)		
101b	Checklist 89-176		
	(#115 is Henry)	7.00	3.50
102	Ed Kirkpatrick	1.50	.75
103a	Dick Groat (No	28.00	14.00
	trade statement)		
103b	Dick Groat (Trade	3.50	1.75
	statement)		
104a	Alex Johnson (No	24.00	12.00
	trade statement)		
104b	Alex Johnson (Trade	2.50	1.25
	statement)	1.50	.75
105	Milt Pappas	1.50	.75
106	Rusty Staub	4.00	2.00
107	Athletics Rookies	1.50	.75
	Larry Stahl (R)		
	Ron Tompkins (R)		

108	Bobby Klaus	1.50	.75
109	Ralph Terry	2.00	1.00
110	Ernie Banks	28.00	14.00
111	Gary Peters	2.50	1.25
112	Manny Mota	3.50	1.75
113	Hank Aguirre	2.50	1.25
114	Jim Gosger	2.50	1.25
115	Bill Henry	2.50	1.25
116	Walt Alston	3.00	1.50
117	Jake Gibbs	2.50	1.25
118	Mike McCormick	2.50	1.25
119	Art Shamsky	2.50	1.25
120	Harmon Killebrew	24.00	12.00
121	Ray Herbert	2.50	1.25
122	Joe Gaines	2.50	1.25
123	Pirates Rookies (R)	2.50	1.25
	Frank Bork		
	Jerry May		
124	Tug McGraw	6.00	3.00
125	Lou Brock	28.00	14.00
126	Jim Palmer (R)	275.00	135.00
127	Ken Berry	2.50	1.25
128	Jim Landis	2.50	1.25
129	Jack Kralick	2.50	1.25
130	Joe Torre	4.50	2.25
131	Angels Team	3.50	1.75
132	Orlando Cepeda	7.00	3.50
133	Don McMahon	2.50	1.25
134	Wes Parker	2.50	1.25
135	Dave Morehead	2.50	1.25
136	Woody Held	2.50	1.25
137	Pat Corrales	2.50	1.25
138	Roger Repoz	2.50	1.25
139	Cubs Rookies	2.50	1.25
	Byron Browne (R)		
	Don Young (R)		
140	Jim Maloney	2.50	1.25
141	Tom McCraw	2.50	1.25
142	Don Dennis	2.50	1.25
143	Jose Tartabull	2.50	1.25
144	Don Schwall	2.50	1.25
145	Bill Freehan	3.50	1.75
146	George Altman	2.50	1.25
147	Lum Harris	2.50	1.25
148	Bob Johnson	2.50	1.25
149	Dick Nen	2.50	1.25
150	Rocky Colavito	6.00	3.00
151	Gary Wagner	2.50	1.25
152	Frank Malzone	2.50	1.25
153	Rico Carty	3.00	1.50
154	Chuck Hiller	2.50	1.25
155	Marcelino Lopez	2.50	1.25
156	DP Combo (Hal	2.50	1.25
	Lanier)		
	Dick Schofield		
157	Rene Lachemann	2.50	1.25
158	Jim Brewer	2.50	1.25
159	Chico Ruiz	2.50	1.25

160	Whitey Ford	28.00	14.00
161	Jerry Lumpe	2.50	1.25
162	Lee Maye	2.50	1.25
163	Tito Francona	2.50	1.25
164	White Sox Rookies	3.00	1.50
	Tommie Agee (R)		
	Marv Staehle (R)		
165	Don Lock	2.50	1.25
166	Chris Krug	2.50	1.25
167	Boog Powell	5.00	2.50
168	Dan Osinski	2.50	1.25
169	Duke Sims	2.50	1.25
170	Cookie Rojas	3.00	1.50
171	Nick Willhite	2.50	1.25
172	Mets Team	3.50	1.75
173	Al Spangler	2.50	1.25
174	Ron Taylor	2.50	1.25
175	Bert Campaneris	3.50	1.75
176	Jim Davenport	2.50	1.25
177	Hector Lopez	2.50	1.25
178	Bob Tillman	2.50	1.25
179	Cardinals Rookies	3.00	1.50
	Dennis Aust (R)		
	Bob Tolan		
180	Vada Pinson	3.00	1.75
181	Al Worthington	2.50	1.25
182	Jerry Lynch	2.50	1.25
183	Checklist 177-264	7.50	3.50
184	Denis Menke	2.50	1.25
185	Bob Buhl	2.50	1.25
186	Ruben Amaro	2.50	1.25
187	Chuck Dressen	2.50	1.25
188	Al Luplow	2.50	1.25
189	John Roseboro	3.00	1.50
190	Jimmie Hall	2.50	1.25
191	Darrell Sutherland	2.50	1.25
192	Vic Power	2.50	1.25
193	Dave McNally	3.00	1.50
194	Senators Team	3.50	1.75
195	Joe Morgan	50.00	25.00
196	Don Pavletich	2.50	1.25
197	Sonny Siebert	2.50	1.25
198	Mickey Stanley (R)	3.50	1.75
199	Chisox Clubbers	2.50	1.25
	Floyd Robinson		
	Johnny Romano		
	Bill Skowron		
200	Ed Mathews	14.00	7.00
201	Jim Dickson	2.50	1.25
202	Clay Dalrymple	2.50	1.25
203	Jose Santiago	2.50	1.25
204	Cubs Team	3.50	1.75
205	Tom Tresh	3.50	1.75
206	Alvin Jackson	2.50	1.25
207	Frank Quilici	2.50	1.25
208	Bob Miller	2.50	1.25
209	Tigers Rookies	3.00	1.50
	Fritz Fisher (R)		

	John Hiller (R)		
210	Bill Mazeroski	4.00	2.00
211	Frank Kreutzer	2.50	1.25
212	Ed Kranepool	3.00	1.50
213	Fred Newman	2.50	1.25
214	Tommy Harper	3.00	1.50
215	N.L. Batting Leaders	26.00	13.00
216	A.L. Batting Leaders	7.00	3.50
217	N.L. HR Leaders	18.00	9.00
218	A.L. HR Leaders	5.00	2.50
219	N.L. RBI Leaders	8.50	4.25
220	A.L. RBI Leaders	4.50	2.25
221	N.L. ERA Leaders	8.50	4.50
222	A.L. ERA Leaders	3.50	1.75
223	N.L. Pitching Leaders	8.50	4.50
224	A.L. Pitching Leaders	3.50	1.75
225	N.L. Strikeout Ldrs	8.50	4.50
226	A.L. Strikeout Ldrs	3.50	1.75
	Siebert)	2.50	1.25
227	Russ Nixon	2.50	1.25
228	Larry Dierker	3.00	1.75
229	Hank Bauer	3.00	1.75
230	Johnny Callison	3.00	1.75
231	Floyd Weaver	2.50	1.25
232	Glenn Beckert	2.50	1.25
233	Dom Zanni	2.50	1.25
234	Yankees Rookies	7.50	3.50
	Rich Beck		
	Roy White (R)		
235	Don Cardwell	2.50	1.25
236	Mike Hershberger	2.50	1.25
237	Billy O'Dell	2.50	1.25
238	Dodgers Team	3.50	1.75
239	Orlando Pena	2.50	1.25
240	Earl Battey	2.50	1.25
241	Dennis Ribant	2.50	1.25
242	Jesue Alou	2.50	1.25
243	Nelson Briles	2.50	1.25
244	Astros Rookies	2.50	1.25
	Chuck Harrison (R)		
	Sonny Jackson (R)		
245	John Buzhardt	2.50	1.25
246	Ed Bailey	2.50	1.25
247	Carl Warwick	2.50	1.25
248	Pete Mikkelsen	2.50	1.25
249	Bill Rigney	2.50	1.25
250	Sam Ellis	2.50	1.25
251	Ed Brinkman	2.50	1.25
252	Denver Lemaster	2.50	1.25
253	Don Wert	2.50	1.25
254	Phillies Rookies	150.00	75.00
	Ferguson Jenkins(R)		
	Bill Sorrell (R)		
255	Willie Stargell	25.00	12.50
256	Lew Krausse	2.50	1.25
257	Jeff Torborg	30.00	1.50
258	Dave Giusti	2.50	1.25
259	Red Sox Team	3.50	1.75

No.	Player		
260	Bob Shaw	2.50	1.25
261	Ron Hansen	2.50	1.25
262	Jack Hamilton	2.50	1.25
263	Tom Egan	2.50	1.25
264	Twins Rookies	2.50	1.25
	Andy Kosco (R)		
	Ted Uhlaender (R)		
265	Stu Miller	2.50	1.25
266	Pedro Gonzalez	2.50	1.25
267	Joe Sparma	2.50	1.25
268	John Blanchard	2.50	1.25
269	Don Heffner	2.50	1.25
270	Claude Osteen	2.50	1.25
271	Hal Lanier	2.50	1.25
272	Jack Baldschun	2.50	1.25
273	Astros Aces (Bob	3.50	1.75
	Aspromonte, Rusty		
	Staub)		
274	Buster Narum	2.50	1.25
275	Tim McCarver	3.50	1.75
276	Jim Bouton	3.00	1.50
277	George Thomas	2.50	1.25
278	Calvin Koonce	2.50	1.25
279	Checklist 265-352	7.00	3.50
280	Bobby Knoop	2.50	1.25
281	Bruce Howard	2.50	1.25
282	Johnny Lewis	2.50	1.25
283	Jim Perry	2.50	1.25
284	Bobby Wine	2.50	1.25
285	Luis Tiant	4.50	2.25
286	Gary Geiger	2.50	1.25
287	Jack Aker	2.50	1.25
288	Dodgers Rookies	160.00	80.00
	Bill Singer (R)		
	Don Sutton (R)		
289	Larry Sherry	2.50	1.25
290	Ron Santo	4.50	2.25
291	Moe Drabowsky	2.50	1.25
292	Jim Coker	2.50	1.25
293	Mike Shannon	2.50	1.25
294	Steve Ridzik	2.50	1.25
295	Jim Hart	2.50	1.25
296	Johnny Keane	2.50	1.25
297	Jim Owens	2.50	1.25
298	Rico Petrocelli	3.00	1.50
299	Lou Burdette	3.50	1.75
300	Roberto Clemente	110.00	55.00
301	Greg Bollo	2.50	1.25
302	Ernie Bowman	2.50	1.25
303	Indians Team	3.50	1.75
304	John Herrnstein	2.50	1.25
305	Camilo Pascual	2.50	1.25
306	Ty Cline	2.50	1.25
307	Clay Carroll	2.50	1.25
308	Tom Haller	2.50	1.25
309	Diego Segui	2.50	1.25
310	Frank Robinson	40.00	20.00
311	Reds Rookies	3.50	1.75
	Tommy Helms (R)		
	Dick Simpson (R)		
312	Bob Saverine	2.50	1.25
313	Chris Zachary	2.50	1.25
314	Hector Valle	2.50	1.25
315	Norm Cash	4.50	2.25
316	Jack Fisher	2.50	1.25
317	Dalton Jones	2.50	1.25
318	Harry Walker	2.50	1.25
319	Gene Freese	2.50	1.25
320	Bob Gibson	30.00	15.00
321	Rick Reichardt	2.50	1.25
322	Bill Faul	2.50	1.25
323	Ray Barker	2.50	1.25
324	John Boozer	2.50	1.25
325	Vic Davalillo	3.00	1.75
326	Braves Team	3.50	1.75
327	Bernie Allen	2.50	1.25
328	Jerry Grote	2.50	1.25
329	Pete Charton	2.50	1.25
330	Ron Fairly	2.50	1.25
331	Ron Herbel	2.50	1.25
332	Billy Bryan	2.50	1.25
333	Senators Rookies	3.00	1.50
	Joe Coleman (R)		
	Jim French (R)		
334	Marty Keough	2.50	1.25
335	Juan Pizarro	2.50	1.25
336	Gene Alley	2.50	1.25
337	Fred Gladding	2.50	1.25
338	Dal Maxvill	2.50	1.25
339	Del Crandall	3.00	1.50
340	Dean Chance	2.50	1.25
341	Wes Westrum	2.50	1.25
342	Bob Humphreys	2.50	1.25
343	Joe Christopher	2.50	1.25
344	Steve Blass	3.00	1.50
345	Bob Allison	2.50	1.25
346	Mike de la Hoz	2.50	1.25
347	Phil Regan	3.00	1.50
348	Orioles Team	3.50	1.75
349	Cap Peterson	2.50	1.25
350	Mel Stottlemyre	4.00	2.00
351	Fred Valentine	2.50	1.25
352	Bob Aspromonte	2.50	1.25
353	Al McBean	2.50	1.25
354	Smoky Burgess	3.00	1.50
355	Wade Blasingame	2.50	1.25
356	Red Sox Rookies	2.50	1.25
	Owen Johnson (R)		
	Ken Sanders (R)		
357	Gerry Arrigo	2.50	1.25
358	Charlie Smith	2.50	1.25
359	Johnny Briggs	2.50	1.25
360	Ron Hunt	3.00	1.50
361	Tom Satriano	2.50	1.25
362	Gates Brown	2.50	1.25
363	Checklist 353-429	7.00	3.50

364	Nate Oliver	2.50	1.25
365	Roger Maris	60.00	30.00
366	Wayne Causey	2.50	1.25
367	Mel Nelson	2.50	1.25
368	Charlie Lau	2.50	1.25
369	Jim King	2.50	1.25
370	Chico Cardenas	2.50	1.25
371	Lee Stange	2.50	1.25
372	Harvey Kuenn	3.50	1.75
373	Giants Rookies	2.50	1.25
	Dick Estelle (R)		
	Jack Hiatt		
374	Bob Locker	2.50	1.25
375	Donn Clendenon	2.50	1.25
376	Paul Schaal	2.50	1.25
377	Turk Farrell	2.50	1.25
378	Dick Tracewski	2.50	1.25
379	Cardinals Team	3.50	1.75
380	Tony Conigliaro	7.00	3.50
381	Hank Fischer	2.50	1.25
382	Phil Roof	2.50	1.25
383	Jackie Brandt	2.50	1.25
384	Al Downing	2.50	1.25
385	Ken Boyer	5.00	2.50
386	Gil Hodges	8.00	4.00
387	Howie Reed	2.50	1.25
388	Don Mincher	2.50	1.25
389	Jim O'Toole	2.50	1.25
390	Brooks Robinson	36.00	18.00
391	Chuck Hinton	2.50	1.25
392	Cubs Rookies	6.00	3.00
	Bill Hands (R)		
	Randy Hundley (R)		
393	George Brunet	2.50	1.25
394	Ron Brand	2.50	1.25
395	Len Gabrielson	2.50	1.25
396	Jerry Stephenson	2.50	1.25
397	Bill White	4.50	2.25
398	Danny Cater	2.50	1.25
399	Ray Washburn	2.50	1.25
400	Zoilo Versalles	3.00	1.50
401	Ken McMullen	2.50	1.25
402	Jim Hickman	2.50	1.25
403	Fred Talbot	2.50	1.25
404	Pirates Team	5.00	2.50
405	Elston Howard	7.00	3.50
406	Joe Jay	2.50	1.25
407	John Kennedy	2.50	1.25
408	Lee Thomas	2.50	1.25
409	Billy Hoeft	2.50	1.25
410	Al Kaline	35.00	17.50
411	Gene Mauch	3.00	1.50
412	Sam Bowens	2.50	1.25
413	John Romano	2.50	1.25
414	Dan Coombs	2.50	1.25
415	Max Alvis	2.50	1.25
416	Phil Ortega	2.50	1.25
417	Angels Rookie	2.50	1.25
	Jim McGlothlin (R)		
	Ed Sukla (R)		
418	Phil Gagliano	2.50	1.25
419	Mike Ryan	2.50	1.25
420	Juan Marichal	14.00	7.00
421	Roy McMillan	2.50	1.25
422	Ed Charles	2.50	1.25
423	Ernie Broglio	2.50	1.25
424	Reds Rookies	7.00	3.50
	Lee May (R)		
	Darrell Osteen		
425	Bob Veale	2.50	1.25
426	White Sox Team	5.00	2.50
427	John Miller	2.50	1.25
428	Sandy Alomar	3.50	1.75
429	Bill Monbouquette	2.50	1.25
430	Don Drysdale	22.00	11.00
431	Walt Bond	2.50	1.25
432	Bob Heffner	2.50	1.25
433	Alvin Dark	2.50	1.25
434	Willie Kirkland	2.50	1.25
435	Jim Bunning	8.00	4.00
436	Julian Javier	2.50	1.25
437	Al Stanek	2.50	1.25
438	Willie Smith	2.50	1.25
439	Pedro Ramos	2.50	1.25
440	Deron Johnson	3.50	1.75
441	Tommie Sisk	2.50	1.25
442	Orioles Rookies	2.50	1.25
	Ed Barnowski (R)		
	Eddie Watt		
443	Bill Wakefield	2.50	1.25
444	Checklist 430-506	7.00	3.50
445	Jim Kaat	8.00	4.00
446	Mack Jones	2.50	1.25
447	Dick Ellsworth (Wrong Photo)	7.00	3.50
448	Eddie Stanky	7.00	3.50
449	Joe Moeller	7.00	3.50
450	Tony Oliva	10.00	5.00
451	Barry Latman	7.00	3.50
452	Joe Azcue	7.00	3.50
453	Ron Kline	7.00	3.50
454	Jerry Buchek	7.00	3.50
455	Mickey Lolich	10.00	5.00
456	Red Sox Rookies	7.00	3.50
	Darrell Brandon (R)		
	Joe Foy (R)		
457	Joe Gibbon	7.00	3.50
458	Manny Jimenez	7.00	3.50
459	Bill McCool	7.00	3.50
460	Curt Blefary	7.00	3.50
461	Roy Face	7.00	3.50
462	Bob Rodgers	7.00	3.50
463	Phillies Team	7.00	3.50
464	Larry Bearnarth	7.00	3.50
465	Don Buford	7.00	3.50
466	Ken Johnson	7.00	3.50

#	Name		
467	Vic Roznovsky	7.00	3.50
468	Johnny Podres	8.00	4.00
469	Yankees Rookies	26.00	13.00
	Bobby Murcer (R)		
	Dooley Womack (R)		
470	Sam McDowell	8.00	4.00
471	Bob Skinner	7.00	3.50
472	Terry Fox	7.00	3.50
473	Rich Rollins	7.00	3.50
474	Dick Schofield	7.00	3.50
475	Dick Radatz	7.00	3.50
476	Bobby Bragan	7.00	3.50
477	Steve Barber	7.00	3.50
478	Tony Gonzalez	7.00	3.50
479	Jim Hannan	7.00	3.50
480	Dick Stuart	7.00	3.50
481	Bob Lee	7.00	3.50
482	Cubs Rookies	7.00	3.50
	John Boccabella (R)		
	Dave Dowling (R)		
483	Joe Nuxhall	7.00	3.50
484	Wes Covington	7.00	3.50
485	Bob Bailey	7.00	3.50
486	Tommy John	12.00	6.00
487	Al Ferrara	7.00	3.50
488	George Banks	7.00	3.50
489	Curt Simmons	7.00	3.50
490	Bobby Richardson	14.00	7.00
491	Dennis Bennett	7.00	3.50
492	Athletics Team	7.00	3.50
493	Johnny Klippstein	7.00	3.50
494	Gordon Coleman	7.00	3.50
495	Dick McAuliffe	7.00	3.50
496	Lindy McDaniel	7.00	3.50
497	Chris Cannizzaro	7.00	3.50
498	Pirates Rookies	7.00	3.50
	Woody Fryman (R)		
	Luke Walker (R)		
499	Wally Bunker	7.00	3.50
500	Hank Aaron	125.00	65.00
501	John O'Donoghue	7.00	3.50
502	Lenny Green	7.00	3.50
503	Steve Hamilton	7.00	3.50
504	Grady Hatton	7.00	3.50
505	Jose Cardenal	7.00	3.50
506	Bo Belinsky	7.00	3.50
507	John Edwards	7.00	3.50
508	Steve Hargan (R)	7.00	3.50
509	Jake Wood	7.00	3.50
510	Hoyt Wilhelm	15.00	7.50
511	Giants Rookies	7.00	3.50
	Bob Barton (R)		
	Tito Fuentes (R)		
512	Dick Stigman	7.00	3.50
513	Camilo Carreon	7.00	3.50
514	Hal Woodeshick	7.00	3.50
515	Frank Howard	10.00	5.00
516	Eddie Bressoud	7.00	3.50
517	Checklist 507-598	12.00	6.00
518	Braves Rookies	7.00	3.50
	Herb Hippauf (R)		
	Arnie Umbach (R)		
519	Bob Friend	7.00	3.50
520	Jim Wynn	8.00	4.00
521	John Wyatt	7.00	3.50
522	Phil Linz	7.00	3.50
523	Bob Sadowski	24.00	12.00
524	Giants Rookies	24.00	12.00
	Ollie Brown (R)		
	Don Mason (R)		
525	Gary Bell	24.00	12.00
526	Twins Team	70.00	40.00
527	Julio Navarro	24.00	12.00
528	Jesse Gonder	24.00	12.00
529	White Sox Rookies	24.00	12.00
	Lee Elia (R)		
	Dennis Higgins (R)		
	Bill Voss (R)		
530	Robin Roberts	48.00	24.00
531	Joe Cunningham	24.00	12.00
532	Aurelio Monteagudo	24.00	12.00
533	Jerry Adair	24.00	12.00
534	Mets Rookies	24.00	12.00
	Dave Eilers (R)		
	Rob Gardner (R)		
535	Willie Davis	32.00	16.00
536	Dick Egan	24.00	12.00
537	Herman Franks	24.00	12.00
538	Bob Allen	24.00	12.00
539	Astros Rookies	24.00	12.00
	Bill Heath (R)		
	Carrol Sembera (R)		
540	Denny McLain	45.00	22.50
541	Gene Oliver	24.00	12.00
542	George Smith	24.00	12.00
543	Roger Craig	24.00	12.00
544	Cardinals Rookies	24.00	12.00
	Joe Hoerner (R)		
	George Kernek (R)		
	Jimmy Williams (R)		
545	Dick Green	24.00	12.00
546	Dwight Siebler	24.00	12.00
547	Horace Clarke	24.00	12.00
548	Gary Kroll	24.00	12.00
549	Senators Rookies	24.00	12.00
	Al Closter (R)		
	Casey Cox (R)		
550	Willie McCovey	125.00	65.00
551	Bob Purkey	24.00	12.00
552	Birdie Tebbets	24.00	12.00
553	M.L. Rookie Stars	24.00	12.00
	Pat Garrett (R)		
	Jackie Warner (R)		
554	Jim Northrup	24.00	12.00
555	Ron Perranoski	24.00	12.00
556	Mel Queen	24.00	12.00

557	Felix Mantilla	24.00	12.00
558	Red Sox Rookies	25.00	12.50
	Guido Grilli(R)		
	Pete Magrini (R)		
	George Scott (R)		
559	Roberto Pena	24.00	12.00
560	Joel Horlen	24.00	12.00
561	Choo Choo Coleman	32.00	16.00
562	Russ Snyder	24.00	12.00
563	Twins Rookies	24.00	12.00
	Pete Cimino (R)		
	Cesar Tovar		
564	Bob Chance	24.00	12.00
565	Jimmy Piersall	36.00	18.00
566	Mike Cuellar	28.00	14.00
567	Dick Howser	25.00	12.50
568	Athletics Rookies	24.00	12.00
	Paul Lindblad (R)		
	Ron Stone (R)		
569	Orlando McFarlane	24.00	12.00
570	Art Mahaffey	24.00	12.00
571	Dave Roberts	24.00	12.00
572	Bob Priddy	24.00	12.00
573	Derrell Griffith	24.00	12.00
574	Mets Rookies	24.00	12.00
	Bill Hepler (R)		
	Bill Murphy		
575	Earl Wilson	24.00	12.00
576	Dave Nicholson	24.00	12.00
577	Jack Lamabe	24.00	12.00
578	Chi Chi Olivo	24.00	12.00
579	Orioles Rookies	24.00	12.00
	Frank Bertaina (R)		
	Gene Brabender (R)		
	Dave Johnson (R)		
580	Billy Williams	100.00	50.00
581	Tony Martinez	24.00	12.00
582	Garry Roggenburk	24.00	12.00
583	Tigers Team	120.00	60.00
584	Yankees Rookies	24.00	12.00
	Frank Fernandez (R)		
	Fritz Peterson (R)		
585	Tony Taylor	24.00	12.00
586	Claude Raymond	24.00	12.00
587	Dick Bertell	24.00	12.00
588	Athletics Rookies	24.00	12.00
	Chuck Dobson (R)		
	Ken Suarez (R)		
589	Lou Klimchock	24.00	12.00
590	Bill Skowron	40.00	20.00
591	N.L. Rookies	28.00	14.00
	Grant Jackson (R)		
	Bart Shirley (R)		
592	Andre Rodgers	24.00	12.00
593	Doug Camilli	24.00	12.00
594	Chico Salmon	24.00	12.00
595	Larry Jackson	24.00	12.00
596	Astros Rookies	24.00	12.00

	Nate Colbert (R)		
	Greg Sims (R)		
597	John Sullivan	24.00	12.00
598	Gaylord Perry	300.00	150.00

1967 Topps

This 609-card set features large color photos on the card fronts framed by a white border. Fascimile autographs appear in the bottom right corner. This is the first Topps issue to sport vertical card backs. Cards measure 2-1/2" by 3-1/2" and the major subsets include League Leaders, World Series Highlights and Rookies.

		NR/MT	EX
Complete Set (609)		5,500.00	2,700.00
Commons (1-110)		1.25	.60
Commons (111-457)		2.50	1.25
Commons (458-533)		6.00	3.00
Commons (534-609)		18.00	9.00
1	The Champs	20.00	8.50
	(Hank Bauer		
	Brooks Robinson		
	Frank Robinson)		
2	Jack Hamilton	1.25	.60
3	Duke Sims	1.25	.60
4	Hal Lanier	1.25	.60
5	Whitey Ford	24.00	12.00
6	Dick Simpson	1.25	.60
7	Don McMahon	1.25	.60
8	Chuck Harrison	1.25	.60
9	Ron Hansen	1.25	.60
10	Matty Alou	2.00	1.00
11	Barry Moore	1.25	.60
12	Dodgers Rookies	2.00	1.25
	Jim Campanis (R)		

	Billy Singer (R)		
13	Joe Sparma	1.25	.60
14	Phil Linz	1.25	.60
15	Earl Battey	1.25	.60
16	Bill Hands	1.25	.60
17	Jim Gosger	1.25	.60
18	Gene Oliver	1.25	.60
19	Jim McGlothlin	1.25	.60
20	Orlando Cepeda	8.50	4.25
21	Dave Bristol	1.25	.60
22	Gene Brabender	1.25	.60
23	Larry Elliot	1.25	.60
24	Bob Allen	1.25	.60
25	Elston Howard	4.50	2.25
26a	Bob Priddy (No trade statement)	24.00	12.00
26b	Bob Priddy (Trade statement)	1.25	.60
27	Bob Saverine	1.25	.60
28	Barry Latman	1.25	.60
29	Tommy McCraw	1.25	.60
30	Al Kaline	20.00	10.00
31	Jim Brewer	1.25	.60
32	Bob Bailey	1.25	.60
33	Athletics Rookies	5.00	2.50
	Sal Bando (R)		
	Randy Schwartz (R)		
34	Pete Cimino	1.25	.60
35	Rico Carty	2.50	1.25
36	Bob Tillman	1.25	.60
37	Rick Wise	1.50	.75
38	Bob Johnson	1.25	.60
39	Curt Simmons	1.25	.60
40	Rick Reichardt	1.25	.60
41	Joe Hoerner	1.25	.60
42	Mets Team	3.00	1.50
43	Chico Salmon	1.25	.60
44	Joe Nuxhall	1.25	.60
45	Roger Maris	48.00	24.00
46	Lindy McDaniel	1.25	.60
47	Ken McMullen	1.25	.60
48	Bill Freehan	1.25	.60
49	Roy Face	1.25	.60
50	Tony Oliva	5.00	2.50
51	Astros Rookies	1.25	.60
	Dave Adlesh (R)		
	Wes Bales (R)		
52	Dennis Higgins	1.25	.60
53	Clay Dalrymple	1.25	.60
54	Dick Green	1.25	.60
55	Don Drysdale	18.00	9.00
56	Jose Tartabull	1.25	.60
57	Pat Jarvis	1.25	.60
58	Paul Schaal	1.25	.60
59	Ralph Terry	1.50	.75
60	Luis Aparicio	7.00	3.50
61	Gordy Coleman	1.25	.60
62	Checklist 1-109	7.00	3.50
63	Cards' Clubbers (Lou Brock/Curt Flood)	8.50	4.25
64	Fred Valentine	1.25	.60
65	Tom Haller	1.25	.60
66	Manny Mota	1.50	.75
67	Ken Berry	1.25	.60
68	Bob Buhl	1.25	.60
69	Vic Davalillo	1.25	.60
70	Ron Santo	4.50	2.25
71	Camilo Pascual	1.25	.60
72	Tigers Rookies	1.25	.60
	George Korince (R)		
	John Matchick (R)		
73	Rusty Staub	4.00	2.00
74	Wes Stock	1.25	.60
75	George Scott	2.50	1.25
76	Jim Barbieri	1.25	.60
77	Dooley Womack	1.25	.60
78	Pat Corrales	1.50	.75
79	Bubba Morton	1.25	.60
80	Jim Maloney	1.25	.60
81	Eddie Stanky	1.25	.60
82	Steve Barber	1.25	.60
83	Ollie Brown	1.25	.60
84	Tommie Sisk	1.25	.60
85	Johnny Callison	1.25	.60
86a	Mike McCormick (No trade statement)	20.00	10.00
86b	Mike McCormick (Trade statement)	1.25	.60
87	George Altman	1.25	.60
88	Mickey Lolich	4.50	2.25
89	Felix Millan (R)	1.50	.75
90	Jim Nash	1.25	.60
91	Johnny Lewis	1.25	.60
92	Ray Washburn	1.25	.60
93	Yankees Rookies	4.00	2.00
	Stan Bahnsen (R)		
	Bobby Murcer		
94	Ron Fairly	1.25	.60
95	Sonny Siebert	1.25	.60
96	Art Shamsky	1.25	.60
97	Mike Cuellar	2.00	1.00
98	Rich Rollins	1.25	.60
99	Lee Stange	1.25	.60
100	Frank Robinson	20.00	10.00
101	Ken Johnson	1.25	.60
102	Phillies Team	3.00	1.50
103	Checklist 110-196	12.00	6.00
104	Minnie Rojas	1.25	.60
105	Ken Boyer	3.50	1.75
106	Randy Hundley	1.25	.60
107	Joel Horlen	1.25	.60
108	Alex Johnson	1.25	.60
109	Tribe Thumpers (Rocky Colavito, Leon Wagner)	2.50	1.25
110	Jack Aker	1.25	.60

111	John Kennedy	2.50	1.25
112	Dave Wickersham	2.50	1.25
113	Dave Nicholson	2.50	1.25
114	Jack Baldschun	2.50	1.25
115	Paul Casanova	2.50	1.25
116	Herman Franks	2.50	1.25
117	Darrell Brandon	2.50	1.25
118	Bernie Allen	2.50	1.25
119	Wade Blasingame	2.50	1.25
120	Floyd Robinson	2.50	1.25
121	Ed Bressoud	2.50	1.25
122	George Brunet	2.50	1.25
123	Pirates Rookies	1.25	.60
	Jim Price (R)		
	Luke Walker		
124	Jim Stewart	2.50	1.25
125	Moe Drabowsky	2.50	1.25
126	Tony Taylor	2.50	1.25
127	John O'Donoghue	2.50	1.25
128	Ed Spiezio	2.50	1.25
129	Phil Roof	2.50	1.25
130	Phil Regan	2.50	1.25
131	Yankees Team	5.00	2.50
132	Ozzie Virgil	2.50	1.25
133	Ron Kline	2.50	1.25
134	Gates Brown	2.50	1.25
135	Deron Johnson	2.50	1.25
136	Carroll Sembera	2.50	1.25
137	Twins Rookies	2.50	1.25
	Ron Clark (R)		
	Jim Ollum (R)		
138	Dick Kelley	2.50	1.25
139	Dalton Jones	2.50	1.25
140	Willie Stargell	20.00	10.00
141	John Miller	2.50	1.25
142	Jackie Brandt	2.50	1.25
143	Sox Sockers	2.50	1.25
	Don Buford		
	Pete Ward		
144	Bill Hepler	2.50	1.25
145	Larry Brown	2.50	1.25
146	Steve Carlton	150.00	75.00
147	Tom Egan	2.50	1.25
148	Adolfo Phillips	2.50	1.25
149	Joe Moeller	2.50	1.25
150	Mickey Mantle	280.00	140.00
151	World Series Game 1	3.50	1.75
152	World Series Game 2	7.00	3.50
153	World Series Game 3	3.50	1.75
154	World Series Game 4	3.50	1.75
155	WS (Celebration)	3.50	1.75
156	Ron Herbel	2.50	1.25
157	Danny Cater	2.50	1.25
158	Jimmy Coker	2.50	1.25
159	Bruce Howard	2.50	1.25
160	Willie Davis	2.50	1.25
161	Dick Williams	2.50	1.25
162	Billy O'Dell	2.50	1.25
163	Vic Roznovsky	2.50	1.25
164	Dwight Siebler	2.50	1.25
165	Cleon Jones	2.50	1.25
166	Eddie Mathews	15.00	7.50
167	Senators Rookies	2.50	1.25
	(Joe Coleman, Tim		
	Cullen)		
168	Ray Culp	2.50	1.25
169	Horace Clarke	2.50	1.25
170	Dick McAuliffe	2.50	1.25
171	Calvin Koonce	2.50	1.25
172	Bill Heath	2.50	1.25
173	Cardinals Team	3.00	1.50
174	Dick Radatz	2.50	1.25
175	Bobby Knoop	2.50	1.25
176	Sammy Ellis	2.50	1.25
177	Tito Fuentes	2.50	1.25
178	John Buzhardt	2.50	1.25
179	Braves Rookies	2.50	1.25
	Cecil Upshaw (R)		
	Charles Vaugan (R)		
180	Curt Blefary	2.50	1.25
181	Terry Fox	2.50	1.25
182	Ed Charles	2.50	1.25
183	Jim Pagliaroni	2.50	1.25
184	George Thomas	2.50	1.25
185	Ken Holtzman (R)	4.00	2.00
186	Mets Maulers (Ed	3.00	1.50
	Kranepool/Ron		
	Swoboda)		
187	Pedro Ramos	2.50	1.25
188	Ken Harrelson	3.00	1.50
189	Chuck Hinton	2.50	1.25
190	Turk Farrell	2.50	1.25
191	Checklist 197-283	7.00	3.50
192	Fred Gladding	2.50	1.25
193	Jose Cardenal	2.50	1.25
194	Bob Allison	2.50	1.25
195	Al Jackson	2.50	1.25
196	Johnny Romano	2.50	1.25
197	Ron Perranoski	2.50	1.25
198	Chuck Hiller	2.50	1.25
199	Billy Hitchcock	2.50	1.25
200	Willie Mays	100.00	50.00
201	Hal Reniff	2.50	1.25
202	Johnny Edwards	2.50	1.25
203	Al McBean	2.50	1.25
204	Orioles Rookies	2.50	1.25
	(Mike Epstein, Tom		
	Phoebus)		
205	Dick Groat	2.50	1.25
206	Dennis Bennett	2.50	1.25
207	John Orsino	2.50	1.25
208	Jack Lamabe	2.50	1.25
209	Joe Nossek	2.50	1.25
210	Bob Gibson	25.00	15.00
211	Twins Team	3.50	1.75
212	Chris Zachary	2.50	1.25

213	Jay Johnstone (R)	3.00	1.75
214	Tom Kelley	2.50	1.25
215	Ernie Banks	24.00	12.00
216	Bengal Belters (Norm Cash/Al Kaline)	9.00	4.50
217	Rob Gardner	2.50	1.25
218	Wes Parker	2.50	1.25
219	Clay Carroll	2.50	1.25
220	Jim Hart	2.50	1.25
221	Woody Fryman	2.50	1.25
222	Reds Rookies (Lee May, Darrell Osteen)	3.50	1.75
223	Mike Ryan	2.50	1.25
224	Walt Bond	2.50	1.25
225	Mel Stottlemyre	3.50	1.75
226	Julian Javier	2.50	1.25
227	Paul Lindblad	2.50	1.25
228	Gil Hodges	6.00	3.00
229	Larry Jackson	2.50	1.25
230	Boog Powell	4.50	2.25
231	John Batema	2.50	1.25
232	Don Buford	2.50	1.25
233	A.L. ERA Leaders	3.00	1.50
234	N.L. ERA Leaders	10.00	5.00
235	A.L. Pitching Leaders	4.50	2.25
236	N.L. Pitching Leaders	15.00	7.50
237	A.L. Strikeout Ldrs	3.00	1.50
238	N.L. Strikeout Ldrs	8.00	4.00
239	A.L. Batting Leaders	8.00	4.00
240	N.L. Batting Leaders	3.00	1.50
241	A.L. RBI Leaders	8.00	4.00
242	N.L. RBI Leaders	10.00	5.00
243	A.L. HR Leaders	8.00	4.00
244	N.L. HR Leaders	12.00	6.00
245	Curt Flood	3.00	1.50
246	Jim Perry	2.50	1.25
247	Jerry Lumpe	2.50	1.25
248	Gene Mauch	2.50	1.25
249	Nick Willhite	2.50	1.25
250	Hank Aaron	110.00	55.00
251	Woody Held	2.50	1.25
252	Bob Bolin	2.50	1.25
253	Indians Rookies Bill Davis (R) Gus Gil (R)	2.50	1.25
254	Milt Pappas	2.50	1.25
255	Frank Howard	4.00	2.50
256	Bob Hendley	2.50	1.25
257	Charley Smith	2.50	1.25
258	Lee Maye	2.50	1.25
259	Don Dennis	2.50	1.25
260	Jim Lefebvre	2.50	1.25
261	John Wyatt	2.50	1.25
262	Athletics Team	3.00	1.50
263	Hank Aguirre	2.50	1.25
264	Ron Swoboda	2.50	1.25
265	Lou Burdette	3.00	1.50
266	Pitt Power (Donn Clendenon, Willie Stargell)	4.50	2.25
267	Don Schwall	2.50	1.25
268	John Briggs	2.50	1.25
269	Don Nottebart	2.50	1.25
270	Zoilo Versalles	3.00	1.50
271	Eddie Watt	2.50	1.25
272	Cubs Rookies Bill Connors (R) Dave Dowling (R)	2.50	1.25
273	Dick Lines	2.50	1.25
274	Bob Aspromonte	2.50	1.25
275	Fred Whitfield	2.50	1.25
276	Bruce Brubaker	2.50	1.25
277	Steve Whitaker	2.50	1.25
278	Checklist 284-370	7.00	3.50
279	Frank Linzy	2.50	1.25
280	Tony Conigliaro	5.00	2.50
281	Bob Rodgers	2.50	1.25
282	Johnny Odom	2.50	1.25
283	Gene Alley	2.50	1.25
284	Johnny Podres	3.00	1.50
285	Lou Brock	25.00	15.00
286	Wayne Causey	2.50	1.25
287	Mets Rookies Greg Gossen (R) Bart Shirley	2.50	1.25
288	Denver Lemaster	2.50	1.25
289	Tom Tresh	3.50	1.75
290	Bill White	3.00	1.50
291	Jim Hannan	2.50	1.25
292	Don Pavletich	2.50	1.25
293	Ed Kirkpatrick	2.50	1.25
294	Walt Alston	3.00	1.50
295	Sam McDowell	3.00	1.50
296	Glenn Beckert	3.00	1.50
297	Dave Morehead	2.50	1.25
298	Ron Davis	2.50	1.25
299	Norm Siebern	2.50	1.25
300	Jim Kaat	5.00	2.50
301	Jesse Gonder	2.50	1.25
302	Orioles Team	4.50	2.25
303	Gil Blanco	2.50	1.25
304	Phil Gagliano	2.50	1.25
305	Earl Wilson	2.50	1.25
306	Bub Harrelson (R)	4.00	2.00
307	Jim Beauchamp	2.50	1.25
308	Al Downing	2.50	1.25
309	Hurlers Beward (Richie Allen, Johnny Callison)	3.50	1.75
310	Gary Peters	2.50	1.25
311	Ed Brinkman	2.50	1.25
312	Don Mincher	2.50	1.25
313	Bob Lee	2.50	1.25
314	Red Sox Rookies Mike Andrews (R) Reggie Smith (R)	8.50	4.25

315	Billy Williams	14.00	7.00
316	Jack Kralick	2.50	1.25
317	Cesar Tovar	2.50	1.25
318	Dave Giusti	2.50	1.25
319	Paul Blair	3.00	1.50
320	Gaylord Perry	15.00	7.50
321	Mayo Smith	2.50	1.25
322	Jose Pagan	2.50	1.25
323	Mike Hershberger	2.50	1.25
324	Hal Woodeshick	2.50	1.25
325	Chico Cardenas	2.50	1.25
326	Bob Uecker	20.00	10.00
327	Angels Team	3.50	1.75
328	Clete Boyer	3.00	1.50
329	Charlie Lau	2.50	1.25
330	Claude Osteen	2.50	1.25
331	Joe Foy	2.50	1.25
332	Jesus Alou	2.50	1.25
333	Ferguson Jenkins	35.00	17.50
334	Twin Terrors (Bob Allison, Harmon Killebrew)	5.00	2.50
335	Bob Veale	2.50	1.25
336	Joe Azcue	2.50	1.25
337	Joe Morgan	25.00	15.00
338	Bob Locker	2.50	1.25
339	Chico Ruiz	2.50	1.25
340	Joe Pepitone	3.50	1.75
341	Giants Rookies Dick Dietz Bill Sorrell (R)	2.50	1.25
342	Hank Fischer	2.50	1.25
343	Tom Satriano	2.50	1.25
344	Ossie Chavarria	2.50	1.25
345	Stu Miller	2.50	1.25
346	Jim Hickman	2.50	1.25
347	Grady Hatton	2.50	1.25
348	Tug McGraw	4.50	2.25
349	Bob Chance	2.50	1.25
350	Joe Torre	4.50	2.25
351	Vern Law	2.50	1.25
352	Ray Oyler	2.50	1.25
353	Bill McCool	2.50	1.25
354	Cubs Team	3.50	1.75
355	Carl Yastrzemski	80.00	50.00
356	Larry Jaster	2.50	1.25
357	Bill Skowron	3.00	1.50
358	Ruben Amaro	2.50	1.25
359	Dick Ellsworth	2.50	1.25
360	Leon Wagner	2.50	1.25
361	Checklist 371-457	7.00	3.50
362	Darold Knowles	2.50	1.25
363	Dave Johnson	2.50	1.25
364	Claude Raymond	2.50	1.25
365	John Roseboro	2.50	1.25
366	Andy Kosco	2.50	1.25
367	Angels Rookies Bill Kelso (R) Don Wallace (R)	2.50	1.25
368	Jack Hiatt	2.50	1.25
369	Jim Hunter	20.00	10.00
370	Tommy Davis	3.50	1.75
371	Jim Lonborg	4.50	2.25
372	Mike de la Hoz	2.50	1.25
373	White Sox Rookies Duane Josephson (R) Fred Klages (R)	2.50	1.25
374	Mel Queen	2.50	1.25
375	Jake Gibbs	2.50	1.25
376	Don Lock	2.50	1.25
377	Luis Tiant	6.00	3.00
378	Tigers Team	3.50	1.75
379	Jerry May	2.50	1.25
380	Dean Chance	2.50	1.25
381	Dick Schofield	2.50	1.25
382	Dave McNally	3.50	1.75
383	Ken Henderson	2.50	1.25
384	Cardinals Rookies Jim Cosman (R) Dick Hughes	2.50	1.25
385	Jim Fregosi	3.00	1.50
386	Dick Selma	2.50	1.25
387	Cap Peterson	2.50	1.25
388	Arnold Earley	2.50	1.25
389	Al Dark	2.50	1.25
390	Jim Wynn	3.00	1.50
391	Wilbur Wood	3.00	1.50
392	Tommy Harper	3.00	1.50
393	Jim Bouton	4.00	2.00
394	Jake Wood	2.50	1.25
395	Chris Short	2.50	1.25
396	Atlanta Aces (Tony Cloninger, Denis Menke)	3.00	1.50
397	Willie Smith		1.25
398	Jeff Torborg	3.00	1.50
399	Al Worthington	2.50	1.25
400	Roberto Clemente	80.00	40.00
401	Jim Coates	2.50	1.25
402	Phillies Rookies Grant Jackson Billy Wilson (R)	2.50	1.25
403	Dick Nen	2.50	1.25
404	Nelson Briles	2.50	1.25
405	Russ Snyder	2.50	1.25
406	Lee Elia	2.50	1.25
407	Reds Team	3.50	1.75
408	Jim Northrup	2.50	1.25
409	Ray Sadecki	2.50	1.25
410	Lou Johnson	2.50	1.25
411	Dick Howser	2.50	1.25
412	Astros Rookies Norm Miller (R) Doug Rader (R)	4.00	2.00
413	Jerry Grote	2.50	1.25
414	Casey Cox	2.50	1.25

No.	Player		
415	Sonny Jackson	2.50	1.25
416	Roger Repoz	2.50	1.25
417	Bob Bruce	2.50	1.25
418	Sam Mele	2.50	1.25
419	Don Kessinger	3.50	1.75
420	Denny McLain	7.00	3.50
421	Dal Maxvill	2.50	1.25
422	Hoyt Wilhelm	10.00	5.00
423	Fence Busters (Willie Mays/Willie McCovey)	25.00	15.00
424	Pedro Gonzalez	2.50	1.25
425	Pete Mikkelsen	2.50	1.25
426	Lou Clinton	2.50	1.25
427	Ruben Gomez	2.50	1.25
428	Dodgers Rookies Tom Hutton (R) Gene Michael (R)	4.00	2.00
429	Garry Roggenburk	2.50	1.25
430	Pete Rose	85.00	42.50
431	Ted Uhlaender	2.50	1.25
432	Jimmie Hall	2.50	1.25
433	AL Luplow	2.50	1.25
434	Eddie Fisher	2.50	1.25
435	Mack Jones	2.50	1.25
436	Pete Ward	2.50	1.25
437	Senators Team	3.50	1.75
438	Chuck Dobson	2.50	1.25
439	Byron Browne	2.50	1.25
440	Steve Hargan	2.50	1.25
441	Jim Davenport	2.50	1.25
442	Yankees Rookies Bill Robinson (R) Joe Verbanic (R)	4.00	2.00
443	Tito Francona	2.50	1.25
444	George Smith	2.50	1.25
445	Don Sutton	36.00	18.00
446	Russ Nixon	2.50	1.25
447	Bo Belinsky	2.50	1.25
448	Harry Walker	2.50	1.25
449	Orlando Pena	2.50	1.25
450	Richie Allen	7.00	3.50
451	Fred Newman	2.50	1.25
452	Ed Kranepool	3.00	1.50
453	Aurelio Monteagudo	2.50	1.25
454	Checklist 458-533	7.00	3.50
455	Tommie Agee	2.50	1.25
456	Phil Niekro	18.00	9.00
457	Andy Etchebarren	2.50	1.25
458	Lee Thomas	6.00	3.00
459	Senators Rookies Dick Bosman (R) Pete Craig	7.00	3.50
460	Harmon Killebrew	55.00	27.50
461	Bob Miller	6.00	3.00
462	Bob Barton	6.00	3.00
463	Tribe Hill Aces (Sam McDowell/Sonny Siebert)	7.00	3.50
464	Dan Coombs	6.00	3.00
465	Willie Horton	7.00	3.50
466	Bobby Wine	6.00	3.00
467	Jim O'Toole	6.00	3.00
468	Ralph Houk	6.00	3.00
469	Len Gabrielson	6.00	3.00
470	Bob Shaw	6.00	3.00
471	Rene Lachemann	6.00	3.00
472	Pirates Rookies John Gelnar (R) George Spriggs (R)	6.00	3.00
473	Jose Santiago	6.00	3.00
474	Bob Tolan	6.00	3.00
475	Jim Palmer	120.00	60.00
476	Tony Perez	90.00	45.00
477	Braves Team	12.00	6.00
478	Bob Humphreys	6.00	3.00
479	Gary Bell	6.00	3.00
480	Willie McCovey	40.00	20.00
481	Leo Durocher	10.00	5.00
482	Bill Monbouquette	6.00	3.00
483	Jim Landis	6.00	3.00
484	Jerry Adair	6.00	3.00
485	Tim McCarver	20.00	10.00
486	Twins Rookies Rich Reese (R) Bill Whitby (R)	6.00	3.00
487	Tom Reynolds	6.00	3.00
488	Gerry Arrigo	6.00	3.00
489	Doug Clemens	6.00	3.00
490	Tony Cloninger	6.00	3.00
491	Sam Bowens	6.00	3.00
492	Pirates Team	12.00	6.00
493	Phil Ortega	6.00	3.00
494	Bill Rigney	6.00	3.00
495	Fritz Peterson	6.00	3.00
496	Orlando McFarlane	6.00	3.00
497	Ron Campbell	6.00	3.00
498	Larry Dierker	6.00	3.00
499	Indians Rookies George Culver (R) Jose Vidal (R)	6.00	3.00
500	Juan Marichal	28.00	14.00
501	Jerry Zimmerman	6.00	3.00
502	Derrell Griffith	6.00	3.00
503	Dodgers Team	12.00	6.00
504	Orlando Martinez	6.00	3.00
505	Tommy Helms	6.00	3.00
506	Smoky Burgess	7.00	3.50
507	Orioles Rookies Ed Barnowski (R) Larry Haney	6.00	3.00
508	Dick Hall	6.00	3.00
509	Jim King	6.00	3.00
510	Bill Mazeroski	12.00	6.00
511	Don Wert	6.00	3.00
512	Red Schoendienst	12.00	6.00
513	Marcelino Lopez	6.00	3.00

514	John Werhas	6.00	3.00
515	Bert Campaneris	7.00	3.50
516	Giants Team	12.00	6.00
517	Fred Talbot	6.00	3.00
518	Denis Menke	6.00	3.00
519	Ted Davidson		
		6.00	3.00
520	Max Alvis	6.00	3.00
521	Bird Bombers (Curt	7.00	3.50
	Blefary/Boog Powell)		
522	John Stephenson	6.00	3.00
523	Jim Merritt	6.00	3.00
524	Felix Mantilla	6.00	3.00
525	Ron Hunt	6.00	3.00
526	Tigers Rookies	8.00	4.00
	Pat Dobson (R)		
	George Korince (R)		
527	Dennis Ribant	6.00	3.00
528	Rico Petrocelli	8.00	4.00
529	Gary Wagner	6.00	3.00
530	Felipe Alou	7.00	3.50
531	Checklist 534-609	10.00	5.00
532	Jim Hicks	6.00	3.00
533	Jack Fisher	6.00	3.00
534	Hank Bauer	18.00	9.00
535	Donn Clendenon	18.00	9.00
536	Cubs Rookies	35.00	17.50
	Joe Niekro (R)		
	Paul Popovich (R)		
537	Chuck Estrada	18.00	9.00
538	J.C. Martin	18.00	9.00
539	Dick Egan	18.00	9.00
540	Norm Cash	45.00	22.50
541	Joe Gibbon	18.00	9.00
542	Athletics Rookies	18.00	9.00
	Rick Monday (R)		
	Tony Pierce (R)		
543	Dan Schneider	18.00	9.00
544	Indians Team	18.00	9.00
545	Jim Grant	18.00	9.00
546	Woody Woodward	18.00	9.00
547	Red Sox Rookies	18.00	9.00
	Russ Gibson (R)		
	Bill Rohr (R)		
548	Tony Gonzalez	18.00	9.00
549	Jack Sanford	18.00	9.00
550	Vada Pinson	18.00	9.00
551	Doug Camilli	18.00	9.00
552	Ted Savage	18.00	9.00
553	Yankees Rookies	18.00	9.00
	Mike Hegan (R)		
	Thad Tillotson (R)		
554	Andre Rodgers	18.00	9.00
555	Don Cardwell	18.00	9.00
556	Al Weis	18.00	9.00
557	Al Ferrara	18.00	9.00
558	Orioles Rookies	45.00	22.50
	Mark Belanger (R)		
	Bill Dillman		
559	Dick Tracewski	18.00	9.00
560	Jim Bunning	45.00	22.50
561	Sandy Alomar	18.00	9.00
562	Steve Blass	18.00	9.00
563	Joe Adcock	20.00	10.00
564	Astros Rookies	18.00	9.00
	Alonzo Harris (R)		
	Aaron Pointer (R)		
565	Lew Krausse	18.00	9.00
566	Gary Geiger	18.00	9.00
567	Steve Hamilton	18.00	9.00
568	John Sullivan	18.00	9.00
569	A.L. Rookies	540.00	270.00
	Hank Allen (R)		
	Rod Carew (R)		
570	Maury Wills	90.00	45.00
571	Larry Sherry	18.00	9.00
572	Don Demeter	18.00	9.00
573	White Sox Team	18.00	9.00
574	Jerry Buchek	18.00	9.00
575	Dave Boswell	18.00	9.00
576	N.L. Rookies		
	Norm Gigon (R)		
	Ramon Hernandez (R)		
577	Bill Short	18.00	9.00
578	John Boccabella	18.00	9.00
579	Bill Henry	18.00	9.00
580	Rocky Colavito	75.00	37.50
581	Mets Rookies	1,500.00	850.00
	Bill Denehy (R)		
	Tom Seaver (R)		
582	Jim Owens	18.00	9.00
583	Ray Barker	18.00	9.00
584	Jim Piersall	24.00	12.00
585	Wally Bunker	18.00	9.00
586	Manny Jimenez	18.00	9.00
587	N.L. Rookies		
	Don Shaw (R)		
	Gary Sutherland (R)		
588	Johnny Klippstein	18.00	9.00
589	Dave Ricketts	18.00	9.00
590	Pete Richert	18.00	9.00
591	Ty Cline	18.00	9.00
592	N.L. Rookies	18.00	9.00
	Jim Shellenback (R)		
	Ron Willis (R)		
593	Wes Westrum	18.00	9.00
594	Dan Osinski	18.00	9.00
595	Cookie Rojas	18.00	9.00
596	Galen Cisco	18.00	9.00
597	Ted Abernathy	18.00	9.00
598	White Sox Rookies	18.00	9.00
	Ed Stroud (R)		
	Walt Williams (R)		
599	Bob Duliba	18.00	9.00
600	Brooks Robinson	250.00	125.00
601	Bill Bryan	18.00	9.00

602	Juan Pizarro	18.00	9.00
603	Athletics Rookies	18.00	9.00
	Tim Talton (R)		
	Ramon Webster (R)		
604	Red Sox Team	120.00	60.00
605	Mike Shannon	45.00	22.50
606	Ron Taylor	18.00	9.00
607	Mickey Stanley	24.00	12.00
608	Cubs Rookies		
	Rich Nye (R)		
	John Upham (R)		
609	Tommy John	120.00	60.00

1968 Topps

This 598-card set features four-color photos on the front printed on a grainy background. Player's names appear below the pictures and team names are printed in a small circle in the lower right corner. Once again, the card backs are vertical and feature bio's, stats and a small cartoon. Cards measure 2-1/2" by 3-1/2" and subsets included League Leaders (1-12), World Series Highlights (151-158) and All-Stars (361-380).

		NR/MT	EX
Complete Set (598)		3,500.00	1,750.00
Commons (1-457)		1.25	.60
Commons (458-598)		3.50	1.75

1	N.L. Batting Leaders	15.00	7.50
2	A.L. Batting Leaders	8.00	4.00
3	N.L. RBI Leaders	8.00	4.00
4	A.L. RBI Leaders	8.00	4.00
5	N.L. HR Leaders	7.00	3.50
6	A.L. HR Leaders	8.00	4.00
7	N.L. ERA Leaders	3.00	1.50
8	A.L. ERA Leaders	3.00	1.50
9	N.L. Pitching Leaders	3.00	1.50
10	A.L. Pitching Leaders	3.00	1.50
11	N.L. Strikeout Ldrs	5.00	2.50
12	A.L. Strikeout Ldrs	3.00	1.50
13	Chuck Hartenstein	1.25	.60
14	Jerry McNertney	1.25	.60
15	Ron Hunt	1.25	.60
16	Indians Rookies	5.00	2.50
	Lou Piniella (R)		
	Richie Scheinblum (R)		
17	Dick Hall	1.25	.60
18	Mike Hershberger	1.25	.60
19	Juan Pizarro	1.25	.60
20	Brooks Robinson	28.00	14.00
21	Ron Davis	1.25	.60
22	Pat Dobson	2.00	1.00
23	Chico Cardenas	1.25	.60
24	Bobby Locke	1.25	.60
25	Julian Javier	1.25	.60
26	Darrell Brandon	1.25	.60
27	Gil Hodges	8.00	4.00
28	Ted Uhlaender	1.25	.60
29	Joe Verbanic	1.25	.60
30	Joe Torre	3.50	1.75
31	Ed Stroud	1.25	.60
32	Joe Gibbon	1.25	.60
33	Pete Ward	1.25	.60
34	Al Ferrara	1.25	.60
35	Steve Hargan	1.25	.60
36	Pirates Rookies	1.50	.75
	Bob Moose (R)		
	Bob Robertson (R)		
37	Billy Williams	12.00	6.00
38	Tony Pierce	1.25	.60
39	Cookie Rojas	1.50	.75
40	Denny McLain	10.00	5.00
41	Julio Gotay	1.25	.60
42	Larry Haney	1.25	.60
43	Gary Bell	1.25	.60
44	Frank Kostro	1.25	.60
45	Tom Seaver	260.00	130.00
46	Dave Ricketts	1.25	.60
47	Ralph Houk	1.50	.75
48	Ted Davidson	1.25	.60
49a	Ed Brinkman (Y)	48.00	24.00
49b	Ed Brinkman (White)	1.25	.60
50	Willie Mays	75.00	38.00
51	Bob Locker	1.25	.60
52	Hawk Taylor	1.25	.60
53	Gene Alley	1.25	.60
54	Stan Williams	1.25	.60
55	Felipe Alou	2.00	1.00
56	Orioles Rookies	1.25	.60
	Dave Leonhard (R)		
	Dave May (R)		
57	Dan Schneider	1.25	.60
58	Eddie Mathews	12.00	6.00

No.	Player		
59	Don Lock	1.25	.60
60	Ken Holtzman	2.00	1.00
61	Reggie Smith	2.50	1.25
62	Chuck Dobson	1.25	.60
63	Dick Kenworthy	1.25	.60
64	Jim Merritt	1.25	.60
65	John Roseboro	1.25	.60
66a	Casey Cox (Yellow)	60.00	30.00
66b	Casey Cox (White)	1.25	.60
67	Checklist 1-109	4.00	2.00
68	Ron Willis	1.25	.60
69	Tom Tresh	1.50	.75
70	Bob Veale	1.25	.60
71	Vern Fuller	1.25	.60
72	Tommy John	5.00	2.50
73	Jim Hart	1.25	.60
74	Milt Pappas	1.25	.60
75	Don Mincher	1.25	.60
76	Braves Rookies	1.25	.60
	Jim Britton (R)		
	Ron Reed (R)		
77	Don Wilson	1.25	.60
78	Jim Northrup	1.25	.60
79	Ted Kubiak	1.25	.60
80	Rod Carew	160.00	80.00
81	Larry Jackson	1.25	.60
82	Sam Bowens	1.25	.60
83	John Stephenson	1.25	.60
84	Bob Tolan	1.25	.60
85	Gaylord Perry	12.00	6.00
86	Willie Stargell	14.00	7.00
87	Dick Williams	1.25	.60
88	Phil Regan	1.25	.60
89	Jake Gibbs	1.25	.60
90	Vada Pinson	2.50	1.25
91	Jim Ollom	1.25	.60
92	Ed Kranepool	1.50	.75
93	Tony Cloninger	1.25	.60
94	Lee Maye	1.25	.60
95	Bob Aspromonte	1.25	.60
96	Senators Rookies	1.25	.60
	Frank Coggins (R)		
	Dick Nold (R)		
97	Tom Phoebus	1.25	.60
98	Gary Sutherland	1.25	.60
99	Rocky Colavito	4.50	2.25
100	Bob Gibson	25.00	12.50
101	Glenn Beckert	1.25	.60
102	Jose Cardenal	1.25	.60
103	Don Sutton	14.00	7.00
104	Dick Dietz	1.25	.60
105	Al Downing	1.25	.60
106	Dalton Jones	1.25	.60
107	Checklist 110-196	5.00	2.50
108	Don Pavletich	1.25	.60
109	Bert Campaneris	2.00	1.00
110	Hank Aaron	80.00	40.00
111	Rich Reese	1.25	.60
112	Woody Fryman	1.25	.60
113	Tigers Rookies	1.25	.60
	Tom Matchick (R)		
	Daryl Patterson (R)		
114	Ron Swoboda	1.50	.75
115	Sam McDowell	1.50	.75
116	Ken McMullen	1.25	.60
117	Larry Jaster	1.25	.60
118	Mark Belanger	1.25	.60
119	Ted Savage	1.25	.60
120	Mel Stotlemyre	2.50	1.25
121	Jimmie Hall	1.25	.60
122	Gene Mauch	1.25	.60
123	Jose Santiago	1.25	.60
124	Nate Oliver	1.25	.60
125	Joe Horlen	1.25	.60
126	Bobby Etheridge	1.25	.60
127	Paul Lindblad	1.25	.60
128	Astros Rookies	1.25	.60
	Tom Dukes (R)		
	Alonzo Harris (R)		
129	Mickey Stanley	2.00	1.25
130	Tony Perez	18.00	9.00
131	Frank Bertaina	1.25	.60
132	Bud Harrelson	2.50	1.25
133	Fred Whitfield	1.25	.60
134	Pat Jarvis	1.25	.60
135	Paul Blair	1.25	.60
136	Randy Hundley	1.25	.60
137	Twins Team	3.00	1.50
138	Ruben Amaro	1.25	.60
139	Chris Short	1.25	.60
140	Tony Conigliaro	4.00	2.00
141	Dal Maxvill	1.25	.60
142	White Sox Rookies	1.25	.60
	Buddy Bradford (R)		
	Bill Voss (R)		
143	Pete Cimino	1.25	.60
144	Joe Morgan	20.00	10.00
145	Don Drysdale	12.00	6.00
146	Sal Bando	2.50	1.25
147	Frank Linzy	1.25	.60
148	Dave Bristol	1.25	.60
149	Bob Saverine	1.25	.60
150	Roberto Clemente	60.00	30.00
151	World Series Game 1	8.00	4.00
152	World Series Game 2	10.00	5.00
153	World Series Game 3	3.50	1.75
154	World Series Game 4	8.00	4.00
155	World Series Game 5	3.50	1.75
156	World Series Game 6	3.50	1.75
157	World Series Game 7	4.50	2.25
158	WS (Celebration)	3.50	1.75
159	Don Kessinger	1.50	.75
160	Earl Wilson	1.25	.60
161	Norm Miller	1.25	.60
162	Cardinals Rookies	1.50	.75
	Hal Gilson (R)		

	Mike Torrez (R)		
163	Gene Brabender	1.25	.60
164	Ramon Webster	1.25	.60
165	Tony Oliva	5.00	2.50
166	Claude Raymond	1.25	.60
167	Elston Howard	4.00	2.00
168	Dodgers Team	4.00	2.00
169	Bob Bolin	1.25	.60
170	Jim Fregosi	1.50	.75
171	Don Nottebart	1.25	.60
172	Walt Williams	1.25	.60
173	John Boozer	1.25	.60
174	Bob Tillman	1.25	.60
175	Maury Wills	4.00	2.00
176	Bob Allen	1.25	.60
177	Mets Rookies	1,650.00	875.00
	Jerry Koosman(R)		
	Nolan Ryan (R)		
178	Don Wert	1.25	.60
179	Bill Stoneman	1.25	.60
180	Curt Flood	2.00	1.00
181	Jerry Zimmerman	1.25	.60
182	Dave Giusti	1.25	.60
183	Bob Kennedy	1.25	.60
184	Lou Johnson	1.25	.60
185	Tom Haller	1.25	.60
186	Eddie Watt	1.25	.60
187	Sonny Jackson	1.25	.60
188	Cap Peterson	1.25	.60
189	Bill Landis	1.25	.60
190	Bill White	1.50	.75
191	Dan Frisella	1.25	.60
192	Checklist 197-283	4.50	2.25
193	Jack Hamilton	1.25	.60
194	Don Buford	1.25	.60
195	Joe Pepitone	1.50	.75
196	Gary Nolan	1.25	.60
197	Larry Brown	1.25	.60
198	Roy Face	1.25	.60
199	A's Rookies	1.25	.60
	Darrell Osteen		
	Roberto Rodriguez (R)		
200	Orlando Cepeda	5.00	2.50
201	Mike Marshall (R)	5.00	2.50
202	Adolfo Phillips	1.25	.60
203	Dick Kelley	1.25	.60
204	Andy Etchebarren	1.25	.60
205	Juan Marichal	10.00	5.00
206	Cal Ermer	1.25	.60
207	Carroll Sembera	1.25	.60
208	Willie Davis	1.50	.75
209	Tim Cullen	1.25	.60
210	Gary Peters	1.25	.60
211	J.C. Martin	1.25	.60
212	Dave Morehead	1.25	.60
213	Chico Ruiz	1.25	.60
214	Yankees Rookies	1.50	.75
	Stan Bahnsen (R)		

	Frank Fernandez (R)		
215	Jim Bunning	4.50	2.25
216	Bubba Morton	1.25	.60
217	Turk Farrell	1.25	.60
218	Ken Suarez	1.25	.60
219	Rob Gardner	1.25	.60
220	Harmon Killebrew	15.00	7.50
221	Braves Team	3.00	1.50
222	Jim Hardin	1.25	.60
223	Ollie Brown	1.25	.60
224	Jack Aker	1.25	.60
225	Richie Allen	4.00	2.00
226	Jimmie Price	1.25	.60
227	Joe Hoerner	1.25	.60
228	Dodgers Rookies	1.50	.75
	Jack Billingham (R)		
	Jim Fairey (R)		
229	Fred Klages	1.25	.60
230	Pete Rose	45.00	22.50
231	Dave Baldwin	1.25	.60
232	Denis Menke	1.25	.60
233	George Scott	2.00	1.00
234	Bill Monbouquette	1.25	.60
235	Ron Santo	4.00	2.00
236	Tug McGraw	3.00	1.50
237	Alvin Dark	1.25	.60
238	Tom Satriano	1.25	.60
239	Bill Henry	1.25	.60
240	Al Kaline	24.00	12.00
241	Felix Millan	1.25	.60
242	Moe Drabowsky	1.25	.60
243	Rich Rollins	1.25	.60
244	John Donaldson	1.25	.60
245	Tony Gonzalez	1.25	.60
246	Fritz Peterson	1.25	.60
247	Red Rookies	280.00	140.00
	Johnny Bench (R)		
	Ron Tompkins (R)		
248	Fred Valentine	1.25	.60
249	Bill Singer	1.25	.60
250	Carl Yastrzemski	40.00	20.00
251	Manny Sanguillen (R)	4.50	2.25
252	Angels Team	3.00	1.50
253	Dick Hughes	1.25	.60
254	Cleon Jones	1.25	.60
255	Dean Chance	1.25	.60
256	Norm Cash	4.50	2.25
257	Phil Niekro	8.50	4.25
258	Cubs Rookies	1.25	.60
	Jose Arcia (R)		
	Bill Schlesinger (R)		
259	Ken Boyer	2.50	1.25
260	Jim Wynn	1.50	.75
261	Dave Duncan	1.25	.60
262	Rick Wise	1.25	.60
263	Horace Clarke	1.25	.60
264	Ted Abernathy	1.25	.60
265	Tommy Davis	2.00	1.00

No.	Player	Price 1	Price 2
266	Paul Popovich	1.25	.60
267	Herman Franks	1.25	.60
268	Bob Humphreys	1.25	.60
269	Bob Tiefenauer	1.25	.60
270	Matty Alou	1.50	.75
271	Bobby Knoop	1.25	.60
272	Ray Culp	1.25	.60
273	Dave Johnson	1.25	.60
274	Mike Cuellar	1.50	.75
275	Tim McCarver	3.50	1.75
276	Jim Roland	1.25	.60
277	Jerry Buchek	1.25	.60
278	Checklist 284-370	3.50	1.75
279	Bill Hands	1.25	.60
280	Mickey Mantle	225.00	115.00
281	Jim Campanis	1.25	.60
282	Rick Monday	2.00	1.00
283	Mel Queen	1.25	.60
284	John Briggs	1.25	.60
285	Dick McAuliffe	1.25	.60
286	Cecil Upshaw	1.25	.60
287	White Sox Rookies	1.25	.60
	Mickey Abarbanel (R)		
	Cisco Carlos (R)		
288	Dave Wickersham	1.25	.60
289	Woody Held	1.25	.60
290	Willie McCovey	14.00	7.00
291	Dick Lines	1.25	.60
292	Art Shamsky	1.25	.60
293	Bruce Howard	1.25	.60
294	Red Schoendienst	4.00	2.00
295	Sonny Siebert	1.25	.60
296	Byron Browne	1.25	.60
297	Russ Gibson	1.25	.60
298	Jim Brewer	1.25	.60
299	Gene Michael	1.50	.75
300	Rusty Staub	3.00	1.50
301	Twins Rookies	1.50	.75
	George Mitterwald(R)		
	Rick Renick (R)		
302	Gery Arrigo	1.25	.60
303	Dick Green	1.25	.60
304	Sandy Valdespino	1.25	.60
305	Minnie Rojas	1.25	.60
306	Mike Ryan	1.25	.60
307	John Hiller	1.25	.60
308	Pirates Team	3.50	1.75
309	Ken Henderson	1.25	.60
310	Luis Aparicio	7.00	3.50
311	Jack Lamabe	1.25	.60
312	Curt Blefary	1.25	.60
313	Al Weis	1.25	.60
314	Red Sox Rookies	1.25	.60
	Bill Rohr (R)		
	George Spriggs (R)		
315	Zolio Versalles	1.50	.75
316	Steve Barber	1.25	.60
317	Ron Brand	1.25	.60
318	Chico Salmno	1.25	.60
319	George Culver	1.25	.60
320	Frank Howard	3.00	1.50
321	Leo Durocher	2.50	1.25
322	Dave Boswell	1.25	.60
323	Deron Johnson	1.50	.75
324	Jim Nash	1.25	.60
325	Manny Mota	1.50	.75
326	Dennis Ribant	1.25	.60
327	Tony Taylor	1.25	.60
328	Angels Rookies	1.25	.60
	Chuck Vinson (R)		
	Jim Weaver (R)		
329	Duane Josephson	1.25	.60
330	Roger Maris	45.00	22.50
331	Dan Osinski	1.25	.60
332	Doug Rader	1.50	.75
333	Ron Herbel	1.25	.60
334	Orioles Team	3.50	1.75
335	Bob Allison	1.25	.60
336	John Purdin	1.25	.60
337	Bill Robinson	1.50	.75
338	Bob Johnson	1.25	.60
339	Rich Nye	1.25	.60
340	Max Alvis	1.25	.60
341	Jim Lemon	1.25	.60
342	Ken Johnson	1.25	.60
343	Jim Gosger	1.25	.60
344	Donn Clendenon	1.50	.75
345	Bob Hendley	1.25	.60
346	Jerry Adair	1.25	.60
347	George Brunet	1.25	.60
348	Phillies Rookies	1.25	.60
	Larry Colton (R)		
	Dick Thoenen (R)		
349	Ed Spiezio	1.25	.60
350	Hoyt Wilhelm	7.00	3.50
351	Bob Barton	1.25	.60
352	Jackie Hernandez	1.25	.60
353	Mack Jones	1.25	.60
354	Pete Richert	1.25	.60
355	Ernie Banks	25.00	12.50
356	Checklist 371-457	3.50	1.75
357	Len Gabrielson	1.25	.60
358	Mike Epstein	1.25	.60
359	Joe Moeller	1.25	.60
360	Willie Horton	1.50	.75
361	Harmon Killebrew AS	7.00	3.50
362	Orlando Cepeda AS	2.50	1.25
363	Rod Carew AS	12.00	6.00
364	Joe Morgan AS	10.00	5.00
365	Brooks Robinson AS	10.00	5.00
366	Ron Santo AS	2.50	1.25
367	Jim Fregosi AS	2.50	1.25
368	Gene Alley AS	2.50	1.25
369	Carl Yastrzemski AS	12.00	6.00
370	Hank Aaron AS	15.00	7.50
371	Tony Oliva AS	2.50	1.25

372	Lou Brock AS	10.00	5.00
373	Frank Robinson AS	10.00	5.00
374	Bob Clemente AS	15.00	7.50
375	Bill Freehan AS	2.50	1.25
376	Tim McCarver AS	2.50	1.25
377	Joe Horlen AS	2.00	1.00
378	Bob Gibson AS	10.00	5.00
379	Gary Peters AS	2.00	1.00
380	Ken Holtzman AS	2.50	1.25
381	Boog Powell	3.50	1.75
382	Ramon Hernandez	1.25	.60
383	Steve Whitaker	1.25	.60
384	Reds Rookies	10.00	5.00
	Bill Henry (R)		
	Hal McRae (R)		
385	Jim Hunter	12.00	6.00
386	Greg Goossen	1.25	.60
387	Joe Foy	1.25	.60
388	Ray Washburn	1.25	.60
389	Jay Johnstone	1.50	.75
390	Bill Mazeroski	3.00	1.50
391	Bob Priddy	1.25	.60
392	Grady Hatton	1.25	.60
393	Jim Perry	1.25	.60
394	Tommie Aaron	1.25	.60
395	Camilo Pascual	1.25	.60
396	Bobby Wine	1.25	.60
397	Vic Davalillo	1.25	.60
398	Jim Grant	1.25	.60
399	Ray Oyler	1.25	.60
400a	Mike McCormick	60.00	30.00
	(White)		
400b	Mike McCormick	1.50	.75
	(Yellow)		
401	Mets Team	3.50	1.75
402	Mike Hegan	1.25	.60
403	John Buzhardt	1.25	.60
404	Floyd Robinson	1.25	.60
405	Tommy Helms	1.25	.60
406	Dick Ellsworth	1.25	.60
407	Gary Kolb	1.25	.60
408	Steve Carlton	70.00	35.00
409	Orioles Rookies	1.25	.60
	Frank Peters (R)		
	Ron Stone (R)		
410	Ferguson Jenkins	20.00	10.00
411	Ron Hansen	1.25	.60
412	Clay Carroll	1.25	.60
413	Tommy McCraw	1.25	.60
414	Mickey Lolich	4.00	2.00
415	Johnny Callison	1.25	.60
416	Bill Rigney	1.25	.60
417	Willie Crawford	1.25	.60
418	Eddie Fisher	1.25	.60
419	Jack Hiatt	1.25	.60
420	Cesar Tovar	1.25	.60
421	Ron Taylor	1.25	.60
422	Rene Lachemann	1.25	.60
423	Fred Gladding	1.25	.60
424	White Sox Team	3.00	1.50
425	Jim Maloney	1.25	.60
426	Hank Allen	1.25	.60
427	Dick Calmus	1.25	.60
428	Vic Roznovsky	1.25	.60
429	Tommie Sisk	1.25	.60
430	Rico Petrocelli	2.00	1.00
431	Dooley Womack	1.25	.60
432	Indians Rookies	1.25	.60
	Bill Davis (R)		
	Jose Vidal (R)		
433	Bob Rodgers		.60
434	Ricardo Joseph	1.25	.60
435	Ron Perranoski	1.25	.60
436	Hal Lanier	1.25	.60
437	Don Cardwell	1.25	.60
438	Lee Thomas	1.25	.60
439	Luman Harris	1.25	.60
440	Claude Osteen	1.50	.75
441	Alex Johnson	1.50	.75
442	Dick Bosman	1.25	.60
443	Joe Azcue	1.25	.60
444	Jack Fisher	1.25	.60
445	Mike Shannon	1.50	.75
446	Ron Kline	1.25	.60
447	Tigers Rookies	1.25	.60
	George Korince (R)		
	Fred Lasher (R)		
448	Gary Wagner	1.25	.60
449	Gene Oliver	1.25	.60
450	Jim Kaat	4.50	2.25
451	Al Spangler	1.25	.60
452	Jesus Alou	1.25	.60
453	Sammy Ellis	1.25	.60
454	Checklist 458-533	5.00	2.50
455	Rico Carty	1.50	.75
456	John O'Donoghue	1.25	.60
457	Jim Lefebvre	1.50	.75
458	Lew Krausse	3.50	1.75
459	Dick Simpson	3.50	1.75
460	Jim Lonborg	4.50	2.25
461	Chuck Hiller	3.50	1.75
462	Barry Moore	3.50	1.75
463	Jimmie Schaffer	3.50	1.75
464	Don McMahon	3.50	1.75
465	Tommie Agee	3.50	1.75
466	Bill Dillman	3.50	1.75
467	Dick Howser	3.50	1.75
468	Larry Sherry	3.50	1.75
469	Ty Cline	3.50	1.75
470	Bill Freehan	4.50	2.25
471	Orlando Pena	3.50	1.75
472	Walt Alston	4.00	2.00
473	Al Worthington	3.50	1.75
474	Paul Schaal	3.50	1.75
475	Joe Niekro	4.00	2.00
476	Woody Woodward	3.50	1.75

477	Phillies Team	4.50	2.25
478	Dave McNally	4.50	2.25
479	Phil Gagliano	3.50	1.75
480	Manager's Dream	36.00	18.00
	(Chico Cardenas,		
	Bob Clemente,		
	Tony Oliva)		
481	John Wyatt	3.50	1.75
482	Jose Pagan	3.50	1.75
483	Darold Knowles	3.50	1.75
484	Phil Roof	3.50	1.75
485	Ken Berry	3.50	1.75
486	Cal Koonce	3.50	1.75
487	Lee May	3.50	1.75
488	Dick Tracewski	3.50	1.75
489	Wally Bunker	3.50	1.75
490	Super Stars	125.00	65.00
	(Harmon Killebrew,		
	Mickey Mantle,		
	Willie Mays)		
491	Denny Lemaster	3.50	1.75
492	Jeff Torborg	4.00	2.00
493	Jim McGlothlin	3.50	1.75
494	Ray Sadecki	3.50	1.75
495	Leon Wagner	3.50	1.75
496	Steve Hamilton	3.50	1.75
497	Cards Team	4.50	2.25
498	Bill Bryan	3.50	1.75
499	Steve Blass	3.50	1.75
500	Frank Robinson	28.00	14.00
501	John Odom	3.50	1.75
502	Mike Andrews	3.50	1.75
503	Al Jackson	3.50	1.75
504	Russ Snyder	3.50	1.75
505	Joe Sparma	3.50	1.75
506	Clarence Jones	3.50	1.75
507	Wade Blasingame	3.50	1.75
508	Duke Sims	3.50	1.75
509	Dennis Higgins	3.50	1.75
510	Ron Fairly	3.50	1.75
511	Bill Kelso	3.50	1.75
512	Grant Jackson	3.50	1.75
513	Hank Bauer	3.50	1.75
514	Al McBean	3.50	1.75
515	Russ Nixon	3.50	1.75
516	Pete Mikkelsen	3.50	1.75
517	Diego Segui	3.50	1.75
518	Checklist 534-598	6.00	3.00
519	Jerry Stephenson	3.50	1.75
520	Lou Brock	25.00	12.50
521	Don Shaw	3.50	1.75
522	Wayne Causey	3.50	1.75
523	John Tsitouris	3.50	1.75
524	Andy Kosco	3.50	1.75
525	Jim Davenport	3.50	1.75
526	Bill Denehy	3.50	1.75
527	Tito Francona	3.50	1.75
528	Tigers Team	50.00	25.00
529	Bruce Von Hoff	3.50	1.75
530	Bird Belters	14.00	7.00
	(Brooks Robinson,		
	Frank Robinson)		
531	Chuck Hinton	3.50	1.75
532	Luis Tiant	5.00	2.50
533	Wes Parker	3.50	1.75
534	Bob Miller	3.50	1.75
535	Danny Cater	3.50	1.75
536	Bill Short	3.50	1.75
537	Norm Siebern	3.50	1.75
538	Manny Jimenez	3.50	1.75
539	Major League Rookies	3.50	1.75
	Mike Ferraro (R)		
	Jim Ray (R)		
540	Nelson Briles	3.50	1.75
541	Sandy Alomar	3.50	1.75
542	John Boccabella	3.50	1.75
543	Bob Lee	3.50	1.75
544	Mayo Smith	3.50	1.75
545	Lindy McDaniel	3.50	1.75
546	Roy White	4.00	2.00
547	Dan Coombs	3.50	1.75
548	Bernie Allen	3.50	1.75
549	Orioles Rookies	3.50	1.75
	Curt Motton (R)		
	Roger Nelson (R)		
550	Clete Boyer	4.00	2.00
551	Darrell Sutherland	3.50	1.75
552	Ed Kirkpatrick	3.50	1.75
553	Hank Aguirre	3.50	1.75
554	A's Team	5.00	2.50
555	Jose Tartabull	3.50	1.75
556	Dick Selma	3.50	1.75
557	Frank Quilici	3.50	1.75
558	John Edwards	3.50	1.75
559	Pirates Rookies	3.50	1.75
	Carl Taylor (R)		
	Luke Walker		
560	Paul Casanova	3.50	1.75
561	Lee Elia	3.50	1.75
562	Jim Bouton	4.00	2.00
563	Ed Charles	3.50	1.75
564	Eddie Stanky	3.50	1.75
565	Larry Dierker	3.50	1.75
566	Ken Harrelson	4.00	2.00
567	Clay Dairymple	3.50	1.75
569	Willie Smith	3.50	1.75
569	N.L. Rookies	3.50	1.75
	Ivan Murrell (R)		
	Les Rohr (R)		
570	Rick Reichardt	3.50	1.75
571	Tony LaRussa	5.00	2.50
572	Don Bosch	3.50	1.75
573	Joe Coleman	3.50	1.75
574	Reds Team	4.50	2.25
575	Jim Palmer	65.00	32.50
576	Dave Adlesh	3.50	1.75

577	Fred Talbot	3.50	1.75
578	Orlando Martinez	3.50	1.75
579	N.L. Rookies	4.50	2.25
	Larry Hisle (R)		
	Mike Lum (R)		
580	Bob Bailey	3.50	1.75
581	Garry Roggenburk	3.50	1.75
582	Jerry Grote	3.50	1.75
583	Gates Brown	3.50	1.75
584	Larry Shepard	3.50	1.75
585	Wilbur Wood	3.50	1.75
586	Jim Pagliaroni	3.50	1.75
587	Roger Repoz	3.50	1.75
588	Dick Schofield	3.50	1.75
589	Twins Rookies	3.50	1.75
	Ron Clark		
	Moe Ogier (R)		
590	Tommy Harper	3.50	1.75
591	Dick Nen	3.50	1.75
592	John Bateman	3.50	1.75
593	Lee Stange	3.50	1.75
594	Phil Linz	3.50	1.75
595	Phil Ortega	3.50	1.75
596	Charlie Smith	3.50	1.75
597	Bill McCool	3.50	1.75
598	Jerry May	3.50	1.75

1969 Topps

This 664-card set marks Topps largest to date. Card fronts contain color player photos with the player's name and position in a circle. Card backs are horizontal. Subsets include League Leaders, World Series Highlights, Rookies and All-Stars. All cards measure 2-1/2" by 3-1/2". Many variations exist in this set. Those are pointed out in the checklist below with the lower valued card included in the complete set price.

		NR/MT	EX
Complete Set (664)		2,500.00	1,250.00
Commons (1-218)		1.25	.60
Commons (219-327)		2.25	1.10
Commons (328-512)		1.25	.60
Commons (513-664)		2.00	1.00
1	A.L. Batting Leaders	10.00	5.00
2	N.L. Batting Leaders	6.00	3.00
3	A.L. RBI Leaders	3.50	1.75
4	N.L. RBI Leaders	5.00	2.50
5	A.L. HR Leaders	3.50	1.75
6	N.L. HR Leaders	5.00	2.50
7	A.L. ERA Leaders	3.00	1.50
8	N.L. ERA Leaders	3.00	1.50
9	A.L. Pitching Leaders	3.00	1.50
10	N.L. Pitching Leaders	6.00	3.00
11	A.L. Strikeout Ldrs	3.00	1.50
12	N.L. Strikeout Ldrs	4.00	2.00
13	Mickey Stanley	1.50	.75
14	Al McBean	1.25	.60
15	Boog Powell	3.50	1.75
16	Giants Rookies	1.25	.60
	Cesar Gutierrez (R)	1.25	.60
	Rich Robinson (R)		
17	Mike Marshall	2.00	1.00
18	Dick Schofield	1.25	.60
19	Ken Suarez	1.25	.60
20	Ernie Banks	24.00	12.00
21	Jose Santiago	1.25	.60
22	Jesus Alou	1.25	.60
23	Lew Krausse	1.25	.60
24	Walt Alston	2.00	1.00
25	Roy White	1.50	.75
26	Clay Carroll	1.25	.60
27	Bernie Allen	1.25	.60
28	Mike Ryan	1.25	.60
29	Dave Morehead	1.25	.60
30	Bob Allison	1.25	.60
31	Mets Rookies	4.00	2.00
	Gary Gentry (R)		
	Amos Otis (R)		
32	Sammy Ellis	1.25	.60
33	Wayne Causey	1.25	.60
34	Gary Peters	1.25	.60
35	Joe Morgan	14.00	7.00
36	Luke Walker	1.25	.60
37	Curt Motton	1.25	.60
38	Zoilo Versalles	1.50	.75
39	Dick Hughes	1.25	.60
40	Mayo Smith	1.25	.60
41	Bob Barton	1.25	.60
42	Tommy Harper	1.25	.60
43	Joe Niekro	2.00	1.00
44	Danny Cater	1.25	.60
45	Maury Wills	2.50	1.25
46	Fritz Peterson	1.25	.60

No.	Player	Value1	Value2
47a	Paul Popovich (No Helmet Logo)	1.25	.60
47b	Paul Popovich (Logo)	5.00	2.50
48	Brant Alyea	1.25	.60
49a	Royals Rookies Steve Jones (R) Eliseo Rodriquez (Er)	5.00	2.50
49b	Royals Rookies Steve Jones (R) Eliseo Rodriguez (R)	1.25	.60
50	Roberto Clemente	45.00	22.50
51	Woody Fryman	1.25	.60
52	Mike Andrews	1.25	.60
53	Sonny Jackson	1.25	.60
54	Cisco Carlos	1.25	.60
55	Jerry Grote	1.25	.60
56	Rich Reese	1.25	.60
57	Checklist 1-109	4.50	2.25
58	Fred Gladding	1.25	.60
59	Jay Johnstone	1.25	.60
60	Nelson Briles	1.25	.60
61	Jimmie Hall	1.25	.60
62	Chico Salmon	1.25	.60
63	Jim Hickman	1.25	.60
64	Billl Monbouquette	1.25	.60
65	Willie Davis	1.50	.75
66	Orioles Rookies Mike Adamson (R) Merv Rettenmund (R)	2.00	1.00
67	Bill Stoneman	1.25	.60
68	Dave Duncan	1.25	.60
69	Steve Hamilton	1.25	.60
70	Tommy Helms	1.25	.60
71	Steve Whitaker	1.25	.60
72	Ron Taylor	1.25	.60
73	Johnny Briggs	1.25	.60
74	Preston Gomez	1.25	.60
75	Luis Aparicio	6.00	3.00
76	Norm Miller	1.25	.60
77a	Ron Perranoski (No Logo On Cap)	1.25	.60
77b	Ron Perranoski (Cor)	5.00	2.50
78	Tom Satriano	1.25	.60
79	Milt Pappas	1.25	.60
80	Norm Cash	3.00	1.50
81	Mel Queen	1.25	.60
82	Pirates Rookies Rich Hebner (R) Al Oliver (R)	12.00	6.00
83	Mike Ferraro	1.25	.60
84	Bob Humphreys	1.25	.60
85	Lou Brock	20.00	10.00
86	Pete Richert	1.25	.60
87	Horace Clarke	1.25	.60
88	Rich Nye	1.25	.60
89	Russ Gibson	1.25	.60
90	Jerry Koosman	5.00	2.50
91	Al Dark	1.25	.60
92	Jack Billigham	1.25	.60
93	Joe Foy	1.25	.60
94	Hank Aguirre	1.25	.60
95	Johnny Bench	175.00	85.00
96	Denver Lemaster	1.25	.60
97	Buddy Bradford	1.25	.60
98	Dave Giusti	1.25	.60
99a	Twins Rookies (Er) Danny Morris (R) Graig Nettles (R)	24.00	12.00
99b	Twins Rookies (Cor) Danny Morris (R) Graig Nettles (R)	12.00	6.00
100	Hank Aaron	65.00	32.50
101	Daryl Patterson	1.25	.60
102	Jim Davenport	1.25	.60
103	Roger Repoz	1.25	.60
104	Steve Blass	1.25	.60
105	Rick Monday	1.50	.75
106	Jim Hannan	1.25	.60
107	Checklist 110-218	5.00	2.50
108	Tony Taylor	1.25	.60
109	Jim Lonborg	2.00	1.00
110	Mike Shannon	1.25	.60
111	Johnny Morris	1.25	.60
112	J.C. Martin	1.25	.60
113	Dave May	1.25	.60
114	Yankees Rookies Alan Closter (R) John Cumberland (R)	1.25	.60
115	Bill Hands	1.25	.60
116	Chuck Harrison	1.25	.60
117	Jim Fairey	1.25	.60
118	Stan Williams	1.25	.60
119	Doug Rader	1.50	.75
120	Pete Rose	35.00	17.50
121	Joe Grzenda	1.25	.60
122	Ron Fairly	1.25	.60
123	Wilbur Wood	1.25	.60
124	Hank Bauer	1.25	.60
125	Ray Sadecki	1.25	.60
126	Dick Tracewski	1.25	.60
127	Kevin Collins	1.25	.60
128	Tommie Aaron	1.25	.60
129	Bill McCool	1.25	.60
130	Carl Yastrzemski	32.00	16.00
131	Chris Cannizzaro	1.25	.60
132	Dave Baldwin	1.25	.60
133	Johnny Callison	1.25	.60
134	Jim Weaver	1.25	.60
135	Tommy Davis	2.00	1.00
136	Cards Rookies Steve Huntz (R) Mike Torrez	1.50	.75
137	Wally Bunker	1.25	.60
138	John Bateman	1.25	.60
139	Andy Kosco	1.25	.60
140	Jim Lefebvre	1.50	.75

141	Bill Dillman	1.25	.60
142	Woody Woodward	1.25	.60
143	Joe Nossek	1.25	.60
144	Bob Hendley	1.25	.60
145	Max Alvis	1.25	.60
146	Jim Perry	1.25	.60
147	Leo Durocher	2.50	1.25
148	Lee Stange	1.25	.60
149	Ollie Brown	1.25	.60
150	Denny McLain	5.00	2.50
151a	Clay Dalrymple (Er) (Phillies)	10.00	5.00
151b	Clay Dalrymple (Cor) (Orioles)	1.25	.60
152	Tommie Sisk	1.25	.60
153	Ed Brinkman	1.25	.60
154	Jim Britton	1.25	.60
155	Pete Ward	1.25	.60
156	Astros Rookies	1.25	.60
	Hal Gilson (R)		
	Leon McFadden (R)		
157	Bob Rodgers	1.25	.60
158	Joe Gibbon	1.25	.60
159	Jerry Adair	1.25	.60
160	Vada Pinson	2.00	1.00
161	John Purdin	1.25	.60
162	World Series Game 1	7.00	3.50
163	World Series Game 2	3.50	1.75
164	World Series Game 3	7.00	3.50
165	World Series Game 4	7.00	3.50
166	World Series Game 5	7.00	3.50
167	World Series Game 6	3.50	1.75
168	World Series Game 7	7.00	3.50
169	WS (Celebration)	3.50	1.75
170	Frank Howard	2.50	1.25
171	Glenn Beckert	1.25	.60
172	Jerry Stephenson	1.25	.60
173	White Sox Rookies	1.25	.60
	Bob Christian (R)		
	Gerry Nyman (R)		
174	Grant Jackson	1.25	.60
175	Jim Bunning	4.00	2.00
176	Joe Azcue	1.25	.60
177	Ron Reed	1.25	.60
178	Ray Oyler	1.25	.60
179	Don Pavletich	1.25	.60
180	Willie Horton	1.50	.75
181	Mel Nelson	1.25	.60
182	Bill Rigney	1.25	.60
183	Don Shaw	1.25	.60
184	Roberto Pena	1.25	.60
185	Tom Phoebus	1.25	.60
186	John Edwards	1.25	.60
187	Leon Wagner	1.25	.60
188	Rick Wise	1.25	.60
189	Red Sox Rookies	1.25	.60
	Joe Lahoud (R)		
	John Thibodeau (R)		
190	Willie Mays	65.00	32.50
191	Lindy McDaniel	1.25	.60
192	Jose Pagan	1.25	.60
193	Don Cardwell	1.25	.60
194	Ted Uhlaender	1.25	.60
195	John Odom	1.25	.60
196	Lum Harris	1.25	.60
197	Dick Selma	1.25	.60
198	Willie Smith	1.25	.60
199	Jim French	1.25	.60
200	Bob Gibson	18.00	9.00
201	Russ Snyder	1.25	.60
202	Don Wilson	1.25	.60
203	Dave Johnson	1.25	.60
204	Jack Hiatt	1.25	.60
205	Rick Reichardt	1.25	.60
206	Phillies Rookies	1.50	.75
	Larry Hisle		
	Barry Lersch (R)		
207	Roy Face	1.25	.60
208a	Donn Clendenon (Er) (Expos)	10.00	5.00
208b	Donn Clendenon (Cor) (Houston)	1.50	.75
209	Larry Haney (Er)	1.25	.60
210	Felix Millan	1.25	.60
211	Galen Cisco	1.25	.60
212	Tom Tresh	1.50	.75
213	Gerry Arrigo	1.25	.60
214	Checklist 219-327	4.50	2.25
215	Rico Petrocelli	1.50	.75
216	Don Sutton	10.00	5.00
217	John Donaldson	1.25	.60
218	John Roseboro	1.25	.60
219	Freddie Patek	2.25	1.10
220	Sam McDowell	2.50	1.25
221	Art Shamsky	2.25	1.10
222	Duane Josephson	2.25	1.10
223	Tom Dukes	2.25	1.10
224	Angels Rookies	2.25	1.10
	Bill Harrelson (R)		
	Steve Kealey (R)		
225	Don Kessinger	2.50	1.25
226	Bruce Howard	2.25	1.10
227	Frank Johnson	2.25	1.10
228	Dave Leonhard	2.25	1.10
229	Don Lock	2.25	1.10
230	Rusty Staub	4.00	2.00
231	Pat Dobson	2.50	1.25
232	Dave Ricketts	2.25	1.10
233	Steve Barber	2.25	1.10
234	Dave Bristol	2.25	1.10
235	Jim Hunter	15.00	7.50
236	Manny Mota	2.50	1.25
237	Bobby Cox	2.25	1.10
238	Ken Johnson	2.25	1.10
239	Bob Taylor	2.25	1.10
240	Ken Harrelson	2.50	1.25

241	Jim Brewer	2.25	1.10	293	Dick Dietz	2.25	1.10
242	Frank Kostro	2.25	1.10	294	Jim Lemon	2.25	1.10
243	Ron Kline	2.25	1.10	295	Tony Perez	15.00	7.50
244	Indians Rookies	2.50	1.25	296	Andy Messersmith (R)	3.00	1.50
	Ray Fosse (R)			297	Deron Johnson	2.50	1.25
	George Woodson (R)			298	Dave Nicholson	2.25	1.10
245	Ed Charles	2.25	1.10	299	Mark Belanger	2.25	1.10
246	Joe Coleman	2.25	1.10	300	Felipe Alou	3.00	1.50
247	Gene Oliver	2.25	1.10	301	Darrell Brandon	2.25	1.10
248	Bob Priddy	2.25	1.10	302	Jim Pagliaroni	2.25	1.10
249	Ed Spiezio	2.25	1.10	303	Cal Koonce	2.25	1.10
250	Frank Robinson	28.00	14.00	304	Padres Rookies	4.50	2.25
251	Ron Herbel	2.25	1.10		Bill Davis (R)		
252	Chuck Cottier	2.25	1.10		Cito Gaston (R)		
253	Jerry Johnson	2.25	1.10	305	Dick McAuliffe	2.25	1.10
254	Joe Schultz	2.25	1.10	306	Jim Grant	2.25	1.10
255	Steve Carlton	60.00	30.00	307	Gary Kolb	2.25	1.10
256	Gates Brown	2.25	1.10	308	Wade Blasingame	2.25	1.10
257	Jim Ray	2.25	1.10	309	Walt Williams	2.25	1.10
258	Jackie Hernandez	2.25	1.10	310	Tom Haller	2.25	1.10
259	Bill Short	2.25	1.10	311	Sparky Lyle (R)	12.00	6.00
260	Reggie Jackson (R)	700.00	350.00	312	Lee Elia	2.25	1.10
261	Bob Johnson	2.25	1.10	313	Bill Robinson	2.50	1.25
262	Mike Kekich	2.25	1.10	314	Checklist 328-425	5.00	2.50
263	Jerry May	2.25	1.10	315	Eddie Fisher	2.25	1.10
264	Bill Landis	2.25	1.10	316	Hal Lanier	2.25	1.10
265	Chico Cardenas	2.25	1.10	317	Bruce Look	2.25	1.10
266	Dodgers Rookies	2.25	1.10	318	Jack Fisher	2.25	1.10
	Alan Foster (R)			319	Ken McMullen	2.25	1.10
	Tom Hutton (R)			320	Dal Maxvill	2.25	1.10
267	Vicente Romo	2.25	1.10	321	Jim McAndrew	2.25	1.10
268	Al Spangler	2.25	1.10	322	Jose Vidal	2.25	1.10
269	Al Weis	2.25	1.10	323	Larry Miller	2.25	1.10
270	Mickey Lolich	4.50	2.25	324	Tigers Rookies	2.25	1.10
271	Larry Stahl	2.25	1.10		Les Cain (R)		
272	Ed Stroud	2.25	1.10		Dave Campbell		
273	Ron Willis	2.25	1.10	325	Jose Cardenal	2.25	1.10
274	Clyde King	2.25	1.10	326	Gary Sutherland	2.25	1.10
275	Vic Davalillo	2.25	1.10	327	Willie Crawford	2.25	1.10
276	Gary Wagner	2.25	1.10	328	Joe Horlen	1.25	.60
277	Elrod Hendricks (R)	4.00	2.00	329	Rick Joseph	1.25	.60
278	Gary Geiger	2.25	1.10	330	Tony Conigliaro	3.00	1.50
279	Roger Nelson	2.25	1.10	331	Braves Rookies	2.00	1.00
280	Alex Johnson	2.50	1.25		Gil Garrido (R)	1.25	.60
281	Ted Kubiak	2.25	1.10		Tom House (R)		
282	Pat Jarvis	2.25	1.10	332	Fred Talbot	1.25	.60
283	Sandy Alomar	2.25	1.10	333	Ivan Murrell	1.25	.60
284	Expos Rookies	2.25	1.10	334	Phil Roof	1.25	.60
	Jerry Robertson			335	Bill Mazeroski	3.00	1.50
	Mike Wegener (R)			336	Jim Roland	1.25	.60
285	Don Mincher	2.25	1.10	337	Marty Martinez	1.25	.60
286	Dock Ellis (R)	2.50	1.25	338	Del Unser	1.25	.60
287	Jose Tartabull	2.25	1.10	339	Reds Rookies	1.25	.60
288	Ken Holtzman	2.50	1.25		Steve Mingori (R)		
289	Bart Shirley	2.25	1.10		Jose Pena		
290	Jim Kaat	4.00	2.00	340	Dave McNally	2.00	1.00
291	Vern Fuller	2.25	1.10	341	Dave Adlesh	1.25	.60
292	Al Downing	2.25	1.10	342	Bubba Morton	1.25	.60

343	Dan Frisella	1.25	.60
344	Tom Matchick	1.25	.60
345	Frank Linzy	1.25	.60
346	Wayne Comer	1.25	.60
347	Randy Hundley	1.25	.60
348	Steve Hargan	1.25	.60
349	Dick Williams	1.25	.60
350	Richie Allen	3.50	1.75
351	Carroll Sembera	1.25	.60
352	Paul Schaal	1.25	.60
353	Jeff Torborg	1.50	.75
354	Nate Oliver	1.25	.60
355	Phil Niekro	7.00	3.50
356	Frank Quilici	1.25	.60
357	Carl Taylor	1.25	.60
358	Athletics Rookies	1.25	.60
	George Lauzerique		
	Roberto Rodriquez (R)		
359	Dick Kelley	1.25	.60
360	Jim Wynn	1.50	.75
361	Gary Holman	1.25	.60
362	Jim Maloney	1.25	.60
363	Russ Nixon	1.25	.60
364	Tommie Agee	1.50	.75
365	Jim Fregosi	1.50	.75
366	Bo Belinsky	1.25	.60
367	Lou Johnson	1.25	.60
368	Vic Roznovsky	1.25	.60
369	Bob Skinner	1.25	.60
370	Juan Marichal	8.00	4.00
371	Sal Bando	1.50	.75
372	Adolfo Phillips	1.25	.60
373	Fred Lasher	1.25	.60
374	Bob Tillman	1.25	.60
375	Harmon Killebrew	22.00	11.00
376	Royals Rookies	1.50	.75
	Mike Flore (R)		
	Jim Rooker (R)		
377	Gary Bell	1.25	.60
378	Jose Herrera	1.25	.60
379	Ken Boyer	2.50	1.25
380	Stan Bahnsen	1.25	.60
381	Ed Kranepool	2.00	1.00
382	Pat Corrales	1.50	.75
383	Casey Cox	1.25	.60
384	Larry Shepard	1.25	.60
385	Orlando Cepeda	3.50	1.75
386	Jim McGlothlin	1.25	.60
387	Bobby Klaus	1.25	.60
388	Tom McCraw	1.25	.60
389	Don Coombs	1.25	.60
390	Bill Freehan	2.00	1.00
391	Ray Culp	1.25	.60
392	Bob Burda	1.25	.60
393	Gene Brabender	1.25	.60
394	Pilots Rookies	4.00	2.00
	Lou Piniella		
	Marv Staehle (R)		

395	Chris Short	1.25	.60
396	Jim Campanis	1.25	.60
397	Chuck Dobson	1.25	.60
398	Tito Francona	1.25	.60
399	Bob Bailey	1.25	.60
400	Don Drysdale	14.00	7.00
401	Jake Gibbs	1.25	.60
402	Ken Boswell	1.25	.60
403	Bob Miller	1.25	.60
404	Cubs Rookies	1.25	.60
	Vic LaRose (R)		
	Gary Ross (R)		
405	Lee May	1.25	.60
406	Phil Ortega	1.25	.60
407	Tom Egan	1.25	.60
408	Nate Colbert	1.25	.60
409	Bob Moose	1.25	.60
410	Al Kaline	22.00	11.00
411	Larry Dierker	1.25	.60
412	Checklist 426-512	7.50	3.75
413	Roland Sheldon	1.25	.60
414	Duke Sims	1.25	.60
415	Ray Washburn	1.25	.60
416	Willie McCovey AS	7.00	3.50
417	Ken Harrelson AS	2.00	1.00
418	Tommy Helms AS	1.50	.75
419	Rod Carew AS	8.50	4.25
420	Ron Santo AS	2.50	1.25
421	Brooks Robinson AS	7.00	3.50
422	Don Kessinger AS	2.00	1.00
423	Bert Campaneris AS	2.00	1.00
424	Pete Rose AS	14.00	7.00
425	Carl Yastrzemski AS	10.00	5.00
426	Curt Flood AS	1.50	.75
427	Tony Oliva AS	2.50	1.25
428	Lou Brock AS	7.00	3.50
429	Willie Horton AS	2.00	1.00
430	Johnny Bench AS	12.00	6.00
431	Bill Freehan AS	1.50	.75
432	Bob Gibson AS	7.00	3.50
433	Denny McLain AS	4.00	2.00
434	Jerry Koosman AS	2.00	1.00
435	Sam McDowell AS	1.50	.75
436	Gene Alley	1.25	.60
437	Luis Alcaraz	1.25	.60
438	Gary Waslewski	1.25	.60
439	White Sox Rookies	1.25	.60
	Ed Herrmann (R)		
	Dan Lazar (R)		
440a	Willie McCovey	100.00	50.00
	(White Lettering)		
440b	Willie McCovey	18.00	9.00
	(Yellow Lettering)		
441a	Dennis Higgins	14.00	7.00
	(White Lettering)		
441b	Dennis Higgins	1.25	.60
	(Yellow Lettering)		
442	Ty Cline	1.25	.60

443	Don Wert	1.25	.60
444a	Joe Moeller (White Lettering)	8.00	4.00
444b	Joe Moeller (Yellow Lettering)	1.25	.60
445	Bobby Knoop	1.25	.60
446	Claude Raymond	1.25	.60
447a	Ralph Houk (White Lettering)	12.00	6.00
447b	Ralph Houk (Yellow Lettering)	1.50	.75
448	Bob Tolan	1.25	.60
449	Paul Lindblad	1.25	.60
450	Billy Williams	8.00	4.00
451a	Rich Rollins (White Lettering)	14.00	7.00
451b	Rich Rollins (Yellow Lettering)	1.25	.60
452a	Al Ferrara (White Lettering)	14.00	7.00
452b	Al Ferrara (Yellow Lettering)	1.25	.60
453	Mike Cuellar	1.50	.75
454a	Phillies Rookies (White Lettering) Larry Colton (R) Don Money (R)	14.00	7.00
454b	Phillies Rookies (Yellow Lettering)	1.50	.75
455	Sonny Siebert	1.25	.60
456	Bud Harrelson	1.50	.75
457	Dalton Jones	1.25	.60
458	Curt Blefary	1.25	.60
459	Dave Boswell	1.25	.60
460	Joe Torre	3.00	1.50
461a	Mike Epstein (White Lettering)	12.00	6.00
461b	Mike Epstein (Yellow Lettering)	1.25	.60
462	Red Schoendienst	2.50	1.25
463	Dennis Ribant	1.25	.60
464a	Dave Marshall (White Lettering)	12.00	6.00
464b	Dave Marshall (Yellow Lettering)	1.25	.60
465	Tommy John	3.50	1.75
466	John Boccabella	1.25	.60
467	Tom Reynolds	1.25	.60
468a	Pirates Rookies (White Lettering) Bruce Dal Canton (R) Bob Robertson	14.00	7.00
468b	Pirates Rookies (Yellow Lettering)	1.50	.75
469	Chico Ruiz	1.25	.60
470a	Mel Stottlemyre (White Lettering)	20.00	10.00
470b	Mel Stottlemyre (Yellow Lettering)	2.00	1.00
471a	Ted Savage (White Lettering)	14.00	7.00
471b	Ted Savage (Yellow Lettering)	1.25	.60
472	Jim Price	1.25	.60
473a	Jose Arcia (White Lettering)	12.00	6.00
473b	Jose Arcia (Yellow Lettering)	1.25	.60
474	Tom Murphy	1.25	.60
475	Tim McCarver	2.50	1.25
476a	Red Sox Rookies (White Lettering) Ken Brett (R) Gerry Moses (R)	14.00	7.00
476b	Red Sox Rookies (Yellow Lettering)	2.00	1.00
477	Jeff James	1.25	.60
478	Don Buford	1.25	.60
479	Richie Scheinblum	1.25	.60
480	Tom Seaver	160.00	80.00
481	Bill Melton (R)	1.50	.75
482a	Jim Gosger (White Lettering)	14.00	7.00
482b	Jim Gosger (Yellow Lettering)	1.25	.60
483	Ted Abernathy	1.25	.60
484	Joe Gordon	1.25	.60
485a	Gaylord Perry (White Lettering)	80.00	40.00
485b	Gaylord Perry (Yellow Lettering)	12.00	6.00
486a	Paul Casanova (White Lettering)	12.00	6.00
486b	Paul Casanova (Yellow Lettering)	1.25	.60
487	Denis Menke	1.25	.60
488	Joe Sparma	1.25	.60
489	Clete Boyer	1.50	.75
490	Matty Alou	1.50	.75
491a	Twins Rookies (White Lettering) Jerry Crider (R) George Mitterwald	14.00	7.00
491b	Twins Rookies (Yellow Lettering)	1.25	.60
492	Tony Cloninger	1.25	.60
493a	Wes Parker (White Lettering)	12.00	6.00
493b	Wes Parker (Yellow Lettering)	1.25	.60
494	Ken Berry	1.25	.60
495	Bert Campaneris	1.50	.75
496	Larry Jaster	1.25	.60
497	Julian Javier	1.25	.60
498	Juan Pizarro	1.25	.60
499	Astros Rookies	1.25	.60

	Don Bryant (R)		
	Steve Shea		
500a	Mickey Mantle (White Lettering)	600.00	300.00
500b	Mickey Mantle (Yellow Lettering)	250.00	125.00
501a	Tony Gonzalez (White Lettering)	14.00	7.00
501b	Tony Gonzalez (Yellow Lettering)		
502	Minnie Rojas	1.25	.60
503	Larry Brown	1.25	.60
504	Checklist 513-588	6.00	3.00
505a	Bobby Bolin (White Lettering)	12.00	6.00
505b	Bobby Bolin (Yellow Lettering)	1.25	.60
506	Paul Blair	1.25	.60
507	Cookie Rojas	1.25	.60
508	Moe Drabowsky	1.25	.60
509	Manny Sanguillen	2.00	1.00
510	Rod Carew	90.00	45.00
511a	Diego Segui (White Lettering)	12.00	6.00
511b	Diego Segui (Yellow Lettering)	1.25	.60
512	Cleon Jones	1.25	.60
513	Camilo Pascual	2.00	1.00
514	Mike Lum	2.00	1.00
515	Dick Green	2.00	1.00
516	Earl Weaver (R)	10.00	5.00
517	Mike McCormick	2.00	1.00
518	Fred Whitfield	2.00	1.00
519	Yankees Rookies	2.00	1.00
	Len Boehmer (R)		
	Gerry Kennedy		
520	Bob Veale	2.00	1.00
521	George Thomas	2.00	1.00
522	Joe Hoerner	2.00	1.00
523	Bob Chance	2.00	1.00
524	Expos Rookies	2.00	1.00
	Jose Laboy (R)		
	Floyd Wicker (R)		
525	Earl Wilson	2.00	1.00
526	Hector Torres	2.00	1.00
527	Al Lopez	2.00	1.00
528	Claude Osteen	2.00	1.00
529	Ed Kirkpatrick	2.00	1.00
530	Cesar Tovar	2.00	1.00
531	Dick Farrell	2.00	1.00
532	Bird Hill Aces (Mike Cuellar, Jim Hardin, Dave McNally, Tom Phoebus)	2.50	1.25
533	Nolan Ryan	550.00	275.00
534	Jerry McNertney	2.00	1.00
535	Phil Regan	2.00	1.00
536	Padres Rookies	2.00	1.00
	Danny Breeden (R)		
	Dave Roberts (R)		
537	Mike Paul	2.00	1.00
538	Charlie Smith	2.00	1.00
539	Ted Shows How (Mike Epstein, Ted Williams)	7.00	3.50
540	Curt Flood	2.50	1.25
541	Joe Verbanic	2.00	1.00
542	Bob Aspromonte	2.00	1.00
543	Fred Newman	2.00	1.00
544	Tigers Rookies	2.00	1.00
	Mike Kilkenny (R)		
	Ron Woods (R)		
545	Willie Stargell	18.00	9.00
546	Jim Nash	2.00	1.00
547	Billy Martin	6.00	3.00
548	Bob Locker	2.00	1.00
549	Ron Brand	2.00	1.00
550	Brooks Robinson	24.00	12.00
551	Wayne Granger	2.00	1.00
552	Dodgers Rookies	2.50	1.25
	Ted Sizemore (R)		
	Bill Sudakis (R)		
553	Ron Davis	2.00	1.00
554	Frank Bertaina	2.00	1.00
555	Jim Hart	2.00	1.00
556	A's Stars (Sal Bando, Bert Campaneris, Danny Cater)	2.50	1.25
557	Frank Fernandez	2.00	1.00
558	Tom Burgmeier	2.00	1.00
559	Cards Rookies	2.00	1.25
	Joe Hague (R)		
	Jim Hicks (R)		
560	Luis Tiant	3.50	1.75
561	Ron Clark	2.00	1.00
562	Bob Watson (R)	5.00	2.50
563	Marty Pattin	2.00	1.00
564	Gil Hodges	8.00	4.00
565	Hoyt Wilhelm	7.00	3.50
566	Ron Hansen	2.00	1.00
567	Pirates Rookies	2.00	1.25
	Elvio Jimenez (R)		
	Jim Shellenback		
568	Cecil Upshaw	2.00	1.00
569	Billy Harris	2.00	1.00
570	Ron Santo	5.00	2.50
571	Cap Peterson	2.00	1.00
572	Giants Heroes (Juan Marichal, Willie McCovey)	12.00	6.00
573	Jim Palmer	45.00	22.50
574	George Scott	2.00	1.00
575	Bill Singer	2.00	1.00
576	Phillies Rookies	2.00	1.25
	Ron Stone (R)		
	Bill Wilson (R)		

577	Mike Hegan	2.00	1.00
578	Don Bosch	2.00	1.00
579	Dave Nelson	2.00	1.00
580	Jim Northrup	2.50	1.25
581	Gary Nolan	2.00	1.00
582	Checklist 589-664	6.00	3.00
583	Clyde Wright	2.00	1.00
584	Don Mason	2.00	1.00
585	Ron Swoboda	2.50	1.25
586	Tim Cullen	2.00	1.00
587	Joe Rudi (R)	4.00	2.00
588	Bill White	2.00	1.00
589	Joe Pepitone	2.50	1.25
590	Rico Carty	2.50	1.25
591	Mike Hedlund	2.00	1.00
592	Padres Rookies	2.00	1.00
	Rafael Robles (R)		
	Al Santorini (R)		
593	Don Nottebart	2.00	1.00
594	Dooley Womack	2.00	1.00
595	Lee Maye	2.00	1.00
596	Chuck Hartenstein	2.00	1.00
597	A.L. Rookies	160.00	80.00
	Larry Burchart (R)		
	Rollie Fingers (R)		
	Bob Floyd (R)		
598	Ruben Amaro	2.00	1.00
599	John Boozer	2.00	1.00
600	Tony Oliva	7.00	3.50
601	Tug McGraw	4.00	2.00
602	Cubs Rookies	2.00	1.00
	Alec Distaco (R)		
	Jim Qualls (R)		
	Don Young (R)		
603	Joe Keough	2.00	1.00
604	Bobby Etheridge	2.00	1.00
605	Dick Ellsworth	2.00	1.00
606	Gene Mauch	2.00	1.00
607	Dick Bosman	2.00	1.00
608	Dick Simpson	2.00	1.00
609	Phil Gagliano	2.00	1.00
610	Jim Hardin	2.00	1.00
611	Braves Rookies	2.00	1.00
	Bob Didier (R)		
	Walt Hriniak (R)		
	Gary Neibauer (R)		
612	Jack Aker	2.00	1.00
613	Jim Beauchamp	2.00	1.00
614	Astros Rookies	2.00	1.00
	Tom Griffin (R)		
	Skip Guinn (R)		
615	Len Gabrielson	2.00	1.00
616	Don McMahon	2.00	1.00
617	Jesse Gonder	2.00	1.00
618	Ramon Webster	2.00	1.00
619	Royals Rookies	2.00	1.00
	Bill Butler (R)		
	Pat Kelly (R)		
	Juan Rios (R)		
620	Dean Chance	2.00	1.00
621	Bill Voss	2.00	1.00
622	Dan Osinski	2.00	1.00
623	Hank Allen	2.00	1.00
624	N.L. Rookies	3.00	1.50
	Darrel Chaney (R)		
	Duffy Dyer (R)		
	Terry Harmon (R)		
625	Mack Jones	2.00	1.00
626	Gene Michael	2.00	1.00
627	George Stone	2.00	1.00
628	Red Sox Rookies	3.00	1.50
	Bill Conigliaro (R)		
	Syd O'Brien (R)		
	Fred Wenz (R)		
629	Jack Hamilton	2.00	1.00
630	Bobby Bonds (R)	36.00	18.00
631	John Kennedy	2.00	1.00
632	Jon Warden	2.00	1.00
633	Harry Walker	2.00	1.00
634	Andy Etchebarren	2.00	1.00
635	George Culver	2.00	1.00
636	Woodie Held	2.00	1.00
637	Padres Rookies	2.00	1.00
	Jerry DaVanon (R)		
	Clay Kirby (R)		
	Frank Reberger (R)		
638	Ed Sprague	2.00	1.00
639	Barry Moore	2.00	1.00
640	Ferguson Jenkins	20.00	10.00
641	N.L. Rookies	2.00	1.00
	Bobby Darwin (R)		
	Tommy Dean (R)		
	John Miller (R)		
642	John Hiller	2.00	1.00
643	Billy Cowan	2.00	1.00
644	Chuck Hinton	2.00	1.00
645	George Brunet	2.00	1.00
646	Expos Rookies	2.50	1.25
	Dan McGinn (R)		
	Carl Morton (R)		
647	Dave Wickersham	2.00	1.00
648	Bobby Wine	2.00	1.00
649	Al Jackson	2.00	1.00
650	Ted Williams	12.00	6.00
651	Gus Gil	2.00	1.00
652	Eddie Watt	2.00	1.00
653	Aurelio Rodriguez (Wrong Photo)	3.50	1.75
654	White Sox Rookies	3.50	1.75
	Carlos May (R)		
	Rich Morales (R)		
	Don Secrist		
655	Mike Hershberger	2.00	1.00
656	Dan Schneider	2.00	1.00
657	Bobby Murcer	5.00	2.50
658	A.L. Rookies	2.00	1.00

	Bill Burbach (R)		
	Tom Hall (R)		
	Jim Miles (R)		
659	Johnny Podres	2.50	1.25
660	Reggie Smith	3.50	1.75
661	Jim Merritt	2.00	1.00
662	Royals Rookies	2.50	1.25
	Dick Drago (R)		
	Bob Oliver (R)		
	George Spriggs (R)		
663	Dick Radatz	2.50	1.25
664	Ron Hunt	3.50	1.75

1970 Topps

This 720-card set features color photos on the card fronts framed by a thin white line and a gray border. Horizontal card backs are blue and yellow. Card measure 2-1/2" by 3-1/2". Major subsets include League Leaders, World Series and Playoff Highlights All-Stars and Rookies.

		NR/MT	EX
Complete Set (720)		2,200.00	1,100.00
Commons (1-459)		.90	.45
Commons (460-546)		1.50	.75
Commons (547-633)		2.50	1.25
Commons (634-720)		5.00	2.50

1	World Champion Mets	12.00	6.00
2	Diego Segui	.90	.45
3	Darrel Chaney	.90	.45
4	Tom Egan	.90	.45
5	Wes Parker	.90	.45
6	Grant Jackson	.90	.45
7	Indians Rookies	.90	.45
	Gary Boyd	.90	.45
	Russ Nagelson (R)	.90	.45
8	Jose Martinez	.90	.45
9	Checklist 1-132	4.00	2.00
10	Carl Yastrzemski	30.00	15.00
11	Nate Colbert	.90	.45
12	John Hiller	.90	.45
13	Jack Hiatt	.90	.45
14	Hank Allen	.90	.45
15	Larry Dierker	.90	.45
16	Charlie Metro	.90	.45
17	Hoyt Wilhelm	4.50	2.25
18	Carlos May	.90	.45
19	John Boccabella	.90	.45
20	Dave McNally	1.25	.60
21	Athletics Rookies	8.00	4.00
	Vida Blue (R)		
	Gene Tenace (R)		
22	Ray Washburn	.90	.45
23	Bill Robinson	1.00	.50
24	Dick Selma	.90	.45
25	Cesar Tovar	.90	.45
26	Tug McGraw	1.50	.75
27	Chuck Hinton	.90	.45
28	Billy Wilson	.90	.45
29	Sandy Alomar	.90	.45
30	Matty Alou	1.25	.60
31	Marty Pattin	.90	.45
32	Harry Walker	.90	.45
33	Don Wert	.90	.45
34	Willie Crawford	.90	.45
35	Joe Horlen	.90	.45
36	Reds Rookies	1.25	.60
	Danny Breeden (R)		
	Bernie Carbo (R)		
37	Dick Drago	.90	.45
38	Mack Jones	.90	.45
39	Mike Nagy	.90	.45
40	Dick Allen	2.50	1.25
41	George Lauzerique	.90	.45
42	Tito Fuentes	.90	.45
43	Jack Aker	.90	.45
44	Roberto Pena	.90	.45
45	Dave Johnson	.90	.45
46	Ken Rudolph	.90	.45
47	Bob Miller	.90	.45
48	Gil Carrido	.90	.45
49	Tim Cullen	.90	.45
50	Tommie Agee	.90	.45
51	Bob Christian	.90	.45
52	Bruce Dal Canton	.90	.45
53	John Kennedy	.90	.45
54	Jeff Torborg	1.00	.50
55	John Odom	.90	.45
56	Phillies Rookies	.90	.45
	Joe Lis (R)		
	Scott Reid (R)		
57	Pat Kelly	.90	.45
58	Dave Marshall	.90	.45
59	Dick Ellsworth	.90	.45
60	Jim Wynn	1.25	.60

61 N.L. Batting Leaders	6.00	3.00	
62 A.L. Batting Leader	4.00	2.00	
63 N.L. RBI Leaders	4.00	2.00	
64 A.L. RBI Leaders	6.00	3.00	
65 N.L. HR Leaders	6.00	3.00	
66 A.L. HR Leaders	6.00	3.00	
67 N.L. ERA Leaders	6.00	3.00	
68 A.L. ERA Leaders	2.50	1.25	
69 N.L. Pitching Leaders	6.00	3.00	
70 A.L. Pitching Leaders	2.50	1.25	
71 N.L. Strikeout Ldrs	4.00	2.00	
72 A.L. Strikeout Ldrs	2.50	1.25	
73 Wayne Granger	.90	.45	
74 Angels Rookies	.90	.45	
Greg Washburn (R)			
Wally Wolf (R)			
75 Jim Kaat	2.00	1.00	
76 Carl Taylor	.90	.45	
77 Frank Linzy	.90	.45	
78 Joe Lahoud	.90	.45	
79 Clay Kirby	.90	.45	
80 Don Kessinger	1.25	.60	
81 Dave May	.90	.45	
82 Frank Fernandez	.90	.45	
83 Don Cardwell	.90	.45	
84 Paul Casanova	.90	.45	
85 Max Alvis	.90	.45	
86 Lum Harris	.90	.45	
87 Steve Renko	.90	.45	
88 Pilots Rookies	.90	.45	
Dick Baney (R)			
Miguel Fuentes (R)			
89 Juan Rios	.90	.45	
90 Tim McCarver	1.25	.60	
91 Rich Morales	.90	.45	
92 George Culver	.90	.45	
93 Rick Renick	.90	.45	
94 Fred Patek	.90	.45	
95 Earl Wilson	.90	.45	
96 Cards Rookies	3.50	1.75	
Leron Lee (R)			
Jerry Reuss (R)			
97 Joe Moeller	.90	.45	
98 Gates Brown	.90	.45	
99 Bobby Pfeil	.90	.45	
100 Mel Stottlemyre	1.50	.75	
101 Bobby Floyd	.90	.45	
102 Joe Rudi	1.25	.60	
103 Frank Reberger	.90	.45	
104 Gerry Moses	.90	.45	
105 Tony Gonzalez	.90	.45	
106 Darold Knowles	.90	.45	
107 Bobby Etheridge	.90	.45	
108 Tom Burgmeier	.90	.45	
109 Expos Rookies	.90	.45	
Garry Jestadt (R)			
Carl Morton			
110 Bob Moose	.90	.45	
111 Mike Hegan	.90	.45	
112 Dave Nelson	.90	.45	
113 Jim Ray	.90	.45	
114 Gene Michael	.90	.45	
115 Alex Johnson	1.00	.50	
116 Sparky Lyle	1.50	.75	
117 Don Young	.90	.45	
118 George Mitterwald	.90	.45	
119 Chuck Taylor	.90	.45	
120 Sal Bando	1.25	.60	
121 Orioles Rookies	1.00	.50	
Fred Beene (R)			
Terry Crowley (R)			
122 George Stone	.90	.45	
123 Don Gutteridge	.90	.45	
124 Larry Jaster	.90	.45	
125 Deron Johnson	1.00	.50	
126 Marty Martinez	.90	.45	
127 Joe Coleman	.90	.45	
128 Checklist 133-263	4.00	2.00	
129 Jimmie Price	.90	.45	
130 Ollie Brown	.90	.45	
131 Dodgers Rookies	.90	.45	
Ray Lamb (R)			
Bob Stinson (R)			
132 Jim McGlothlin	.90	.45	
133 Clay Carroll	.90	.45	
134 Danny Walton	.90	.45	
135 Dick Dietz	.90	.45	
136 Steve Hargan	.90	.45	
137 Art Shamsky	.90	.45	
138 Joe Foy	.90	.45	
139 Rich Nye	.90	.45	
140 Reggie Jackson	185.00	95.00	
141 Pirates Rookies	1.25	.60	
Dave Cash (R)			
Johnny Jeter (R)			
142 Fritz Peterson	.90	.45	
143 Phil Gagliano	.90	.45	
144 Ray Culp	.90	.45	
145 Rico Carty	1.00	.50	
146 Danny Murphy	.90	.45	
147 Angel Hermoso	.90	.45	
148 Earl Weaver	2.50	1.25	
149 Billy Champion	.90	.45	
150 Harmon Killebrew	10.00	5.00	
151 Dave Roberts	.90	.45	
152 Ike Brown	.90	.45	
153 Gary Gentry	.90	.45	
154 Senators Rookies	.90	.45	
Jan Dukes (R)			
Jim Miles			
155 Denis Menke	.90	.45	
156 Eddie Fisher	.90	.45	
157 Manny Mota	1.00	.50	
158 Jerry McNertney	.90	.45	
159 Tommy Helms	.90	.45	
160 Phil Niekro	6.00	3.00	

161 Richie Scheinblum	.90	.45	213 Andy Etchebarren	.90	.45
162 Jerry Johnson	.90	.45	214 Ken Boswell	.90	.45
163 Syd O'Brien	.90	.45	215 Reggie Smith	1.00	.50
164 Ty Cline	.90	.45	216 Chuck Hartenstein	.90	.45
165 Ed Kirkpatrick	.90	.45	217 Ron Hansen	.90	.45
166 Al Oliver	2.50	1.25	218 Ron Stone	.90	.45
167 Bill Burbach	.90	.45	219 Jerry Kenney	.90	.45
168 Dave Watkins	.90	.45	220 Steve Carlton	42.00	21.00
169 Tom Hall	.90	.45	221 Ron Brand	.90	.45
170 Billy Williams	8.00	4.00	222 Jim Rooker	.90	.45
171 Jim Nash	.90	.45	223 Nate Oliver	.90	.45
172 Braves Rookies	2.00	1.00	224 Steve Barber	.90	.45
Ralph Garr (R)			225 Lee May	.90	.45
Garry Hill (R)			226 Ron Perranoski	.90	.45
173 Jim Hicks	.90	.45	227 Astros Rookies	1.25	.60
174 Ted Sizemore	1.00	.50	John Mayberry (R)		
175 Dick Bosman	.90	.45	Bob Watkins		
176 Jim Hart	.90	.45	228 Aurelio Rodriquez	.90	.45
177 Jim Northrup	1.00	.50	229 Rich Robertson	.90	.45
178 Denny Lemaster	.90	.45	230 Brooks Robinson	15.00	7.50
179 Ivan Murrell	.90	.45	231 Luis Tiant	2.50	1.25
180 Tommy John	2.50	1.25	232 Bob Didier	.90	.45
181 Sparky Anderson	2.00	1.00	233 Lew Krausse	.90	.45
182 Dick Hall	.90	.45	234 Tommy Dean	.90	.45
183 Jerry Grote	.90	.45	235 Mike Epstein	.90	.45
184 Ray Fosse	.90	.45	236 Bob Veale	.90	.45
185 Don Mincher	.90	.45	237 Russ Gibson	.90	.45
186 Rick Joseph	.90	.45	238 Jose Laboy	.90	.45
187 Mike Hedlund	.90	.45	239 Ken Berry	.90	.45
188 Manny Sanguillen	1.00	.50	240 Fergie Jenkins	10.00	5.00
189 Yankees Rookies	90.00	45.00	241 Royals Rookies	.90	.45
Dave McDonald (R)			Al Fitzmorris		
Thurman Munson (R)			Scott Northey (R)		
190 Joe Torre	2.00	1.00	242 Walter Alston	1.25	.60
191 Vicente Romo	.90	.45	243 Joe Sparma	.90	.45
192 Jim Qualls	.90	.45	244 Checklist 264-372	4.00	2.00
193 Mike Wegener	.90	.45	245 Leo Cardenas	.90	.45
194 Chuck Manuel	.90	.45	246 Jim McAndrew	.90	.45
195 N.L. Playoff Game 1	8.00	4.00	247 Lou Klimchock	.90	.45
196 N.L. Playoff Game 2	2.00	1.00	248 Jesus Alou	.90	.45
197 N.L. Playoff Game 3	18.00	9.00	249 Bob Locker	.90	.45
198 N.L. (Celebration)	5.00	2.50	250 Willie McCovey	12.00	6.00
199 A.L. Playoff Game 1	2.00	1.00	251 Dick Schofield	.90	.45
200 A.L. Playoff Game 2	2.00	1.00	252 Lowell Palmer	.90	.45
201 A.L. Playoff Game 3	2.00	1.00	253 Ron Woods	.90	.45
202 A.L. (Celebration)	2.00	1.00	254 Camilo Pascual	.90	.45
203 Rudy May	.90	.45	255 Jim Spencer (R)	.90	.45
204 Len Gabrielson	.90	.45	256 Vic Davalillo	.90	.45
205 Bert Campaneris	1.25	.60	257 Dennis Higgins	.90	.45
206 Clete Boyer	1.00	.50	258 Paul Popovich	.90	.45
207 Tigers Rookies	.90	.45	259 Tommie Reynolds	.90	.45
Norman McRae (R)			260 Claude Osteen	.90	.45
Bob Reed (R)			261 Curt Motton	.90	.45
208 Fred Gladding	.90	.45	262 Padres Rookies	1.25	.60
209 Ken Suarez	.90	.45	Jerry Morales (R)		
210 Juan Marichal	7.00	3.50	Jim Williams (R)		
211 Ted Williams	8.00	4.00	263 Duane Josephson	.90	.45
212 Al Santorini	.90	.45	264 Rich Hebner	1.00	.50

265 Randy Hundley	1.00	.50
266 Wally Bunker	.90	.45
267 Twins Rookies	.90	.45
Herman Hill (R)		
Paul Ratliff (R)		
268 Claude Raymond	.90	.45
269 Cesar Gutierrez	.90	.45
270 Chris Short	.90	.45
271 Greg Goossen	.90	.45
272 Hector Torres	.90	.45
273 Ralph Houk	1.00	.50
274 Gerry Arrigo	.90	.45
275 Duke Sims	.90	.45
276 Ron Hunt	.90	.45
277 Paul Doyle	.90	.45
278 Tommie Aaron	.90	.45
279 Bill Lee (R)	2.00	1.00
280 Donn Clendenon	.90	.45
281 Casey Cox	.90	.45
282 Steve Huntz	.90	.45
283 Angel Bravo	.90	.45
284 Jack Baldschun	.90	.45
285 Paul Blair	.90	.45
286 Dodgers Rookies	8.00	4.00
Bill Buckner (R)		
Jack Jenkins (R)		
287 Fred Talbot	.90	.45
288 Larry Hisle	1.25	.60
289 Gene Brabender	.90	.45
290 Rod Carew	50.00	25.00
291 Leo Durocher	1.25	.60
292 Eddie Leon	.90	.45
293 Bob Bailey	.90	.45
294 Jose Azcue	.90	.45
295 Cecil Upshaw	.90	.45
296 Woody Woodward	.90	.45
297 Curt Blefary	.90	.45
298 Ken Henderson	.90	.45
299 Buddy Bradford	.90	.45
300 Tom Seaver	125.00	65.00
301 Chico Salmon	.90	.45
302 Jeff James	.90	.45
303 Brant Alyea	.90	.45
304 Bill Russell (R)	4.00	2.00
305 World Series Game 1	3.50	1.75
306 World Series Game 2	3.50	1.75
307 World Series Game 3	3.50	1.75
308 World Series Game 4	3.50	1.75
309 World Series Game 5	3.50	1.75
310 WS (Celebration)	5.00	2.50
311 Dick Green	.90	.45
312 Mike Torrez	.90	.45
313 Mayo Smith	.90	.45
314 Bill McCool	.90	.45
315 Luis Aparicio	5.00	2.50
316 Skip Guinn	.90	.45
317 Red Sox Rookies	1.25	.60
Luis Alvarado (R)		
Billy Conigliaro		
318 Willie Smith	.90	.45
319 Clayton Dalrymple	.90	.45
320 Jim Maloney	.90	.45
321 Lou Piniella	2.00	1.00
322 Luke Walker	.90	.45
323 Wayne Comer	.90	.45
324 Tony Taylor	.90	.45
325 Dave Boswell	.90	.45
326 Bill Voss	.90	.45
327 Hal King	.90	.45
328 George Brunet	.90	.45
329 Chris Cannizzaro	.90	.45
330 Lou Brock	12.00	6.00
331 Chuck Dobson	.90	.45
332 Bobby Wine	.90	.45
333 Bobby Murcer	2.50	1.25
334 Phil Regan	.90	.45
335 Bill Freehan	1.25	.60
336 Del Unser	.90	.45
337 Mike McCormick	.90	.45
338 Paul Schaal	.90	.45
339 Johnny Edwards	.90	.45
340 Tony Conigliaro	1.50	.75
341 Bill Sudakis	.90	.45
342 Wilbur Wood	.90	.45
343 Checklist 373-459	4.00	2.00
344 Marcelino Lopez	.90	.45
345 Al Ferrara	.90	.45
346 Red Schoendienst	1.50	.90
347 Russ Snyder	.90	.45
348 Mets Rookies	1.25	.60
Jesse Hudson (R)		
Mike Jorgensen (R)		
349 Steve Hamilton	.90	.45
350 Roberto Clemente	55.00	27.50
351 Tom Murphy	.90	.45
352 Bob Barton	.90	.45
353 Stan Williams	.90	.45
354 Amos Otis	2.00	1.00
355 Doug Rader	1.00	.50
256 Fred Lasher	.90	.45
357 Bob Burda	.90	.45
358 Pedro Borbon (R)	1.25	.60
359 Phil Roof	.90	.45
360 Curt Flood	1.00	.50
361 Ray Jarvis	.90	.45
362 Joe Hague	.90	.45
363 Tom Shopay	.90	.45
364 Dan McGinn	.90	.45
365 Zoilo Versalles	1.00	.50
366 Barry Moore	.90	.45
367 Mike Lum	.90	.45
368 Ed Herrmann	.90	.45
369 Alan Foster	.90	.45
370 Tommy Harper	.90	.45
371 Rod Gaspar	.90	.45
372 Dave Giusti	.90	.45

No.	Name	Price 1	Price 2
373	Roy White	.90	.45
374	Tommie Sisk	.90	.45
375	Johnny Callison	.90	.45
376	Lefty Phillips	.90	.45
377	Bill Butler	.90	.45
378	Jim Davenport	.90	.45
379	Tom Tischinski	.90	.45
380	Tony Perez	10.00	5.00
381	Athletics Rookies	.90	.45
	Bobby Brooks (R)		
	Mike Olivo (R)		
382	Jack DiLauro	.90	.45
383	Mickey Stanley	1.00	.50
384	Gary Neibauer	.90	.45
385	George Scott	1.00	.50
386	Bill Dillman	.90	.45
387	Orioles Team	2.00	1.00
388	Byron Browne	.90	.45
389	Jim Shellenback	.90	.45
390	Willie Davis	.90	.45
391	Larry Brown	.90	.45
392	Walt Hriniak	.90	.45
393	John Gelnar	.90	.45
394	Gil Hodges	5.00	2.50
395	Walt Williams	.90	.45
396	Steve Blass	.90	.45
397	Roger Repoz	.90	.45
398	Bill Stoneman	.90	.45
399	Yankees Team	4.00	2.00
400	Denny McLain	1.50	.75
401	Giants Rookie	.90	.45
	John Harrell (R)		
	Bernie Williams (R)		
402	Ellie Rodriguez	.90	.45
403	Jim Bunning	3.00	1.50
404	Rich Reese	.90	.45
405	Bill Hands	.90	.45
406	Mike Andrews	.90	.45
407	Bob Watson	2.00	1.00
408	Paul Lindblad	.90	.45
409	Bob Tolan	.90	.45
410	Boog Powell	3.00	1.50
411	Dodgers Team	2.00	1.00
412	Larry Burchart	.90	.45
413	Sonny Jackson	.90	.45
414	Paul Edmondson	.90	.45
415	Julian Javier	.90	.45
416	Joe Verbanic	.90	.45
417	John Bateman	.90	.45
418	John Donaldson	.90	.45
419	Ron Taylor	.90	.45
420	Ken McMullen	.90	.45
421	Pat Dobson	1.00	.50
422	Royals Team	2.00	1.00
423	Jerry May	.90	.45
424	Mike Kilkenny	.90	.45
425	Bobby Bonds	8.50	4.25
426	Bill Rigney	.90	.45
427	Fred Norman	.90	.45
428	Don Buford	.90	.45
429	Cubs Rookies	.90	.45
	Randy Bobb (R)		
	Jim Cosman		
430	Andy Messersmith	.90	.45
431	Ron Swoboda	1.25	.60
432	Checklist 460-546	4.00	2.00
433	Ron Bryant	.90	.45
434	Felipe Alou	2.50	1.25
435	Nelson Briles	.90	.45
436	Phillies Team	2.00	1.00
437	Danny Cater	.90	.45
438	Pat Jarvis	.90	.45
439	Lee Maye	.90	.45
440	Bill Mazeroski	2.00	1.00
441	John O'Donoghue	.90	.45
442	Gene Mauch	.90	.45
443	Al Jackson	.90	.45
444	White Sox Rookies	.90	.45
	Bill Farmer		
	John Matias (R)		
445	Vada Pinson	2.00	1.00
446	Billy Grabarkewitz (R)	.90	.45
447	Lee Stange	.90	.45
448	Astros Team	2.00	1.00
449	Jim Palmer	25.00	12.50
450	Willie McCovey AS	6.00	3.00
451	Boog Powell AS	1.50	.90
452	Felix Millan AS	1.25	.60
453	Rod Carew AS	7.00	3.50
454	Ron Santo AS	1.50	.75
455	Brooks Robinson AS	6.00	3.00
456	Don Kessinger AS	1.25	.60
457	Rico Petrocelli AS	1.25	.60
458	Pete Rose AS	15.00	7.50
459	Reggie Jackson AS	25.00	12.50
460	Matty Alou AS	1.50	.75
461	Carl Yastrzemski AS	10.00	5.00
462	Hank Aaron AS	15.00	7.50
463	Frank Robinson AS	6.00	3.00
464	Johnny Bench AS	15.00	7.50
465	Bill Freehan AS	1.50	.75
466	Juan Marichal AS	6.00	3.00
467	Denny McLain AS	2.50	1.25
468	Jerry Koosman AS	1.50	.75
469	Sam McDowell AS	1.50	.75
470	Willie Stargell	12.00	6.00
471	Chris Zachary	1.50	.75
472	Braves Team	2.00	1.00
473	Don Bryant	1.50	.75
474	Dick Kelley	1.50	.75
475	Dick McAuliffe	1.50	.75
476	Don Shaw	1.50	.75
477	Orioles Rookies	1.50	.75
	Roger Freed (R)		
	Al Severinsen (R)		
478	Bob Heise	1.50	.75

479 Dick Woodson	1.50	.75
480 Glenn Beckert	1.50	.75
481 Jose Tartabull	1.50	.75
482 Tom Hilgendorf	1.50	.75
483 Gail Hopkins	1.50	.75
484 Gary Nolan	1.50	.75
485 Jay Johnstone	2.00	1.00
486 Terry Harmon	1.50	.75
487 Cisco Carlos	1.50	.75
488 J.C. Martin	1.50	.75
489 Eddie Kasko	1.50	.75
490 Bill Singer	1.50	.75
491 Graig Nettles	1.50	.75
492 Astros Rookies	1.50	.75
Keith Lampard (R)		
Scipio Spinks (R)		
493 Lindy McDaniel	1.50	.75
494 Larry Stahl	1.50	.75
495 Dave Morehead	1.50	.75
496 Steve Whitaker	1.50	.75
497 Eddie Watt	1.50	.75
498 Al Weis	1.50	.75
499 Skip Lockwood	1.50	.75
500 Hank Aaron	60.00	30.00
501 White Sox Team	2.00	1.00
502 Rollie Fingers	40.00	20.00
503 Dal Maxvill	1.50	.75
504 Don Pavletich	1.50	.75
505 Ken Holtzman	2.00	1.00
506 Ed Stroud	1.50	.75
507 Pat Corrales	1.50	.75
508 Joe Niekro	2.00	1.00
509 Expos Team	2.00	1.00
510 Tony Oliva	3.00	1.50
511 Joe Hoerner	1.50	.75
512 Billy Harris	1.50	.75
513 Preston Gomez	1.50	.75
514 Steve Hovley	1.50	.75
515 Don Wilson	1.50	.75
516 Yankees Rookies	1.50	.75
John Ellis (R)		
Jim Lyttle (R)		
517 Joe Gibbon	1.50	.75
518 Bill Melton	1.50	.75
519 Don McMahon	1.50	.75
520 Willie Horton	2.00	1.00
521 Cal Koonce	1.50	.75
522 Angels Team	2.00	1.00
523 Jose Pena	1.50	.75
524 Alvin Dark	1.50	.75
525 Jerry Adair	1.50	.75
526 Ron Herbel	1.50	.75
527 Don Bosch	1.50	.75
528 Elrod Hendricks	2.00	1.00
529 Bob Aspromonte	1.50	.75
530 Bob Gibson	15.00	7.50
531 Ron Clark	1.50	.75
532 Danny Murtaugh	1.50	.75

533 Buzz Stephen	1.50	.75
534 Twins Team	2.00	1.00
535 Andy Kosco	1.50	.75
536 Mike Kekich	1.50	.75
537 Joe Morgan	15.00	7.50
538 Bob Humphreys	1.50	.75
539 Phillies Rookies	5.00	2.50
Larry Bowa (R)		
Dennis Doyle (R)		
540 Gary Peters	1.50	.75
541 Bill Heath	1.50	.75
542 Checklist 547-633	4.00	2.00
543 Clyde Wright	1.50	.75
544 Reds Team	2.00	1.00
545 Ken Harrelson	2.00	1.00
546 Ron Reed	1.50	.75
547 Rick Monday	3.00	1.50
548 Howie Reed	2.50	1.25
549 Cardinals Team	3.00	1.50
550 Frank Howard	2.50	1.25
551 Dock Ellis	2.50	1.25
552 Royals Rookies	2.50	1.25
Don O'Riley (R)		
Dennis Paepke (R)		
Fred Rico (R)		
553 Jim Lefebvre	3.00	1.50
554 Tom Timmermann	2.50	1.25
555 Orlando Cepeda	5.00	2.50
556 Dave Bristol	2.50	1.25
557 Ed Kranepool	3.50	1.75
558 Vern Fuller	2.50	1.25
559 Tommy Davis	3.50	1.75
560 Gaylord Perry	16.00	8.00
561 Tom McCraw	2.50	1.25
562 Ted Abernathy	2.50	1.25
563 Red Sox Team	3.00	1.50
564 Johnny Briggs	2.50	1.25
565 Jim Hunter	15.00	7.50
566 Gene Alley	2.50	1.25
567 Bob Oliver	2.50	1.25
568 Stan Bahnsen	2.50	1.25
569 Cookie Rojas	2.50	1.25
570 Jim Fregosi	3.00	1.50
571 Jim Brewer	2.50	1.25
572 Frank Quilici	2.50	1.25
573 Padres Rookies	2.50	1.25
Mike Corkins (R)		
Rafael Robles (R)		
Ron Slocum (R)		
574 Bobby Bolin	2.50	1.25
575 Cleon Jones	2.50	1.25
576 Milt Pappas	2.50	1.25
577 Bernie Allen	2.50	1.25
578 Tom Griffin	2.50	1.25
579 Tigers Team	3.00	1.50
580 Pete Rose	70.00	35.00
581 Tom Satriano	2.50	1.25
582 Mike Paul	2.50	1.25

583	Hal Lanier	2.50	1.25
584	Al Downing	2.50	1.25
585	Rusty Staub	4.00	2.00
586	Rickey Clark	2.50	1.25
587	Jose Arcia	2.50	1.25
588a	Checklist 634-720 (Er) (Aldolfo)	6.00	3.00
588b	Checklist 634-720 (Cor) (Aldolpho)	4.00	2.00
589	Joe Keough	2.50	1.25
590	Mike Cuellar	3.00	1.50
591	Mike Ryan	2.50	1.25
592	Daryl Patterson	2.50	1.25
593	Cubs Team	3.00	1.50
594	Jake Gibbs	2.50	1.25
595	Maury Wills	4.00	2.00
596	Mike Hershberger	2.50	1.25
597	Sonny Siebert	2.50	1.25
598	Joe Pepitone	3.00	1.50
599	Senators Rookies	2.50	1.25
	Gene Martin (R)		
	Dick Stelmaszek (R)		
	Dick Such (R)		
600	Willie Mays	85.00	42.50
601	Pete Richert	2.50	1.25
602	Ted Savage	2.50	1.25
603	Ray Oyler	2.50	1.25
604	Cito Gaston	3.00	1.50
605	Rick Wise	3.00	1.50
606	Chico Ruiz	2.50	1.25
607	Gary Waslewski	2.50	1.25
608	Pirates Team	3.00	1.50
609	Buck Martinez (R)	3.00	1.50
610	Jerry Koosman	4.50	2.25
611	Norm Cash	2.50	1.25
612	Jim Hickman	2.50	1.25
613	Dave Baldwin	2.50	1.25
614	Mike Shannon	2.50	1.25
615	Mark Belanger	3.00	1.50
616	Jim Merritt	2.50	1.25
617	Jim French	2.50	1.25
618	Billy Wynne	2.50	1.25
619	Norm Miller	2.50	1.25
620	Jim Perry	4.00	2.00
621	Braves Rookies	28.00	14.00
	Darrell Evans (R)		
	Rick Kester (R)		
	Mike McQueen		
622	Don Sutton	15.00	7.50
623	Horace Clarke	2.50	1.25
624	Clyde King	2.50	1.25
625	Dean Chance	2.50	1.25
626	Dave Ricketts	2.50	1.25
627	Gary Wagner	2.50	1.25
628	Wayne Garrett	2.50	1.25
629	Merv Rettenmund	2.50	1.25
630	Ernie Banks	38.00	19.00
631	Athletics Team	3.00	1.50

632	Gary Sutherland	2.50	1.25
633	Roger Nelson	2.50	1.25
634	Bud Harrelson	5.00	2.50
635	Bob Allison	5.00	2.50
636	Jim Stewart	5.00	2.50
637	Indians Team	8.00	4.00
638	Frank Bertaina	5.00	2.50
639	Dave Campbell	5.00	2.50
640	Al Kaline	55.00	27.50
641	Al McBean	5.00	2.50
642	Angels Rookies	5.00	2.50
	Greg Garrett (R)		
	Gordon Lund (R)		
	Jarvis Tatum (R)		
643	Jose Pagan	5.00	2.50
644	Gerry Nyman	5.00	2.50
645	Don Money	5.00	2.50
646	Jim Britton	5.00	2.50
647	Tom Matchick	5.00	2.50
648	Larry Haney	5.00	2.50
649	Jimmie Hall	5.00	2.50
650	Sam McDowell	6.00	3.00
651	Jim Gosger	5.00	2.50
652	Rich Rollins	5.00	2.50
653	Moe Drabowsky	5.00	2.50
654	N.L. Rookies	6.00	3.00
	Boots Day (R)		
	Oscar Gamble (R)		
	Angel Mangual (R)		
655	John Roseboro	5.00	2.50
656	Jim Hardin	5.00	2.50
657	Padres Team	8.00	4.00
658	Ken Tatum	5.00	2.50
659	Pete Ward	5.00	2.50
660	Johnny Bench	180.00	90.00
661	Jerry Robertson	5.00	2.50
662	Frank Lucchesi	5.00	2.50
663	Tito Francona	5.00	2.50
664	Bob Robertson	5.00	2.50
665	Jim Lonborg	6.00	3.00
666	Adolpho Phillips	5.00	2.50
667	Bob Meyer	5.00	2.50
668	Bob Tillman	5.00	2.50
669	White Sox Rookies	5.00	2.50
	Bart Johnson (R)		
	Dan Lazar (R)		
	Mickey Scott (R)		
670	Ron Santo	7.00	3.50
671	Jim Campanis	5.00	2.50
672	Leon McFadden	5.00	2.50
673	Ted Uhlaender	5.00	2.50
674	Dave Leonhard	5.00	2.50
675	Jose Cardenal	5.00	2.50
676	Senators Team	8.00	4.00
677	Woodie Fryman	5.00	2.50
678	Dave Duncan	5.00	2.50
679	Ray Sadecki	5.00	2.50
680	Rico Petrocelli	5.00	2.50

681	Bob Garibaldi	5.00	2.50
682	Dalton Jones	5.00	2.50
683	Reds Rookies	8.00	4.00
	Vern Geishert (R)		
	Hal McRae		
	Wayne Simpson (R)		
684	Jack Fisher	5.00	2.50
685	Tom Haller	5.00	2.50
686	Jackie Hernandez	5.00	2.50
687	Bob Priddy	5.00	2.50
688	Ted Kubiak	5.00	2.50
689	Frank Tepedino	5.00	2.50
690	Ron Fairly	5.00	2.50
691	Joe Grzenda	5.00	2.50
692	Duffy Dyer	5.00	2.50
693	Bob Johnson	5.00	2.50
694	Gary Ross	5.00	2.50
695	Bobby Knoop	5.00	2.50
696	Giants Team	8.00	4.00
697	Jim Hannan	5.00	2.50
698	Tom Tresh	6.00	3.00
699	Hank Aguirre	5.00	2.50
700	Frank Robinson	45.00	22.50
701	Jack Billingham	5.00	2.50
702	A.L. Rookies	5.00	2.50
	Bob Johnson (R)		
	Ron Klimkowski (R)		
	Bill Zepp (R)		
703	Lou Marone	5.00	2.50
704	Frank Baker	5.00	2.50
705	Tony Cloninger	5.00	2.50
706	John McNamara	5.00	2.50
707	Kevin Collins	5.00	2.50
708	Jose Santiago	5.00	2.50
709	Mike Fiore	5.00	2.50
710	Felix Millan	5.00	2.50
711	Ed Brinkman	5.00	2.50
712	Nolan Ryan	575.00	290.00
713	Pilots Team	20.00	10.00
714	Al Spangler	5.00	2.50
715	Mickey Lolich	7.00	3.50
716	Cards Rookies	5.00	2.50
	Sal Campisi (R)		
	Reggie Cleveland (R)		
	Santiago Guzman (R)		
717	Tom Phoebus	5.00	2.50
718	Ed Spiezio	5.00	2.50
719	Jim Roland	5.00	2.50
720	Rick Reichardt	6.00	3.00

1971 Topps

Topps increased the size of their set in 1971 to 752-cards. All cards measure 2-1/2" by 3-1/2". Card fronts feature large color photographs surrounded by a black border. Card backs are horizontal and include a black and white head shot of the player. Popular subsets include League Leaders, World Series and Playoff Highlights and Rookies.

	NR/MT	EX
Complete Set (752)	2,400.00	1,200.00
Commons (1-393)	1.00	.50
Commons (394-523)	1.50	.75
Commons (524-643)	3.50	1.75
Commons (644-752)	5.00	2.50

1	World Champions	12.00	6.00
	(Orioles)		
2	Dock Ellis	1.00	.50
3	Dick McAuliffe	1.00	.50
4	Vic Davalillo	1.00	.50
5	Thurman Munson	38.00	19.00
6	Ed Spiezio	1.00	.50
7	Jim Holt	1.00	.50
8	Mike McQueen	1.00	.50
9	George Scott	1.25	.60
10	Claude Osteen	1.25	.60
11	Elliott Maddox (R)	1.00	.50
12	Johnny Callison	1.00	.50
13	White Sox Rookies	1.00	.50
	Charlie Brinkman (R)		
	Dick Moloney (R)		
14	Dave Concepcion(R)	24.00	12.00
15	Andy Messersmith	1.00	.50
16	Ken Singleton (R)	3.00	1.50
17	Billy Sorrell	1.00	.50
18	Norm Miller	1.00	.50
19	Skip Pitlock	1.00	.50
20	Reggie Jackson	125.00	60.00
21	Dan McGinn	1.00	.50

22	Phil Roof	1.00	.50
23	Oscar Gamble	1.25	.60
24	Rich Hand	1.00	.50
25	Clarence Gaston	1.00	.50
26	Bert Blyleven (R)	55.00	27.50
27	Pirates Rookies	1.00	.50
	Fred Cambria (R)		
	Gene Clines (R)		
28	Ron Kimkowski	1.00	.50
29	Don Buford	1.00	.50
30	Phil Niekro	6.00	3.00
31	Eddie Kasko	1.00	.50
32	Jerry DaVanon	1.00	.50
33	Del Unser	1.00	.50
34	Sandy Vance	1.00	.50
35	Lou Piniella	2.00	1.00
36	Dean Chance	1.00	.50
37	Rich McKinney	1.00	.50
38	Jim Colborn	1.00	.50
39	Tigers Rookies	1.25	.60
	Gene Lamont (R)		
	Lerrin LaGrow (R)		
40	Lee May	1.00	.50
41	Rick Austin	1.00	.50
42	Boots Day	1.00	.50
43	Steve Kealey	1.00	.50
44	Johnny Edwards	1.00	.50
45	Jim Hunter	7.50	3.75
46	Dave Campbell	1.00	.50
47	Johnny Jeter	1.00	.50
48	Dave Baldwin	1.00	.50
49	Don Money	1.00	.50
50	Willie McCovey	12.00	6.00
51	Steve Kline	1.00	.50
52	Braves Rookies	1.25	.60
	Oscar Brown (R)		
	Earl Williams (R)		
53	Paul Blair	1.00	.50
54	Checklist 1-132	3.50	1.75
55	Steve Carlton	35.00	17.50
56	Duane Josephson	1.00	.50
57	Von Joshua	1.00	.50
58	Bill Lee	1.25	.60
59	Gene Mauch	1.00	.50
60	Dick Bosman	1.00	.50
61	A.L. Batting Leaders	4.00	2.00
62	N.L. Batting Leaders	2.00	1.00
63	A.L. RBI Leaders	2.00	1.00
64	N.L. RBI Leaders	4.00	2.00
65	A.L. HRLeaders	4.00	2.00
66	N.L. HRLeaders	5.00	2.50
67	A.L. ERA Leaders	2.00	1.00
68	N.L. ERA Leaders	4.00	2.00
69	A.L. Pitching Leaders	2.00	1.00
70	N.L. Pitching Leaders	4.00	2.00
71	A.L. Strikeout Ldrs	2.00	1.00
72	N.L. Strikeout Ldrs	5.00	2.00
73	George Brunet	1.00	.50
74	Twins Rookies	1.00	.50
	Pete Hamm (R)		
	Jim Nettles (R)		
75	Gary Nolan	1.00	.50
76	Ted Savage	1.00	.50
77	Mike Compton	1.00	.50
78	Jim Spencer	1.00	.50
79	Wade Blasingame	1.00	.50
80	Bill Melton	1.00	.50
81	Felix Millan	1.00	.50
82	Casey Cox	1.00	.50
83	Mets Rookies	1.50	.75
	Randy Bobb (R)		
	Tim Foli (R)		
84	Marcel Lachemann	1.25	.60
85	Billy Grabarkewitz	1.00	.50
86	Mike Kilkenny	1.00	.50
87	Jack Heidemann	1.00	.50
88	Hal King	1.00	.50
89	Ken Brett	1.00	.50
90	Joe Pepitone	1.25	.60
91	Bob Lemon	1.50	.75
92	Fred Wenz	1.00	.50
93	Senators Rookies	1.00	.50
	Norm McRae		
	Denny Riddleberger(R)		
94	Don Hahn	1.00	.50
95	Luis Tiant	2.50	1.25
96	Joe Hague	1.00	.50
97	Floyd Wicker	1.00	.50
98	Joe Decker	1.00	.50
99	Mark Belanger	1.25	.60
100	Pete Rose	48.00	24.00
101	Les Cain	1.00	.50
102	Astros Rookies	1.25	.60
	Ken Forsch (R)		
	Larry Howard (R)		
103	Rich Severson	1.00	.50
104	Dan Frisella	1.00	.50
105	Tony Conigliaro	1.50	.75
106	Tom Dukes	1.00	.50
107	Roy Foster	1.00	.50
108	John Cumberland	1.00	.50
109	Steve Hovley	1.00	.50
110	Bill Mazeroski	2.00	1.00
111	Yankees Rookies	1.00	.50
	Loyd Colson (R)		
	Bobby Mitchell (R)		
112	Manny Mota	1.25	.60
113	Jerry Crider	1.00	.50
114	Billy Conigliaro	1.00	.50
115	Donn Clendenon	1.00	.50
116	Ken Sanders	1.00	.50
117	Ted Simmons (R)	24.00	12.00
118	Cookie Rojas	1.00	.50
119	Frank Lucchesi	1.00	.50
120	Willie Horton	1.25	.60
121	1971 Rookie Stars	1.00	.50

Jim Dunegan (R)			
Roe Skidmore (R)			
122 Eddie Watt	1.00	.50	
123 Checklist 133-263	3.50	1.75	
124 Don Gullett (R)	1.50	.75	
125 Ray Fosse	1.00	.50	
126 Danny Coombs	1.00	.50	
127 Danny Thompson (R)	1.00	.50	
128 Frank Johnson	1.00	.50	
129 Aurelio Monteagudo	1.00	.50	
130 Denis Menke	1.00	.50	
131 Curt Blefary	1.00	.50	
132 Jose Laboy	1.00	.50	
133 Mickey Lolich	2.50	1.25	
134 Jose Arcia	1.00	.50	
135 Rick Monday	1.25	.60	
136 Duffy Dyer	1.00	.50	
137 Marcelino Lopez	1.00	.50	
138 Phillies Rookies	1.25	.60	
Joe Lis			
Willie Montanez (R)			
139 Paul Casanova	1.00	.50	
140 Gaylord Perry	10.00	5.00	
141 Frank Quilici	1.00	.50	
142 Mack Jones	1.00	.50	
143 Steve Blass	1.00	.50	
144 Jackie Hernandez	1.00	.50	
145 Bill Singer	1.00	.50	
146 Ralph Houk	1.25	.60	
147 Bob Priddy	1.00	.50	
148 John Mayberry	1.00	.50	
149 Mike Hershberger	1.00	.50	
150 Sam McDowell	1.25	.60	
151 Tommy Davis	1.50	.75	
152 Angels Rookies	1.00	.50	
Lloyd Allen (R)			
Winston Llenas (R)			
153 Gary Ross	1.00	.50	
154 Cesar Gutierrez	1.00	.50	
155 Ken Henderson	1.00	.50	
156 Bart Johnson	1.00	.50	
157 Bob Bailey	1.00	.50	
158 Jerry Reuss	2.00	1.00	
159 Jarvis Tatum	1.00	.50	
160 Tom Seaver	70.00	35.00	
161 Coins Checklist	3.00	1.50	
162 Jack Billingham	1.00	.50	
163 Buck Martinez	1.00	.50	
164 Reds Rookies	1.25	.60	
Frank Duffy (R)			
Milt Wilcox (R)			
165 Cesar Tovar	1.00	.50	
166 Joe Hoerner	1.00	.50	
167 Tom Grieve (R)	1.25	.60	
168 Bruce Dal Canton	1.00	.50	
169 Ed Herrmann	1.00	.50	
170 Mike Cuellar	1.50	.75	
171 Bobby Wine	1.00	.50	
172 Duke Sims	1.00	.50	
173 Gil Garrido	1.00	.50	
174 Dave LaRoche	1.00	.50	
175 Jim Hickman	1.00	.50	
176 Red Sox Rookies	1.00	.50	
Doug Griffin (R)			
Bob Montgomery (R)			
177 Hal McRae	3.00	1.50	
178 Dave Duncan	1.00	.50	
179 Mike Corkins	1.00	.50	
180 Al Kaline	22.00	11.00	
181 Hal Lanier	1.00	.50	
182 Al Downing	1.00	.50	
183 Gil Hodges	6.00	3.00	
184 Stan Bahnsen	1.00	.50	
185 Julian Javier	1.00	.50	
186 Bob Spence	1.00	.50	
187 Ted Abernathy	1.00	.50	
188 Dodgers Rookies	3.50	1.75	
Mike Strahler (R)			
Bob Valentine (R)			
189 George Mitterwald	1.00	.50	
190 Bob Tolan	1.00	.50	
191 Mike Andrews	1.00	.50	
192 Billy Wilson	1.00	.50	
193 Bob Grich (R)	6.00	3.00	
194 Mike Lum	1.00	.50	
195 A.L. Playoff Game 1	2.00	1.00	
196 A.L. Playoff Game 2	2.00	1.00	
197 A.L. Playoff Game 3	4.00	2.00	
198 A.L. (Celebration)	2.00	1.00	
199 N.L. Playoff Game 1	2.00	1.00	
200 N.L. Playoff Game 2	2.00	1.00	
201 N.L. Playoff Game 3	2.00	1.00	
202 N.L. (Celebration)	2.00	1.00	
203 Larry Gura	1.00	.50	
204 Brewers Rookies	1.00	.50	
George Kopacz (R)			
Bernie Smith (R)			
205 Gerry Moses	1.00	.50	
206 Checklist 264-393	3.50	1.75	
207 Alan Foster	1.00	.50	
208 Billy Martin	4.00	2.00	
209 Steve Renko	1.00	.50	
210 Rod Carew	50.00	25.00	
211 Phil Hennigan	1.00	.50	
212 Rich Hebner	1.00	.50	
213 Frank Baker	1.00	.50	
214 Al Ferrara	1.00	.50	
215 Diego Segui	1.00	.50	
216 Cards Rookies	1.00	.50	
Reggie Cleveland			
Luis Melendez (R)			
217 Ed Stroud	1.00	.50	
218 Tony Cloninger	1.00	.50	
219 Elrod Hendricks	1.00	.50	
220 Ron Santo	2.50	1.25	
221 Dave Morehead	1.00	.50	

222 Bob Watson	1.50	.75
223 Cecil Upshaw	1.00	.50
224 Alan Gallagher	1.00	.50
225 Gary Peters	1.00	.50
226 Bill Russell	2.00	1.00
227 Floyd Weaver	1.00	.50
228 Wayne Garrett	1.00	.50
229 Jim Hannan	1.00	.50
230 Willie Stargell	12.00	6.00
231 Indians Rookies	1.25	.60
Vince Colbert (R)		
John Lowenstein (R)		
232 John Strohmayer	1.00	.50
233 Larry Bowa	2.50	1.25
234 Jim Lyttle	1.00	.50
235 Nate Colbert	1.00	.50
236 Bob Humphreys	1.00	.50
237 Cesar Cedeno (R)	3.50	1.75
238 Chuck Dobson	1.00	.50
239 Red Schoendienst	2.00	1.00
240 Clyde Wright	1.00	.50
241 Dave Nelson	1.00	.50
242 Jim Ray	1.00	.50
243 Carlos May	1.00	.50
244 Bob Tillman	1.00	.50
245 Jim Kaat	3.50	1.75
246 Tony Taylor	1.00	.50
247 Royals Rookies	2.00	1.00
Jerry Cram (R)		
Paul Splittorff (R)		
248 Hoyt Wilhelm	4.50	2.25
249 Chico Salmon	1.00	.50
250 Johnny Bench	60.00	30.00
251 Frank Reberger	1.00	.50
252 Eddie Leon	1.00	.50
253 Bill Sudakis	1.00	.50
254 Cal Koonce	1.00	.50
255 Bob Robertson	1.00	.50
256 Tony Gonzalez	1.00	.50
257 Nelson Briles	1.00	.50
258 Dick Green	1.00	.50
259 Dave Marshall	1.00	.50
260 Tommy Harper	1.00	.50
261 Darold Knowles	1.00	.50
262 Padres Rookies	1.00	.50
Dave Robinson (R)		
Jim Williams (R)		
263 John Ellis	1.00	.50
264 Joe Morgan	12.00	6.00
265 Jim Northrup	1.00	.50
266 Bill Stoneman	1.00	.50
267 Rich Morales	1.00	.50
268 Phillies Team	2.00	1.00
269 Gail Hopkins	1.00	.50
270 Rico Carty	1.25	.60
271 Bill Zepp	1.00	.50
272 Tommy Helms	1.00	.50
273 Pete Richert	1.00	.50
274 Ron Slocum	1.00	.50
275 Vada Pinson	2.00	1.00
276 Giants Rookies	10.00	5.00
Mike Davison (R)		
George Foster (R)		
277 Gary Waslewski	1.00	.50
278 Jerry Grote	1.00	.50
279 Lefty Phillips	1.00	.50
280 Ferguson Jenkins	12.00	6.00
281 Danny Walton	1.00	.50
282 Jose Pagan	1.00	.50
283 Dick Such	1.00	.50
284 Jim Gosger	1.00	.50
285 Sal Bando	1.25	.60
286 Jerry McNertney	1.00	.50
287 Mike Fiore	1.00	.50
288 Joe Moeller	1.00	.50
289 White Sox Team	2.00	1.00
290 Tony Oliva	4.00	2.00
291 George Culver	1.00	.50
292 Jay Johnstone	1.25	.60
293 Pat Corrales	1.25	.60
294 Steve Dunning	1.00	.50
295 Bobby Bonds	4.00	2.00
296 Tom Timmermann	1.00	.50
297 Johnny Briggs	1.00	.50
298 Jim Nelson	1.00	.50
299 Ed Kirkpatrick	1.00	.50
300 Brooks Robinson	20.00	10.00
301 Earl Wilson	1.00	.50
302 Phil Gagliano	1.00	.50
303 Lindy McDaniel	1.00	.50
304 Ron Brand	1.00	.50
305 Reggie Smith	1.25	.60
306 Jim Nash	1.00	.50
307 Don Wert	1.00	.50
308 Cardinals Team	2.00	1.00
309 Dick Ellsworth	1.00	.50
310 Tommie Agee	1.00	.50
311 Lee Stange	1.00	.50
312 Harry Walker	1.00	.50
313 Tom Hall	1.00	.50
314 Jeff Torborg	1.25	.60
315 Ron Fairly	1.00	.50
316 Fred Scherman	1.00	.50
317 Athletics Rookies	1.00	.50
Jim Driscoll (R)		
Angel Mangual		
318 Rudy May	1.00	.50
319 Ty Cline	1.00	.50
320 Dave McNally	1.25	.60
321 Tom Matchick	1.00	.50
322 Jim Beauchamp	1.00	.50
323 Billy Champion	1.00	.50
324 Graig Nettles	3.50	1.75
325 Juan Marichal	7.00	3.50
326 Richie Scheinblum	1.00	.50
327 World Series Game 1	2.00	1.00

328	World Series Game 2	2.00	1.00
329	World Series Game 3	4.00	2.00
330	World Series Game 4	2.00	1.00
331	World Series Game 5	4.00	2.00
332	WS (Celebration)	2.00	1.00
333	Clay Kirby	1.00	.50
334	Roberto Pena	1.00	.50
335	Jerry Koosman	2.50	1.25
336	Tigers Team	2.00	1.00
337	Jesus Alou	1.00	.50
338	Gene Tenace	2.00	1.00
339	Wayne Simpson	1.00	.50
340	Rico Petrocelli	1.25	.60
341	Steve Garvey (R)	90.00	45.00
342	Frank Tepedino	1.00	.50
343	Pirates Rookies	1.25	.60
	Ed Acosta (R)		
	Milt May (R)		
344	Ellie Rodriguez	1.00	.50
345	Joe Horlen	1.00	.50
346	Lum Harris	1.00	.50
347	Ted Uhlaender	1.00	.50
348	Fred Norman	1.00	.50
349	Rich Reese	1.00	.50
350	Billy Williams	7.00	3.50
351	Jim Shellenback	1.00	.50
352	Denny Doyle	1.00	.50
353	Carl Taylor	1.00	.50
354	Don McMahon	1.00	.50
355	Bud Harrelson	1.25	.60
356	Bob Locker	1.00	.50
357	Reds Team	2.00	1.00
358	Danny Cater	1.00	.50
359	Ron Reed	1.00	.50
360	Jim Fregosi	1.25	.60
361	Don Sutton	8.00	4.00
362	Orioles Rookies	1.00	.50
	Mike Adamson (R)		
	Roger Freed		
363	Mike Nagy	1.00	.50
364	Tommy Dean	1.00	.50
365	Bob Johnson	1.00	.50
366	Ron Stone	1.00	.50
367	Dalton Jones	1.00	.50
368	Bob Veale	1.00	.50
369	Checklist 394-523	3.50	1.75
370	Joe Torre	4.00	2.00
371	Jack Hiatt	1.00	.50
372	Lew Krausse	1.00	.50
373	Tom McCraw	1.00	.50
374	Clete Boyer	1.25	.60
375	Steve Hargan	1.00	.50
376	Expos Rookies	1.00	.50
	Clyde Mashore (R)		
	Ernie McAnally (R)		
377	Greg Garrett	1.00	.50
378	Tito Fuentes	1.00	.50
379	Wayne Granger	1.00	.50
380	Ted Williams	8.00	4.00
381	Fred Gladding	1.00	.50
382	Jake Gibbs	1.00	.50
383	Rod Gaspar	1.00	.50
384	Rollie Fingers	18.00	9.00
385	Maury Wills	2.50	1.25
386	Red Sox Team	2.00	1.00
387	Ron Herbel	1.00	.50
388	Al Oliver	3.00	1.50
389	Ed Brinkman	1.00	.50
390	Glenn Beckert	1.00	.50
391	Twins Rookies	1.00	.60
	Steve Brye (R)		
	Cotton Nash (R)		
392	Grant Jackson	1.00	.50
393	Merv Rettenmund	1.00	.50
394	Clay Carroll	1.50	.75
395	Roy White	1.50	.75
396	Dick Schofield	1.50	.75
397	Alvin Dark	1.50	.75
398	Howie Reed	1.50	.75
399	Jim French	1.50	.75
400	Hank Aaron	60.00	30.00
401	Tom Murphy	1.50	.75
402	Dodgers Team	3.00	1.50
403	Joe Coleman	1.50	.75
404	Astros Rookies	2.00	1.00
	Buddy Harris		
	Roger Metzger (R)		
405	Leo Cardenas	1.50	.75
406	Ray Sadecki	1.50	.75
407	Joe Rudi	2.00	1.00
408	Rafael Robles	1.50	.75
409	Don Pavletich	1.50	.75
410	Ken Holtzman	1.50	.75
411	George Spriggs	1.50	.75
412	Jerry Johnson	1.50	.75
413	Pat Kelly	1.50	.75
414	Woodie Fryman	1.50	.75
415	Mike Hegan	1.50	.75
416	Gene Alley	1.50	.75
417	Dick Hall	1.50	.75
418	Adolfo Phillips	1.50	.75
419	Ron Hansen	1.50	.75
420	Jim Merritt	1.50	.75
421	John Stephenson	1.50	.75
422	Frank Bertaina	1.50	.75
423	Tigers Rookies	1.50	.75
	Tim Marting (R)		
	Dennis Saunders (R)		
424	Roberto Rodriguez	1.50	.75
425	Doug Rader	1.50	.75
426	Chris Canizzaro	1.50	.75
427	Bernie Allen	1.50	.75
428	Jim McAndrew	1.50	.75
429	Chuck Hinton	1.50	.75
430	Wes Parker	1.50	.75
431	Tom Burgmeier	1.50	.75

432 Bob Didier	1.50	.75
433 Skip Lockwood	1.50	.75
434 Gary Sutherland	1.50	.75
435 Jose Cardenal	1.50	.75
436 Wilbur Wood	1.50	.75
437 Danny Murtaugh	1.50	.75
438 Mike McCormick	1.50	.75
439 Phillies Rookies	5.00	2.50
Greg Luzinski (R)		
Scott Reid (R)		
440 Bert Campaneris	2.00	1.00
441 Milt Pappas	1.50	.75
442 Angels Team	3.00	1.50
443 Rich Robertson	1.50	.75
444 Jimmie Price	1.50	.75
445 Art Shamsky	1.50	.75
446 Bobby Bolin	1.50	.75
447 Cesar Geronimo (R)	2.00	1.00
448 Dave Roberts	1.50	.75
449 Brant Alyea	1.50	.75
450 Bob Gibson	18.00	9.00
451 Joe Keough	1.50	.75
452 John Boccabella	1.50	.75
453 Terry Crowley	1.50	.75
454 Mike Paul	1.50	.75
455 Don Kessinger	2.00	1.00
456 Bob Meyer	1.50	.75
457 Willie Smith	1.50	.75
458 White Sox Rookies(R)	1.50	.75
Dave Lemond (R)		
Ron Lolich (R)		
459 Jim Lefebvre	2.00	1.00
460 Fritz Peterson	1.50	.75
461 Jim Hart	1.50	.75
462 Senators Team	3.00	1.50
463 Tom Kelley	1.50	.75
464 Aurelio Rodriguez	1.50	.75
465 Tim McCarver	2.00	1.00
466 Ken Berry	1.50	.75
467 Al Santorini	1.50	.75
468 Frank Fernandez	1.50	.75
469 Bob Aspromonte	1.50	.75
470 Bob Oliver	1.50	.75
471 Tom Griffin	1.50	.75
472 Ken Rudolph	1.50	.75
473 Gary Wagner	1.50	.75
474 Jim Fairey	1.50	.75
475 Ron Perranoski	1.50	.75
476 Dal Maxvill	1.50	.75
477 Earl Weaver	2.00	1.00
478 Bernie Carbo	1.50	.75
479 Dennis Higgins	1.50	.75
480 Many Sanguillen	2.00	1.00
481 Daryl Patterson	1.50	.75
482 Padres Team	3.00	1.50
483 Gene Michael	1.50	.75
484 Don Wilson	1.50	.75
485 Ken McMullen	1.50	.75
486 Steve Huntz	1.50	.75
487 Paul Schaal	1.50	.75
488 Jerry Stephenson	1.50	.75
489 Luis Alvarado	1.50	.75
490 Deron Johnson	1.50	.75
491 Jim Hardin	1.50	.75
492 Ken Boswell	1.50	.75
493 Dave May	1.50	.75
494 Braves Rookies	2.00	1.00
Ralph Garr		
Rick Kester (R)		
495 Felipe Alou	2.50	1.25
496 Woody Woodward	1.50	.75
497 Horacio Pina	1.50	.75
498 John Kennedy	1.50	.75
499 Checklist 524-643	3.50	1.75
500 Jim Perry	1.50	.75
501 Andy Etchebarren	1.50	.75
502 Cubs Team	3.00	1.50
503 Gates Brown	1.50	.75
504 Ken Wright	1.50	.75
505 Ollie Brown	1.50	.75
506 Bobby Knoop	1.50	.75
507 George Stone	1.50	.75
508 Roger Repoz	1.50	.75
509 Jim Grant	1.50	.75
510 Ken Harrelson	2.00	1.00
511 Chris Short	1.50	.75
512 Red Sox Rookies	1.50	.75
Mike Garman (R)		
Dick Mills (R)		
513 Nolan Ryan	275.00	140.00
514 Ron Woods	1.50	.75
515 Carl Morton	1.50	.75
516 Ted Kubiak	1.50	.75
517 Charlie Fox	1.50	.75
518 Joe Grzenda	1.50	.75
519 Willie Crawford	1.50	.75
520 Tommy John	4.00	2.00
521 Leron Lee	1.50	.75
522 Twins Team	3.00	1.50
523 John Odom	1.50	.75
524 Mickey Stanley	2.00	1.00
525 Ernie Banks	40.00	20.00
526 Ray Jarvis	3.50	1.75
527 Cleon Jones	3.50	1.75
528 Wally Bunker	3.50	1.75
529 N.L. Rookies	4.50	2.25
Bill Buckner,		
Enzo Hernandez		
Marty Perez (R)		
530 Carl Yastrzemski	40.00	20.00
531 Mike Torrez	3.50	1.75
532 Bill Rigney	3.50	1.75
533 Mike Ryan	3.50	1.75
534 Luke Walker	3.50	1.75
535 Curt Flood	4.00	2.00
536 Claude Raymond	3.50	1.75

537 Tom Egan	3.50	1.75
538 Angel Bravo	3.50	1.75
539 Larry Brown	3.50	1.75
540 Larry Dierker	3.50	1.75
541 Bob Burda	3.50	1.75
542 Bob Miller	3.50	1.75
543 Yankees Team	5.00	2.50
544 Vida Blue	5.00	2.50
545 Dick Dietz	3.50	1.75
546 John Matias	3.50	1.75
547 Pat Dobson	3.50	1.75
548 Don Mason	3.50	1.75
549 Jim Brewer	3.50	1.75
550 Harmon Killebrew	25.00	12.50
551 Frank Linzy	3.50	1.75
552 Buddy Bradford	3.50	1.75
553 Kevin Collins	3.50	1.75
554 Lowell Palmer	3.50	1.75
555 Walt Williams	3.50	1.75
556 Jim McGlothlin	3.50	1.75
557 Tom Satriano	3.50	1.75
558 Hector Torres	3.50	1.75
559 A.L. Rookies	3.50	1.75
Terry Cox		
Bill Gogolewski		
Gary Jones		
560 Rusty Staub	4.50	2.25
561 Syd O'Brien	3.50	1.75
562 Dave Giusti	3.50	1.75
563 Giants Team	5.00	2.50
564 Al Fitzmorris	3.50	1.75
565 Jim Wynn	4.50	2.25
566 Tim Cullen	3.50	1.75
567 Walt Alston	4.00	2.00
568 Sal Campisi	3.50	1.75
569 Ivan Murrell	3.50	1.75
570 Jim Palmer	40.00	20.00
571 Ted Sizemore	3.50	1.75
572 Jerry Kenney	3.50	1.75
573 Ed Kranepool	4.00	2.00
574 Jim Bunning	5.00	2.50
575 Bill Freehan	4.00	2.00
576 Cubs Rookies	3.50	1.75
Brock Davis (R)		
Adrian Garrett (R)		
Garry Jestadt (R)		
577 Jim Lonborg	4.00	2.00
578 Ron Hunt	3.50	1.75
579 Marty Pattin	3.50	1.75
580 Tony Perez	14.00	7.00
581 Roger Nelson	3.50	1.75
582 Dave Cash	3.50	1.75
583 Ron Cook	3.50	1.75
584 Indians Team	5.00	2.50
585 Willie Davis	3.50	1.75
586 Dick Woodson	3.50	1.75
587 Sonny Jackson	3.50	1.75
588 Tom Bradley	3.50	1.75
589 Bob Barton	3.50	1.75
590 Alex Johnson	3.50	1.75
591 Jackie Brown	3.50	1.75
592 Randy Hundley	3.50	1.75
593 Jack Aker	3.50	1.75
594 Cards Rookies	5.00	2.50
Bob Chlupsa (R)		
Al Hrabosky (R)		
Bob Stinson		
595 Dave Johnson	3.50	1.75
596 Mike Jorgensen	3.50	1.75
597 Ken Suarez	3.50	1.75
598 Rick Wise	3.50	1.75
599 Norm Cash	6.00	3.00
600 Willie Mays	90.00	45.00
601 Ken Tatum	3.50	1.75
602 Marty Martinez	3.50	1.75
603 Pirates Team	5.00	2.50
604 John Gelnar	3.50	1.75
605 Orlando Cepeda	6.00	3.00
606 Chuck Taylor	3.50	1.75
607 Paul Ratliff	3.50	1.75
608 Mike Wegener	3.50	1.75
609 Leo Durocher	4.50	2.25
610 Amos Otis	4.50	2.25
611 Tom Phoebus	3.50	1.75
612 Indians Rookies	3.50	1.75
Lou Camilli (R)		
Ted Ford (R)		
Steve Mingori (R)		
613 Pedro Borbon	3.50	1.75
614 Billy Cowan	3.50	1.75
615 Mel Stottlemyre	4.50	2.25
616 Larry Hisle	3.50	1.75
617 Clay Dairymple	3.50	1.75
618 Tug McGraw	5.00	2.50
619 Checklist 644-752	4.50	2.25
620 Frank Howard	5.00	2.50
621 Ron Bryant	3.50	1.75
622 Joe Lahoud	3.50	1.75
623 Pat Jarvis	3.50	1.75
624 Athletics Team	4.00	2.00
625 Lou Brock	32.00	16.00
626 Freddie Patek	3.50	1.75
627 Steve Hamilton	3.50	1.75
628 John Bateman	3.50	1.75
629 John Hiller	3.50	1.75
630 Roberto Clemente	68.00	34.00
631 Eddie Fisher	3.50	1.75
632 Darrel Chaney	3.50	1.75
633 A.L. Rookies	3.50	1.75
Bobby Brooks (R)		
Pete Koegel		
Scott Northey		
634 Phil Regan	3.50	1.75
635 Bobby Murcer	7.50	3.75
636 Denny Lemaster	3.50	1.75
637 Dave Bristol	3.50	1.75

638 Stan Williams	3.50	1.75	689 Frank Baker	5.00	2.50
639 Tom Haller	3.50	1.75	690 Bob Moose	5.00	2.50
640 Frank Robinson	38.00	19.00	691 Bob Heise	5.00	2.50
641 Mets Team	5.00	2.50	692 A.L. Rookies	5.00	2.50
642 Jim Roland	3.50	1.75	Hal Haydel (R)		
643 Rick Reichardt	3.50	1.75	Rogelio Moret (R)		
644 Jim Stewart	5.00	2.50	Wayne Twitchel		
645 Jim Maloney	5.00	2.50	693 Jose Pena	5.00	2.50
646 Bobby Floyd	5.00	2.50	694 Rick Renick	5.00	2.50
647 Juan Pizarro	5.00	2.50	695 Joe Niekro	6.00	3.00
648 Mets Rookies	7.00	3.50	696 Jerry Morales	5.00	2.50
Rich Folkers (R)			697 Rickey Clark	5.00	2.50
Ted Martinez (R)			698 Brewers Team	8.00	4.00
Jon Matlack (R)			699 Jim Britton	5.00	2.50
649 Sparky Lyle	7.50	3.75	700 Boog Powell	8.50	4.25
650 Richie Allen	12.00	6.00	701 Bob Garibaldi	5.00	2.50
651 Jerry Robertson	5.00	2.50	702 Milt Ramirez	5.00	2.50
652 Braves Team	8.00	4.00	703 Mike Kekich	5.00	2.50
653 Russ Snyder	5.00	2.50	704 J.C. Martin	5.00	2.50
654 Don Shaw	5.00	2.50	705 Dick Selma	5.00	2.50
655 Mike Epstein	5.00	2.50	706 Joe Foy	5.00	2.50
656 Gerry Nyman	5.00	2.50	707 Fred Lasher	5.00	2.50
657 Jose Azcue	5.00	2.50	708 Russ Nagelson	5.00	2.50
658 Paul Lindblad	5.00	2.50	709 Major League	40.00	20.00
659 Byron Browne	5.00	2.50	Rookies		
660 Ray Culp	5.00	2.50	Dusty Baker (R)		
661 Chuck Tanner	5.00	2.50	Don Baylor (R)		
662 Mike Hedlund	5.00	2.50	Tom Paciorek (R)		
663 Marv Staehle	5.00	2.50	710 Sonny Siebert	5.00	2.50
664 MajorLeague	5.00	2.50	711 Larry Stahl	5.00	2.50
Rookies			712 Jose Martinez	5.00	2.50
Archie Reynolds (R)			713 Mike Marshall	5.00	2.50
Bob Reynolds (R)			714 Dick Williams	5.00	2.50
Ken Reynolds (R)			715 Horace Clarke	5.00	2.50
665 Ron Swoboda	7.50	3.75	716 Dave Leonhard	5.00	2.50
666 Gene Brabender	5.00	2.50	717 Tommie Aaron	5.00	2.50
667 Pete Ward	5.00	2.50	718 Billy Wynne	5.00	2.50
668 Gary Neibauer	5.00	2.50	719 Jerry May	5.00	2.50
669 Ike Brown	5.00	2.50	720 Matty Alou	5.00	2.50
670 Bill Hands	5.00	2.50	721 John Morris	5.00	2.50
671 Bill Voss	5.00	2.50	722 Astros Team	8.00	4.00
672 Ed Crosby	5.00	2.50	723 Vicente Romo	5.00	2.50
673 Gerry Janeski	5.00	2.50	724 Tom Tischinski	5.00	2.50
674 Expos Team	8.00	4.00	725 Gary Gentry	5.00	2.50
675 Dave Boswell	5.00	2.50	726 Paul Popovich	5.00	2.50
676 Tommie Reynolds	5.00	2.50	727 Ray Lamb	5.00	2.50
677 Jack DiLauro	5.00	2.50	728 N.L. Rookies	5.00	2.50
678 George Thomas	5.00	2.50	Keith Lampard (R)		
679 Don O'Riley	5.00	2.50	Wayne Redmond (R)		
680 Don Mincher	5.00	2.50	Bernie Williams		
681 Bill Butler	5.00	2.50	729 Dick Billings	5.00	2.50
682 Terry Harmon	5.00	2.50	730 Jim Rooker	5.00	2.50
683 Bill Burbach	5.00	2.50	731 Jim Qualls	5.00	2.50
684 Curt Motton	5.00	2.50	732 Bob Reed	5.00	2.50
685 Moe Drabowsky	5.00	2.50	733 Lee Maye	5.00	2.50
686 Chico Ruiz	5.00	2.50	734 Rob Gardner	5.00	2.50
687 Ron Taylor	5.00	2.50	735 Mike Shannon	5.00	2.50
688 Sparky Anderson	8.00	4.00	736 Mel Queen	5.00	2.50

737	Preston Gomez	5.00	2.50
738	Russ Gibson	5.00	2.50
739	Barry Lersch	5.00	2.50
740	Luis Aparicio	18.00	9.00
741	Skip Guinn	5.00	2.50
742	Royals Team	8.00	4.00
743	John O'Donoghue	5.00	2.50
744	Chuck Manuel	5.00	2.50
745	Sandy Alomar	5.00	2.50
746	Andy Kosco	5.00	2.50
747	N.L. Rookies	5.00	2.50
	Balor Moore (R)		
	Al Severinsen		
	Scipio Spinks		
748	John Purdin	5.00	2.50
749	Ken Szotkiewicz	5.00	2.50
750	Denny McLain	8.00	4.00
751	Al Weis	6.00	3.00
752	Dick Drago	6.00	3.00

1972 Topps

This 787-card set features several Topps innovations. Card fronts include large color photos wrapped in an arch-style frame. Team names appear in multi-colored letters at the top of the photo across the arch. Players' names are found at the bottom of the photograph. With this set Topps introduced their "In-Action" subset (IA), Traded cards (TR), Trophy cards and Childhood photos. Regular features include League Leaders, World Series and Playoff highlights. All cards measure 2-1/2" by 3-1/2".

	NR/MT	EX
Complete Set (787)	2,100.00	1,050.00
Commons (1-394)	.80	.40
Commons (395-525)	1.25	.60

		NR/MT	EX
Commons (526-656)		3.00	1.50
Commons (657-787)		6.00	3.00
1	World Champions (Pirates)	7.50	3.75
2	Ray Culp	.80	.40
3	Bobby Tolan	.80	.40
4	Checklist 1-132	3.00	1.50
5	John Bateman	.80	.40
6	Fred Scherman	.80	.40
7	Enzo Hernandez	.80	.40
8	Ron Swoboda	1.00	.50
9	Stan Williams	.80	.40
10	Amos Otis	1.00	.50
11	Bobby Valentine	1.00	.50
12	Jose Cardenal	.80	.40
13	Joe Grzenda	.80	.40
14	Phillies Rookies	.80	.40
	Pete Koegel		
	Mike Anderson (R)		
	Wayne Twitchell		
15	Walt Williams	.80	.40
16	Mike Jorgensen	.80	.40
17	Dave Duncan	.80	.40
18a	Juan Pizarro (Green Line Unders C and S)	3.00	1.50
18b	Juan Pizarro (Yellow Line Under C and S)	.80	.40
19	Billy Cowan	.80	.40
20	Don Wilson	.80	.40
21	Braves Team	1.50	.75
22	Rob Gardner	.80	.40
23	Ted Kubiak	.80	.40
24	Ted Ford	.80	.40
25	Bill Singer	.80	.40
26	Andy Etchebarren	.80	.40
27	Bob Johnson	.80	.40
28	Twins Rookies	.80	.40
	Steve Brye (R)		
	Bob Gebhard (R)		
	Hal Haydel (R)		
29a	Bill Bonham (Green Line)	3.00	1.50
29b	Bill Bonham (Yellow Line)	.80	.40
30	Rico Petrocelli	.90	.45
31	Cleon Jones	.80	.40
32	Cleon Jones IA	.80	.40
33	Billy Martin	4.00	2.00
34	Billy Martin IA	1.50	.75
35	Jerry Johnson	.80	.40
36	Jerry Johnson IA	.80	.40
37	Carl Yastrzemski	15.00	7.50
38	Carl Yastrzemski IA	7.50	3.25
39	Bob Barton	.80	.40
40	Bob Barton IA	.80	.40

41	Tommy Davis	1.25	.60
42	Tommy Davis IA	1.00	.50
43	Rick Wise	.80	.40
44	Rick Wise IA	.80	.40
45a	Glenn Beckert (Green Line)	3.00	1.50
45b	Glenn Beckert (Yellow Line)	.80	.40
46	Glenn Beckert IA	.80	.40
47	John Ellis	.80	.40
48	John Ellis IA	.80	.40
49	Willie Mays	28.00	14.00
50	Willie Mays IA	12.00	6.00
51	Harmon Killebrew	7.00	3.50
52	Harmon Killebrew IA	3.00	1.50
53	Bud Harrelson	.90	.60
54	Bud Harrelson IA	.80	.40
55	Clyde Wright	.80	.40
56	Rich Chiles	.80	.40
57	Bob Oliver	.80	.40
58	Ernie McAnally	.80	.40
59	Fred Stanley	.80	.40
60	Manny Sanguillen	1.00	.50
61	Cubs Rookies Gene Hiser Burt Hooton (R) Earl Stephenson (R)	1.25	.60
62	Angel Mangual	.80	.40
63	Duke Sims	.80	.40
64	Pete Broberg	.80	.40
65	Cesar Cedeno	1.50	.75
66	Ray Corbin	.80	.40
67	Red Schoendienst	1.00	.50
68	Jim York	.80	.40
69	Roger Freed	.80	.40
70	Mike Cuellar	1.00	.50
71	Angels Team	1.50	.75
72	Bruce Kison (R)	.80	.40
73	Steve Huntz	.80	.40
74	Cecil Upshaw	.80	.40
75	Bert Campaneris	1.25	.60
76	Don Carrithers	.80	.40
77	Ron Theobald	.80	.40
78	Steve Arlin	.80	.40
79	Red Sox Rookies Cecil Cooper (R) Carlton Fisk (R) Mike Garman (R)	130.00	65.00
80	Tony Perez	6.00	3.00
81	Mike Hedlund	.80	.40
82	Ron Woods	.80	.40
83	Dalton Jones	.80	.40
84	Vince Colbert	.80	.40
85	N.L. Batting Leaders	1.00	.50
86	A.L. Batting Leaders	1.25	.60
87	N.L. RBI Leaders	4.00	2.00
88	A.L. RBI Leaders	4.00	2.00
89	N.L. HR Leaders	4.00	2.00
90	A.L. HR Leaders	5.00	2.50
91	N.L. ERA Leaders	3.50	1.75
92	A.L. ERA Leaders	3.50	1.75
93	N.L. Pitching Leaders	4.00	2.00
94	A.L. Pitching Leaders	4.00	2.00
95	N.L. Strikeout Ldrs	4.00	2.00
96	A.L. Strikeout Ldrs	3.50	1.75
97	Tom Kelley	.80	.40
98	Chuck Tanner	.80	.40
99	Ross Grimsley	.80	.40
100	Frank Robinson	7.00	3.50
101	Astros Rookies Ray Busse (R) Bill Grief (R) J.R. Richard (R)	2.00	1.00
102	Lloyd Allen	.80	.40
103	Checklist 133-263	3.00	1.50
104	Toby Harrah (R)	2.00	1.00
105	Gary Gentry	.80	.40
106	Brewers Team	1.25	.60
107	Jose Cruz (R)	2.50	1.25
108	Gary Waslewski	.80	.40
109	Jerry May	.80	.40
110	Ron Hunt	.80	.40
111	Jim Grant	.80	.40
112	Greg Luzinski	1.50	.75
113	Rogelio Moret	.80	.40
114	Bill Buckner	2.00	1.00
115	Jim Fregosi	1.00	.50
116	Ed Farmer (R)	.80	.40
117a	Cleo James (Green Line)	3.00	1.50
117b	Cleo James (Yellow Line)	.80	.50
118	Skip Lockwood	.80	.40
119	Marty Perez	.80	.40
120	Bill Freehan	1.00	.50
121	Ed Sprague	.80	.40
122	Larry Biittner	.80	.40
123	Ed Acosta	.80	.40
124	Yankees Rookies Alan Closter (R) Roger Hambright (R) Rusty Torres (R)	.80	.50
125	Dave Cash	.80	.40
126	Bary Johnson	.80	.40
127	Duffy Dyer	.80	.40
128	Eddie Watt	.80	.40
129	Charlie Fox	.80	.40
130	Bob Gibson	7.50	3.25
131	Jim Nettles	.80	.40
132	Joe Morgan	7.50	3.25
133	Joe Keough	.80	.40
134	Carl Morton	.80	.40
135	Vada Pinson	1.25	.60
136	Darrel Chaney	.80	.40
137	Dick Williams	.80	.40
138	Mike Kekich	.80	.40

139 Tim McCarver	1.00	.50
140 Pat Dobson	.80	.40
141 Mets Rookies	1.25	.60
Buzz Capra (R)		
Jon Matlack		
Leroy Stanton		
142 Chris Chambliss (R)	3.50	1.75
143 Garry Jestadt	.80	.40
144 Marty Pattin	.80	.40
145 Don Kessinger	1.00	.80
146 Steve Kealey	.80	.40
147 Dave Kingman (R)	6.00	3.00
148 Dick Billings	.80	.40
149 Gary Neibauer	.80	.40
150 Norm Cash	1.50	.75
151 Jim Brewer	.80	.40
152 Gene Clines	.80	.40
153 Rick Auerbach	.80	.40
154 Ted Simmons	2.50	1.25
155 Larry Dierker	.80	.40
156 Twins Team	1.25	.60
157 Don Gullett	1.00	.50
158 Jerry Kenney	.80	.40
159 John Boccabela	.80	.40
160 Andy Messersmith	.80	.40
161 Brock Davis	.80	.40
162 Brewers Rookies	1.25	.60
Jerry Bell (R)		
Darrell Porter (R)		
Bob Reynolds (R)		
163 Tug McGraw	1.50	.75
164 Tug McGraw IA	1.00	.50
165 Chris Speier (R)	1.50	.75
166 Chris Speier IA	1.00	.50
167 Deron Johnson	.80	.40
168 Deron Johnson IA	.80	.40
169 Vida Blue	2.00	1.00
170 Vida Blue IA	1.25	.60
171 Darrell Evans	2.50	1.25
172 Darrell Evans IA	1.25	.60
173 Clay Kirby	.80	.40
174 Clay Kirby IA	.80	.40
175 Tom Haller	.80	.40
176 Tom Haller IA	.80	.40
177 Paul Schaal	.80	.40
178 Paul Schaal IA	.80	.40
179 Dock Ellis	.80	.40
180 Dock Ellis IA	.80	.40
181 Ed Kranepool	1.00	.50
182 Ed Kranepool IA	.80	.40
183 Bill Melton	.80	.40
184 Bill Melton IA	.80	.40
185 Ron Bryant	.80	.40
186 Ron Bryant IA	.80	.40
187 Gates Brown	.80	.40
188 Frank Lucchesi	.80	.40
189 Gene Tenace	1.00	.50
190 Dave Giusti	.80	.40
191 Jeff Burroughs (R)	1.50	.75
192 Cubs Team	1.25	.60
193 Kurt Bevacqua (R)	.80	.40
194 Fred Norman	.80	.40
195 Orlando Cepeda	3.00	1.50
196 Mel Queen	.80	.40
197 Johnny Briggs	.80	.40
198 Dodgers Rookies	4.00	2.00
Charlie Hough (R)		
Bob O'Brien (R)		
Mike Strahler (R)		
199 Mike Fiore	.80	.40
200 Lou Brock	7.50	3.25
201 Phil Roof	.80	.40
202 Scipio Spinks	.80	.40
203 Ron Blomberg (R)	.80	.40
204 Tommy Helms	.80	.40
205 Dick Drago	.80	.40
206 Dal Maxvill	.80	.40
207 Tom Egan	.80	.40
208 Milt Pappas	.80	.40
209 Joe Rudi	1.00	.50
210 Denny McLain	1.50	.75
211 Gary Sutherland	.80	.40
212 Grant Jackson	.80	.40
213 Angels Rookies	.80	.50
Art Kusnyer (R)		
Billy Parker (R)		
Tom Silverio (R)		
214 Mike McQueen	.80	.40
215 Alex Johnson	.80	.40
216 Joe Niekro	1.00	.50
217 Roger Metzger	.80	.40
218 Eddie Kasko	.80	.40
219 Rennie Stennett (R)	1.50	.75
220 Jim Perry	.80	.40
221 N.L. Playoffs (Bucs)	1.25	.60
222 A.L. Playoffs (Orioles)	2.00	1.00
223 World Series Game 1	1.25	.60
224 World Series Game 2	1.25	.60
225 World Series Game 3	1.25	.60
226 World Series Game 4	2.50	1.25
227 World Series Game 5	1.25	.60
228 World Series Game 6	1.25	.60
229 World Series Game 7	1.25	.60
230 WS (Celebration)	1.25	.60
231 Casey Cox	.80	.40
232 Giants Rookies	.80	.50
Chris Arnold (R)		
Jim Barr (R)		
Dave Rader (R)		
233 Jay Johnstone	1.00	.50
234 Ron Taylor	.80	.40
235 Merv Rettenmund	.80	.40
236 Jim McGlothlin	.80	.40
237 Yankees Team	1.25	.60
238 Leron Lee	.80	.40
239 Tom Timmermann	.80	.40

240 Rich Allen	3.00	1.50	293 Danny Frisella	.80	.40
241 Rollie Fingers	8.00	4.00	294 Danny Frisella IA	.80	.40
242 Don Mincher	.80	.40	295 Dick Dietz	.80	.40
243 Frank Linzy	.80	.40	296 Dick Dietz IA	.80	.40
244 Steve Braun	.80	.40	297 Claude Osteen	1.00	.50
245 Tommie Agee	.80	.40	298 Claude Osteen IA	.80	.40
246 Tom Burgmeier	.80	.40	299 Hank Aaron	36.00	18.00
247 Milt May	.80	.40	300 Hank Aaron IA	16.00	8.00
248 Tom Bradley	.80	.40	301 George Mitterwald	.80	.40
249 Harry Walker	.80	.40	302 George Mitterwald IA	.80	.40
250 Boog Powell	1.25	.60	303 Joe Pepitone	1.00	.50
251 Checklist 264-394	3.00	1.50	304 Joe Pepitone IA	.80	.40
252 Ken Reynolds	.80	.40	305 Ken Boswell	.80	.40
253 Sandy Alomar	.80	.40	306 Ken Boswell IA	.80	.40
254 Boots Day	.80	.40	307 Steve Renko	.80	.40
255 Jim Lonborg	1.00	.50	308 Steve Renko IA	.80	.40
256 George Foster	2.50	1.25	309 Roberto Clemente	35.00	17.50
257 Tigers Rookies	.80	.40	310 Roberto Clemente IA	15.00	7.50
Jim Foor (R)			311 Clay Carroll	.80	.40
Tim Hosley (R)			312 Clay Carroll IA	.80	.40
Paul Jata (R)			313 Luis Aparicio	3.50	1.75
258 Randy Hundley	.80	.40	314 Luis Aparicio IA	1.50	.75
259 Sparky Lyle	1.50	.75	315 Paul Splittorff	.80	.40
260 Ralph Garr	.80	.40	316 Cardinals Rookies	1.25	.60
261 Steve Mingori	.80	.40	Jim Bibby (R)		
262 Padres Team	1.25	.60	Santiago Guzman (R)		
263 Felipe Alou	1.50	.75	Jorge Roque (R)		
264 Tommy John	2.50	1.25	317 Rich Hand	.80	.40
265 Wes Parker	.80	.40	318 Sonny Jackson	.80	.40
266 Bobby Bolin	.80	.40	319 Aurelio Rodriguez	.80	.40
267 Dave Concepcion	4.00	2.00	320 Steve Blass	.80	.40
268 A's Rookies	.80	.50	321 Joe Lohoud	.80	.40
Dwain Anderson (R)			322 Jose Pena	.80	.40
Chris Floethe (R)			323 Earl Weaver	1.50	.75
269 Don Hahn	.80	.40	324 Mike Ryan	.80	.40
270 Jim Palmer	16.00	8.00	325 Mel Stottlemyre	1.00	.50
271 Ken Rudolph	.80	.40	326 Pat Kelly	.80	.40
272 Mickey Rivers (R)	1.50	.75	327 Steve Stone (R)	1.50	.75
273 Bobby Floyd	.80	.40	328 Red Sox Team	1.25	.80
274 Al Severinsen	.80	.40	329 Roy Foster	.80	.40
275 Cesar Tovar	.80	.40	330 Jim Hunter	5.00	2.50
276 Gene Mauch	.80	.40	331 Stan Swanson	.80	.40
277 Elliott Maddox	.80	.40	332 Buck Martinez	.80	.40
278 Dennis Higgins	.80	.40	333 Steve Barber	.80	.40
279 Larry Brown	.80	.40	334 Rangers Rookies	.80	.40
280 Willie McCovey	7.50	3.25	Bill Fahey (R)		
281 Bill Parsons	.80	.40	Jim Mason (R)		
282 Astros Team	1.25	.60	Tom Ragland (R)		
283 Darrell Brandon	.80	.40	335 Bill Hands	.80	.40
284 Ike Brown	.80	.40	336 Marty Martinez	.80	.40
285 Gaylord Perry	8.00	4.00	337 Mike Kilkenny	.80	.40
286 Gene Alley	.80	.40	338 Bob Grich	1.50	.75
287 Jim Hardin	.80	.40	339 Ron Cook	.80	.40
288 Johnny Jeter	.80	.40	340 Roy White	.80	.40
289 Syd O'Brien	.80	.40	341 Joe Torre (Child)	1.00	.50
290 Sonny Siebert	.80	.40	342 Wilbur Wood (Child)	.80	.50
291 Hal McRae	2.00	1.00	343 Willie Stargell (Child)	1.50	.75
292 Hal McRae IA	1.00	.50	344 Dave McNally (Child)	.80	.40

345 Rick Wise (Child)	.80	.40	396 Paul Lindblad	1.25	.60
346 Jim Fregosi (Child)	.80	.40	397 Phillies Team	2.00	1.00
347 Tom Seaver (Child)	3.50	1.75	398 Larry Hisle	1.25	.60
348 Sal Bando (Child)	.80	.50	399 Milt Wilcox	1.25	.60
349 Al Fitzmorris	.80	.40	400 Tony Oliva	2.50	1.25
350 Frank Howard	1.25	.60	401 Jim Nash	1.25	.60
351 Braves Rookies	1.00	.50	402 Bobby Heise	1.25	.60
Jimmy Britton (R)			403 John Cumberland	1.25	.60
Tom House			404 Jeff Torborg	1.50	.75
Rick Kester			405 Ron Fairly	1.25	.60
352 Dave LaRoche	.80	.40	406 George Hendrick (R)	2.00	1.00
353 Art Shamsky	.80	.40	407 Chuck Taylor	1.25	.60
354 Tom Murphy	.80	.40	408 Jim Northrup	1.25	.60
355 Bob Watson	1.25	.60	409 Frank Baker	1.25	.60
356 Gerry Moses	.80	.40	410 Ferguson Jenkins	8.00	4.00
357 Woodie Fryman	.80	.40	411 Bob Montgomery	1.25	.60
358 Sparky Anderson	1.25	.60	412 Dick Kelley	1.25	.60
359 Don Pavletich	.80	.40	413 White Sox Rookies	1.25	.60
360 Dave Roberts	.80	.40	Don Eddy (R)		
361 Mike Andrews	.80	.40	Dave Lemonds (R)		
362 Mets Team	1.25	.60	414 Bob Miller	1.25	.60
363 Ron Klimkowski	.80	.40	415 Cookie Rojas	1.25	.60
364 Johnny Callison	.80	.40	416 Johnny Edwards	1.25	.60
365 Dick Bosman	.80	.40	417 Tom Hall	1.25	.60
366 Jimmy Rosario	.80	.40	418 Tom Shopay	1.25	.60
367 Ron Perranoski	.80	.40	419 Jim Spencer	1.25	.60
368 Danny Thompson	.80	.40	420 Steve Carlton	30.00	15.00
369 Jim Lefebvre	1.00	.50	421 Ellie Rodriguez	1.25	.60
370 Don Buford	.80	.40	422 Ray Lamb	1.25	.60
371 Denny Lemaster	.80	.40	423 Oscar Gamble	1.50	.75
372 Royals Rookies	.80	.40	424 Bill Gogolewski	1.25	.60
Lance Clemons (R)			425 Ken Singleton	2.00	1.00
Monty Montgomery			426 Ken Singleton IA	1.50	.75
373 John Mayberry	1.25	.60	427 Tito Fuentes	1.25	.60
374 Jack Heidemann	.80	.40	428 Tito Fuentes IA	1.25	.60
375 Reggie Cleveland	.80	.40	429 Bob Robertson	1.25	.60
376 Andy Kosco	.80	.40	430 Bob Robertson IA	1.25	.60
377 Terry Harmon	.80	.40	431 Cito Gaston	1.25	.60
378 Checklist 395-525	3.00	1.50	432 Cito Gaston IA	1.25	.60
379 Ken Berry	.80	.40	433 Johnny Bench	48.00	24.00
380 Earl Williams	.80	.40	434 Johnny Bench IA	20.00	10.00
381 White Sox Team	1.25	.60	435 Reggie Jackson	55.00	27.50
382 Joe Gibbon	.80	.40	436 Reggie Jackson IA	24.00	12.00
383 Brant Alyea	.80	.40	437 Maury Wills	2.50	1.25
384 Dave Campbell	.80	.40	438 Maury Wills IA	1.50	.75
385 Mickey Stanley	1.00	.50	439 Billy Williams	7.00	3.50
386 Jim Colborn	.80	.40	440 Billy Williams IA	2.50	1.25
387 Horace Clarke	.80	.40	441 Thurman Munson	18.00	9.00
388 Charlie Williams	.80	.40	442 Thurman Munson IA	8.50	4.25
389 Bill Rigney	.80	.40	443 Ken Henderson	1.25	.60
390 Willie Davis	1.00	.50	444 Ken Henderson IA	1.25	.60
391 Ken Sanders	.80	.40	445 Tom Seaver	45.00	22.50
392 Pirates Rookies	1.25	.60	446 Tom Seaver IA	20.00	10.00
Fred Cambria (R)			447 Willie Stargell	7.50	3.25
Richie Zisk (R)			448 Willie Stargell IA	3.00	1.50
393 Curt Motton	.80	.40	449 Bob Lemon	1.50	.75
394 Ken Forsch	.80	.40	450 Mickey Lolich	2.00	1.00
395 Matty Alou	1.50	.75	451 Tony LaRussa	1.50	.75

452 Ed Herrmann	1.25	.60
453 Barry Lersch	1.25	.60
454 A's Team	2.00	1.00
455 Tommy Harper	1.25	.60
456 Mark Belanger	1.50	.75
457 Padres Rookies	1.25	.60
Darcy Fast (R)		
Mike Ivie (R)		
Derrell Thomas (R)		
458 Aurelio Monteagudo	1.25	.60
459 Rick Renick	1.25	.60
460 Al Downing	1.25	.60
461 Tim Cullen	1.25	.60
462 Rickey Clark	1.25	.60
463 Bernie Carbo	1.25	.60
464 Jim Roland	1.25	.60
465 Gil Hodges	5.00	2.50
466 Norm Miller	1.25	.60
467 Steve Kline	1.25	.60
468 Richie Scheinblum	1.25	.60
469 Ron Herbel	1.25	.60
470 Ray Fosse	1.25	.60
471 Luke Walker	1.25	.60
472 Phil Gagliano	1.25	.60
473 Dan McGinn	1.25	.60
474 Orioles Rookies	4.50	2.25
Don Baylor		
Roric Harrison (R)		
Johnny Oates (R)		
475 Gary Nolan	1.25	.60
476 Lee Richard	1.25	.60
477 Tom Phoebus	1.25	.60
478 Checklist 526-656	3.00	1.50
479 Don Shaw	1.25	.60
480 Lee May	1.25	.60
481 Billy Conigliaro	1.25	.60
482 Joe Hoerner	1.25	.60
483 Ken Suarez	1.25	.60
484 Lum Harris	1.25	.60
485 Phil Regan	1.25	.60
486 John Lowenstein	1.25	.60
487 Tigers Team	2.00	1.25
488 Mike Nagy	1.25	.60
489 Expos Rookies	1.25	.60
Terry Humphrey (R)		
Keith Lampard		
490 Dave McNally	1.50	.75
491 Lou Piniella (Child)	1.50	.75
492 Mel Stottlemyre(Child)	1.25	.60
493 Bob Bailey (Child)	1.25	.60
494 Willie Horton (Child)	1.25	.60
495 Bill Melton (Child)	1.25	.60
496 Bud Harrelson (Child)	1.25	.60
497 Jim Perry (Child)	1.25	.60
498 Brooks Robinson	2.50	1.25
(Child)		
499 Vicente Romo	1.25	.60
500 Joe Torre	2.00	1.00

501 Pete Hamm	1.25	.60
502 Jackie Hernandez	1.25	.60
503 Gary Peters	1.25	.60
504 Ed Spiezio	1.25	.60
505 Mike Marshall	1.50	.75
506 Indians Rookies	1.25	.60
Terry Ley (R)		
Jim Moyer (R)		
Dick Tidrow (R)		
507 Fred Gladding	1.25	.60
508 Ellie Hendricks	1.25	.60
509 Don McMahon	1.25	.60
510 Ted Williams	8.00	4.00
511 Tony Taylor	1.25	.60
512 Paul Popovich	1.25	.60
513 Lindy McDaniel	1.25	.60
514 Ted Sizemore	1.25	.60
515 Bert Blyleven	14.00	7.00
516 Oscar Brown	1.25	.60
517 Ken Brett	1.25	.60
518 Wayne Garrett	1.25	.60
519 Ted Abernathy	1.25	.60
520 Larry Bowa	1.50	.75
521 Alan Foster	1.25	.60
522 Dodgers Team	2.00	1.00
523 Chuck Dobson	1.25	.60
524 Reds Rookies	1.25	.60
Ed Armbrister (R)		
Mel Behney (R)		
525 Carlos May	1.25	.60
526 Bob Bailey	3.00	1.50
527 Dave Leonhard	3.00	1.50
528 Ron Stone	3.00	1.50
529 Dave Nelson	3.00	1.50
530 Don Sutton	7.50	3.25
531 Freddie Patek	3.00	1.50
532 Fred Kendall	3.00	1.50
533 Ralph Houk	4.00	2.00
534 Jim Hickman	3.00	1.50
535 Ed Brinkman	3.00	1.50
536 Doug Rader	3.00	1.50
537 Bob Locker	3.00	1.50
538 Charlie Sands	3.00	1.50
539 Terry Forster (R)	3.50	1.75
540 Felix Milan	3.00	1.50
541 Roger Repoz	3.00	1.50
542 Jack Billingham	3.00	1.50
543 Duane Josephson	3.00	1.50
544 Ted Martinez	3.00	1.50
545 Wayne Granger	3.00	1.50
546 Joe Hague	3.00	1.50
547 Indians Team	4.50	2.25
548 Frank Reberger	3.00	1.50
549 Dave May	3.00	1.50
550 Brooks Robinson	26.00	13.00
551 Ollie Brown	3.00	1.50
552 Ollie Brown IA	3.00	1.50
553 Wilbur Wood	3.00	1.50

554	Wilbur Wood IA	3.00	1.50	612	Joe Decker	3.00	1.50
555	Ron Santo	5.00	2.50	613	Mike Ferraro	3.00	1.50
556	Ron Santo IA	3.50	1.75	614	Ted Uhlaender	3.00	1.50
557	John Odom	3.00	1.50	615	Steve Hargan	3.00	1.50
558	John Odom IA	3.00	1.50	616	Joe Ferguson (R)	3.50	1.75
559	Pete Rose	48.00	24.00	617	Royals Team	4.50	2.25
560	Pete Rose IA	20.00	10.00	618	Rich Robertson	3.00	1.50
561	Leo Cardenas	3.00	1.50	619	Rich McKinney	3.00	1.50
562	Leo Cardenas IA	3.00	1.50	620	Phil Niekro	8.00	4.00
563	Ray Sadecki	3.00	1.50	621	Commissioners	3.00	1.50
564	Ray Sadecki IA	3.00	1.50		Award		
565	Reggie Smith	3.00	1.50	622	MVP Award	3.00	1.50
566	Reggie Smith IA	3.00	1.50	623	Cy Young Award	3.00	1.50
567	Juan Marichal	7.00	3.50	624	Minor League Player	3.00	1.50
568	Juan Marichal IA	3.50	1.75	625	Rookie Of the Year	3.00	1.50
569	Ed Kirkpatrick	3.00	1.50	626	Babe Ruth Award	3.00	1.50
570	Ed Kirkpatrick IA	3.00	1.50	627	Moe Drabowsky	3.00	1.50
571	Nate Colbert	3.00	1.50	628	Terry Crowley	3.00	1.50
572	Nate Colbert IA	3.00	1.50	629	Paul Doyle	3.00	1.50
573	Fritz Peterson	3.00	1.50	630	Rich Hebner	3.00	1.50
574	Fritz Peterson IA	3.00	1.50	631	John Strohmayer	3.00	1.50
575	Al Oliver	3.50	1.75	632	Mike Hegan	3.00	1.50
576	Leo Durocher	3.50	1.75	633	Jack Hiatt	3.00	1.50
577	Mike Paul	3.00	1.50	634	Dick Woodson	3.00	1.50
578	Billy Grabarkewitz	3.00	1.50	635	Don Money	3.00	1.50
579	Doyle Alexander (R)	3.50	1.75	636	Bill Lee	3.00	1.50
580	Lou Piniella	3.50	1.75	637	Preston Gomez	3.00	1.50
581	Wade Blasingame	3.00	1.50	638	Ken Wright	3.00	1.50
582	Expos Team	4.50	2.25	639	J.C. Martin	3.00	1.50
583	Darold Knowles	3.00	1.50	640	Joe Coleman	3.00	1.50
584	Jerry McNertney	3.00	1.50	641	Mike Lum	3.00	1.50
585	George Scott	3.50	1.75	642	Denny Riddleberger	3.00	1.50
586	Denis Menke	3.00	1.50	643	Russ Gibson	3.00	1.50
587	Billy Wilson	3.00	1.50	644	Bernie Allen	3.00	1.50
588	Jim Holt	3.00	1.50	645	Jim Maloney	3.00	1.50
589	Hal Lanier	3.00	1.50	646	Chico Salmon	3.00	1.50
590	Graig Nettles	4.50	2.25	647	Bob Moose	3.00	1.50
591	Paul Casanova	3.00	1.50	648	Jim Lyttle	3.00	1.50
592	Lew Krausse	3.00	1.50	649	Pete Richert	3.00	1.50
593	Rich Morales	3.00	1.50	650	Sal Bando	3.50	1.75
594	Jim Beauchamp	3.00	1.50	651	Reds Team	4.50	2.25
595	Nolan Ryan	250.00	125.00	652	Marcelino Lopez	3.00	1.50
596	Manny Mota	3.50	1.75	653	Jim Fairey	3.00	1.50
597	Jim Magnuson	3.00	1.50	654	Horacio Pina	3.00	1.50
598	Hal King	3.00	1.50	655	Jerry Grote	3.00	1.50
599	Billy Champion	3.00	1.50	656	Rudy May	3.00	1.50
600	Al Kaline	24.00	12.00	657	Bobby Wine	6.00	3.00
601	George Stone	3.00	1.50	658	Steve Dunning	6.00	3.00
602	Dave Bristol	3.00	1.50	659	Bob Aspromonte	6.00	3.00
603	Jim Ray	3.00	1.50	660	Paul Blair	6.00	3.00
604	Checklist 657-787	4.00	2.00	661	Bill Virdon	6.00	3.00
605	Nelson Briles	3.00	1.50	662	Stan Bahnsen	6.00	3.00
606	Luis Melendez	3.00	1.50	663	Fran Healy	6.00	3.00
607	Frank Duffy	3.00	1.50	664	Bobby Knoop	6.00	3.00
608	Mike Corkins	3.00	1.50	665	Chris Short	6.00	3.00
609	Tom Grieve	3.00	1.50	666	Hector Torres	6.00	3.00
610	Bill Stoneman	3.00	1.50	667	Ray Newman	6.00	3.00
611	Rich Reese	3.00	1.50	668	Rangers Team	10.00	5.00

669 Willie Crawford	6.00	3.00		John Curtis (R)		
670 Ken Holtzman	6.00	3.00		Rich Hinton (R)		
671 Donn Clendenon	6.00	3.00		Mickey Scott (R)		
672 Archie Reynolds	6.00	3.00	725 Dick McAuliffe	6.00	3.00
673 Dave Marshall	6.00	3.00	726 Dick Selma	6.00	3.00
674 John Kennedy	6.00	3.00	727 Jose Laboy	6.00	3.00
675 Pat Jarvis	6.00	3.00	728 Gail Hopkins	6.00	3.00
676 Danny Cater	6.00	3.00	729 Bob Veale	6.00	3.00
677 Ivan Murrell	6.00	3.00	730 Rick Monday	6.50	3.25
678 Steve Luebber	6.00	3.00	731 Orioles Team	10.00	5.00
679 Astros Rookies	6.00	3.00	732 George Culver	6.00	3.00
Bob Fenwick (R)			733 Jim Hart	6.00	3.00
Bob Stinson			734 Bob Burda	6.00	3.00
680 Dave Johnson	6.00	3.00	735 Diego Segui	6.00	3.00
681 Bobby Pfeil	6.00	3.00	736 Bill Russell	7.00	3.50
682 Mike McCormick	6.00	3.00	737 Lenny Randle (R)	6.00	3.00
683 Steve Hovley	6.00	3.00	738 Jim Merritt	6.00	3.00
684 Hal Breeden	6.00	3.00	739 Don Mason	6.00	3.00
685 Joe Horlen	6.00	3.00	740 Rico Carty	6.00	3.00
686 Steve Garvey	80.00	40.00	741 Major League	8.50	4.25
687 Del Unser	6.00	3.00	Rookies		
688 Cardinals Team	8.50	4.25	Tom Hutton		
689 Eddie Fisher	6.00	3.00	Rick Miller (R)		
690 Willie Montanez	6.00	3.00	John Milner (R)		
691 Curt Blefary	6.00	3.00	742 Jim Rooker	6.00	3.00
692 Curt Blefary IA	6.00	3.00	743 Cesar Gutierrez	6.00	3.00
693 Alan Gallagher	6.00	3.00	744 Jim Slaton (R)	6.00	3.00
694 Alan Gallagher IA	6.00	3.00 ·	745 Julian Javier	6.00	3.00
695 Rod Carew	110.00	55.00	746 Lowell Palmer	6.00	3.00
696 Rod Carew IA	48.00	24.00	747 Jim Stewart	6.00	3.00
697 Jerry Koosman	10.00	5.00	748 Phil Hennigan	6.00	3.00
698 Jerry Koosman IA	7.00	3.50	749 Walter Alston	7.50	3.75
699 Bobby Murcer	10.00	5.00	750 Willie Horton	6.50	3.25
700 Bobby Murcer IA	7.00	3.50	751 Steve Carlton	65.00	32.50
701 Jose Pagan	6.00	3.00	752 Joe Morgan	48.00	24.00
702 Jose Pagan IA	6.00	·3.00	753 Denny McLain	12.00	6.00
703 Doug Griffin	6.00	3.00	754 Frank Robinson	40.00	20.00
704 Doug Griffin IA	6.00	3.00	755 Jim Fregosi	6.00	3.00
705 Pat Corrales	6.00	3.00	756 Rick Wise	6.00	3.00
706 Pat Corrales IA	6.00	3.00	757 Jose Cardenal	6.00	3.00
707 Tim Foli	6.00	3.00	758 Gil Garrido	6.00	3.00
708 Tim Foli IA	6.00	3.00	759 Chris Cannizzaro	6.00	3.00
709 Jim Kaat	9.00	4.50	760 Bill Mazeroski	8.00	4.00
710 Jim Kaat IA	6.50	3.25	761 Major League	18.00	9.00
711 Bobby Bonds	15.00	7.50	Rookies		
712 Bobby Bonds IA	9.00	4.50	Ron Cey (R)		
713 Gene Michael	6.00	3.00	Ben Oglivie (R)		
714 Gene Michael IA	6.00	3.00	Bernie Williams		
715 Mike Epstein	6.00	3.00	762 Wayne Simpson	6.00	3.00
716 Jesus Alou	6.00	3.00	763 Ron Hansen	6.00	3.00
717 Bruce Dal Canton	6.00	3.00	764 Dusty Baker	7.50	3.75
718 Del Rice	6.00	3.00	765 Ken McMullen	6.00	3.00
719 Cesar Geronimo	6.00	3.00	766 Steve Hamilton	6.00	3.00
720 Sam McDowell	6.50	3.25	767 Tom McCraw	6.00	3.00
721 Eddie Leon	6.00	3.00	768 Denny Doyle	6.00	3.00
722 Bill Sudakis	6.00	3.00	769 Jack Aker	6.00	3.00
723 Al Santorini	6.00	3.00	770 Jim Wynn	7.00	3.50
724 A.L. Rookies	6.00	3.00	771 Giants Team	8.50	4.25

		NR/MT	EX
772	Ken Tatum	6.00	3.00
773	Ron Brand	6.00	3.00
774	Luis Alvarado	6.00	3.00
775	Jerry Reuss	6.00	3.00
776	Bill Voss	6.00	3.00
777	Hoyt Wilhelm	18.00	9.00
778	Twins Rookies	8.50	4.25
	Vic Albury (R)		
	Rick Dempsey (R)		
	Jim Strickland (R)		
779	Tony Cloninger	6.00	3.00
780	Dick Green	6.00	3.00
781	Jim McAndrew	6.00	3.00
782	Larry Stahl	6.00	3.00
783	Les Cain	6.00	3.00
784	Ken Aspromonte	6.00	3.00
785	Vic Davalillo	6.00	3.00
786	Chuck Brinkman	6.00	3.00
787	Ron Reed	6.00	3.00

1973 Topps

Topps reduced the size of their set to 660-cards in 1973. The 2-1/2" by 3-1/2" cards feature color photos on the card fronts and vertical card backs. Topps introduced a new subset called All-Time Leaders. Other key subsets include League Leaders, World Series and Playoff Highlights, Childhood Cards and Rookies.

	NR/MT	EX
Complete Set (660)	1,250.00	600.00
Commons (1-396)	.50	.25
Commons (397-528)	1.10	.55
Commons (529-660)	2.50	1.25

		NR/MT	EX
1	All Time HR Leaders	32.00	16.00
	(Hank Aaron, Willie		
	Mays, Babe Ruth)		
2	Rich Hebner	.50	.25
3	Jim Lonborg	.75	.35
4	John Milner	.50	.25
5	Ed Brinkman	.50	.25
6	Mac Scarce	.50	.25
7	Rangers Team	.50	.25
8	Tom Hall	.50	.25
9	Johnny Oates	.75	.35
10	Don Sutton	3.50	1.75
11	Chris Chambliss	.75	.35
12	Padres Mgr/Coaches	.75	.35
13	George Hendrick	.75	.35
14	Sonny Siebert	.50	.25
15	Ralph Garr	.60	.30
16	Steve Braun	.50	.25
17	Fred Gladding	.50	.25
18	Leroy Stanton	.50	.25
19	Tim Foli	.50	.25
20	Stan Bahnsen	.50	.25
21	Randy Hundley	.50	.25
22	Ted Abernathy	.50	.25
23	Dave Kingman	1.25	.60
24	Al Santorini	.50	.25
25	Roy White	.50	.25
26	Pirates Team	1.00	.50
27	Bill Gogolewski	.50	.25
28	Hal McRae	1.50	.75
29	Tony Taylor	.50	.25
30	Tug McGraw	1.25	.60
31	Buddy Bell (R)	3.00	1.50
32	Fred Norman	.50	.25
33	Jim Breazeale	.50	.25
34	Pat Dobson	.60	.30
35	Willie Davis	.60	.30
36	Steve Barber	.50	.25
37	Bill Robinson	.60	.30
38	Mike Epstein	.50	.25
39	Dave Roberts	.50	.25
40	Reggie Smith	.80	.40
41	Tom Walker	.50	.25
42	Mike Andrews	.50	.25
43	Randy Moffitt (R)	.50	.25
44	Rick Monday	.75	.35
45	Ellie Rodriguez	.50	.25
	(Wrong Photo)		
46	Lindy McDaniel	.50	.25
47	Luis Melendez	.50	.25
48	Paul Splittorff	.50	.25
49	Twins Mgr./Coaches	.75	.45
50	Roberto Clemente	36.00	18.00
51	Chuck Seelbach	.50	.25
52	Denis Menke	.50	.25
53	Steve Dunning	.50	.25
54	Checklist 1-132	2.00	1.00
55	Jon Matlack	.75	.35

No.	Player	Price	Price
56	Merv Rettenmund	.50	.25
57	Derrel Thomas	.50	.25
58	Mike Paul	.50	.25
59	Steve Yeager (R)	1.25	.60
60	Ken Holtzman	.50	.25
61	Batting Leaders	3.00	1.50
62	Home Run Leaders	3.00	1.50
63	RBI Leaders	3.00	1.50
64	Stolen Base Leaders	2.00	1.00
65	ERA Leaders	2.00	1.00
66	Victory Leaders	3.00	1.50
67	Strikeout Leaders	12.00	6.00
	(Ryan/Carlton)		
68	Leading Firemen	1.50	.75
69	Phil Gagliano	.50	.25
70	Milt Pappas	.50	.25
71	Johnny Briggs	.50	.25
72	Ron Reed	.50	.25
73	Ed Herrmann	.50	.25
74	Billy Champion	.50	.25
75	Vada Pinson	1.00	.50
76	Doug Rader	.75	.35
77	Mike Torrez	.50	.25
78	Richie Scheinblum	.50	.25
79	Jim Willoughby	.50	.25
80	Tony Oliva	1.50	.75
81a	Cubs Mgr./Coaches	1.25	.60
82	Fritz Peterson	.50	.25
83	Leron Lee	.50	.25
84	Rollie Fingers	7.50	3.75
85	Ted Simmons	2.00	1.00
86	Tom McCraw	.50	.25
87	Ken Boswell	.50	.25
88	Mickey Stanley	.60	.30
89	Jack Billingham	.50	.25
90	Brooks Robinson	8.00	4.00
91	Dodgers Team	1.25	.60
92	Jerry Bell	.50	.25
93	Jesus Alou	.50	.25
94	Dick Billings	.50	.25
95	Steve Blass	.50	.25
96	Doug Griffin	.50	.25
97	Willie Montanez	.50	.25
98	Dick Woodson	.50	.25
99	Carl Taylor	.50	.25
100	Hank Aaron	30.00	15.00
101	Ken Henderson	.50	.25
102	Rudy May	.50	.25
103	Celerino Sanchez	.50	.25
104	Reggie Cleveland	.50	.25
105	Carlos May	.50	.25
106	Terry Humphrey	.50	.25
107	Phil Hennigan	.50	.25
108	Bill Russell	.80	.40
109	Doyle Alexander	.60	.30
110	Bob Watson	1.00	.50
111	Dave Nelson	.50	.25
112	Gary Ross	.50	.25
113	Jerry Grote	.50	.25
114	Lynn McGlothen	.50	.25
115	Ron Santo	1.25	.60
116	Yankees Mgr/	1.00	.50
	Coaches		
117	Ramon Hernandez	.50	.25
118	John Mayberry	.75	.35
119	Larry Bowa	.90	.45
120	Joe Coleman	.50	.25
121	Dave Rader	.50	.25
122	Jim Strickland	.50	.25
123	Sandy Alomar	.50	.25
124	Jim Hardin	.50	.25
125	Ron Fairly	.50	.25
126	Jim Brewer	.50	.25
127	Brewers Team	1.25	.60
128	Ted Sizemore	.60	.30
129	Terry Forster	.50	.25
130	Pete Rose	20.00	10.00
131	Red Sox Mgr/Coaches	.75	.35
132	Matty Alou	.90	.45
133	Dave Roberts	.50	.25
134	Milt Wilcox	.50	.25
135	Lee May	.50	.25
136	Orioles Mgr/Coaches	.90	.45
137	Jim Beauchamp	.50	.25
138	Horacio Pina	.50	.25
139	Carmen Fanzone	.50	.25
140	Lou Piniella	1.25	.60
141	Bruce Kison	.50	.25
142	Thurman Munson	8.50	4.25
143	John Curtis	.50	.25
144	Marty Perez	.50	.25
145	Bobby Bonds	3.00	1.50
146	Woodie Fryman	.50	.25
147	Mike Anderson	.50	.25
148	Dave Goltz	.50	.25
149	Ron Hunt	.50	.25
150	Wilbur Wood	.50	.25
151	Wes Parker	.50	.25
152	Dave May	.50	.25
153	Al Hrabosky	.75	.35
154	Jeff Torborg	.75	.35
155	Sal Bando	.75	.35
156	Cesar Geronimo	.50	.25
157	Denny Riddleberger	.50	.25
158	Astros Team	1.25	.60
159	Cito Gaston	.50	.25
160	Jim Palmer	12.00	6.00
161	Ted Martinez	.50	.25
162	Pete Broberg	.50	.25
163	Vic Davalillo	.50	.25
164	Monty Montgomery	.50	.25
165	Luis Aparicio	3.00	1.50
166	Terry Harmon	.50	.25
167	Steve Stone	.75	.45
168	Jim Northrup	.50	.25
169	Ron Schueler	.50	.25

No.	Player	Price 1	Price 2
170	Harmon Killebrew	6.50	3.25
171	Bernie Carbo	.50	.25
172	Steve Kline	.50	.25
173	Hal Breeden	.50	.25
174	Rich Gossage (R)	24.00	12.00
175	Frank Robinson	7.50	3.75
176	Chuck Taylor	.50	.25
177	Bill Plummer (R)	.75	.35
178	Don Rose	.50	.25
179	A's Mgr./Coaches	.75	.35
180	Fergie Jenkins	6.00	3.00
181	Jack Brohamer	.50	.25
182	Mike Caldwell	.50	.25
183	Don Buford	.50	.25
184	Jerry Koosman	1.00	.50
185	Jim Wynn	.75	.35
186	Bill Fahey	.50	.25
187	Luke Walker	.50	.25
188	Cookie Rojas	.50	.25
189	Greg Luzinski	.80	.40
190	Bob Gibson	7.00	3.50
191	Tigers Team	1.25	.60
192	Pat Jarvis	.50	.25
193	Carlton Fisk	48.00	24.00
194	Jorge Orta	.50	.25
195	Clay Carroll	.50	.25
196	Ken McMullen	.50	.25
197	Ed Goodson	.50	.25
198	Horace Clarke	.50	.25
199	Bert Blyleven	5.00	2.50
200	Billy Williams	5.00	2.50
201	A.L. Playoffs	1.00	.50
202	N.L. Playoffs	1.00	.50
203	World Series Game 1	1.25	.60
204	World Series Game 2	1.25	.60
205	World Series Game 3	1.25	.60
206	World Series Game 4	1.25	.60
207	World Series Game 5	1.25	.60
208	World Series Game 6	1.25	.60
209	World Series Game 7	1.25	.60
210	WS Champions	1.25	.60
211	Balor Moore	.50	.25
212	Joe Lohoud	.50	.25
213	Steve Garvey	16.00	8.00
214	Dave Hamilton	.50	.25
215	Dusty Baker	1.00	.50
216	Toby Harrah	.60	.30
217	Don Wilson	.50	.25
218	Aurelio Rodriguez	.50	.25
219	Cardinals Team	1.25	.60
220	Nolan Ryan	100.00	50.00
221	Fred Kendall	.50	.25
222	Rob Gardner	.50	.25
223	Bud Harrelson	.75	.35
224	Bill Lee	.60	.30
225	Al Oliver	1.25	.60
226	Ray Fosse	.50	.25
227	Wayne Twitchell	.50	.25
228	Bobby Darwin	.50	.25
229	Roric Harrison	.50	.25
230	Joe Morgan	7.00	3.50
231	Bill Parsons	.50	.25
232	Ken Singleton	.75	.35
233	Ed Kirkpatrick	.50	.25
234	Bill North (R)	.75	.45
235	Jim Hunter	5.00	2.50
236	Tito Fuentes	.50	.25
237	Braves Mgr/Coaches	1.00	.50
238	Tony Muser	.50	.25
239	Pete Richert	.50	.25
240	Bobby Murcer	.90	.45
241	Dwain Anderson	.50	.25
242	George Culver	.50	.25
243	Angels Team	1.25	.60
244	Ed Acosta	.50	.25
245	Carl Yastrzemski	15.00	7.50
246	Ken Sanders	.50	.25
247	Del Unser	.50	.25
248	Jerry Johnson	.50	.25
249	Larry Bittner	.50	.25
250	Manny Sanguillen	.75	.35
251	Roger Nelson	.50	.25
252	Giants Mgr/Coaches	.75	.35
253	Mark Belanger	.80	.40
254	Bill Stoneman	.50	.25
255	Reggie Jackson	38.00	19.00
256	Chris Zachary	.50	.25
257	Mets Mgr/Coaches	2.00	1.00
258	Tommy John	1.50	.75
259	Jim Holt	.50	.25
260	Gary Nolan	.50	.25
261	Pat Kelly	.50	.25
262	Jack Aker	.50	.25
263	George Scott	.60	.35
264	Checklist 133-264	2.00	1.00
265	Gene Michael	.50	.25
266	Mike Lum	.50	.25
267	Lloyd Allen	.50	.25
268	Jerry Morales	.50	.25
269	Tim McCarver	1.00	.50
270	Luis Tiant	1.25	.60
271	Tom Hutton	.50	.25
272	Ed Farmer	.50	.25
273	Chris Speier	.50	.25
274	Darold Knowles	.50	.25
275	Tony Perez	5.00	2.50
276	Joe Lovitto	.50	.25
277	Bob Miller	.50	.25
278	Orioles Team	1.25	.60
279	Mike Strahler	.50	.25
280	Al Kaline	7.00	3.50
281	Mike Jorgensen	.50	.25
282	Steve Hovley	.50	.25
283	Ray Sadecki	.50	.25
284	Glenn Borgmann	.50	.25
285	Don Kessinger	.75	.35

286 Frank Linzy	.50	.25	
287 Eddie Leon	.50	.25	
288 Gary Gentry	.50	.25	
289 Bob Oliver	.50	.25	
290 Cesar Cedeno	1.00	.50	
291 Rogelio Moret	.50	.25	
292 Jose Cruz	1.25	.60	
293 Bernie Allen	.50	.25	
294 Steve Arlin	.50	.25	
295 Bert Campaneris	1.00	.50	
296 Reds Mgr/Coaches	1.25	.60	
297 Walt Williams	.50	.25	
298 Ron Bryant	.50	.25	
299 Ted Ford	.50	.25	
300 Steve Carlton	18.00	9.00	
301 Billy Grabarkewitz	.50	.25	
302 Terry Crowley	.50	.25	
303 Nelson Briles	.50	.25	
304 Duke Sims	.50	.25	
305 Willie Mays	38.00	19.00	
306 Tom Burgmeier	.50	.25	
307 Boots Day	.50	.25	
308 Skip Lockwood	.50	.25	
309 Paul Popovich	.50	.25	
310 Dick Allen	1.50	.75	
311 Joe Decker	.50	.25	
312 Oscar Brown	.50	.25	
313 Jim Ray	.50	.25	
314 Ron Swoboda	.75	.35	
315 John Odom	.50	.25	
316 Padres Team	1.25	.60	
317 Danny Cater	.50	.25	
318 Jim McGlothlin	.50	.25	
319 Jim Spencer	.50	.25	
320 Lou Brock	7.50	3.75	
321 Rich Hinton	.50	.25	
322 Garry Maddox (R)	1.25	.60	
323 Tigers Mgr/Coaches	1.25	.60	
324 Al Downing	.50	.25	
325 Boog Powell	1.00	.50	
326 Darrell Brandon	.50	.25	
327 John Lowenstein	.50	.25	
328 Bill Bonham	.50	.25	
329 Ed Kranepool	1.00	.50	
330 Rod Carew	18.00	9.00	
331 Carl Morton	.50	.25	
332 John Felski	.50	.25	
333 Gene Clines	.50	.25	
334 Freddie Patek	.50	.25	
335 Bob Tolan	.50	.25	
336 Tom Bradley	.50	.25	
337 Dave Duncan	.50	.25	
338 Checklist 265-396	2.00	1.00	
339 Dick Tidrow	.50	.25	
340 Nate Colbert	.50	.25	
341 Jim Palmer (Child)	1.50	.75	
342 Sam McDowell (Child)	.60	.30	
343 Bobby Murcer (Child)	.75	.35	
344 Jim Hunter (Child)	1.25	.60	
345 Chris Speier (Child)	.60	.30	
346 Gaylord Perry (Child)	1.50	.75	
347 Royals Team	1.25	.60	
348 Rennie Stennett	.90	.45	
349 Dick McAuliffe	.50	.25	
350 Tom Seaver	32.00	16.00	
351 Jimmy Stewart	.50	.25	
352 Don Stanhouse	.50	.25	
353 Steve Brye	.50	.25	
354 Billy Parker	.50	.25	
355 Mike Marshall	.60	.30	
356 White Sox Mgr/Coaches	.75	.35	
357 Ross Grimsley	.50	.25	
358 Jim Nettles	.50	.25	
359 Cecil Upshaw	.50	.25	
360 Joe Rudi (Wrong Photo)	1.25	.60	
361 Fran Healy	.50	.25	
362 Eddie Watt	.50	.25	
363 Jackie Hernandez	.50	.25	
364 Rick Wise	.60	.30	
365 Rico Petrocelli	.60	.30	
366 Brock Davis	.50	.25	
367 Burt Hooton	.60	.30	
368 Bill Buckner	1.25	.60	
369 Lerrin LaGrow	.50	.25	
370 Willie Stargell	7.00	3.50	
371 Mike Kekich	.50	.25	
372 Oscar Gamble	.60	.30	
373 Clyde Wright	.50	.25	
374 Darrell Evans	1.25	.60	
375 Larry Dierker	.50	.25	
376 Frank Duffy	.50	.25	
377 Expos Mgr/Coaches	.75	.35	
378 Lenny Randle	.50	.25	
379 Cy Acosta	.50	.25	
380 Johnny Bench	32.00	16.00	
381 Vincente Romo	.50	.25	
382 Mike Hegan	.50	.25	
383 Diego Segui	.50	.25	
384 Don Baylor	2.50	1.25	
385 Jim Perry	.75	.35	
386 Don Money	.50	.25	
387 Jim Barr	.50	.25	
388 Ben Oglivie	.60	.30	
389 Mets Team	2.50	1.25	
390 Mickey Lolich	.50	.25	
391 Lee Lacy (R)	.80	.50	
392 Dick Drago	.50	.25	
393 Jose Cardenal	.50	.25	
394 Sparky Lyle	1.00	.50	
395 Roger Metzger	.60	.30	
396 Grant Jackson	.50	.25	
397 Dave Cash	1.10	.55	
398 Rich Hand	1.10	.55	
399 George Foster	2.00	1.00	

No.	Player	Price	Price
400	Gaylord Perry	6.00	3.00
401	Clyde Mashore	1.10	.55
402	Jack Hiatt	1.10	.55
403	Sonny Jackson	1.10	.55
404	Chuck Brinkman	1.10	.55
405	Cesar Tovar	1.10	.55
406	Paul Lindblad	1.10	.55
407	Felix Millan	1.10	.55
408	Jim Colborn	1.10	.55
409	Ivan Murrell	1.10	.55
410	Willie McCovey	7.00	3.50
411	Ray Corbin	1.10	.55
412	Manny Mota	1.50	.75
413	Tom Timmermann	1.10	.55
414	Ken Rudolph	1.10	.55
415	Marty Pattin	1.10	.55
416	Paul Schaal	1.10	.55
417	Scipio Spinks	1.10	.55
418	Bobby Grich	1.50	.75
419	Casey Cox	1.10	.55
420	Tommie Agee	1.10	.55
421	Angels Mgr/Coaches	1.50	.75
422	Bob Robertson	1.10	.55
423	Johnny Jeter	1.10	.55
424	Denny Doyle	1.10	.55
425	Alex Johnson	1.10	.55
426	Dave LaRoche	1.10	.55
427	Rick Auerbach	1.10	.55
428	Wayne Simpson	1.10	.55
429	Jim Fairey	1.10	.55
430	Vida Blue	2.00	1.00
431	Gerry Moses	1.10	.55
432	Dan Frisella	1.10	.55
433	Willie Horton	1.50	.75
434	Giants Team	2.00	1.00
435	Rico Carty	1.50	.75
436	Jim McAndrew	1.10	.55
437	John Kennedy	1.10	.55
438	Enzo Hernandez	1.10	.55
439	Eddie Fisher	1.10	.55
440	Glenn Beckert	1.10	.55
441	Gail Hopkins	1.10	.55
442	Dick Dietz	1.10	.55
443	Danny Thompson	1.10	.55
444	Ken Brett	1.10	.55
445	Ken Berry	1.10	.55
446	Jerry Reuss	1.50	.75
447	Joe Hague	1.10	.55
448	John Hiller	1.10	.55
449	Indians Mgr/Coaches	2.50	1.25
450	Joe Torre	1.50	.75
451	John Vukovich	1.10	.55
452	Paul Casanova	1.10	.55
453	Checklist 397-528	2.00	1.00
454	Tom Haller	1.10	.55
455	Bill Melton	1.10	.55
456	Dick Green	1.10	.55
457	John Strohmayer	1.10	.55
458	Jim Mason	1.10	.55
459	Jimmy Howarth	1.10	.55
460	Bill Freehan	1.50	.75
461	Mike Corkins	1.10	.55
462	Ron Blomberg	1.10	.55
463	Ken Tatum	1.10	.55
464	Cubs Team	2.00	1.00
465	Dave Giusti	1.10	.55
466	Jose Arcia	1.10	.55
467	Mike Ryan	1.10	.55
468	Tom Griffin	1.10	.55
469	Dan Monzon	1.10	.55
470	Mike Cuellar	1.50	.75
471	Hit Leader (Ty Cobb)	5.00	2.50
472	Grand Slam Leader (Lou Gehrig)	6.00	3.00
473	Total Base Leader (Hank Aaron)	6.00	3.00
474	R.B.I. Leader (Babe Ruth)	7.50	3.75
475	Batting Leader (Ty Cobb)	5.00	2.50
476	Shutout Leader (Walter Johnson)	3.50	1.75
477	Victory Leader (Cy Young)	3.50	1.75
478	Strikeout Leader (Walter Johnson)	3.50	1.75
479	Hal Lanier	1.10	.55
480	Juan Marichal	5.00	2.50
481	White Sox Team	2.00	1.00
482	Rick Reuschel (R)	4.50	2.25
483	Dal Maxvill	1.10	.55
484	Ernie McAnally	1.10	.55
485	Norm Cash	1.50	.75
486	Phillies Mgr/Coaches	1.50	.75
487	Bruce Dal Canton	1.10	.55
488	Dave Campbell	1.10	.55
489	Jeff Burroughs	1.50	.75
490	Claude Osteen	1.10	.55
491	Bob Montgomery	1.10	.55
492	Pedro Borbon	1.10	.55
493	Duffy Dyer	1.10	.55
494	Rich Morales	1.10	.55
495	Tommy Helms	1.10	.55
496	Ray Lamb	1.10	.55
497	Cardinals Mgr/Coaches	1.50	.75
498	Graig Nettles	3.00	1.50
499	Bob Moose	1.10	.55
500	A's Team	2.00	1.00
501	Larry Gura	1.10	.55
502	Bobby Valentine	1.50	.75
503	Phil Niekro	7.00	3.50
504	Earl Williams	1.10	.55
505	Bob Bailey	1.10	.55
506	Bart Johnson	1.10	.55

507 Darrel Chaney	1.10	.55
508 Gates Brown	1.10	.55
509 Jim Nash	1.10	.55
510 Amos Otis	1.50	.75
511 Sam McDowell	1.25	.60
512 Dalton Jones	1.10	.55
513 Dave Marshall	1.10	.55
514 Jerry Kenney	1.10	.55
515 Andy Messersmith	1.10	.55
516 Danny Walton	1.10	.55
517 Pirates Mgr/Coaches	1.50	.75
518 Bob Veale	1.10	.55
519 John Edwards	1.10	.55
520 Mel Stottlemyre	1.50	.75
521 Braves Team	2.00	1.00
522 Leo Cardenas	1.10	.55
523 Wayne Granger	1.10	.55
524 Gene Tenace	1.50	.75
525 Jim Fregosi	1.25	.60
526 Ollie Brown	1.10	.55
527 Dan McGinn	1.10	.55
528 Paul Blair	1.10	.55
529 Milt May	2.50	1.25
530 Jim Kaat	4.00	2.00
531 Ron Woods	2.50	1.25
532 Steve Mingori	2.50	1.25
533 Larry Stahl	2.50	1.25
534 Dave Lemonds	2.50	1.25
535 John Callison	2.50	1.25
536 Phillies Team	4.00	2.00
537 Bill Slayback	2.50	1.25
538 Jim Hart	2.50	1.25
539 Tom Murphy	2.50	1.25
540 Cleon Jones	2.50	1.25
541 Bob Bolin	2.50	1.25
542 Pat Corrales	2.50	1.25
543 Alan Foster	2.50	1.25
544 Von Joshua	2.50	1.25
545 Orlando Cepeda	4.00	2.00
546 Jim York	2.50	1.25
547 Bobby Heise	2.50	1.25
548 Don Durham	2.50	1.25
549 Rangers Mgr/Coaches	3.50	1.75
550 Dave Johnson	2.50	1.25
551 Mike Kilkenny	2.50	1.25
552 J.C. Martin	2.50	1.25
553 Mickey Scott	2.50	1.25
554 Dave Concepcion	5.00	2.50
555 Bill Hands	2.50	1.25
556 Yankees Team	6.00	3.00
557 Bernie Williams	2.50	1.25
558 Jerry May	2.50	1.25
559 Barry Lersch	2.50	1.25
560 Frank Howard	4.00	2.00
561 Jim Geddes	2.50	1.25
562 Wayne Garrett	2.50	1.25
563 Larry Haney	2.50	1.25
564 Mike Thompson	2.50	1.25
565 Jim Hickman	2.50	1.25
566 Lew Krause	2.50	1.25
567 Bob Fenwick	2.50	1.25
568 Ray Newman	2.50	1.25
569 Dodgers Mgr/Coaches	4.50	2.25
570 Bill Singer	2.50	1.25
571 Rusty Torres	2.50	1.25
572 Gary Sutherland	2.50	1.25
573 Fred Beene	2.50	1.25
574 Bob Didier	2.50	1.25
575 Dock Ellis	2.50	1.25
576 Expos Team	4.00	2.00
577 Eric Soderholm (R)	2.50	1.25
578 Ken Wright	2.50	1.25
579 Tom Grieve	2.50	1.25
580 Joe Pepitone	3.00	1.50
581 Steve Kealey	2.50	1.25
582 Darrell Porter	2.50	1.25
583 Bill Greif	2.50	1.25
584 Chris Arnold	2.50	1.25
585 Joe Niekro	2.50	1.25
586 Bill Sudakis	2.50	1.25
587 Rich McKinney	2.50	1.25
588 Checklist 529-660	2.50	1.25
589 Ken Forsch	2.50	1.25
590 Deron Johnson	2.50	1.25
591 Mike Hedlund	2.50	1.25
592 John Boccabella	2.50	1.25
593 Royals Mgr/Coaches	3.00	1.50
594 Vic Harris	2.50	1.25
595 Don Gullett	3.00	1.50
596 Red Sox Team	4.00	2.00
597 Mickey Rivers	3.50	1.75
598 Phil Roof	2.50	1.25
599 Ed Crosby	2.50	1.25
600 Dave McNally	3.00	1.50
601 Rookie Catchers	2.50	1.25
George Pena (R)		
Sergio Robles (R)		
Rick Stelmaszek (R)		
602 Rookie Pitchers	2.50	1.25
Mel Behney (R)		
Ralph Garcia (R)		
Doug Rau (R)		
603 Rookie Third Basemen	2.50	1.25
Terry Hughes (R)		
Bill McNulty (R)		
Ken Reitz (R)		
604 Rookie Pitchers	2.50	1.25
Jesse Jefferson (R)		
Dennis O'Toole (R)		
Bob Strampe (R)		
605 Rookie First Basemen	3.00	1.50
Pat Bourque (R)		

Enos Cabell (R)
Gonzalo Marquez (R)

606 Rookie Outfielders 5.00 2.50
Gary Matthews (R)
Tom Paciorek
Jorge Roque (R)

607 Rookie Shortstops 2.50 1.25
Ray Busse (R)
Pepe Frias (R)
Mario Guerrero (R)

608 Rookie Pitchers 3.00 1.50
Steve Busby (R)
Dick Colpaert (R)
George Medich (R)

609 Rookie 5.00 2.50
Second Basemen
Larvell Blanks (R)
Pedro Garcia (R)
Davey Lopes (R)

610 Rookie Pitchers 3.00 1.50
Jimmy Freeman (R)
Charlie Hough
Hank Webb (R)

611 Rookie Outfielders 3.00 1.50
Rich Coggins (R)
Jim Wohlford (R)
Richie Zisk

612 Rookie Pitchers 2.50 1.25
Steve Lawson (R)
Bob Reynolds (R)
Brent Strom (R)

613 Rookie Catchers 45.00 22.50
Bob Boone (R)
Mike Ivie (R)
Skip Jutze (R)

614 Rookie Outfielders 70.00 35.00
Al Bumbry (R)
Dwight Evans (R)
Charlie Spikes (R)

615 Rookie Third- 500.00 250.00
Basemen
Ron Cey
John Hilton (R)
Mike Schmidt (R)

616 Rookie Pitchers 2.50 1.25
Norm Angelini (R)
Steve Blateric (R)
Mike Garman (R)

617 Rich Chiles 2.50 1.25
618 Andy Etchebarren 2.50 1.25
619 Billy Wilson 2.50 1.25
620 Tommy Harper 2.50 1.25
621 Joe Ferguson 2.80 1.40
622 Larry Hisle 2.50 1.25
623 Steve Renko 2.50 1.25
624 Astros Mgr/Coaches 4.00 2.00
625 Angel Mangual 2.50 1.25
626 Bob Barton 2.50 1.25

627 Luis Alvarado 2.50 1.25
628 Jim Slaton 2.50 1.25
629 Indians Team 4.00 2.00
630 Denny McLain 4.00 2.00
631 Tom Matchick 2.50 1.25
632 Dick Selma 2.50 1.25
633 Ike Brown 2.50 1.25
634 Alan Closter 2.50 1.25
635 Gene Alley 2.50 1.25
636 Rick Clark 2.50 1.25
637 Norm Niller 2.50 1.25
638 Ken Reynolds 2.50 1.25
639 Willie Crawford 2.50 1.25
640 Dick Bosman 2.50 1.25
641 Reds Team 4.00 2.00
642 Jose Laboy 2.50 1.25
643 Al Fitzmorris 2.50 1.25
644 Jack Heidemann 2.50 1.25
645 Bob Locker 2.50 1.25
646 Brewers 4.00 2.00
Mgr/Coaches
647 George Stone 2.50 1.25
648 Tom Egan 2.50 1.25
649 Rich Folkers 2.50 1.25
650 Felipe Alou 3.50 1.75
651 Don Carrithers 2.50 1.25
652 Ted Kubiak 2.50 1.25
653 Joe Hoerner 2.50 1.25
654 Twins Team 4.00 2.00
655 Clay Kirby 2.50 1.25
656 John Ellis 2.50 1.25
657 Bob Johnson 2.50 1.25
658 Elliott Maddox 2.50 1.25
659 Jose Pagan 2.50 1.25
660 Fred Scherman 2.50 1.25

1974 Topps

This 660-card set marks the first time
Topps released their cards all at once,
rather than in series. Card fronts feature

four-color photos framed by white borders. Card backs are horizontal. Cards meaurse 2-1/2" by 3-1/2". The set contains fifteen variations concerning the San Diego Padres who were on the verge of moving to Washington D.C. Cards with Washington printed on them are worth considerably more than those with San Diego. Those variations are noted in the checklist below but the higher valued cards are not included in the Complete Set price. The 1974 Topps set includes a 6-card tribute to Hank Aaron. Other notable subsets are League Leaders, World Series and Playoff Highlights, All-Stars and Rookies.

		NR/MT	EX
Complete Set (660)		650.00	330.00
Commons (1-660)		.50	.25
1	Hank Aaron	35.00	18.00
2	Hank Aaron (1954-57)	5.00	2.50
3	Hank Aaron (1958-61)	5.00	2.50
4	Hank Aaron (1962-65)	5.00	2.50
5	Hank Aaron (1966-69)	5.0	2.50
6	Hank Aaron (1970-73)	5.00	2.50
7	Jim Hunter	5.00	2.50
8	George Theodore	.50	.25
9	Mickey Lolich	.80	.40
10	Johnny Bench	15.00	7.50
11	Jim Bibby	.50	.25
12	Dave May	.50	.25
13	Tom Hilgendorf	.50	.25
14	Paul Popovich	.50	.25
15	Joe Torre	.80	.40
16	Orioles Team	.80	.40
17	Doug Bird	.50	.25
18	Gary Thomasson	.50	.25
19	Gerry Moses	.50	.25
20	Nolan Ryan	70.00	35.00
21	Bob Gallagher	.50	.25
22	Cy Acosta	.50	.25
23	Craig Robinson	.50	.25
24	John Hiller	.50	.25
25	Ken Singleton	.75	.35
26	Bill Campbell (R)	.50	.25
27	George Scott	.60	.30
28	Manny Sanguillen	.60	.30
29	Phil Niekro	4.50	2.25
30	Bobby Bonds	2.00	1.00
31	Astros Mgr/Coaches	.60	.30
32a	John Grubb (Wash)	7.50	3.75
32b	John Grubb (SD)	.50	.25
33	Don Newhauser	.50	.25
34	Andy Kosco	.50	.25
35	Gaylord Perry	5.00	2.50
36	Cardinals Team	.80	.40
37	Dave Sells	.50	.25
38	Don Kessinger	.60	.30
39	Ken Suarez	.50	.25
40	Jim Palmer	10.00	5.00
41	Bobby Floyd	.50	.25
42	Claude Osteen	.50	.25
43	Jim Wynn	.75	.35
44	Mel Stottlemyre	.60	.30
45	Dave Johnson	.50	.25
46	Pat Kelly	.50	.25
47	Dick Ruthven (R)	.50	.25
48	Dick Sharon	.50	.25
49	Steve Renko	.50	.25
50	Rod Carew	15.00	7.50
51	Bobby Heise	.50	.25
52	Al Oliver	1.00	.50
53a	Fred Kendall (Wash)	7.50	3.75
53b	Fred Kendall (SD)	.50	.25
54	Elias Sosa	.50	.25
55	Frank Robinson	7.00	3.50
56	Mets Team	.80	.50
57	Darold Knowles	.50	.25
58	Charlie Spikes	.50	.25
59	Ross Grimsley	.50	.25
60	Lou Brock	6.00	3.00
61	Luis Aparicio	2.50	1.25
62	Bob Locker	.50	.25
63	Bill Sudakis	.50	.25
64	Doug Rau	.50	.25
65	Amos Otis	.60	.30
66	Sparky Lyle	.75	.35
67	Tommy Helms	.50	.25
68	Grant Jackson	.50	.25
69	Del Unser	.50	.25
70	Dick Allen	1.00	.50
71	Danny Frisella	.50	.25
72	Aurleio Rodriguez	.50	.25
73	Mike Marshall	.60	.30
74	Twins Team	.80	.50
75	Jim Colburn	.50	.25
76	Mickey Rivers	.60	.30
77a	Rich Troedson (Wash)	7.50	3.75
77b	Rich Troedson (SD)	.50	.25
78	Giants Mgr/Coaches	.60	.30
79	Gene Tenace	.75	.35
80	Tom Seaver	24.00	12.00
81	Frank Duffy	.50	.25
82	Dave Giusti	.50	.25
83	Orlando Cepeda	1.25	.60
84	Rick Wise	.60	.30

85	Joe Morgan	7.00	3.50
86	Joe Ferguson	.60	.30
87	Ferguson Jenkins	6.00	3.00
88	Freddie Patek	.50	.25
89	Jackie Brown	.50	.25
90	Bobby Murcer	.75	.35
91	Ken Forsch	.50	.25
92	Paul Blair	.50	.25
93	Rod Gilbreath	.50	.25
94	Tigers Team	.80	.40
95	Steve Carlton	15.00	7.50
96	Jerry Hairston (R)	.50	.25
97	Bob Bailey	.50	.25
98	Bert Blyleven	3.50	1.75
99	Brewers Mgr/Coaches	.60	.30
100	Willie Stargell	6.00	3.00
101	Bobby Valentine	.60	.30
102a	Bill Greif (Wash)	7.50	3.75
102b	Bill Greif (SD)	.50	.25
103	Sal Bando	.60	.30
104	Ron Bryant	.50	.25
105	Carlton Fisk	28.00	14.00
106	Harry Parker	.50	.25
107	Alex Johnson	.50	.25
108	Al Hrabosky	.60	.30
109	Bob Grich	.75	.35
110	Billy Williams	4.50	2.25
111	Clay Carroll	.50	.25
112	Dave Lopes	1.00	.50
113	Dick Drago	.50	.25
114	Angels Team	.80	.50
115	Willie Horton	.60	.30
116	Jerry Reuss	.60	.30
117	Ron Blomberg	.50	.25
118	Bill Lee	.50	.25
119	Phillies Mgr/Coaches	.60	.30
120	Wilbur Wood	.50	.25
121	Larry Lintz	.50	.25
122	Jim Holt	.50	.25
123	Nelson Briles	.50	.25
124	Bob Coluccio	.50	.25
125a	Nate Colbert (Wash)	7.50	3.75
125b	Nate Colbert (SD)	.50	.25
126	Checklist 1-132	1.50	.75
127	Tom Paciorek	.50	.25
128	John Ellis	.50	.25
129	Chris Speier	.50	.25
130	Reggie Jackson	30.00	15.00
131	Bob Boone	4.50	2.25
132	Felix Milan	.50	.25
133	David Clyde (R)	.50	.25
134	Denis Menke	.50	.25
135	Roy White	.50	.25
136	Rick Reuschel	1.00	.50
137	Al Bumbry	.60	.30
138	Ed Brinkman	.50	.25
139	Aurelio Monteagudo	.50	.25
140	Darrell Evans	.75	.35
141	Pat Bourque	.50	.25
142	Pedro Garcia	.50	.25
143	Dick Woodson	.50	.25
144	Dodgers Mgr/Coaches	1.25	.60
145	Dock Ellis	.50	.25
146	Ron Fairly	.50	.25
147	Bart Johnson	.50	.25
148a	Dave Hilton (Wash)	7.50	3.75
148b	Dave Hilton (SD)	.50	.25
149	Mac Scarce	.50	.25
150	John Mayberry	.60	.30
151	Diego Segui	.50	.25
152	Oscar Gamble	.60	.30
153	Jon Matlack	.75	.45
154	Astros Team	.80	.40
155	Bert Campaneris	.75	.45
156	Randy Moffitt	.50	.25
157	Vic Harris	.50	.25
158	Jack Billingham	.50	.25
159	Jim Ray Hart	.50	.25
160	Brooks Robinson	8.00	4.00
161	Ray Burris (R)	.75	.45
162	Bill Freehan	.60	.30
163	Ken Berry	.50	.25
164	Tom House	.50	.25
165	Willie Davis	.60	.30
166	Royals Mgr/Coaches	.80	.40
167	Luis Tiant	.75	.35
168	Danny Thompson	.50	.25
169	Steve Rogers (R)	.75	.35
170	Bill Melton	.50	.25
171	Eduardo Rodriguez	.50	.25
172	Gene Clines	.50	.25
173a	Randy Jones (Wash)	10.00	5.00
173b	Randy Jones (SD)	.50	.25
174	Bill Robinson	.60	.30
175	Reggie Cleveland	.50	.25
176	John Lowenstein	.50	.25
177	Dave Roberts	.50	.25
178	Garry Maddox	.60	.30
179	Mets Mgr/Coaches	1.50	.75
180	Ken Holtzman	.50	.25
181	Cesar Geronimo	.50	.25
182	Lindy McDaniel	.50	.25
183	Johnny Oates	.60	.30
184	Rangers Team	.80	.40
185	Jose Cardenal	.50	.25
186	Fred Scherman	.50	.25
187	Don Baylor	2.00	1.00
188	Rudy Meoli	.50	.25
189	Jim Brewer	.50	.25
190	Tony Oliva	1.50	.75
191	Al Fitzmorris	.50	.25
192	Mario Guerrero	.50	.25
193	Tom Walker	.50	.25
194	Darrell Porter	.50	.25
195	Carlos May	.50	.25
196	Jim Fregosi	.60	.30

197aVincente Romo (Wash)	7.50	3.75	
197bVincente Romo (SD)	.50	.25	
198 Dave Cash	.50	.25	
199 Mike Kekich	.50	.25	
200 Cesar Cedeno	.60	.30	
201 Batting Leaders (Rod Carew, Pete Rose)	6.50	3.25	
202 HR Leaders (Reggie Jackson, Willie Stargell)	7.50	3.25	
203 RBI Leaders (Reggie Jackson, Willie Stargell)	7.50	3.25	
204 Stolen Base Leaders (Lou Brock, Tommy Harper)	1.25	.60	
205 Victory Leaders (Ron Bryant, Wilbur Wood)	1.25	.60	
206 ERA Leaders (Jim Palmer, Tom Seaver)	6.00	3.00	
207 Strikeout Leaders (Nolan Ryan, Tom Seaver)	12.00	6.00	
208 Leading Firemen (John Hiller, Mike Marshall)	1.00	.50	
209 Ted Sizemore	.50	.25	
210 Bill Singer	.50	.25	
211 Cubs Team	.60	.30	
212 Rollie Fingers	7.50	3.75	
213 Dave Rader	.50	.25	
214 Billy Grabarkewitz	.50	.25	
215 Al Kaline	7.00	3.50	
216 Ray Sadecki	.50	.25	
217 Tim Foli	.50	.25	
218 Johnny Briggs	.50	.25	
219 Doug Griffin	.50	.25	
220 Don Sutton	4.50	2.25	
221 White Sox Mgr/Coaches	.80	.50	
222 Ramon Hernandez	.50	.25	
223 Jeff Burroughs	.60	.30	
224 Roger Metzger	.50	.25	
225 Paul Splittorff	.50	.25	
226aWashington Team	10.00	5.00	
226bPadres Team	1.25	.60	
227 Mike Lum	.50	.25	
228 Ted Kubiak	.50	.25	
229 Fritz Peterson	.50	.25	
230 Tony Perez	4.50	2.25	
231 Dick Tidrow	.50	.25	
232 Steve Brye	.50	.25	
233 Jim Barr	.50	.25	
234 John Milner	.50	.25	
235 Dave McNally	.60	.30	
236 Cardinals	.80	.40	

Mgr/Coaches Barney Schultz)	.50	.25	
237 Ken Brett	.50	.25	
238 Fran Healy	.50	.25	
239 Bill Russell	.75	.35	
240 Joe Coleman	.50	.25	
241aGlenn Beckert (Wash)	7.50	3.50	
241bGlenn Beckert (SD)	.50	.25	
242 Bill Gogolewski	.50	.25	
243 Bob Oliver	.50	.25	
244 Carl Morton	.50	.25	
245 Cleon Jones	.50	.25	
246 A's Team	.80	.50	
247 Rick Miller	.50	.25	
248 Tom Hall	.50	.25	
249 George Mitterwald	.50	.25	
250aWillie McCovey (Wash)	32.00	16.00	
250bWillie McCovey (SD)	7.00	3.50	
251 Graig Nettles	2.00	1.00	
252 Dave Parker (R)	36.00	18.00	
253 John Boccabella	.50	.25	
254 Stan Bahnsen	.50	.25	
255 Larry Bowa	.75	.35	
256 Tom Griffin	.50	.25	
257 Buddy Bell	.50	.25	
258 Jerry Morales	.50	.25	
259 Bob Reynolds	.50	.25	
260 Ted Simmons	2.00	1.00	
261 Jerry Bell	.50	.25	
262 Ed Kirkpatrick	.50	.25	
263 Checklist 133-264	1.50	.75	
264 Joe Rudi	.75	.35	
265 Tug McGraw	1.25	.60	
266 Jim Northrup	.50	.25	
267 Andy Messersmith	.50	.25	
268 Tom Grieve	.50	.25	
269 Bob Johnson	.50	.25	
270 Ron Santo	1.00	.50	
271 Bill Hands	.50	.25	
272 Paul Casanova	.50	.25	
273 Checklist 265-396	1.50	.75	
274 Fred Beene	.50	.25	
275 Ron Hunt	.50	.25	
276 Angels Mgr/Coaches	.60	.30	
277 Gary Nolan	.50	.25	
278 Cookie Rojas	.50	.25	
279 Jim Crawford	.50	.25	
280 Carl Yastrzemski	14.00	7.00	
281 Giants Team	.80	.40	
282 Doyle Alexander	.50	.25	
283 Mike Schmidt	100.00	50.00	
284 Dave Duncan	.50	.25	
285 Reggie Smith	.60	.30	
286 Tony Muser	.50	.25	
287 Clay Kirby	.50	.25	
288 Gorman Thomas (R)	2.00	1.00	

289 Rick Auerbach	.50	.25	
290 Vida Blue	.80	.40	
291 Don Hahn	.50	.25	
292 Chuck Seelbach	.50	.25	
293 Milt May	.50	.25	
294 Rick Monday	.75	.45	
296 Ray Corbin	.50	.25	
297 Hal Breeden	.50	.25	
298 Roric Harrison	.50	.25	
299 Gene Michael	.50	.25	
300 Pete Rose	14.00	7.00	
301 Bob Montgomery	.50	.25	
302 Rudy May	.50	.25	
303 George Hendrick	.60	.30	
304 Don Wilson	.50	.25	
305 Tito Fuentes	.50	.25	
306 Orioles Mgr/Coaches	.75	.35	
307 Luis Melendez	.50	.25	
308 Bruce Dal Canton	.50	.25	
309aDave Roberts (Wash)	7.50	3.75	
309bDave Roberts (SD)	.50	.25	
310 Terry Forster	.50	.25	
311 Jerry Grote	.50	.25	
312 Deron Johnson	.50	.25	
313 Barry Lersch	.50	.25	
314 Brewers Team	.80	.40	
315 Ron Cey	1.00	.50	
316 Jim Perry	.60	.30	
317 Richie Zisk	.50	.25	
318 Jim Merritt	.50	.25	
319 Randy Hundley	.50	.25	
320 Dusty Baker	.75	.35	
321 Steve Braun	.50	.25	
322 Ernie McAnally	.50	.25	
323 Richie Scheinblum	.50	.25	
324 Steve Kline	.50	.25	
325 Tommy Harper	.50	.25	
326 Reds Mgr/Coaches	.75	.35	
327 Tom Timmermann	.50	.25	
328 Skip Jutze	.50	.25	
329 Mark Belanger	.75	.35	
330 Juan Marichal	4.00	2.00	
331 All Star Catchers	7.00	3.50	
(Johnny Bench,			
Carlton Fisk)			
332 All Star First Base	5.00	2.50	
(Hank Aaron,			
Dick Allen)			
333 All Star Second Base	4.00	2.00	
(Rod Carew,			
Joe Morgan)			
334 All Star Third Base	4.00	2.00	
(Brooks Robinson,			
Ron Santo)			
335 All Star Shortstops	2.00	1.00	
(Bert Campaneris,			
Chris Speier)			
336 All Star Left Field	4.00	2.00	

(Bobby Murcer,			
Pete Rose)			
337 All Star Center Field	2.00	1.00	
(Cesar Cedeno,			
Amos Otis)			
338 All Star Right Field	5.00	2.50	
(Reggie Jackson,			
Billy Williams)			
339 All Star Pitchers	2.50	1.25	
(Jim Hunter,			
Rick Wise)			
340 Thurman Munson	8.00	4.00	
341 Dan Driessen (R)	1.00	.50	
342 Jim Lonborg	.60	.30	
343 Royals Team	.80	.40	
344 Mike Caldwell	.50	.25	
345 Bill North	.50	.25	
346 Ron Reed	.50	.25	
347 Sandy Alomar	.50	.25	
348 Pete Richert	.50	.25	
349 John Vukovich	.50	.25	
350 Bob Gibson	7.00	3.50	
351 Dwight Evans	16.00	8.00	
352 Bill Stoneman	.50	.25	
353 Rich Coggins	.50	.25	
354 Cubs Mgr/Coaches	.60	.30	
355 Dave Nelson	.50	.25	
356 Jerry Koosman	.75	.35	
357 Buddy Bradford	.50	.25	
358 Dal Maxvill	.50	.25	
359 Brent Strom	.50	.25	
360 Greg Luzinski	.80	.40	
361 Don Carrithers	.50	.25	
362 Hal King	.50	.25	
363 Yankees Team	.80	.40	
364aCito Gaston (Wash)	7.50	3.25	
364bCito Gaston (SD	.50	.25	
365 Steve Busby	.50	.25	
366 Larry Hisle	.50	.25	
367 Norm Cash	.80	.40	
368 Manny Mota	.75	.35	
369 Paul Lindblad	.50	.25	
370 Bob Watson	.75	.35	
371 Jim Slaton	.50	.25	
372 Ken Reitz	.50	.25	
373 John Curtis	.50	.25	
374 Marty Perez	.50	.25	
375 Earl Williams	.50	.25	
376 Jorge Orta	.50	.25	
377 Ron Woods	.50	.25	
378 Burt Hooton	.60	.30	
379 Rangers Mgr/Coaches	1.00	.50	
380 Bud Harrelson	.60	.30	
381 Charlie Sands	.50	.25	
382 Bob Moose	.50	.25	
383 Phillies Team	.80	.40	
384 Chris Chambliss	.60	.30	
385 Don Gullett	.60	.30	

386 Gary Matthews	.60	.30	443 Tom Hutton	.50	.25
387a Rich Morales (Wash)	7.50	3.75	444 Vic Davalillo	.50	.25
387b Rich Morales (SD)	.50	.25	445 George Medich	.50	.25
388 Phil Roof	.50	.25	446 Len Randle	.50	.25
389 Gates Brown	.50	.25	447 Twins Mgr/Coaches	.60	.30
390 Lou Piniella	1.00	.50	448 Ron Hodges	.50	.25
391 Billy Champion	.50	.25	449 Tom McCraw	.50	.25
392 Dick Green	.50	.25	450 Rich Hebner	.50	.25
393 Orlando Pena	.50	.25	451 Tommy John	1.50	.75
394 Ken Henderson	.50	.25	452 Gene Hiser	.50	.25
395 Doug Rader	.50	.25	453 Balor Moore	.50	.25
396 Tommy Davis	.80	.40	454 Kurt Bevacqua	.50	.25
397 George Stone	.50	.25	455 Tom Bradley	.50	.25
398 Duke Sims	.50	.25	456 Dave Winfield (R)	110.00	55.00
399 Mike Paul	.50	.25	457 Chuck Goggin	.50	.25
400 Harmon Killebrew	6.00	3.00	458 Jim Ray	.50	.25
401 Elliott Maddox	.50	.25	459 Reds Team	.80	.40
402 Jim Rooker	.50	.25	460 Boog Powell	.80	.40
403 Red Sox Mgr/Coaches	.60	.30	461 John Odom	.50	.25
404 Jim Howarth	.50	.25	462 Luis Alvarado	.50	.25
405 Ellie Rodriguez	.50	.25	463 Pat Dobson	.50	.25
406 Steve Arlin	.50	.25	464 Jose Cruz	.80	.40
407 Jim Wohlford	.50	.25	465 Dick Bosman	.50	.25
408 Charlie Hough	.60	.30	466 Dick Billings	.50	.25
409 Ike Brown	.50	.25	467 Winston Llenas	.50	.25
410 Pedro Borbon	.50	.25	468 Pepe Frias	.50	.25
411 Frank Baker	.50	.25	469 Joe Decker	.50	.25
412 Chuck Taylor	.50	.25	470 A.L. Playoffs	6.00	3.00
413 Don Money	.50	.25	471 N.L. Playoffs	1.25	.60
414 Checklist 397-528	1.50	.75	472 World Series Game 1	1.25	.60
415 Gary Gentry	.50	.25	473 World Series Game 2	6.00	3.00
416 White Sox Team	.80	.50	474 World Series Game 3	1.25	.60
417 Rich Folkers	.50	.25	475 World Series Game 4	1.25	.60
418 Walt Williams	.50	.25	476 World Series Game 5	1.25	.60
419 Wayne Twitchell	.50	.25	477 World Series Game 6	6.00	3.00
420 Ray Fosse	.50	.25	478 World Series Game 7	1.25	.60
421 Dan Fife	.50	.25	479 WS (Celebration)	1.25	.60
422 Gonzalo Marquez	.50	.25	480 Willie Crawford	.50	.25
423 Fred Stanley	.50	.25	481 Jerry Terrell	.50	.25
424 Jim Beauchamp	.50	.25	482 Bob Didier	.50	.25
425 Pete Broberg	.50	.25	483 Braves Team	.80	.40
426 Rennie Stennett	.60	.30	484 Carmen Fanzone	.50	.25
427 Bobby Bolin	.50	.25	485 Felipe Alou	1.00	.50
428 Gary Sutherland	.50	.25	486 Steve Stone	.60	.30
429 Dick Lange	.50	.25	487 Ted Martinez	.50	.25
430 Matty Alou	.60	.30	488 Andy Etchebarren	.50	.25
431 Gene Garber	.60	.30	489 Pirates Mgr/Coaches	.75	.35
432 Chris Arnold	.50	.25	490 Vada Pinson	.80	.40
433 Lerrin LaGrow	.50	.25	491 Roger Nelson	.50	.25
434 Ken McMullen	.50	.25	492 Mike Rogodzinski	.50	.25
435 Dave Concepcion	2.50	1.25	493 Joe Hoerner	.50	.25
436 Don Hood	.50	.25	494 Ed Goodson	.50	.25
437 Jim Lyttle	.50	.25	495 Dick McAuliffe	.50	.25
438 Ed Herrmann	.50	.25	496 Tom Murphy	.50	.25
439 Norm Miller	.50	.25	497 Bobby Mitchell	.50	.25
440 Jim Kaat	1.00	.50	498 Pat Corrales	.50	.25
441 Tom Ragland	.50	.25	499 Rusty Torres	.50	.25
442 Alan Foster	.50	.25	500 Lee May	.50	.25

501 Eddie Leon	.50	.25
502 Dave LaRoche	.50	.25
503 Eric Soderholm	.50	.25
504 Joe Niekro	.50	.25
505 Bill Buckner	1.00	.50
506 Ed Farmer	.50	.25
507 Larry Stahl	.50	.25
508 Expos Team	.80	.40
509 Jesse Jefferson	.50	.25
510 Wayne Garrett	.50	.25
511 Toby Harrah	.50	.25
512 Joe Lahoud	.50	.25
513 Jim Campanis	.50	.25
514 Paul Schaal	.50	.25
515 Willie Montanez	.50	.25
516 Horacio Pina	.50	.25
517 Mike Hegan	.50	.25
518 Derrel Thomas	.50	.25
519 Bill Sharp	.50	.25
520 Tim McCarver	.75	.35
521 Indians Mgr/Coaches	.60	.30
522 J.R. Richard	.80	.40
523 Cecil Cooper	.60	.30
524 Bill Plummer	.50	.25
525 Clyde Wright	.50	.25
526 Frank Tepedino	.50	.25
527 Bobby Darwin	.50	.25
528 Bill Bonham	.50	.25
529 Horace Clarke	.50	.25
530 Mickey Stanley	.50	.25
531 Expos Mgr/Coaches	.60	.30
532 Skip Lockwood	.50	.25
533 Mike Phillips	.50	.25
534 Eddie Watt	.50	.25
535 Bob Tolan	.50	.25
536 Duffy Dyer	.50	.25
537 Steve Mingori	.50	.25
538 Cesar Tovar	.50	.25
539 Lloyd Allen	.50	.25
540 Bob Robertson	.50	.25
541 Indians Team	.80	.40
542 Rich Gossage	2.50	1.25
543 Danny Cater	.50	.25
544 Ron Schueler	.50	.25
545 Billy Conigliaro	.50	.25
546 Mike Corkins	.50	.25
547 Glenn Borgmann	.50	.25
548 Sonny Siebert	.50	.25
549 Mike Jorgensen	.50	.25
550 Sam McDowell	.60	.30
551 Von Joshua	.50	.25
552 Denny Doyle	.50	.25
553 Jim Willoughby	.50	.25
554 Tim Johnson	.50	.25
555 Woodie Fryman	.50	.25
556 Dave Campbell	.50	.25
557 Jim McGlothin	.50	.25
558 Bill Fahey	.50	.25
559 Darrel Chaney	.50	.25
560 Mike Cuellar	.60	.30
561 Ed Kranepool	.75	.35
562 Jack Aker	.50	.25
563 Hal McRae	.80	.40
564 Mike Ryan	.50	.25
565 Milt Wilcox	.50	.25
566 Jackie Hernandez	.50	.25
567 Red Sox Team	.80	.40
568 Mike Torrez	.50	.25
569 Rick Dempsey	.50	.25
570 Ralph Garr	.60	.30
571 Rich Hand	.50	.25
572 Enzo Hernandez	.50	.25
573 Mike Adams	.50	.25
574 Bill Parsons	.50	.25
575 Steve Garvey	12.00	6.00
576 Scipio Spinks	.50	.25
577 Mike Sadek	.50	.25
578 Ralph Houk	.60	.30
579 Cecil Upshaw	.50	.25
580 Jim Spencer	.50	.25
581 Fred Norman	.50	.25
582 Bucky Dent (R)	2.00	1.00
583 Marty Pattin	.50	.25
584 Ken Rudolph	.50	.25
585 Merv Rettenmund	.50	.25
586 Jack Brohamer	.50	.25
587 Larry Christenson	.50	.25
588 Hal Lanier	.50	.25
589 Boots Day	.50	.25
590 Rogelio Moret	.50	.25
591 Sonny Jackson	.50	.25
592 Ed Bane	.50	.25
593 Steve Yeager	.60	.30
594 Leroy Stanton	.50	.25
595 Steve Blass	.50	.25
596 Rookie Pitchers	.50	.25
Wayne Garland (R)		
Fred Holdsworth (R)		
Mark Littell (R)		
Dick Pole (R)		
597 Rookie Shortstops	.60	.30
Dave Chalk (R)		
John Gamble (R)		
Pete Mackanin (R)		
Manny Trillo (R)		
598 Rookie Outfielders	25.00	12.50
Dave Augustine (R)		
Ken Griffey (R)		
Steve Ontiveros (R)		
Jim Tyrone (R)		
599a Rookie Pitchers	7.50	3.75
Ron Diorio (R)		
Dave Freisleben (R)		
(Wash)		
Frank Riccelli (R)		
Greg Shanahan (R)		

599b Rookie Pitchers	.50	.25	
Ron Diorio (R)			
Dave Freisleben (R)			
(SD)			
Frank Riccelli (R)			
Greg Shanahan (R)			
600 Rookie Infielders	5.00	2.50	
Ron Cash (R)			
Jim Cox (R)			
Bill Madlock (R)			
Reggie Sanders (R)			
601 Rookie Outfielders	5.00	2.50	
Ed Armbrister			
Rich Bladt (R)			
Brian Downing (R)			
Bake McBride (R)			
602 Rookie Pitchers	.50	.25	
Glenn Abbott (R)			
Rick Henninger (R)			
Craig Swan (R)			
Dan Vossler (R)			
603 Rookie Catchers	.75	.35	
Barry Foote (R)			
Tom Lundstedt (R)			
Charlie Moore (R)			
Sergio Robles (R)			
604 Rookie Infielders	4.00	2.00	
Terry Hughes (R)			
John Knox (R)			
Andy Thornton (R)			
Frank White (R)			
605 Rookie Pitchers	3.00	1.50	
Vic Albury (R)			
Ken Frailing (R)			
Kevin Kobel (R)			
Frank Tanana (R)			
606 Rookie Outfielders	.50	.25	
Jim Fuller (R)			
Wilbur Howard (R)			
Tommy Smith (R)			
Otto Velez (R)			
607 Rookie Shortstops	.50	.25	
Leo Foster (R)			
Tom Heintzelman (R)			
Dave Rosello (R)			
Frank Taveras (R)			
608 Rookie Pitchers	.50	.25	
Bob Apodaca (R)			
Dick Baney (R)			
John D'Acquisto (R)			
Mike Wallace (R)			
609 Rico Petrocelli	.60	.30	
610 Dave Kingman	1.25	.60	
611 Rick Stelmaszek	.50	.25	
612 Luke Walker	.50	.25	
613 Dan Monzon	.50	.25	
614 Adrian Devine	.50	.25	
615 Johnny Jeter	.50	.25	
616 Larry Gura	.50	.25
617 Ted Ford	.50	.25
618 Jim Mason	.50	.25
619 Mike Anderson	.50	.25
620 Al Downing	.50	.25
621 Bernie Carbo	.50	.25
622 Phil Gagliano	.50	.25
623 Celerino Sanchez	.50	.25
624 Bob Miller	.50	.25
625 Ollie Brown	.50	.25
626 Pirates Team	.80	.40
627 Carl Taylor	.50	.25
628 Ivan Murrell	.50	.25
629 Rusty Staub	1.00	.50
630 Tommie Agee	.50	.25
631 Steve Barber	.50	.25
632 George Culver	.50	.25
633 Dave Hamilton	.50	.25
634 Braves Mgr/Coaches	1.00	.50
635 John Edwards	.50	.25
636 Dave Goltz	.50	.25
637 Checklist 529-660	1.50	.75
638 Ken Sanders	.50	.25
639 Joe Lovitto	.50	.25
640 Milt Pappas	.50	.25
641 Chuck Brinkman	.50	.25
642 Terry Harmon	.50	.25
643 Dodgers team	.80	.40
644 Wayne Granger	.50	.25
645 Ken Boswell	.50	.25
646 George Foster	1.50	.75
647 Juan Beniquez (R)	.60	.30
648 Terry Crowley	.50	.25
649 Fernando Gonzalez	.50	.25
650 Mike Epstein	.50	.25
651 Leron Lee	.50	.25
652 Gail Hopkins	.50	.25
653 Bob Stinson	.50	.25
654a Jesus Alou	6.00	3.00
(NoPosition Listed)		
654b Jesus Alou (Outfield)	.50	.25
655 Mike Tyson	.50	.25
656 Adrian Garrett	.50	.25
657 Jim Shellenback	.50	.25
658 Lee Lacy	.50	.25
659 Joe Lis	.50	.25
660 Larry Dierker	.50	.25

1974 Topps Traded

This 44-card set marks Topps first baseball update set and features players who changed teams during the season. The 2-1/2" by 3-1/2" cards feature color photos on the front with the word "Traded" printed in bold type below the photographs. Card backs resemble newspaper print. Card numbers are followed by the letter "T" and coincide with the numbers assigned to the traded players in Topps regular edition.

	NR/MT	EX
Complete Set (44)	12.50	6.25
Commons (23-649)	.30	.15
23T Craig Robinson	.30	.15
42T Claude Osteen	.30	.15
43T Jim Wynn	.50	.25
51T Bobby Heise	.30	.15
59T Ross Grimsley	.30	.15
62T Bob Locker	.30	.15
63T Bill Sudakis	.30	.15
73T Mike Marshall	.50	.25
123T Nelson Briles	.30	.15
139T Aurelio Monteagudo	.30	.15
151T Diego Segui	.30	.15
165T Willie Davis	.40	.20
175T Reggie Cleveland	.30	.15
182T Lindy McDaniel	.30	.15
186T Fred Scherman	.30	.15
249T George Mitterwald	.30	.15
262T Ed Kirkpatrick	.30	.15
269T Bob Johnson	.30	.15
270T Ron Santo	.75	.35
313T Barry Lersch	.30	.15
319T Randy Hundley	.30	.15
330T Juan Marichal	2.50	1.25
348T Pete Richert	.30	.15
373T John Curtis	.30	.15
390T Lou Piniella	.75	.35
428T Gary Sutherland	.30	.15
454T Kurt Bevacqua	.30	.15
458T Jim Ray	.30	.15
485T Felipe Alou	.50	.25
486T Steve Stone	.35	.18
496T Tom Murphy	.30	.15
516T Horacio Pina	.30	.15
534T Eddie Watt	.30	.15
538T Cesar Tovar	.30	.15
544T Ron Schueler	.30	.15
579T Cecil Upshaw	.30	.15
585T Merv Rettenmund	.30	.15
612T Luke Walker	.30	.15
616T Larry Gura	.30	.15
618T Jim Mason	.30	.15
530T Tommie Agee	.30	.15
648T Terry Crowley	.30	.15
649T Fernando Gonzalez	.30	.15
____ Traded Checklist	.80	.40

1975 Topps

The cards in this 660-card set feature large color player photos with a fascimile autograph at the bottom of each picture. The photos are surrounded by two-color borders. Card backs are vertical and features red and green type on a gray paper stock. All cards measure 2-1/2" by 3-1/2". Subsets include Highlights (HL) (1-7), a 24-card MVP Series (189-212) that depicts MVP's from 1951 through 1974, League Leaders, World Series Highlights and Rookies. Topps also issued a Mini Set in 1975 which is valued at twice the price quoted for the regular editon below.

	NR/MT	EX
Complete Set (660)	950.00	475.00
Commons (1-660)	.50	.25

#	Name		
1	Hank Aaron (HL)	32.00	16.00
2	Lou Brock (HL)	3.00	1.50
3	Bob Gibson (HL)	3.50	1.75
4	Al Kaline (HL)	3.00	1.50
5	Nolan Ryan (HL)	15.00	7.50
6	Mike Marshall (HL)	.50	.25
7	Dick Bosman, Steve Busby, Nolan Ryan (HL)	3.00	1.50
8	Rogelio Moret	.50	.25
9	Frank Tepedino	.50	.25
10	Willie Davis	.60	.30
11	Bill Melton	.50	.25
12	David Clyde	.50	.25
13	Gene Locklear	.50	.25
14	Milt Wilcox	.50	.25
15	Jose Cardenal	.50	.25
16	Frank Tanana	1.25	.60
17	Dave Concepcion	2.00	1.00
18	Tigers Team	1.25	.60
19	Jerry Koosman	.75	.35
20	Thurman Munson	8.00	4.00
21	Rollie Fingers	6.00	3.00
22	Dave Cash	.50	.25
23	Bill Russell	.75	.35
24	Al Fitzmorris	.50	.25
25	Lee May	.50	.25
26	Dave McNally	.60	.30
27	Ken Reitz	.50	.25
28	Tom Murphy	.50	.25
29	Dave Parker	10.00	5.00
30	Bert Blyleven	3.00	1.50
31	Dave Rader	.50	.25
32	Reggie Cleveland	.50	.25
33	Dusty Baker	.60	.30
34	Steve Renko	.50	.25
35	Ron Santo	1.00	.50
36	Joe Lovitto	.50	.25
37	Dave Freisleben	.50	.25
38	Buddy Bell	.60	.30
39	Andy Thornton	.50	.25
40	Bill Singer	.50	.25
41	Cesar Geronimo	.50	.25
42	Joe Coleman	.50	.25
43	Cleon Jones	.50	.25
44	Pat Dobson	.50	.25
45	Joe Rudi	.60	.30
46	Phillies Team	1.25	.60
47	Tommy John	1.50	.75
48	Freddie Patek	.50	.25
49	Larry Dierker	.50	.25
50	Brooks Robinson	7.00	3.50
51	Bob Forsch	.50	.25
52	Darrell Porter	.50	.25
53	Dave Giusti	.50	.25
54	Eric Soderholm	.50	.25
55	Bobby Bonds	1.50	.75
56	Rick Wise	.60	.30
57	Dave Johnson	.50	.25
58	Chuck Taylor	.50	.25
59	Ken Henderson	.50	.25
60	Ferguson Jenkins	5.50	2.25
61	Dave Winfield	38.00	19.00
62	Fritz Peterson	.50	.25
63	Steve Swisher	.50	.25
64	Dave Chalk	.50	.25
65	Don Gullett	.60	.30
66	Willie Horton	.60	.30
67	Tug McGraw	1.25	.60
68	Ron Blomberg	.50	.25
69	John Odom	.50	.25
70	Mike Schmidt	80.00	40.00
71	Charlie Hough	.60	.30
72	Royals Team	1.25	.60
73	J. R. Richard	.75	.35
74	Mark Belanger	.60	.30
75	Ted Simmons	2.00	1.00
76	Ed Sprague	.50	.25
77	Richie Zisk	.50	.25
78	Ray Corbin	.50	.25
79	Gary Matthews	.60	.30
80	Carlton Fisk	20.00	10.00
81	Ron Reed	.50	.25
82	Pat Kelly	.50	.25
83	Jim Merritt	.50	.25
84	Enzo Hernandez	.50	.25
85	Bill Bonham	.50	.25
86	Joe Lis	.50	.25
87	George Foster	1.50	.75
88	Tom Egan	.50	.25
89	Jim Ray	.50	.25
90	Rusty Staub	1.00	.50
91	Dick Green	.50	.25
92	Cecil Upshaw	.50	.25
93	Dave Lopes	1.00	.50
94	Jim Lonborg	.60	.30
95	John Mayberry	.60	.30
96	Mike Cosgrove	.50	.25
97	Earl Williams	.50	.25
98	Rich Folkers	.50	.25
99	Mike Hegan	.50	.25
100	Willie Stargell	5.00	2.50
101	Expos Team	1.25	.60
102	Joe Decker	.50	.25
103	Rick Miller	.50	.25
104	Bill Madlock	1.50	.75
105	Buzz Capra	.50	.25
106	Mike Hargrove (R)	.75	.35
107	Jim Barr	.50	.25
108	Tom Hall	.50	.25
109	George Hendrick	.60	.30
110	Wilbur Wood	.50	.25
111	Wayne Garrett	.50	.25
112	Larry Hardy	.50	.25
113	Elliott Maddox	.50	.25
114	Dick Lange	.50	.25
115	Joe Ferguson	.60	.30

116 Lerrin LaGrow	.50	.25
117 Orioles Team	1.25	.60
118 Mike Anderson	.50	.25
119 Tommy Helms	.50	.25
120 Steve Busby	.50	.25
(Wrong Photo)		
121 Bill North	.50	.25
122 Al Hrabosky	.60	.30
123 Johnny Briggs	.50	.25
124 Jerry Reuss	.75	.35
125 Ken Singleton	.60	.30
126 Checklist 1-132	1.50	.75
127 Glen Borgmann	.50	.25
128 Bill Lee	.50	.25
129 Rick Monday	.60	.30
130 Phil Niekro	4.50	2.25
131 Toby Harrah	.50	.25
132 Randy Moffitt	.50	.25
133 Dan Driessen	.75	.35
134 Ron Hodges	.50	.25
135 Charlie Spikes	.50	.25
136 Jim Mason	.50	.25
137 Terry Forster	.50	.25
138 Del Unser	.50	.25
139 Horacio Pina	.50	.25
140 Steve Garvey	8.50	4.25
141 Mickey Stanley	.60	.30
142 Bob Reynolds	.50	.25
143 Cliff Johnson (R)	.75	.35
144 Jim Wohlford	.50	.25
145 Ken Holtzman	.50	.25
146 Padres Team	1.25	.60
147 Pedro Garcia	.50	.25
148 Jim Rooker	.50	.25
149 Tim Foli	.50	.25
150 Bob Gibson	6.50	3.25
151 Steve Brye	.50	.25
152 Mario Guerrero	.50	.25
153 Rick Reuschel	.75	.35
154 Mike Lum	.50	.25
155 Jim Bibby	.50	.25
156 Dave Kingman	1.00	.50
157 Pedro Borbon	.50	.25
158 Jerry Grote	.50	.25
159 Steve Arlin	.50	.25
160 Graig Nettles	1.50	.75
161 Stan Bahnsen	.50	.25
162 Willie Montanez	.50	.25
163 Jim Brewer	.50	.25
164 Mickey Rivers	.50	.25
165 Doug Rader	.50	.25
166 Woodie Fryman	.50	.25
167 Rich Coggins	.50	.25
168 Bill Greif	.50	.25
169 Cookie Rojas	.50	.25
170 Bert Campaneris	.75	.35
171 Ed Kirkpatrick	.50	.25
172 Red Sox Team	1.25	.60

173 Steve Rogers	.60	.30
174 Bake McBride	.50	.25
175 Don Money	.50	.25
176 Burt Hooton	.50	.25
177 Vic Correll	.50	.25
178 Cesar Tovar	.50	.25
179 Tom Bradley	.50	.25
180 Joe Morgan	7.50	3.25
181 Fred Beene	.50	.25
182 Don Hahn	.50	.25
183 Mel Stottlemyre	.60	.30
184 Jorge Orta	.50	.25
185 Steve Carlton	14.00	7.00
186 Wllie Crawford	.50	.25
187 Denny Doyle	.50	.25
188 Tom Griffin	.50	.25
189 1951 MVPs	3.00	1.50
(Yogi Berra,		
Roy Campanella)		
190 1952 MVPs	1.25	.60
(Hank Sauer,		
Bobby Shantz)		
191 1953 MVPs	1.25	.60
(Roy Campanella,		
Al Rosen)		
192 1954 MVPs	3.50	1.75
(YogiBerra,		
Willie Mays)		
193 1955 MVPs	3.00	1.50
(Yogi Berra,		
Roy Campanella)		
194 1956 MVPs	8.00	4.00
(Mickey Mantle,		
Don Newcombe)		
195 1957 MVPs	12.50	6.25
(Hank Aaron,		
Mickey Mantle)		
196 1958 MVPs	2.50	1.25
(Ernie Banks,		
Jackie Jensen)		
197 1959 MVPs	2.50	1.25
(ErnieBanks,		
Nellie Fox)		
198 1960 MVPs	2.00	1.00
(Dick Groat,		
Roger Maris)		
199 1961 MVPs	3.00	1.50
(Roger Maris,		
Frank Robinson)		
200 1962 MVPs	8.00	4.00
(Mickey Mantle,		
Maury Wills)		
201 1963 MVPs	2.50	1.25
(Elston Howard,		
Sandy Koufax)		
202 1964 MVPs	2.00	1.00
(Ken Boyer,		
Brooks Robinson)		

203	1965 MVPs (Willie Mays, Zoilo Versalles)	2.50	1.25
204	1966 MVPs (Bo Clemente, Frank Robinson)	3.50	1.75
205	1967 MVPs (Orlando Cepeda, Carl Yastrzemski)	2.50	1.25
206	1968 MVPs (Bob Gibson, Denny McLain)	2.50	1.25
207	1969 MVPs (Harmon Killebrew, Willie McCovey)	3.00	1.50
208	1970 MVPs (Johnny Bench, Boog Powell)	2.50	1.25
209	1971-MVPs (Vida Blue, Joe Torre)	2.00	1.00
210	1972 MVPs (Rich Allen, JohnnyB ench)	2.00	1.00
211	1973 MVPs (Reggie Jackson, Pete Rose)	7.50	3.75
212	1974 MVPs (Jeff Burroughs, Steve Garvey)	1.50	.75
213	Oscar Gamble	.50	.25
214	Harry Parker	.50	.25
215	Bobby Valentine	.60	.30
216	Giants Team	1.25	.60
217	Lou Piniella	1.00	.50
218	Jerry Johnson	.50	.25
219	Ed Herrmann	.50	.25
220	Don Sutton	4.50	2.25
221	Aurelio Rodriquez	.50	.25
222	Dan Spillner	.50	.25
223	Robin Yount (R)	240.00	120.00
224	Ramon Hernandez	.50	.30
225	Bob Grich	.60	.30
226	Bill Campbell	.50	.25
227	Bob Watson	.75	.35
228	George Brett (R)	240.00	120.00
229	Barry Foote	.50	.25
230	Jim Hunter	4.50	2.25
231	Mike Tyson	.50	.25
232	Diego Segui	.50	.25
233	Billy Grabarkewitz	.50	.25
234	Tom Grieve	.50	.25
235	Jack Billingham	.50	.25
236	Angels Team	1.25	.60
237	Carl Morton	.50	.25
238	Dave Duncan	.50	.25
239	George Stone	.50	.25
240	Garry Maddox	.60	.30
241	Dick Tidrow	.50	.25
242	Jay Johnstone	.50	.25
243	Jim Kaat	1.00	.50
244	Bill Buckner	1.00	.50
245	Mickey Lolich	.80	.40
246	Cardinals Team	1.25	.60
247	Enos Cabell	.50	.25
248	Randy Jones	.60	.30
249	Danny Thompson	.50	.25
250	Ken Brett	.50	.25
251	Fran Healy	.50	.25
252	Fred Scherman	.50	.25
253	Jesus Alou	.50	.25
254	Mike Torrez	.50	.25
255	Dwight Evans	7.00	3.50
256	Billy Champion	.50	.25
257	Checklist 133-264	1.50	.75
258	Dave LaRoche	.50	.25
259	Len Randle	.50	.25
260	Johnny Bench	18.00	9.00
261	Andy Hassler	.50	.25
262	Rowland Office	.50	.25
263	Jim Perry	.50	.25
264	John Milner	.50	.25
265	Ron Bryant	.50	.25
266	Sandy Alomar	.50	.25
267	Dick Ruthven	.50	.25
268	Hal McRae	.80	.40
269	Doug Rau	.50	.25
270	Ron Fairly	.50	.25
271	Jerry Moses	.50	.25
272	Lynn McGlothen	.50	.25
273	Steve Braun	.50	.25
274	Vicente Romo	.50	.25
275	Paul Blair	.50	.25
276	White Sox Team	1.25	.60
277	Frank Taveras	.50	.25
278	Paul Lindblad	.50	.25
279	Milt May	.50	.25
280	Carl Yastrzemski	12.00	6.00
281	Jim Slaton	.50	.25
282	Jerry Morales	.50	.25
283	Steve Foucault	.50	.25
284	Ken Griffey	4.00	2.00
285	Ellie Rodriguez	.50	.25
286	Mike Jorgensen	.50	.25
287	Roric Harrison	.50	.25
288	Bruce Ellingsen	.50	.25
289	Ken Rudolph	.50	.25
290	Jon Matlack	.60	.30
291	Bill Sudakis	.50	.25
292	Ron Schueler	.50	.25
293	Dick Sharon	.50	.25
294	Geoff Zahn (R)	.50	.25
295	Vada Pinson	.75	.35
296	Alan Foster	.50	.25
297	Craig Kusick	.50	.25
298	Johnny Grubb	.50	.25

299	Bucky Dent	.75	.35	339 Jim Fregosi	.60	.30
300	Reggie Jackson	28.00	14.00	340 Paul Splittorff	.50	.25
301	Dave Roberts	.50	.25	341 Hal Breeden	.50	.25
302	Rick Burleson (R)	.75	.35	342 Leroy Stanton	.50	.25
303	Grant Jackson	.50	.25	343 Danny Frisella	.50	.25
304	Pirates Team	1.25	.60	344 Ben Oglivie	.50	.25
305	Jim Colborn	.50	.25	345 Clay Carroll	.50	.25
306	Batting Leaders	1.50	.75	346 Bobby Darwin	.50	.25
	(Rod Carew,			347 Mike Caldwell	.50	.25
	Ralph Garr)			348 Tony Muser	.50	.25
307	HR Leaders	4.00	2.00	349 Ray Sadecki	.50	.25
	(Dick Allen,			350 Bobby Murcer	.80	.40
	Mike Schmidt)			351 Bob Boone	2.00	1.00
308	RBI Leaders	2.50	1.25	352 Darold Knowles	.50	.25
	(Johnny Bench,			353 Luis Melendez	.50	.25
	Jeff Burroughs)			354 Dick Bosman	.50	.25
309	Stolen Base Leaders	1.50	.75	355 Chris Cannizzaro	.50	.25
	(Lou Brock,			356 Rico Petrocelli	.50	.25
	Bill North)			357 Ken Forsch	.50	.25
310	Victory Leaders	1.50	.75	358 Al Bumbry	.50	.25
	(Jim Hunter,			359 Paul Popovich	.50	.25
	Fergie Jenkins			360 George Scott	.60	.30
	Andy Messersmith,			361 Dodgers Team	1.25	.60
	Phil Niekro)			362 Steve Hargan	.50	.25
311	ERA Leaders	1.25	.60	363 Carmen Fanzone	.50	.25
	(Buzz Capra,			364 Doug Bird	.50	.25
	Jim Hunter)			365 Bob Bailey	.50	.25
312	Strikeout Leaders	12.00	6.00	366 Ken Sanders	.50	.25
	(Steve Carlton,			367 Craig Robinson	.50	.25
	Nolan Ryan)			368 Vic Albury	.50	.25
313	Leading Firemen	1.00	.50	369 Merv Rettenmund	.50	.25
	(Terry Forster,			370 Tom Seaver	24.00	12.00
	Mike Marshall)			371 Gates Brown	.50	.25
314	Buck Martinez	.50	.25	372 John D'Acquisto	.50	.25
315	Don Kessinger	.60	.30	373 Bill Sharp	.50	.25
316	Jackie Brown	.50	.25	374 Eddie Watt	.50	.25
317	Joe Lahoud	.50	.25	375 Roy White	.50	.25
318	Ernie McAnally	.50	.25	376 Steve Yeager	.60	.30
319	Johnny Oates	.50	.25	377 Tom Hilgendorf	.50	.25
320	Pete Rose	16.00	8.00	378 Derrel Thomas	.50	.25
321	Rudy May	.50	.25	379 Bernie Carbo	.50	.25
322	Ed Goodson	.50	.25	380 Sal Bando	.60	.30
323	Fred Holdsworth	.50	.25	381 John Curtis	.50	.25
324	Ed Kranepool	.75	.35	382 Don Baylor	1.50	.75
325	Tony Oliva	1.50	.75	383 Jim York	.50	.25
326	Wayne Twitchell	.50	.25	384 Brewers Team	1.25	.60
327	Jerry Hairston	.50	.25	385 Dock Ellis	.50	.25
328	Sonny Siebert	.50	.25	386 Checklist 265-396	1.50	.75
329	Ted Kubiak	.50	.25	387 Jim Spencer	.50	.25
330	Mike Marshall	.60	.30	388 Steve Stone	.50	.25
331	Indians Team	1.50	.75	389 Tony Spolaita	.50	.25
332	Fred Kendall	.50	.25	390 Ron Cey	1.00	.50
333	Dick Drago	.50	.25	391 Don DeMola	.50	.25
334	Greg Gross (R)	.50	.25	392 Bruce Bochte	.50	.25
335	Jim Palmer	10.00	5.00	393 Gary Gentry	.50	.25
336	Rennie Stennett	.50	.25	394 Larvell Blanks	.50	.25
337	Kevin Kobel	.50	.25	395 Bud Harrelson	.60	.30
338	Rick Stelmaszek	.50	.25	396 Fred Norman	.50	.25

397 Bill Freehan	.60	.30
398 Elias Sosa	.50	.25
399 Terry Harmon	.50	.25
400 Dick Allen	1.00	.50
401 Mike Wallace	.50	.25
402 Bob Tolan	.50	.25
403 Tom Buskey	.50	.25
404 Ted Sizemore	.50	.25
405 John Montague	.50	.25
406 Bob Gallagher	.50	.25
407 Herb Washington (R)	.50	.25
408 Clyde Wright	.50	.25
409 Bob Robertson	.50	.25
410 Mike Cuellar	.60	.30
411 George Mitterwald	.50	.25
412 Bill Hands	.50	.25
413 Marty Pattin	.50	.25
414 Manny Mota	.60	.30
415 John Hiller	.50	.25
416 Larry Lintz	.50	.25
417 Skip Lockwood	.50	.25
418 Leo Foster	.50	.25
419 Dave Goltz	.50	.25
420 Larry Bowa	.60	.30
421 Mets Team	1.50	.75
422 Brian Downing	.60	.30
423 Clay Kirby	.50	.25
424 John Lowenstein	.50	.25
425 Tito Fuentes	.50	.25
426 George Medich	.50	.25
427 Cito Gaston	.50	.25
428 Dave Hamilton	.50	.25
429 Jim Dwyer (R)	.50	.25
430 Luis Tiant	.80	.40
431 Rod Gilbreath	.50	.25
432 Ken Berry	.50	.25
433 Larry Demery	.50	.25
434 Bob Locker	.50	.25
435 Dave Nelson	.50	.25
436 Ken Frailing	.50	.25
437 Al Cowens	.50	.25
438 Don Carrithers	.50	.25
439 Ed Brinkman	.50	.25
440 Andy Messersmith	.50	.25
441 Bobby Heise	.50	.25
442 Maximino Leon	.50	.25
443 Twins Team	1.25	.60
444 Gene Garber	.50	.25
445 Felix Millan	.50	.25
446 Bart Johnson	.50	.25
447 Terry Crowley	.50	.25
448 Frank Duffy	.50	.25
449 Charlie Williams	.50	.25
450 Willie McCovey	5.00	2.50
451 Rick Dempsey	.50	.25
452 Angel Mangual	.50	.25
453 Claude Osteen	.50	.25
454 Doug Griffin	.50	.25
455 Don Wilson	.50	.25
456 Bob Coluccio	.50	.25
457 Mario Mendoza	.50	.25
458 Ross Grimsley	.50	.25
459 A.L. Championships	.80	.40
460 N.L. Championships	1.25	.60
461 World Series Game 1	4.00	2.00
462 World Series Game 2	1.25	.60
463 World Series Game 3	1.25	.60
464 World Series Game 4	1.25	.60
465 World Series Game 5	1.25	.60
466 WS (Celebration)	1.00	.50
467 Ed Halicki	.50	.25
468 Bobby Mitchell	.50	.25
469 Tom Dettore	.50	.25
470 Jeff Burroughs	.50	.25
471 Bob Stinson	.50	.25
472 Bruce Dal Canton	.50	.25
473 Ken McMullen	.50	.25
474 Luke Walker	.50	.25
475 Darrell Evans	.75	.35
476 Ed Figueroa (R)	.60	.30
477 Tom Hutton	.50	.25
478 Tom Burgmeier	.50	.25
479 Ken Boswell	.50	.25
480 Carlos May	.50	.25
481 Will McEnaney (R)	.50	.25
482 Tom McCraw	.50	.25
483 Steve Ontiveros	.50	.25
484 Glenn Beckert	.50	.25
485 Sparky Lyle	.60	.30
486 Ray Fosse	.50	.25
487 Astros Team	1.25	.60
488 Bill Travers	.50	.25
489 Cecil Cooper	.50	.25
490 Reggie Smith	.75	.35
491 Doyle Alexander	.50	.25
492 Rich Hebner	.50	.25
493 Don Stanhouse	.50	.25
494 Pete LaCock (R)	.50	.25
495 Nelson Briles	.50	.25
496 Pepe Frias	.50	.25
497 Jim Nettles	.50	.25
498 Al Downing	.50	.25
499 Marty Perez	.50	.25
500 Nolan Ryan	70.00	35.00
501 Bill Robinson	.60	.30
502 Pat Bourque	.50	.25
503 Fred Stanley	.50	.25
504 Buddy Bradford	.50	.25
505 Chris Speier	.50	.25
506 Leron Lee	.50	.25
507 Tom Carroll	.50	.25
508 Bob Hansen	.50	.25
509 Dave Hilton	.50	.25
510 Vida Blue	.75	.35
511 Rangers Team	1.50	.75
512 Larry Milbourne	.50	.25

513 Dick Pole	.50	.25	572 Dave Lemanczyk	.50	.25
514 Jose Cruz	.75	.35	573 Orlando Pena	.50	.25
515 Manny Sanguillen	.60	.30	574 Tony Taylor	.50	.25
516 Don Hood	.50	.25	575 Gene Clines	.50	.25
517 Checklist 397-528	1.50	.75	576 Phil Roof	.50	.25
518 Leo Cardenas	.50	.25	577 John Morris	.50	.25
519 Jim Todd	.50	.25	578 Dave Tomlin	.50	.25
520 Amos Otis	.60	.30	579 Skip Pitlock	.50	.25
521 Dennis Blair	.50	.25	580 Frank Robinson	6.50	3.25
522 Gary Sutherland	.50	.25	581 Darrel Chaney	.50	.25
523 Tom Paciorek	.50	.25	582 Eduardo Rodriguez	.50	.25
524 John Doherty	.50	.25	583 Andy Etchebarren	.50	.25
525 Tom House	.50	.25	584 Mike Garman	.50	.25
526 Larry Hisle	.50	.25	585 Chris Chambliss	.60	.30
527 Mac Scarce	.50	.25	586 Tim McCarver	.75	.35
528 Eddie Leon	.50	.25	587 Chris Ward	.50	.25
529 Gary Thomasson	.50	.25	588 Rick Auerbach	.50	.25
530 Gaylord Perry	5.00	2.50	589 Braves Team	1.25	.60
531 Reds Team	1.50	.75	590 Cesar Cedeno	.60	.30
532 Gorman Thomas	.60	.30	591 Glenn Abbott	.50	.25
533 Rudy Meoli	.50	.25	592 Balor Moore	.50	.25
534 Alex Johnson	.50	.25	593 Gene Lamont	.50	.25
535 Gene Tenace	.60	.30	594 Jim Fuller	.50	.25
536 Bob Moose	.50	.25	595 Joe Niekro	.50	.25
537 Tommy Harper	.50	.25	596 Ollie Brown	.50	.25
538 Duffy Dyer	.50	.25	597 Winston Llenas	.50	.25
539 Jesse Jefferson	.50	.25	598 Bruch Kison	.50	.25
540 Lou Brock	6.00	3.00	599 Nate Colbert	.50	.25
541 Roger Metzger	.50	.25	600 Rod Carew	12.00	6.00
542 Pete Broberg	.50	.25	601 Juan Beniquez	.50	.25
543 Larry Bittner	.50	.25	602 John Vukovich	.50	.25
544 Steve Mingori	.50	.25	603 Lew Krausse	.50	.25
545 Billy Williams	4.50	2.25	604 Oscar Zamora	.50	.25
546 John Knox	.50	.25	605 John Ellis	.50	.25
547 Von Joshua	.50	.25	606 Bruce Miller	.50	.25
548 Charlie Sands	.50	.25	607 Jim Holt	.50	.25
549 Bill Butler	.50	.25	608 Gene Michael	.50	.25
550 Ralph Garr	.60	.30	609 Ellie Hendricks	.50	.25
551 Larry Christenson	.50	.25	610 Ron Hunt	.50	.25
552 Jack Brohamer	.50	.25	611 Yankees Team	1.25	.60
553 John Boccabella	.50	.25	612 Terry Hughes	.50	.25
554 Rich Gossage	3.50	1.75	613 Bill Parsons	.50	.25
555 Al Oliver	1.00	.50	614 Rookie Pitchers	.50	.25
556 Tim Johnson	.50	.25	Jack Kucek (R)		
557 Larry Gura	.50	.25	Dyar Miller (R)		
558 Dave Roberts	.50	.25	Vern Ruhle (R)		
559 Bob Montgomery	.50	.25	Paul Siebert (R)		
560 Tony Perez	4.50	2.25	615 Rookie Pitchers	1.00	.50
561 A's Team	1.25	.60	Pat Darcy (R)		
562 Gary Nolan	.50	.25	Dennis Leonard (R)		
563 Wilbur Howard	.50	.25	Tom Underwood (R)		
564 Tommy Davis	.60	.30	Hank Webb (R)		
565 Joe Torre	.80	.40	616 Rookie Outfielders	24.00	12.00
566 Ray Burris	.50	.25	Dave Augustine (R)		
567 Jim Sundberg (R)	1.25	.60	Pepe Mangual (R)		
568 Dale Murray	.50	.25	Jim Rice (R)		
569 Frank White	.80	.40	John Scott (R)		
570 Jim Wynn	.60	.30	617 Rookie Infielders	1.50	.75

Mike Cubbage (R)
Doug DeCinces (R)
Reggie Sanders
Manny Trillo
618 Rookie Pitchers 1.50 .75
Jamie Easterly (R)
Tom Johnson (R)
Scott McGregor (R)
Rick Rhoden (R)
619 Rookie Outfielders .50 .25
Benny Ayala (R)
Nyls Nyman (R)
Tommy Smith (R)
Jerry Turner (R)
620 Rookie Catchers-OF 50.00 25.00
Gary Carter (R)
Marc Hill (R)
Danny Meyer (R)
Leon Roberts (R)
621 Rookie Pitchers .80 .40
John Denny (R)
Rawly Eastwick (R)
Jim Kern (R)
Juan Veintidos (R)
622 Rookie Outfielders 12.00 6.00
Ed Armbrister (R)
Fred Lynn (R)
Tom Poquette (R)
Terry Whitfield (R)
623 Rookie Infielders 18.00 9.00
Phil Garner (R)
Keith Hernandez (R)
Bob Sheldon (R)
Tom Veryzer (R)
624 Rookie Pitchers .50 .25
Doug Konieczny (R)
Gary Lavelle (R)
Jim Otten (R)
Eddie Solomon (R)
625 Boog Powell .80 .40
626 Larry Haney .50 .25
627 Tom Walker .50 .25
628 Ron LeFlore (R) .80 .50
629 Joe Hoerner .50 .25
630 Greg Luzinski .60 .30
631 Lee Lacy .50 .25
632 Morris Nettles .50 .25
633 Paul Casanova .50 .25
634 Cy Acosta .50 .25
635 Chuck Dobson .50 .25
636 Charlie Moore .50 .25
637 Ted Martinez .50 .25
638 Cubs Team 1.25 .60
639 Steve Kline .50 .25
640 Harmon Killebrew 6.00 3.00
641 Jim Northrup .50 .25
642 Mike Phillips .50 .25
643 Brent Storm .50 .25
644 Bill Fahey .50 .25
645 Danny Cater .50 .25
646 Checklist 529-660 1.50 .75
647 Claudell Washington 1.00 .50
(R)
648 Dave Pagan .50 .25
649 Jack Heidemann .50 .25
650 Dave May .50 .25
651 John Morlan .50 .25
652 Lindy McDaniel .50 .25
653 Lee Richards .50 .25
654 Jerry Terrell .50 .25
655 Rico Carty .50 .25
656 Bill Plummer .50 .25
657 Bob Oliver .50 .25
658 Vic Harris .50 .25
659 Bob Apodaca .50 .25
660 Hank Aaron 30.00 15.00

1976 Topps

Topps improved the quality of their photographs with this 660-card set which features large color photos on the card fronts with a small drawing of a player in the bottom left corner. Cards measure 2-1/2" by 3-1/2". The major subsets include Record Breakers (RB)(1-6), a new Father and Sons subset (66-70) and an All Time All-Stars series (341-350). Also present are League Leaders, World Series and Playoff Highlights and Rookies.

	NR/MT	EX
Complete Set (660)	480.00	240.00
Commons (1-660)	.30	.15
1 Hank Aaron (RB)	15.00	7.50
2 Bobby Bonds (RB)	.50	.25
3 Mickey Lolich (RB)	.50	.25

No.	Player	Val1	Val2
4	Dave Lopes (RB)	.50	.25
5	Tom Seaver (RB)	4.00	2.00
6	Rennie Stennett (RB)	.50	.25
7	Jim Umbarger	.30	.15
8	Tito Fuentes	.30	.15
9	Paul Lindblad	.30	.15
10	Lou Brock	6.00	3.00
11	Jim Hughes	.30	.15
12	Richie Zisk	.30	.15
13	Johnny Wockenfuss	.30	.15
14	Gene Garber	.30	.15
15	George Scott	.40	.20
16	Bob Apodaca	.30	.15
17	Yankees Team	1.50	.75
18	Dale Murray	.30	.15
19	George Brett	70.00	35.00
20	Bob Watson	.60	.30
21	Dave LaRoche	.30	.15
22	Bill Russell	.40	.20
23	Brian Downing	.80	.40
24	Cesar Geronimo	.30	.15
25	Mike Torrez	.30	.15
26	Andy Thornton	.30	.15
27	Ed Figueroa	.30	.15
28	Dusty Baker	.60	.30
29	Rick Burleson	.40	.20
30	John Montefusco (R)	.50	.25
31	Lenny Randle	.30	.15
32	Danny Frisella	.30	.15
33	Bill North	.30	.15
34	Mike Garman	.30	.15
35	Tony Oliva	1.25	.60
36	Frank Taveras	.30	.15
37	John Hiller	.30	.15
38	Garry Maddox	.40	.20
39	Pete Broberg	.30	.15
40	Dave Kingman	1.00	.50
41	Tippy Martinez (R)	.40	.20
42	Barry Foote	.30	.15
43	Paul Splittorff	.30	.15
44	Doug Rader	.30	.15
45	Boog Powell	.60	.30
46	Dodgers Team	1.25	.60
47	Jesse Jefferson	.30	.15
48	Dave Concepcion	1.50	.75
49	Dave Duncan	.30	.15
50	Fred Lynn	2.00	1.00
51	Ray Burris	.30	.15
52	Dave Chalk	.30	.15
53	Mike Beard	.30	.15
54	Dave Rader	.30	.15
55	Gaylord Perry	4.00	2.00
56	Bob Tolan	.30	.15
57	Phil Garner	.80	.40
58	Ron Reed	.30	.15
59	Larry Hisle	.30	.15
60	Jerry Reuss	.50	.25
61	Ron LeFlore	.50	.25
62	Johnny Oates	.30	.15
63	Bobby Darwin	.30	.15
64	Jerry Koosman	.50	.25
65	Chris Chambliss	.40	.20
66	Buddy & Gus Bell	.60	.30
67	Bob & Ray Boone	1.00	.50
68	Joe Coleman & Jr.	.50	.25
69	Jim & Mike Hegan	.50	.25
70	Roy Smalley & Jr.	.50	.25
71	Steve Rogers	.30	.15
72	Hal McRae	.80	.40
73	Orioles Team	1.25	.60
74	Oscar Gamble	.30	.15
75	Larry Dierker	.30	.15
76	Willie Crawford	.30	.15
77	Pedro Borbon	.30	.15
78	Cecil Cooper	.40	.20
79	Jerry Morales	.30	.15
80	Jim Kaat	1.00	.50
81	Darrell Evans	.50	.25
82	Von Joshua	.30	.15
83	Jim Spencer	.30	.15
84	Brent Strom	.30	.15
85	Mickey Rivers	.30	.15
86	Mike Tyson	.30	.15
87	Tom Burgmeier	.30	.15
88	Duffy Dyer	.30	.15
89	Vern Ruhle	.30	.15
90	Sal Bando	.50	.25
91	Tom Hutton	.30	.15
92	Eduardo Rodriguez	.30	.15
93	Mike Phillips	.30	.15
94	Jim Dwyer	.30	.15
95	Brooks Robinson	6.50	3.25
96	Doug Bird	.30	.15
97	Wilbur Howard	.30	.15
98	Dennis Eckersley (R)	50.00	25.00
99	Lee Lacy	.30	.15
100	Jim Hunter	3.50	1.75
101	Pete LaCock	.30	.15
102	Jim Willoughby	.30	.15
103	Biff Pocoroba	.30	.15
104	Reds Team	1.25	.60
105	Gary Lavelle	.30	.15
106	Tom Grieve	.30	.15
107	Dave Roberts	.30	.15
108	Don Kirkwood	.30	.15
109	Larry Lintz	.30	.15
110	Carlos May	.30	.15
111	Danny Thompson	.30	.15
112	Kent Tekulve (R)	1.25	.60
113	Gary Sutherland	.30	.15
114	Jay Johnstone	.40	.20
115	Ken Holtzman	.40	.20
116	Charlie Moore	.30	.15
117	Mike Jorgensen	.30	.15
118	Red Sox Team	1.00	.50

#	Name		
119	Checklist 1-132	1.25	.60
120	Rusty Staub	.75	.35
121	Tony Solaita	.30	.15
122	Mike Cosgrove	.30	.15
123	Walt Williams	.30	.15
124	Doug Rau	.30	.15
125	Don Baylor	1.50	.75
126	Tom Dettore	.30	.15
127	Larvell Blanks	.30	.15
128	Ken Griffey	2.50	1.25
129	Andy Etchebarren	.30	.15
130	Luis Tiant	.60	.30
131	Bill Stein	.30	.15
132	Don Hood	.30	.15
133	Gary Matthews	.40	.20
134	Mike Ivie	.30	.15
135	Bake McBride	.30	.15
136	Dave Goltz	.30	.15
137	Bill Robinson	.50	.25
138	Lerrin LaGrow	.30	.15
139	Gorman Thomas	.50	.25
140	Vida Blue	.60	.30
141	Larry Parrish (R)	1.50	.75
142	Dick Drago	.30	.15
143	Jerry Grote	.30	.15
144	Al Fitzmorris	.30	.15
145	Larry Bowa	.50	.25
146	George Medich	.30	.15
147	Astros Team	1.00	.50
148	Stan Thomas	.30	.15
149	Tommy Davis	.50	.25
150	Steve Garvey	7.00	3.50
151	Bill Bonham	.30	.15
152	Leroy Stanton	.30	.15
153	Buzz Capra	.30	.15
154	Bucky Dent	.50	.25
155	Jack Billingham	.30	.15
156	Rico Carty	.40	.20
157	Mike Caldwell	.30	.15
158	Ken Reitz	.30	.15
159	Jerry Terrell	.30	.15
160	Dave Winfield	20.00	10.00
161	Bruce Kison	.30	.15
162	Jack Pierce	.30	.15
163	Jim Slaton	.30	.15
164	Pepe Mangual	.30	.15
165	Gene Tenace	.40	.20
166	Skip Lockwood	.30	.15
167	Freddie Patek	.30	.15
168	Tom Hilgendorf	.30	.15
169	Graig Nettles	1.00	.50
170	Rick Wise	.40	.20
171	Greg Gross	.30	.15
172	Rangers Team	1.00	.50
173	Steve Swisher	.30	.15
174	Charlie Hough	.50	.25
175	Ken Singleton	.40	.20
176	Dick Lange	.30	.15
177	Marty Perez	.30	.15
178	Tom Buskey	.30	.15
179	George Foster	1.00	.50
180	Rich Gossage	3.00	1.50
181	Willie Montanez	.30	.15
182	Harry Rasmussen	.30	.15
183	Steve Braun	.30	.15
184	Bill Greif	.30	.15
185	Dave Parker	5.00	2.50
186	Tom Walker	.30	.15
187	Pedro Garcia	.30	.15
188	Fred Scherman	.30	.15
189	Claudell Washington	.40	.20
190	Jon Matlack	.50	.25
191	N.L. Batting Leaders	.80	.40
192	A.L. Batting Leaders	3.00	1.50
193	N.L. HR Leaders	4.00	2.00
194	A.L. HR Leaders	4.00	2.00
195	N.L. RBI Leaders	2.00	1.00
196	A.L. RBI Leaders	1.00	.50
197	N.L. Stolen Base Leaders	2.00	1.00
198	A.L. Stolen Base Leaders	.80	.50
199	N.L. Victory Ldrs	2.50	1.25
200	A.L Victory Ldrs	2.50	1.25
201	N.L. ERA Leaders	2.00	1.00
202	A.L. ERA Leaders	3.00	1.50
203	N.L. Strikeout Leaders	2.00	1.00
204	A.L. Strikeout Leaders	2.00	1.00
205	Major League Fireman	.80	.50
206	Manny Trillo	.30	.15
207	Andy Hassler	.30	.15
208	Mike Lum	.30	.15
209	Alan Ashby	.30	.15
210	Lee May	.30	.15
211	Clay Carroll	.30	.15
212	Pat Kelly	.30	.15
213	Dave Heaverlo	.30	.15
214	Eric Soderholm	.30	.15
215	Reggie Smith	.40	.20
216	Expos Team	1.00	.50
217	Dave Freisleben	.30	.15
218	John Knox	.30	.15
219	Tom Murphy	.30	.15
220	Manny Sanguillen	.50	.25
221	Jim Todd	.30	.15
222	Wayne Garrett	.30	.15
223	Ollie Brown	.30	.15
224	Jim York	.30	.15
225	Roy White	.30	.15
226	Jim Sundberg	.30	.15
227	Oscar Zamora	.30	.15
228	John Hale	.30	.15
229	Jerry Remy (R)	.40	.20

230	Carl Yastrzemski	8.50	4.25
231	Tom House	.30	.15
232	Frank Duffy	.30	.15
233	Grant Jackson	.30	.15
234	Mike Sadek	.30	.15
235	Bert Blyleven	3:00	1.50
236	Royals Team	1.25	.60
237	Dave Hamilton	.30	.15
238	Larry Biittner	.30	.15
239	John Curtis	.30	.15
240	Pete Rose	14.00	7.00
241	Hector Torres	.30	.15
242	Dan Meyer	.30	.15
243	Jim Rooker	.30	.15
244	Bill Sharp	.30	.15
245	Felix Millan	.30	.15
246	Cesar Tovar	.30	.15
247	Terry Harmon	.30	.15
248	Dick Tidrow	.30	.15
249	Cliff Johnson	.30	.15
250	Ferguson Jenkins	4.00	2.00
251	Rick Monday	.50	.25
252	Tim Nordbrook	.30	.15
253	Bill Buckner	.60	.30
254	Rudy Meoli	.30	.15
255	Fritz Peterson	.30	.15
256	Rowland Office	.30	.15
257	Ross Grimsley	.30	.15
258	Nyls Nyman	.30	.15
259	Darrel Chaney	.30	.15
260	Steve Busby	.30	.15
261	Gary Thomasson	.30	.15
262	Checklist 133-265	1.50	.75
263	Lyman Bostock (R)	.60	.30
264	Steve Renko	.30	.15
265	Willie Davis	.40	.20
266	Alan Foster	.30	.15
267	Aurelio Rodriguez	.30	.15
268	Del Unser	.30	.15
269	Rick Austin	.30	.15
270	Willie Stargell	4.00	2.00
271	Jim Lonborg	.50	.25
272	Rick Dempsey	.30	.15
273	Joe Niekro	.30	.15
274	Tommy Harper	.30	.15
275	Rick Manning (R)	.40	.20
276	Mickey Scott	.30	.15
277	Cubs Team	1.00	.50
278	Bernie Carbo	.30	.15
279	Roy Howell	.30	.15
280	Burt Hooton	.30	.15
281	Dave May	.30	.15
282	Dan Osborn	.30	.15
283	Merv Rettenmund	.30	.15
284	Steve Ontiveros	.30	.15
285	Mike Cuellar	.50	.25
286	Jim Wohlford	.30	.15
287	Pete Mackanin	.30	.15

288	Bill Campbell	.30	.15
289	Enzo Hernandez	.30	.15
290	Ted Simmons	1.00	.50
291	Ken Sanders	.30	.15
292	Leon Roberts	.30	.15
293	Bill Castro	.30	.15
294	Ed Kirkpatrick	.30	.15
295	Dave Cash	.30	.15
296	Pat Dobson	.30	.15
297	Roger Metzger	.30	.15
298	Dick Bosman	.30	.15
299	Champ Summers	.30	.15
300	Johnny Bench	12.00	6.00
301	Jackie Brown	.30	.15
302	Rick Miller	.30	.15
303	Steve Foucault	.30	.15
304	Angels Team	1.00	.50
305	Andy Messersmith	.30	.15
306	Rod Gilbreath	.30	.15
307	Al Bumbry	.30	.15
308	Jim Barr	.30	.15
309	Bill Melton	.30	.15
310	Randy Jones	.40	.20
311	Cookie Rojas	.30	.15
312	Don Carrithers	.30	.15
313	Dan Ford (R)	.30	.15
314	Ed Kranepool	.50	.25
315	Al Hrabosky	.30	.15
316	Robin Yount	70.00	35.00
317	John Candelaria(R)	2.50	1.25
318	Bob Boone	1.25	.60
319	Larry Gura	.30	.15
320	Willie Horton	.40	.20
321	Jose Cruz	.50	.25
322	Glenn Abbott	.30	.15
323	Rob Sperring	.30	.15
324	Jim Bibby	.30	.15
325	Tony Perez	3.00	1.50
326	Dick Pole	.30	.15
327	Dave Moates	.30	.15
328	Carl Morton	.30	.15
329	Joe Ferguson	.30	.15
330	Nolan Ryan	55.00	27.50
331	Padres Team	1.00	.50
332	Charlie Williams	.30	.15
333	Bob Coluccio	.30	.15
334	Dennis Leonard	.40	.20
335	Bob Grich	.50	.25
336	Vic Albury	.30	.15
337	Bud Harrelson	.50	.25
338	Bob Bailey	.30	.15
339	John Denny	.30	.15
340	Jim Rice	7.50	3.75
341	Lou Gehrig (AS)	7.50	3.75
342	Rogers Hornsby (AS)	3.50	1.75
343	Pie Traynor (AS)	1.50	.75
344	Honus Wagner(AS)	5.00	2.50

345	Babe Ruth (AS)	10.00	5.00
346	Ty Cobb (AS)	7.50	3.75
347	Ted Williams (AS)	8.50	4.25
348	Mickey Cochrane (AS)	1.50	.75
349	Walter Johnson	3.50	1.75
350	Lefty Grove (AS)	1.50	.75
351	Randy Hundley	.30	.15
352	Dave Giusti	.30	.15
353	Sixto Lezcano (R)	.40	.20
354	Ron Blomberg	.30	.15
355	Steve Carlton	8.50	4.25
356	Ted Martinez	.30	.15
357	Ken Forsch	.30	.15
358	Buddy Bell	.40	.20
359	Rick Reuschel	.50	.25
360	Jeff Burroughs	.40	.20
361	Tigers Team	1.00	.50
362	Will McEnaney	.30	.15
363	Dave Collins	.30	.15
364	Elias Sosa	.30	.15
365	Carlton Fisk	14.00	7.00
366	Bobby Valentine	.40	.20
367	Bruce Miller	.30	.15
368	Wilbur Wood	.30	.15
369	Frank White	.50	.25
370	Ron Cey	.75	.35
371	Ellie Hendricks	.30	.15
372	Rick Baldwin	.30	.15
373	Johnny Briggs	.30	.15
374	Dan Warthen	.30	.15
375	Ron Fairly	.30	.15
376	Rich Hebner	.30	.15
377	Mike Hegan	.30	.15
378	Steve Stone	.40	.20
379	Ken Boswell	.30	.15
380	Bobby Bonds	1.50	.75
381	Denny Doyle	.30	.15
382	Matt Alexander	.30	.15
383	John Ellis	.30	.15
384	Phillies Team	1.00	.50
385	Mickey Lolich	.50	.25
386	Ed Goodson	.30	.15
387	Mike Miley	.30	.15
388	Stan Perzanowski	.30	.15
389	Glenn Adams	.30	.15
390	Don Gullett	.40	.20
391	Jerry Hairston	.30	.15
392	Checklist 265-396	1.50	.75
393	Paul Mitchell	.30	.15
394	Fran Healy	.30	.15
395	Jim Wynn	.50	.25
396	Bill Lee	.30	.15
397	Tim Foli	.30	.15
398	Dave Tomlin	.30	.15
399	Luis Melendez	.30	.15
400	Rod Carew	10.00	5.00
401	Ken Brett	.30	.15
402	Don Money	.30	.15
403	Geoff Zahn	.30	.15
404	Enos Cabell	.30	.15
405	Rollie Fingers	5.00	2.50
406	Ed Herrmann	.30	.15
407	Tom Underwood	.30	.15
408	Charlie Spikes	.30	.15
409	Dave Lemancyzk	.30	.15
410	Ralph Garr	.40	.20
411	Bill Singer	.30	.15
412	Toby Harrah	.30	.15
413	Pete Varney	.30	.15
414	Wayne Garland	.30	.15
415	Vada Pinson	.60	.30
416	Tommy John	1.25	.60
417	Gene Clines	.30	.15
418	Jose Morales	.30	.15
419	Reggie Cleveland	.30	.15
420	Joe Morgan	6.50	3.25
421	A's Team	1.00	.50
422	Johnny Grubb	.30	.15
423	Ed Halicki	.30	.15
424	Phil Roof	.30	.15
425	Rennie Stennett	.30	.15
426	Bob Forsch	.30	.15
427	Kurt Bevacqua	.30	.15
428	Jim Crawford	.30	.15
429	Fred Stanley	.30	.15
430	Jose Cardenal	.30	.15
431	Dick Ruthven	.30	.15
432	Tom Veryzer	.30	.15
433	Rick Waits	.30	.15
434	Morris Nettles	.30	.15
435	Phil Niekro	3.50	1.75
436	Bill Fahey	.30	.15
437	Terry Forster	.30	.15
438	Doug DeCinces	.40	.20
439	Rick Rhoden	.30	.15
440	John Mayberry	.40	.20
441	Gary Carter	12.00	6.00
442	Hank Webb	.30	.15
443	Giants Team	1.00	.50
444	Gary Nolan	.30	.15
445	Rico Petrocelli	.40	.20
446	Larry Haney	.30	.15
447	Gene Locklear	.30	.15
448	Tom Johnson	.30	.15
449	Bob Robertson	.30	.15
450	Jim Palmer	8.50	4.25
451	Buddy Bradford	.30	.15
452	Tom Hausman	.30	.15
453	Lou Piniella	.50	.25
454	Tom Griffin	.30	.15
455	Dick Allen	.75	.35
456	Joe Coleman	.30	.15
457	Ed Crosby	.30	.15
458	Earl Williams	.30	.15
459	Jim Brewer	.30	.15

460	Cesar Cedeno	.40	.20
461	NL & AL Champs	.75	.35
462	1975 World Series	.75	.35
463	Steve Hargan	.30	.15
464	Ken Henderson	.30	.15
465	Mike Marshall	.40	.20
466	Bob Stinson	.30	.15
467	Woodie Fryman	.30	.15
468	Jesus Alou	.30	.15
469	Rawly Eastwick	.30	.15
470	Bobby Murcer	.50	.25
471	Jim Burton	.30	.15
472	Bob Davis	.30	.15
473	Paul Blair	.30	.15
474	Ray Corbin	.30	.15
475	Joe Rudi	.50	.25
476	Bob Moose	.30	.15
477	Indians Team	1.50	.75
478	Lynn McGlothen	.30	.15
479	Bobby Mitchell	.30	.15
480	Mike Schmidt	42.00	21.00
481	Rudy May	.30	.15
482	Tim Hosley	.30	.15
483	Mickey Stanley	.30	.15
484	Eric Raich	.30	.15
485	Mike Hargrove	.30	.15
486	Bruce Dal Canton	.30	.15
487	Leron Lee	.30	.15
488	Claude Osteen	.40	.20
489	Skip Jutze	.30	.15
490	Frank Tanana	.60	.30
491	Terry Crowley	.30	.15
492	Marty Pattin	.30	.15
493	Derrel Thomas	.30	.15
494	Craig Swan	.30	.15
495	Nate Colbert	.30	.15
496	Juan Beniquez	.30	.15
497	Joe McIntosh	.30	.15
498	Glenn Borgmann	.30	.15
499	Mario Guerrero	.30	.15
500	Reggie Jackson	25.00	12.50
501	Billy Champion	.30	.15
502	Tim McCarver	.50	.25
503	Elliott Maddox	.30	.15
504	Pirates Team	1.00	.50
505	Mark Belanger	.50	.25
506	George Mitterwald	.30	.15
507	Ray Bare	.30	.15
508	Duane Kuiper (R)	.30	.15
509	Bill Hands	.30	.15
510	Amos Otis	.40	.20
511	Jamie Easterly	.30	.15
512	Ellie Rodriguez	.30	.15
513	Bart Johnson	.30	.15
514	Dan Driessen	.40	.20
515	Steve Yeager	.40	.20
516	Wayne Granger	.30	.15
517	John Milner	.30	.15
518	Doug Flynn (R)	.30	.15
519	Steve Brye	.30	.15
520	Willie McCovey	5.00	2.50
521	Jim Colborn	.30	.15
522	Ted Sizemore	.30	.15
523	Bob Montgomery	.30	.15
524	Pete Falcone	.30	.15
525	Billy Williams	4.50	2.25
526	Checklist 397-528	1.50	.75
527	Mike Anderson	.30	.15
528	Dock Ellis	.30	.15
529	Deron Johnson	.30	.15
530	Don Sutton	3.50	1.75
531	Mets Team	1.00	.50
532	Milt May	.30	.15
533	Lee Richard	.30	.15
534	Stan Bahnsen	.30	.15
535	Dave Nelson	.30	.15
536	Mike Thompson	.30	.15
537	Tony Muser	.30	.15
538	Pat Darcy	.30	.15
539	John Balaz	.30	.15
540	Bill Freehan	.40	.20
541	Steve Mingori	.30	.15
542	Keith Hernandez	3.50	1.75
543	Wayne Twitchell	.30	.15
544	Pepe Frias	.30	.15
545	Sparky Lyle	.50	.25
546	Dave Rosello	.30	.15
547	Roric Harrison	.30	.15
548	Manny Mota	.40	.20
549	Randy Tate	.30	.15
550	Hank Aaron	28.00	14.00
551	Jerry DaVanon	.30	.15
552	Terry Humphrey	.30	.15
553	Randy Moffitt	.30	.15
554	Ray Fosse	.30	.15
555	Dyar Miller	.30	.15
556	Twins Team	1.00	.50
557	Dan Spillner	.30	.15
558	Cito Gaston	.40	.20
559	Clyde Wright	.30	.15
560	Jorge Orta	.30	.15
561	Tom Carroll	.30	.15
562	Adrian Garrett	.30	.15
563	Larry Demery	.30	.15
564	Bubble Gum Champ (Kurt Bevacqua)	.50	.25
565	Tug McGraw	.75	.35
566	Ken McMullen	.30	.15
567	George Stone	.30	.15
568	Rob Andrews	.30	.15
569	Nelson Briles	.30	.15
570	George Hendrick	.40	.20
571	Don DeMola	.30	.15
572	Rich Coggins	.30	.15
573	Bill Travers	.30	.15
574	Don Kessinger	.30	.15

575	Dwight Evans	4.50	2.25
576	Maximino Leon	.30	.15
577	Marc Hill	.30	.15
578	Ted Kubiak	.30	.15
579	Clay Kirby	.30	.15
580	Bert Campaneris	.50	.25
581	Cardinals Team	1.25	.60
582	Mike Kekich	.30	.15
583	Tommy Helms	.30	.15
584	Stan Wall	.30	.15
585	Joe Torre	.50	.25
586	Ron Schueler	.30	.15
587	Leo Cardenas	.30	.15
588	Kevin Kobel	.30	.15
589	Rookie Pitchers	2.00	1.00
	Santo Alcala (R)		
	Mike Flanagan (R)		
	Joe Pactwa (R)		
	Pablo Torrealba (R)		
590	Rookie Outfielders	.75	.35
	Henry Cruz (R)		
	Chet Lemon (R)		
	Ellis Valentine (R)		
	Terry Whitfield		
591	Rookie Pitchers	.30	.15
	Steve Grilli (R)		
	Craig Mitchell (R)		
	Jose Sosa (R)		
	George Throop (R)		
592	Rookie Infielders	10.00	5.00
	Dave McKay (R)		
	Willie Randolph (R)		
	Jerry Royster (R)		
	Roy Staiger (R)		
593	Rookie Pitchers	.30	.15
	Larry Anderson (R)		
	Ken Crosby (R)		
	Mark Littell (R)		
	Butch Metzger (R)		
594	Rookie Catchers	.40	.20
	& Outfielders		
	Andy Merchant (R)		
	Ed Ott (R)		
	Royle Stillman (R)		
	Jerry White (R)		
595	Rookie Pitchers	.40	.20
	Steve Barr (R)		
	Art DeFilippi (R)		
	Randy Lerch (R)		
	Sid Monge (R)		
596	Rookie Infielders	.40	.20
	Lamar Johnson (R)		
	Johnny LeMaster (R)		
	Jerry Manuel (R)		
	Craig Reynolds (R)		
597	Rookie Pitchers	.40	.20
	Don Aase (R)		
	Jack Kucek (R)		
	Frank LaCorte (R)		
	Mike Pazik (R)		
598	Rookie Outfielders	.40	.20
	Hector Cruz (R)		
	Jamie Quirk (R)		
	Jerry Turner (R)		
	Joe Wallis (R)		
599	Rookie Pitchers	8.00	4.00
	Rob Dressler (R)		
	Ron Guidry (R)		
	Bob McClure (R)		
	Pat Zachry (R)		
600	Tom Seaver	18.00	9.00
601	Ken Rudolph	.30	.15
602	Doug Konieczny	.30	.15
603	Jim Holt	.30	.15
604	Joe Lovitto	.30	.15
605	Al Downing	.40	.20
606	Brewers Team	1.00	.50
607	Rich Hinton	.30	.15
608	Vic Correll	.30	.15
609	Fred Norman	.30	.15
610	Greg Luzinski	.60	.30
611	Rick Folkers	.30	.15
612	Joe Lahoud	.30	.15
613	Tim Johnson	.30	.15
614	Fernando Arroyo	.30	.15
615	Mike Cubbage	.30	.15
616	Buck Martinez	.30	.15
617	Darold Knowles	.30	.15
618	Jack Brohamer	.30	.15
619	Bill Butler	.30	.15
620	Al Oliver	.75	.35
621	Tom Hall	.30	.15
622	Rick Auerbach	.30	.15
623	Bob Allietta	.30	.15
624	Tony Taylor	.30	.15
625	J.R. Richard	.50	.25
626	Bob Sheldon	.30	.15
627	Bill Plummer	.30	.15
628	John D'Acquisto	.30	.15
629	Sandy Alomar	.30	.15
630	Chris Speier	.30	.15
631	Braves Team	1.00	.50
632	Rogelio Moret	.30	.15
633	John Stearns (R)	.40	.20
634	Larry Christenson	.30	.15
635	Jim Fregosi	.40	.20
636	Joe Decker	.30	.15
637	Bruce Bochte	.30	.15
638	Doyle Alexander	.30	.15
639	Fred Kendall	.30	.15
640	Bill Madlock	1.25	.60
641	Tom Paciorek	.30	.15
642	Dennis Blair	.30	.15
643	Checklist 529-660	1.50	.75
644	Tom Bradley	.30	.15
645	Darrell Porter	.30	.15

646	John Lowenstein	.30	.15
647	Ramon Hernandez	.30	.15
648	Al Cowens	.30	.15
649	Dave Roberts	.30	.15
650	Thurman Munson	7.50	3.75
651	John Odom	.30	.15
652	Ed Armbrister	.30	.15
653	Mike Norris	.30	.15
654	Doug Griffin	.30	.15
655	Mike Vail	.30	.15
656	White Sox Team	1.00	.50
657	Roy Smalley (R)	.40	.20
658	Jerry Johnson	.30	.15
659	Ben Oglivie	.30	.15
660	Dave Lopes	.80	.40

1976 Topps Traded

This update set consists of 44 cards including an unnumbered checklist. Cards measure 2-1/2" by 3-1/2". Card fronts feature color photos with a newspaper headline design. Card backs include a newspaper type graphic which contains biographical information about the player. Card numbers carry a "T" suffix and coincide with the players number in Topps 1976 regular edition.

		NR/MT	EX
Complete Set (44)		10.50	5.25
Commons		.30	.15
27T	Ed Figueroa	.30	.15
28T	Dusty Baker	.40	.20
44T	Doug Rader	.30	.15
58T	Ron Reed	.30	.15
74T	Oscar Gamble	.40	.25
80T	Jim Kaat	1.00	.50

83T	Jim Spencer	.30	.15
85T	Mickey Rivers	.30	.15
99T	Lee Lacy	.30	.15
120T	Rusty Staub	.60	.30
127T	Larvell Blanks	.30	.15
146T	George Medich	.30	.15
158T	Ken Reitz	.30	.15
208T	Mike Lum	.30	.15
211T	Clay Carroll	.30	.15
231T	Tom House	.30	.15
250T	Ferguson Jenkins	3.00	1.50
259T	Darrel Chaney	.30	.15
292T	Leon Roberts	.30	.15
296T	Pat Dobson	.30	.15
309T	Bill Melton	.30	.15
338T	Bob Bailey	.30	.15
380T	Bobby Bonds	.75	.35
383T	John Ellis	.30	.15
385T	Mickey Lolich	.50	.25
401T	Ken Brett	.30	.15
410T	Ralph Garr	.30	.15
411T	Bill Singer	.30	.15
428T	Jim Crawford	.30	.15
434T	Morris Nettles	.30	.15
464T	Ken Henderson	.30	.15
497T	Joe McIntosh	.30	.15
524T	Pete Falcone	.30	.15
527T	Mike Anderson	.30	.15
528T	Dock Ellis	.30	.15
532T	Milt May	.30	.15
554T	Ray Fosse	.30	.15
579T	Clay Kirby	.30	.15
583T	Tommy Helms	.30	.15
592T	Willie Randolph	4.00	2.00
618T	Jack Brohamer	.30	.15
632T	Rogelio Moret	.30	.15
649T	Dave Roberts	.30	.15
____	Traded Checklist	.75	.35

1977 Topps

This 660-card set features full color photos on the card fronts with fascimile autographs. The player's name, team and position are printed above the photo. All cards measure 2-1/2" by 3-1/2". New subsets include "Turn Back The Clock" (433-437) and "Brothers" (631-634). Other subsets are League Leaders, Record Breakers, World Series and Playoff Highlights and Rookies.

		NR/MT	EX
	Complete Set (660)	440.00	220.00
	Commons	.25	.12
1	Batting Leaders (George Brett, Bill Madlock)	5.00	2.50
2	HR Leaders (Graig Nettles, Mike Schmidt)	2.50	1.25
3	RBI Leaders (George Foster, Lee May)	.50	.25
4	Stolen Base Leaders (Dave Lopes, Bill North)	.40	.20
5	Victory Leaders (Randy Jones, Jim Palmer)	.80	.50
6	Strikeout Leaders (Nolan Ryan, Tom Seaver)	8.00	4.00
7	ERA Leaders (John Denny, Mark Fidrych)	.50	.25
8	Leading Firemen (Bill Campbell, Rawly Eastwick)	.40	.20
9	Doug Rader	.25	.12
10	Reggie Jackson	18.00	9.00
11	Rob Dressler	.25	.12
12	Larry Haney	.25	.12
13	Luis Gomez	.25	.12
14	Tommy Smith	.25	.12
15	Don Gullett	.35	.18
16	Bob Jones	.25	.12
17	Steve Stone	.35	.18
18	Indians Team	1.25	.60
19	John D'Acquisto	.25	.12
20	Graig Nettles	1.00	.50
21	Ken Forsch	.25	.12
22	Bill Freehan	.35	.18
23	Dan Driessen	.30	.15
24	Carl Morton	.25	.12
25	Dwight Evans	3.00	1.50
26	Ray Sadecki	.25	.12
27	Bill Buckner	.40	.20
28	Woodie Fryman	.25	.12
29	Bucky Dent	.50	.25
30	Greg Luzinski	.45	.22
31	Jim Todd	.25	.12
32	Checklist 1-132	1.00	.50
33	Wayne Garland	.25	.12
34	Angels Team	.75	.35
35	Rennie Stennett	.25	.12
36	John Ellis	.25	.12
37	Steve Hargan	.25	.12
38	Craig Kusick	.25	.12
39	Tom Griffin	.25	.12
40	Bobby Murcer	.40	.20
41	Jim Kern	.25	.12
42	Jose Cruz	.40	.20
43	Ray Bare	.25	.12
44	Bud Harrelson	.30	.15
45	Rawly Eastwick	.25	.12
46	Buck Martinez	.25	.12
47	Lynn McGlothen	.25	.12
48	Tom Paciorek	.25	.12
49	Grant Jackson	.25	.12
50	Ron Cey	.40	.20
51	Brewers Team	.75	.35
52	Ellis Valentine	.25	.12
53	Paul Mitchell	.25	.12
54	Sandy Alomar	.25	.12
55	Jeff Burroughs	.30	.15
56	Rudy May	.25	.12
57	Marc Hill	.25	.12
58	Chet Lemon	.35	.18
59	Larry Christenson	.25	.12
60	Jim Rice	3.50	1.75
61	Manny Sanguillen	.40	.20
62	Eric Raich	.25	.12
63	Tito Fuentes	.25	.12
64	Larry Bittner	.25	.12
65	Skip Lockwood	.25	.12
66	Roy Smalley	.25	.12
67	Joaquin Andujar (R)	.75	.35
68	Bruce Bochte	.25	.12
69	Jim Crawford	.25	.12
70	Johnny Bench	12.00	6.00
71	Dock Ellis	.25	.12
72	Mike Anderson	.25	.12
73	Charlie Williams	.25	.12
74	A's Team	.75	.35
75	Dennis Leonard	.35	.18
76	Tim Foli	.25	.12
77	Dyar Miller	.25	.12
78	Bob Davis	.25	.12
79	Don Money	.25	.12
80	Andy Messersmith	.25	.12
81	Juan Beniquez	.25	.12
82	Jim Rooker	.25	.12
83	Kevin Bell	.25	.12

84	Ollie Brown	.25	.12	141	Mark Littell	.25	.12
85	Duane Kuiper	.25	.12	142	Steve Dillard	.25	.12
86	Pat Zachry	.25	.12	143	Ed Herrmann	.25	.12
87	Glenn Borgmann	.25	.12	144	Bruce Sutter (R)	5.00	2.50
88	Stan Wall	.25	.12	145	Tom Veryzer	.25	.12
89	Butch Hobson (R)	.75	.35	146	Dusty Baker	.35	.18
90	Cesar Cedeno	.35	.18	147	Jackie Brown	.25	.12
91	John Verhoeven	.25	.12	148	Fran Healy	.25	.12
92	Dave Rosello	.25	.12	149	Mike Cubbage	.25	.12
93	Tom Poquette	.25	.12	150	Tom Seaver	12.50	6.25
94	Craig Swan	.25	.12	151	Johnnie LeMaster	.25	.12
95	Keith Hernandez	2.00	1.00	152	Gaylord Perry	3.50	1.75
96	Lou Piniella	.40	.20	153	Ron Jackson	.25	.12
97	Dave Heaverlo	.25	.12	154	Dave Giusti	.25	.12
98	Milt May	.25	.12	155	Joe Rudi	.30	.15
99	Tom Hausman	.25	.12	156	Pete Mackanin	.25	.12
100	Joe Morgan	5.00	2.50	157	Ken Brett	.25	.12
101	Dick Bosman	.25	.12	158	Ted Kubiak	.25	.12
102	Jose Morales	.25	.12	159	Bernie Carbo	.25	.12
103	Mike Bacsik	.25	.12	160	Will McEnaney	.25	.12
104	Omar Moreno (R)	.25	.12	161	Garry Templeton (R)	1.00	.50
105	Steve Yeager	.30	.15	162	Mike Cuellar	.30	.15
106	Mike Flanagan	.40	.20	163	Dave Hilton	.25	.12
107	Bill Melton	.25	.12	164	Tug McGraw	.50	.25
108	Alan Foster	.25	.12	165	Jim Wynn	.35	.18
109	Jorge Orta	.25	.12	166	Bill Campbell	.25	.12
110	Steve Carlton	9.00	4.50	167	Rich Hebner	.25	.12
111	Rico Petrocelli	.30	.18	169	Charlie Spikes	.25	.12
112	Bill Greif	.25	.12	170	Thurman Munson	6.00	3.00
113	Blue Jays Mgr/	.75	.35	171	Ken Sanders	.25	.12
	Coaches			172	John Milner	.25	.12
114	Bruce Dal Canton	.25	.12	173	Chuck Scrivener	.25	.12
115	Rick Manning	.25	.12	174	Nelson Briles	.25	.12
116	Joe Niekro	.30	.15	175	Butch Wynegar (R)	.35	.18
117	Frank White	.35	.18	176	Bob Robertson	.25	.12
118	Rick Jones	.25	.12	177	Bart Johnson	.25	.12
119	John Stearns	.25	.12	178	Bombo Rivera	.25	.12
120	Rod Carew	8.00	4.00	179	Paul Hartzell	.25	.12
121	Gary Nolan	.25	.12	180	Dave Lopes	.35	.18
122	Ben Oglivie	.35	.18	181	Ken McMullen	.25	.12
123	Fred Stanley	.25	.12	182	Dan Spillner	.25	.12
124	George Mitterwald	.25	.12	183	Cardinals Team	.75	.35
125	Bill Travers	.25	.12	184	Bo McLaughlin	.25	.12
126	Rod Gilbreath	.25	.12	185	Sixto Lezcano	.25	.12
127	Ron Fairly	.25	.12	186	Doug Flynn	.25	.12
128	Tommy John	1.00	.50	187	Dick Pole	.25	.12
129	Mike Sadek	.25	.12	188	Bob Tolan	.25	.12
130	Al Oliver	.75	.35	189	Rick Dempsey	.35	.18
131	Orlando Ramirez	.25	.12	190	Ray Burris	.25	.12
132	Chip Lang	.25	.12	191	Doug Griffin	.25	.12
133	Ralph Garr	.25	.12	192	Cito Gaston	.25	.12
134	Padres Team	.75	.35	193	Larry Gura	.25	.12
135	Mark Belanger	.35	.18	194	Gary Matthews	.35	.18
136	Jerry Mumphrey (R)	.35	.18	195	Ed Figueroa	.25	.12
137	Jeff Terpko	.25	.12	196	Len Randle	.25	.12
138	Bob Stinson	.25	.12	197	Ed Ott	.25	.12
139	Fred Norman	.25	.12	198	Wilbur Wood	.25	.12
140	Mike Schmidt	28.00	14.00	199	Pepe Frias	.25	.12

200	Frank Tanana	.45	.22
201	Ed Kranepool	.35	.18
202	Tom Johnson	.25	.12
203	Ed Armbrister	.25	.12
204	Jeff Newman	.25	.12
205	Pete Falcone	.25	.12
206	Boog Powell	.50	.25
207	Glenn Abbott	.25	.12
208	Checklist 133-264	1.00	.50
209	Rob Andrews	.25	.12
210	Fred Lynn	1.50	.75
211	Giants Team	.75	.35
212	Jim Mason	.25	.12
213	Maximino Leon	.25	.12
214	Darrell Porter	.25	.12
215	Butch Metzger	.25	.12
216	Doug DeCinces	.30	.15
217	Tom Underwood	.25	.12
218	John Wathan (R)	.75	.35
219	Joe Coleman	.25	.12
220	Chris Chambliss	.40	.20
221	Bob Bailey	.25	.12
222	Francisco Barrios	.25	.12
223	Earl Williams	.25	.12
224	Rusty Torres	.25	.12
225	Bob Apodaca	.25	.12
226	Leroy Stanton	.25	.12
227	Joe Sambito (R)	.25	.12
228	Twins Team	.75	.35
229	Don Kessinger	.35	.18
230	Vida Blue	.40	.20
231	George Brett (RB)	8.00	4.00
232	Minnie Minoso (RB)	.75	.35
233	Jose Morales (RB)	.35	.18
234	Nolan Ryan (RB)	10.00	5.00
235	Cecil Cooper	.45	.22
236	Tom Buskey	.25	.12
237	Gene Clines	.25	.12
238	Tippy Martinez	.25	.12
239	Bill Plummer	.25	.12
240	Ron LeFlore	.40	.20
241	Dave Tomlin	.25	.12
242	Ken Henderson	.25	.12
243	Ron Reed	.25	.12
244	John Mayberry	.30	.15
245	Rick Rhoden	.25	.12
246	Mike Vail	.25	.12
247	Chris Knapp	.25	.12
248	Wilbur Howard	.25	.12
249	Pete Redfern	.25	.12
250	Bill Madlock	.75	.35
251	Tony Muser	.25	.12
252	Dale Murray	.25	.12
253	John Hale	.25	.12
254	Doyle Alexander	.25	.12
255	George Scott	.30	.15
256	Joe Hoerner	.25	.12
257	Mike Miley	.25	.12
258	Luis Tiant	.60	.30
259	Mets Team	.75	.35
260	J.R. Richard	.35	.18
261	Phil Garner	.45	.22
262	Al Cowens	.25	.12
263	Mike Marshall	.30	.18
264	Tom Hutton	.25	.12
265	Mark Fidrych (R)	1.25	.60
266	Derrel Thomas	.25	.12
267	Ray Fosse	.25	.12
268	Rick Sawyer	.25	.12
269	Joe Lis	.25	.12
270	Dave Parker	4.00	2.00
271	Terry Forster	.25	.12
272	Lee Lacy	.25	.12
273	Eric Soderholm	.25	.12
274	Don Stanhouse	.25	.12
275	Mike Hargrove	.25	.12
276	A.L. Championship	.75	.35
277	N.L. Championship	1.50	.75
278	Danny Frisella	.25	.12
279	Joe Wallis	.25	.12
280	Jim Hunter	2.50	1.25
281	Roy Staiger	.25	.12
282	Sid Monge	.25	.12
283	Jerry DaVanon	.25	.12
284	Mike Norris	.25	.12
285	Brooks Robinson	5.00	2.50
286	Johnny Grubb	.25	.12
287	Reds Team	.75	.35
288	Bob Montgomery	.25	.12
289	Gene Garber	.25	.12
290	Amos Otis	.35	.18
291	Jason Thompson (R)	.35	.18
292	Rogelio Moret	.25	.12
293	Jack Brohamer	.25	.12
294	George Medich	.25	.12
295	Gary Carter	7.00	3.50
296	Don Hood	.25	.12
297	Ken Reitz	.25	.12
298	Charlie Hough	.35	.18
299	Otto Velez	.25	.12
300	Jerry Koosman	.45	.22
301	Toby Harrah	.25	.12
302	Mike Garman	.25	.12
303	Gene Tenace	.35	.18
304	Jim Hughes	.25	.12
305	Mickey Rivers	.30	.15
306	Rick Waits	.25	.12
307	Gary Sutherland	.25	.12
308	Gene Pentz	.25	.12
309	Red Sox Team	.75	.35
310	Larry Bowa	.30	.15
311	Vern Ruhle	.25	.12
312	Rob Belloir	.25	.12
313	Paul Blair	.25	.12
314	Steve Mingori	.25	.12
315	Dave Chalk	.25	.12

316	Steve Rogers	.25	.12
317	Kurt Bevacqua	.25	.12
318	Duffy Dyer	.25	.12
319	Rich Gossage	1.50	.75
320	Ken Griffey	1.25	.60
321	Dave Goltz	.25	.12
322	Bill Russell	.35	.18
323	Larry Lintz	.25	.12
324	John Curtis	.25	.12
325	Mike Ivie	.25	.12
326	Jesse Jefferson	.25	.12
327	Astros Team	.75	.35
328	Tommy Boggs	.25	.12
329	Ron Hodges	.25	.12
330	George Hendrick	.30	.15
331	Jim Colborn	.25	.12
332	Elliott Maddox	.25	.12
333	Paul Reuschel	.25	.12
334	Bill Stein	.25	.12
335	Bill Robinson	.30	.15
336	Denny Doyle	.25	.12
337	Ron Schueler	.25	.12
338	Dave Duncan	.25	.12
339	Adrian Devine	.25	.12
340	Hal McRae	.40	.20
341	Joe Kerrigan	.25	.12
342	Jerry Remy	.25	.12
343	Ed Halicki	.25	.12
344	Brian Downing	.50	.25
345	Reggie Smith	.30	.15
346	Bill Singer	.25	.12
347	George Foster	1.00	.50
348	Brent Strom	.25	.12
349	Jim Holt	.25	.12
350	Larry Dierker	.25	.12
351	Jim Sundberg	.30	.15
352	Mike Phillips	.25	.12
353	Stan Thomas	.25	.12
354	Pirates Team	.75	.35
355	Lou Brock	5.00	2.50
356	Checklist 265-396	1.00	.50
357	Tim McCarver	.35	.18
358	Tom House	.25	.12
359	Willie Randolph	2.50	1.25
360	Rick Monday	.30	.15
361	Eduardo Rodriguez	.25	.12
362	Tommy Davis	.30	.15
363	Dave Roberts	.25	.12
364	Vic Correll	.25	.12
365	Mike Torrez	.25	.12
366	Ted Sizemore	.25	.12
367	Dave Hamilton	.25	.12
368	Mike Jorgensen	.25	.12
369	Terry Humphrey	.25	.12
370	John Montefusco	.25	.12
371	Royals Team	.90	.45
372	Rich Folkers	.25	.12
373	Bert Campaneris	.35	.18
374	Kent Tekulve	.25	.12
375	Larry Hisle	.25	.12
376	Nino Espinosa	.25	.12
377	Dave McKay	.25	.12
378	Jim Umbarger	.25	.12
379	Larry Cox	.25	.12
380	Lee May	.25	.12
381	Bob Forsch	.25	.12
382	Charlie Moore	.25	.12
383	Stan Bahnsen	.25	.12
384	Darrel Chaney	.25	.12
385	Dave LaRoche	.25	.12
386	Manny Mota	.30	.15
387	Yankees Team	1.50	.75
388	Terry Harmon	.25	.12
389	Ken Kravec	.25	.12
390	Dave Winfield	14.00	7.00
391	Don Warthen	.25	.12
392	Phil Roof	.25	.12
393	John Lowenstein	.25	.12
394	Bill Laxton	.25	.12
395	Manny Trillo	.25	.12
396	Tom Murphy	.25	.12
397	Larry Herndon (R)	.25	.12
398	Tom Burgmeier	.25	.12
399	Bruce Boisclair	.25	.12
400	Steve Garvey	4.50	2.25
401	Mickey Scott	.25	.12
402	Tommy Helms	.25	.12
403	Tom Grieve	.25	.12
404	Eric Rasmussen	.25	.12
405	Claudell Washington	.30	.15
406	Tim Johnson	.25	.12
407	Dave Freisleben	.25	.12
408	Cesar Tovar	.25	.12
409	Pete Broberg	.25	.12
410	Willie Montanez	.25	.12
411	WS Games 1 & 2	1.50	.75
412	WS Games 3 & 4	1.25	.60
413	WS Summary	1.00	.50
414	Tommy Harper	.25	.12
415	Jay Johnstone	.30	.15
416	Chuck Hartenstein	.25	.12
417	Wayne Garrett	.25	.12
418	White Sox Team	.90	.45
419	Steve Swisher	.25	.12
420	Rusty Staub	.40	.20
421	Doug Rau	.25	.12
422	Freddie Patek	.25	.12
423	Gary Lavelle	.25	.12
424	Steve Brye	.25	.12
425	Joe Torre	.40	.20
426	Dick Drago	.25	.12
427	Dave Rader	.25	.12
428	Rangers Team	.75	.35
429	Ken Boswell	.25	.12
430	Ferguson Jenkins	3.50	1.75
431	Dave Collins	.25	.12

432	Buzz Capra	.25	.12
433	Nate Colbert (Clock)	.30	.15
434	Carl Yastrzemski (Clock)	1.25	.60
435	Maury Wills (Clock)	.50	.25
436	Bob Keegan (Clock)	.30	.15
437	Ralph Kiner (Clock)	.75	.35
438	Marty Perez	.25	.12
439	Gorman Thomas	.35	.18
440	Jon Matlack	.30	.15
441	Larvell Blanks	.25	.12
442	Braves Team	.75	.35
443	Lamar Johnson	.25	.12
444	Wayne Twitchell	.25	.12
445	Ken Singleton	.30	.15
446	Bill Bonham	.25	.12
447	Jerry Turner	.25	.12
448	Ellie Rodriguez	.25	.12
449	Al Fitzmorris	.25	.12
450	Pete Rose	12.00	6.00
451	Checklist 397-528	1.00	.50
452	Mike Caldwell	.25	.12
453	Pedro Garcia	.25	.12
454	Andy Etchebarren	.25	.12
455	Rick Wise	.30	.15
456	Leon Roberts	.25	.12
457	Steve Luebber	.25	.12
458	Leo Foster	.25	.12
459	Steve Foucault	.25	.12
460	Willie Stargell	4.00	2.00
461	Dick Tidrow	.25	.12
462	Don Baylor	1.00	.50
463	Jamie Quirk	.25	.12
464	Randy Moffitt	.25	.12
465	Rico Carty	.30	.15
466	Fred Holdsworth	.25	.12
467	Phillies Team	.75	.35
468	Ramon Hernandez	.25	.12
469	Pat Kelly	.25	.12
470	Ted Simmons	.75	.35
471	Del Unser	.25	.12
472	Rookie Pitchers	.30	.15
	Don Aase		
	Bob McClure		
	Gil Patterson (R)		
	Dave Wehrmeister		
473	Rookie Outfielders	75.00	37.50
	Andre Dawson (R)		
	Gene Richards (R)		
	John Scott (R)		
	Denny Walling (R)		
474	Rookie Shortstops	.35	.18
	Bob Bailor		
	Kiko Garcia (R)		
	Craig Reynolds		
	Alex Taveras		
475	Rookie Pitchers	.30	.15
	Chris Batton (R)		

	Rick Camp (R)		
	Scott McGregor		
	Manny Sarmiento		
476	Rookie Catchers	40.00	20.00
	Gary Alexander		
	Rick Cerone (R)		
	Dale Murphy (R)		
	Kevin Pasley (R)		
477	Rookie Infielders	.30	.15
	Doug Ault (R)		
	Rich Dauer (R)		
	Orlando Gonzalez (R)		
	Phil Mankowski (R)		
478	Rookie Pitchers	.30	.15
	Jim Gideon (R)		
	Leon Hooten (R)		
	Dave Johnson (R)		
	Mark Lemongello (R)		
479	Rookie Outfielders	.30	.15
	Brian Asselstine (R)		
	Wayne Gross (R)		
	Sam Mejia (R)		
	Alvis Woods (R)		
480	Carl Yastrzemski	7.00	3.50
481	Roger Metzger	.25	.12
482	Tony Solaita	.25	.12
483	Richie Zisk	.25	.12
484	Burt Hooton	.25	.12
485	Roy White	.25	.12
486	Ed Bane	.25	.12
487	Rookie Pitchers	.25	.12
	Larry Anderson		
	Ed Glynn (R)		
	Joe Henderson (R)		
	Greg Terlecky (R)		
488	Rookie Outfielders	10.00	5.00
	Jack Clark (R)		
	Ruppert Jones (R)		
	Lee Mazzilli (R)		
	Dan Thomas (R)		
489	Rookie Pitchers (R)	.45	.22
	Len Barker (R)		
	Randy Lerch		
	Greg Minton (R)		
	Mike Overy (R)		
490	Rookie Shortstops	.30	.15
	Billy Almon (R)		
	Mickey Klutts (R)		
	Tommy McMillan (R)		
	Mark Wagner (R)		
491	Rookie Pitchers	6.00	3.00
	Mike Dupree (R)		
	Denny Martinez (R)		
	Craig Mitchell (R)		
	Bob Sykes (R)		
492	Rookie Outfielders	.75	.35
	Tony Armas (R)		
	Steve Kemp (R)		

	Carlos Lopez (R)		
	Gary Woods (R)		
493	Rookie Pitchers	.35	.18
	Mike Krukow (R)		
	Jim Otten		
	Gary Wheelock (R)		
	Mike Willis (R)		
494	Rookie Infielders	1.50	.75
	Juan Bernhardt (R)		
	Mike Champion		
	Jim Gantner (R)		
	Bump Wills (R)		
495	Al Hrabosky	.35	.18
496	Gary Thomasson	.25	.12
497	Clay Carroll	.25	.12
498	Sal Bando	.35	.18
499	Pablo Torrealba	.25	.12
500	Dave Kingman	.75	.35
501	Jim Bibby	.25	.12
502	Randy Hundley	.25	.12
503	Bill Lee	.25	.12
504	Dodgers Team	1.00	.50
505	Oscar Gamble	.35	.18
506	Steve Grilli	.25	.12
507	Mike Hegan	.25	.12
508	Dave Pagan	.25	.12
409	Cookie Rojas	.25	.12
510	John Candelaria	.50	.25
511	Bill Fahey	.25	.12
512	Jack Billingham	.25	.12
513	Jerry Terrell	.25	.12
514	Cliff Johnson	.25	.12
515	Chris Speier	.25	.12
516	Bake McBride	.25	.12
517	Pete Vuckovich (R)	.50	.25
518	Cubs Team	.75	.35
519	Don Kirkwood	.25	.12
520	Garry Maddox	.30	.15
521	Bob Grich	.35	.18
522	Enzo Hernandez	.25	.12
523	Rollie Fingers	4.50	2.25
524	Rowland Office	.25	.12
525	Dennis Eckersley	16.00	8.00
526	Larry Parrish	.30	.15
527	Dan Meyer	.25	.12
528	Bill Castro	.25	.12
529	Jim Essian	.25	.12
530	Rick Reuschel	.35	.18
531	Lyman Bostock	.35	.18
532	Jim Willoughby	.25	.12
533	Mickey Stanley	.25	.12
534	Paul Splittorff	.25	.12
535	Cesar Geronimo	.25	.12
536	Vic Albury	.25	.12
537	Dave Roberts	.25	.12
538	Frank Taveras	.25	.12
539	Mike Wallace	.25	.12
540	Bob Watson	.40	.20
541	John Denny	.25	.12
542	Frank Duffy	.25	.12
543	Ron Blomberg	.25	.12
544	Gary Ross	.25	.12
545	Bob Boone	1.00	.50
546	Orioles Team	.80	.40
547	Willie McCovey	5.00	2.50
548	Joel Youngblood (R)	.30	.15
549	Jerry Royster	.25	.12
550	Randy Jones	.30	.15
551	Bill North	.30	.15
552	Pepe Mangual	.25	.12
553	Jack Heidemann	.25	.12
554	Bruce Kimm	.25	.12
555	Dan Ford	.25	.12
556	Doug Bird	.25	.12
557	Jerry White	.25	.12
558	Elias Sosa	.25	.12
559	Alan Bannister	.25	.12
560	Dave Concepcion	1.25	.60
561	Pete LaCock	.25	.12
562	Checklist 529-660	1.00	.50
563	Bruce Kison	.25	.12
564	Alan Ashby	.25	.12
565	Mickey Lolich	.45	.22
566	Rick Miller	.25	.12
567	Enos Cabell	.25	.12
568	Carlos May	.25	.12
569	Jim Lonborg	.30	.15
570	Bobby Bonds	.75	.35
571	Darrell Evans	.45	.22
572	Ross Grimsley	.25	.12
573	Joe Ferguson	.25	.12
574	Aurelio Rodriguez	.25	.12
575	Dick Ruthven	.25	.12
576	Fred Kendall	.25	.12
577	Jerry Augustine	.25	.12
578	Bob Randall	.25	.12
579	Don Carrithers	.25	.12
580	George Brett	36.00	18.00
581	Pedro Borbon	.25	.12
582	Ed Kirkpatrick	.25	.12
583	Paul Lindblad	.25	.12
584	Ed Goodson	.25	.12
585	Rick Burleson	.30	.15
586	Steve Renko	.25	.12
587	Rick Baldwin	.25	.12
588	Dave Moates	.25	.12
589	Mike Cosgrove	.25	.12
590	Buddy Bell	.30	.15
591	Chris Arnold	.25	.12
592	Dan Briggs	.25	.12
593	Dennis Blair	.25	.12
594	Biff Pocoroba	.25	.12
495	John Hiller	.25	.12
596	Jerry Martin (R)	.25	.12
597	Mariners Mgr/ Coaches	.60	.30

598	Sparky Lyle	.60	.30
599	Mike Tyson	.25	.12
600	Jim Palmer	7.00	3.50
601	Mike Lum	.25	.12
602	Andy Hassler	.25	.12
603	Willie Davis	.30	.15
604	Jim Slaton	.25	.12
605	Felix Millan	.25	.12
606	Steve Braun	.25	.12
607	Larry Demery	.25	.12
608	Roy Howell	.25	.12
609	Jim Barr	.25	.12
610	Jose Cardenal	.25	.12
611	Dave Lemanczyk	.25	.12
612	Barry Foote	.25	.12
613	Reggie Cleveland	.25	.12
614	Greg Gross	.25	.12
615	Phil Niekro	3.50	1.75
616	Tommy Sandt	.25	.12
617	Bobby Darwin	.25	.12
618	Pat Dobson	.30	.15
619	Johnny Oates	.30	.15
620	Don Sutton	3.00	1.75
621	Tigers Team	.75	.35
622	Jim Wohlford	.25	.12
623	Jack Kucek	.25	.12
624	Hector Cruz	.25	.12
625	Ken Holtzman	.25	.12
626	Al Bumbry	.25	.12
627	Bob Myrick	.25	.12
628	Mario Guerrero	.25	.12
629	Bobby Valentine	.35	.18
630	Bert Blyleven	2.50	1.25
631	George & Ken Brett	5.00	2.50
632	Bob & Ken Forsch	.35	.18
633	Carlos & Lee May	.35	.18
634	Paul & Rick Reuschel	.35	.18
635	Robin Yount	36.00	18.00
636	Santo Alcala	.25	.12
637	Alex Johnson	.25	.12
638	Jim Kaat	.75	.35
639	Jerry Morales	.25	.12
640	Carlton Fisk	9.00	4.50
641	Dan Larson	.25	.12
642	Willie Crawford	.25	.12
643	Mike Pazik	.25	.12
644	Matt Alexander	.25	.12
645	Jerry Reuss	.35	.18
646	Andres Mora	.25	.12
647	Expos Team	.75	.35
648	Jim Spencer	.25	.12
649	Dave Cash	.25	.12
650	Nolan Ryan	42.00	21.00
651	Von Joshua	.25	.12
652	Tom Walker	.25	.12
653	Diego Segui	.25	.12
654	Ron Pruitt	.25	.12
655	Tony Perez	2.50	1.25

656	Ron Guidry	2.00	1.00
657	Mick Kelleher	.25	.12
658	Marty Pattin	.25	.12
659	Merv Rettenmund	.25	.12
660	Willie Horton	.40	.20

1978 Topps

Topps increased the size of their set to 726-cards in 1978. Cards measure 2-1/2" by 3-1/2". Card fronts include large color photos with the player's name and team located in the border below the photo. The player's position is printed in a small baseball design at the top right corner. Key subsets include Record Breakers (RB) (1-7), League Leaders, World Series and Playoff Highlights, All-Stars and Rookies.

		NR/MT	EX
Complete Set (726)		360.00	180.00
Commons (1-726)		.15	.08

1	Lou Brock (RB)	3.00	1.50
2	Sparky Lyle (RB)	.50	.25
3	Willie McCovey(RB)	1.50	.75
4	Brooks Robinson (RB)	1.50	.75
5	Pete Rose (RB)	3.50	1.75
6	Nolan Ryan (RB)	8.50	4.25
7	Reggie Jackson (RB)	4.50	2.25
8	Mike Sadek	.15	.08
9	Doug DeCinces	.20	.10
10	Phil Niekro	3.00	1.50
11	Rick Manning	.15	.08
12	Don Aase	.15	.08

13	Art Howe (R)	.35	.18	71	Terry Humphrey	.15	.08
14	Lerrin LaGrow	.15	.08	72	Andre Dawson	22.00	11.00
15	Tony Perez	1.00	.50	73	Andy Hassler	.15	.08
16	Roy White	.15	.08	74	Checklist 1-121	.75	.35
17	Mike Krukow	.15	.08	75	Dick Ruthven	.15	.08
18	Bob Grich	.25	.12	76	Steve Ontiveros	.15	.08
19	Darrell Porter	.15	.08	77	Ed Kirkpatrick	.15	.08
20	Pete Rose	5.00	2.50	78	Pablo Torrealba	.15	.08
21	Steve Kemp	.15	.08	79	Darrell Johnson	.15	.08
22	Charlie Hough	.20	.10	80	Ken Griffey	1.00	.50
23	Bump Wills	.15	.08	81	Pete Redfern	.15	.08
24	Don Money	.15	.08	82	Giants Team	.75	.35
25	Jon Matlack	.20	.10	83	Bob Montgomery	.15	.08
26	Rich Hebner	.15	.08	84	Kent Tekulve	.20	.10
27	Geoff Zahn	.15	.08	85	Ron Fairly	.15	.08
28	Ed Ott	.15	.08	86	Dave Tomlin	.15	.08
29	Bob Lacey	.15	.08	87	John Lowenstein	.15	.08
30	George Hendrick	.20	.10	88	Mike Phillipsk	.15	.08
31	Glenn Abbott	.15	.08	89	Ken Clay	.15	.08
32	Garry Templeton	.40	.20	90	Larry Bowa	.30	.15
33	Dave Lemanczyk	.15	.08	91	Oscar Zamora	.15	.08
34	Willie McCovey	3.50	1.75	92	Adrian Devine	.15	.08
35	Sparky Lyle	.35	.18	93	Bobby Cox	.15	.08
36	Eddie Murray (R)	90.00	45.00	94	Chuck Scrivener	.15	.08
37	Rich Waits	.15	.08	95	Jamie Quirk	.15	.08
38	Willie Montanez	.15	.08	96	Orioles Team	.75	.35
39	Floyd Bannister (R)	.50	.25	97	Stan Bahnsen	.15	.08
40	Carl Yastrzemski	5.00	2.50	98	Jim Essian	.15	.08
41	Burt Hooton	.15	.08	99	Willie Hernandez (R)	.50	.25
42	Jorge Orta	.15	.08	100	George Brett	24.00	12.00
43	Bill Atkinson	.15	.08	101	Sid Monge	.15	.08
44	Toby Harrah	.15	.08	102	Matt Alexander	.15	.08
45	Mark Fidrych	.40	.20	103	Tom Murphy	.15	.08
46	Al Cowens	.15	.08	104	Lee Lacy	.15	.08
47	Jack Billingham	.15	.08	105	Reggie Cleveland	.15	.08
48	Don Baylor	.80	.40	106	Bill Plummer	.15	.08
49	Ed Kranepool	.25	.12	107	Ed Halicki	.15	.08
50	Rick Reuschel	.25	.12	108	Von Joshua	.15	.08
51	Charlie Moore	.15	.08	109	Joe Torre	.35	.18
52	Jim Lonborg	.25	.12	110	Richie Zisk	.15	.08
53	Phil Garner	.20	.10	111	Mike Tyson	.15	.08
54	Tom Johnson	.15	.08	112	Astros Team	.75	.35
55	Mitchell Page	.15	.08	113	Don Carrithers	.15	.08
56	Randy Jones	.20	.10	114	Paul Blair	.15	.08
57	Dan Meyer	.15	.08	115	Gary Nolan	.15	.08
58	Bob Forsch	.15	.08	116	Tucker Ashford	.15	.08
59	Otto Velez	.15	.08	117	John Montague	.15	.08
60	Thurman Munson	4.50	2.25	118	Terry Harmon	.15	.08
61	Larvell Blanks	.15	.08	119	Denny Martinez	1.50	.75
62	Jim Barr	.15	.08	120	Gary Carter	4.50	2.25
63	Don Zimmer	.20	.10	121	Alvis Woods	.15	.08
64	Gene Pentz	.15	.08	122	Dennis Eckersley	8.50	4.25
65	Ken Singleton	.25	.12	123	Manny Trillo	.15	.08
66	White Sox Team	.75	.35	124	Dave Rozema (R)	.20	.10
67	Claudell Washington	.25	.12	125	George Scott	.25	.12
68	Steve Foucault	.15	.08	126	Paul Moskau	.15	.08
69	Mike Vail	.15	.08	127	Chet Lemon	.25	.12
70	Rich Gossage	1.25	.60	128	Bill Russell	.30	.15

129	Jim Colborn	.15	.08	187	Jerry Royster	.15	.08
130	Jeff Burroughs	.15	.08	188	Al Bumbry	.15	.08
131	Bert Blyleven	1.25	.60	189	Tom Lasorda	.35	.18
132	Enos Cabell	.20	.10	190	John Candelaria	.30	.15
133	Jerry Augustine	.15	.08	191	Rodney Scott	.15	.08
134	Steve Henderson (R)	.15	.08	192	Padres Team	.75	.35
135	Ron Guidry	.80	.40	193	Rich Chiles	.15	.08
136	Ted Sizemore	.15	.08	194	Derrel Thomas	.15	.08
137	Craig Kusick	.15	.08	195	Larry Dierker	.15	.08
138	Larry Demery	.15	.08	196	Bob Bailor	.15	.08
139	Wayne Gross	.15	.08	197	Nino Espinosa	.15	.08
140	Rollie Fingers	4.00	2.00	198	Ron Pruitt	.15	.08
141	Rupert Jones	.15	.08	199	Craig Reynolds	.15	.08
142	John Montefusco	.15	.08	200	Reggie Jackson	12.50	6.25
143	Keith Hernandez	2.00	1.00	201	Batting Leaders	1.25	.60
144	Jesse Jefferson	.15	.08	202	Home Run Leaders	.75	.35
145	Rick Monday	.25	.12	203	RBI Leaders	.40	.20
146	Doyle Alexander	.15	.08	204	Stolen Base Leaders	.25	.12
147	Lee Mazzilli	.15	.08	205	Victory Leaders	1.50	.75
148	Andre Thornton	.25	.12	206	Strikeout Leaders	3.00	1.50
149	Dale Murray	.15	.08	207	ERA Leaders	.25	.12
150	Bobby Bonds	.60	.30	208	Leading Firemen	1.00	.50
151	Milt Wilcox	.15	.08	209	Dock Ellis	.15	.08
152	Ivan DeJesus (R)	.25	.12	210	Jose Cardenal	.15	.08
153	Steve Stone	.25	.12	211	Earl Weaver	.15	.08
154	Cecil Cooper	.25	.12	212	Mike Caldwell	.15	.08
155	Butch Hopson	.25	.12	213	Alan Bannister	.15	.08
156	Andy Messersmith	.15	.08	214	Angels Team	.75	.35
157	Pete LaCock	.15	.08	215	Darrell Evans	.30	.15
158	Joaquin Andujar	.30	.18	216	Mike Paxton	.15	.08
159	Lou Piniella	.35	.18	217	Rod Gilbreath	.15	.08
160	Jim Palmer	6.00	3.00	218	Marty Pattin	.15	.08
161	Bob Boone	.80	.40	219	Mike Cubbage	.15	.08
162	Paul Thormodsgard	.15	.08	220	Pedro Borbon	.15	.08
163	Bill North	.15	.08	221	Chris Speier	.15	.08
164	Bob Owchinko	.15	.08	222	Jerry Martin	.15	.08
165	Rennie Stennett	.15	.08	223	Bruce Kison	.15	.08
166	Carlos Lopez	.15	.08	224	Jerry Tabb	.15	.08
167	Tim Foli	.15	.08	225	Don Gullett	.25	.12
168	Reggie Smith	.30	.15	226	Joe Ferguson	.20	.10
169	Jerry Johnson	.15	.08	227	Al Fitzmorris	.15	.08
170	Lou Brock	4.00	2.00	228	Manny Mota	.20	.10
171	Pat Zachry	.15	.08	229	Leo Foster	.15	.08
172	Mike Hargrove	.15	.08	230	Al Hrabosky	.20	.10
173	Robin Yount	24.00	12.00	231	Wayne Nordhagen	.15	.08
174	Wayne Garland	.15	.08	232	Mickey Stanley	.20	.10
175	Jerry Morales	.25	.12	233	Dick Pole	.15	.08
176	Milt May	.15	.08	234	Herman Franks	.15	.08
177	Gene Garber	.15	.08	235	Tim McCarver	.25	.12
178	Dave Chalk	.15	.08	236	Terry Whitfield	.15	.08
179	Dick Tidrow	.15	.08	237	Rich Dauer	.15	.08
180	Dave Concepcion	.80	.40	238	Juan Beniquez	.15	.08
181	Ken Forsch	.15	.08	239	Dyar Miller	.15	.08
182	Jim Spencer	.15	.08	240	Gene Tenace	.25	.12
183	Doug Bird	.15	.08	241	Pete Vuckovich	.25	.12
184	Checklist 122-242	.75	.35	242	Barry Bonnell	.15	.08
185	Ellis Valentine	.15	.08	243	Bob McClure	.15	.08
186	Bob Stanley	.15	.08	244	Expos Team	.75	.35

245	Rick Burleson	.25	.12
246	Dan Driessen	.25	.12
247	Larry Christenso	.15	.08
248	Frank White	.20	.10
249	Dave Goltz	.15	.08
250	Graig Nettles	.35	.18
251	Don Kirkwood	.15	.08
252	Steve Swisher	.15	.08
253	Jim Kern	.15	.08
254	Dave Collins	.15	.08
255	Jerry Reuss	.25	.12
256	Joe Altobelli	.15	.08
257	Hector Cruz	.15	.08
258	John Hiller	.15	.08
259	Dodgers Team	.75	.35
260	Bert Campaneris	.25	.12
261	Tim Hosley	.15	.08
262	Rudy May	.15	.08
263	Danny Walton	.15	.08
264	Jamie Easterly	.15	.08
265	Sal Bando	.20	.10
266	Bob Shirley	.15	.08
267	Doug Ault	.15	.08
268	Gil Flores	.15	.08
269	Wayne Twitchell	.15	.08
270	Carlton Fisk	7.00	3.50
271	Randy Lerch	.15	.08
272	Royle Stillman	.15	.08
273	Fred Norman	.15	.08
274	Freddie Patek	.15	.08
275	Dan Ford	.15	.08
276	Bill Bonham	.15	.08
277	Bruce Boisclair	.15	.08
278	Enrique Romo	.15	.08
279	Bill Virdon	.15	.08
280	Buddy Bell	.20	.10
281	Eric Rasmussen	.15	.08
282	Yankees Team	1.25	.60
283	Omar Moreno	.15	.08
284	Randy Moffitt	.15	.08
285	Steve Yeager	.20	.10
286	Ben Oglivie	.25	.12
287	Kiko Garcia	.15	.08
288	Dave Hamilton	.15	.08
289	Checklist 243-363	.75	.35
290	Willie Horton	.25	.12
291	Gary Ross	.15	.08
292	Gene Richard	.15	.08
293	Mike Willis	.15	.08
294	Larry Parrish	.25	.12
295	Bill Lee	.20	.10
296	Biff Pocoroba	.15	.08
297	Warren Brusstar	.15	.08
298	Tony Armas	.25	.12
299	Whitey Herzog	.20	.10
300	Joe Morgan	4.00	2.00
301	Buddy Schultz	.15	.08
302	Cubs Team	.75	.35
303	Sam Hinds	.15	.08
304	John Milner	.15	.08
305	Rico Carty	.20	.10
306	Joe Niekro	.20	.10
307	Glenn Borgmann	.15	.08
308	Jim Rooker	.15	.08
309	Cliff Johnson	.15	.08
310	Don Sutton	2.50	1.25
311	Jose Baez	.15	.08
312	Greg Minton	.15	.08
313	Andy Etchebarren	.15	.08
314	Paul Lindblad	.15	.08
315	Mark Belanger	.25	.12
316	Henry Cruz	.15	.08
317	Dave Johnson	.15	.08
318	Tom Griffin	.15	.08
319	Alan Ashby	.15	.08
320	Fred Lynn	1.25	.60
321	Santo Alcala	.15	.08
322	Tom Paciorek	.15	.08
323	Jim Fregosi	.20	.10
324	Vern Rapp	.15	.08
325	Bruce Sutter	1.00	.50
326	Mike Lum	.15	.08
327	Rick Langford	.15	.08
328	Brewers Team	.75	.35
329	John Verhoeven	.15	.08
330	Bob Watson	.40	.20
331	Mark Littell	.15	.08
332	Duane Kuiper	.15	.08
333	Jim Todd	.15	.08
334	John Stearns	.15	.08
335	Bucky Dent	.50	.25
336	Steve Busby	.15	.08
337	Tom Grieve	.15	.08
338	Dave Heaverlo	.15	.08
339	Mario Guerrero	.15	.08
340	Bake McBride	.15	.08
341	Mike Flanagan	.30	.15
342	Aurelio Rodriguz	.15	.08
343	John Wathan	.15	.08
344	Sam Ewing	.15	.08
345	Luis Tiant	.40	.20
346	Larry Biittner	.15	.08
347	Terry Forster	.15	.08
348	Del Unser	.15	.08
349	Rick Camp	.15	.08
350	Steve Garvey	3.50	1.75
351	Jeff Torborg	.20	.10
352	Tony Scott	.15	.08
353	Doug Bair	.15	.08
354	Cesar Geronimo	.15	.08
355	Bill Travers	.15	.08
356	Mets Team	.75	.35
357	Tom Poquette	.15	.08
358	Mark Lemongello	.15	.08
359	Marc Hill	.15	.08
360	Mike Schmidt	18.00	9.00

361	Chris Knapp	.15	.08
362	Dave May	.15	.08
363	Bob Randall	.15	.08
364	Jerry Turner	.15	.08
365	Ed Figueroa	.15	.08
366	Larry Milbourne	.15	.08
367	Rick Dempsey	.20	.10
368	Balor Moore	.15	.08
369	Tim Nordbrook	.15	.08
370	Rusty Staub	.40	.20
371	Ray Burris	.15	.08
372	Brian Asselstine	.15	.08
373	Jim Willoughby	.15	.08
374	Jose Morales	.15	.08
375	Tommy John	1.00	.50
376	Jim Wohlford	.15	.08
377	Manny Sarmiento	.15	.08
378	Bobby Winkles	.15	.08
379	Skip Lockwood	.15	.08
380	Ted Simmons	.75	.35
381	Phillies Team	.75	.35
382	Joe Lahoud	.15	.08
383	Mario Mendoza	.15	.08
384	Jack Clark	2.00	1.00
385	Tito Fuentes	.15	.08
386	Bob Gorinski	.15	.08
387	Ken Holtzman	.20	.10
388	Bill Fahey	.15	.08
389	Julio Gonzalez	.15	.08
390	Oscar Gamble	.20	.10
391	Larry Haney	.15	.08
392	Billy Almon	.15	.08
393	Tippy Martinez	.15	.08
394	Roy Howell	.15	.08
395	Jim Hughes	.15	.08
396	Bob Stinson	.15	.08
397	Greg Gross	.15	.08
398	Don Hood	.15	.08
399	Pete Mackanin	.15	.08
400	Nolan Ryan	32.00	16.00
401	Sparky Anderson	.25	.12
402	Dave Campbell	.15	.08
403	Bud Harrelson	.25	.12
404	Tigers Team	.75	.35
405	Rawly Eastwick	.15	.08
406	Mike Jorgensen	.15	.08
407	Odell Jones	.15	.08
408	Joe Zdeb	.15	.08
409	Ron Schueler	.15	.08
410	Bill Madlock	.75	.35
411	A.L. Championships	.75	.35
412	N.L. Championships	.60	.30
413	World Series	3.50	1.75
414	Darold Knowles	.15	.08
415	Ray Fosse	.15	.08
416	Jack Brohamer	.15	.08
417	Mike Garman	.15	.08
418	Tony Muser	.15	.08
419	Jerry Garvin	.15	.08
420	Greg Luzinski	.40	.20
421	Junior Moore	.15	.08
422	Steve Braun	.15	.08
423	Dave Rosello	.15	.08
424	Red Sox Team	.75	.35
425	Steve Rogers	.20	.10
426	Fred Kendall	.15	.08
427	Mario Soto (R)	.50	.25
428	Joel Youngblood	.15	.08
429	Mike Barlow	.15	.08
430	Al Oliver	.50	.25
431	Butch Metzger	.15	.08
432	Terry Bulling	.15	.08
433	Fernando Gonzalez	.15	.08
434	Mike Norris	.15	.08
435	Checklist 364-484	.75	.35
436	Vic Harris	.15	.08
437	Bo McLaughlin	.15	.08
438	John Ellis	.15	.08
439	Ken Kravec	.15	.08
440	Dave Lopes	.30	.15
441	Larry Gura	.15	.08
442	Elliott Maddox	.15	.08
443	Darrel Chaney	.15	.08
444	Roy Hartsfield	.15	.08
445	Mike Ivie	.15	.08
446	Tug McGraw	.40	.20
447	Leroy Stanton	.15	.08
448	Bill Castro	.15	.08
449	Tim Blackwell	.15	.08
450	Tom Seaver	8.50	4.25
451	Twins Team	.75	.35
452	Jerry Mumphrey	.15	.08
453	Doug Flyn	.15	.08
454	Dave LaRoche	.15	.08
455	Bill Robinson	.25	.12
456	Vern Ruhle	.15	.08
457	Bob Bailey	.15	.08
458	Jeff Newman	.15	.08
459	Charlie Spikes	.15	.08
460	Jim Hunter	3.00	1.50
461	Rob Andrews	.15	.08
462	Rogelio Moret	.15	.08
463	Kevin Bell	.15	.08
464	Jerry Grote	.15	.08
465	Hal McRae	.35	.18
466	Dennis Blair	.15	.08
467	Alvin Dark	.15	.08
468	Warren Cromartie (R)	.35	.18
469	Rick Cerone	.25	.12
470	J.R. Richard	.30	.18
471	Roy Smalley	.15	.08
472	Ron Reed	.15	.08
473	Bill Buckner	.40	.20
474	Jim Slaton	.15	.08
475	Gary Matthews	.25	.12
476	Bill Stein	.15	.08

477	Doug Capilla	.15	.08
478	Jerry Remy	.15	.08
479	Cardinals Team	.75	.35
480	Ron LeFlore	.25	.12
481	Jackson Todd	.15	.08
482	Rick Miller	.15	.08
483	Ken Macha	.15	.08
484	Jim Norris	.15	.08
485	Chris Chambliss	.25	.12
486	John Curtis	.15	.08
487	Jim Tyrone	.15	.08
488	Dan Spillner	.15	.08
489	Rudy Meoli	.15	.08
490	Amos Otis	.30	.15
491	Scott McGregor	.25	.15
492	Jim Sundberg	.20	.10
493	Steve Renko	.15	.08
494	Chuck Tanner	.15	.08
495	Dave Cash	.15	.08
496	Jim Clancy (R)	.25	.12
497	Glenn Adams	.15	.08
498	Joe Sambito	.15	.08
499	Mariners Team	.75	.35
500	George Foster	.75	.35
501	Dave Roberts	.15	.08
502	Pat Rockett	.15	.08
503	Ike Hampton	.15	.08
504	Roger Freed	.15	.08
505	Felix Millan	.15	.08
506	Ron Blomberg	.15	.08
507	Willie Crawford	.15	.08
508	Johnny Oates	.20	.10
509	Brent Strom	.15	.08
510	Willie Stargell	3.50	1.75
511	Frank Duffy	.15	.08
512	Larry Herndon	.15	.08
513	Barry Foote	.15	.08
514	Rob Sperring	.15	.08
515	Tim Corcoran	.15	.08
516	Gary Beare	.15	.08
517	Andres Mora	.15	.08
518	Tommy Boggs	.15	.08
519	Brian Downing	.30	.15
520	Larry Hisle	.20	.10
521	Steve Staggs	.15	.08
522	Dick Williams	.15	.08
523	Donnie Moore (R)	.20	.10
524	Bernie Carbo	.15	.08
525	Jerry Terrell	.15	.08
526	Reds Team	.75	.35
527	Vic Correll	.15	.08
528	Rob Picciolo	.15	.08
529	Paul Hartzell	.15	.08
530	Dave Winfield	10.00	5.00
531	Tom Underwood	.15	.08
532	Skip Jutze	.15	.08
533	Sandy Alomar	.15	.08
534	Wilbur Howard	.15	.08
535	Checklist 485-606	.75	.35
536	Roric Harrison	.15	.08
537	Bruce Bochte	.15	.08
538	Johnnie LeMaster	.15	.08
539	Vic Davalillo	.15	.08
540	Steve Carlton	7.50	3.50
541	Larry Cox	.15	.08
542	Tim Johnson	.15	.08
543	Larry Harlow	.15	.08
544	Len Randle	.15	.08
545	Bill Campbell	.15	.08
546	Ted Martinez	.15	.08
547	John Scott	.15	.08
548	Billy Hunter	.15	.08
549	Joe Kerrigan	.15	.08
550	John Mayberry	.25	.12
551	Braves Team	.75	.35
552	Francisco Barrios	.15	.08
553	Terry Puhl (R)	.35	.18
554	Joe Coleman	.15	.08
555	Butch Wynegar	.15	.08
556	Ed Armbrister	.15	.08
557	Tony Solaita	.15	.08
558	Paul Mitchell	.15	.08
559	Phil Mankowski	.15	.08
560	Dave Parker	3.00	1.50
561	Charlie Williams	.15	.08
562	Glenn Burke	.15	.08
563	Dave Rader	.15	.08
564	Mick Kelleher	.15	.08
565	Jerry Koosman	.40	.20
566	Merv Rettenmund	.15	.08
567	Dick Drago	.15	.08
568	Tom Hutton	.15	.08
569	Lary Sorensen (R)	.15	.08
570	Dave Kingman	.45	.22
571	Buck Martinez	.15	.08
572	Rick Wise	.20	.10
573	Luis Gomez	.15	.08
574	Bob Lemon	.30	.15
575	Pat Dobson	.15	.08
576	Sam Mejias	.15	.08
577	A's Team	.75	.35
578	Buzz Capra	.15	.08
579	Rance Mulliniks (R)	.20	.10
580	Rod Carew	6.00	3.00
581	Lynn McGlothen	.15	.08
582	Fran Healy	.15	.08
583	George Medich	.15	.08
584	John Hale	.15	.08
585	Woodie Fryman	.15	.08
586	Ed Goodson	.15	.08
587	John Urrea	.15	.08
588	Jim Mason	.15	.08
589	Bob Knepper (R)	.35	.18
590	Bobby Murcer	.40	.20
591	George Zeber	.15	.08
592	Bob Apodaca	.15	.08

593	Dave Skaggs	.15	.08
594	Dave Freisleben	.15	.08
595	Sixto Lezcano	.15	.08
596	Gary Wheelock	.15	.08
597	Steve Dillard	.15	.08
598	Eddie Solomon	.15	.08
599	Gary Woods	.15	.08
600	Frank Tanana	.30	.15
601	Gene Mauch	.15	.08
602	Eric Soderholm	.15	.08
603	Will McEnaney	.15	.08
604	Earl Williams	.15	.08
605	Rick Rhoden	.15	.08
606	Pirates Team	.75	.35
607	Fernando Arroyo	.15	.08
608	Johnny Grubb	.15	.08
609	John Denny	.20	.10
610	Garry Maddox	.25	.12
611	Pat Scanlon	.15	.08
612	Ken Henderson	.15	.08
613	Marty Perez	.15	.08
614	Joe Wallis	.15	.08
615	Clay Carroll	.15	.08
616	Pat Kelly	.15	.08
617	Joe Nolan	.15	.08
618	Tommy Helms	.20	.10
619	Thad Bosley (R)	.15	.08
620	Willie Randolph	1.25	.60
621	Craig Swan	.15	.08
622	Champ Summers	.15	.08
623	Eduardo Rodriguez	.15	.08
624	Gary Alexander	.15	.08
625	Jose Cruz	.30	.15
626	Blue Jays Team	.75	.35
627	Dave Johnson	.15	.08
628	Ralph Garr	.20	.10
629	Don Stanhouse	.15	.08
630	Ron Cey	.35	.18
631	Danny Ozark	.15	.08
632	Rowland Office	.15	.08
633	Tom Veryzer	.15	.08
634	Len Barker	.20	.10
635	Joe Rudi	.25	.12
636	Jim Bibby	.15	.08
637	Duffy Dyer	.15	.08
638	Paul Splittorff	.15	.08
639	Gene Clines	.15	.08
640	Lee May	.15	.08
641	Doug Rau	.15	.08
642	Denny Doyle	.15	.08
643	Tom House	.15	.08
644	Jim Dwyer	.15	.08
645	Mike Torrez	.15	.08
646	Rick Auerbach	.15	.08
647	Steve Dunning	.15	.08
648	Gary Thomasson	.15	.08
649	Moose Haas (R)	.15	.08
650	Cesar Cedeno	.25	.12
651	Doug Rader	.15	.08
652	Checklist 606-726	.75	.35
653	Ron Hodges	.15	.08
654	Pepe Frias	.15	.08
655	Lyman Bostock	.20	.10
656	Dave Garcia	.15	.08
657	Bombo Rivera	.15	.08
658	Manny Sanguillen	.25	.12
659	Rangers Team	.75	.35
660	Jason Thompson	.15	.08
661	Grant Jackson	.15	.08
662	Paul Dade	.15	.08
663	Paul Reuschel	.15	.08
664	Fred Stanley	.15	.08
665	Dennis Leonard	.20	.10
666	Billy Smith	.15	.08
667	Jeff Byrd	.15	.08
668	Dusty Baker	.30	.15
669	Pete Falcone	.15	.08
670	Jim Rice	3.00	1.50
671	Gary Lavelle	.15	.08
672	Don Kessinger	.20	.10
673	Steve Brye	.15	.08
674	Ray Knight (R)	1.50	.75
675	Jay Johnstone	.20	.10
676	Bob Myrick	.15	.08
677	Ed Herrmann	.15	.08
678	Tom Burgmeier	.15	.08
679	Wayne Garrett	.15	.08
680	Vida Blue	.30	.15
681	Rob Belloir	.15	.08
682	Ken Brett	.15	.08
683	Mike Champion	.15	.08
684	Ralph Houk	.15	.08
685	Frank Taveras	.15	.08
686	Gaylord Perry	3.00	1.50
687	Julio Cruz (R)	.20	.10
688	George Mitterwald	.15	.08
689	Indians Team	.75	.35
690	Mickey Rivers	.15	.08
691	Ross Grimsley	.15	.08
692	Ken Reitz	.15	.08
693	Lamar Johnson	.15	.08
694	Elias Sosa	.15	.08
695	Dwight Evans	2.50	1.25
696	Steve Mingori	.15	.08
697	Roger Metzger	.15	.08
698	Juan Bernhardt	.15	.08
699	Jackie Brown	.15	.08
700	Johnny Bench	6.00	3.00
701	Rookie Pitchers	.20	.10
	Tom Hume (R)		
	Larry Landreth (R)		
	Steve McCatty (R)		
	Bruce Taylor (R)		
702	Rookie Catchers	.15	.08
	Bill Nahorodny (R)		
	Kevin Pasley		

	Rick Sweet (R)		
	Don Werner (R)		
703	Rookie Pitchers	18.00	9.00
	Larry Andersen (R)		
	Tim Jones (R)		
	Mickey Mahler (R)		
	Jack Morris (R)		
704	Rookie 2nd Base	15.00	7.50
	Garth Iorg (R)		
	Dave Oliver (R)		
	Sam Perlozzo (R)		
	Lou Whitaker (R)		
705	Rookie Outfielders	.50	.25
	Dave Bergman (R)		
	Miguel Dilone (R)		
	Clint Hurdle (R)		
	Willie Norwood (R)		
706	Rookie 1st Basemen	.20	.10
	Wayne Cage (R)		
	Ted Cox (R)		
	Pat Putnam (R)		
	Dave Revering (R)		
707	Rookie Shortstops	50.00	25.00
	Mickey Klutts		
	Paul Molitor (R)		
	Alan Trammell (R)		
	U.L. Washington (R)		
708	Rookie Catchers	15.00	7.50
	Bo Diaz (R)		
	Dale Murphy		
	Lance Parrish (R)		
	Ernie Whitt		
709	Rookie Pitchers	.25	.12
	Steve Burke (R)		
	Matt Keough		
	Lance Rautzhan (R)		
	Dan Schatzeder		
710	Rookie Outfielders	.50	.25
	Dell Alston		
	Rick Bosetti (R)		
	Mike Easler (R)		
	Keith Smith (R)		
711	Rookie Pitchers	.15	.08
	Cardell Camper		
	Dennis Lamp		
	Craig Mitchell (R)		
	Roy Thomas (R)		
712	Bobby Valentine	.20	.10
713	Bob Davis	.15	.08
714	Mike Anderson	.15	.08
715	Jim Kaat	.60	.30
716	Cito Gaston	.20	.10
717	Nelson Briles	.15	.08
718	Ron Jackson	.15	.08
719	Randy Elliott	.15	.08
720	Ferguson Jenkins	3.00	1.50
721	Billy Martin	.75	.35
722	Pete Broberg	.15	.08
723	Johnny Wockenfuss	.15	.08
724	Royals Team	.75	.35
725	Kurt Bevacqua	.15	.08
726	Wilbur Wood	.25	.12

1979 Topps

The cards in this 726-card set are similar in design to the 1978 Topps set. Card fronts feature large color photos. The player's name and team are in horizontal stripes below the photos. A small baseball in the lower left corner contains the player's position. Cards measure 2-1/2" by 3-1/2". The set contains League Leaders (1-8), 1978 Record Breakers, All-Time Record Breakers and Rookie Prospects.

		NR/MT	EX
Complete Set (726)		270.00	135.00
Commons (1-726)		.15	.08
1	Batting Leaders	2.50	1.25
2	Home Run Leaders	.50	.25
3	RBI Leaders	.50	.25
4	Stolen Base Leaders	.20	.10
5	Victory Leaders	.50	.25
6	Strikeout Leaders	4.00	2.00
7	ERA Leaders	.30	.15
8	Leading Firemen	.50	.25
9	Dave Campbell	.15	.08
10	Lee May	.15	.08
11	Marc Hill	.15	.08
12	Dick Drago	.15	.08
13	Paul Dade	.15	.08
14	Rafael Landestoy	.15	.08
15	Ross Grimsley	.15	.08

16	Fred Stanley	.15	.08
17	Donnie Moore	.15	.08
18	Tony Solaita	.15	.08
19	Larry Gura	.15	.08
20	Joe Morgan	1.00	.50
21	Kevin Kobel	.15	.08
22	Mike Jorgensen	.15	.08
23	Terry Forster	.15	.08
24	Paul Molitor	10.00	5.00
25	Steve Carlton	5.00	2.50
26	Jamie Quirk	.15	.08
27	Dave Goltz	.15	.08
28	Steve Brye	.15	.08
29	Rick Langford	.15	.08
30	Dave Winfield	8.50	4.25
31	Tom House	.15	.08
32	Jerry Mumphrey	.15	.08
33	Dave Rozema	.15	.08
34	Rob Andrews	.15	.08
35	Ed Figueroa	.15	.08
36	Alan Ashby	.15	.08
37	Joe Kerrigan	.15	.08
38	Bernie Carbo	.15	.08
39	Dale Murphy	7.00	3.50
40	Dennis Eckersley	6.50	3.25
41	Twins Team	.50	.25
42	Ron Blomberg	.15	.08
43	Wayne Twitchell	.15	.08
44	Kurt Bevacqua	.15	.08
45	Al Hrabosky	.20	.10
46	Ron Hodges	.15	.08
47	Fred Norman	.15	.08
48	Merv Rettenmund	.15	.08
49	Vern Ruhle	.15	.08
50	Steve Garvey	1.50	.75
51	Ray Fosse	.15	.08
52	Randy Lerch	.15	.08
53	Mick Kelleher	.15	.08
54	Dell Alston	.15	.08
55	Willie Stargell	3.00	1.50
56	John Hale	.15	.08
57	Eric Rasmussen	.15	.08
58	Bob Randall	.15	.08
59	John Denny	.15	.08
60	Mickey Rivers	.15	.08
61	Bo Diaz	.15	.08
62	Randy Moffitt	.15	.08
63	Jack Brohamer	.15	.08
64	Tom Underwood	.15	.08
65	Mark Balanger	.25	.12
66	Tigers Team	.50	.25
67	Jim Mason	.15	.08
68	Joe Niekro	.20	.10
69	Elliott Maddox	.15	.08
70	John Candelaria	.25	.12
71	Brian Downing	.40	.20
72	Steve Mingori	.15	.08
73	Ken Henderson	.15	.08
74	Shane Rawley (R)	.30	.15
75	Steve Yeager	.15	.08
76	Warren Cromartie	.15	.08
77	Dan Briggs	.15	.08
78	Elias Sosa	.15	.08
79	Ted Cox	.15	.08
80	Jason Thompson	.15	.08
81	Roger Erickson	.15	.08
82	Mets Team	.50	.25
83	Fred Kendall	.15	.08
84	Greg Minton	.15	.08
85	Gary Matthews	.20	.10
86	Rodney Scott	.15	.08
87	Pete Falcone	.15	.08
88	Bob Molinaro	.15	.08
89	Dick Tidrow	.15	.08
90	Bob Boone	.75	.35
91	Terry Crowley	.15	.08
92	Jim Bibby	.15	.08
93	Phil Mankowski	.15	.08
94	Len Barker	.15	.08
95	Robin Yount	15.00	7.50
96	Indians Team	.50	.25
97	Sam Mejias	.15	.08
98	Ray Burris	.15	.08
99	John Wathan	.20	.10
100	Tom Seaver	4.50	2.25
101	Roy Howell	.15	.08
102	Mike Anderson	.15	.08
103	Jim Todd	.15	.08
104	Johnny Oates	.20	.10
105	Rick Camp	.15	.08
106	Frank Duffy	.15	.08
107	Jesus Alou	.15	.08
108	Eduardo Rodriguez	.15	.08
109	Joel Youngblood	.15	.08
110	Vida Blue	.25	.12
111	Roger Freed	.15	.08
112	Phillies Team	.50	.25
113	Pete Redfern	.15	.08
114	Cliff Johnson	.15	.08
115	Nolan Ryan	28.00	14.00
116	Ozzie Smith (R)	75.00	37.50
117	Grant Jackson	.15	.08
118	Bud Harrelson	.20	.10
119	Don Stanhouse	.15	.08
120	Jim Sundberg	.15	.08
121	Checklist 1-121	.35	.18
122	Mike Paxton	.15	.08
123	Lou Whitaker	5.00	2.50
124	Dan Schatzeder	.15	.08
125	Rick Burleson	.20	.10
126	Doug Bair	.15	.08
127	Thad Bosley	.15	.08
128	Ted Martinez	.15	.08
129	Marty Pattin	.15	.08
130	Bob Watson	.30	.15
131	Jim Clancy	.15	.08

#	Player	Price	Price		#	Player	Price	Price
132	Rowland Office	.15	.08		190	Ron Cey	.35	.18
133	Bill Castro	.15	.08		191	Mike Norris	.15	.08
134	Alan Bannister	.15	.08		192	Cardinals Team	.60	.30
135	Bobby Murcer	.30	.15		193	Glenn Adams	.15	.08
136	Jim Kaat	.50	.25		194	Randy Jones	.15	.08
137	Larry Wolfe	.15	.08		195	Bill Madlock	.50	.25
138	Mark Lee	.15	.08		196	Steve Kemp	.15	.08
139	Luis Pujols	.15	.08		197	Bob Apodaca	.15	.08
140	Don Gullett	.20	.10		198	Johnny Grubb	.15	.08
141	Tom Paciorek	.15	.08		199	Larry Milbourne	.15	.08
142	Charlie Williams	.15	.08		200	Johnny Bench	3.50	1.75
143	Tony Scott	.15	.08		201	Mike Edwards (RB)	.15	.08
144	Sandy Alomar	.15	.08		202	Ron Guidry (RB)	.25	.12
145	Rick Rhoden	.15	.08		203	J.R. Richards (RB)	.20	.10
146	Duane Kuiper	.15	.08		204	Pete Rose (RB)	2.50	1.25
147	Dave Hamilton	.15	.08		205	John Stearns (RB)	.15	.08
148	Bruce Boisclair	.15	.08		206	Sammy Stewart (RB)	.15	.08
149	Manny Sarmiento	.15	.08		207	Dave Lemanczyk	.15	.08
150	Wayne Cage	.15	.08		208	Cito Gaston	.15	.08
151	John Hiller	.15	.08		209	Reggie Cleveland	.15	.08
152	Rick Cerone	.25	.12		210	Larry Bowa	.25	.12
153	Dennis Lamp	.15	.08		211	Denny Martinez	.15	.08
154	Jim Gantner	.30	.15		212	Carney Lansford (R)	5.00	2.50
155	Dwight Evans	1.50	.75		213	Bill Travers	.15	.08
156	Buddy Solomon	.15	.08		214	Red Sox Team	.50	.25
157	U.L. Washington	.15	.08		215	Willie McCovey	3.00	1.50
158	Joe Sambito	.15	.08		216	Wilbur Wood	.25	.12
159	Roy White	.15	.08		217	Steve Dillard	.15	.08
160	Mike Flanagan	.25	.12		218	Dennis Leonard	.15	.08
161	Barry Foote	.15	.08		219	Roy Smalley	.15	.08
162	Tom Johnson	.15	.08		220	Cesar Geronimo	.15	.08
163	Glenn Burke	.15	.08		221	Jesse Jefferson	.15	.08
164	Mickey Lolich	.35	.18		222	Bob Beall	.15	.08
165	Frank Taveras	.15	.08		223	Kent Tekulve	.20	.10
166	Leon Roberts	.15	.08		224	Dave Revering	.15	.08
167	Roger Metzger	.15	.08		225	Rich Gossage	1.25	.60
168	Dave Freisleben	.15	.08		226	Ron Pruitt	.15	.08
169	Bill Nahorodny	.15	.08		227	Steve Stone	.25	.12
170	Don Sutton	2.00	1.00		228	Vic Davalillo	.15	.08
171	Gene Clines	.15	.08		229	Doug Flynn	.15	.08
172	Mike Bruhert	.15	.08		230	Bob Forsch	.15	.08
173	John Lowenstein	.15	.08		231	Johnny Wockenfuss	.15	.08
174	Rick Auerbach	.15	.08		232	Jimmy Sexton	.15	.08
175	George Hendrick	.20	.10		233	Paul Mitchell	.15	.08
176	Aurelio Rodriguez	.15	.08		234	Toby Harrah	.15	.08
177	Ron Reed	.15	.08		235	Steve Rogers	.20	.10
178	Alvis Woods	.15	.08		236	Jim Dwyer	.15	.08
179	Jim Beattie	.15	.08		237	Billy Smith	.15	.08
180	Larry Hisle	.15	.08		238	Balor Moore	.15	.08
181	Mike Garman	.15	.08		239	Willie Horton	.25	.12
182	Tim Johnson	.15	.08		240	Rick Reuschel	.25	.12
183	Paul Splittorff	.20	.10		241	Checklist 122-242	.35	.18
184	Darrel Chaney	.15	.08		242	Pablo Torrealba	.15	.08
185	Mike Torrez	.15	.08		243	Buck Martinez	.15	.08
186	Eric Soderholm	.15	.08		244	Pirates Team	.50	.25
187	Mark Lemongello	.15	.08		245	Jeff Burroughs	.20	.10
188	Pat Kelly	.15	.08		246	Darrell Jackson	.15	.08
189	Eddie Whitson (R)	.75	.35		247	Tucker Ashford	.15	.08

248	Pete LaCock	.15	.08	306	Floyd Bannister	.15	.08
249	Paul Thormodsgard	.15	.08	307	Larvell Blanks	.15	.08
250	Willie Randolph	.80	.40	308	Bert Blyleven	1.00	.50
251	Jack Morris	7.50	3.75	309	Ralph Garr	.15	.08
252	Bob Stinson	.15	.08	310	Thurman Munson	3.50	1.75
253	Rick Wise	.20	.12	311	Gary Lavelle	.15	.08
254	Luis Gomez	.15	.08	312	Bob Robertson	.15	.08
255	Tommy John	1.00	.50	313	Dyar Miller	.15	.08
256	Mike Sadek	.15	.08	314	Larry Harlow	.15	.08
257	Adrian Devine	.15	.08	315	Jon Matlack	.20	.10
258	Mike Phillips	.15	.08	316	Milt May	.15	.08
259	Reds Team	.60	.30	317	Jose Cardenal	.15	.08
260	Richie Zisk	.15	.08	318	Bob Welch (R)	6.00	3.00
261	Mario Guerrero	.15	.08	319	Wayne Garrett	.15	.08
262	Nelson Briles	.15	.08	320	Carl Yastrzemski	4.00	2.00
263	Oscar Gamble	.20	.10	321	Gaylord Perry	3.00	1.50
264	Don Robinson (R)	.50	.25	322	Danny Goodwin	.15	.08
265	Don Money	.15	.08	323	Lynn McGlothen	.15	.08
266	Jim Willoughby	.15	.08	324	Mike Tyson	.15	.08
267	Joe Rudi	.20	.10	325	Cecil Cooper	.25	.12
268	Julio Gonzalez	.15	.08	326	Pedro Borbon	.15	.08
269	Woodie Fryman	.15	.08	327	Art Howe	.20	.10
270	Butch Hopson	.20	.10	328	A's Team	.50	.25
271	Rawly Eastwick	.15	.08	329	Joe Coleman	.15	.08
272	Tim Corcoran	.15	.08	330	George Brett	15.00	7.50
273	Jerry Terrell	.15	.08	331	Mickey Mahler	.15	.08
274	Willie Norwood	.15	.08	332	Gary Alezander	.15	.08
275	Junior Moore	.15	.08	333	Chet Lemon	.20	.10
276	Jim Colburn	.15	.08	334	Craig Swan	.15	.08
277	Tom Grieve	.15	.08	335	Chris Chambliss	.25	.12
278	Andy Messersmith	.15	.08	336	Bobby Thompson	.15	.08
279	Jerry Grote	.15	.08	337	John Montague	.15	.08
280	Andre Thornton	.25	.12	338	Vic Harris	.15	.08
281	Vic Correll	.15	.08	339	Ron Jackson	.15	.08
282	Blue Jays Team	.50	.25	340	Jim Palmer	4.00	2.00
283	Ken Kravec	.15	.08	341	Willie Upshaw (R)	.30	.15
284	Johnnie LeMaster	.15	.08	342	Dave Roberts	.15	.08
285	Bobby Bonds	.50	.25	343	Ed Glynn	.15	.08
286	Duffy Dyer	.15	.08	344	Jerry Royster	.15	.08
287	Andres Mora	.15	.08	345	Tug McGraw	.35	.18
288	Milt Wilcox	.15	.08	346	Bill Buckner	.40	.20
289	Jose Cruz	.25	.12	347	Doug Rau	.15	.08
290	Dave Lopes	.30	.15	348	Andre Dawson	14.00	7.00
291	Tom Griffin	.15	.08	349	Jim Wright	.15	.08
292	Don Reynolds	.15	.08	350	Garry Templeton	.25	.12
293	Jerry Garvin	.15	.08	351	Wayne Nordhagen	.15	.08
294	Pepe Frias	.15	.08	352	Steve Renko	.15	.08
295	Mitchell Page	.15	.08	353	Checklist 243-363	.50	.25
296	Preston Hanna	.15	.08	354	Bill Bonham	.15	.08
297	Ted Sizemore	.15	.08	355	Lee Mazzilli	.15	.08
298	Rich Gale	.15	.08	356	Giants Team	.50	.25
299	Steve Ontiveros	.15	.08	357	Jerry Augustine	.15	.08
300	Rod Carew	4.00	2.00	358	Alan Trammell	10.00	5.00
301	Tom Hume	.15	.08	359	Dan Spilner	.15	.08
302	Braves Team	.50	.25	360	Amos Otis	.20	.10
303	Lary Sorensen	.15	.08	361	Tom Dixon	.15	.08
304	Steve Swisher	.15	.08	362	Mike Cubbage	.15	.08
305	Willie Montanez	.15	.08	363	Craig Skok	.15	.08

364	Gene Richards	.15	.08
365	Sparky Lyle	.35	.18
366	Juan Bernhardt	.15	.08
367	Dave Skaggs	.15	.08
368	Daon Aase	.15	.08
369a	Bump Wills(Tor))	2.50	1.25
369b	Bump Wills (Tex)	3.00	1.50
370	Dave Kingman	.45	.22
371	Jeff Holly	.15	.08
372	Lamar Johnson	.15	.08
373	Lance Rautzhan	.15	.08
374	Ed Herrmann	.15	.08
375	Bill Campbell	.15	.08
376	Gorman Thomas	.25	.12
377	Paul Moskau	.15	.08
378	Rob Picciolo	.15	.08
379	Dale Murray	.15	.08
380	John Mayberry	.20	.10
381	Astros Team	.50	.25
382	Jerry Martin	.15	.08
383	Phil Garner	.20	.10
384	Tommy Boggs	.15	.08
385	Dan Ford	.15	.08
386	Francisco Barrios	.15	.08
387	Gary Tomasson	.15	.08
388	Jack Billingham	.15	.08
389	Joe Zdeb	.15	.08
390	Rollie Fingers	2.50	1.25
391	Al Oliver	.45	.22
392	Doug Ault	.15	.08
393	Scott McGregor	.20	.10
394	Randy Stein	.15	.08
395	Dave Cash	.15	.08
396	Bill Plummer	.15	.08
397	Sergio Ferrer	.15	.08
398	Ivan DeJesus	.15	.08
399	David Clyde	.15	.08
400	Jim Rice	2.50	1.25
401	Ray Knight	.35	.18
402	Paul Hartzell	.15	.08
403	Tim Foli	.15	.08
404	White Sox Team	.50	.25
405	Butch Wynegar	.15	.08
406	Joe Wallis	.15	.08
407	Pete Vuckovich	.20	.10
408	Charlie Moore	.15	.08
409	Willie Wilson	2.00	1.00
410	Darrell Evans	.35	.18
411	Ty Cobb, George Sisler (Hits Record)	.60	.30
412	Hank Aaron, Hack Wilson (RBI Records)	1.00	.50
413	Hank Aaron, Roger Maris (HR Records)	1.50	.75
414	Ty Cobb, Roger Hornsby (Batting Avg Records)	.75	.35
415	Lou Brock (SB Record)	.60	.30
416	Jack Chesbro, Cy Young (Wins Record)	.40	.20
417	Walter Johnson, Nolan Ryan (Strikeout Records)	.75	.35
418	Walter Johnson, Dutch Leonard (ERA Records)	.40	.25
419	Dick Ruthven	.15	.08
420	Ken Griffey	.75	.35
421	Doug DeCinces	.20	.10
422	Ruppert Jones	.15	.08
423	Bob Montgomery	.15	.08
424	Angels Team	.50	.25
425	Rick Manning	.15	.08
426	Chris Speier	.15	.08
427	Andy Replogle	.15	.08
428	Bobby Valentine	.20	.10
429	John Urrea	.15	.08
430	Dave Parker	2.00	1.00
431	Glenn Borgmann	.15	.08
432	Dave Heaverlo	.15	.08
433	Larry Bittner	.15	.08
434	Ken Clay	.15	.08
435	Gene Tenace	.25	.12
436	Hector Cruz	.15	.08
437	Rick Williams	.15	.08
438	Horace Speed	.15	.08
439	Frank White	.20	.10
440	Rusty Staub	.35	.18
441	Lee Lacy	.15	.08
442	Doyle Alexander	.15	.08
443	Bruce Bochte	.15	.08
444	Aurelio Lopez	.15	.08
445	Steve Henderson	.15	.08
446	Jim Lonborg	.20	.10
447	Manny Sanguillen	.20	.10
448	Moose Haas	.15	.08
449	Bombo Rivera	.15	.08
450	Dave Concepcion	.75	.35
451	Royals Team	.60	.30
452	Jerry Morales	.15	.08
453	Chris Knapp	.15	.08
454	Len Randle	.15	.08
455	Bill Lee	.15	.08
456	Chuck Baker	.15	.08
457	Bruce Sutter	.75	.35
458	Jim Essian	.15	.08
459	Sid Monge	.15	.08
460	Graig Nettles	.50	.25
461	Jim Barr	.15	.08
462	Otto Velez	.15	.08
463	Steve Comer	.15	.08
464	Joe Nolan	.15	.08
465	Reggie Smith	.20	.10

466	Mark Littell	.15	.08	523	John Milner	.15	.08
467	Don Kessinger	.15	.08	524	Tom Burgmeier	.15	.08
468	Stan Bahnsen	.15	.08	525	Freddie Patek	.15	.08
469	Lance Parrish	2.50	1.25	526	Dodgers Team	.75	.35
470	Garry Maddox	.20	.10	527	Lerrin LaGrow	.15	.08
471	Joaquin Andujar	.25	.12	528	Wayne Gross	.15	.08
472	Craig Kusick	.15	.08	529	Brian Asselstine	.15	.08
473	Dave Roberts	.15	.08	530	Frank Tanana	.25	.12
474	Dick Davis	.15	.08	531	Fernando Gonzalez	.15	.08
475	Dan Driessen	.20	.10	532	Buddy Schultz	.15	.08
476	Tom Poquette	.15	.08	533	Leroy Stanton	.15	.08
477	Bob Grich	.20	.10	534	Ken Forsch	.15	.08
478	Juan Beniquez	.15	.08	535	Ellis Valentine	.15	.08
479	Padres Team	.50	.25	536	Jerry Reuss	.20	.10
480	Fred Lynn	.80	.40	537	Tom Veryzer	.15	.08
481	Skip Lockwood	.15	.08	538	Mike Ivie	.15	.08
482	Craig Reynolds	.15	.08	539	John Ellis	.15	.08
483	Checklist 364-484	.50	.25	540	Greg Luzinski	.35	.18
484	Rick Waits	.15	.08	541	Jim Slaton	.15	.08
485	Bucky Dent	.30	.15	542	Rick Bosetti	.15	.08
486	Bob Knepper	.15	.08	543	Kiko Garcia	.15	.08
487	Miguel Dilone	.15	.08	544	Ferguson Jenkins	2.00	1.00
488	Bob Owchinko	.15	.08	545	John Stearns	.15	.08
489	Larry Cox (Wrong Photo)	.15	.08	546	Bill Russell	.25	.12
				547	Clint Hurdle	.15	.08
490	Al Cowens	.15	.08	548	Enrique Romo	.15	.08
491	Tippy Martinez	.15	.08	549	Bob Bailey	.15	.08
492	Bob Bailor	.15	.08	550	Sal Bando	.20	.10
493	Larry Christenson	.15	.08	551	Cubs Team	.50	.25
494	Jerry White	.15	.08	552	Jose Morales	.15	.08
495	Tony Perez	1.25	.60	553	Denny Walling	.15	.08
496	Barry Bonnell	.15	.08	554	Matt Keough	.15	.08
497	Glenn Abbott	.15	.08	555	Biff Pocoroba	.15	.08
498	Rich Chiles	.15	.08	556	Mike Lum	.15	.08
499	Rangers Team	.50	.25	557	Ken Brett	.15	.08
500	Ron Guidry	.50	.25	558	Jay Johnstone	.20	.10
501	Junior Kennedy	.15	.08	559	Greg Pryor	.15	.08
502	Steve Braun	.15	.08	560	John Montefusco	.15	.08
503	Terry Humphrey	.15	.08	561	Ed Ott	.15	.08
504	Larry McWilliams (R)	.20	.10	562	Dusty Baker	.25	.12
505	Ed Kranepool	.20	.10	563	Roy Thomas	.15	.08
506	John D'Acquisto	.15	.08	564	Jerry Turner	.15	.08
507	Tony Armas	.20	.10	565	Rico Carty	.20	.10
508	Charlie Hough	.15	.08	566	Nino Espinosa	.15	.08
509	Mario Mendoza	.15	.08	567	Rich Hebner	.15	.08
510	Ted Simmons	.45	.22	568	Carlos Lopez	.15	.08
511	Paul Reuschel	.15	.08	569	Bob Sykes	.15	.08
512	Jack Clark	1.25	.60	570	Cesar Cedeno	.20	.10
513	Dave Johnson	.15	.08	571	Darrell Porter	.15	.08
514	Mike Proly	.15	.08	572	Rod Gilbreath	.15	.08
515	Enos Cabell	.15	.08	573	Jim Kern	.15	.08
516	Champ Summers	.15	.08	574	Claudell Washington	.20	.10
517	Al Bumbry	.15	.08	575	Luis Tiant	.40	.20
518	Jim Umbarger	.15	.08	576	Mike Parrott	.15	.08
519	Ben Oglivie	.15	.08	577	Brewers Team	.50	.25
520	Gary Carter	3.50	1.75	578	Pete Broberg	.15	.08
521	Sam Ewing	.15	.08	579	Greg Gross	.15	.08
522	Ken Holtzman	.20	.10	580	Ron Fairly	.15	.08

#	Player	Price	Price
581	Darold Knowles	.15	.08
582	Paul Blair	.15	.08
583	Julio Cruz	.15	.08
584	Jim Rooker	.15	.08
585	Hal McRae	.35	.18
586	Bob Horner (R)	1.25	.60
587	Ken Reitz	.15	.08
588	Tom Murphy	.15	.08
589	Terry Whitfield	.15	.08
590	J.R. Richard	.25	.12
591	Mike Hargrove	.15	.08
592	Mike Krukow	.15	.08
593	Rick Dempsey	.20	.10
594	Bob Shirley	.15	.08
595	Phil Niekro	2.00	1.00
596	Jim Wohlford	.15	.08
597	Bob Stanley	.15	.08
598	Mark Wagner	.15	.08
599	Jim Spencer	.15	.08
600	George Foster	.50	.25
601	Dave LaRoche	.15	.08
602	Checklist 485-605	.50	.25
603	Rudy May	.15	.08
604	Jeff Newman	.15	.08
605	Rick Monday	.20	.10
606	Expos Team	.50	.25
607	Omar Moreno	.15	.08
608	Dave McKay	.15	.08
609	Silvio Martinez	.15	.08
610	Mike Schmidt	12.00	6.00
611	Jim Norris	.15	.08
612	Rick Honeycutt (R)	.40	.20
613	Mike Edwards	.15	.08
614	Willie Hernandez	.25	.12
615	Ken Singleton	.20	.10
616	Billy Almon	.15	.08
617	Terry Puhl	.15	.08
618	Jerry Remy	.15	.08
619	Ken Landreaux (R)	.25	.12
620	Bert Campaneris	.25	.12
621	Pat Zachry	.15	.08
622	Dave Collins	.15	.08
623	Bob McClure	.15	.08
624	Larry Herndon	.15	.08
625	Mark Fidrych	.25	.15
626	Yankees Team	.75	.35
627	Gary Serum	.15	.08
628	Del Unser	.15	.08
629	Gene Garber	.15	.08
630	Bake McBride	.15	.08
631	Jorge Orta	.15	.08
632	Don Kirkwood	.15	.08
633	Rob Wilfong	.15	.08
634	Paul Lindblad	.15	.08
635	Don Baylor	.75	.35
636	Wayne Garland	.15	.08
637	Bill Robinson	.20	.10
638	Al Fitzmorris	.15	.08
639	Manny Trillo	.15	.08
640	Eddie Murray	26.00	13.00
641	Bobby Castillo (R)	.15	.08
642	Wilbur Howard	.15	.08
643	Tom Hausman	.15	.08
644	Manny Mota	.20	.10
645	George Scott	.15	.08
646	Rick Sweet	.15	.08
647	Bob Lacey	.15	.08
648	Lou Piniella	.25	.12
649	John Curtis	.15	.08
650	Pete Rose	6.50	3.25
651	Mike Caldwell	.15	.08
652	Stan Papi	.15	.08
653	Warren Brusstar	.15	.08
654	Rick Miller	.15	.08
655	Jerry Koosman	.35	.18
656	Hosken Powell	.15	.08
657	George Medich	.15	.08
658	Taylor Duncan	.15	.08
659	Mariners Team	.50	.25
660	Ron LeFlore	.20	.10
661	Bruce Kison	.15	.08
662	Kevin Bell	.15	.08
663	Mike Vail	.15	.08
664	Doug Bird	.15	.08
665	Lou Brock	3.50	1.75
666	Rich Dauer	.15	.08
667	Ron Hood	.15	.08
668	Bill North	.15	.08
669	Checklist 606-726	.50	.25
670	Jim Hunter	.80	.40
671	Joe Ferguson	.15	.08
672	Ed Halicki	.15	.08
673	Tom Hutton	.15	.08
674	Dave Tomlin	.15	.08
675	Tim McCarver	.25	.12
676	Johnny Sutton	.15	.08
677	Larry Parrish	.20	.10
678	Geoff Zahn	.15	.08
679	Derrel Thomas	.15	.08
680	Carlton Fisk	6.50	3.25
681	John Henry Johnson	.15	.08
682	Dave Chalk	.15	.08
683	Dan Meyer	.15	.08
684	Jamie Easterly	.15	.08
685	Sixto Lezcano	.15	.08
686	Ron Schueler	.15	.08
687	Rennie Stennett	.15	.08
688	Mike Willis	.15	.08
689	Orioles Team	.60	.30
690	Buddy Bell	.15	.08
691	Dock Ellis	.15	.08
692	Mickey Stanley	.15	.08
693	Dave Rader	.15	.08
694	Burt Hooton	.15	.08
695	Keith Hernandez	1.50	.75
696	Andy Hassler	.15	.08
697	Dave Bergman	.15	.08

698	Bill Stein	.15	.08
699	Hal Dues	.15	.08
700	Reggie Jackson	5.00	2.50
701	Orioles Prospects	.25	.12
	Mark Corey (R)		
	John Flinn (R)		
	Sammy Stewart (R)		
702	Red Sox Prospects	.15	.08
	Joel Finch (R)		
	Garry Hancock (R)		
	Allen Ripley (R)		
703	Angels Prospects	.15	.08
	Jim Anderson (R)		
	Dave Frost (R)		
	Bob Slater (R)		
704	White Sox Prospects	.15	.08
	Ross Baumgarten (R)		
	Mike Colbern (R)		
	Mike Squires (R)		
705	Indians Prospects	.50	.25
	Alfredo Griffin (R)		
	Tim Norrid (R)		
	Dave Oliver (R)		
706	Tigers Prospects	.15	.08
	Dave Stegman (R)		
	Dave Tobik (R)		
	Kip Young (R)		
707	Royals Prospects	.25	.12
	Randy Bass (R)		
	Jim Gaudet (R)		
	Randy McGilberry (R)		
708	Brewers Prospects	.80	.40
	Kevin Bass (R)		
	Eddie Romero (R)		
	Ned Yost (R)		
709	Twins Prospects	.15	.08
	Sam Perlozzo,		
	Rick Sofield (R)		
	Kevin Stanfield (R)		
710	Yankees Prospects	.20	.10
	Brian Doyle (R)		
	Mike Heath		
	Dave Rajsich (R)		
711	A's Prospects	.25	.12
	Dwayne Murphy (R)		
	Bruce Robinson (R)		
	Alan Wirth		
712	Mariners Prospects	.15	.08
	Bud Anderson (R)		
	Greg Biercevicz (R)		
	Byron McLaughlin (R)		
713	Rangers Prospects	.50	.25
	Danny Darwin (R)		
	Pat Putnam (R)		
	Billy Sample (R)		
714	Blue Jays Prospects	.25	.12
	Victor Cruz (R)		
	Pat Kelly		
	Ernie Whitt		
715	Braves Prospects	.25	.12
	Bruce Benedict (R)		
	Glenn Hubbard (R)		
	Larry Whisenton (R)		
716	Cubs Prospects	.15	.08
	Dave Geisel (R)		
	Karl Pagel		
	Scot Thompson (R)		
717	Reds Prospects	.35	.18
	Mike LaCoss (R)		
	Ron Oester (R)		
	Harry Spilman (R)		
718	Astros Prospects	.15	.08
	Bruce Bochy (R)		
	Mike Fischlin (R)		
	Don Pisker (R)		
719	Dodger Prospects	5.00	2.50
	Pedro Guerrero (R)		
	Rudy Law (R)		
	Joe Simpson		
720	Expos Prospects	1.25	.60
	Jerry Fry (R)		
	Jerry Pirtle (R)		
	Scott Sanderson (R)		
721	Mets Prospects	.35	.18
	Juan Berenguer (R)		
	Dwight Bernard (R)		
	Dan Norman (R)		
722	Phillies Prospects	1.25	.60
	Jim Morrison (R)		
	Lonnie Smith (R)		
	Jim Wright (R)		
723	Pirates Prospects	.25	.12
	Dale Berra (R)		
	Eugenio Cotes (R)		
	Ben Wiltbank (R)		
724	Cardinals Prospects	.40	.20
	Tom Bruno (R)		
	George Frazier (R)		
	Terry Kennedy (R)		
725	Padres Prospects	.15	.08
	Jim Beswick (R)		
	Steve Mura (R)		
	Broderick Perkins		
726	Giants Prospects	.25	.12
	Greg Johnston (R)		
	Joe Strain (R)		
	John Tamargo (R)		

1980 Topps

This 726-card set marks another design change for Topps. Card fronts feature full color pictures with the player's name above the photo. The player's position appears in a pennant in the top left corner while his team is listed in another pennant at the lower right corner. Cards measure 2-1/2" by 3-1/2". Subsets include Hightlights (HL) (1-6), League Leaders and Team Rookie cards.

		NR/MT	EX
Complete Set (726)		290.00	145.00
Commons (1-726)		.12	.06

		NR/MT	EX
1	Lou Brock, Carl Yastrzemski (HL)	3.00	1.50
2	Willie McCovey(HL)	1.25	.60
3	Manny Mota (HL)	.15	.08
4	Pete Rose (HL)	2.50	1.25
5	Garry Templeton(HL)	.15	.08
6	Del Unser (HL)	.15	.08
7	Mike Lum	.12	.06
8	Craig Swan	.12	.06
9	Steve Braun	.12	.06
10	Denny Martinez	.80	.40
11	Jimmy Sexton	.12	.06
12	John Curtis	.12	.06
13	Ron Pruitt	.12	.06
14	Dave Cash	.12	.06
15	Bill Campbell	.12	.06
16	Jerry Narron	.12	.06
17	Bruce Sutter	.75	.35
18	Ron Jackson	.12	.06
19	Balor Moore	.12	.06
20	Dan Ford	.12	.06
21	Manny Sarmiento	.12	.06
22	Pat Putnam	.12	.06
23	Derrel Thomas	.12	.06
24	Jim Slaton	.12	.06
25	Lee Mazzilli	.12	.06
26	Marty Pattin	.12	.06
27	Del Unser	.12	.06
28	Bruce Kison	.12	.06
29	Mark Wagner	.12	.06
30	Vida Blue	.25	.12
31	Jay Johnstone	.15	.08
32	Julio Cruz	.12	.06
33	Tony Scott	.12	.06
34	Jeff Newman	.12	.06
35	Luis Tiant	.30	.15
36	Rusty Torres	.12	.06
37	Kiko Garcia	.12	.06
38	Dan Spillner	.12	.06
39	Rowland Office	.12	.06
40	Carlton Fisk	5.00	2.50
41	Rangers Team	.40	.20
42	Dave Palmer	.12	.06
43	Bombo Rivera	.12	.06
44	Bill Fahey	.12	.06
45	Frank White	.20	.10
46	Rico Carty	.15	.08
47	Bill Bonham	.12	.06
48	Rick Miller	.12	.06
49	Mario Guerrero	.12	.06
50	J.R. Richard	.25	.12
51	Joe Ferguson	.12	.06
52	Warren Brusstar	.12	..06
53	Ben Oglivie	.12	.06
54	Dennis Lamp	.12	.06
55	Bill Madlock	.50	.25
56	Bobby Valentine	.15	.08
57	Pete Vuckovich	.12	.06
58	Doug Flynn	.12	.06
59	Eddy Putman	.12	.06
60	Bucky Dent	.20	.10
61	Gary Serum	.12	.06
62	Mike Ivie	.12	.06
63	Bob Stanley	.12	.06
64	Joe Nolan	.12	.06
65	Al Bumbry	.12	.06
66	Royals Team	.40	.20
67	Doyle Alexander	.12	.06
68	Larry Harlow	.12	.06
69	Rick Williams	.12	.06
70	Gary Carter	3.50	1.75
71	John Milner	.12	.06
72	Fred Howard	.12	.06
73	Dave Collins	.12	.06
74	Sid Monge	.12	.06
75	Bill Russell	.20	.10
76	John Stearns	.12	.06
77	Dave Stieb (R)	4.00	2.00
78	Ruppert Jones	.12	.06
79	Bob Owchinko	.12	.06
80	Ron LeFlore	.15	.08
81	Ted Sizemore	.12	.06
82	Astros Team	.40	.20
83	Steve Trout (R)	.20	.10

84	Gary Lavelle	.12	.06	142	Phil Huffman	.12	.06
85	Ted Simmons	.40	.20	143	Bruce Bochte	.12	.06
86	Dave Hamilton	.12	.06	144	Steve Comer	.12	.06
87	Pepe Frias	.12	.06	145	Darrell Evans	.30	.15
88	Ken Landreaux	.15	.08	146	Bob Welch	.60	.30
89	Don Hood	.12	.06	147	Terry Puhl	.12	.06
90	Manny Trillo	.12	.06	148	Manny Sanguillen	.15	.08
91	Rick Dempsey	.15	.08	149	Tom Hume	.12	.06
92	Rick Rhoden	.12	.06	150	Jason Thompson	.12	.06
93	Dave Roberts	.12	.06	151	Tom Hausman	.12	.06
94	Neil Allen (R)	.15	.08	152	John Fulgham	.12	.06
95	Cecil Cooper	.15	.08	153	Tim Blackwell	.12	.06
96	A's Team	.40	.20	154	Lary Sorensen	.12	.06
97	Bill Lee	.12	.06	155	Jerry Remy	.12	.06
98	Jerry Terrell	.12	.06	156	Tony Brizzolara	.12	.06
99	Victor Cruz	.12	.06	157	Willie Wilson	.12	.06
100	Johnny Bench	5.00	2.50	158	Rob Picciolo	.12	.06
101	Aurelio Lopez	.12	.06	159	Ken Clay	.12	.06
102	Rich Dauer	.12	.06	160	Eddie Murray	14.00	7.00
103	Bill Caudill (R)	.15	.08	161	Larry Christenson	.12	.06
104	Manny Mota	.15	.08	162	Bob Randall	.12	.06
105	Frank Tanana	.20	.10	163	Steve Swisher	.12	.06
106	Jeff Leonard (R)	.30	.15	164	Greg Pryor	.12	.06
107	Francisco Barrios	.12	.06	165	Omar Moreno	.12	.06
108	Bob Horner	.20	.10	166	Glenn Abbott	.12	.06
109	Bill Travers	.12	.06	167	Jack Clark	1.00	.50
110	Fred Lynn	.30	.15	168	Rick Waits	.12	.06
111	Bob Knepper	.12	.06	169	Luis Gomez	.12	.06
112	White Sox Team	.50	.25	170	Burt Hooton	.12	.06
113	Geoff Zahn	.12	.06	171	Fernando Gonzalez	.12	.06
114	Juan Beniquez	.12	.06	172	Ron Hodges	.12	.06
115	Sparky Lyle	.15	.08	173	John Henry Johnson	.12	.06
116	Larry Cox	.12	.06	174	Ray Knight	.25	.12
117	Dock Ellis	.12	.06	175	Rick Reuschel	.15	.08
118	Phil Garner	.15	.08	176	Champ Summers	.12	.06
119	Sammy Stewart	.12	.06	177	Dave Heaverlo	.12	.06
120	Greg Luzinski	.25	.12	178	Tim McCarver	.20	.10
121	Checklist 1-121	.50	.25	179	Ron Davis (R)	.20	.10
122	Dave Rosello	.12	.06	180	Warren Cromartie	.12	.06
123	Lynn Jones	.12	.06	181	Moose Haas	.12	.06
124	Dave Lemanczyk	.12	.06	182	Ken Reitz	.12	.06
125	Tony Perez	1.50	.75	183	Jim Anderson	.12	.06
126	Dave Tomlin	.12	.06	184	Steve Renko	.12	.06
127	Gary Thomasson	.12	.06	185	Hal McRae	.30	.15
128	Tom Burgmeier	.12	.06	186	Junior Moore	.12	.06
129	Craig Reynolds	.12	.06	187	Alan Ashby	.12	.06
130	Amos Otis	.15	.08	188	Terry Crowley	.12	.06
131	Paul Mitchell	.12	.06	189	Kevin Kobel	.12	.06
132	Biff Pocoroba	.12	.06	190	Buddy Bell	.15	.08
133	Jerry Turner	.12	.06	191	Ted Martinez	.12	.06
134	Matt Keough	.12	.06	192	Braves Team	.40	.20
135	Bill Buckner	.25	.12	193	Dave Goltz	.12	.06
136	Dick Ruthven	.12	.06	194	Mike Easler	.12	.06
137	John Castino (R)	.12	.06	195	John Montefusco	.12	.06
138	Ross Baumgarten	.12	.06	196	Lance Parrish	.80	.40
139	Dane Iorg	.12	.06	197	Byron McLaughlin	.12	.06
140	Rich Gossage	.80	.40	198	Dell Alston	.12	.06
141	Gary Alexander	.12	.06	199	Mike LaCoss	.12	.06

200	Jim Rice	1.25	.60
201	Batting Leaders	.40	.20
202	Home Run Leaders	.40	.20
203	RBI Leaders	.80	.40
204	Stolen Base Leaders	.25	.12
205	Victory Leaders	.40	.20
206	Strikeout Leaders	4.00	2.00
207	ERA Leaders	.40	.20
208	Wayne Cage	.12	.06
209	Von Joshua	.12	.06
210	Steve Carlton	5.00	2.50
211	Dave Skaggs	.12	.06
212	Dave Roberts	.12	.06
213	Mike Jorgensen	.12	.06
214	Angels Team	.40	.20
215	Sixto Lezcano	.12	.06
216	Phil Mankowski	.12	.06
217	Ed Halicki	.12	.06
218	Jose Morales	.12	.06
219	Steve Mingori	.12	.06
220	Dave Concepcion	.60	.30
221	Joe Cannon	.12	.06
222	Ron Hassey (R)	.40	.20
223	Bob Sykes	.12	.06
224	Willie Montanez	.12	.06
225	Lou Piniella	.20	.10
226	Bill Stein	.12	.06
227	Len Barker	.12	.06
228	Johnny Oates	.12	.06
229	Jim Bibby	.12	.06
230	Dave Winfield	7.00	3.50
231	Steve McCatty	.12	.06
232	Alan Trammell	3.00	1.50
233	LaRue Washington	.12	.06
234	Vern Ruhle	.12	.06
235	Andre Dawson	10.00	5.00
236	Marc Hill	.12	.06
237	Scott McGregor	.12	.06
238	Rob Wilfong	.12	.06
239	Don Aase	.12	.06
240	Dave Kingman	.30	.15
241	Checklist 122-242	.50	.25
242	Lamar Johnson	.12	.06
243	Jerry Augustine	.12	.06
244	Cardinals Team	.40	.20
245	Phil Niekro	2.50	1.25
246	Tim Foli	.12	.06
247	Frank Riccelli	.12	.06
248	Jamie Quirk	.12	.06
249	Jim Clancy	.12	.06
250	Jim Kaat	.35	.18
251	Kip Young	.12	.06
252	Ted Cox	.12	.06
253	John Montague	.12	.06
254	Paul Dade	.12	.06
255	Dusty Baker	.15	.08
256	Roger Erickson	.12	.06
257	Larry Herndon	.12	.06
258	Paul Moskau	.12	.06
259	Mets Team	.40	.20
260	Al Oliver	.40	.20
261	Dave Chalk	.12	.06
262	Benny Ayala	.12	.06
263	Dave LaRoche	.12	.06
264	Bill Robinson	.15	.08
265	Robin Yount	12.50	6.25
266	Bernie Carbo	.12	.06
267	Dan Schatzeder	.12	.06
268	Rafael Landestoy	.12	.06
269	Dave Tobik	.12	.06
270	Mike Schmidt	7.00	3.50
271	Dick Drago	.12	.06
272	Ralph Garr	.12	.06
273	Eduardo Rodriguez	.12	.06
274	Dale Murphy	4.00	2.00
275	Jerry Koosman	.25	.12
276	Tom Veryzer	.12	.06
277	Rick Bosetti	.12	.06
278	Jim Spencer	.12	.06
279	Rob Andrews	.12	.06
280	Gaylord Perry	2.00	1.00
281	Paul Blair	.12	.06
282	Mariners Team	.40	.20
283	John Ellis	.12	.06
284	Larry Murray	.12	.06
285	Don Baylor	.60	.30
286	Darold Knowles	.12	.06
287	John Lowenstein	.12	.06
288	Dave Rozema	.12	.06
289	Bruce Bochy	.12	.06
290	Steve Garvey	1.50	.75
291	Randy Scarbery	.12	.06
292	Dale Berra	.12	.06
293	Elias Sosa	.12	.06
294	Charlie Spikes	.12	.06
295	Larry Gura	.12	.06
296	Dave Rader	.12	.06
297	Tim Johnson	.12	.06
298	Ken Holtzman	.12	.06
299	Steve Henderson	.12	.06
300	Ron Guidry	.75	.35
301	Mike Edwards	.12	.06
302	Dodgers Team	.60	.30
303	Bill Castro	.12	.06
304	Butch Wynegar	.12	.06
305	Randy Jones	.15	.08
306	Denny Walling	.12	.06
307	Rick Honeycutt	.15	.08
308	Mike Hargrove	.12	.06
309	Larry McWilliams	.12	.06
310	Dave Parker	1.50	.75
311	Roger Metzger	.12	.06
312	Mike Barlow	.12	.06
313	Johnny Oates	.12	.06
314	Tim Stoddard (R)	.15	.08
315	Steve Kemp	.12	.06

316	Bob Lacey	.12	.06
317	Mike Anderson	.12	.06
318	Jerry Reuss	.20	.10
319	Chris Speier	.12	.06
320	Dennis Eckersley	3.00	1.50
321	Keith Hernandez	1.00	.50
322	Claudell Washington	.15	.08
323	Mick Kelleher	.12	.06
324	Tom Underwood	.12	.06
325	Dan Driessen	.15	.08
326	Bo McLaughlin	.12	.06
327	Ray Fosse	.12	.06
328	Twins Team	.40	.20
329	Bert Roberge	.12	.06
330	Al Cowens	.12	.06
331	Rich Hebner	.12	.06
332	Enrique Romo	.12	.06
333	Jim Norris	.12	.06
334	Jim Beattie	.12	.06
335	Willie McCovey	3.00	1.50
336	George Medich	.12	.06
337	Carney Lansford	.80	.40
338	Johnny Wockenfuss	.12	.06
339	John D'Acquisto	.12	.06
340	Ken Singleton	.15	.08
341	Jim Essian	.12	.06
342	Odell Jone	.12	.06
343	Mike Vail	.12	.06
344	Randy Lerch	.12	.06
345	Larry Parrish	.15	.08
346	Buddy Solomon	.12	.06
347	Harry Chappas	.12	.06
348	Checklist 243-363	.50	.25
349	Jack Brohamer	.12	.06
350	George Hendrick	.15	.08
351	Bob Davis	.12	.06
352	Dan Briggs	.12	.06
353	Andy Hassler	.12	.06
354	Rick Auerbach	.12	.06
355	Gary Matthews	.15	.08
356	Padres Team	.40	.20
357	Bob McClure	.12	.06
358	Lou Whitaker	3.00	1.50
359	Randy Moffitt	.12	.06
360	Darrell Porter	.12	.06
361	Wayne Garland	.12	.06
362	Danny Goodwin	.12	.06
363	Wayne Gross	.12	.06
364	Ray Burris	.12	.06
365	Bobby Murcer	.25	.12
366	Rob Dressler	.12	.06
367	Billy Smith	.12	.06
368	Willie Aikens (R)	.20	.12
369	Jim Kern	.12	.06
370	Cesar Cedeno	.15	.08
371	Jack Morris	5.00	2.50
372	Joel Youngblood	.12	.06
373	Dan Petry (R)	.35	.18
374	Jim Gantner	.15	.08
375	Ross Grimsley	.12	.06
376	Gary Allenson	.12	.06
377	Junior Kennedy	.12	.06
378	Jerry Mumphrey	.12	.06
379	Kevin Bell	.12	.06
380	Garry Maddox	.15	.08
381	Cubs Team	.40	.20
382	Dave Freisleben	.12	.06
383	Ed Ott	.12	.06
384	Joey McLaughlin	.12	.06
385	Enos Cabell	.12	.06
386	Darrell Jackson	.12	.06
387a	Fred Stanley (Name in red)	.12	.06
387b	Fred Stanley (Name in yellow)	1.50	.75
388	Mike Paxton	.12	.06
389	Pete LaCock	.12	.06
390	Ferguson Jenkins	2.00	1.00
391	Tony Armas	.15	.08
392	Milt Wilcox	.12	.06
393	Ozzie Smith	16.00	8.00
394	Reggie Cleveland	.12	.06
395	Ellis Valentine	.12	.06
396	Dan Meyer	.12	.06
397	Roy Thomas	.12	.06
398	Barry Foote	.12	.06
399	Mike Proly	.12	.06
400	George Foster	.40	.20
401	Pete Falcone	.12	.06
402	Merv Rettenmund	.12	.06
403	Pete Redfern	.12	.06
404	Orioles Team	.50	.25
405	Dwight Evans	1.50	.75
406	Paul Molitor	5.00	2.50
407	Tony Solaita	.12	.06
408	Bill North	.12	.06
409	Paul Splittorff	.12	.06
410	Bobby Bonds	.40	.20
411	Frank LaCorte	.12	.06
412	Thad Bosley	.12	.06
413	Allen Ripley	.12	.06
414	George Scott	.15	.08
415	Bill Atkinson	.12	.06
416	Tom Brookens (R)	.15	.08
417	Craig Chamberlain	.12	.06
418	Roger Freed	.12	.06
419	Vic Correll	.12	.06
420	Butch Hobson	.15	.08
421	Doug Bird	.12	.06
422	Larry Milbourne	.12	.06
423	Dave Frost	.12	.06
424	Yankees Team	.40	.20
425	Mark Belanger	.20	.10
426	Grant Jackson	.12	.06
427	Tom Hutton	.12	.06
428	Pat Zachry	.12	.06

429	Duane Kuiper	.12	.06
430	Larry Hisle	.15	.08
431	Mike Krukow	.12	.06
432	Willie Norwood	.12	.06
433	Rich Gale	.12	.06
434	Johnnie LeMaster	.12	.06
435	Don Gullett	.15	.08
436	Billy Almon	.12	.06
437	Joe Niekro	.15	.08
438	Dave Revering	.12	.06
439	Mike Phillips	.12	.06
440	Don Sutton	1.50	.75
441	Eric Soderholm	.12	.06
442	Jorge Orta	.12	.06
443	Mike Parrott	.12	.06
444	Alvis Woods	.12	.06
445	Mark Fidrych	.20	.10
446	Duffy Dyer	.12	.06
447	Nino Espinosa	.12	.06
448	Jim Wohlford	.12	.06
449	Doug Bair	.12	.06
450	George Brett	14.00	7.00
451	Indians Team	.40	.20
452	Steve Dillard	.12	.06
453	Mike Bacsik	.12	.06
454	Tom Donohue	.12	.06
455	Mike Torrez	.12	.06
456	Frank Taveras	.12	.06
457	Bert Blyleven	.80	.40
458	Billy Sample	.12	.06
459	Mickey Lolich	.20	.10
460	Willie Randolph	.75	.35
461	Dwayne Murphy	.12	.06
462	Mike Sadek	.12	.06
463	Jerry Royster	.12	.06
464	John Denny	.12	.06
465	Rick Monday	.15	.08
466	Mike Squires	.12	.06
467	Jesse Jefferson	.12	.06
468	Aurelio Rodriguez	.12	.06
469	Randy Niemann	.12	.06
470	Bob Boone	.60	.30
471	Hosken Powell	.12	.06
472	Willie Hernandez	.20	.10
473	Bump Wills	.12	.06
474	Steve Busby	.12	.06
475	Cesar Geronimo	.12	.06
476	Bob Shirley	.12	.06
477	Buck Martinez	.12	.06
478	Gil Flores	.12	.06
479	Expos Team	.40	.20
480	Bob Watson	.30	.15
481	Tom Paciorek	.12	.06
482	Rickey Henderson (R)	140.00	70.00
483	Bo Diaz	.12	.06
484	Checklist 364-484	.50	.25
485	Mickey Rivers	.12	.06

486	Mike Tyson	.12	.06
487	Wayne Nordhagen	.12	.06
488	Roy Howell	.12	.06
489	Preston Hanna	.12	.06
490	Lee May	.12	.06
491	Steve Mura	.12	.06
492	Todd Cruz	.12	.06
493	Jerry Martin	.12	.06
494	Craig Minetto	.12	.06
495	Bake McBride	.12	.06
496	Silvio Martinez	.12	.06
497	Jim Mason	.12	.06
498	Danny Darwin	.15	.08
499	Giants Team	.40	.20
500	Tom Seaver	6.00	3.00
501	Rennis Stennett	.12	.06
502	Rich Wortham	.12	.06
503	Mike Cubbage	.12	.06
504	Gene Garber	.12	.06
505	Bert Campaneris	.20	.10
506	Tom Buskey	.12	.06
507	Leon Roberts	.12	.06
508	U.L. Washington	.12	.06
509	Ed Glynn	.12	.06
510	Ron Cey	.25	.12
511	Eric Wilkins	.12	.06
512	Jose Cardenal	.12	.06
513	Tom Dixon	.12	.06
514	Steve Ontiveros	.12	.06
515	Mike Caldwell	.12	.06
516	Hector Cruz	.12	.06
517	Don Stanhouse	.12	.06
518	Nelson Norman	.12	.06
519	Steve Nicosia	.12	.06
520	Steve Rogers	.15	.08
521	Ken Brett	.12	.06
522	Jim Morrison	.12	.06
523	Ken Henderson	.12	.06
524	Jim Wright	.12	.06
525	Clint Hurdle	.12	.06
526	Phillies Team	.40	.20
527	Doug Rau	.12	.06
528	Adrian Devine	.12	.06
529	Jim Barr	.12	.06
530	Jim Sundberg	.12	.06
531	Eric Rasmussen	.12	.06
532	Willie Horton	.15	.08
533	Checklist 485-605	.50	.25
534	Andre Thornton	.15	.08
535	Bob Forsch	.12	.06
536	Lee Lacy	.12	.06
537	Alex Trevino (R)	.15	.08
538	Joe Strain	.12	.06
539	Rudy May	.12	.06
540	Pete Rose	5.50	2.75
541	Miguel Dilone	.12	.06
542	Joe Coleman	.12	.06
543	Pat Kelly	.12	.06

544	Rick Sutcliffe (R)	4.50	2.25
545	Jeff Burroughs	.15	.08
546	Rick Langford	.12	.06
547	John Wathan	.12	.06
548	Dave Rajsich	.12	.06
549	Larry Wolfe	.12	.06
550	Ken Griffey	.50	.25
551	Pirates Team	.40	.20
552	Bill Nahorodny	.12	.06
553	Dick Davis	.12	.06
554	Art Howe	.12	.06
555	Ed Figueroa	.12	.06
556	Joe Rudi	.15	.08
557	Mark Lee	.12	.06
558	Alfredo Griffin	.20	.10
559	Dale Murray	.12	.06
560	Dave Lopes	.20	.10
561	Eddie Whitson	.15	.08
562	Joe Wallis	.12	.06
563	Will McEnaney	.12	.06
564	Rick Manning	.12	.06
565	Dennis Leonard	.12	.06
566	Bud Harrelson	.15	.08
567	Skip Lockwood	.12	.06
568	Gary Roenicke (R)	.12	.06
569	Terry Kennedy	.15	.08
570	Roy Smalley	.12	.06
571	Joe Sambito	.12	.06
572	Jerry Morales	.12	.06
573	Kent Tekulve	.12	.06
574	Scot Thompson	.12	.06
575	Ken Kravec	.12	.06
576	Jim Dwyer	.12	.06
577	Blue Jays Team	.40	.20
578	Scott Sanderson	.25	.12
579	Charlie Moore	.12	.06
580	Nolan Ryan	24.00	12.00
581	Bob Bailor	.12	.06
582	Brian Doyle	.12	.06
583	Bob Stinson	.12	.06
584	Kurt Bevacqua	.12	.06
585	Al Hrabosky	.15	.08
586	Mitchell Page	.12	.06
587	Gerry Templeton	.15	.08
588	Greg Minton	.12	.06
589	Chet Lemon	.12	.06
590	Jim Palmer	4.00	2.00
591	Rick Cerone	.15	.08
592	Jon Matlack	.12	.06
593	Jesus Alou	.12	.06
594	Dick Tidrow	.12	.06
595	Don Money	.12	.06
596	Rick Matula	.12	.06
597	Tom Poquette	.12	.06
598	Fred Kendall	.12	.06
599	Mike Norris	.12	.06
600	Reggie Jackson	8.50	4.25
601	Buddy Schultz	.12	.06
602	Brian Downing	.15	.08
603	Jack Billingham	.12	.06
604	Glenn Adams	.12	.06
605	Terry Forster	.12	.06
606	Reds Team	.40	.20
607	Woodie Fryman	.12	.06
608	Alan Bannister	.12	.06
609	Ron Reed	.12	.06
610	Willie Stargell	2.50	1.25
611	Jerry Garvin	.12	.06
612	Cliff Johnson	.12	.06
613	Randy Stein	.12	.06
614	John Hiller	.12	.06
615	Doug DeCinces	.15	.08
616	Gene Richards	.12	.06
617	Joaquin Andujar	.20	.10
618	Bob Montgomery	.12	.06
619	Sergio Ferrer	.12	.06
620	Richie Zisk	.12	.06
621	Bob Grich	.15	.08
622	Mario Soto	.15	.08
623	Gorman Thomas	.15	.08
624	Lerrin LaGrow	.12	.06
625	Chris Chambliss	.15	.08
626	Tigers Team	.50	.25
627	Pedro Borbon	.12	.06
628	Doug Capilla	.12	.06
629	Jim Todd	.12	.06
630	Larry Bowa	.15	.08
631	Mark Littell	.12	.06
632	Barry Bonnell	.12	.06
633	Bob Apodaca	.12	.06
634	Glenn Borgmann	.12	.06
635	John Candelaria	.25	.12
636	Toby Harrah	.12	.06
637	Joe Simpson	.12	.06
638	Mark Clear (R)	.15	.08
639	Larry Blittner	.12	.06
640	Mike Flanagan	.15	.08
641	Ed Kranepool	.20	.10
642	Ken Forsch	.12	.06
643	John Mayberry	.15	.08
644	Charlie Hough	.15	.08
645	Rick Burleson	.15	.08
646	Checklist 606-726	.50	.25
647	Milt May	.12	.06
648	Roy White	.12	.06
649	Tom Griffin	.12	.06
650	Joe Morgan	2.50	1.25
651	Rollie Fingers	2.00	1.00
652	Mario Mendoza	.12	.06
653	Stan Bahnsen	.12	.06
654	Bruce Boisclair	.12	.06
655	Tug McGraw	.35	.18
656	Larvell Blanks	.12	.06
657	Dave Edwards	.12	.06
658	Chris Knapp	.12	.06
659	Brewers Team	.40	.20

660	Rusty Staub	.35	.18
661	Orioles Future Star	.12	.06
	Mark Corey (R)		
	Dave Ford (R)		
	Wayne Krenchicki (R)		
662	Red Sox Future Stars	.12	.06
	Joel Finch (R)		
	Mike O'Berry (R)		
	Chuck Rainey (R)		
663	Angels Future Stars	.80	.40
	Ralph Botting (R)		
	Bob Clark (R)		
	Dickie Thon (R)		
664	White Sox Future Stars	.12	.06
	Mike Colbern		
	Guy Hoffman (R)		
	Dewey Robinson (R)		
665	Indians Future Stars	.20	.10
	Larry Andersen		
	Bobby Cuellar (R)		
	Sandy Wihtol (R)		
666	Tigers Future Stars	.12	.06
	Mike Chris (R)		
	Al Greene (R)		
	Bruce Robbins (R)		
667	Royals Future Stars	2.50	1.25
	Renie Martin (R)		
	Bill Paschall (R)		
	Dan Quisenberry (R)		
668	Brewers Future Stars	.12	.06
	Danny Boitano		
	Willie Mueller (R)		
	Lenn Sakata (R)		
669	Twins Future Stars	.15	.08
	Dan Graham (R)		
	Rick Sofield (R)		
	Gary Ward		
670	Yankees Future Stars	.15	.08
	Bobby Brown (R)		
	Brad Gulden (R)		
	Darryl Jones (R)		
671	A's Future Stars	2.00	1.00
	Derek Bryant (R)		
	Brian Kingman (R)		
	Mike Morgan (R)		
672	Mariners Future Stars	.12	.06
	Charlie Beamon (R)		
	Rodney Craig		
	Rafael Vasquez (R)		
673	Rangers Future Stars	.12	.06
	Brian Allard (R)		
	Jerry Don Gleaton (R)		
	Greg Mahlberg (R)		
674	Blue Jays Future Stars	.12	.06
	Butch Edge (R)		
	Pat Kelly (R)		
675	Braves Future Stars	.12	.06
	Bruce Benedict		
	Larry Bradford (R)		
	Eddie Miller (R)		
676	Cubs Future Stars	.12	.06
	Dave Geisel		
	Steve Macko (R)		
	Karl Pagel		
677	Reds Future Stars	.12	.06
	Art DeFreites (R)		
	Frank Pastore (R)		
	Harry Spilman		
678	Astros Future Stars	.12	.06
	Reggie Baldwin (R)		
	Alan Knicely (R)		
	Pete Ladd		
679	Dodgers Future Stars	.25	.12
	Joe Beckwith		
	Mickey Hatcher (R)		
	Dave Patterson (R)		
680	Expos Future Stars	.12	.06
	Tony Bernazard (R)		
	Randy Miller (R)		
	John Tamargo (R)		
681	Mets Future Stars	2.50	1.25
	Dan Norman		
	Jesse Orosco (R)		
	Mike Scott (R)		
682	Phillies Future Stars	.15	.08
	Ramon Aviles		
	Dickie Noles		
	Kevin Saucier (R)		
683	Pirates Future Stars	.12	.06
	Dorian Boyland (R)		
	Alberto Lois (R)		
	Harry Saferight (R)		
684	Cardinals Future Stars	.50	.25
	George Frazier		
	Tom Herr (R)		
	Dan O'Brien (R)		
685	Padres Future Stars	.12	.06
	Tim Flannery (R)		
	Brian Greer (R)		
	Jim Wilhelm (R)		
686	Giants Future Stars	.12	.06
	Greg Johnston (R)		
	Dennis Littlejohn (R)		
	Phil Nastu (R)		
687	Mike Heath	.12	.06
688	Steve Stone	.12	.06
689	Red Sox Team	.40	.20
690	Tommy John	.50	.25
691	Ivan DeJesus	.12	.06
692	Rawly Eastwick	.12	.06
693	Craig Kusick	.12	.06
694	Jim Rooker	.12	.06

695	Reggie Smith	.15	.08
696	Julio Gonzalez	.12	.06
697	David Clyde	.12	.06
698	Oscar Gamble	.15	.08
699	Floyd Bannister	.12	.06
700	Rod Carew	2.50	1.25
701	Ken Oberkfell (R)	.20	.10
702	Ed Farmer	.12	.06
703	Otto Velez	.12	.06
704	Gene Tenace	.15	.08
705	Freddie Patek	.12	.06
706	Tippy Martinez	.12	.06
707	Elliott Maddox	.12	.06
708	Bob Tolan	.12	.06
709	Pat Underwood	.12	.06
710	Graig Nettles	.25	.12
711	Bob Galasso	.12	.06
712	Rodney Scott	.12	.06
713	Terry Whitfield	.12	.06
714	Fred Norman	.12	.06
715	Sal Bando	.15	.08
716	Lynn McGlothen	.12	.06
717	Mickey Klutts	.12	.06
718	Greg Gross	.12	.06
719	Don Robinson	.15	.08
720	Carl Yastrzemski	2.00	1.00
721	Paul Hartzell	.12	.06
722	Jose Cruz	.20	.10
723	Shane Rawley	.12	.06
724	Jerry White	.12	.06
725	Rick Wise	.15	.08
726	Steve Yeager	.15	.08

1981 Topps

This 726-card set features full color photos on the card fronts with multi colored borders with each team assigned a different border color. The player's name appears below the photo with his position and team printed in a small baseball cap graphic in the lower left corner. Cards measure 2-1/2" by 3-1/2". Key subsets include League Leaders (1-8), Record Breakers, World Series and Playoff Highlights and Rookies.

		NR/MT	EX
Complete Set (726)		110.00	55.00
Commons (1-726)		.10	.05

1	Batting Leaders	2.00	1.00
2	Home Run Leaders	.75	.35
3	RBI Leaders	.75	.35
4	SB Leaders	1.50	.75
5	Victory Leaders	.35	.18
6	Strikeout Leaders	.25	.12
7	ERA Leaders	.25	.12
8	Leading Firemen	.35	.18
9	Pete LaCock	.10	.05
10	Mike Flanagan	.15	.08
11	Jim Wohlford	.10	.05
12	Mark Clear	.10	.05
13	Joe Charboneau (R)	.15	.08
14	John Tudor (R)	.40	.20
15	Larry Parrish	.10	.05
16	Ron Davis	.10	.05
17	Cliff Johnson	.10	.05
18	Glenn Adams	.10	.05
19	Jim Clancy	.10	.05
20	Jeff Burroughs	.12	.06
21	Ron Oester	.10	.05
22	Danny Darwin	.12	.06
23	Alex Trevino	.10	.05
24	Don Stanhouse	.10	.05
25	Sixto Lezcano	.10	.05
26	U.L. Washington	.10	.05
27	Champ Summers	.10	.05
28	Enrique Romo	.10	.05
29	Gene Tenace	.12	.06
30	Jack Clark	.50	.25
31	Checklist 1-121	.12	.06
32	Ken Oberkfell	.10	.05
33	Rick Honeycutt	.12	.06
34	Aurelio Rodriguez	.10	.05
35	Mitchell Page	.10	.05
36	Ed Farmer	.10	.05
37	Gary Roenicke	.10	.05
38	Win Remmerswaal	.10	.05
39	Tom Veryzer	.10	.05
40	Tug McGraw	.25	.12
41	Rangers Future Stars	.10	.05
	Bob Babock (R)		
	John Butcher (R)		
	Jerry Don Gleaton		
42	Jerry White	.10	.05
43	Jose Morales	.10	.05

44	Larry McWilliams	.10	.05	96	A's Future Stars	.15	.08
45	Enos Cabell	.10	.05		Dave Beard		
46	Rick Bosetti	.10	.05		Ernie Camacho (R)		
47	Ken Brett	.10	.05		Pat Dempsey (R)		
48	Dave Skaggs	.10	.05	97	Chris Speier	.10	.05
49	Bob Shirley	.10	.05	98	Clint Hurdle	.10	.05
50	Dave Lopes	.20	.10	99	Eric Wilkins	.10	.05
51	Bill Robinson	.12	.06	100	Rod Carew	3.50	1.75
52	Hector Cruz	.10	.05	101	Benny Ayala	.10	.05
53	Kevin Saucier	.10	.05	102	Dave Tobik	.10	.05
54	Ivan DeJesus	.10	.05	103	Jerry Martin	.10	.05
55	Mike Norris	.10	.05	104	Terry Forster	.10	.05
56	Buck Martinez	.10	.05	105	Jose Cruz	.15	.08
57	Dave Roberts	.10	.05	106	Don Money	.10	.05
58	Joel Youngblood	.10	.05	107	Rich Wortham	.10	.05
59	Dan Petry	.15	.08	108	Bruce Benedict	.10	.05
60	Willie Randolph	.40	.20	109	Mike Scott	.30	.15
61	Butch Wynegar	.10	.05	110	Carl Yastrzemski	3.50	1.75
62	Joe Pettini	.10	.05	111	Greg Minton	.10	.05
63	Steve Renko	.10	.05	112	White Sox Future	.10	.05
64	Brian Asselstine	.10	.05		Stars		
65	Scott McGregor	.10	.05		Rusty Kuntz		
66	Royals Future Stars	.12	.06		Fran Mullins (R)		
	Manny Castillo (R)				Leo Sutherland (R)		
	Tim Ireland (R)			113	Mike Phillips	.10	.05
	Mike Jones (R)			114	Tom Underwood	.10	.05
67	Ken Kravec	.10	.05	115	Roy Smalley	.10	.05
68	Matt Alexander	.10	.05	116	Joe Simpson	.10	.05
69	Ed Halicki	.10	.05	117	Pete Falcone	.10	.05
70	Al Oliver	.20	.10	118	Kurt Bevacqua	.10	.05
71	Hal Dues	.10	.05	119	Tippy Martinez	.10	.05
72	Barry Evans	.10	.05	120	Larry Bowa	.15	.08
73	Doug Bair	.10	.05	121	Larry Harlow	.10	.05
74	Mike Hargrove	.10	.05	122	John Denny	.10	.05
75	Reggie Smith	.15	.08	123	Al Cowens	.10	.05
76	Mario Mendoza	.10	.05	124	Jerry Garvin	.10	.05
77	Mike Barlow	.10	.05	125	Andre Dawson	4.50	2.25
78	Steve Dillard	.10	.05	126	Charlie Leibrandt(R)	1.00	.50
79	Bruce Robbins	.10	.05	127	Rudy Law	.10	.05
80	Rusty Staub	.30	.15	128	Gary Allenson	.10	.05
81	Dave Stapleton	.10	.05	129	Art Howe	.10	.05
82	Astros Future Stars	.15	.08	130	Larry Gura	.10	.05
	Danny Heep			131	Keith Moreland (R)	.15	.08
	Alan Knicely			132	Tommy Boggs	.10	.05
	Bobby Sprowl (R)			133	Jeff Cox	.10	.05
83	Mike Proly	.10	.05	134	Steve Mura	.10	.05
84	Johnnie LeMaster	.10	.05	135	Gorman Thomas	.12	.06
85	Mike Caldwell	.10	.05	136	Doug Capilla	.10	.05
86	Wayne Gross	.10	.05	137	Hosken Powell	.10	.05
87	Rick Camp	.10	.05	138	Rich Dotson (R)	.12	.06
88	Joe Lefebvre	.10	.05	139	Oscar Gamble	.12	.06
89	Darrell Jackson	.10	.05	140	Bob Forsch	.10	.05
90	Bake McBride	.10	.05	141	Miguel Dilone	.10	.05
91	Tim Stoddard	.10	.05	142	Jackson Todd	.10	.05
92	Mike Easler	.10	.05	143	Dan Meyer	.10	.05
93	Ed Glynn	.10	.05	144	Allen Ripley	.10	.05
94	Harry Spilman	.10	.05	145	Mickey Rivers	.10	.05
95	Jim Sundberg	.10	.05	146	Bobby Castillo	.10	.05

147	Dale Berra	.10	.05	202	Steve Carlton (RB)	1.00	.50
148	Randy Niemann	.10	.05	203	Bill Gullickson (RB)	.20	.10
149	Joe Nolan	.10	.05	204	Ron LeFlore/Rodney	.20	.10
150	Mark Fidrych	.15	.08		Scott (RB)		
151	Claudell Washington	.12	.06	205	Pete Rose (RB)	1.00	.50
152	John Urrea	.10	.05	206	Mike Schmidt (RB)	1.25	.60
153	Tom Poquette	.10	.05	207	Ozzie Smith (RB)	1.00	.50
154	Rick Langford	.10	.05	208	Willie Wilson (RB)	.20	.10
155	Chris Chambliss	.15	.08	209	Dickie Thon	.10	.05
156	Bob McClure	.10	.05	210	Jim Palmer	3.00	1.50
157	John Wathan	.10	.05	211	Derrel Thomas	.10	.05
158	Ferguson Jenkins	1.25	.60	212	Steve Nicosia	.10	.05
159	Brian Doyle	.10	.05	213	Al Holland (R)	.10	.05
160	Garry Maddox	.12	.06	214	Angels Future Stars	.10	.05
161	Dan Graham	.10	.05		Ralph Botting		
162	Doug Corbett	.10	.05		Jim Dorsey (R)		
163	Billy Almon	.10	.05		John Harris (R)		
164	LaMarr Hoyt	.15	.08	215	Larry Hisle	.10	.05
165	Tony Scott	.10	.05	216	John Henry Johnson	.10	.05
166	Floyd Bannister	.10	.05	217	Rich Hebner	.10	.05
167	Terry Whitfield	.10	.05	218	Paul Splittorff	.12	.06
168	Don Robinson	.12	.06	219	Ken Landreaux	.10	.05
169	John Mayberry	.12	.06	220	Tom Seaver	4.00	2.00
170	Ross Grimsley	.10	.05	221	Bob Davis	.10	.05
171	Gene Richards	.10	.05	222	Jorge Orta	.10	.05
172	Gary Woods	.10	.05	223	Roy Lee Jackson	.10	.05
173	Bump Wills	.10	.05	224	Pat Zachry	.10	.05
174	Doug Rau	.10	.05	225	Ruppert Jones	.10	.05
175	Dave Collins	.10	.05	226	Manny Sanguillen	.15	.08
176	Mike Krukow	.10	.05	227	Fred Martinez	.10	.05
177	Rick Peters	.10	.05	228	Tom Paciorek	.10	.05
178	Jim Essian	.10	.05	229	Rollie Fingers	2.50	1.25
179	Rudy May	.10	.05	230	George Hendrick	.12	.06
180	Pete Rose	4.50	2.25	231	Joe Beckwith	.10	.05
181	Elias Sosa	.10	.05	232	Mickey Klutts	.10	.05
182	Bob Grich	.15	.08	233	Skip Lockwood	.10	.05
183	Dick Davis	.10	.05	234	Lou Whitaker	1.00	.50
184	Jim Dwyer	.10	.05	235	Scott Sanderson	.20	.10
185	Dennis Leonard	.10	.05	236	Mike Ivie	.10	.05
186	Wayne Nordhagen	.10	.05	237	Charlie Moore	.10	.05
187	Mike Parrott	.10	.05	238	Willie Hernandez	.15	.08
188	Doug DeCinces	.12	.06	239	Rick Miller	.10	.05
189	Craig Swan	.10	.05	240	Nolan Ryan	14.00	7.00
190	Cesar Cedeno	.15	.08	241	Checklist 122-242	.12	.06
191	Rick Sutcliffe	.50	.25	242	Chet Lemon	.12	.06
192	Braves Future Stars	.20	.10	243	Sal Butera	.10	.05
	Terry Harper (R)			244	Cardinals Future	.10	.05
	Ed Miller				Stars		
	Rafael Ramirez (R)				Tito Landrum (R)		
193	Pete Vuckovich	.12	.06		Al Olmsted (R)		
194	Rod Scurry (R)	.10	.05		Andy Rincon		
195	Rich Murray	.10	.05	245	Ed Figueroa	.10	.05
196	Duffy Dyer	.10	.05	246	Ed Ott	.10	.05
197	Jim Kern	.10	.05	247	Glenn Hubbard	.10	.05
198	Jerry Dybzinski	.10	.05	248	Joey McLaughlin	.10	.05
199	Chuck Rainey	.10	.05	249	Larry Cox	.10	.05
200	George Foster	.25	.12	250	Ron Guidry	.50	.25
201	Johnny Bench (RB)	.80	.40	251	Tom Brookens	.10	.05

252	Victor Cruz	.10	.05
253	Dave Bergman	.10	.05
254	Ozzie Smith	6.50	3.25
255	Mark Littell	.10	.05
256	Bombo Rivera	.10	.05
257	Rennie Stenett	.10	.05
258	Joe Price (R)	.10	.05
259	Mets Future Stars	1.25	.60
	Juan Berenguer		
	Hubie Brooks (R)		
	Mookie Wilson (R)		
260	Ron Cey	.25	.12
261	Rickey Henderson	20.00	10.00
262	Sammy Stewart	.10	.05
263	Brian Downing	.10	.05
264	Jim Norris	.10	.05
265	John Candelaria	.15	.08
266	Tom Herr	.15	.08
267	Stan Bahnsen	.10	.05
268	Jerry Royster	.10	.05
269	Ken Forsch	.10	.05
270	Greg Luzinski	.25	.12
271	Bill Castro	.10	.05
272	Bruce Kimm	.10	.05
273	Stan Papi	.10	.05
274	Craig Chamberlain	.10	.05
275	Dwight Evans	.60	.30
276	Dan Spillner	.10	.05
277	Alfredo Griffin	.15	.08
278	Rick Sofield	.10	.05
279	Bob Knepper	.10	.05
280	Ken Griffey	.40	.20
281	Fred Stanley	.10	.05
282	Mariners Future Stars	.10	.05
	Rick Anderson		
	Greg Biercevicz		
	Rodney Craig		
283	Billy Sample	.10	.05
284	Brian Kingman	.10	.05
285	Jerry Turner	.10	.05
286	Dave Frost	.10	.05
287	Lenn Sakata	.10	.05
288	Bob Clark	.10	.05
289	Mickey Hatcher	.10	.05
290	Bob Boone	.25	.12
291	Aurelio Lopez	.10	.05
292	Mike Squiers	.10	.05
293	Charlie Lea (R)	.12	.06
294	Mike Tyson	.10	.05
295	Hal McRae	.25	.12
296	Bill Nahorodny	.10	.05
297	Bob Bailor	.10	.05
298	Buddy Solomon	.10	.05
299	Elliott Maddox	.10	.05
300	Paul Molitor	2.00	1.00
301	Matt Keough	.10	.05
302	Dodgers Future Stars	2.50	1.25

	Jack Perconte		
	Mike Scioscia(R)		
	Fernando Valenzuela (R)		
303	Johnny Oates	.12	.06
304	John Castino	.10	.05
305	Ken Clay	.10	.05
306	Juan Beniquez	.10	.05
307	Gene Garber	.10	.05
308	Rick Manning	.10	.05
309	Luis Salazar (R)	.15	.08
310	Vida Blue	.15	.08
311	Freddie Patek	.10	.05
312	Rick Rhoden	.10	.05
313	Luis Pujols	.10	.05
314	Rich Dauer	.10	.05
315	Kirk Gibson (R)	3.00	1.50
316	Criag Minetto	.10	.05
317	Lonnie Smith	.25	.12
318	Steve Yeager	.10	.05
319	Rowland Office	.10	.05
320	Tom Burgmeier	.10	.05
321	Leon Durham (R)	.15	.08
322	Neil Allen	.10	.05
323	Jim Morrison	.10	.05
324	Mike Willis	.10	.05
325	Ray Knight	.20	.10
326	Biff Pocoroba	.10	.05
327	Moose Haas	.10	.05
328	Twins Future Stars	.12	.06
	Dave Engle		
	Greg Johnston (R)		
	Gary Ward		
329	Joaquin Andujar	.15	.08
330	Frank White	.15	.08
331	Dennis Lamp	.10	.05
332	Lee Lacy	.10	.05
333	Sid Monge	.10	.05
334	Dane Jorg	.10	.05
335	Rick Cerone	.15	.08
336	Eddie Whitson	.12	.06
337	Lynn Jones	.10	.05
338	Checklist 243-363	.30	.15
339	John Ellis	.10	.05
340	Bruce Kison	.10	.05
341	Dwayne Murphy	.10	.05
342	Eric Rasmussen	.10	.05
343	Frank Taveras	.10	.05
344	Byron McLaughlin	.10	.05
345	Warren Cromartie	.10	.05
346	Larry Christenson	.10	.05
347	Harold Baines (R)	3.50	1.75
348	Bob Sykes	.10	.05
349	Glenn Hoffman	.10	.05
350	J.R. Richard	.20	.10
351	Otto Velez	.10	.05
352	Dick Tidrow	.10	.05
353	Terry Kennedy	.15	.08

354	Mario Soto	.15	.08
355	Bob Horner	.25	.12
356	Padres Future Stars	.10	.05
	George Stablein (R)		
	Craig Stimac (R)		
	Tom Tellmann (R)		
357	Jim Slaton	.10	.05
358	Mark Wagner	.10	.05
359	Tom Hausman	.10	.05
360	Willie Wilson	.20	.10
361	Joe Strain	.10	.05
362	Bo Diaz	.10	.05
363	Geoff Zahn	.10	.05
364	Mike Davis (R)	.12	.06
365	Graig Nettles	.20	.10
366	Mike Ramsey	.10	.05
367	Denny Martinez	.30	.15
368	Leon Roberts	.10	.05
369	Frank Tanana	.15	.08
370	Dave Winfield	4.00	2.00
371	Charlie Hough	.15	.08
372	Jay Johnstone	.12	.06
373	Pat Underwood	.10	.05
374	Tom Hutton	.10	.05
375	Dave Concepcion	.35	.18
376	Ron Reed	.10	.05
377	Jerry Morales	.10	.05
378	Dave Rader	.10	.05
379	Lary Sorensen	.10	.05
380	Willie Stargell	2.00	1.00
381	Cubs Future Stars	.10	.05
	Carlos Lezcano		
	Steve Macko		
	Randy Martz		
382	Paul Mirabella (R)	.10	.05
383	Eric Soderholm	.10	.05
384	Mike Sadek	.10	.05
385	Joe Sambito	.10	.05
386	Dave Edwards	.10	.05
387	Phil Niekro	1.25	.60
388	Andre Thornton	.15	.08
389	Marty Pattin	.10	.05
390	Cesar Geronimo	.10	.05
391	Dave Lemanczyk	.10	.05
392	Lance Parrish	.40	.20
393	Broderick Perkins	.10	.05
394	Woodie Fryman	.10	.05
395	Scot Thompson	.10	.05
396	Bill Campbell	.10	.05
397	Julio Cruz	.10	.05
398	Ross Baumgarten	.10	.05
399	Orioles Future Stars	.75	.35
	Mike Boddicker (R)		
	Mark Corey (R)		
	Floyd Rayford (R)		
400	Reggie Jackson	4.50	2.25
401	A.L. Championships	1.25	.60
402	N.L. Championships	.25	.12
403	World Series	.25	.12
404	World Series		
	Summary	.25	.12
405	Nino Espinosa	.10	.05
406	Dickie Noles	.10	.05
407	Ernie Whitt	.10	.05
408	Fernando Arroyo	.10	.05
409	Larry Herndon	.10	.05
410	Bert Campaneris	.15	.08
411	Terry Puhl	.10	.05
412	Britt Burns (R)	.12	.06
413	Tony Bernazard	.10	.05
414	John Pacella	.10	.05
415	Ben Oglivie	.10	.05
416	Gary Alexander	.10	.05
417	Dan Schatzeder	.10	.05
418	Bobby Brown	.10	.05
419	Tom Hume	.10	.05
420	Keith Hernandez	.40	.20
421	Bob Stanley	.10	.05
422	Dan Ford	.10	.05
423	Shane Rawley	.10	.05
424	Yankees Future Stars	.10	.05
	Tim Lollar (R)		
	Bruce Robinson (R)		
	Dennis Werth		
425	Al Bumbry	.10	.05
426	Warren Brusstar	.10	.05
427	John D'Acquisto	.10	.05
428	John Stearns	.10	.05
429	Mick Kelleher	.10	.05
430	Jim Bibby	.10	.05
431	Dave Roberts	.10	.05
432	Len Barker	.10	.05
433	Rance Mulliniks	.10	.05
434	Roger Erickson	.10	.05
435	Jim Spencer	.10	.05
436	Gary Lucas	.10	.05
437	Mike Heath	.10	.05
438	John Montefusco	.10	.05
439	Denny Walling	.10	.05
440	Jerry Reuss	.15	.08
441	Ken Reitz	.10	.05
442	Ron Pruitt	.10	.05
443	Jim Beattie	.10	.05
444	Garth Iorg	.10	.05
445	Ellis Valentine	.10	.05
446	Checklist 364-484	.30	.15
447	Junior Kennedy	.10	.05
448	Tim Corcoran	.10	.05
449	Paul Mitchell	.10	.05
450	Dave Kingman	.20	.10
451	Indians Future Stars	.10	.05
	Chris Bando (R)		
	Tom Brennan		
	Sandy Wihtol		
452	Renie Martin	.10	.05
453	Rob Wilfong	.10	.05

454	Andy Hassler	.10	.05
455	Rick Burleson	.12	.06
456	Jeff Reardon (R)	14.00	7.00
457	Mike Lum	.10	.05
458	Randy Jones	.12	.06
459	Greg Gross	.10	.05
460	Rich Gossage	.40	.20
461	Dave McKay	.10	.05
462	Jack Brohamer	.10	.05
463	Milt May	.10	.05
464	Adrian Devine	.10	.05
465	Bill Russell	.15	.08
466	Bob Molinaro	.10	.05
467	Dave Stieb	.60	.30
468	Johnny Wockenfuss	.10	.05
469	Jeff Leonard	.20	.10
470	Manny Trillo	.10	.05
471	Mike Vail	.10	.05
472	Dyar Miller	.10	.05
473	Jose Cardenal	.10	.05
474	Mike LaCoss	.10	.05
475	Buddy Bell	.12	.06
476	Jerry Koosman	.15	.08
477	Luis Gomez	.10	.05
478	Juan Eichelberger	.10	.05
479	Expos Future Stars	6.00	3.00
	Bobby Pate (R)		
	Tim Raines (R)		
	Roberto Ramos		
480	Carlton Fisk	3.50	1.75
481	Bob Lacey	.10	.05
482	Jim Gantner	.10	.05
483	Mike Griffin	.10	.05
484	Max Venable	.10	.05
485	Garry Templeton	.15	.08
486	Marc Hill	.10	.05
487	Dewey Robinson	.10	.05
488	Damaso Garcia	.12	.06
489	John Littlefield	.10	.05
490	Eddie Murray	4.50	2.25
491	Gordy Pladson	.10	.05
492	Barry Foote	.10	.05
493	Dan Quisenberry	.35	.18
494	Bob Walk (R)	.35	.18
495	Dusty Baker	.15	.08
496	Paul Dade	.10	.05
497	Fred Norman	.10	.05
498	Pat Putnam	.10	.05
499	Frank Pastore	.10	.05
500	Jim Rice	.50	.25
501	Tim Foli	.10	.05
502	Giants Future Stars	.10	.05
	Chris Bourjos		
	Al Hargesheimer (R)		
	Mike Rowland		
503	Steve McCatty	.10	.05
504	Dale Murphy	1.50	.75
505	Jason Thompson	.10	.05
506	Phil Huffman	.10	.05
507	Jamie Quirk	.10	.05
508	Rob Dressler	.10	.05
509	Pete Mackanin	.10	.05
510	Lee Mazzilli	.10	.05
511	Wayne Garland	.10	.05
512	Gary Thomasson	.10	.05
513	Frank LaCorte	.10	.05
514	George Riley	.10	.05
515	Robin Yount	7.00	3.50
516	Doug Bird	.10	.05
517	Richie Zisk	.10	.05
518	Grant Jackson	.10	.05
519	John Tamargo	.10	.05
520	Steve Stone	.15	.08
521	Sam Mejias	.10	.05
522	Mike Colbern	.10	.05
523	John Fulgham	.10	.05
524	Willie Aikens	.10	.05
525	Mike Torrez	.10	.05
526	Phillies Future Stars	.12	.06
	Marty Bystrom		
	Jay Loviglio (R)		
	Jim Wright		
527	Danny Goodwin	.10	.05
528	Gary Matthews	.15	.08
529	Dave LaRoche	.10	.05
530	Steve Garvey	1.25	.60
531	John Curtis	.10	.05
532	Bill Stein	.10	.05
533	Jesus Figueroa	.10	.05
534	Dave Smith (R)	.25	.12
535	Omar Moreno	.10	.05
536	Bob Owchinko	.10	.05
537	Ron Hodges	.10	.05
538	Tom Griffin	.10	.05
539	Rodney Scott	.10	.05
540	Mike Schmidt	4.50	2.25
541	Steve Swisher	.10	.05
542	Larry Bradford	.10	.05
543	Terry Crowley	.10	.05
544	Rich Gale	.10	.05
545	Johnny Grubb	.10	.05
546	Paul Moskau	.10	.05
547	Mario Guerrero	.10	.05
548	Dave Goltz	.10	.05
549	Jerry Remy	.10	.05
550	Tommy John	.25	.12
551	Pirates Future Stars	1.25	.60
	Vance Law (R)		
	Tony Pena (R)		
	Pascual Perez (R)		
552	Steve Trout	.10	.05
553	Tim Blackwell	.10	.05
554	Bert Blyleven	.75	.35
555	Cecil Cooper	.15	.08
556	Jerry Mumphrey	.10	.05
557	Chris Knapp	.10	.05

No.	Name		
558	Barry Bonnell	.10	.05
559	Willie Montanez	.10	.05
560	Joe Morgan	2.00	1.00
561	Dennis Littlejohn	.10	.05
562	Checklist 485-605	.30	.15
563	Jim Kaat	.25	.12
564	Ron Hassey	.10	.05
565	Burt Hooton	.10	.05
566	Del Unser	.10	.05
567	Mark Bomback	.10	.05
568	Dave Revering	.10	.05
569	Al Williams	.10	.05
570	Ken Singleton	.12	.06
571	Todd Cruz	.10	.05
572	Jack Morris	3.00	1.50
573	Phil Garner	.12	.06
574	Bill Caudill	.10	.05
575	Tony Perez	.75	.35
576	Reggie Cleveland	.10	.05
577	Blue Jays Future Stars	.12	.06
	Luis Leal (R)		
	Brian Milner		
	Ken Schrom		
578	Bill Gullickson (R)	1.25	.60
579	Tim Flannery	.10	.05
580	Don Baylor	.30	.15
581	Roy Howell	.10	.05
582	Gaylord Perry	1.25	.60
583	Larry Milbourne	.10	.05
584	Randy Lerch	.10	.05
585	Amos Otis	.12	.06
586	Silvio Martinez	.10	.05
587	Jeff Newman	.10	.05
588	Gary Lavelle	.10	.05
589	Lamar Johnson	.10	.05
590	Bruce Sutter	.25	.12
591	John Lowenstein	.10	.05
592	Steve Comer	.10	.05
593	Steve Kemp	.10	.05
594	Preston Hanna	.10	.05
595	Butch Hobson	.10	.05
596	Jerry Augustine	.10	.05
597	Rafael Landestoy	.10	.05
598	George Vukovich	.10	.05
599	Dennis Kinney	.10	.05
600	Johnny Bench	3.50	1.75
601	Don Aase	.10	.05
602	Bobby Murcer	.20	.10
603	John Verhoeven	.10	.05
604	Rob Picciolo	.10	.05
605	Don Sutton	1.00	.50
606	Reds Future Stars	.10	.05
	Bruce Berenyi (R)		
	Geoff Combe (R)		
	Paul Householder (R)		
607	Dave Palmer	.10	.05
608	Greg Pryor	.10	.05
609	Lynn McGlothen	.10	.05
610	Darrell Porter	.10	.05
611	Rick Matula	.10	.05
612	Duane Kuiper	.10	.05
613	Jim Anderson	.10	.05
614	Dave Rozema	.10	.05
615	Rick Dempsey	.12	.06
616	Rick Wise	.12	.06
617	Craig Reynolds	.10	.05
618	John Milner	.10	.05
619	Steve Henderson	.10	.05
620	Dennis Eckersley	2.50	1.25
621	Tom Donohue	.10	.05
622	Randy Moffitt	.10	.05
623	Sal Bando	.12	.06
624	Bob Welch	.40	.20
625	Bill Buckner	.20	.10
626	Tigers Future Stars	.10	.05
	Dave Steffen		
	Jerry Ujdur (R)		
	Roger Weaver (R)		
627	Luis Tiant	.25	.12
628	Vic Correll	.10	.05
629	Tony Armas	.12	.06
630	Steve Carlton	3.50	1.75
631	Ron Jackson	.10	.05
632	Alan Bannister	.10	.05
633	Bill Lee	.10	.05
634	Doug Flynn	.10	.05
635	Bobby Bonds	.25	.12
636	Al Hrabosky	.12	.06
637	Jerry Narron	.10	.05
638	Checklist 606-726	.30	.15
639	Carney Lansford	.35	.18
640	Dave Parker	.50	.25
641	Mark Belanger	.15	.08
642	Vern Ruhle	.10	.05
643	Lloyd Moseby (R)	.25	.12
644	Ramon Aviles	.10	.05
645	Rick Reuschel	.15	.08
646	Marvis Foley	.10	.05
647	Dick Drago	.10	.05
648	Darrell Evans	.25	.12
649	Many Sarmiento	.10	.05
650	Bucky Dent	.12	.06
651	Pedro Guerrero	.60	.30
652	John Montague	.10	.05
653	Bill Fahey	.10	.05
654	Ray Burris	.10	.05
655	Dan Driessen	.10	.05
656	Jon Matlack	.10	.05
657	Mike Cubbage	.10	.05
658	Milt Wilcox	.10	.05
659	Brewers Future Stars	.10	.05
	John Flinn (R)		
	Ed Romero		
	Ned Yost		
660	Gary Carter	1.50	.75

661	Orioles Team	.30	.15
662	Red Sox Team	.20	.10
663	Angels Team	.20	.10
664	White Sox Team	.30	.15
665	Indians Team	.20	.10
666	Tigers Team	.30	.15
667	Royals Team	.20	.10
668	Brewers Team	.20	.10
669	Twins Team	.20	.10
670	Yankees Team	.30	.15
671	A's Team	.35	.18
672	Mariners Team	.30	.15
673	Rangers Team	.20	.10
674	Blue Jays Team	.20	.10
675	Braves Team	.20	.10
676	Cubs Team	.20	.10
677	Reds Team	.20	.10
678	Astros Team	.20	.10
679	Dodgers Team	.30	.15
680	Expos Team	.20	.10
681	Mets Team	.30	.15
682	Phillies Team	.20	.10
683	Pirates Team	.20	.10
684	Cardinals Team	.30	.15
685	Padres Team	.20	.10
686	Giants Team	.20	.10
687	Jeff Jones	.10	.05
688	Kiko Garcia	.10	.05
689	Red Sox Future Stars	2.00	1.00
	Bruce Hurst (R)		
	Keith MacWhorter (R)		
	Reid Nichols		
690	Bob Watson	.30	.15
691	Dick Ruthven	.10	.05
692	Lenny Randle	.10	.05
693	Steve Howe (R)	.15	.08
694	Bud Harrelson	.10	.05
695	Kent Tekulve	.10	.05
696	Alan Ashby	.10	.05
697	Rick Waits	.10	.05
698	Mike Jorgensen	.10	.05
699	Glenn Abbott	.10	.05
700	George Brett	7.50	3.75
701	Joe Rudi	.12	.06
702	George Medich	.10	.05
703	Alvis Woods	.10	.05
704	Bill Travers	.10	.05
705	Ted Simmons	.25	.12
706	Dave Ford	.10	.05
707	Dave Cash	.10	.05
708	Doyle Alexander	.10	.05
709	Alan Trammell	.80	.40
710	Ron LeFlore	.12	.06
711	Joe Ferguson	.10	.05
712	Bill Bonham	.10	.05
713	Bill North	.10	.05
714	Pete Redfern	.10	.05

715	Bill Madlock	.25	.12
716	Glenn Borgmann	.10	.05
717	Jim Barr	.10	.05
718	Larry Bittner	.10	.05
719	Sparky Lyle	.15	.08
720	Fred Lynn	.30	.15
721	Toby Harrah	.10	.05
722	Joe Niekro	.12	.06
723	Bruce Bochte	.10	.05
724	Lou Piniella	.15	.08
725	Steve Rogers	.12	.06
726	Rick Monday	.15	.08

1981 Topps Traded

This 132-card set marks Topps first update set since 1976. Card numbers pick up where the regular edition left off (727-858). The set features players who were traded during the season and rookies.

		MINT	NR/MT
Complete Set (132)		34.00	22.00
Commons		.10	.05
727	Danny Ainge	3.00	1.50
728	Doyle Alexander	.10	.05
729	Gary Alexander	.10	.05
730	Bill Almon	.10	.05
731	Joaquin Andujar	.20	.10
732	Bob Bailor	.10	.05
733	Juan Beniquez	.10	.05
734	Dave Bergman	.10	.05
735	Tony Bernazard	.10	.05
736	Larry Biittner	.10	.05
737	Doug Bird	.10	.05
739	Bert Blyleven	1.50	.75
739	Mark Bomback	.10	.05

740	Bobby Bonds	.25	.12
741	Rick Bosetti	.10	.05
742	Hubie Brooks	.80	.40
743	Rick Burleson	.15	.08
744	Ray Burris	.10	.05
745	Jeff Burroughs	.12	.06
746	Enos Cabell	.10	.05
747	Ken Clay	.10	.05
748	Mark Clear	.10	.05
749	Larry Cox	.10	.05
750	Hector Cruz	.10	.05
751	Victor Cruz	.10	.05
752	Mike Cubbage	.10	.05
753	Dick Davis	.10	.05
754	Brian Doyle	.10	.05
755	Dick Drago	.10	.05
756	Leon Durham	.10	.05
757	Jim Dwyer	.10	.05
758	Dave Edwards	.10	.05
759	Jim Essian	.10	.05
760	Bill Fahey	.10	.05
761	Rollie Fingers	4.00	2.00
762	Carlton Fisk	7.50	3.75
763	Barry Foote	.10	.05
764	Ken Forsch	.10	.05
765	Kiko Garcia	.10	.05
766	Cesar Geronimo	.10	.05
767	Gary Gray	.10	.05
768	Mickey Hatcher	.10	.05
769	Steve Henderson	.10	.05
770	Marc Hill	.10	.05
771	Butch Hobson	.12	.06
772	Rick Honeycutt	.12	.06
773	Roy Howell	.10	.05
774	Mike Ivie	.10	.05
775	Roy Lee Jackson	.10	.05
776	Cliff Johnson	.10	.05
777	Randy Jones	.10	.05
778	Ruppert Jones	.10	.05
779	Mick Kelleher	.10	.05
780	Terry Kennedy	.15	.08
781	Dave Kingman	.30	.15
782	Bob Knepper	.10	.05
783	Ken Kravec	.10	.05
784	Bob Lacey	.10	.05
785	Dennis Lamp	.10	.05
786	Rafael Landestoy	.10	.05
787	Ken Landreaux	.10	.05
788	Carney Lansford	.60	.30
789	Dave LaRoche	.10	.05
790	Joe Lefebvre	.10	.05
791	Ron LeFlore	.12	.06
792	Randy Lerch	.10	.05
793	Sixto Lezcano	.10	.05
794	John Littlefield	.10	.05
795	Mike Lum	.10	.05
796	Greg Luzinski	.30	.15
797	Fred Lynn	.35	.18
798	Jerry Martin	.10	.05
799	Buck Martinez	.10	.05
800	Gary Matthews	.12	.06
801	Mario Mendoza	.10	.05
802	Larry Milbourne	.10	.05
803	Rick Miller	.10	.05
804	John Montefusco	.10	.05
805	Jerry Morales	.10	.05
806	Jose Morales	.10	.05
807	Joe Morgan	3.50	1.75
808	Jerry Mumphrey	.10	.05
809	Gene Nelson	.10	.05
810	Ed Ott	.10	.05
811	Bob Owchinko	.10	.05
812	Gaylord Perry	2.50	1.25
813	Mike Phillips	.10	.05
814	Darrell Porter	.10	.05
815	Mike Proly	.10	.05
816	Tim Raines	10.00	5.00
817	Lenny Randle	.10	.05
818	Doug Rau	.10	.05
819	Jeff Reardon	24.00	12.00
820	Ken Reitz	.10	.05
821	Steve Renko	.10	.05
822	Rick Reuschel	.20	.10
823	Dave Revering	.10	.05
824	Dave Roberts	.10	.05
825	Leon Roberts	.10	.05
826	Joe Rudi	.12	.06
827	Kevin Saucier	.10	.05
828	Tony Scott	.10	.05
829	Bob Shirley	.10	.05
830	Ted Simmons	.40	.20
831	Lary Sorensen	.10	.05
832	Jim Spencer	.10	.05
833	Harry Spilman	.10	.05
834	Fred Stanley	.10	.05
835	Rusty Staub	.25	.12
836	Bill Stein	.10	.05
837	Joe Strain	.10	.05
838	Bruce Sutter	.60	.30
839	Don Sutton	3.00	1.50
840	Steve Swisher	.10	.05
841	Frank Tanana	.25	.12
842	Gene Tenace	.15	.08
843	Jason Thompson	.10	.05
844	Dickie Thon	.10	.05
845	Bill Travers	.10	.05
846	Tom Underwood	.10	.05
847	John Urrea	.10	.05
848	Mike Vail	.10	.05
849	Ellis Valentine	.10	.05
850	Fernando Valenzuela	2.50	1.25
851	Pete Vuckovich	.15	.08
852	Mark Wagner	.10	.05
853	Bob Walk	.25	.12
854	Claudell Washington	.12	.06
855	Dave Winfield	10.00	5.00

856	Geoff Zahn	.10	.05
857	Richie Zisk	.10	.05
858	Checklist 727-858	.10	.05

1982 Topps

At 792-cards, this is the largest set Topps produced to this point. Cards measure 2-1/2" by 3-1/2" and feature large color photos on the fronts with a fascimile autograph beneath the picture. Subsets include Highlights (HL) (1-6), League Leaders, All-Stars, In-Action (IA), Future Stars (Rookies) and Team Leaders (TL).

		MINT	NR/MT
Complete Set(792)		155.00	110.00
Commons		.10	.06
1	Steve Carlton (HL)	1.00	.70
2	Ron Davis (HL)	.10	.06
3	Tim Raines (HL)	.25	.15
4	Pete Rose (HL)	1.00	.70
5	Nolan Ryan (HL)	3.50	2.50
6	Fernando Valenzuela (HL)	.20	.12
7	Scott Sanderson	.12	.07
8	Rich Dauer	.10	.06
9	Ron Guidry	.40	.25
10	Ron Guidry IA	.15	.10
11	Gary Alexander	.10	.06
12	Moose Haas	.10	.06
13	Lamar Johnson	.10	.06
14	Steve Howe	.10	.06
15	Ellis Valentine	.10	.06
16	Steve Comer	.10	.06
17	Darrell Evans	.15	.10
18	Fernando Arroyo	.10	.06
19	Ernie Whitt	.10	.06
20	Garry Maddox	.10	.06
21	Orioles Future Stars	90.00	45.00
	Bob Bonner (R)		
	Cal Ripken (R)		
	Jeff Schneider (R)		
22	Jim Beattie	.10	.06
23	Willie Hernandez	.15	.10
24	Dave Frost	.10	.06
25	Jerry Remy	.10	.06
26	Jorge Orta	.10	.06
27	Tom Herr	.12	.07
28	John Urrea	.10	.06
29	Dwayne Murphy	.10	.06
30	Tom Seaver	3.00	2.00
31	Tom Seaver IA	1.50	.90
32	Gene Garber	.10	.06
33	Jerry Morales	.10	.06
34	Joe Sambito	.10	.06
35	Willie Aikens	.10	.06
36	Rangers (TL)	.25	.15
	George Medich		
	Al Oliver		
37	Dan Graham	.10	.06
38	Charlie Lea	.10	.06
39	Lou Whitaker	.50	.30
40	Dave Parker	.50	.30
41	Dave Parker IA	.25	.15
42	Rick Sofield	.10	.06
43	Mike Cubbage	.10	.06
44	Britt Burns	.10	.06
45	Rick Cerone	.12	.07
46	Jerry Augustine	.10	.06
47	Jeff Leonard	.12	.07
48	Bobby Castillo	.10	.06
49	Alvis Woods	.10	.06
50	Buddy Bell	.12	.07
51	Cubs Future Stars	.20	.12
	Jay Howell (R)		
	Carlos Lezcano		
	Ty Waller (R)		
52	Larry Andersen	.10	.06
53	Greg Gross	.10	.06
54	Ron Hassey	.12	.07
55	Rick Burleson	.12	.07
56	Mark Littell	.10	.06
57	Craig Reynolds	.10	.06
58	John D'Acquisto	.10	.06
59	Rich Gedman (R)	.15	.10
60	Tony Armas	.12	.07
61	Tommy Boggs	.10	.06
62	Mike Tyson	.10	.06
63	Mario Soto	.15	.10
64	Lynn Jones	.10	.06
65	Terry Kennedy	.12	.07
66	Astros (TL) (Art Howe, Nolan Ryan)	1.25	.60

67	Rich Gale	.10	.06
68	Roy Howell	.10	.06
69	Al Williams	.10	.06
70	Tim Raines	1.25	.60
71	Roy Lee Jackson	.10	.06
72	Rick Auerbach	.10	.06
73	Buddy Solomon	.10	.06
74	Bob Clark	.10	.06
75	Tommy John	.25	.15
76	Greg Pryor	.10	.06
77	Miguel Dilone	.10	.06
78	George Medich	.10	.06
79	Bob Bailor	.10	.06
80	Jim Palmer	2.00	1.25
81	Jim Palmer IA	1.00	.70
82	Bob Welch	.30	.20
83	Yankees Future Stars	.15	.10
	Steve Balboni (R)		
	Andy McGaffigan (R)		
	Andre Robertson		
84	Rennie Stennett	.10	.06
85	Lynn McGlothen	.10	.06
86	Dane Iorg	.10	.06
87	Matt Keough	.10	.06
88	Biff Pocoroba	.10	.06
89	Steve Henderson	.10	.06
90	Nolan Ryan	12.50	8.25
91	Carney Lansford	.20	.12
92	Brad Havens	.10	.06
93	Larry Hisle	.10	.06
94	Andy Hassler	.10	.06
95	Ozzie Smith	3.00	2.00
96	Royals (TL) (George	.50	.30
	Brett, Larry Gura)		
97	Paul Moskau	.10	.06
98	Terry Bulling	.10	.06
99	Bary Bonnell	.10	.06
100	Mike Schmidt	4.50	3.00
101	Mike Schmidt IA	2.00	1.25
102	Dan Briggs	.10	.06
103	Bob Lacey	.10	.06
104	Rance Mulliniks	.10	.06
105	Kirk Gibson	.60	.35
106	Enrique Romo	.10	.06
107	Wayne Krenchicki	.10	.06
108	Bob Sykes	.10	.06
109	Dave Revering	.10	.06
110	Carlton Fisk	2.50	1.50
111	Carlton Fisk IA	1.50	.90
112	Billy Sample	.10	.06
113	Steve McCatty	.10	.06
114	Ken Landreaux	.10	.06
115	Gaylord Perry	.80	.50
116	Jim Wohlford	.10	.06
117	Rawly Eastwick	.10	.06
118	Expos Future Stars	.20	.12
	Terry Francona (R)		
	Brad Mills		
	Bryn Smith (R)		

119	Joe Pittman	.10	.06
120	Gary Lucas	.10	.06
121	Ed Lynch	.10	.06
122	Jamie Easterly	.10	.06
123	Danny Goodwin	.10	.06
124	Reid Nichols	.10	.06
125	Danny Ainge	1.00	.70
126	Braves (TL)(Rick	.12	.07
	Mahler, Claudell		
	Washington)		
127	Lonnie Smith	.10	.06
128	Frank Pastore	.10	.06
129	Checklist 1-132	.10	.06
130	Julio Cruz	.10	.06
131	Stan Bahnsen	.10	.06
132	Lee May	.10	.06
133	Pat Underwood	.10	.06
134	Dan Ford	.10	.06
135	Andy Rincon	.10	.06
136	Lenn Sakata	.10	.06
137	George Cappuzzello	.10	.06
138	Tony Pena	.20	.12
139	Jeff Jones	.10	.06
140	Ron LeFlore	.12	.07
141	Indians Future Stars	.40	.25
	Chris Bando		
	Tom Brennan (R)		
	Von Hayes (R)		
142	Dave Laroche	.10	.06
143	Mookie Wilson	.15	.10
144	Fred Breining	.10	.06
145	Bob Horner	.15	.10
146	Mike Griffin	.10	.06
147	Denny Walling	.10	.06
148	Mickey Klutts	.10	.06
149	Pat Putnam	.10	.06
150	Ted Simmons	.20	.15
151	Dave Edwards	.10	.06
152	Ramon Aviles	.10	.06
153	Roger Erickson	.10	.06
154	Dennis Werth	.10	.06
155	Otto Velez	.10	.06
156	A's (TL) (Rickey	.80	.50
	Henderson, Steve		
	McCatty (R)		
157	Steve Crawford	.10	.06
158	Brian Downing	.12	.07
159	Larry Bittner	.10	.06
160	Luis Tiant	.20	.12
161	Batting Leaders	.25	.15
162	Home Run Leaders	.50	.30
163	RBI Leaders	1.25	.60
164	SB Leaders	1.25	.60
165	Victory Leaders	.80	.50
166	Strikeout Leaders	.20	.12
167	ERA Leaders	2.00	1.25
168	Leading Firemen	.35	.20
169	Charlie Leibrandt	.10	.06

170	Jim Bibby	.10	.06
171	Giants Future Stars	1.50	.90
	Bob Brenly (R)		
	Chili Davis (R)		
	Bob Tufts (R)		
172	Bill Gullickson	.12	.07
173	Jamie Quirk	.10	.06
174	Dave Ford	.10	.06
175	Jerry Mumphrey	.10	.06
176	Dewey Robinson	.10	.06
177	John Ellis	.10	.06
178	Dyar Miller	.10	.06
179	Steve Garvey	1.25	.80
180	Steve Garvey IA	.60	.35
181	Silvio Martinez	.10	.06
182	Larry Herndon	.10	.06
183	Mike Proly	.10	.06
184	Mick Kelleher	.10	.06
185	Phil Niekro	.80	.50
186	Cardinals (TL)(Bob	.25	.15
	Forsch, Keith		
	Hernandez)		
187	Jeff Newman	.10	.06
188	Randy Martz	.10	.06
189	Glenn Hoffman	.10	.06
190	J.R. Richard	.20	.12
191	Tim Wallach (R)	2.00	1.25
192	Broderick Perkins	.10	.06
193	Darrell Jackson	.10	.06
194	Mike Vail	.10	.06
195	Paul Molitor	2.00	1.25
196	Willie Upshaw	.10	.06
197	Shane Rawley	.10	.06
198	Chris Speier	.10	.06
199	Don Aase	.10	.06
200	George Brett	4.50	3.00
201	George Brett IA	2.00	1.25
202	Rick Maning	.10	.06
203	Blue Jays Future	.80	.50
	Stars		
	Jesse Barfield (R)		
	Brian Milner		
	Boomer Wells (R)		
204	Gary Roenicke	.10	.06
205	Neil Allen	.10	.06
206	Tony Bernazard	.10	.06
207	Rod Scurry	.10	.06
208	Bobby Murcer	.15	.10
209	Gary Lavelle	.10	.06
210	Keith Hernandez	.30	.20
211	Dan Petry	.10	.06
212	Mario Mendoza	.10	.06
213	Dave Stewart (R)	3.50	2.50
214	Brian Asselstine	.10	.06
215	Mike Krukow	.10	.06
216	White Sox (TL)	.15	.10
	(Dennis Lamp,		
	Chet Lemon)		

217	Bo McLaughlin	.10	.06
218	Dave Roberts	.10	.06
219	John Curtis	.10	.06
220	Manny Trillo	.10	.06
221	Jim Slaton	.10	.06
222	Butch Wynegar	.10	.06
223	Lloyd Moseby	.10	.06
224	Bruce Bochte	.15	.10
225	Mike Torrez	.10	.06
226	Checklist 133-264	.10	.06
227	Ray Burris	.10	.06
228	Sam Mejias	.10	.06
229	Geoff Zahn	.10	.06
230	Willie Wilson	.15	.10
231	Phillies Future Stars	.20	.12
	Mark Davis (R)		
	Bob Dernier		
	Ozzie Virgil (R)		
232	Terry Crowley	.10	.06
233	Duane Kuiper	.10	.06
234	Ron Hodges	.10	.06
235	Mike Easler	.10	.06
236	John Martin	.10	.06
237	Rusty Kuntz	.10	.06
238	Kevin Saucier	.10	.06
239	Jon Matlack	.12	.07
240	Bucky Dent	.15	.10
241	Bucky Dent IA	.10	.06
242	Milt May	.10	.06
243	Bob Owchinko	.10	.06
244	Rufino Linares	.10	.06
245	Ken Reitz	.10	.06
246	Mets (TL)(Hubie	.25	.15
	Brooks, Mike Scott)		
247	Pedro Guerrero	.35	.20
248	Frank LaCorte	.10	.06
249	Tim Flannery	.10	.06
250	Tug McGraw	.20	.12
251	Fred Lynn	.30	.20
252	Fred Lynn IA	.15	.10
253	Chuck Baker	.10	.06
254	Jorge Bell (R)	10.00	5.00
255	Tony Perez	.80	.50
256	Tony Perez IA	.40	.25
257	Larry Harlow	.10	.06
258	Bo Diaz	.10	.06
259	Rodney Scott	.10	.06
260	Bruce Sutter	.20	.12
261	Tigers Future Stars	.12	.07
	Howard Bailey		
	Marty Castillo		
	Dave Rucker (R)		
262	Doug Bair	.10	.06
263	Victor Cruz	.10	.06
264	Dan Quisenberry	.20	.12
265	Al Bumbry	.10	.06
266	Rick Leach	.10	.06
267	Kurt Bevacqua	.10	.06

268	Rickey Keeton	.10	.06
269	Jim Esian	.10	.06
270	Rusty Staub	.25	.15
271	Larry Bradford	.10	.06
272	Bump Wills	.10	.06
273	Doug Bird	.10	.06
274	Bob Ojeda (R)	.40	.25
275	Bob Watson	.25	.15
276	Angels (TL) (Rod Carew, Ken Forsch)	.40	.25
277	Terry Puhl	.10	.06
278	John Littlefield	.10	.06
279	Bill Russell	.15	.10
280	Ben Oglivie	.10	.06
281	John Verhoeven	.10	.06
282	Ken Macha	.10	.06
283	Brian Allard	.10	.06
284	Bob Grich	.15	.10
285	Sparky Lyle	.15	.10
286	Bill Fahey	.10	.06
287	Alan Bannister	.10	.06
288	Garry Templeton	.12	.07
289	Bob Stanley	.10	.06
290	Ken Singleton	.12	.07
291	Pirates Future Stars Vance Law Bob Long (R) Johnny Ray (R)	.25	.15
292	Dave Palmer	.10	.06
293	Rob Picciolo	.10	.06
294	Mike LaCoss	.10	.06
295	Jason Thompson	.10	.06
296	Bob Walk	.10	.06
297	Clint Hurdle	.10	.06
298	Danny Darwin	.12	.07
299	Steve Trout	.10	.06
300	Reggie Jackson	3.50	2.50
301	Reggie Jackson IA	2.00	1.25
302	Doug Flynn	.10	.06
303	Bill Caudill	.10	.06
304	Johnnie LeMaster	.10	.06
305	Don Sutton	.80	.50
306	Don Sutton IA	.40	.25
307	Randy Bass	.10	.06
308	Charlie Moore	.10	.06
309	Pete Redfern	.10	.06
310	Mike Hargrove	.10	.06
311	Dodgers (TL)(Dusty Baker, Burt Hooton)	.25	.15
312	Lenny Randle	.10	.06
313	John Harris	.10	.06
314	Buck Martinez	.10	.06
315	Burt Hooton	.10	.06
316	Steve Braun	.10	.06
317	Dick Ruthven	.10	.06
318	Mike Heath	.10	.06
319	Dave Rozema	.10	.06
320	Chris Chambliss	.15	.10
321	Chris Chambliss IA	.10	.06
322	Garry Hancock	.10	.06
323	Bill Lee	.10	.06
324	Steve Dillard	.10	.06
325	Jose Cruz	.15	.10
326	Pete Falcone	.10	.06
327	Joe Nolan	.10	.06
328	Ed Farmer	.10	.06
329	U.L. Washington	.10	.06
330	Rick Wise	.12	.07
331	Benny Ayala	.10	.06
332	Don Robinson	.10	.06
333	Brewers Future Stars Frank DiPino Marshall Edwards (R) Chuck Porter (R)	.12	.07
334	Aurelio Rodriguez	.10	.06
335	Jim Sundberg	.10	.06
336	Mariners (TL)(Glenn Abbott, Tom Paciorek)	.12	.07
337	Pete Rose AS	1.00	.50
338	Dave Lopes AS	.12	.07
339	Mike Schmidt AS	1.75	1.00
340	Dave Concepcion AS	.20	.12
341	Andre Dawson AS	1.25	.80
342a	George Foster AS (No Autograph)	.80	.50
342b	George Foster AS (Autograph)	.25	.15
343	Dave Parker AS	.25	.15
344	Gary Carter AS	.50	.30
345	Fernando Valenzuela AS	.25	.15
346	Tom Seaver AS	1.50	.90
347	Bruce Sutter AS	.25	.15
348	Derrel Thomas	.10	.06
349	George Frazier	.10	.06
350	Thad Bosley	.10	.06
351	Reds Future Stars Scott Brown (R) Geoff Combe (R) Paul Householder	.10	.06
352	Dick Davis	.10	.06
353	Jack O'Connor	.10	.06
354	Roberto Ramos	.10	.06
355	Dwight Evans	.40	.25
356	Denny Lewallyn	.10	.06
357	Butch Hobson	.10	.06
358	Mike Parrott	.10	.06
359	Jim Dwyer	.10	.06
360	Len Barker	.10	.06
361	Rafael Landestoy	.10	.06
362	Jim Wright	.10	.06
363	Bob Molinaro	.10	.06
364	Doyle Alexander	.10	.06
365	Bill Madlock	.25	.15
366	Padres (TL)(Juan Eichelberger, Luis Salazar)	.12	.07

367	Jim Kaat	.20	.12
368	Alex Trevino	.10	.06
369	Champ Summers	.10	.06
370	Mike Norris	.10	.06
371	Jerry Don Gleaton	.10	.06
372	Luis Gomez	.10	.06
373	Gene Nelson	.10	.06
374	Tim Blackwell	.10	.06
375	Dusty Baker	.15	.10
376	Chris Welsh	.10	.06
377	Kiko Garcia	.10	.06
378	Mike Caldwell	.10	.06
379	Rob Wllfong	.10	.06
380	Dave Stieb	.25	.15
381	Red Sox Future Stars	.40	.25
	Bruce Hurst		
	Dave Schmidt		
	Julio Valdez		
382	Joe Simpson	.10	.06
383a	Pascual Perez	28.00	18.00
	(No position on front)		
383b	Pascual Perez (Cor)	.20	.12
384	Keith Moreland	.10	.06
385	Ken Forsch	.10	.06
386	Jerry White	.10	.06
387	Tom Veryzer	.10	.06
388	Joe Rudi	.12	.07
389	George Vukovich	.10	.06
390	Eddie Murray	3.50	2.50
391	Dave Tobik	.10	.06
392	Rick Bosetti	.10	.06
393	Al Hrabosky	.12	.07
394	Checklist 265-396	.10	.06
395	Omar Moreno	.10	.06
396	Twins (TL)(Fernando	.12	.07
	Arroyo, John Castino)		
397	Ken Brett	.10	.06
398	Mike Squires	.10	.06
399	Pat Zachry	.10	.06
400	Johnny Bench	2.50	1.50
401	Johnny Bench IA	1.50	.90
402	Bill Stein	.10	.06
403	Jim Tracy	.10	.06
404	Dickie Thon	.10	.06
405	Rick Reuschel	.12	.07
406	Al Hollard	.10	.06
407	Danny Boone	.10	.06
408	Ed Romero	.10	.06
409	Don Cooper	.10	.06
410	Ron Cey	.15	.10
411	Ron Cey IA	.10	.06
412	Luis Leal	.10	.06
413	Dan Meyer	.10	.06
414	Elias Sosa	.10	.06
415	Don Baylor	.20	.12
416	Marty Bystrom	.10	.06
417	Pat Kelly	.10	.06
418	Rangers Future Stars	.12	.07

	John Butcher		
	Bobby Johnson (R)		
	Dave Schmidt		
419	Steve Stone	.12	.07
420	George Hendrick	.12	.07
421	Mark Clear	.10	.06
422	Cliff Johnson	.10	.06
423	Stan Papi	.10	.06
424	Bruce Benedict	.10	.06
425	John Candelaria	.12	.07
426	Orioles (TL) (Eddie	.50	.30
	Murray, Sammy		
	Stewart)		
427	Ron Oester	.10	.06
428	LaMarr Hoyt	.10	.06
429	John Wathan	.10	.06
430	Vida Blue	.25	.15
431	Vida Blue IA	.15	.10
432	Mike Scott	.25	.15
433	Alan Ashby	.10	.06
434	Joe Lefebvre	.10	.06
435	Robin Yount	4.50	3.00
436	Joe Strain	.10	.06
437	Juan Berenguer	.10	.06
438	Pete Mackanin	.10	.06
439	Dave Righetti (R)	.60	.35
440	Jeff Burroughs	.10	.06
441	Astros Future Stars	.15	.10
	Danny Heep		
	Billy Smith (R)		
	Bobby Sprowl		
442	Bruce Kison	.10	.06
443	Mark Wagner	.10	.06
444	Terry Forster	.10	.06
445	Larry Parrish	.10	.06
446	Wayne Garland	.10	.06
447	Darrell Porter	.10	.06
448	Darrell Porter IA	.10	.06
449	Luis Aguayo	.10	.06
450	Jack Morris	2.50	1.50
451	Ed Miller	.10	.06
452	Lee Smith	14.00	7.00
453	Art Howe	.10	.06
454	Rick Langford	.10	.06
455	Tom Burgmeier	.10	.06
456	Cubs (TL)(Bill	.20	.12
	Buckner, Randy		
	Martz)		
457	Tim Stoddard	.10	.06
458	Willie Montanez	.10	.06
459	Bruce Berenyi	.10	.06
460	Jack Clark	.25	.15
461	Rich Dotson	.10	.06
462	Dave Chalk	.10	.06
463	Jim Kern	.10	.06
464	Juan Bonilla	.10	.06
465	Lee Mazzilli	.10	.06
466	Randy Lerch	.10	.06

No.	Name		
467	Mickey Hatcher	.10	.06
468	Floyd Bannister	.10	.06
469	Ed Ott	.10	.06
470	John Mayberry	.12	.07
471	Royals Future Stars	.15	.10
	Atlee Hammaker (R)		
	Mike Jones (R)		
	Darryl Motley (R)		
472	Oscar Gamble	.12	.07
473	Mike Stanton	.10	.06
474	Ken Oberkfell	.10	.06
475	Alan Trammell	1.00	.70
476	Brian Kingman	.10	.06
477	Steve Yeager	.10	.06
478	Ray Searage	.10	.06
479	Rowland Office	.10	.06
480	Steve Carlton	3.00	2.00
481	Steve Carlton IA	1.75	1.00
482	Glenn Hubbard	.10	.06
483	Gary Woods	.10	.06
484	Ivan DeJesus	.10	.06
485	Kent Tekulve	.10	.06
486	Yankees (TL)	.25	.15
	(Tommy John,		
	Jerry Mumphrey)		
487	Bob McClure	.10	.06
488	Ron Jackson	.10	.06
489	Rick Dempsey	.12	.07
490	Dennis Eckersley	2.50	1.50
491	Checklist 397-528	.10	.06
492	Joe Price	.10	.06
493	Chet Lemon	.12	.07
494	Hubie Brooks	.50	.30
495	Dennis Leonard	.10	.06
496	Johnny Grubb	.10	.06
497	Jim Anderson	.10	.06
498	Dave Bergman	.10	.06
499	Paul Mirabella	.10	.06
500	Rod Carew	2.00	1.25
501	Rod Carew IA	1.00	.70
502	Braves Future Stars	3.00	2.00
	Steve Bedrosian (R)		
	Brett Butler (R)		
	Larry Owen (R)		
503	Julio Gonzalez	.10	.06
504	Rick Peters	.10	.06
505	Graig Nettles	.25	.15
506	Graig Nettles IA	.12	.07
507	Terry Harper	.10	.06
508	Jody Davis	.10	.06
509	Harry Spillman	.10	.06
510	Fernando Valenzuela	.25	.15
511	Ruppert Jones	.10	.06
512	Jerry Dybzinski	.10	.06
513	Rick Rhoden	.10	.06
514	Joe Ferguson	.10	.06
515	Larry Bowa	.15	.10
516	Larry Bowa IA	.10	.06
517	Mark Brouhard	.10	.06
518	Garth Iorg	.10	.06
519	Glenn Adams	.10	.06
520	Mike Flanagan	.15	.10
521	Billy Almon	.10	.06
522	Chuck Rainey	.10	.06
523	Gary Gray	.10	.06
524	Tom Hausman	.10	.06
525	Ray Knight	.15	.10
526	Expos (TL) (Warren	.15	.10
	Cromartie, Bill		
	Gullickson)		
527	John Henry Johnson	.10	.06
528	Matt Alexander	.10	.06
529	Allen Ripley	.10	.06
530	Dickie Noles	.10	.06
531	A's Future Stars	.10	.06
	Rich Bordi		
	Mark Budaska (R)		
	Kelvin Moore		
532	Toby Harrah	.10	.06
533	Joaquin Andujar	.15	.10
534	Dave McKay	.10	.06
535	Lance Parrish	.25	.15
536	Rafael Ramirez	.10	.06
537	Doug Capilla	.10	.06
538	Lou Piniella	.15	.10
539	Vern Ruhle	.10	.06
540	Andre Dawson	3.50	2.50
541	Barry Evans	.10	.06
542	Ned Yost	.10	.06
543	Bill Robinson	.10	.06
544	Larry Christenson	.10	.06
545	Reggie Smith	.15	.10
546	Reggie Smith IA	.10	.06
547	Rod Carew AS	.80	.50
548	Willie Randolph AS	.20	.12
549	George Brett AS	1.50	.90
550	Bucky Dent AS	.15	.10
551	Reggie Jackson AS	1.50	.90
552	Ken Singleton AS	.12	.07
553	Dave Winfield AS	1.25	.80
554	Carlton Fisk AS	.90	.60
555	Scott McGregor AS	.15	.10
556	Jack Morris AS	.75	.45
557	Rich Gossage AS	.15	.10
558	John Tudor	.15	.10
559	Indians (TL)(Bert	.25	.15
	Blyleven, Mike		
	Hargrove)		
560	Doug Corbett	.10	.06
561	Cardinals Future	.10	.06
	Stars		
	Glenn Brummer		
	Luis DeLeon		
	Gene Roof		
562	Mike O'Berry	.10	.06
563	Ross Baumgarten	.10	.06

564	Doug DeCinces	.12	.07
565	Jackson Todd	.10	.06
566	Mike Jorgensen	.10	.06
567	Bob Babcock	.10	.06
568	Joe Pettini	.10	.06
569	Willie Randolph	.20	.12
570	Willie Randolph IA	.12	.07
571	Glenn Abbott	.10	.06
572	Juan Beniquez	.10	.06
573	Rick Waits	.10	.06
574	Mike Ramsey	.10	.06
575	Al Cowens	.10	.06
576	Giants (TL) (Vida Blue, Milt May)	.25	.15
577	Rick Monday	.15	.10
578	Shooty Babitt	.10	.06
579	Rick Mahler (R)	.20	.12
580	Bobby Bonds	.20	.12
581	Ron Reed	.10	.06
582	Luis Pujols	.10	.06
583	Tippy Martinez	.10	.06
584	Hosken Powell	.10	.06
585	Rollie Fingers	1.50	.90
586	Rollie Fingers IA	.75	.45
587	Tim Lollar	.10	.06
588	Dale Berra	.10	.06
589	Dave Stapleton	.10	.06
590	Al Oliver	.20	.12
591	Al Oliver IA	.12	.07
592	Craig Swan	.10	.06
593	Billy Smith	.10	.06
594	Renie Martin	.10	.06
595	Dave Collins	.10	.06
596	Damaso Garcia	.10	.06
597	Wayne Nordhagen	.10	.06
598	Bob Galasso	.10	.06
599	White Sox Future Stars Jay Loviglio Reggie Patterson (R) Leo Sutherland	.10	.06
600	Dave Winfield	3.50	2.50
601	Sid Monge	.10	.06
602	Freddie Patek	.10	.06
603	Rich Hebner	.10	.06
604	Orlando Sanchez	.10	.06
605	Steve Rogers	.10	.06
606	Blue Jays (TL)(John Mayberry, Dave Stieb)	.20	.12
607	Leon Durham	.10	.06
608	Jerry Royster	.10	.06
609	Rick Sutcliffe	.25	.15
610	Rickey Henderson	8.50	5.50
611	Joe Niekro	.10	.06
612	Gary Ward	.10	.06
613	Jim Gantner	.10	.06
614	Juan Eichelberger	.10	.06
615	Bob Boone	.25	.15
616	Bob Boone IA	.15	.10
617	Scott McGregor	.12	.07
618	Tim Foli	.10	.06
619	Bill Campbell	.10	.06
620	Ken Griffey	.35	.20
621	Ken Griffey IA	.20	.12
622	Dennis Lamp	.10	.06
623	Mets Future Stars Ron Gardenhire (R) Terry Leach (R) Tim Leary (R)	.30	.20
624	Ferguson Jenkins	.80	.50
625	Hal McRae	.20	.12
626	Randy Jones	.10	.06
627	Enos Cabell	.10	.06
628	Bill Travers	.10	.06
629	Johnny Wockenfuss	.10	.06
630	Joe Charboneau	.10	.06
631	Gene Tenace	.12	.07
632	Bryan Clark	.10	.06
633	Mitchell Page	.10	.06
634	Checklist 529-660	.10	.06
635	Ron Davis	.10	.06
636	Phillies (TL)(Steve Carlton, Pete Rose)	1.00	.70
637	Rick Camp	.10	.06
638	John Milner	.10	.06
639	Ken Kravec	.10	.06
640	Cesar Cedeno	.15	.10
641	Steve Mura	.10	.06
642	Mike Scioscia	.25	.15
643	Pete Vuckovich	.10	.06
644	John Castino	.10	.06
645	Frank White	.10	.06
646	Frank White IA	.10	.06
647	Warren Brusstar	.10	.06
648	Jose Morales	.10	.06
649	Ken Clay	.10	.06
650	Carl Yastrzemski	2.00	1.25
651	Carl Yastrzemski IA	1.25	.80
652	Steve Nicosia	.10	.06
653	Angels Future Stars Tom Brunansky (R) Luis Sanchez (R) Daryl Sconiers (R)	1.25	.80
654	Jim Morrison	.10	.06
655	Joel Youngblood	.10	.06
656	Eddie Whitson	.10	.06
657	Tom Poquette	.10	.06
658	Tito Landrum	.10	.06
659	Fred Martinez	.10	.06
660	Dave Concepcion	.25	.15
661	Dave Concepcion IA	.15	.10
662	Luis Salazar	.10	.06
663	Hector Cruz	.10	.06
664	Dan Spillner	.10	.06
665	Jim Clancy	.10	.06
666	Tigers (TL)(Steve Kemp, Dan Petry)	.15	.10

667	Jeff Reardon	4.50	3.00
668	Dale Murphy	1.50	.90
669	Larry Milbourne	.10	.06
670	Steve Kemp	.10	.06
671	Mike Davis	.10	.06
672	Bob Knepper	.10	.06
673	Keith Drumright	.10	.06
674	Dave Goltz	.10	.06
675	Cecil Cooper	.15	.10
676	Sal Butera	.10	.06
677	Alfredo Griffin	.10	.06
678	Tom Paciorek	.10	.06
679	Sammy Stewart	.10	.06
680	Gary Matthews	.12	.07
681	Dodgers Future Stars	4.50	3.00
	Mike Marshall (R)		
	Ron Roenicke		
	Steve Sax (R)		
682	Jesse Jefferson	.10	.06
683	Phil Garner	.12	.07
684	Harold Baines	.80	.50
685	Bert Blyleven	.75	.45
686	Gary Allenson	.10	.06
687	Greg Minton	.10	.06
688	Leon Roberts	.10	.06
689	Larry Sorensen	.10	.06
690	Dave Kingman	.20	.12
691	Dan Schatzeder	.10	.06
692	Wayne Gross	.10	.06
693	Cesar Geronimo	.10	.06
694	Dave Wehrmeister	.10	.06
695	Warren Cromartie	.10	.06
696	Pirates (TL) (Bill Madlock, Buddy Solomon)	.20	.12
697	John Montefusco	.10	.06
698	Tony Scott	.10	.06
699	Dick Tidrow	.10	.06
700	George Foster	.25	.15
701	George Foster IA	.15	.10
702	Steve Renko	.10	.06
703	Brewers (TL) (Cecil Cooper, Pete Vuckovich)	.20	.12
704	Mickey Rivers	.10	.06
705	Mickey Rivers IA	.10	.06
706	Barry Foote	.10	.06
707	Mark Bomback	.10	.06
708	Gene Richards	.10	.06
709	Don Money	.10	.06
710	Jerry Reuss	.12	.07
711	Mariners Future Stars	1.25	.80
	Dave Edler (R)		
	Dave Henderson (R)		
	Reggie Walton (R)		
712	Denny Martinez	.50	.30
713	Del Unser	.10	.06
714	Jerry Koosman	.15	.10
715	Willie Stargell	1.25	.80
716	Willie Stargell IA	.60	.35
717	Rick Miller	.10	.06
718	Charlie Hough	.12	.07
719	Jerry Narron	.10	.06
720	Greg Luzinski	.20	.12
721	Greg Luzinski IA	.12	.07
722	Jerry Martin	.10	.06
723	Junior Kennedy	.10	.06
724	Dave Rosello	.10	.06
725	Amos Otis	.12	.07
726	Amos Otis IA	.10	.06
727	Sixto Lezcano	.10	.06
728	Aurelio Lopez	.10	.06
729	Jim Spencer	.10	.06
730	Gary Carter	1.25	.80
731	Padres Future Stars	.10	.06
	Mike Armstrong (R)		
	Doug Gwosdz (R)		
	Fred Kuhaulua		
632	Mike Lum	.10	.06
733	Larry McWilliams	.10	.06
734	Mike Ivie	.10	.06
735	Rudy May	.10	.06
736	Jerry Turner	.10	.06
737	Reggie Cleveland	.10	.06
738	Dave Engle	.10	.06
739	Joey McLaughlin	.10	.06
740	Dave Lopes	.15	.10
741	Dave Lopes IA	.10	.06
742	Dick Drago	.10	.06
743	John Stearns	.10	.06
744	Mike Witt (R)	.20	.12
745	Bake McBride	.10	.06
746	Andre Thornton	.15	.10
747	John Lowenstein	.10	.06
748	Marc Hill	.10	.06
749	Bob Shirley	.10	.06
750	Jim Rice	.50	.30
751	Rick Honeycutt	.12	.07
752	Lee Lacy	.10	.06
753	Tom Brookens	.10	.06
754	Joe Morgan	1.25	.80
755	Joe Morgan IA	.60	.35
756	Reds (TL) (Ken Griffey, Tom Seaver)	.75	.45
757	Tom Underwood	.10	.06
758	Claudell Washington	.10	.06
759	Paul Splittorff	.12	.07
760	Bill Buckner	.20	.12
761	Dave Smith	.15	.10
762	Mike Phillips	.10	.06
763	Tom Hume	.10	.06
764	Steve Swisher	.10	.06
765	Gorman Thomas	.15	.10
766	Twins Future Stars	2.50	1.50

Lenny Faedo (R)
Kent Hrbek (R)
Tim Laudner (R)

767	Roy Smalley	.10	.06
768	Jerry Garvin	.10	.06
769	Richie Zisk	.10	.06
770	Rich Gossage	.30	.20
771	Rish Gossage IA	.15	.10
772	Bert Campaneris	.15	.10
773	John Denny	.10	.06
774	Jay Johnstone	.12	.07
775	Bob Forsch	.10	.06
776	Mark Belanger	.15	.10
777	Tom Griffin	.10	.06
778	Kevin Hickey	.10	.06
779	Grant Jackson	.10	.06
780	Pete Rose	3.00	2.00
781	Pete Rose IA	1.75	1.00
782	Frank Taveras	.10	.06
783	Greg Harris (R)	.25	.15
784	Milt Wilcox	.10	.06
785	Dan Driessen	.10	.06
786	Red Sox (TL)	.15	.10
	(Carney Lansford,		
	Mike Torrez)		
787	Fred Stanley	.10	.06
788	Woodie Fryman	.10	.06
789	Checklist 661-792	.10	.06
790	Larry Gura	.10	.06
791	Bobby Brown	.10	.06
792	Frank Tanana	.15	.10

1982 Topps Traded

Patterned after Topps 1982 regular edition, this update set features players who changed teams during the season and a selection of rookies. Players are listed in alphabetical order and card numbers carry the letter "T". Cards measure 2-1/2" by 3-1/2". The production figures for this set are lower than the total cards produced in Topps regular edition.

		MINT	NR/MT
Complete Set (132)		325.00	250.00
Commons (1-132)		.25	.15

1T	Doyle Alexander	.25	.15
2T	Jesse Barfield	1.25	.80
3T	Ross Baumgarten	.25	.15
4T	Steve Bedrosian	.40	.25
5T	Mark Belanger	.30	.20
6T	Kurt Bevacqua	.25	.15
7T	Tim Blackwell	.25	.15
8T	Vida Blue	.30	.20
9T	Bob Boone	.50	.30
10T	Larry Bowa	.30	.20
11T	Don Briggs	.25	.15
12T	Bobby Brown	.25	.15
13T	Tom Brunansky	1.75	1.00
14T	Jeff Burroughs	.25	.15
15T	Enos Cabell	.25	.15
16T	Bill Campbell	.25	.15
17T	Bobby Castillo	.25	.15
18T	Bill Caudill	.25	.15
19T	Cesar Cedeno	.30	.20
20T	Dave Collins	.25	.15
21T	Doug Corbett	.25	.15
22T	Al Cowens	.25	.15
23T	Chili Davis	1.75	1.00
24T	Dick Davis	.25	.15
25T	Ron Davis	.25	.15
26T	Doug DeCinces	.25	.15
27T	Ivan DeJesus	.25	.15

28T	Bob Dernier	.25	.15	86T	Larry Parrish	.25	.15
29T	Bo Diaz	.25	.15	87T	Jack Perconte	.25	.15
30T	Roger Erickson	.25	.15	88T	Gaylord Perry	2.50	1.50
31T	Jim Essian	.25	.15	89T	Rob Picciolo	.25	.15
32T	Ed Farmer	.25	.15	90T	Joe Pittman	.25	.15
33T	Doug Flynn	.25	.15	91T	Hosken Powell	.25	.15
34T	Tim Foli	.25	.15	92T	Mike Proly	.25	.15
35T	Dan Ford	.25	.15	93T	Greg Pryor	.25	.15
36T	George Foster	.40	.25	94T	Charlie Puleo (R)	.25	.15
37T	Dave Frost	.25	.15	95T	Shane Rawley	.25	.15
38T	Rich Gale	.25	.15	96T	Johnny Ray	.30	.20
39T	Ron Gardenhire	.25	.15	97T	Dave Revering	.25	.15
40T	Ken Griffey	.75	.45	98T	Cal Ripken	300.00	225.00
41T	Greg Harris	.30	.20	99T	Allen Ripley	.25	.15
42T	Von Hayes	.80	.50	100T	Bill Robinson	.25	.15
43T	Larry Herndon	.25	.15	101T	Aurelio Rodriguez	.25	.15
44T	Kent Hrbek	4.50	3.00	102T	Joe Rudi	.30	.20
45T	Mike Ivie	.25	.15	103T	Steve Sax	8.00	5.00
46T	Grant Jackson	.25	.15	104T	Dan Schatzeder	.25	.15
47T	Reggie Jackson	12.00	8.50	105T	Bob Shirley	.25	.15
48T	Ron Jackson	.25	.15	106T	Eric Show (R)	.30	.20
49T	Ferguson Jenkins	2.50	1.50	107T	Roy Smalley	.25	.15
50T	Lamar Johnson	.25	.15	108T	Lonnie Smith	.25	.15
51T	Randy Johnson	.25	.15	109T	Ozzie Smith	18.00	9.00
52T	Jay Johnstone	.25	.15	110T	Reggie Smith	.30	.20
53T	Mick Kelleher	.25	.15	111T	Lary Sorensen	.25	.15
54T	Steve Kemp	.25	.15	112T	Elias Sosa	.25	.15
55T	Junior Kennedy	.25	.15	113T	Mike Stanton	.25	.15
56T	Jim Kern	.25	.15	114T	Steve Stroughter	.25	.15
57T	Ray Knight	.40	.25	115T	Champ Summers	.25	.15
58T	Wayne Krenchicki	.25	.15	116T	Rick Sutcliffe	.60	.35
59T	Mike Krukow	.25	.15	117T	Frank Tanana	.30	.20
60T	Duane Kuiper	.25	.15	117T	Frank Taveras	.25	.15
61T	Mike LaCoss	.25	.15	119T	Garry Templeton	.30	.20
62T	Chet Lemon	.25	.15	120T	Alex Trevino	.25	.15
63T	Sixto Lezcano	.25	.15	121T	Jerry Turner	.25	.15
64T	Dave Lopes	.30	.20	122T	Ed Vande Berg	.25	.15
65T	Jerry Martin	.25	.15	123T	Tom Veryzer	.25	.15
66T	Renie Martin	.25	.15	124T	Ron Washington	.25	.15
67T	John Mayberry	.30	.20	125T	Bob Watson	.35	.20
68T	Lee Mazzilli	.25	.15	126T	Dennis Werth	.25	.15
69T	Bake McBride	.25	.15	127T	Eddie Whitson	.25	.15
70T	Dan Meyer	.25	.15	128T	Rob Wilfong	.25	.15
71T	Larry Milbourne	.25	.15	129T	Bump Wills	.25	.15
72T	Edie Milner	.25	.15	130T	Gary Woods	.25	.15
73T	Sid Monge	.25	.15	131T	Butch Wynegar	.25	.15
74T	Jose Morales	.25	.15	132T	Checklist 1-132	.25	.15
75T	Keith Moreland	.25	.15				
76T	John Montefusco	.25	.15				
77T	Jim Morison	.25	.15				
78T	Rance Mulliniks	.25	.15				
79T	Steve Mura	.25	.15				
80T	Gene Nelson	.25	.15				
81T	Joe Nolan	.25	.15				
82T	Dickie Noles	.25	.15				
83T	Al Oliver	.40	.25				
84T	Jorge Orta	.25	.15				
85T	Tom Paciorek	.25	.15				

1983 Topps

This 792-card set features two photos on the card fronts. A large color action shot and a small head shot located in a circle in the lower right corner. Cards measure 2-1/2" by 3-1/2". Subsets include Record Breakers (1-6), League Leaders, All-Stars, Team Leaders (TL) and a new category called Super Veterans (SV) with a horizontal format on the front.

		MINT	NR/MT
Complete Set (792)		175.00	105.00
Commons		.10	.06
1	Tony Armas (RB)	.15	.10
2	Rickey Henderson (RB)	1.50	.90
3	Greg Minton (RB)	.10	.06
4	Lance Parrish (RB)	.10	.06
5	Manny Trillo (RB)	.10	.06
6	John Wathan (RB)	.10	.06
7	Gene Richards	.10	.06
8	Steve Balboni	.10	.06
9	Joey McLaughlin	.10	.06
10	Gorman Thomas	.15	.10
11	Billy Gardner	.10	.06
12	Paul Mirabella	.10	.06
13	Larry Herndon	.10	.06
14	Frank LaCorte	.10	.06
15	Ron Cey	.15	.10
16	George Vukovich	.10	.06
17	Kent Tekulve	.10	.06
18	Kent Tekulve (SV)	.10	.06
19	Oscar Gamble	.12	.07
20	Carlton Fisk	2.50	1.50
21	Orioles (TL)	.75	.45
	(Eddie Murray,		
	Jim Palmer)		
22	Randy Martz	.10	.06
23	Mike Heath	.10	.06
24	Steve Mura	.10	.06
25	Hal McRae	.20	.12
26	Jerry Royster	.10	.06
27	Doug Corbett	.10	.06
28	Bruce Bochte	.10	.06
29	Randy Jones	.10	.06
30	Jim Rice	.35	.20
31	Bill Gullickson	.15	.10
32	Dave Bergman	.10	.06
33	Jack O'Connor	.10	.06
34	Paul Householder	.10	.06
35	Rollie Fingers	1.25	.80
36	Rollie Fingers (SV)	.60	.35
37	Darrell Johnson	.10	.06
38	Tim Flannery	.10	.06
39	Terry Puhl	.10	.06
40	Fernando Valenzuela	.25	.15
41	Jerry Turner	.10	.06
42	Dale Murray	.10	.06
43	Bob Dernier	.10	.06
44	Don Robinson	.10	.06
45	John Mayberry	.12	.07
46	Richard Dotson	.10	.06
47	Dave McKay	.10	.06
48	Lary Sorensen	.10	.06
49	Willie McGee (R)	5.00	3.50
50	Bob Horner	.10	.06
51	Cubs (TL)	.35	.20
	(Leon Durham,		
	Fergie Jenkins)		
52	Onix Concepcion	.10	.06
53	Mike Witt	.10	.06
54	Jim Maler	.10	.06
55	Mookie Wilson	.15	.10
56	Chuck Rainey	.10	.06
57	Tim Blackwelll	.10	.06
58	Al Holland	.10	.06
59	Benny Ayala	.10	.06
60	Johnny Bench	2.50	1.25
61	Johnny Bench (SV)	1.25	.80
62	Bob McClure	.10	.06
63	Rick Monday	.12	.07
64	Bill Stein	.10	.06
65	Jack Morris	2.00	1.25
66	Bob Lillis	.10	.06
67	Sal Butera	.10	.06
68	Eric Show	.12	.07
69	Lee Lacy	.10	.06
70	Steve Carlton	2.50	1.25
71	Steve Carlton	1.25	.80
72	Tom Paciorek	.10	.06
73	Allen Ripley	.10	.06
74	Julio Gonzalez	.10	.06
75	Amos Otis	.15	.10
76	Rick Mahler	.12	.07
77	Hosken Powell	.10	.06
78	Bill Caudill	.10	.06
79	Mick Kelleher	.10	.06

No.	Player		
80	George Foster	.25	.15
81	Yankees (TL)	.20	.12
	(Jerry Mumphrey,		
	Dave Righetti)		
82	Bruce Hurst	.25	.15
83	Ryne Sandberg(R)	70.00	48.00
84	Milt May	.10	.06
85	Ken Singleton	.12	.07
86	Tom Hume	.10	.06
87	Joe Rudi	.12	.07
88	Jim Gantner	.10	.06
89	Leon Roberts	.10	.06
90	Jerry Reuss	.12	.07
91	Larry Milbourne	.10	.06
92	Mike LaCoss	.10	.06
93	John Castino	.10	.06
94	Dave Edwards	.10	.06
95	Alan Trammell	1.00	.70
96	Dick Howser	.10	.06
97	Ross Baumgarten	.10	.06
98	Vance Law	.10	.06
99	Dickie Noles	.10	.06
100	Pete Rose	3.00	2.00
101	Pete Rose (SV)	1.50	.75
102	Dave Beard	.10	.06
103	Darrell Porter	.10	.06
104	Bob Walk	.10	.06
105	Don Baylor	.20	.12
106	Gene Nelson	.10	.06
107	Mike Jorgensen	.10	.06
108	Glenn Hoffman	.10	.06
109	Luis Leal	.10	.06
110	Ken Griffey	.30	.20
111	Expos (TL)	.20	.12
	(Al Oliver,		
	Steve Rogers)		
112	Bob Shirley	.10	.06
113	Ron Roenicke	.10	.06
114	Jim Slaton	.10	.06
115	Chili Davis	.40	.25
116	Dave Schmidt	.10	.06
117	Alan Knicely	.10	.06
118	Chris Welsh	.10	.06
119	Tom Brookens	.10	.06
120	Len Barker	.10	.06
121	Mickey Hatcher	.10	.06
122	Jimmy Smith	.10	.06
123	George Frazier	.10	.06
124	Marc Hill	.10	.06
125	Leon Durham	.12	.07
126	Joe Torre	.12	.07
127	Preston Hanna	.10	.06
128	Mike Ramsey	.10	.06
129	Checklist 1-132	.12	.07
130	Dave Stieb	.25	.15
131	Ed Ott	.10	.06
132	Todd Cruz	.10	.06
133	Jim Barr	.10	.06
134	Hubie Brooks	.25	.15
135	Dwight Evans	.50	.30
136	Willie Aikens	.10	.06
137	Woodie Fryman	.10	.06
138	Rick Dempsey	.10	.06
139	Bruce Berenyi	.10	.06
140	Willie Randolph	.15	.10
141	Indians (TL)	.20	.12
	(Toby Harrah,		
	Rick Sutcliffe)		
142	Mike Caldwell	.10	.06
143	Joe Pettini	.10	.06
144	Mark Wagner	.10	.06
145	Don Sutton	.75	.45
146	Don Sutton (SV)	.35	.20
147	Rick Leach	.10	.06
148	Dave Roberts	.10	.06
149	Johnny Ray	.12	.07
150	Bruce Sutter	.20	.12
151	Bruce Sutter	.12	.07
152	Jay Johnstone	.12	.07
153	Jerry Koosman	.15	.10
154	Johnnie LeMaster	.10	.06
155	Dan Quisenberry	.15	.10
156	Billy Martin	.25	.15
157	Steve Bedrosian	.15	.10
158	Rob Wilfong	.10	.06
159	Mike Stanton	.10	.06
160	Dave Kingman	.15	.10
161	Dave Kingman (SV)	.10	.06
162	Mark Clear	.10	.06
163	Cal Ripken	30.00	20.00
164	Dave Palmer	.10	.06
165	Dan Driessen	.10	.06
166	John Pacella	.10	.06
167	Mark Brouhard	.10	.06
168	Juan Eichelberger	.10	.06
169	Doug Flynn	.10	.06
170	Steve Howe	.10	.06
171	Giants (TL)	.30	.20
	(Bill Laskey,		
	Joe Morgan)		
172	Vern Ruhle	.10	.06
173	Jim Morrison	.10	.06
174	Jerry Ujdur	.10	.06
175	Bo Diaz	.10	.06
176	Dave Righetti	.20	.12
177	Harold Baines	.60	.35
178	Luis Tiant	.20	.12
179	Luis Tiant (SV)	.12	.07
180	Rickey Henderson	6.00	4.00
181	Terry Felton	.10	.06
182	Mike Fischin	.10	.06
183	Ed Vande Berg	.10	.06
184	Bob Clark	.10	.06
185	Tim Lollar	.10	.06
186	Whitey Herzog	.15	.10
187	Terry Leach	.10	.06

188	Rick Miller	.10	.06
189	Dan Schatzeder	.10	.06
190	Cecil Cooper	.15	.10
191	Joe Price	.10	.06
192	Floyd Rayford	.10	.06
193	Harry Spilman	.10	.06
194	Cesar Geronimo	.10	.06
195	Bob Stoddard	.10	.06
196	Bill Fahey	.10	.06
197	Jim Eisenreich (R)	.30	.20
198	Kiko Garcia	.10	.06
199	Marty Bystrom	.10	.06
200	Rod Carew	2.00	1.25
201	Rod Carew (SV)	1.25	.80
202	Blue Jays (TL)	.15	.10
	(Damaso Garcia,		
	Dave Stieb)		
203	Mike Morgan	.35	.20
204	Junior Kennedy	.10	.06
205	Dave Parker	.45	.28
206	Ken Oberkfell	.10	.06
207	Rick Camp	.10	.06
208	Dan Meyer	.10	.06
209	Mike Moore (R)	1.50	.90
210	Jack Clark	.20	.12
211	John Denny	.10	.06
212	John Stearns	.10	.06
213	Tom Burgmeier	.10	.06
214	Jerry White	.10	.06
215	Mario Soto	.12	.07
216	Tony LaRussa	.15	.10
217	Tim Stoddard	.10	.06
218	Roy Howell	.10	.06
219	Mike Armstrong	.10	.06
220	Dusty Baker	.15	.10
221	Joe Niekro	.12	.07
222	Damaso Garcia	.10	.06
223	John Montefusco	.10	.06
224	Mickey Rivers	.10	.06
225	Enos Cabell	.10	.06
226	Enrique Romo	.10	.06
227	Chris Bando	.10	.06
228	Joaquin Andujar	.15	.10
229	Phillies (TL)	.50	.30
	(Steve Carlton,		
	Bo Diaz)		
230	Ferguson Jenkins	.75	.45
231	Ferguson Jenkins	.35	.20
	(SV)		
232	Tom Brunansky	.25	.15
233	Wayne Gross	.10	.06
234	Larry Andersen	.10	.06
235	Claudell Washington	.12	.07
236	Steve Renko	.10	.06
237	Dan Norman	.10	.06
238	Bud Black (R)	.50	.30
239	Dave Stapleton	.10	.06
240	Rich Gossage	.30	.20
241	Rich Gossage (SV)	.15	.10
242	Joe Nolan	.10	.06
243	Duane Walker	.10	.06
244	Dwight Bernard	.10	.06
245	Steve Sax	1.00	.70
246	George Bamberger	.10	.06
247	Dave Smith	.10	.06
248	Bake McBride	.10	.06
249	Checklist 133-264	.12	.07
250	Bill Buckner	.20	.12
251	Alan Wiggins (R)	.10	.06
252	Luis Aguayo	.10	.06
253	Larry McWilliams	.10	.06
254	Rick Cerone	.12	.07
255	Gene Garber	.10	.06
256	Gene Garber	.10	.06
257	Jesse Barfield	.15	.10
258	Manny Castillo	.10	.06
259	Jeff Jones	.10	.06
260	Steve Kemp	.10	.06
261	Tigers (TL)	.12	.07
	(Larry Herndon,		
	Dan Petry)		
262	Ron Jackson	.10	.06
263	Renie Martin	.10	.06
264	Jamie Quirk	.10	.06
265	Joel Youngblood	.10	.06
266	Paul Boris	.10	.06
267	Terry Francona	.10	.06
268	Storm Davis (R)	.25	.15
269	Ron Oester	.10	.06
270	Dennis Eckersley	1.75	1.00
271	Ed Romero	.10	.06
272	Frank Tanana	.12	.07
273	Mark Belanger	.15	.10
274	Terry Kennedy	.10	.06
275	Ray Knight	.15	.10
276	Gene Mauch	.10	.06
277	Rance Mulliniks	.10	.06
278	Kevin Hickey	.10	.06
279	Greg Gross	.10	.06
280	Bert Blyleven	.60	.35
281	Andre Robertson	.10	.06
282	Reggie Smith	.15	.10
283	Reggie Smith (SV)	.10	.06
284	Jeff Lahti	.10	.06
285	Lance Parrish	.20	.12
286	Rick Langford	.10	.06
287	Bobby Brown	.10	.06
288	Joe Cowley	.10	.06
289	Jerry Dybzinski	.10	.06
290	Jeff Reardon	3.50	2.50
291	Pirates (TL)	.25	.15
	(John Candelaria,		
	Bill Madlock)		
292	Craig Swan	.10	.06
293	Glenn Gulliver	.10	.06
294	Dave Engle	.10	.06

#	Player		
295	Jerry Remy	.10	.06
296	Greg Harris	.10	.06
297	Ned Yost	.10	.06
298	Floyd Chiffer	.10	.06
299	George Wright	.10	.06
300	Mike Schmidt	4.00	2.75
301	Mike Schmidt (SV)	2.50	1.50
302	Ernie Whitt	.10	.06
303	Miguel Dilone	.10	.06
304	Dave Rucker	.10	.06
305	Larry Bowa	.15	.10
306	Tom Lasorda	.15	.10
307	Lou Piniella	.20	.12
308	Jesus Vega	.10	.06
309	Jeff Leonard	.12	.07
310	Greg Luzinski	.20	.12
311	Glenn Brummer	.10	.06
312	Brian Kingman	.10	.06
313	Gary Gray	.10	.06
314	Ken Dayley (R)	.10	.06
315	Rick Burleson	.12	.07
316	Paul Splittorff	.12	.07
317	Gary Rajsich	.10	.06
318	John Tudor	.15	.10
319	Lenn Sakata	.10	.06
320	Steve Rogers	.10	.06
321	Brewers (TL)	.60	.35
	(Pet Vuckovich,		
	Robin Yount)		
322	Dave Van Gorder	.10	.06
323	Luis DeLeon	.10	.06
324	Mike Marshall	.12	.07
325	Von Hayes	.15	.10
326	Garth Iorg	.10	.06
327	Bobby Castillo	.10	.06
328	Craig Reynolds	.10	.06
329	Randy Niemann	.10	.06
330	Buddy Bell	.10	.06
331	Mike Krukow	.10	.06
332	Glenn Wilson (R)	.12	.07
333	Dave LaRoche	.10	.06
334	Dave LaRoche (SV)	.10	.06
335	Steve Henderson	.10	.06
336	Rene Lachemann	.10	.06
337	Tito Landrum	.10	.06
338	Bob Owchinko	.10	.06
339	Terry Harper	.10	.06
340	Larry Gura	.10	.06
341	Doug DeCinces	.12	.07
342	Atlee Hammaker	.10	.06
343	Bob Bailor	.10	.06
344	Roger LaFrancois	.10	.06
345	Jim Clancy	.10	.06
346	Joe Pittman	.10	.06
347	Sammy Stewart	.10	.06
348	Alan Bannister	.10	.06
349	Checklist 265-396	.12	.07
350	Robin Yount	4.00	2.75
351	Reds (TL)	.20	.12
	(Cesar Cedeno,		
	Mario Soto)		
352	Mike Scioscia	.15	.10
353	Steve Comer	.10	.06
354	Randy Johnson	.10	.06
355	Jim Bibby	.10	.06
356	Gary Woods	.10	.06
357	Len Matuszek (R)	.10	.06
358	Jerry Garvin	.10	.06
359	Dave Collins	.10	.06
360	Nolan Ryan	10.00	5.00
361	Nolan Ryan	6.00	4.00
362	Bill Almon	.10	.06
363	John Stuper	.10	.06
364	Brett Butler	.75	.45
365	Dave Lopes	.15	.10
366	Dick Williams	.10	.06
367	Bud Anderson	.10	.06
368	Richie Zisk	.10	.06
369	Jesse Orosco	.10	.06
370	Gary Carter	1.00	.70
371	Mike Richardt	.10	.06
372	Terry Crowley	.10	.06
373	Kevin Saucier	.10	.06
374	Wayne Krenchicki	.10	.06
375	Pete Vuckovich	.12	.07
376	Ken Landreaux	.10	.06
377	Lee May	.10	.06
378	Lee May (SV)	.10	.06
379	Guy Sularz	.10	.06
380	Ron Davis	.10	.06
381	Red Sox (TL)	.20	.12
	(Jim Rice,		
	Bob Stanley)		
382	Bob Knepper	.10	.06
383	Ozzie Virgil	.10	.06
384	Dave Dravecky (R)	.60	.35
385	Mike Easler	.10	.06
386	Rod Carew AS	.75	.45
387	Bob Grich AS	.15	.10
388	George Brett AS	1.25	.80
389	Robin Yount AS	1.25	.80
390	Reggie Jackson AS	1.50	.90
391	Rickey Henderson AS	1.75	1.00
392	Fred Lynn AS	.25	.15
393	Carlton Fisk AS	.75	.45
394	Pete Vuckovich AS	.15	.10
395	Larry Gura AS	.10	.06
396	Dan Quisenberry AS	.12	.07
397	Pete Rose AS	1.00	.70
398	Manny Trillo AS	.10	.06
399	Mike Schmidt AS	1.50	.90
400	Dave Concepcion AS	.25	.15
401	Dale Murphy AS	.35	.20
402	Andre Dawson AS	.60	.35
403	Tim Raines AS	.25	.15

404	Gary Carter AS	.30	.20
405	Steve Rogers AS	.12	.07
406	Steve Carlton AS	1.25	.80
407	Bruce Sutter AS	.15	.10
408	Rudy May	.10	.06
409	Marvis Foley	.10	.06
410	Phil Niekro	.80	.50
411	Phil Niekro (SV)	.45	.28
412	Rangers (TL)	.15	.10
	(Buddy Bell,		
	Charlie Hough)		
413	Matt Keough	.10	.06
414	Julio Cruz	.10	.06
415	Bob Forsch	.10	.06
416	Joe Ferguson	.10	.06
417	Tom Hausman	.10	.06
418	Greg Pryor	.10	.06
419	Steve Crawford	.10	.06
420	Al Oliver	.20	.12
421	Al Oliver (R)	.12	.07
422	George Cappuzzello	.10	.06
423	Tom Lawless (R)	.10	.06
424	Jerry Augustine	.10	.06
425	Pedro Guerrero	.30	.20
426	Earl Weaver	.15	.10
427	Roy Lee Jackson	.10	.06
428	Champ Summers	.10	.06
429	Eddie Whitson	.10	.06
430	Kirk Gibson	.50	.30
431	Gary Gaetti (R)	.40	.25
432	Porfirio Altamirano	.10	.06
433	Dale Berra	.10	.06
434	Dennis Lamp	.10	.06
435	Tony Armas	.12	.07
436	Bill Campbell	.10	.06
437	Rick Sweet	.10	.06
438	Dave LaPoint	.10	.06
439	Rafael Ramirez	.10	.06
440	Ron Guidry	.35	.20
441	Astros (TL)	.15	.10
	(Ray Knight,		
	Joe Niekro)		
442	Brian Downing	.12	.07
443	Don Hood	.10	.06
444	Wally Backman	.15	.10
445	Mike Flanagan	.15	.10
446	Reid Nichols	.10	.06
447	Bryn Smith	.10	.06
448	Darrell Evans	.15	.10
449	Eddie Milner	.10	.06
450	Ted Simmons	.15	.10
451	Ted Simmons (SV)	.10	.06
452	Lloyd Moseby	.12	.07
453	Lamar Johnson	.10	.06
454	Bob Welch	.35	.20
455	Sixto Lezcano	.10	.06
456	Lee Elia	.10	.06
457	Milt Wilcox	.10	.06
458	Ron Washington	.10	.06
459	Ed Farmer	.10	.06
460	Roy Smalley	.10	.06
461	Steve Trout	.10	.06
462	Steve Nicosia	.10	.06
463	Gaylord Perry	.75	.45
464	Gaylord Perry (SV)	.40	.25
465	Lonnie Smith	.10	.06
466	Tom Underwood	.10	.06
467	Rufino Linares	.10	.06
468	Dave Goltz	.10	.06
469	Ron Gardenhire	.10	.06
470	Greg Minton	.10	.06
471	Royals (TL)	.20	.12
	(Vida Blue,		
	Willie Wilson)		
472	Gary Allenson	.10	.06
473	John Lowenstein	.10	.06
474	Ray Burris	.10	.06
475	Cesar Cedeno	.15	.10
476	Rob Picciolo	.10	.06
477	Tom Niedenfuer	.10	.06
478	Phil Garner	.12	.07
479	Charlie Hough	.12	.07
480	Toby Harrah	.10	.06
481	Scot Thompson	.10	.06
482	Tony Gwynn (R)	45.00	32.00
483	Lynn Jones	.10	.06
484	Dick Ruthven	.10	.06
485	Omar Moreno	.10	.06
486	Clyde King	.10	.06
487	Jerry Hairston	.10	.06
488	Alfredo Griffin	.10	.06
489	Tom Herr	.12	.07
490	Jim Palmer	2.00	1.25
491	Jim Palmer (SV)	1.25	.80
492	Paul Serna	.10	.06
493	Steve McCatty	.10	.06
494	Bob Brenly	.10	.06
495	Warren Cromartie	.10	.06
496	Tom Veryzer	.10	.06
497	Rick Sutcliffe	.25	.15
498	Wade Boggs (R)	38.00	19.00
499	Jeff Little	.10	.06
500	Reggie Jackson	3.50	2.50
501	Reggie Jackson (SV)	2.00	1.25
502	Braves (TL)	.45	.28
	(Dale Murphy,		
	Phil Niekro)		
503	Moose Haas	.10	.06
504	Don Werner	.10	.06
505	Garry Templeton	.10	.06
506	Jim Gott (R)	.15	.10
507	Tony Scott	.10	.06
508	Tom Filer	.10	.06
509	Lou Whitaker	.60	.35
510	Tug McGraw	.20	.12
511	Tug McGraw (SV)	.12	.07

512	Doyle Alexander	.10	.06	565	Bucky Dent	.15	.10
513	Fred Stanley	.10	.06	566	Manny Sarmiento	.10	.06
514	Rudy Law	.10	.06	567	Joe Simpson	.10	.06
515	Gene Tenace	.12	.07	568	Willie Hernandez	.12	.07
516	Bill Virdon	.10	.06	569	Jack Perconte	.10	.06
517	Gary Ward	.10	.06	570	Vida Blue	.20	.12
518	Bill Laskey	.10	.06	571	Mickey Klutts	.10	.06
519	Terry Bulling	.10	.06	572	Bob Watson	.25	.15
520	Fred Lynn	.25	.15	573	Andy Hassler	.10	.06
521	Bruce Benedict	.10	.06	574	Glenn Adams	.10	.06
522	Pat Zachry	.10	.06	575	Neil Allen	.10	.06
523	Carney Lansford	.15	.10	576	Frank Robinson	.40	.25
524	Tom Brennan	.10	.06	577	Luis Aponte	.10	.06
525	Frank White	.10	.06	578	David Green	.10	.06
526	Checklist 397-528	.12	.07	579	Rich Dauer	.10	.06
527	Larry Biittner	.10	.06	580	Tom Seaver	2.50	1.50
528	Jamie Easterly	.10	.06	581	Tom Seaver (SV)	1.25	.80
529	Tim Laudner	.10	.06	582	Marshall Edwards	.10	.06
530	Eddie Murray	3.00	2.00	583	Terry Forster	.10	.06
531	Athletics (TL)	.60	.35	584	Dave Hostetler	.10	.06
	(Rickey Henderson,			585	Jose Cruz	.15	.10
	Rick Langford)			586	Frank Viola (R)	6.00	4.00
532	Dave Stewart	.80	.50	587	Ivan DeJesus	.10	.06
533	Luis Salazar	.10	.06	588	Pat Underwood	.10	.06
534	John Butcher	.10	.06	589	Alvis Woods	.10	.06
535	Manny Trillo	.10	.06	590	Tony Pena	.15	.10
536	Johnny Wockenfuss	.10	.06	591	White Sox (TL)	.20	.12
537	Rod Scurry	.10	.06		(LaMarr Hoyt,		
538	Danny Heep	.10	.06		Greg Luzinski)		
539	Roger Erickson	.10	.06	592	Shane Rawley	.10	.06
540	Ozzie Smith	2.50	1.50	593	Broderick Perkins	.10	.06
541	Britt Burns	.10	.06	594	Eric Rasmussen	.10	.06
542	Jody Davis	.10	.06	595	Tim Raines	.80	.50
543	Alan Fowlkes	.10	.06	596	Randy Johnson	.10	.06
544	Larry Whisenton	.10	.06	597	Mike Proly	.10	.06
545	Floyd Bannister	.10	.06	598	Dwayne Murphy	.10	.06
546	Dave Garcia	.10	.06	599	Don Aase	.10	.06
547	Geoff Zahn	.10	.06	600	George Brett	4.00	2.75
548	Brian Giles	.10	.06	601	Ed Lynch	.10	.06
549	Charlie Puleo	.10	.06	602	Rich Gedman	.10	.06
550	Carl Yastrzemski	2.50	1.50	603	Joe Morgan	1.25	.80
551	Carl Yastrzemski	1.25	.80	604	Joe Morgan (SV)	.60	.35
	(SV)			605	Gary Roenicke	.10	.06
552	Tim Wallach	.35	.20	606	Bobby Cox	.10	.06
553	Denny Martinez	.20	.12	607	Charlie Leibrandt	.12	.07
554	Mike Vail	.10	.06	608	Don Money	.10	.06
555	Steve Yeager	.10	.06	609	Danny Darwin	.10	.06
556	Willie Upshaw	.10	.06	610	Steve Garvey	.80	.50
557	Rick Honeycutt	.10	.06	611	Bert Roberge	.10	.06
558	Dickie Thon	.10	.06	612	Steve Swisher	.10	.06
559	Pete Redfern	.10	.06	613	Mike Ivie	.10	.06
560	Ron LeFlore	.10	.06	614	Ed Glynn	.10	.06
561	Cardinals (R)	.15	.10	615	Garry Maddox	.10	.06
	(Joaquin Andujar,			616	Bill Nahorodny	.10	.06
	Lonnis Smith)			617	Butch Wynegar	.10	.06
562	Dave Rozema	.10	.06	618	LaMarr Hoyt	.10	.06
563	Juan Bonilla	.10	.06	619	Keith Moreland	.10	.06
564	Sid Monge	.10	.06	620	Mike Norris	.10	.06

621	Mets (TL)	.15	.10		675	Jim Beattie	.10	.06
	(Craig Swan,				676	Biff Pocoroba	.10	.06
	Mookie Wilson)				677	Dave Revering	.10	.06
622	Dave Edler	.10	.06		678	Juan Beniquez	.10	.06
623	Luis Sanchez	.10	.06		679	Mike Scott	.15	.10
624	Glenn Hubbard	.10	.06		680	Andre Dawson	3.00	2.00
625	Ken Forsch	.10	.06		681	Dodgers (TL)	.20	.12
626	Jerry Martin	.10	.06			(Pedro Guerrero,		
627	Doug Bair	.10	.06			Fernando Valenzuela)		
628	Julio Valdez	.10	.06		682	Bob Stanley	.10	.06
629	Charlie Lea	.10	.06		683	Dan Ford	.10	.06
630	Paul Molitor	1.75	1.00		684	Rafael Landestoy	.10	.06
631	Tippy Martinez	.10	.06		685	Lee Mazzilli	.10	.06
632	Alex Trevino	.10	.06		686	Randy Lerch	.10	.06
633	Vicente Romo	.10	.06		687	U.L. Washington	.10	.06
634	Max Venable	.10	.06		688	Jim Wohlford	.10	.06
635	Graig Nettles	.15	.10		689	Ron Hassey	.10	.06
636	Graig Nettles (SV)	.10	.06		690	Kent Hrbek	.50	.30
637	Pat Corrales	.10	.06		691	Dave Tobik	.10	.06
638	Dan Petry	.12	.07		692	Denny Walling	.10	.06
639	Art Howe	.10	.06		693	Sparky Lyle	.15	.10
640	Andre Thornton	.12	.07		694	Sparky Lyle (SV)	.10	.06
641	Billy Sample	.10	.06		695	Ruppert Jones	.10	.06
642	Checklist 529-660	.12	.07		696	Chuck Tanner	.10	.06
643	Bump Wills	.10	.06		697	Barry Foote	.10	.06
644	Joe Lefebvre	.10	.06		698	Tony Bernazard	.10	.06
645	Bill Madlock	.20	.12		699	Lee Smith	3.50	2.00
646	Jim Essian	.10	.06		700	Keith Hernandez	.25	.15
647	Bobby Mitchell	.10	.06		701	Batting Leaders	.20	.12
648	Jeff Burroughs	.10	.06		702	Home Run Leaders	1.25	.80
649	Tommy Boggs	.10	.06		703	Runs Batted	.25	.15
650	George Hendrick	.12	.07			In Leaders		
651	Angels (TL)	.35	.20		704	Stolen Base Leaders	1.00	.70
	(Rod Carew,				705	Victory Leaders	.75	.45
	Mike Witt)				706	Strikeout Leaders	.75	.45
652	Butch Hobson	.10	.06		707	ERA Leaders	.15	.10
653	Ellis Valentine	.10	.06		708	Leading Firemen	.20	.12
654	Bob Ojeda	.15	.10		709	Jimmy Sexton	.10	.06
655	Al Bumbry	.10	.06		710	Willie Wilson	.12	.07
656	Dave Frost	.10	.06		711	Mariners (TL)	.10	.06
657	Mike Gates	.10	.06			(Jim Beattie,		
658	Frank Pastore	.10	.06			Bruce Bochte)		
659	Charlie Moore	.10	.06		712	Bruce Kison		.06
660	Mike Hargrove	.10	.06		713	Ron Hodges	.10	.06
661	Bill Russell	.12	.07		714	Wayne Nordhagen	.10	.06
662	Joe Sambito	.10	.06		715	Tony Perez	.75	.45
663	Tom O'Malley	.10	.06		716	Tony Perez (SV)	.40	.25
664	Bob Molinaro	.10	.06		717	Scott Sanderson	.12	.07
665	Jim Sundberg	.10	.06		718	Jim Dwyer	.10	.06
666	Sparky Anderson	.15	.10		719	Rich Gale	.10	.06
667	Dick Davis	.10	.06		720	Dave Concepcion	.25	.15
668	Larry Christenson	.10	.06		721	John Martin	.10	.06
669	Mike Squires	.10	.06		722	Jorge Orta	.10	.06
670	Jerry Mumphrey	.10	.06		723	Randy Moffitt	.10	.06
671	Lenny Faedo	.10	.06		724	Johnny Grubb	.10	.06
672	Jim Kaat	.20	.12		725	Dan Spillner	.10	.06
673	Jim Kaat (SV)	.12	.07		726	Harvey Kuenn	.10	.06
674	Kurt Bevacqua	.10	.06		727	Chet Lemon	.10	.06

728	Ron Reed	.10	.06
729	Jerry Morales	.10	.06
730	Jason Thompson	.10	.06
731	Al Williams	.10	.06
732	Dave Henderson	.30	.20
733	Buck Martinez	.10	.06
734	Steve Braun	.10	.06
735	Tommy John	.15	.10
736	Tommy John (SV)	.10	.06
737	Mitchell Page	.10	.06
738	Tim Foli	.10	.06
739	Rick Ownbey	.10	.06
740	Rusty Staub	.20	.12
741	Rusty Staub (SV)	.12	.07
742	Padres (TL) (Terry Kennedy, Tim Lollar)	.12	.07
743	Mike Torrez	.10	.06
744	Brad Mills	.10	.06
745	Scott McGregor	.10	.06
746	John Wathan	.10	.06
747	Fred Breining	.10	.06
748	Derrel Thomas	.10	.06
749	Jon Matlack	.10	.06
750	Ben Oglivie	.10	.06
751	Brad Havens	.10	.06
752	Luis Pujols	.10	.06
753	Elias Sosa	.10	.06
754	Bill Robinson	.10	.06
755	John Candelaria	.12	.07
756	Russ Nixon	.10	.06
757	Rick Manning	.10	.06
758	Aurelio Rodriguez	.10	.06
759	Doug Bird	.10	.06
760	Dale Murphy	1.25	.80
761	Gary Lucas	.10	.06
762	Cliff Johnson	.10	.06
763	Al Cowens	.10	.06
764	Pete Falcone	.10	.06
765	Bob Boone	.25	.15
766	Barry Bonnell	.10	.06
767	Duane Kuiper	.10	.06
768	Chris Speier	.10	.06
769	Checklist 661-792	.12	.07
770	Dave Winfield	3.50	2.50
771	Twins (TL) (Bobby Castillo, Kent Hrbek)	.20	.12
772	Jim Kern	.10	.06
773	Larry Hisle	.10	.06
774	Alan Ashby	.10	.06
775	Burt Hooton	.10	.06
776	Larry Parrish	.10	.06
777	John Curtis	.10	.06
778	Rich Hebner	.10	.06
779	Rick Waits	.10	.06
780	Gary Matthews	.12	.07

781	Rick Rhoden	.10	.06
782	Bobby Murcer	.15	.10
783	Bobby Murcer (SV)	.10	.06
784	Jeff Newman	.10	.06
785	Dennis Leonard	.10	.06
786	Ralph Houk	.10	.06
787	Dick Tidrow	.10	.06
788	Dane Iorg	.10	.06
789	Bryan Clark	.10	.06
790	Bob Grich	.12	.07
791	Gary Lavelle	.10	.06
792	Chris Chambliss	.12	.07

1983 Topps Traded

This 132-card update set is an extension of Topps regular 1983 edition in design and features cards of players traded during the regular season and rookies who joined their club during the season. Cards measure 2-1/2" by 3-1/2" and carry the suffix "T" after the card number.

	MINT	NR/MT
Complete Set (132)	125.00	80.00
Commons	.12	.07

1T	Neil Allen	.15	.10
2T	Bill Almon	.12	.07
3T	Joe Altobelli	.12	.07
4T	Tony Armas	.12	.07
5T	Doug Bair	.12	.07
6T	Steve Baker	.12	.07
7T	Floyd Bannister	.12	.07
8T	Don Baylor	.30	.20
9T	Tony Bernazard	.12	.07
10T	Larry Biittner	.12	.07

11T	Dann Bilardello	.12	.07	69T	Craig McMurtry (R)	.15	.10
12T	Doug Bird	.12	.07	70T	John McNamara	.12	.07
13T	Steve Boros	.12	.07	71T	Orlando Mercado	.12	.07
14T	Greg Brock (R)	.25	.15	72T	Larry Milbourne	.12	.07
15T	Mike Brown	.12	.07	73T	Randy Moffitt	.12	.07
16T	Tom Burgmeier	.12	.07	74T	Sid Monge	.12	.07
17T	Randy Bush (R)	.15	.10	75T	Jose Morales	.12	.07
18T	Bert Campaneris	.20	.12	76T	Omar Moreno	.12	.07
19T	Ron Cey	.20	.12	77T	Joe Morgan	2.00	1.25
20T	Chris Codiroli (R)	.12	.07	78T	Mike Morgan	.40	.25
21T	Dave Collins	.12	.07	79T	Dale Murray	.12	.07
22T	Terry Crowley	.12	.07	80T	Jeff Newman	.12	.07
23T	Julio Cruz	.12	.07	81T	Pete O'Brien (R)	.80	.50
24T	Mike Davis	.12	.07	82T	Jorge Orta	.12	.07
25T	Frank DiPino	.12	.07	83T	Alejandro Pena (R)	.80	.50
26T	Bill Doran (R)	1.75	1.00	84T	Pascual Perez	.25	.15
27T	Jerry Dybzinski	.12	.07	85T	Tony Perez	1.75	1.00
28T	Jamie Easterly	.12	.07	86T	Broderick Perkins	.12	.07
29T	Juan Elchelberger	.12	.07	87T	Tony Phillips (R)	1.75	1.00
30T	Jim Essian	.12	.07	88T	Charlie Puleo	.12	.07
31T	Pete Falcone	.12	.07	89T	Pat Putnam	.12	.07
32T	Mike Ferraro	.12	.07	90T	Jamie Quirk	.12	.07
33T	Terry Forster	.12	.07	91T	Doug Rader	.12	.07
34T	Julio Franco (R)	10.00	7.00	92T	Chuck Rainey	.12	.07
35T	Rich Gale	.12	.07	93T	Bobby Ramos	.12	.07
36T	Kiko Garcia	.12	.07	94T	Gary Redus	.40	.25
37T	Steve Garvey	1.75	1.00	95T	Steve Renko	.12	.07
38T	Johnny Grubb	.12	.07	96T	Leon Roberts	.12	.07
39T	Mel Hall (R)	3.00	2.00	97T	Aurelio Rodriguez	.12	.07
40T	Von Hayes	.25	.15	98T	Dick Ruthven	.12	.07
41T	Danny Heep	.12	.07	99T	Daryl Sconiers	.12	.07
42T	Steve Henderson	.12	.07	100T	Mike Scott	.30	.20
43T	Keith Hernandez	.40	.25	101T	Tom Seaver	10.00	7.00
44T	Leo Hernandez	.12	.07	102T	John Shelby (R)	.15	.10
45T	Willie Hernandez	.15	.10	103T	Bob Shirley	.12	.07
46T	Al Holland	.12	.07	104T	Joe Simpson	.12	.07
47T	Frank Howard	.12	.07	105T	Doug Sisk (R)	.12	.07
48T	Bobby Johnson	.12	.07	106T	Mike Smithson (R)	.12	.07
49T	Cliff Johnson	.12	.07	107T	Elias Sosa	.12	.07
50T	Odell Jones	.12	.07	108T	Darryl Strawberry (R)	95.00	75.00
51T	Mike Jorgensen	.12	.07				
52T	Bob Kearney	.12	.07	109T	Tom Tellmann	.12	.07
53T	Steve Kemp	.12	.07	110T	Gene Tenace	.20	.12
54T	Matt Keough	.12	.07	111T	Gorman Thomas	.20	.12
55T	Ron Kittle (R)	.25	.15	112T	Dick Tidrow	.12	.07
56T	Mickey Klutts	.12	.07	113T	Dave Tobik	.12	.07
57T	Alan Knicely	.12	.07	114T	Wayne Tolleson (R)	.12	.07
58T	Mike Krukow	.12	.07	115T	Mike Torrez	.12	.07
59T	Rafael Landestoy	.12	.07	116T	Manny Trillo	.12	.07
60T	Carney Lansford	.25	.15	117T	Steve Trout	.12	.07
61T	Joe Lefebvre	.12	.07	118T	Lee Tunnell (R)	.12	.07
62T	Bryan Little	.12	.07	119T	Mike Vail	.12	.07
63T	Aurelio Lopez	.12	.07	120T	Ellis Valentine	.12	.07
64T	Mike Madden	.12	.07	121T	Tom Veryzer	.12	.07
65T	Rick Manning	.12	.07	122T	George Vukovich	.12	.07
66T	Billy Martin	.30	.20	123T	Rick Waits	.12	.07
67T	Lee Mazzilli	.12	.07	124T	Greg Walker (R)	.15	.10
68T	Andy McGaffigan	.12	.07	125T	Chris Welsh	.12	.07

126T	Len Whiethouse	.12	.07
127T	Eddie Whitson	.12	.07
128T	Jim Wohlford	.12	.07
129T	Matt Young (R)	.20	.12
130T	Joel Youngblood	.12	.07
131T	Pat Zachry	.12	.07
132T	Checklist 1-132	.12	.07

1984 Topps

This 792-card set has some of the same features of the 1983 set including the use of two photos on the card fronts, a large color action photo and a small head shot in the lower left corner. Cards measure 2-1/2" by 3-1/2". Key subsets include Highlights (HL) (1-6), League Leaders, All-Stars and Team Leaders. A new feature, Active Career Leaders, has been added to this set. A specially boxed glossy set, called Topps Tiffany, was also issued. Limited to 10,000 sets, the Tiffany Edition mirrors the regular issue except for the paper stock and the glossy coating. Those cards are valued at eight times the price of the redular edition.

		MINT	NR/MT
Complete Set (792)		100.00	70.00
Commons		.07	.04
1	Steve Carlton (HL)	.50	.30
2	Rickey Henderson (HL)	.80	.50
3	Dan Quisenberry (HL)	.10	.06
4	Steve Carlton, Gaylord Perry, Nolan Ryan (HL)	1.25	.80

5	Bob Forsch, Dave Righetti, Mike Warren (HL)	.10	.06
6	Johnny Bench, Gaylord Perry, Carl Yastrzemski (HL)	.60	.35
7	Gary Lucas	.07	.04
8	Don Mattingly (R)	20.00	10.00
9	Jim Gott	.10	.06
10	Robin Yount	2.50	1.50
11	Twins (TL) (Kent Hrbek, Ken Schrom)	.12	.07
12	Billy Sample	.07	.04
13	Scott Holman	.07	.04
14	Tom Brookens	.07	.04
15	Burt Hooton	.07	.04
16	Omar Moreno	.07	.04
17	John Denny	.07	.04
18	Dale Berra	.07	.04
19	Ray Fontenot (R)	.07	.04
20	Greg Luzinski	.15	.10
21	Joe Altobelli	.07	.04
22	Bryan Clark	.07	.04
23	Keith Moreland	.07	.04
24	John Martin	.07	.04
25	Glenn Hubbard	.07	.04
26	Bud Black	.12	.07
27	Daryl Sconiers	.07	.04
28	Frank Viola	.50	.30
29	Danny Heep	.07	.04
30	Wade Boggs	4.00	2.75
31	Andy McGaffigan	.07	.04
32	Bobby Ramos	.07	.04
33	Tom Burgmeier	.07	.04
34	Eddie Milner	.07	.04
35	Don Sutton	.50	.30
36	Denny Walling	.07	.04
37	Rangers (TL) (Buddy Bell, Rick Honeycutt)	.12	.07
38	Luis DeLeon	.07	.04
39	Garth Iorg	.07	.04
40	Dusty Baker	.12	.07
41	Tony Bernazard	.07	.04
42	Johnny Grubb	.07	.04
43	Ron Reed	.07	.04
44	Jim Morrison	.07	.04
45	Jerry Mumphrey	.07	.04
46	Ray Smith	.07	.04
47	Rudy Law	.07	.04
48	Julio Franco	1.25	.75
49	John Stuper	.07	.04
50	Chris Chambliss	.10	.06
51	Jim Frey	.07	.04
52	Paul Splittorff	.10	.06
53	Juan Beniquez	.07	.04
54	Jesse Orosco	.07	.04

#	Player			#	Player		
55	Dave Concepcion *	.20	.12	109	Brad Wellman	.07	.04
56	Gary Allenson	.07	.04	110	Ron Guidry	.20	.12
57	Dan Schatzeder	.07	.04	111	Bill Virdon	.07	.04
58	Max Venable	.07	.04	112	Tom Niedenfuer	.07	.04
59	Sammy Stewart	.07	.04	113	Kelly Paris	.07	.04
60	Paul Molitor	.80	.50	114	Checklist 1-132	.10	.06
61	Chris Codiroli	.07	.04	115	Andre Thornton	.10	.06
62	Dave Hostetler	.07	.04	116	George Bjorkman	.07	.04
63	Ed Vande Berg	.07	.04	117	Tom Veryzer	.07	.04
64	Mike Scioscia	.12	.07	118	Charlie Hough	.10	.06
65	Kirk Gibson	.30	.18	119	Johnny Wockenfuss	.07	.04
66	Astros (TL)	.80	.50	120	Keith Hernandez	.15	.10
	(Jose Cruz,			121	Pat Sheridan (R)	.10	.06
	Nolan Ryan)			122	Cecilio Guante	.07	.04
67	Gary Ward	.07	.04	123	Butch Wynegar	.07	.04
68	Luis Salazar	.07	.04	124	Damaso Garcia	.07	.04
69	Rod Scurry	.07	.04	125	Britt Burns	.07	.04
70	Gary Matthews	.07	.04	126	Braves (TL)	.15	.10
71	Leo Hernandez	.07	.04		(Craig McMurtry,		
72	Mike Squires	.07	.04		Dale Murphy)		
73	Jody Davis	.07	.04	127	Mike Madden	.07	.04
74	Jerry Martin	.07	.04	128	Rick Manning	.07	.04
75	Bob Forsch	.07	.04	129	Bill Laskey	.07	.04
76	Alfredo Griffin	.07	.04	130	Ozzie Smith	1.50	.90
77	Brett Butler	.35	.20	131	Batting Leaders	.75	.45
78	Mike Torrez	.07	.04	132	Home Run Leaders	.75	.45
79	Rob Wilfong	.07	.04	133	RBI Leaders Leaders	.30	.18
80	Steve Rogers	.07	.04	134	Stolen Base Leaders	.75	.45
81	Billy Martin	.20	.12	135	Victory Leaders	.12	.07
82	Doug Bird	.07	.04	136	Strikeout Leaders	.75	.45
83	Richie Zisk	.07	.04	137	ERA Leaders	.10	.06
84	Lenny Faedo	.07	.04	138	Leading Firemen	.10	.06
85	Atlee Hammaker	.07	.04	139	Bert Campaneris	.12	.07
86	John Shelby	.07	.04	140	Storm Davis	.12	.07
87	Frank Pastore	.10	.06	141	Pat Corrales	.07	.04
88	Rob Picciolo	.07	.04	142	Rich Gale	.07	.04
89	Mike Smithson	.07	.04	143	Jose Morales	.07	.04
90	Pedro Guerrero	.25	.15	144	Brian Harper	.75	.45
91	Dan Spillner	.07	.04	145	Gary Lavelle	.07	.04
92	Lloyd Moseby	.07	.04	146	Ed Romero	.07	.04
93	Bob Knepper	.07	.04	147	Dan Petry	.07	.04
94	Mario Ramirez	.07	.04	148	Joe Lefebvre	.07	.04
95	Aurelio Lopez	.07	.04	149	Jon Matlack	.07	.04
96	Royals (TL)	.12	.07	150	Dale Murphy	.75	.45
	(Larry Gura,			151	Steve Trout	.07	.04
	Hal McRae)			152	Glenn Brummer	.07	.04
97	LaMarr Hoyt	.07	.04	153	Dick Tidrow	.07	.04
98	Steve Nicosia	.07	.04	154	Dave Henderson	.15	.10
99	Craig Lefferts (R)	.15	.10	155	Frank White	.07	.04
100	Reggie Jackson	2.00	1.25	156	A''s (TL)	.40	.25
101	Porfirio Altamirano	.07	.04		(Tim Conroy,	.40	.25
102	Ken Oberkfell	.07	.04		Rickey Henderson)		
103	Dwayne Murphy	.07	.04	157	Gary Gaetti	.12	.07
104	Ken Dayley	.07	.04	158	John Curtis	.07	.04
105	Tony Armas	.10	.06	159	Darryl Cias	.07	.04
106	Tim Stoddard	.07	.04	160	Mario Soto	.10	.06
107	Ned Yost	.07	.04	161	Junior Ortiz (R)	.10	.06
108	Randy Moffitt	.07	.04	162	Bob Ojeda	.07	.04

163	Lorenzo Gray	.07	.04
164	Scott Sanderson	.12	.07
165	Ken Singleton	.10	.06
166	Jamie Nelson	.07	.04
167	Marshall Edwards	.07	.04
168	Juan Bonilla	.07	.04
169	Larry Parrish	.07	.04
170	Jerry Reuss	.10	.06
171	Frank Robinson	.10	.06
172	Frank DiPino	.07	.04
173	Marvell Wynne (R)	.10	.06
174	Juan Berenguer	.07	.04
175	Graig Nettles	.10	.06
176	Lee Smith	.90	.60
177	Jerry Hairston	.07	.04
178	Bill Krueger	.07	.04
179	Buck Martinez	.07	.04
180	Manny Trillo	.07	.04
181	Roy Thomas	.07	.04
182	Darryl Strawberry	18.00	12.50
183	Al Williams	.07	.04
184	Mike O'Berry	.07	.04
185	Sixto Lezcano	.07	.04
186	Cardinals (TL)	.10	.06
	(Lonni Smith,		
	John Stuper)		
187	Luis Aponte	.07	.04
188	Bryan Little	.07	.04
189	Tim Conroy (R)	.07	.04
190	Ben Oglivie	.07	.04
191	Mike Boddicker	.10	.06
192	Nick Esasky (R)	.10	.06
193	Darrell Brown	.07	.04
194	Domingo Ramos	.07	.04
195	Jack Morris	1.25	.80
196	Don Slaught	.10	.06
197	Garry Hancock	.07	.04
198	Bill Doran	.40	.25
199	Willie Hernandez	.10	.06
200	Andre Dawson	1.75	1.00
201	Bruce Kison	.07	.04
202	Bobby Cox	.07	.04
203	Matt Keough	.07	.04
204	Bobby Meacham (R)	.07	.04
205	Greg Minton	.07	.04
206	Andy Van Slyke (R)	3.50	2.50
207	Donnie Moore	.07	.04
208	Jose Oquendo (R)	.12	.07
209	Manny Sarmiento	.07	.04
210	Joe Morgan	.60	.35
211	Rick Sweet	.07	.04
212	Broderick Perkins	.07	.04
213	Bruce Hurst	.15	.10
214	Paul Householder	.07	.04
215	Tippy Martinez	.07	.04
216	White Sox (TL)	.25	.15
	(Richard Dotson		
	Carlton Fisk)		
217	Alan Ashby	.07	.04
218	Rick Waits	.07	.04
219	Joe Simpson	.07	.04
220	Fernando Valenzuela	.15	.10
221	Cliff Johnson	.07	.04
222	Rick Honeycutt	.07	.04
223	Wayne Krenchicki	.07	.04
224	Sid Monge	.07	.04
225	Lee Mazzilli	.07	.04
226	Juan Eichelberger	.07	.04
227	Steve Braun	.07	.04
228	John Rabb	.07	.04
229	Paul Owens	.07	.04
230	Rickey Henderson	4.00	2.75
231	Gary Woods	.07	.04
232	Tim Wallach	.20	.12
233	Checklist 133-264	.10	.06
234	Rafael Ramirez	.07	.04
235	Matt Young	.12	.07
236	Ellis Valentine	.07	.04
237	John Castino	.07	.04
238	Reid Nichols	.07	.04
239	Jay Howell	.10	.06
240	Eddie Murray	1.75	1.00
241	Billy Almon	.07	.04
242	Alex Trevino	.07	.04
243	Pete Ladd	.07	.04
244	Candy Maldonado	.25	.15
245	Rick Sutcliffe	.20	.12
246	Mets (TL)	.35	.20
	(Tom Seaver,		
	Mookie Wilson)		
247	Onix Concepcion	.07	.04
248	Bill Dawley (R)	.07	.04
249	Jay Johnstone	.10	.06
250	Bill Madlock	.15	.10
251	Tony Gwynn	5.00	3.00
252	Larry Christenson	.07	.04
253	Jim Wohlford	.07	.04
254	Shane Rawley	.07	.04
255	Bruce Benedict	.07	.04
256	Dave Geisel	.07	.04
257	Julio Cruz	.07	.04
258	Luis Sanchez	.07	.04
259	Sparky Anderson	.10	.06
260	Scott McGregor	.07	.04
261	Bobby Brown	.07	.04
262	Tom Candiotti (R)	.40	.25
263	Jack Fimple	.07	.04
264	Doug Frobel	.07	.04
265	Donnie Hill (R)	.07	.04
266	Steve Lubratich	.07	.04
267	Carmelo Martinez (R)	.12	.07
268	Jack O'Connor	.07	.04
269	Aurelio Rodriguez	.07	.04
270	Jeff Russell (R)	.25	.15
271	Moose Haas	.07	.04
272	Rick Dempsey	.10	.06

273	Charlie Puleo	.07	.04
274	Rick Monday	.10	.06
275	Len Matuszek	.07	.04
276	Angels (TL)	.25	.15
	(Rod Carew,		
	Geoff Zahn)		
277	Eddie Whitson	.07	.04
278	Jorge Bell	1.00	.70
279	Ivan DeJesus	.07	.04
280	Floyd Bannister	.07	.04
281	Larry Milbourne	.07	.04
282	Jim Barr	.07	.04
283	Larry Biittner	.07	.04
284	Howard Bailey	.07	.04
285	Darrell Porter	.07	.04
286	Lary Sorensen	.07	.04
287	Warren Cromartie	.07	.04
288	Jim Beattie	.07	.04
289	Randy Johnson	.07	.04
290	Dave Dravecky	.12	.07
291	Chuck Tanner	.07	.04
292	Tony Scott	.07	.04
293	Ed Lynch	.07	.04
294	U.L. Washington	.07	.04
295	Mike Flanagan	.15	.10
296	Jeff Newman	.07	.04
297	Bruce Berenyl	.07	.04
298	Jim Gantner	.07	.04
299	John Butcher	.07	.04
300	Pete Rose	1.75	1.00
301	Frank LaCorte	.07	.04
302	Barry Bonnell	.07	.04
303	Marty Castillo	.07	.04
304	Warren Brusstar	.07	.04
305	Roy Smalley	.07	.04
306	Dodgers (TL)	.15	.10
	(Pedro Guerrero,		
	Bob Welch)		
307	Bobby Mitchell	.07	.04
308	Ron Hassey	.07	.04
309	Tony Phillips	.40	.25
310	Willie McGee	.50	.30
311	Jerry Koosman	.15	.10
312	Jorge Orta	.07	.04
313	Mike Jorgensen	.07	.04
314	Orlando Mercado	.07	.04
315	Bob Grich	.10	.06
316	Mark Bradley	.07	.04
317	Greg Pryor	.07	.04
318	Bill Gullickson	.10	.06
319	Al Bumbry	.07	.04
320	Bob Stanley	.07	.04
321	Harvey Kuenn	.07	.04
322	Ken Schrom	.07	.04
323	Alan Knicely	.07	.04
324	Alejandro Pena	.20	.12
325	Darrell Evans	.15	.10
326	Bob Kearney	.07	.04
327	Ruppert Jones	.07	.04
328	Vern Ruhle	.07	.04
329	Pat Tabler	.10	.06
330	John Candelaria	.10	.06
331	Bucky Dent	.10	.06
332	Kevin Gross (R)	.15	.10
333	Larry Herndon	.07	.04
334	Chuck Rainey	.07	.04
335	Don Baylor	.15	.10
336	Mariners (TL)	.10	.06
	(Pat Putnam,		
	Matt Young)		
337	Kevin Hagen	.07	.04
338	Mike Warren	.07	.04
339	Roy Lee Jackson	.07	.04
340	Hal McRae	.15	.10
341	Dave Tobik	.07	.04
342	Tim Foli	.07	.04
343	Mark Davis	.07	.04
344	Rick Miller	.07	.04
345	Kent Hrbek	.30	.18
346	Kurt Bevacqua	.07	.04
347	Allan Ramirez	.07	.04
348	Toby Harrah	.07	.04
349	Bob Gibson	.07	.04
350	George Foster	.15	.10
351	Russ Nixon	.07	.04
352	Dave Stewart	.25	.15
353	Jim Anderson	.07	.04
354	Jeff Burroughs	.07	.04
355	Jason Thompson	.07	.04
356	Glenn Abbott	.07	.04
357	Ron Cey	.10	.06
358	Bob Dernier	.07	.04
359	Jim Acker (R)	.07	.04
360	Willie Randolph	.15	.10
361	Dave Smith	.07	.04
362	David Green	.07	.04
363	Tim Laudner	.07	.04
364	Scott Fletcher (R)	.12	.07
365	Steve Bedrosian	.10	.06
366	Padres (TL)	.10	.06
	(Dave Dravecky,		
	Terry Kennedy)		
367	Jamie Easterly	.07	.04
368	Hubie Brooks	.12	.07
369	Steve McCatty	.07	.04
370	Tim Raines	.30	.18
371	Dave Gumpert	.07	.04
372	Gary Roenicke	.07	.04
373	Bill Scherrer	.07	.04
374	Don Money	.07	.04
375	Dennis Leonard	.07	.04
376	Dave Anderson (R)	.10	.06
377	Danny Darwin	.10	.06
378	Bob Brenly	.07	.04
379	Checklist 265-396	.10	.06
380	Steve Garvey	.45	.28

No.	Player	Price 1	Price 2
381	Ralph Houk	.07	.04
382	Chris Hyman	.07	.04
383	Terry Puhl	.07	.04
384	Lee Tunnell	.07	.04
385	Tony Perez	.35	.20
386	George Hendrick AS	.10	.06
387	Johnny Ray AS	.07	.04
388	Mike Schmidt AS	1.00	.70
389	Ozzie Smith AS	.35	.20
390	Tim Raines AS	.15	.10
391	Dale Murphy AS	.20	.12
392	Andre Dawson AS	.50	.30
393	Gary Carter AS	.15	.10
394	Steve Rogers AS	.07	.04
395	Steve Carlton AS	.50	.30
396	Jesse Orosco AS	.07	.04
397	Eddie Murray AS	.50	.30
398	Lou Whitaker AS	.15	.10
399	George Brett AS	.80	.50
400	Cal Ripken AS	2.50	1.50
401	Jim Rice AS	.15	.10
402	Dave Winfield AS	.60	.35
403	Lloyd Moseby AS	.07	.04
404	Ted Simmons AS	.10	.06
405	LaMarr Hoyt AS	.07	.04
406	Ron Guidry AS	.15	.10
407	Dan Quisenberry AS	.07	.04
408	Lou Piniella	.10	.06
409	Juan Agosto (R)	.10	.06
410	Claudell Washington	.10	.06
411	Houston Jimenez	.07	.04
412	Doug Rader	.07	.04
413	Spike Owen (R)	.20	.12
414	Mitchell Page	.07	.04
415	Tommy John	.15	.10
416	Dane Iorg	.07	.04
417	Mike Armstrong	.07	.04
418	Ron Hodges	.07	.04
419	John Henry Johnson	.07	.04
420	Cecil Cooper	.10	.06
421	Charlie Lea	.07	.04
422	Jose Cruz	.12	.07
423	Mike Morgan	.07	.04
424	Dann Bilardello	.07	.04
425	Steve Howe	.07	.04
426	Orioles (TL)	1.25	.80
	(Mike Boddicker, Cal Ripken)		
427	Rick Leach	.07	.04
428	Fred Breining	.07	.04
429	Randy Bush	.10	.06
430	Rusty Staub	.15	.10
431	Chris Bando	.07	.04
432	Charlie Hudson (R)	.07	.04
433	Rich Hebner	.07	.04
434	Harold Baines	.15	.10
435	Neil Allen	.07	.04
436	Rick Peters	.07	.04
437	Mike Proly	.07	.04
438	Biff Pocoroba	.07	.04
439	Bob Stoddard	.07	.04
440	Steve Kemp	.07	.04
441	Bob Lillis	.07	.04
442	Byron McLaughlin	.07	.04
443	Benny Ayala	.07	.04
444	Steve Renko	.07	.04
445	Jerry Remy	.07	.04
446	Luis Pujols	.07	.04
447	Tom Brunansky	.12	.07
448	Ben Hayes	.07	.04
449	Joe Pettini	.07	.04
450	Gary Carter	.40	.25
451	Bob Jones	.07	.04
452	Chuck Porter	.07	.04
453	Willie Upshaw	.07	.04
454	Joe Beckwith	.07	.04
455	Terry Kennedy	.07	.04
456	Cubs (TL)	.20	.12
	(Ferguso Jenkins, Keith Moreland)		
457	Dave Rozema	.07	.04
458	Kiko Garcia	.07	.04
459	Kevin Hickey	.07	.04
460	Dave Winfield	2.00	1.25
461	Jim Maler	.07	.04
462	Lee Lacy	.07	.04
463	Dave Engle	.07	.04
464	Jeff Jones	.07	.04
465	Mookie Wilson	.10	.06
466	Gene Garber	.07	.04
467	Mike Ramsey	.07	.04
468	Geoff Zahn	.07	.04
469	Tom O'Malley	.07	.04
470	Nolan Ryan	7.50	4.50
471	Dick Howser	.07	.04
472	Mike Brown	.07	.04
473	Jim Dwyer	.07	.04
474	Greg Bargar	.07	.04
475	Gary Redus	.12	.07
476	Tom Tellmann	.07	.04
477	Rafael Landestoy	.07	.04
478	Alan Bannister	.07	.04
479	Frank Tanana	.10	.06
480	Ron Kittle	.10	.06
481	Mark Thurmond (R)	.07	.04
482	Enos Cabell	.07	.04
483	Ferguson Jenkins	.50	.30
484	Ozzie Virgil	.07	.04
485	Rick Rhoden	.07	.04
486	Yankees (TL)	.15	.10
	(Don Baylor, Ron Guidry)		
487	Ricky Adams	.07	.04
488	Jesse Barfield	.15	.10
489	Dave Von Ohlen	.07	.04
490	Cal Ripken	12.00	8.50

491	Bobby Castillo	.07	.04		(Mike Hargrove,			
492	Tucker Ashford	.07	.04		Lary Sorensen)			
493	Mike Norris	.07	.04	547	Mike Moore	.12	.07	
494	Chili Davis	.07	.04	548	Ron Jackson	.07	.04	
495	Rollie Fingers	.75	.45	549	Walt Terrell	.07	.04	
496	Terry Francona	.07	.04	550	Jim Rice	.15	.10	
497	Bud Anderson	.07	.04	551	Scott Ullger	.07	.04	
498	Rich Gedman	.07	.04	552	Ray Burris	.07	.04	
499	Mike Witt	.07	.04	553	Joe Nolan	.07	.04	
500	George Brett	3.00	2.00	554	Ted Power	.10	.06	
501	Steve Henderson	.07	.04	555	Greg Brock	.07	.04	
502	Joe Torre	.10	.06	556	Joey McLaughlin	.07	.04	
503	Elias Sosa	.07	.04	557	Wayne Tolleson	.07	.04	
504	Mickey Rivers	.07	.04	558	Mike Davis	.07	.04	
505	Pete Vuckovich	.07	.04	559	Mike Scott	.12	.07	
506	Ernie Whitt	.07	.04	560	Carlton Fisk	1.50	.90	
507	Mike LaCoss	.07	.04	561	Whitey Herzog	.10	.06	
508	Mel Hall	.60	.35	562	Manny Castillo	.07	.04	
509	Brad Havens	.07	.04	563	Glenn Wilson	.07	.04	
510	Alan Trammell	.75	.45	564	Al Holland	.07	.04	
511	Marty Bystrom	.07	.04	565	Leon Durham	.07	.04	
512	Oscar Gamble	.07	.04	566	Jim Bibby	.07	.04	
513	Dave Beard	.07	.04	567	Mike Heath	.07	.04	
514	Floyd Rayford	.07	.04	568	Pete Filson	.07	.04	
515	Gorman Thomas	.10	.06	569	Bake McBride	.07	.04	
516	Expos (TL)	.12	.07	570	Dan Quisenberry	.10	.06	
	(Charlie Lea,			571	Bruce Bochy	.07	.04	
	Al Oliver)			572	Jerry Royster	.07	.04	
517	John Moses	.07	.04	573	Dave Kingman	.12	.07	
518	Greg Walker	.07	.04	574	Brian Downing	.10	.06	
519	Ron Davis	.07	.04	575	Jim Clancy	.07	.04	
520	Bob Boone	.20	.12	576	Giants (TL)	.10	.06	
521	Pete Falcone	.07	.04		(Atlee Hammaker,			
522	Dave Bergman	.07	.04		Jeff Leonard)			
523	Glenn Hoffman	.07	.04	577	Mark Clear	.07	.04	
524	Carlos Diaz	.07	.04	578	Lenn Sakata	.07	.04	
525	Willie Wilson	.10	.06	579	Bob James	.07	.04	
526	Ron Oester	.07	.04	580	Lonnie Smith	.12	.07	
527	Checklist 397-528	.10	.06	581	Jose DeLeon (R)	.10	.06	
528	Mark Brouhard	.07	.04	582	Bob McClure	.07	.04	
529	Keith Atherton	.07	.04	583	Derrel Thomas	.07	.04	
530	Dan Ford	.07	.04	584	Dave Schmidt	.07	.04	
531	Steve Boros	.07	.04	585	Dan Driessen	.07	.04	
532	Eric Show	.07	.04	586	Joe Niekro	.07	.04	
533	Ken Landreaux	.07	.04	587	Von Hayes	.10	.06	
534	Pete O'Brien	.20	.12	588	Milt Wilcox	.07	.04	
535	Bo Diaz	.07	.04	589	Mike Easler	.07	.04	
536	Doug Bair	.07	.04	590	Dave Stieb	.12	.07	
537	Johnny Ray	.07	.04	591	Tony LaRussa	.10	.06	
538	Kevin Bass	.10	.06	592	Andre Robertson	.07	.04	
539	George Frazier	.07	.04	593	Jeff Lahti	.07	.04	
540	George Hendrick	.10	.06	594	Gene Richards	.07	.04	
541	Dennis Lamp	.07	.04	595	Jeff Reardon	1.25	.80	
542	Duane Kuiper	.07	.04	596	Ryne Sandberg	12.00	8.50	
543	Craig McMurtry	.10	.06	597	Rick Camp	.07	.04	
544	Cesar Geronimo	.07	.04	598	Rusty Kuntz	.07	.04	
545	Bill Buckner	.12	.07	599	Doug Sisk	.07	.04	
546	Indians (TL)	.07	.04	600	Rod Carew	1.00	.70	

601	John Tudor	.10	.06
602	John Wathan	.07	.04
603	Renie Martin	.07	.04
604	John Lowenstein	.07	.04
605	Mike Caldwell	.07	.04
606	Blue Jays (TL)	.12	.07
	(Lloyd Moseby,		
	Dave Stieb)		
607	Tom Hume	.07	.04
608	Bobby Johnson	.07	.04
609	Dan Meyer	.07	.04
610	Steve Sax	.35	.20
611	Chet Lemon	.07	.04
612	Harry Spilman	.07	.04
613	Greg Gross	.07	.04
614	Len Barker	.07	.04
615	Garry Templeton	.10	.06
616	Don Robinson	.07	.04
617	Rick Cerone	.07	.04
618	Dickie Noles	.07	.04
619	Jerry Dybzinski	.07	.04
620	Al Oliver	.12	.07
621	Frank Howard	.07	.04
622	Al Cowens	.07	.04
623	Ron Washington	.07	.04
624	Terry Harper	.07	.04
625	Larry Gura	.07	.04
626	Bob Clark	.07	.04
627	Dave LaPoint	.07	.04
628	Ed Jurak	.07	.04
629	Rick Langford	.07	.04
630	Ted Simmons	.10	.06
631	Denny Martinez	.15	.10
632	Tom Foley	.07	.04
633	Mike Krukow	.07	.04
634	Mike Marshall	.07	.04
635	Dave Righetti	.12	.07
636	Pat Putnam	.07	.04
637	Phillies (TL)	.10	.06
	(John Denny,		
	Gary Matthews)		
638	George Vukovich	.07	.04
639	Rick Lysander	.07	.04
640	Lance Parrish	.12	.07
641	Mike Richardt	.07	.04
642	Tom Underwood	.07	.04
643	Mike Brown	.07	.04
644	Tim Lollar	.07	.04
645	Tony Pena	.10	.06
646	Checklist 529-660	.10	.06
647	Ron Roenicke	.07	.04
648	Len Whitehouse	.07	.04
649	Tom Herr	.10	.06
650	Phil Niekro	.50	.30
651	John McNamara	.07	.04
652	Rudy May	.07	.04
653	Dave Stapleton	.07	.04
654	Bob Bailor	.07	.04

655	Amos Otis	.10	.06
656	Bryn Smith	.10	.06
657	Thad Bosley	.07	.04
658	Jerry Augustine	.07	.04
659	Duane Walker	.07	.04
660	Ray Knight	.10	.06
661	Steve Yeager	.07	.04
662	Tom Brennan	.07	.04
663	Johnnie LeMaster	.07	.04
664	Dave Stegman	.07	.04
665	Buddy Bell	.07	.04
666	Tigers (TL)	.30	.18
	(Jack Morris,		
	Lou Whitaker)		
667	Vance Law	.07	.04
668	Larry McWilliams	.07	.04
669	Dave Lopes	.10	.06
670	Rich Gossage	.20	.12
671	Jamie Quirk	.07	.04
672	Ricky Nelson	.07	.04
673	Mike Walters	.07	.04
674	Tim Flannery	.07	.04
675	Pascual Perez	.10	.06
676	Brian Giles	.07	.04
677	Doyle Alexander	.07	.04
678	Chris Speier	.07	.04
679	Art Howe	.07	.04
680	Fred Lynn	.15	.10
681	Tom Lasorda	.10	.06
682	Dan Morogiello	.07	.04
683	Marty Barrett (R)	.20	.12
684	Bob Shirley	.07	.04
685	Willie Aikens	.07	.04
686	Joe Price	.07	.04
687	Roy Howell	.07	.04
688	George Wright	.07	.04
689	Mike Fischlin	.07	.04
690	Jack Clark	.12	.07
691	Steve Lake (R)	.07	.04
692	Dickie Thon	.10	.06
693	Alan Wiggins	.07	.04
694	Mike Stanton	.07	.04
695	Lou Whitaker	.35	.20
696	Pirates (TL)	.12	.07
	(Bill Madlock,		
	Rick Rhoden)		
697	Dale Murray	.07	.04
698	Marc Hill	.07	.04
699	Dave Rucker	.07	.04
700	Mike Schmidt	3.50	2.50
701	NL Active	.35	.20
	Batting Leaders		
	(Bill Madlock, Dave		
	Parker, Pete Rose)		
702	NL Active Hit Leaders	.35	.20
	(Tony Perez,		
	Pete Rose,		
	Rusty Staub)		

703	NL Active HR Leaders (Dave Kingman, Tony Perez, Mike Schmidt)	.40	.25
704	NL Active RBI Leaders (Al Oliver, Tony Perez, Rusty Staub)	.20	.12
705	NL Active SB Leaders (Larry Bowa, Cesar Cedeno, Joe Morgan)	.25	.15
706	NL Active Victory Ldrs (Steve Carlton, Fergie Jenkins, Tom Seaver)	.75	.45
707	NL Active Strikeout Leaders (SteveCarlton, Nolan Ryan, Tom Seaver)	1.00	.70
708	NL Active ERA Leaders (Steve Carlton, Steve Rogers, Tom Seaver)	.75	.45
709	NL Active Save Leaders (Gene Garber, Tug McGraw, Bruce Sutter)	.25	.15
710	AL Active Batting Ldrs (George Brett, Rod Carew, Cecil Cooper)	.75	.45
711	AL Active Hit Leaders (Bert Campaneris, Rod Carew, Reggie Jackson)	1.00	.70
712	AL Active HR Leaders (Reggie Jackson, Greg Luzinski, Graig Nettles)	.75	.45
713	AL Active RBI Leaders (Reggie Jackson, Graig Nettles, Ted Simmons)	.75	.45
714	AL Active SB Leaders (Bert Campaneris, Dave Lopes, Omar Moreno)	.20	.12
715	AL Active Victory Leaders (Tommy John, Jim Palmer, Don Sutton)	.35	.20
716	AL Active Strikeout Leaders (Bert Blyleven, Jerry Koosman, Don Sutton)	.25	.15
717	AL Active ERA Leaders (Rollie Fingers, Ron Guidry, Jim Palmer)	.40	.25
718	AL Active Save Leaders (Rollie Ringers, Rich Gossage, Dan Quisenberry)	.35	.20
719	Andy Hassler	.07	.04
720	Dwight Evans	.30	.18
721	Del Crandall	.07	.04
722	Bob Welch	.15	.10
723	Rich Dauer	.07	.04
724	Eric Rasmussen	.07	.04
725	Cesar Cedeno	.10	.06
726	Brewers (TL) (Moose Haas, Ted Simmons)	.12	.07
727	Joel Youngblood	.07	.04
728	Tug McGraw	.12	.07
729	Gene Tenace	.10	.06
730	Bruce Sutter	.15	.10
731	Lynn Jones	.07	.04
732	Terry Crowley	.07	.04
733	Dave Collins	.07	.04
734	Odell Jones	.07	.04
735	Rick Burleson	.10	.06
736	Dick Ruthven	.07	.04
737	Jim Essian	.07	.04
738	Bill Schroeder	.07	.04
739	Bob Watson	.15	.10
740	Tom Seaver	1.25	.80
741	Wayne Gross	.07	.04
742	Dick Williams	.07	.04
743	Don Hood	.07	.04
744	Jamie Allen	.07	.04
745	Dennis Eckersley	1.00	.70
746	Mickey Hatcher	.07	.04
747	Pat Zachry	.07	.04
478	Jeff Leonard	.10	.06
749	Doug Flynn	.07	.04
750	Jim Palmer	1.25	.80
751	Charlie Moore	.07	.04
752	Phil Garner	.10	.06
753	Doug Gwosdz	.07	.04
754	Kent Tekulve	.07	.04
755	Garry Maddox	.07	.04
756	Reds (TL) (Ron Oester, Mario Soto)	.10	.06
757	Larry Bowa	.10	.06

758	Bill Stein	.07	.04
759	Richard Dotson	.07	.04
760	Bob Horner	.10	.06
761	John Montefusco	.07	.04
762	Rance Mulliniks	.07	.04
763	Craig Swan	.07	.04
764	Mike Hargrove	.07	.04
765	Ken Forsch	.07	.04
766	Mike Vail	.07	.04
767	Carney Lansford	.10	.06
768	Champ Summers	.07	.04
769	Bill Caudill	.07	.04
770	Ken Griffey	.15	.10
771	Billy Gardner	.07	.04
772	Jim Slaton	.07	.04
773	Todd Cruz	.07	.04
774	Tom Gorman	.07	.04
775	Dave Parker	.25	.15
776	Craig Reynolds	.07	.04
777	Tom Paciorek	.07	.04
778	Andy Hawkins	.07	.04
779	Jim Sundberg	.07	.04
780	Steve Carlton	1.50	.90
781	Checklist 661-792	.10	.06
782	Steve Balboni	.07	.04
783	Luis Leal	.07	.04
784	Leon Roberts	.07	.04
785	Joaquin Andujar	.10	.06
786	Red Sox (TL) (Wade Boggs, Bob Ojeda)	.40	.25
787	Bill Campbell	.07	.04
788	Milt May	.07	.04
789	Bert Blyleven	.30	.18
790	Doug DeCinces	.10	.06
791	Terry Forster	.07	.04
792	Bill Russell	.12	.07

1984 Topps Traded

This 132-card update set is identical to the 1984 Topps regular edition. Cards measure 2-1/2" by 3-1/2" and the set features players traded during the season, rookies called up after the start of the season and new managers.

		MINT	NR/MT
Complete Set (132)		100.00	75.00
Commons		.12	.07
1T	Willie Aikens	.12	.07
2T	Luis Aponte	.12	.07
3T	Mike Armstrong	.12	.07
4T	Bob Bailor	.12	.07
5T	Dusty Baker	.15	.10
6T	Steve Balboni	.12	.07
7T	Alan Bannister	.12	.07
8T	Dave Beard	.12	.07
9T	Joe Beckwith	.12	.07
10T	Bruce Berenyi	.12	.07
11T	Dave Bergman	.12	.07
12T	Tony Bernazard	.12	.07
13T	Yogi Berra	1.25	.80
14T	Barry Bonnell	.12	.07
15T	Phil Bradley (R)	.30	.18
16T	Ferd Breining	.12	.07
17T	Bill Buckner	.25	.15
18T	Ray Burris	.12	.07
19T	John Butcher	.12	.07
20T	Brett Butler	.80	.50
21T	Enos Cabell	.12	.07
22T	Bill Campbell	.12	.07
23T	Bill Caudill	.12	.07
24T	Bob Clark	.12	.07
25T	Bryan Clark	.12	.07
26T	Jaime Cocanower	.12	.07
27T	Ron Darling (R)	3.00	2.00
28T	Alvin Davis (R)	1.00	.70
29T	Ken Dayley	.12	.07
30T	Jeff Dedmon (R)	.15	.10

No.	Player			No.	Player		
31T	Bob Dernier	.12	.07	89T	Amos Otis	.15	.10
32T	Carlos Diaz	.12	.07	90T	Dave Parker	1.50	.90
33T	Mike Easler	.12	.07	91T	Tony Perez	2.00	1.25
34T	Dennis Eckersley	7.00	4.50	92T	Gerald Perry (R)	.25	.15
35T	Jim Essian	.12	.07	93T	Gary Pettis (R)	.25	.15
36T	Darrell Evans	.35	.20	94T	Rob Piccioo	.12	.07
37T	Mike Fitzgerald	.12	.07	95T	Vern Rapp	.12	.07
38T	Tim Foli	.12	.07	96T	Floyd Rayford	.12	.07
39T	George Frazier	.12	.07	97T	Randy Ready (R)	.15	.10
40T	Rich Gale	.12	.07	98T	Ron Reed	.12	.07
41T	Barbaro Garbey	.12	.07	99T	Gene Richards	.12	.07
42T	Dwight Gooden(R)	32.00	24.00	100T	Jose Rijo (R)	8.50	5.50
43T	Rich Gossage	.60	.35	101T	Jeff Robinson (R)	.15	.10
44T	Wayne Gross	.12	.07	102T	Ron Romanick (R)	.12	.07
45T	Mark Gubicza (R)	1.50	.90	103T	Pete Rose	8.00	5.00
46T	Jackie Gutierrez	.12	.07	104T	Bret Saberhagen (R)	15.00	11.00
47T	Mel Hall	1.00	.70				
48T	Toby Harrah	.12	.07	105T	Juan Samuel (R)	1.00	.70
49T	Ron Hassey	.15	.10	106T	Scott Sanderson	.25	.15
50T	Rich Hebner	.12	.07	107T	Dick Schofield (R)	.30	.18
51T	Willie Hernandez	.20	.12	108T	Tom Seaver	8.50	5.50
52T	Ricky Horton (R)	.20	.12	109T	Jim Slaton	.12	.07
53T	Art Howe	.15	.10	110T	Mike Smithson	.12	.07
54T	Dane Iorg	.12	.07	111T	Lary Sorensen	.12	.07
55T	Brook Jacoby (R)	.30	.18	112T	Tim Stoddard	.12	.07
56T	Mike Jeffcoat (R)	.15	.10	113T	Champ Summers	.12	.07
57T	Dave Johnson	.15	.10	114T	Jim Sundberg	.12	.07
58T	Lynn Jones	.12	.07	115T	Rick Sutcliffe	.40	.25
59T	Ruppert Jones	.12	.07	116T	Craig Swan	.12	.07
60T	Mike Jorgensen	.12	.07	117T	Tim Teufel (T)	.20	.12
61T	Bob Kearney	.12	.07	118T	Derrel Thomas	.12	.07
62T	Jimmy Key (R)	2.50	1.50	119T	Gorman Thomas	.20	.12
63T	Dave Kingman	.25	.15	120T	Alex Trevino	.12	.07
64T	Jerry Koosman	.20	.12	121T	Manny Trillo	.12	.07
65T	Wayne Krenchicki	.12	.07	122T	John Tudor	.20	.12
66T	Rusty Kuntz	.12	.07	123T	Tom Underwood	.12	.07
67T	Rene Lachemann	.12	.07	124T	Mike Vail	.12	.07
68T	Frank LaCorte	.12	.07	125T	Tom Waddell	.12	.07
69T	Dennis Lamp	.12	.07	126T	Gary Ward	.12	.07
70T	Mark Langston (R)	8.00	5.00	127T	Curt Wilkerson	.12	.07
71T	Rick Leach	.12	.07	128T	Frank Williams (R)	.15	.10
72T	Craig Lefferts	.25	.15	129T	Glenn Wilson	.12	.07
73T	Gary Lucas	.12	.07	130T	Johnny Wockenfuss	.12	.07
74T	Jerry Martin	.12	.07	131T	Ned Yost	.12	.07
75T	Carmelo Martinez	.12	.07	132T	Checklist 1-132	.12	.07
76T	Mike Mason	.12	.07				
77T	Gary Matthews	.15	.10				
78T	Andy McGaffigan	.12	.07				
79T	Larry Milbourne	.12	.07				
80T	Sid Monge	.12	.07				
81T	Jackie Moore	.12	.07				
82T	Joe Morgan	2.50	1.50				
83T	Graig Nettles	.35	.20				
84T	Phil Niekro	2.50	1.50				
85T	Ken Oberkfell	.12	.07				
86T	Mike O'Berry	.12	.07				
87T	Al Oliver	.20	.12				
88T	Jorge Orta	.12	.07				

1985 Topps

In this 792-card set Topps reverted to one large photo on the card front. Card backs are horizontal and printed in green and burgundy on a gray paper stock. All cards measure 2-1/2" by 3-1/2". Topps introduced several new subsets in 1985 including members of the 1984 U.S.A. Olympic Baseball Team and First Round Draft Picks. Topps also brought back the popular Fathers and Sons subset which last appeared in 1976. Other subsets include Record Breakers (RB) and All-Stars. For the second year in a row Topps produced a "glossy" edition called the Tiffany Set. Limited to 5,000 sets, the Tiffany edition is valued at five to six times the current price of the regular set.

		MINT	NR/MT
Complete Set(792)		110.00	75.00
Commons		.07	.04
1	Carlton Fisk (RB)	.35	.20
2	Steve Garvey (RB)	.25	.15
3	Dwight Gooden (RB)	.80	.50
4	Cliff Johnson (RB)	.10	.06
5	Joe Morgan (RB)	.20	.12
6	Pete Rose (RB)	.50	.30
7	Nolan Ryan (RB)	1.50	.90
8	Juan Samuel (RB)	.10	.06
9	Bruce Sutter (RB)	.12	.07
10	Don Sutton (RB)	.20	.12
11	Ralph Houk	.07	.04
12	Dave Lopes	.10	.06
13	Tim Lollar	.07	.04
14	Chris Bando	.07	.04
15	Jerry Koosman	.10	.06
16	Bobby Meacham	.07	.04
17	Mike Scott	.12	.07
18	Mickey Hatcher	.07	.04
19	George Frazier	.07	.04
20	Chet Lemon	.07	.04
21	Lee Tunnell	.07	.04
22	Duane Kuiper	.07	.04
23	Bret Saberhagen	3.00	2.00
24	Jesse Barfield	.15	.10
25	Steve Bedrosian	.10	.06
26	Roy Smalley	.07	.04
27	Bruce Berenyl	.07	.04
28	Dann Bilardello	.07	.04
29	Odell Jones	.07	.04
30	Cal Ripken	5.00	3.00
31	Terry Whitfield	.07	.04
32	Chuck Porter	.07	.04
33	Tito Landrum	.07	.04
34	Ed Nunez (R)	.07	.04
35	Graig Nettles	.12	.07
36	Fred Breining	.07	.04
37	Reid Nichols	.07	.04
38	Jackie Moore	.07	.04
39	Johnny Wockenfuss	.07	.04
40	Phil Niekro	.30	.18
41	Mike Fischlin	.07	.04
42	Luis Sanchez	.07	.04
43	Andre David	.07	.04
44	Dickie Thon	.10	.06
45	Greg Minton	.07	.04
46	Gary Woods	.07	.04
47	Dave Rozema	.07	.04
48	Tony Fernandez (R)	.80	.50
49	Butch Davis	.07	.04
50	John Candelaria	.10	.06
51	Bob Watson	.20	.12
52	Jerry Dybzinski	.07	.04
53	Tom Gorman	.07	.04
54	Cesar Cedeno	.10	.06
55	Frank Tanana	.10	.06
56	Jim Dwyer	.07	.04
57	Pat Zachry	.07	.04
58	Orlando Mercado	.07	.04
59	Rick Waits	.07	.04
60	George Hendrick	.10	.06
61	Curt Kaufman	.07	.04
62	Mike Ramsey	.07	.04
63	Steve McCatty	.07	.04
64	Mark Bailey	.07	.04
65	Bill Buckner	.12	.07
66	Dick Williams	.07	.04
67	Rafael Santana (R)	.10	.06
68	Von Hayes	.10	.06
69	Jim Winn	.07	.04
70	Don Baylor	.15	.10
71	Tim Laudner	.07	.04
72	Rick Sutcliffe	.12	.07
73	Rusty Kuntz	.07	.04
74	Mike Krukow	.07	.04
75	Willie Upshaw	.07	.04
76	Alan Bannister	.07	.04
77	Joe Beckwith	.07	.04

78	Scott Fletcher	.07	.04
79	Rick Mahler	.07	.04
80	Keith Hernandez	.12	.07
81	Lenn Sakata	.07	.04
82	Joe Price	.07	.04
83	Charlie Moore	.07	.04
84	Spike Owen	.07	.04
85	Mike Marshall	.07	.04
86	Don Aase	.07	.04
87	David Green	.07	.04
88	Bryn Smith	.10	.06
89	Jackie Gutierrez	.07	.04
90	Rich Gossage	.15	.10
91	Jeff Burroughs	.07	.04
92	Paul Owens	.07	.04
93	Don Schulze	.07	.04
94	Toby Harrah	.07	.04
95	Jose Cruz	.12	.07
96	Johnny Ray	.07	.04
97	Pete Filson	.07	.04
98	Steve Lake	.07	.04
99	Milt Wilcox	.07	.04
100	George Brett	1.75	1.00
101	Jim Acker	.07	.04
102	Tommy Dunbar	.07	.04
103	Randy Lerch	.07	.04
104	Mike Fitzgerald	.07	.04
105	Ron Kittle	.10	.06
106	Pascual Perez	.10	.06
107	Tom Foley	.07	.04
108	Darnell Coles	.10	.06
109	Gary Roenicke	.07	.04
110	Alejandro Pena	.12	.07
111	Doug DeCinces	.10	.06
112	Tom Tellmann	.07	.04
113	Tom Herr	.10	.06
114	Bob James	.07	.04
115	Rickey Henderson	2.00	1.25
116	Dennis Boyd	.10	.06
117	Greg Gross	.07	.04
118	Eric show	.07	.04
119	Pat Corrales	.07	.04
120	Steve Kemp	.07	.04
121	Checklist 1-132	.10	.06
122	Tom Brunansky	.12	.07
123	Dave Smith	.07	.04
124	Rich Hebner	.07	.04
125	Kent Tekulve	.07	.04
126	Ruppert Jones	.07	.04
127	Mark Gubicza	.35	.20
128	Ernie Whitt	.07	.04
129	Gene Garber	.07	.04
130	Al Oliver	.12	.07
131	Buddy & Gus Bell	.10	.06
132	Dale & Yogi Berra	.20	.12
133	Bob & Ray Boone	.12	.07
134	Terry & Tito Francona	.07	.04
135	Bob & Terry Kennedy	.07	.04
136	Bill & Jeff Kunkel	.07	.04
137	Vance & Vern Law	.07	.04
138	Dick Jr & Dick Schofield	.07	.04
139	Bob & Joel Skinner	.07	.04
140	Roy Jr & Roy Smalley	.07	.04
141	Dave & Mike Stenhouse	.07	.04
142	Dizzy & Steve Trout	.07	.04
143	Ossie Jr & Ossie Virgil	.07	.04
144	Ron Gardenhier	.07	.04
145	Alvin Davis	.20	.12
146	Gary Redus	.07	.04
147	Bill Swaggerty	.07	.04
148	Steve Yeager	.07	.04
149	Dickie Noles	.07	.04
150	Jim Rice	.15	.10
151	Moose Haas	.07	.04
152	Steve Braun	.07	.04
153	Frank LaCorte	.07	.04
154	Argenis Salazar	.07	.04
155	Yogi Berra	.20	.12
156	Craig Reynolds	.07	.04
157	Tug McGraw	.10	.06
158	Pat Tabler	.07	.04
159	Carlos Diaz	.07	.04
160	Lance Parrish	.10	.06
161	Ken Schrom	.07	.04
162	Benny Distefano (R)	.07	.04
163	Dennis Eckersley	.50	.30
164	Jorge Orta	.07	.04
165	Dusty Baker	.10	.06
166	Keith Atherton	.07	.04
167	Rufino Linares	.07	.04
168	Garth Iorg	.07	.04
169	Dan Spillner	.07	.04
170	George Foster	.10	.06
171	Bill Stein	.07	.04
172	Jack Perconte	.07	.04
173	Mike Young	.07	.04
174	Rick Honeycutt	.07	.04
175	Dave Parker	.15	.10
176	Bill Schroeder	.07	.04
177	Dave Von Ohlen	.07	.04
178	Miguel Dilone	.07	.04
179	Tommy John	.12	.07
180	Dave Winfield	1.25	.80
181	Roger Clemens(R)	28.00	14.00
182	Tim Flannery	.07	.04
183	Larry McWilliams	.07	.04
184	Carmen Castillo	.07	.04
185	Al Holland	.07	.04
186	Bob Lillis	.07	.04
187	Mike Waters	.07	.04
188	Greg Pryor	.07	.04

189	Warren Brusstar	.07	.04
190	Rusty Staub	.12	.07
191	Steve Nicosia	.07	.04
192	Howard Johnson	2.50	1.25
193	Jimmy Key	.40	.25
194	Dave Stegman	.07	.04
195	Glenn Hubbard	.07	.04
196	Pete O'Brien	.10	.06
197	Mike Warren	.07	.04
198	Eddie Milner	.07	.04
199	Denny Martinez	.20	.12
200	Reggie Jackson	1.00	.70
201	Burt Hooton	.07	.04
202	Gorman Thomas	.10	.06
203	Bob McClure	.07	.04
204	Art Howe	.07	.04
205	Steve Rogers	.07	.04
206	Phil Garner	.10	.06
207	Mark Clear	.07	.04
208	Champ Summers	.07	.04
209	Bill Campbell	.07	.04
210	Gary Matthews	.07	.04
211	Clay Christiansen	.07	.04
212	George Vukovich	.07	.04
213	Billy Gardner	.07	.04
214	John Tudor	.10	.06
215	Bob Brenly	.07	.04
216	Jerry Don Gleaton	.07	.04
217	Leon Roberts	.07	.04
218	Doyle Alexander	.07	.04
219	Gerald Perry	.10	.06
220	Fred Lynn	.12	.07
221	Ron Reed	.07	.04
222	Hubie Brooks	.12	.07
223	Tom Hume	.07	.04
224	Al Cowens	.07	.04
225	Mike Boddicker	.10	.06
226	Juan Beniquez	.07	.04
227	Danny Darwin	.10	.06
228	Dion James	.07	.04
229	Dave LaPoint	.07	.04
230	Gary Carter	.30	.18
231	Dwayne Murphy	.07	.04
232	Dave Beard	.07	.04
233	Ed Jurak	.07	.04
234	Jerry Narron	.07	.04
235	Garry Maddox	.07	.04
236	Mark Thurmond	.07	.04
237	Julio Franco	.60	.35
238	Jose Rijo	1.50	.90
239	Tim Teufel	.10	.06
240	Dave Stieb	.15	.10
241	Jim Frey	.07	.04
242	Greg Harris	.07	.04
243	Barbaro Garbey	.07	.04
244	Mike Jones	.07	.04
245	Chili Davis	.12	.07
246	Mike Norris	.07	.04
247	Wayne Tolleson	.07	.04
248	Terry Forster	.07	.04
249	Harold Baines	.15	.10
250	Jesse Orosco	.07	.04
251	Brad Gulden	.07	.04
252	Dan Ford	.07	.04
253	Sid Bream (R)	.30	.18
254	Pete Vuckovich	.10	.06
255	Lonnie Smith	.10	.06
256	Mike Stanton	.07	.04
257	Bryan Little	.07	.04
258	Mike Brown	.07	.04
259	Gary Allenson	.07	.04
260	Dave Righetti	.12	.07
261	Checklist 133-264	.10	.06
262	Greg Booker	.07	.04
263	Mel Hall	.15	.10
264	Joe Sambito	.07	.04
265	Juan Samuel	.15	.10
266	Frank Viola	.25	.15
267	Henry Cotto (R)	.10	.06
268	Chuck Tanner	.07	.04
269	Doug Baker	.07	.04
270	Dan Quisenberry	.10	.06
271	1968 #1 DP (Tim Foli)	.07	.04
272	1969 #1 DP (Jeff Burroughs)	.07	.04
273	1974 #1 DP (Bill Almon)	.07	.04
274	1976 #1 DP (Floyd Bannister)	.07	.04
275	1977 #1 DP (Harold Baines)	.10	.06
276	1978 #1 DP (Bob Horner)	.10	.06
277	1979 #1 DP (Al Chambers)	.07	.04
278	1980 #1 DP (Darryl Strawberry)	1.75	1.00
279	1981 #1 DP (Mike Moore)	.10	.06
280	1982 #1 DP (Shawon Dunston)	.80	.50
281	1983 #1 DP (Tim Belcher) (R)	1.25	.80
282	1984 #1 DP (Shawn Abner) (R)	.12	.07
283	Frank Mullins	.07	.04
284	Marty Bystrom	.07	.04
285	Dan Driessen	.07	.04
286	Rudy Law	.07	.04
287	Walt Terrell	.07	.04
288	Jeff Kunkel (R)	.07	.04
289	Tom Underwood	.07	.04
290	Cecil Cooper	.10	.06
291	Bob Welch	.10	.06
292	Brad Komminsk	.07	.04
293	Curt Young (R)	.10	.06

294	Tom Nieto (R)	.07	.04	352	Joe Morgn	.35	.20
295	Joe Niekro	.07	.04	353	Julio Solano	.07	.04
296	Ricky Nelson	.07	.04	354	Andre Robertson	.07	.04
297	Gary Lucas	.07	.04	355	Bert Blyleven	.20	.12
298	Marty Barrett	.10	.06	356	Dave Meier	.07	.04
299	Andy Hawkins	.07	.04	357	Rich Bordi	.07	.04
300	Rod Carew	.80	.50	358	Tony Pena	.10	.06
301	John Montefusco	.07	.04	359	Pat Sheridan	.07	.04
302	Tim Corcoran	.07	.04	360	Steve Carlton	.80	.50
303	Mike Jeffcoat	.10	.06	361	Alfredo Griffin	.07	.04
304	Gary Gaetti	.10	.06	362	Craig McMurtry	.07	.04
305	Dale Berra	.07	.04	363	Ron Hodges	.07	.04
306	Rick Reuschel	.07	.04	364	Richard Dotson	.07	.04
307	Sparky Anderson	.10	.06	365	Danny Ozark	.07	.04
308	John Wathan	.07	.04	366	Todd Cruz	.07	.04
309	Mike Witt	.07	.04	367	Keefe Cato	.07	.04
310	Manny Trillo	.07	.04	368	Dave Bergman	.07	.04
311	Jim Gott	.07	.04	369	R.J. Reynolds (R)	.10	.06
312	Marc Hill	.07	.04	370	Bruce Sutter	.10	.06
313	Dave Schmidt	.07	.04	371	Mickey Rivers	.07	.04
314	Ron Oester	.07	.04	372	Roy Howell	.07	.04
315	Doug Sisk	.07	.04	373	Mike Moore	.10	.06
316	John Lowenstein	.07	.04	374	Brian Downing	.10	.06
317	Jack Lazorko (R)	.07	.04	375	Jeff Reardon	.50	.30
318	Ted Simmons	.10	.06	376	Jeff Newman	.07	.04
319	Jeff Jones	.07	.04	377	Checklist 265-396	.10	.06
320	Dale Murphy	.40	.25	378	Alan Wiggins	.07	.04
321	Ricky Horton	.07	.04	379	Charles Hudson	.07	.04
322	Dave Stapleton	.07	.04	380	Ken Griffey	.12	.07
323	Andy McGaffigan	.07	.04	381	Roy Smith	.07	.04
324	Bruce Bochy	.07	.04	382	Denny Walling	.07	.04
325	John Denny	.07	.04	383	Rick Lysaner	.07	.04
326	Kevin Bass	.10	.06	384	Jody Davis	.07	.04
327	Brook Jacoby	.10	.06	385	Jose DeLeon	.07	.04
328	Bob Shirley	.07	.04	386	Dan Gladden (R)	.20	.12
329	Ron Washington	.07	.04	387	Buddy Biancalana (R)	.07	.04
330	Leon Durham	.07	.04				
331	Bill Laskey	.07	.04	388	Bert Roberge	.07	.04
332	Brian Harper	.20	.12	389	Rod Dedeaux (USA)	.07	.04
333	Willie Hernandez	.10	.06	390	Sid Akins (USA)(R)	.07	.04
334	Dick Howser	.07	.04	391	Flavio Alfaro (USA)(R)	.07	.04
335	Bruce Benedict	.07	.04				
336	Rance Mulliniks	.07	.04	392	Don August (USA)(R)	.10	.06
337	Billy Sample	.07	.04				
338	Britt Burns	.07	.04	393	Scott Bankhead (USA) (R)	.30	.18
339	Danny Heep	.07	.04				
340	Robin Yount	2.00	1.25	394	Bob Caffrey (USA)(R)	.07	.04
341	Floyd Rayford	.07	.04	395	Mike Dunne (USA) (R)	.12	.07
342	Ted Power	.07	.04				
343	Bill Russell	.10	.06	396	Gary Green (USA)(R)	.07	.04
344	Dave Henderson	.12	.07	397	John Hoover (USA) (R)	.07	.04
345	Charlie Lea	.07	.04				
346	Terry Pendleton (R)	3.50	2.50	398	Shane Mack (USA) (R)	5.00	3.00
347	Rick Langford	.07	.04				
348	Bob Boone	.15	.10	399	John Marzano (USA) (R)	.15	.10
349	Domnigo Ramos	.07	.04				
350	Wade Boggs	2.00	1.25	400	Oddibe McDowell (USA) (R)	.12	.07
351	Juan Agosto	.07	.04				

401	Mark McGwire (USA) (R)	34.00	26.00	457	Cecilio Guante	.07	.04
402	Pat Pacillo (USA)(R)	.10	.06	458	Randy Johnson	.07	.04
403	Cory Snyder (USA) (R)	1.00	.70	459	Charlie Leibrandt	.07	.04
404	Billy Swift (USA)(R)	1.25	.80	460	Ryne Sandberg	5.00	3.00
405	Tom Veryzer	.07	.04	461	Marty Castillo	.07	.04
406	Len Whitehouse	.07	.04	462	Gary Lavelle	.07	.04
407	Bobby Ramos	.07	.04	463	Dave Collins	.07	.04
408	Sid Monge	.07	.04	464	Mike Mason	.07	.04
409	Brad Wellman	.07	.04	465	Bob Grich	.10	.06
410	Bob Horner	.10	.06	466	Tony LaRussa	.10	.06
411	Bobby Cox	.07	.04	467	Ed Lynch	.07	.04
412	Bud Black	.10	.06	468	Wayne Krenchicki	.07	.04
413	Vance Law	.07	.04	469	Sammy Stewart	.07	.04
414	Gary Ward	.07	.04	470	Steve Sax	.20	.12
415	Ron Darling	.25	.15	471	Pete Ladd	.07	.04
416	Wayne Gross	.07	.04	472	Jim Essian	.07	.04
417	John Franco (R)	1.00	.70	473	Tim Wallach	.12	.07
418	Ken Landreaux	.07	.04	474	Kurt Kepshire	.07	.04
419	Mike Caldwell	.07	.04	475	Andre Thornton	.10	.06
420	Andre Dawson	1.25	.80	476	Jeff Stone	.07	.04
421	Dave Rucker	.07	.04	477	Bob Ojeda	.10	.06
422	Carney Lansford	.10	.06	478	Kurt Bevacqua	.07	.04
423	Barry Bonnell	.07	.04	479	Mike Madden	.07	.04
424	Al Nipper (R)	.07	.04	480	Lou Whitaker	.20	.12
425	Mike Hargrove	.07	.04	481	Dale Murray	.07	.04
426	Verne Ruhle	.07	.04	482	Harry Spillman	.07	.04
427	Mario Ramirez	.07	.04	483	Mike Smithson	.07	.04
428	Larry Andersen	.07	.04	484	Larry Bowa	.10	.06
429	Rick Cerone	.10	.06	485	Matt Young	.07	.04
430	Ron Davis	.07	.04	486	Steve Balboni	.07	.04
431	U.L. Washington	.07	.04	487	Frank Williams	.07	.04
432	Thad Bosley	.07	.04	488	Joel Skinner	.07	.04
433	Jim Morrison	.07	.04	489	Bryan Clark	.07	.04
434	Gene Richards	.07	.04	490	Jason Thompson	.07	.04
435	Dan Petry	.07	.04	491	Rick Camp	.07	.04
436	Willie Aikens	.07	.04	492	Dave Johnson	.10	.06
437	Al Jones	.07	.04	493	Orel Hershiser (R)	1.75	1.00
438	Joe Torre	.10	.06	494	Rich Dauer	.07	.04
439	Junior Ortiz	.07	.04	495	Mario Soto	.10	.06
440	Fernando Valenzuela	.15	.10	496	Donnie Scott	.07	.04
441	Duane Walker	.07	.04	497	Gary Pettis	.10	.06
442	Ken Forsch	.07	.04	498	Ed Romero	.07	.04
443	George Wright	.07	.04	499	Danny Cox	.07	.04
444	Tony Phillips	.10	.06	500	Mike Schmidt	2.50	1.50
445	Tippy Martinez	.07	.04	501	Dan Schatzeder	.07	.04
446	Jim Sundberg	.07	.04	502	Rick Miller	.07	.04
447	Jeff Lahti	.07	.04	503	Tim Conroy	.07	.04
448	Derrel Thomas	.07	.04	504	Jerry Willard	.07	.04
449	Phil Bradley	.10	.06	505	Jim Beattie	.07	.04
450	Steve Garvey	.30	.18	506	Franklin Stubbs (R)	.12	.07
451	Bruce Hurst	.12	.07	507	Ray Fontenot	.07	.04
452	John Castino	.07	.04	508	John Shelby	.07	.04
453	Tom Waddell	.07	.04	509	Milt May	.07	.04
454	Glenn Wilson	.07	.04	510	Kent Hrbek	.15	.10
455	Bob Knepper	.07	.04	511	Lee Smith	.50	.30
456	Tim Foli	.07	.04	512	Tom Brookens	.07	.04
				513	Lynn Jones	.07	.04
				514	Jeff Cornell	.07	.04

515	Dave Concepcion	.15	.10
516	Roy Lee Jackson	.07	.04
517	Jerry Martin	.07	.04
518	Chris Chamblis	.10	.06
519	Doug Rader	.07	.04
520	LaMarr Hoyt	.07	.04
521	Rick Dempsey	.07	.04
522	Paul Molitor	.40	.25
523	Candy Maldonado	.10	.06
524	Rob Wilfong	.07	.04
525	Darrell Porter	.07	.04
526	Dave Palmer	.07	.04
527	Checklist 397-528	.10	.06
528	Bill Kruegar	.07	.04
529	Rich Gedman	.07	.04
530	Dave Dravecky	.10	.06
531	Joe Lefebvre	.07	.04
532	Frank DiPino	.07	.04
533	Tony Bernazard	.07	.04
534	Brian Dayett	.07	.04
535	Pat Putnam	.07	.04
536	Kirby Puckett (R)	26.00	13.00
537	Don Robinson	.07	.04
538	Keith Moreland	.07	.04
539	Aurelio Lopez	.07	.04
540	Claudell Washington	.07	.04
541	Mark Davis	.10	.06
542	Don Slaught	.07	.04
543	Mike Squires	.07	.04
544	Bruce Kison	.07	.04
545	Lloyd Moseby	.10	.06
546	Brent Gaff	.07	.04
547	Pete Rose	.60	.35
548	Larry Parrish	.07	.04
549	Mike Scioscia	.10	.06
550	Scott McGregor	.07	.04
551	Andy Van Slyke	.80	.50
552	Chris Codiroli	.07	.04
553	Bob Clark	.07	.04
554	Doug Flynn	.07	.04
555	Bob Stanley	.07	.04
556	Sixto Lezcano	.07	.04
557	Len Barker	.07	.04
558	Carmelo Martinez	.07	.04
559	Jay Howell	.10	.06
560	Bill Madlock	.15	.10
561	Darryl Motley	.07	.04
562	Houston Jimenez	.07	.04
563	Dick Ruthven	.07	.04
564	Alan Ashby	.07	.04
565	Kirk Gibson	.12	.07
566	Ed Vande Berg	.07	.04
567	Joel Youngblood	.07	.04
568	Cliff Johnson	.07	.04
569	Ken Oberkfell	.07	.04
570	Darryl Strawberry	4.00	2.00
571	Charlie Hough	.10	.06
572	Tom Paciorek	.07	.04

573	Jay Tibbs (R)	.07	.04
574	Joe Altobelli	.07	.04
575	Pedro Guerrero	.12	.07
576	Jaime Cocanower	.07	.04
577	Chris Speier	.07	.04
578	Terry Francona	.07	.04
579	Ron Romanick	.07	.04
580	Dwight Evans	.20	.12
581	Mark Wagner	.07	.04
582	Ken Phelps	.07	.04
583	Bobby Brown	.07	.04
584	Kevin Gross	.07	.04
585	Butch Wynegar	.07	.04
586	Bill Scherrer	.07	.04
587	Doug Frobel	.07	.04
588	Bobby Castillo	.07	.04
589	Bob Dernier	.07	.04
590	Ray Knight	.10	.06
591	Larry Herndon	.07	.04
592	Jeff Robinson	.07	.04
593	Rick Leach	.07	.04
594	Curt Wilkerson	.07	.04
595	Larry Gura	.07	.04
596	Jerry Hairston	.07	.04
597	Brad Lesley	.07	.04
598	Jose Oquendo	.07	.04
599	Storm Davis	.07	.04
600	Pete Rose	1.00	.70
601	Tom Lasorda	.10	.06
602	Jeff Dedman	.07	.04
603	Rick Manning	.07	.04
604	Daryl Sconiers	.07	.04
605	Ozzie Smith	.80	.50
606	Rich Gale	.07	.04
607	Bill Almon	.07	.04
608	Craig Lefferts	.10	.06
609	Broderick Perkins	.07	.04
610	Jack Morris	.60	.35
611	Ozzie Virgil	.07	.04
612	Mike Armstrong	.07	.04
613	Terry Puhl	.07	.04
614	Al Williams	.07	.04
615	Marvell Wynne	.07	.04
616	Scott Sanderson	.10	.06
617	Willie Wilson	.10	.06
618	Pete Falcone	.07	.04
619	Jeff Leonard	.10	.06
620	Dwight Gooden	5.00	3.00
621	Marvis Foley	.07	.04
622	Luis Leal	.07	.04
623	Greg Walker	.07	.04
624	Benny Ayala	.07	.04
625	Mark Langston	1.25	.80
626	German Rivera	.07	.04
627	Eric Davis (R)	5.00	3.00
628	Rene Lacheman	.07	.04
629	Dick Schofield	.07	.04
630	Tim Raines	.15	.10

631	Bob Forsch	.07	.04	689	Luis DeLeon	.07	.04
632	Bruce Bochte	.07	.04	690	Alan Trammell	.40	.25
633	Glenn Hoffman	.07	.04	691	Dennis Rasmussen	.10	.06
634	Bill Dawley	.07	.04	692	Randy Bush	.07	.04
635	Terry Kennedy	.07	.04	693	Tim Stoddard	.07	.04
636	Shane Rawley	.07	.04	694	Joe Carter (R)	6.00	4.00
637	Brett Butler	.25	.15	695	Rick Rhoden	.07	.04
638	Mike Pagliarulo (R)	.15	.10	696	John Rabb	.07	.04
639	Ed Hodge	.07	.04	697	Onix Concepcion	.07	.04
640	Steve Henderson	.07	.04	698	Jorge Bell	.40	.25
641	Rod Scurry	.07	.04	699	Donnie Moore	.07	.04
642	Dave Owen	.07	.04	700	Eddie Murray	1.25	.80
643	Johnny Grubb	.07	.04	701	Eddie Murray AS	.40	.25
644	Mark Huismann	.07	.04	702	Damaso Garcia AS	.07	.04
645	Damaso Garcia	.07	.04	703	George Brett AS	.75	.45
646	Scot Thompson	.07	.04	704	Cal Ripken AS	1.50	.90
647	Rafael Ramirez	.07	.04	705	Dave Winfield AS	.50	.30
648	Bob Jones	.07	.04	706	Rickey Henderson AS	.75	.45
649	Sid Fernandez	.35	.20				
650	Greg Luzinski	.12	.07	707	Tony Armas AS	.10	.06
651	Jeff Russell	.10	.06	708	Lance Parrish AS	.10	.06
652	Joe Nolan	.07	.04	709	Mike Boddicker AS	.10	.06
653	Mark Brouhard	.07	.04	710	Frank Viola AS	.15	.10
654	Dave Anderson	.07	.04	711	Dan Quisenberry AS	.10	.06
655	Joaquin Andujar	.10	.06	712	Keith Hernandez AS	.12	.07
656	Chuck Cottier	.07	.04	713	Ryne Sandberg AS	1.25	.80
657	Jim Slaton	.07	.04	714	Mike Schmidt AS	1.00	.70
658	Mike Stenhouse	.07	.04	715	Ozzie Smith AS	.75	.45
659	Checklist 529-660	.10	.06	716	Dale Murphy AS	.25	.15
660	Tony Gwynn	3.50	2.50	717	Tony Gwynn AS	.80	.50
661	Steve Crawford	.07	.04	718	Jeff Leonard AS	.10	.06
662	Mike Heath	.07	.04	719	Gary Carter AS	.15	.10
663	Luis Aguayo	.07	.04	720	Rick Sutcliffe AS	.10	.06
664	Steve Farr (R)	.10	.06	721	Bob Knepper AS	.07	.04
665	Don Mattingly	3.50	2.50	722	Bruce Sutter AS	.10	.06
666	Mike LaCoss	.07	.04	723	Dave Stewart	.12	.07
667	Dave Engle	.07	.04	724	Oscar Gamble	.07	.04
668	Steve Trout	.07	.04	725	Floyd Bannister	.07	.04
669	Lee Lacy	.07	.04	726	Al Bumbry	.07	.04
670	Tom Seaver	1.00	.70	727	Frank Pastore	.07	.04
671	Dane Iorg	.07	.04	728	Bob Bailor	.07	.04
672	Juan Berenguer	.07	.04	729	Don Sutton	.25	.15
673	Buck Martinez	.07	.04	730	Dave Kingman	.10	.06
674	Atlee Hammaker	.07	.04	731	Neil Allen	.07	.04
675	Tony Perez	.25	.15	732	John McNamara	.07	.04
676	Albert Hall (R)	.10	.06	733	Tony Scott	.07	.04
677	Wally Backman	.07	.04	734	John Henry Johnson	.07	.04
678	Joey McLaughlin	.07	.04	735	Garry Templeton	.10	.06
679	Bob Kearney	.07	.04	736	Jerry Mumphrey	.07	.04
680	Jerry Reuss	.10	.06	737	Bo Diaz	.07	.04
681	Ben Oglivie	.07	.04	738	Omar Moreno	.07	.04
682	Doug Corbett	.07	.04	739	Ernie Camacho	.07	.04
683	Whitey Herzog	.10	.06	740	Jack Clark	.10	.06
684	Bill Doran	.10	.06	741	John Butcher	.07	.04
685	Bill Caudill	.07	.04	742	Ron Hassey	.07	.04
686	Mike easler	.07	.04	743	Frank White	.10	.06
687	Bill Gullickson	.10	.06	744	Doug Bair	.07	.04
688	Len Matuszek	.07	.04	745	Budy Bell	.07	.04

746	Jim Clancy	.07	.04
747	Alex Trevino	.07	.04
748	Lee Mazzilli	.07	.04
749	Julio Cruz	.07	.04
750	Rollie Fingers	.25	.15
751	Kelvin Chapman	.07	.04
752	Bob Owchinko	.07	.04
753	Greg Brock	.07	.04
754	Larry Milbourne	.07	.04
755	Ken Singleton	.07	.04
756	Rob Picciolo	.07	.04
757	Willie McGee	.20	.12
758	Ray Burris	.07	.04
759	Jim Fanning	.07	.04
760	Nolan Ryan	6.00	4.00
761	Jerry Remy	.07	.04
762	Eddie Whitson	.07	.04
763	Kiko Garcia	.07	.04
764	Jamie Easterly	.07	.04
765	Willie Randolph	.12	.07
766	Paul Mirabella	.07	.04
767	Darrell Brown	.07	.04
768	Ron Cey	.10	.06
769	Joe Cowley	.07	.04
770	Carlton Fisk	.80	.50
771	Geoff Zahn	.07	.04
772	Johnnie LeMaster	.07	.04
773	Hal McRae	.12	.07
774	Dennis Lamp	.07	.04
775	Mookie Wilson	.10	.06
776	Jerry Royster	.07	.04
777	Ned Yost	.07	.04
778	Mike Davis	.07	.04
779	Nick Esasky	.07	.04
780	Mike Flanagan	.10	.06
781	Jim Gantner	.07	.04
782	Tom Niedenfuer	.07	.04
783	Mike Jorgensen	.07	.04
784	Checklist 661-792	.10	.06
785	Tony Armas	.07	.04
786	Enos Cabell	.07	.04
787	Jim Wohlford	.07	.04
788	Steve Comer	.07	.04
789	Luis Salazar	.07	.04
790	Ron Guidry	.15	.10
791	Ivan DeJesus	.07	.04
792	Darrell Evans	.12	.07

1985 Topps Traded

The 132-cards in this update set carry the "T" designation after the card numbers but otherwise, the set is identical to the Topps 1985 regular edition. The set contains players who were traded during the year and rookies who joined their clubs after this seaon began.

		MINT	NR/MT
Complete Set (132)		32.00	24.00
Commons		.10	.06
1T	Don Aase	.10	.06
2T	Bill Almon	.10	.06
3T	Benny Ayala	.10	.06
4T	Dusty Baker	.12	.07
5T	George Bamberger	.10	.06
6T	Dale Berra	.10	.06
7T	Rich Bordi	.10	.06
8T	Daryl Boston (R)	.20	.12
9T	Hubie Brooks	.25	.15
10T	Chris Brown (R)	.12	.07
11T	Tom Browning (R)	1.00	.70
12T	Al Bumbry	.10	.06
13T	Ray Burris	.10	.06
14T	Jeff Burroughs	.10	.06
15T	Bill Campbell	.10	.06
16T	Don Carman (R)	.10	.06
17T	Gary Carter	1.00	.70
18T	Bobby Castillo	.10	.06
19T	Bill Caudill	.10	.06
20T	Rick Cerone	.10	.06
21T	Bryan Clark	.10	.06
22T	Jack Clark	.25	.15
23T	Pat Clements (R)	.10	.06
24T	Vince Coleman (R)	4.50	3.00
25T	Dave Collins	.10	.06
26T	Danny Darwin	.12	.07
27T	Jim Davenport	.10	.06
28T	Jerry Davis	.10	.06

29T	Brian Dayett	.10	.06	87T	Steve Nicosia	.10	.06
30T	Ivan DeJesus	.10	.06	88T	Al Oliver	.25	.15
31T	Ken Dixon	.10	.06	89T	Joe Orsulak (R)	.50	.30
32T	Mariano Duncan (R)	.40	.25	90T	Rob Picciolo	.10	.06
33T	John Felske	.10	.06	91T	Chris Pittaro	.10	.06
34T	Mike Fitzgerald	.10	.06	92T	Jim Presley (R)	.12	.07
35T	Ray Fontenot	.10	.06	93T	Rick Reuschel	.15	.10
36T	Greg Gagne (R)	.40	.25	94T	Bert Roberge	.10	.06
37T	Oscar Gamble	.12	.07	95T	Bob Rodgers	.10	.06
38T	Scott Garrelts (R)	.20	.12	96T	Jerry Royster	.10	.06
39T	Bob Gibson	.10	.06	97T	Dave Rozema	.10	.06
40T	Jim Gott	.12	.07	98T	Dave Rucker	.10	.06
41T	David Green	.10	.06	99T	Vern Ruhl	.10	.06
42T	Alfredo Griffin	.12	.07	100T	Paul Runge (R)	.10	.06
43T	Ozzie Guillen (R)	1.00	.70	101T	Mark Salas (R)	.12	.07
44T	Eddie Haas	.10	.06	102T	Luis Salazar	.10	.06
45T	Terry Harper	.10	.06	103T	Joe Sambito	.10	.06
46T	Toby Harrah	.10	.06	104T	Rick Schu (R)	.12	.07
47T	Greg Harris	.10	.06	105T	Donnie Scott	.10	.06
48T	Ron Hassey	.10	.06	106T	Larry Sheets (R)	.12	.07
49T	Rickey Henderson	5.00	3.00	107T	Don Slaught	.10	.06
50T	Steve Henderson	.10	.06	108T	Roy Smalley	.10	.06
51T	George Hendrick	.12	.07	109T	Lonnie Smith	.15	.10
52T	Joe Hesketh (R)	.25	.15	110T	Nate Snell	.10	.06
53T	Teddy Higuera (R)	.35	.20	111T	Chris Speier	.10	.06
54T	Donnie Hill	.10	.06	112T	Mike Stenhouse	.10	.06
55T	Al Holland	.10	.06	113T	Tim Stoddard	.10	.06
56T	Burt Hooton	.10	.06	114T	Jim Sundberg	.10	.06
57T	Jay Howell	.12	.07	115T	Bruce Sutter	.30	.15
58T	Ken Howell (R)	.10	.06	116T	Don Sutton	.75	.45
59T	LaMarr Hoyt	.10	.06	117T	Kent Tekulve	.10	.06
60T	Tim Hulett (R)	.12	.07	118T	Tom Tellmann	.10	.06
61T	Bob James	.10	.06	119T	Walt Terrell	.10	.06
62T	Steve Jeltz (R)	.10	.06	120T	Mickey Tettleton (R)	4.50	3.00
63T	Cliff Johnson	.10	.06	121T	Derrel Thomas	.10	.06
64T	Howard Johnson	2.00	1.25	122T	Rich Thompson	.10	.06
65T	Ruppert Jones	.10	.06	123T	Alex Trevino	.10	.06
66T	Steve Kemp	.10	.06	124T	John Tudor	.15	.10
67T	Bruce Kison	.10	.06	125T	Jose Uribe (R)	.15	.10
68T	Alan Knicely	.10	.06	126T	Bobby Valentine	.12	.07
69T	Mike LaCoss	.10	.06	127T	Dave Von Ohlen	.10	.06
70T	Lee Lacy	.10	.06	128T	U.L. Washington	.10	.06
71T	Dave LaPoint	.10	.06	129T	Earl Weaver	.15	.10
72T	Gary Lavelle	.10	.06	130T	Eddie Whitson	.10	.06
73T	Vance Law	.10	.06	131T	Herm Winningham (R)	.20	.12
74T	Johnnie LeMaster	.10	.06	132T	Checklist 1-132	.10	.06
75T	Sixto Lezcano	.10	.06				
76T	Tim Lollar	.10	.06				
77T	Fred Lynn	.20	.12				
78T	Billy Martin	.20	.12				
79T	Ron Mathis	.10	.06				
80T	Len Matuszek	.10	.06				
81T	Gene Mauch	.10	.06				
82T	Oddibe McDowell	.12	.07				
83T	Roger McDowell	.30	.18				
84T	John McNamara	.10	.06				
85T	Donnie Moore	.10	.06				
86T	Gene Nelson	.10	.06				

1986 Topps

DODGERS

FERNANDO VALENZUELA

This set features 792-cards which measure 2-1/2" by 3-1/2". Card fronts consist of large color photos with team names in bold block letters above the photos while the player's name is printed under the photo. Card backs are horizontal. Topps honors Pete Rose with the first seven cards in the set and brings back the popular Turn Back The Clock series. Other subsets include Record Breakers, All-Stars and Team Leaders.

		MINT	NR/MT
Complete Set (792)		42.00	34.00
Commons		.05	.02

1	Pete Rose	1.25	.80
2	Pete Rose(1963-66)	.35	.20
3	Pete Rose(1967-70)	.35	.20
4	Pete Rose(1971-74)	.35	.20
5	Pete Rose(1975-78)	.35	.20
6	Pete Rose(1979-82)	.35	.30
7	Pete Rose(1983-85)	.35	.20
8	Dwayne Murphy	.05	.03
9	Roy Smith	.05	.03
10	Tony Gwynn	1.75	1.00
11	Bob Ojeda	.07	.04
12	Jose Uribe	.10	.06
13	Bob Kearney	.05	.03
14	Julio Cruz	.05	.03
15	Eddie Whitson	.05	.03
16	Rick Schu	.05	.03
17	Mike Stenhouse	.05	.03
18	Brent Gaff	.05	.03
19	Rich Hebner	.05	.03
20	Lou Whitaker	.15	.10
21	George Bamberger	.05	.03
22	Duane Walker	.05	.03
23	Manny Lee (R)	.15	.10
24	Len Barker	.05	.03
25	Willie Wilson	.07	.04
26	Frank DiPino	.05	.03
27	Ray Knight	.10	.06
28	Eric Davis	.75	.45
29	Tony Phillips	.10	.06
30	Eddie Murray	.75	.45
31	Jamie Easterly	.05	.03
32	Steve Yeager	.05	.03
33	Jeff Lahti	.05	.03
34	Ken Phelps	.10	.06
35	Jeff Reardon	.40	.25
36	Tigers	.10	.06
	(Lance Parrish)		
37	Mark Thurmond	.05	.03
38	Glenn Hoffman	.05	.03
39	Dave Rucker	.05	.03
40	Ken Griffey	.10	.06
41	Brad Wellman	.05	.03
42	Geoff Zahn	.05	.03
43	Dave Engle	.05	.03
44	Lance McCullers (R)	.10	.06
45	Damaso Garcia	.05	.03
46	Billy Hatcher	.05	.03
47	Juan Berenguer	.05	.03
48	Bill Almon	.05	.03
49	Rick Manning	.05	.03
50	Dan Quisenberry	.10	.06
51	Never Issued	.00	.00
52	Chris Welsh	.05	.03
53	Len Dykstra (R)	.80	.50
54	John Franco	.12	.07
55	Fred Lynn	.15	.10
56	Tom Niedenfuer	.05	.03
57a	Bobby Wine	.08	.05
57b	Bill Doran	.10	.06
58	Bill Krueger	.05	.03
59	Andre Thornton	.08	.05
60	Dwight Evans	.15	.10
61	Karl Best	.05	.03
62	Bob Boone	.12	.07
63	Ron Roenicke	.05	.03
64	Floyd Bannister	.05	.03
65	Dan Driessen	.05	.03
66	Cardinals Leaders	.08	.05
67	Carmelo Martinez	.07	.04
68	Ed Lynch	.05	.03
69	Luis Aguayo	.05	.03
70	Dave Winfield	.80	.50
71	Ken Schrom	.05	.03
72	Shawon Dunston	.20	.12
73	Randy O'Neal	.05	.03
74	Rance Mulliniks	.05	.03
75	Jose DeLeon	.05	.03
76	Dion James	.05	.03
77	Charlie Leibrandt	.07	.04
78	Bruce Benedict	.05	.03
79	Dave Schmidt	.05	.03
80	Darryl Strawberry	1.75	1.00
81	Gene Mauch	.05	.03

82	Tippy Martinez	.05	.03
83	Phil Garner	.08	.05
84	Curt Young	.05	.03
85	Tony Perez	.20	.12
86	Tom Waddell	.05	.03
87	Candy Maldonado	.08	.05
88	Tom Nieto	.05	.03
89	Randy St. Claire	.05	.03
90	Garry Templeton	.08	.05
91	Steve Crawford	.05	.03
92	Al Cowens	.05	.03
93	Scot Thompson	.05	.03
94	Rick Bordi	.05	.03
95	Ozzie Virgil	.05	.03
96	Blue Jay Leaders	.08	.05
97	Gary Gaetti	.08	.05
98	Dick Ruthven	.05	.03
99	Buddy Biancalana	.05	.03
100	Nolan Ryan	4.00	2.75
101	Dave Bergman	.05	.03
102	Joe Orsulak	.15	.10
103	Luis Salazar	.05	.03
104	Sid Fernandez	.12	.07
105	Gary Ward	.05	.03
106	Ray Burris	.05	.03
107	Rafael Ramirez	.05	.03
108	Ted Power	.05	.03
109	Len Matuszek	.05	.03
110	Scott McGregor	.05	.03
111	Roger Craig	.05	.03
112	Bill Campbell	.05	.03
113	U.L. Washington	.05	.03
114	Mike Brown	.05	.03
115	Jay Howell	.08	.05
116	Brook Jacoby	.07	.04
117	Bruce Kison	.05	.03
118	Jerry Royster	.05	.03
119	Barry Bonnell	.05	.03
120	Steve Carlton	.75	.45
121	Nelson Simmons	.05	.03
122	Pete Filson	.05	.03
123	Greg Walker	.05	.03
124	Luis Sanchez	.05	.03
125	Dave Lopes	.08	.05
126	Mets Leaders	.10	.06
127	Jack Howell (R)	.10	.06
128	John Wathan	.05	.03
129	Jeff Dedmon	.05	.03
130	Alan Trammell	.25	.15
131	Checklist 1-132	.08	.05
132	Razor Shines	.05	.03
133	Andy McGaffigan	.05	.03
134	Carney Lansford	.10	.06
135	Joe Niekro	.05	.03
136	Mike Hargrove	.05	.03
137	Charlie Moore	.05	.03
138	Mark Davis	.07	.04
139	Daryl Boston	.08	.05
140	John Candelaria	.05	.03
141a	Bob Rogers	.05	.03
141b	Chuck Cottier	.05	.03
142	Bob Jones	.05	.03
143	Dave Van Gorder	.05	.03
144	Doug Sisk	.05	.03
145	Pedro Guerrero	.10	.06
146	Jack Perconte	.05	.03
147	Larry Sheets	.05	.03
148	Mike Heath	.05	.03
149	Brett Butler	.12	.07
150	Joaquin Andujar	.08	.05
151	Dave Stapleton	.05	.03
152	Mike Morgan	.08	.05
153	Ricky Adams	.05	.03
154	Bert Roberge	.05	.03
155	Bob Grich	.08	.05
156	White Sox Leaders	.07	.04
157	Ron Hassey	.05	.03
158	Derrel Thomas	.05	.03
159	Orel Hershiser	.25	.15
160	Chet Lemon	.05	.03
161	Lee Tunnell	.05	.03
162	Greg Gagne	.10	.06
163	Pete Ladd	.05	.03
164	Steve Balboni	.05	.03
165	Mike Davis	.05	.03
166	Dickie Thon	.05	.03
167	Zane Smith (R)	.20	.12
168	Jeff Burroughs	.05	.03
169	George Wright	.05	.03
170	Gary Carter	.25	.15
171	Never issued	.00	.00
172	Jerry Reed	.05	.03
173	Wayne Gross	.05	.03
174	Brian Snyder	.05	.03
175	Steve Sax	.12	.07
176	Jay Tibbs	.05	.03
177	Joel Youngblood	.05	.03
178	Ivan DeJesus	.05	.03
179	Stu Cliburn	.05	.03
180	Don Mattingly	1.25	.80
181	Al Nipper	.05	.03
182	Bobby Brown	.05	.03
183	Larry Andersen	.05	.03
184	Tim Laudner	.05	.03
185	Rollie Fingers	.25	.15
186	Astros Leaders	.10	.06
187	Scott Fletcher	.05	.03
188	Bob Dernier	.05	.03
189	Mike Mason	.05	.03
190	George Hendrick	.07	.04
191	Wally Backman	.05	.03
192	Milt Wilcox	.05	.03
193	Daryl Sconiers	.05	.03
194	Craig McMurtry	.05	.03
195	Dave Concepcion	.15	.10
196	Doyle Alexander	.05	.03

197	Enos Cabell	.05	.03	253	Dann Bilardello	.05	.03
198	Ken Dixon	.05	.03	254	Ozzie Guillen	.25	.15
199	Dick Howser	.05	.03	255	Tony Armas	.05	.03
200	Mike Schmidt	1.75	1.00	256	Kurt Kepshire	.05	.03
201	Vince Coleman (RB)	.15	.10	257	Doug DeCinces	.05	.03
202	Dwight Gooden (RB)	.25	.15	258	Tim Burke (R)	.10	.06
203	Keith Hernandez (RB)	.10	.06	259	Dan Pasqua (R)	.15	.10
				260	Tony Pena	.08	.05
204	Phil Niekro (RB)	.15	.10	261	Bobby Valentine	.05	.03
205	Tony Perez (RB)	.15	.10	262	Mario Ramirez	.05	.03
206	Pete Rose (RB)	.30	.18	263	Checklist 133-264	.08	.05
207	Fernando Valenzuela (RB)	.10	.06	264	Darren Daulton (R)	1.50	.90
				265	Ron Davis	.05	.03
208	Ramon Romero	.05	.03	266	Keith Moreland	.05	.03
209	Randy Ready	.05	.03	267	Paul Molitor	.25	.15
210	Calvin Schiraldi (R)	.10	.06	268	Mike Scott	.08	.05
211	Ed Wojna	.05	.03	269	Dane Iorg	.05	.03
212	Chris Speier	.05	.03	270	Jack Morris	.45	.28
213	Bob Shirley	.05	.03	271	Dave Collins	.05	.03
214	Randy Bush	.05	.03	272	Tim Tolman	.05	.03
215	Frank White	.07	.04	273	Jerry Willard	.05	.03
216	A's Leaders	.07	.04	274	Ron Gardenhire	.05	.03
217	Bill Scherrer	.05	.03	275	Charlie Hough	.08	.05
218	Randy Hunt	.05	.03	276	Yankees Leaders	.10	.06
219	Dennis Lamp	.05	.03	277	Jaime Cocanower	.05	.03
220	Bob Horner	.10	.06	278	Sixto Lezcano	.05	.03
221	Dave Henderson	.10	.06	279	Al Pardo	.05	.03
222	Craig Gerber	.05	.03	280	Tim Raines	.15	.10
223	Atlee Hammaker	.05	.03	281	Steve Mura	.05	.03
224	Cesar Cedeno	.07	.04	282	Jerry Mumphrey	.05	.03
225	Ron Darling	.10	.06	283	Mike Fischlin	.05	.03
226	Lee Lacy	.05	.03	284	Brian Dayett	.05	.03
227	Al Jones	.05	.03	285	Buddy Bell	.05	.03
228	Tom Lawless	.05	.03	286	Luis DeLeon	.05	.03
229	Bill Gullickson	.08	.05	287	John Christensen (R)	.05	.03
230	Terry Kennedy	.05	.03	288	Don Aase	.05	.03
231	Jim Frey	.05	.03	289	Johnnie LeMaster	.05	.03
232	Rick Rhoden	.05	.03	290	Carlton Fisk	.60	.35
233	Steve Lyons (R)	.05	.03	291	Tom Lasorda	.08	.05
234	Doug Corbett	.05	.03	292	Chuck Porter	.05	.03
235	Butch Wynegar	.05	.03	293	Chris Chambliss	.08	.05
236	Frank Eufemia	.05	.03	294	Danny Cox	.05	.03
237	Ted Simmons	.08	.05	295	Kirk Gibson	.10	.06
238	Larry Parrish	.05	.03	296	Gino Petralli	.05	.03
239	Joel Skinner	.05	.03	297	Tim Lollar	.05	.03
240	Tommy John	.10	.06	298	Craig Reynolds	.05	.03
241	Tony Fernandez	.12	.07	299	Bryn Smith	.07	.04
242	Rich Thompson	.05	.03	300	George Brett	1.00	.70
243	Johnny Grubb	.05	.03	301	Dennis Rasmussen	.05	.03
244	Craig Lefferts	.08	.05	302	Greg Gross	.05	.03
245	Jim Sundberg	.05	.03	303	Curt Wardle	.05	.03
246	Phillies Leaders	.25	.15	304	Mike Gallego (R)	.10	.06
247	Terry Harper	.05	.03	305	Phil Bradley	.05	.03
248	Spike Owen	.05	.03	306	Padres Leaders	.07	.04
249	Rob Deer (R)	.25	.15	307	Dave Sax	.05	.03
250	Dwight Gooden	.60	.35	308	Ray Fontenot	.05	.03
251	Rich Dauer	.05	.03	309	John Shelby	.05	.03
252	Bobby Castillo	.05	.03	310	Greg Minton	.05	.03

311	Dick Schofield	.05	.03
312	Tom Filer	.05	.03
313	Joe DeSa	.05	.03
314	Frank Pastore	.05	.03
315	Mookie Wilson	.08	.05
316	Sammy Khalifa	.05	.03
317	Ed Romero	.05	.03
318	Terry Whitfield	.05	.03
319	Rick Camp	.05	.03
320	Jim Rice	.12	.07
321	Earl Weaver	.08	.05
322	Bob Forsch	.05	.03
323	Jerry Davis	.05	.03
324	Dan Schatzeder	.05	.03
325	Juan Beniquez	.05	.03
326	Kent Tekulve	.05	.03
327	Mike Pagliarulo	.08	.05
328	Pete O'Brien	.08	.05
329	Kirby Puckett	5.50	3.75
330	Rick Sutcliffe	.10	.06
331	Alan Ashby	.05	.03
332	Darryl Motley	.05	.03
333	Tom Henke (R)	.25	.15
334	Ken Oberkfell	.05	.03
335	Don Sutton	.20	.12
336	Indians Leaders	.08	.05
337	Darnell Coles	.05	.03
338	George Bell	.35	.20
339	Bruce Berenyi	.05	.03
340	Cal Ripken	3.00	2.00
341	Frank Williams	.05	.03
342	Gary Redus	.05	.03
343	Carlos Diaz	.05	.03
344	Jim Wohlford	.05	.03
345	Donnie Moore	.05	.03
346	Bryan Little	.05	.03
347	Teddy Higuera	.10	.06
348	Cliff Johnson	.05	.03
349	Mark Clear	.05	.03
350	Jack Clark	.08	.05
351	Chuck Tanner	.05	.03
352	Harry Spilman	.05	.03
353	Keith Atherton	.05	.03
354	Tony Bernazard	.05	.03
355	Lee Smith	.35	.20
356	Mickey Hatcher	.05	.03
357	Ed Vande Berg	.05	.03
358	Rick Dempsey	.05	.03
359	Mike LaCoss	.05	.03
360	Lloyd Moseby	.05	.03
361	Shane Rawley	.05	.03
362	Tom Paciorek	.05	.03
363	Terry Forster	.05	.03
364	Reid Nichols	.05	.03
365	Mike Flanagan	.08	.05
366	Reds Leaders	.10	.06
367	Aurelio Lopez	.05	.03
368	Greg Brock	.05	.03
369	Al Holland	.05	.03
370	Vince Coleman	1.00	.70
371	Bell Stein	.05	.03
372	Ben Oglivie	.05	.03
373	Urbano Lugo (R)	.05	.03
374	Terry Francona	.05	.03
375	Rich Gedman	.05	.03
376	Bill Dawley	.05	.03
377	Joe Carter	1.50	.90
378	Bruce Bochte	.05	.03
379	Bobby Meacham	.05	.03
380	LaMarr Hoyt	.05	.03
381	Ray Miller	.05	.03
382	Ivan Calderon (R)	.50	.30
383	Chris Brown	.05	.03
384	Steve Trout	.05	.03
385	Cecil Cooper	.08	.05
386	Cecil Fielder (R)	9.00	6.00
387	Steve Kemp	.05	.03
388	Dickie Noles	.05	.03
389	Glenn Davis (R)	.40	.25
390	Tom Seaver	.60	.35
391	Julio Franco	.25	.15
392	John Russell	.05	.03
393	Chris Pittaro	.05	.03
394	Checklist 265-396	.08	.05
395	Scott Garrelts	.10	.06
396	Red Sox Leaders	.12	.07
397	Steve Buechele (R)	.25	.15
398	Earnie Riles (R)	.12	.07
399	Bill Swift	.10	.06
400	Rod Carew	.60	.35
401	Fernando Valenzuela (Clock)	.10	.06
402	Tom Seaver (Clock)	.25	.15
403	Willie Mays (Clock)	.25	.15
404	Frank Robinson (Clock)	.15	.10
405	Roger Maris (Clock)	.20	.12
406	Scott Sanderson	.08	.05
407	Sal Butera	.05	.03
408	Dave Smith	.05	.03
409	Paul Runge	.05	.03
410	Dave Kingman	.10	.06
411	Sparky Anderson	.08	.05
412	Jim Clancy	.05	.03
413	Tim Flannery	.05	.03
414	Tom Gorman	.05	.03
415	Hal McRae	.10	.06
416	Denny Martinez	.12	.07
417	R. J. Reynolds	.05	.03
418	Alan Knicely	.05	.03
419	Frank Wills	.05	.03
420	Von Hayes	.07	.04
421	Dave Palmer	.05	.03
422	Mike Jorgensen	.05	.03
423	Dan Spillner	.05	.03
424	Rick Miller	.05	.03

425	Larry McWilliams	.05	.03	483	George Vukovich	.05	.03
426	Brewers Leaders	.05	.03	484	Donnie Hill	.05	.03
427	Joe Cowley	.05	.03	485	Gary Matthews	.05	.03
428	Max Venable	.05	.03	486	Angels Leaders	.08	.05
429	Greg Booker	.05	.03	487	Bret Saberhagen	.60	.35
430	Kent Hrbek	.15	.10	488	Lou Thornton	.05	.03
431	George Frazier	.05	.03	489	Jim Winn	.05	.03
432	Mark Bailey	.05	.03	490	Jeff Leonard	.05	.03
433	Chris Codiroli	.05	.03	491	Pascual Perez	.07	.04
434	Curt Wilkerson	.05	.03	492	Kelvin Chapman	.05	.03
435	Bill Caudill	.05	.03	493	Gene Nelson	.05	.03
436	Doug Flynn	.05	.03	494	Gary Roenicke	.05	.03
437	Rick Mahler	.05	.03	495	Mark Langston	.35	.20
438	Clint Hurdle	.05	.03	496	Jay Johnstone	.05	.03
439	Rick Honeycutt	.05	.03	497	John Stuper	.05	.03
440	Alvin Davis	.10	.06	498	Tito Landrum	.05	.03
441	Whitey Herzog	.08	.05	499	Bob Gibson	.05	.03
442	Ron Robinson (R)	.05	.03	500	Rickey Henderson	1.25	.80
443	Bill Buckner	.08	.05	501	Dave Johnson	.05	.03
444	Alex Trevino	.05	.03	502	Glen Cook	.05	.03
445	Bert Blyleven	.15	.10	503	Mike Fitzgerald	.05	.03
446	Lenn Sakata	.05	.03	504	Denny Walling	.05	.03
447	Jerry Don Gleaton	.05	.03	505	Jerry Koosman	.08	.05
448	Herm Winningham	.05	.03	506	Bill Russell	.08	.05
449	Rod Scurry	.05	.03	507	Steve Ontiveros (R)	.05	.03
450	Graig Nettles	.08	.05	508	Alan Wiggins	.05	.03
451	Mark Brown	.05	.03	509	Ernie Camacho	.05	.03
452	Bob Clark	.05	.03	510	Wade Boggs	1.50	.90
453	Steve Jeltz	.05	.03	511	Ed Nunez	.05	.03
454	Burt Hooton	.05	.03	512	Thad Bosley	.05	.03
455	Willie Randolph	.08	.05	513	Ron Washington	.05	.03
456	Braves Leaders	.12	.07	514	Mike Jones	.05	.03
457	Mickey Tettleton	1.00	.70	515	Darrell Evans	.08	.05
458	Kevin Bass	.07	.04	516	Giants Leaders	.05	.03
459	Luis Leal	.05	.03	517	Milt Thompson (R)	.15	.10
460	Leon Durham	.05	.03	518	Buck Martinez	.05	.03
461	Walt Terrell	.05	.03	519	Danny Darwin	.07	.04
462	Domingo Ramos	.05	.03	520	Keith Hernandez	.10	.06
463	Jim Gott	.07	.04	521	Nate Snell	.05	.03
464	Ruppert Jones	.05	.03	522	Bob Bailor	.05	.03
465	Jesse Orosco	.05	.03	523	Joe Price	.05	.03
466	Tom Foley	.05	.03	524	Darrell Miller	.05	.03
467	Bob James	.05	.03	525	Marvell Wynne	.05	.03
468	Mike Scioscia	.08	.05	526	Charlie Lea	.05	.03
469	Storm Davis	.05	.03	527	Checklist 397-528	.08	.05
470	Bill Madlock	.12	.07	528	Terry Pendleton	.80	.50
471	Bobby Cox	.05	.03	529	Marc Sullivan	.05	.03
472	Joe Hesketh	.07	.04	530	Rich Gossage	.12	.07
473	Mark Brouhard	.05	.03	531	Tony LaRussa	.08	.05
474	John Tudor	.08	.05	532	Don Carman	.05	.03
475	Juan Samuel	.05	.03	533	Billy Sample	.05	.03
476	Ron Mathis	.05	.03	534	Jeff Calhoun	.05	.03
477	Mike Easler	.05	.03	535	Toby Harrah	.05	.03
478	Andy Hawkins	.05	.03	536	Jose Rijo	.30	.18
479	Bob Melvin (R)	.08	.05	537	Mark Salas	.05	.03
480	Oddibe McDowell	.05	.03	538	Dennis Eckersley	.45	.28
481	Scott Bradley (R)	.05	.03	539	Glenn Hubbard	.05	.03
482	Rick Lysander	.05	.03	540	Dan Petry	.07	.04

541	Jorge Orta	.05	.03
542	Don Schulze	.05	.03
543	Jerry Narron	.05	.03
544	Eddie Milner	.05	.03
545	Jimmy Key	.10	.06
546	Mariners Leaders	.08	.05
547	Roger McDowell	.10	.06
548	Mike Young	.05	.03
549	Bob Welch	.10	.06
550	Tom Herr	.07	.04
551	Dave LaPoint	.05	.03
552	Marc Hill	.05	.03
553	Jim Morrison	.05	.03
554	Paul Householder	.05	.03
555	Hubie Brooks	.10	.06
556	John Denny	.05	.03
557	Gerald Perry	.07	.04
558	Tim Stoddard	.05	.03
559	Tommy Dunbar	.05	.03
560	Dave Righetti	.08	.05
561	Bob Lillis	.05	.03
562	Joe Beckwith	.05	.03
563	Alejandro Sanchez	.05	.03
564	Warren Brusstar	.05	.03
565	Tom Brunansky	.10	.06
566	Alfredo Griffin	.05	.03
567	Jeff Barkley	.05	.03
568	Donnie Scott	.05	.03
569	Jim Acker	.05	.03
570	Rusty Staub	.08	.05
571	Mike Jeffcoat	.05	.03
572	Paul Zuvella	.05	.03
573	Tom Hume	.05	.03
574	Ron Kittle	.07	.04
575	Mike Boddicker	.08	.05
576	Expos Leaders	.20	.12
577	Jerry Reuss	.07	.04
578	Lee Mazzilli	.05	.03
579	Jim Slaton	.05	.03
580	Willie McGee	.12	.07
581	Bruce Hurst	.08	.05
582	Jim Gantner	.05	.03
583	Al Bumbry	.05	.03
584	Brian Fisher	.05	.03
585	Garry Maddox	.05	.03
586	Greg Harris	.05	.03
587	Rafael Santana	.05	.03
588	Steve Lake	.05	.03
589	Sid Bream	.08	.05
590	Bob Knepper	.05	.03
591	Jackie Moore	.05	.03
592	Frank Tanana	.08	.05
593	Jesse Barfield	.08	.05
594	Chris Bando	.05	.03
595	Dave Parker	.10	.06
596	Onix Concepcion	.05	.03
597	Sammy Stewart	.05	.03
598	Jim Presley	.05	.03
599	Rick Aguilera (R)	.50	.30
600	Dale Murphy	.25	.15
601	Gary Lucas	.05	.03
602	Mariano Duncan	.15	.10
603	Bill Laskey	.05	.03
604	Gary Pettis	.05	.03
605	Dennis Boyd	.05	.03
606	Royals Leaders	.10	.06
607	Ken Dayley	.05	.03
608	Bruce Bochy	.05	.03
609	Barbaro Garbey	.05	.03
610	Ron Guidry	.12	.07
611	Gary Woods	.05	.03
612	Richard Dotson	.05	.03
613	Roy Smalley	.05	.03
614	Rick Waits	.05	.03
615	Johnny Ray	.05	.03
616	Glenn Brummer	.05	.03
617	Lonnie Smith	.08	.05
618	Jim Pankovits	.05	.03
619	Danny Heep	.05	.03
620	Bruce Sutter	.10	.06
621	John Felski	.05	.03
622	Gary Lavelle	.05	.03
623	Floyd Rayford	.05	.03
624	Steve McCatty	.05	.03
625	Bob Brenly	.05	.03
626	Roy Thomas	.05	.03
627	Ron Oester	.05	.03
628	Kirk McCaskill (R)	.25	.15
629	Mitch Webster (R)	.15	.10
630	Fernando Valenzuela	.10	.06
631	Steve Braun	.05	.03
632	Dave Von Ohlen	.05	.03
633	Jackie Gutierrez	.05	.03
634	Roy Lee Jackson	.05	.03
635	Jason Thompson	.05	.03
636	Cubs Leaders	.12	.07
637	Rudy Law	.05	.03
638	John Butcher	.05	.03
639	Bo Diaz	.05	.03
640	Jose Cruz	.10	.06
641	Wayne Tolleson	.05	.03
642	Ray Searage	.05	.03
643	Tom Brookens	.05	.03
644	Mark Gubicza	.12	.07
645	Dusty Baker	.08	.05
646	Mike Moore	.08	.05
647	Mel Hall	.10	.06
648	Steve Bedrosian	.10	.06
649	Ronn Reynolds	.05	.03
650	Dave Stieb	.12	.07
651	Billy Martin	.12	.07
652	Tom Browning	.15	.10
653	Jim Dwyer	.05	.03
654	Ken Howell	.05	.03
655	Manny Trillo	.05	.03
656	Brian Harper	.05	.03

657	Juan Agosto	.05	.03
658	Rob Wilfong	.05	.03
659	Checklist 529-660	.08	.05
660	Steve Garvey	.25	.15
661	Roger Clemens	5.50	3.75
662	Bill Schroeer	.05	.03
663	Neil Allen	.05	.03
664	Tim Corcoran	.05	.03
665	Alejandro Pena	.08	.05
666	Rangers Leaders	.07	.04
667	Tim Teufel	.05	.03
668	Cecilio Guante	.05	.03
669	Ron Cey	.07	.04
670	Willie Hernandez	.07	.04
671	Lynn Jones	.05	.03
672	Rob Picciolo	.05	.03
673	Ernie Whitt	.05	.03
674	Pat Tabler	.05	.03
675	Claudell Washington	.05	.03
676	Matt Young	.05	.03
677	Nick Esasky	.05	.03
678	Dan Gladden	.05	.03
679	Britt Burns	.05	.03
680	George Foster	.08	.05
681	Dick Williams	.05	.03
682	Junior Ortiz	.05	.03
683	Andy Van Slyke	.45	.28
684	Bob McClure	.05	.03
685	Tim Wallach	.10	.06
686	Jeff Stone	.05	.03
687	Mike Trujillo	.05	.03
688	Larry Herndon	.05	.03
689	Dave Stewart	.10	.06
690	Ryne Sandberg	3.00	2.00
691	Mike Madden	.05	.03
692	Dale Berra	.05	.03
693	Tom Tellmann	.05	.03
694	Garth Iorg	.05	.03
695	Mike Smithson	.05	.03
696	Dodgers Leaders	.07	.04
697	Bud Black	.07	.04
698	Brad Komminsk	.05	.03
699	Pat Corrales	.05	.03
700	Reggie Jackson	.80	.50
701	Keith Hernandez AS	.10	.06
702	Tom Herr AS	.07	.04
703	Tim Wallach AS	.10	.06
704	Ozzie Smith AS	.20	.12
705	Dale Murphy AS	.20	.12
706	Pedro Guerrero AS	.10	.06
707	Willie McGee As	.10	.06
708	Gary Carter As	.15	.10
709	Dwight Gooden AS	.20	.12
710	John Tudor AS	.07	.04
711	Jeff Reardon AS	.15	.10
712	Don Mattingly AS	.35	.20
713	Damaso Garcia AS	.07	.04
714	George Brett AS	.45	.28

715	Cal Ripken AS	1.25	.80
716	Rickey Henderson AS	.40	.25
717	Dave Winfield AS	.35	.20
718	George Bell AS	.15	.10
719	Carlton Fisk AS	.20	.12
720	Bret Saberhagen AS	.15	.10
721	Ron Guidry AS	.12	.07
722	Dan Quisenberry AS	.08	.05
723	Marty Bystrom	.05	.03
724	Tim Hulett	.05	.03
725	Mario Soto	.07	.04
726	Orioles Leaders	.07	.04
727	David Green	.05	.03
728	Mike Marshall	.05	.03
729	Jim Beattie	.05	.03
730	Ozzie Smith	.70	.40
731	Don Robinson	.05	.03
732	Floyd Youmans (R)	.05	.02
733	Ron Romanick	.05	.03
734	Marty Barrett	.08	.05
735	Dave Dravecky	.08	.05
736	Glenn Wilson	.05	.03
737	Pete Vuckovich	.07	.04
738	Andre Robertson	.05	.03
739	Dave Rozema	.05	.03
740	Lance Parrish	.12	.07
741	Pete Rose	.45	.28
742	Frank Viola	.12	.07
743	Pat Sheridan	.05	.03
744	Lary Sorensen	.05	.03
745	Willie Upshaw	.05	.03
746	Denny Gonzalez	.05	.03
747	Rick Cerone	.07	.04
748	Steve Henderson	.05	.03
749	Ed Jurak	.05	.03
750	Gorman Thomas	.08	.05
751	Howard Johnson	.40	.25
752	Mike Krukow	.05	.03
753	Dan Ford	.05	.03
754	Pat Clements	.05	.03
755	Harold Baines	.10	.06
756	Pirates Leaders	.07	.04
757	Darrell Porter	.05	.03
758	Dave Anderson	.05	.03
759	Moose Haas	.05	.03
760	Andre Dawson	.75	.45
761	Don Slaught	.05	.03
762	Eric Show	.05	.03
763	Terry Puhl	.05	.03
764	Kevin Gross	.05	.03
765	Don Baylor	.10	.06
767	Jody Davis	.05	.03
768	Vern Ruhle	.05	.03
769	Harold Reynolds (R)	.25	.15
770	Vida Blue	.10	.06
771	John McNamara	.05	.03
772	Brian Downing	.08	.05

773	Greg Pryor	.05	.03
774	Terry Leach	.05	.03
775	Al Oliver	.08	.05
776	Gene Garber	.05	.03
777	Wayne Krenchicki	.05	.03
778	Jerry Hairston	.05	.03
779	Rick Reuschel	.07	.04
780	Robin Yount	1.25	.80
781	Joe Nolan	.05	.03
782	Ken Landreaux	.05	.03
783	Ricky Horton	.05	.03
784	Alan Bannister	.05	.03
785	Bob Stanley	.05	.03
786	Twins Leaders	.07	.04
787	Vance Law	.05	.03
788	Marty Castillo	.05	.03
789	Kurt Bevacqua	.05	.03
790	Phil Niekro	.25	.15
791	Checklsit 661-792	.08	.05
792	Charles Hudson	.05	.03

1986 Topps Traded

The cards in this 132-card update set are identical to the 1986 Topps regular edition. Cards measure 2-1/2" by 3-1/2" and card numbers carry the letter "T". The set features players who were traded since the beginning of the year and a number of rookies who made their first Major League appearance during the 1986 season.

		MINT	NR/MT
Complete Set (132)		28.50	20.00
Commons		.07	.04
1T	Andy Allanson (R)	.10	.06
2T	Neil Allen	.07	.04

3T	Joaquin Andujar	.10	.06
4T	Paul Assenmacher (R)	.12	.07
5T	Scott Bailes (R)	.10	.06
6T	Don Baylor	.15	.10
7T	Steve Bedrosian	.10	.06
8T	Juan Beniquez	.07	.04
9T	Juan Berenguer	.07	.04
10T	Mike Bielecki (R)	.15	.10
11T	Barry Bonds (R)	5.50	3.75
12T	Bobby Bonilla (R)	3.00	2.00
13T	Juan Bonilla	.07	.04
14T	Rich Bordi	.07	.04
15T	Steve Boros	.07	.04
16T	Rick Burleson	.07	.04
17T	Bill Campbell	.07	.04
18T	Tom Candiotti	.15	.10
19T	John Cangelosi (R)	.10	.06
20T	Jose Canseco (R)	8.00	5.00
21T	Carmen Castillo	.07	.04
22T	Rick Cerone	.10	.06
23T	John Cerutti (R)	.10	.06
24T	Will Clark (R)	7.50	4.50
25T	Mark Clear	.07	.04
26T	Darnell Coles	.07	.04
27T	Dave Collins	.07	.04
28T	Tim Conroy	.07	.04
29T	Joe Cowley	.07	.04
30T	Joel Davis (R)	.07	.04
31T	Rob Deer	.12	.07
32T	John Denny	.07	.04
33T	Mike Easler	.07	.04
34T	Mark Eichhorn (R)	.12	.07
35T	Steve Farr	.07	.04
36T	Scott Fletcher	.07	.04
37T	Terry Forster	.07	.04
38T	Terry Francona	.07	.04
39T	Jim Fregosi	.07	.04
40T	Andres Galarraga (R)	.25	.15
41T	Ken Griffey	.15	.10
42T	Bill Gullickson	.10	.06
43T	Jose Guzman (R)	.25	.15
44T	Moose Haas	.07	.04
45T	Billy Hatcher	.15	.10
46T	Mike Heath	.07	.04
47T	Tom Hume	.07	.04
48T	Pete Incaviglia (R)	.25	.15
49T	Dane Iorg	.07	.04
50T	Bo Jackson (R)	3.50	2.50
51T	Wally Joyner (R)	1.25	.80
52T	Charlie Kerfeld (R)	.07	.04
53T	Eric King (R)	.12	.07
54T	Bob Kipper (R)	.10	.06
55T	Wayne Krenchicki	.07	.04
56T	John Kruk (R)	1.00	.70
57T	Mike LaCoss	.07	.04
58T	Pete Ladd	.07	.04
59T	Mike Laga	.07	.04

		MINT	NR/MT
60T	Hal Lanier	.07	.04
61T	Dave LaPoint	.07	.04
62T	Rudy Law	.07	.04
63T	Rick Leach	.07	.04
64T	Tim Leary	.10	.06
65T	Dennis Leonard	.07	.04
66T	Jim Leyland (R)	.15	.10
67T	Steve Lyons	.07	.04
68T	Mickey Mahler	.07	.04
69T	Candy Maldonado	.15	.10
70T	Roger Mason (R)	.12	.07
71T	Bob McClure	.07	.04
72T	Andy McGaffigan	.07	.04
73T	Gene Michael	.07	.04
74T	Kevin Mitchell (R)	1.25	.80
75T	Omar Moreno	.07	.04
76T	Jerry Mumphrey	.07	.04
77T	Phil Niekro	.35	.20
78T	Randy Niemann	.07	.04
79T	Juan Nieves (R)	.15	.10
80T	Otis Nixon (R)	.40	.25
81T	Bob Ojeda	.10	.06
82T	Jose Oquendo	.10	.06
83T	Tom Paciorek	.07	.04
84T	Dave Palmer	.07	.04
85T	Frank Pastore	.07	.04
86T	Lou Piniella	.10	.06
87T	Dan Plesac (R)	.15	.10
88T	Darrell Porter	.07	.04
89T	Rey Quinones (R)	.08	.05
90T	Gary Redus	.07	.04
91T	Bip Roberts (R)	.75	.45
92T	Billy Jo Robidoux	.07	.04
93T	Jeff Robinson	.10	.06
94T	Gary Roenicke	.07	.04
95T	Ed Romero	.07	.04
96T	Argenis Salazar	.07	.04
97T	Joe Sambito	.07	.04
98T	Billy Sample	.07	.04
99T	Dave Schmidt	.07	.04
100T	Ken Schrom	.07	.04
101T	Tom Seaver	.75	.45
102T	Ted Simmons	.12	.07
103T	Sammy Stewart	.07	.04
104T	Kurt Stillwell (R)	.15	.10
105T	Franklin Stubbs	.10	.06
106T	Dale Sveum	.15	.10
107T	Chuck Tanner	.07	.04
108T	Danny Tartabull (R)	1.25	.80
109T	Tim Teufel	.10	.06
110T	Bob Tewksbury (R)	.45	.28
111T	Andres Thomas (R)	.08	.05
112T	Milt Thompson	.12	.07
113T	Robby Thompson (R)	.25	.15
114T	Jay Tibbs	.07	.04
115T	Wayne Tolleson	.07	.04
116T	Alex Trevino	.07	.04
117T	Manny Trillo	.07	.04

		MINT	NR/MT
118T	Ed Vande Berg	.07	.04
119T	Ozzie Virgil	.07	.04
120T	Bob Walk	.07	.04
121T	Gene Walter (R)	.07	.04
122T	Claudell Washington	.07	.04
123T	Bill Wegman (R)	.25	.15
124T	Dick Williams	.07	.04
125T	Mitch Williams (R)	.20	.12
126T	Bobby Witt (R)	.35	.20
127T	Todd Worrell (R)	.25	.15
128T	Geroge Wright	.07	.04
129T	Ricky Wright	.07	.04
130T	Steve Yeager	.07	.04
131T	Paul Zuvella	.07	.04
132T	Checklist	.07	.04

1987 Topps

This 792-card set features mostly action photos surrounded by wood grain borders that are similar to the 1962 Topps set. Card backs are horizontal with blue and yellow colors on a gray paper stock. Cards measure 2-1/2" by 3-1/2". Key subsets include Record Breakers, Turn Back The Clock, Team Leaders and All-Stars.

		MINT	NR/MT
Complete Set (792)		35.00	26.00
Commons		.05	.03
1	Roger Clemens (RB)	.50	.30
2	Jim Deshaies (RB)	.05	.03
3	Dwight Evans (RB)	.12	.07
4	Dave Lopes (RB)	.07	.04
5	Dave Righetti (RB)	.07	.04
6	Ruben Sierra (RB)	.40	.25
7	Todd Worrell (RB)	.07	.04

8	Terry Pendleton	.35	.20
9	Jay Tibbs	.05	.03
10	Cecil Cooper	.07	.04
11	Indians Leaders	.10	.06
12	Jeff Sellers	.05	.03
13	Nick Esasky	.05	.03
14	Dave Stewart	.10	.06
15	Claudell Washington	.07	.04
16	Pat Clements	.05	.03
17	Pete O'Brien	.05	.03
18	Dick Howser	.05	.03
19	Matt Young	.05	.03
20	Gary Carter	.15	.10
21	Mark Davis	.05	.03
22	Doug DeCinces	.05	.03
23	Lee Smith	.20	.12
24	Tony Walker	.05	.03
25	Bert Blyleven	.15	.10
26	Greg Brock	.05	.03
27	Joe Cowley	.05	.03
28	Rick Dempsey	.05	.03
29	Jimmy Key	.08	.05
30	Tim Raines	.10	.06
31	Braves Leaders	.05	.03
32	Tim Leary	.07	.04
33	Andy Van Slyke	.25	.15
34	Jose Rijo	.15	.10
35	Sid Bream	.08	.05
36	Eric King	.05	.03
37	Marvell Wynne	.05	.03
38	Dennis Leonard	.05	.03
39	Marty Barrett	.07	.04
40	Dave Righetti	.08	.05
41	Bo Diaz	.05	.03
42	Gary Redus	.05	.03
43	Gene Michael	.05	.03
44	Greg Harris	.05	.03
45	Jim Presley	.05	.03
46	Danny Gladden	.08	.05
47	Dennis Powell	.05	.03
48	Wally Backman	.05	.03
49	Terry Harper	.05	.03
50	Dave Smith	.05	.03
51	Mel Hall	.10	.06
52	Keith Atherton	.05	.03
53	Ruppert Jones	.05	.03
54	Bill Dawley	.05	.03
55	Tim Wallach	.10	.06
56	Brewers Leaders	.10	.06
57	Scott Nielsen	.05	.03
58	Thad Bosley	.05	.03
59	Ken Dayley	.05	.03
60	Tony Pena	.08	.05
61	Bobby Thigpen (R)	.35	.20
62	Bobby Meacham	.05	.03
63	Fred Toliver	.05	.03
64	Harry Spilman	.05	.03
65	Tom Browning	.10	.06
66	Marc Sullivan	.05	.03
67	Bill Swift	.10	.06
68	Tony LaRussa	.08	.05
69	Lonnie Smith	.07	.04
70	Charlie Hough	.05	.03
71	Mike Aldrete (R)	.08	.05
72	Walt Terrell	.05	.03
73	Dave Anderson	.05	.03
74	Dan Pasqua	.08	.05
75	Ron Darling	.10	.06
76	Rafael Ramirez	.05	.03
77	Bryan Oelkers	.05	.03
78	Tom Foley	.05	.03
79	Juan Nieves	.10	.06
80	Wally Joyner	.75	.45
81	Padres Leaders	.05	.03
82	Rob Murphy (R)	.08	.05
83	Mike Davis	.05	.03
84	Steve Lake	.05	.03
85	Kevin Bass	.08	.05
86	Nate Snell	.05	.03
87	Mark Salas	.05	.03
88	Ed Wojna	.05	.03
89	Ozzie Guillen	.10	.06
90	Dave Stieb	.12	.07
91	Harold Reynolds	.12	.07
92	Urbano Lugo	.05	.03
93	Jim Leyland	.10	.06
94	Calvin Schiraldi	.05	.03
95	Oddibe McDowell	.05	.03
96	Frank Williams	.05	.03
97	Glenn Wilson	.05	.03
98	Bill Scherrer	.05	.03
99	Darryl Motley	.05	.03
100	Steve Garvey	.20	.12
101	Carl Willis (R)	.08	.05
102	Paul Zuvella	.05	.03
103	Rick Aguilera	.12	.07
104	Billy Sample	.05	.03
105	Floyd Youmans	.05	.03
106	Blue Jays Leaders	.10	.06
107	John Butcher	.05	.03
108	Jim Gantner (Photo reversed)	.05	.03
109	R.J. Reynolds	.05	.03
110	John Tudor	.07	.04
111	Alfredo Griffin	.05	.03
113	Neil Allen	.05	.03
114	Billy Beane	.05	.03
115	Donnie Moore	.05	.03
116	Bill Russell	.07	.04
117	Jim Beattie	.05	.03
118	Bobby Valentine	.05	.03
119	Ron Robinson	.05	.03
120	Eddie Murray	.35	.20
121	Kevin Romine	.05	.03
122	Jim Clancy	.05	.03
123	John Kruk	.75	.45

124	Ray Fontenot	.05	.03	182	Lee Lacy	.05	.03
125	Bob Brenly	.05	.03	183	Andy Hawkins	.05	.03
126	Mike Loynd (R)	.05	.03	184	Bobby Bonilla	1.25	.80
127	Vance Law	.05	.03	185	Roger McDowell	.05	.03
128	Checklist 1-132	.05	.03	186	Bruce Benedict	.05	.03
129	Rick Cerone	.05	.03	187	Mark Huismann	.05	.03
130	Dwight Gooden	.25	.15	188	Tony Phillips	.07	.04
131	Pirates Leaders	.07	.04	189	Joe Hesketh	.05	.03
132	Paul Assenmacher	.05	.03	190	Jim Sundberg	.05	.03
133	Jose Oquendo	.05	.03	191	Charles Hudson	.05	.03
134	Rich Yett (R)	.07	.04	192	Cory Snyder	.08	.05
135	Mike Easler	.05	.03	193	Roger Craig	.05	.03
136	Ron Romanick	.05	.03	194	Kirk McCaskill	.07	.04
137	Jerry Willard	.05	.03	195	Mike Pagliarulo	.05	.03
138	Roy Lee Jackson	.05	.03	196	Randy O'Neal	.05	.03
139	Devon White (R)	.25	.15	197	Mark Bailey	.05	.03
140	Bret Saberhagen	.20	.12	198	Lee Mazzilli	.05	.03
141	Herm Winningham	.05	.03	199	Mariano Duncan	.07	.04
142	Rick Sutcliffe	.08	.05	200	Pete Rose	.40	.25
143	Steve Boros	.05	.03	201	John Cangelosi	.05	.03
144	Mike Scioscia	.07	.04	202	Ricky Wright	.05	.03
145	Charlie Kerfeld	.05	.03	203	Mike Kingery (R)	.08	.05
146	Tracy Jones (R)	.08	.05	204	Sammy Stewart	.05	.03
147	Randy Niemann	.05	.03	205	Graig Nettles	.08	.05
148	Dave Collins	.05	.03	206	Twins Leaders	.08	.05
149	Ray Searage	.05	.03	207	George Frazier	.05	.03
150	Wade Boggs	.50	.30	208	John Shelby	.05	.03
151	Mike LaCoss	.05	.03	209	Rich Schu	.05	.03
152	Toby Harrah	.05	.03	210	Lloyd Moseby	.05	.03
153	Duane Ward (R)	.20	.12	211	John Morris	.05	.03
154	Tom O'Malley	.05	.03	212	Mike Fitzgerald	.05	.03
155	Eddie Whitson	.05	.03	213	Randy Myers (R)	.20	.12
156	Mariners Leaders	.05	.03	214	Omar Moreno	.05	.03
157	Danny Darwin	.05	.03	215	Mark Langston	.20	.12
158	Tim Teufel	.05	.03	216	B.J. Surhoff (R)	.15	.10
159	Ed Olwine	.05	.03	217	Chris Codiroli	.05	.03
160	Julio Franco	.15	.10	218	Sparky Anderson	.08	.05
161	Steve Ontiveros	.05	.03	219	Cecilio Guante	.05	.03
162	Mike LaValliere	.15	.10	220	Joe Carter	.40	.25
163	Kevin Gross	.05	.03	221	Vern Ruhle	.05	.03
164	Sammy Khalifa	.05	.03	222	Denny Walling	.05	.03
165	Jeff Reardon	.30	.18	223	Charlie Liebrandt	.07	.04
166	Bob Boone	.12	.07	224	Wayne Tolleson	.05	.03
167	Jim Deshaies	.10	.06	225	Mike Smithson	.05	.03
168	Lou Piniella	.08	.05	226	Max Venable	.05	.03
169	Ron Washington	.05	.03	227	Jamie Moyer	.05	.03
170	Bo Jackson	1.25	.80	228	Curt Wilkerson	.05	.03
171	Chuck Cary	.05	.03	229	Mike Birkbeck (R)	.05	.03
172	Ron Oester	.05	.03	230	Don Baylor	.10	.06
173	Alex Trevino	.05	.03	231	Giants Leaders	.07	.04
174	Henry Cotto	.05	.03	232	Reggie Williams	.05	.03
175	Bob Stanley	.05	.03	233	Russ Morman	.05	.03
176	Steve Buechele	.08	.05	234	Pat Sheridan	.05	.03
177	Keith Moreland	.05	.03	235	Alvin Davis	.07	.04
178	Cecil Fielder	1.25	.80	236	Tommy John	.10	.06
179	Bill Wegman	.07	.04	237	Jim Morrison	.05	.03
180	Chris Brown	.05	.03	238	Bill Krueger	.05	.03
181	Cardinals Leaders	.10	.06	239	Juan Espino	.05	.03

240	Steve Balboni	.05	.03
241	Danny Heep	.05	.03
242	Rick Mahler	.05	.03
243	Whitey Herzog	.08	.05
244	Dickie Noles	.05	.03
245	Willie Upshaw	.05	.03
246	Jim Dwyer	.05	.03
247	Jeff Reed	.05	.03
248	Gene Walter	.05	.03
249	Jim Pankovits	.05	.03
250	Teddy Higuera	.08	.05
251	Rob Wilfong	.05	.03
252	Denny Martinez	.10	.06
253	Eddie Milner	.05	.03
254	Bob Tewksbury	.25	.15
255	Juan Samuel	.05	.03
256	Royals Leaders	.20	.12
257	Bob Forsch	.05	.03
258	Steve Yeager	.05	.03
259	Mike Greenwell (R)	.50	.30
260	Vida Blue	.08	.05
261	Ruben Sierra (R)	3.00	2.00
262	Jim Winn	.05	.03
263	Stan Javier	.05	.03
264	Checklist 133-264	.05	.03
265	Darrell Evans	.08	.05
266	Jeff Hamilton	.05	.03
267	Howard Johnson	.25	.15
268	Pat Corrales	.05	.03
269	Cliff Speck	.05	.03
270	Jody Davis	.05	.03
271	Mike Brown	.05	.03
272	Andres Galarraga	.12	.07
273	Gene Nelson	.05	.03
274	Jeff Hearron (R)	.05	.03
275	LaMarr Hoyt	.05	.03
276	Jackie Gutierrez	.05	.03
277	Juan Agosto	.05	.03
278	Gary Pettis	.10	.06
279	Dan Plesac	.08	.05
280	Jeffrey Leonard	.08	.05
281	Reds Leaders	.25	.15
282	Jeff Calhuon	.05	.03
283	Doug Drabek (R)	.70	.40
284	John Moses	.05	.03
285	Dennis Boyd	.05	.03
286	Mike Woodard	.05	.03
287	Dave Von Ohlen	.05	.03
288	Tito Landrum	.05	.03
289	Bob Kipper	.05	.03
290	Leon Durham	.05	.03
291	Mitch Williams	.15	.10
292	Franklin Stubbs	.05	.03
293	Bob Rodgers	.05	.03
294	Steve Jeltz	.05	.03
295	Len Dykstra	.12	.07
296	Andres Thomas	.05	.03
297	Don Schulze	.05	.03
298	Terry Herndon	.05	.03
299	Joel Davis	.05	.03
300	Reggie Jackson	.60	.35
301	Luis Aquino	.05	.03
302	Bill Schroeder	.05	.03
303	Juan Berenguer	.07	.04
304	Phil Garner	.07	.04
305	John Franco	.10	.06
306	Red Sox Leaders	.20	.12
307	Lee Guetterman	.05	.03
308	Don Slaught	.05	.03
309	Mike Young	.05	.03
310	Frank Viola	.15	.10
311	Rickey Henderson (Clock)	.25	.15
312	Reggie Jackson (Clock)	.20	.12
313	Roberto Clemente (Clock)	.10	.06
314	Carl Yastrzemski (Clock)	.10	.06
315	Maury Wills (Clock)	.08	.05
316	Brian Fisher	.05	.03
317	Clint Hurdle	.05	.03
318	Jim Fregosi	.05	.03
319	Greg Swindell	.60	.35
320	Barry Bonds	3.00	2.00
321	Mike Laga	.05	.03
322	Chris Bando	.05	.03
323	Al Newman	.05	.03
324	Dave Palmer	.05	.03
325	Garry Templeton	.08	.05
326	Mark Gubicza	.10	.06
327	Dale Sveum	.08	.05
328	Bob Welch	.08	.05
329	Ron Roenicke	.05	.03
330	Mike Scott	.08	.05
331	Mets Leaders	.25	.15
332	Joe Price	.05	.03
333	Ken Phelps	.05	.03
334	Ed Correa	.05	.03
335	Candy Maldonado	.08	.05
336	Allan Anderson	.07	.04
337	Darrell Miller	.05	.03
338	Tim Conroy	.05	.03
339	Donnie Hill	.05	.03
340	Roger Clemens	1.75	1.00
341	Mike Brown	.05	.03
342	Bob James	.05	.03
343	Hal Lanier	.05	.03
344	Joe Niekro	.05	.03
345	Andre Dawson	.30	.18
346	Shawon Dunston	.15	.10
347	Mickey Brantley	.05	.03
348	Carmelo Martinez	.05	.03
349	Storm Davis	.05	.03
350	Keith Hernandez	.08	.05
351	Gene Garber	.05	.03

352	Mike Felder	.08	.05	410	Fernando Valenzuela	.10		.06
353	Ernie Camacho	.05	.03	411	Darnell Coles	.07		.04
354	Jamie Quirk	.05	.03	412	Eric Davis	.20		.12
355	Don Carman	.05	.03	413	Moose Haas	.05		.03
356	White Sox Leaders	.05	.03	414	Joe Orsulak	.08		.05
357	Steve Fireovid (R)	.05	.03	415	Bobby Witt	.25		.15
358	Sal Butera	.05	.03	416	Tom Nieto	.05		.03
359	Doug Corbett	.05	.03	417	Pat Perry (R)	.07		.04
360	Pedro Guerrero	.10	.06	418	Dick Williams	.05		.03
361	Mark Thurmond	.05	.03	419	Mark Portugal (R)	.10		.06
362	Luis Quinones (R)	.07	.04	420	Will Clark	3.50		2.50
363	Jose Guzman	.07	.04	421	Jose DeLeon	.05		.03
364	Randy Bush	.07	.04	422	Jack Howell	.05		.03
365	Rick Rhoden	.05	.03	423	Jaime Cocanower	.05		.03
366	Mark McGwire	3.00	2.00	424	Chris Speier	.05		.03
367	Jeff Lahti	.05	.03	425	Tom Seaver	.30		.18
368	John McNamara	.05	.03	426	Floyd Rayford	.05		.03
369	Brian Dayett	.05	.03	427	Ed Nunez	.05		.03
370	Fred Lynn	.08	.05	428	Bruce Bochy	.05		.03
371	Mark Eichhorn	.08	.05	429	Tim Pyznarski (R)	.05		.03
372	Jerry Mumphrey	.05	.03	430	Mike Schmidt	.80		.50
373	Jeff Dedmon	.05	.03	431	Dodgers Leaders	.08		.05
374	Glenn Hoffman	.05	.03	432	Jim Slaton	.05		.03
375	Ron Guidry	.10	.06	433	Ed Hearn	.05		.03
376	Scott Bradley	.05	.03	434	Mike Fischlin	.05		.03
377	John Henry Johnson	.05	.03	435	Bruce Sutter	.08		.05
378	Rafael Santana	.05	.03	436	Andy Allanson	.05		.03
379	John Russell	.05	.03	437	Ted Power	.05		.03
380	Rich Gossage	.10	.06	438	Kelly Downs (R)	.10		.06
381	Expos Leaders	.05	.03	439	Karl Best	.05		.03
382	Rudy Law	.05	.03	440	Willie McGee	.10		.06
383	Ron Davis	.05	.03	441	Dave Leiper (R)	.07		.04
384	Johnny Grubb	.05	.03	442	Mitch Webster	.05		.03
385	Orel Hershiser	.12	.07	443	John Felske	.05		.03
386	Dickie Thon	.05	.03	444	Jeff Russell	.08		.05
387	T.R. Bryden	.05	.03	445	Dave Lopes	.07		.04
388	Geno Petralli	.05	.03	446	Chuck Finley (R)	.35		.20
389	Jeff Robinson	.05	.03	447	Bill Almon	.05		.03
390	Gary Matthews	.05	.03	448	Chris Bosio (R)	.25		.15
391	Jay Howell	.05	.03	449	Pat Dodson (R)	.07		.04
392	Checklist 265-396	.05	.03	450	Kirby Puckett	1.50		.90
393	Pete Rose	.25	.15	451	Joe Sambito	.05		.03
394	Mike Bielecki	.08	.05	452	Dave Henderson	.08		.05
395	Damaso Garcia	.05	.03	453	Scott Terry (R)	.07		.04
396	Tim Lollar	.05	.03	454	Luis Salazar	.05		.03
397	Greg Walker	.05	.03	455	Mike Boddicker	.08		.05
398	Brad Havens	.05	.03	456	A's Leaders	.10		.06
399	Curt Ford (R)	.07	.04	457	Len Matuszak	.05		.03
400	George Brett	.50	.30	458	Kelly Gruber (R)	.35		.20
401	Billy Jo Robidoux	.05	.03	459	Dennis Eckersley	.25		.15
402	Mike Trujillo	.05	.03	460	Darryl Strawberry	.75		.45
403	Jerry Royster	.05	.03	461	Craig McMurtry	.05		.03
404	Doug Sisk	.05	.03	462	Scott Fletcher	.05		.03
405	Brook Jacoby	.05	.03	463	Tom Candiotti	.10		.06
406	Yankees Leaders	.35	.20	464	Butch Wynegar	.05		.03
407	Jim Acker	.05	.03	465	Todd Worrell	.10		.06
408	John Mizerock	.05	.03	466	Kal Daniels (R)	.15		.10
409	Milt Thompson	.05	.03	467	Randy St. Claire	.05		.03

468	George Bamberger	.05	.03
469	Mike Diaz (R)	.05	.03
470	Dave Dravecky	.08	.05
471	Ronn Reynolds	.05	.03
472	Bill Doran	.08	.05
473	Steve Farr	.05	.03
474	Jerry Narron	.05	.03
475	Scott Garrelts	.08	.05
476	Danny Tartabull	.60	.35
477	Ken Howell	.05	.03
478	Tim Laudner	.05	.03
479	Bob Sebra	.05	.03
480	Jim Rice	.10	.06
481	Phillies Leaders	.07	.04
482	Daryl Boston	.05	.03
483	Dwight Lowry	.05	.03
484	Jim Traber	.05	.03
485	Tony Fernandez	.08	.05
486	Otis Nixon	.15	.10
487	Dave Gumpert	.05	.03
488	Ray Knight	.07	.04
489	Bill Gullickson	.07	.04
490	Dale Murphy	.20	.12
491	Ron Karkovice (R)	.08	.05
492	Mike Heath	.05	.03
493	Tom Lasorda	.08	.05
494	Barry Jones	.05	.03
495	Gorman Thomas	.07	.04
496	Bruce Bochte	.05	.03
497	Dale Mohorcic (R)	.07	.04
498	Bob Kearney	.05	.03
499	Bruce Ruffin	.05	.03
500	Don Mattingly	.70	.40
501	Craig Lefferts	.07	.04
502	Dick Schofield	.05	.03
503	Larry Andersen	.05	.03
504	Mickey Hatcher	.05	.03
505	Bryn Smith	.07	.04
506	Orioles Leaders	.08	.05
507	Dave Stapleton	.05	.03
508	Scott Bankhead	.05	.03
509	Enos Cabell	.05	.03
510	Tom Henke	.10	.06
511	Steve Lyons	.05	.03
512	Dave Magadan (R)	.20	.12
513	Carmen Castillo	.05	.03
514	Orlando Mercado	.05	.03
515	Willie Hernandez	.07	.04
516	Ted Simmons	.08	.05
517	Mario Soto	.05	.03
518	Gene Mauch	.05	.03
519	Curt Young	.05	.03
520	Jack Clark	.08	.05
521	Rick Reuschel	.05	.03
522	Checklist 397-528	.05	.03
523	Earnie Riles	.05	.03
524	Bob Shirley	.05	.03
525	Phil Bradley	.05	.03
526	Roger Mason	.05	.03
527	Jim Wohlford	.05	.03
528	Ken Dixon	.05	.03
529	Alvaro Espinoza (R)	.08	.05
530	Tony Gwynn	.60	.35
531	Astros Leaders	.12	.07
532	Jeff Stone	.05	.03
533	Argenis Salazar	.05	.03
534	Scott Sanderson	.05	.03
535	Tony Armas	.05	.03
536	Terry Mulholland (R)	.25	.15
537	Rance Mulliniks	.05	.03
538	Tom Niedenfuer	.05	.03
539	Reid Nichols	.05	.03
540	Terry Kennedy	.05	.03
541	Rafael Belliard (R)	.10	.06
542	Ricky Horton	.05	.03
543	Dave Johnson	.05	.03
544	Zane Smith	.10	.06
545	Buddy Bell	.05	.03
546	Mike Morgan	.08	.05
547	Rob Deer	.10	.06
548	Bill Mooneyham (R)	.05	.03
549	Bob Melvin	.05	.03
550	Pete Incaviglia	.15	.10
551	Frank Wills	.05	.03
552	Larry Sheets	.05	.03
553	Mike Maddux (R)	.07	.04
554	Buddy Biancalana	.05	.03
555	Dennis Rasmussen	.05	.03
556	Angels Leaders	.08	.05
557	John Cerutti	.05	.03
558	Greg Gagne	.07	.04
559	Lance McCullers	.05	.03
560	Glenn Davis	.10	.06
561	Rey Quinones	.05	.03
562	Bryan Clutterbuck (R)	.05	.03
563	John Stefero	.05	.03
564	Larry McWilliams	.05	.03
565	Dusty Baker	.07	.04
566	Tim Hulett	.05	.03
567	Greg Mathews	.05	.03
568	Earl Weaver	.08	.05
569	Wade Rowdon (R)	.05	.03
570	Sid Fernandez	.05	.03
571	Ozzie Virgil	.05	.03
572	Pete Ladd	.05	.03
573	Hal McRae	.08	.05
574	Manny Lee	.07	.04
575	Pat Tabler	.05	.03
576	Frank Pastore	.05	.03
577	Dann Bilardello	.05	.03
578	Billy Hatcher	.05	.03
579	Rick Burleson	.05	.03
580	Mike Krukow	.05	.03
581	Cubs Leaders	.07	.04
582	Bruce Berenyi	.05	.03
583	Junior Ortiz	.05	.03

584	Ron Kittle	.07	.04
585	Scott Bailes	.05	.03
586	Ben Oglivie	.05	.03
587	Eric Plunk	.08	.05
588	Wallace Johnson	.05	.03
589	Steve Crawford	.05	.03
590	Vince Coleman	.10	.06
591	Spike Owen	.05	.03
592	Chris Welsh	.05	.03
593	Chuck Tanner	.05	.03
594	Rick Anderson	.05	.03
595	Keith Hernandez AS	.08	.05
596	Steve Sax AS	.08	.05
597	Mike Schmidt AS	.35	.20
598	Ozzie Smith AS	.12	.07
599	Tony Gwynn AS	.20	.12
600	Dave Parker AS	.10	.06
601	Darryl Strawberry AS	.25	.15
602	Gary Carter AS	.10	.06
603a	Dwight Gooden AS (No trademark on front)	.40	.25
603b	Dwight Gooden AS (Cor)	.15	.10
604	Fernando Valenzuela AS	.08	.05
605	Todd Worrell As	.07	.04
606a	Don Mattingly AS (No. trademark on front)	.50	.30
606b	Don Mattingly AS	.15	.10
607	Tony Bernazard	.05	.03
608	Wade Boggs AS	.15	.10
609	Cal Ripken AS	.50	.30
610	Jim Rice AS	.08	.05
611	Kirby Puckett AS	.50	.30
612	George Bell AS	.10	.06
613	Lance Parrish AS	.08	.05
614	Rogers Clemens AS	.70	.40
615	Teddy Higuera AS	.08	.05
616	Dave Righetti AS	.08	.05
617	Al Nipper	.05	.03
618	Tom Kelly	.05	.03
619	Jerry Reed	.05	.03
620	Jose Canseco	3.50	2.50
621	Danny Cox	.05	.03
622	Glenn Braggs (R)	.10	.06
623	Kurt Stillwell	.07	.04
624	Tim Burke	.05	.03
625	Mookie Wilson	.08	.05
626	Joel Skinner	.05	.03
627	Ken Oberkfell	.05	.03
628	Bob Walk	.05	.03
629	Larry Parrish	.05	.03
630	John Candelaria	.05	.03
631	Tigers Leaders	.08	.05
632	Rob Woodward	.05	.03
633	Jose Uribe	.08	.05
634	Rafael Palmeiro (R)	1.25	.80
635	Ken Schrom	.05	.03
636	Darren Daulton	.35	.20
637	Bip Roberts	.30	.18
638	Rich Bordi	.05	.03
639	Gerald Perry	.05	.03
640	Mark Clear	.05	.03
641	Domingo Ramos	.05	.03
642	Al Pulido	.05	.03
643	Ron Shepherd	.05	.03
644	John Denny	.05	.03
645	Dwight Evans	.12	.07
646	Mike Mason	.05	.03
647	Tom Lawless	.05	.03
648	Barry Larkin (R)	1.75	1.00
649	Mickey Tettleton	.15	.10
650	Hubie Brooks	.08	.05
651	Benny Distefano	.05	.03
652	Terry Forster	.05	.03
653	Kevin Mitchell	.70	.40
654	Checklist 529-660	.05	.03
655	Jesse Barfield	.10	.06
656	Rangers Leaders	.07	.04
657	Tom Waddell	.05	.03
658	Robby Thompson	.20	.12
659	Aurelio Lopez	.05	.03
660	Bob Horner	.10	.06
661	Lou Whitaker	.10	.06
662	Frank DiPino	.05	.03
663	Cliff Johnson	.05	.03
664	Mike Marshall	.05	.03
665	Rod Scurry	.05	.03
666	Von Hayes	.07	.04
667	Ron Hassey	.05	.03
668	Juan Bonilla	.05	.03
669	Bud Black	.05	.03
670	Jose Cruz	.08	.05
671	Ray Soff	.05	.03
672	Chili Davis	.08	.05
673	Don Sutton	.12	.07
674	Bill Campbell	.05	.03
675	Ed Romero	.05	.03
676	Charlie Moore	.05	.03
677	Bob Grich	.07	.04
678	Carney Lansford	.08	.05
679	Kent Hrbek	.10	.06
680	Ryne Sandberg	1.25	.80
681	George Bell	.12	.07
682	Jerry Reuss	.05	.03
683	Gary Roenicke	.05	.03
684	Kent Tekulve	.05	.03
685	Jerry Hairston	.05	.03
686	Doyle Alexander	.05	.03
687	Alan Trammell	.20	.12
688	Juan Beniquez	.05	.03
689	Darrell Porter	.05	.03
690	Dane Iorg	.05	.03
691	Dave Parker	.10	.06
692	Frank White	.05	.03

693	Terry Puhl	.05	.03
694	Phil Niekro	.15	.10
695	Chico Walker	.05	.03
696	Gary Lucas	.05	.03
697	Ed Lynch	.05	.03
698	Ernie Whitt	.05	.03
699	Ken Landreaux	.05	.03
700	Dave Bergman	.05	.03
701	Willie Randolph	.08	.05
702	Greg Gross	.05	.03
703	Dave Schmidt	.05	.03
704	Jesse Orosco	.05	.03
705	Bruce Hurst	.08	.05
706	Rick Manning	.05	.03
707	Bob McClure	.05	.03
708	Scott McGregor	.05	.03
709	Dave Kingman	.08	.05
710	Gary Gaetti	.05	.03
711	Ken Griffey	.10	.06
712	Don Robinson	.05	.03
713	Tom Brookens	.05	.03
714	Dan Quisenberry	.07	.04
715	Bob Dernier	.05	.03
716	Rick Leach	.05	.03
717	Ed Vande Berg	.05	.03
718	Steve Carlton	.40	.25
719	Tom Hume	.05	.03
720	Richard Dotson	.05	.03
721	Tom Herr	.05	.03
722	Bob Knepper	.05	.03
723	Brett Butler	.15	.10
724	Greg Minton	.05	.03
725	George Hendrick	.07	.04
726	Frank Tanana	.07	.04
727	Mike Moore	.07	.04
728	Tippy Martinez	.05	.03
729	Tom Paciorek	.05	.03
730	Eric Show	.05	.03
731	Dave Concepcion	.12	.07
732	Manny Trillo	.05	.03
733	Bill Caudill	.05	.03
734	Bill Madlock	.10	.06
735	Rickey Henderson	.60	.35
736	Steve Bedrosian	.08	.05
737	Floyd Bannister	.05	.03
738	Jorge Orta	.05	.03
739	Chet Lemon	.05	.03
740	Rich Gedman	.05	.03
741	Paul Molitor	.20	.12
742	Andy McGaffigan	.05	.03
743	Dwayne Murphy	.05	.03
744	Roy Smalley	.05	.03
745	Glenn Hubbard	.05	.03
746	Bob Ojeda	.05	.03
747	Johnny Ray	.05	.03
748	Mike Flanagan	.07	.04
749	Ozzie Smith	.30	.18
750	Steve Trout	.05	.03
751	Garth Iorg	.05	.03
752	Dan Petry	.05	.03
753	Rick Honeycutt	.05	.03
754	Dave LaPoint	.05	.03
755	Luis Aguayo	.05	.03
756	Carlton Fisk	.40	.25
757	Nolan Ryan	2.00	1.25
758	Tony Bernazard	.05	.03
759	Joel Youngblood	.05	.03
760	Mike Witt	.05	.03
761	Greg Pryor	.05	.03
762	Gary Ward	.05	.03
763	Tim Flannery	.05	.03
764	Bill Buckner	.08	.05
765	Kirk Gibson	.08	.05
766	Don Aase	.05	.03
767	Ron Cey	.05	.03
768	Dennis Lamp	.05	.03
769	Steve Sax	.12	.07
770	Dave Winfield	.40	.25
771	Shane Rawley	.05	.03
772	Harold Baines	.08	.05
773	Robin Yount	.60	.35
774	Wayne Krenchicki	.05	.03
775	Joaquin Andujar	.07	.04
776	Tom Brunansky	.08	.05
777	Chris Chambliss	.07	.04
778	Jack Morris	.25	.15
779	Craig Reynolds	.05	.03
780	Andre Thornton	.05	.03
781	Atlee Hammaker	.05	.03
782	Brian Downing	.07	.04
783	Willie Wilson	.07	.04
784	Cal Ripken	1.75	1.00
785	Terry Francona	.05	.03
786	Jimy Williams	.05	.03
787	Alejandro Pena	.08	.05
788	Tim Stoddard	.05	.03
789	Dan Schatzeder	.05	.03
790	Julio Cruz	.05	.03
791	Lance Parrish	.12	.07
792	Checklist 661-792	.05	.03

1987 Topps Traded

This update set consists of 132-cards identical in design to those found in Topps regular 1987 edition. Cards measure 2-1/2" by 3-1/2" and card numbers are followed by the letter "T". The set features player's traded during the year and some up and coming rookie prospects not included in Topps regular set.

		MINT	NR/MT
Complete Set (132)		12.00	8.50
Commons		.05	.03
1T	Bill Almon	.05	.03
2T	Scott Bankhead	.05	.03
3T	Eric Bell (R)	.12	.07
4T	Juan Beniquez	.05	.03
5T	Juan Berenguer	.05	.03
6T	Greg Booker	.05	.03
7T	Thad Bosley	.05	.03
8T	Larry Bowa	.08	.05
9T	Greg Brock	.05	.03
10T	Bob Brower (R)	.05	.03
11T	Jerry Browne (R)	.12	.07
12T	Ralph Bryant (R)	.08	.05
13T	DeWayne Buice (R)	.05	.03
14T	Ellis Burks (R)	.50	.30
15T	Ivan Calderon	.12	.07
16T	Jeff Calhoun	.05	.03
17T	Casey Candaele	.05	.03
18T	John Cangelosi	.05	.03
19T	Steve Carlton	.50	.30
20T	Juan Castillo (R)	.05	.03
21T	Rick Cerone	.05	.03
22T	Ron Cey	.05	.03
23T	John Christensen	.08	.05
24T	Dave Cone (R)	3.00	2.00
25T	Chuck Crim (R)	.07	.04
26T	Storm Davis	.07	.04
27T	Andre Dawson	.35	.20
28T	Rick Dempsey	.05	.03
29T	Doug Drabek	.30	.18
30T	Mike Dunne	.08	.05
31T	Dennis Eckersley	.40	.25
32T	Lee Elia	.05	.03
33T	Brian Fisher	.05	.03
34T	Terry Francona	.05	.03
35T	Willie Fraser (R)	.07	.04
36T	Billy Gardner	.05	.03
37T	Ken Gerhart (R)	.07	.04
38T	Danny Gladden	.10	.06
39T	Jim Gott	.08	.04
40T	Cecilio Guante	.05	.03
41T	Albert Hall	.05	.03
42T	Terry Harper	.05	.03
43T	Mickey Hatcher	.05	.03
44T	Brad Havens	.05	.03
45T	Neal Heaton	.05	.03
46T	Mike Henneman (R)	.20	.12
47T	Donnie Hill	.05	.03
48T	Guy Hoffman	.05	.03
49T	Brian Holton (R)	.12	.07
50T	Charles Hudson	.05	.03
51T	Danny Jackson (R)	.25	.15
52T	Reggie Jackson	.50	.30
53T	Chris James (R)	.12	.07
54T	Dion James	.05	.03
55T	Stan Jefferson (R)	.08	.05
56T	Joe Johnson (R)	.07	.04
57T	Terry Kennedy	.05	.03
58T	Mike Kingery	.08	.05
59T	Ray Knight	.10	.06
60T	Gene Larkin (R)	.15	.10
61T	Mike LaValliere	.10	.06
62T	Jack Lazorko	.05	.03
63T	Terry Leach	.05	.03
64T	Tim Leary	.10	.06
65T	Jim Lindeman (R)	.10	.06
66T	Steve Lombardozzi (R)	.15	.10
67T	Bill Long (R)	.12	.07
68T	Barry Lyons (R)	.12	.07
69T	Shane Mack	.80	.50
70T	Greg Maddux (R)	3.00	2.00
71T	Bill Madlock	.12	.07
72T	Joe Magrane (R)	.12	.07
73T	Dave Martinez (R)	.15	.10
74T	Fred McGriff (R)	4.50	2.75
75T	Mark McLemore (R)	.12	.07
76T	Kevin McReynolds	.12	.07
77T	Dave Meads (R)	.10	.06
78T	Eddie Milner	.05	.03
79T	Greg Minton	.05	.03
80T	John Mitchell (R)	.08	.05
81T	Kevin Mitchell	.50	.30
82T	Charlie Moore	.05	.03
83T	Jeff Musselman (R)	.10	.06
84T	Gene Nelson	.05	.03

1988 Topps

This 792-card set features card fronts with large color photographs surrounded by a thin yellow line and a white border. Card backs are horizontal and printed in orange and black on a white card stock. Cards measure 2-1/2" by 3-1/2". Key subsets include Record Breakers, Turn Back The Clock, Team Leaders and All-Stars.

		MINT	NR/MT
Complete Set (792)		21.50	14.00
Commons		.05	.03

1	Vince Coleman (RB)	.10	.06
2	Don Mattingly (RB)	.15	.10
3	Mark McGwire (RB) (Er) (Spot behind left foot)	.50	.30
3b	Mark McGwire (RB) (Cor)	.25	.15
4a	Eddie Murray (RB) (Er) (No Record on front)	.35	.20
4b	Eddie Murray (RB) (Cor)	.15	.10
5	Joe & Phil Niekro (RB)	.12	.07
6	Nolan Ryan (RB)	.50	.30
7	Benito Santiago (RB)	.12	.07
8	Kevin Elster	.10	.06
9	Andy Hawkins	.05	.03
10	Ryne Sandberg	.75	.45
11	Mike Young	.05	.03
12	Bill Schroeder	.05	.03
13	Andres Thomas	.05	.03
14	Sparky Anderson	.07	.04
15	Chili Davis	.08	.05
16	Kirk McCaskill	.05	.03
17	Ron Oester	.05	.03
18a	Al Leiter (R) (Er)	.15	.10

85T	Graig Nettles	.12	.07
86T	Al Newman	.05	.03
87T	Reid Nichols	.05	.03
88T	Tom Niedenfuer	.05	.03
89T	Joe Niekro	.08	.05
90T	Tom Nieto	.05	.03
91T	Matt Nokes (R)	.25	.15
92T	Dickie Noles	.05	.03
93T	Pat Pacillo	.05	.03
94T	Lance Parrish	.15	.10
95T	Tony Pena	.12	.07
96T	Luis Polonia (R)	.35	.20
97T	Randy Ready	.05	.03
98T	Jeff Reardon	.35	.20
99T	Gary Redus	.05	.03
100T	Jeff Reed	.05	.03
101T	Rick Rhoden	.05	.03
102T	Cal Ripken, Sr.	.08	.05
103T	Wally Ritchie	.08	.05
104T	Jeff Robinson	.10	.06
105T	Gary Roenicke	.05	.03
106T	Jerry Royster	.05	.03
107T	Mark Salas	.05	.03
108T	Luis Salazar	.05	.03
109T	Benny Santiago (R)	.40	.25
110T	Dave Schmidt	.05	.03
111T	Kevin Seitzer (R)	.25	.15
112T	John Shelby	.05	.03
113T	Steve Shields (R)	.05	.03
114T	John Smiley (R)	.75	.45
115T	Chris Speier	.05	.03
116T	Mike Stanley (R)	.10	.06
117T	Terry Steinbach (R)	.35	.20
118T	Les Straker (R)	.08	.05
119T	Jim Sundberg	.05	.03
120T	Danny Tartabull	.25	.15
121T	Tom Trebelhorn	.05	.03
122T	Dave Valle	.12	.07
123T	Ed Vande Berg	.05	.03
124T	Andy Van Slyke	.25	.15
125T	Gary Ward	.05	.03
126T	Alan Wiggins	.05	.03
127T	Bill Wilkinson (R)	.07	.04
128T	Frank Williams	.05	.03
129T	Matt Williams (R)	2.00	1.25
130T	Jim Winn	.05	.03
131T	Matt Young	.05	.03
132T	Checklist 1T-132T	.05	.03

	(Wrong Photo)		
18b	Al Leiter (R) (Cor)	.08	.05
19	Mark Davidson (R)	.08	.05
20	Kevin Gross	.05	.03
21	Red Sox Leaders	.10	.06
22	Greg Swindell	.20	.12
23	Ken Landreaux	.05	.03
24	Jim Deshaies	.05	.03
25	Andres Galarraga	.10	.06
26	Mitch Williams	.10	.06
27	R.J. Reynolds	.05	.03
28	Jose Nunez (R)	.07	.04
29	Argenis Salazar	.05	.03
30	Sid Fernandez	.08	.05
31	Bruce Bochy	.05	.03
32	Mike Morgan	.05	.03
33	Rob Deer	.07	.04
34	Ricky Horton	.05	.03
35	Harold Baines	.08	.05
36	Jamie Moyer	.05	.03
37	Ed Romero	.05	.03
38	Jeff Calhoun	.05	.03
39	Gerald Perry	.05	.03
40	Orel Hershiser	.10	.06
41	Bob Melvin	.05	.03
42	Bill Landrum (R)	.08	.05
43	Dick Schofield	.05	.03
44	Lou Piniella	.08	.05
45	Kent Hrbek	.08	.05
46	Darnell Coles	.05	.03
47	Joaquin Andujar	.07	.04
48	Alan Ashby	.05	.03
49	Dave Clark	.05	.03
50	Hubie Brooks	.08	.05
51	Orioles Leaders	.35	.20
	(Eddie Murray		
	Cal Ripken)		
52	Don Robinson	.05	.03
53	Curt Wilkerson	.05	.03
54	Jim Clancy	.05	.03
55	Phil Bradley	.05	.03
56	Ed Hearn	.05	.03
57	Tim Crews (R)	.08	.05
58	Dave Magadan	.10	.06
59	Danny Cox	.05	.03
60	Ricky Henderson	.35	.20
61	Mark Knudson (R)	.08	.05
62	Jeff Hamilton	.05	.03
63	Jimmy Jones	.05	.03
64	Ken Caminiti (R)	.25	.15
65	Leon Durham	.05	.03
66	Shane Rawley	.05	.03
67	Ken Oberkfell	.05	.03
68	Dave Dravecky	.07	.04
69	Mike Hart (R)	.05	.03
70	Roger Clemens	.75	.45
71	Gary Pettis	.07	.04
72	Dennis Eckersley	.25	.15
73	Randy Bush	.05	.03
74	Tom Lasorda	.08	.05
75	Joe Carter	.30	.18
76	Denny Martinez	.10	.06
77	Tom O'Malley	.05	.03
78	Dan Petry	.05	.03
79	Ernie Whitt	.05	.03
80	Mark Langston	.12	.07
81	Reds Leaders	.05	.03
82	Darrel Akerfelds (R)	.05	.02
83	Jose Oquendo	.05	.03
84	Cecilio Guante	.05	.03
85	Howard Johnson	.10	.06
86	Ron Karkovice	.05	.03
87	Mike Mason	.05	.03
88	Earnie Riles	.05	.03
89	Gary Thurman (R)	.10	.06
90	Dale Murphy	.12	.07
91	Joey Cora (R)	.10	.06
92	Len Matuszek	.05	.03
93	Bob Sebra	.05	.03
94	Chuck Jackson	.05	.03
95	Lance Parrish	.08	.05
96	Todd Benzinger (R)	.10	.06
97	Scott Garrelts	.07	.04
98	Rene Gonzales (R)	.15	.10
99	Chuck Finley	.12	.07
100	Jack Clark	.08	.05
101	Allan Anderson	.05	.03
102	Barry Larkin	.25	.15
103	Curt Young	.05	.03
104	Dick Williams	.05	.03
105	Jesse Orosco	.05	.03
106	Jim Walewander (R)	.05	.03
107	Scott Bailes	.05	.03
108	Steve Lyons	.05	.03
109	Joel Skinner	.05	.03
110	Teddy Higuera	.07	.04
111	Expos Leaders	.07	.04
112	Les Lancaster (R)	.10	.06
113	Kelly Gruber	.12	.07
114	Jeff Russell	.08	.05
115	Johnny Ray	.05	.03
116	Jerry Don Gleaton	.05	.03
117	James Steels (R)	.05	.03
118	Bob Welch	.08	.05
119	Robbie Wine (R)	.05	.03
120	Kirby Puckett	.60	.35
121	Checklist 1-132	.05	.03
122	Tony Bernazard	.05	.03
123	Tom Candiotti	.07	.04
124	Ray Knight	.07	.04
125	Bruce Hurst	.08	.05
126	Steve Jeltz	.05	.03
127	Jim Gott	.05	.03
128	Johnny Grubb	.05	.03
129	Greg Minton	.05	.03
130	Buddy Bell	.05	.03

131	Don Schulze	.05	.03
132	Donnie Hill	.05	.03
133	Greg Mathews	.05	.03
134	Chuck Tanner	.05	.03
135	Dennis Rasmussen	.05	.03
136	Brian Dayett	.05	.03
137	Chris Bosio	.07	.04
138	Mitch Webster	.05	.03
139	Jerry Browne	.08	.05
140	Jesse Barfield	.08	.05
141	Royals Leaders	.25	.15
	(George Brett		
	Bret Saberhagen)		
142	Andy Van Slyke	.15	.10
143	Mickey Tettleton	.10	.06
144	Don Gordon (R)	.05	.03
145	Bill Madlock	.08	.05
146	Donell Nixon (R)	.10	.06
147	Bill Buckner	.07	.04
148	Carmelo Martinez	.05	.03
149	Ken Howell	.05	.03
150	Eric Davis	.15	.10
151	Bob Knepper	.05	.03
152	Jody Reed (R)	.20	.12
153	John Habyan	.05	.03
154	Jeff Stone	.05	.03
155	Bruce Sutter	.08	.05
156	Gary Matthews	.05	.03
157	Atlee Hammaker	.05	.03
158	Tim Hulett	.05	.03
159	Brad Arnsberg (R)	.05	.03
160	Willie McGee	.10	.06
161	Bryn Smith	.05	.03
162	Mark McLemore	.05	.03
163	Dale Mohorcic	.05	.03
164	Dave Johnson	.07	.04
165	Robin Yount	.40	.25
166	Rick Rodriquez (R)	.08	.05
167	Rance Mulliniks	.05	.03
168	Barry Jones	.05	.03
169	Ross Jones (R)	.05	.03
170	Rich Gossage	.08	.05
171	Cubs Leaders	.08	.05
172	Lloyd McClendon (R)	.08	.05
173	Eric Plunk	.05	.03
174	Phil Garner	.07	.04
175	Kevin Bass	.07	.04
176	Jeff Reed	.05	.03
177	Frank Tanana	.07	.04
178	Dwayne Henry	.05	.03
179	Charlie Puleo	.05	.03
180	Terry Kennedy	.05	.03
181	Dave Cone	.70	.40
182	Ken Phelps	.05	.03
183	Tom Lawless	.05	.03
184	Ivan Calderon	.10	.06
185	Rick Rhoden	.05	.03
186	Rafael Palmeiro	.25	.15
187	Steve Kiefer	.05	.03
188	John Russell	.05	.03
189	Wes Gardner (R)	.08	.05
190	Candy Maldonado	.08	.05
191	John Cerutti	.05	.03
192	Devon White	.10	.06
193	Brian Fisher	.05	.03
194	Tom Kelly	.05	.03
195	Dan Quisenberry	.05	.03
196	Dave Engle	.05	.03
197	Lance McCullers	.05	.03
198	Franklin Stubbs	.05	.03
199	Dave Meads	.05	.03
200	Wade Boggs	.25	.15
201	Rangers Leaders	.07	.04
202	Glenn Hoffman	.05	.03
203	Fred Toliver	.05	.03
204	Paul O'Neill	.15	.10
205	Nelson Liriano (R)	.10	.06
206	Domingo Ramos	.05	.03
207	John Mitchell	.05	.03
208	Steve Lake	.05	.03
209	Richard Dotson	.05	.03
210	Willie Randolph	.08	.05
211	Frank DiPino	.05	.03
212	Greg Brock	.05	.03
213	Albert Bell	.05	.03
214	Dave Schmidt	.05	.03
215	Von Hayes	.05	.03
216	Jerry Reuss	.05	.03
217	Harry Spilman	.05	.03
218	Dan Schatzeder	.05	.03
219	Mike Stanley	.05	.03
220	Tom Henke	.08	.05
221	Rafael Belliard	.05	.03
222	Steve Farr	.05	.03
223	Stan Jefferson	.05	.03
224	Tom Trebelhorn	.05	.03
225	Mike Scioscia	.07	.04
226	Dave Lopes	.05	.03
227	Ed Correa	.05	.03
228	Wallace Johnson	.05	.03
229	Jeff Musselman	.05	.03
230	Pat Tabler	.05	.03
231	Pirates Leaders	.25	.15
	(Barry Bobds		
	Bobby Bonilla)		
232	Bob James	.05	.03
233	Rafael Santana	.05	.03
234	Ken Dayley	.05	.03
235	Gary Ward	.05	.03
236	Ted Power	.05	.03
237	Mike Heath	.05	.03
238	Luis Polonia	.20	.12
239	Roy Smalley	.05	.03
240	Lee Smith	.20	.12
241	Damaso Garcia	.05	.03
242	Tom Niedenfuer	.05	.03

243	Mike Ryal	.05	.03	301	Bud Black	.08	.05
244	Jeff Robinson	.05	.03	302	Jose Uribe	.07	.04
245	Rich Gedman	.05	.03	303	Eric Show	.05	.03
246	Mike Campbell	.05	.03	304	George Hendrick	.05	.03
247	Thad Bosley	.05	.03	305	Steve Sax	.12	.07
248	Storm Davis	.05	.03	306	Billy Hatcher	.05	.03
249	Mike Marshall	.05	.03	307	Mike Trujillo	.05	.03
250	Nolan Ryan	1.00	.70	308	Lee Mazilli	.05	.03
251	Tom Foley	.05	.03	309	Bill Long	.05	.03
252	Bob Brower	.05	.03	310	Tom Herr	.05	.03
253	Checklist 133-264	.05	.03	311	Scott Sanderson	.05	.03
254	Lee Elia	.05	.03	312	Joey Meyer	.05	.03
255	Mookie Wilson	.08	.05	313	Bob McClure	.05	.03
256	Ken Schrom	.05	.03	314	Jimy Williams	.05	.03
257	Jerry Royster	.05	.03	315	Dave Parker	.08	.05
258	Ed Nunez	.05	.03	316	Jose Rijo	.10	.06
259	Ron Kittle	.05	.03	317	Tom Nieto	.05	.03
260	Vince Coleman	.10	.06	318	Mel Hall	.08	.05
261	Giants Leaders	.12	.07	319	Mike Loynd	.05	.03
262	Drew Hall	.05	.03	320	Alan Trammell	.15	.10
263	Glenn Braggs	.05	.03	321	White Sox Leaders	.10	.06
264	Les Straker	.05	.03	322	Vicente Palacios (R)	.08	.05
265	Bo Diaz	.05	.03	323	Rick Leach	.05	.03
266	Paul Assenmacher	.05	.03	324	Danny Jackson	.08	.05
267	Billy Bean (R)	.07	.04	325	Glenn Hubbard	.05	.03
268	Bruce Ruffin	.05	.03	326	Al Nipper	.05	.03
269	Ellis Burks	.25	.15	327	Larry Sheets	.05	.03
270	Mike Witt	.05	.03	328	Greg Cadaret (R)	.08	.05
271	Ken Gerhart	.05	.03	329	Chris Speier	.05	.03
272	Steve Ontiveros	.05	.03	330	Eddie Whitson	.05	.03
273	Garth Iorg	.05	.03	331	Brian Downing	.05	.03
274	Junior Ortiz	.05	.03	332	Jerry Reed	.05	.03
275	Kevin Seitzer	.10	.06	333	Wally Backman	.05	.03
276	Luis Salazar	.05	.03	334	Dave LaPoint	.05	.03
277	Alejandro Pena	.05	.03	335	Claudell Washington	.05	.03
278	Jose Cruz	.05	.03	336	Ed Lynch	.05	.03
279	Randy St. Claire	.05	.03	337	Jim Gantner	.05	.03
280	Pete Incaviglia	.08	.05	338	Brian Holton	.08	.05
281	Jerry Hairston	.05	.03	339	Kurt Stillwell	.07	.04
282	Pat Perry	.05	.03	340	Jack Morris	.15	.10
283	Phil Lombardi	.05	.03	341	Carmen Castillo	.05	.03
284	Larry Bowa	.05	.03	342	Larry Andersen	.05	.03
285	Jim Presley	.05	.03	343	Greg Gagne	.07	.04
286	Chuck Crim	.05	.03	344	Tony LaRussa	.08	.05
287	Manny Trillo	.05	.03	345	Scott Fletcher	.05	.03
288	Pat Pacillo	.05	.03	346	Vance Law	.05	.03
289	Dave Bergman	.05	.03	347	Joe Johnson	.05	.03
290	Tony Fernandez	.08	.05	348	Jim Eisenreich	.07	.04
291	Astros Leaders	.07	.04	349	Bob Walk	.05	.03
292	Carney Lansford	.07	.04	350	Will Clark	1.00	.70
293	Doug Jones (R)	.20	.12	351	Cardinals Leaders	.08	.05
294	Al Pedrique (R)	.07	.04	352	Billy Ripken (R)	.12	.07
295	Bert Blyleven	.12	.07	353	Ed Olwine	.05	.03
296	Floyd Rayford	.05	.03	354	Marc Sullivan	.05	.03
297	Zane Smith	.07	.04	355	Roger McDowell	.05	.03
298	Milt Thompson	.05	.03	356	Luis Aguayo	.05	.03
299	Steve Crawford	.05	.03	357	Floyd Bannister	.05	.03
300	Don Mattingly	.35	.20	358	Rey Quinones	.05	.03

359	Tim Stoddard	.05	.03	417	Mark Ciardi (R)	.05	.03
360	Tony Gwynn	.35	.20	418	Joel Youngblood	.05	.03
361	Greg Maddux	.75	.45	419	Scott McGregor	.05	.03
362	Juan Castillo	.05	.03	420	Wally Joyner	.15	.10
363	Willie Fraser	.05	.03	421	Ed Vande Berg	.05	.03
364	Nick Esasky	.05	.03	422	Dave Concepcion	.08	.05
365	Floyd Youmans	.05	.03	423	John Smiley	.50	.30
366	Chet Lemon	.05	.03	424	Dwayne Murphy	.05	.03
367	Tim Leary	.07	.04	425	Jeff Reardon	.20	.12
368	Gerald Young (R)	.10	.06	426	Randy Ready	.05	.03
369	Greg Harris	.05	.03	427	Paul Kilgus (R)	.08	.05
370	Jose Canseco	1.00	.70	428	John Shelby	.05	.03
371	Joe Hesketh	.05	.03	429	Tigers Leaders	.08	.05
372	Matt Williams	1.25	.80	430	Glenn Davis	.10	.06
373	Checklist 265-396	.05	.03	431	Casey Candaele	.05	.03
374	Doc Edwards	.05	.03	432	Mike Moore	.07	.04
375	Tom Brunansky	.08	.05	433	Bill Pecota	.08	.05
376	Bill Wilkinson	.05	.03	434	Rick Aguilera	.08	.05
377	Sam Horn	.12	.07	435	Mike Pagliarulo	.05	.03
378	Todd Frohwirth (R)	.07	.04	436	Mike Bielecki	.07	.04
379	Rafael Ramirez	.05	.03	437	Fred Manrique (R)	.07	.04
380	Joe Magrane	.10	.06	438	Rob Ducey (R)	.08	.05
381	Angels Leaders	.08	.05	439	Dave Martinez	.08	.05
382	Keith Miller (R)	.15	.10	440	Steve Bedrosian	.07	.04
383	Eric Bell	.05	.03	441	Rick Manning	.05	.03
384	Neil Allen	.05	.03	442	Tom Bolton (R)	.12	.07
385	Carlton Fisk	.25	.15	443	Ken Griffey	.08	.05
386	Don Mattingly AS	.15	.10	444	Cal Ripken Sr.	.08	.05
387	Willie Randolph AS	.08	.05	445	Mike Krukow	.05	.03
388	Wade Boggs AS	.12	.07	446	Doug DeCinces	.05	.03
389	Alan Trammell AS	.10	.06	447	Jeff Montgomery (R)	.35	.20
390	George Bell AS	.10	.06	448	Mike Davis	.05	.03
391	Kirby Puckett AS	.25	.15	449	Jeff Robinson	.05	.03
392	Dave Winfield AS	.20	.12	450	Barry Bonds	.60	.35
393	Matt Nokes AS	.08	.05	451	Keith Atherton	.05	.03
394	Roger Clemens AS	.30	.18	452	Willie Wilson	.07	.04
395	Jimmy Key AS	.08	.05	453	Dennis Powell	.05	.03
396	Tom Henke AS	.08	.05	454	Marvell Wynne	.05	.03
397	Jack Clark AS	.08	.05	455	Shawn Hillegas (R)	.12	.07
398	Juan Samuel AS	.07	.04	456	Dave Anderson	.05	.03
399	Tim Wallach AS	.08	.05	457	Terry Leach	.05	.03
400	Ozzie Smith AS	.12	.07	458	Ron Hassey	.05	.03
401	Andre Dawson AS	.15	.10	459	Yankees Leaders	.10	.06
402	Tony Gwynn AS	.15	.10	460	Ozzie Smith	.25	.15
403	Tim Raines AS	.08	.05	461	Danny Darwin	.05	.03
404	Benny Santiago AS	.08	.05	462	Don Slaught	.05	.03
405	Dwight Gooden AS	.12	.07	463	Fred McGriff	1.00	.70
406	Shane Rawley AS	.07	.04	464	Jay Tibbs	.05	.03
407	Steve Bedrosian AS	.07	.04	465	Paul Molitor	.15	.10
408	Dion James	.05	.03	466	Jerry Mumphrey	.05	.03
409	Joel McKeon	.05	.03	467	Dan Aase	.05	.03
410	Tony Pena	.07	.04	468	Darren Dalton	.15	.10
411	Wayne Tolleson	.05	.03	469	Jeff Dedmon	.05	.03
412	Randy Myers	.10	.06	470	Dwight Evans	.10	.06
413	John Christensen	.05	.03	471	Donnie Moore	.05	.03
414	John McNamara	.05	.03	472	Robby Thompson	.08	.05
415	Don Carman	.05	.03	473	Joe Niekro	.05	.03
416	Keith Moreland	.05	.03	474	Tom Brookens	.05	.03

475	Pete Rose	.20	.12
476	Dave Stewart	.10	.06
477	Jamie Quirk	.05	.03
478	Sid Bream	.05	.03
479	Brett Butler	.12	.07
480	Dwight Gooden	.15	.10
481	Mariano Duncan	.05	.03
482	Mark Davis	.07	.04
483	Rod Booker (R)	.05	.03
484	Pat Clements	.05	.03
485	Harold Reynolds	.07	.04
486	Pat Keedy (R)	.05	.03
487	Jim Pankovits	.05	.03
488	Andy McGaffigan	.05	.03
489	Dodgers Leaders	.07	.04
490	Larry Parrish	.05	.03
491	B.J. Surhoff	.07	.04
492	Doyle Alexander	.05	.03
493	Mike Greenwell	.12	.07
494	Wally Ritchie	.05	.03
495	Eddie Murray	.25	.15
496	Guy Hoffman	.05	.03
497	Kevin Mitchell	.12	.07
498	Bob Boone	.08	.05
499	Eric King	.05	.03
500	Andre Dawson	.25	.15
501	Tim Birtsas	.07	.04
502	Danny Gladden	.05	.03
503	Junior Noboa (R)	.08	.05
504	Bob Rodgers	.05	.03
505	Willie Upshaw	.05	.03
506	John Cangelosi	.05	.03
507	Mark Gubicza	.10	.06
508	Tim Teufel	.05	.03
509	Bill Dawley	.05	.03
510	Dave Winfield	.30	.20
511	Joel Davis	.05	.03
512	Alex Trevino	.05	.03
513	Tim Flannery	.05	.03
514	Pat Sherdian	.05	.03
515	Juan Nieves	.07	.04
516	Jim Sundberg	.05	.03
517	Ron Robinson	.05	.03
518	Greg Gross	.05	.03
519	Mariners Leaders	.07	.04
520	Dave Smith	.05	.03
521	Jim Dwyer	.05	.03
522	Bob Patterson (R)	.07	.04
523	Gary Roenicke	.05	.03
524	Gary Lucas	.05	.03
525	Marty Barrett	.07	.04
526	Juan Berenguer	.05	.03
527	Steve Henderson	.05	.03
528	Checklist 397-528	.05	.03
529	Tim Burke	.05	.03
530	Gary Carter	.12	.07
531	Rich Yett	.05	.03
532	Mike Kingery	.05	.03
533	John Farrell (R)	.08	.05
534	John Wathan	.05	.03
535	Ron Guidry	.10	.06
536	John Morris	.05	.03
537	Steve Buchele	.08	.05
538	Bill Wegman	.05	.03
539	Mike LaValliere	.07	.04
540	Bret Saberhagen	.15	.10
541	Juan Beniquez	.05	.03
542	Paul Noce (R)	.07	.04
543	Kent Tekulve	.05	.03
544	Jim Traber	.05	.03
545	Don Baylor	.08	.05
546	John Candelaria	.05	.03
547	Felix Fermin (R)	.07	.04
548	Shane Mack	.30	.18
549	Braves Leaders	.10	.06
550	Pedro Guerrero	.08	.05
551	Terry Steinbach	.08	.05
552	Mark Thurmond	.05	.03
553	Tracy Jones	.05	.03
554	Mike Smithson	.05	.03
555	Brook Jacoby	.05	.03
556	Stan Clarke	.05	.03
557	Craig Reynolds	.05	.03
558	Bob Ojeda	.05	.03
559	Ken Williams (R)	.07	.04
560	Tim Wallach	.10	.06
561	Rick Cerone	.05	.03
562	Jim Lindeman	.05	.03
563	Jose Guzman	.05	.03
564	Frank Lucchesi	.05	.03
565	Lloyd Moseby	.05	.03
566	Charlie O'Brien (R)	.08	.05
567	Mike Diaz	.05	.03
568	Chris Brown	.05	.03
569	Charlie Leibrandt	.05	.03
570	Jeffrey Leonard	.07	.04
571	Mark Williamson (R)	.10	.06
572	Chris James	.05	.03
573	Bob Stanley	.05	.03
574	Graig Nettles	.08	.05
575	Don Sutton	.12	.07
576	Tommy Hinzo (R)	.05	.03
577	Tom Browning	.08	.05
578	Gary Gaetti	.05	.03
579	Mets Leaders	.08	.05
580	Mark McGwire	.70	.40
581	Tito Landrum	.05	.03
582	Mike Henneman	.05	.03
583	Dave Valle	.05	.03
584	Steve Trout	.05	.03
585	Ozzie Guillen	.08	.05
586	Bob Forsch	.05	.03
587	Terry Puhl	.05	.03
588	Jeff Parrett (R)	.10	.06
589	Geno Petralli	.05	.03
590	George Bell	.12	.07

591	Doug Drabek	.15	.10
592	Dale Sveum	.07	.04
593	Bob Tewksbury	.10	.06
594	Bobby Valentine	.05	.03
595	Frank White	.07	.04
596	John Kruk	.15	.10
597	Gene Garber	.05	.03
598	Lee Lacy	.05	.03
599	Calvin Schiraldi	.05	.03
600	Mike Schmidt	.60	.35
601	Jack Lazorko	.05	.03
602	Mike Aldrete	.05	.03
603	Rob Murphy	.05	.03
604	Chris Bando	.05	.03
605	Kirk Gibson	.08	.05
606	Moose Haas	.05	.03
607	Mickey Hatcher	.05	.03
608	Charlie Kerfeld	.05	.03
609	Twins Leaders	.08	.05
610	Keith Hernandez	.08	.05
611	Tommy John	.08	.05
612	Curt Ford	.05	.03
613	Bobby Thigpen	.10	.06
614	Herm Winningham	.05	.03
615	Jody Davis	.05	.03
616	Jay Aldrich	.05	.03
617	Oddibe McDowell	.05	.03
618	Cecil Fielder	.40	.25
619	Mike Dunne	.05	.03
620	Cory Snyder	.07	.04
621	Gene Nelson	.05	.03
622	Kal Daniels	.07	.04
623	Mike Flanagan	.07	.04
624	Jim Leyland	.08	.05
625	Frank Viola	.08	.05
626	Glenn Wilson	.05	.03
627	Joe Boever (R)	.08	.05
628	Dave Henderson	.07	.04
629	Kelly Downs	.07	.04
630	Darrell Evans	.08	.05
631	Jack Howell	.05	.03
632	Steve Shields	.05	.03
633	Barry Lyons	.05	.03
634	Jose DeLeon	.05	.03
635	Terry Pendleton	.25	.15
636	Charles Hudson	.05	.03
637	Jay Bell (R)	.40	.25
638	Steve Balboni	.05	.03
639	Brewers Leaders	.07	.04
640	Garry Templeton	.07	.04
641	Rick Honeycutt	.05	.03
642	Bob Dernier	.05	.03
643	Rocky Childress (R)	.08	.05
644	Terry McGriff	.05	.03
645	Matt Nokes	.05	.03
646	Checklist 529-660	.05	.03
647	Pascual Perez	.05	.03
648	Al Newman	.05	.03
649	DeWayne Buice	.05	.03
650	Cal Ripken	.80	.50
651	Mike Jackson (R)	.12	.07
652	Bruce Benedict	.05	.03
653	Jeff Sellers	.05	.03
654	Roger Craig	.05	.03
655	Len Dykstra	.08	.05
656	Lee Guetterman	.05	.03
657	Gary Redus	.05	.03
658	Tim Conroy	.05	.03
659	Bobby Meacham	.05	.03
660	Rick Reuschel	.05	.03
661	Nolan Ryan (Clock)	.50	.30
662	Jim Rice (Clock)	.08	.05
663	Ron Blomberg (Clock)	.05	.03
664	Bob Gibson (Clock)	.15	.10
665	Stan Musial (Clock)	.15	.10
666	Mario Soto	.05	.03
667	Luis Quinones	.05	.03
668	Walt Terrell	.05	.03
669	Phillies Leaders	.07	.04
670	Dan Plesac	.07	.04
671	Tim Laudner	.05	.03
672	John Davis (R)	.07	.04
673	Tony Phillips	.07	.04
674	Mike Fitzgerald	.05	.03
675	Jim Rice	.08	.05
676	Ken Dixon	.05	.03
677	Eddie Milner	.05	.03
678	Jim Acker	.05	.03
679	Darrell Miller	.05	.03
680	Charlie Hough	.07	.04
681	Bobby Bonilla	.30	.18
682	Jimmy Key	.07	.04
683	Julio Franco	.10	.06
684	Hal Lanier	.05	.03
685	Ron Darling	.05	.03
686	Terry Francona	.05	.03
687	Mickey Brantley	.05	.03
688	Jim Winn	.05	.03
689	Tom Pagnozzi (R)	.25	.15
690	Jay Howell	.05	.03
691	Dan Pasqua	.05	.03
692	Mike Birkbeck	.05	.03
693	Benny Santiago	.15	.10
694	Eric Nolte (R)	.08	.05
695	Shawon Dunston	.12	.07
696	Duane Ward	.05	.03
697	Steve Lombardozzi	.07	.04
698	Brad Havens	.05	.03
699	Padres Leaders	.15	.10
700	George Brett	.35	.20
701	Sammy Stewart	.05	.03
702	Mike Gallego	.05	.03
703	Bob Brenly	.05	.03
704	Dennis Boyd	.05	.03
705	Juan Samuel	.05	.03

706	Rick Mahler	.05	.03
707	Fred Lynn	.07	.04
708	Gus Polidor	.05	.03
709	George Frazier	.05	.03
710	Darryl Strawberry	.35	.20
711	Bill Gullickson	.07	.04
712	John Moses	.05	.03
713	Willie Hernandez	.05	.03
714	Jim Fregosi	.05	.03
715	Todd Worrell	.07	.04
716	Lenn Sakata	.05	.03
717	Jay Baller	.05	.03
718	Mike Felder	.05	.03
719	Denny Walling	.05	.03
720	Tim Raines	.08	.05
721	Pete O'Brien	.07	.04
722	Manny Lee	.05	.03
723	Bob Kipper	.05	.03
724	Danny Tartabull	.20	.12
725	Mike Boddicker	.05	.03
726	Alfredo Griffin	.05	.03
727	Greg Booker	.05	.03
728	Andy Allanson	.05	.03
729	Blue Jays Leaders	.12	.07
730	John Franco	.05	.03
731	Rick Schu	.05	.03
732	Dave Palmer	.05	.03
733	Spike Owen	.05	.03
734	Craig Lefferts	.05	.03
735	Kevin McReynolds	.08	.05
736	Matt Young	.05	.03
737	Butch Wynegar	.05	.03
738	Scott Bankhead	.05	.03
739	Daryl Boston	.05	.03
740	Rick Sutcliffe	.08	.05
741	Mike Easler	.05	.03
742	Mark Clear	.05	.03
743	Larry Herndon	.05	.03
744	Whitey Herzog	.08	.05
745	Bill Doran	.05	.03
746	Gene Larkin	.10	.06
747	Bobby Witt	.12	.07
748	Reid Nichols	.05	.03
749	Mark Eichhorn	.05	.03
750	Bo Jackson	.30	.18
751	Jim Morrison	.05	.03
752	Mark Grant	.05	.03
753	Danny Heep	.05	.03
754	Mike LaCoss	.05	.03
755	Ozzie Virgil	.05	.03
756	Mike Maddux	.05	.03
757	John Marzano	.05	.03
758	Eddie Williams (R)	.05	.03
759	A's Leaders (Canseco, McGwire)	.35	.20
760	Mike Scott	.07	.04
761	Tony Armas	.05	.03
762	Scott Bradley	.05	.03

763	Doug Sisk	.05	.03
764	Greg Walker	.05	.03
765	Neal Heaton	.05	.03
766	Henry Cotto	.05	.03
767	Jose Lind (R)	.20	.12
768	Dickie Noles	.05	.03
769	Cecil Cooper	.07	.04
770	Lou Whitaker	.08	.05
771	Ruben Sierra	.60	.35
772	Sal Butera	.05	.03
773	Frank Williams	.05	.03
774	Gene Mauch	.05	.03
775	Dave Stieb	.10	.06
776	Checklist 661-792	.05	.03
777	Lonnie Smith	.07	.04
778a	Keith Comstock (White Team Letters)	2.50	1.50
778b	Keith Comstock (Blue Letters)	.05	.03
779	Tom Glavine (R)	4.00	2.75
780	Fernando Valenzuela	.08	.05
781	Keith Hughes (R)	.07	.04
782	Jeff Ballard (R)	.10	.06
783	Ron Roenicke	.05	.03
784	Joe Sambito	.05	.03
785	Alvin Davis	.05	.03
786	Joe Price	.05	.03
787	Bill Almon	.05	.03
788	Ray Searage	.05	.03
789	Indians Leaders	.12	.07
790	Dave Righetti	.08	.05
791	Ted Simmons	.08	.05
792	John Tudor	.08	.05

1988 Topps Traded

The cards in this 132-card set are identical to Topps regular 1988 edition. Measuring 2-1/2" by 3-1/2" the cards feature players traded during the season and up and coming rookie prospects. The set also includes members of the 1988 U.S. Olympic Team (USA). Players are listed in alphabetical order and card numbers carry the "T" designation.

		MINT	NR/MT
Complete Set (132)		36.50	26.00
Commons		.06	.03
1T	Jim Abbott (R)(USA)	5.50	3.50
2T	Juan Agosto	.06	.03
3T	Luis Alicea (R)	.15	.10
4T	Roberto Alomar (R)	8.00	5.00
5T	Brady Anderson (R)	2.00	1.25
6T	Jack Armstrong (R)	.15	.10
7T	Don August	.06	.03
8T	Floyd Bannister	.06	.03
9T	Bret Barberie (R) (USA)	.35	.20
10T	Jose Bautista (R)	.07	.04
11T	Don Baylor	.10	.06
12T	Tim Belcher	.15	.10
13T	Buddy Bell	.06	.03
14T	Andy Benes (R) (USA)	3.00	2.00
15T	Damon Berryhill (R)	.15	.10
16T	Bud Black	.06	.03
17T	Pat Borders (R)	.40	.25
18T	Phil Bradley	.06	.03
19T	Jeff Branson (R) (USA)	.15	.10
20T	Tom Brunansky	.10	.06
21T	Jay Buhner (R)	.60	.35
22T	Brett Butler	.12	.07
23T	Jim Campanis (R) (USA)	.25	.15
24T	Sil Campusano	.08	.05
25T	John Candelaria	.06	.03
26T	Jose Cecena (R)	.07	.04
27T	Rick Cerone	.06	.03
28T	Jack Clark	.08	.05
29T	Kevin Coffman (R)	.08	.05
30T	Pat Combs (R)(USA)	.25	.15
31T	Henry Cotto	.06	.03
32T	Chili Davis	.10	.06
33T	Mike Davis	.06	.03
34T	Jose DeLeon	.06	.03
35T	Richard Dotson	.06	.03
36T	Cecil Espy (R)	.15	.10
37T	Tom Filer	.06	.03
38T	Mike Fiore (R)(USA)	.10	.06
39T	Ron Gant (R)	3.00	2.00
40T	Kirk Gibson	.10	.06
41T	Rich Gossage	.12	.07
42T	Mark Grace (R)	2.50	1.50
43T	Alfredo Griffin	.06	.03
44T	Ty Griffin (R)(USA)	.10	.06
45T	Bryan Harvey (R)	.50	.30
46T	Ron Hassey	.06	.03
47T	Ray Hayward (R)	.06	.03
48T	Dave Henderson	.10	.06
49T	Tom Herr	.08	.05
50T	Bob Horner	.10	.06
51T	Ricky Horton	.06	.03
52T	Jay Howell	.06	.03
53T	Glenn Hubbard	.06	.03
54T	Jeff Innis (R)	.12	.07
55T	Danny Jackson	.08	.05
56T	Darrin Jackson (R)	.50	.30
57T	Roberto Kelly (R)	1.25	.80
58T	Ron Kittle	.08	.05
59T	Ray Knight	.08	.05
60T	Vance Law	.06	.03
61T	Jeffrey Leonard	.08	.05
62T	Mike Macfarlane (R)	.35	.20
63T	Scotti Madison (R)	.08	.05
64T	Kirt Manwaring (R)	.12	.07
65T	Mark Marquess (USA)	.06	.03
66T	Tino Martinez (R) (USA)	2.00	1.25
67T	Billy Masse (R)(USA)	.12	.07
68T	Jack McDowell (R)	3.50	2.50
69T	Jack McKeon	.06	.03
70T	Larry McWilliams	.06	.03
71T	Mickey Morandini (R) (USA)	.75	.45
72T	Keith Moreland	.06	.03
73T	Mike Morgan	.08	.05
74T	Charles Nagy (R) (USA)	3.50	2.50
75T	Al Nipper	.06	.03
76T	Russ Nixon	.06	.03
77T	Jesse Orosco	.06	.03

78T	Joe Orsulak	.06	.03
79T	Dave Palmer	.06	.03
80T	Mark Parent	.08	.05
81T	Dave Parker	.10	.06
82T	Dan Pasqua	.08	.05
83T	Melido Perez (R)	.60	.35
84T	Steve Peters (R)	.10	.06
85T	Dan Petry	.06	.03
86T	Gary Pettis	.06	.03
87T	Jeff Pico	.12	.07
88T	Jim Poole (R)(USA)	.10	.06
89T	Ted Power	.06	.03
90T	Rafael Ramirez	.06	.03
91T	Dennis Rasmussen	.06	.03
92T	Jose Rijo	.15	.10
93T	Earnie Riles	.06	.03
94T	Luis Rivera	.06	.03
95T	Doug Robbins (R) (USA)	.10	.06
96T	Frank Robinson	.10	.06
97T	Cookie Rojas	.06	.03
98T	Chris Sabo (R)	.75	.45
99T	Mark Salas	.06	.03
100T	Luis Salazar	.06	.03
101T	Rafael Santana	.06	.03
102T	Nelson Santovenia (R)	.10	.06
103T	Mackey Sasser (R)	.12	.07
104T	Calvin Schiraldi	.06	.03
105T	Mike Schooler (R)	.12	.07
106T	Scott Servais (R) (USA)	.20	.12
107T	Dave Silvestri (R) (USA)	.20	.12
108T	Don Slaught	.06	.03
109T	Joe Slusarski (R) (USA)	.25	.15
110T	Lee Smith	.25	.15
111T	Pete Smith (R)	.75	.45
112T	Jim Snyder	.06	.03
113T	Ed Sprague (R)(USA)	.50	.30
114T	Pete Stanicek (R)	.10	.06
115T	Kurt Stillwell	.08	.05
116T	Todd Stottlemyre (R)	.40	.25
117T	Bill Swift	.15	.10
118T	Pat Tabler	.06	.03
119T	Scott Terry	.06	.03
120T	Mickey Tettleton	.15	.10
121T	Dickie Thon	.06	.03
122T	Jeff Treadway	.06	.03
123T	Willie Upshaw	.06	.03
124T	Robin Ventura (R) (USA)	14.00	9.75
125T	Ron Washington	.06	.03
126T	Walt Weiss (R)	.20	.12
127T	Bob Welch	.12	.07
128T	David Wells (R)	.15	.10
129T	Glenn Wilson	.06	.03
130T	Ted Wood (R)(USA)	.25	.15
131T	Dom Zimmer	.06	.03
132T	Checklist 1T-132T	.06	.03

1989 Topps

This 792-card set features standard size cards measuring 2-1/2" by 3-1/2". Card fronts consist of full color photos with the players name listed in a banner below the photo. Card backs are horizontal and printed in light red and black. Key subsets include Record Breakers, All-Stars, Future Stars, Turn Back The Clock and First Round Draft Picks.

		MINT	NR/MT
Complete Set (792)		21.00	14.00
Commons		.05	.03

1	George Bell (RB)	.10	.06
2	Wade Boggs (RB)	.10	.06
3	Gary Carter (RB)	.08	.05
4	Andre Dawson (RB)	.10	.06
5	Orel Hershiser (RB)	.08	.05
6	Doug Jones (RB)	.05	.03
7	Kevin McReynolds (RB)	.07	.04
8	Dave Eiland (R)	.12	.07
9	Tim Teufel	.05	.03
10	Andre Dawson	.20	.12
11	Bruce Sutter	.08	.05
12	Dale Sveum	.05	.03
13	Doug Sisk	.05	.03
14	Tom Kelly	.05	.03
15	Robby Thompson	.08	.05
16	Ron Robinson	.05	.03
17	Brian Downing	.07	.04

18	Rick Rhoden	.05	.03
19	Greg Gagne	.05	.03
20	Steve Bedrosian	.07	.04
21	White Sox Leaders	.05	.03
22	Tim Crews	.05	.03
23	Mike Fitzgerald	.05	.03
24	Larry Andersen	.05	.03
25	Frank White	.05	.03
26	Dale Mohorcic	.05	.03
27	Orestes Destrade (R)	.10	.06
28	Mike Moore	.07	.04
29	Kelly Gruber	.08	.05
30	Dwight Gooden	.15	.10
31	Terry Francona	.05	.03
32	Dennis Rasmussen	.05	.03
33	B.J. Surhoff	.05	.03
34	Ken Williams	.05	.03
35	John Tudor	.05	.03
36	Mitch Webster	.05	.03
37	Bob Stanley	.05	.03
38	Paul Runge	.05	.03
39	Mike Maddux	.05	.03
40	Steve Sax	.08	.05
41	Terry Mulholland	.07	.04
42	Jim Eppard	.05	.03
43	Guillermo Hernandez	.05	.03
44	Jim Snyder	.05	.03
45	Kal Daniels	.07	.04
46	Mark Portugal	.05	.03
47	Carney Lansford	.08	.05
48	Tim Burke	.05	.03
49	Craig Biggio	.40	.25
50	George Bell	.12	.07
51	Angels Leaders	.05	.03
52	Bob Brenly	.05	.03
53	Reuben Sierra	.40	.25
54	Steve Trout	.05	.03
55	Julio Franco	.08	.05
56	Pat Tabler	.05	.03
57	Alejandro Pena	.07	.04
58	Lee Mazzilli	.05	.03
59	Mark Davis	.05	.03
60	Tom Brunansky	.07	.04
61	Neil Allen	.05	.03
62	Alfredo Griffin	.05	.03
63	Mark Clear	.05	.03
64	Alex Trevino	.05	.03
65	Rick Reuschel	.05	.03
66	Manny Trillo	.05	.03
67	Dave Palmer	.05	.03
68	Darrell Miller	.05	.03
69	Jeff Ballard	.05	.03
70	Mark McGwire	.50	.30
71	Mike Boddicker	.05	.03
72	John Moses	.05	.03
73	Pascual Perez	.05	.03
74	Nick Leyva	.05	.03
75	Tom Henke	.08	.05
76	Terry Blocker (R)	.08	.05
77	Doyle Alexander	.05	.03
78	Jim Sundberg	.05	.03
79	Scott Bankhead	.05	.03
80	Cory Snyder	.07	.04
81	Expos Leaders	.05	.03
82	Dave Leiper	.05	.03
83	Jeff Blauser	.08	.05
84	Bill Bene (#1 Pick)	.05	.03
85	Kevin McReynolds	.07	.04
86	Al Nipper	.05	.03
87	Larry Owen	.05	.03
88	Darryl Hamilton (R)	.20	.12
89	Dave LaPoint	.05	.03
90	Vince Coleman	.07	.04
91	Floyd Youmans	.05	.03
92	Jeff Kunkel	.05	.03
93	Ken Howell	.05	.03
94	Chris Speier	.05	.03
95	Gerald Young	.05	.03
96	Rick Cerone	.05	.03
97	Greg Mathews	.05	.03
98	Larry Sheets	.05	.03
99	Sherman Corbett (R)	.05	.03
100	Mike Schmidt	.50	.30
101	Les Straker	.05	.03
102	Mike Gallego	.05	.03
103	Tim Birtsas	.05	.03
104	Dallas Green	.05	.03
105	Ron Darling	.07	.04
106	Willie Upshaw	.05	.03
107	Jose DeLeon	.05	.03
108	Fred Manrique	.05	.03
109	Hipolito Pena (R)	.05	.03
110	Paul Molitor	.12	.07
111	Reds Leaders	.07	.04
112	Jim Presley	.05	.03
113	Lloyd Moseby	.05	.03
114	Bob Kipper	.05	.03
115	Jody Davis	.05	.03
116	Jeff Montgomery	.07	.04
117	Dave Anderson	.05	.03
118	Checklist 1-132	.05	.03
119	Terry Puhl	.05	.03
120	Frank Viola	.08	.05
121	Garry Templeton	.07	.04
122	Lance Johnson	.07	.04
123	Spike Owen	.05	.03
124	Jim Traber	.05	.03
125	Mike Krukow	.05	.03
126	Sid Bream	.05	.03
127	Walt Terrell	.05	.03
128	Milt Thompson	.05	.03
129	Terry Clark (R)	.07	.04
130	Gerald Perry	.05	.03
131	Dave Otto	.05	.03
132	Curt Ford	.05	.03
133	Bill Long	.05	.03

134	Don Zimmer	.05	.03
135	Jose Rijo	.12	.07
136	Joey Meyer	.05	.03
137	Geno Petralli	.05	.03
138	Wallace Johnson	.05	.03
139	Mike Flanagan	.07	.04
140	Shawon Dunston	.10	.06
141	Indians Leaders	.05	.03
142	Mike Diaz	.05	.03
143	Mike Campbell	.05	.03
144	Jay Bell	.08	.05
145	Dave Stewart	.10	.06
146	Gary Pettis	.05	.03
147	DeWayne Buice	.05	.03
148	Bill Pecota	.05	.03
149	Doug Dascenzo (R)	.10	.06
150	Fernando Valenzuela	.08	.05
151	Terry McGriff	.05	.03
152	Mark Thurmond	.05	.03
153	Jim Pankovits	.05	.03
154	Don Carman	.05	.03
155	Marty Barrett	.05	.03
156	Dave Gallagher (R)	.08	.05
157	Tom Glavine	.75	.45
158	Mike Aldrete	.05	.03
159	Pat Clements	.05	.03
160	Jeffrey Leonard	.07	.04
161	Gregg Olson (#1 Pick)	.35	.20
162	John Davis	.05	.03
163	Bob Forsch	.05	.03
164	Hal Lanier	.05	.03
165	Mike Dunne	.05	.03
166	Doug Jennings (R)	.08	.05
167	Steve Searcy (R)	.15	.10
168	Willie Wilson	.07	.04
169	Mike Jackson	.05	.03
170	Tony Fernandez	.08	.05
171	Braves Leaders	.05	.03
172	Frank Williams	.05	.03
173	Mel Hall	.08	.05
174	Todd Burns (R)	.12	.07
175	John Shelby	.05	.03
176	Jeff Parrett	.05	.03
177	Monty Fariss (#1 Pick)	.25	.15
178	Mark Grant	.05	.03
179	Ozzie Virgil	.05	.03
180	Mike Scott	.08	.05
181	Craig Worthington (R)	.07	.04
182	Bob McClure	.05	.03
183	Oddibe McDowell	.05	.03
184	John Costello	.05	.03
185	Claudell Washington	.05	.03
186	Pat Perry	.05	.03
187	Darren Daulton	.15	.10
188	Dennis Lamp	.05	.03
189	Kevin Mitchell	.12	.07
190	Mike Witt	.05	.03
191	Sil Campusano	.05	.03
192	Paul Mirabella	.05	.03
193	Sparky Anderson	.07	.04
194	Greg Harris (R)	.15	.10
195	Ozzie Guillen	.08	.05
196	Denny Walling	.05	.03
197	Neal Heaton	.05	.03
198	Danny Heep	.05	.03
199	Mike Schooler	.10	.06
200	George Brett	.30	.18
201	Blue Jays Leaders	.05	.03
202	Brad Moore (R)	.08	.05
203	Rob Ducey	.05	.03
204	Brad Havens	.05	.03
205	Dwight Evans	.12	.07
206	Roberto Alomar	1.00	.70
207	Terry Leach	.05	.03
208	Tom Pagnozzi	.08	.05
209	Jeff Bittiger (R)	.08	.05
210	Dale Murphy	.12	.07
211	Mike Pagliarulo	.05	.03
212	Scott Sanderson	.05	.03
213	Rene Gonzales	.08	.05
214	Charlie O'Brien	.05	.03
215	Kevin Gross	.05	.03
216	Jack Howell	.05	.03
217	Joe Price	.05	.03
218	Mike LaValliere	.05	.03
219	Jim Clancy	.05	.03
220	Gary Gaetti	.05	.03
221	Cecil Espy	.05	.03
222	Mark Lewis (#1 Pick)	.35	.20
223	Jay Buhner	.12	.07
224	Tony LaRussa	.07	.04
225	Ramon Martinez (R)	.50	.30
226	Bill Doran	.05	.03
227	John Farrell	.05	.03
228	Nelson Santovenia	.07	.04
229	Jimmy Key	.07	.04
230	Ozzie Smith	.20	.12
231	Padres Leaders	.15	.10
232	Ricky Horton	.05	.03
233	Gregg Jefferies (R)	.40	.25
234	Tom Browning	.08	.05
235	John Kruk	.08	.05
236	Charles Hudson	.05	.03
237	Glenn Hubbard	.05	.03
238	Eric King	.05	.03
239	Tim Laudner	.05	.03
240	Greg Maddux	.25	.15
241	Brett Butler	.10	.06
242	Ed Vande Berg	.05	.03
243	Bob Boone	.08	.05
244	Jim Acker	.05	.03
245	Jim Rice	.08	.05
246	Rey Quinones	.05	.03

No.	Player	Price	Price
247	Shawn Hillegas	.05	.03
248	Tony Phillips	.05	.03
249	Tim Leary	.05	.03
250	Cal Ripken	.70	.40
251	John Dopson (R)	.10	.06
252	Billy Hatcher	.05	.03
253	Jose Alvarez	.05	.03
254	Tom Lasorda	.07	.04
255	Ron Guidry	.08	.05
256	Benny Santiago	.10	.06
257	Rick Aguilera	.08	.05
258	Checklist 133-264	.05	.03
259	Larry McWilliams	.05	.03
260	Dave Winfield	.25	.15
261	Cardinals Leaders	.05	.03
262	Jeff Pico	.07	.04
263	Mike Felder	.05	.03
264	Rob Dibble (R)	.20	.12
265	Kent Hrbek	.08	.05
266	Luis Aquino	.05	.03
267	Jeff Robinson	.05	.03
268	Keith Miller	.05	.03
269	Tom Bolton	.05	.03
270	Wally Joyner	.12	.07
271	Jay Tibbs	.05	.03
272	Ron Hassey	.05	.03
273	Jose Lind	.07	.04
274	Mark Eichhorn	.05	.03
275	Danny Tartabull	.15	.10
276	Paul Kilgus	.05	.03
277	Mike Davis	.05	.03
278	Andy McGaffigan	.05	.03
279	Scott Bradley	.05	.03
280	Bob Knepper	.05	.03
281	Gary Redus	.05	.03
282	Cris Carpenter (R)	.15	.10
283	Andy Allanson	.05	.03
284	Jim Leyland	.07	.04
285	John Candelaria	.05	.03
286	Darrin Jackson	.12	.07
287	Juan Nieves	.05	.03
288	Pat Sheridan	.05	.03
289	Ernie Whitt	.05	.03
290	John Franco	.05	.03
291	Mets Leaders	.12	.07
292	Jim Corsi (R)	.08	.05
293	Glenn Wilson	.05	.03
294	Juan Berenguer	.07	.04
295	Scott Flethcer	.05	.03
296	Ron Gant	.75	.45
297	Oswald Peraza (R)	.08	.05
298	Chris James	.05	.03
299	Steve Ellsworth (R)	.08	.05
300	Darryl Strawberry	.25	.15
301	Charlie Liebrandt	.05	.03
302	Gary Ward	.05	.03
303	Felix Fermin	.05	.03
304	Joel Youngblood	.05	.03
305	Dave Smith	.05	.03
306	Tracy Woodson	.05	.03
307	Lance McCullers	.05	.03
308	Ron Karkovice	.05	.03
309	Mario Diaz	.07	.04
310	Rafael Palmeiro	.25	.15
311	Chris Bosio	.08	.05
312	Tom Lawless	.05	.03
313	Denny Martinez	.10	.06
314	Bobby Valentine	.05	.03
315	Greg Swindell	.10	.06
316	Walt Weiss	.10	.06
317	Jack Armstrong	.08	.05
318	Gene Larkin	.05	.03
319	Greg Booker	.05	.03
320	Lou Whitaker	.08	.05
321	Red Sox Leaders	.05	.03
322	John Smiley	.12	.07
323	Gary Thurman	.05	.03
324	Bob Milacki (R)	.10	.06
325	Jesse Barfield	.08	.05
326	Dennis Boyd	.05	.03
327	Mark Lemke (R)	.15	.10
328	Rick Honeycutt	.05	.03
329	Bob Melvin	.05	.03
330	Eric Davis	.12	.07
331	Curt Wilkerson	.05	.03
332	Tony Armas	.05	.03
333	Bob Ojeda	.05	.03
334	Steve Lyons	.05	.03
335	Dave Righetti	.07	.04
336	Steve Balboni	.05	.03
337	Calvin Schiraldi	.05	.03
338	Jim Adduci	.05	.03
339	Scott Bailes	.05	.03
340	Kirk Gibsosn	.08	.05
341	Jim Deshaies	.07	.04
342	Tom Brookens	.05	.03
343	Gary Sheffield	3.00	2.00
344	Tom Trebelhorn	.05	.03
345	Charlie Hough	.05	.03
346	Rex Hudler	.05	.03
347	John Cerutti	.05	.03
348	Ed Hearn	.05	.03
349	Ron Jones (R)	.08	.05
350	Andy Van Slyke	.15	.10
351	Giants Leaders	.05	.03
352	Rick Schu	.05	.03
353	Marvell Wynne	.05	.03
354	Larry Parrish	.05	.03
355	Mark Langston	.10	.06
356	Kevin Elster	.05	.03
357	Jerry Reuss	.05	.03
358	Ricky Jordan (R)	.15	.10
359	Tommy John	.08	.05
360	Ryne Sandberg	.50	.30
361	Kelly Downs	.05	.03
362	Jack Lazorko	.05	.03

363	Rich Yett	.05	.03
364	Rob Deer	.08	.05
365	Mike Henneman	.05	.03
366	Herm Winningham	.05	.03
367	Johnny Paredes (R)	.07	.04
368	Brian Holton	.05	.03
369	Ken Caminiti	.10	.06
370	Dennis Eckersley	.15	.10
371	Manny Lee	.05	.03
372	Craig Lefferts	.05	.03
373	Tracy Jones	.05	.03
374	John Wathan	.05	.03
375	Terry Pendleton	.20	.12
376	Steve Lombardozzi	.05	.03
377	Mike Smithson	.05	.03
378	Checklist 265-396	.05	.03
379	Tim Flannery	.05	.03
380	Rickey Henderson	.35	.20
381	Orioles Leaders	.05	.03
382	John Smoltz (R)	.80	.50
383	Howard Johnson	.12	.07
384	Mark Salas	.05	.03
385	Von Hayes	.05	.03
386	Andres Galarraga AS	.05	.03
387	Ryne Sandberg AS	.25	.15
388	Bobby Bonilla AS	.10	.06
389	Ozzie Smith AS	.12	.07
390	Darryl Strawberry AS	.15	.10
391	Andre Dawson AS	.12	.07
392	Andy Van Slyke AS	.08	.05
393	Gary Carter AS	.08	.05
394	Orel Hershiser AS	.08	.05
395	Danny Jackson AS	.05	.03
396	Kirk Gibson AS	.08	.05
397	Don Mattingly AS	.12	.07
398	Julio Franco AS	.08	.05
399	Wade Boggs AS	.10	.06
400	Alan Trammell AS	.08	.05
401	Jose Canseco AS	.25	.15
402	Mike Greenwell AS	.08	.05
403	Kirby Puckett AS	.15	.10
404	Bob Boone AS	.08	.05
405	Roger Clemens AS	.25	.15
406	Frank Viola AS	.08	.05
407	Dave Winfield AS	.12	.07
408	Greg Walker	.05	.03
409	Ken Dayley	.05	.03
410	Jack Clark	.07	.04
411	Mitch Williams	.05	.03
412	Barry Lyons	.05	.03
413	Mike Kingery	.05	.03
414	Jim Fregosi	.05	.03
415	Rich Gossage	.08	.05
416	Fred Lynn	.08	.05
417	Mike LaCoss	.05	.03
418	Bob Dernier	.05	.03
419	Tom Filer	.05	.03
420	Joe Carter	.20	.12
421	Kirk McCaskill	.05	.03
422	Bo Diaz	.05	.03
423	Brian Fisher	.05	.03
424	Luis Polonia	.08	.05
425	Jay Howell	.05	.03
426	Danny Gladden	.05	.03
427	Eric Show	.05	.03
428	Craig Reynolds	.05	.03
429	Twins Leaders	.05	.03
430	Mark Gubicza	.08	.05
431	Luis Rivera	.05	.03
432	Chat Kreuter (R)	.08	.05
433	Albert Hall	.05	.03
434	Ken Patterson (R)	.08	.05
435	Len Dykstra	.07	.04
436	Bobby Meacham	.05	.03
437	Andy Benes	.50	.30
438	Greg Gross	.05	.03
439	Frank DiPino	.05	.03
440	Bobby Bonilla	.20	.12
441	Jerry Reed	.05	.03
442	Jose Oquendo	.05	.03
443	Rod Nichols (R)	.10	.06
444	Moose Stubing	.05	.03
445	Matt Nokes	.07	.04
446	Rob Murphy	.05	.03
447	Donell Nixon	.05	.03
448	Eric Plunk	.05	.03
449	Carmelo Martinez	.05	.03
450	Roger Clemens	.60	.35
451	Mark Davidson	.05	.03
452	Israel Sanchez	.05	.03
453	Tom Prince	.05	.03
454	Paul Assenmacher	.05	.03
455	Johnny Ray	.05	.03
456	Tim Belcher	.08	.05
457	Mackey Sasser	.05	.03
458	Donn Paul (R)	.10	.06
459	Mariners Leaders	.05	.03
460	Dave Stieb	.08	.05
461	Buddy Bell	.05	.03
462	Jose Guzman	.05	.03
463	Steve Lake	.05	.03
464	Bryn Smith	.05	.03
465	Mark Grace	.50	.30
466	Chuck Crim	.05	.03
467	Jim Walewander	.05	.03
468	Henry Cotto	.05	.03
469	Jose Bautista	.05	.03
470	Lance Parrish	.07	.04
471	Steve Curry (R)	.08	.05
472	Brian Harper	.08	.05
473	Don Robinson	.05	.03
474	Bob Rodgers	.05	.03
475	Dave Parker	.08	.05
476	Jon Perlman	.05	.03
477	Dick Schofield	.05	.03
478	Doug Drabek	.12	.07

479	Mike MacFarlane	.15	.10
480	Keith Hernandez	.07	.04
481	Chris Brown	.05	.03
482	Steve Peters	.05	.03
483	Mickey Hatcher	.05	.03
484	Steve Shields	.05	.03
485	Hubie Brooks	.07	.04
486	Jack McDowell	.70	.40
487	Scott Lusader	.05	.03
488	Kevin Coffman	.05	.03
489	Phillies Leaders	.20	.12
490	Chris Sabo	.25	.15
491	Mike Birkbeck	.05	.03
492	Alan Ashby	.05	.03
493	Todd Benzinger	.05	.03
494	Shane Rawley	.05	.03
495	Candy Maldonado	.05	.03
496	Dwayne Henry	.05	.03
497	Pete Stanicek	.05	.03
498	Dave Valle	.05	.03
499	Don Heinkel (R)	.07	.04
500	Jose Canseco	.50	.30
501	Vance Law	.05	.03
502	Duane Ward	.05	.03
503	Al Newman	.05	.03
504	Bob Walk	.05	.03
505	Pete Rose	.15	.10
506	Kirt Manwaring	.05	.03
507	Steve Farr	.05	.03
508	Wally Backman	.05	.03
509	Bud Black	.05	.03
510	Bob Horner	.08	.05
511	Richard Dotson	.05	.03
512	Donnie Hill	.05	.03
513	Jesse Orosco	.05	.03
514	Chet Lemon	.05	.03
515	Barry Larkin	.20	.12
516	Eddie Whitson	.05	.03
517	Greg Brock	.05	.03
518	Bruce Ruffin	.05	.03
519	Yankees Leaders	.05	.03
520	Rick Sutcliffe	.07	.04
521	Mickey Tettleton	.08	.05
522	Randy Kramer (R)	.08	.05
523	Andres Thomas	.05	.03
524	Checklist 397-528	.05	.03
525	Chili Davis	.07	.04
526	Wes Gardner	.05	.03
527	Dave Henderson	.07	.04
528	Luis Medina (R)	.10	.06
529	Tom Foley	.05	.03
530	Nolan Ryan	.80	.50
531	Dave Hengel (R)	.07	.04
532	Jerry Browne	.07	.04
533	Andy Hawkins	.05	.03
534	Doc Edwards	.05	.03
535	Todd Worrell	.08	.05
536	Joel Skinner	.05	.03
537	Pete Smith	.20	.12
538	Juan Castillo	.05	.03
539	Barry Jones	.05	.03
540	Bo Jackson	.20	.12
541	Cecil Fielder	.30	.18
542	Todd Frohwirth	.05	.03
543	Damon Berryhill	.05	.03
544	Jeff Sellers	.05	.03
545	Mookie Wilson	.07	.04
546	Mark Williamson	.05	.03
547	Mark McLemore	.05	.03
548	Bobby Witt	.08	.05
549	Cubs Leaders	.05	.03
550	Orel Hershiser	.10	.06
551	Randy Ready	.05	.03
552	Greg Cadaret	.05	.03
553	Luis Salazar	.05	.03
554	Nick Esasky	.05	.03
555	Bert Blyleven	.08	.05
556	Bruce Fields	.05	.03
557	Keith Miller (R)	.08	.05
558	Dan Pasqua	.05	.03
559	Juan Agosto	.05	.03
560	Tim Raines	.08	.05
561	Luis Aguayo	.05	.03
562	Danny Cox	.05	.03
563	Bill Schroeder	.05	.03
564	Russ Nixon	.05	.03
565	Jeff Russell	.07	.04
566	Al Pedrique	.05	.03
567	David Wells	.08	.05
568	Mickey Brantley	.05	.03
569	German Jimenez (R)	.07	.04
570	Tony Gwynn	.25	.15
571	Billy Ripken	.05	.03
572	Atlee Hammaker	.05	.03
573	Jim Abbott (#1 Pick)	1.25	.80
574	Dave Clark	.05	.03
575	Juan Samuel	.05	.03
576	Greg Minton	.05	.03
577	Randy Bush	.05	.03
578	John Morris	.05	.03
579	Astros Leaders	.05	.03
580	Harold Reynolds	.05	.03
581	Gene Nelson	.05	.03
582	Mike Marshall	.05	.03
583	Paul Gibson (R)	.08	.05
584	Randy Velarde	.05	.03
585	Harold Baines	.08	.05
586	Joe Boever	.05	.03
587	Mike Stanley	.05	.03
588	Luis Alicea	.05	.03
589	Dave Meads	.05	.03
590	Andres Galarraga	.07	.04
591	Jeff Musselman	.05	.03
592	John Cangelosi	.05	.03
593	Drew Hall	.05	.03
594	Jimy Williams	.05	.03

595	Teddy Higuera	.07	.04
596	Kurt Stillwell	.05	.03
597	Terry Taylor (R)	.08	.05
598	Ken Gerhart	.05	.03
599	Tom Candiotti	.07	.04
600	Wade Boggs	.20	.12
601	Dave Dravecky	.05	.03
602	Devon White	.07	.04
603	Frank Tanana	.07	.04
604	Paul O'Neill	.12	.07
605a	Bob Welch	3.50	2.50
	(Missing Major		
	League Pitching		
	Record line)		
605b	Bob Welch (Cor)	.08	.05
606	Rick Dempsey	.05	.03
607	Willie Ansley (R)	.15	.10
	(#1 Pick)	.05	.03
608	Phil Bradley	.05	.03
609	Tigers Leaders	.05	.03
610	Randy Myers	.07	.04
611	Don Slaught	.05	.03
612	Dan Quisenberry	.05	.03
613	Gary Varsho (R)	.10	.06
614	Joe Hesketh	.05	.03
615	Robin Yount	.30	.18
616	Steve Rosenberg (R)	.07	.04
617	Mark Parent	.05	.03
618	Rance Mulliniks	.05	.03
619	Checklist 529-660	.05	.03
620	Barry Bonds	.45	.28
621	Rick Mahler	.05	.03
622	Stan Javier	.05	.03
623	Fred Toliver	.05	.03
624	Jack McKeon	.05	.03
625	Eddie Murray	.20	.12
626	Jeff Reed	.05	.03
627	Greg Harris	.05	.03
628	Matt Williams	.25	.15
629	Pete O'Brien	.05	.03
630	Mike Greenwell	.10	.06
631	Dave Bergman	.05	.03
632	Bryan Harvey	.15	.10
633	Daryl Boston	.05	.03
634	Marvin Freeman	.05	.03
635	Willie Randolph	.07	.04
636	Bill Wilkinson	.05	.03
637	Carmen Castillo	.05	.03
638	Floyd Bannister	.05	.03
639	Athletics Leaders	.05	.03
640	Willie McGee	.08	.05
641	Curt Young	.05	.03
642	Argenis Salazar	.05	.03
643	Louie Meadows (R)	.07	.04
644	Lloyd McClendon	.05	.03
645	Jack Morris	.15	.10
646	Kevin Bass	.07	.04
647	Randy Johnson (R)	.60	.35
648	Sandy Alomar Jr. (R)	.30	.18
649	Stewart Cliburn	.05	.03
650	Kirby Puckett	.40	.25
651	Tom Niedenfuer	.05	.03
652	Rich Gedman	.05	.03
653	Tommy Barrett (R)	.07	.04
654	Whitey Herzog	.07	.04
655	Dave Magadan	.08	.05
656	Ivan Calderon	.08	.05
657	Joe Magrane	.08	.05
658	R.J. Reynolds	.05	.03
659	Al Leiter	.05	.03
660	Will Clark	.50	.30
661	Dwight Gooden	.10	.06
	(Clock)		
662	Lou Brock (Clock)	.12	.07
663	Hank Aaron (Clock)	.15	.10
664	Gil Hodges (Clock)	.10	.06
665	Tony Oliva (Clock)	.10	.06
666	Randy St.Claire	.05	.03
667	Dwayne Murphy	.05	.03
668	Mike Bielecki	.07	.04
669	Dodgers Leaders	.08	.05
670	Kevin Seitzer	.12	.07
671	Jim Gantner	.05	.03
672	Allan Anderson	.05	.03
673	Don Baylor	.08	.05
674	Otis Nixon	.07	.04
675	Bruce Hurst	.07	.04
676	Ernie Riles	.05	.03
677	Dave Schmidt	.05	.03
678	Dion James	.05	.03
679	Willie Fraser	.05	.03
680	Gary Carter	.10	.06
681	Jeff Robinson	.05	.03
682	Rick Leach	.05	.03
683	Jose Cecena	.05	.03
684	Dave Johnson	.07	.04
685	Jeff Treadway	.05	.03
686	Scott Terry	.05	.03
687	Alvin Davis	.07	.04
688	Zane Smith	.07	.04
689	Stan Jefferson	.05	.03
690	Doug Jones	.07	.04
691	Roberto Kelly	.30	.18
692	Steve Ontiveros	.05	.03
693	Pat Borders	.15	.10
694	Les Lancaster	.05	.03
695	Carlton Fisk	.20	.12
696	Don August	.05	.03
697	Franklin Stubbs	.05	.03
698	Keith Atherton	.05	.03
699	Pirates Leaders	.05	.03
700	Don Mattingly	.25	.15
701	Storm Davis	.05	.03
702	Jamie Quirk	.05	.03
703	Scott Garrelts	.05	.03
704	Carlos Quintana (R)	.15	.10

705	Terry Kennedy	.05	.03
706	Pete Incaviglia	.07	.04
707	Steve Jeltz	.05	.03
708	Chuck Finley	.10	.06
709	Tom Herr	.05	.03
710	Dave Cone	.20	.12
711	Candy Sierra (R)	.07	.04
712	Bill Swift	.08	.05
713	Ty Griffin (#1 Pick)	.08	.05
714	Joe Morgan	.08	.05
715	Tony Pena	.05	.03
716	Wayne Tolleson	.05	.03
717	Jamie Moyer	.05	.03
718	Glenn Braggs	.05	.03
719	Danny Darwin	.05	.03
720	Tim Wallach	.08	.05
721	Ron Tingley (R)	.08	.05
722	Todd Stottlemyre	.15	.10
723	Rafael Belliard	.05	.03
724	Jerry Don Gleaton	.05	.03
725	Terry Steinbach	.08	.05
726	Dickie Thon	.05	.03
727	Joe Orsulak	.05	.03
728	Charlie Puleo	.05	.03
729	Rangers Leaders	.05	.03
730	Danny Jackson	.07	.04
731	Mike Young	.05	.03
732	Steve Buechele	.08	.05
733	Randy Bockus (R)	.07	.04
734	Jody Reed	.05	.03
735	Roger McDowell	.05	.03
736	Jeff Hamilton	.05	.03
737	Norm Charlton (R)	.25	.15
738	Darnell Coles	.05	.03
739	Brook Jacoby	.05	.03
740	Dan Plesac	.05	.03
741	Ken Phelps	.07	.04
742	Mike Harkey (R)	.20	.12
743	Mike Heath	.05	.03
744	Roger Craig	.05	.03
745	Fred McGriff	.40	.25
746	German Gonzalez (R)	.07	.04
747	Wil Tejada	.05	.03
748	Jimmy Jones	.05	.03
749	Rafael Ramirez	.05	.03
750	Bret Saberhagen	.12	.07
751	Ken Oberkfell	.05	.03
752	Jim Gott	.05	.03
753	Jose Uribe	.05	.03
754	Bob Brower	.05	.03
755	Mike Scioscia	.07	.04
756	Scott Medvin (R)	.08	.05
757	Brady Anderson	1.00	.70
758	Gene Walter	.05	.03
759	Brewers Leaders	.05	.03
760	Lee Smith	.12	.07
761	Dante Bichette (R)	.15	.10
762	Bobby Thigpen	.10	.06
763	Dave Martinez	.05	.03
764	Robin Ventura (#1 Pick)	1.50	.90
765	Glenn Davis	.07	.04
766	Cecilio Guante	.05	.03
767	Mike Capel (R)	.08	.05
768	Bill Wegman	.05	.03
769	Junior Ortiz	.05	.03
770	Alan Trammell	.12	.07
771	Ron Kittle	.07	.04
772	Ron Oester	.05	.03
773	Keith Moreland	.05	.03
774	Frank Robinson	.08	.05
775	Jeff Reardon	.12	.07
776	Nelson Liriano	.05	.03
777	Ted Power	.05	.03
778	Bruce Benedict	.05	.03
779	Craig McMurtry	.05	.03
780	Pedro Guerrero	.08	.05
781	Greg Briley (R)	.12	.07
782	Checklist 661-792	.05	.03
783	Trevor Wilson (R)	.15	.10
784	Steve Avery (#1 Pick)	1.75	1.00
785	Ellis Burks	.10	.06
786	Melido Perez	.07	.04
787	Dave West (R)	.12	.07
788	Mike Morgan	.07	.04
789	Royals Leaders (Bo Jackson)	.15	.10
790	Sid Fernandez	.07	.04
791	Jim Lindeman	.05	.03
792	Rafael Santana	.05	.03

1989 Topps Traded

This update set contains 132-cards that are identical to the 1989 Topps regular issue. The featured players include those traded to new teams since the beginning of the year and a number of promising rookies. Cards measure 2-1/2" by 3-1/2" and numbers carry the "T" designation to distinguish it from the regular set.

		MINT	NR/MT
	Complete Set (132)	10.00	7.00
	Commons	.05	.03
1T	Don Aase	.05	.03
2T	Jim Abbott	1.00	.70
3T	Kent Anderson (R)	.12	.07
4T	Keith Atherton	.05	.03
5T	Wally Backman	.05	.03
6T	Steve Balboni	.05	.03
7T	Jesse Barfield	.08	.05
8T	Steve Bedrosian	.07	.04
9T	Todd Benzinger	.07	.04
10T	Geronimo Berroa (R)	.10	.06
11T	Bert Blyleven	.15	.10
12T	Bob Boone	.10	.06
13T	Phil Bradley	.05	.03
14T	Jeff Brantley (R)	.15	.10
15T	Kevin Brown (R)	.20	.12
16T	Jerry Browne	.05	.03
17T	Chuck Cary	.05	.03
18T	Carmen Castillo	.05	.03
19T	Jim Clancy	.05	.03
20T	Jack Clark	.08	.05
21T	Bryan Clutterbuck	.05	.03
22T	Jody Davis	.05	.03
23T	Mike Devereaux (R)	.35	.20
24T	Frank DiPino	.05	.03
25T	Benny Distefano	.05	.03
26T	John Dopson	.08	.05
27T	Len Dykstra	.08	.05
28T	Jim Eisenreich	.05	.03
29T	Nick Esasky	.05	.03
30T	Alvaro Espinoza	.08	.05
31T	Darrell Evans	.08	.05
32T	Junior Felix (R)	.15	.10
33T	Felix Fermin	.05	.03
34T	Julio Franco	.15	.10
35T	Terry Francona	.05	.03
36T	Cito Gaston	.05	.03
37T	Bob Geren (R) (Wrong Photo)	.25	.15
38T	Tom Gordon (R)	.15	.10
39T	Tommy Gregg (R)	.08	.05
40T	Ken Griffey	.10	.06
41T	Ken Griffey, Jr. (R)	5.00	3.00
42T	Kevin Gross	.05	.03
43T	Lee Guetterman	.05	.03
44T	Mel Hall	.10	.06
45T	Erik Hanson (R)	.25	.15
46T	Gene Harris (R)	.12	.07
47T	Andy Hawkins	.05	.03
48T	Rickey Henderson	.35	.20
49T	Tom Herr	.05	.03
50T	Ken Hill (R)	.50	.30
51T	Brian Holman (R)	.12	.07
52T	Brian Holton	.07	.04
53T	Art Howe	.05	.03
54T	Ken Howell	.05	.03
55T	Bruce Hurst	.08	.05
56T	Chris James	.05	.03
57T	Randy Johnson	.35	.20
58T	Jimmy Jones	.05	.03
59T	Terry Kennedy	.05	.03
60T	Paul Kilgus	.05	.03
61T	Eric King	.05	.03
62T	Ron Kittle	.05	.03
63T	John Kruk	.10	.06
64T	Randy Kutcher (R)	.07	.04
65T	Steve Lake	.05	.03
66T	Mark Langston	.10	.06
67T	Dave LaPoint	.05	.03
68T	Rick Leach	.05	.03
69T	Terry Leach	.05	.03
70T	Jim Levebvre	.05	.03
71T	Al Leiter	.05	.03
72T	Jeffrey Leonard	.05	.03
73T	Derek Lilliquist (R)	.08	.05
74T	Rick Mahler	.05	.03
75T	Tom McCarthy (R)	.08	.05
76T	Lloyd McClendon	.07	.04
77T	Lance McCullers	.05	.03
78T	Oddibe McDowell	.05	.03
79T	Roger McDowell	.05	.03
80T	Larry McWilliams	.05	.03
81T	Randy Milligan	.08	.05
82T	Mike Moore	.08	.05
83T	Keith Moreland	.05	.03
84T	Mike Morgan	.08	.05
85T	Jamie Moyer	.05	.03

86T	Rob Murphy	.05	.03
87T	Eddie Murray	.15	.10
88T	Pete O'Brien	.05	.03
89T	Gregg Olson	.30	.18
90T	Steve Ontiveros	.05	.03
91T	Jesse Orosco	.05	.03
92T	Spike Owen	.05	.03
93T	Rafael Palmeiro	.25	.15
94T	Clay Parker (R)	.10	.06
95T	Jeff Parrett	.05	.03
96T	Lance Parrish	.08	.05
97T	Dennis Powell	.05	.03
98T	Rey Quinones	.05	.03
99T	Doug Rader	.05	.03
100T	Willie Randolph	.08	.05
101T	Shane Rawley	.05	.03
102T	Randy Ready	.05	.03
103T	Bip Roberts	.12	.07
104T	Kenny Rogers (R)	.15	.10
105T	Ed Romero	.05	.03
106T	Nolan Ryan	1.75	1.00
107T	Luis Salazar	.05	.03
108T	Juan Samuel	.05	.03
109T	Alex Sanchez (R)	.08	.05
110T	Deion Sanders (R)	1.75	1.00
111T	Steve Sax	.10	.06
112T	Rick Schu	.05	.03
113T	Dwight Smith (R)	.10	.06
114T	Lonnie Smith	.08	.05
115T	Billy Spiers	.05	.03
116T	Kent Tekulve	.05	.03
117T	Walt Terrell	.05	.03
118T	Milt Thompson	.05	.03
119T	Dickie Thon	.05	.03
120T	Jeff Torborg	.05	.03
121T	Jeff Treadway	.05	.03
122T	Omar Vizquel (R)	.10	.06
123T	Jerome Walton (R)	.10	.06
124T	Gary Ward	.05	.03
125T	Claudell Washington	.05	.03
126T	Curt Wilkerson	.05	.03
127T	Eddie Williams	.05	.03
128T	Frank Williams	.05	.03
129T	Ken Williams	.05	.03
130T	Mitch Williams	.10	.06
131T	Steve Wilson (R)	.10	.06
132T	Checklist	.05	.03

1990 Topps

The 1990 Topps set consists of 792 cards and features multi-colored borders surrounding full color player photos. Cards measure 2-1/2" by 3-1/2". The set contains a special salute to Nolan Ryan (2-5), Record Breakers (6-9), All-Stars (385-407), Number One Draft Picks and a Turn Back The Clock subset.

		MINT	NR/MT
Complete Set (792)		24.00	16.50
Commons		.05	.03
1	Nolan Ryan	.80	.50
2	Nolan Ryan (Mets)	.25	.15
3	Nolan Ryan (Angels)	.25	.15
4	Nolan Ryan (Astros)	.25	.15
5	Nolan Ryan (Rangers)	.25	.15
6	Vince Coleman (RB)	.07	.04
7	Rickey Henderson (RB)	.15	.10
8	Cal Ripken (RB)	.25	.15
9	Eric Plunk	.05	.03
10	Barry Larkin	.15	.10
11	Paul Gibson	.05	.03
12	Joe Girardi	.08	.05
13	Mark Williamson	.05	.03
14	Mike Fetters (R)	.10	.06
15	Teddy Higuera	.07	.04
16	Kent Anderson	.05	.03
17	Kelly Downs	.05	.03
18	Carlos Quintana	.10	.06
19	Al Newman	.05	.03
20	Mark Gubicza	.08	.05
21	Jeff Torborg	.05	.03
22	Bruce Ruffin	.05	.03
23	Randy Velarde	.05	.03
24	Joe Hesketh	.05	.03
25	Willie Randolph	.07	.04
26	Don Slaught	.05	.03

27	Rick Leach	.05	.03	83	Hensley Meulens	.10		.06
28	Duane Ward	.05	.03	84	Ray Searage	.05		.03
29	John Cangelosi	.05	.03	85	Juan Samuel	.05		.03
30	David Cone	.15	.10	86	Paul Kilgus	.05		.03
31	Henry Cotto	.05	.03	87	Rick Luecken (R)	.08		.05
32	John Farrell	.05	.03	88	Glenn Braggs	.05		.03
33	Greg Walker	.05	.03	89	Clint Zavaras (R)	.10		.06
34	Tony Fossas (R)	.10	.06	90	Jack Clark	.07		.04
35	Benito Santiago	.08	.05	91	Steve Frey	.05		.03
36	John Costello	.05	.03	92	Mike Stanley	.05		.03
37	Domingo Ramos	.05	.03	93	Shawn Hillegas	.05		.03
38	Wes Gardner	.05	.03	94	Herm Winningham	.05		.03
39	Curt Ford	.05	.03	95	Todd Worrell	.07		.04
40	Jay Howell	.05	.03	96	Jody Reed	.05		.03
41	Matt Williams	.15	.10	97	Curt Schilling	.08		.05
42	Jeff Robinson	.05	.03	98	Jose Gonzalez	.07		.04
43	Dante Bichette	.08	.05	99	Rich Monteleone (R)	.08		.05
44	Roger Salkeld (R) (#1 Pick)	.35	.20	100	Will Clark	.35		.20
45	Dave Parker	.08	.05	101	Shane Rawley	.05		.03
46	Rob Dibble	.08	.05	102	Stan Javier	.05		.03
47	Brian Harper	.07	.04	103	Marvin Freeman	.05		.03
48	Zane Smith	.07	.04	104	Bob Knepper	.05		.03
49	Tom Lawless	.05	.03	105	Randy Myers	.05		.03
50	Glenn Davis	.05	.03	106	Charlie O'Brien	.05		.03
51	Doug Rader	.05	.03	107	Fred Lynn	.07		.04
52	Jack Daugherty (R)	.12	.07	108	Rod Nichols	.05		.03
53	Mike LaCoss	.05	.03	109	Roberto Kelly	.15		.10
54	Joel Skinner	.05	.03	110	Tommy Helms	.05		.03
55	Darrell Evans	.07	.04	111	Ed Whited	.05		.03
56	Franklin Stubbs	.05	.03	112	Glenn Wilson	.05		.03
57	Greg Vaughn (R)	.25	.15	113	Manny Lee	.05		.03
58	Keith Miller	.05	.03	114	Mike Bielecki	.05		.03
59	Ted Power	.05	.03	115	Tony Pena	.05		.03
60	George Brett	.25	.15	116	Floyd Bannister	.05		.03
61	Deion Sanders	.40	.25	117	Mike Sharperson	.05		.03
62	Ramon Martinez	.15	.10	118	Erik Hanson	.10		.06
63	Mike Pagliarulo	.05	.03	119	Billy Hatcher	.05		.03
64	Danny Darwin	.05	.03	120	John Franco	.05		.03
65	Devon White	.07	.04	121	Robin Ventura	.90		.60
66	Greg Litton (R)	.10	.06	122	Shawn Abner	.05		.03
67	Scott Sanderson	.05	.03	123	Rich Gedman	.05		.03
68	Dave Henderson	.07	.04	124	Dave Dravecky	.05		.03
69	Todd Frohwirth	.05	.03	125	Kent Hrbek	.08		.05
70	Mike Greenwell	.08	.05	126	Randy Kramer	.05		.03
71	Allan Anderson	.05	.03	127	Mike Devereaux	.08		.05
72	Jeff Huson (R)	.10	.06	128	Checklist 1-132	.05		.03
73	Bob Milacki	.05	.03	129	Ron Jones	.05		.03
74	Jeff Jackson (R) (#1 Pick)	.12	.07	130	Bert Blyleven	.08		.05
				131	Matt Nokes	.07		.04
75	Doug Jones	.05	.03	132	Lance Blankenship	.05		.03
76	Dave Valle	.05	.03	133	Ricky Horton	.05		.03
77	Dave Bergman	.05	.03	134	Earl Cunningham (R) (#1 Pick)	.20		.12
78	Mike Flanagan	.05	.03					
79	Ron Kittle	.05	.03	135	Dave Magadan	.07		.04
80	Jeff Russell	.07	.04	136	Kevin Brown	.05		.03
81	Bob Rodgers	.05	.03	137	Marty Pevey (R)	.08		.05
82	Scott Terry	.05	.03	138	Al Leiter	.05		.03
				139	Greg Brock	.05		.03

140	Andre Dawson	.15	.10	197	Doug Drabek	.12	.07
141	John Hart	.05	.03	198	Mike Marshall	.05	.03
142	Jeff Wetherby (R)	.08	.05	199	Sergio Valdez (R)	.10	.06
143	Rafael Belliard	.05	.03	200	Don Mattingly	.20	.12
144	Bud Black	.07	.04	201	Cito Gaston	.05	.03
145	Terry Steinbach	.07	.04	202	Mike Macfarlane	.05	.03
146	Rob Richie (R)	.07	.04	203	Mike Roesler (R)	.08	.05
147	Chuck Finley	.08	.05	204	Bob Dernier	.05	.03
148	Edgar Martinez	.35	.20	205	Mark Davis	.05	.03
149	Steve Farr	.05	.03	206	Nick Esasky	.05	.03
150	Kirk Gibson	.07	.04	207	Bob Ojeda	.05	.03
151	Rick Mahler	.05	.03	208	Brook Jacoby	.05	.03
152	Lonnie Smith	.07	.04	209	Greg Mathews	.05	.03
153	Randy Milligan	.07	.04	210	Ryne Sandberg	.35	.20
154	Mike Maddux	.05	.03	211	John Cerutti	.05	.03
155	Ellis Burks	.08	.05	212	Joe Orsulak	.05	.03
156	Ken Patterson	.05	.03	213	Scott Bankhead	.05	.03
157	Craig Biggio	.10	.06	214	Terry Francona	.05	.03
158	Craig Lefferts	.05	.03	215	Kirk McCaskill	.05	.03
159	Mike Felder	.05	.03	216	Ricky Jordan	.07	.04
160	Dave Righetti	.07	.04	217	Don Robinson	.05	.03
161	Harold Reynolds	.05	.03	218	Wally Backman	.05	.03
162	Todd Zeile (R)	.25	.15	219	Donn Pall	.05	.03
163	Phil Bradley	.05	.03	220	Barry Bonds	.35	.20
164	Jeff Juden (R) (#1 Pick)	.25	.15	221	Gary Mielke (R)	.08	.05
				222	Kurt Stillwell	.05	.03
165	Walt Weiss	.05	.03	223	Tommy Gregg	.05	.03
166	Bobby Witt	.08	.05	224	Delino DeShields (R)	.80	.50
167	Kevin Appier (R)	.40	.25	225	Jim Deshaies	.05	.03
168	Jose Lind	.05	.03	226	Mickey Hatcher	.05	.03
169	Richard Dotson	.05	.03	227	Kevin Tapani (R)	.30	.18
170	George Bell	.10	.06	228	Dave Martinez	.05	.03
171	Russ Nixon	.05	.03	229	David Wells	.05	.03
172	Tom Lampkin	.05	.03	230	Keith Hernandez	.07	.04
173	Tim Belcher	.07	.04	231	Jack McKeon	.05	.03
174	Jeff Kunkel	.05	.03	232	Darnell Coles	.05	.03
175	Mike Moore	.05	.03	233	Ken Hill	.15	.10
176	Luis Quinones	.05	.03	234	Mariano Duncan	.05	.03
177	Mike Henneman	.05	.03	235	Jeff Reardon	.12	.07
178	Chris James	.05	.03	236	Hal Morris (R)	.25	.15
179	Brian Holton	.05	.03	237	Kevin Ritz (R)	.10	.06
180	Tim Raines	.08	.05	238	Felix Jose (R)	.25	.15
181	Juan Agosto	.05	.03	239	Eric Show	.05	.03
182	Mookie Wilson	.05	.03	240	Mark Grace	.15	.10
183	Steve Lake	.05	.03	241	Mike Krukow	.05	.03
184	Danny Cox	.05	.03	242	Fred Manrique	.05	.03
185	Ruben Sierra	.25	.15	243	Barry Jones	.05	.03
186	Dave LaPoint	.05	.03	244	Bill Schroeder	.05	.03
187	Rick Wrona (R)	.08	.05	245	Roger Clemens	.35	.20
188	Mike Smithson	.05	.03	246	Jim Eisenreich	.05	.03
189	Dick Schofield	.05	.03	247	Jerry Reed	.05	.03
190	Rick Reuschel	.05	.03	248	Dave Anderson	.05	.03
191	Pat Borders	.05	.03	249	Mike Smith (R)	.08	.05
192	Don August	.05	.03	250	Jose Canseco	.45	.28
193	Andy Benes	.20	.12	251	Jeff Blauser	.05	.03
194	Glenallen Hill	.10	.06	252	Otis Nixon	.07	.04
195	Tim Burke	.05	.03	253	Mark Portugal	.05	.03
196	Gerald Young	.05	.03	254	Francisco Cabrera	.12	.07

#	Player	Price 1	Price 2
255	Bobby Thigpen	.08	.05
256	Marvell Wynne	.05	.03
257	Jose DeLeon	.05	.03
258	Barry Lyons	.05	.03
259	Lance McCullers	.05	.03
260	Eric Davis	.10	.06
261	Whitey Herzog	.07	.04
262	Checklist 133-264	.05	.03
263	Mel Stottlemyre Jr (R)	.08	.05
264	Bryan Clutterbuck	.05	.03
265	Pete O'Brien	.05	.03
266	German Gonzalez	.05	.03
267	Mark Davidson	.05	.03
268	Rob Murphy	.05	.03
269	Dickie Thon	.05	.03
270	Dave Stewart	.10	.06
271	Chet Lemon	.05	.03
272	Bryan Harvey	.10	.06
273	Bobby Bonilla	.15	.10
274	Mauro Gozzo (R)	.10	.06
275	Mickey Tettleton	.08	.05
276	Gary Thurman	.05	.03
277	Lenny Harris	.05	.03
278	Pascual Perez	.05	.03
279	Steve Buechele	.07	.04
280	Lou Whitaker	.07	.04
281	Kevin Bass	.05	.03
282	Derek Lilliquist	.05	.03
283	Joey Belle (R)	.80	.50
284	Mark Gardner (R)	.20	.12
295	Willie McGee	.08	.05
286	Lee Guetterman	.05	.03
287	Vance Law	.05	.03
288	Greg Briley	.05	.03
289	Norm Charlton	.08	.05
290	Robin Yount	.25	.15
291	Dave Johnson	.05	.03
292	Jim Gott	.05	.03
293	Mike Gallego	.05	.03
294	Craig McMurtry	.05	.03
295	Fred McGriff	.30	.18
296	Jeff Ballard	.05	.03
297	Tom Herr	.05	.03
298	Danny Gladden	.05	.03
299	Adam Peterson	.05	.03
300	Bo Jackson	.20	.12
301	Don Aase	.05	.03
302	Marcus Lawton (R)	.12	.07
303	Rick Cerone	.05	.03
304	Marty Clary	.05	.03
305	Eddie Murray	.12	.07
306	Tom Niedenfuer	.05	.03
307	Bip Roberts	.08	.05
308	Jose Guzman	.05	.03
309	Eric Yelding (R)	.10	.06
310	Steve Bedrosian	.07	.04
311	Dwight Smith	.07	.04
312	Dan Quisenberry	.05	.03
313	Gus Polidor	.05	.03
314	Donald Harris (R) (#1 Pick)	.12	.07
315	Bruce Hurst	.07	.04
316	Carney Lansford	.07	.04
317	Mark Guthrie (R)	.10	.06
318	Wallace Johnson	.05	.03
319	Dion James	.05	.03
320	Dave Steib	.08	.05
321	Joe Morgan	.08	.05
322	Junior Ortiz	.05	.03
323	Willie Wilson	.05	.03
324	Pete Harnisch (R)	.12	.07
325	Robby Thompson	.07	.04
326	Tom McCarthy	.05	.03
327	Ken Williams	.05	.03
328	Curt Young	.05	.03
329	Oddibe McDowell	.05	.03
330	Ron Darling	.07	.04
331	Juan Gonzalez (R)	2.50	1.50
332	Paul O'Neill	.10	.06
333	Bill Wegman	.05	.03
334	Johnny Ray	.05	.03
335	Andy Hawkins	.05	.03
336	Ken Griffey, Jr.	1.50	.90
337	Lloyd McClendon	.05	.03
338	Dennis Lamp	.05	.03
339	Dave Clark	.05	.03
340	Fernando Valenzuela	.08	.05
341	Tom Foley	.05	.03
342	Alex Trevino	.05	.03
343	Frank Tanana	.05	.03
344	George Canale (R)	.10	.06
345	Harold Baines	.08	.05
346	Jim Presley	.05	.03
347	Junior Felix	.07	.04
348	Gary Wayne (R)	.10	.06
349	Steve Finley (R)	.12	.07
350	Bret Saberhagen	.12	.07
351	Roger Craig	.05	.03
352	Bryn Smith	.05	.03
353	Sandy Alomar	.12	.07
354	Stan Belinda (R)	.12	.07
355	Marty Barrett	.05	.03
356	Randy Ready	.05	.03
357	Dave West	.05	.03
358	Andres Thomas	.05	.03
359	Jimmy Jones	.05	.03
360	Paul Molitor	.12	.07
361	Randy McCament (R)	.07	.04
362	Damon Berryhill	.05	.03
363	Dan Petry	.05	.03
364	Rolando Roomes	.07	.04
365	Ozzie Guillen	.07	.04
366	Mike Heath	.05	.03
367	Mike Morgan	.05	.03
368	Bill Doran	.05	.03

369	Todd Burns	.05	.03
370	Tim Wallach	.08	.05
371	Jimmy Key	.07	.04
372	Terry Kennedy	.05	.03
373	Alvin Davis	.05	.03
374	Steve Cummings (R)	.10	.06
375	Dwight Evans	.08	.05
376	Checklist 265-396	.05	.03
377	Mickey Weston (R)	.08	.05
378	Luis Salazar	.05	.03
379	Steve Rosenberg	.05	.03
380	Dave Winfield	.20	.12
381	Frank Robinson	.08	.05
382	Jeff Musselman	.05	.03
383	John Morris	.05	.03
384	Pat Combs	.12	.07
385	Fred McGriff AS	.15	.10
386	Julio Franco AS	.07	.04
387	Wade Boggs AS	.08	.05
388	Cal Ripken AS	.20	.12
389	Robin Yount AS	.15	.10
390	Ruben Sierra AS	.12	.07
391	Kirby Puckett AS	.15	.10
392	Carlton Fisk AS	.10	.06
393	Bret Saberhagen AS	.08	.05
394	Jeff Ballard AS	.05	.03
395	Jeff Russell AS	.05	.03
396	A. Bartlett Giamatti	.10	.06
397	Will Clark AS	.15	.10
398	Ryne Sandberg AS	.15	.10
399	Howard Johnson AS	.08	.05
400	Ozzie Smith AS	.10	.06
401	Kevin Mitchell AS	.08	.05
402	Eric Davis AS	.08	.05
403	Tony Gwynn AS	.10	.06
404	Craig Biggio AS	.07	.04
405	Mike Scott AS	.05	.03
406	Joe Magrane AS	.05	.03
407	Mark Davis AS	.05	.03
408	Trevor Wilson	.05	.03
409	Tom Brunansky	.07	.04
410	Joe Boever	.05	.03
411	Ken Phelps	.05	.03
412	Jamie Moyer	.05	.03
413	Brian DuBois (R)	.08	.05
414	Frank Thomas (R) (#1 Pick)	4.00	3.00
415	Shawon Dunston	.10	.06
416	Dave Johnson (R)	.08	.05
417	Jim Gantner	.05	.03
418	Tom Browning	.07	.04
419	Beau Allred (R)	.12	.07
420	Carlton Fisk	.12	.07
421	Greg Minton	.05	.03
422	Pat Sheridan	.05	.03
423	Fred Oliver	.05	.03
424	Jerry Reuss	.05	.03
425	Bill Landrum	.05	.03
426	Jeff Hamilton	.05	.03
427	Carmen Castillo	.05	.03
428	Steve Davis (R)	.08	.05
429	Tom Kelly	.05	.03
430	Pete Incaviglia	.07	.04
431	Randy Johnson	.25	.15
432	Damaso Garcia	.05	.03
433	Steve Olin (R)	.15	.10
434	Mark Carreon	.05	.03
435	Kevin Seitzer	.08	.05
436	Mel Hall	.07	.04
437	Les Lancaster	.05	.03
438	Greg Myers	.05	.03
439	Jeff Parrett	.05	.03
440	Alan Trammell	.10	.06
441	Bob Kipper	.05	.03
442	Jerry Browne	.07	.04
443	Cris Carpenter	.08	.05
444	Kyle Abbott (R) (#1 Pick)	.20	.12
445	Danny Jackson	.05	.03
446	Dan Pasqua	.05	.03
447	Atlee Hammaker	.05	.03
448	Greg Gagne	.05	.03
449	Dennis Rasmussen	.05	.03
450	Rickey Henderson	.25	.15
451	Mark Lemke	.07	.04
452	Luis de los Santos (R)	.07	.04
453	Jody Davis	.05	.03
454	Jeff King (R)	.12	.07
455	Jeffrey Leonard	.05	.03
456	Chris Gwynn	.05	.03
457	Gregg Jefferies	.12	.07
458	Bob McClure	.05	.03
459	Jim Lefebvre	.05	.03
460	Mike Scott	.07	.04
461	Carlos Martinez (R)	.08	.05
462	Denny Walling	.05	.03
463	Drew Hall	.05	.03
464	Jerome Walton	.10	.06
465	Kevin Gross	.05	.03
466	Rance Mulliniks	.05	.03
467	Juan Nieves	.05	.03
468	Billy Ripken	.05	.03
469	John Kruk	.08	.05
470	Frank Viola	.08	.05
471	Mike Brumley	.05	.03
472	Jose Uribe	.05	.03
473	Joe Price	.05	.03
474	Rich Thompson	.05	.03
475	Bob Welch	.08	.05
476	Brad Komminsk	.05	.03
477	Willie Fraser	.05	.03
478	Mike LaValliere	.05	.03
479	Frank White	.05	.03
480	Sid Fernandez	.07	.04
481	Garry Templeton	.07	.04

482	Steve Carter	.05	.03	540	Danny Tartabull	.12	.07
483	Alejandro Pena	.07	.04	541	Pat Perry	.05	.03
484	Mike Fitzgerald	.05	.03	542	Darren Daulton	.12	.07
485	John Candelaria	.05	.03	543	Nelson Liriano	.05	.03
486	Jeff Treadway	.05	.03	544	Dennis Boyd	.05	.03
487	Steve Searcy	.05	.03	545	Kevin McReynolds	.07	.04
488	Ken Oberkfell	.05	.03	546	Kevin Hickey	.05	.03
489	Nick Leyva	.05	.03	547	Jack Howell	.05	.03
490	Dan Plesac	.05	.03	548	Pat Clements	.05	.03
491	Dave Cochrane (R)	.10	.06	549	Don Zimmer	.05	.03
492	Ron Oester	.05	.03	550	Julio Franco	.08	.05
493	Jason Grimsley (R)	.12	.07	551	Tim Crews	.05	.03
494	Terry Puhl	.05	.03	552	Mike Smith	.05	.03
495	Lee Smith	.10	.06	553	Scott Scudder (R)	.12	.07
496	Cecil Espy	.05	.03	554	Jay Buhner	.08	.05
497	Dave Schmidt	.05	.03	555	Jack Morris	.12	.07
498	Rick Schu	.05	.03	556	Gene Larkin	.05	.03
499	Bill Long	.05	.03	557	Jeff Innis	.10	.06
500	Kevin Mitchell	.10	.06	558	Rafael Ramirez	.05	.03
501	Matt Young	.05	.03	559	Andy McGaffigan	.05	.03
502	Mitch Webster	.05	.03	560	Steve Sax	.08	.05
503	Randy St. Claire	.05	.03	561	Ken Dayley	.05	.03
504	Tom O'Malley	.05	.03	562	Chad Kreuter	.05	.03
505	Kelly Gruber	.08	.05	563	Alex Sanchez	.05	.03
506	Tom Glavine	.40	.25	564	Tyler Houston (R)	.12	.07
507	Gary Redus	.05	.03		(#1 Pick)		
508	Terry Leach	.05	.03	565	Scott Fletcher	.05	.03
509	Tom Pagnozzi	.08	.05	566	Mark Knudson	.05	.03
510	Dwight Gooden	.12	.07	567	Ron Gant	.30	.18
511	Clay Parker	.05	.03	568	John Smiley	.10	.06
512	Gary Pettis	.05	.03	569	Ivan Calderon	.08	.05
513	Mark Eichhorn	.05	.03	570	Cal Ripken	.50	.30
514	Andy Allanson	.05	.03	571	Brett Butler	.08	.05
515	Len Dykstra	.07	.04	572	Greg Harris	.05	.03
516	Tim Leary	.05	.03	573	Danny Heep	.05	.03
517	Roberto Alomar	.50	.30	574	Bill Swift	.07	.04
518	Bill Krueger	.05	.03	575	Lance Parrish	.07	.04
519	Bucky Dent	.05	.03	576	Mike Dyer	.05	.03
520	Mitch Williams	.05	.03	577	Charlie Hayes (R)	.10	.06
521	Craig Worthington	.05	.03	578	Joe Magrane	.07	.04
522	Mike Dunne	.05	.03	579	Art Howe	.05	.03
523	Jay Bell	.05	.03	580	Joe Carter	.20	.12
524	Daryl Boston	.05	.03	581	Ken Griffey	.08	.05
525	Wally Joyner	.10	.06	582	Rick Honeycutt	.05	.03
526	Checklist 397-528	.05	.03	583	Bruce Benedict	.05	.03
527	Ron Hassey	.05	.03	584	Phil Stephenson (R)	.07	.04
528	Kevin Wickander (R)	.08	.05	585	Kal Daniels	.05	.03
529	Greg Harris	.05	.03	586	Ed Nunez	.05	.03
530	Mark Langston	.10	.06	587	Lance Johnson	.05	.03
531	Ken Caminiti	.08	.05	588	Rick Rhoden	.05	.03
532	Cecilio Guante	.05	.03	589	Mike Aldrete	.05	.03
533	Tim Jones	.05	.03	590	Ozzie Smith	.12	.07
534	Louie Meadows	.05	.03	591	Todd Stottlemyre	.08	.05
535	John Smoltz	.35	.20	592	R.J. Reynolds	.05	.03
536	Bob Geren	.05	.03	593	Scott Bradley	.05	.03
537	Mark Grant	.05	.03	594	Luis Sojo (R)	.15	.10
538	Billy Spiers	.08	.05	595	Greg Swindell	.08	.05
539	Neal Heaton	.05	.03	596	Jose DeJesus	.05	.03

597	Chris Bosio	.07	.04
598	Brady Anderson	.20	.12
599	Frank Williams	.05	.03
600	Darryl Strawberry	.25	.15
601	Luis Rivera	.05	.03
602	Scott Garrelts	.05	.03
603	Tony Armas	.05	.03
604	Ron Robinson	.05	.03
605	Mike Scioscia	.05	.03
606	Storm Davis	.05	.03
607	Steve Jeltz	.05	.03
608	Eric Anthony (R)	.40	.25
609	Sparky Anderson	.07	.04
610	Pedro Guerrero	.07	.04
611	Walt Terrell	.05	.03
612	Dave Gallagher	.05	.03
613	Jeff Pico	.05	.03
614	Nelson Santovenia	.05	.03
615	Rob Deer	.07	.04
616	Brian Holman	.05	.03
617	Geronimo Berroa	.05	.03
618	Eddie Whitson	.05	.03
619	Rob Ducey	.05	.03
620	Tony Castillo (R)	.07	.04
621	Melido Perez	.07	.04
622	Sid Bream	.05	.03
623	Jim Corsi	.05	.03
624	Darrin Jackson	.07	.04
625	Roger McDowell	.05	.03
626	Bob Melvin	.05	.03
627	Jose Rijo	.10	.06
628	Candy Maldonado	.05	.03
629	Eric Hetzel	.08	.05
630	Gary Gaetti	.05	.03
631	John Wetteland (R)	.25	.15
632	Scott Lusader	.05	.03
633	Dennis Cook	.05	.03
634	Luis Polonia	.07	.04
635	Brian Downing	.07	.04
636	Jesse Orosco	.05	.03
637	Craig Reynolds	.05	.03
638	Jeff Montgomery	.07	.04
639	Tony LaRussa	.07	.04
640	Rick Sutcliffe	.07	.04
641	Doug Strange (R)	.10	.06
642	Jack Armstrong	.07	.04
643	Alfredo Griffin	.05	.03
644	Paul Assenmacher	.05	.03
645	Jose Oquendo	.05	.03
646	Checklist 529-660	.05	.03
647	Rex Hudler	.05	.03
648	Jim Clancy	.05	.03
649	Dan Murphy (R)	.08	.05
650	Mike Witt	.05	.03
651	Rafael Santana	.05	.03
652	Mike Boddicker	.05	.03
653	John Moses	.05	.03
654	Paul Coleman (R)	.15	.10

	(#1 Pick)		
655	Gregg Olson	.10	.06
656	Mackey Sasser	.05	.03
657	Terry Mulholland	.05	.03
658	Donell Nixon	.05	.03
659	Greg Cadaret	.05	.03
660	Vince Coleman	.07	.04
661	Dick Howser (Clock)	.05	.03
662	Mike Schmidt (Clock)	.15	.10
663	Fred Lynn Clock)	.08	.05
664	Johnny Bench (Clock)	.10	.06
665	Sandy Koufax (Clock)	.15	.10
666	Brian Fisher	.05	.03
667	Curt Wilkerson	.05	.03
668	Joe Oliver (R)	.15	.10
669	Tom Lasorda	.07	.04
670	Dennis Eckersley	.15	.10
671	Bob Boone	.08	.05
672	Roy Smith	.05	.03
673	Joey Meyer	.05	.03
674	Spike Owen	.05	.03
675	Jim Abbott	.25	.15
676	Randy Kutcher	.05	.03
677	Jay Tibbs	.05	.03
678	Kirt Manwaring	.05	.03
679	Gary Ward	.05	.03
680	Howard Johnson	.08	.05
681	Mike Schooler	.05	.03
682	Dan Bilardello	.05	.03
683	Kenny Rogers	.05	.03
684	Julio Machado (R)	.10	.06
685	Tony Fernandez	.08	.05
686	Carmelo Martinez	.05	.03
687	Tim Birtsas	.05	.03
688	Milt Thompson	.05	.03
689	Rich Yett	.05	.03
690	Mark McGwire	.35	.20
691	Chuck Cary	.05	.03
692	Sammy Sosa (R)	.25	.15
693	Calvin Schiraldi	.05	.03
694	Mike Stanton (R)	.15	.10
695	Tom Henke	.08	.05
696	B.J. Surhoff	.05	.03
697	Mike Davis	.05	.03
698	Omar Vizquel	.05	.03
699	Jim Leyland	.07	.04
700	Kirby Puckett	.30	.18
701	Bernie Williams (R)	.35	.20
702	Tony Phillips	.05	.03
703	Jeff Brantley	.08	.05
704	Chip Hale (R)	.10	.06
705	Claudell Washington	.05	.03
706	Geno Petralli	.05	.03
707	Luis Aquino	.05	.03
708	Larry Sheets	.05	.03
709	Juan Berenguer	.05	.03
710	Von Hayes	.05	.03

711	Rick Aguilera	.07	.04
712	Todd Benzinger	.05	.03
713	Tim Drummond (R)	.10	.06
714	Marquis Grissom (R)	.80	.50
715	Greg Maddux	.20	.12
716	Steve Balboni	.05	.03
717	Ron Karkovice	.05	.03
718	Gary Sheffield	.60	.35
719	Wally Whitehurst (R)	.15	.10
720	Andres Galarraga	.07	.04
721	Lee Mazzilli	.05	.03
722	Felix Fermin	.05	.03
723	Jeff Robinson	.05	.03
724	Juan Bell	.10	.06
725	Terry Pendleton	.15	.10
726	Gene Nelson	.05	.03
727	Pat Tabler	.05	.03
728	Jim Acker	.05	.03
729	Bobby Valentine	.05	.03
730	Tony Gwynn	.25	.15
731	Don Carman	.05	.03
732	Ernie Riles	.05	.03
733	John Dopson	.05	.03
734	Kevin Elster	.05	.03
735	Charlie Hough	.05	.03
736	Rick Dempsey	.05	.03
737	Chris Sabo	.08	.05
738	Gene Harris	.05	.03
739	Dale Sveum	.05	.03
740	Jesse Barfield	.07	.04
741	Steve Wilson	.05	.03
742	Ernie Whitt	.05	.03
743	Tom Candiotti	.07	.04
744	Kelly Mann (R)	.08	.05
745	Hubie Brooks	.07	.04
746	Dave Smith	.05	.03
747	Randy Bush	.05	.03
748	Doyle Alexander	.05	.03
749	Mark Parent	.05	.03
750	Dale Murphy	.12	.07
751	Steve Lyons	.05	.03
752	Tom Gordon	.10	.06
753	Chris Speier	.05	.03
754	Bob Walk	.05	.03
755	Rafael Palmeiro	.12	.07
756	Ken Howell	.05	.03
757	Larry Walker (R)	.75	.45
758	Mark Thurmond	.05	.03
759	Tom Trebelhorn	.05	.03
760	Wade Boggs	.15	.10
761	Mike Jackson	.05	.03
762	Doug Dascenzo	.05	.03
763	Denny Martinez	.10	.06
764	Tim Teufel	.05	.03
765	Chili Davis	.07	.04
766	Brian Meyer	.08	.05
767	Tracy Jones	.05	.03
768	Chuck Crim	.05	.03

769	Greg Hibbard (R)	.15	.10
770	Cory Snyder	.07	.04
771	Pete Smith	.12	.07
772	Jeff Reed	.05	.03
773	Dave Leiper	.05	.03
774	Ben McDonald (R)	.75	.45
775	Andy Van Slyke	.15	.10
776	Charlie Leibrandt	.05	.03
777	Tim Laudner	.05	.03
778	Mike Jeffcoat	.05	.03
779	Lloyd Moseby	.05	.03
780	Orel Hershiser	.10	.06
781	Mario Diaz	.05	.03
782	Jose Alvarez	.05	.03
783	Checklist 661-792	.05	.03
784	Scott Bailes	.05	.03
785	Jim Rice	.08	.05
786	Eric King	.05	.03
787	Rene Gonzales	.08	.05
788	Frank DiPino	.05	.03
789	John Wathan	.05	.03
790	Gary Carter	.10	.06
791	Alvaro Espinoza	.05	.03
792	Gerald Perry	.05	.03

1990 Topps Traded

This 132-card set marks the tenth straight year that Topps issued an end-of-year Traded set. It also marks the first time the cards in the Traded Series were available in wax packs. Cards measure 2-1/2" by 3-1/2" and the set features a combination of players who were traded during the season and promising rookies.

	MINT	NR/MT
Complete Set (132)	7.00	4.50
Commons	.05	.03

1T	Darrel Akerfelds	.05	.03
2T	Sandy Alomar, Jr.	.12	.07
3T	Brad Arnsberg	.08	.05
4T	Steve Avery	.80	.50
5T	Wally Backman	.05	.03
6T	Carlos Baerga (R)	1.25	.80
7T	Kevin Bass	.05	.03
8T	Willie Blair (R)	.15	.10
9T	Mike Blowers (R)	.10	.06
10T	Shawn Boskie (R)	.10	.06
11T	Daryl Boston	.05	.03
12T	Dennis Boyd	.05	.03
13T	Glenn Braggs	.05	.03
14T	Hubie Brooks	.08	.05
15T	Tom Brunansky	.08	.05
16T	John Burkett (R)	.10	.06
17T	Casey Candaele	.05	.03
18T	John Candelaria	.05	.03
19T	Gary Carter	.10	.06
20T	Joe Carter	.20	.12
21T	Rick Cerone	.05	.03
22T	Scott Coolbaugh (R)	.08	.05
23T	Bobby Cox	.05	.03
24T	Mark Davis	.08	.05
25T	Storm Davis	.05	.03
26T	Edgar Diaz (R)	.10	.06
27T	Wayne Edwards (R)	.10	.06
28T	Mark Eichhorn	.05	.03
29T	Scott Erickson (R)	.80	.05
30T	Nick Esasky	.05	.03
31T	Cecil Fielder	.25	.15
32T	John Franco	.05	.03
33T	Travis Fryman (R)	1.25	.80
34T	Bill Gullickson	.08	.05
35T	Darryl Hamilton	.08	.05
36T	Mike Harkey	.15	.10
37T	Bud Harrelson	.05	.03
38T	Billy Hatcher	.05	.03
39T	Keith Hernandez	.08	.05
40T	Joe Hesketh	.05	.03
41T	Dave Hollins (R)	.75	.45
42T	Sam Horn	.10	.06
43T	Steve Howard (R)	.10	.06
44T	Todd Hundley (R)	.20	.12
45T	Jeff Huson	.05	.03
46T	Chris James	.05	.03
47T	Stan Javier	.05	.03
48T	Dave Justice (R)	1.50	.90
49T	Jeff Kaiser (R)	.08	.05
50T	Dana Kiecker (R)	.12	.07
51T	Joe Klink	.05	.03
52T	Brent Knackert (R)	.12	.07
53T	Brad Komminsk	.05	.03
54T	Mark Langston	.10	.06
55T	Tim Layana (R)	.15	.10
56T	Rick Leach	.05	.03
57T	Terry Leach	.05	.03
58T	Tim Leary	.08	.05
59T	Craig Lefferts	.05	.03
60T	Charlie Leibrandt	.05	.03
61T	Jim Leyritz (R)	.10	.06
62T	Fred Lynn	.08	.05
63T	Kevin Maas (R)	.30	.18
64T	Shane Mack	.15	.10
65T	Candy Maldonado	.07	.04
66T	Fred Manrique	.05	.03
67T	Mike Marshall	.05	.03
68T	Carmelo Martinez	.05	.03
69T	John Marzano	.05	.03
70T	Ben McDonald	.60	.35
71T	Jack McDowell	.35	.20
72T	John McNamara	.05	.03
73T	Orlando Mercado	.05	.03
74T	Stump Merrill	.05	.03
75T	Alan Mills (R)	.12	.07
76T	Hal Morris	.20	.12
77T	Lloyd Moseby	.07	.04
78T	Randy Myers	.07	.04
79T	Tim Naehring (R)	.15	.10
80T	Junior Noboa	.05	.03
81T	Matt Nokes	.08	.05
82T	Pete O'Brien	.05	.03
83T	John Olerud (R)	.60	.35
84T	Greg Olson (R)	.10	.06
85T	Junior Ortiz	.05	.03
86T	Dave Parker	.08	.05
87T	Rick Parker	.10	.06
88T	Bob Patterson	.05	.03
89T	Alejandro Pena	.07	.04
90T	Tony Pena	.08	.05
91T	Pascual Perez	.07	.04
92T	Gerald Perry	.05	.03
93T	Dan Petry	.05	.03
94T	Gary Pettis	.05	.03
95T	Tony Phillips	.05	.03
96T	Lou Pinella	.08	.05
97T	Luis Polonia	.08	.05
98T	Jim Presley	.05	.03
99T	Scott Radinsky (R)	.15	.10
100T	Willie Randolph	.08	.05
101T	Jeff Reardon	.12	.07
102T	Greg Riddoch	.05	.03
103T	Jeff Robinson	.05	.03
104T	Ron Robinson	.05	.03
105T	Kevin Romine	.05	.03
106T	Scott Ruskin (R)	.12	.07
107T	John Russell	.05	.03
108T	Bill Sampen (R)	.12	.07
109T	Juan Samuel	.05	.03
110T	Scott Sanderson	.07	.04
111T	Jack Savage (R)	.10	.06
112T	Dave Schmidt	.05	.03
113T	Red Schoendienst	.07	.04
114T	Terry Shumpert (R)	.15	.10
115T	Matt Sinatro	.05	.03
116T	Don Slaught	.05	.03

117T	Bryn Smith	.05	.03
118T	Lee Smith	.12	.07
119T	Paul Sorrento (R)	.30	.18
120T	Franklin Stubbs	.05	.03
121T	Russ Swan (R)	.12	.07
122T	Bob Tewksbury	.10	.06
123T	Wayne Tolleson	.05	.03
124T	John Tudor	.07	.04
125T	Randy Veres (R)	.08	.05
126T	Hector Villanueva (R)	.12	.07
127T	Mitch Webster	.07	.04
128T	Ernie Whitt	.05	.03
129T	Frank Wills	.05	.03
130T	Dave Winfield	.15	.10
131T	Matt Young	.05	.03
132T	Checklist	.05	.03

1991 Topps

This 792-card set marks Topps 40th Anniversary and the card fronts reflect that milestone with a special "Topps 40th" logo above the photo. As part of their celebration Topps randomly inserted into wax packs one of each card they issued since 1952. Card fronts feature full color player photos and different color borders with each team assigned the same border colors. Card backs are horizontal. Special subsets include Record Breakers, All-Stars, Number One Draft Picks and Future Stars.

	MINT	NR/MT
Complete Set (792)	22.00	16.00
Commons	.05	.03

1	Nolan Ryan	.60	.35
2	George Brett (RB)	.12	.07

3	Carlton Fisk (RB)	.08	.05
4	Kevin Maas (RB)	.08	.05
5	Cal Ripken (RB)	.20	.12
6	Nolan Ryan (RB)	.30	.18
7	Ryne Sandberg (RB)	.15	.10
8	Bobby Thigpen (RB)	.07	.04
9	Darrin Fletcher	.05	.03
10	Gregg Olson	.08	.05
11	Roberto Kelly	.12	.07
12	Paul Assenmacher	.05	.03
13	Mariano Duncan	.05	.03
14	Dennis Lamp	.05	.03
15	Von Hayes	.05	.03
16	Mike Heath	.05	.03
17	Jeff Brantley	.05	.03
18	Nelson Liriano	.05	.03
19	Jeff Robinson	.05	.03
20	Pedro Guerrero	.07	.04
21	Joe Morgan	.05	.03
22	Storm Davis	.05	.03
23	Jim Gantner	.05	.03
24	Dave Martinez	.05	.03
25	Tim Belcher	.07	.04
26	Luis Sojo	.07	.04
27	Bobby Witt	.08	.05
28	Alvaro Espinoza	.05	.03
29	Bob Walk	.05	.03
30	Gregg Jefferies	.10	.06
31	Colby Ward (R)	.08	.05
32	Mike Simms (R)	.10	.06
33	Barry Jones	.05	.03
34	Atlee Hammaker	.05	.03
35	Greg Maddux	.15	.10
36	Donnie Hill	.05	.03
37	Tom Bolton	.05	.03
38	Scott Bradley	.05	.03
39	Jim Neidlinger (R)	.10	.06
40	Kevin Mitchell	.08	.05
41	Ken Dayley	.05	.03
42	Chris Hoiles (R)	.25	.15
43	Roger McDowell	.05	.03
44	Mike Felder	.05	.03
45	Chris Sabo	.08	.05
46	Tim Drummond	.05	.03
47	Brook Jacoby	.05	.03
48	Dennis Boyd	.05	.03
49a	Pat Borders (Er) (40 stolen bases)	.20	.12
49b	Pat Borders (Cor)	.05	.03
50	Bob Welch	.08	.05
51	Art Howe	.05	.03
52	Francisco Oliveras	.05	.03
53	Mike Sharperson	.05	.03
54	Gary Mielke	.05	.03
55	Jeffrey Leonard	.05	.03
56	Jeff Parrett	.05	.03
57	Jack Howell	.05	.03
58	Mel Stottlemyre	.05	.03

59	Eric Yelding	.07	.04
60	Frank Viola	.08	.05
61	Stan Javier	.05	.03
62	Lee Guetterman	.05	.03
63	Milt Thompson	.05	.03
64	Tom Herr	.05	.03
65	Bruce Hurst	.07	.04
66	Terry Kennedy	.05	.03
67	Rick Honeycutt	.05	.03
68	Gary Sheffield	.40	.25
69	Steve Wilson	.05	.03
70	Ellis Burks	.08	.05
71	Jim Acker	.05	.03
72	Junior Ortiz	.05	.03
73	Craig Worthington	.05	.03
74	Shane Andrews (R) (#1 Pick)	.25	.15
75	Jack Morris	.12	.07
76	Jerry Browne	.05	.03
77	Drew Hall	.05	.03
78	Geno Petralli	.05	.03
79	Frank Thomas	1.50	.90
80	Fernando Valenzuela	.08	.05
81	Cito Gaston	.05	.03
82	Tom Galvine	.25	.15
83	Daryl Boston	.05	.03
84	Bob McClure	.05	.03
85	Jesse Barfield	.07	.04
86	Les Lancaster	.05	.03
87	Tracy Jones	.05	.03
88	Bob Tewksbury	.08	.05
89	Darren Dalton	.10	.06
90	Danny Tartabull	.12	.07
91	Greg Colbrunn (R)	.25	.15
92	Danny Jackson	.05	.03
93	Ivan Calderon	.07	.04
94	John Dopson	.05	.03
95	Paul Molitor	.10	.06
96	Trevor Wilson	.05	.03
97	Brady Anderson	.15	.10
98	Sergio Valdez	.05	.03
99	Chris Gwynn	.05	.03
100a	Don Mattingly (Er) (10 hits in 1990)	.50	.30
100b	Don Mattingly (Cor) (101 hits in 1990)	.15	.10
101	Ron Ducey	.05	.03
102	Gene Larkin	.05	.03
103	Tim Costo (R) (#1 Pick)	.25	.15
104	Don Robinson	.05	.03
105	Keith Miller	.05	.03
106	Ed Nunez	.05	.03
107	Luis Polonia	.07	.04
108	Matt Young	.05	.03
109	Greg Riddoch	.05	.03
110	Tom Henke	.07	.04
111	Andres Thomas	.05	.03
112	Frank DiPino	.05	.03
113	Carl Everett (R) (#1 Pick)	.15	.10
114	Lance Dickson (R)	.20	.12
115	Hubie Brooks	.07	.04
116	Mark Davis	.05	.03
117	Dion James	.05	.03
118	Tom Edens (R)	.08	.05
119	Carl Nichols	.05	.03
120	Joe Carter	.15	.10
121	Eric King	.05	.03
122	Paul O'Neill	.08	.05
123	Greg Harris	.05	.03
124	Randy Bush	.05	.03
125	Steve Bedrosian	.07	.04
126	Bernard Gilkey (R)	.25	.15
127	Joe Price	.05	.03
128	Travis Fryman	.40	.25
129	Mark Eichhorn	.05	.03
130	Ozzie Smith	.12	.07
131	Checklist 1	.05	.03
132	Jamie Quirk	.05	.03
133	Greg Briley	.05	.03
134	Kevin Elster	.05	.03
135	Jerome Walton	.08	.05
136	Dave Schmidt	.05	.03
137	Randy Ready	.05	.03
138	Jamie Moyer	.05	.03
139	Jeff Treadway	.05	.03
140	Fred McGriff	.20	.12
141	Nick Leyva	.05	.03
142	Curtis Wilkerson	.05	.03
143	John Smiley	.08	.05
144	Dave Henderson	.07	.04
145	Lou Whitaker	.07	.04
146	Dan Plesac	.05	.03
147	Carlos Baerga	.30	.18
148	Rey Palacios	.05	.03
149	Al Osuna (R)	.15	.10
150	Cal Ripken	.40	.25
151	Tom Browning	.08	.05
152	Mickey Hatcher	.05	.03
153	Bryan Harvey	.07	.04
154	Jay Buhner	.07	.04
155	Dwight Evans	.08	.05
156	Carlos Martinez	.05	.03
157	John Smoltz	.15	.10
158	Jose Uribe	.05	.03
159	Joe Boever	.05	.03
160	Vince Coleman	.07	.04
161	Tim Leary	.05	.03
162	Ozzie Canseco (R)	.12	.07
163	Dave Johnson	.05	.03
164	Edgar Diaz	.05	.03
165	Sandy Alomar	.10	.06
166	Harold Baines	.08	.05
167	Randy Tomlin (R)	.25	.15
168	John Olerud	.15	.10

169	Luis Aquino	.05	.03
170	Carlton Fisk	.12	.07
171	Tony LaRussa	.07	.04
172	Pete Incaviglia	.05	.03
173	Jason Grimsley	.05	.03
174	Ken Caminiti	.07	.04
175	Jack Armstrong	.05	.03
176	John Orton	.08	.05
177	Reggie Harris (R)	.10	.06
178	Dave Valle	.05	.03
179	Pete Harnisch	.07	.04
180	Tony Gwynn	.12	.07
181	Duane Ward	.05	.03
182	Junior Noboa	.05	.03
183	Clay Parker	.05	.03
184	Gary Green	.05	.03
185	Joe Magrane	.07	.04
186	Rod Booker	.05	.03
187	Greg Cadaret	.05	.03
188	Damon Berryhill	.05	.03
189	Daryl Irvine (R)	.10	.06
190	Matt Williams	.12	.07
191	Willie Blair	.08	.05
192	Rob Deer	.07	.04
193	Felix Fermin	.05	.03
194	Xavier Hernandez (R)	.10	.06
195	Wally Joyner	.10	.06
196	Jim Vatcher	.08	.05
197	Chris Nabholz (R)	.20	.12
198	R.J. Reynolds	.05	.03
199	Mike Hartley	.05	.03
200	Darryl Strawberry	.15	.10
201	Tom Kelly	.05	.03
202	Jim Leyritz	.05	.03
203	Gene Harris	.05	.03
204	Herm Winningham	.05	.03
205	Mike Perez (R)	.15	.10
206	Carlos Quintana	.08	.05
207	Gary Wayne	.05	.03
208	Willie Wilson	.07	.04
209	Ken Howell	.05	.03
210	Lance Parrish	.07	.04
211	Brian Barnes (R)	.20	.12
212	Steve Finley	.07	.04
213	Frank Wills	.05	.03
214	Joe Girardi	.05	.03
215	Dave Smith	.05	.03
216	Greg Gagne	.05	.03
217	Chris Bosio	.07	.04
218	Rick Parker	.05	.03
219	Jack McDowell	.20	.12
220	Tim Wallach	.08	.05
221	Don Slaught	.05	.03
222	Brian McRae (R)	.25	.15
223	Allan Anderson	.05	.03
224	Juan Gonzalez	.50	.30
225	Randy Johnson	.25	.15
226	Alfredo Griffin	.05	.03
227	Steve Avery	.30	.18
228	Rex Hudler	.05	.03
229	Rance Mulliniks	.05	.03
230	Sid Fernandez	.07	.04
231	Doug Rader	.05	.03
232	Jose DeJesus	.05	.03
233	Al Leiter	.05	.03
234	Scott Erickson	.30	.18
235	Dave Parker	.08	.05
236	Frank Tanana	.05	.03
237	Rick Cerone	.05	.03
238	Mike Dunne	.05	.03
239	Darren Lewis (R)	.12	.07
240	Mike Scott	.07	.04
241	Dave Clark	.05	.03
242	Mike LaCoss	.05	.03
243	Lance Johnson	.07	.04
244	Mike Jeffcoat	.05	.03
245	Kal Daniels	.05	.03
246	Kevin Wickander	.05	.03
247	Jody Reed	.05	.03
248	Tom Gordon	.08	.05
249	Bob Melvin	.05	.03
250	Dennis Eckersley	.12	.07
251	Mark Lemke	.05	.03
252	Mel Rojas (R)	.10	.06
253	Garry Templeton	.07	.04
254	Shawn Boskie	.05	.03
255	Brian Downing	.05	.03
256	Greg Hibbard	.05	.03
257	Tom O'Malley	.05	.03
258	Chris Hammond (R)	.15	.10
259	Hensley Meulens	.08	.05
260	Harold Reynolds	.05	.03
261	Bud Harrelson	.05	.03
262	Tim Jones	.05	.03
263	Checklist 2	.05	.03
264	Dave Hollins	.25	.15
265	Mark Gubicza	.08	.05
266	Carmen Castillo	.05	.03
267	Mark Knudson	.05	.03
268	Tom Brookens	.05	.03
269	Joe Hesketh	.05	.03
270	Mark McGwire	.30	.18
271	Omar Olivares (R)	.12	.07
272	Jeff King	.08	.05
273	Johnny Ray	.05	.03
274	Ken Williams	.05	.03
275	Alan Trammell	.08	.05
276	Bill Swift	.07	.04
277	Scott Coolbaugh	.05	.03
278	Alex Fernandez (R)	.15	.10
279a	Jose Gonzalez (Wrong Photo)	.20	.12
279b	Jose Gonzalez (Cor)	.05	.03
280	Bret Saberhagen	.10	.06
281	Larry Sheets	.05	.03
282	Don Carman	.05	.03

283	Marquis Grissom	.20	.12
284	Bill Spiers	.05	.03
285	Jim Abbott	.12	.07
286	Ken Oberkfell	.05	.03
287	Mark Grant	.05	.03
288	Derrick May	.12	.07
289	Tim Birtsas	.05	.03
290	Steve Sax	.08	.05
291	John Wathan	.05	.03
292	Bud Black	.05	.03
293	Jay Bell	.05	.03
294	Mike Moore	.05	.03
295	Rafael Palmeiro	.10	.06
296	Mark Williamson	.05	.03
297	Manny Lee	.05	.03
298	Omar Vizquel	.05	.03
299	Scott Radinsky	.08	.05
300	Kirby Puckett	.25	.15
301	Steve Farr	.05	.03
302	Tim Teufel	.05	.03
303	Mike Boddicker	.05	.03
304	Kevin Reimer	.12	.07
305	Mike Scioscia	.07	.04
306	Lonnie Smith	.07	.04
307	Andy Benes	.12	.07
308	Tom Pagnozzi	.07	.04
309	Norm Charlton	.08	.05
310	Gary Carter	.10	.06
311	Jeff Pico	.05	.03
312	Charlie Hayes	.05	.03
313	Ron Robinson	.05	.03
314	Gary Pettis	.05	.03
315	Roberto Alomar	.20	.12
316	Gene Nelson	.05	.03
317	Mike Fitzgerald	.05	.03
318	Rick Aguilera	.05	.03
319	Jeff McKnight	.05	.03
320	Tony Fernandez	.08	.05
321	Bob Rodgers	.05	.03
322	Terry Shumpert	.08	.05
323	Cory Snyder	.07	.04
324	Ron Kittle	.05	.03
325	Brett Butler	.08	.05
326	Ken Patterson	.05	.03
327	Ron Hassey	.05	.03
328	Walt Terrell	.05	.03
329	Dave Justice	.35	.20
330	Dwight Gooden	.10	.06
331	Eric Anthony	.15	.10
332	Kenny Rogers	.05	.03
333	Clipper Jones (R) (#1 Pick)	.60	.35
334	Todd Benzinger	.05	.03
335	Mitch Williams	.05	.03
336	Matt Nokes	.05	.03
337	Keith Comstock	.05	.03
338	Luis Rivera	.05	.03
339	Larry Walker	.20	.12
340	Ramon Martinez	.12	.07
341	John Moses	.05	.03
342	Mickey Morandini	.12	.07
343	Jose Oquendo	.05	.03
344	Jeff Russell	.07	.04
345	Jose DeJesus	.05	.03
346	Jesse Orosco	.05	.03
347	Greg Vaughn	.12	.07
348	Todd Stottlemyre	.08	.05
349	Dave Gallagher	.05	.03
350	Glenn Davis	.05	.03
351	Joe Torre	.07	.04
352	Frank White	.05	.03
353	Tony Castillo	.05	.03
354	Sid Bream	.05	.03
355	Chili Davis	.07	.04
356	Mike Marshall	.05	.03
357	Jack Savage	.05	.03
358	Mark Parent	.05	.03
359	Chuck Cary	.05	.03
360	Tim Raines	.07	.03
361	Scott Garrelts	.05	.03
362	Hector Villanueva	.08	.05
363	Rick Mahler	.05	.03
364	Dan Pasqua	.05	.03
365	Mike Schooler	.05	.03
366	Checklist 3	.05	.03
367	Dave Walsh (R)	.10	.06
368	Felix Jose	.15	.10
369	Steve Searcy	.05	.03
370	Kelly Gruber	.08	.05
371	Jeff Montgomery	.05	.03
372	Spike Owen	.05	.03
373	Darrin Jackson	.07	.04
374	Larry Casian (R)	.08	.05
375	Tony Pena	.05	.03
376	Mike Harkey	.08	.05
377	Rene Gonzales	.08	.05
378	Wilson Alvarez (R)	.25	.15
379	Randy Velarde	.05	.03
380	Willie McGee	.08	.05
381	Jose Lind	.05	.03
382	Mackey Sasser	.05	.03
383	Pete Smith	.10	.06
384	Gerald Perry	.05	.03
385	Mickey Tettleton	.07	.04
386	Cecil Fielder (AS)	.12	.07
387	Julio Franco (AS)	.07	.04
388	Kelly Gruber (AS)	.07	.04
389	Alan Trammell (AS)	.08	.05
390	Jose Canseco (AS)	.15	.10
391	Rickey Henderson (AS)	.12	.07
392	Ken Griffey Jr. (AS)	.25	.15
393	Carlton Fisk (AS)	.10	.06
394	Bob Welch (AS)	.07	.04
395	Chuck Finley (AS)	.07	.04
396	Bobby Thigpen (AS)	.07	.04

397	Eddie Murray (AS)	.10	.06		454	Kevin Appier	.12	.07
398	Ryne Sandberg (AS)	.12	.07		455	Walt Weiss	.05	.03
399	Matt Williams (AS)	.10	.06		456	Charlie Leibrandt	.05	.03
400	Barry Larkin (AS)	.10	.06		457	Todd Handley	.10	.06
401	Barry Bonds (AS)	.12	.07		458	Brian Holman	.05	.03
402	Darryl Strawberry (AS)	.12	.07		459	Tom Trebelhorn	.05	.03
403	Bobby Bonilla (AS)	.08	.05		460	Dave Steib	.08	.05
404	Mike Scoscia (AS)	.07	.04		461	Robin Ventura	.25	.15
405	Doug Drabek (AS)	.08	.05		462	Steve Frey	.05	.03
406	Frank Viola (AS)	.08	.05		463	Dwight Smith	.07	.04
407	John Franco (AS)	.07	.04		464	Steve Buechele	.07	.04
408	Ernie Riles	.05	.03		465	Ken Griffey	.07	.04
409	Mike Stanley	.05	.03		466	Charles Nagy	.50	.30
410	Dave Righetti	.07	.04		467	Dennis Cook	.05	.03
411	Lance Blankenship	.05	.03		468	Tim Hulett	.05	.03
412	Dave Bergman	.05	.03		469	Chet Lemon	.05	.03
413	Terry Mulholland	.05	.03		470	Howard Johnson	.08	.05
414	Sammy Sosa	.10	.06		471	Mike Lieberthal (R) (#1 Pick)	.25	.15
415	Rick Sutcliffe	.07	.04		472	Kirt Manwaring	.05	.03
416	Randy Milligan	.07	.04		473	Curt Young	.05	.03
417	Bill Krueger	.05	.03		474	Phil Plantier (R)	.50	.30
418	Nick Esasky	.05	.03		475	Teddy Higuera	.07	.04
419	Jeff Reed	.05	.03		476	Glenn Wilson	.05	.03
420	Bobby Thigpen	.07	.04		477	Mike Fetters	.05	.03
421	Alex Cole	.08	.05		478	Kurt Stillwell	.05	.03
422	Rick Rueschel	.05	.03		479	Bob Patterson	.05	.03
423	Rafael Ramirez	.05	.03		480	Dave Magadan	.07	.04
424	Calvin Schiraldi	.05	.03		481	Eddie Whitson	.05	.03
425	Andy Van Slyke	.12	.07		482	Tino Martinez	.15	.10
426	Joe Grahe (R)	.15	.10		483	Mike Aldrete	.05	.03
427	Rick Dempsey	.05	.03		484	Dave LaPoint	.05	.03
428	John Barfield	.05	.03		485	Terry Pendleton	.15	.10
429	Stump Merill	.05	.03		486	Tommy Greene	.12	.07
430	Gary Gaetti	.05	.03		487	Rafael Belliard	.05	.03
431	Paul Gibson	.05	.03		488	Jeff Manto	.08	.05
432	Delino DeShields	.20	.12		489	Bobby Valentine	.05	.03
433	Pat Tabler	.05	.03		490	Kirk Gibson	.07	.04
434	Julio Machado	.07	.04		491	Kurt Miller (R) (#1 Pick)	.40	.25
435	Kevin Mass	.10	.06					
436	Scott Bankhead	.05	.03		492	Ernie Whitt	.05	.03
437	Doug Dascenzo	.05	.03		493	Jose Rijo	.08	.05
438	Vicente Palacios	.05	.03		494	Chris James	.05	.03
439	Dickie Thon	.05	.03		495	Charlie Hough	.05	.03
440	George Bell	.08	.05		496	Marty Barrett	.05	.03
441	Zane Smith	.05	.03		497	Ben McDonald	.15	.10
442	Charlie O'Brien	.05	.03		498	Mark Salas	.05	.03
443	Jeff Innis	.05	.03		499	Melido Perez	.05	.03
444	Glenn Braggss	.05	.03		500	Will Clark	.25	.15
445	Greg Swindell	.08	.05		501	Mike Bielecki	.05	.03
446	Craig Grebeck (R)	.10	.06		502	Carney Lansford	.07	.04
447	John Burkett	.05	.03		503	Roy Smith	.05	.03
448	Craig Lefferts	.05	.03		504	Julio Valera (R)	.08	.05
449	Juan Berenguer	.05	.03		505	Chuck Finley	.08	.05
450	Wade Boggs	.12	.07		506	Darnell Coles	.05	.03
451	Neal Heaton	.05	.03		507	Steve Jeltz	.05	.03
452	Bill Schroeder	.05	.03		508	Mike York (R)	.05	.03
453	Lenny Harris	.05	.03		509	Glenallen Hill	.10	.06

510	John Franco	.05	.03
511	Steve Balboni	.05	.03
512	Jose Mesa	.05	.03
513	Jerald Clark	.08	.05
514	Mike Stanton	.05	.03
515	Alvin Davis	.05	.03
516	Karl Rhodes (R)	.12	.07
517	Joe Oliver	.08	.05
518	Cris Carpenter	.07	.04
519	Sparky Anderson	.07	.04
520	Mark Grace	.12	.07
521	Joe Orsulak	.05	.03
522	Stan Belinda	.07	.04
523	Rodney McCray (R)	.07	.04
524	Darrel Akerfelds	.05	.03
525	Willie Randolph	.07	.04
526	Moises Alou (R)	.35	.20
527	Checklist 4	.05	.03
528	Denny Martinez	.10	.06
529	Marc Newfield (R)	.60	.35
530	Roger Clemens	.25	.15
531	Dave Rhode (R)	.10	.06
532	Kirk McCaskill	.05	.03
533	Oddibe McDowell	.05	.03
534	Mike Jackson	.05	.03
535	Ruben Sierra	.20	.12
536	Mike Witt	.05	.03
537	Mike LaValliere	.05	.03
538	Bip Roberts	.08	.05
539	Scott Terry	.05	.03
540	George Brett	.15	.10
541	Domingo Ramos	.05	.03
542	Rob Murphy	.05	.03
543	Junior Felix	.07	.04
544	Alejandro Pena	.07	.04
545	Dale Murphy	.10	.06
546	Jeff Ballard	.05	.03
547	Mike Pagliarulo	.05	.03
548	Jaime Navarro	.12	.07
549	John McNamara	.05	.03
550	Eric Davis	.10	.06
551	Bob Kipper	.05	.03
552	Jeff Hamilton	.05	.03
553	Joe Klink	.05	.03
554	Brian Harper	.05	.03
555	Turner Ward (R)	.12	.07
556	Gary Ward	.05	.03
557	Wally Whitehurst	.05	.03
558	Otis Nixon	.07	.04
559	Adam Peterson	.05	.03
560	Greg Smith	.08	.05
561	Tim McIntosh	.12	.07
562	Jeff Kunkel	.05	.03
563	Brent Knackert	.08	.05
564	Dante Bichette	.05	.03
565	Craig Biggio	.10	.06
566	Craig Wilson (R)	.10	.06
567	Dwayne Henry	.05	.03
568	Ron Karkovice	.05	.03
569	Curt Schilling	.07	.04
570	Barry Bonds	.20	.12
571	Pat Combs	.07	.04
572	Dave Anderson	.05	.03
573	Rich Rodriguez (R)	.12	.07
574	John Marzano	.05	.03
575	Robin Yount	.20	.12
576	Jeff Kaiser	.05	.03
577	Bill Doran	.05	.03
578	Dave West	.05	.03
579	Roger Craig	.05	.03
580	Dave Stewart	.08	.05
581	Luis Quinones	.05	.03
582	Marty Clary	.05	.03
583	Tony Phillips	.05	.03
584	Kevin Brown	.10	.06
585	Pete O'Brien	.05	.03
586	Fred Lynn	.07	.04
587	Jose Offerman	.15	.10
588	Mark Whiten (R)	.20	.12
589	Scott Ruskin	.10	.06
590	Eddie Murray	.12	.07
591	Ken Hill	.10	.06
592	B.J. Surhoff	.05	.03
593	Mike Walker (R)	.08	.05
594	Rich Garces (R)	.12	.07
595	Bill Landrum	.05	.03
596	Ronnie Walden (R) (#1 Pick)	.12	.07
597	Jerry Don Gleaton	.05	.03
598	Sam Horn	.07	.04
599	Greg Myers	.05	.03
600	Bo Jackson	.15	.10
601	Bob Ojeda	.05	.03
602	Casey Candaele	.05	.03
603a	Wes Chamberlain (Wrong Photo)	.60	.35
603b	Wes Chamberlain (Cor)	.25	.15
604	Billy Hatcher	.05	.03
605	Jeff Reardon	.10	.06
606	Jim Gott	.05	.03
607	Edgar Martinez	.12	.07
608	Todd Burns	.05	.03
609	Jeff Torborg	.05	.03
610	Andres Galarraga	.07	.04
611	Dave Eiland	.07	.04
612	Steve Lyons	.05	.03
613	Eric Show	.05	.03
614	Luis Salazar	.05	.03
615	Bert Blyleven	.08	.05
616	Todd Zeile	.10	.06
617	Bill Wegman	.05	.03
618	Sil Campusano	.05	.03
619	David Wells	.05	.03
620	Ozzie Guillen	.07	.04
621	Ted Power	.05	.03

622	Jack Daugherty	.05	.03
623	Jeff Blauser	.05	.03
624	Tom Candiotti	.07	.04
625	Terry Steinbach	.07	.04
626	Gerald Young	.05	.03
627	Tim Layana	.05	.03
628	Greg Litton	.05	.03
629	Wes Gardner	.05	.03
630	Dave Winfield	.15	.10
631	Mike Morgan	.07	.04
632	Lloyd Moseby	.05	.03
633	Kevin Tapani	.08	.05
634	Henry Cotto	.05	.03
635	Andy Hawkins	.05	.03
636	Geronimo Pena (R)	.12	.07
637	Bruce Ruffin	.05	.03
638	Mike Macfarlane	.05	.03
639	Frank Robinson	.08	.05
640	Andre Dawson	.12	.07
641	Mike Henneman	.05	.03
642	Hal Morris	.10	.06
643	Jim Presley	.05	.03
644	Chuck Crim	.05	.03
645	Juan Samuel	.05	.03
646	Andujar Cedeno (R)	.15	.10
647	Mark Portugal	.05	.03
648	Lee Stevens	.10	.06
649	Bill Sampen	.05	.03
650	Jack Clark	.07	.04
651	Alan Mills	.05	.03
652	Kevin Romine	.05	.03
653	Anthony Telford (R)	.15	.10
654	Paul Sorrento	.08	.05
655	Erik Hanson	.08	.05
656	Checklist 5	.05	.03
657	Mike Kingery	.05	.03
658	Scott Aldred (R)	.10	.06
659	Oscar Azocar (R)	.12	.07
660	Lee Smith	.12	.07
661	Steve Lake	.05	.03
662	Rob Dibble	.07	.04
663	Greg Brock	.05	.03
664	John Farrell	.05	.03
665	Jim Leyland	.07	.04
666	Danny Darwin	.05	.03
667	Kent Anderson	.05	.03
668	Bill Long	.05	.03
669	Lou Pinella	.07	.04
670	Rickey Henderson	.15	.10
671	Andy McGaffigan	.05	.03
672	Shane Mack	.10	.06
673	Greg Olson	.05	.03
674	Kevin Gross	.07	.04
675	Tom Brunansky	.07	.04
676	Scott Chiamparino (R)	.10	.06
677	Billy Ripken	.05	.03
678	Mark Davidson	.05	.03
679	Bill Bathe	.05	.03
680	Dave Cone	.15	.10
681	Jeff Schaefer (R)	.08	.05
682	Ray Lankford (R)	.40	.25
683	Derek Lilliquist	.05	.03
684	Milt Cuyler (R)	.30	.18
685	Doug Drabek	.10	.06
686	Mike Gallego	.05	.03
687	John Cerutti	.05	.03
688	Rosario Rodriguez	.05	.03
689	John Kruk	.08	.05
690	Orel Hershiser	.10	.06
691	Mike Blowers	.05	.03
692	Efrain Valdez (R)	.10	.06
693	Francisco Cabrera	.05	.03
694	Randy Veres	.05	.03
695	Kevin Seitzer	.08	.05
696	Steve Olin	.05	.03
697	Shawn Abner	.05	.03
698	Mark Guthrie	.05	.03
699	Jim Lefebvre	.05	.03
700	Jose Canseco	.25	.15
701	Pascual Perez	.05	.03
702	Tim Naehring	.10	.06
703	Juan Agosto	.05	.03
704	Devon White	.07	.04
705	Robby Thompson	.07	.04
706	Brad Arnsberg	.05	.03
707	Jim Eisenreich	.05	.03
708	John Mitchell	.05	.03
709	Matt Sinatro	.05	.03
710	Kent Hrbek	.08	.05
711	Jose DeLeon	.05	.03
712	Ricky Jordan	.05	.03
713	Scott Scudder	.08	.05
714	Marvell Wynne	.05	.03
715	Tim Burke	.05	.03
716	Bob Geren	.05	.03
717	Phil Bradley	.05	.03
718	Steve Crawford	.05	.03
719	Kevin McReynolds	.07	.04
720	Cecil Fielder	.15	.10
721	Mark Lee (R)	.12	.07
722	Wally Backman	.05	.03
723	Candy Maldonado	.05	.03
724	David Segui (R)	.15	.10
725	Ron Gant	.15	.10
726	Phil Stephenson	.05	.03
727	Mookie Wilson	.05	.03
728	Scott Sanderson	.05	.03
729	Don Zimmer	.05	.03
730	Barry Larkin	.12	.07
731	Jeff Gray (R)	.12	.07
732	Franklin Stubbs	.05	.03
733	Kelly Downs	.05	.03
734	John Russell	.05	.03
735	Ron Darling	.07	.04
736	Dick Schofield	.05	.03

737	Tim Crews	.05	.03
738	Mel Hall	.07	.04
739	Russ Swan	.05	.03
740	Ryne Sandberg	.20	.12
741	Jimmy Key	.07	.04
742	Tommy Gregg	.05	.03
743	Bryn Smith	.05	.03
744	Nelson Santovenia	.05	.03
745	Doug Jones	.05	.03
746	John Shelby	.05	.03
747	Tony Fossas	.05	.03
748	Al Newman	.05	.03
749	Greg Harris	.05	.03
750	Bobby Bonilla	.10	.06
751	Wayne Edwards	.05	.03
752	Kevin Bass	.05	.03
753	Paul Marak (R)	.10	.06
754	Bill Pecota	.05	.03
755	Mark Langston	.08	.05
756	Jeff Huson	.05	.03
757	Mark Gardner	.10	.06
758	Mike Devereaux	.08	.05
759	Bobby Cox	.05	.03
760	Benny Santiago	.08	.05
761	Larry Andersen	.05	.03
762	Mitch Webster	.05	.03
763	Dana Kiecker	.05	.03
764	Mark Carreon	.05	.03
765	Shawon Dunston	.08	.05
766	Jeff Robinson	.05	.03
767	Dan Wilson (R) (#1 Pick)	.20	.12
768	Donn Paul	.05	.03
769	Tim Sherrill (R)	.08	.05
770	Jay Howell	.05	.03
771	Gary Redus	.05	.03
772	Kent Mercker	.10	.06
773	Tom Foley	.05	.03
774	Dennis Rasmussen	.05	.03
775	Julio Franco	.08	.05
776	Brent Mayne (R)	.10	.06
777	John Candelaria	.05	.03
778	Dan Gladden	.05	.03
779	Carmelo Martinez	.05	.03
780	Randy Myers	.05	.03
781	Darryl Hamilton	.05	.03
782	Jim Deshaies	.05	.03
783	Joel Skinner	.05	.03
784	Willie Fraser	.05	.03
785	Scott Fletcher	.05	.03
786	Eric Plunk	.05	.03
787	Checklist 6	.05	.03
788	Bob Milacki	.05	.03
789	Tom Lasorda	.07	.04
790	Ken Griffey Jr.	.60	.35
791	Mike Benjamin	.08	.05
792	Mike Greenwell	.10	.06

1991 Topps Stadium Club

This 600-card set marks Topps entrance into the upscale premium baseball card market. The set was released in two 300-card series and sold only in foil packs. Card fronts feature a high gloss, borderless design with full-bleed photos. Card backs include a small player photo, a player evaluation chart and biographical information. Cards measure 2-1/2" by 3-1/2".

		MINT	NR/MT
Complete Set (600)		240.00	185.00
Commons		.20	.12
1	Dave Stewart	.80	.50
2	Wally Joyner	.30	.18
3	Shawon Dunston	.25	.15
4	Darren Daulton	.30	.18
5	Will Clark	3.00	2.00
6	Sammy Sosa	.30	.18
7	Dan Plesac	.20	.12
8	Marquis Grissom	2.50	1.50
9	Erik Hanson	.25	.15
10	Geno Petralli	.20	.12
11	Jose Rijo	.25	.15
12	Carlos Quintana	.25	.15
13	Junior Ortiz	.20	.12
14	Bob Walk	.20	.12
15	Mike Macfarlane	.20	.12
16	Eric Yelding	.20	.12
17	Bryn Smith	.20	.12
18	Bip Roberts	.20	.12
19	Mike Scioscia	.20	.12
20	Mark Williamson	.20	.12
21	Don Mattingly	1.50	.90
22	John Franco	.20	.12
23	Chet Lemon	.20	.12
24	Tom Henke	.20	.12

#	Name		
25	Jerry Browne	.20	.12
26	Dave Justice	8.50	5.50
27	Mark Langston	.35	.20
28	Damon Berryhill	.20	.12
29	Kevin Bass	.20	.12
30	Scott Fletcher	.20	.12
31	Moises Alou	1.25	.80
32	Dave Valle	.20	.12
33	Jody Reed	.20	.12
34	Dave West	.20	.12
35	Kevin McReynolds	.25	.15
36	Pat Combs	.25	.15
37	Eric Davis	.40	.25
38	Bret Saberhagen	.30	.18
39	Stan Javier	.20	.12
40	Chuck Cary	.20	.12
41	Tony Phillips	.20	.12
42	Lee Smith	.30	.18
43	Tim Teufel	.20	.12
44	Lance Dickson	.35	.20
45	Greg Litton	.20	.12
46	Teddy Higuera	.20	.12
47	Edgar Martinez	.80	.05
48	Steve Avery	4.50	3.00
49	Walt Weiss	.20	.12
50	David Segui	.25	.15
51	Andy Benes	1.00	.70
52	Karl Rhodes	.20	.12
53	Neal Heaton	.20	.12
54	Danny Gladden	.20	.12
55	Luis Rivera	.20	.12
56	Kevin Brown	.35	.20
57	Frank Thomas	32.00	25.00
58	Terry Mulholland	.20	.12
59	Dick Schofield	.20	.12
60	Ron Darling	.25	.15
61	Sandy Alomar, Jr.	.25	.15
62	Dave Stieb	.25	.15
63	Alan Trammell	.30	.18
64	Matt Nokes	.20	.12
65	Lenny Harris	.20	.12
66	Milt Thompson	.20	.12
67	Storm Davis	.20	.12
68	Joe Oliver	.20	.12
69	Andres Galarraga	.25	.15
70	Ozzie Guillen	.25	.15
71	Ken Howell	.20	.12
72	Garry Templeton	.20	.12
73	Derrick May	.25	.15
74	Xavier Hernandez	.20	.12
75	Dave Parker	.25	.15
76	Rick Aguilera	.25	.15
77	Robby Thompson	.25	.15
78	Pete Incaviglia	.20	.12
79	Bob Welch	.25	.15
80	Randy Milligan	.25	.15
81	Chuck Finley	.25	.15
82	Alvin Davis	.20	.12
83	Tim Naehring	.25	.15
84	Jay Bell	.20	.12
85	Joe Magrane	.20	.12
86	Howard Johnson	.25	.15
87	Jack McDowell	1.50	.90
88	Kevin Seitzer	.25	.15
89	Bruce Ruffin	.20	.12
90	Fernando Valenzuela	.25	.15
91	Terry Kennedy	.20	.12
92	Barry Larkin	1.00	.70
93	Larry Walker	1.75	1.00
94	Luis Salazar	.20	.12
95	Gary Sheffield	7.00	4.50
96	Bobby Witt	.25	.15
97	Lonnie Smith	.20	.12
98	Bryan Harvey	.25	.15
99	Mookie Wilson	.20	.12
100	Dwight Gooden	.50	.30
101	Lou Whitaker	.25	.15
102	Ron Karkovice	.20	.12
103	Jesse Barfield	.25	.15
104	Jose DeJesus	.20	.12
105	Benito Santiago	.25	.15
106	Brian Holman	.25	.15
107	Rafael Ramirez	.20	.12
108	Ellis Burks	.25	.15
109	Mike Bielecki	.20	.12
110	Kirby Puckett	3.50	2.50
111	Terry Shumpert	.20	.12
112	Chuck Crim	.20	.12
113	Todd Benzinger	.20	.12
114	Brian Barnes	.30	.18
115	Carlos Baerga	2.50	1.50
116	Kal Daniels	.20	.12
117	Dave Johnson	.20	.12
118	Andy Van Slyke	.50	.30
119	John Burkett	.20	.12
120	Rickey Henderson	1.75	1.00
121	Tim Jones	.20	.12
122	Daryl Irvine	.25	.15
123	Ruben Sierra	2.50	1.50
124	Jim Abbott	1.25	.80
125	Daryl Boston	.20	.12
126	Greg Maddux	1.00	.70
127	Von Hayes	.20	.12
128	Mike Fitzgerald	.20	.12
129	Wayne Edwards	.20	.12
130	Greg Briley	.20	.12
131	Rob Dibble	.25	.15
132	Gene Larkin	.20	.12
133	David Wells	.20	.12
134	Steve Balboni	.20	.12
135	Greg Vaughn	.50	.30
136	Mark Davis	.20	.12
137	Dave Rohde	.25	.15
138	Eric Show	.20	.12
139	Bobby Bonilla	1.25	.80
140	Dana Kiecker	.20	.12

141	Gary Pettis	.20	.12
142	Dennis Boyd	.20	.12
143	Mike Benjamin	.20	.12
144	Luis Polonia	.20	.12
145	Doug Jones	.20	.12
146	Al Newman	.20	.12
147	Alex Fernandez	.75	.45
148	Bill Doran	.20	.12
149	Kevin Elster	.20	.12
150	Len Dykstra	.25	.15
151	Mike Gallego	.20	.12
152	Tim Belcher	.25	.15
153	Jay Buhner	.25	.15
154	Ozzie Smith	1.00	.70
155	Jose Canseco	3.50	2.50
156	Gregg Olson	.25	.15
157	Charlie O'Brien	.20	.12
158	Frank Tanana	.20	.12
159	George Brett	1.75	1.00
160	Jeff Huson	.20	.12
161	Kevin Tapani	.30	.18
162	Jerome Walton	.20	.12
163	Charlie Hayes	.20	.12
164	Chris Bosio	.20	.12
165	Chris Sabo	.25	.15
166	Lance Parrish	.25	.15
167	Don Robinson	.20	.12
168	Manuel Lee	.20	.12
169	Dennis Rasmussen	.20	.12
170	Wade Boggs	1.50	.90
171	Bob Geren	.20	.12
172	Mackey Sasser	.20	.12
173	Julio Franco	.35	.20
174	Otis Nixon	.25	.15
175	Bert Blyleven	.25	.15
176	Craig Biggio	.50	.30
177	Eddie Murray	1.00	.70
178	Randy Tomlin	.80	.50
179	Tino Martinez	.80	.50
180	Carlton Fisk	1.00	.70
181	Dwight Smith	.20	.12
182	Scott Garrelts	.20	.12
183	Jim Gantner	.20	.12
184	Dickie Thon	.20	.12
185	John Farrell	.20	.12
186	Cecil Fielder	1.50	.90
187	Glenn Braggs	.20	.12
188	Allan Anderson	.20	.12
189	Kurt Stillwell	.20	.12
190	Jose Oquendo	.20	.12
191	Joe Orsulak	.20	.12
192	Ricky Jordan	.20	.12
193	Kelly Downs	.20	.12
194	Delino DeShields	2.50	1.50
195	Omar Vizquel	.20	.12
196	Mark Carreon	.20	.12
197	Mike Harkey	.25	.15
198	Jack Howell	.20	.12
199	Lance Johnson	.20	.12
200	Nolan Ryan	18.00	12.50
201	John Marzano	.20	.12
202	Doug Drabek	.30	.18
203	Mark Lemke	.20	.12
204	Steve Sax	.25	.15
205	Greg Harris	.20	.12
206	B.J. Surhoff	.20	.12
207	Todd Burns	.20	.12
208	Jose Gonzalez	.20	.12
209	Mike Scott	.20	.12
210	Dave Magadan	.20	.12
211	Dante Bichette	.20	.12
212	Trevor Wilson	.20	.12
213	Hector Villanueva	.20	.12
214	Dan Pasqua	.20	.12
215	Greg Colbrunn (R)	1.25	.80
216	Mike Jeffcoat	.20	.12
217	Harold Reynolds	.25	.15
218	Paul O'Neill	.25	.15
219	Mark Guthrie	.20	.12
220	Barry Bonds	3.00	2.00
221	Jimmy Key	.20	.12
222	Billy Ripken	.20	.12
223	Tom Pagnozzi	.25	.15
224	Bo Jackson	1.50	.90
225	Sid Fernandez	.25	.15
226	Mike Marshall	.20	.12
227	John Kruk	.25	.15
228	Mike Fetters	.20	.12
229	Eric Anthony	.35	.20
230	Ryne Sandberg	3.50	2.50
231	Carney Lansford	.25	.15
232	Melido Perez	.20	.12
233	Jose Lind	.20	.12
234	Darryl Hamilton	.25	.15
235	Tom Browning	.25	.15
236	Spike Owen	.20	.12
237	Juan Gonzalez	18.00	12.50
238	Felix Fermin	.20	.12
239	Keith Miller	.20	.12
240	Mark Gubicza	.25	.15
241	Kent Anderson	.20	.12
242	Alvaro Espinoza	.20	.12
243	Dale Murphy	.40	.25
244	Orel Hershiser	.30	.18
245	Paul Molitor	.35	.20
246	Eddie Whitson	.20	.12
247	Joe Girardi	.20	.12
248	Kent Hrbek	.25	.15
249	Bill Sampen	.20	.12
250	Kevin Mitchell	.30	.18
251	Mariano Duncan	.20	.12
252	Scott Bradley	.20	.12
253	Mike Greenwell	.40	.25
254	Tom Gordon	.25	.15
255	Todd Zeile	.50	.30
256	Bobby Thigpen	.25	.15

257	Gregg Jefferies	.70	.40	315	Walt Terrell	.20	.12
258	Kenny Rogers	.20	.12	316	Sam Horn	.20	.12
259	Shane Mack	.50	.30	317	Wes Chamberlain	1.00	.70
260	Zane Smith	.20	.12	318	Pedro Munoz (R)	1.50	.90
261	Mitch Williams	.20	.12	319	Roberto Kelly	.50	.30
262	Jim DeShaies	.20	.12	320	Mark Portugal	.20	.12
263	Dave Winfield	1.25	.80	321	Tim McIntosh	.25	.15
264	Ben McDonald	1.25	.80	322	Jesse Orosco	.20	.12
265	Randy Ready	.20	.12	323	Gary Green	.20	.12
266	Pat Borders	.20	.12	324	Greg Harris	.20	.12
267	Jose Uribe	.20	.12	325	Hubie Brooks	.25	.15
268	Derek Lilliquist	.20	.12	326	Chris Nabholz	.60	.35
269	Greg Brock	.20	.12	327	Terry Pendleton	.75	.45
270	Ken Griffey, Jr.	18.00	12.50	328	Eric King	.20	.12
271	Jeff Gray	.25	.15	329	Chili Davis	.25	.15
272	Danny Tartabull	.50	.30	330	Anthony Telford	.25	.15
273	Dennis Martinez	.25	.15	331	Kelly Gruber	.25	.15
274	Robin Ventura	4.50	3.00	332	Dennis Eckersley	.75	.45
275	Randy Myers	.20	.12	333	Mel Hall	.25	.15
276	Jack Daugherty	.20	.12	334	Bob Kipper	.20	.12
277	Greg Gagne	.20	.12	335	Willie McGee	.25	.15
278	Jay Howell	.20	.12	336	Steve Olin	.20	.12
279	Mike LaValliere	.20	.12	337	Steve Buechele	.20	.12
280	Rex Hudler	.20	.12	338	Scott Leius	.20	.12
281	Mike Simms (R)	.25	.15	339	Hal Morris	.60	.35
282	Kevin Maas	.50	.30	340	Jose Offerman	.25	.15
283	Jeff Ballard	.20	.12	341	Kent Mercker	.25	.15
284	Dave Henderson	.25	.15	342	Ken Griffey	.25	.15
285	Pete O'Brien	.20	.12	343	Pete Harnisch	.25	.15
286	Brook Jacoby	.20	.12	344	Kirk Gibson	.25	.15
287	Mike Henneman	.20	.12	345	Dave Smith	.20	.12
288	Greg Olson	.20	.12	346	Dave Martinez	.20	.12
289	Greg Myers	.20	.12	347	Atlee Hammaker	.20	.12
290	Mark Grace	1.00	.70	348	Brian Downing	.20	.12
291	Shawn Abner	.20	.12	349	Todd Hundley	.25	.15
292	Frank Viola	.30	.18	350	Candy Maldonado	.20	.12
293	Lee Stevens	.25	.15	351	Dwight Evans	.25	.15
294	Jason Grimsley	.25	.15	352	Steve Searcy	.20	.12
295	Matt Williams	.60	.35	353	Gary Gaetti	.20	.12
296	Ron Robinson	.20	.12	354	Jeff Reardon	.50	.30
297	Tom Brunansky	.25	.15	355	Travis Fryman	7.50	4.50
298	Checklist	.20	.12	356	Dave Righetti	.20	.12
299	Checklist	.20	.12	357	Fred McGriff	2.50	1.50
300	Checklist	.20	.12	358	Don Slaught	.20	.12
301	Darryl Strawberry	1.50	.90	359	Gene Nelson	.20	.12
302	Bud Black	.20	.12	360	Billy Spiers	.20	.12
303	Harold Baines	.25	.15	361	Lee Guetterman	.20	.12
304	Roberto Alomar	5.00	3.50	362	Darren Lewis	.25	.15
305	Norm Charlton	.25	.15	363	Duane Ward	.20	.12
306	Gary Thurman	.20	.12	364	Lloyd Moseby	.20	.12
307	Mike Felder	.20	.12	365	John Smoltz	1.25	.80
308	Tony Gwynn	1.75	1.00	366	Felix Jose	1.25	.80
309	Roger Clemens	5.00	3.50	367	David Cone	.75	.45
310	Andre Dawson	1.25	.80	368	Wally Backman	.20	.12
311	Scott Radinsky	.25	.15	369	Jeff Montgomery	.20	.12
312	Bob Melvin	.20	.12	370	Rich Garces (R)	.25	.15
313	Kirk McCaskill	.20	.12	371	Billy Hatcher	.20	.12
314	Pedro Guerrero	.25	.15	372	Bill Swift	.20	.12

373	Jim Eisenreich	.20	.12	429	Scott Aldred	.25	.15
374	Rob Ducey	.20	.12	430	Cal Ripken	6.50	4.50
375	Tim Crews	.20	.12	431	Bill Landrum	.20	.12
376	Steve Finley	.20	.12	432	Ernie Riles	.20	.12
377	Jeff Blauser	.20	.12	433	Danny Jackson	.20	.12
378	Willie Wilson	.20	.12	434	Casey Candaele	.20	.12
379	Gerald Perry	.20	.12	435	Ken Hill	.25	.15
380	Jose Mesa	.20	.12	436	Jaime Navarro	.80	.50
381	Pat Kelly (R)	.60	.35	437	Lance Blankenship	.20	.12
382	Matt Merullo (R)	.25	.15	438	Randy Velarde	.20	.12
383	Ivan Calderon	.25	.15	439	Frank DiPino	.20	.12
384	Scott Chiamparino (R)	.25	.15	440	Carl Nichols	.20	.12
				441	Jeff Robinson	.20	.12
385	Lloyd McClendon	.20	.12	442	Deion Sanders	3.00	2.00
386	Dave Bergman	.20	.12	443	Vincente Palacios	.20	.12
387	Ed Sprague	.50	.30	444	Devon White	.20	.12
388	Jeff Bagwell (R)	8.50	5.50	445	John Cerutti	.20	.12
389	Brett Butler	.25	.15	446	Tracy Jones	.20	.12
390	Larry Andersen	.20	.12	447	Jack Morris	.60	.35
391	Glenn Davis	.20	.12	448	Mitch Webster	.20	.12
392	Alex Cole (Wrong Photo)	.20	.12	449	Bob Ojeda	.20	.12
				450	Oscar Azocar	.20	.12
393	Mike Heath	.20	.12	451	Luis Aquino	.20	.12
394	Danny Darwin	.20	.12	452	Mark Whiten	.60	.35
395	Steve Lake	.20	.12	453	Stan Belinda	.20	.12
396	Tim Layana	.20	.12	454	Ron Gant	2.00	1.25
397	Terry Leach	.20	.12	455	Jose DeLeon	.20	.12
398	Bill Wegman	.20	.12	456	Mark Salas	.20	.12
399	Mark McGwire	4.00	2.75	457	Junior Felix	.20	.12
400	Mike Boddicker	.20	.12	458	Wally Whitehurst	.20	.12
401	Steve Howe	.20	.12	459	Phil Plantier (R)	6.50	4.50
402	Bernard Gilkey	.60	.35	460	Juan Berenguer	.20	.12
403	Thomas Howard	.25	.15	461	Franklin Stubbs	.20	.12
404	Rafael Belliard	.20	.12	462	Joe Boever	.20	.12
405	Tom Candiotti	.20	.12	463	Tim Wallach	.25	.15
406	Rene Gonzalez	.20	.12	464	Mike Moore	.25	.15
407	Chuck McElroy	.20	.12	465	Albert Belle	3.00	2.00
408	Paul Sorrento	.40	.25	466	Mike Witt	.20	.12
409	Randy Johnson	.75	.45	467	Craig Worthington	.20	.12
410	Brady Anderson	.80	.50	468	Jerald Clark	.25	.15
411	Dennis Cook	.20	.12	469	Scott Terry	.20	.12
412	Mickey Tettleton	.25	.15	470	Milt Cuyler	.40	.25
413	Mike Stanton	.25	.15	471	John Smiley	.30	.18
414	Ken Oberkfell	.20	.12	472	Charles Nagy	2.50	1.50
415	Rick Honeycutt	.20	.12	473	Alan Mills	.25	.15
416	Nelson Santovenia	.20	.12	474	John Russell	.20	.12
417	Bob Tewksbury	.20	.12	475	Bruce Hurst	.25	.15
418	Brent Mayne	.25	.15	476	Andujar Cedeno	1.25	.80
419	Steve Farr	.20	.12	477	Dave Eiland	.20	.12
420	Phil Stephenson	.20	.12	478	Brian McRae (R)	1.25	.80
421	Jeff Russell	.20	.12	479	Mike LaCoss	.20	.12
422	Chris James	.20	.12	480	Chris Gwynn	.20	.12
423	Tim Leary	.20	.12	481	Jamie Moyer	.20	.12
424	Gary Carter	.40	.25	482	John Olerud	1.50	.90
425	Glenallen Hill	.25	.15	483	Efrain Valdez	.25	.15
426	Matt Young	.20	.12	484	Sil Campusano	.20	.12
427	Sid Bream	.20	.12	485	Pascual Perez	.20	.12
428	Greg Swindell	.25	.15	486	Gary Redus	.20	.12

487	Andy Hawkins	.20	.12
488	Cory Snyder	.20	.12
489	Chris Hoiles	.80	.50
490	Ron Hassey	.20	.12
491	Gary Wayne	.20	.12
492	Mark Lewis	.75	.45
493	Scott Coolbaugh	.20	.12
494	Gerald Young	.20	.12
495	Juan Samuel	.20	.12
496	Willie Fraser	.20	.12
497	Jeff Treadway	.20	.12
498	Vince Coleman	.25	.15
499	Cris Carpenter	.20	.12
500	Jack Clark	.25	.15
501	Kevin Appier	1.50	.90
502	Rafael Palmeiro	1.00	.70
503	Hensley Meulens	.25	.15
504	George Bell	.50	.30
505	Tony Pena	.20	.12
506	Roger McDowell	.20	.12
507	Luis Sojo	.25	.15
508	Mike Schooler	.20	.12
509	Robin Yount	2.00	1.25
510	Jack Armstrong	.20	.12
511	Rick Cerone	.20	.12
512	Curt Wilkerson	.20	.12
513	Joe Carter	1.50	.90
514	Tim Burke	.20	.12
515	Tony Fernandez	.25	.15
516	Ramon Martinez	.50	.30
517	Tim Hulett	.20	.12
518	Terry Steinbach	.25	.15
519	Pete Smith	.50	.30
520	Ken Caminiti	.25	.15
521	Shawn Boskie	.20	.12
522	Mike Pagliarulo	.20	.12
523	Tim Raines	.25	.15
524	Alfredo Griffin	.20	.12
525	Henry Cotto	.20	.12
526	Mike Stanley	.20	.12
527	Charlie Leibrandt	.20	.12
528	Jeff King	.25	.15
529	Eric Plunk	.20	.12
530	Tom Lampkin	.20	.12
531	Steve Bedrosian	.20	.12
532	Tom Herr	.20	.12
533	Craig Lefferts	.20	.12
534	Jeff Reed	.20	.12
535	Mickey Morandini	.50	.30
536	Greg Cadaret	.20	.12
537	Ray Lankford	3.00	2.00
538	John Candelaria	.20	.12
539	Rob Deer	.25	.15
540	Brad Arnsberg	.20	.12
541	Mike Sharperson	.20	.12
542	Jeff Robinson	.20	.12
543	Mo Vaughn	1.25	.80
544	Jeff Parrett	.20	.12
545	Willie Randolph	.25	.15
546	Herm Winningham	.20	.12
547	Jeff Innis	.20	.12
548	Chuck Knoblauch	6.50	4.50
549	Tommy Greene	.25	.15
550	Jeff Hamilton	.20	.12
551	Barry Jones	.20	.12
552	Ken Dayley	.20	.12
553	Rick Dempsey	.20	.12
554	Greg Smith	.20	.12
555	Mike Devereaux	.40	.25
556	Keith Comstock	.20	.12
557	Paul Faries	.20	.12
558	Tom Glavine	3.50	2.50
559	Craig Grebeck (R)	.25	.15
560	Scott Erickson	2.00	1.25
561	Joel Skinner	.20	.12
562	Mike Morgan	.25	.15
563	Dave Gallagher	.20	.12
564	Todd Stottlemyre	.25	.15
565	Rich Rodriguez (R)	.25	.15
566	Craig Wilson (R)	.25	.15
567	Jeff Brantley	.25	.15
568	Scott Kamieniecki (R)	.25	.15
569	Steve Decker (R)	.25	.15
570	Juan Agosto	.20	.12
571	Tommy Gregg	.20	.12
572	Kevin Wickander	.20	.12
573	Jamie Quirk	.20	.12
574	Jerry Don Gleaton	.20	.12
575	Chris Hammond	.40	.25
576	Luis Gonzalez (R)	1.00	.70
577	Russ Swan	.20	.12
578	Jeff Conine (R)	1.00	.70
579	Charlie Hough	.20	.12
580	Jeff Kunkel	.20	.12
581	Darrel Akerfelds	.20	.12
582	Jeff Manto (R)	.25	.15
583	Alejandro Pena	.25	.15
584	Mark Davidson	.20	.12
585	Bob MacDonald (R)	.25	.15
586	Paul Assenmacher	.20	.12
587	Dan Wilson	.80	.50
588	Tom Bolton	.20	.12
589	Brian Harper	.20	.12
590	John Habyan	.20	.12
591	John Orton	.20	.12
592	Mark Gardner (R)	.25	.15
593	Turner Ward (R)	.35	.20
594	Bob Patterson	.20	.12
595	Edwin Nunez	.20	.12
596	Gary Scott	.35	.20
597	Scott Bankhead	.20	.12
598	Checklist	.20	.12
599	Checklist	.20	.12
600	Checklist	.20	.12

1991 Topps Traded

This 132-card set is identical in design to the 1991 Topps regular edition. The cards measure 2-1/2" by 3-1/2". Card fronts carry the "Topps 40th" logo in honor of Topps 40th Anniversary. The set contains cards of players who were traded during the year plus some promising rookie prospects and a 25-card Team USA subset.

	MINT	NR/MT
Complete Set (132)	13.00	8.50
Commons	.05	.03

1	Juan Agosto	.05	.03
2	Roberto Alomar	.25	.15
3	Wally Backman	.05	.03
4	Jeff Bagwell (R)	1.25	.80
5	Skeeter Barnes (R)	.10	.06
6	Steve Bedrosian	.07	.04
7	Derek Bell (R)	.25	.15
8	George Bell	.10	.06
9	Rafael Belliard	.05	.03
10	Dante Bichette	.05	.03
11	Bud Black	.05	.03
12	Mike Boddicker	.07	.04
13	Sid Bream	.05	.03
14	Hubie Brooks	.07	.04
15	Brett Butler	.10	.06
16	Ivan Calderon	.08	.05
17	John Candelaria	.05	.03
18	Tom Candiotti	.07	.04
19	Gary Carter	.10	.06
20	Joe Carter	.20	.12
21	Rick Cerone	.05	.03
22	Jack Clark	.07	.04
23	Vince Coleman	.07	.04
24	Scott Coolbaugh	.05	.03
25	Danny Cox	.05	.03
26	Danny Darwin	.05	.03
27	Chili Davis	.07	.04

28	Glenn Davis	.07	.04
29	Steve Decker (R)	.12	.07
30	Rob Deer	.07	.04
31	Rich DeLucia (R)	.12	.07
32	John Dettmer (R) (USA)	.12	.07
33	Brian Downing	.05	.03
34	Darren Dreifort (R) (USA)	.15	.10
35	Kirk Dressendorfer (R)	.15	.10
36	Jim Essian	.05	.03
37	Dwight Evans	.08	.05
38	Steve Farr	.05	.03
39	Jeff Fassero (R)	.10	.06
40	Junior Felix	.08	.05
41	Tony Fernandez	.08	.05
42	Steve Finley	.08	.05
43	Jim Fregosi	.05	.03
44	Gary Gaetti	.05	.03
45	Jason Giambi (R) (USA)	.30	.18
46	Kirk Gibson	.07	.04
47	Leo Gomez (R)	.35	.20
48	Luis Gonzalez (R)	.25	.15
49	Jeff Granger (R) (USA)	.20	.12
50	Todd Greene (R) (USA)	.15	.10
51	Jeffrey Hammonds (R) (USA)	1.75	1.00
52	Mike Hargrove	.05	.03
53	Pete Harnisch	.08	.05
54	Rick Helling (R)(USA)	.15	.10
55	Glenallen Hill	.10	.06
56	Charlie Hough	.05	.03
57	Pete Incaviglia	.07	.04
58	Bo Jackson	.20	.12
59	Danny Jackson	.07	.04
60	Reggie Jefferson (R)	.20	.12
61	Charles Johnson (R) (USA)	1.75	1.00
62	Jeff Johnson (R)	.10	.06
63	Todd Johnson (R) (USA)	.15	.10
64	Barry Jones		.03
65	Chris Jones (R)	.15	.10
66	Scott Kamieniecki (R)	.12	.07
67	Pat Kelly (R)		.10
68	Darryl Kile (R)	.15	.10
69	Chuck Knoblauch (R)	.60	.35
70	Bill Krueger	.05	.03
71	Scott Leius (R)	.10	.06
72	Donnie Leshnock (R) (USA)	.15	.10
73	Mark Lewis	.12	.07
74	Candy Maldonado	.07	.04

75	Jason McDonald (R) (USA)	.15	.10
76	Willie McGee	.08	.05
77	Fred McGriff	.20	.12
78	Billy McMillon (R) (USA)	.15	.10
79	Hal McRae	.08	.05
80	Dan Melendez (R) (USA)	.35	.20
81	Orlando Merced (R)	.20	.12
82	Jack Morris	.12	.07
83	Phil Nevin (R)(USA)	2.50	1.50
84	Otis Nixon	.07	.04
85	Johnny Oates	.05	.03
86	Bob Ojeda	.05	.03
87	Mike Pagliarulo	.05	.03
88	Dean Palmer (R)	.40	.25
89	Dave Parker	.08	.05
90	Terry Pendleton	.15	.10
91	Tony Phillips (R) (USA)	.15	.10
92	Doug Piatt (R)	.10	.06
93	Ron Polk (USA)	.05	.03
94	Tim Raines	.08	.05
95	Willie Randolph	.08	.05
96	Dave Righetti	.07	.04
97	Ernie Riles	.05	.03
98	Chris Roberts (R) (USA)	.40	.25
99	Jeff Robinson (Angels)	.05	.03
100	Jeff Robinson (Orioles)	.05	.03
101	Ivan Rodriguez (R)	1.50	.90
102	Steve Rodriguez (R) (USA)	.15	.10
103	Tom Runnells	.05	.03
104	Scott Sanderson	.07	.04
105	Bob Scanlan (R)	.10	.06
106	Pete Schourek (R)	.12	.07
107	Gary Scott (R)	.12	.07
108	Paul Shuey (R)(USA)	.35	.20
109	Doug Simons (R)	.10	.06
110	Dave Smith	.05	.03
111	Cory Snyder	.07	.04
112	Luis Sojo	.07	.04
113	Kennie Steenstra (R) (USA)	.15	.10
114	Darryl Strawberry	.15	.10
115	Franklin Stubbs	.05	.03
116	Todd Taylor (R) (USA)	.15	.10
117	Wade Taylor (R)	.15	.10
118	Garry Templeton	.08	.05
119	Mickey Tettleton	.08	.05
120	Tim Teufel	.05	.03
121	Mike Timlin (R)	.12	.07
122	David Tuttle (R) (USA)	.15	.10
123	Mo Vaughn (R)	.25	.15
124	Jeff Ware (R)(USA)	.15	.10
125	Devon White	.07	.04
126	Mark Whiten	.15	.10
127	Mitch Williams	.08	.05
128	Craig Wilson (R) (USA)	.15	.10
129	Willie Wilson	.07	.03
130	Chris Wimmer (R) (USA)	.20	.12
131	Ivan Zweig (R)(USA)	.15	.10
132	Checklist	.05	.03

1992 Topps

This 792-card set is similar to the 1991 Topps regular edition. Card fronts feature large full color photos surrounded by multi-colored borders. Card backs are horizontal with the usual stats and bio's. Some card backs feature type printed over an image of a ball park. Cards measure 2-1/2" by 3-1/2". Key subsets include Record Breakers (2-5), All-Stars, Top Prospects and Number One Draft Picks.

		MINT	NR/MT
Complete Set (792)		22.00	15.00
Commons		.05	.03
1	Nolan Ryan	.50	.30
2	Rickey Henderson (RB)	.12	.07
3	Jeff Reardon (RB)	.10	.06
4	Nolan Ryan (RB)	.30	.18
5	Dave Winfield (RB)	.12	.07
6	Brien Taylor (#1 Pick)	2.50	1.50

7	Jim Olander (R)	.10	.06
8	Bryan Hickerson (R)	.12	.07
9	John Farrell (R)	.10	.06
10	Wade Boggs	.12	.07
11	Jack McDowell	.15	.10
12	Luis Gonzalez	.12	.07
13	Mike Scioscia	.07	.04
14	Wes Chamberlain	.12	.07
15	Denny Martinez	.10	.06
16	Jeff Montgomery	.05	.03
17	Randy Milligan	.07	.04
18	Greg Cadaret	.05	.03
19	Jamie Quirk	.05	.03
20	Bip Roberts	.08	.05
21	Buck Rogers	.05	.03
22	Bill Wegman	.05	.03
23	Chuck Knoblauch	.30	.18
24	Randy Myers	.05	.03
25	Ron Gant	.12	.07
26	Mike Bielecki	.05	.03
27	Juan Gonzalez	.40	.25
28	Mike Schooler	.05	.03
29	Mickey Tettleton	.07	.04
30	John Kruk	.08	.05
31	Bryn Smith	.05	.03
32	Chris Nabholz	.10	.06
33	Carlos Baerga	.20	.12
34	Jeff Juden	.12	.07
35	Dave Righetti	.05	.03
36	Scott Ruffcorn (R) (#1 Pick)	.35	.20
37	Luis Polonia	.07	.04
38	Tom Candiotti	.07	.04
39	Greg Olson	.05	.03
40	Cal Ripken	.25	.15
41	Craig Lefferts	.05	.03
42	Mike Macfarlane	.05	.03
43	Jose Lind	.05	.03
44	Rick Aguilera	.05	.03
45	Gary Carter	.08	.05
46	Steve Farr	.05	.03
47	Rex Hudler	.05	.03
48	Scott Scudder	.08	.05
49	Damon Berryhill	.05	.03
50	Ken Griffey, Jr.	.60	.35
51	Tom Runnells	.05	.03
52	Juan Bell	.05	.03
53	Tommy Gregg	.05	.03
54	David Wells	.05	.03
55	Rafael Palmeiro	.10	.06
56	Charlie O'Brien	.05	.03
57	Donn Pall	.05	.03
58	Top Prospects-Catcher (Brad Ausmus (R) Jim Campanis, Dave Nilsson, Doug Robbins (R)	.30	.18
59	Mo Vaughn	.15	.10
60	Tony Fernandez	.08	.05
61	Paul O'Neill	.08	.05
62	Gene Nelson	.05	.03
63	Randy Ready	.05	.03
64	Bob Kipper	.05	.03
65	Willie McGee	.08	.05
66	Scott Stahoviak (R) (#1 Pick)	.25	.15
67	Luis Salazar	.05	.03
68	Marvin Freeman	.05	.03
69	Kenny Lofton (R)	.60	.35
70	Gary Gaetti	.05	.03
71	Erik Hanson	.07	.04
72	Eddie Zosky	.05	.03
73	Brian Barnes	.10	.06
74	Scott Leius	.07	.04
75	Bret Saberhagen	.08	.05
76	Mike Gallego	.05	.03
77	Jack Armstrong	.05	.03
78	Ivan Rodriguez	.40	.25
79	Jesse Orosco	.05	.03
80	David Justice	.20	.12
81	Ced Landrum	.05	.03
82	Doug Simons	.07	.04
83	Tommy Greene	.08	.05
84	Leo Gomez	.10	.06
85	Jose DeLeon	.05	.03
86	Steve Finley	.07	.04
87	Bob MacDonald	.07	.04
88	Darrin Jackson	.05	.03
89	Neal Heaton	.05	.03
90	Robin Yount	.15	.10
91	Jeff Reed	.05	.03
92	Lenny Harris	.05	.03
93	Reggie Jefferson	.10	.06
94	Sammy Sosa	.10	.06
95	Scott Bailes	.05	.03
96	Tom McKinnon (R) (#1 Pick)	.10	.06
97	Luis Rivera	.05	.03
98	Mike Harkey	.08	.05
99	Jeff Treadway	.05	.03
100	Jose Canseco	.20	.12
101	Omar Vizquel	.05	.03
102	Scott Kamieniecki	.08	.05
103	Ricky Jordan	.05	.03
104	Jeff Ballard	.05	.03
105	Felix Jose	.10	.06
106	Mike Boddicker	.05	.03
107	Dan Pasqua	.05	.03
108	Mike Timlin	.10	.06
109	Roger Craig	.05	.03
110	Ryne Sandberg	.20	.12
111	Mark Carreon	.05	.03
112	Oscar Azocar	.05	.03
113	Mike Greenwell	.08	.05
114	Mark Portugal	.05	.03
115	Terry Pendleton	.12	.07

116	Willie Randolph	.05	.03
117	Scott Terry	.05	.03
118	Chili Davis	.07	.04
119	Mark Gardner	.05	.03
120	Alan Trammell	.08	.05
121	Derek Bell	.15	.10
122	Gary Varsho	.05	.03
123	Bob Ojeda	.05	.03
124	Shawn Livsey (R) (#1 Pick)	.15	.10
125	Chris Hoiles	.08	.05
126	Top Prospects- 1st Base Rico Brogna (R) John Jaha, Ryan Klesko(R) Dave Staton (R)	1.00	.70
127	Carols Quintana	.07	.04
128	Kurt Stillwell	.05	.03
129	Melido Perez	.05	.03
130	Alvin Davis	.05	.03
131	Checklist 1	.05	.03
132	Eric Show	.05	.03
133	Rance Mulliniks	.05	.03
134	Darryl Kile	.08	.05
135	Von Hayes	.05	.03
136	Bill Doran	.05	.03
137	Jeff Robinson	.05	.03
138	Monty Fariss	.08	.05
139	Jeff Innis	.05	.03
140	Mark Grace	.10	.06
141	Jim Leyland	.07	.04
142	Todd Van Poppel (R)	.30	.18
143	Paul Gibson	.05	.03
144	Bill Swift	.05	.03
145	Danny Tartabull	.10	.06
146	Al Newman	.05	.03
147	Cris Carpenter	.05	.03
148	Anthony Young (R)	.25	.15
149	Brian Bohanon (R)	.12	.07
150	Roger Clemens	.25	.15
151	Jeff Hamilton	.05	.03
152	Charlie Leibrandt	.05	.03
153	Ron Karkovice	.05	.03
154	Hensley Meulens	.08	.05
155	Scott Bankhead	.05	.03
156	Manny Ramirez (R) (#1 Pick)	.80	.50
157	Keith Miller	.05	.03
158	Todd Frohwirth	.05	.03
159	Darrin Fletcher	.05	.03
160	Bobby Bonilla	.10	.06
161	Casey Candaele	.05	.03
162	Paul Faries	.05	.03
163	Dana Kiecker	.05	.03
164	Shane Mack	.08	.05
165	Mark Langston	.08	.05
166	Geronimo Pena	.05	.03
167	Andy Allanson	.05	.03
168	Dwight Smith	.05	.03
169	Chuck Crim	.05	.03
170	Alex Cole	.05	.03
171	Bill Plummer	.05	.03
172	Juan Berenguer	.05	.03
173	Brian Downing	.05	.03
174	Steve Frey	.05	.03
175	Orel Hershiser	.08	.05
176	Ramon Garcia (R)	.12	.07
177	Danny Gladden	.05	.03
178	Jim Acker	.05	.03
179	Top Prospects- 2nd Base Cesar Bernhardt (R) Bobby DeJardin (R) Armando Moreno (R) Andy Stankiewicz	.25	.15
180	Kevin Mitchell	.08	.05
181	Hector Villanueva	.05	.03
182	Jeff Reardon	.10	.06
183	Brent Mayne	.07	.04
184	Jimmy Jones	.05	.03
185	Benny Santiago	.08	.05
186	Cliff Floyd (R) (#1 Pick)	.75	.45
187	Ernie Riles	.05	.03
188	Jose Guzman	.05	.03
189	Junior Felix	.05	.03
190	Glenn Davis	.07	.04
191	Charlie Hough	.05	.03
192	Dave Fleming (R)	.75	.45
193	Omar Oliveras	.08	.05
194	Eric Karros	.75	.45
195	David Cone	.12	.07
196	Frank Castillo	.05	.03
197	Glenn Braggs	.05	.03
198	Scott Aldred	.07	.04
199	Jeff Blauser	.05	.03
200	Len Dykstra	.07	.04
201	Buck Showalter	.05	.03
202	Rick Honeycutt	.05	.03
203	Greg Myers	.05	.03
204	Trevor Wilson	.05	.03
205	Jay Howell	.05	.03
206	Luis Sojo	.07	.04
207	Jack Clark	.07	.04
208	Julio Machado	.05	.03
209	Lloyd McClendon	.05	.03
210	Ozzie Guillen	.05	.03
211	Jeremy Hernandez (R)	.12	.07
212	Randy Velarde	.05	.03
213	Les Lancaster	.05	.03
214	Andy Mota (R)	.08	.05
215	Rich Gossage	.08	.05
216	Brent Gates (R) (#1 Pick)	.40	.25
217	Brian Harper	.05	.03

218	Mike Flanagan	.05	.03
219	Jerry Browne	.05	.03
220	Jose Rijo	.08	.05
221	Skeeter Barnes	.05	.03
222	Jaime Navarro	.08	.05
223	Mel Hall	.12	.07
225	Roberto Alomar	.20	.12
226	Pete Smith	.12	.07
227	Daryl Boston	.05	.03
228	Eddie Whitson	.05	.03
229	Shawn Boskie	.05	.03
230	Dick Schofield	.05	.03
231	Brian Drahman (R)	.10	.06
232	John Smiley	.08	.05
233	Mitch Webster	.05	.03
234	Terry Steinbach	.07	.04
235	Jack Morris	.10	.06
236	Bill Pecota	.05	.03
237	Jose Hernandez (R)	.08	.05
238	Greg Litton	.05	.03
239	Brian Holman	.05	.03
240	Andres Galarraga	.07	.04
241	Gerald Young	.05	.03
242	Mike Mussina	.70	.40
243	Alvaro Espinoza	.05	.03
244	Darren Daulton	.08	.05
245	John Smoltz	.12	.07
246	Jason Pruitt (R) (#1 Pick)	.15	.10
247	Chuck Finley	.08	.05
248	Jim Gantner	.05	.03
249	Tony Fossas	.05	.03
250	Ken Griffey	.07	.04
251	Kevin Elster	.05	.03
252	Dennis Rasmussen	.05	.03
253	Terry Kennedy	.05	.03
254	Ryan Bowen (R)	.12	.07
255	Robin Ventura	.25	.15
256	Mike Aldrete	.05	.03
257	Jeff Russell	.07	.04
258	Jim Lindeman	.05	.03
259	Ron Darling	.07	.04
260	Devon White	.07	.04
261	Tom Lasorda	.07	.04
262	Terry Lee	.05	.03
263	Bob Patterson	.05	.03
264	Checklist 2	.05	.03
265	Teddy Higuera	.05	.03
266	Roberto Kelly	.10	.06
267	Steve Bedrosian	.05	.03
268	Brady Anderson	.10	.06
269	Ruben Amaro (R)	.12	.07
270	Tony Gwynn	.15	.10
271	Tracy Jones	.05	.03
272	Jerry Don Gleaton	.05	.03
273	Craig Grebeck	.05	.03
274	Bob Scanlan	.07	.04
275	Todd Zeile	.10	.06
276	Shawn Green (R) (#1 Pick)	.30	.18
277	Scott Chiamparino	.05	.03
278	Darryl Hamilton	.05	.03
279	Jim Clancy	.05	.03
280	Carlos Martinez	.05	.03
281	Kevin Appier	.08	.05
282	John Wehner (R)	.10	.06
283	Reggie Sanders (R)	.35	.20
284	Gene Larkin	.05	.03
285	Bob Welch	.07	.04
286	Gilberto Reyes	.05	.03
287	Pete Schourek	.05	.03
288	Andujar Cedeno	.12	.07
289	Mike Morgan	.07	.04
290	Bo Jackson	.15	.10
291	Phil Garner	.05	.03
292	Ray Lankford	.15	.10
293	Mike Henneman	.05	.03
294	Dave Valle	.05	.03
295	Alonzo Powell	.07	.04
296	Tom Brunansky	.07	.04
297	Kevin Brown	.10	.06
298	Kelly Gruber	.07	.04
299	Charles Nagy	.15	.10
300	Don Mattingly	.15	.10
301	Kirk McCaskill	.05	.03
302	Joey Cora	.05	.03
303	Dan Plesac	.05	.03
304	Joe Oliver	.05	.03
305	Tom Glavine	.12	.07
306	Al Shirley (R) (#1 Pick)	.35	.20
307	Bruce Ruffin	.05	.03
308	Craig Shipley (R)	.08	.05
309	Dave Martinez	.05	.03
310	Jose Mesa	.05	.03
311	Henry Cotto	.05	.03
312	Mike LaValliere	.05	.03
313	Kevin Tapani	.08	.05
314	Jeff Huson	.05	.03
315	Juan Samuel	.05	.03
316	Curt Schilling	.05	.03
317	Mike Bordick	.12	.07
318	Steve Howe	.05	.03
319	Tony Phillips	.05	.03
320	George Bell	.08	.05
321	Lou Piniella	.07	.04
322	Tim Burke	.05	.03
323	Milt Thompson	.05	.03
324	Danny Darwin	.05	.03
325	Joe Orsulak	.05	.03
326	Eric King	.05	.03
327	Jay Buhner	.07	.04
328	Joel Johnson (R)	.10	.06
329	Franklin Stubbs	.05	.03
330	Will Clark	.20	.12
331	Steve Lake	.05	.03

332	Chris Jones	.05	.03
333	Pat Tabler	.05	.03
334	Kevin Gross	.05	.03
335	Dave Henderson	.07	.04
336	Greg Anthony (R) (#1 Pick)	.15	.10
337	Alejandro Pena	.05	.03
338	Shawn Abner	.05	.03
339	Tom Browning	.07	.04
340	Otis Nixon	.07	.04
341	Bob Geren	.05	.03
342	Tim Spehr (R)	.10	.06
343	Jon Vander Wal (R)	.12	.07
344	Jack Daugherty	.05	.03
345	Zane Smith	.05	.03
346	Rheal Cormier (R)	.15	.10
347	Kent Hrbek	.08	.05
348	Rick Wilkins (R)	.12	.07
349	Steve Lyons	.05	.03
350	Gregg Olson	.07	.04
351	Greg Riddoch	.05	.03
352	Ed Nunez	.05	.03
353	Braulio Castillo (R)	.08	.05
354	Dave Bergman	.05	.03
355	Warren Newson (R)	.08	.05
356	Luis Quinones	.05	.03
357	Mike Witt	.05	.03
358	Ted Wood	.12	.07
359	Mike Moore	.07	.04
360	Lance Parrish	.07	.04
361	Barry Jones	.05	.03
362	Javier Ortiz (R)	.08	.05
363	John Candelaria	.05	.03
364	Glenallen Hill	.08	.05
365	Duane Ward	.05	.03
366	Checklist 3	.05	.03
367	Rafael Belliard	.05	.03
368	Bill Kruegar	.05	.03
369	Steve Whitaker (R) (#1 Pick)	.15	.10
370	Shawon Dunston	.08	.05
371	Dante Bichette	.05	.03
372	Kip Gross	.05	.03
373	Don Robinson	.05	.03
374	Bernie Williams	.15	.10
375	Bert Blyleven	.08	.05
376	Chris Donnels (R)	.12	.07
377	Bob Zupcic (R)	.25	.15
378	Joel Skinner	.05	.03
379	Steve Chitren	.05	.03
380	Barry Bonds	.20	.12
381	Sparky Anderson	.07	.04
382	Sid Fernandez	.07	.04
383	Dave Hollins	.10	.06
384	Mark Lee	.05	.03
385	Tim Wallach	.08	.05
386	Will Clark (AS)	.12	.07
387	Ryne Sandberg (AS)	.15	.10
388	Howard Johnson (AS)	.07	.04
389	Barry Larkin (AS)	.08	.05
390	Barry Bonds (AS)	.10	.06
391	Ron Gant (AS)	.08	.05
392	Bobby Bonilla (AS)	.08	.05
393	Craig Biggio (AS)	.07	.04
394	Denny Martinez (AS)	.07	.04
395	Tom Glavine (AS)	.10	.06
396	Ozzie Smith (AS)	.10	.06
397	Cecil Fielder (AS)	.10	.06
398	Julio Franco (AS)	.07	.04
399	Wade Boggs (AS)	.08	.05
400	Cal Ripken (AS)	.15	.10
401	Jose Canseco (AS)	.12	.07
402	Joe Carter (AS)	.10	.06
403	Ruben Sierra (AS)	.10	.06
404	Matt Nokes (AS)	.07	.04
405	Roger Clemens (AS)	.12	.07
406	Jim Abbott (AS)	.08	.05
407	Bryan Harvey (AS)	.07	.04
408	Bob Milacki	.05	.03
409	Geno Petralli	.05	.03
410	Dave Stewart	.08	.05
411	Mike Jackson	.05	.03
412	Luis Aquino	.05	.03
413	Tim Teufel	.05	.03
414	Jeff Ware (#1 Pick)	.12	.07
415	Jim Deshaies	.05	.03
416	Ellis Burks	.08	.05
417	Allan Anderson	.05	.03
418	Alfredo Griffin	.05	.03
419	Wally Whitehurst	.05	.03
420	Sandy Alomar	.08	.05
421	Juan Agosto	.05	.03
422	Sam Horn	.05	.03
423	Jeff Fassero	.05	.03
424	Paul McClellan (R)	.10	.06
425	Cecil Fielder	.15	.10
426	Tim Raines	.07	.04
427	Eddie Taubensee (R)	.12	.07
428	Dennis Boyd	.05	.03
429	Tony LaRussa	.07	.04
430	Steve Sax	.07	.04
431	Tom Gordon	.07	.04
432	Billy Hatcher	.05	.03
433	Cal Eldred	.15	.10
434	Wally Backman	.05	.03
435	Mark Eichhorn	.05	.03
436	Mookie Wilson	.05	.03
437	Scott Servais	.08	.05
438	Mike Maddux	.05	.03
439	Chico Walker	.05	.03
440	Doug Drabek	.10	.06
441	Rob Deer	.07	.04
442	Dave West	.05	.03
443	Spike Owen	.05	.03
444	Tyrone Hill (R)	.35	.20

	(#1 Pick)		
445	Matt Williams	.10	.06
446	Mark Lewis	.08	.05
447	David Segui	.07	.04
448	Tom Pagnozzi	.07	.04
449	Jeff Johnson	.07	.04
450	Mark McGwire	.25	.15
451	Tom Henke	.05	.03
452	Wilson Alvarez	.08	.05
453	Gary Redus	.05	.03
454	Darren Holmes	.07	.04
455	Pete O'Brien	.05	.03
456	Pat Combs	.07	.04
457	Hubie Brooks		
		.005	.03
458	Frank Tanana	.05	.03
459	Tom Kelly	.05	.03
460	Andre Dawson	.12	.07
461	Doug Jones	.05	.03
462	Rich Rodriguez	.07	.04
463	Mike Simms	.07	.04
464	Mike Jeffcoat	.05	.03
465	Barry Larkin	.10	.06
466	Stan Belinda	.05	.03
467	Lonnie Smith	.07	.04
468	Greg Harris	.05	.03
469	Jim Eisenreich	.05	.03
470	Pedro Guerrero	.07	.04
471	Jose DeJesus	.05	.03
472	Rich Rowland (R)	.12	.07
473	Top Prospects-	.20	.12
	3rd Base		
	Frank Bolick (R)		
	Craig Paquette (R)		
	Tom Redington (R)		
	Paul Russo (R)		
474	Mike Rossiter (R)	.12	.07
	(#1 Pick)		
475	Robby Thompson	.05	.03
476	Randy Bush	.05	.03
477	Greg Hibbard	.05	.03
478	Dale Sveum	.05	.03
479	Chito Martinez (R)	.15	.10
480	Scott Sanderson	.05	.03
481	Tino Martinez	.08	.05
482	Jimmy Key	.05	.03
483	Terry Shumpert	.05	.03
484	Mike Hartley	.05	.03
485	Chris Sabo	.08	.05
486	Bob Walk	.05	.03
487	John Cerutti	.05	.03
488	Scott Cooper	.12	.07
489	Bobby Cox	.05	.03
490	Julio Franco	.08	.05
491	Jeff Brantley	.05	.03
492	Mike Devereaux	.08	.05
493	Jose Offerman	.08	.05
494	Gary Thurman	.05	.03
495	Carney Lansford	.07	.04
496	Joe Grahe	.07	.04
497	Andy Ashby	.05	.03
498	Gerald Perry	.05	.03
499	Dave Otto	.05	.03
500	Vince Coleman	.07	.04
501	Rob Mallicoat (R)	.08	.05
502	Greg Briley	.05	.03
503	Pascual Perez	.05	.03
504	Aaron Sele (R)	.40	.25
	(#1 Pick)		
505	Bobby Thigpen	.07	.04
506	Todd Benzinger	.05	.03
507	Candy Maldonado	.05	.03
508	Bill Gullickson	.05	.03
509	Doug Dascenzo	.05	.03
510	Frank Viola	.08	.05
511	Kenny Rogers	.05	.03
512	Mike Heath	.05	.03
513	Kevin Bass	.05	.03
514	Kim Batiste	.08	.05
515	Delino DeShields	.15	.10
516	Ed Sprague	.10	.06
517	Jim Gott	.05	.03
518	Jose Melendez	.05	.03
519	Hal McRae	.07	.04
520	Jeff Bagwell	.35	.20
521	Joe Hesketh	.05	.03
522	Milt Cuyler	.08	.05
523	Shawn Hillegas	.05	.03
524	Don Slaught	.05	.03
525	Randy Johnson	.12	.07
526	Doug Piatt	.05	.03
527	Checklist 4	.05	.03
528	Steve Foster (R)	.08	.05
529	Joe Girardi	.05	.03
530	Jim Abbott	.12	.07
531	Larry Walker	.12	.07
532	Mike Huff	.05	.03
533	Mackey Sasser	.05	.03
534	Benji Gil (R)	.25	.15
	(#1 Pick)		
535	Dave Stieb	.07	.04
536	Willie Wilson	.05	.03
537	Mark Leiter (R)	.08	.05
538	Jose Uribe	.05	.03
539	Thomas Howard	.08	.05
540	Ben McDonald	.12	.07
541	Jose Tolentino (R)	.08	.05
542	Keith Mitchell	.10	.06
543	Jerome Walton	.07	.04
544	Cliff Brantley (R)	.10	.06
545	Andy Van Slyke	.08	.05
546	Paul Sorrento	.08	.05
547	Herm Winningham	.05	.03
548	Mark Guthrie	.05	.03
549	Joe Torre	.07	.04
550	Darryl Strawberry	.15	.10

551	Top Prospects-SS	.70	.40
	Manny Alexander (R)		
	Alex Arias (R)		
	Wil Cordero (R)		
	Chipper Jones		
552	Dave Gallagher	.05	.03
553	Edgar Martinez	.12	.07
554	Donald Harris	.08	.05
555	Frank Thomas	.80	.05
556	Storm Davis	.05	.03
557	Dickie Thon	.05	.03
558	Scott Garrelts	.05	.03
559	Steve Olin	.05	.03
560	Rickey Henderson	.15	.10
561	Jose Vizcaino	.05	.03
562	Wade Taylor	.05	.03
563	Pat Borders	.05	.03
564	Jimmy Gonzalez (R)	.10	.06
	(#1 Pick)		
565	Lee Smith	.10	.06
566	Bill Sampen	.05	.03
567	Dean Palmer	.15	.10
568	Bryan Harvey	.07	.04
569	Tony Pena	.05	.03
570	Lou Whitaker	.08	.05
572	Greg Vaughn	.08	.05
573	Kelly Downs	.05	.03
574	Steve Avery	.15	.10
575	Kirby Puckett	.20	.12
576	Heathcliff Slocumb	.10	.06
	(R)		
577	Kevin Seitzer	.07	.04
578	Lee Guetterman	.05	.03
579	Johnny Oates	.05	.03
580	Greg Maddux	.12	.07
581	Stan Javier	.05	.03
582	Vicente Palacios	.05	.03
583	Mel Rojas	.07	.04
584	Wayne Rosenthal (R)	.08	.05
585	Lenny Webster	.05	.03
586	Rod Nichols	.05	.03
587	Mickey Morandini	.08	.05
588	Russ Swan	.05	.03
589	Mariano Duncan	.05	.03
590	Howard Johnson	.08	.05
591	Top Prospects-OF	.35	.20
	Jacob Brumfield (R)		
	Jeromy Burnitz (R)		
	Alan Cockrell (R)		
	D.J. Dozier (R)		
592	Denny Neagle (R)	.12	.07
593	Steve Decker	.08	.05
594	Brian Barber (R)	.25	.15
	(#1 Pick)		
595	Bruce Hurst	.07	.04
596	Kent Mercker	.07	.04
597	Mike Magnante (R)	.10	.06
598	Jody Reed	.05	.03
599	Steve Searcy	.05	.03
600	Paul Molitor	.08	.05
601	Dave Smith	.05	.03
602	Mike Fetters	.05	.03
603	Luis Mercedes	.12	.07
604	Chris Gwynn	.05	.03
605	Scott Erickson	.12	.07
606	Brook Jacoby	.05	.03
607	Todd Stottlemyre	.07	.04
608	Scott Bradley	.05	.03
609	Mike Hargrove	.05	.03
610	Eric Davis	.08	.05
611	Brian Hunter (R)	.15	.10
612	Pat Kelly	.08	.05
613	Pedro Munoz	.10	.06
614	Al Osuna	.05	.03
615	Matt Merullo	.05	.03
616	Larry Andersen	.05	.03
617	Junior Ortiz	.05	.03
618	Top Prospects-OF	.30	.18
	Cesar Hernandez (R)		
	Steve Hosey (R)		
	Dan Peltier (R)		
	Jeff McNeely (R)		
619	Danny Jackson	.05	.03
620	George Brett	.20	.12
621	Dan Gakeler (R)	.10	.06
622	Steve Buechele	.05	.03
623	Bob Tewksbury	.05	.03
624	Shawn Estes (R)	.25	.15
	(#1 Pick)		
625	Kevin McReynolds	.07	.04
626	Chris Haney (R)	.10	.06
627	Mike Sharperson	.05	.03
628	Mark Williamson	.05	.03
629	Wally Joyner	.08	.05
630	Carlton Fisk	.10	.06
631	Armando Reynoso	.08	.05
	(R)		
632	Felix Fermin	.05	.03
633	Mitch Williams	.05	.03
634	Manuel Lee	.05	.03
635	Harold Baines	.07	.04
636	Greg Harris	.05	.03
637	Orlando Merced	.10	.06
638	Chris Bosio	.05	.03
639	Wayne Housie (R)	.10	.06
640	Xavier Hernandez	.05	.03
641	David Howard	.05	.03
642	Tim Crews	.05	.03
643	Rick Cerone	.05	.03
644	Terry Leach	.05	.03
645	Deion Sanders	.15	.10
646	Craig Wilson	.07	.04
647	Marquis Grissom	.15	.10
648	Scott Fletcher	.05	.03
649	Norm Charlton	.07	.04
650	Jesse Barfield	.07	.04

No.	Player		
651	Joe Slusarski	.07	.04
652	Bobby Rose	.07	.04
653	Dennis Lamp	.05	.03
654	Allen Watson (R) (#1 Pick)	.25	.15
655	Brett Butler	.07	.04
656	Top Prospects-OF Rudy Pemberton (R) Henry Rodriguez (R) Lee Tinsley (R) Gerald Williams (R)	.30	.18
657	Dave Johnson	.05	.03
658	Checklist 5	.05	.03
659	Brian McRae	.12	.07
660	Fred McGriff	.20	.12
661	Bill Landrum	.05	.03
662	Juan Guzman	1.00	.70
663	Greg Gagne	.05	.03
664	Ken Hill	.08	.05
665	Dave Haas (R)	.10	.06
666	Tom Foley	.05	.03
667	Roberto Hernandez (R)	.10	.06
668	Dwayne Henry	.05	.03
669	Jim Fregosi	.05	.03
670	Harold Reynolds	.05	.03
671	Mark Whiten	.10	.06
672	Eric Plunk	.05	.03
673	Todd Hundley	.08	.05
674	Mo Sanford (R)	.12	.07
675	Bobby Witt	.07	.04
676	Top Prospects-P Pat Mahomes (R) Sam Militello (R) Roger Salkeld Turk Wendell (R)	1.25	.80
677	John Marzano	.05	.03
678	Joe Klink	.05	.03
679	Pete Incaviglia	.05	.03
680	Dale Murphy	.10	.06
681	Rene Gonzales	.07	.04
682	Andy Benes	.10	.06
683	Jim Poole	.08	.05
684	Trever Miller (R) (#1 Pick)	.12	.07
685	Scott Livingstone (R)	.12	
686	Rich DeLucia	.07	.04
687	Harvy Pulliam (R)	.12	.07
688	Tim Belcher	.07	.04
689	Mark Lemke	.05	.03
690	John Franco	.05	.03
691	Walt Weiss	.05	.03
692	Scott Ruskin	.07	.04
693	Jeff King	.07	.04
694	Mike Gardiner	.07	.04
695	Gary Sheffield	.35	.20
696	Joe Boever	.05	.03
697	Mike Felder	.05	.03
698	John Habyan	.05	.03
699	Cito Gaston	.05	.03
700	Ruben Sierra	.20	.12
701	Scott Radinsky	.07	.04
702	Lee Stevens	.07	.04
703	Mark Wohlers (R)	.20	.12
704	Curt Young	.05	.03
705	Dwight Evans	.07	.04
706	Rob Murphy	.05	.03
707	Gregg Jefferies	.10	.06
708	Tom Bolton	.05	.03
709	Chris James	.05	.03
710	Kevin Maas	.10	.06
711	Ricky Bones (R)	.12	.07
712	Curt Wilkerson	.05	.03
713	Roger McDowell	.05	.03
714	Calvin Reese (R) (#1 Pick)	.25	.15
715	Craig Biggio	.08	.05
716	Kirk Dressendorfer	.08	.05
717	Ken Dayley	.05	.03
718	B.J. Surhoff	.05	.03
719	Terry Mulholland	.05	.03
720	Kirk Gibson	.05	.03
721	Mike Pagliarulo	.05	.03
722	Walt Terrell	.05	.03
723	Jose Oquendo	.05	.03
724	Kevin Morton	.05	.03
725	Dwight Gooden	.10	.06
726	Kirt Manwaring	.05	.03
727	Chuck McElroy	.05	.03
728	Dave Burba	.05	.03
729	Art Howe	.05	.03
730	Ramon Martinez	.10	.06
731	Donnie Hill	.05	.03
732	Nelson Santovenia	.05	.03
733	Bob Melvin	.05	.03
734	Scott Hatteberg (R) (#1 Pick)	.20	.12
735	Greg Swindell	.07	.04
736	Lance Johnson	.05	.03
737	Kevin Reimer	.05	.03
738	Dennis Eckersley	.10	.06
739	Rob Ducey	.05	.03
740	Ken Caminiti	.07	.04
741	Mark Gubicza	.07	.04
742	Billy Spiers	.05	.03
743	Darren Lewis	.08	.05
744	Chris Hammond	.08	.05
745	Dave Magadan	.05	.03
746	Bernard Gilkey	.10	.06
747	Willie Banks	.08	.05
748	Matt Nokes	.05	.03
749	Jerald Clark	.05	.03
750	Travis Fryman	.15	.10
751	Steve Wilson	.05	.03
752	Billy Ripken	.05	.03
753	Paul Assenmacher	.05	.03

754	Charlie Hayes	.05	.03
755	Alex Fernandez	.10	.06
756	Gary Pettis	.05	.03
757	Rob Dibble	.07	.04
758	Tim Naehring	.07	.04
759	Jeff Torborg	.05	.03
760	Ozzie Smith	.10	.06
761	Mike Fitzgerald	.05	.03
762	John Burkett	.05	.03
763	Kyle Abbott	.10	.06
764	Tyler Green (R) (#1 Pick)	.40	.25
765	Pete Harnisch	.07	.04
766	Mark Davis	.05	.03
767	Kal Daniels	.05	.03
768	Jim Thome (R)	.15	.10
769	Jack Howell	.05	.03
770	Sid Bream	.05	.03
771	Arthur Rhodes	.15	.10
772	Garry Templeton	.05	.03
773	Hal Morris	.10	.06
774	Bud Black	.05	.03
775	Ivan Calderon	.07	.04
776	Doug Henry (R)	.12	.07
777	John Olerud	.12	.07
778	Tim Leary	.05	.03
779	Jay Bell	.05	.03
780	Eddie Murray	.12	.07
781	Paul Abbott (R)	.10	.06
782	Phil Plantier	.20	.12
783	Joe Magrane	.05	.03
784	Ken Patterson	.05	.03
785	Albert Belle	.15	.10
786	Royce Clayton (R)	.20	.12
787	Checklist 6	.05	.03
788	Mike Stanton	.10	.06
789	Bobby Valentine	.05	.03
790	Joe Carter	.15	.10
791	Danny Cox	.05	.03
792	Dave Winfield	.15	.10

1992 Topps Traded

As in previous years this update set features 132-cards consisting of traded players and rookie prospects. The set is identical to the Topps regular issue except for the "T" designation on the card numbers. The key subset includes players from Team USA. All cards measure 2-1/2" by 3-1/2".

		MINT	NR/MT
Complete Set (132)		15.00	10.00
Commons		.05	.02

1	Willie Adams (USA)	.20	.12
2	Jeff Alkire (USA)	.20	.12
3	Felipe Alou	.05	.02
4	Moises Alou	.12	.07
5	Ruben Amaro	.08	.05
6	Jack Armstrong	.05	.02
7	Scott Bankhead	.05	.02
8	Tim Belcher	.07	.04
9	George Bell	.08	.05
10	Freddie Benavides	.05	.02
11	Todd Benzinger	.05	.02
12	Joe Boever	.05	.02
13	Ricky Bones	.10	.06
14	Bobby Bonilla	.12	.07
15	Hubie Brooks	.05	.02
16	Jerry Browne	.05	.02
17	Jim Bullinger	.08	.05
18	Dave Burba	.05	.02
19	Kevin Campbell (R)	.10	.06
20	Tom Candiotti	.05	.02
21	Mark Carreon	.05	.02
22	Gary Carter	.10	.06
23	Archi Cianfrocco (R)	.20	.12
24	Phil Clark	.08	.05
25	Chad Curtis (R)	.20	.12
26	Eric Davis	.08	.05
27	Tim Davis (USA)	.20	.12
28	Gary DiSarcina	.07	.04

29	Darren Dreifort (USA)	.15	.10
30	Mariano Duncan	.05	.02
31	Mike Fitzgerald	.05	.02
32	John Flaherty (R)	.12	.07
33	Darrin Fletcher	.05	.02
34	Scott Fletcher	.05	.02
35	Ron Fraser (USA)	.10	.06
36	Andres Galarraga	.07	.04
37	Dave Gallagher	.05	.02
38	Mike Gallego	.05	.02
39	Nomar Garciaparra (USA)	.25	.15
40	Jason Giambi (USA)	.15	.10
41	Dan Gladden	.05	.02
42	Rene Gonzales	.05	.02
43	Jeff Granger (USA)	.15	.10
44	Rick Greene (USA)	.20	.12
45	Jeffrey Hammonds (USA)	1.00	.70
46	Charlie Hayes	.05	.02
47	Von Hayes	.05	.02
48	Rick Helling (USA)	.15	.10
49	Butch Henry (R)	.20	.12
50	Carlos Hernandez	.08	.05
51	Ken Hill	.08	.05
52	Butch Hobson	.05	.02
53	Vince Horsman (R)	.15	.10
54	Pete Incaviglia	.05	.02
55	Gregg Jefferies	.12	.07
56	Charles Johnson (USA)	.50	.30
57	Doug Jones	.05	.02
58	Brian Jordan (R)	.20	.12
59	Wally Joyner	.08	.05
60	Daron Kirkreit (USA)	.20	.12
61	Bill Krueger	.05	.02
62	Gene Lamont	.05	.02
63	Jim Lefebvre	.05	.02
64	Danny Leon (R)	.10	.06
65	Pat Listach (R)	1.25	.80
66	Kenny Lofton	.30	.18
67	Dave Martinez	.05	.02
68	Derrick May	.08	.05
69	Kirk McCaskill	.05	.02
70	Chad McConnell (USA)	.25	.15
71	Kevin McReynolds	.07	.04
72	Rusty Meacham	.08	.05
73	Keith Miller	.05	.02
74	Kevin Mitchell	.08	.05
75	Jason Moler (USA)	.20	.12
76	Mike Morgan	.05	.02
77	Jack Morris	.10	.06
78	Calvin Murray (USA)	.75	.45
79	Eddie Murray	.12	.07
80	Randy Myers	.05	.02
81	Denny Neagle	.08	.05
82	Phil Nevin (USA)	1.25	.80
83	Dave Nilsson	.15	.10
84	Junior Ortiz	.05	.02
85	Donovan Osborne	.35	.20
86	Bill Pecota	.05	.02
87	Melido Perez	.08	.05
88	Mike Perez	.05	.02
89	Hipolito Pichardo (R)	.15	.10
90	Willie Randolph	.07	.04
91	Darren Reed	.05	.02
92	Bip Roberts	.05	.02
93	Chris Roberts (USA)	.20	.12
94	Steve Rodriquez (USA)	.15	.10
95	Bruce Ruffin	.05	.02
96	Scott Ruskin	.05	.02
97	Bret Saberhagen	.10	.06
98	Rey Sanchez (R)	.20	.12
99	Steve Sax	.07	.04
100	Curt Schilling	.05	.02
101	Dick Schofield	.05	.02
102	Gary Scott	.07	.04
103	Kevin Seitzer	.05	.02
104	Frank Seminara (R)	.20	.12
105	Gary Sheffield	.20	.12
106	John Smiley	.08	.05
107	Cory Snyder	.05	.02
108	Paul Sorrento	.10	.06
109	Sammy Sosa	.07	.04
110	Matt Stairs (R)	.20	.12
111	Andy Stankiewicz	.12	.07
112	Kurt Stillwell	.05	.02
113	Rick Sutcliffe	.05	.02
114	Bill Swift	.07	.04
115	Jeff Tackett	.08	.05
116	Danny Tartabull	.10	.06
117	Eddie Taubensee	.08	.05
118	Dickie Thon	.05	.02
119	Michael Tucker (USA)	1.00	.70
120	Scooter Tucker (R)	.12	.07
121	Marc Valdes (USA)	.20	.12
122	Julio Valera	.05	.02
123	Jason Varitek (USA)	.35	.20
124	Ron Villone (USA)	.20	.12
125	Frank Viola	.07	.04
126	B.J. Wallace (USA)	.80	.50
127	Dan Walters (R)	.12	.07
128	Craig Wilson (USA)	.15	.10
129	Chris Wimmer (USA)	.15	.10
130	Dave Winfield	.20	.12
131	Herm Winningham	.05	.02
132	Checklist	.05	.02

1992 Topps Stadium Club

This is Topps second annual upscale premium baseball set and the design is similar to 1991 Stadium Club. The fronts feature full color action shots with the player's name and Stadium Club logo at the bottom of the card. Card backs include a small full color player photo. Cards measure 2-1/2" by 3-1/2" and the set was issued in three 300-card series. The set includes the Members Choice Subset (591-610) and three special First Round Draft Pick insert cards. The Draft Pick cards are included at the end of this checklist but are not part of the complete set price.

		MINT	NR/MT
Complete Set (900)		110.00	75.00
Commons		.15	.10
1	Cal Ripken	3.00	2.00
2	Eric Yelding	.10	.10
3	Geno Petralli	.15	.10
4	Wally Backman	.15	.10
5	Milt Cuyler	.20	.12
6	Kevin Bass	.15	.10
7	Dante Bichette	.15	.10
8	Ray Lankford	.75	.45
9	Mel Hall	.15	.10
10	Joe Carter	.75	.45
11	Juan Samuel	.15	.10
12	Jeff Montgomery	.15	.10
13	Glenn Braggs	.15	.10
14	Henry Cotto	.15	.10
15	Deion Sanders	.80	.50
16	Dick Schofield	.15	.10
17	David Cone	.40	.25
18	Chili Davis	.15	.10
19	Tom Foley	.15	.10
20	Ozzie Guillen	.15	.10
21	Luis Salazar	.15	.10
22	Terry Steinbach	.15	.10
23	Chris James	.15	.10
24	Jeff King	.20	.12
25	Carlos Quintana	.20	.12
26	Mike Maddux	.15	.10
27	Tommy Greene	.20	.12
28	Jeff Russell	.15	.10
29	Steve Finley	.20	.12
30	Mike Flanagan	.20	.12
31	Darren Lewis	.20	.12
32	Mark Lee	.15	.10
33	Willie Fraser	.15	.10
34	Mike Henneman	.15	.10
35	Kevin Maas	.20	.12
36	Dave Hansen	.20	.12
37	Erik Hansen	.20	.12
38	Bill Doran	.15	.10
39	Mike Boddicker	.15	.10
40	Vince Coleman	.25	.15
41	Devon White	.15	.10
42	Mark Gardner	.20	.12
43	Scott Lewis	.15	.10
44	Juan Berenguer	.15	.10
45	Carney Lansford	.20	.12
46	Curt Wilkerson	.15	.10
47	Shane Mack	.30	.18
48	Bip Roberts	.15	.10
49	Greg Harris	.15	.10
50	Ryne Sandberg	1.75	1.00
51	Mark Whiten	.20	.12
52	Jack McDowell	.50	.30
53	Jimmy Jones	.15	.10
54	Steve Lake	.15	.10
55	Bud Black	.15	.10
56	Dave Valle	.15	.10
57	Kevin Reimer	.15	.10
58	Rich Gedman	.15	.10
59	Travis Fryman	1.00	.70
60	Steve Avery	1.00	.70
61	Francisco de la Rosa(R)	.15	.10
62	Scott Hemond	.15	.10
63	Hal Morris	.20	.12
64	Hensley Muelens	.20	.12
65	Frank Castillo	.15	.10
66	Gene Larkin	.15	.10
67	Jose DeLeon	.15	.10
68	Al Osuna	.15	.10
69	Dave Cochrane	.20	.12
70	Robin Ventura	1.25	.80
71	John Cerutti	.15	.10
72	Kevin Gross	.15	.10
73	Ivan Calderon	.20	.12
74	Mike Macfarlane	.15	.10
75	Stan Belinda	.15	.10
76	Shawn Hillegas	.15	.10

77	Pat Borders	.15	.10
78	Jim Vatcher	.15	.10
79	Bobby Rose	.15	.10
80	Roger Clemens	2.00	1.25
81	Craig Worthington	.15	.10
82	Jeff Treadway	.15	.10
83	Jamie Quirk	.15	.10
84	Randy Bush	.15	.10
85	Anthony Young	.30	.18
86	Trevor Wilson	.15	.10
87	Jaime Navarro	.30	.18
88	Les Lancaster	.15	.10
89	Pat Kelly	.20	.12
90	Alvin Davis	.15	.10
91	Larry Anderson	.15	.10
92	Rob Deer	.15	.10
93	Mike Sharperson	.15	.10
94	Lance Parrish	.15	.10
95	Cecil Espy	.15	.10
96	Tim Spehr	.15	.10
97	Dave Stieb	.15	.10
98	Terry Mulholland	.15	.10
99	Dennis Boyd	.15	.10
100	Barry Larkin	.40	.25
101	Ryan Bowen	.20	.12
102	Felix Fermin	.15	.10
103	Luis Alicea	.15	.10
104	Tim Hulett	.15	.10
105	Rafael Belliard	.15	.10
106	Mike Gallego	.15	.10
107	Dave Righetti	.15	.10
108	Jeff Schaefer	.15	.10
109	Ricky Bones	.20	.12
110	Scott Erickson	.35	.20
111	Matt Nokes	.15	.10
112	Bob Scanlan	.15	.10
113	Tom Candiotti	.15	.10
114	Sean Berry	.20	.12
115	Kevin Morton	.20	.12
116	Scott Fletcher	.15	.10
117	B.J. Surhoff	.15	.10
118	Dave Magadan	.15	.10
119	Bill Gullickson	.15	.10
120	Marquis Grissom	.75	.45
121	Lenny Harris	.15	.10
122	Wally Joyner	.25	.15
123	Kevin Brown	.20	.12
124	Braulio Castillo (R)	.20	.12
125	Eric King	.15	.10
126	Mark Portugal	.15	.10
127	Calvin Jones (R)	.20	.12
128	Mike Heath	.15	.10
129	Todd Van Poppel	.80	.50
130	Benny Santiago	.25	.15
131	Gary Thurman	.15	.10
132	Joe Girardi	.15	.10
133	Dave Eiland	.15	.10
134	Orlando Merced	.25	.15
135	Joe Orsulak	.15	.10
136	John Burkett	.15	.10
137	Ken Dayley	.15	.10
138	Ken Hill	.20	.12
139	Walt Terrell	.15	.10
140	Mike Scioscia	.15	.10
141	Junior Felix	.15	.10
142	Ken Caminiti	.15	.10
143	Carlos Baerga	.75	.45
144	Tony Fossas	.15	.10
145	Craig Grebeck	.15	.10
146	Scott Bradley	.15	.10
147	Kent Mercker	.20	.12
148	Derrick May	.20	.12
149	Jerald Clark	.15	.10
150	George Brett	.75	.45
151	Luis Quinones	.15	.10
152	Mike Pagliarulo	.15	.10
153	Jose Guzman	.15	.10
154	Charlie O'Brien	.15	.10
155	Darren Holmes	.15	.10
156	Joe Boever	.15	.10
157	Rick Monteleone	.15	.10
158	Reggie Harris	.15	.10
159	Roberto Alomar	1.25	.80
160	Robby Thompson	.15	.10
161	Chris Hoiles	.25	.15
162	Tom Pagnozzi	.20	.12
163	Omar Vizquel	.15	.10
164	John Candiotti	.15	.10
165	Terry Shumpert	.15	.10
166	Andy Mota	.15	.10
167	Scott Bailes	.15	.10
168	Jeff Blauser	.15	.10
169	Steve Olin	.15	.10
170	Doug Drabek	.35	.20
171	Dave Bergman	.15	.10
172	Eddie Whitson	.15	.10
173	Gilberto Reyes	.15	.10
174	Mark Grace	.40	.25
175	Paul O'Neill	.20	.12
176	Greg Cadaret	.15	.10
177	Mark Williamson	.15	.10
178	Casey Candaele	.15	.10
179	Candy Maldonado	.15	.10
180	Lee Smith	.25	.15
181	Harold Reynolds	.15	.10
182	David Justice	1.50	.90
183	Lenny Webster	.15	.10
184	Donn Pall	.15	.10
185	Gary Alexander	.15	.10
186	Jack Clark	.20	.12
187	Stan Javier	.15	.10
188	Ricky Jordan	.15	.10
189	Franklin Stubbs	.15	.10
190	Dennis Eckersley	.40	.25
191	Danny Tartabull	.35	.20
192	Pete O'Brien	.15	.10

193	Mark Lewis	.25	.15
194	Mike Felder	.15	.10
195	Mickey Tettleton	.20	.12
196	Dwight Smith	.15	.10
197	Shawn Abner	.15	.10
198	Jim Leyritz	.15	.10
199	Mike Devereaux	.20	.12
200	Craig Biggio	.20	.12
201	Kevin Elster	.15	.10
202	Rance Mulliniks	.15	.10
203	Tony Fernandez	.20	.12
204	Allan Anderson	.15	.10
205	Herm Winningham	.15	.10
206	Tim Jones	.15	.10
207	Ramon Martinez	.25	.15
208	Teddy Higuera	.15	.10
209	John Kruk	.20	.12
210	Jim Abbott	.40	.25
211	Dean Palmer	.80	.50
212	Mark Davis	.15	.10
213	Jay Buhner	.15	.10
214	Jesse Barfield	.15	.10
215	Kevin Mitchell	.20	.12
216	Mike LaValliere	.15	.10
217	Mark Wohlers	.30	.18
218	Dave Henderson	.15	.10
219	Dave Smith	.15	.10
220	Albert Belle	.80	.50
221	Spike Owen	.15	.10
222	Jeff Gray	.15	.10
223	Paul Gibson	.15	.10
224	Bobby Thigpen	.20	.12
225	Mike Mussina	4.50	2.75
226	Darrin Jackson	.15	.10
227	Luis Gonzalez	.20	.12
228	Greg Briley	.15	.10
229	Brent Mayne	.20	.12
230	Paul Molitor	.20	.12
231	Al Leiter	.15	.10
232	Andy Van Slyke	.30	.18
233	Ron Tingley	.15	.10
234	Bernard Gilkey	.20	.12
235	Kent Hrbek	.20	.12
236	Eric Karros	3.50	2.50
237	Randy Velarde	.15	.10
238	Andy Allanson	.15	.10
239	Willie McGee	.20	.12
240	Juan Gonzalez	3.00	2.00
241	Karl Rhodes	.20	.12
242	Luis Mercedes	.35	.20
243	Billy Swift	.15	.10
244	Tommy Gregg	.15	.10
245	David Howard	.15	.10
246	Dave Hollins	.60	.35
247	Kip Gross	.15	.10
248	Walt Weiss	.15	.10
249	Mackey Sasser	.15	.10
250	Cecil Fielder	.75	.45
251	Jerry Browne	.15	.10
252	Doug Dascenzo	.15	.10
253	Darryl Hamilton	.20	.12
254	Dan Bilardello	.15	.10
255	Luis Rivera	.15	.10
256	Larry Walker	.60	.35
257	Ron Karkovice	.15	.10
258	Bob Tewksbury	.15	.10
259	Jimmy Key	.15	.10
260	Bernie Williams	.50	.30
261	Gary Wayne	.20	.12
262	Mike Simms	.15	.10
263	John Orton	.20	.12
264	Marvin Freeman	.15	.10
265	Mike Jeffcoat	.15	.10
266	Roger Mason	.15	.10
267	Edgar Martinez	.40	.25
268	Henry Rodriquez	.25	.15
269	Sam Horn	.15	.10
270	Brian McRae	.20	.12
271	Kirt Manwaring	.15	.10
272	Mike Bordick	.20	.12
273	Chris Sabo	.15	.10
274	Jim Olander	.15	.10
275	Greg Harris	.15	.10
276	Dan Gakeler	.15	.10
277	Bill Sampen	.15	.10
278	Joel Skinner	.15	.10
279	Curt Schilling	.15	.10
280	Dale Murphy	.25	.15
281	Lee Stevens	.20	.12
282	Lonnie Smith	.15	.10
283	Manual Lee	.15	.10
284	Shawn Boskie	.15	.10
285	Kevin Seitzer	.20	.12
286	Stan Royer	.20	.12
287	John Dopson	.15	.10
288	Scott Bullett (R)	.30	.18
289	Ken Patterson	.15	.10
290	Todd Hundley	.20	.12
291	Tim Leary	.15	.10
292	Brett Butler	.25	.15
293	Gregg Olson	.25	.15
294	Jeff Brantley	.15	.10
295	Brian Holman	.20	.12
296	Brian Harper	.15	.10
297	Brian Bohanon	.15	.10
298	Checklist	.15	.10
299	Checklist	.15	.10
300	Checklist	.15	.10
301	Frank Thomas	5.00	3.50
302	Lloyd McClendon	.15	.10
303	Brady Anderson	.40	.25
304	Julio Valera	.15	.10
305	Mike Aldrete	.15	.10
306	Joe Oliver	.15	.10
307	Todd Stottlemyre	.20	.12
308	Rey Sanchez (R)	.25	.15

309	Gary Sheffield	2.00	1.25
310	Andujar Cedeno	.30	.18
311	Kenny Rogers	.15	.10
312	Bruce Hurst	.20	.12
313	Mike Schooler	.20	.12
314	Mike Benjamin	.15	.10
315	Chuck Finley	.20	.12
316	Mark Lemke	.15	.10
317	Scott Livingstone	.30	.18
318	Chris Nabholz	.25	.15
319	Mike Humphreys	.20	.12
320	Pedro Guerrero	.20	.12
321	Willie Banks	.30	.18
322	Tom Goodwin	.25	.15
323	Hector Warner (R)	.20	.12
324	Wally Ritchie	.15	.10
325	Mo Vaughn	.35	.20
326	Jo Klink	.15	.10
327	Cal Eldred	1.75	1.00
328	Daryl Boston	.15	.10
329	Mike Huff	.15	.10
330	Jeff Bagwell	1.50	.90
331	Bob Milacki	.15	.10
332	Tom Prince (R)	.15	.10
333	Pat Tabler	.15	.10
334	Ced Landrum	.15	.10
335	Reggie Jefferson	.25	.15
336	Mo Sanford	.20	.12
337	Kevin Ritz	.20	.12
338	Gerald Perry	.15	.10
339	Jeff Hamilton	.15	.10
340	Tim Wallach	.20	.12
341	Jeff Huson	.20	.12
342	Jose Melendez	.15	.10
343	Willie Wilson	.15	.10
344	Mike Stanton	.20	.12
345	Joel Johnston	.15	.10
346	Lee Guetterman	.15	.10
347	Francisco Oliveras	.15	.10
348	Dave Burba (R)	.20	.12
349	Tim Crews	.15	.10
350	Scott Leius	.15	.10
351	Danny Cox	.15	.10
352	Wayne Housie (R)	.20	.12
353	Chris Donnels	.20	.12
354	Chris George	.20	.12
355	Gerald Young	.15	.10
356	Roberto Hernandez	.20	.12
357	Neal Heaton	.15	.10
358	Todd Frohwirth	.15	.10
359	Jose Vizcaino	.15	.10
360	Jim Thome	.40	.25
361	Craig Wilson	.20	.12
362	Dave Haas	.15	.10
363	Billy Hatcher	.15	.10
364	John Barfield	.15	.10
365	Luis Aquino	.15	.10
366	Charlie Leibrandt	.15	.10
367	Howard Farmer	.15	.10
368	Bryn Smith	.15	.10
369	Mickey Morandini	.25	.15
370	Jose Canseco	1.75	1.00
371	Jose Uribe	.15	.10
372	Bob MacDonald (R)	.20	.12
373	Luis Sojo	.15	.10
374	Craig Shipley (R)	.20	.12
375	Scott Bankhead	.15	.10
376	Greg Gagne	.15	.10
377	Scott Cooper	.30	.18
378	Jose Offerman	.20	.12
379	Billy Spiers	.15	.10
380	John Smiley	.20	.12
381	Jeff Carter (R)	.15	.10
382	Heathcliff Slocumb	.15	.10
383	Jeff Tackett	.20	.12
384	John Kiely (R)	.20	.12
385	John Vander Wal (R)	.25	.15
386	Omar Olivares	.15	.10
387	Ruben Sierra	1.25	.80
388	Tom Gordon	.20	.12
389	Charles Nagy	.60	.35
390	Dave Stewart	.20	.12
391	Pete Harnisch	.20	.12
392	Tim Burke	.15	.10
393	Roberto Kelly	.25	.15
394	Freddie Benavides	.15	.10
395	Tom Glavine	.75	.45
396	Wes Chamberlain	.20	.12
397	Eric Gunderson	.15	.10
398	Dave West	.15	.10
399	Ellis Burks	.20	.12
400	Ken Griffey, Jr.	4.50	3.50
401	Thomas Howard	.20	.12
402	Juan Guzman	4.00	3.00
403	Mitch Webster	.15	.10
404	Matt Merullo	.20	.12
405	Steve Buechele	.20	.12
406	Danny Jackson	.15	.10
407	Felix Jose	.25	.15
408	Doug Piatt (R)	.15	.10
409	Jim Eisenreich	.15	.10
410	Bryan Harvey	.20	.12
411	Jim Austin (R)	.15	.10
412	Jim Poole	.15	.10
413	Glenallen Hill	.20	.12
414	Gene Nelson	.15	.10
415	Ivan Rodriguez	2.00	1.25
416	Frank Tanana	.15	.10
417	Steve Decker	.20	.12
418	Jason Grimsley	.15	.10
419	Tim Layana	.15	.10
420	Don Mattingly	.50	.30
421	Jerome Walton	.15	.10
422	Rob Ducey	.15	.10
423	Andy Benes	.25	.15
424	John Marzano	.15	.10

425	Gene Harris	.15	.10	483	Jim Gott	.15	.10
426	Tim Raines	.20	.12	484	Bob McClure	.15	.10
427	Bret Barberie	.20	.12	485	Tim Teufel	.15	.10
428	Harvey Pulliam	.20	.12	486	Vicente Palacios	.15	.10
429	Cris Carpenter	.15	.10	487	Jeff Reed	.15	.10
430	Howard Johnson	.25	.15	488	Tony Phillips	.15	.10
431	Orel Hershiser	.25	.15	489	Mel Rojas	.20	.12
432	Brain Hunter	.30	.18	490	Ben McDonald	.35	.20
433	Kevin Tapani	.20	.12	491	Andres Santana	.20	.12
434	Rick Reed	.15	.10	492	Chris Beasley (R)	.20	.12
435	Ron Witmeyer (R)	.15	.10	493	Mike Timlin	.20	.12
436	Gary Gaetti	.15	.10	494	Brian Downing	.15	.10
437	Alex Cole	.15	.10	495	Kirk Gibson	.20	.12
438	Chito Martinez	.20	.12	496	Scott Sanderson	.15	.10
439	Greg Litton	.15	.10	497	Nick Esasky	.15	.10
440	Julio Franco	.25	.15	498	Johnny Guzman (R)	.25	.15
441	Mike Munoz	.15	.10	499	Mitch Wiliams	.15	.10
442	Erik Pappas	.15	.10	500	Kirby Puckett	1.75	1.00
443	Pat Combs	.15	.10	501	Mike Harkey	.20	.12
444	Lance Johnson	.15	.10	502	Jim Gantner	.15	.10
445	Ed Sprague	.20	.12	503	Bruce Egloff	.20	.12
446	Mike Greenwell	.20	.12	504	Josias Manzanillo (R)	.20	.12
447	Milt thompson	.15	.10	505	Delino DeShields	.75	.45
448	Mike Magnante (R)	.20	.12	506	Rheal Cormier	.20	.12
449	Chris Haney	.25	.15	507	Jay Bell	.15	.10
450	Robin Yount	.75	.45	508	Rich Rowland (R)	.25	.15
451	Rafael Ramirez	.15	.10	509	Scott Servais	.15	.10
452	Gino Minutelli	.15	.10	510	Terry Pendleton	.35	.20
453	Tom Lampkin	.15	.10	511	Rich DeLucia	.20	.12
454	Tony Perezchica	.15	.10	512	Warren Newson	.20	.12
455	Dwight Gooden	.30	.18	513	Paul Faries	.15	.10
456	Mark Guthrie	.20	.12	514	Kal Daniels	.15	.10
457	Jay Howell	.15	.10	515	Jarvis Brown (R)	.20	.12
458	Gary DiSarcina	.20	.12	516	Rafael Palmeiro	.35	.20
459	John Smoltz	.50	.30	517	Kelly Downs	.15	.10
460	Will Clark	1.50	.90	518	Steve Chitren	.15	.10
461	Dave Otto	.15	.10	519	Moises Alou	.40	.25
462	Rob Maurer (R)	.30	.18	520	Wade Boggs	.75	.45
463	Dwight Evans	.20	.12	521	Pete Schourek	.20	.12
464	Tom Brunansky	.20	.12	522	Scott Terry	.20	.12
465	Shawn Hare (R)	.30	.18	523	Kevin Appier	.25	.15
466	Geronimo Pena	.15	.10	524	Gary Redus	.15	.10
467	Alex Fernandez	.25	.15	525	George Bell	.35	.20
468	Greg Myers	.15	.10	526	Jeff Kaiser (R)	.20	.12
469	Jeff Fassero	.15	.10	527	Alvaro Espinoza	.15	.10
470	Len Dykstra	.20	.12	528	Luis Polonia	.20	.12
471	Jeff Johnson	.15	.10	529	Darren Daulton	.25	.15
472	Russ Swan	.15	.10	530	Norm Charlton	.20	.12
473	Archie Corbin (R)	.25	.15	531	John Olerud	.50	.30
474	Chuck McElroy	.15	.10	532	Dan Plesac	.15	.10
475	Mark McGwire	1.75	1.00	533	Billy Ripken	.15	.10
476	Wally Whitehurst	.15	.10	534	Rod Nichols	.15	.10
477	Tim McIntosh	.20	.12	535	Joey Cora	.15	.10
478	Sid Bream	.15	.10	536	Harold Baines	.20	.12
479	Jeff Juden	.30	.18	537	Bob Ojeda	.15	.10
480	Carlton Fisk	.40	.25	538	Mark Leonard	.15	.10
481	Jeff Plympton (R)	.20	.12	539	Danny Darwin	.15	.10
482	Carlos Martinez	.15	.10	540	Shawon Dunston	.20	.12

541	Pedro Munoz	.30	.18
542	Mark Gubicza	.20	.12
543	Kevin Baez (R)	.20	.12
544	Todd Zeile	.25	.15
545	Don Slaught	.15	.10
546	Tony Eusebio (R)	.20	.12
547	Alonzo Powell	.20	.12
548	Gary Pettis	.15	.10
549	Brian Barnes	.20	.12
550	Lou Whitaker	.20	.12
551	Keith Mitchell	.20	.12
552	Oscar Azocar	.15	.10
553	Stu Cole (R)	.20	.12
554	Steve Wapnick (R)	.20	.12
555	Derek Bell	.35	.20
556	Luis Lopez	.15	.10
557	Anthony Telford	.25	.15
558	Tim Mauser (R)	.20	.12
559	Glenn Sutko (R)	.20	.12
560	Darryl Strawberry	.60	.35
561	Tom Bolton	.15	.10
562	Cliff Young	.15	.10
563	Bruce Walton (R)	.15	.10
564	Chico Walker	.15	.10
565	John Franco	.15	.10
566	Paul McClellan	.15	.10
567	Paul Abbott	.15	.10
568	Gary Varsho	.15	.10
569	Carlos Maldonado (R)	.20	.12
570	Kelly Gruber	.20	.12
571	Jose Oquendo	.15	.10
572	Steve Frey	.15	.10
573	Tino Martinez	.20	.12
574	Bill Haselman	.15	.10
575	Eric Anthony	.25	.15
576	John Habyan	.15	.10
577	Jeffrey McNeely	.50	.30
578	Chris Bosio	.15	.10
579	Joe Grahe	.20	.12
580	Fred McGriff	.80	.50
581	Rick Honeycutt	.15	.10
582	Matt Williams	.30	.18
583	Cliff Brantley (R)	.25	.15
584	Rob Dibble	.20	.12
585	Skeeter Barnes	.15	.10
586	Greg Hibbard	.15	.10
587	Randy Milligan	.15	.10
588	Checklist 301-400	.15	.10
589	Checklist 401-500	.15	.10
590	Checklist 501-600	.15	.10
591	Frank Thomas (MC)	5.00	3.50
592	David Justice (MC)	1.50	.90
593	Roger Clemens (MC)	2.00	1.25
594	Steve Avery (MC)	1.25	.80
595	Cal Ripken (MC)	2.50	1.50
596	Barry Larkin (MC)	.50	.30
597	Jose Canseco (MC)	1.75	1.00
598	Will Clark (MC)	1.50	.90
599	Cecil Fielder (MC)	.75	.45
600	Ryne Sandberg (MC)	1.50	.90
601	Chuck Knoblauch (MC)	1.00	.70
602	Dwight Gooden (MC)	.35	.20
603	Ken Griffey, Jr. (MC)	4.50	3.50
604	Barry Bonds (MC)	1.50	.90
605	Nolan Ryan (MC)	4.00	3.00
606	Jeff Bagwell (MC)	1.50	.90
607	Robin Yount (MC)	.75	.45
608	Bobby Bonilla (MC)	.35	.20
609	George Brett (MC)	.75	.45
610	Howard Johnson (MC)	.25	.15
611	Esteban Beltre (R)	.25	.15
612	Mike Christopher (R)	.20	.15
613	Troy Afenir	.15	.10
614	Mariano Duncan	.15	.10
615	Doug Henry (R)	.35	.20
616	Doug Jones	.15	.10
617	Alvin Davis	.15	.10
618	Craig Lefferts	.15	.10
619	Kevin McReynolds	.20	.12
620	Barry Bonds	1.50	.90
621	Turner Ward	.15	.10
622	Joe Magrane	.15	.10
623	Mark Parent	.15	.10
624	Tom Browning	.20	.12
625	John Smiley	.20	.12
626	Steve Wilson	.15	.10
627	Mike Gallego	.15	.10
628	Sammy Sosa	.20	.12
629	Rico Rossy (R)	.20	.12
630	Royce Clayton	.60	.35
631	Clay Parker	.15	.10
632	Pete Smith	.30	.18
633	Jeff McKnight	.15	.10
634	Jack Daugherty	.15	.10
635	Steve Sax	.25	.15
636	Joe Hesketh	.15	.10
637	Vince Horsman (R)	.20	.12
638	Eric King	.15	.10
639	Joe Boever	.15	.10
640	Jack Morris	.35	.20
641	Arthur Rhodes	.50	.30
642	Bob Melvin	.15	.10
643	Rick Wilkins	.15	.10
744	Scott Scudder	.15	.10
645	Bip Roberts	.15	.10
646	Julio Valera	.20	.12
647	Kevin Campbell (R)	.20	.12
648	Steve Searcey	.15	.10
649	Scott Kamieniecki	.20	.12
650	Kurt Stillwell	.15	.10
651	Bob Welch	.20	.12
652	Andres Galarraga	.20	.12
653	Mike Jackson	.15	.10

654	Bo Jackson	.60	.35
655	Sid Fernandez	.20	.12
656	Mike Bielecki	.15	.10
657	Jeff Reardon	.25	.15
658	Wayne Rosenthal(R)	.20	.12
659	Eric Bullock	.15	.10
660	Eric Davis	.25	.15
661	Randy Tomlin	.25	.15
662	Tom Edens (R)	.20	.12
663	Rob Murphy	.15	.10
664	Leo Gomez	.35	.20
665	Greg Maddux	.40	.25
666	Greg Vaughn	.25	.15
667	Wade Taylor	.15	.10
668	Brad Arnsberg	.15	.10
669	Mike Moore	.15	.10
670	Mark Langston	.25	.15
671	Barry Jones	.15	.10
672	Bill Landrum	.15	.10
673	Greg Swindell	.20	.12
674	Wayne Edwards	.15	.10
675	Greg Olson	.15	.10
676	Bill Pulsipher (R)	.20	.12
677	Bobby Witt	.20	.12
678	Mark Carreon	.15	.10
679	Patrick Lennon	.25	.15
680	Ozzie Smith	.45	.28
681	John Briscoe	.20	.12
682	Matt Young	.15	.10
683	Jeff Conine	.25	.15
684	Phil Stephenson	.15	.10
685	Ron Darling	.15	.10
686	Bryan Hickerson (R)	.20	.12
687	Dale Sveum	.15	.10
688	Kirk McCaskill	.15	.10
689	Rich Amaral (R)	.20	.12
690	Danny Tartabull	.35	.20
691	Donald Harris	.20	.12
692	Doug Davis (R)	.20	.12
693	John Farrell	.15	.10
694	Paul Gibson	.15	.10
695	Kenny Lofton	2.50	1.50
696	Mike Fetters	.15	.10
697	Rosario Rodriquez	.15	.10
698	Chris Jones	.15	.10
699	Jeff Manto	.20	.12
700	Rick Sutcliffe	.20	.12
701	Scott Bankhead	.20	.12
702	Donnie Hill	.15	.10
703	Todd Worrell	.20	.12
704	Rene Gonzales	.25	.15
705	Rick Cerone	.15	.10
706	Tony Pena	.15	.10
707	Paul Sorrento	.25	.15
708	Gary Scott	.20	.12
709	Junior Noboa	.15	.10
710	Wally Joyner	.25	.15
711	Charlie Hayes	.15	.10
712	Rich Rodriquez	.20	.12
713	Rudy Seanez	.25	.15
714	Jim Bullinger (R)	.25	.15
715	Jeff Robinson	.15	.10
716	Jeff Branson	.15	.10
717	Andy Ashby	.20	.12
718	Dave Burba	.20	.12
719	Rich Gossage	.20	.12
720	Randy Johnson	.50	.30
721	David Wells	.15	.10
722	Paul Kilgus	.15	.10
723	Dave Martinez	.15	.10
724	Denny Neagle	.20	.12
725	Andy Stankiewicz (R)	.30	.18
726	Rick Aguilera	.15	.10
727	Junior Noboa	.15	.10
728	Storm Davis	.15	.10
729	Don Robinson	.15	.10
730	Ron Gant	.60	.35
731	Paul Assenmacher	.15	.10
732	Mike Gardiner	.20	.12
733	Milt Hill (R)	.20	.12
734	Jeremy Hernandez (R)	.20	.12
735	Ken Hill	.25	.15
736	Xavier Hernandez	.15	.10
737	Gregg Jefferies	.30	.18
738	Dick Schofield	.15	.10
739	Ron Robinson	.15	.10
740	Sandy Alomar	.20	.12
741	Mike Stanley	.15	.10
742	Butch Henry (R)	.30	.18
743	Floyd Bannister	.15	.10
744	Brian Drahman (R)	.20	.12
745	Dave Winfield	.75	.45
746	Bob Walk	.15	.10
747	Chris James	.15	.10
748	Don Prybylinski (R)	.20	.12
749	Dennis Rasmussen	.15	.10
750	Rickey Henderson	.77	.45
751	Chris Hammond	.25	.15
752	Bob Kipper	.15	.10
753	Dave Rohde	.20	.12
754	Hubie Brooks	.15	.10
755	Bret Saberhagen	.25	.15
756	Jeff Robinson	.15	.10
757	Pat Listach (R)	3.50	2.50
758	Bill Wegman	.15	.10
759	John Wettland	.25	.15
760	Phil Plantier	1.00	.70
761	Wilson Alvarez	.20	.12
762	Scott Aldred	.20	.12
763	Armando Reynoso (R)	.25	.15
764	Todd Benzinger	.15	.10
765	Kevin Mitchell	.25	.15
766	Gary Sheffield	2.50	1.50
767	Allan Anderson	.15	.10

768	Rusty Meacham (R)	.20	.12
769	Rick Parker	.15	.10
770	Nolan Ryan	4.00	3.00
771	Jeff Ballard	.15	.10
772	Cory Snyder	.20	.12
773	Denis Boucher	.20	.12
774	Jose Gonzalez	.15	.10
775	Juan Guerrero (R)	.35	.20
776	Scott Ruskin	.15	.10
778	Terry Leach	.15	.10
779	Carl Willis	.15	.10
780	Bobby Bonilla	.35	.20
781	Duane Ward	.15	.10
782	Joe Slusarski	.15	.10
783	David Segui	.20	.12
784	Kirk Gibson	.20	.12
785	Frank Viola	.25	.15
786	Keith Miller	.15	.10
787	Mike Morgan	.15	.10
788	Kim Batiste	.20	.12
789	Sergio Valdez (R)	.20	.12
790	Eddie Taubensee (R)	.20	.12
791	Jack Armstrong	.20	.12
792	Scott Fletcher	.15	.10
793	Steve Farr	.15	.10
794	Dan Pasqua	.15	.10
795	Eddie Murray	.60	.35
796	John Morris	.15	.10
797	Francisco Cabrera	.15	.10
798	Mike Perez	.25	.15
799	Ted Wood	.30	.18
800	Jose Rijo	.30	.18
801	Danny Gladden	.15	.10
802	Archi Ciafrocco (R)	.50	.30
803	Monty Fariss	.25	.15
804	Roger McDowell	.15	.10
805	Randy Myers	.15	.10
806	Kirk Dressendorfer	.20	.12
807	Zane Smith	.15	.10
808	Glenn Davis	.20	.12
809	Torey Lovullo	.20	.12
810	Andre Dawson	.60	.35
811	Bill Pecota	.15	.10
812	Ted Power	.15	.10
813	Willie Blair	.25	.15
814	Dave Fleming	2.50	1.50
815	Chris Gwynn	.15	.10
816	Jody Reed	.15	.10
817	Mark Dewey (R)	.20	.12
818	Kyle Abbott	.20	.12
819	Tom Henke	.15	.10
820	Kevin Seitzer	.20	.12
821	Al Newman	.15	.10
822	Tim Sherrill (R)	.20	.12
823	Chuck Crim	.20	.12
824	Darren Reed	.20	.12
825	Tony Gwynn	1.00	.70
826	Steve Foster (R)	.20	.12
827	Steve Howe	.15	.10
828	Brook Jacoby	.15	.10
829	Rodney McCray (R)	.20	.12
830	Chuck Knoblauch	1.25	.80
831	John Wehner	.20	.12
832	Scott Garrelts	.15	.10
833	Alejandro Pena	.15	.10
834	Jeff Parrett	.15	.10
835	Juan Bell	.15	.10
836	Lance Dickson	.25	.15
837	Darryl Kile	.20	.12
838	Efrain Valdez	.20	.12
839	Bob Zupcic (R)	.80	.50
840	George Bell	.30	.18
841	Dave Gallagher	.15	.10
842	Tim Belcher	.20	.12
843	Jeff Shaw	.20	.12
844	Mike Fitzgerald	.15	.10
845	Gary Carter	.30	.18
846	John Russell	.15	.10
847	Eric Hillman (R)	.25	.15
848	Mike Witt	.15	.10
849	Curt Wilkerson	.15	.10
850	Alan Trammell	.30	.18
851	Rex Hudler	.15	.10
852	Mike Walkden (R)	.20	.12
853	Kevin Ward (R)	.20	.12
854	Tim Naehring	.20	.12
855	Bill Swift	.15	.10
856	Damon Berryhill	.15	.10
857	Mark Eichhorn	.15	.10
858	Hector Villanueva	.15	.10
859	Jose Lind	.15	.10
860	Denny Martinez	.25	.15
861	Bill Krueger	.15	.10
862	Mike Kingery	.15	.10
863	Jeff Innis	.15	.10
864	Derek Lilliquist	.15	.10
865	Reggie Sanders	1.75	1.00
866	Ramon Garcia	.20	.12
867	Bruce Ruffin	.15	.10
868	Dickie Thon	.15	.10
869	Merlido Perez	.20	.12
870	Ruben Amaro	.20	.12
871	Alan Mills	.20	.12
872	Matt Sinatro	.15	.10
873	Eddie Zosky	.20	.12
874	Pete Incaviglia	.15	.10
875	Tom Candiotti	.15	.10
876	Bob Patterson	.15	.10
877	Neal Heaton	.15	.10
878	Terrel Hansen (R)	.30	.18
879	Dave Eiland	.15	.10
880	Von Hayes	.15	.10
881	Tim Scott (R)	.20	.12
882	Otis Nixon	.20	.12
883	Herm Winningham	.15	.10
884	Dion James	.15	.10

885	Dave Wainhouse	.20	.12
886	Frank DiPino	.15	.10
887	Dennis Cook	.15	.10
888	Jose Mesa	.15	.10
889	Mark Leiter	.15	.10
890	Willie Randolph	.20	.12
891	Craig Colbert (R)	.20	.12
892	Dwayne Henry	.20	.12
893	Jim Lindeman	.15	.10
894	Charlie Hough	.15	.10
895	Gil Heredia (R)	.20	.12
896	Scott Chiamparino	.20	.12
897	Lance Blankenship	.15	.10
898	Checklist	.15	.10
899	Checklist	.15	.10
900	Checklist	.15	.10
SP1	Chipper Jones	12.00	9.00
SP2	Brien Taylor	20.00	15.00
SP3	Phil Nevin	15.00	11.00

1993 Topps

The cards in this 825-card set were issued in two series and feature full color photos on the card fronts framed by a white border. The player's name appears in a color bar below the photo while the team name is centered at the bottom. Card backs include a color photo, personal data and complete stats. The set includes random gold inserts valued at 6 to 10 times the price of the player's regular card. All cards measure 2-1/2" by 3-1/2".

	MINT	NR/MT
Complete Set (825)	28.00	18.00
Commons	.05	.02

1	Robin Yount	.15	.10
2	Barry Bonds	.20	.12
3	Ryne Sandberg	.20	.12
4	Roger Clemens	.20	.12
5	Tony Gwynn	.12	.07
6	Jeff Tackett	.12	.07
7	Pete Incaviglia	.05	.02
8	Mark Wohlers	.12	.07
9	Kent Hrbek	.05	.02
10	Will Clark	.20	.12
11	Eric Karros	.35	.20
12	Lee Smith	.10	.06
13	Esteban Beltre	.07	.04
14	Greg Briley	.05	.02
15	Marquis Grissom	.15	.10
16	Dan Plesac	.05	.02
17	Dave Hollins	.10	.06
18	Terry Steinbach	.05	.02
19	Ed Nunez	.05	.02
20	Tim Salmon	.25	.15
21	Luis Salazar	.05	.02
22	Jim Eisenreich	.05	.02
23	Todd Stottlemyre	.05	.02
24	Tim Naehring	.05	.02
25	John Franco	.05	.02
26	Skeeter Barnes	.05	.02
27	Carlos Garcia	.12	.07
28	Joe Orsulak	.05	.02
29	Dwayne Henry	.05	.02
30	Fred McGriff	.15	.10
31	Derek Lilliquist	.05	.02
32	Don Mattingly	.15	.10
33	B.J. Wallace	.30	.18
34	Juan Gonzalez	.25	.15
35	John Smoltz	.12	.07
36	Scott Servais	.05	.02
37	Lenny Webster	.05	.02
38	Chris James	.05	.02
39	Roger McDowell	.05	.02
40	Ozzie Smith	.10	.06
41	Alex Fernandez	.08	.05
42	Spike Owen	.05	.02
43	Ruben Amaro	.08	.05
44	Kevin Seitzer	.05	.02
45	Dave Fleming	.25	.15
46	Eric Fox	.07	.04
47	Bob Scanlan	.05	.02
48	Bert Blyleven	.08	.05
49	Brian McRae	.08	.05
50	Roberto Alomar	.20	.12
51	Mo Vaughn	.12	.07
52	Bobby Bonilla	.12	.07
53	Frank Tanana	.05	.02
54	Mike LaValliere	.05	.02
55	Mark McLemore	.05	.02
56	Chad Mottola (R)	.50	.30
57	Norm Charlton	.05	.02
58	Jose Melendez	.05	.02

#	Player		
59	Carlos Martinez	.05	.02
60	Roberto Kelly	.10	.06
61	Gene Larkin	.05	.02
62	Rafael Belliard	.05	.02
63	Al Osuna	.05	.02
64	Scott Chiamparino	.05	.02
65	Brett Butler	.07	.04
66	John Burkett	.05	.02
67	Felix Jose	.08	.05
68	Omar Vizquel	.05	.02
69	John Vander Wal	.07	.04
70	Roberto Hernandez	.05	.02
71	Ricky Bones	.07	.04
72	Jeff Grotewold	.05	.02
73	Mike Moore	.05	.02
74	Steve Buechele	.05	.02
75	Juan Guzman	.25	.15
76	Kevin Appier	.08	.05
77	Junior Felix	.05	.02
78	Greg Harris	.05	.02
79	Dick Schofield	.05	.02
80	Cecil Fielder	.15	.10
81	Lloyd McClendon	.05	.02
82	David Segui	.07	.04
83	Reggie Sanders	.15	.10
84	Kurt Stillwell	.05	.02
85	Sandy Alomar	.07	.04
86	John Habyan	.05	.02
87	Kevin Reimer	.07	.04
88	Mike Stanton	.05	.02
89	Eric Anthony	.10	.06
90	Scott Erickson	.12	.07
91	Craig Colbert	.05	.02
92	Tom Pagnozzi	.07	.04
93	Pedro Astacio	.15	.10
94	Lance Johnson	.05	.02
95	Larry Walker	.10	.06
96	Russ Swan	.05	.02
97	Scott Fletcher	.05	.02
98	Derek Jeter (R)	.35	.20
99	Mike Williams	.10	.06
100	Mark McGwire	.25	.15
101	Jim Bullinger	.05	.02
102	Brian Hunter	.10	.06
103	Jody Reed	.05	.02
104	Mike Butcher	.05	.02
105	Gregg Jefferies	.10	.06
106	Howard Johnson	.08	.05
107	John Kiely	.08	.05
108	Jose Lind	.05	.02
109	Sam Horn	.05	.02
110	Barry Larkin	.12	.07
111	Bruce Hurst	.07	.04
112	Brian Barnes	.07	.04
113	Thomas Howard	.08	.05
114	Mel Hall	.07	.04
115	Robby Thompson	.05	.02
116	Mark Lemke	.05	.02
117	Eddie Taubensee	.05	.02
118	David Hulse (R)	.12	.07
119	Pedro Munoz	.08	.05
120	Ramon Martinez	.10	.06
121	Todd Worrell	.05	.02
122	Joey Cora	.05	.02
123	Moises Alou	.12	.07
124	Franklin Stubbs	.05	.02
125	Pete O'Brien	.05	.02
126	Bob Ayrault	.08	.05
127	Carney Lansford	.05	.02
128	Kal Daniels	.05	.02
129	Joe Drake	.05	.02
130	Jeff Montgomery	.05	.02
131	Dave Winfield	.15	.10
132	Preston Wilson (R)	.50	.30
133	Steve Wilson	.05	.02
134	Lee Guetterman	.05	.02
135	Mickey Tettleton	.07	.04
136	Jeff King	.07	.04
137	Alan Mills	.05	.02
138	Joe Oliver	.05	.02
139	Gary Gaetti	.05	.02
140	Gary Sheffield	.15	.10
141	Dennis Cook	.05	.02
142	Charlie Hayes	.05	.02
143	Jeff Huson	.05	.02
144	Kent Mercker	.05	.02
145	Eric Young	.10	.06
146	Scott Leius	.05	.02
147	Bryan Hickerson	.05	.02
148	Steve Finley	.05	.02
149	Rheal Cormier	.05	.02
150	Frank Thomas	.75	.45
151	Archi Cianfrocco	.12	.07
152	Rich DeLucia	.05	.02
153	Greg Vaughn	.10	.06
154	Wes Chamberlain	.10	.06
155	Dennis Eckersley	.12	.07
156	Sammy Sosa	.05	.02
157	Gary DiSarcina	.07	.04
158	Kevin Koslofski	.08	.05
159	Doug Linton	.08	.05
160	Lou Whitaker	.07	.04
161	Chad McConnell	.15	.10
162	Joe Hesketh	.05	.02
163	Tim Wakefield	.70	.40
164	Leo Gomez	.08	.05
165	Jose Rijo	.08	.05
166	Tim Scott	.05	.02
167	Steve Olin	.07	.04
168	Kevin Maas	.10	.06
169	Kevin Rogers	.05	.02
170	David Justice	.15	.10
171	Doug Jones	.05	.02
172	Jeff Reboulet	.10	.06
173	Andres Galarraga	.07	.04
174	Randy Velarde	.05	.02

175	Kirk McCaskill	.05	.02	233	Rick Greene	.12	.07	
176	Darren Lewis	.07	.04	234	Tim McIntosh	.10	.06	
177	Lenny Harris	.05	.02	235	Mitch Williams	.05	.02	
178	Jeff Fassero	.05	.02	236	Kevin Campbell	.07	.04	
179	Ken Griffey, Jr.	.60	.35	237	Jose Vizcaino	.05	.02	
180	Darren Daulton	.12	.07	238	Chris Donnels	.07	.04	
181	John Jaha	.10	.06	239	Mike Bodicker	.05	.02	
182	Ron Darling	.05	.02	240	John Olerud	.10	.06	
183	Greg Maddux	.15	.10	241	Mike Gardiner	.05	.02	
184	Damion Easley	.12	.07	242	Charlie O'Brien	.05	.02	
185	Jack Morris	.15	.10	243	Rob Deer	.07	.04	
186	Mike Magnante	.07	.04	244	Denny Neagle	.07	.04	
187	John Dopson	.05	.02	245	Chris Sabo	.07	.04	
188	Sid Fernandez	.07	.04	246	Gregg Olson	.07	.04	
189	Tony Phillips	.05	.02	247	Frank Seminara	.10	.06	
190	Doug Drabek	.10	.06	248	Scott Scudder	.07	.04	
191	Sean Lowe (R)	.20	.12	249	Tim Burke	.05	.02	
192	Bob Milacki	.05	.02	250	Chuck Knoblauch	.15	.10	
193	Steve Foster	.05	.02	251	Mike Bielecki	.05	.02	
194	Jerald Clark	.07	.04	252	Xavier Hernandez	.05	.02	
195	Pete Harnisch	.07	.04	253	Jose Guzman	.07	.04	
196	Pat Kelly	.08	.05	254	Cory Snyder	.05	.02	
197	Jeff Frye	.05	.02	255	Orel Hershiser	.10	.06	
198	Alejandro Pena	.05	.02	256	Wil Cordero	.15	.10	
199	Junior Ortiz	.05	.02	257	Luis Alicea	.05	.02	
200	Kirby Puckett	.20	.12	258	Mike Schooler	.05	.02	
201	Jose Uribe	.05	.02	259	Craig Grebeck	.05	.02	
202	Mike Scioscia	.05	.02	260	Duane Ward	.05	.02	
203	Bernard Gilkey	.10	.06	261	Bill Wegman	.05	.02	
204	Dan Pasqua	.05	.02	262	Mickey Morandini	.07	.04	
205	Gary Carter	.10	.06	263	Vince Horsman	.10	.06	
206	Henry Cotto	.05	.02	264	Paul Sorrento	.08	.05	
207	Paul Molitor	.10	.06	265	Andre Dawson	.15	.10	
208	Mike Hartley	.05	.02	266	Rene Gonzales	.07	.04	
209	Jeff Parrett	.05	.02	267	Keith Miller	.05	.02	
210	Mark Langston	.08	.05	268	Derek Bell	.10	.06	
211	Doug Dascenzo	.05	.02	269	Todd Steverson (R)	.25	.15	
212	Rick Reed	.05	.02	270	Frank Viola	.07	.04	
213	Candy Maldonado	.05	.02	271	Wally Whitehurst	.05	.02	
214	Danny Darwin	.05	.02	272	Kurt Knudsen	.10	.06	
215	Pat Howell	.08	.05	273	Dan Walters	.08	.05	
216	Mark Leiter	.05	.02	274	Rick Sutcliffe	.05	.02	
217	Kevin Mitchell	.08	.05	275	Andy Van Slyke	.12	.07	
218	Ben McDonald	.12	.07	276	Paul O'Neill	.12	.07	
219	Bip Roberts	.05	.02	277	Mark Whiten	.08	.05	
220	Benito Santiago	.08	.05	278	Chris Nabholz	.07	.04	
221	Carlos Baerga	.15	.10	279	Todd Burns	.05	.02	
222	Bernie Williams	.10	.06	280	Tom Glavine	.15	.10	
223	Roger Pavlik	.10	.06	281	Butch Henry	.05	.02	
224	Sid Bream	.05	.02	282	Shane Mack	.08	.05	
225	Matt Williams	.12	.07	283	Mike Jackson	.05	.02	
226	Willie Banks	.08	.05	284	Henry Rodriquez	.08	.05	
227	Jeff Bagwell	.20	.12	285	Bob Tewksbury	.05	.02	
228	Tom Goodwin	.08	.05	286	Ron Karkovice	.05	.02	
229	Mike Perez	.07	.04	287	Mike Gallego	.05	.02	
230	Carlton Fisk	.15	.10	288	Dave Cochrane	.05	.02	
231	John Wetteland	.07	.04	289	Jesse Orosco	.05	.02	
232	Tino Martinez	.08	.05	290	Dave Stewart	.08	.05	

#	Player		
291	Tommy Greene	.07	.04
292	Rey Sanchez	.10	.06
293	Rob Ducey	.05	.02
294	Brent Mayne	.07	.04
295	Dave Stieb	.08	.05
296	Luis Rivera	.05	.02
297	Jeff Innis	.05	.02
298	Scott Livingstone	.07	.04
299	Bob Patterson	.05	.02
300	Cal Ripken	.25	.15
301	Cesar Hernandez	.08	.05
302	Randy Myers	.05	.02
303	Brook Jacoby	.05	.02
304	Melido Perez	.07	.04
305	Rafael Palmeiro	.10	.06
306	Damon Berryhill	.05	.02
307	Dan Serafini (R)	.25	.15
308	Darryl Kile	.05	.02
309	J.T. Bruett	.08	.05
310	Dave Righetti	.05	.02
311	Jay Howell	.05	.02
312	Geronimo Pena	.05	.02
313	Greg Hibbard	.05	.02
314	Mark Gardner	.05	.02
315	Edgar Martinez	.12	.07
316	Dave Nilsson	.10	.06
317	Kyle Abbott	.07	.04
318	Willie Wilson	.05	.02
319	Paul Assenmacher	.05	.02
320	Tim Fortugno	.05	.02
321	Rusty Meacham	.08	.05
322	Pat Borders	.07	.04
323	Mike Greenwell	.08	.05
324	Willie Randolph	.07	.04
325	Bill Gullickson	.05	.02
326	Gary Varsho	.05	.02
327	Tim Hulett	.07	.04
328	Scott Ruskin	.07	.04
329	Mike Maddux	.05	.02
330	Danny Tartabull	.10	.06
331	Kenny Lofton	.20	.12
332	Gino Petralli	.05	.02
333	Otis Nixon	.08	.05
334	Jason Kendall (R)	.25	.15
335	Mark Portugal	.05	.02
336	Mike Pagliarulo	.05	.02
337	Kirk Manwaring	.05	.02
338	Bob Ojeda	.05	.02
339	Mark Clark	.08	.05
340	John Kruk	.07	.04
341	Mel Rojas	.05	.02
342	Erik Hanson	.05	.02
343	Doug Henry	.05	.02
344	Jack McDowell	.12	.07
345	Harold Baines	.07	.04
346	Chuck McElroy	.05	.02
347	Luis Sojo	.05	.02
348	Andy Stankiewicz	.07	.04
349	Hipolito Pichardo	.10	.06
350	Joe Carter	.15	.10
351	Ellis Burks	.07	.04
352	Pete Schourek	.05	.02
353	Buddy Groom (R)	.12	.07
354	Jay Bell	.05	.02
355	Brady Anderson	.12	.07
356	Freddie Benavides	.05	.02
357	Phil Stephenson	.05	.02
358	Kevin Wickander	.05	.02
359	Mike Stanley	.05	.02
360	Ivan Rodriguez	.20	.12
361	Scott Bankhead	.05	.02
362	Luis Gonzalez	.08	.05
363	John Smiley	.08	.05
364	Trevor Wilson	.05	.02
365	Tom Candiotti	.05	.02
366	Craig Wilson	.08	.05
367	Steve Sax	.07	.04
368	Delino DeShields	.12	.07
369	Jaime Navarro	.08	.05
370	Dave Valle	.05	.02
371	Mariano Duncan	.05	.02
372	Rod Nichols	.05	.02
373	Mike Morgan	.05	.02
374	Julio Valera	.05	.02
375	Wally Joyner	.08	.05
376	Tom Henke	.05	.02
377	Herm Winningham	.05	.02
378	Orlando Merced	.08	.05
379	Mike Munoz	.07	.04
380	Todd Hundley	.07	.04
381	Mike Flannigan	.05	.02
382	Tim Belcher	.07	.04
383	Jerry Browne	.05	.02
384	Mike Benjamin	.07	.04
385	Jim Leyritz	.05	.02
386	Ray Lankford	.15	.10
387	Devon White	.05	.02
388	Jeremy Hernandez	.08	.05
389	Brian Harper	.05	.02
390	Wade Boggs	.12	.07
391	Derrick May	.08	.05
392	Travis Fryman	.15	.10
393	Ron Gant	.12	.07
394	Checklist I-132	.05	.02
395	Checklist 133-264	.05	.02
396	Checklist 265-396	.05	.02
397	George Brett	.20	.12
398	Bobby Witt	.07	.04
399	Daryl Boston	.05	.02
400	Bo Jackson	.25	.15
401	McGriff/Thomas	.60	.35
402	Sandberg/Baerga	.20	.12
403	Sheffield/E. Martinez	.15	.10
404	Larkin/Fryman	.12	.07
405	Van Slyke/Griffey Jr.	.50	.30
406	L. Walker/Puckett	.20	.12

407	B. Bonds/J. Carter	.20	.12
408	Daulton/Harper	.07	.04
409	G. Maddux/Clemens	.20	.12
410	Glavine/Fleming	.15	.10
411	L. Smith/Eckersley	.12	.07
412	Jamie McAndrew	.05	.02
413	Pete Smith	.10	.06
414	Juan Guerrero	.08	.05
415	Todd Frohwirth	.07	.04
416	Randy Tomlin	.08	.05
417	B.J. Surhoff	.05	.02
418	Jim Gott	.05	.02
419	Mark Thompson	.05	.02
420	Kevin Tapani	.07	.04
421	Curt Schilling	.05	.02
422	J.T. Snow (R)	.75	.45
423	1993 Prospects	.35	.20
424	John Valentin (R)	.20	.12
425	Joe Girardi	.05	.02
426	Nigel Wilson (R)	1.25	.80
427	Bob MacDonald (R)	.20	.12
428	Todd Zeile	.08	.05
429	Milt Cuyler	.07	.04
430	Eddie Murray	.12	.07
431	Rich Amaral (R)	.15	.10
432	Pete Young (R)	.15	.10
433	Bailey/Schmidt	.20	.12
434	Jack Armstrong	.05	.02
435	Willie McGee	.08	.05
436	Greg Harris	.05	.02
437	Chris Hammond	.07	.04
438	Ritchie Moody (R)	.15	.10
439	Bryan Harvey	.07	.04
440	Ruben Sierra	.20	.12
441	D. Lemon/T. Pridy	.20	.12
442	Kevin McReynolds	.08	.05
443	Terry Leach	.05	.02
444	David Nied (R)	2.50	1.50
445	Dale Murphy	.10	.06
446	Luis Mercedes	.08	.05
447	Keith Shepherd (R)	.20	.12
448	Ken Caminiti	.05	.02
449	James Austin (R)	.15	.10
450	Darryl Strawberry	.15	.10
451	1993 Prospects	.35	.20
452	Bob Wickman	.20	.12
453	Victor Cole	.05	.02
454	John Johnstone	.10	.06
455	Chili Davis	.07	.04
456	Scott Taylor (R)	.15	.10
457	Tracy Woodson	.05	.02
458	David Wells	.05	.02
459	Derek Wallace (R)	.20	.12
460	Randy Johnson	.10	.06
461	Steve Reed (R)	.15	.10
462	Felix Fermin	.05	.02
463	Scott Aldred	.08	.05
464	Greg Colbrunn	.12	.07
465	Tony Fernandez	.07	.04
466	Mike Felder	.05	.02
467	Lee Stevens	.12	.07
468	Matt Whiteside (R)	.15	.10
469	Dave Hansen	.05	.02
470	Rob Dibble	.07	.04
471	Dave Gallagher	.05	.02
472	Chris Gwynn	.05	.02
473	Dave Henderson	.07	.04
474	Ozzie Guillen	.05	.02
475	Jeff Reardon	.08	.05
476	Voisard/Scalzitti	.35	.20
477	Jimmy Jones	.05	.02
478	Greg Cadaret	.05	.02
479	Todd Pratt	.05	.02
480	Pat Listach	.75	.45
481	Ryan Luzinsky (R)	.40	.25
482	Darren Reed	.05	.02
483	Brian Griffiths (R)	.20	.12
484	John Wehner	.05	.02
485	Glenn Davis	.08	.05
486	Eric Wedge (R)	.40	.25
487	Jesse Hollins (R)	.25	.15
488	Manuel Lee	.05	.02
489	Scott Fredrickson (R)	.15	.10
490	Omar Olivares	.05	.02
491	Shawn Hare (R)	.30	.18
492	Tom Lampkin	.05	.02
493	Jeff Nelson	.05	.02
494	1993 Prospects	.35	.20
495	Ken Hill	.08	.05
496	Reggie Jefferson	.10	.06
497	Petersen/Brown	.20	.12
498	Bud Black	.05	.02
499	Chuck Crim	.05	.02
500	Jose Canseco	.25	.15
501	Johnny Oates	.05	.02
502	Butch Hobson	.05	.02
503	Buck Rodgers	.05	.02
504	Gene Lamont	.05	.02
505	Mike Hargrove	.05	.02
506	Sparky Anderson	.07	.04
507	Hal McRae	.05	.02
508	Phil Garner	.05	.02
509	Tom Kelly	.05	.02
510	Buck Showalter	.05	.02
511	Tony LaRussa	.07	.04
512	Lou Piniella	.05	.02
513	Toby Harrah	.05	.02
514	Cito Gaston	.05	.02
515	Greg Swindell	.07	.04
516	Alex Arias (R)	.15	.10
517	Bill Pecota	.05	.02
518	Benji Grigsby (R)	.25	.15
519	David Howard	.08	.05
520	Charlie Hough	.05	.02
521	Kevin Flora (R)	.15	.10
522	Shane Reynolds (R)	.20	.12

523	Doug Bochtler	.05	.02
524	Chris Hoiles	.08	.05
525	Scott Sanderson	.05	.02
526	Mike Sharperson	.05	.02
527	Mike Fetters	.05	.02
528	Paul Quantrill (R)	.25	.15
529	1993 Prospects	.35	.20
530	Sterling Hitchcock (R)	.40	.25
531	Joe Millette (R)	.15	.10
532	Tom Brunansky	.07	.04
533	Frank Castillo	.05	.02
534	Randy Knorr	.05	.02
535	Jose Oquendo	.05	.02
536	Dave Haas	.05	.02
537	Hutchins/Turner	.20	.12
538	Jimmy Baron (R)	.20	.12
539	Kerry Woodson (R)	.25	.15
540	Ivan Calderon	.07	.04
541	Denis Boucher	.05	.02
542	Royce Clayton	.12	.07
543	Reggie Williams (R)	.15	.10
544	Steve Decker	.08	.05
545	Dean Palmer	.12	.07
546	Hal Morris	.10	.06
547	Ryan Thompson (R)	.40	.25
548	Lance Blankenship	.05	.02
549	Hensley Meulens	.08	.05
550	Scott Radinsky	.05	.02
551	Eric Young (R)	.30	.18
552	Jeff Blauser	.05	.02
553	Andujar Cedeno	.12	.07
554	Arthur Rhodes	.10	.06
555	Terry Mulholland	.05	.02
556	Darryl Hamilton	.07	.04
557	Pedro Martinez (R)	.60	.35
558	R. Whitman/Skeels	.25	.15
559	Jamie Arnold (R)	.20	.12
560	Zane Smith	.05	.02
561	Matt Nokes	.05	.02
562	Bob Zupcic	.08	.05
563	Shawn Boskie	.05	.02
564	Mike Timlin	.08	.05
565	Jerald Clark	.08	.05
566	Rod Brewer	.05	.02
567	Mark Carreon	.05	.02
568	Andy Benes	.10	.06
569	Shawn Barton (R)	.20	.12
570	Tim Wallach	.07	.04
571	Dave Mlicki (R)	.20	.12
572	Trevor Hoffman (R)	.15	.10
573	John Patterson	.07	.04
574	Shawn Warren (R)	.20	.12
575	Monty Fariss	.08	.05
576	1993 Prospects	.35	.20
577	Tim Costo	.15	.10
578	Dave Magadan	.05	.02
579	N. Garrett/Bates	.25	.15
580	Walt Weiss	.05	.02
581	Chris Haney	.07	.04
582	Shawn Abner	.05	.02
583	Marvin Freeman	.05	.02
584	Casey Candaele	.05	.02
585	Ricky Jordan	.07	.04
586	Jeff Tabaka (R)	.20	.12
587	Manny Alexander	.15	.10
588	Mike Trombley	.07	.04
589	Carlos Hernandez (R)	.15	.10
590	Cal Eldred	.30	.18
591	Alex Cole	.05	.02
592	Phil Plantier	.12	.07
593	Brett Merriman (R)	.15	.10
594	Jerry Nielsen (R)	.15	.10
595	Shawon Dunston	.08	.05
596	Jimmy Key	.05	.02
597	Gerald Perry	.05	.02
598	Rico Brogna	.15	.10
599	Nunez/Robinson	.15	.10
600	Bret Saberhagen	.10	.06
601	Craig Shipley	.05	.02
602	Henry Mercedes (R)	.15	.10
603	Jim Thome	.12	.07
604	Rod Beck	.08	.05
605	Chuck Finley	.08	.05
606	J. Owens (R)	.20	.12
607	Dan Smith (R)	.25	.15
608	Bill Doran	.05	.02
609	Lance Parrish	.05	.02
610	Denny Martinez	.08	.05
611	Tom Gordon	.07	.04
612	Bryon Mathews (R)	.20	.12
613	Joel Adamson (R)	.20	.12
614	Brian Williams	.25	.15
615	Steve Avery	.15	.10
616	1993 Prospects	.35	.20
617	Craig Lefferts	.05	.02
618	Tony Pena	.05	.02
619	Billy Spiers	.05	.02
620	Todd Benzinger	.05	.02
621	Kotarski/Boyd	.20	.12
622	Ben Rivera	.08	.05
623	Al Martin (R)	.20	.12
624	Sam Militello	.40	.25
625	Rick Aguilera	.05	.02
626	Dan Gladden	.05	.02
627	Andres Berumen (R)	.15	.10
628	Kelly Gruber	.07	.04
629	Cris Carpenter	.07	.04
630	Mark Grace	.10	.06
631	Jeff Brantley	.05	.02
632	Chris Widger (R)	.15	.10
633	Three Russians	.15	.10
634	Mo Sanford	.07	.04
635	Albert Belle	.15	.10
636	Tim Teufel	.05	.02
637	Greg Myers	.05	.02
638	Brian Bohanon	.05	.02

639	Mike Bordick	.08	.05
640	Dwight Gooden	.12	.07
641	Leahy/Baugh	.20	.12
642	Milt Hill	.05	.02
643	Luis Aquino	.05	.02
644	Dante Bichette	.05	.02
645	Bobby Thigpen	.07	.04
646	Rich Scheid (R)	.15	.10
647	Brian Sackinsky (R)	.15	.10
648	Ryan Howblitzel (R)	.25	.15
649	Tom Marsh (R)	.15	.10
650	Terry Pendleton	.15	.10
651	Rafael Bournigal (R)	.15	.10
652	Dave West	.05	.02
653	Steve Hosey	.25	.15
654	Gerald Williams	.20	.12
655	Scott Cooper	.08	.05
656	Gary Scott	.07	.04
657	Mike Harkey	.07	.04
658	1993 Prospects	.35	.20
659	Ed Sprague	.08	.05
660	Alan Trammell	.10	.06
661	Alston/Case	.20	.12
662	Donovan Osborne	.25	.15
663	Jeff Gardner	.08	.05
664	Calvin Jones	.15	.10
665	Darrin Fletcher	.05	.02
666	Glenallen Hill	.08	.05
667	Jim Rosenbohm (R)	.15	.10
668	Scott Leius	.05	.02
669	Kip Vaughn (R)	.15	.10
670	Julio Franco	.08	.05
671	Dave Martinez	.05	.02
672	Kevin Bass	.05	.02
673	Todd Van Poppel	.20	.12
674	Mark Gubicza	.07	.04
675	Tim Raines	.07	.04
676	Rudy Seanez	.08	.05
677	Charlie Leibrandt	.05	.02
678	Randy Milligan	.05	.02
679	Kim Batiste	.10	.06
680	Craig Biggio	.08	.05
681	Darren Holmes	.05	.02
682	John Candelaria	.05	.02
683	Stafford/Christian	.20	.12
684	Pat Mahomes	.25	.15
685	Bob Walk	.05	.02
686	Russ Springer (R)	.15	.10
687	Tony Sheffield (R)	.12	.07
688	Dwight Smith	.05	.02
689	Eddie Zosky	.08	.05
690	Bien Figueroa (R)	.12	.07
691	Jim Tatum (R)	.12	.07
692	Chad Kreuter	.05	.02
693	Rich Rodriquez	.07	.04
694	Shane Turner (R)	.15	.10
695	Kent Bottenfield (R)	.15	.10
696	Jose Mesa	.05	.02
697	Darrell Whitmore (R)	.12	.07
698	Ted Wood	.10	.06
699	Chad Curtis	.15	.10
700	Nolan Ryan	.40	.25
701	1993 Prospects	.35	.20
702	Tim Pugh (R)	.20	.12
703	Jeff Kent (R)	.50	.30
704	Goodrich/D. Figueroa	.20	.12
705	Bob Welch	.07	.04
706	Sherard Clinkscales (R)	.25	.15
707	Donn Paul	.05	.02
708	Greg Olson	.05	.02
709	Jeff Juden	.08	.05
710	Mike Mussina	.40	.25
711	Scott Chiamparino	.07	.04
712	Stan Javier	.05	.02
713	John Doherty	.05	.02
714	Kevin Gross	.05	.02
715	Greg Gagne	.05	.02
716	Steve Cooke (R)	.20	.12
717	Steve Farr	.05	.02
718	Jay Buhner	.07	.04
719	Butch Henry	.08	.05
720	David Cone	.12	.07
721	Rick Wilkins	.05	.02
722	Chuck Carr	.12	.07
723	Kenny Felder (R)	.15	.10
724	Guillermo Valesquez (R)	.12	.07
725	Billy Hatcher	.05	.02
726	Venezaile/Kendrena	.20	.12
727	Jonathan Hurst (R)	.20	.12
728	Steve Frey	.05	.02
729	Mark Leonard	.05	.02
730	Charles Nagy	.10	.06
731	Donald Harris	.15	.10
732	Travis Buckley (R)	.15	.10
733	Tom Browning	.07	.04
734	Anthony Young	.10	.06
735	Steve Shifflett (R)	.15	.10
736	Jeff Russell	.05	.02
737	Wilson Alvarez	.08	.05
738	Lance Painter	.15	.10
739	Dave Weathers (R)	.15	.10
740	Len Dykstra	.07	.04
741	Mike Devereaux	.07	.04
742	1993 Prospects	.20	.12
743	Dave Landaker (R)	.15	.10
744	Chris George (R)	.20	.12
745	Eric Davis	.08	.05
746	Strittmatter/Rogers	.20	.12
747	Carl Willis	.05	.02
748	Stan Belinda	.05	.02
749	Scott Kamieniecki	.07	.04
750	Rickey Henderson	.15	.10
751	Eric Hillman (R)	.15	.10
752	Pat Hentgen	.05	.02
753	Jim Corsi	.05	.02
754	Brian Jordan	.12	.07

755	Bill Swift	.07	.04
756	Mike Henneman	.05	.02
757	Harold Reynolds	.05	.02
758	Sean Berry	.15	.10
759	Charlie Hayes	.05	.02
760	Luis Polonia	.07	.04
761	Darrin Jackson	.07	.04
762	Mark Lewis	.07	.04
763	Rob Maurer	.08	.05
764	Willie Greene (R)	.50	.30
765	Vince Coleman	.07	.04
766	Todd Revenig (R)	.15	.10
767	Rich Ireland (R)	.15	.10
768	Mike Macfarlane	.05	.02
769	Francisco Cabrera	.05	.02
770	Robin Ventura	.15	.10
771	Kevin Ritz	.07	.04
772	Chito Martinez	.08	.05
773	Cliff Brantley	.07	.04
774	Curtis Leskanic (R)	.15	.10
775	Chris Bosio	.07	.04
776	Jose Offerman	.10	.06
777	Mark Guthrie	.05	.02
778	Don Slaught	.05	.02
779	Rich Monteleone	.05	.02
780	Jim Abbott	.12	.07
781	Jack Clark	.07	.04
782	Mendoza/Roman	.15	.10
784	Jeff Branson	.05	.02
785	Kevin Brown	.08	.05
786	1993 Prospects	.35	.20
787	Mike Matthews (R)	.15	.10
788	Mackey Sasser	.05	.02
789	Jeff Conine	.12	.07
790	George Bell	.10	.06
791	Pat Rapp (R)	.15	.10
792	Joe Boever	.05	.02
793	Jim Poole	.05	.02
794	Andy Ashby	.07	.04
795	Deion Sanders	.15	.10
796	Scott Brosius	.05	.02
797	Brad Pennington (R)	.12	.07
798	Greg Blosser (R)	.35	.20
799	Jim Edmonds (R)	.12	.07
800	Shawn Jeter (R)	.25	.15
801	Jesse Levis (R)	.15	.10
802	Phil Clark (R)	.10	.06
803	Ed Pierce (R)	.12	.07
804	Jose Valentin (R)	.10	.06
805	Terry Jorgensen (R)	.10	.06
806	Mark Hutton (R)	.12	.07
807	Troy Neel (R)	.15	.10
808	Bret Boone (R)	.75	.45
809	Cris Colon (R)	.20	.12
810	Domingo Martinez (R)	.25	.15
811	Javy Lopez (R)	.30	.18
812	Matt Walbeck (R)	.12	.07
813	Dan Wilson	.25	.15

814	Scooter Tucker	.08	.05
815	Billy Ashley (R)	.50	.30
816	Tim Laker (R)	.20	.12
817	Bobby Jones (R)	.30	.18
818	Brad Brink (R)	.20	.12
819	William Pennyfeather	.20	.12
820	Stan Royer	.07	.04
821	Doug Brocail (R)	.12	.07
822	Kevin Rogers	.05	.02
823	Checklist	.05	.02
824	Checklist	.05	.02
825	Checklist	.05	.02

UPPER DECK

1989 Upper Deck

This 800-card set marks Upper Deck's entrance into the baseball card field. The cards, which measure 2-1/2" by 3-1/2", feature full color photographs on both the card fronts and card backs. The backs also contain a small hologram that makes the card counterfeit-proof. The first 26-cards are "Star Rookies". A high-number series, (701-800) was released later in the year and consists of additional rookies and traded players. The complete set prices includes values for both the low and high number series.

	MINT	NR/MT
Complete Set (800)	165.00	110.00
Commons (1-800)	.10	.06

1	Ken Griffey, Jr (R)	60.00	42.00
2	Luis Medina (R)	.15	.08
3	Tony Chance (R)	.12	.07
4	Dave Otto (R)	.10	.06

5	Sandy Alomar, Jr. (R)	.80	.50
6	Rolando Roomes (R)	.12	.07
7	David West (R)	.20	.12
8	Cris Carpenter (R)	.20	.12
9	Gregg Jefferies	1.00	.70
10	Doug Dascenzo	.12	.07
11	Ron Jones (R)	.12	.07
12	Luis de los Santos (R)	.10	.06
13	Gary Sheffield (R)	16.00	10.00
14	Mike Harkey (R)	.30	.18
15	Lance Blankenship (R	.20	.12
16	John Smoltz (R)	6.00	4.00
18	Ramon Martinez (R)	3.50	2.25
19	Mark Lemke (R)	.25	.15
20	Juan Bell (R)	.12	.07
21	Rey Palacios (R)	.12	.07
22	Felix Jose (R)	3.00	2.00
23	Van Snider (R)	.15	.08
24	Dante Bichette (R)	.30	.18
25	Randy Johnson (R)	2.00	1.25
26	Carlos Quintana (R)	.25	.15
27	Checklist 1-26	.10	.06
28	Mike Schooler (R)	.20	.12
29	Randy St. Claire	.10	.06
30	Jerald Clark (R)	.20	.12
31	Kevin Gross	.10	.06
32	Dan Firova (R)	.12	.07
33	Jeff Calhoun (R)	.10	.06
34	Tommy Hinzo (R)	.12	.07
35	Ricky Jordan (R)	.20	.12
36	Larry Parrish	.10	.06
37	Bret Saberhagen	.30	.18
38	Mike Smithson	.10	.06
39	Dave Dravecky	.10	.06
40	Ed Romero	.10	.06
41	Jeff Musselman	.10	.06
42	Ed Hearn	.10	.06
43	Rance Mulliniks	.10	.06
44	Jim Eisenreich	.10	.06
45	Sil Campusano (R)	.15	.08
46	Mike Krukow	.10	.06
47	Paul Gibson	.10	.06
48	Mike LaCoss	.10	.06
49	Larry Herndon	.10	.06
50	Scott Garretts	.10	.06
51	Dwayne Henry	.12	.07
52	Jim Acker	.10	.06
53	Steve Sax	.10	.06
54	Pete O'Brien	.10	.06
55	Paul Runge	.10	.06
56	Rick Rhoden	.10	.06
57	John Dopson (R)	.15	.08
58	Casey Candaele	.10	.06
59	Dave Righetti	.10	.06
60	Joe Hesketh	.10	.06
61	Frank DiPino	.10	.06

62	Tim Laudner	.10	.06
63	Jamie Moyer	.10	.06
64	Fred Toliver	.10	.06
65	Mitch Webster	.10	.06
66	John Tudor	.10	.06
67	John Gangelosi	.10	.06
68	Mike Devereaux	.30	.18
69	Brian Fisher	.10	.06
70	Mike Marshall	.10	.06
71	Zane Smith	.10	.06
72a	Brian Holton (Wrong Photo)	1.50	.90
72b	Brian Holton (Cor)	.10	.06
73	Jose Guzman	.10	.06
74	Rick Mahler	.10	.06
75	John Shelby	.10	.06
76	Jim Deshaies	.10	.06
77	Bobby Meacham	.10	.06
78	Bryn Smith	.10	.06
79	Joaquin Andujar	.10	.06
80	Richard Dotson	.10	.06
81	Charlie Lea	.10	.06
82	Calvin Schiraldi	.10	.06
83	Les Straker	.10	.06
84	Les Lancaster	.10	.06
85	Allan Anderson	.10	.06
86	Junior Ortiz	.10	.06
87	Jesse Orosco	.10	.06
88	Felix Fermin	.10	.06
89	Dave Anderson	.10	.06
90	Rafael Belliard	.10	.06
91	Franklin Stubbs	.10	.06
92	Cecil Espy	.10	.06
93	Albert Hall	.10	.06
94	Tim Leary	.10	.06
95	Mitch Williams	.10	.06
96	Tracy Jones	.10	.06
97	Danny Darwin	.10	.06
98	Gary Ward	.10	.06
99	Neal Heaton	.10	.06
100	Jim Pankovitz	.10	.06
101	Bill Doran	.10	.06
102	Tim Wallach	.15	.08
103	Joe Magrane	.12	.07
104	Ozzie Virgil	.10	.06
105	Alvin Davis	.10	.06
106	Tom Brookens	.15	.08
108	Tracy Woodson	.10	.06
109	Nelson Liriano	.10	.06
110	Devon White	.10	.06
111	Steve Balboni	.10	.06
112	Buddy Bell	.10	.06
113	German Jimenez (R)	.12	.07
114	Ken Dayley	.10	.06
115	Andres Galarraga	.12	.07
116	Mike Scioscia	.10	.06
117	Gary Pettis	.10	.06
118	Ernie Whitt	.10	.06

119	Bob Boone	.15	.08
120	Ryne Sandberg	2.00	1.25
121	Bruce Benedict	.10	.06
122	Hubie Brooks	.12	.07
123	Mike Moore	.10	.06
124	Wallace Johnson	.10	.06
125	Bob Horner	.10	.06
126	Chili Davis	.10	.06
127	Manny Trillo	.10	.06
128	Chet Lemon	.10	.06
129	John Cerutti	.10	.06
130	Orel Hershiser	.15	.08
131	Terry Pendleton	.50	.30
132	Jeff Blauser	.10	.06
133	Mike Fitzgerald	.10	.06
134	Henry Cotto	.10	.06
135	Gerald Young	.12	.07
136	Luis Salazar	.10	.06
137	Alejandro Pena	.10	.06
138	Jack Howell	.10	.06
139	Tony Fernandez	.12	.07
140	Mark Grace	1.50	.90
141	Ken Caminiti	.12	.07
142	Mike Jackson	.10	.06
143	Larry McWilliams	.10	.06
144	Andres Thomas	.10	.06
145	Nolan Ryan	5.00	3.50
146	Mike Davis	.10	.06
147	DeWayne Buice	.10	.06
148	Jody Davis	.10	.06
149	Jesse Barfield	.12	.07
150	Matt Nokes	.12	.07
151	Jerry Reuss	.10	.06
152	Rick Cerone	.10	.06
153	Storm Davis	.10	.06
154	Marvell Wynne	.10	.06
155	Will Clark	2.00	1.25
156	Luis Aguayo	.10	.06
157	Willie Upshaw	.10	.06
158	Randy Bush	.10	.06
159	Ron Darling	.12	.07
160	Kal Daniels	.10	.06
161	Spike Owen	.10	.06
162	Luis Polonia	.12	.07
163	Kevin Mitchell	.20	.12
164	Dave Gallagher (R)	.12	.07
165	Benito Santiago	.15	.08
166	Greg Gagne	.10	.06
167	Ken Phelps	.10	.06
168	Sid Fernandez	.12	.07
169	Bo Diaz	.10	.06
170	Cory Snyder	.10	.06
171	Eric Show	.10	.06
172	Rob Thompson	.10	.06
173	Marty Barrett	.10	.06
174	Dave Henderson	.10	.06
175	Ozzie Guillen	.12	.07
176	Barry Lyons	.10	.06
177	Kevin Torve (R)	.12	.07
178	Don Slaught	.10	.06
179	Steve Lombardozzi	.10	.06
180	Chris Sabo (R)	.80	.50
181	Jose Uribe	.10	.06
182	Shane Mack	.20	.12
183	Ron Karkovice	.10	.06
184	Todd Benzinger	.10	.06
185	Dave Stewart	.15	.08
186	Julio Franco	.25	.15
187	Ron Robinson	.10	.06
188	Wally Backman	.10	.06
189	Randy Velarde	.10	.06
190	Joe Carter	.80	.50
191	Bob Welch	.12	.07
192	Kelly Paris	.10	.06
193	Chris Brown	.10	.06
194	Rick Reuschel	.10	.06
195	Roger Clemens	2.50	1.50
196	Dave Concepcion	.10	.06
197	Al Newman	.10	.06
198	Brook Jacoby	.10	.06
199	Mookie Wilson	.10	.06
200	Don Mattingly	1.00	.70
201	Dick Schofield	.10	.06
202	Mark Gubicza	.12	.07
203	Gary Gaetti	.10	.06
204	Dan Pasqua	.10	.06
205	Andre Dawson	.60	.35
206	Chris Speier	.10	.06
207	Kent Tekulve	.10	.06
208	Rod Scurry	.10	.06
209	Scott Bailes	.10	.06
210	Rickey Henderson	1.75	1.00
211	Harold Baines	.12	.07
212	Tony Armas	.10	.06
213	Kent Hrbek	.12	.07
214	Darrin Jackson	.12	.07
215	George Brett	.90	.60
216	Rafael Santana	.12	.07
217	Andy Allanson	.10	.06
218	Brett Butler	.15	.08
219	Steve Jeltz	.10	.06
220	Jay Buhner	.15	.08
221	Bo Jackson	1.25	.80
222	Angel Salazar	.10	.06
223	Kirk McCaskill	.10	.06
224	Steve Lyons	.10	.06
225	Bert Blyleven	.15	.08
226	Scott Bradley	.10	.06
227	Bob Melvin	.10	.06
228	Ron Kittle	.10	.06
229	Phil Bradley	.10	.06
230	Tommy John	.12	.07
231	Greg Walker	.10	.06
232	Juan Berenguer	.10	.06
233	Pat Tabler	.10	.06
234	Terry Clark (R)	.10	.06

235	Rafael Palmeiro	.60	.35
236	Paul Zuvella	.10	.06
237	Willie Randolph	.12	.07
238	Bruce Fields	.10	.06
239	Mike Aldrete	.10	.06
240	Lance Parrish	.10	.06
241	Greg Maddux	.75	.45
242	John Moses	.10	.06
243	Melido Perez	.12	.07
244	Willie Wilson	.10	.06
245	Mark McLemore	.10	.06
246	Von Hayes	.10	.06
247	Matt Williams	.80	.50
248	John Candelaria	.10	.06
249	Harold Reynolds	.12	.07
250	Greg Swindell	.15	.08
251	Juan Agosto	.10	.06
252	Mike Felder	.10	.06
253	Vince Coleman	.12	.07
254	Larry Sheets	.10	.06
255	George Bell	.35	.20
256	Terry Steinbach	.12	.07
257	Jack Armstrong (R)	.20	.12
258	Dickie Thon	.10	.06
259	Ray Knight	.10	.06
260	Darryl Strawberry	1.25	.80
261	Doug Sisk	.10	.06
262	Alex Trevino	.10	.06
263	Jeff Leonard	.10	.06
264	Tom Henke	.12	.07
266	Dave Bergman	.10	.06
267	Tony Phillips	.12	.07
268	Mark Davis	.10	.06
269	Kevin Elster	.10	.06
270	Barry Larkin	.75	.45
271	Manny Lee	.10	.06
272	Tom Brunansky	.15	.08
273	Craig Biggio (R)	1.00	.70
274	Jim Gantner	.10	.06
275	Eddie Murray	.60	.35
276	Jeff Reed	.10	.06
277	Tim Teufel	.10	.06
278	Rick Honeycutt	.10	.06
279	Guillermo Hernandez	.10	.06
280	John Kruk	.15	.08
281	Luis Alicea (R)	.15	.08
282	Jim Clancy	.10	.06
283	Billy Ripken	.10	.06
284	Craig Reynolds	.10	.06
285	Robin Yount	1.00	.70
286	Jimmy Jones	.10	.06
287	Ron Oester	.10	.06
288	Terry Leach	.10	.06
289	Dennis Eckersley	.40	.25
290	Alan Trammell	.30	.18
291	Jimmy Key	.12	.07
292	Chris Bosio	.12	.07
293	Jose DeLeon	.10	.06
294	Jim Traber	.10	.06
295	Mike Scott	.10	.06
296	Roger McDowell	.10	.06
297	Garry Templeton	.10	.06
298	Doyle Alexander	.10	.06
299	Nick Esasky	.10	.06
300	Mark McGwire	2.50	1.50
301	Darryl Hamilton (R)	.35	.20
302	Dave Smith	.10	.06
303	Rick Sutcliffe	.10	.06
304	Dave Stapleton	.10	.06
305	Alan Ashby	.10	.06
306	Pedro Guerrero	.12	.07
307	Ron Guidry	.12	.07
308	Steve Farr	.10	.06
309	Curt Ford	.10	.06
310	Claudell Washington	.10	.06
311	Tom Prince	.10	.06
312	Chad Kreuter (R)	.12	.07
313	Ken Oberkfell	.10	.06
314	Jerry Browne	.10	.06
315	R.J. Reynolds	.10	.06
316	Scott Bankhead	.10	.06
317	Milt Thompson	.10	.06
318	Mario Diaz	.10	.06
319	Bruce Ruffin	.10	.06
320	Dave Valle	.10	.06
321a	Gary Varsho (Wrong Photo)	1.75	1.00
321b	Gary Varsho (R) (Cor)	.12	.07
322	Paul Mirabella	.10	.06
323	Chuck Jackson	.10	.06
324	Drew Hall	.10	.06
325	Don August	.10	.06
326	Israel Sanchez (R)	.12	.07
327	Denny Walling	.10	.06
328	Joel Skinner	.10	.06
329	Danny Tartabull	.50	.30
330	Tony Pena	.12	.07
331	Jim Sundberg	.10	.06
332	Jeff Robinson	.10	.06
333	Odibbe McDowell	.10	.06
334	Jose Lind	.10	.06
335	Paul Kilgus	.10	.06
336	Juan Samuel	.10	.06
337	Mike Campbell	.10	.06
338	Mike Maddux	.10	.06
339	Darnell Coles	.10	.06
340	Bob Dernier	.10	.06
341	Rafael Ramirez	.10	.06
342	Scott Sanderson	.10	.06
343	B.J. Surhoff	.10	.06
344	Billy Hatcher	.10	.06
345	Pat Perry	.10	.06
346	Jack Clark	.12	.07
347	Gary Thurman	.10	.06
348	Timmy Jones (R)	.12	.07

349	Dave Winfield	.75	.45
350	Frank White	.10	.06
351	Dave Collins	.10	.06
352	Jack Morris	.50	.25
353	Eric Plunk	.10	.06
354	Leon Durham	.10	.06
355	Ivan DeJesus	.10	.06
356	Brian Holman (R)	.20	.12
357a	Dale Murphy	50.00	30.00
	(Photo Reversed)		
357b	Dale Murphy (Cor)	.40	.25
358	Mark Portugal	.10	.06
359	Andy McGaffigan	.10	.06
360	Tom Glavine	4.00	2.75
361	Keith Moreland	.10	.06
362	Todd Stottlemyre	.25	.15
363	Dave Leiper	.12	.07
364	Cecil Fielder	1.75	1.00
355	Carmelo Martinez	.10	.06
356	Dwight Evans	.12	.07
357	Kevin McReynolds	.12	.07
358	Rich Gedman	.10	.06
359	Len Dykstra	.15	.08
370	Jody Reed	.10	.06
371	Jose Canseco	2.50	1.50
372	Rob Murphy	.10	.06
373	Mike Henneman	.10	.06
374	Walt Weiss	.12	.07
375	Rob Dibble (R)	.60	.35
376	Kirby Puckett	2.00	1.25
377	Denny Martinez	.25	.15
378	Ron Gant	2.00	1.25
379	Brian Harper	.10	.06
380	Nelson Santovenia (R)	.12	.07
381	Lloyd Moseby	.10	.06
382	Lance McCullers	.10	.06
383	Dave Stieb	.12	.07
384	Tony Gwynn	1.50	.90
385	Mike Flanagan	.10	.06
386	Bob Ojeda	.12	.07
387	Bruce Hurst	.12	.07
388	Dave Magadan	.12	.07
389	Wade Boggs	1.25	.80
390	Gary Carter	.25	.15
391	Frank Tanana	.10	.06
392	Curt Young	.10	.06
383	Jeff Treadway	.10	.06
384	Darrell Evans	.12	.07
385	Glenn Hubbard	.10	.06
386	Chuck Cary	.10	.06
387	Frank Viola	.12	.07
388	Jeff Parrett	.10	.06
389	Terry Blocker (R)	.12	.07
400	Dan Gladden	.10	.06
401	Louie Meadows (R)	.12	.07
402	Tim Raines	.12	.07
403	Joey Meyer	.10	.06
404	Larry Andersen	.10	.06
405	Rex Hudler	.10	.06
406	Mike Schmidt	2.00	1.25
407	John Franco	.10	.06
408	Brady Anderson (R)	1.75	1.00
409	Don Carman	.10	.06
410	Eric Davis	.35	.20
411	Bob Stanley	.10	.06
412	Pete Smith	.30	.18
413	Jim Rice	.15	.08
414	Bruce Sutter	.12	.07
415	Oil Can Boyd	.10	.06
416	Ruben Sierra	1.75	1.00
417	Mike LaValliere	.10	.06
418	Steve Buechele	.10	.06
419	Gary Redus	.10	.06
420	Scott Fletcher	.10	.06
421	Dale Sveum	.10	.06
422	Bob Knepper	.10	.06
423	Luis Rivera	.10	.06
424	Ted Higuera	.10	.06
425	Kevin Bass	.10	.06
426	Ken Gerhart	.10	.06
427	Shane Rawley	.10	.06
428	Paul O'Neill	.20	.12
429	Joe Orsulak	.12	.07
430	Jackie Gutierrez	.10	.06
431	Gerald Perry	.10	.06
432	Mike Greenwell	.20	.12
433	Jerry Royster	.10	.06
434	Ellis Burks	.20	.12
435	Ed Olwine	.10	.06
436	Dave Rucker	.10	.06
437	Charlie Hough	.10	.06
438	Bob Walk	.10	.06
439	Bob Brower	.10	.06
440	Barry Bonds	2.00	1.25
441	Tom Foley	.10	.06
442	Rob Deer	.12	.07
443	Glenn Davis	.12	.07
444	Dave Martinez	.10	.06
445	Bill Wegman	.10	.06
446	Lloyd McClendon	.10	.06
447	Dave Schmidt	.10	.06
448	Darren Daulton	.20	.12
449	Frank Williams	.10	.06
450	Don Aase	.10	.06
451	Lou Whitaker	.12	.07
452	Goose Gossage	.12	.07
453	Ed Whison	.10	.06
454	Jim Walewander	.10	.06
455	Damon Berryhill	.10	.06
456	Tim Burke	.10	.06
457	Barry Jones	.10	.06
458	Joel Youngblood	.10	.06
459	Floyd Youmans	.10	.06
460	Mark Salas	.10	.06
461	Jeff Russell	.10	.06

462	Darrell Miller	.10	.06	520	Bob Kipper	.10	.06
463	Jeff Kunkel	.10	.06	521	Lee Smith	.20	.12
464	Sherman Corbett (R)	.12	.07	522	Juan Castillo	.10	.06
465	Curtis Wilkerson	.10	.06	523	Don Robinson	.10	.06
466	Bud Black	.10	.06	524	Kevin Romine	.10	.06
467	Cal Ripken, Jr.	3.00	2.00	525	Paul Molitor	.30	.18
468	John Farrell	.10	.06	526	Mark Langston	.15	.08
469	Terry Kennedy	.10	.06	527	Donnie Hill	.10	.06
470	Tom Candiotti	.12	.07	528	Larry Owen	.10	.06
471	Roberto Alomar	5.00	3.50	529	Jerry Reed	.10	.06
472	Jeff Robinson	.10	.06	530	Jack McDowell	2.00	1.25
473	Vance Law	.10	.06	531	Greg Matthews	.10	.06
474	Randy Ready	.10	.06	532	John Russell	.10	.06
475	Walt Terrell	.10	.06	533	Don Quisenberry	.10	.06
476	Kelly Downs	.10	.06	534	Greg Gross	.10	.06
477	Johnny Paredes (R)	.10	.06	535	Danny Cox	.10	.06
478	Shawn Hillegas	.10	.06	536	Terry Francona	.10	.06
479	Bob Brenly	.10	.06	537	Andy Van Slyke	.35	.20
480	Otis Nixon	.12	.07	538	Mel Hall	.15	.08
481	Johnny Ray	.10	.06	539	Jim Gott	.10	.06
482	Geno Petralli	.10	.06	540	Doug Jones	.10	.06
483	Stu Cliburn	.10	.06	541	Craig Lefferts	.10	.06
484	Pete Incaviglia	.10	.06	542	Mike Boddicker	.10	.06
485	Brian Downing	.12	.07	543	Greg Brock	.10	.06
486	Jeff Stone	.10	.06	544	Atlee Hammaker	.10	.06
487	Carmen Castillo	.10	.06	545	Tom Bolton	.10	.06
488	Tom Niedenfuer	.10	.06	546	Mike Macfarlane (R)	.30	.18
489	Jay Bell	.15	.08	547	Rich Renteria (R)	.12	.07
490	Rick Schu	.10	.06	548	John Davis	.10	.06
491	Jeff Pico (R)	.12	.07	549	Floyd Bannister	.10	.06
492	Mark Parent (R)	.10	.06	550	Mickey Brantley	.10	.06
493	Eric King	.10	.06	551	Duane Ward	.10	.06
494	Al Nipper	.10	.06	552	Dan Petry	.10	.06
495	Andy Hawkins	.10	.06	553	Mickey Tettleton	.15	.08
496	Daryl Boston	.10	.06	554	Rick Leach	.10	.06
497	Ernie Riles	.10	.06	555	Mike Witt	.10	.06
498	Pascual Perez	.10	.06	556	Sid Bream	.10	.06
499	Bill Long	.10	.06	557	Bobby Witt	.15	.08
500	Kirt Manwaring	.10	.06	558	Tommy Herr	.10	.06
501	Chuck Crim	.10	.06	559	Randy Milligan	.12	.07
502	Candy Maldonado	.10	.06	560	Jose Cecena (R)	.10	.06
503	Dennis Lamp	.10	.06	561	Mackey Sasser	.10	.06
504	Glenn Braggs	.10	.06	562	Carney Lansford	.12	.07
505	Joe Price	.10	.06	563	Rick Aguilera	.10	.06
506	Ken Williams	.10	.06	564	Ron Hassey	.10	.06
507	Bill Pecota	.10	.06	565	Dwight Gooden	.50	.30
508	Rey Quinones	.10	.06	566	Paul Assenmacher	.10	.06
509	Jeff Bittiger (R)	.12	.07	567	Neil Allen	.10	.06
510	Kevin Seitzer	.15	.08	568	Jim Morrison	.10	.06
511	Steve Bedrosian	.10	.06	569	Mike Pagliarulo	.10	.06
512	Todd Worrell	.15	.08	570	Ted Simmons	.12	.07
513	Chris James	.10	.06	571	Mark Thurmond	.10	.06
514	Jose Oquendo	.10	.06	572	Fred McGriff	1.75	1.00
515	David Palmer	.10	.06	573	Wally Joyner	.30	.18
516	John Smiley	.15	.08	574	Jose Bautista (R)	.12	.07
517	Dave Clark	.10	.06	575	Kelly Gruber	.15	.08
518	Mike Dunne	.10	.06	576	Cecilio Guane	.10	.06
519	Ron Washington	.10	.06	577	Mark Davidson	.10	.06

578	Bobby Bonilla	.80	.50
579	Mike Stanley	.10	.06
580	Gene Larkin	.10	.06
581	Stan Javier	.10	.06
582	Howard Johnson	.30	.18
583a	Mike Gallego (Photo Reversed On Back)	1.00	.07
583b	Mike Gallego (Cor)	.10	.06
584	David Cone	.20	.12
585	Doug Jennings (R)	.12	.07
586	Charlie Hudson	.10	.06
587	Dion James	.10	.06
588	Al Leiter	.10	.06
589	Charlie Puleo	.10	.06
590	Roberto Kelly	.80	.50
591	Thad Bosley	.10	.06
592	Pete Stanicek	.10	.06
593	Pat Borders (R)	.40	.25
594	Bryan Harvey (R)	.50	.30
595	Jeff Ballard	.10	.06
596	Jeff Reardon	.25	.15
597	Doug Drabek	.20	.12
598	Edwin Correa	.10	.06
599	Keith Atherton	.10	.06
600	Dave LaPoint	.10	.06
601	Don Baylor	.15	.08
602	Tom Pagnozzi	.12	.07
603	Tim Flannery	.10	.06
604	Gene Walter	.10	.06
605	Dave Parker	.15	.08
606	Mike Diaz	.10	.06
607	Chris Gwynn	.10	.06
608	Odell Jones	.10	.06
609	Carlton Fisk	.50	.30
610	Jay Howell	.10	.06
611	Tim Crews	.10	.06
612	Keith Hernandez	.12	.07
613	Willie Fraser	.10	.06
614	Jim Eppard	.10	.06
615	Jeff Hamilton	.10	.06
616	Kurt Stillwell	.10	.06
617	Tom Browning	.12	.07
618	Jeff Montgomery	.10	.06
619	Jose Rijo	.15	.08
620	Jamie Quirk	.10	.06
621	Willie McGee	.15	.08
622	Mark Grant	.10	.06
623	Bill Swift	.12	.07
624	Orlando Mercado	.10	.06
625	John Costello (R)	.12	.07
626	Jose Gonzalez	.10	.06
627a	Bill Schroder (Wrong Photo)	1.00	.70
627b	Bill Schroder (Cor)	.10	.06
628a	Fred Manrique (Wrong Photo On Back)	.25	.15
628b	Fred Manrique (Cor)	.10	.06
629	Ricky Horton	.10	.06
630	Dan Plesac	.10	.06
631	Alfredo Griffin	.10	.06
632	Chuck Finley	.15	.08
633	Kirk Gibson	.12	.07
634	Randy Myers	.10	.06
635	Greg Minton	.10	.06
636	Herm Winningham	.10	.06
637	Charlie Leibrandt	.10	.06
638	Tim Birtsas	.10	.06
639	Bill Buckner	.12	.07
640	Danny Jackson	.12	.07
641	Greg Booker	.10	.06
642	Jim Presley	.10	.06
643	Gene Nelson	.10	.06
644	Rod Booker	.10	.06
645	Dennis Rasmussen	.10	.06
646	Juan Nieves	.10	.06
647	Bobby Thigpen	.12	.07
648	Tim Belcher	.12	.07
649	Mike Young	.10	.06
650	Ivan Calderon	.12	.07
651	Oswaldo Peraza (R)	.12	.07
652a	Pat Sheridan (No Position On Front)	24.00	12.00
652b	Pat Sheridan (Cor)	.10	.06
653	Mike Morgan	.10	.06
654	Mike Heath	.10	.06
655	Jay Tibbs	.10	.06
656	Fernando Valenzuela	.12	.07
657	Lee Mazzilli	.10	.06
658	Frank Viola (CY)	.15	.08
659	Jose Canseco (MVP)	.50	.30
660	Walt Weiss (ROY)	.12	.07
661	Orel Hershiser (CY)	.15	.08
662	Kirk Gibson (MVP)	.12	.07
663	Chris Sabo (ROY)	.12	.07
664	Dennis Eckersley (ALCS)	.15	.08
665	Orel Hershiser (NLCS)	.15	.08
666	Kirk Gibson (WS)	.12	.07
667	Orel Hershiser (WS)	.15	.08
668	Wally Joyner (CL)	.10	.06
669	Nolan Ryan (CL)	.80	.50
670	Jose Canseco (CL)	.50	.30
671	Fred McGriff (CL)	.30	.18
672	Dale Murphy (CL)	.15	.08
673	Paul Molitor (CL)	.12	.07
674	Ozzie Smith (CL)	.15	.08
675	Ryne Sandberg (CL)	.40	.25
676	Kirk Gibson (CL)	.12	.07
677	Andres Galarraga (CL)	.10	.06
678	Will Clark (CL)	.40	.25
679	Cory Snyder (CL)	.10	.06
680	Alvin Davis (CL)	.10	.06

681	Darryl Strawberry (CL)	.25	.15
682	Cal Ripken (CL)	.75	.45
683	Tony Gwynn (CL)	.25	.15
684	Mike Schmidt (CL)	.60	.35
685	Andy Van Slyke (CL)	.12	.07
686	Ruben Sierra (CL)	.25	.15
687	Wade Boggs (CL)	.20	.12
688	Eric Davis (CL)	.15	.08
689	George Brett (CL)	.25	.15
690	Alan Trammell (CL)	.12	.07
691	Frank Viola (CL)	.12	.07
692	Harold Baines (CL)	.12	.07
693	Don Mattingly (CL)	.25	.15
694	Checklist 1-100	.10	.06
695	Checklist 101-200	.10	.06
696	Checklist 201-300	.10	.06
697	Checklist 301-400	.10	.06
698	Checklist 401-500	.10	.06
699	Checklist 501-600	.10	.06
700	Checklist 601-700	.10	.06
701	Checklist 701-800	.10	.06
702	Jessie Barfield	.10	.06
703	Walt Terrell	.10	.06
704	Dickie Thon	.10	.06
705	Al Leiter	.10	.06
706	Dave LaPoint	.10	.06
707	Charlie Hayes (R)	.20	.12
708	Andy Hawkins	.10	.06
709	Mickey Hatcher	.10	.06
710	Lance McCullers	.10	.06
711	Ron Kittle	.10	.06
712	Bert Blyleven	.12	.07
713	Rick Dempsey	.10	.06
714	Ken Williams	.10	.06
715	Steve Rosenberg (R)	.12	.07
716	Joe Skalski (R)	.10	.06
717	Spike Owen	.10	.06
718	Todd Burns	.10	.06
719	Kevin Gross	.10	.06
720	Tommy Herr	.10	.06
721	Rob Ducey	.10	.06
722	Gary Green (R)	.12	.07
723	Gregg Olson (R)	1.25	.80
724	Greg Harris (R)	.20	.12
725	Craig Worthington (R)	.12	.07
726	Thomas Howard (R)	.30	.18
727	Dale Mohorcic	.10	.06
728	Rich Yett	.10	.06
729	Mel Hall	.12	.07
730	Floyd Youmans	.10	.06
731	Lonnie Smith	.10	.06
732	Wally Backman	.10	.06
733	Trevor Wilson (R)	.20	.12
734	Jose Alvarez (R)	.12	.07
735	Bob Milacki (R)	.12	.07
736	Tom Gordon (R)	.20	.12
737	Wally Whitehurst (R)	.12	.07
738	Mike Aldrete	.10	.06
739	Keith Miller	.10	.06
740	Randy Milligan	.10	.06
741	Jeff Parrett	.10	.06
742	Steve Finley (R)	.60	.35
743	Junior Felix (R)	.25	.15
744	Pete Harnisch (R)	.70	.40
745	Bill Spiers (R)	.20	.12
746	Hensley Meulens (R)	.20	.12
747	Juan Bell	.10	.06
748	Steve Sax	.12	.07
749	Phil Bradley	.10	.06
750	Rey Quinones	.12	.07
751	Tommy Gregg (R)	.10	.06
752	Kevin Brown (R)	.60	.35
753	Derek Lilliquist (R)	.12	.07
754	Todd Zeile (R)	1.25	.80
755	Jim Abbott (R)	4.00	2.75
756	Ozzie Canseco (R)	.25	.15
757	Nick Esasky	.10	.06
758	Mike Moore	.10	.06
759	Rob Murphy	.10	.06
760	Rick Mahler	.10	.06
761	Fred Lynn	.12	.07
762	Kevin Blankenship (R)	.12	.07
763	Eddie Murray	.50	.30
764	Steve Searcy (R)	.12	.07
765	Jerome Walton (R)	.20	.12
766	Erik Hanson (R)	.35	.20
767	Bob Boone	.15	.08
768	Edgar Martinez (R)	2.00	1.25
769	Jose DeJesus (R)	.15	.08
770	Greg Briley (R)	.15	.08
771	Steve Peters (R)	.12	.07
772	Rafael Palmeiro	.50	.30
773	Jack Clark	.12	.07
774	Nolan Ryan	4.00	2.75
775	Lance Parrish	.10	.06
776	Joe Girardi	.15	.08
777	Willie Randolph	.12	.07
778	Mitch Williams	.12	.07
779	Dennis Cook (R)	.12	.07
780	Dwight Smith (R)	.15	.08
781	Lenny Harris (R)	.20	.12
782	Torey Lovullo (R)	.12	.07
783	Norm Charlton (R)	.40	.25
784	Chris Brown	.10	.06
785	Todd Benzinger	.10	.06
786	Shane Rawley	.10	.06
787	Omar Vizquel (R)	.20	.12
788	LaVel Freeman (R)	.10	.06
789	Jeffrey Leonard	.10	.06
790	Eddie Williams (R)	.10	.06
791	Jamie Moyer	.10	.06
792	Bruce Hurst	.12	.07
793	Julio Franco	.25	.15

794	Claudell Washington	.10	.06
795	Jody Davis	.10	.06
796	Odibbe McDowell	.10	.06
797	Paul Kilgus	.10	.06
798	Tracy Jones	.10	.06
799	Steve Wilson (R)	.12	.07
800	Pete O'Brien	.12	.07

1990 Upper Deck

Upper Deck follows up their premier issue with another 800-card set. The cards measure 2-1/2" by 3-1/2" and feature full color photos on the front and back. With this edition Upper Deck introduces their Heroes Of Baseball Inserts. 10 special Reggie Jackson Heroes cards were inserted randomly into the company's foil packs. Those cards are listed at the end of this checklist. Upper Deck issued a separate high-number series (701-800) at mid-season featuring rookies and traded players. Those card values are included in the complete set price below.

		MINT	NR/MT
Complete Set (800)		48.00	34.00
Commons (1-800)		.05	.02

1	Star Rookie Checklist	.05	.02
2	Randy Nosek (R)	.08	.05
3	Tom Drees (R)	.05	.02
4	Curt Young	.08	.05
5	Devon White (CL)	.05	.02
6	Luis Salazar	.05	.02
7	Von Hayes (CL)	.05	.02
8	Jose Bautista	.08	.05
9	Marquis Grissom(R)	2.00	1.25
10	Orel Hershiser (CL)	.07	.04
11	Rick Aguilera	.05	.02

12	Benito Santiago (CL)	.07	.04
13	Deion Sanders (R)	2.00	1.25
14	Marvell Wynne	.05	.02
15	David West	.05	.02
16	Bobby Bonilla (CL)	.08	.05
17	Sammy Sosa (R)	.25	.15
18	Steve Sax (CL)	.07	.04
19	Jack Howell	.05	.02
20	Mike Schmidt (SP)	.60	.35
21	Robin Ventura (R)	2.75	1.75
22	Brian Meyer (R)	.12	.07
23	Blaine Beatty (R)	.10	.06
24	Ken Griffey Jr. (CL)	.50	.30
25	Greg Vaughn (R)	.40	.25
26	Xavier Hernandez (R)	.12	.07
27	Jason Grimsley (R)	.15	.07
28	Eric Anthony (R)	.70	.40
29	Tim Raines (CL)	.07	.04
30	David Wells	.07	.04
31	Hal Morris (R)	.50	.30
32	Bo Jackson (CL)	.20	.12
33	Kelly Mann (R)	.12	.07
34	Nolan Ryan (SP)	.80	.50
35	Scott Service (R)	.10	.06
36	Mark McGwire (CL)	.25	.15
37	Tino Martinez (R)	.60	.35
38	Chili Davis	.07	.04
39	Scott Sanderson	.05	.02
40	Kevin Mitchell (CL)	.10	.06
41	Lou Whitaker (CL)	.07	.04
42	Scott Coolbaugh (R)	.07	.04
43	Jose Cano (R)	.10	.06
44	Jose Vizcaino (R)	.10	.06
45	Bob Hamelin (R)	.12	.07
46	Jose Offerman (R)	.35	.20
47	Kevin Blankenship	.05	.02
48	Kirby Puckett (CL)	.25	.15
49	Tommy Greene (R)	.20	.12
50	Will Clark (SP)	.25	.15
51	Rob Nelson (R)	.07	.04
52	Chris Hammond (R)	.40	.25
53	Joe Carter (CL)	.15	.08
54a	Ben McDonald (No Rookie Logo)	18.00	9.00
54b	Ben McDonald (Cor)	2.50	1.25
55	Andy Benes (R)	.80	.50
56	John Olerud (R)	1.25	.80
57	Roger Clemens (CL)	.25	.15
58	Tony Armas	.05	.02
59	George Canale (R)	.10	.06
60a	Mickey Tettleton(CL) (Lists Jamie Weston)	2.00	1.00
60b	Mickey Tettleton (CL) (Lists Mickey Weston)	.08	.05
61	Mike Stanton (R)	.12	.07
62	Dwight Gooden (CL)	.10	.06
63	Kent Mercker (R)	.15	.08
64	Francisco Cabrera	.12	.07

(R)

65	Steve Avery (R)	2.50	1.50
66	Jose Canseco	.50	.30
67	Matt Merullo (R)	.10	.06
68	Vince Coleman (CL)	.07	.04
69	Ron Karkovice	.05	.02
70	Kevin Maas (R)	.80	.50
71	Dennis Cook	.05	.02
72	Juan Gonzalez (R)	10.00	7.00
73	Andre Dawson (CL)	.10	.06
74	Dean Palmer (R)	2.00	1.25
75	Bo Jackson (SP)	.25	.15
76	Rob Richie (R)	.07	.04
77	Bobby Rose (R)	.15	.08
78	Brian DuBois (R)	.12	.07
79	Ozzie Guillen (CL)	.07	.04
80	Gene Nelson	.05	.02
81	Bob McClure	.05	.02
82	Julio Franco (CL)	.08	.05
83	Greg Minton	.05	.02
84	John Smoltz (CL)	.15	.08
85	Willie Fraser	.05	.02
86	Neal Heaton	.05	.02
87	Kevin Tapani (R)	.75	.45
88	Mike Scott (CL)	.07	.04
89a	Jim Gott	5.00	2.50
	(Wrong Photo)		
89b	Jim Gott (Cor)	.07	.04
90	Lance Johnson (R)	.08	.05
91	Robin Yount (CL)	.20	.12
92	Jeff Parrett	.05	.02
93	Julio Machado (R)	.08	.05
94	Ron Jones	.05	.02
95	George Bell (CL)	.08	.05
96	Jerry Reuss	.05	.02
97	Brian Fisher	.05	.02
98	Kevin Ritz (R)	.10	.06
99	Barry Larkin (CL)	.10	.06
100	Checklist 1-100	.05	.02
101	Gerald Perry	.05	.02
102	Kevin Appier (R)	1.25	.80
103	Julio Franco	.15	.08
104	Craig Biggio	.15	.08
105	Bo Jackson	.30	.18
106	Junior Felix	.08	.05
107	Mike Harkey (R)	.10	.06
108	Fred McGriff	.50	.30
109	Rick Sutcliffe	.07	.04
110	Pete O'Brien	.05	.02
111	Kelly Gruber	.07	.04
112	Pat Borders	.07	.04
113	Dwight Evans	.07	.04
114	Dwight Gooden	.15	.08
115	Kevin Batiste (FC)	.15	.08
116	Eric Davis	.15	.08
117	Kevin Mitchell	.12	.07
118	Ron Oester	.05	.02
119	Brett Butler	.10	.06
120	Danny Jackson	.07	.04
121	Tommy Gregg	.05	.02
122	Ken Caminiti	.07	.04
123	Kevin Brown	.10	.06
124	George Brett	.30	.18
125	Mike Scott	.05	.02
126	Cory Snyder	.05	.02
127	George Bell	.15	.08
128	Mark Grace	.20	.12
129	Devon White	.05	.02
130	Tony Fernandez	.07	.04
131	Dan Aase	.05	.02
132	Rance Mulliniks	.05	.02
133	Marty Barrett	.05	.02
134	Nelson Liriano	.05	.02
135	Mark Carreon (R)	.07	.04
136	Candy Maldonado	.05	.02
137	Tim Birtsas	.05	.02
138	Tom Brookens	.05	.02
139	John Franco	.05	.02
140	Mike LaCoss	.05	.02
141	Jeff Treadway	.05	.02
142	Pat Tabler	.05	.02
143	Darrell Evans	.07	.04
144	Rafael Ramirez	.05	.02
145	Oddibe McDowell	.05	.02
146	Brian Downing	.05	.02
147	Curtis Wilkerson	.05	.02
148	Ernie Whitt	.05	.02
149	Bill Schroeder	.05	.02
150	Domingo Ramos	.05	.02
151	Rick Honeycutt	.05	.02
152	Don Slaught	.05	.02
153	Mitch Webster	.05	.02
154	Tony Phillips	.05	.02
155	Paul Kilgus	.05	.02
156	Ken Griffey, Jr.	5.00	3.50
157	Gary Sheffield	1.50	.90
158	Wally Backman	.05	.02
159	B.J. Surhoff	.05	.02
160	Louie Meadows	.05	.02
161	Paul O'Neill	.15	.08
162	Jeff McKnight (R)	.15	.08
163	Alvaro Espinoza (R)	.12	.07
164	Scott Scudder (R)	.15	.08
165	Jeff Reed	.05	.02
166	Gregg Jefferies	.25	.15
167	Barry Larkin	.20	.12
168	Gary Carter	.10	.06
169	Robby Thompson	.05	.02
170	Rolando Roomes	.05	.02
171	Mark McGwire	.60	.35
172	Steve Sax	.07	.04
173	Mark Williamson	.05	.02
174	Mitch Williams	.05	.02
175	Brian Holton	.05	.02
176	Rob Deer	.07	.04
177	Tim Raines	.07	.05

#	Player	Val1	Val2
178	Mike Felder	.05	.02
179	Harold Reynolds	.07	.04
180	Terry Francona	.05	.02
181	Chris Sabo	.15	.08
182	Darryl Strawberry	.30	.18
183	Willie Randolph	.07	.04
184	Billy Ripken	.05	.02
185	Mackey Sasser	.05	.02
186	Todd Benzinger	.05	.02
187	Kevin Elster	.05	.02
188	Jose Uribe	.05	.02
189	Tom Browning	.07	.04
190	Keith Miller	.05	.02
191	Don Mattingly	.30	.18
192	Dave Parker	.07	.04
193	Roberto Kelly	.25	.15
194	Phil Bradley	.05	.02
195	Ron Hassey	.05	.02
196	Gerald Young	.05	.02
197	Hubie Brooks	.05	.02
198	Bill Doran	.05	.02
199	Al Newman	.05	.02
200	Checklist 101-200	.05	.02
201	Terry Puhl	.05	.02
202	Frank DiPino	.05	.02
203	Jim Clancy	.05	.02
204	Bob Ojeda	.05	.02
205	Alex Trevino	.05	.02
206	Dave Henderson	.05	.02
207	Henry Cotto	.05	.02
208	Rafael Belliard	.05	.02
209	Stan Javier	.05	.02
210	Jerry Reed	.05	.02
211	Doug Dascenzo	.07	.04
212	Andres Thomsa	.05	.02
213	Greg Maddux	.15	.08
214	Mike Schooler	.05	.02
215	Lonnie Smith	.05	.02
216	Jose Rijo	.08	.05
217	Greg Gagne	.05	.02
218	Jim Gantner	.05	.02
219	Allan Anderson	.05	.02
220	Rick Mahler	.05	.02
221	Jim Deshaies	.05	.02
222	Keith Hernandez	.07	.04
223	Vince Coleman	.07	.04
224	David Cone	.12	.07
225	Ozzie Smith	.20	.12
226	Matt Nokes	.05	.02
227	Barry Bonds	.80	.50
228	Felix Jose	.35	.20
229	Dennis Powell	.05	.02
230	Mike Gallego	.05	.02
231	Shawon Dunston	.08	.05
232	Ron Gant	.50	.30
233	Omar Vizquel	.08	.05
234	Derek Lilliquist	.05	.02
235	Erik Hanson	.08	.05
236	Kirby Puckett	.75	.45
237	Bill Spiers	.08	.05
238	Dan Gladden	.05	.02
239	Bryan Clutterbuck(R)	.07	.04
240	John Moses	.05	.02
241	Ron Darling	.07	.04
242	Joe Magrane	.07	.04
243	Dave Magadan	.07	.04
244	Pedro Guerrero	.07	.04
245	Glenn Davis	.07	.04
246	Terry Steinbach	.07	.04
247	Fred Lynn	.07	.04
248	Gary Redus	.05	.02
249	Kenny Williams	.05	.02
250	Sid Bream	.05	.02
251	Bob Welch	.07	.04
252	Bill Buckner	.07	.04
253	Carney Lansford	.07	.04
254	Paul Molitor	.15	.08
255	Jose DeJesus	.05	.02
256	Orel Hershiser	.10	.06
257	Tom Brunansky	.07	.04
258	Mike Davis	.05	.02
259	Jeff Ballard	.05	.02
260	Scott Terry	.05	.02
261	Sid Fernandez	.07	.04
263	Howard Johnson	.12	.07
264	Kirk Gibson	.07	.04
265	Kevin McReynolds	.07	.04
266	Cal Ripken, Jr.	1.50	.90
267	Ozzie Guillen	.07	.04
268	Jim Traber	.05	.02
269	Bobby Thigpen	.07	.04
270	Joe Orsulak	.05	.02
271	Bob Boone	.08	.05
272	Dave Stewart	.08	.05
273	Tim Wallach	.08	.05
274	Luis Aquino	.05	.02
275	Mike Moore	.05	.02
276	Tony Pena	.07	.04
277	Eddie Murray	.20	.12
278	Milt Thompson	.05	.02
279	Alejandro Pena	.05	.02
280	Ken Dayley	.05	.02
281	Carmen Castillo	.05	.02
282	Tom Henke	.05	.02
283	Mickey Hatcher	.05	.02
284	Roy Smith	.07	.04
285	Manny Lee	.05	.02
286	Dan Pasqua	.05	.02
287	Larry Sheets	.05	.02
288	Garry Templeton	.05	.02
289	Eddie Williams	.05	.02
290	Brady Anderson	.25	.15
291	Spike Owen	.05	.02
292	Storm Davis	.05	.02
293	Chris Bosio	.07	.04
294	Jim Eisenreich	.05	.02

#	Player		
295	Don August	.05	.02
296	Jeff Hamilton	.05	.02
297	Mickey Tettleton	.07	.04
298	Mike Scioscia	.05	.02
299	Kevin Hickey	.05	.02
300	Checklist 201-300	.05	.02
301	Shawn Abner	.05	.02
302	Kevin Bass	.05	.02
303	Bip Roberts	.10	.06
304	Joe Girardi	.08	.05
305	Danny Darwin	.05	.02
306	Mike Heath	.05	.02
307	Mike Macfarlane	.07	.04
308	Ed Whitson	.05	.02
309	Tracy Jones	.05	.02
310	Scott Fletcher	.05	.02
311	Darnell Coles	.05	.02
312	Mike Brumley	.05	.02
313	Bill Swift	.07	.04
314	Charlie Hough	.05	.02
315	Jim Presley	.05	.02
316	Luis Polonia	.07	.04
317	Mike Morgan	.05	.02
318	Lee Guetterman	.05	.02
319	Jose Oquendo	.07	.04
320	Wayne Tollenson	.05	.02
321	Jody Reed	.05	.02
322	Damon Berryhill	.05	.02
323	Roger Clemens	.75	.45
324	Ryne Sandberg	.70	.40
325	Benito Santiago	.10	.06
326	Bret Saberhagen	.10	.06
327	Lou Whitaker	.07	.04
328	Dave Gallagher	.05	.02
329	Mike Pagliarulo	.05	.02
330	Doyle Alexander	.05	.02
331	Jeffrey Leonard	.05	.02
332	Torey Lovullo	.05	.02
333	Pete Incaviglia	.05	.02
334	Rickey Henderson	.50	.30
335	Rafael Palmeiro	.20	.12
336	Ken Hill (R)	.70	.40
337	Dave Winfield	.25	.15
338	Alfredo Griffin	.05	.02
339	Andy Hawkins	.05	.02
340	Ted Power	.05	.02
341	Steve Wilson	.05	.02
342	Jack Clark	.07	.04
343	Ellis Burks	.10	.06
344	Tony Gwynn	.40	.25
345	Jerome Walton	.10	.06
346	Roberto Alomar	1.25	.80
347	Carlos Martinez (R)	.12	.07
348	Chet Lemon	.05	.02
349	Willie Wilson	.05	.02
350	Greg Walker	.05	.02
351	Tom Bolton	.05	.02
352	German Gonzalez	.07	.04
353	Harold Baines	.07	.04
354	Mike Greenwell	.10	.06
355	Ruben Sierra	.50	.30
356	Andres Galarraga	.07	.04
357	Andre Dawson	.20	.12
358	Jeff Brantley (R)	.15	.08
359	Mike Bielecki	.05	.02
360	Ken Oberkfell	.05	.02
361	Kurt Stillwell	.05	.02
362	Brian Holman	.07	.04
363	Kevin Seitzer	.07	.04
364	Alvin Davis	.05	.02
365	Tom Gordon	.10	.06
366	Bobby Bonilla	.25	.15
367	Carlton Fisk	.20	.12
368	Steve Carter (R)	.08	.05
369	Joel Skinner	.05	.02
370	John Cangelosi	.05	.02
371	Cecil Espy	.05	.02
372	Gary Wayne (R)	.12	.07
373	Jim Rice	.08	.05
374	Mike Dyer (R)	.08	.05
375	Joe Carter	.30	.18
376	Dwight Smith	.08	.05
377	John Wetteland (R)	.35	.20
378	Ernie Riles	.05	.02
379	Otis Nixon	.07	.04
380	Vance Law	.05	.02
381	Dave Bergman	.05	.02
382	Frank White	.05	.02
383	Scott Bradley	.05	.02
384	Israel Sanchez	.05	.02
385	Gary Pettis	.05	.02
386	Donn Pall	.08	.05
387	John Smiley	.10	.06
388	Tom Candiotti	.07	.04
389	Junior Ortiz	.05	.02
390	Steve Lyons	.05	.02
391	Brian Harper	.05	.02
392	Fred Manrique	.05	.02
393	Lee Smith	.12	.07
394	Jeff Kunkel	.05	.02
395	John Tudor	.05	.02
397	Terry Kennedy	.05	.02
398	Lloyd McClendon	.05	.02
399	Craig Lefferts	.05	.02
400	Checklist 301-400	.05	.02
401	Keith Moreland	.05	.02
402	Rich Gedman	.05	.02
403	Jeff Robinson	.05	.02
404	Randy Ready	.05	.02
405	Rick Cerone	.05	.02
406	Jeff Blauser	.05	.02
407	Larry Anderson	.05	.02
408	Joe Boever	.05	.02
409	Felix Fermin	.05	.02
410	Glenn Wilson	.05	.02
411	Rex Hudler	.05	.02

412	Mark Grant	.05	.02
413	Dennis Martinez	.10	.06
414	Darrin Jackson	.05	.02
415	Mike Aldrete	.05	.02
416	Roger McDowell	.05	.02
417	Jeff Reardon	.15	.08
418	Darren Daulton	.20	.12
419	Tim Laudner	.05	.02
420	Don Carman	.05	.02
421	Lloyd Moseby	.05	.02
422	Doug Drabek	.10	.06
423	Lenny Harris	.05	.02
424	Jose Lind	.05	.02
425	Dave Johnson (R)	.10	.06
426	Jerry Browne	.05	.02
427	Eric Yelding ((R)	.15	.08
428	Brad Komminsk	.07	.04
429	Jody Davis	.05	.02
430	Mariano Duncan	.07	.04
431	Mark Davis	.05	.02
432	Nelson Santovenia	.05	.02
433	Bruce Hurst	.007	.04
434	Jeff Huson (R)	.10	.06
435	Chris James	.05	.02
436	Mark Guthrie (R)	.12	.07
437	Charlie Hayes	.07	.04
438	Shane Rawley	.05	.02
439	Dickie Thon	.05	.02
440	Juan Berenguer	.05	.02
441	Kevin Romine	.05	.02
442	Bill Landrum	.05	.02
443	Todd Frohwirth	.05	.02
444	Craig Worthington	.05	.02
445	Fernando Valenzuela	.07	.04
446	Joey Belle (R)	2.50	1.50
447	Ed Whited (R)	.10	.06
448	Dave Smith	.05	.02
449	Dave Clark	.05	.02
450	Juan Agosto	.05	.02
451	Dave Valle	.05	.02
452	Kent Hrbek	.07	.04
453	Von Hayes	.05	.02
454	Gary Gaetti	.05	.02
455	Greg Briley	.05	.02
456	Glenn Braggs	.05	.02
457	Kirt Manwaring	.05	.02
458	Mel Hall	.07	.04
459	Brook Jacoby	.05	.02
460	Pat Sheridan	.05	.02
461	Rob Murphy	.05	.02
462	Jimmy Key	.05	.02
463	Nick Esasky	.05	.02
464	Rob Ducey	.05	.02
465	Carlos Quintana	.07	.04
466	Larry Walker (R)	1.75	1.00
467	Todd Worrell	.07	.04
468	Kevin Gross	.05	.02
469	Terry Pendleton	.25	.15
470	Dave Martinez	.05	.02
471	Gene Larkin	.05	.02
472	Len Dykstra	.07	.04
473	Barry Lyons	.05	.02
474	Terry Mulholland	.15	.08
475	Chip Hale (R)	.10	.06
476	Jesse Barfield	.05	.02
477	Dan Plesac	.05	.02
478a	Scott Garrelts (Wrong Photo)	3.00	1.50
478b	Scott Garrelts (Cor)	.10	.06
479	Dave Righetti	.05	.02
480	Gus Polidor	.07	.04
481	Mookie Wilson	.05	.02
482	Luis Rivera	.05	.02
483	Mike Flanagan	.05	.02
484	Dennis "Oil Can" Boyd	.05	.02
485	John Cerutti	.05	.02
486	John Costello	.05	.02
487	Pascual Perez	.05	.02
488	Tommy Herr	.05	.02
489	Tom Foley	.05	.02
490	Curt Ford	.05	.02
491	Steve Lake	.05	.02
492	Tim Teufel	.05	.02
493	Randy Bush	.05	.02
494	Mike Jackson	.05	.02
495	Steve Jeltz	.05	.02
496	Paul Gibson	.05	.02
497	Steve Balboni	.05	.02
498	Bud Black	.07	.04
499	Dale Sveum	.05	.02
500	Checklist 401-500	.05	.02
501	Timmy Jones	.05	.02
502	Mark Portugal	.05	.02
503	Ivan Calderon	.08	.05
504	Rick Rhoden	.05	.02
505	Willie McGee	.08	.05
506	Kirk McCaskill	.05	.02
507	Dave LaPoint	.05	.02
508	Jay Howell	.05	.02
509	Johnny Ray	.05	.02
510	Dave Anderson	.05	.02
511	Chuck Crim	.05	.02
512	Joe Hesketh	.05	.02
513	Dennis Eckersley	.20	.12
514	Greg Brock	.05	.02
515	Tim Burke	.05	.02
516	Frank Tanana	.05	.02
517	Jay Bell	.07	.04
518	Guillermo Hernandez	.05	.02
519	Randy Kramer	.08	.05
520	Charles Hudson	.05	.02
521	Jim Corsi	.08	.05
522	Steve Rosenberg	.05	.02
523	Cris Carpenter	.05	.02
524	Matt Winters (R)	.08	.05

525	Melido Perez	.07	.04
526	Chris Gwynn	.05	.02
527	Bert Blyleven	.10	.06
528	Chuck Cary	.05	.02
529	Daryl Boston	.05	.02
530	Dale Mohorcic	.05	.02
531	Geronimo Berroa	.07	.04
532	Edgar Martinez	.50	.30
533	Dale Murphy	.15	.08
534	Jay Buhner	.08	.05
535	John Smoltz	.50	.30
536	Andy Van Slyke	.15	.08
537	Mike Henneman	.05	.02
538	Miguel Garcia (R)	.10	.06
539	Frank Williams	.05	.02
540	R.J. Reynolds	.05	.02
541	Shawn Hillegas	.05	.02
542	Walt Weiss	.05	.02
543	Greg Hibbard (R)	.25	.15
544	Nolan Ryan	1.75	1.00
545	Todd Zeile	.25	.15
546	Hensley Meulens	.10	.06
547	Tim Belcher	.07	.04
548	Mike Witt	.05	.02
549	Greg Cadaret	.05	.02
550	Franklin Stubbs	.05	.02
551	Tony Castillo (R)	.15	.08
552	Jeff Robinson	.05	.02
553	Steve Olin (R)	.35	.20
554	Alan Trammell	.10	.06
555	Wade Boggs	.35	.20
556	Will Clark	.70	.40
557	Jeff King (R)	.12	.07
558	Mike Fitzgerald	.05	.02
559	Ken Howell	.05	.02
560	Bob Kipper	.05	.02
561	Scott Bankhead	.05	.02
562a	Jeff Innis (Wrong Photo)	3.00	1.50
562b	Jeff Innis (Cor)	.12	.07
563	Randy Johnson	.40	.25
564	Wally Whithurst	.05	.02
565	Gene Harris (R)	.08	.05
566	Norm Charlton	.07	.04
567	Robin Yount	.30	.18
568	Joe Oliver (R)	.25	.15
569	Mark Parent	.05	.02
570	John Farrell	.05	.02
571	Tom Glavine	.80	.50
572	Rod Nichols	.07	.04
573	Jack Morris	.20	.12
574	Greg Swindell	.07	.04
575	Steve Searcy	.08	.05
576	Ricky Jordan	.07	.04
577	Matt Williams	.25	.15
578	Mike LaValliere	.05	.02
579	Bryn Smith	.05	.02
580	Bruce Ruffin	.05	.02

581	Randy Myers	.05	.02
582	Rick Wrona (R)	.15	.08
583	Juan Samuel	.05	.02
584	Les Lancaster	.05	.02
585	Jeff Musselman	.05	.02
586	Rob Dibble	.12	.07
587	Eric Show	.05	.02
588	Jesse Orosco	.05	.02
589	Herm Winningham	.05	.02
590	Andy Allanson	.05	.02
591	Dion James	.05	.02
592	Carmelo Martinez	.05	.02
593	Luis Quinones	.07	.04
594	Dennis Rasmussen	.05	.02
595	Rich Yett	.05	.02
596	Bob Walk	.05	.02
597	Andy McGaffigan	.05	.02
598	Billy Hatcher	.05	.02
599	Bob Knepper	.05	.02
600	Checklist 501-600	.05	.02
601	Joey Cora	.07	.04
602	Steve Finley	.12	.07
603	Kal Daniels	.05	.02
604	Gregg Olson	.12	.07
605	Dave Steib	.07	.04
606	Kenny Rogers (R)	.10	.06
607	Zane Smith	.05	.02
608	Bob Geren (R)	.10	.06
609	Chad Kreuter	.05	.02
610	Mike Smithson	.05	.02
611	Jeff Wetherby (R)	.12	.07
612	Gary Mielke (R)	.08	.05
613	Pete Smith	.15	.08
614	Jack Daugherty (R)	.10	.06
615	Lance McCullers	.05	.02
616	Don Robinson	.05	.02
617	Jose Guzman	.05	.02
618	Steve Bedrosian	.05	.02
619	Jamie Moyer	.05	.02
620	Atlee Hammaker	.05	.02
621	Rick Luecken (R)	.10	.06
622	Greg W. Harris	.05	.02
623	Pete Harnisch	.10	.06
624	Jerald Clark	.07	.04
625	Jack McDowell	.50	.30
626	Frank Viola	.08	.05
627	Ted Higuera	.05	.02
628	Marty Pevey (R)	.10	.06
629	Bill Wegman	.05	.02
630	Eric Plunk	.05	.02
631	Drew Hall	.05	.02
632	Doug Jones	.05	.02
633	Geno Petralli	.05	.02
634	Jose Alvarez	.05	.02
635	Bob Milacki	.07	.04
636	Bobby Witt	.08	.05
637	Trevor Wilson	.08	.05
638	Jeff Russell	.05	.02

639	Mike Krukow	.05	.02
640	Rick Leach	.05	.02
641	Dave Schmidt	.05	.02
642	Terry Leach	.05	.02
643	Calvin Schiraldi	.05	.02
644	Bob Melvin	.05	.02
645	Jim Abbott	.40	.25
646	Jaime Navarro (R)	.70	.40
647	Mark Langston	.10	.06
648	Juan Nieves	.05	.02
649	Damaso Garcia	.05	.02
650	Charlie O'Brien	.05	.02
651	Eric King	.05	.02
652	Mike Boddicker	.05	.02
653	Duane Ward	.05	.02
654	Bob Stanley	.05	.02
655	Sandy Alomar, Jr.	.15	.08
656	Danny Tartabull	.20	.12
657	Randy McCament	.05	.02
658	Charlie Leibrandt	.05	.02
659	Dan Quisenberry	.05	.02
660	Paul Assenmacher	.05	.02
661	Walt Terrell	.05	.02
662	Tim Leary	.05	.02
663	Randy Milligan	.07	.04
664	Bo Diaz	.05	.02
665	Mark Lemke	.05	.02
666	Jose Gonzalez	.05	.02
667	Chuck Finley	.10	.06
668	John Kruk	.12	.07
669	Dick Schofield	.05	.02
670	Tim Crews	.05	.02
671	John Dopson	.05	.02
672	John Orton (R)	.12	.07
673	Eric Hetzel	.08	.05
674	Lance Parrish	.05	.02
675	Ramon Martinez	.25	.15
676	Mark Gubicza	.07	.04
677	Greg Litton	.05	.02
678	Greg Mathews	.05	.02
679	Dave Dravecky	.05	.02
680	Steve Farr	.05	.02
681	Mike Deveraux	.12	.07
682	Ken Griffey, Sr.	.10	.06
683a	Mickey Weston (Jamie)	3.00	1.50
683b	Mickey Weston (Cor)	.15	.08
684	Jack Armstrong	.07	.04
685	Steve Buechele	.05	.02
686	Bryan Harvey	.10	.06
687	Lance Blankenship	.05	.02
688	Dante Bichette	.05	.02
689	Todd Burns	.05	.02
690	Dan Petry	.05	.02
691	Kent Anderson (R)	.10	.06
692	Todd Stottlemyre	.08	.05
693	Wally Joyner	.15	.08
694	Mike Rochford	.08	.05

695	Floyd Bannister	.05	.02
696	Rick Reuschel	.05	.02
697	Jose DeLeon	.05	.02
698	Jeff Montgomery	.05	.02
699	Kelly Downs	.05	.02
700a	Checklist 601-700 (Jamie Weston Listed)	3.00	1.50
700b	Checklist 601-700 (Mickey Weston Listed)	.12	.07
701	Jim Gott	.05	.02
702	Rookie Threats Delino DeShields Larry Walker Marquis Grissom	.80	.50
703	Alejandro Pena	.05	.02
704	Willie Randolph	.07	.04
705	Tim Leary	.05	.02
706	Chuck McElroy (R)	.20	.12
707	Gerald Perry	.05	.02
708	Tom Brunansky	.07	.04
709	John Franco	.05	.02
710	Mark Davis	.05	.02
711	Dave Justice (R)	5.00	3.50
712	Storm Davis	.05	.02
713	Scott Ruskin (R)	.20	.12
714	Glenn Braggs	.05	.02
715	Kevin Bearse (R)	.12	.07
716	Jose Nunez (R)	.12	.07
717	Tim Layana (R)	.15	.08
718	Greg Myers (R)	.15	.08
719	Pete O'Brien	.05	.02
720	John Candelaria	.05	.02
721	Craig Grebeck (R)	.25	.15
722	Shawn Boskie (R)	.15	.08
723	Jim Leyritz (R)	.15	.08
724	Bill Sampen (R)	.12	.07
725	Scott Radinsky (R)	.20	.12
726	Todd Hundley (R)	.20	.12
727	Scott Hemond (R)	.12	.07
728	Lenny Webster (R)	.10	.06
729	Jeff Reardon	.15	.08
730	Mitch Webster	.05	.02
731	Brian Bohanon (R)	.10	.06
732	Rick Parker (R)	.12	.07
733	Terry Shumpert (R)	.15	.08
734a	Nolan Ryan (6th No Hitter)	10.00	5.00
734b	Nolan Ryan (6th No Hitter/300 Win)	1.50	.90
735	John Burkett (R)	.25	.15
736	Derrick May (R)	.40	.25
737	Carlos Baerga (R)	3.00	2.00
738	Greg Smith (R)	.10	.06
739	Joe Kraemer (R)	.10	.06
740	Scott Sanderson	.05	.02
741	Hector Villanueva (R)	.12	.07
742	Mike Fetters (R)	.12	.07

743	Mark Gardner (R)	.20	.12
744	Matt Nokes	.05	.02
745	Dave Winfield	.25	.15
746	Delino DeShields(R)	2.00	1.25
747	Dann Howitt (R)	.15	.08
748	Tony Pena	.05	.02
749	Oil Can Boyd	.05	.02
750	Mike Benjamin (R)	.10	.06
751	Alex Cole (R)	.25	.15
752	Eric Gunderson (R)	.15	.08
753	Howard Farmer (R)	.12	.07
754	Joe Carter	.30	.18
755	Ray Lankford (R)	2.00	1.25
756	Sandy Alomar, Jr.	.15	.08
757	Alex Sanchez (R)	.10	.06
758	Nick Esasky	.05	.02
759	Stan Belinda (R)	.25	.15
760	Jim Presley	.05	.02
761	Gary DiSarcina (R)	.50	.30
762	Wayne Edwards (R)	.12	.07
763	Pat Combs (R)	.12	.07
764	Mickey Pina (R)	.08	.05
765	Wilson Alvarez (R)	.40	.25
766	Dave Parker	.07	.04
767	Mike Blowers (R)	.10	.06
768	Tony Phillips	.07	.04
769	Pascual Perez	.05	.02
770	Gary Pettis	.05	.02
771	Fred Lynn	.07	.04
772	Mel Rojas (R)	.25	.15
773	David Segui (R)	.20	.12
774	Gary Carter	.10	.06
775	Rafael Valdez (R)	.12	.07
776	Glenallen Hill (R)	.20	.12
777	Keith Hernandez	.07	.04
778	Billy Hatcher	.05	.02
779	Marty Clary (R)	.10	.06
780	Candy Maldonado	.05	.02
781	Mike Marshall	.05	.02
782	Billy Jo Robidoux (R)	.10	.06
783	Mark Langston	.10	.06
784	Paul Sorrento (R)	.50	.30
785	Dave Hollins (R)	1.00	.70
786	Cecil Fielder	.35	.20
787	Matt Young	.05	.02
788	Jeff Huson	.07	.04
789	Lloyd Moseby	.05	.02
790	Ron Kittle	.05	.02
791	Hubie Brooks	.05	.02
792	Craig Lefferts	.05	.02
793	Kevin Bass	.05	.02
794	Bryn Smith	.05	.02*
795	Juan Samuel	.05	.02
796	Sam Horn (R)	.15	.08
797	Randy Myers	.05	.02
798	Chris James	.05	.02
799	Bill Gullickson	.05	.02
800	Checklist 701-800	.05	.02

BH1	Reggie Jackson (Hero)	5.00	3.50
BH2	Reggie Jackson (Hero)	5.00	3.50
BH3	Reggie Jackson (Hero)	5.00	3.50
BH4	Reggie Jackson (Hero)	5.00	3.50
BH5	Reggie Jackson (Hero)	5.00	3.50
BH6	Reggie Jackson (Hero)	5.00	3.50
BH7	Reggie Jackson (Hero)	5.00	3.50
BH8	Reggie Jackson (Hero)	5.00	3.50
BH9	Reggie Jackson (Hero)	5.00	3.50
___	Reggie Jackson (Cover)	7.50	4.50
___	Heroes Checklist	5.00	3.50
___	Reggie Jackson (Hero) (Autographed)	400.00	200.00

1991 Upper Deck

This **800-card set** features color photos on both the card fronts and backs. The cards measure 2-1/2" by 3-1/2". The first 26-cards belong to the Star Rookies Subset. Special insert cards include a Michael Jordan Bonus card, a 9-card Heroes of Baseball set featuring Nolan Ryan, a 9-card Hank Aaron Heroes of Baseball Set, 4-Hall of Fame Heroes, and 18- Silver Sluggers. All of these inserts are listed at the end of this checklist. A high-number series (701-800) includes additional rookies and traded players. The complete set price below includes the high number series but not the special Jordan card or Heroes sets.

		MINT	NR/MT
	Complete Set (800)	38.00	28.00
	Commons	.05	.02
1	Star Rookie Checklist	.05	.02
2	Phil Plantier (R)	1.75	1.00
3	D.J. Dozier (R)	.12	.07
4	Dave Hansen (R)	.15	.08
5	Maurice Vaughn (R)	.40	.25
6	Leo Gomez (R)	.40	.25
7	Scott Aldred (R)	.10	.06
8	Scott Chiamparino (R)	.10	.06
9	Lance Dickson (R)	.25	.15
10	Sean Berry (R)	.15	.08
11	Bernie Williams (R)	.40	.25
12	Brian Barnes (R)	.25	.15
13	Narciso Elvira (R)	.10	.06
14	Mike Gardiner (R)	.15	.08
15	Greg Colbrunn (R)	.25	.15
16	Bernard Gilkey (R)	.35	.20
17	Mark Lewis (R)	.25	.15
18	Mickey Morandini (R)	.20	.12
19	Charles Nagy (R)	1.00	.70
20	Geronimo Pena (R)	.12	.07
21	Henry Rodriguez (R)	.30	.18
22	Scott Cooper (R)	.30	.18
23	Andujar Cedeno (R)	.40	.25
24	Eric Karros (R)	2.50	1.50
25	Steve Decker (R)	.15	.08
26	Kevin Belcher (R)	.12	.07
27	Jeff Conine (R)	.20	.12
28	Dave Stewart (TC)	.05	.02
29	Carlton Fisk (TC)	.05	.02
30	Rafael Palmeiro (TC)	.05	.02
31	Chuck Finley (TC)	.05	.02
32	Harold Reynolds (TC)	.05	.02
33	Bret Saberhagen (TC)	.05	.02
34	Gary Gaetti (TC)	.05	.02
35	Scott Leius	.15	.08
36	Neal Heaton	.05	.02
37	Terry Lee (R)	.10	.06
38	Gary Redus	.05	.02
39	Barry Jones	.05	.02
40	Chuck Knoblauch	1.25	.80
41	Larry Andersen	.05	.02
42	Darryl Hamilton	.05	.02
43	Mike Greenwell (TC)	.05	.02
44	Kelly Gruber (TC)	.05	.02
45	Jack Morris (TC)	.05	.02
46	Sandy Alomar Jr. (TC)	.05	.02
47	Gregg Olson (TC)	.05	.02
48	Dave Parker (TC)	.05	.02
49	Roberto Kelly (TC)	.05	.02
50	Top Prospect	.05	.02

	Checklist		
51	Kyle Abbott	.15	.08
52	Jeff Juden	.25	.15
53	Todd Van Poppel (R)	1.50	.90
54	Steve Karsay (R)	.25	.15
55	Chipper Jones (R)	.80	.05
56	Chris Johnson (R)	.12	.08
57	John Ericks	.15	.08
58	Gary Scott (R)	.15	.08
59	Kiki Jones	.10	.06
60	Wilfredo Cordero (R)	.80	.05
61	Royce Clayton (R)	.60	.35
62	Tim Costo (R)	.40	.25
63	Roger Salkeld	.70	.40
64	Brook Fordyce	.15	.08
65	Mike Mussina	3.00	2.00
66	Dave Staton	.30	.18
67	Mike Lieberthal (R)	.50	.30
68	Kurt Miller (R)	.50	.30
69	Dan Peltier (R)	.15	.08
70	Greg Blosser	.20	.12
71	Reggie Sanders (R)	2.50	1.50
72	Brent Mayne	.10	.06
73	Rico Brogna	.20	.12
74	Willie Banks	.20	.12
75	Len Brutcher (R)	.12	.07
76	Pat Kelly (R)	.30	.18
77	Chris Sabo (TC)	.05	.02
78	Ramon Martinez (TC)	.07	.04
79	Matt Williams (TC)	.07	.04
80	Roberto Alomar (TC)	.15	.08
81	Glenn Davis (TC)	.05	.02
82	Ron Gant (TC)	.07	.04
83	Cecil Fielder (Feat)	.15	.08
84	Orlando Merced (R)	.30	.18
85	Domingo Ramos	.05	.02
86	Tom Bolton	.05	.02
87	Andres Santana	.12	.07
88	John Dopson	.05	.02
89	Kenny Williams	.05	.02
90	Marty Barrett	.05	.02
91	Tom Pagnozzi	.07	.04
92	Carmelo Martinez	.05	.02
93	Bobby Thigpen (Save)	.08	.05
94	Barry Bonds (TC)	.15	.08
95	Gregg Jefferies (TC)	.05	.02
96	Tim Wallach (TC)	.05	.02
97	Len Dykstra (TC)	.05	.02
98	Pedro Guerrero (TC)	.05	.02
99	Mark Grace (TC)	.05	.02
100	Checklist 1-100	.05	.02
101	Kevin Elster	.05	.02
102	Tom Brookens	.05	.02
103	Mackey Sasser	.05	.02
104	Felix Fermin	.05	.02
105	Kevin McReynolds	.07	.04
106	Dave Steib	.07	.04

107	Jeffrey Leonard	.05	.02	165	Mike Greenwell	.08	.05
108	Dave Henderson	.05	.02	166	Kal Daniels	.05	.02
109	Sid Bream	.05	.02	167	Kent Hrbek	.07	.04
110	Henry Cotto	.05	.02	168	Franklin Stubbs	.05	.02
111	Shawon Dunston	.08	.05	169	Dick Schofield	.05	.02
112	Mariano Duncan	.05	.02	170	Junior Ortiz	.05	.02
113	Joe Girardi	.05	.02	171	Hector Villanueva	.05	.02
114	Billy Hatcher	.05	.02	172	Dennis Eckersley	.20	.12
115	Greg Maddux	.15	.08	173	Mitch Williams	.05	.02
116	Jerry Browne	.05	.02	174	Mark McGwire	.30	.18
117	Juan Samuel	.05	.02	175	Fernando Valenzuela	.05	.02
118	Steve Olin	.07	.04	176	Gary Carter	.08	.05
119	Alfredo Griffin	.05	.02	177	Dave Magadan	.05	.02
120	Mitch Webster	.05	.02	178	Robby Thompson	.05	.02
121	Joel Skinner	.05	.02	179	Bob Ojeda	.05	.02
122	Frank Viola	.08	.05	180	Ken Caminiti	.07	.04
123	Cory Snyder	.05	.02	181	Don Slaught	.05	.02
124	Howard Johnson	.10	.06	182	Luis Rivera	.05	.02
125	Carlos Baerga	.35	.20	183	Jay Bell	.05	.02
126	Tony Fernandez	.07	.04	184	Jody Reed	.05	.02
127	Dave Stewart	.08	.05	185	Wally Backman	.05	.02
128	Jay Buhner	.07	.04	186	Dave Martinez	.05	.02
129	Mike LaValliere	.05	.02	187	Luis Polonia	.05	.02
130	Scott Bradley	.05	.02	188	Shane Mack	.10	.06
131	Tony Phillips	.05	.02	189	Spike Owen	.05	.02
132	Ryne Sandberg	.25	.15	190	Scott Bailes	.05	.02
133	Paul O'Neill	.08	.05	191	John Russell	.05	.02
134	Mark Grace	.12	.07	192	Walt Weiss	.05	.02
135	Chris Sabo	.10	.06	193	Jose Oquendo	.05	.02
136	Ramon Martinez	.12	.07	194	Carney Lansford	.07	.04
137	Brook Jacoby	.05	.02	195	Jeff Huson	.05	.02
138	Candy Maldonado	.05	.02	196	Keith Miller	.05	.02
139	Mike Scioscia	.05	.02	197	Eric Yelding	.05	.02
140	Chris James	.05	.02	198	Ron Darling	.07	.04
141	Craig Worthington	.05	.02	199	John Kruk	.08	.05
142	Manny Lee	.05	.02	200	Checklist 101-200	.05	.02
143	Tim Raines	.07	.04	201	John Shelby	.05	.02
144	Sandy Alomar, Jr.	.08	.05	202	Bob Geren	.05	.02
145	John Olerud	.25	.15	203	Lance McCullers	.05	.02
146	Ozzie Canseco	.10	.06	204	Alvaro Espinoza	.05	.02
147	Pat Borders	.05	.02	205	Mark Salas	.05	.02
148	Harold Reynolds	.05	.02	206	Mike Pagliarulo	.05	.02
149	Tom Henke	.05	.02	207	Jose Uribe	.05	.02
150	R.J. Reynolds	.05	.02	208	Jim Deshaies	.05	.02
151	Mike Gallego	.05	.02	209	Ron Karkovice	.05	.02
152	Bobby Bonilla	.15	.08	210	Rafael Ramirez	.05	.02
153	Terry Steinbach	.07	.04	211	Donnie Hill	.05	.02
154	Barry Bonds	.30	.18	212	Brian Harper	.05	.02
155	Jose Canseco	.30	.18	213	Jack Howell	.05	.02
156	Gregg Jeffries	.10	.06	214	Wes Gardner	.05	.02
157	Matt Williams	.12	.07	215	Tim Burke	.05	.02
158	Craig Biggio	.08	.05	216	Doug Jones	.05	.02
159	Daryl Boston	.05	.02	217	Hubie Brooks	.07	.04
160	Ricky Jordan	.05	.02	218	Tom Candiotti	.07	.04
161	Stan Belinda	.05	.02	219	Gerald Perry	.05	.02
162	Ozzie Smith	.15	.08	220	Jose DeLeon	.05	.02
163	Tom Brunansky	.07	.04	221	Wally Whitehurst	.05	.02
164	Todd Zeile	.10	.06	222	Alan Mills	.15	.08

223	Alan Trammell	.10	.06
224	Dwight Gooden	.15	.08
225	Travis Fryman (R)	2.00	1.25
226	Joe Carter	.20	.12
227	Julio Franco	.08	.05
228	Craig Lefferts	.05	.02
229	Gary Pettis	.05	.02
230	Dennis Rasmussen	.05	.02
231	Brian Downing	.05	.02
232	Carlos Quintana	.08	.05
233	Gary Gaetti	.05	.02
234	Mark Langston	.10	.06
235	Tim Wallach	.08	.05
236	Greg Swindell	.08	.05
237	Eddie Murray	.15	.08
238	Jeff Manto	.12	.07
239	Lenny Harris	.05	.02
240	Jesse Orosco	.05	.02
241	Scott Lusader	.05	.02
242	Sid Fernandez	.07	.04
243	Jim Leyritz (R)	.12	.07
244	Cecil Fielder	.25	.15
245	Darryl Strawberry	.25	.15
246	Frank Thomas	4.50	3.50
247	Kevin Mitchell	.10	.06
248	Lance Johnson	.05	.02
249	Rick Rueschel	.05	.02
250	Mark Portugal	.05	.02
251	Derek Lilliquest	.05	.02
252	Brian Holman	.08	.05
253	Rafael Valdez	.08	.05
254	B.J. Surhoff	.05	.02
255	Tony Gwynn	.25	.15
256	Andy Van Slyke	.15	.08
257	Todd Stottlemyre	.07	.04
258	Jose Lind	.05	.02
259	Greg Myers	.05	.02
260	Jeff Ballard	.05	.02
261	Bobby Thigpen	.05	.02
262	Jimmy Kremers (R)	.08	.05
263	Robin Ventura	.50	.30
264	John Smoltz	.25	.15
265	Sammy Sosa	.08	.05
266	Gary Sheffield	.60	.35
267	Lenny Dykstra	.07	.04
268	Bill Spiers	.05	.02
269	Charlie Hayes	.05	.02
270	Brett Butler	.08	.05
271	Bip Roberts	.05	.02
272	Rob Deer	.07	.04
273	Fred Lynn	.07	.04
274	Dave Parker	.07	.04
275	Andy Benes	.15	.08
276	Glenallen Hill	.08	.05
277	Steve Howard (R)	.10	.06
278	Doug Drabek	.15	.08
279	Joe Oliver	.05	.02
280	Todd Benzinger	.05	.02
281	Eric King	.05	.02
282	Jim Presley	.05	.02
283	Ken Patterson	.05	.02
284	Jack Daugherty	.05	.02
285	Ivan Calderon	.07	.04
286	Edgar Diaz (R)	.08	.05
287	Kevin Bass	.05	.02
288	Don Carman	.05	.02
289	Greg Brock	.05	.02
290	John Franco	.05	.02
291	Joey Cora	.05	.02
292	Bill Wegman	.05	.02
293	Eric Show	.05	.02
294	Scott Bankhead	.05	.02
295	Garry Templeton	.05	.02
296	Mickey Tettleton	.07	.04
297	Luis Sojo	.08	.05
298	Jose Rijo	.10	.06
299	Dave Johnson	.05	.02
300	Checklist 201-300	.05	.02
301	Mark Grant	.05	.02
302	Pete Harnisch	.10	.06
303	Greg Olson	.10	.06
304	Anthony Telford	.12	.07
305	Lonnie Smith	.05	.02
306	Chris Hoiles	.20	.12
307	Bryn Smith	.05	.02
308	Mike Devereaux	.10	.06
309	Milt Thompson	.05	.02
310	Bob Melvin	.05	.02
311	Luis Salazar	.05	.02
312	Ed Whitson	.05	.02
313	Charlie Hough	.05	.02
314	Dave Clark	.05	.02
315	Eric Gunderson	.07	.04
316	Dan Petry	.05	.02
317	Dante Bichette	.05	.02
318	Mike Heath	.05	.02
319	Damon Berryhill	.05	.02
320	Walt Terrell	.05	.02
321	Scott Fletcher	.05	.02
322	Dan Plesac	.05	.02
323	Jack McDowell	.20	.12
324	Paul Molitor	.10	.06
325	Ozzie Guillen	.07	.04
326	Gregg Olson	.08	.05
327	Pedro Guerrero	.05	.02
328	Bob Milacki	.05	.02
329	John Tudor	.05	.02
330	Steve Finley	.07	.04
331	Jack Clark	.07	.04
332	Jerome Walton	.07	.04
333	Andy Hawkins	.05	.02
334	Derrick May	.12	.07
335	Roberto Alomar	.40	.25
336	Jack Morris	.15	.07
337	Dave Winfield	.20	.12
338	Steve Searcy	.05	.02

339	Chili Davis	.05	.02
340	Larry Sheets	.05	.02
341	Ted Higuera	.05	.02
342	David Segui	.15	.08
343	Greg Cadaret	.05	.02
344	Robin Yount	.25	.15
345	Nolan Ryan	.80	.50
346	Ray Lankford	.50	.30
347	Cal Ripken, Jr.	.75	.45
348	Lee Smith	.12	.07
349	Brady Anderson	.40	.25
350	Frank DiPino	.05	.02
351	Hal Morris	.15	.08
352	Deion Sanders	.35	.20
353	Barry Larkin	.15	.08
354	Don Mattingly	.25	.05
355	Eric Davis	.10	.06
356	Jose Offerman	.10	.06
357	Mel Rojas	.08	.05
358	Rudy Seanez (R)	.15	.08
359	Oil Can Boyd	.05	.02
360	Nelson Liriano	.05	.02
361	Ron Gant	.25	.15
362	Howard Farmer	.08	.05
363	David Justice	.50	.30
364	Delino DeShields	.30	.18
365	Steve Avery	.50	.30
366	David Cone	.15	.08
367	Lou Whitaker	.07	.04
368	Von Hayes	.05	.02
369	Frank Tanana	.05	.02
370	Tim Teufel	.05	.02
371	Randy Myers	.05	.02
372	Roberto Kelly	.20	.12
373	Jack Armstrong	.07	.04
374	Kelly Gruber	.07	.04
375	Kevin Maas	.15	.08
376	Randy Johnson	.25	.15
377	David West	.05	.02
378	Brent Knackert (R)	.12	.07
379	Rick Honeycutt	.05	.02
380	Kevin Gross	.05	.02
381	Tom Foley	.05	.02
382	Jeff Blauser	.05	.02
383	Scott Ruskin	.05	.02
384	Andres Thomas	.05	.02
385	Dennis Martinez	.10	.06
386	Mike Henneman	.05	.02
387	Felix Jose	.15	.08
388	Alejandro Pena	.05	.02
389	Chet Lemon	.05	.02
390	Craig Wilson (R)	.10	.06
391	Chuck Crim	.07	.04
392	Mel Hall	.07	.04
393	Mark Knudson	.05	.02
394	Norm Charlton	.05	.02
395	Mike Felder	.05	.02
396	Tim Layana	.05	.02
397	Steve Frey	.07	.04
398	Bill Doran	.05	.02
399	Dion James	.05	.02
400	Checklist 301-400	.05	.02
401	Ron Hassey	.05	.02
402	Don Robinson	.05	.02
403	Gene Nelson	.05	.02
404	Terry Kennedy	.05	.02
405	Todd Burns	.05	.02
406	Roger McDowell	.05	.02
407	Bob Kipper	.05	.02
408	Darren Daulton	.10	.06
409	Chuck Cary	.05	.02
410	Bruce Ruffin	.05	.02
411	Juan Berenguer	.05	.02
412	Gary Ward	.05	.02
413	Al Newman	.05	.02
414	Danny Jackson	.05	.02
415	Greg Gagne	.05	.02
416	Tom Herr	.05	.02
417	Jeff Parrett	.05	.02
418	Jeff Reardon	.12	.07
419	Mark Lemke	.05	.02
420	Charlie O'Brien	.05	.02
421	Willie Randolph	.07	.04
422	Steve Bedrosian	.05	.02
423	Mike Moore	.05	.02
424	Jeff Brantley	.08	.05
425	Bob Welch	.07	.04
426	Terry Mulholland	.05	.02
427	Willie Blair	.15	.08
428	Darrin Fletcher	.12	.07
429	Mike Witt	.05	.02
430	Joe Boever	.05	.02
431	Tom Gordon	.07	.04
432	Pedro Munoz (R)	.70	.40
433	Kevin Seitzer	.07	.04
434	Kevin Tapani	.08	.05
435	Bret Saberhagen	.08	.05
436	Ellis Burks	.08	.05
437	Chuck Finley	.10	.06
438	Mike Boddicker	.05	.02
439	Francisco Cabrera	.05	.02
440	Todd Hundley	.10	.06
441	Kelly Downs	.05	.02
442	Dann Howitt	.08	.05
443	Scott Garrelts	.05	.02
444	Rickey Henderson	.25	.15
445	Will Clark	.30	.18
446	Ben McDonald	.25	.15
447	Dale Murphy	.12	.07
448	Dave Righetti	.05	.02
449	Dickie Thon	.05	.02
450	Ted Power	.05	.02
451	Scott Coolbaugh	.05	.02
452	Dwight Smith	.07	.04
453	Pete Incaviglia	.05	.02
454	Andre Dawson	.20	.12

455	Ruben Sierra	.25	.15	513	Dave Smith	.05	.02
456	Andres Galarraga	.07	.04	514	Chuck Carr (R)	.10	.06
457	Alvin Davis	.05	.02	515	Glenn Wilson	.05	.02
458	Tony Castillo	.05	.02	516	Mike Fitzgerald	.05	.02
459	Pete O'Brien	.05	.02	517	Devon White	.05	.02
460	Charlie Leibrandt	.05	.02	518	Dave Hollins	.25	.15
461	Vince Coleman	.07	.04	519	Mark Eichhorn	.05	.02
462	Steve Sax	.08	.05	520	Otis Nixon	.07	.04
463	Omar Oliveras (R)	.15	.08	521	Terry Shumpert	.10	.06
464	Oscar Azocar (R)	.10	.06	522	Scott Erickson	.80	.50
465	Joe Magrane	.07	.04	523	Danny Tartabull	.15	.08
466	Karl Rhodes (R)	.20	.12	524	Orel Hershiser	.10	.06
467	Benito Santiago	.08	.05	525	George Brett	.30	.18
468	Joe Klink (R)	.15	.08	526	Greg Vaughn	.10	.06
469	Sil Campusano	.05	.02	527	Tim Naehring	.10	.06
470	Mark Parent	.05	.02	528	Curt Schilling	.08	.05
471	Shawn Boskie	.07	.04	529	Chris Bosio	.07	.04
472	Kevin Brown	.12	.07	530	Sam Horn	.05	.02
473	Rick Sutcliffe	.07	.04	531	Mike Scott	.05	.02
474	Rafael Palmeiro	.12	.07	532	George Bell	.12	.08
475	Mike Harkey	.10	.06	533	Eric Anthony	.20	.12
476	Jaime Navarro	.15	.08	534	Julio Valera	.12	.07
477	Marquis Grissom	.35	.20	535	Glenn Davis	.07	.04
478	Marty Clary	.05	.02	536	Larry Walker	.30	.18
479	Greg Briley	.05	.02	537	Pat Combs	.07	.04
480	Tom Glavine	.30	.18	538	Chris Nabholz (R)	.25	.15
481	Lee Guetterman	.05	.02	539	Kirk McCaskill	.05	.02
482	Rex Hudler	.05	.02	540	Randy Ready	.05	.02
483	Dave LaPoint	.05	.02	541	Mark Gubicza	.07	.04
484	Terry Pendleton	.20	.12	542	Rick Aguilera	.05	.02
485	Jesse Barfield	.07	.04	543	Brian McRae (R)	.30	.18
486	Jose DeJesus	.05	.02	544	Kirby Puckett	.30	.18
487	Paul Abbott (R)	.12	.07	545	Bo Jackson	.25	.15
488	Ken Howell	.05	.02	546	Wade Boggs	.20	.12
489	Greg W. Harris	.05	.02	547	Tim McIntosh	.10	.06
490	Roy Smith	.05	.02	548	Randy Milligan	.07	.04
491	Paul Assenmacher	.05	.02	549	Dwight Evans	.07	.04
492	Geno Petralli	.05	.02	550	Billy Ripken	.05	.02
493	Steve Wilson	.05	.02	551	Erik Hanson	.07	.04
494	Kevin Reimer	.08	.05	552	Lance Parrish	.05	.02
495	Bill Long	.05	.02	553	Tino Martinez	.15	.08
496	Mike Jackson	.05	.02	554	Jim Abbott	.20	.12
497	Oddibe McDowell	.05	.02	555	Ken Griffey, Jr.	1.25	.80
498	Bill Swift	.07	.04	556	Milt Cuyler	.15	.08
499	Jeff Treadway	.05	.02	557	Mark Leonard (R)	.12	.07
500	Checklist 401-500	.05	.02	558	Jay Howell	.05	.02
501	Gene Larkin	.05	.02	559	Lloyd Moseby	.05	.02
502	Bob Boone	.08	.05	560	Chris Gwynn	.05	.02
503	Allan Anderson	.05	.02	561	Mark Whiten (R)	.30	.18
504	Luis Aquino	.05	.02	562	Harold Baines	.07	.04
505	Mark Guthrie	.05	.02	563	Junior Felix	.05	.02
506	Joe Orsulak	.05	.02	564	Darren Lewis (R)	.20	.12
507	Dana Kiecker (R)	.12	.07	565	Fred McGriff	.25	.15
508	Dave Gallagher	.05	.02	566	Kevin Appier	.10	.06
509	Greg W. Harris	.05	.02	567	Luis Gonzalez (R)	.30	.18
510	Mark Williamson	.05	.02	568	Frank White	.05	.02
511	Casey Candaele	.05	.02	569	Juan Agosto	.05	.02
512	Mookie Wilson	.05	.02	570	Mike Macfarlane	.05	.02

571	Bert Blyleven	.10	.06
572	Ken Griffey, Sr.	.20	.12
573	Lee Stevens	.12	.07
574	Edgar Martinez	.20	.12
575	Wally Joyner	.12	.07
576	Tim Belcher	.07	.04
577	John Burkett	.07	.04
578	Mike Morgan	.05	.02
579	Paul Gibson	.05	.02
580	Jose Vizcaino	.05	.02
581	Duane Ward	.05	.02
582	Scott Sanderson	.05	.02
583	David Wells	.05	.02
584	Willie McGee	.08	.05
585	John Cerutti	.05	.02
586	Danny Darwin	.05	.02
587	Kurt Stillwell	.05	.02
588	Rich Gedman	.05	.02
589	Mark Davis	.05	.02
590	Bill Gullickson	.05	.02
591	Matt Young	.05	.02
592	Bryan Harvey	.08	.05
593	Omar Vizquel	.05	.02
594	Scott Lewis (R)	.12	.07
595	Dave Valle	.05	.02
596	Tim Crews	.05	.02
597	Mike Bielecki	.05	.02
598	Mike Sharperson	.05	.02
599	Dave Bergman	.05	.02
600	Checklist 501-600	.05	.02
601	Steve Lyons	.05	.02
602	Bruce Hurst	.08	.05
603	Donn Pall	.05	.02
604	Jim Vatcher (R)	.12	.07
605	Dan Pasqua	.05	.02
606	Kenny Rogers	.05	.02
607	Jeff Schulz (R)	.10	.06
608	Brad Arnsberg (R)	.10	.06
609	Willie Wilson	.05	.02
610	Jamie Moyer	.05	.02
611	Ron Oester	.05	.02
612	Dennis Cook	.05	.02
613	Rick Mahler	.05	.02
614	Bill Landrum	.05	.02
615	Scott Scudder	.05	.02
616	Tom Edens (R)	.10	.06
617	1917 Revisited	.08	.05
618	Jim Gantner	.05	.02
619	Darrel Akerfelds (R)	.10	.06
620	Ron Robinson	.05	.02
621	Scott Radinsky	.15	.08
622	Pete Smith	.25	.15
623	Melido Perez	.07	.04
624	Jerald Clark	.07	.04
625	Carlos Martinez	.05	.02
626	Wes Chamberlain (R)	.25	.15
627	Bobby Witt	.08	.05
628	Ken Dayley	.05	.02
629	John Barfield (R)	.10	.06
630	Bob Tewksbury	.05	.02
631	Glenn Braggs	.05	.02
632	Jim Neidlinger (R)	.10	.06
633	Tom Browning	.07	.04
634	Kirk Gibson	.07	.04
635	Rob Dibble	.10	.06
636	R. Henderson/	.50	.30
	L. Brock		
637	Jeff Montgomery	.05	.02
638	Mike Schooler	.05	.02
639	Storm Davis	.05	.02
640	Rich Rodriguez (R)	.10	.06
641	Phil Bradley	.05	.02
642	Kent Mercker	.07	.04
643	Carlton Fisk	.15	.08
644	Mike Bell (R)	.12	.07
645	Alex Fernandez	.25	.15
646	Juan Gonzalez	1.00	.70
647	Ken Hill	.12	.07
648	Jeff Russell	.05	.02
649	Chuck Malone (R)	.12	.07
650	Steve Buechele	.05	.02
651	Mike Benjamin	.07	.04
652	Tony Pena	.07	.04
653	Trevor Wilson	.07	.04
654	Alex Cole	.10	.06
655	Roger Clemens	.35	.20
656	Mark McGwire(Bash)	.20	.12
657	Joe Grahe (R)	.15	.08
658	Jim Eisenreich	.05	.02
659	Dan Gladden	.05	.02
660	Steve Farr	.05	.02
661	Bill Sampen	.07	.04
662	Dave Rohde (R)	.10	.06
663	Matt Nokes	.07	.04
664	Mike Simms (R)	.10	.06
665	Moises Alou (R)	.30	.18
666	Mickey Hatcher	.05	.02
667	Jimmy Key	.07	.04
668	John Wetteland	.10	.06
669	John Smiley	.12	.07
670	Jim Acker	.05	.02
671	Pascual Perez	.05	.02
672	Reggie Harris (FC)	.15	.08
673	Matt Nokes	.05	.02
674	Rafael Novoa (R)	.08	.05
675	Hensley Meulens	.08	.05
676	Jeff M. Robinson	.05	.02
677	Carlton Fisk/	.15	.08
	Robin Ventura		
	(New Comiskey)		
678	Johnny Ray	.05	.02
679	Greg Hibbard	.05	.02
680	Paul Sorrento	.12	.07
681	Mike Marshall	.05	.02
682	Jim Clancy	.05	.02
683	Rob Murphy	.05	.02

684	Dave Schmidt	.05	.02	736	Jack Morris	.12	.07
685	Jeff Gray (R)	.12	.07	737	Kirk Gibson	.07	.04
686	Mike Hartley	.08	.05	738	Steve Bedrosian	.05	.02
687	Jeff King	.07	.04	739	Candy Maldonado	.05	.02
688	Stan Javier	.05	.02	740	Matt Young	.05	.02
689	Bob Walk	.05	.02	741	Rich Garces (R)	.12	.07
690	Jim Gott	.05	.02	742	George Bell	.12	.07
691	Mike LaCoss	.05	.02	743	Deion Sanders	.25	.15
692	John Farrell	.05	.02	744	Bo Jackson	.25	.15
693	Tim Leary	.05	.02	745	Luis Mercedes (R)	.25	.15
694	Mike Walker (R)	.08	.05	746	Reggie Jefferson	.25	.15
695	Eric Plunk	.05	.02	747	Pete Incaviglia	.05	.02
696	Mike Fetters	.10	.06	748	Chris Hammond	.10	.06
697	Wayne Edwards	.05	.02	749	Mike Stanton	.07	.04
698	Tim Drummond	.07	.04	750	Scott Sanderson	.05	.02
699	Willie Fraser	.05	.02	751	Paul Faries (R)	.08	.05
700	Checklist 601-700	.05	.02	752	Al Osuna (R)	.12	.07
701	Mike Heath	.05	.02	753	Steve Chitren (R)	.12	.07
702	Rookie Threats	.50	.30	754	Tony Fernandez	.07	.04
	Jeff Bagwell			755	Jeff Bagwell (R)	2.00	1.25
	Luis Gonzalez			756	Kirk Dressendorfer (R)	.20	.12
	Karl Rhodes						
703	Jose Mesa	.05	.02	757	Glenn Davis	.07	.04
704	Dave Smith	.05	.02	758	Gary Carter	.10	.06
705	Danny Darwin	.05	.02	759	Zane Smith	.05	.02
706	Rafael Belliard	.05	.02	760	Vance Law	.05	.02
707	Rob Murphy	.05	.02	761	Denis Boucher (R)	.10	.06
708	Terry Pendleton	.15	.08	762	Turner Ward (R)	.15	.08
709	Mike Pagilarulo	.05	.02	763	Roberto Alomar	.40	.25
710	Sid Bream	.05	.02	764	Albert Belle	.35	.20
711	Junior Felix	.05	.02	765	Joe Carter	.25	.15
712	Dante Bichette	.05	.02	766	Pete Schourek (R)	.20	.12
713	Kevin Gross	.05	.02	767	Heathcliff Slocumb	.08	.05
714	Luis Sojo	.05	.02	768	Vince Coleman	.07	.04
715	Bob Ojeda	.05	.02	769	Mitch Williams	.05	.02
716	Julio Machado	.05	.02	770	Brian Downing	.05	.02
717	Steve Farr	.05	.02	771	Dana Allison (R)	.10	.06
718	Franklin Stubbs	.05	.02	772	Pete Harnisch	.10	.06
719	Mike Boddicker	.05	.02	773	Tim Raines	.07	.04
720	Willie Randolph	.07	.04	774	Darryl Kile (FC)	.12	.07
721	Willie McGee	.08	.05	775	Fred McGriff	.25	.15
722	Chili Davis	.07	.04	776	Dwight Evans	.08	.05
723	Danny Jackson	.07	.04	777	Joe Slusarski (R)	.15	.08
724	Cory Snyder	.05	.02	778	Dave Righetti	.05	.02
725	MVP Lineup	.20	.12	779	Jeff Hamilton	.05	.02
	George Bell			780	Ernest Riles	.05	.02
	Andre Dawson			781	Ken Dayley	.05	.02
	Ryne Sandberg			782	Eric King	.05	.02
726	Rob Deer	.07	.04	783	Devon White	.05	.02
727	Rich DeLucia (R)	.12	.07	784	Beau Allred	.05	.02
728	Mike Perez (R)	.12	.07	785	Mike Timlin (R)	.12	.07
729	Mickey Tettleton	.07	.04	786	Ivan Calderon	.07	.04
730	Mike Blowers	.05	.02	787	Hubie Brooks	.07	.04
731	Gary Gaetti	.05	.02	788	Juan Agosto	.05	.02
732	Brett Butler	.08	.05	789	Barry Jones	.05	.02
733	Dave Parker	.07	.04	790	Wally Backman	.05	.02
734	Eddie Zosky	.10	.06	791	Jim Presley	.05	.02
735	Jack Clark	.07	.04	792	Charlie Hough	.05	.02

793	Larry Andersen	.05	.02
794	Steve Finley	.07	.04
795	Shawn Abner	.05	.02
796	Jeff M. Robinson	.05	.02
797	Joe Bitker (R)	.08	.05
798	Eric Show	.05	.02
799	Bud Black	.07	.04
800	Checklist 701-800	.05	.02
SP	Michael Jordan	10.00	7.00
BH10	Nolan Ryan (Hero)	.80	.50
BH11	Nolan Ryan (Hero)	.80	.50
BH12	Nolan Ryan (Hero)	.80	.50
BH13	Nolan Ryan (Hero)	.80	.50
BH14	Nolan Ryan (Hero)	.80	.50
BH15	Nolan Ryan (Hero)	.80	.50
BH16	Nolan Ryan (Hero)	.80	.50
BH17	Nolan Ryan (Hero)	.80	.50
BH18	Nolan Ryan (Hero)	.80	.50
____	Nolan Ryan (Cover)	3.50	2.50
____	Nolan Ryan Checklist	.80	.50
____	Nolan Ryan (Signed)	500.00	375.00
BH19	Hank Aaron (Hero)	.80	.50
BH20	Hank Aaron (Hero)	.80	.50
BH21	Hank Aaron (Hero)	.80	.50
BH22	Hank Aaron (Hero)	.80	.50
BH23	Hank Aaron (Hero)	.80	.50
BH24	Hank Aaron (Hero)	.80	.50
BH25	Hank Aaron (Hero)	.80	.50
BH26	Hank Aaron (Hero)	.80	.50
BH27	Hank Aaron (Hero)	.80	.50
____	Hank Aaron (Cover)	3.50	2.50
____	Hank Aaron Checklist	.80	.50
____	Hank Aaron (Signed)	450.00	350.00
HOF1a	Harmon Killebrew	12.00	8.00
HOF1b	(Hero) (Signed)	175.00	125.00
HOF2a	Gaylord Perry (Hero)	12.00	8.00
HOF2b	(Signed)	140.00	100.00
HOF3a	Ferguson Jenkins	12.00	8.00
HOF3b	(Hero) (Signed)	140.00	100.00
HOF4	Hall of Fame Cover	12.00	8.00
SS1	Julio Franco	.75	.45
SS2	Allan Trammell	.80	.50
SS3	Rickey Henderson	3.00	2.00
SS4	Jose Canseco	5.00	3.50
SS5	Barry Bonds	3.50	2.50
SS6	Eddie Murray	1.50	.90
SS7	Kelly Gruber	.75	.45
SS8	Ryne Sandberg	6.50	4.50
SS9	Darryl Strawberry	3.00	2.00
SS10	Ellis Burks	.80	.50
SS11	Lance Parrish	.75	.45
SS12	Cecil Fielder	3.50	2.50
SS13	Matt Williams	1.00	.70

SS14	Dave Parker	.80	.50
SS15	Bobby Bonilla	2.00	1.25
SS16	Don Robinson	.75	.45
SS17	Benito Santiago	.80	.50
SS18	Barry Larkin	1.50	.90

1991 Upper Deck Final Edition

Patterned after Upper Deck's 1991 regular edition, this 100-card boxed set includes additional rookies and traded players. New subsets include Diamond Skills (1-21) and All-Stars (80-99). The standard-size cards measure 2-1/2" by 3-1/2" and card numbers on the back carry the "F" designation.

		MINT	NR/MT
Complete Set (100)		18.50	13.50
Commons		.05	.02

1	Diamond Skills (CL) Ryan Klesko/ Deion Sanders	.50	.30
2	Pedro Martinez	1.25	.80
3	Lance Dickson	.12	.07
4	Royce Clayton	.25	.15
5	Scott Bryant (R)	.20	.12
6	Dan Wilson (R)	.40	.25
7	Dmitri Young (R)	1.75	1.00
8	Ryan Klesko (R)	2.00	1.25
9	Tom Goodwin (R)	.25	.15
10	Rondell White (R)	.25	.15
11	Reggie Sanders	.60	.35
12	Todd Van Poppel	.30	.18
13	Arthur Rhodes (R)	.40	.25
14	Eddie Zosky	.20	.12
15	Gerald Williams (R)	.75	.45
16	Robert Eenhorn (R)	.12	.07

17	Jim Thome (R)	.75	.45
18	Marc Newfield (R)	1.50	.90
19	Kerwin Moore (R)	.25	.15
20	Jeff McNeely (R)	.75	.45
21	Frankie Rodriguez (R)	1.75	1.00
22	Andy Mota (R)	.20	.12
23	Chris Haney (R)	.15	.08
24	Kenny Lofton (R)	1.50	.90
25	Dave Nilsson (R)	.50	.35
26	Derek Bell (R)	.40	.25
27	Frank Castillo (R)	.15	.08
28	Candy Maldonado	.05	.02
29	Chuck McElroy	.07	.04
30	Chito Martinez (R)	.20	.12
31	Steve Howe	.05	.02
32	Freddie Benavides (R)	.08	.05
33	Scott Kamienieck (R)	.12	.07
34	Denny Neagle (R)	.20	.12
35	Mike Humphreys (R)	.12	.07
36	Mike Remlinger (R)	.10	.06
37	Scott Coolbaugh	.05	.02
38	Darren Lewis	.08	.05
39	Thomas Howard (R)	.20	.12
40	John Candelaria	.05	.02
41	Todd Benzinger	.05	.02
42	Wilson Alvarez	.08	.05
43	Patrick Lennon	.20	.12
44	Rusty Meacham (R)	.15	.08
45	Ryan Bowen (R)	.20	.12
46	Rick Wilkins	.15	.08
47	Ed Sprague	.12	.07
48	Bob Scanlan (R)	.12	.07
49	Tom Candiotti	.05	.02
50	Dennis Martinez (Perfecto)	.10	.06
51	Oil Can Boyd	.05	.02
52	Glenallen Hill	.08	.05
53	Scott Livingstone (R)	.25	.15
54	Brian Hunter (R)	.25	.15
55	Ivan Rodriguez (R)	2.50	1.50
56	Keith Mitchell (R)	.25	.15
57	Roger McDowell	.05	.02
58	Otis Nixon	.07	.04
59	Juan Bell	.07	.04
60	Bill Krueger	.05	.02
61	Chris Donnels (R)	.10	.06
62	Tommy Greene	.08	.05
63	Doug Simons R)	.10	.06
64	Andy Ashby (R)	.12	.07
65	Anthony Young (R)	.25	.15
66	Kevin Morton (R)	.20	.12
67	Bret Barberie	.12	.07
68	Scott Servais	.10	.06
69	Ron Darling	.05	.02
70	Vincente Palacios	.05	.02
71	Tim Burke	.05	.02
72	Gerald Alexander (R)	.10	.06
73	Reggie Jefferson	.10	.06
74	Dean Palmer	.35	.20
75	Mark Whiten	.15	.08
76	Randy Tomlin (R)	.40	.25
77	Mark Wohlers (R)	.25	.15
78	Brook Jacoby	.05	.02
79	All-Star Checklist Ken Griffey Jr/ Ryne Sandberg	.60	.35
80	Jack Morris (AS)	.10	.06
81	Sandy Alomar, Jr. (AS)	.07	.04
82	Cecil Fielder (AS)	.15	.08
83	Roberto Alomar (AS)	.25	.15
84	Wade Boggs (AS)	.12	.07
85	Cal Ripken, Jr. (AS)	.40	.25
86	Rickey Henderson (AS)	.15	.08
87	Ken Griffey, Jr. (AS)	.50	.30
88	Dave Henderson (AS)	.05	.02
89	Danny Tartabull (AS)	.10	.06
90	Tom Glavine (AS)	.20	.12
91	Benito Santiago (AS)	.08	.05
92	Will Clark (AS)	.20	.12
93	Ryne Sandberg (AS)	.20	.12
94	Chris Sabo (AS)	.07	.04
95	Ozzie Smith (AS)	.10	.06
96	Ivan Calderon (AS)	.07	.04
97	Tony Gwynn (AS)	.15	.08
98	Andre Dawson (AS)	.12	.07
99	Bobby Bonilla (AS)	.10	.06
100	Checklist	.05	.02

1992 Upper Deck

This 800-card set is styled after previous Upper Deck issues and includes five major subsets; Star Rookies, Top Prospects, Bloodlines, Diamond Skills and Diamond Debuts. This edition contains two 9-card Heroes of Baseball insert sets. The first features Ted

Williams, the second Johnny Bench and Joe Morgan. A 4-card Hall of Fame Heroes Insert set was randomly packed in high-number foil packs. All cards measure 2-1/2" by 3-1/2". The high-number series (701-800) was released later in the season. Those cards are included in the Complete Set Price below. The Heroes Inserts are priced at the end of this checklist but are not included in the complete set price.

		MINT	NR/MT
	Complete Set (800)	38.00	28.00
	Commons	.05	.02
1	Star Rookie Checklist (R. Klesko/J. Thome)	.25	.15
2	Royce Clayton	.20	.12
3	Brian Jordan (R)	.75	.45
4	Dave Fleming	1.25	.80
5	Jim Thome	.25	.15
6	Jeff Juden	.12	.07
7	Roberto Hernandez	.10	.06
8	Kyle Abbott (R)	.20	.12
9	Chris George (R)	.10	.06
10	Rob Maurer (R)	.20	.12
11	Donald Harris (R)	.05	.02
12	Ted Wood (R)	.20	.12
13	Patrick Lennon	.10	.06
14	Willie Banks	.15	.08
15	Roger Salkeld	.20	.12
16	Wilfredo Cordero	.30	.18
17	Arthur Rhodes	.20	.12
18	Pedro Martinez	.30	.18
19	Andy Ashby	.10	.06
20	Tom Goodwin	.12	.07
21	Braulio Castillo (R)	.20	.12
22	Todd Van Poppel	.30	.18
23	Brian Williams (R)	.60	.35
24	Ryan Klesko	.80	.05
25	Kenny Lofton	.50	.30
26	Derek Bell	.20	.12
27	Reggie Sanders	.40	.25
28	Winfield's 400th	.15	.08
29	Dave Justice (CL)	.15	.08
30	Rob Dibble (CL)	.07	.04
31	Craig Biggio (CL)	.07	.04
32	Eddie Murray (CL)	.08	.05
33	Fred McGriff (CL)	.10	.06
34	Willie McGee (CL)	.07	.04
35	Shawon Dunston (CL)	.07	.04
36	Delino DeShields (CL)	.08	.05
37	Howard Johnson (CL)	.07	.04
38	John Kruk (CL)	.05	.02
39	Doug Drabek (CL)	.07	.04
40	Todd Zeile (CL)	.07	.04
41	Steve Avery (Playoff)	.15	.08
42	Jeremy Hernandez (R)	.10	.06
43	Doug Henry (R)	.15	.08
44	Chris Donnels	.05	.02
45	Mo Sanford	.08	.05
46	Scott Kamieniecki	.07	.04
47	Mark Lemke	.05	.02
48	Steve Farr	.05	.02
49	Francisco Oliveras	.05	.02
50	Ced Landrum	.08	.05
51	Top Prospect Checklist Rondell White/ Craig Griffey	.25	.15
52	Eduardo Perez (R)	.60	.35
53	Tom Nevers	.12	.07
54	David Zancanaro (R)	.15	.08
55	Shawn Green (R)	.40	.25
56	Mark Wholers	.15	.08
57	Dave Nilsson	.25	.15
58	Dmitri Young	.75	.45
59	Ryan Hawblitzel (R)	.25	.15
60	Raul Mondesi	.60	.30
61	Rondell White	.35	.20
62	Steve Hosey	.35	.20
63	Manny Ramirez (R)	1.00	.70
64	Marc Newfield	.50	.30
65	Jeromy Burnitz	.75	.45
66	Mark Smith (R)	.40	.25
67	Joey Hamilton (R)	.40	.25
68	Tyler Green (R)	.60	.35
69	John Farrell (R)	.20	.12
70	Kurt Miller	.20	.12
71	Jeff Plympton (R)	.20	.12
72	Dan Wilson	.12	.07
73	Joe Vitiello (R)	.60	.35
74	Rico Brogna	.15	.08
75	David McCarty (R)	1.75	1.00
76	Bob Wickman (R)	.35	.20
77	Carlos Rodriquez (R)	.20	.12
78	Jim Abbott (School)	.10	.06
79	Ramon & Pedro Martinez	.30	.18
80	Kevin & Keith Mitchell	.10	.06
81	Sandy & Roberto Alomar	.25	.15
82	Cal Jr. & Billy Ripken	.25	.15
83	Tony & Chris Gwynn	.15	.08
84	Dwight Gooden & Gary Sheffield	.30	.18
85	Ken, Ken Jr. & Craig Griffey	.80	.50
86	Jim Abbott (CL)	.10	.06
87	Frank Thomas (CL)	.25	.15

88	Danny Tartabull (CL)	.07	.04
89	Scott Erickson (CL)	.10	.06
90	Rickey Henderson (CL)	.12	.07
91	Edgar Martinez (CL)	.10	.06
92	Nolan Ryan (CL)	.25	.15
93	Ben McDonald (CL)	.10	.06
94	Ellis Burks (CL)	.07	.04
95	Greg Swindell (CL)	.05	.02
96	Cecil Fielder (CL)	.12	.07
97	Greg Vaughn (CL)	.07	.04
98	Kevin Maas (CL)	.08	.05
99	Dave Stieb (CL)	.05	.02
100	Checklist 1-100	.05	.02
101	Joe Oliver	.05	.02
102	Hector Villanueva	.05	.02
103	Ed Whitson	.05	.02
104	Danny Jackson	.07	.04
105	Chris Hammond	.07	.04
106	Ricky Jordan	.05	.02
107	Kevin Bass	.05	.02
108	Darrin Fletcher	.05	.02
109	Junior Ortiz	.05	.02
110	Tom Bolton	.05	.02
111	Jeff King	.05	.02
112	Dave Magadan	.05	.02
113	Mike LaValliere	.05	.02
114	Hubie Brooks	.05	.02
115	Jay Bell	.05	.02
116	David Wells	.05	.02
117	Jim Leyritz	.05	.02
118	Manuel Lee	.05	.02
119	Alvaro Espinoza	.05	.02
120	B. J. Surhoff	.05	.02
121	Hal Morris	.10	.06
122	Shawon Dunston	.08	.05
123	Chris Sabo	.07	.04
124	Andre Dawson	.15	.08
125	Eric Davis	.08	.05
126	Chili Davis	.07	.04
127	Dale Murphy	.08	.05
128	Kirk McCaskill	.05	.02
129	Terry Mulholland	.05	.02
130	Rick Aguilera	.05	.02
131	Vince Coleman	.05	.02
132	Andy Van Slyke	.10	.06
133	Gregg Jefferies	.10	.06
134	Barry Bonds	.25	.15
135	Dwight Gooden	.12	.07
136	Dave Stieb	.07	.04
137	Albert Belle	.12	.07
138	Teddy Higuera	.05	.02
139	Jesse Barfield	.05	.02
140	Pat Borders	.05	.02
141	Bip Roberts	.05	.02
142	Rob Dibble	.07	.04
143	Mark Grace	.12	.07
144	Barry Larkin	.12	.07
145	Ryne Sandberg	.25	.15
146	Scott Erickson	.20	.12
147	Luis Polonia	.07	.04
148	John Burkett	.05	.02
149	Luis Sojo	.05	.02
150	Dickie Thon	.05	.02
151	Walt Weiss	.05	.02
152	Mike Scioscia	.05	.02
153	Mark McGwire	.25	.15
154	Matt Williams	.12	.07
155	Rickey Henderson	.15	.08
156	Sandy Alomar, Jr.	.07	.04
157	Brian McRae	.08	.05
158	Harold Baines	.05	.02
159	Kevin Appier	.10	.06
160	Felix Fermin	.05	.02
161	Leo Gomez	.12	.07
162	Craig Biggio	.07	.04
163	Ben McDonald	.15	.08
164	Randy Johnson	.15	.08
165	Cal Ripken, Jr.	.30	.18
166	Frank Thomas	1.00	.70
167	Delino Deshields	.20	.12
168	Greg Gagne	.05	.02
169	Ron Karkovice	.05	.02
170	Charlie Leibrandt	.05	.02
171	Dave Righetti	.05	.02
172	Dave Henderson	.05	.02
173	Steve Decker	.08	.05
174	Darryl Strawberry	.20	.12
175	Will Clark	.25	.15
176	Ruben Sierra	.20	.12
177	Ozzie Smith	.12	.07
178	Charles Nagy	.20	.12
179	Gary Pettis	.05	.02
180	Kirk Gibson	.07	.04
181	Randy Milligan	.05	.02
182	Dave Valle	.05	.02
183	Chris Hoiles	.08	.05
184	Tony Phillips	.05	.02
185	Brady Anderson	.15	.08
186	Scott Fletcher	.05	.02
187	Gene Larkin	.05	.02
188	Lance Johnson	.05	.02
189	Greg Olson	.05	.02
190	Melido Perez	.05	.02
191	Lenny Harris	.05	.02
192	Terry Kennedy	.05	.02
193	Mike Gallego	.05	.02
194	Willie McGee	.08	.05
195	Juan Samuel	.05	.02
196	Jeff Huson	.05	.02
197	Alex Cole	.07	.04
198	Ron Robinson	.05	.02
199	Joel Skinner	.05	.02
200	Checklist 101-200	.05	.02
201	Kevin Reimer	.05	.02
202	Stan Belinda	.05	.02

203	Pat Tabler	.05	.02	261	Orel Hershiser	.10	.06
204	Jose Guzman	.05	.02	262	Ray Lankford	.15	.08
205	Jose Lind	.05	.02	263	Robin Ventura	.20	.12
206	Spike Owen	.05	.02	264	Felix Jose	.10	.06
207	Joe Orsulak	.07	.04	265	Eddie Murray	.12	.07
208	Charlie Hayes	.05	.02	266	Kevin Mitchell	.08	.05
209	Mike Devereaux	.08	.05	267	Gary Carter	.10	.06
210	Mike Fitzgerald	.05	.02	268	Mike Benjamin	.07	.04
211	Willie Randolph	.07	.04	269	Dick Schofield	.05	.02
212	Rod Nichols	.05	.02	270	Jose Uribe	.05	.02
213	Mike Boddicker	.05	.02	271	Pete Incaviglia	.05	.02
214	Bill Spiers	.05	.02	272	Tony Fernandez	.07	.04
215	Steve Olin	.07	.04	273	Alan Trammell	.08	.05
216	David Howard (R)	.15	.08	274	Tony Gwynn	.20	.12
217	Gary Varsho	.05	.02	275	Mike Greenwell	.08	.05
218	Mike Harkey	.08	.05	276	Jeff Bagwell	.50	.30
219	Luis Aquino	.05	.02	277	Frank Viola	.08	.05
220	Chuck McElroy	.05	.02	278	Randy Myers	.05	.02
221	Doug Drabek	.10	.06	279	Ken Caminiti	.05	.02
222	Dave Winfield	.15	.08	280	Bill Doran	.05	.02
223	Rafael Palmeiro	.08	.05	281	Dan Pasqua	.05	.02
224	Joe Carter	.15	.08	282	Alfredo Griffin	.05	.02
225	Bobby Bonilla	.12	.07	283	Jose Oquendo	.05	.02
226	Ivan Calderon	.07	.04	284	Kal Daniels	.05	.02
227	Gregg Olson	.08	.05	285	Bobby Thigpen	.07	.04
228	Tim Wallach	.07	.04	286	Robby Thompson	.05	.02
229	Terry Pendleton	.15	.08	287	Mark Eichhorn	.05	.02
230	Gilberto Reyes	.05	.02	288	Mike Felder	.05	.02
231	Carlos Baerga	.20	.12	289	Dave Gallagher	.05	.02
232	Greg Vaughn	.08	.05	290	Dave Anderson	.05	.02
233	Bret Saberhagen	.08	.05	291	Mel Hall	.07	.04
234	Gary Sheffield	.50	.30	292	Jerald Clark	.05	.02
235	Mark Lewis	.10	.06	293	Al Newman	.05	.02
236	George Bell	.10	.06	294	Rob Deer	.07	.04
237	Danny Tartabull	.12	.07	295	Matt Nokes	.05	.02
238	Willie Wilson	.05	.02	296	Jack Armstrong	.05	.02
239	Doug Dascenzo	.05	.02	297	Jim Deshaies	.05	.02
240	Bill Pecota	.05	.02	298	Jeff Innis	.05	.02
241	Julio Franco	.08	.05	299	Jeff Reed	.05	.02
242	Ed Sprague	.07	.04	300	Checklist 201-300	.05	.02
243	Juan Gonzalez	.60	.35	301	Lonnie Smith	.05	.02
244	Chuck Finley	.10	.06	302	Jimmy Key	.07	.04
245	Ivan Rodriguez	.50	.30	303	Junior Felix	.05	.02
246	Lenny Dykstra	.07	.04	304	Mike Heath	.05	.02
247	Deion Sanders	.20	.12	305	Mark Langston	.10	.06
248	Dwight Evans	.07	.04	306	Greg W. Harris	.05	.02
249	Larry Walker	.10	.06	307	Brett Butler	.08	.05
250	Billy Ripken	.05	.02	308	Luis Rivera	.05	.02
251	Mickey Tettleton	.07	.04	309	Bruce Ruffin	.05	.02
252	Tony Pena	.05	.02	310	Paul Faries	.05	.02
253	Benito Santiago	.08	.05	311	Terry Leach	.05	.02
254	Kirkby Puckett	.25	.15	312	Scott Brosius (R)	.10	.06
255	Cecil Fielder	.25	.15	313	Scott Leius	.05	.02
256	Howard Johnson	.08	.05	314	Harold Reynolds	.05	.02
257	Andujar Cedeno	.10	.06	315	Jack Morris	.12	.07
258	Jose Rijo	.08	.05	316	David Segui	.07	.04
259	Al Osuna	.05	.02	317	Bill Gullickson	.05	.02
260	Todd Hundley	.07	.04	318	Todd Frohwirth	.05	.02

319	Mark Leiter (FC)	.05	.02
320	Jeff M. Robinson	.05	.02
321	Gary Gaetti	.05	.02
322	John Smoltz	.15	.08
323	Andy Benes	.10	.06
324	Kelly Gruber	.07	.04
325	Jim Abbott	.15	.08
326	John Kruk	.08	.05
327	Kevin Seitzer	.07	.04
328	Darrin Jackson	.05	.02
329	Kurt Stillwell	.05	.02
330	Mike Maddux	.05	.02
331	Dennis Eckersley	.15	.08
332	Dan Gladden	.05	.02
333	Jose Canseco	.25	.15
334	Kent Hrbek	.07	.04
335	Ken Griffey, Sr.	.07	.04
336	Greg Swindell	.07	.04
337	Trevor Wilson	.07	.04
338	Sam Horn	.05	.02
339	Mike Henneman	.05	.02
340	Jerry Browne	.05	.02
341	Glenn Braggs	.05	.02
342	Tom Glavine	.25	.15
343	Wally Joyner	.08	.05
344	Fred McGriff	.20	.12
345	Ron Gant	.12	.07
346	Ramon Martinez	.10	.06
347	Wes Chamberlain	.12	.07
348	Terry Shumpert	.05	.02
349	Tim Teufel	.05	.02
350	Wally Backman	.05	.02
351	Joe Girardi	.05	.02
352	Devon White	.05	.02
353	Greg Maddux	.15	.08
354	Ryan Bowen	.08	.05
355	Roberto Alomar	.25	.15
356	Don Mattingly	.20	.12
357	Pedro Guerrero	.05	.02
358	Steve Sax	.08	.05
359	Joey Cora	.05	.02
360	Jim Gantner	.05	.02
361	Brian Barnes	.08	.05
362	Kevin McReynolds	.07	.04
363	Bret Barberie	.15	.08
364	David Cone	.12	.07
365	Dennis Martinez	.10	.06
366	Brian Hunter	.10	.06
367	Edgar Martinez	.12	.07
368	Steve Finley	.07	.04
369	Greg Briley	.05	.02
370	Jeff Blauser	.05	.02
371	Todd Stottlemyre	.05	.02
372	Luis Gonzalez	.08	.05
373	Rick Wilkins	.05	.02
374	Darryl Kile	.08	.05
375	John Olerud	.15	.08
376	Lee Smith	.12	.07
377	Kevin Maas	.08	.05
378	Danta Bichette	.05	.02
379	Tom Pagnozzi	.05	.02
380	Mike Flanagan	.05	.02
381	Charlie O'Brien	.05	.02
382	Dave Martinez	.05	.02
383	Keith Miller	.05	.02
384	Scott Ruskin	.05	.02
385	Kevin Elster	.05	.02
386	Alvin Davis	.05	.02
387	Casey Candaele	.05	.02
388	Pete O'Brien	.05	.02
389	Jeff Treadway	.05	.02
390	Scott Bradley	.05	.02
391	Mookie Wilson	.05	.02
392	Jimmy Jones	.05	.02
393	Candy Maldonado	.05	.02
394	Eric Yelding	.05	.02
395	Tom Henke	.05	.02
396	Franklin Stubbs	.05	.02
397	Milt Thompson	.05	.02
398	Mark Carreon	.05	.02
399	Randy Velarde	.05	.02
400	Checklist 301-400	.05	.02
401	Omar Vizquel	.05	.02
402	Joe Boever	.05	.02
403	Bill Krueger	.05	.02
404	Jody Reed	.05	.02
405	Mike Schooler	.05	.02
406	Jason Grimsley	.05	.02
407	Greg Myers	.05	.02
408	Randy Ready	.05	.02
409	Mike Timlin	.07	.04
410	Mitch Williams	.05	.02
411	Garry Templeton	.05	.02
412	Greg Cadaret	.05	.02
413	Donnie Hill	.05	.02
414	Wally Whitehurst	.05	.02
415	Scott Sanderson	.05	.02
416	Thomas Howard	.10	.06
417	Neal Heaton	.05	.02
418	Charlie Hough	.05	.02
419	Jack Howell	.05	.02
420	Greg Hibbard	.05	.02
421	Carlos Quintana	.08	.05
422	Kim Batiste	.10	.06
423	Paul Molitor	.10	.06
424	Ken Griffey, Jr.	.80	.05
425	Phil Plantier	.25	.15
426	Denny Neagle	.15	.08
427	Von Hayes	.05	.02
428	Shane Mack	.08	.05
429	Darren Daulton	.10	.06
430	Dwayne Henry	.08	.05
431	Lance Parrish	.05	.02
432	Mike Humphreys	.10	.06
433	Tim Burke	.05	.02
434	Bryan Harvey	.07	.04

435	Pat Kelly	.15	.08
436	Ozzie Guillen	.05	.02
437	Bruce Hurst	.07	.04
438	Sammy Sosa	.08	.05
439	Dennis Rasmussen	.05	.02
440	Ken Patterson	.05	.02
441	Jay Buhner	.07	.04
442	Pat Combs	.07	.04
443	Wade Boggs	.15	.08
444	George Brett	.20	.12
445	Mo Vaughn	.20	.12
446	Chuck Knoblauch	.25	.15
447	Tom Candiotti	.05	.02
448	Mark Portugal	.05	.02
449	Mickey Morandini	.07	.04
450	Duane Ward	.05	.02
451	Otis Nixon	.07	.04
452	Bob Welch	.07	.04
453	Rusty Meacham	.08	.05
454	Keith Mitchell	.10	.06
455	Marquis Grissom	.20	.12
456	Robin Yount	.25	.15
457	Harvey Pulliam	.12	.07
458	Jose DeLeon	.05	.02
459	Mark Gubicza	.07	.04
460	Darryl Hamilton	.05	.02
461	Tom Browning	.07	.04
462	Monty Fariss	.10	.06
463	Jerome Walton	.07	.04
464	Paul O'Neill	.10	.06
465	Dean Palmer	.15	.08
466	Travis Fryman	.30	.18
467	John Smiley	.10	.06
468	Lloyd Moseby	.05	.02
469	John Wehner (R)	.15	.08
470	Skeeter Barnes	.05	.02
471	Steve Chitren	.05	.02
472	Kent Mercker	.05	.02
473	Terry Steinbach	.07	.04
474	Andres Galarraga	.07	.04
475	Steve Avery	.20	.12
476	Tom Gordon	.07	.04
477	Cal Eldred	.35	.20
478	Omar Olivares	.08	.05
479	Julio Machado	.05	.02
480	Bob Milacki	.05	.02
481	Les Lancaster	.05	.02
482	John Candelaria	.05	.02
483	Brian Downing	.05	.02
484	Roger McDowell	.05	.02
485	Scott Scudder	.05	.02
486	Zane Smith	.05	.02
487	John Cerutti	.05	.02
488	Steve Buechele	.05	.02
489	Paul Gibson	.05	.02
490	Curtis Wilkerson	.05	.02
491	Marvin Freemen	.05	.02
492	Tom Foley	.05	.02
493	John Berenguer	.05	.02
494	Ernest Riles	.05	.02
495	Sid Bream	.05	.02
496	Chuck Crim	.05	.02
497	Mike Macfarlane	.05	.02
498	Dale Sveum	.05	.02
499	Storm Davis	.05	.02
500	Checklist 401-500	.05	.02
501	Jeff Reardon	.12	.07
502	Shawn Abner	.05	.02
503	Tony Fossas	.05	.02
504	Cory Snyder	.05	.02
505	Matt Young	.05	.02
506	Allan Anderson	.05	.02
507	Mark Lee	.05	.02
508	Gene Nelson	.05	.02
509	Mike Pagliarulo	.05	.02
510	Rafael Belliard	.05	.02
511	Jay Howell	.05	.02
512	Bob Tewksbury	.05	.02
513	Mike Morgan	.05	.02
514	John Franco	.05	.02
515	Kevin Gross	.05	.02
516	Lou Whitaker	.07	.04
517	Orlando Merced	.10	.06
518	Todd Benzinger	.05	.02
519	Gary Redus	.05	.02
520	Walt Terrell	.05	.02
521	Jack Clark	.07	.04
522	Dave Parker	.07	.04
523	Tim Naehring	.08	.05
524	Mark Whiten	.12	.07
525	Ellis Burks	.08	.05
526	Frank Castillo	.08	.05
527	Brian Harper	.05	.02
528	Brook Jacoby	.05	.02
529	Rick Sutcliffe	.07	.04
530	Joe Klink	.05	.02
531	Terry Bross	.05	.02
532	Jose Offerman	.10	.06
533	Todd Zeile	.08	.05
534	Eric Karros	.60	.35
535	Anthony Young	.15	.08
536	Milt Cuyler	.10	.06
537	Randy Tomlin	.08	.05
538	Scott Livingstone	.10	.06
539	Jim Eisenreich	.05	.02
540	Don Slaught	.05	.02
541	Scott Cooper (FC)	.15	.08
542	Joe Grahe	.08	.05
543	Tom Brunansky	.07	.04
544	Eddie Zosky	.07	.04
545	Roger Clemens	.25	.15
546	David Justice	.25	.15
547	Dave Stewart	.08	.05
548	David West	.05	.02
549	Dave Smith	.05	.02
550	Dan Plesac	.05	.02

No.	Name		
551	Alex Fernandez	.10	.06
552	Bernard Gilkey	.12	.07
553	Jack McDowell	.20	.12
554	Tino Martinez	.10	.06
555	Bo Jackson	.20	.12
556	Bernie Williams	.12	.07
557	Mark Gardner	.08	.05
558	Glenallen Hill	.07	.04
559	Oil Can Boyd	.05	.02
560	Chris James	.05	.02
561	Scott Servais	.07	.04
562	Rey Sanchez (R)	.12	.07
563	Paul McClellan (R)	.10	.06
564	Andy Mota	.07	.04
565	Darren Lewis	.10	.06
566	Jose Melendez (R)	.10	.06
567	Tommy Greene	.12	.07
568	Rich Rodriguez	.07	.04
569	Heathcliff Slocumb	.07	.04
570	Joe Hesketh	.05	.02
571	Carlton Fisk	.12	.07
572	Erik Hanson	.07	.04
573	Wilson Alvarez	.07	.04
574	Rheal Cormier	.12	.07
575	Tim Raines	.07	.04
576	Bobby Witt	.08	.05
577	Roberto Kelly	.15	.08
578	Kevin Brown	.12	.07
579	Chris Nabholz	.10	.06
580	Jesse Orosco	.05	.02
581	Jeff Brantley	.07	.04
582	Rafael Ramirez	.05	.02
583	Kelly Downs	.05	.02
584	Mike Simms	.05	.02
585	Mike Remlinger	.07	.04
586	Dave Hollins	.12	.07
587	Larry Andersen	.05	.02
588	Mike Gardiner	.07	.04
589	Craig Lefferts	.05	.02
590	Paul Assenmacher	.05	.02
591	Bryn Smith	.05	.02
592	Donn Pall	.05	.02
593	Mike Jackson	.05	.02
594	Scott Radinsky	.05	.02
595	Brian Holman	.07	.04
596	Geronimo Pena	.05	.02
597	Mike Jeffcoat	.05	.02
598	Carlos Martinez	.05	.02
599	Geno Petralli	.05	.02
600	Checklist 501-600	.05	.02
601	Jerry Don Gleaton	.05	.02
602	Adam Peterson	.05	.02
603	Craig Grebeck	.05	.02
604	Mark Guthrie	.05	.02
605	Frank Tanana	.05	.02
606	Hensley Meulens	.07	.04
607	Mark Davis	.05	.02
608	Eric Plunk	.05	.02
609	Mark Williamson	.05	.02
610	Lee Guetterman	.05	.02
611	Bobby Rose	.08	.05
612	Bill Wegman	.05	.02
613	Mike Hartley	.05	.02
614	Chris Beasley (R)	.10	.06
615	Chris Bosio	.05	.02
616	Henry Cotto	.05	.02
617	Chico Walker (R)	.10	.06
618	Russ Swan	.05	.02
619	Bob Walk	.05	.02
620	Billy Swift	.07	.04
621	Warren Newson	.05	.02
622	Steve Bedrosian	.05	.02
623	Ricky Bones	.12	.07
624	Kevin Tapani	.07	.04
625	Juan Guzman	1.00	.70
626	Jeff Johnson	.08	.05
627	Jeff Montgomery	.05	.02
628	Ken Hill	.10	.06
629	Gary Thurman	.05	.02
630	Steve Howe	.05	.02
631	Jose DeJesus	.05	.02
632	Bert Blyleven	.08	.05
633	Jaime Navarro	.10	.06
634	Lee Stevens	.10	.06
635	Pete Harnisch	.08	.05
636	Bill Landrum	.05	.02
637	Rich DeLucia	.05	.02
638	Luis Salazar	.05	.02
639	Rob Murphy	.05	.02
640	Diamond Skills (CL) (Jose Canseco/ Rickey Henderson)	.25	.15
641	Roger Clemens (DS)	.20	.12
642	Jim Abbott (DS)	.08	.05
643	Travis Fryman (DS)	.15	.08
644	Jesse Barfield (DS)	.05	.02
645	Cal Ripken, Jr. (DS)	.20	.12
646	Wade Boggs (DS)	.12	.07
647	Cecil Fielder (DS)	.15	.08
648	Rickey Henderson (DS)	.15	.08
649	Jose Canseco (DS)	.20	.12
650	Ken Griffey, Jr. (DS)	.35	.20
651	Kenny Rogers	.05	.02
652	Luis Mercedes	.20	.12
653	Mike Stanton	.07	.04
654	Glenn Davis	.07	.04
655	Nolan Ryan	.60	.35
656	Reggie Jefferson	.12	.07
657	Javier Ortiz (R)	.12	.07
658	Greg A. Harris	.05	.02
659	Mariano Duncan	.05	.02
660	Jeff Shaw	.05	.02
661	Mike Moore	.05	.02
662	Chris Haney	.07	.04
663	Joe Slusarski	.08	.05

664	Wayne Housie (R)	.10	.06
665	Carlos Garcia	.12	.07
666	Bob Ojeda	.05	.02
667	Bryan Hickerson (R)	.10	.06
668	Tim Belcher	.07	.04
669	Ron Darling	.07	.04
670	Rex Hudler	.05	.02
671	Sid Fernandez	.07	.04
672	Chito Martinez	.25	.15
673	Pete Schourek	.12	.07
674	Armando Reynoso (R)	.10	.06
675	Mike Mussina	.75	.45
676	Kevin Morton	.10	.06
677	Norm Charlton	.07	.04
678	Danny Darwin	.05	.02
679	Eric King	.05	.02
680	Ted Power	.05	.02
681	Barry Jones	.05	.02
682	Carney Lansford	.07	.04
683	Mel Rojas	.07	.04
684	Rick Honeycutt	.05	.02
685	Jeff Fassero (R)	.10	.06
686	Cris Carpenter	.05	.02
687	Tim Crews	.05	.02
688	Scott Terry	.05	.02
689	Chris Gwynn	.05	.02
690	Gerald Perry	.05	.02
691	John Barfield	.05	.02
692	Bob Melvin	.05	.02
693	Juan Agosto	.05	.02
694	Alejandro Pena	.05	.02
695	Jeff Russell	.05	.02
696	Carmelo Martinez	.05	.02
697	Bud Black	.07	.04
698	Dave Otto	.05	.02
699	Billy Hatcher	.05	.02
700	Checklist 601-700	.05	.02
701	Clemente Nunez (R)	.50	.30
702	Rookie Threats (Clark/Jordan/ Osborne)	.25	.15
703	Mike Morgan	.05	.02
704	Keith Miller	.05	.02
705	Kurt Stillwell	.05	.02
706	Damon Berryhill	.05	.02
707	Von Hayes	.05	.02
708	Rick Sutcliffe	.07	.04
709	Hubie Brooks	.05	.02
710	Ryan Turner (R)	.50	.35
711	Barry Bonds/Andy Van Slyke (CL)	.15	.08
712	Jose Rijo (DS)	.08	.05
713	Tom Glavine (DS)	.15	.08
714	Shawon Dunston (DS)	.08	.05
715	Andy Van Slyke (DS)	.10	.06
716	Ozzie Smith (DS)	.12	.07
717	Tony Gwynn (DS)	.15	.08
718	Will Clark (DS)	.25	.15
719	Marquis Grissom (DS)	.20	.12
720	Howard Johnson (DS)	.08	.05
721	Barry Bonds (DS)	.25	.15
722	Kirk McCaskill	.05	.02
723	Sammy Sosa	.08	.05
724	George Bell	.10	.06
725	Gregg Jefferies	.10	.06
726	Gary DiSarcina	.12	.07
727	Mike Bordick	.12	.07
728	Eddie Murray (400 HR)	.12	.07
729	Alvin Davis	.05	.02
730	Mike Bielecki	.05	.02
731	Calvin Jones (R)	.12	.07
732	Jack Morris	.12	.07
733	Frank Viola	.08	.05
734	Dave Winfield	.15	.08
735	Kevin Mitchell	.08	.05
736	Billy Swift	.07	.04
737	Dan Gladden	.05	.02
738	Mike Jackson	.05	.02
739	Mark Carreon	.05	.02
740	Kirt Manwaring	.05	.02
741	Randy Myers	.05	.02
742	Kevin McReynolds	.07	.04
743	Steve Sax	.08	.05
744	Wally Joyner	.08	.05
745	Gary Sheffield	.50	.30
746	Danny Tartabull	.10	.06
747	Julio Valera	.05	.02
748	Danny Neagle	.08	.05
749	Lance Blankenship	.05	.02
750	Mike Gallego	.05	.02
751	Bret Saberhagen	.08	.05
752	Ruben Amaro	.08	.05
753	Eddie Murray	.12	.07
754	Kyle Abbott	.07	.04
755	Bobby Bonilla	.12	.07
756	Eric Davis	.08	.05
757	Eddie Taubensee	.12	.07
758	Andres Galarraga	.07	.04
759	Pete Incaviglia	.05	.02
760	Tom Candiotti	.05	.02
761	Tim Belcher	.07	.04
762	Ricky Bones	.08	.05
763	Bip Roberts	.05	.02
764	Pedro Munoz	.10	.06
765	Greg Swindell	.07	.04
766	Kenny Lofton	.35	.20
767	Gary Carter	.10	.06
768	Charlie Hayes	.05	.02
769	Dickie Thon	.05	.02
770	Donovan Osborne (CL)	.15	.08

771	Bret Boone (R)	.75	.45
772	Archi Cianfroco (R)	.30	.18
773	Mark Clark (R)	.15	.08
774	Chad Curtis (R)	.30	.18
775	Pat Listach (R)	2.00	1.25
776	Pat Mahomes (R)	.40	.25
777	Donovan Osborne (R)	.30	.18
778	John Patterson (R)	.15	.08
779	Andy Stankiewicz (R)	.30	.18
780	Turk Wendell (R)	.40	.25
781	Bill Krueger	.05	.02
782	Rickey Henderson Grand Theft)	.15	.08
783	Kevin Seitzer	.07	.04
784	Dave Martinez	.05	.02
785	John Smiley	.10	.06
786	Matt Stairs (R)	.30	.18
787	Scott Scudder	.05	.02
788	John Wetteland	.08	.05
789	Jack Armstrong	.07	.04
790	Ken Hill	.12	.07
791	Dick Schofield	.05	.02
792	Mariano Duncan	.05	.02
793	Bill Pecota	.05	.02
794	Mike Kelly (R)	1.25	.80
795	Willie Randolph	.07	.04
796	Butch Henry	.05	.02
797	Carlos Hernandez	.05	.02
798	Doug Jones	.05	.02
799	Melido Perez	.07	.04
800	Checklist 701-800	.07	.04
BH28	Ted Williams (Hero)	1.25	.80
BH29	Ted Williams (Hero)	1.25	.80
BH30	Ted Williams (Hero)	1.25	.80
BH31	Ted Williams (Hero)	1.25	.80
BH32	Ted Williams (Hero)	1.25	.80
BH33	Ted Williams (Hero)	1.25	.80
BH34	Ted Williams (Hero)	1.25	.80
BH35	Ted Williams (Hero)	1.25	.80
BH36	Ted Williams (Hero)	1.25	.80
____	Ted Williams (Cover)	10.00	7.00
BH37	Johnny Bench/Joe Morgan (Hero)	1.25	.80
BH38	Johnny Bench/Joe Morgan (Hero)	1.25	.80
BH39	Johnny Bench/Joe Morgan (Hero)	1.25	.80
BH40	Johnny Bench/Joe Morgan (Hero)	1.25	.80
BH41	Johnny Bench/Joe Morgan (Hero)	1.25	.80
BH42	Johnny Bench/Joe Morgan (Hero)	1.25	.80
BH43	Johnny Bench/Joe Morgan (Hero)	1.25	.80
BH44	Johnny Bench/Joe Morgan (Hero)	1.25	.80
BH45	Johnny Bench/Joe Morgan (Hero)	1.25	.80
____	Bench/Morgan (Cover)	10.00	7.00
HOF5	Vida Blue (Hero)	4.00	2.75
HOF6	Lou Brock (Hero)	8.00	5.50
HOF7	Rollie Fingers (Hero)	7.00	4.50
HOF8	Blue/Brock/Fingers	8.00	5.50

1993 Upper Deck

For the first time Upper Deck divided their baseball set into two series. Series I contains 420-cards. Card fronts feature full color action photos framed by a white border. Upper Deck appears in white type across the top with the player's name, team and position centered under the photo. Card backs include another full color action shot and a stats box. The set includes numerous subsets including Star Rookies, Community Heroes (CH) and Teammates (41-55). Limited inserts consists of a Willie Mays Heroes set, Home Run Heroes and Triple Crown Contenders. All cards measure 2-1/2" by 3-1/2".

		MINT	NR/MT
Complete Set (420)		24.00	16.00
Commons		.05	.02
1	Star Rookie (CL)	.15	.10
2	Mike Piazza (R)	.80	.50
3	Rene Arocha (R)	.40	.25
4	Willie Greene (R)	.75	.45
5	Manny Alexander (R)	.25	.15

#	Player		
6	Dan Wilson	.15	.10
7	Dan Smith (R)	.40	.25
8	Kevin Rogers	.20	.12
9	Nigel Wilson (R)	.80	.50
10	Joe Vitko (R)	.35	.20
11	Tim Costo	.15	.10
12	Alan Embree (R)	.20	.12
13	Jim Tatum (R)	.15	.10
14	Cris Colon (R)	.30	.18
15	Steve Hosey	.25	.15
16	Sterling Hitchcock (R)	.40	.25
17	Dave Mlicki (R)	.15	.10
18	Jessie Hollins (R)	.20	.12
19	Bobby Jones (R)	.25	.15
20	Kurt Miller	.10	.06
21	Melvin Nieves (R)	.75	.45
22	Billy Ashley (R)	.60	.35
23	J.T. Snow (R)	.75	.45
24	Chipper Jones (R)	.40	.25
25	Tim Simon (R)	.15	.10
26	Tim Pugh (R)	.20	.12
27	Dave Nied (R)	1.25	.80
28	Mike Trombley (R)	.15	.10
29	Javy Lopez (R)	.20	.12
30	Checklist	.07	.04
31	Jim Abbott (CH)	.10	.06
32	Dale Murphy (CH)	.10	.06
33	Tony Pena (CH)	.06	.03
34	Kirby Puckett (CH)	.12	.07
35	Harold Reynolds (CH)	.06	.03
36	Cal Ripken, Jr. (CH)	.20	.12
37	Nolan Ryan (CH)	.30	.18
38	Ryne Sandberg (CH)	.20	.12
39	Dave Stewart (CH)	.07	.04
40	Dave Winfield (CH)	.10	.06
41	Checklist	.07	.04
42	Blockbuster	.15	.10
43	Brew Crew	.20	.12
44	Iron And Steal	.15	.10
45	Young Tribe	.20	.12
46	Motown Mashers	.12	.07
47	Yankee Pride	.12	.07
48	Boston Cy Sox	.15	.10
49	Bash Brothers	.20	.12
50	Twin Titles	.12	.07
51	Southside Sluggers	.60	.35
52	Latin Stars	.50	.30
53	Lethal Lefties	.10	.06
54	Royal Family	.10	.06
55	Pacific Sox	.25	.15
56	George Brett	.15	.10
57	Scott Cooper	.10	.06
58	Mike Maddux	.05	.02
59	Rusty Meacham	.08	.05
60	Wilfredo Cordero	.40	.25
61	Tim Teufel	.05	.02
62	Jeff Montgomery	.05	.02
63	Scott Livingstone	.07	.04
64	Doug Dascenzo	.05	.02
65	Bret Boone	.40	.25
66	Tim Wakefield (R)	3.50	2.00
67	Curt Schilling	.05	.02
68	Frank Tanana	.05	.02
69	Lenny Dykstra	.07	.04
70	Derek Lilliquist	.05	.02
71	Anthony Young	.10	.06
72	Hipolito Pichardo (R)	.15	.10
73	Rod Beck (R)	.15	.10
74	Kent Hrbek	.05	.02
75	Tom Glavine	.20	.12
76	Kevin Brown	.10	.06
77	Chuck Finley	.08	.05
78	Bob Walk	.05	.02
79	Rheal Cormier	.08	.05
80	Rick Sutcliffe	.05	.02
81	Harold Baines	.07	.04
82	Lee Smith	.10	.06
83	Geno Petralli	.05	.02
84	Jose Oquendo	.05	.02
85	Mark Gubicza	.07	.04
86	Mickey Tettleton	.07	.04
87	Bobby Witt	.07	.04
88	Mark Lewis	.07	.04
89	Kevin Appier	.07	.04
90	Mike Stanton	.05	.02
91	Rafael Belliard	.05	.02
92	Kenny Rogers	.05	.02
93	Randy Velarde	.05	.02
94	Luis Sojo	.05	.02
95	Mark Leiter	.05	.02
96	Jody Reed	.05	.02
97	Pete Harnisch	.07	.04
98	Tom Candiotti	.05	.02
99	Mark Portugal	.05	.02
100	Dave Valle	.05	.02
101	Shawon Dunston	.08	.05
102	B.J. Surhoff	.05	.02
103	Jay Bell	.05	.02
104	Sid Bream	.05	.02
105	Checklist 1-105	.05	.02
106	Mike Morgan	.05	.02
107	Bill Doran	.05	.02
108	Lance Blankenship	.05	.02
109	Mark Lemke	.05	.02
110	Brian Harper	.05	.02
111	Brady Anderson	.12	.07
112	Bip Roberts	.05	.02
113	Mitch Williams	.05	.02
114	Craig Biggio	.07	.04
115	Eddie Murray	.15	.10
116	Matt Nokes	.05	.02
117	Lance Parrish	.05	.02
118	Bill Swift	.07	.04
119	Jeff Innis	.05	.02
120	Mike LaValliere	.05	.02
121	Hal Morris	.08	.05

#	Player			#	Player		
122	Walt Weiss	.05	.02	180	Mike Magnante	.07	.04
123	Ivan Rodriguez	.30	.18	181	Billy Ripken	.05	.02
124	Andy Van Slyke	.10	.06	182	Mike Moore	.05	.02
125	Roberto Alomar	.25	.15	183	Eric Anthony	.15	.10
126	Robby Thompson	.05	.02	184	Lenny Harris	.05	.02
127	Sammy Sosa	.07	.04	185	Tony Pena	.05	.02
128	Mark Langston	.10	.06	186	Mike Felder	.05	.02
129	Jerry Browne	.05	.02	187	Greg Olson	.05	.02
130	Chuck McElroy	.05	.02	188	Rene Gonzales	.08	.05
131	Frank Viola	.08	.05	189	Mike Bordick	.08	.05
132	Leo Gomez	.10	.06	190	Mel Rojas	.05	.02
133	Ramon Martinez	.10	.06	191	Todd Frohwirth	.07	.04
134	Don Mattingly	.15	.10	192	Darryl Hamilton	.08	.05
135	Roger Clemens	.30	.18	193	Mike Fetters	.07	.04
136	Rickey Henderson	.20	.12	194	Omar Olivares	.05	.02
137	Darren Daulton	.12	.07	195	Tony Phillips	.05	.02
138	Ken Hill	.08	.05	196	Paul Sorrento	.10	.06
139	Ozzie Guillen	.05	.02	197	Trevor Wilson	.05	.02
140	Jerald Clark	.08	.05	198	Kevin Gross	.05	.02
141	Dave Fleming	.40	.25	199	Ron Karkovice	.05	.02
142	Delino DeShields	.15	.10	200	Brook Jacoby	.05	.02
143	Matt Williams	.12	.07	201	Mariano Duncan	.05	.02
144	Larry Walker	.20	.12	202	Dennis Cook	.05	.02
145	Ruben Sierra	.20	.12	203	Daryl Boston	.05	.02
146	Ozzie Smith	.15	.10	204	Mike Perez	.10	.06
147	Chris Sabo	.08	.05	205	Manuel Lee	.05	.02
148	Carlos Hernandez	.15	.10	206	Steve Olin	.08	.05
149	Pat Borders	.07	.04	207	Charlie Hough	.05	.02
150	Orlando Merced	.08	.05	208	Scott Scudder	.05	.02
151	Royce Clayton	.20	.12	209	Charlie O'Brien	.05	.02
152	Kurt Stillwell	.05	.02	210	Checklist 106-210	.05	.02
153	Dave Hollins	.15	.10	211	Jose Vizcaino	.05	.02
154	Mike Greenwell	.08	.05	212	Scott Leius	.05	.02
155	Nolan Ryan	.50	.30	213	Kevin Mitchell	.12	.07
156	Felix Jose	.08	.05	214	Brian Barnes	.07	.04
157	Junior Felix	.05	.02	215	Pat Kelly	.10	.06
158	Derek Bell	.15	.10	216	Chris Hammond	.08	.05
159	Steve Buechele	.05	.02	217	Rob Deer	.08	.05
160	John Burkett	.05	.02	218	Cory Snyder	.05	.02
161	Pat Howell (R)	.20	.12	219	Gary Carter	.10	.06
162	Milt Cuyler	.08	.05	220	Danny Darwin	.05	.02
163	Terry Pendleton	.12	.07	221	Tom Gordon	.08	.05
164	Jack Morris	.05	.02	222	Gary Sheffield	.30	.18
165	Tony Gwynn	.12	.07	223	Joe Carter	.25	.15
166	Deion Sanders	.25	.15	224	Jay Buhner	.08	.05
167	Mike Deavereaux	.07	.04	225	Jose Offerman	.10	.06
168	Ron Darling	.07	.04	226	Jose Rijo	.08	.05
169	Orel Hershiser	.10	.06	227	Mark Whiten	.10	.06
170	Mike Jackson	.05	.02	228	Randy Milligan	.05	.02
171	Doug Jones	.05	.02	229	Bud Black	.05	.02
172	Dan Walters	.08	.05	230	Gary DiSarcina	.08	.05
173	Darren Lewis	.08	.05	231	Steve Finley	.05	.02
174	Carlos Baerga	.20	.12	232	Dennis Martinez	.10	.06
175	Ryne Sandberg	.30	.18	233	Mike Mussina	.50	.30
176	Gregg Jefferies	.15	.10	234	Joe Oliver	.07	.04
177	John Jaha (R)	.25	.15	235	Chad Curtis	.10	.06
178	Luis Polonia	.07	.04	236	Shane Mack	.10	.06
179	Kirt Manwaring	.05	.02	237	Jaime Navarro	.10	.06

238	Brian McRae	.08	.05
239	Chili Davis	.07	.04
240	Jeff King	.07	.04
241	Dean Palmer	.15	.10
242	Danny Tartabull	.12	.07
243	Charles Nagy	.12	.07
244	Ray Lankford	.20	.12
245	Barry Larkin	.12	.07
246	Steve Avery	.20	.12
247	John Kruk	.07	.04
248	Derrick May	.15	.10
249	Stan Javier	.05	.02
250	Roger McDowell	.05	.02
251	Dan Gladden	.05	.02
252	Wally Joyner	.10	.06
253	Pat Listach	1.00	.70
254	Chuck Knoblauch	.20	.12
255	Sandy Alomar, Jr.	.08	.05
256	Jeff Bagwell	.25	.15
257	Andy Stankiewicz	.10	.06
258	Darrin Jackson	.07	.04
259	Brett Butler	.08	.05
260	Joe Orsulak	.05	.02
261	Andy Benes	.12	.07
262	Kenny Lofton	.30	.18
263	Robin Ventura	.20	.12
264	Ron Gant	.15	.10
265	Ellis Burks	.08	.05
266	Juan Guzman	.50	.30
267	Wes Chamberlain	.10	.06
268	John Smiley	.08	.05
269	Franklin Stubbs	.05	.02
270	Tom Browning	.07	.04
271	Dennis Eckersley	.20	.12
272	Carlton Fisk	.15	.10
273	Lou Whitaker	.07	.04
274	Phil Plantier	.20	.12
275	Bobby Bonilla	.15	.10
276	Ben McDonald	.15	.10
277	Bob Zupcic (R)	.25	.15
278	Terry Steinbach	.07	.04
279	Terry Mulholland	.05	.02
280	Lance Johnson	.05	.02
281	Willie McGee	.08	.05
282	Bret Saberhagen	.10	.06
283	Randy Myers	.05	.02
284	Randy Tomlin	.10	.06
285	Mickey Morandini	.08	.05
286	Brian Williams	.25	.15
287	Tino Martinez	.15	.10
288	Jose Melendez	.10	.06
289	Jeff Huson	.07	.04
290	Joe Grahe	.07	.04
291	Mel Hall	.07	.04
292	Otis Nixon	.10	.06
293	Todd Hundley	.10	.06
294	Casey Candaele	.05	.02
295	Kevin Seitzer	.05	.02
296	Eddie Taubensee	.08	.05
297	Moises Alou	.20	.12
298	Scott Radinsky	.05	.02
299	Thomas Howard	.08	.05
300	Kyle Abbott	.08	.05
301	Omar Vizquel	.05	.02
302	Keith Miller	.05	.02
303	Rick Aguilera	.05	.02
304	Bruce Hurst	.08	.05
305	Ken Caminiti	.07	.04
306	Mike Pagliarulo	.05	.02
307	Frank Seminara (R)	.25	.15
308	Andre Dawson	.15	.10
309	Jose Lind	.05	.02
310	Joe Boever	.05	.02
311	Jeff Parrett	.05	.02
312	Alan Mills	.08	.05
313	Kevin Tapani	.08	.05
314	Daryl Kile	.08	.05
315	Checklist 211-315	.05	.02
316	Mike Sharperson	.05	.02
317	John Orton	.07	.04
318	Bob Tewksbury	.05	.02
319	Xavier Hernandez	.05	.02
320	Paul Assenmacher	.05	.02
321	John Franco	.07	.04
322	Mike Timlin	.07	.04
323	Jose Guzman	.05	.02
324	Pedro Martinez	.25	.15
325	Bill Spiers	.05	.02
326	Melido Perez	.08	.05
327	Mike Macfarlane	.05	.02
328	Ricky Bones	.08	.05
329	Scott Bankhead	.05	.02
330	Rich Rodriguez	.08	.05
331	Geronimo Pena	.05	.02
332	Bernie Williams	.12	.07
333	Paul Molitor	.10	.06
334	Roger Mason	.05	.02
335	David Cone	.15	.10
336	Randy Johnson	.12	.07
337	Pat Mahomes	.25	.15
338	Erik Hanson	.07	.04
339	Duane Ward	.05	.02
340	Al Martin	.10	.06
341	Pedro Munoz	.12	.07
342	Greg Colbrunn	.20	.12
343	Julio Valera	.05	.02
344	John Olerud	.12	.07
345	George Bell	.10	.06
346	Devon White	.07	.04
347	Donovan Osborne	.30	.18
348	Mark Gardner	.07	.04
349	Zane Smith	.05	.02
350	Wilson Alvarez	.07	.04
351	Kevin Koslofski (R)	.25	.15
352	Roberto Hernandez	.08	.05
353	Glenn Davis	.07	.04

354	Reggie Sanders	.25	.15
355	Ken Griffey, Jr.	.77	.45
356	Marquis Grissom	.15	.10
357	Jack McDowell	.20	.12
358	Jimmy Key	.05	.02
359	Stan Belinda	.05	.02
360	Gerald Williams	.12	.07
361	Sid Fernandez	.07	.04
362	Alex Fernandez	.12	.07
363	John Smoltz	.15	.10
364	Travis Fryman	.25	.15
365	Jose Canseco	.30	.18
366	David Justice	.25	.15
367	Pedro Astacio (R)	.50	.30
368	Tim Belcher	.07	.04
369	Steve Sax	.08	.05
370	Gary Gaetti	.05	.02
371	Jeff Frye (R)	.20	.12
372	Bob Wickman	.20	.12
373	Ryan Thompson (R)	.20	.12
374	David Hulse (R)	.20	.12
375	Cal Eldred	.50	.30
376	Ryan Klesko	.60	.35
377	Damion Easley (R)	.25	.15
378	John Kiely (R)	.20	.12
379	Jim Bullinger (R) (R)	.20	.12
380	Brian Bohanon	.05	.02
381	Rod Brewer	.05	.02
382	Fernando Ramsey (R)	.20	.12
383	Sam Militello (R)	1.50	.90
384	Arthur Rhodes	.12	.07
385	Eric Karros	.75	.45
386	Rico Brogna	.10	.06
387	John Valentin (R)	.25	.15
388	Kerry Woodson (R)	.20	.12
389	Ben Rivera	.10	.06
390	Matt Whiteside (R)	.15	.10
391	Henry Rodriquez	.12	.07
392	John Wetteland	.08	.05
393	Kent Mercker	.05	.02
394	Bernard Gilkey	.12	.07
395	Doug Henry	.10	.06
396	Mo Vaughn	.15	.10
397	Scott Erickson	.15	.10
398	Bill Gullickson	.05	.02
399	Mark Guthrie	.05	.02
400	Dave Martinez	.05	.02
401	Jeff Kent (R)	.60	.35
402	Chris Hoiles	.10	.06
403	Mike Henneman	.05	.02
404	Chris Nabholz	.07	.04
405	Tom Pagnozzi	.08	.05
406	Kelly Gruber	.07	.04
407	Bob Welch	.07	.04
408	Frank Castillo	.05	.02
409	John Dopson	.05	.02
410	Steve Farr	.05	.02
411	Henry Cotto	.05	.02

412	Bob Patterson	.05	.02
413	Todd Stottlemyre	.07	.04
414	Greg Harris	.05	.02
415	Denny Neagle	.08	.05
416	Bill Wegman	.05	.02
417	Willie Wilson	.07	.04
418	Terry Leach	.05	.02
419	Willie Randolph	.07	.04
420	Checklist 316-420	.05	.02
BC	Willie Mays Heroes(ea)	1.75	1.00

1993 Upper Deck I Home Run Heroes

	MINT	NR/MT
Complete Set (28)	28.00	18.00
Commons	.50	.30

		MINT	NR/MT
HR1	Juan Gonzalez	3.50	2.50
HR2	Mark McGwire	2.00	1.25
HR3	Cecil Fielder	1.25	.80
HR4	Fred McGriff	1.25	.80
HR5	Albert Belle	1.00	.70
HR6	Barry Bonds	2.00	1.25
HR7	Joe Carter	1.25	.80
HR8	Darren Daulton	.50	.30
HR9	Ken Griffey, Jr.	4.50	3.00
HR10	Dave Hollins	.75	.50
HR11	Ryne Sandberg	3.00	2.00
HR12	George Bell	.75	.50
HR13	Danny Tartabull	.75	.50
HR14	Mike Devereaux	.50	.30
HR15	Greg Vaughn	.75	.50
HR16	Larry Walker	1.00	.70
HR17	David Justice	1.50	.90
HR18	Terry Pendleton	1.00	.70
HR19	Eric Karros	2.00	1.25
HR20	Ray Lankford	1.25	.80
HR21	Matt Williams	1.25	.80
HR22	Eric Anthony	.75	.45
HR23	Bobby Bonilla	1.25	.80
HR24	Kirby Puckett	3.00	2.00
HR25	Mike Macfarlane	.50	.30
HR26	Tom Brunansky	.50	.30
HR27	Paul O'Neill	.75	.45
HR28	Gary Gaetti	.50	.30

1993 Upper Deck I
Triple Crown

		MINT	NR/MT
Complete Set (10)		40.00	28.00
Commons		2.50	1.50
TC1	Barry Bonds	3.50	2.50
TC2	Jose Canseco	5.00	3.50
TC3	Will Clark	3.50	2.50
TC4	Ken Griffey, Jr.	6.00	4.50
TC5	Fred McGriff	3.00	2.00
TC6	Kirby Puckett	4.00	2.75
TC7	Cal Ripken, Jr.	4.00	2.75
TC8	Gary Sheffield	3.50	2.50
TC9	Frank Thomas	7.50	5.00
TC10	Larry Walker	2.50	1.50